M	Maturity value of a bond
n	Life of a project; also terminal year of decision or planning horizon
N	Number of shares outstanding
p	Price of a security
P	Sales price per unit of product sold
P_o	Present value; also $P_{r,n}$
$P_{r,t}$	Present value of an annuity
P_s	Probability of state-of-the world s
PVIF	Present value interest factor
PVIFA	Present value interest factor for an annuity
Q	Quantity produced or sold
r	Interest rate (usually real rate)
R_M	Return on the market portfolio
R_F	Risk-free rate of interest
R_j	Returns to individual firm or security
R	Expected rate of return on new investment; also internal rate of return (IRR); also R is nominal interest rate
R^*	Required rate of return
ρ_{jk}(rho)	Correlation coefficient
s	Subscript referring to alternative states-of-the-world
S	Market value of a firm's common equity; also sales when indicated
σ (sigma)	Standard deviation
σ^2	Variance; also Var( )
t	Time period; t^* is time to maturity in OPM
T	Marginal corporate income tax rate
v	Variable costs per unit
V	Market value of a firm; also total variable costs
$V_{r,n}$	Compound sum
$V_{r,t}$	Sum of an annuity
w	Weights in capital structure or portfolio proportions
X	Net operating income (EBIT = NOI); also exercise price in OPM
Z	Estimated salvage value

ESSENTIALS OF MANAGERIAL FINANCE

ESSENTIALS OF MANAGERIAL FINANCE

J. FRED WESTON
University of California, Los Angeles

EUGENE F. BRIGHAM
University of Florida

Sixth Edition

THE DRYDEN PRESS
Chicago New York Philadelphia San Francisco Montreal Toronto London Sydney Tokyo Mexico City Rio de Janeiro Madrid

Acquisitions Editor: Glenn Turner
Developmental Editor: Elizabeth Widdicombe
Project Editor: Kathy Richmond
Design Director: Alan Wendt
Production Manager: Mary Jarvis

Text and cover design by: James Buddenbaum
Copy editing by Kathryn Jandeska
Permissions by Gertrude Fitzpatrick, Naples Editing Services

Address orders to:

383 Madison Avenue
New York, New York 10017

Address editorial correspondence to:

901 North Elm Street
Hinsdale, Illinois 60521

Library of Congress Catalog Card Number: 81-67245
ISBN: 0-03-059548-7
Printed in the United States of America
234-032-987654321

CBS College Publishing
The Dryden Press
Holt, Rinehart and Winston
Saunders College Publishing

PREFACE

Managerial finance continues to reflect important new developments. The changing value of the U.S. dollar dramatizes the increased importance of international finance. Strong inflationary pressures have pushed interest rates to unprecedented heights, and the resulting high cost of capital has led to profound changes in corporate financial policies and practices. Academic researchers have made significant advances, especially in the areas of capital budgeting and the cost of capital. At the same time, business practitioners are making increased use of financial theory, and feedback from the "real world" has led to revisions in this theory. These trends have dictated the revisions made in this edition of *Essentials of Managerial Finance.*

The changes reflect our experience and that of others in teaching business finance. Organizational changes have been made to provide for smoother flow and greater continuity; points that, historically, have proved troublesome to students have been clarified; and, of course, descriptive materials have been updated.

Much of the book's content is the result of our experience in executive development programs and in consulting with business firms on financial problems and policies over a number of years. This experience has helped us identify the significant responsibilities of financial managers, the fundamental problems facing firms, and the most feasible approaches to practical decision making. Some topics are conceptually difficult, but so are the issues faced. Financial managers must be prepared to handle complex problems, and solving the problems necessarily involves the use of advanced tools and techniques.

We acknowledge that the level and difficulty of the material is somewhat uneven. Certain sections simply provide descriptions of the institutional features of the financial environment and are not difficult to understand. Others—notably the material on capital budgeting, uncertainty, and the cost of capital—are by nature difficult for those unaccustomed to thinking in abstract terms. Although we could have simplified the text in many places by avoiding complex issues, we prefer to provide a basic framework based on the received doctrine, and then to present materials on a number of important but controversial issues. We hope that our presentation will stimulate the reader to further inquiry.

Changes in the Sixth Edition

The sixth edition of *Essentials of Managerial Finance* incorporates important new developments. Some of the more significant changes are described below:

1. The material on goals in Chapter 1 has been reoriented, and the discussion of managers versus stockholders has been placed in the agency-cost framework.
2. The chapter on the time value of money has been moved forward so that the material on compound interest relationships can be used in the chapters on financial ratio analysis and on working capital management.
3. A simplified presentation of continuous discounting is presented in Appendix A to Chapter 4 and some key compound interest relationships for application in subsequent topics are presented.
4. In Chapter 5, "Financial Ratio Analysis," studies on the determinants of a firm's required rate of return have suggested two more categories of financial ratios—growth measures and valuation measures. The two are logically related; they also provide a basis for integration with the later chapters on the cost of capital and valuation.
5. Appendix A to Chapter 5, "Effects of Changing Price Levels," incorporates recent developments, particularly FASB Statement No. 33, issued in December 1979.
6. Appendix B to Chapter 5, "Use of Financial Ratios in Discriminant Analysis," presents some simplified practical procedures.
7. The section on working capital management has been completely reworked. The coverage has been expanded from three chapters to five chapters. The sequence of the material has been reorganized using inventory models as a foundation for further applications. The materials include the latest materials on cash gathering methods, including concentration banking and evaluation of alternative transfer systems. New materials on credit management include the payments pattern approach and recent literature on credit decisions.
8. Appendix A to Chapter 11 presents materials on the interest rate futures markets and summarizes the literature on "riding the yield curve."
9. The materials on investment decisions under uncertainty have been streamlined and regrouped. The chapter title is "Risk and Investment Decisions" to emphasize the broader setting in which the material is placed.
10. Chapter 15 on the use of leverage has been rewritten and clarified.
11. The valuation materials are brought together in Chapter 18 after all necessary background material has been presented.
12. Chapter 19, "Capital Markets: Institutions and Behavior," incorporates the material formerly treated in a later chapter on the timing of financial decisions.
13. Appendix A to Chapter 21 reflects the recent literature on refunding decisions.
14. Appendix B to Chapter 21 includes materials on floating rate notes and other new financial instruments which have been devised in response to persistent inflation.

15. The materials on leasing (Chapter 22) incorporate the important developments in recent articles.
16. Appendix A to Chapter 23 is a simplified presentation of the basic option pricing model with illustrations of how to use it.
17. Current developments in merger activity are highlighted in Chapter 24.
18. Chapter 25, "Reorganization and Bankruptcy," discusses the new bankruptcy law, effective October 1979.
19. Chapter 27, "International Business Finance," has been reworked. The new end-of-chapter problems are particularly useful in summarizing the basic concepts.
20. All materials that have a time aspect have been updated.
21. About one-third of the end-of-chapter problems for the entire text have been changed. On all of the problems, the interest rate levels now reflect the changed conditions that the economy has experienced in recent years. We have also added new problems to round out the coverage of concepts and to provide appropriate emphasis on areas of central importance.
22. A listing of frequently used symbols is contained for convenient reference in the inside front covers of the book. Some symbols in specialized areas have been changed from previous editions so the reader can be assured that each set of symbols is used consistently in the main conceptual flow of the book.
23. A summary of the key formulas used in financial decisions is provided in the inside back covers of the book. This helps the reader obtain an overview of the entire subject matter.
24. In previous editions, we have rounded to the even number to avoid the bias of rounding upward. However, hand calculators are programmed to round upward. Since hand calculators are now so widely used, we have changed to rounding upward to avoid the discrepancies that would otherwise occur.
25. Particular attention has been given to the glossary and index. Their completeness will ease any problems occurring when instructors assign chapters out of sequence.

Ancillary Materials

Several items are available to supplement *Essentials of Managerial Finance.* First, the *Study Guide* highlights the key points in the text and presents a comprehensive set of problems similar to those at the end of each chapter. Each problem is solved in detail, so a student who has difficulty working the end-of-chapter problems can be aided by careful use of the *Study Guide.*

For the professor there is a very thorough 400-page *Instructor's Manual.* It contains alternative subject sequences and teaching methods, course outlines, answers to all text questions, solutions to all text problems, and an extensive array of test questions and problems. Also available to the instructor is a comprehensive set of acetates for use with overhead projectors, featuring solutions to selected end-of-chapter problems. As a supplement to those in the text, an additional set of problems and solutions is available to adopters. These were developed with the assistance of Roger Bey, Keith Johnson, and Ramon Johnson.

In a further attempt to keep this text up-to-date, we will publish an annual *Newsletter*. This will be provided to all adopters and will contain, among other things, fresh problems, summaries of important new research, the latest changes in tax rates, and any other available material that is relevant to teaching corporate finance.

A casebook, *Cases in Managerial Finance,* Fourth Edition, by Eugene Brigham, Roy Crum, Timothy Nantell, Robert Aubey, and Richard Pettway, is available. Books of readings can be used to supplement the text. *Issues in Managerial Finance,* Second Edition, edited by Eugene Brigham and Ramon Johnson, is a particularly useful accompaniment to *Essentials of Managerial Finance.*

Acknowledgments

In its many revisions, *Essentials* has been worked on and critically reviewed by numerous individuals. We have also received detailed comments and suggestions from instructors and students using the book. We are deeply indebted to them and to the following individuals in particular: M. Adler, E. Altman, J. Andrews, R. Aubey, P. Bacon, W. Beranek, V. Brewer, W. Brueggeman, R. Carleson, S. Choudhury, P. Cooley, C. Cox, L. Dann, H. DeAngelo, D. Fischer, R. Gray, J. Griggs, R. Haugen, S. Hawk, R. Hehre, J. Henry, A. Herrmann, G. Hettenhouse, R. Himes, C. Johnson, R. Jones, D. Kaplan, D. Knight, H. Krogh, W. Lee, D. Longmore, J. Longstreet, H. Magee, P. Malone, R. Masulis, R. Moore, T. Morton, T. Nantell, R. Nelson, R. Norgaard, J. Pappas, R. Pettit, R. Pettway, J. Pinkerton, G. Pogue, W. Regan, F. Reilly, R. Rentz, R. Richards, C. Rini, R. Roenfeldt, W. Sharpe, K. Smith, P. Smith, D. Sorenson, M. Tysseland, P. Vanderheiden, D. Woods, J. Yeakel, and D. Ziegenbein.

For providing us with detailed reviews of the fifth edition, we owe special thanks to Adrian C. Edwards, Western Michigan University; R. Larry Johnson, New Hampshire College; Larry Lang, University of Wisconsin–Oshkosh; Richard Nelson, Central Connecticut State College; R. Richardson Pettit, University of Houston; Frederick C. Scherr, West Virginia University; C. Lankford Walker, New Mexico Highlands University; and Michael E. Solt, University of Cincinnati. For their in-depth work on the manuscript of the sixth edition, we are very grateful to George Granger, East Tennessee State University; Jack S. Rader, University of South Florida; M. J. Scheuer, California State University at Northridge; Dr. Richard Ball, University of Cincinnati; Gary Simpson, Oklahoma State University; and Jonathan Welch, Northeastern University.

We are particularly indebted to John M. Wachowicz, Jr., of the University of Tennessee at Knoxville, for his work on both the fifth edition and the manuscript of the sixth edition, and to Daniel McCarty of the University of Louisville, James Gentry of the University of Illinois, and (again) Frederick Scherr of West Virginia University for their thorough review of the new working capital management section. We owe our very special thanks to Robert J. Porter of the University of South Carolina for his fine work evaluating the appropriateness and accuracy of the text's problem material.

Considerable help in preparing the sixth edition of *Essentials* was also provided by Susan Hoag, Geoffry Stern, Marilyn McElroy, and Lynn Hickman.

We would also like to thank C. Barngrover, S. Mansinghka, W. Eckardt, H. Rollins, H. Alwan, D. Wort, and J. Zumwalt for their assistance in developing the transparency program. Special thanks to Bob LeClair and The American College for their help as well.

Finally, we are indebted to the Dryden Press staff—principally Glenn Turner, Liz Widdicombe, Alan Wendt, and Kathy Richmond—for their special efforts in getting the manuscript into production and for following through to the bound book. The contributions of both Liz Widdicombe in managing the writing and reviewing of this book and Kathy Richmond in managing its production were invaluable.

The field of finance will continue to experience significant changes. It is stimulating to participate in these exciting developments, and we hope that *Essentials of Managerial Finance* will contribute to continued advances in the theory and practice of finance.

J. Fred Weston — *Los Angeles, California*
Eugene F. Brigham — *Gainesville, Florida*

January 1982

CONTENTS

Part Two
Financial Analysis, Planning, and Control 73

Part Three
Working Capital Management 163

PART ONE

FUNDAMENTAL CONCEPTS OF MANAGERIAL FINANCE

Part 1 consists of four chapters. Chapter 1, which describes the scope and nature of managerial finance, serves as an introduction to the book. Chapter 2 develops an overview of the total financial environment within which decisions are made. It deals with the role of the money and capital markets—the major financing sources and their international dimensions—and views the functions of financial managers in the perspective of this broad framework. Chapter 3 examines the tax system. It emphasizes that since a high percentage of business income is paid to the government, taxes have an important influence on many kinds of business decisions—particularly the form of business organization chosen (proprietorship, partnership, or corporation). Chapter 4 examines the role of the interest rate, or time value of money, in financial decisions.

CHAPTER 1

THE FINANCE FUNCTION

What is the finance function of the firm? What specific tasks are assigned to financial managers, and what tools and techniques are available to them for improving the performance of the firm? On a broader scale, what is the role of finance in the U.S. economy, and how can managerial finance be used to further national goals? Providing at least tentative answers to these questions is the principal purpose of this book.

The Finance Function

The financial manager's main functions are to plan for, obtain, and use funds to maximize the value of a firm. In short, the financial manager makes decisions on alternative sources and uses of funds. This definition involves several important activities. First, in planning and forecasting, the financial manager must look ahead and interact with the executives who are responsible for the general planning activities of the firm.

Second, a financial manager is concerned with investment and financing decisions and their interactions. A successful firm usually achieves a high rate of growth in sales, which requires the support of increased investments by the firm. Financial managers must determine a sound rate of sales growth and must rank alternative investment opportunities. They help decide on the specific investments to be made, and the alternative sources and forms of funds for financing these investments. Decisions must be made about the use of internal versus external funds, the use of debt versus owners' funds, and the use of long-term versus short-term financing.

Third, the financial manager interacts with other parts of the business to help the firm operate as efficiently as possible. All business decisions have financial implications, and all managers—financial and otherwise—need to take this into account. For example, marketing will affect sales growth, which will change investment requirements. Thus, marketing decisions need to take into account how they affect (and are affected by) the availability of funds, inventory policies, plant capacity utilization, etc.

The fourth aspect involves the use of the money and capital markets. As we shall explain in the following chapter, the financial manager links his firm to the financial markets in which funds are raised and in which the firm's securities are traded.

In sum, the central responsibilities of financial managers relate to decisions on investments, and how they are financed. In the performance of these functions, the financial manager's responsibilities have a direct bearing on the key decisions affecting the value of the firm.

Finance in the Organizational Structure of the Firm

Specific finance functions are typically divided between two top financial officers—the treasurer and controller. The *treasurer* handles the acquisition and custody of funds. The areas of responsibility for the *controller* are accounting, reporting, and control. In addition to these core responsibilities, the two positions often include related activities. For example, the treasurer is typically responsible for the acquisition of cash and, therefore, the relationships with commercial banks and investment bankers. The treasurer is likely to provide reports on the daily cash position of the firm and its working capital position; he is also responsible for the formulation of cash budgets. Although the controller has the main reporting responsibilities, the treasurer generally reports on cash flows and cash conservation. The treasurer is also usually responsible for credit management, insurance, and pensions management.

The controller's central function includes the recording and reporting of financial information. This typically involves the preparation of budgets and financial statements, two instruments for carrying out control responsibility. Other duties of the controller include payroll, taxes, and internal auditing.

Many variations occur in the job descriptions outlined above. In smaller organizations, the owner of the firm may carry out (or supervise the execution of) the treasurer and controller functions. Also in small firms, one financial officer may perform both functions under the title of treasurer, controller, or vice president of finance.

Larger organizations often have additional financial officers. Typically, the *vice president of finance* reports directly to the president. The treasurer and controller in turn report to the vice president of finance. Characteristically, the vice president of finance is the representative to the president and chairman of the board and formulates general financial policy. The vice president of finance is also responsible for the analytical aspects of the treasurer's and controller's work.

Some large firms include a fourth corporate officer, whose activities are sometimes considered to be financial in nature—the *corporate secretary*. The corporate secretary is responsible for communications relating to the company's financial instruments. These encompass legal affairs and recording in connection with top-level committee meetings. The corporate secretary's duties include record keeping in connection with the instruments of ownership, and financial records related to the borrowing activities of the company.

The job descriptions of these four financial officers vary from company to company. Company history and the abilities of individual officers also figure heavily in this variation. A very able and active financial officer will be involved in all top management policies and decisions. Such involvement often provides a training ground for the movement of the chief financial officer into the top management position of the company—the president or chief executive officer.

In addition to individual financial officers, larger enterprises use *finance committees*. Ideally, a committee assembles persons of different backgrounds and abilities to formulate policies and decisions. Finance committees are used for two broad types of reasons. The first is that in the acquisition of funds significant aspects of major financial market developments must be understood. These involve developments of broad significance and require a wide scope of knowledge and sound judgment. For example, obtaining outside funds represents a major decision. The difference of a quarter- or half-percent in interest rates may represent a large amount of money in absolute terms. When such firms as IBM, General Motors, and Kellogg borrow $600 million, a difference of one-half of one percent amounts to $3 million per year. Therefore, the judgments of senior managers with a financial background are valuable in arriving at decisions with bankers on the terms of a loan.

Second, the finance committee will characteristically have major responsibility for administering the capital and the operating budgets. It will work closely with the board of directors in this connection. Typically in a successful company, the operating and investment programs proposed will exceed the amount of funds the company has available. Thus some programs will be denied funding. By using a committee, decisions are made on the input of many minds, and dissatisfactions will not be centered on any one person.

Finance committees are classified into further subgroups in larger firms. In addition to the general finance committee, there may be a *capital appropriations committee* responsible primarily for capital budgets and expenditures. A *budget committee* may deal primarily with the operating budgets of the forthcoming year. There may also be a *pension committee* because the amounts of funds involved are so large.

In addition, there may be a *salary and profit-sharing committee*. Such a group would be responsible for planning the salary administration objectives as well as for setting classifications and compensation for top-level officers. The work of the salary and profit-sharing committee is usually tied to the general planning and control processes of the firm and seeks to provide the rewards and penalties necessary to make the planning and control system work effectively.

The finance function is typically close to the top in the organizational structure of the firm because financial decisions are crucial to the survival and success of the firm. Finance typically plays an important role in the major planning and control activities of the firm. All important episodes in the life of a corporation have major financial implications. Such decisions include adding a new product line or reducing participation in an old one; expanding or adding a plant or changing locations; selling additional new securities; and entering into leasing arrangements. These decisions have a lasting effect upon the long-run profitability of the firm and, therefore, require top management consideration. Hence, finance is typically involved in high-level decisions of the firm.

Goals of the Firm

The goal of financial management is to maximize the value of the firm. Financial managers should seek to balance the interests of owners and creditors and other constituencies of the firm (labor, consumers, suppliers).

There are potential conflicts between a firm's owners and its creditors. For example, consider a firm financed half from the owners' funds and half from debt funds borrowed at a fixed interest rate (such as 10 percent). No matter how high the firm's earnings, the bondholders still receive only their 10 percent return. Yet if the firm is fantastically successful, the market value of the ownership funds (the common stock of the company) is likely to rise greatly.

Thus, if the company does very well, the value of its common stock will increase, while the "value" of the firm's debt is not likely to be greatly affected. On the other hand, if the firm does poorly, the claims of the debtholders will have to be honored first and the value of the common stock will decline greatly. Thus, the value of the ownership shares provides a good index for measuring the degree of a company's effectiveness in performance. It is for this reason that the goal of financial management is generally expressed in terms of maximizing the value of the ownership shares of the firm—in short, maximizing share price.

By formulating clear objectives in terms of stock price values, the discipline of the financial markets is implemented. Thus, firms that perform better than others have higher stock prices and can raise additional funds under more favorable terms. When funds go to firms with favorable stock price trends, the economy's resources are thereby directed to their most efficient uses. For this reason, finance literature has generally adopted the basic postulate of maximizing the price of the firm's common stock. Financial theories have been developed from this axiom and receive considerable support from empirical studies. Shareholder wealth maximization also provides a basis for rational decision making with respect to a wide range of financial issues faced by the firm. Within this general framework of share-price maximization, a number of important distinctions should be kept in mind.

Shareholders versus Bondholders

The goal of maximizing share price does not imply that managers should seek to improve the value of common stock at the expense of bondholders. For example, managers should not substantially alter the riskiness of the firm's product-market investment activities. Riskier investments, if they are successful, will benefit the shareholders greatly. On the other hand, risky investments that fail will reduce the security to bondholders and decrease bond values. As a practical matter, if a firm does not give strong assurances to bondholders that investment policies will not be changed to their disadvantage, it must pay interest rates high enough to compensate bondholders against the possibility of such adverse policy changes.

Managers versus Securities Owners

Another concern is that managers may place their own goals and welfare ahead of the interests of shareholders and bondholders. M. C. Jensen and W. H. Meckling have developed the most analytical treatment of the relationship between managers and owners of securities.[1] In their formulation, an agency problem arises when a manager owns less than the total common stock of the firm. This partial ownership can lead a manager to work less strenuously than he might otherwise and to consume more perquisites (luxurious offices, first-class travel, company car) because other owners bear part of the costs.

Counterarguments assert that various incentives stimulate managers to operate in the best interests of the firm. Compensation for managers often takes the form of bonuses tied to profits, or stock options tied to increasing the value of the firm's common stock. Moreover, shareholders have the ultimate power to replace

[1] M. C. Jensen and W. H. Meckling, "Theory of the Firm: Managerial Behavior, Agency Costs and Ownership Structure," *Journal of Financial Economics* 3 (October 1976), pp. 350–60.

unsatisfactory managers; they do, in fact, exercise this power. Just the threat of its use may keep managers functioning in the best interests of the firm. E. F. Fama observes that these pressures are reinforced by the managerial labor market through its continuing reassessments of the value of the human capital of managers on the basis of the relationships between their potential or contracted performance and their actual performance.[2]

Social Responsibility

A third and highly important aspect of the goals of the firm and the goals of financial management is consideration of social responsibility. There are a number of dimensions to be taken into account. First, if financial management seeks to maximize share price, this requires efficient, well-managed operations related to consumer demand patterns. Successful firms are at the forefront of efficiency and innovation so that value maximization leads to new products, new technologies, and greater employment. Hence, the more successful the firm in value maximization, the better the quality and quantity of the total "pie" to be distributed.

But in recent years "externalities" (such as pollution, product safety, and job safety) have increased in importance. As economic agents whose actions have considerable impact, business firms must take into account the effects of their policies and actions on society as a whole. No one—least of all large firms—can ignore the obligations of responsible citizenship.

It has long been recognized that the external economic environment is highly important to a firm's decision making. Fluctuations in the overall level of business activity and related changes in the conditions of financial markets are important aspects of the external environment. In a like manner, the expectations of workers, consumers, and various interest groups create other dimensions of the external environment that firms must respond to in order to achieve long-run wealth maximization. Indeed, responsiveness to these new and powerful constituencies may be required for the survival of the private enterprise system. This point of view argues that business firms simply must recognize a wider range of influences in the external environment.

But there are many different viewpoints on what is best for society. By what authority do businesses have the right to allocate funds in terms of their own views of the social good? In addition, if some firms attempt to be socially responsible and their costs thereby increase substantially, they will be at a disadvantage if their competitors do not incur the same costs. Because of these considerations, some would argue that social programs should be formulated through the processes of representative government. This implies that most cost-increasing programs should be enacted by the government and put on a mandatory rather than a voluntary basis, at least initially, to ensure that their burden rests uniformly on all businesses. However, what is first imposed by government may be too much and too fast, and after some experience the requirements may need modification. An example is the former requirement that seat belts be installed in such a way that a car could not be started unless the belts were fastened. This requirement was later modified.

[2] E. F. Fama, "Agency Problems and the Theory of the Firm," *Journal of Political Economy* 88 (April 1980), pp. 288–307.

It is critical that industry and government cooperate in establishing rules for corporate behavior and that firms follow the spirit as well as the letter of the law in their actions. Thus, constraints become the rules of the game, and firms should strive to maximize shareholder wealth within the external constraints. Throughout this book, we shall assume that managements operate in this manner.

Value Maximization as a Goal

We have discussed some broad and general aspects of value maximization as a goal. Now we turn to a consideration of some technical distinctions and some implementation aspects of the role of financial management in value maximization.

It is important to recognize that value maximization is broader than "profit maximization." This is true for several reasons. First, maximizing value takes the time value of money into account. Funds that are received this year have more value than funds that may be received ten years from now. Second, value takes the riskiness of the income stream into account. For example, the rate of return required on riskless government securities would be lower than the rate of return required on an investment in starting a new business.

Third, the "quality" of the expected future fund flows may vary. Profit figures can vary widely depending upon the accounting rules and conventions used. Value maximization avoids some of these problems by emphasizing cash or fund flows rather than being dependent on the way that profits or net income are measured. There is considerable evidence that the financial markets "see through" differences in accounting procedures and get closer to "true, underlying values."

Thus, value maximization is broader and more general than profit maximization. It provides a basis for rigorous analysis for making choices among alternatives. It provides a solid basis for decision making. Hence, value maximization is the unifying conceptual idea used throughout the book.

Performance Measurement by the Financial Markets

The basic finance functions must be performed in all types of organizations. What is unique about business organizations is that they are directly and measurably subject to the discipline of the financial markets. These markets are continuously determining the valuations of business firms' securities, thereby providing measures of the firms' performance.[3] A consequence of this continuous assessment of a firm by the capital markets is the change in its valuation level (stock market price).

The presence of the capital market's continuous assessment therefore stimulates efficiency and provides incentive to business managers to improve their performance.

The Risk-Return Tradeoff

Financial decisions affect the level of a firm's stock prices by influencing the size of the cash flow stream and the riskiness of the firm. These relationships are diagramed in Figure 1.1. Policy decisions, which are subject to government con-

[3] The financial markets discussed in Chapter 2 provide valuation of firms whose shares are traded. The relationships between return and risk also provide the basis for the valuation of companies whose ownership shares are not actively traded.

Figure 1.1 **Valuation as the Central Focus of the Finance Function**

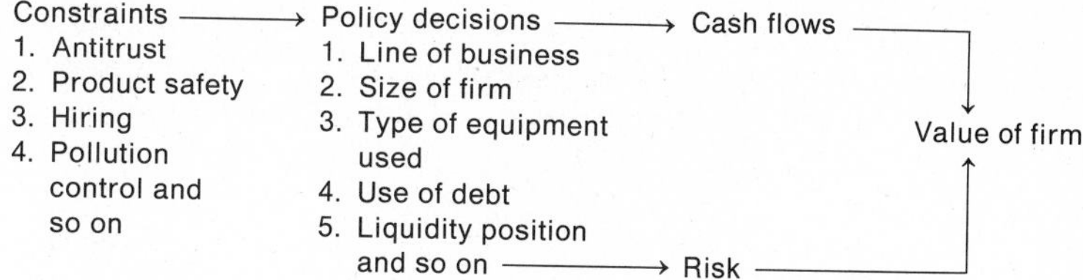

straints, affect both profitability and risk; these two factors jointly determine the value of the firm.

The primary policy decision is choosing the industry in which the firm will operate. When this choice has been made, profitability and risk are further influenced by decisions relating to the size of the firm, its growth rate, the types and amounts of equipment used, the extent to which debt is employed, the firm's liquidity position, and so on.

Such decisions generally affect both risk and profitability. An increase in the cash position, for instance, reduces risk; however, since cash is not an earning asset, converting other assets to cash also reduces profitability. Similarly, the use of additional debt raises the rate of return, or the profitability, on the stockholders' net worth; at the same time, more debt means more risk. The financial manager seeks to strike the particular balance between risk and profitability that will maximize the wealth of the firm's stockholders—called the *risk-return tradeoff.* Most financial decisions involve such tradeoffs.

The Changing Role of Financial Management

As with many things in the contemporary world, financial management has undergone significant changes over the years. When finance first emerged as a separate field of study in the early 1900s, the emphasis was on legalistic matters such as mergers, consolidations, the formation of new firms, and the various types of securities issued by corporations. Industrialization was sweeping the country, and the critical problem faced by firms was obtaining capital for expansion. The capital markets were relatively primitive, and transfers of funds from individual savers to businesses were quite difficult. Accounting statements of earnings and asset values were unreliable, and stock trading by insiders and manipulators caused prices to fluctuate wildly; consequently, investors were reluctant to purchase stocks and bonds. In this environment, it is easy to see why finance concentrated so heavily on legal issues relating to the issuance of securities.

The emphasis remained on securities through the 1920s; however, radical changes occurred during the depression of the 1930s. Business failures during that period caused finance to focus on bankruptcy and reorganization, corporate liquidity, and government regulation of securities markets. Finance was still a descriptive, legalistic subject, but the emphasis shifted to survival rather than expansion.

During the 1940s and early 1950s, finance continued to be taught as a descriptive, institutional subject, viewed from the outside rather than from within the firm's management. However, some effort was devoted to budgeting and other internal control procedures, and, stimulated by the work of Joel Dean, capital budgeting began to receive attention.[4]

The evolutionary pace quickened during the late 1950s. While the right-hand side of the balance sheet (liabilities and capital) had received more attention in the earlier era, increasing emphasis was placed on asset analysis during the last half of that decade. Mathematical models were developed and applied to inventories, cash, accounts receivable, and fixed assets. Increasingly, the focus of finance shifted from the outsider's to the insider's point of view, as financial decisions within the firm were recognized to be the critical issues in corporate finance. Descriptive, institutional materials on capital markets and financing instruments were still studied, but these topics were considered within the context of corporate financial decisions.

The emphasis on decision making has continued in recent years. First, there has been increasing belief that sound capital budgeting procedures require accurate measurements of the cost of capital. Accordingly, ways of quantifying the cost of capital now play a key role in finance. Second, capital has been in short supply, rekindling the old interest in ways of raising funds. Third, there has been continued merger activity, which has led to renewed interest in takeovers. Fourth, accelerated progress in transportation and communications has brought the countries of the world closer together; this in turn has stimulated interest in international finance. Fifth, there is an increasing awareness of social problems such as air and water pollution, work safety, urban blight, and unemployment among minorities. Finding the firm's appropriate role in efforts to solve these problems demands an increasing proportion of the time of financial managers. Finally, another important change in the economic environment is the persistent high rate of inflation.

The Impact of Inflation on Financial Management

Inflation has become such a pervasive part of the economic environment that it must be taken into account as an important new influence on business financial decisions. During the 1950s and 1960s prices rose at an average rate of about 1 to 2 percent per year, but in the 1970s the rate of inflation in some years rose to more than 10 percent. The U.S. economy entered the 1980s with inflation again above 10 percent. This "double-digit" inflation rate has had a tremendous impact on business firms, especially on their financial operations. As a result, many traditional financial policies and practices are changing. The many influences of inflation will be taken into account throughout the book. Some major effects of inflation are briefly sketched here.

Interest Rates The rate of interest on U.S. government securities (called the *default-free rate*) consists of a "real rate of interest" of 2 to 3 percent plus an "inflation premium" that reflects the expected long-run rate of inflation. Accordingly, an increase in the rate of inflation is quickly translated into higher default-free interest rates. The cost of money to firms is the default-free rate plus a risk premium, so inflation-induced increases in the default-free rate are also reflected in business borrowing rates.

[4] Joel Dean, *Capital Budgeting* (New York: Columbia University Press, 1951).

Planning Difficulties Businesses operate on the basis of long-run plans. For example, a firm builds a plant only after making a thorough analysis of expected costs and revenues over the life of the plant. Reaching such estimates is not easy under the best of conditions. During rapid inflation, when labor and materials costs are changing unevenly, accurate forecasts are especially important yet exceedingly difficult to make.

Demand for Capital Inflation increases the amount of capital required to conduct a given volume of business. When inventories are sold, they must be replaced with more expensive goods. The costs of expanding or replacing plants are also greater, while workers demand higher wages. All these things put pressure on financial managers to raise additional capital. At the same time, in an effort to hold down the rate of inflation, the Federal Reserve System may restrict the supply of loanable funds. The ensuing scramble for limited funds drives interest rates still higher.

Bond Price Declines Long-term bond prices fall as interest rates rise. In the effort to protect themselves against such capital losses, lenders are beginning (1) to put more funds into short-term rather than long-term debt, and (2) to insist upon bonds whose interest rates vary with "the general level of interest rates" as measured by an index of interest rates. Brazil and other inflation-plagued South American countries have used such indexed bonds for years. Unless inflation in the United States is controlled, their use is likely to increase in this country.

Accounting Problems With high rates of inflation, reported profits are distorted. The sale of low-cost inventories results in higher reported profits, but cash flows are held down as firms restock with higher-cost inventories. Similarly, depreciation charges are inadequate, since they do not reflect the new costs of replacing plant and equipment. Higher reported profits caused by inadequate inventory valuation and depreciation charges result in higher income taxes and reduced cash flows. If a firm plans dividends and capital expenditures based on these "paper" profits, it may develop serious financial problems.

Inflation is a disturbing and challenging new experience for United States financial managers. If it persists, financial policies and practices will undergo still further modifications.

Organization of This Book

The aim of this book is to explain the procedures, practices, and policies by which financial management can contribute to the successful performance of organizations. We begin with an emphasis on the tradeoffs between risk and return in seeking to make decisions that will maximize the value of the firm. Each subsequent topic is treated within this basic framework.

The seven major parts of the book are as follows:

1. Fundamental Concepts of Managerial Finance
2. Financial Analysis, Planning and Control
3. Working Capital Management
4. Investment Decisions
5. The Cost of Capital and Valuation

6. Long-Term Financing Decisions
7. Integrated Topics in Managerial Finance

Part 1 includes basic background material on financial markets, tax laws, and the use of interest rates. Part 2 covers financial analysis, financial models of the firm, and planning and control systems. It provides a foundation for Part 3, which covers all aspects of working capital management.

Part 4 discusses the investment decisions of the firm in the framework of capital budgeting under certainty and uncertainty. Part 5 deals with the cost of capital concepts required both for capital budgeting analysis and for the valuation of the firm.

With the analytic framework established, the long-term financing decisions of the firm are treated in Part 6. This section builds on the financial structure issues discussed in the cost of capital materials, but in a setting related to individual financial decisions. Also, the increasingly important uses of warrants, convertibles, and other forms of options are developed. Finally, in Part 7, the general concepts and principles of managerial finance are applied in the areas of mergers, reorganization, small firm finance, and international business finance.

Summary

The main functions of financial managers are to plan for, acquire, and utilize funds to make the maximum contribution to the efficient operation of an organization. This requires knowledge of the financial markets from which funds are drawn. It requires a knowledge of how to make sound investment decisions and how to stimulate efficient operations in the organization. A large number of alternative sources and uses of funds will have to be considered. There are always alternative choices involved in financial decisions. The choices include the use of internal versus external funds, long-term versus short-term projects, long-term versus short-term fund sources, a higher rate of growth versus a lower rate of growth, and so on.

Questions

1.1 What are the main functions of financial managers?

1.2 Why is value maximization a better operating goal than profit maximization?

1.3 What are the issues in the conflict of interest between managers and the suppliers of funds and how can they be resolved?

1.4 What are the potential conflicts of interest between shareholders and bondholders? How can they be resolved?

1.5 What role does social responsibility have in formulating business and financial goals?

1.6 What have been the major developmental periods in the field of finance, and what circumstances led to the evolution of the emphasis in each period?

1.7 What is the nature of the risk-return tradeoff faced in financial decision making?

CHAPTER 2

THE FINANCIAL ENVIRONMENT

An important part of the environment within which financial managers function is the financial sector of the economy, which consists of financial markets, financial institutions, and financial instruments. This chapter will discuss each of these three major aspects of the financial environment.

Financial Markets

The financial manager functions in a complex financial network because the savings and investment functions in a modern economy are performed by different economic agents. For savings surplus units, savings exceed their investment in real assets, and they own financial assets. For savings deficit units, current savings are less than investment in real assets so they issue financial liabilities. The savings deficit units issue a wide variety of financial claims, including promissory notes, bonds, and common stocks.

The process by which financial assets and liabilities are created is illustrated by Figure 2.1. The savings account owner makes a deposit in a bank (financial institution). This deposit represents an asset to the depositor and a liability to the bank. The bank may in turn invest the funds in liquid assets such as government bonds. Now, suppose a potential home owner borrows from the bank in order to buy a house. The house is a real asset on which the home owner incurs a financial liability—a mortgage—in order to complete the purchase. The home owner's mortgage (a financial liability) represents a financial asset to the bank.

Figure 2.1

Financial Assets and Financial Liabilities[a]

A. The effect of a deposit

Savings account owner (lender)	
Deposit in FI	Net worth

Bank—financial institution (borrower)	
Government bonds	Deposits

B. The effect of a mortgage loan

Home owner (borrower)	
Real asset House	*Financial liability* Mortgage

Bank—financial institution (lender)	
Financial asset Mortgage	*Financial liability* Deposits

[a] From a suggestion by Professor Larry Lang, University of Wisconsin–Oshkosh, Oshkosh, Wisconsin.

Consider another example. When a person buys goods on credit from a department store, the purchase price is added to "accounts receivable" on the store's books. The amount payable by the person who has purchased goods on credit represents a financial liability to that person.

A financial transaction results in the simultaneous creation of a financial asset and a financial liability. The creation and transfer of such assets and liabilities constitute *financial markets*. The nature of financial markets can be further explained by analogy to the market for actual goods, such as automobiles. The "automobile market" is defined by all transactions in automobiles, whether they occur at the auto dealer's showroom, at wholesale auctions of used cars, or at individuals' homes. These transactions all constitute the automobile market because they make up part of the total demand and supply curves for autos.

Similarly, financial markets are comprised of all trades that result in the creation of financial assets and financial liabilities. Some trades are made through organized institutions such as the New York Stock Exchange or the regional stock exchanges. A large number are made through the thousands of brokers and dealers who buy and sell securities (comprising what is called the "over-the-counter market"). Individual transactions with department stores, savings banks, or other financial institutions also create financial assets and financial liabilities. Thus financial markets are not specific physical structures; nor are they remote. Everyone is involved in them to some degree.

Continuing the auto analogy, just as a distinction is made between a new car market and a used car market because somewhat different demand and supply influences operate in each, different segments of the financial markets are also categorized and named. When the financial claims and obligations bought and sold have a maturity of less than one year, the transactions constitute *money markets*. When maturities of the instruments traded are more than one year, the markets are referred to as *capital markets*. The latter term is somewhat confusing because real capital in an economy is represented by things such as plants, machinery, and equipment. But long-term financial instruments are regarded as ultimately representing claims on the real resources in an economy, and for that reason the markets in which these instruments are traded are referred to as capital markets.

Financing Sources and Financial Intermediation

The financial markets, composed of money markets and capital markets, provide a mechanism through which the financial manager obtains funds from a wide range of financing sources.

Commercial banks are defined by their ability to accept demand deposits subject to transfer by depositors' checks. Such checks represent a widely accepted medium of exchange, accounting for more than 90 percent of the transactions that take place. Savings and loan associations receive funds mainly from passbook savings and invest them primarily in real estate mortgages representing long-term borrowing (mostly by individuals). Finance companies are business firms whose main activity is making loans to other business firms and to individuals. Life insurance companies sell protection against the loss of income from premature death or disability. The insurance policies they sell typically have a savings element in them. Pension funds collect contributions from employees and/or employers to make periodic payments upon employees' retirement. Investment funds or mutual funds sell shares to investors and use the proceeds to purchase already existing equity securities.

Investment bankers buy new issues of securities from business firms at a guaranteed agreed-upon price and immediately resell them to investors. As shown in Figure 2.2, the investment banker is an intermediary between business firms and investors. The business firms issue securities (certificates of debt or ownership, i.e., bonds or stock) and receive funds; the investors use their funds to purchase securities.

Figure 2.2

The Role of the Investment Banker[a]

[a] Figures 2.2 and 2.3 appear courtesy of Professor Larry Lang, University of Wisconsin–Oshkosh, Oshkosh, Wisconsin.

Financial firms that act simply as agents linking buyers and sellers are called investment brokers. Investment dealers are those who purchase from sellers for their own accounts and ultimately resell to other buyers. While investment bankers (discussed in Chapter 19) operate in the new issues market, brokers and dealers trade already issued securities. Other potential sources of funds are households, other business firms, and governments. At any point in time some of these will be borrowers and others lenders.

Financial intermediation is accomplished through transactions in the financial markets that bring the savings surplus units together with the savings deficit units so that savings can be redistributed into their most productive uses. The specialized business firms whose activities include the creation of financial assets and liabilities are called *financial intermediaries*. The process of financial intermediation is illustrated in Figure 2.3. The financial intermediary provides a link between borrowers and lenders. The financial intermediary may simply buy a firm's securities and resell them (as do investment bankers and dealers) or create its own financial instruments based on deposits by investors (the mortgages of savings and loan associations).

Figure 2.3

The Role of the Financial Intermediary

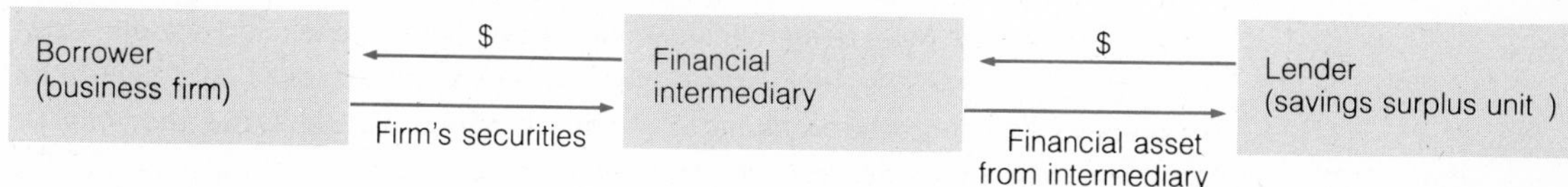

Without these intermediaries and the processes of financial intermediation, the allocation of savings into real investment would be limited by whatever the distribution of savings happened to be. With financial intermediation, savings are transferred to economic units that have opportunities for profitable investment. In the process, real resources are allocated more effectively, and real output for the economy as a whole is increased.

Financial managers have important responsibilities in the financial intermediation process. They are the part of the process by which funds are allocated to their most productive uses. Therefore, the functions of financial managers can now be restated in the perspective of this broader social framework. In the aggregate, business firms are savings deficit units that obtain funds to make investments to increase the supply of goods and services. Financial managers utilize financial markets to obtain external funds. How should the funds be acquired efficiently? What is the most economical mix of financing to be obtained? From what alternative sources and in what specific forms should the funds be raised? What should be the timing and forms of returns and repayments to financing sources?

Since funds are acquired as part of the process by which resources are allocated to their most productive uses, financial managers have responsibility for effectively using funds. To what projects and products should the funds be allocated? What assets and resources should the organization acquire in order to produce its products and services? What standards and controls should monitor the effective utilization of funds allocated among the segments of operating activities? How should the planning and control of funds be managed so the organization will produce and sell its products and services most efficiently? The financial manager's major responsibility is to implement these choices in the various financial markets to meet the firm's capital requirements.

The Federal Reserve System

Fundamental to an understanding of the behavior of the money and capital markets is an analysis of the role of the Federal Reserve System. The Fed, as it is called, has a set of instruments with which to influence the operations of commercial banks, whose loan and investment activities in turn have an important influence on the cost and availability of money. The most powerful of the Fed's instruments, hence the one used most sparingly, is changing reserve requirements (the percentage of deposits that must be kept in reserve with the Fed). The one most often used is changing the pattern of open-market operations (the Fed's buying and selling of securities, which expands and contracts the amount of funds in the public's hands).

Changes in the discount rate (the interest rate charged to commercial banks when they borrow from Federal Reserve banks) are likely to have more psychological influence than direct quantitative effect. These changes represent an implicit announcement by Federal Reserve authorities that a change in economic conditions has occurred and that the new conditions call for a tightening or easing of monetary conditions. The data demonstrate that increases in the Federal Reserve bank discount rate have been followed by rising interest rate levels and decreases by lowered levels. When the Federal Reserve System purchases or sells securities in the open market, makes changes in the discount rate, or varies the reserve requirement, interest rates on most securities will consequently change.

Fiscal Policy

The fiscal policy of the federal government has great impact on movements in interest rates. A cash budget deficit represents a stimulating influence by the federal government, and a cash surplus exerts a restraining influence. However, this generalization must be modified to reflect the way a deficit is financed and the way a surplus is used. To have the most stimulating effect, a deficit should be financed by a sale of securities through the banking system, particularly the central bank; this provides a maximum amount of bank reserves and permits a multiple expansion in the money supply. To have the most restrictive effect, the surplus should be used to retire bonds held by the banking system, particularly the central bank, thereby reducing bank reserves and causing a multiple contraction in the supply of money.

The impact of Treasury financing programs varies. Ordinarily, when the Treasury needs to draw funds from the money market, it competes with other potential users of funds; the result may be a rise in interest rate levels. However, the desire to hold down interest rates also influences Treasury and Federal Reserve policy. To ensure the success of a large new offering, Federal Reserve authorities may temporarily ease money conditions—a procedure that tends to soften interest rates. If the Treasury encounters resistance in selling securities in the nonbanking sector, it may sell them in large volume to the commercial banking system, which expands its reserves and thereby increases the monetary base. This change in turn tends to lower the level of interest rates.

Securities Markets

Other important institutions in the operation of the financial system are the securities markets. One basis for classifying securities markets is the distinction between *primary markets*, in which stocks and bonds are initially sold, and *secondary markets*, in which they are subsequently traded. Initial sales of securities are made by investment banking firms, which purchase them from the issuing firm and sell them through an underwriting syndicate or group (see Figure 2.2). Subsequent transactions can take place on organized securities exchanges or in less formal markets. The operations of securities markets provide a framework within which the nature of investment banking and the new issues market (discussed in Chapter 19) can be understood. The secondary market—the organized security exchanges, and the over-the-counter markets, the third market, and the fourth market—will be discussed in this section.

The major exchange is the New York Stock Exchange (NYSE), on which about 1,500 common stocks are listed, accounting for more than 80 percent of the almost $200 billion of annual dollar volume of trading and somewhat less than 80 percent of the more than 6 billion annual share volume of trading. The American Stock Exchange, with 1,300 stocks traded, is second in volume, accounting for under 10 percent of dollar volume and somewhat over 10 percent of share volume. About 350 stocks are traded on one or more of the eleven registered regional exchanges, accounting for about 2 to 5 percent of volume in the three largest regional exchanges and less than 1 percent of total volume in the remaining ones.

The organized security exchanges are tangible physical entities. Each of the larger ones occupies its own building and has specifically designated members and an elected governing body—its board of governors. Only members have the right to trade on the exchange. Memberships, called "seats," are regularly bought and sold. In 1968 seats on the NYSE sold at a record high of $515,000; in 1974 they sold for about $85,000. During 1977 they ranged between $35,000 and $95,000.[1]

Like other markets, a security exchange facilitates communication between buyers and sellers. For example, Merrill Lynch, Pierce, Fenner & Smith (the largest brokerage firm), may receive an order in its Atlanta office from a customer who wants to buy 100 shares of General Motors stock. Simultaneously, a brokerage house in Denver may receive an order from a customer wishing to sell 100 shares of GM stock. Each broker communicates with his or her firm's representative on the NYSE. Other brokers throughout the country are also communicating with their own exchange members. Members with sell orders offer the shares for sale, and they are bid for by members with buy orders. Thus, the exchanges operate as *auction markets*.[2]

Benefits Provided by Security Exchanges

Organized security exchanges are said to provide at least four important benefits to businesses.

1. Security exchanges facilitate the investment process by providing a marketplace in which to conduct efficient and relatively inexpensive transactions. Investors are thus assured that they will have a place in which to sell their securities if they decide to do so. The increased liquidity provided by the exchanges makes investors willing to accept a lower rate of return on securities than they would otherwise require. This means that exchanges lower the cost of capital to businesses.
2. By providing a market, exchanges create an institution in which continuous transactions test the values of securities. The purchases and sales of securities record judgments on the values and prospects of companies. Those whose prospects are judged favorably by the investment community have higher values, which facilitate new financing and growth.
3. Security prices are relatively more stable because of the operation of the security exchanges. Organized markets improve liquidity by providing continuous markets that make for more frequent but smaller price changes. In the absence of organized markets, price changes are less frequent but larger.
4. The securities markets aid in the digestion of new security issues and facilitate their successful flotation.

Although these benefits are important, not all firms can use them. However, some firms that cannot utilize the exchanges can get many of the same benefits by having their securities traded in the over-the-counter market.

The securities markets are in a state of flux. After four years of research and investigation, Congress enacted the Securities Acts Amendments of 1975.[3] These statutes depart from the concept of self-regulation that had previously been followed

[1] New York Stock Exchange, *1978 Fact Book* (New York: New York Stock Exchange, 1978), p. 58.

[2] This discussion is highly simplified. The exchanges have members, known as "specialists," who facilitate the trading process by keeping an inventory of shares of the stocks in which they specialize. If a buy order comes in at a time when no sell order arrives, the specialist may sell off some inventory. Similarly, if a sell order comes in, the specialist will buy and add to inventory.

[3] The original Securities Acts of 1933 and 1934 which established the Securities and Exchange Commission (SEC) for federal regulation of the financial markets are discussed in Chapter 19.

in the relationships between the government and the securities industry. They state that no national securities exchange can impose a schedule of minimum fixed commission rates. While it is still too early to judge their impact, one likely effect of the laws is the "unbundling" of joint services such as research reports from the buying and selling activities provided by brokerage firms.

The amendments also provide for the development of a national market system. Two concepts of a central market system have emerged. One, sponsored by the NYSE, envisions a single trading exchange. The other sees competitive trading in a number of places linked together by a system of communications, including clearing and settlement facilities. The SEC is empowered to exercise leadership in developing a central market system.

Over-the-Counter (OTC) Security Markets

Over-the-counter security markets is the term used for all the buying and selling activity in securities that does not take place on a stock exchange. The OTC market includes stocks of all types and for all sizes of U.S. corporations, as well as some foreign issues. There are approximately 30,000 common stocks of public corporations in the OTC market but only about 10,000 are actively traded. This is about three times the number of companies listed on the organized exchanges. In addition, the OTC market is where transactions take place in (1) almost all bonds of U.S. corporations; (2) almost all bonds of federal, state, and local governments; (3) open-end investment company shares of mutual funds; (4) new issues of securities; (5) most secondary distributions of large blocks of stock, regardless of whether they are listed on an exchange; and (6) stocks of most of the country's banks and insurance companies.

The exchanges operate as auction markets; the trading process is achieved through agents making transactions at one geographically centralized exchange location. On an exchange, members known as specialists are responsible for matching buy and sell orders and for maintaining an orderly market in a particular security. In contrast, the OTC market is a dealer market—that is, business is conducted across the country by broker/dealers known as market makers. These dealers stand ready to buy and sell securities in a manner similar to wholesale suppliers of goods or merchandise. The exchanges are used to match buy and sell orders that come in more or less simultaneously. But if a stock is traded less frequently, perhaps because it is a new or small firm, matching buy and sell orders might require an extended period of time. To avoid this problem, some broker/dealer firms maintain an inventory of stocks. They buy when individual investors want to sell and sell when investors want to buy. At one time these securities were kept in a safe; when they were bought and sold, they were literally passed "over the counter."

The brokers and dealers operating in the OTC markets communicate through a network of private wires and telephone lines and, since 1971, by an electronic quotation system called NASDAQ, whose letters stand for the National Association of Securities Dealers Automated Quotation system. NASDAQ is a computerized system that enables current price quotations to be displayed on terminals in subscribers' offices.

The term *third market* refers to OTC trading in listed securities by nonmembers of an exchange. It also includes trades of large blocks of listed stocks off the floor of the exchange, with a brokerage house acting as intermediary between two institutional investors.

The *fourth market* refers to direct transfers of blocks of stock among institutional investors without an intermediary broker. A well-known example is the arrangement between the Ford Foundation and the Rockefeller Foundation to exchange the common stocks of the Ford Motor Co. and Standard Oil of New Jersey. Such transactions have led to the development of *Instinet*, a computerized quotation system with display terminals to provide communications among major institutional investors.

The development of the third and fourth markets reflects the increased importance of institutional investors in stock trading. During the decade of the 1960s, for example, the equity holdings of private, noninsured pension funds rose by over 500 percent, of state and local retirement funds by over 2,800 percent, and of investment companies (mutual funds) by over 300 percent. New York Stock Exchange studies indicate that by the mid-1970s these institutions held a third of NYSE-listed stocks and accounted for over half the dollar volume on the NYSE.

In terms of numbers of issues, the majority of stocks are traded over the counter. However, because the stocks of larger companies are listed on the exchanges, it is estimated that two-thirds of the dollar volume of stock trading takes place on the exchanges. The situation is reversed in the bond market. Although the bonds of a number of the larger companies are listed on the NYSE bond list, over 95 percent of bond transactions take place in the OTC market. The reason for this is that bonds typically are traded among the large financial institutions (for example, life insurance companies and pension funds), which deal in very large blocks of securities. It is relatively easy for the OTC bond dealers to arrange the transfer of large blocks of bonds among the relatively few holders of the bonds. It would be impossible to conduct similar operations in the stock market among the literally millions of large and small stockholders.

Decision to List Stock

The exchanges have certain requirements that firms must meet before their stock can be listed; these requirements relate to size of company, number of years in business, earnings record, number of shares outstanding and their market value, and the like. In general, requirements become more stringent as we move from the regional exchanges toward the NYSE.

The firm itself makes the decision on whether to seek to list its securities on an exchange. Typically, the stock of a new and small company is traded over the counter; there is simply not enough activity to justify the use of an auction market for such stocks. As the company grows and establishes an earnings record, expands the number of shares outstanding, and increases its list of stockholders, it may decide to apply for listing on one of the regional exchanges. For example, a Chicago company may list on the Midwest Stock Exchange and a West Coast company on the Pacific Stock Exchange. As the company grows still more and its stock becomes distributed throughout the country, it may seek a listing on the American Stock Exchange, the smaller of the two national exchanges. Finally, if it becomes one of the nation's leading firms, it may switch to the Big Board, the New York Stock Exchange—if it qualifies.

Many people believe that listing is beneficial to both the company and its stockholders. Listed companies receive a certain amount of free advertising and publicity, and the status of being listed enhances their prestige and reputation. This probably has a beneficial effect on the sales of the firms' products, and is advantageous in terms of lowering the required rate of return on the common stock. Investors respond favorably to increased information, increased liquidity, and increased prestige; by providing investors with these services in the form of listing their companies' stocks, financial managers lower their firms' costs of capital.[4]

Stock Market Reporting

Securities traded on the organized security exchanges are called *listed securities;* they are distinguished from *unlisted securities*, which are traded in the over-the-counter market.

Considerable information is available on transactions among listed securities, and the very existence of this information reduces the uncertainty inherent in security investments. This reduction of uncertainty, of course, makes listed securities relatively attractive to investors, and it lowers the cost of capital to firms. We cannot delve deeply into the matter of financial reporting (which is more properly the field of investment analysis), but we will attempt to explain the most widely used service—the New York Stock Exchange reporting system.

Figure 2.4 is a section of the "stock market page" taken from the *Wall Street Journal* reporting of NYSE-Composite Transactions, which include trades on five regional exchanges and those reported by the National Association of Securities Dealers and Instinet. Stocks are listed alphabetically, with those whose names consist of capital letters listed first. The items are explained by reference to the information on Abbott Labs, a drug company. The two columns on the left show the highest and the lowest prices at which the stocks have sold during the year; Abbott has traded in the range from $\$34\frac{1}{8}$ to $\$61\frac{1}{4}$ (or \$34.125 to \$61.25). The figure just to the right of the company's abbreviated name is the dividend rate based on the most recent regular quarterly payment. Abbott Labs was expected to pay \$1.20 a share in 1981. The next column gives the dividend yield, 2.1 percent for Abbott, which is the dividend divided by the closing stock price. Next comes the price/earnings (P/E) ratio, or the current price of the stock divided by its earnings per share during the last year; Abbott had a P/E ratio of 17.

After the P/E ratio comes the volume of trading for the day; 14,700 shares of Abbott Labs stock were traded on March 6, 1981. Following the volume are the high and low prices for the day and the closing price. On March 6, Abbott traded as high as $\$58\frac{7}{8}$ and as low as $\$58\frac{3}{8}$, while the last trade was at $\$58\frac{1}{2}$. The last column gives the change from the closing price on the previous day. Abbott Labs was up $\frac{1}{4}$, so the previous close must have been $\$58\frac{1}{4}$ (since $\$58\frac{1}{4} + \$\frac{1}{4} = \$58\frac{1}{2}$, the closing price on March 6). A set of footnotes giving additional information about specific issues always accompanies the stock market quotes.

[4] Banks earlier had a tradition against listing their stocks. The historic reason was fear that a falling market price for their stocks could lead depositors to think a particular bank was in danger, causing a run on the bank. Some basis for such fears may have existed before the creation of the Federal Deposit Insurance Corporation in 1935, but that fear is no longer justified.

Figure 2.4

Stock Market Transactions

52 Weeks High	52 Weeks Low	Stock	Div.	Yld %	P-E Ratio	Sales 100s	High	Low	Close	Net Chg.
				—A—A—A—						
15	$9\frac{1}{8}$	AAR	.40	3.7	7	22	$10\frac{7}{8}$	$10\frac{3}{4}$	$10\frac{7}{8}$	$+\frac{1}{8}$
$52\frac{1}{4}$	$27\frac{1}{2}$	ACF	2.50	5.1	10	259	49	$48\frac{3}{4}$	$48\frac{7}{8}$	$+\frac{1}{8}$
$24\frac{1}{2}$	$11\frac{1}{2}$	AMF	1.24	5.3	8	491	$23\frac{3}{8}$	$22\frac{3}{4}$	$23\frac{1}{4}$	$-\frac{1}{8}$
$24\frac{3}{4}$	$10\frac{7}{8}$	AM Intl	..	..	..	510	$15\frac{3}{8}$	$14\frac{7}{8}$	$15\frac{1}{8}$	$+\frac{1}{8}$
$11\frac{3}{8}$	$6\frac{7}{8}$	APL	..	..	..	12	$7\frac{5}{8}$	$7\frac{1}{2}$	$7\frac{1}{2}$	.....
$37\frac{5}{8}$	$24\frac{3}{4}$	ARA	1.94	5.6	7	71	35	$34\frac{1}{2}$	$34\frac{1}{2}$	$-\frac{1}{2}$
$91\frac{1}{2}$	$35\frac{5}{8}$	ASA	5a	11.	..	700	$46\frac{1}{2}$	45	45	.....
23	$8\frac{1}{2}$	ATO	.60	3.4	6	38	18	$17\frac{3}{4}$	$17\frac{3}{4}$	$-\frac{1}{8}$
45	$18\frac{1}{4}$	AVX	.32	1.0	18	45	$32\frac{1}{2}$	32	32	$+\frac{3}{8}$
$61\frac{1}{4}$	$34\frac{1}{8}$	AbbtLb	1.20	2.1	17	147	$58\frac{7}{8}$	$58\frac{3}{8}$	$58\frac{1}{2}$	$+\frac{1}{4}$
$35\frac{5}{8}$	$18\frac{3}{4}$	AcmeC	1.40	5.8	7	5	$24\frac{1}{4}$	$24\frac{1}{8}$	$24\frac{1}{8}$	$-\frac{3}{8}$
$5\frac{3}{4}$	$2\frac{3}{4}$	AdmDg	.04	.9	7	55	$4\frac{5}{8}$	$4\frac{1}{4}$	$4\frac{1}{4}$	$-\frac{1}{4}$
17	11	AdaEx	1.88e	14.	..	105	$13\frac{1}{2}$	$13\frac{1}{4}$	$13\frac{3}{8}$	.....
$7\frac{1}{2}$	$3\frac{5}{8}$	AdmMI	.20e	3.6	5	41	$5\frac{5}{8}$	$5\frac{1}{2}$	$5\frac{1}{2}$	$-\frac{1}{8}$
$44\frac{1}{2}$	20	AMD s	..	..	14	254	$23\frac{1}{8}$	$22\frac{3}{8}$	23	$+\frac{1}{2}$
$40\frac{1}{8}$	$29\frac{7}{8}$	AetnLf	2.32	6.8	5	988	$34\frac{1}{4}$	$33\frac{5}{8}$	$34\frac{1}{8}$	$+\frac{5}{8}$
25	15	Ahmns	1.20	6.5	9	10	$18\frac{3}{8}$	$18\frac{3}{8}$	$18\frac{3}{8}$	.....
$6\frac{1}{8}$	2	Aileen	..	..	7	51	$3\frac{1}{2}$	$3\frac{1}{4}$	$3\frac{1}{2}$	$+\frac{1}{4}$
$54\frac{1}{4}$	$32\frac{1}{4}$	AirPrd	.80	1.9	10	99	$42\frac{1}{2}$	$41\frac{7}{8}$	$41\frac{7}{8}$	$-\frac{5}{8}$
$26\frac{1}{2}$	$15\frac{3}{4}$	AirbFrt	1.20	7.3	10	66	$16\frac{1}{2}$	$16\frac{3}{8}$	$16\frac{1}{2}$	.....
$14\frac{3}{4}$	$7\frac{3}{4}$	Akzona	.80	5.4	37	84	$14\frac{3}{4}$	$14\frac{3}{8}$	$14\frac{3}{4}$	$+\frac{1}{8}$
$7\frac{5}{8}$	$5\frac{1}{2}$	AlaP dpf	.87	15.	..	×5	6	$5\frac{7}{8}$	6	.....

Source: *Wall Street Journal*, March 9, 1981 (reporting transactions on March 6, 1981). Reprinted by permission of *The Wall Street Journal*.

Margin Trading and Short Selling

Margin trading and short selling are two practices that are said to contribute to the efficiency of securities markets. *Margin trading* involves the buying of securities on credit. For example, when margin requirements are 60 percent, 100 shares of a stock selling for $100 a share can be bought by putting up, in cash, only $6,000, or 60 percent of the purchase price, and borrowing the remaining $4,000. The stockbroker lends the margin purchaser the funds, retaining custody of the stock as collateral. Margin requirements are determined by the Federal Reserve Board. When the Fed judges that stock market activity and prices are unduly stimulated by easy credit, it raises margin requirements and thus reduces the amount of credit available for the purchase of stocks. On the other hand, if the Fed wants to stimulate the market as part of its overall monetary policy operations, it reduces margin requirements.

Short selling means selling a security that is not owned by the seller. Suppose you own 100 shares of ZN, which is currently selling for $80 a share. If you become convinced that ZN is overpriced and that it is going to fall to $40 within the next year, you will probably sell your stock. Now suppose you do not own any ZN, but you still think the price will fall from $80 to $40. If you are really convinced that this drop will occur, you can *go short* in ZN, or *sell ZN short*. This involves borrowing ZN shares from your broker and selling them at the $80 price, anticipating that when the price falls to $40 you will purchase ZN shares to replace the ones you borrowed.

Margin trading, whether in a long position or in a short position, magnifies the gains and losses from a given percentage of price swings in securities. It is a form of leverage that will be discussed at some length in connection with the financial policies of business firms.

Insofar as margin trading and short selling make for a more continuous market, they encourage stock ownership and have two other benefits: (1) they broaden ownership of securities by increasing the ability of people to buy them, and (2) they provide for a more active market—and more active trading makes for narrower price fluctuations. However, when a strong speculative psychology grips the market, margin trading can be a fuel that feeds the speculative fervor, while short selling can aggravate pessimism on the downside. However, the downside effects of short selling are somewhat restricted, because by SEC rules, a short sale cannot be made at a price lower than that of the last previously recorded sale. If a stock is in a continuous decline, short selling cannot occur; hence it cannot be used to push the stock down. In the 1920s, before this rule was put into effect, market manipulators could and did use short sales to drive prices down. Today most short selling occurs when stocks are rising rapidly, and this has a stabilizing influence.

Interest-Bearing Business Securities

Within the framework of the financial markets and financial institutions we have described, financial managers have a wide range of possibilities with respect to financial instruments in which they can invest or forms of financing by which they can raise funds. The range of business financial instruments is set forth in Table 2.1, which is organized by issuer, maturity, and other such characteristics.

Table 2.1

Overview of Interest-Bearing Securities Traded in Financial Markets

I. Corporate issues

- A. Short-term
  1. Commercial banks
     - a. Federal funds
     - b. Certificates of deposit (CDs)
     - c. Bankers' acceptances
     - d. Prime rate loans
  2. Finance companies
     - a. Direct commercial paper
     - b. Dealers' commercial paper
  3. Other corporations
     - a. Commercial paper
     - b. Bank loans
- B. Long-term (utilities and industrials)
  1. Term loans
  2. Bonds
  3. Mortgages

II. International instruments

- A. Eurocurrency deposits
- B. Eurocurrency CDs
- C. Euromarket bonds

Short-Term Financial Instruments

Federal Funds Trading in federal funds has developed as a way of adjusting the reserve position of commercial banks. Commercial banks that are members of the Federal Reserve System account for more than three-fourths of the bank deposits in the United States. Their required reserves are held on deposit in the Federal Reserve banks. In the ebb and flow of daily commercial transactions throughout the United States, funds are withdrawn from some sectors and accumulate in others. Some banks accumulate more deposits with the Federal Reserve banks than they need to meet their reserve requirements, while others need to increase their deposits to meet their reserve requirements.

The federal funds market represents purchases and sales of member bank deposits held at the Federal Reserve banks. A sale of federal funds is a loan by one bank to another. The basic trading unit is $1 million, and the volume of such loans can be in excess of $20 billion per day. Transactions in federal funds can be accomplished within minutes by wire. The loans are for overnight or over the weekend. The interest rate on federal funds is the most sensitive of money market rates. It is not unusual for it to fluctuate as much as 25 percent on either side of its average level for the day. The federal funds rate reflects the many changes taking place in the economy and in the financial markets. It provides a highly sensitive index of the impact the Fed has on the money markets. Sharp movements in the rate may reflect the market's judgment that the Fed has embarked on a shift in its policies with regard to tightening or relaxing conditions in the money markets. The Depository Institutions Deregulation and Monetary Control Act of 1980 requires on a phased-in basis that all depository institutions be subject to reserve requirements.

Certificates of Deposit In 1961, major New York commercial banks began to issue interest-bearing negotiable certificates of deposit (CDs) to domestic business corporations. These certificates are a form of savings deposit, except that they cannot be withdrawn before their maturity date. However, since they are negotiable, they can be sold in the money market prior to maturity—and there is an active secondary market for them. CDs give banks an opportunity to compete for corporate and other funds that in the past were invested in Treasury bills and other types of short-term paper. They bear rates of interest in line with money rates at the time of issuance. However, during periods of tight money market conditions, when banks are aggressively seeking to add to their deposits, CD rates may rise sharply.

Prime Rate Loans Prime rate loans are loans made by commercial banks to customers who qualify for the best rate available on short-term bank lending. The result of direct negotiation between the bank and the borrower, they usually are part of a continuing financial relationship. Commercial bank rates to borrowers other than those qualifying for the prime rate are usually higher than that rate. Prime rate loans compete on a rate basis with commercial paper borrowing.

Commercial Paper Unsecured promissory notes called commercial paper are issued by firms to finance short-term credit needs. In recent years commercial paper has become an increasingly important source of short-term financing for many types of corporations, including utilities, finance companies, insurance companies, bank holding companies, and manufacturing companies. It is used increasingly not only to finance seasonal working capital needs but also as a method of interim financing of major projects such as bank buildings, ships, pipelines, nuclear fuel cores, and plant expansion.

Some commercial paper—especially the large volume of it issued by finance companies—is sold directly to investors, including business corporations, commercial banks, insurance companies, and state and local government units. At the end of 1976 about 60 percent of the commercial paper outstanding had been sold directly to investors. The remainder had been sold through commercial paper dealers, who function as intermediaries in the commercial paper market.

The commercial paper market is generally available only to the best credits. Commercial paper sold through dealers is rated as to quality by Moody's or Standard & Poor's. Surprises do occur, however; witness the Penn Central bankruptcy in 1970, which happened with more than $80 million of commercial paper outstanding. In March 1978, when Standard & Poor's reduced its rating on the senior long-term debt of Chrysler Corporation from BBB to BBB–, S&P maintained its existing ratings on the company's short-term instruments, including commercial paper. While commercial paper rates are generally somewhat higher than the rates on Treasury bills, they are somewhat lower than the prime bank loan rate.

Bankers' Acceptances A banker's acceptance is a check, drawn by a business firm, whose payment is guaranteed by a bank's acceptance of it. That is, the bank accepts the obligation to cover the check at maturity. These instruments are especially important in foreign trade because the seller of goods has less certainty that the buyer's check will actually have funds backing it up.

Long-Term Corporate Borrowing

Like government units and financial institutions, nonfinancial business firms issue various forms of long-term debt. Some forms are arranged with financial institutions such as banks or insurance companies; others are sold with the help of investment bankers to a wider range of buyers. The many different kinds of corporate bonds are discussed in Chapter 21.

Technically, *bonds* are any form of long-term debt. When secured by real estate, they are referred to as *mortgage bonds* or simply *mortgages*. The long-term loans on individual residences are referred to as mortgages, but mortgage financing exists for commercial properties as well. The federal government has established a number of organizations that provide a secondary market in mortgages by purchasing them from the financial institutions that originally made the loans. In the mortgage and related fields considerable interaction exists between private financial institutions and government agencies.

International Markets

Next we turn to increasingly important international dimensions of financial markets and the instruments that have been developed. The international dimension of financial markets has been stimulated through the mechanism of the Eurocurrency market. The Eurocurrency deposit is created when a banking office in one country accepts a deposit denominated in the currency of another country. The development of this market began in the late 1950s, and by the mid-1970s the volume of

Eurocurrency accounts had grown to more than $250 billion, at least three-fourths of it in U.S. dollars. The Eurocurrency market denominated in dollars is referred to as the Eurodollar market. While the main instrument of the Eurocurrency market is the deposit, other forms include certificates of deposit, bankers' acceptances, commercial paper, and loans of various maturities.

A bank, corporation, or government unit owning foreign currency in excess of its working needs will seek to earn interest on these temporary surplus funds. If the amount is large, it is worthwhile for the financial manager to seek the best rate available. This may include the use of a banking office in a foreign country and the deposit of funds denominated in the appropriate currency. When foreign money markets provide more favorable terms than U.S. markets, the lender and the banking office that accepts the deposit exchange letters detailing the terms of the deposit, and the transfer of funds is acknowledged. The normal deposit unit is 1 million currency units. The lender who needs short-term funds prior to the maturity of the deposit can become a borrower for the necessary period by initiating an offsetting transaction in the Eurocurrency market.

The rate paid on these deposits among the largest and best-known international banks is called the London Inter-Bank Offer Rate (LIBOR). Deposit rates are generally fixed for shorter-term deposits but may float on longer-term deposits. Floating rates are usually adjusted semiannually in response to changes in the LIBOR short-term rate to which they are tied.

The Eurocurrency market has participants located throughout the world; transactions are negotiated by Telex, cable, and telephone. Trading is normally done for settlement on the second business day following the trade date. Funds are transferred either directly through correspondent banks in the home country of the currency involved or according to the broker's instructions against delivery of the required instrument.

In addition to conventional interbank deposits, there are Eurodollar certificates of deposit (similar to the CDs in our domestic market), negotiable instruments that enjoy an active secondary trading market. Many branches of U.S. banks compete for Eurodollar funds through the issuance of Eurodollar certificates of deposit.

Besides placing temporary surplus funds in Eurocurrency deposits or Eurodollar CDs, many U.S. firms utilize the Euromarket as borrowers. The rates on long-term borrowing in the Euromarket are sometimes below the rates on comparable securities in the United States. The relative rates depend on supply and demand conditions in the U.S. capital market as compared with conditions in the Euromarket. A situation that illustrates this point developed at the end of 1976.

> "Fierce competition among banks across the Atlantic for loan business is driving down the cost of credit to the point where U.S. corporations and their overseas subsidiaries can now borrow five-year money in Europe for nearly the same price that they have to pay for short-term bank loans at home."[5]

Of course, if interest rates are relatively lower in Europe, the increased borrowing abroad tends to bring rates back into balance. Sometimes foreign firms find it

[5] "Big Loan Bargains in the Euromart," *BusinessWeek*, December 13, 1976, pp. 10–11.

attractive to sell "'Yankee' bonds—bonds issued by foreign governments and corporations but sold in the United States and denominated in U.S. dollars."[6]

Increasingly the financial manager (whether in the United States or in a foreign country) is looking at the whole world as a relevant financial market. With the ebb and flow of changing economic and financial conditions throughout the world, the financial manager is sometimes an investor and sometimes a borrower abroad. Transportation and communication systems now link nations together directly and closely. For this reason further analysis of the international dimensions of financial markets will be developed later in the book (see Chapter 27).

Summary

The financial sector of the economy, an important part of the financial manager's environment, is comprised of financial markets, financial institutions, and financial instruments.

Financial markets involve the creation and transfer of financial assets and liabilities. The financial manager uses these markets to obtain needed funds for the operation and growth of the business and to employ funds temporarily not needed by the business. Funds are provided by savings surplus units to be used by savings deficit units. This transfer of funds creates a financial asset for the surplus unit and a financial liability for the deficit unit. Transfers can occur directly between a surplus and a deficit unit or can involve a financial intermediary, such as a bank. Intermediaries take on financial liabilities in order to create financial assets, typically profiting from their expertise in packaging these assets and liabilities. The operations of intermediaries and financial markets in general bring about a more efficient allocation of real resources.

The money markets involve financial assets and liabilities with maturities of less than one year, and the capital markets involve transfers for longer periods. Since most businesses are savings deficit units, the financial manager is concerned with the choice of financial markets, the intermediaries, and instruments best suited to the needs of the firm and with the decision of how best to employ excess funds for short periods.

The initial sale of stocks and bonds is known as the primary market. Subsequent trading takes place in the secondary markets, which include the organized exchanges and the over-the-counter market. In over-the-counter trading, broker-dealers throughout the United States act as market makers. Sometimes large blocks of stock are traded directly among institutional investors, which represent the fourth market.

In addition to the ordinary purchase or sale of stocks or bonds, margin trading involves borrowing. Margin requirements, set by the Fed, change from time to time. Short selling is the practice of borrowing securities and selling them immediately, while anticipating an opportunity to repurchase them later at a lower price to repay the loan. (That is, the short seller benefits if the price of the stock falls.) Short selling and margin trading make the stock market more active and thus may contribute to the ability to buy or sell securities with smaller price swings than otherwise would occur.

[6] " 'Yankee' Bonds Are Doing Just Dandy," *BusinessWeek*, December 6, 1976, pp. 76–77.

Two major forms of financing are used by business firms: equity financing through common stock and various forms of debt financing. There are numerous alternative types of debt instruments; they differ in duration and in the degree of risk of the borrower (the issuer of the debt) being unable to meet the obligation.

International financial markets extend the range of alternatives available to financial managers. Surplus funds can be invested at advantageous rates in the many different types of international financial instruments. Financing can be obtained in the Eurocurrency market for short-term borrowing or in the Eurobond market for longer-term debt financing.

Questions

2.1 What are financial intermediaries, and what economic functions do they perform?

2.2 How could each tool of the Fed be used to slow down expansion?

2.3 Evaluate each of the arguments in favor of organized securities exchanges relative to OTC markets 100 years ago versus today.

2.4 One day the New York Stock Exchange reporting system showed XYZ Corporation as follows:

49 27 XYZ 1.20 3.8 8 60 33 30 32 +1

a. Is XYZ trading near its high or its low for the year?

b. What was yesterday's closing price?

c. What is the dividend yield on XYZ stock?

d. Based on the information given in the report, what would you estimate XYZ's annual earnings to be?

2.5 Why might an investor want to sell short?

2.6 As the financial manager of a business, what factors would you want to consider in deciding how to invest some temporary surplus funds?

2.7 If your firm needs more long-term capital, can you think of a situation where you might want to use a short-term source of funds?

Problems

2.1 Walter Jones has two investment opportunities available to him.

Investment	Number of shares	$ price per share	Margin requirement	Interest rate on borrowed funds
A	100	$38\frac{1}{4}$	50%	10%
B	250	20	45%	12%

a. How much cash must Jones put up to make Investment A? Investment B?

b. If he sells the stock at the end of one year, how much interest will Jones owe on Investment A? Investment B?

2.2 Stock in XYZ Company is currently selling for $26 per share.

a. Calculate the gain or loss to an investor who sells short 100 shares of XYZ if the price falls to $20 per share.

b. Calculate the gain or loss to an investor who sells short 100 shares of XYZ if the price rises to $30 per share.

2.3 In a recent issue of the *Federal Reserve Bulletin*, locate the table giving information on margin requirements for margin stocks, convertible bonds, and short sales.

a. Does the term *margin requirements* refer to the percentage of borrowing to market value of the collateral or to the percentage of funds provided by the investor?
b. Are the requirements always the same for the three types of securities?
c. What has been the trend in margin requirements since 1968?
d. What are current margin requirements?

2.4 Using a recent issue of the *Wall Street Journal*, answer the following questions about Dow Chemical Company common stock:

a. On what exchange is it listed?
b. What is the annual dollar amount of dividends based on the last quarterly or semiannual distribution?
c. What percentage yield is represented by this dollar amount of dividend based on the closing price of the stock?
d. How does this compare with the rate of interest the same funds could earn in a savings account?
e. What is the indicated price/earnings ratio of the stock based on the closing price and the most recent twelve months' earnings?
f. By what percentage is the closing price below the high price for the previous fifty-two weeks?
g. By what percentage is the closing price above the low price for the previous fifty-two weeks?
h. Would you say that the common stock of Dow Chemical Company has experienced high, low, or moderate volatility during the previous fifty-two weeks?

2.5 Using a recent issue of the *Wall Street Journal*, answer the following questions about the $9\frac{1}{2}$ percent bonds of the International Business Machines Corporation:

a. On what exchange are they listed?
b. What is their maturity date?
c. What is their current yield?
d. What was their closing price?
e. Was their closing price below or above their par value of 100?

CHAPTER 3

BUSINESS ORGANIZATION AND TAXES

The federal government is often called the most important stockholder in the U.S. economy. This is not literally true, since the government does not "own" corporate shares in the strict sense of the word. It is, however, by far the largest recipient of business profits. Income of unincorporated businesses has been subject to tax rates ranging up to 70 percent (50 percent on earned income), while corporate income in excess of $100,000 is taxed at a 46 percent rate. Furthermore, dividends received by stockholders are subject to personal income taxes at the stockholders' individual tax rates. State and sometimes city or county taxes must be added to these federal taxes.

With such a large percentage of business income going to the government, it is not surprising that taxes play an important role in financial decisions. To lease or to buy, to use common stock or debt, to make or not to make a particular investment, to merge or not to merge—all these decisions are influenced by tax factors. This chapter summarizes some basic elements of the tax structure relating to financial decisions and the choice of form of business organization. Since the new tax law, the Economic Recovery Tax Act of 1981, was passed by Congress on August 4, 1981, the Internal Revenue Service regulations interpreting the act were not issued in time to be included in this chapter. Some aspects of implementation will be subject to the rules issued by the IRS.

Corporate Income Tax

Under the Economic Recovery Tax Act of 1981, the corporate tax rates for the years 1981 through 1983 are as follows:

Rate Structure

Taxable income	1981	1982	1983
First $25,000	17%	16%	15%
Second $25,000	20%	19%	18%
Third $25,000	30%	30%	30%
Fourth $25,000	40%	40%	40%
Over $100,000	46%	46%	46%

For example, if in 1981 a corporation has a taxable net income of $110,000, its tax will be computed as follows:

$$
\begin{aligned}
0.17(\$25{,}000) &= \$\ 4{,}250 \\
0.20(\$25{,}000) &= 5{,}000 \\
0.30(\$25{,}000) &= 7{,}500 \\
0.40(\$25{,}000) &= 10{,}000 \\
0.46(\$10{,}000) &= \underline{4{,}600} \\
\text{Total tax} &= 31{,}350
\end{aligned}
$$

Thus the corporation's average tax rate will be $31,350 ÷ $110,000 = 28.5 percent. However, on any amount over $100,000, the marginal tax rate on this incremental income will be 46 percent. Table 3.1 shows that the average corporate income tax is moderately progressive up to $11 million, after which it becomes virtually a flat 46 percent.

Table 3.1

Marginal and Average Corporate Tax Rates for 1981

Taxable corporate income (in dollars)	Marginal tax rate (percent)	Incremental taxes paid	Total taxes paid	Average tax rate (percent)[a]
0–25,000	17	4,250	4,250	17.00
25,001–50,000	20	5,000	9,250	18.50
50,001–75,000	30	7,500	16,750	22.33
75,001–100,000	40	10,000	26,750	26.75
100,001–200,000	46	46,000	72,750	36.38
200,001–1,000,000	46	368,000	440,750	44.08
1,000,001–11,000,000	46	4,600,000	5,040,750	45.82
11,000,001–111,000,000	46	46,000,000	51,040,750	45.98

[a] Based on upper limit of income range.

This relatively simple tax structure has wide implications for business planning. Because the tax rate increases sharply when corporate income rises above $100,000, it clearly will seem advantageous to break moderate-sized companies into two or more separate corporations in order to make the lower corporate income tax rates applicable. In fact, this was done for many years by a number of firms, with some groups (such as retail chains and small loan companies) having literally thousands of separate corporations. However, the Tax Reform Act of 1969 eliminated the advantages of multiple corporations from a tax standpoint.

Payment of Tax in Installments

Firms must estimate their taxable income for the current year and, if reporting on a calendar year basis, pay one-fourth of the estimated tax on April 15, June 15, September 15, and December 15 of that year. In general, the estimated taxes paid must be identical to the previous year or at least 80 percent of actual tax liability for the current year, or the firm will be subject to penalties. Any differences between estimated and actual taxes are payable by March 15 of the following year. For example, if a firm expects to earn $100,000 in 1981 and to owe a tax of $26,750 on this income, then it must file an estimated income statement and pay $6,688 on the

15th of April, June, September, and December of 1981. By March 15, 1982, it must file a final income statement and pay any shortfall (or receive a refund for overages) between estimated and actual taxes.

Net Operating Losses Carryover

For most businesses, net operating losses incurred in taxable years ending after 1975 can now be carried forward for fifteen years (up from the former seven-year carryforward provision). The allowable carryback period for net operating losses remains at three years, thereby giving firms an eighteen-year period in which to absorb their losses against future profits or to recoup taxes paid on past profits. The purpose of permitting this loss averaging is to avoid penalizing firms whose incomes fluctuate widely.

Deductibility of Interest and Dividends Paid

Interest payments made by a corporation are a deductible expense to the firm, but dividends paid on its own stock are not. Thus, if a firm raises $100,000 and contracts to pay the suppliers of this money 7 percent, or $7,000 a year, the $7,000 is deductible if the $100,000 is debt. It is not deductible if the $100,000 is raised as stock and the $7,000 is paid as dividends.[1] This differential treatment of dividends and interest payments has an important effect on the manner in which firms raise capital, as later chapters will show.

Depreciation and Taxes

Another deductible expense is depreciation on assets. There are four main methods of depreciation—straight line, double declining balance, sum-of-years'-digits, and units of production. The double declining balance and sum-of-years'-digits methods are referred to as *accelerated* depreciation methods; they generally have favorable tax effects. Each method of depreciation is illustrated in Table 3.2. Assume that a

Table 3.2

Comparison of Depreciation Methods for a 10-year, $1,100 Asset with a $100 Salvage Value

	Depreciation methods			
Year	Straight line	Double declining balance	Sum-of-years'-digits	Units of production[a]
1	$ 100	$220	$ 182	$ 200
2	100	176	164	180
3	100	141	145	150
4	100	113	127	130
5	100	90	109	100
6	100	72	91	80
7	100	58	73	60
8	100	46	55	50
9	100	37	36	30
10	100	29	18	20
Total	$1,000	$982	$1,000	$1,000

[a] The assumption is made that the machine is used the following number of hours: first year, 2,000; second year, 1,800; third year, 1,500; fourth year, 1,300; fifth year, 1,000; sixth year, 800; seventh year, 600; eighth year, 500; ninth year, 300; tenth year, 200.

[1] Limits have been placed on the deductibility of interest payments on some forms of securities issued in connection with mergers.

machine is purchased for $1,100 and has an estimated useful life of ten years or ten thousand hours. It will have a scrap value of $100 after ten years of use or after ten thousand hours, whichever comes first. Table 3.2 compares the depreciation charges of each method over the ten-year period.

With the straight line method, a uniform annual depreciation charge of $100 a year is provided. This figure is arrived at by simply dividing the economic life into the total cost of the machine minus the estimated salvage value:

$$\frac{(\$1{,}100 \text{ cost} - \$100 \text{ salvage value})}{10 \text{ years}} = \$100 \text{ a year depreciation charge}$$

The double declining balance (DDB) method of accelerated depreciation requires the application of a cost rate of depreciation each year to the undepreciated value of the asset at the close of the previous year. In this case, since the annual straight line rate is 10 percent a year ($100 ÷ $1,000), the double declining rate would be 20 percent (2 × 10 percent). This rate is applied to the full purchase price of the machine, not to the cost less salvage value. Therefore, depreciation under the DDB method is $220 during the first year (20 percent × $1,100). Depreciation amounts to $176 in the second year and is calculated by applying the 20 percent rate to the undepreciated value of the asset,

$$20\% \times (\$1{,}100 - \$220) = \$176,$$

and so on, as the undepreciated balance declines. Notice that under DDB the asset is not fully depreciated at the end of the tenth year. In our example the remaining depreciation would be taken in the tenth year.[2]

Under the sum-of-years'-digits method, the yearly depreciation allowance is determined as follows:

1. Calculate the sum of the years' digits; in our example, the digits total 55: $1 + 2 + 3 + 4 + 5 + 6 + 7 + 8 + 9 + 10 = 55$. This figure can also be arrived at by means of the sum of an algebraic progression equation where n is the life of the asset:

$$\text{Sum} = n\left(\frac{n+1}{2}\right)$$
$$= 10\left(\frac{10+1}{2}\right) = 55$$

2. Divide the number of remaining years by the sum-of-years'-digits and multiply this fraction by the depreciable cost (total cost minus salvage value) of the asset:

$$\text{Year 1: } \frac{10}{55}(\$1{,}000) = \$182 \text{ depreciation}$$

$$\text{Year 2: } \frac{9}{55}(\$1{,}000) = \$164 \text{ depreciation}$$

$$\text{Year 10: } \frac{1}{55}(\$1{,}000) = \$18 \text{ depreciation}$$

[2] Actually, the company would switch from DDB to straight line whenever straight line depreciation on the remaining book value of the asset exceeds the DDB amount. Thus, in the ninth year the book value is $84, so straight line depreciation would be $42 versus $37 if the change were not made.

Under the units of production method, the expected useful life of 10,000 hours is divided into the depreciable cost (purchase price minus salvage value) to arrive at an hourly depreciation rate of ten cents. Since, in our example, the machine is run for 2,000 hours in the first year, the depreciation in that year is $200; in the second year, $180; and so on. With this method, depreciation charges cannot be estimated precisely ahead of time; the firm must wait until the end of the year to determine what usage has been made of the machine and hence its depreciation.

The effect of the accelerated methods on a firm's income tax payment is easily demonstrated. In the first year, should the firm choose to use the straight line method, only $100 may be deducted from its earnings to arrive at earnings before taxes (the amount of earnings to which the tax rate applies). However, using any one of the other three methods, the firm would have a much greater deduction and, therefore, a lower tax liability. Under the Economic Recovery Tax Act of 1981, companies can rapidly recoup capital expenditures made after 1980 under a system called the "accelerated cost recovery system." Under this system, it is no longer necessary to select a depreciation method, neither is it necessary to determine an asset's useful life or its salvage value. The system provides statutory recovery periods and depreciation methods for four classes of assets that result in high deductions in the early years and low deductions in the latter years of an asset's life. The specific rules are quite technical and beyond the scope of this book.

Investment Tax Credit

The concept of an investment tax credit was first incorporated into the federal income tax laws in 1962. Under the investment tax credit program, business firms could deduct, as a credit against their income tax, a specified percentage of the dollar amount of new investment in each of certain categories of assets. The 1981 tax law specifies a 6 percent investment tax credit for qualifying property with a life of three years or less and a 10 percent credit for all qualifying property with a life of more than three years. Thus, if a firm that otherwise will have a $100,000 tax bill purchases an asset costing $200,000 and having a twenty-year life, it will receive a tax credit of $20,000 (10 percent of $200,000), and its adjusted tax bill will be $80,000. There are rules that impose a recapture tax on investment credit property not held for a specified minimum period of time.

Dividend Income

Another important rule is that 85 percent of the dividends received by one corporation from another are exempt from taxation.[3] For example, if Corporation H owns stock in Corporation J and receives $100,000 in dividends from that corporation, it must pay taxes on only $15,000 of the $100,000. Assuming H is in the 46 percent tax bracket, the tax is $6,900 or 6.9 percent of the dividends received. The reason for this reduced tax is that to subject intercorporate dividends to the full corporate tax rate would eventually lead to triple taxation. First, Corporation J would pay its regular taxes. Then, Corporation H would pay a second tax. Finally, H's own stockholders would be subject to taxes on their dividends. The 85 percent dividend deduction thus reduces the multiple taxation of corporate income.

[3] If the corporation receiving the dividends owns 80 percent or more of the stock of a dividend-paying firm, it can file a consolidated tax return. In this situation there are no dividends as far as the Internal Revenue Service is concerned, so there is obviously no tax on dividends received. The internal books of the related corporations may show an accounting entry entitled "dividends," which is used for transferring funds from the subsidiary to the parent; but this is of no concern to the IRS.

Corporate Capital Gains and Losses

Corporate taxable income consists of two components: profits from the sale of capital assets and all other income (defined as *ordinary income). Capital assets* (for example, security investments) are defined as assets not bought and sold in the ordinary course of a firm's business. Gains and losses on the sale of capital assets are defined as capital gains and losses, and under certain circumstances they receive special tax treatment.[4] Real and depreciable property used in the business is not defined as a capital asset, although the Internal Revenue Code specifies that such property is treated as a capital asset in the event of a net gain. (However, the recapture of depreciation provisions may eliminate much of this benefit.) If there is a net loss, the full amount can be deducted from ordinary income without any of the limitations described below for capital loss treatment.[5]

Before 1977, the distinction between short-term and long-term capital gains was based on a six-month holding period. Assets held six months or less gave rise to short-term capital gains or losses on their sale. If held more than six months, the gain or loss was considered long-term. The Tax Reform Act of 1976 increased the period assets must be held for purposes of determining long-term capital gain or loss from six months to nine months in 1977 and to twelve months thereafter. Thus, from 1978 on, the sale of a capital asset held for twelve months or less gives rise to a short-term capital gain or loss. When held for more than twelve months, its disposal produces a long-term gain or loss. Short-term capital gains less short-term capital losses equals net short-term gains, which are added to the firm's ordinary income and taxed at regular corporate income tax rates. For net long-term capital gains (long-term gains less long-term losses), the tax is limited to 28 percent plus a minimum tax factor on part of a corporation's gains, which makes the maximum rate on corporate capital gains slightly higher. For example, if a corporation holds the common stock of another corporation as an investment for more than twelve months and then sells it at a profit, the gain is subject to a maximum tax of 28+ percent. Of course, if income is below $50,000, the lower, regular tax rates (17 and 20 percent in 1981) apply.

Deductibility of Capital Losses

A corporation's net capital loss is not deductible from ordinary income. For example, if in 1981 a corporation had ordinary income of $100,000 and a net capital loss of $25,000 (that is, capital losses for the year exceeded capital gains for the year by $25,000), it still paid a tax of $26,750 on the $100,000 ordinary income. The net capital loss, however, can be carried back three years and forward five years and can be used to offset capital gains during that period.

Improper Accumulation

A special surtax on improperly accumulated income is provided for by Section 531 of the Internal Revenue Code, which states that earnings accumulated by a corporation are subject to penalty rates *if the purpose of the accumulation is to enable*

[4] Corporate capital gains and losses (as well as most other tax matters) are subject to many technical provisions. This section and the others dealing with tax matters include only the most general provisions. For special cases see *Federal Tax Course* (Englewood Cliffs, N.J.: Prentice-Hall, 1981).

[5] The special treatment of depreciable properties should be kept in mind in connection with the material in Chapter 13 on capital budgeting. The difference between the book value of an asset and its salvage or abandonment value (if lower than book value) can be deducted from ordinary income; thus the full amount of this difference is a deductible expense.

the stockholders to avoid the personal income tax. The penalty rate is 27.5 percent on the first $100,000 of improperly accumulated taxable income for the current year and 38.5 percent on all amounts over $100,000. Of income not paid out in dividends, a cumulative total of $250,000 (the balance sheet item of retained earnings) is prima facie retainable for the reasonable needs of the business; this benefits small corporations. Of course, most companies have legitimate reasons for retaining earnings over $250,000, and they are not subject to the penalty.

Retained earnings are used to pay off debt, to finance growth, and to provide the corporation with a cushion against possible cash drains caused by losses. How much a firm should properly accumulate for uncertain contingencies is a matter of judgment. Fear of the penalty taxes that can be imposed under Section 531 may cause a firm to pay out a higher rate of dividends than it otherwise would.[6]

Sometimes Section 531 stimulates mergers. A clear illustration is provided by the purchase of the Toni Company (home permanents) by the Gillette Safety Razor Company.[7] The sale was made at a time when Toni's sales volume had begun to level off. Since earnings retention might have been difficult to justify, Toni's owners—the Harris brothers—were faced with the alternatives of paying penalty rates for improper accumulation of earnings or of paying out the income as dividends. Toni's income after corporate taxes was $4 million a year; with the Harris brothers' average personal income tax of 75 percent, only $1 million a year would have been left after they had paid personal taxes on dividends. By selling Toni for $13 million, they realized a $12 million capital gain (their book value was $1 million). After paying the 25 percent capital gains tax on the $12 million—$3 million—the Harrises realized $10 million after taxes ($13 million sale price minus $3 million tax). Thus Gillette paid the equivalent of three and one-quarter years' after-corporate-tax earnings for Toni, while the Harris brothers received ten years' after-personal-income-tax net income for it. The tax factor made the transaction advantageous to both parties.

The broad aspects of the federal corporate income tax have now been covered. Because the federal income tax on individuals is equally important for many business decisions, the individual tax structure will now be examined and compared with the corporate tax structure. This will provide a basis for making an intelligent choice as to which form of organization a firm should elect for tax purposes.

Personal Income Tax

Of some 5 million firms in the United States, more than 4 million are organized as sole proprietorships or partnerships. The income of these firms is taxed as personal income to the owners or the partners. The net income of a proprietorship or partnership provides a basis for determining the individual's income tax liability. Thus, as a business tax, the individual income tax can be as important as the corporate income tax.

[6] See materials in James K. Hall, *The Taxation of Corporate Surplus Accumulations* (Washington, D.C.: U.S. Government Printing Office, 1952), especially app. 3.

[7] See J. K. Butters, J. Lintner, and W. L. Cary, *Effects of Taxation on Corporate Mergers* (Boston: Harvard Business School, 1951), pp. 96–111. The lucid presentation by these authors has been drawn on for the general background, but the data have been approximated to simplify the illustration. The principle involved is not affected by the modifications of the facts.

The personal income tax is conceptually straightforward, although many taxpayers find it confusing. Virtually all the income a person or family receives goes into determining the tax liability. For tax purposes income is classified as *earned* (wages or salary) or *unearned* (primarily capital gains, rents, interest, and dividends). Under existing tax laws different kinds of income may be taxed in different ways or at different rates.

Total income from all sources is called gross income. All taxpayers are permitted to deduct part of their gross income before computing any tax. These deductions are of two types: standard deductions and personal exemptions.

Deductions State and local taxes, medical expenses, interest payments, and charitable contributions are tax-deductible expenses. The standard deduction can be claimed in lieu of these actual expenses. Effective in 1979, the standard deduction was $3,400 for joint returns of married couples and $2,300 for single taxpayers. Taxpayers with actual expenses in excess of the standard deduction reduce the amount of taxable income by itemizing their deductible expenses.

Personal Exemptions A $1,000 deduction is allowed for the taxpayer and each of that person's dependents. These are built into some tax tables. The deduction is doubled for any taxpayer who is over sixty-five years old or blind. In 1981, a family of four—husband, wife, and two dependent children, none blind or over sixty-five—had personal exemptions totaling $4,000. The apparent intent of the personal exemption is to exempt the first part of income from taxation, thereby enabling the family to obtain the basic necessities of life, such as food and shelter. The same intent appears in the form of the graduated income tax, where the highest tax rates are levied against "discretionary" income.

The following classifications are used in connection with calculating an individual's income tax liability:

Income
Wages, salaries, tips, and so on
Interest income
Dividends less exclusion
Business income
Applicable capital gains or losses
Pensions, annuities, rents, royalties, partnerships, and so on
Alimony received
Several other categories

Total income (the sum of the above)

Adjustments to income
Moving expenses
Employee business expenses
Payments to an individual retirement arrangement
Alimony paid
Several other categories

Total adjustments (the sum of the above)

Adjusted gross income =
Total income less adjustments to income

Less: number of personal exemptions times $1,000

Less: excess itemized deductions (itemized deductions in excess of the applicable standard deduction)

Equals taxable income

A number of aspects of tax liability have significance for corporate financial policy. Among the itemized deductions that enable gross income to be reduced is interest paid on borrowings by individuals. Thus, for both corporations and individuals, interest expenses paid are deductible for tax purposes. There are also special rules that allow exclusions for some dividends received and interest income under certain circumstances.

Tax Rates for the Personal Income Tax Tax rates that became effective with the Revenue Act of 1978 are indicated in Table 3.3. Effective October 31, 1981, the tax law of 1981 reduces these rates by 5 percent in 1981, and by 10 percent in each of the years 1982 and 1983. The tax rates presented are for the joint return of a married couple or surviving spouse. The taxable income is adjusted gross income less personal exemptions less the excess of itemized deductions over the applicable

Table 3.3

Marginal and Average Personal Income Tax Rates for 1981[a]

Taxable income		Tax liability		
Over (1)	Not over (2)	Tax (3)	Percent of excess over column (1) (4)	Average percent tax on upper limit of bracket (5)
$ 3,400	$ 5,500	$ 0	14	5.35
5,500	7,600	294	16	8.29
7,600	11,900	630	18	11.80
11,900	16,000	1,404	21	14.16
16,000	20,200	2,265	24	16.20
20,200	24,600	3,273	28	18.31
24,600	29,900	4,505	32	20.74
29,900	35,200	6,201	37	23.19
35,200	45,800	8,162	43	27.77
45,800	60,000	12,720	49	32.80
60,000	85,600	19,678	54	39.14
85,600	109,400	33,502	59	43.46
109,400	162,400	47,544	64	50.16
162,400	215,400	81,464	68	54.55
215,400	and over	117,504	70	—[b]

The table shows a joint return for a married couple or surviving spouse.

[a] This table does not include the tax reductions of the Economic Recovery Tax Act of 1981.

[b] Not calculable.

Source: *Revenue Act of 1978* (Washington, D.C.: Government Printing Office, 1978)

standard deduction. The average tax rate rises relatively slowly, but the marginal rate reaches 49 percent for taxable income of $60,000. For other than earned income, the marginal tax goes up to a maximum of 70 percent on income of $215,400. Under the 1981 tax law, the maximum will be 50 percent as of January 31, 1982. Table 3.3 will be used in subsequent comparisons of sole proprietorships, partnerships, and corporations.

Individual Capital Gains and Losses

As with corporations, the distinction between short-term and long-term gains and losses is the twelve-month holding period. Net short-term gains are taxed at regular rates. The tax on net long-term capital gains is computed by deducting 60 percent of the amount, with the remaining 40 percent subject to tax at the marginal tax rate on ordinary income.

Dividend and Interest Income

Under the former tax law, $200 of qualifying interest and/or dividend income received by an individual could be excluded from taxable income. Starting in 1982, the new law provides a $100 dividend exclusion, plus an interest exclusion of up to fifteen percent of net interest income by 1985 (to a maximum of $450). In addition, the new tax law provides another incentive to saving in the form of a $1,000 interest exclusion on qualifying savings certificates. (All of these exclusions may be doubled on a joint return whether the interest and dividends are received by either one or both spouses.)

Choices Among Alternative Forms of Business Organization

Taxes exert an important influence in choosing among alternative forms of business organization. In the following sections the nature of the alternatives and their advantages and disadvantages will be described. Then, the tax aspects will be considered.

From a technical and legal standpoint, there are three major forms of business organization: the sole proprietorship, the partnership, and the corporation.[8] In terms of numbers, 70 percent of business firms are operated as sole proprietorships, 8 percent are partnerships, and 14 percent are corporations. By dollar value of sales, however, about 80 percent of business is conducted by corporations, about 13 percent by sole proprietorships, and about 7 percent by partnerships. The remainder of this section describes and compares the characteristics of these alternative forms of business organization.

Sole Proprietorship

A sole proprietorship is a business owned by one individual. Going into business as a sole proprietor is very simple; a person merely begins business operations. However, cities or counties may require even the smallest establishments to be licensed or registered. State licenses may also be required.

The proprietorship has key advantages for small operations. It is easily and inexpensively formed, requires no formal charter for operations, and is subject to few government regulations. Further, it pays no corporate income taxes, although all earnings of the firm are subject to personal income taxes, regardless of whether they are reinvested in the business or withdrawn from it.

[8] Other less common forms of organization include business trusts, joint stock companies, and cooperatives.

The proprietorship also has important limitations. Most significant is its inability to obtain large sums of capital. Further, the proprietor has unlimited personal liability for business debts; creditors can look to both business assets and personal assets to satisfy their claims. Finally, the proprietorship is limited to the life of the individual who creates it. For all these reasons, the sole proprietorship is limited primarily to small-business operations. However, businesses frequently are started as proprietorships and converted to corporations when their growth causes the disadvantages of the proprietorship form to outweigh its advantages.

Partnership

When two or more persons associate to conduct a business enterprise, a partnership is said to exist. Partnerships can operate under different degrees of formality, ranging from an informal oral understanding to a written partnership agreement to a formal agreement filed with the local secretary of state. Like the proprietorship, the partnership has the advantages of ease and economy of formation as well as freedom from special government regulations. Partnership profits are taxed as personal income in proportion to the partners' claims, whether or not they are distributed to them.

One of the advantages of the partnership over the proprietorship is that it makes possible a pooling of various types of resources. Some partners contribute particular skills or contacts, while others contribute funds. However, there are practical limits to the number of co-owners who can join in an enterprise without destructive conflict, so most partnership agreements provide that the individual partners cannot sell their share in the business unless all the partners agree to accept the new partner (or partners).

If a new partner comes into the business, the old partnership ceases to exist and a new one is created. The withdrawal or death of any of the partners also dissolves the partnership. To prevent disputes under such circumstances, the articles of the partnership agreement should include terms and conditions under which assets are to be distributed upon dissolution. Of course, dissolution of the partnership does not necessarily mean the end of the business; the remaining partners may simply buy out the one who left the firm. To avoid financial pressures caused by the death of one of the partners, it is a common practice for each partner to carry life insurance naming the remaining partners as beneficiaries. The proceeds of such policies can be used to buy out the investment of the deceased partner.

A number of drawbacks stemming from the characteristics of the partnership limit its use. They include impermanence, difficulty of transferring ownership, and unlimited liability (except for limited partners). Partners risk their personal assets as well as their investments in the business. Further, under partnership law, the partners are jointly and separately liable for business debts. This means that if any partner is unable to meet the claims resulting from the liquidation of the partnership, the remaining partners must take over the unsatisfied claims, drawing on their personal assets if necessary.[9]

[9] However, it is possible to limit the liabilities of some partners by establishing a limited partnership, wherein certain partners are designated general partners and others limited partners. Limited partnerships are quite common in the area of real estate investment.

Corporation

A corporation is a legal entity created under state law.[10] It is a separate entity, distinct from its owners and managers. This separateness gives the corporation three major advantages: (1) it has an unlimited life—it can continue after its original owners and managers are dead; (2) it permits limited liability—stockholders are not personally liable for the debts of the firm; and (3) it permits easy transferability of ownership interest in the firm—ownership interests can be divided into shares of stock, which can be transferred far more easily than partnership interests.[11]

While a proprietorship or a partnership can commence operations without much paperwork, the chartering of a corporation involves a complicated, but routinized, process. First, a certificate of incorporation is drawn up; in most states it includes the following information: (1) name of proposed corporation, (2) purposes, (3) amount of capital stock, (4) number of directors, (5) names and addresses of directors, and (6) duration (if limited). The certificate is notarized and sent to the secretary of the state in which the business seeks incorporation. If it is satisfactory, the corporation officially exists.

The actual operations of the firm are governed by two documents, the charter and the bylaws. The corporate charter technically consists of a certificate of incorporation and, by reference, the general corporation laws of the state. Thus the corporation is bound by the general corporation laws of the state as well as by the unique provisions of its certificate of incorporation. The bylaws are a set of rules drawn up by the founders of the corporation to aid in governing the internal management of the company. Included are such points as (1) how directors are to be elected (all elected each year or, say, one-third each year, and whether cumulative voting will be used); (2) whether the preemptive right is granted to existing stockholders in the event new securities are sold; and (3) provisions for management committees, such as an executive committee or a finance committee, and their duties. Also included is the procedure for changing the bylaws themselves should conditions require this.

Tax Aspects of the Forms of Organization

To a small, growing firm, the advantage of the corporate form of organization is that the tax rate is low for income up to $100,000. There is "double taxation" of dividends, but salaries paid to the principals in the corporation are a tax-deductible expense and so are not sibject to double taxation. The entire income of a proprietorship or partnership is subject to the higher personal tax rates. Thus the influence of taxes involves more than just a comparison of the personal tax rates with the corporate tax rates.

A specific example will illustrate the application of the several factors influencing the amount of taxes under alternative forms of business organization. Craig Vernon, a married man with two children, is planning to start a new business, CV Manufacturing. He is trying to decide between a corporation or a sole proprietorship as the form of organization. Under either form, he will initially own 100 percent of the firm. Tax considerations are very important to him because he plans to finance the

[10] Certain types of firms (for example, banks) are also chartered by the federal government.

[11] In the case of small corporations, the limited liability feature is often a fiction, since bankers and credit managers frequently require personal guarantees from the stockholders of small, weak businesses.

expected growth of the firm by drawing a salary sufficient for living expenses for his family (about $30,000) and plowing the remainder back into the enterprise.

Vernon will have no outside income, since he is liquidating all his investments in order to initially finance CV Manufacturing. He estimates that his itemized deductions will be $5,800 in excess of the standard deduction. He expects the following income before deducting his salary:

1979	$ 50,000
1980	80,000
1981	100,000

To determine whether Vernon should form the new business as a corporation or a proprietorship, we will first calculate the total taxes to be paid if it is organized as a corporation (see Table 3.4). Then we will calculate total taxes on the basis of a proprietorship (see Table 3.5).

The taxes are lower for a corporation in each of the years. The corporate form of ownership allows Vernon to split his income so it is taxed at low marginal rates

Table 3.4

Total Taxes for CV as a Corporation

	1979	1980	1981
Income before salary and tax	$50,000	$80,000	$100,000
Less salary	30,000	30,000	30,000
Taxable income, corporate	$20,000	$50,000	$ 70,000
Corporate taxes:			
$25,000 at 17%	3,400	4,250	4,250
$25,000 at 20%	0	5,000	5,000
Balance at 30%	0	0	6,000
Total corporate tax	$ 3,400	$ 9,250	$ 15,250
Salary	$30,000	$30,000	$ 30,000
Less exemptions	4,000	4,000	4,000
Total	$26,000	$26,000	$ 26,000
Less excess deductions	5,800	5,800	5,800
Taxable income, personal	$20,200	$20,200	$ 20,200
Total personal tax	$ 3,273	$ 3,273	$ 3,273
Combined total tax	$ 6,673	$12,523	$ 18,523

Table 3.5

Total Taxes for CV as a Sole Proprietorship

	1979	1980	1981
Total income	$50,000	$80,000	$100,000
Less exemptions	4,000	4,000	4,000
Total	$46,000	$76,000	$ 96,000
Less excess deductions	5,800	5,800	5,800
Taxable income	$40,200	$70,200	$ 90,200
Tax liability	$10,312	$25,186	$ 36,216

(most of it at less than 30 percent). Under the single proprietorship, much of his income is subject to higher rates.

To a certain extent, the advantage to the corporate form of organization is somewhat illusory. The figures shown for the corporation deal with dollars that have not yet come into the hands of the shareholders. If the earnings are distributed as a dividend, there will be further taxes to be borne by the shareholders individually. If a shareholder sells his or her stock and gets the benefit of corporate earnings in the form of a capital gain, the person will have to pay a capital gains tax. The extent of the ultimate additional tax is currently unknown, but the shareholder does benefit from having at least temporary use of the tax dollars saved. We can now compare the results:

	1979	1980	1981
Taxes paid as a proprietorship	$10,312	$25,186	$36,216
Taxes paid as a corporation	6,673	12,523	18,523
Advantage as a corporation	$ 3,639	$12,663	$17,693

(We have also performed these calculations assuming the scheduled full 25 percent reduction in personal income tax rates and the reduced tax rates for the lower corporate income brackets. The advantage to the corporate form is reduced, but still persists because it enables income to be "split" and subject to lower marginal rates.) Of course, for a large enterprise with income of several hundred million dollars, the "tax splitting" effect does not have as great an influence. However, in that case, the corporation's effectiveness in raising large sums of capital from a large number of sources becomes the major consideration in selecting the corporate form of organization.

While broad generalizations are not possible, these are factors that should at least be taken into account in making the decision about the form of organization for any business enterprise.

Special Provisions for Small Business

A number of provisions of the Internal Revenue Code favor small business firms. Two in particular are of practical importance.

Subchapter S Corporations

Subchapter S of the Internal Revenue Code provides that some small, incorporated businesses may still elect to be taxed as proprietorships or partnerships if some technical requirements are met. Thus the firm may enjoy the protection of the limited liability provided by incorporation, but still retain some tax advantages.

These benefits are particularly important to a small new firm, which may incur losses while it seeks to become established in its beginning years. Its operating losses may be used on a pro rata basis by its stockholders as deductions against their ordinary income. This would stimulate persons in high marginal personal income tax brackets to invest in small, new, risky enterprises. Similarly, investment tax credits (deductions against tax liabilities and therefore very valuable) can be taken by the stockholders. New firms making large capital investments may not have income sufficient to fully utilize such tax credits. But the deductions would be very valuable to individuals with high incomes. In circumstances in which an analysis favored the use of a sole proprietorship, the owners can still gain the benefits of limited liability, but pay taxes as a sole proprietorship. This would avoid the double taxation involved in the payment of a corporate income tax.

Section 1244 Provisions

Section 1244 of the Revenue Act of 1978 provides that individuals who invest in the stock of small corporations and suffer a loss on that stock may, for tax purposes, treat such a loss up to $25,000 a year ($50,000 on a joint return) as an ordinary loss rather than as a capital loss. A corporation is defined for this purpose as a small corporation, and the loss on its stock can be treated as an ordinary loss, if its common stock does not exceed $500,000 and if its total shareholders' equity—common stock plus retained earnings—does not exceed $1 million. This provision also encourages the formation of, and investment in, small corporations.

Although the foregoing special provisions make it difficult to generalize on whether the corporate or the noncorporate form is more advantageous from a tax standpoint, the essential variables for making an analysis are provided. In general, the advantage now seems to be on the side of the corporation, particularly since a small firm may obtain the many benefits of its corporate status and yet elect to be taxed as a proprietorship or a partnership.

Tax Considerations and Financial Policy

The object of tax planning should be to minimize the burden of taxation. To achieve this objective, the following guideposts should be used:

1. Keep income stable to avoid top rate brackets.
2. Speed up or defer income and expenses to take advantage of anticipated higher or lower tax rates.
3. Spread income over several years to keep out of higher tax brackets and postpone tax.
4. Use tax-free money to expand business operations.
5. Select the best form for your business operations.
6. Set up business deals along lines that make the best overall use of tax rates, earning potential, losses, and depreciable assets.

Many transactions can be arranged or structured to minimize tax burdens. Tax planning should form an integral part of corporate financial policy.

Summary

This chapter provides some background on the tax environment within which business firms operate. The corporate tax rate structure is relatively simple. The tax rate is 17 percent on income up to $25,000; 20, 30, and 40 percent respectively on the next three increments of $25,000; and 46 percent on all income over $100,000. (As of 1983, the rates on the first two $25,000 increments drop to 15 and 18 percent respectively.) Estimated taxes are paid in quarterly installments during the year in which the income is earned; when the returns are filed, the actual tax liability results either in additional payments or in a refund due. Any operating loss incurred by the corporation can be carried back three years and forward fifteen years against income in those years.

Assets that are not bought and sold in the ordinary course of business are subject to capital gains tax on disposition. If an asset is held more than twelve months, any gain on the sale is classified as long-term and taxed at a maximum rate of 28+ percent. Gains on assets held fewer than twelve months are subject to taxation at the company's regular rate. Capital losses can be offset against capital gains to arrive at net long-term gains and net short-term gains. These losses can be carried back against gains for three years and carried forward for five years but cannot be offset against ordinary income.

Of the dividends received by a corporation owning stock in another firm, 85 percent are excluded from the receiving firm's taxable income, but the firm must pay full taxes on the remaining 15 percent. Dividends paid are not treated as a tax-deductible expense. Regardless of the size of its earnings, a corporation does not have to pay dividends if it needs funds for expansion. If, however, the funds are not used for a legitimate purpose—if earnings are retained merely to enable stockholders to avoid paying personal income taxes on dividends received—the firm is subject to an improper accumulations tax. Interest received is taxable as ordinary income; interest paid is a deductible expense.

Unincorporated business income is taxed at the personal tax rate of the owner. Personal income tax rates for both individuals and married persons filing jointly are progressive—the higher the income, the higher the tax rate. The rates start at 14 percent of taxable income and rise to a maximum of 50 percent.

The holding period for long-term capital gains and losses is twelve months, which is the same as that for corporations. Short-term gains are taxed as ordinary income, and 40 percent of long-term gains are taxed at the regular tax rate.

The information presented here on the tax system is not designed to make the reader a tax expert. It merely provides a few essentials for recognizing the tax aspects of business financial problems and for developing an awareness of the kinds of situations that should be dealt with by tax specialists. These basics are, however, referred to frequently throughout the text, because income taxes are often an important factor in business financial decisions.

Sole proprietorships and partnerships are easily formed. All earnings are taxed at the rate of the owner or partner as regular income. Owners and partners are also personally liable for the debts of the business.

The corporation has the advantage of limiting the liability of the participants, but it is generally more expensive to organize. Once organized it is easy to transfer ownership to others. Corporate earnings paid as dividends are subject to double taxation. The other tax differences between corporations and proprietorships or partnerships depend on the facts of individual cases.

Questions

3.1 Compare the marginal and the average 1981 tax rates of corporations for taxable incomes of $5,000, $50,000, $500,000, and $50,000,000. Can you make such a comparison for sole proprietorships or for partnerships?

3.2 Which is the more relevant tax rate—the marginal or the average—in determining the form of organization for a new firm? Have recent changes in the tax laws made the form of organization more or less important than formerly? Explain.

3.3 For tax purposes, how does the treatment of interest expense compare with the treatment of common stock dividends from each of the following standpoints: a firm paying the interest or dividends, an individual recipient, and a corporate recipient?

3.4 What is the purpose of the Internal Revenue Code provision dealing with improper accumulation of corporate surplus revenue?

3.5 Why is personal income tax information important for a study of business finance?

3.6 How do the tax rates for capital gains and losses affect an individual's investment policies and opportunities for financing a small business?

3.7 What are the advantages and disadvantages of the use of a sole proprietorship versus a partnership for conducting the operations of a small business firm?

3.8 Under what circumstances does it become advantageous for the small business to incorporate?

3.9 In what sense is the corporation a person?

3.10 Would it be practical for General Motors to be organized as a partnership?

Problems

3.1 A corporation had net income of $73,500 in 1981.
a. How much income tax must the corporation pay?
b. What is the marginal tax rate?
c. What is the average tax rate?

3.2 The J. K. Allen Corporation had net income from operations of $30,000. It also had $10,000 of interest expense and $25,000 of interest revenue during the 1981 fiscal year.
a. How much income tax must the corporation pay?
b. What is the marginal tax rate?
c. What is the average tax rate?

3.3 The Moonstone Corporation had net income of $140,000 in 1981, including $20,000 in dividend income on stocks of various major publicly held corporations. Moonstone paid out $25,000 in dividends to its own shareholders.
a. How much tax must the corporation pay?
b. What is the average tax rate on net income?

3.4 Determine the marginal and average 1981 income tax rates for a corporation earning (a) $10,000; (b) $100,000; (c) $1,000,000, and (d) $100,000,000.

3.5 The taxable income of the Baer Corporation, formed in 1977, is indicated below. (Losses are shown as minuses.)

Year	Taxable income
1977	−$80,000
1978	60,000
1979	50,000
1980	70,000
1981	−120,000

What is the corporate tax liability for each year? (Use 1981 rates.)

3.6 John Alexander has operated his small machine shop as a sole proprietorship for several years, but recent changes in the corporate tax structure have led him to consider incorporating.

Alexander is married and has two children. His family's only income, an annual salary of $40,000, is from operating the business. He reinvests any additional earnings in the business. His itemized deductions in excess of the applicable standard deduction are $6,100. Alexander estimates that his proprietorship earnings before salary and taxes for the period of 1983 to 1985 will be:

Year	Income before salary and taxes
1983	$50,000
1984	70,000
1985	90,000

a. What will his total taxes be under:
   1. a corporate form of organization?
   2. a proprietorship?

   Hint: Assume a 25 percent reduction in personal income tax rates as of 1983.

b. Should Alexander incorporate? Discuss.

3.7 During 1981 Wilbraham Corporation purchased industrial equipment costing $45,000. The equipment is expected to last eight years. Wilbraham's net income before taxes for the year was $85,000. How much income tax must Wilbraham pay?

3.8 The Germaine Corporation has purchased an asset for $5,200. It has an estimated salvage value of $200 at the end of its five-year life. The annual hours of use for the machine are estimated as follows:

Year	Hours of use
1	1,500
2	1,400
3	1,200
4	900
5	500

Calculate the annual depreciation under each of the following methods:

a. Straight line method
b. Double declining balance method
c. Sum-of-years'-digits method
d. Units of production method

CHAPTER 4

THE TIME VALUE OF MONEY

A clear view of the time value of money is essential to an understanding of many topics throughout this book. Financial structure decisions, lease versus purchase decisions, bond refunding operations, security valuation techniques, and the whole question of the cost of capital are subjects that cannot be understood without a knowledge of compound interest.

Many people are afraid of the subject and simply avoid it. It is certainly true that many successful business persons—even some bankers—know very little about it. However, as technology advances, as more engineers become involved in general management, and as modern business administration programs turn out more highly qualified graduates, this pattern—success in spite of yourself—will become more difficult to achieve. Furthermore, a fear of compound interest relationships is quite unfounded; the subject matter is not inherently difficult. Almost all problems involving compound interest can be handled with only a few basic formulas.

Compound Value

A person invests $1,000 in a security that pays 10 percent interest compounded annually. How much will this person have at the end of one year? To treat the matter systematically, let us define the following terms:

$$P_0 = \text{principal, or beginning amount, at time 0}$$

$$r = \text{interest rate}$$

$$P_0 r = \text{total dollar amount of interest earned}$$

$$V_{r,n} = \text{value at the end of } n \text{ periods}$$

When n equals 1, $V_{r,n}$ can be calculated as follows:

$$\begin{aligned} V_{r,1} &= P_0 + P_0 r \\ &= P_0(1 + r) \end{aligned} \tag{4.1}$$

Equation 4.1 shows that the ending amount ($V_{r,1}$) is equal to the beginning amount (P_0) times the factor $(1 + r)$. In the example, where P_0 is $1,000, r is 10 percent, and n is one year, $V_{r,n}$ is determined as follows:

$$V_{10\%,\,1\text{ yr.}} = \$1{,}000(1.0 + 0.10) = \$1{,}000(1.10) = \$1{,}100$$

Multiple Periods

If the person leaves the $1,000 on deposit for five years, to what amount will it have grown at the end of that period? Equation 4.1 can be used to construct Table 4.1,

Table 4.1 **Compound Interest Calculations**

Period	Beginning amount	× (1 + r) =	Ending amount ($V_{r,n}$)
1	$1,000.00	1.10	$1,100.00
2	1,100.00	1.10	1,210.00
3	1,210.00	1.10	1,331.00
4	1,331.00	1.10	1,464.10
5	1,464.10	1.10	1,610.51

which indicates the answer. Note that $V_{r,2}$, the balance at the end of the second year, is found as follows:

$$V_{r,2} = V_{r,1}(1 + r) = P_0(1 + r)(1 + r) = P_0(1 + r)^2$$

Similarly, $V_{r,3}$, the balance after three years, is found as:

$$V_{r,3} = V_{r,2}(1 + r) = P_0(1 + r)^3$$

In general, $V_{r,n}$, the compound amount at the end of any year n, is found as:

$$V_{r,n} = P_0(1 + r)^n \tag{4.2}$$

Equation 4.2 is the fundamental equation of compound interest. Equation 4.1 is simply a special case of Equation 4.2, where $n = 1$.

While an understanding of the derivation of Equation 4.2 will help in understanding much of the remaining material in this chapter (and in subsequent chapters), the concept can be applied quite readily in a mechanical sense. Tables have been constructed for values of $(1 + r)^n$ for wide ranges of r and n. (See Table A.1 in Appendix A at the end of the book.)

Letting CVIF (compound value interest factor) $= (1 + r)^n$, we can write Equation 4.2 as $V_{r,n} = P_0[\text{CVIF}(r, n)]$. It is necessary only to go to an appropriate interest table to find the proper interest factor. For example, the correct interest factor for the illustration given in Table 4.1 can be found in Table A.1. Look down the period column to 5, then across this row to the appropriate number in the 10 percent column to find the interest factor, 1.6105. Then, using this interest factor, the compound value of the $1,000 after five years is:

$$V_{10\%,\ 5\text{ yrs.}} = P_0\text{CVIF}(10\%, 5\text{ yrs.}) = \$1{,}000(1.6105) = \$1{,}610.50$$

This is precisely the same figure that was obtained by the long method in Table 4.1.

Graphic View of the Compounding Process: Growth

Figure 4.1 shows how the interest factors for compounding grow as the compounding period increases. Curves can be drawn for any interest rate, including fractional rates; we have plotted curves for 0 percent, 5 percent, and 10 percent from data in Table A.1.

Figure 4.1 also shows how $1 (or any other sum) grows over time at various rates of interest. The higher the rate of interest, the faster the rate of growth. The interest rate is, in fact, the growth rate; if a deposited sum earns 5 percent, then the funds on deposit grow at the rate of 5 percent per year.

Figure 4.1

Relationships among Compound Value Interest Factors, Interest Rates, and Time

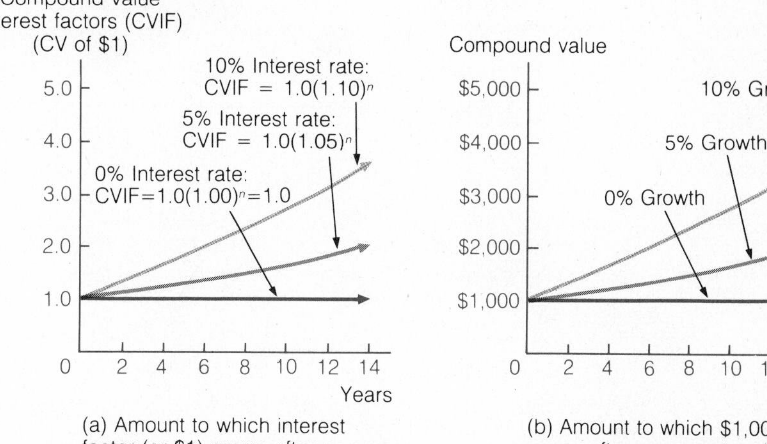

Present Value

Suppose you are offered the alternative of either $1,610.50 at the end of five years or X dollars today. There is no question that the $1,610.50 will be paid in full (perhaps the payer is the United States government). Having no current need for the money, you deposit the X dollars in a savings association paying 10 percent interest; the 10 percent is your *opportunity cost*. How small must X be to induce you to accept the promise of $1,610.50 five years hence?

Table 4.1 shows that the initial amount of $1,000 growing at 10 percent a year yields $1,610.50 at the end of five years. Thus, you should be indifferent about the choice between $1,000 today and $1,610.50 at the end of five years. The $1,000 is the present value of $1,610.50 due in five years when the applicable interest rate is 10 percent. The subscript zero in the term P_0 indicates the present. Hence present value quantities can be identified by either P_0 or $P_{r,n}$.

Finding present values (*discounting*, as it is commonly called) is simply the reverse of compounding, and Equation 4.2 can readily be transformed into a present value formula.

$$\text{Present value} = P_0 = \frac{V_{r,n}}{(1+r)^n} = V_{r,n}\left[\frac{1}{(1+r)^n}\right] = V_{r,n}\text{PVIF}(r, n) \qquad \textbf{(4.3)}$$

Tables have been constructed for the bracketed term for various values of r and n. (See Table A.2 in Appendix A at the end of the book.) For the case being considered, look down the 10 percent column in Table A.2 to the fifth row. The figure shown there, 0.6209, is the present value interest factor (PVIF) used to determine the present value of $1,610.50 payable in five years, discounted at 10 percent.

$$\begin{aligned} P_0 &= V_{10\%,\ 5\text{ yrs.}}\ (\text{PVIF}) \\ &= \$1{,}610.50(0.6209) \\ &= \$1{,}000 \end{aligned}$$

Figure 4.2 **Relationships among Present Value Interest Factors, Interest Rates, and Time**

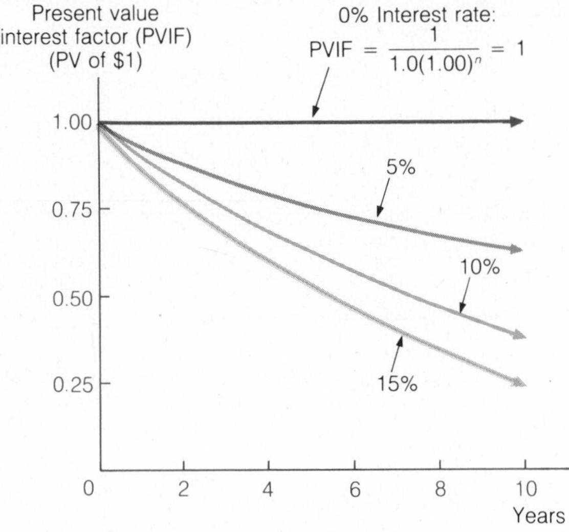

Graphic View of the Discounting Process

Figure 4.2 shows how the interest factors for discounting decrease as the discounting period increases. The curves in the figure, plotted from data in Table A.2, show that the present value of a sum to be received at some future date decreases (1) as the payment date is extended further into the future and (2) as the discount rate increases. If relatively high discount rates apply, funds due in the future are worth very little today; even at relatively low discount rates, funds due in the distant future are not worth much today. For example, $1,000 due in ten years is worth $247 today if the discount rate is 15 percent, but it is worth $614 today at a 5 percent discount rate. Similarly, $1,000 due in ten years at 10 percent is worth $386 today, but the same amount at the same discount rate due in five years is worth $621 today.[1]

Compound Value versus Present Value

Because a thorough understanding of compound value concepts is vital to understanding the remainder of this book and because the subject gives many students trouble, it will be useful to examine in more detail the relationship between compounding and discounting.

Notice that Equation 4.2, the basic equation for compounding, is developed from the logical sequence set forth in Table 4.1; the equation merely presents in mathematical form the steps outlined in the table. The present value interest factor [PVIF(r, n)] in Equation 4.3 (the basic equation for discounting or finding present values) is the reciprocal of the compound value interest factor [CVIF(r, n)] for the same r, n combination:

$$\text{PVIF}(r, n) = \frac{1}{\text{CVIF}(r, n)}$$

[1] Note that Figure 4.2 is not a mirror image of Figure 4.1. The curves in Figure 4.1 approach ∞ as n increases; in Figure 4.2, the curves approach zero, not $-\infty$, as n increases.

For example, the *compound value* interest factor for 10 percent over five years is seen in Table A.1 to be 1.6105. The *present value* interest factor for 10 percent over five years must therefore be the reciprocal of 1.6105:

$$\text{PVIF}(10\%, 5 \text{ yrs.}) = \frac{1}{1.6105} = 0.6209$$

The PVIF found in this manner must, of course, correspond with the PVIF shown in Table A.2 at the end of this book.

The reciprocal nature of the relationship between present value and compound value permits us to find present values in two ways—by multiplying or by dividing. Thus the present value of $1,000 due in five years and discounted at 10 percent can be found as:

$$P_0 = P_{r,n} = V_{r,n}[\text{PVIF}(r, n)] = V_{r,n}\left(\frac{1}{1+r}\right)^n = \$1{,}000(0.6209) = \$620.90$$

or

$$P_0 = P_{r,n} = \frac{V_{r,n}}{\text{CVIF}(r, n)} = \frac{V_{r,n}}{(1+r)^n} = \frac{\$1{,}000}{1.6105} = \$620.90$$

In the second form, it is easy to see why the present value of a given future amount ($V_{r,n}$) declines as the discount rate increases.

To conclude this comparison of present and compound values, compare Figures 4.1 and 4.2. Notice that the vertical intercept is at 1.0 in each case, but compound value interest factors rise while present value interest factors decline. The reason for this divergence is, of course, that present value factors are reciprocals of compound factors.

Compound Value of an Annuity

An *annuity* is defined as a series of payments of a fixed amount for a specified number of years. Each payment occurs at the end of the year.[2] For example, a promise to pay $1,000 a year for three years is a three-year annuity. If you were to receive such an annuity and were to invest each annual payment in a security paying 10 percent interest, how much would you have at the end of three years? The answer is shown graphically in Figure 4.3. The first payment is made at the end of Year 1, the second at the end of Year 2, and the third at the end of Year 3. The last payment is not compounded at all; the next to the last is compounded for one year; the first is compounded for two years, that is, for $n - 1$ years. When the compound values of each of the payments are added, their total is the sum of the annuity. In the example, this total is $3,310.

Expressed algebraically, with $V_{r,t}$ defined as the compound sum, a as the periodic receipt, t as the length of the annuity, and CVIFA as the compound value

[2] Had the payment been made at the beginning of the period, each receipt would simply have been shifted back one year. The annuity would have been called an *annuity due*; the one in the present discussion, where payments are made at the end of each period, is called a *regular annuity* or, sometimes, a *deferred annuity*.

Figure 4.3 **Graphic Illustration of an Annuity: Compound Sum**

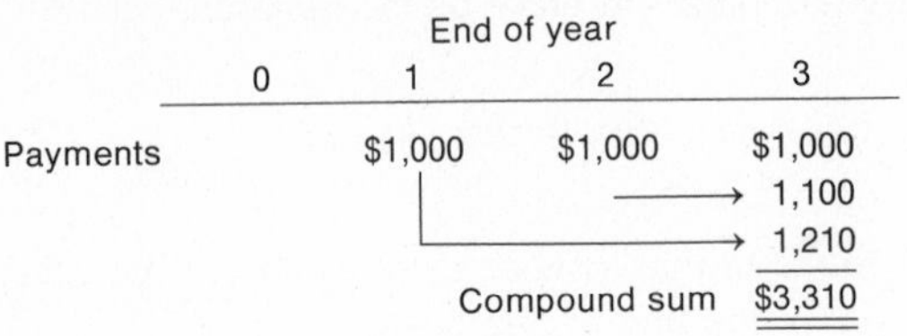

interest factor for an annuity, the formula for $V_{r,t}$ is:

$$V_{r,t} = a(1+r)^{n-1} + a(1+r)^{n-2} + \cdots + a(1+r)^1 + a(1+r)^0$$
$$= a[(1+r)^{n-1} + (1+r)^{n-2} + \cdots + (1+r)^1 + (1+r)^0]$$
$$V_{r,t} = a\text{CVIFA}(r,t) \quad \textbf{(4.4)}$$

CVIFA has been given values for various combinations of r and t. To find these, see Table A.3 in Appendix A. To find the answer to the three-year, $1,000 annuity problem, simply refer to Table A.3, look down the 10 percent column to the row for the third year, and multiply the factor 3.3100 by $1,000. The answer is the same as the one derived by the long method illustrated in Figure 4.3:

$$V_{r,t} = a \times \text{CVIFA}\ (r,t)$$
$$V_{10\%,\ 3\ \text{yrs.}} = \$1{,}000 \times 3.3100 = \$3{,}310$$

Notice that the CVIFA for the sum of an annuity is always larger than the number of years the annuity runs.

It is useful to recognize some relationships between the formulas for a compound sum and for the sum of an annuity by looking at them together.

$$\text{Compound sum: } V_{r,n} = P_0\text{CVIF}(r,n)$$
$$\text{Compound value of an annuity: } V_{r,t} = a \times \text{CVIFA}(r,t)$$

Both formulas involve an interest rate, r. But time is indexed as n in the compound sum and as t in the compound value of an annuity. An example will illustrate the reason. You place $1,000 in a savings account and want to know what its value will be at the end of 3 years at a compound interest rate of 10 percent. The compound interest factor at 10% for 3 years is 1.3310 as shown by Table A.1. So the compound value at the end of 3 years is $1,331.

The sum of an annuity formula is based on making a deposit of $1,000 at the end of the first year and also at the end of the second and third years. So we have to use t to indicate that the annuity deposits are made at the end of each of the years 1, 2, and 3. The third year in this example is the nth year, or the terminal (final) year. This is the reason n is used in the compound sum and present value formulas, but t is used in the formulas involving annuities. In Table A.3 we find that the sum of an annuity factor at 10% for 3 years is 3.3100, giving a compound future sum of $3,310. This is much larger than the result for the compound sum because three deposits (rather than one) were made. Even at a zero interest rate the compound sum factor for the three deposits (three annuity payments) would be 3, which is much larger than the compound sum factor of 1.3310 with a ten percent interest rate.

Present Value of an Annuity

Suppose you were offered the following alternatives: a three-year annuity of $1,000 a year or a lump-sum payment today. You have no need for the money during the next three years, so if you accept the annuity you will simply invest the funds in a security paying 10 percent interest. How large must the lump-sum payment be to make it equivalent to the annuity? Figure 4.4 helps explain the problem.

Figure 4.4

Graphic Illustration of an Annuity: Present Value

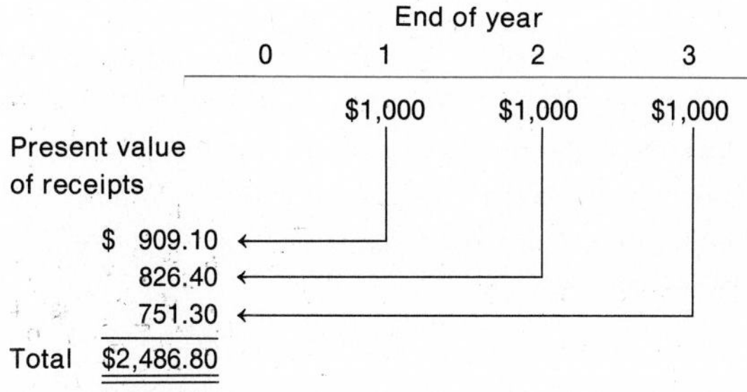

The present value of the first receipt is $a[1/(1+r)]$, that of the second is $a[1/(1+r)]^2$, and so on. Defining the present value of an annuity of t years as $P_{r,t}$ and the present value interest factor for an annuity as PVIFA, we can write the following equation:

$$P_{r,t} = a\left[\frac{1}{1+r}\right] + a\left[\frac{1}{1+r}\right]^2 + \cdots + a\left[\frac{1}{1+r}\right]^t$$

$$= a\left[\frac{1}{(1+r)} + \frac{1}{(1+r)^2} + \cdots + \frac{1}{(1+r)^t}\right]$$

$$P_{r,t} = a\text{PVIFA}(r, t) \quad \textbf{(4.5)}$$

Again, tables have been worked out for the PVIFA, the term in the brackets. (See Table A.4 in Appendix A.) From Table A.4, the PVIFA for a three-year, 10 percent annuity is found to be 2.4869. Multiplying this factor by the $1,000 annual receipt gives $2,486.90, the present value of the annuity:

$$P_{r,t} = a \times \text{PVIFA}(r, t)$$

$$P_{10\%,\ 3\text{ yrs.}} = \$1{,}000 \times 2.4869 = \$2{,}486.90$$

Notice that the PVIFA for the present value of an annuity is always less than the number of years the annuity runs, whereas the CVIFA for the sum of an annuity is larger than the number of years.

Annual Payments for Accumulation of a Future Sum

Thus far in the chapter all the equations have been based on Equation 4.2. The present value equation merely involves a transposition of Equation 4.2, and the annuity equations simply take the sum of the basic compound interest equation for different values of t. We now examine some additional modifications of the equations.

Suppose we want to know the amount of money that must be deposited at 10 percent for each of the next five years in order to have $10,000 available to pay off a debt at the end of the fifth year. Dividing both sides of Equation 4.4 by the CVIFA, we obtain:

$$a = \frac{V_{r,t}}{\text{CVIFA}(r, t)} \tag{4.6}$$

Looking up the sum of an annuity interest factor for five years at 10 percent in Table A.3 at the end of the book and dividing that figure into $10,000 we find:

$$a = \frac{\$10,000}{6.1051} = \$1,638$$

Thus, if $1,638 is deposited each year in an account paying a 10 percent return, at the end of five years the account will have accumulated $10,000. The procedure is called setting up a sinking fund; such funds are used, for example, to provide for bond retirements.

Annual Receipts from an Annuity

Suppose that on September 1, 1981, you receive an inheritance of $7,000. The money is to be used for your education and is to be spent during the academic years beginning September 1982, 1983, and 1984. If you place the money in a bank account paying 10 percent annual interest and make three equal withdrawals on each of the specified dates, how large can each withdrawal be to leave you with exactly a zero balance after the last one has been made?

The solution requires application of the present value of an annuity formula, Equation 4.5. Here, however, we know that the present value of the annuity is $7,000, and the problem is to find the three equal annual payments when the interest rate is 10 percent. This calls for dividing both sides of Equation 4.5 by the PVIFA to make Equation 4.7.

$$P_{r,t} = a \times \text{PVIFA}(r, t) \tag{4.5}$$

$$a = \frac{P_{r,t}}{\text{PVIFA}(r, t)} \tag{4.7}$$

The interest factor (PVIFA) is found in Appendix A, Table A.4 to be 2.4869. Substituting this value in Equation 4.7, we find the three equal annual withdrawals to be $2,814.75:

$$a = \frac{\$7,000}{2.4869} = \$2,814.75$$

This particular kind of calculation frequently is used in setting up insurance and pension plan benefit schedules; it is also used to find the periodic payments necessary to retire a loan within a specified period. For example, if you want to retire a \$7,000 bank loan, bearing interest at 10 percent on the unpaid balance, in three equal annual installments, the amount of each payment is \$2,814.75. In this case, you are the borrower, and the bank is "buying" an annuity with a present value of \$7,000.

Determining Interest Rates

In many instances the present values and cash flows associated with a payment stream are known, but the interest rate is not known. Suppose a bank offers to lend you \$1,000 today if you sign a note agreeing to pay the bank \$1,762.30 at the end of five years. What rate of interest would you be paying on the loan? To answer the question, we use Equation 4.2:

$$V_{r,n} = P_0(1 + r)^n = P_0\text{CVIF}(r, n) \tag{4.2}$$

We simply solve for the CVIF, then look up this value of the CVIF in Table A.1 under the row for the fifth year:

$$\text{CVIF}(r, n) = \frac{V_{r,\,5\text{ yrs.}}}{P_0} = \frac{\$1{,}762.30}{\$1{,}000} = 1.7623$$

Looking across the row for the fifth year, we find the value 1.7623 in the 12 percent column; therefore, the interest rate on the loan is 12 percent.

Precisely the same approach is taken to determine the interest rate implicit in an annuity. For example, suppose a bank will lend you \$2,401.80 if you sign a note in which you agree to pay the bank \$1,000 at the end of each of the next three years. What interest rate is the bank charging you? To answer the question, we solve Equation 4.5 for PVIFA and then look up the PVIFA in Table A.4:

$$P_{r,t} = a \times \text{PVIFA}(r, t) \tag{4.5}$$

$$\text{PVIFA}(r, t) = \frac{P_{r,\,3\text{ yrs.}}}{a} = \frac{\$2{,}401.8}{\$1{,}000} = 2.4018$$

Looking across the third-year row, we find the factor 2.4018 under the 12 percent column; therefore, the bank is lending you money at 12 percent interest.

Linear Interpolation

The tables give values for even interest rates (such as 8 percent or 9 percent). Suppose you need to find the present value of \$1,000 due in ten years and discounted at $8\frac{1}{4}$ percent. The appropriate PVIF is not in the tables, but a very close approximation to the correct factor can be estimated by the method of *linear interpolation*. The PVIF for 8 percent, ten years, is 0.4632; that for 9 percent is 0.4224. The difference is 0.0408. Since $8\frac{1}{4}$ is 25 percent of the way between 8 and 9, we can subtract 25 percent of 0.0408 from 0.4632 and obtain 0.453 as the PVIF for $8\frac{1}{4}$ percent due in ten years. Thus, if the appropriate discount rate is $8\frac{1}{4}$ percent, \$1,000 due in ten years is worth \$453 today.

In general, the formula used for interpolation is as follows:

$$\text{IF for intermediate interest rate} = \left(\frac{r - r_L}{r_H - r_L}\right)(\text{IF}_H - \text{IF}_L) + \text{IF}_L \tag{4.8}$$

Here r is the interest rate in question, r_L is the interest rate in the table just lower than r, r_H is the interest rate in the table just higher than r, and IF_H and IF_L are the interest factors for r_H and r_L, respectively. Using the equation with the preceding example, we have:

$$\text{PVIF for } 8\tfrac{1}{4}\% \text{ due in 10 years} = \left(\frac{8.25 - 8}{9 - 8}\right)(0.4224 - 0.4632) + 0.4632$$
$$= \left(\frac{0.25}{1}\right)(-0.0408) + 0.4632 = 0.453,$$

which is the PVIF found before. The equation can be used for each type of factor expression, PVIF, CVIF, PVIFA, or CVIFA.

Interpolation can also be used to determine interest rates if interest factors are provided. For example, suppose an investment that costs $163,500 promises to yield $50,000 per year for four years, and we want to know the rate of return on the investment. We use Equation 4.5 to find the PVIFA:

$$\text{PVIFA} = \frac{\$163{,}500}{\$50{,}000} = 3.27$$

Looking this value up in Table A.4, Period 4, we see that it lies between 8 and 9 percent. Applying the interpolation formula, but solving for r, we have:[3]

$$\text{PVIFA for } r\% = 3.27 = \left(\frac{r - 8}{9 - 8}\right)(3.2397 - 3.3121) + 3.3121$$
$$3.27 = (r - 8)(-0.0724) + 3.3121$$
$$-0.0421 = -0.0724r + 0.5792$$
$$0.0724r = 0.6213$$
$$r = 8.58\%$$

Present Value of an Uneven Series of Receipts

The definition of an annuity includes the words *fixed amount*; in other words, annuities deal with constant, or level, payments or receipts. Although many financial decisions do involve constant payments, many others (especially those dealt with in Chapter 13) are concerned with *uneven flows* of cash. Consequently it is necessary to expand our analysis to deal with varying payment streams. Since most of

[3] Alternatively, the interest factors can be calculated using the formulas at the top of each table. For example, using an 8.25 percent interest rate and a ten-year period:

$$\text{CVIF} = (1 + k)^n = 1.0825^{10} = 2.2094$$
$$\text{PVIF} = 1/(1 + k)^n = 1/1.0825^{10} = 0.4526$$
$$\text{CVIFA} = [(1 + k)^n - 1]/k = (1.0825^{10} - 1)/0.0825$$
$$= 14.6597$$
$$\text{PVIFA} = [1 + (1 - k)^{-n}]/k = (1 - 1.0825^{-10})/0.0825$$

In this book, the formulas will be used for interest rates not given in the tables. Of course, all of this can be done directly on a hand calculator.

the applications call for present values, not compound sums or other figures, this section is restricted to the present value (PV).

To do the calculating procedure, suppose someone offers to sell you a series of payments consisting of $300 after one year, $100 after two years, and $200 after three years. How much will you be willing to pay for the series, assuming the appropriate discount rate (interest rate) is 10 percent? To determine the purchase price, we simply compute the present value of the series; the calculations are worked out in Table 4.2. The receipts for each year are shown in the second column; the discount factors are given in the third column; and the product of these two columns, the present value of each individual receipt, is given in the last column. When the individual present values in the last column are added together, the sum is the present value of the investment—$505.63. Under the assumptions of the example, you should be willing to pay this amount for the investment.

Table 4.2

Calculating the Present Value of an Uneven Series of Payments

Period	Receipt ×	Interest factor (PVIF)	=	Present value (PV or P_0)
1	$300	0.9091		$272.73
2	100	0.8264		82.64
3	200	0.7513		150.26
		PV of investment		$505.63

If the series of payments are somewhat different—say $300 at the end of the first year, $200 at the end of the second year, then eight annual payments of $100 each—we will probably want to use a different procedure for finding the investment's present value. We can, of course, set up a calculating table such as Table 4.2, but because most of the payments are part of an annuity, we can use a shortcut. The calculating procedure is shown in Table 4.3, and the logic of the table is diagramed in Figure 4.5.

Table 4.3

Calculating Procedure for an Uneven Series of Payments That Includes an Annuity

1. PV of $300 due in one year = $300(0.9091) = $272.73
   PV of $200 due in two years = $200(0.8264) = 165.28
2. PV of eight-year annuity with $100 receipts
   a. PV at beginning of Year 3:
      $100(5.3349) = $533.49
   b. PV of $533.49 = $533.49(0.8264) = 440.88
3. PV of total series $878.89

Section 1 of Table 4.3 deals with the $300 and the $200 received at the end of the first and second years, respectively; their present values are found to be $272.73 and $165.28. Section 2 deals with the eight $100 payments. In Part a, the value of a $100, eight-year, 10 percent annuity is found to be $533.49. However, $533.49 is the

Figure 4.5 **Graphic Illustration of Present Value Calculations for an Uneven Series of Payments That Includes an Annuity**

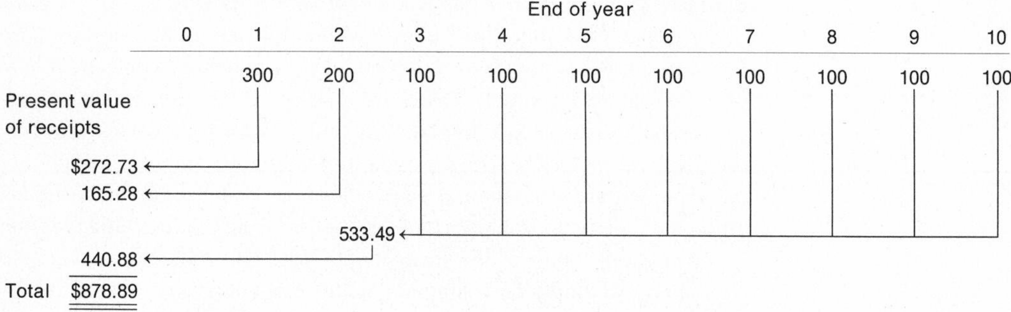

value of the annuity at the beginning of Year 3, that is, at the end of Year 2, so it is worth less than $533.49 today. Specifically, it is worth the present value of $533.49, discounted back two years at 10 percent, or $440.88. This calculation is shown in Part b of Section 2.[4] When the present values of the first two payments are added to the present value of the annuity component, the sum is the present value of the entire investment, or $878.89.

Semiannual and Other Compounding Periods[5]

In all the examples used thus far, it has been assumed that returns were received annually. For example, in the section dealing with compound values, it was assumed that the funds earned 10 percent a year. However, suppose the earnings rate had been 10 percent compounded semiannually (that is, every six months). What would this have meant? Consider the following example.

Table 4.4 **Compound Interest Calculations with Semiannual Compounding**

Period	Beginning amount (P_0)	×	$(1 + r)$	=	Ending amount ($V_{r,n}$)
1	$1,000.00		1.05		$1,050.00
2	1,050.00		1.05		1,102.50

You invest $1,000 in a security to receive a return of 10 percent compounded semiannually. How much will you have at the end of one year? Since semiannual compounding means that interest is actually paid each six months, this fact is taken into account in the tabular calculations in Table 4.4. Here, the annual interest rate is divided by two, but twice as many compounding periods are used because interest is paid twice a year. Comparing the amount on hand at the end of the second six-month period, $1,102.50, with what would have been on hand under annual compounding, $1,100.00, shows that semiannual compounding is better for the

[4] The present value of the annuity portion, $440.88, could also have been found by subtracting the PVIFA for a two-year annuity from the PVIFA for a ten-year annuity, then multiplying the result by $100.

[5] This section can be omitted without loss of continuity.

saver. This result occurs, of course, because the saver earns interest on interest more frequently. General formulas can be developed for use when compounding periods are more frequent than once a year. To demonstrate this, Equation 4.2 is modified as follows:

$$V_{r,n} = P_0(1 + r)^n \quad \textbf{(4.2)}$$

$$V_{r,n} = P_0\left(1 + \frac{r}{q}\right)^{qn} \quad \textbf{(4.9)}$$

Here, q is the number of times per year that compounding occurs. When banks compute daily interest, the value of q is set at 365, and Equation 4.9 is applied.

The interest tables can be used when compounding occurs more than once a year. Simply divide the nominal, or stated, interest rate by the number of times compounding occurs, and multiply the years by the number of compounding periods per year. For example, to find the amount to which $1,000 will grow after five years if semiannual compounding is applied to a stated 10 percent interest rate, divide 10 percent by two and multiply the five years by two. Then look in Table A.1 at the end of the book under the 5 percent column and in the row for the tenth period, where you will find an interest factor of 1.6289. Multiplying this by the initial $1,000 gives a value of $1,628.90, the amount to which $1,000 will grow in five years at 10 percent compounded semiannually. This compares with $1,610.50 for annual compounding.

The same procedure is applied in all the cases covered—compounding, discounting, single payments, and annuities. To illustrate semiannual compounding in finding the present value of an annuity, for example, consider the case described in the section on present value of an annuity; $1,000 a year for three years, discounted at 10 percent. With annual discounting or compounding the interest factor is 2.4869, and the present value of the annuity is $2,486.90. For semiannual compounding, look under the 5 percent column and in the Year 6 row of Table A.4 to find an interest factor of 5.0757. Then multiply by half of $1,000, or the $500 received each six months, to get the present value of the annuity, $2,537.85. The payments come a little more rapidly (the first $500 is paid after only six months), so the annuity is a little more valuable if payments are received semiannually rather than annually.

By letting q approach infinity, Equation 4.9 can be modified to the special case of *continuous compounding*. Continuous compounding is extremely useful in theoretical finance, and it also has practical applications. For example, some banks and savings and loan associations pay interest on a continuous basis.

A Special Case of Semiannual Compounding: Bond Values

Most bonds pay interest semiannually, so semiannual compounding procedures are appropriate for determining bond values. To illustrate: Suppose a particular bond pays interest in the amount of $50 each six months, or $100 a year. The bond will mature in ten years, paying $1,000 (the principal) at that time. Thus, if you buy the bond you will receive an annuity of $50 each six months, or twenty payments in total, plus $1,000 at the end of ten years (or twenty six-month periods). What is the bond worth, assuming that the appropriate market discount (or interest) rate is (a) 10 percent; (b) higher than 10 percent, say 12 percent; and (c) lower than 10 percent, say 8 percent?

At 10 Percent Interest

Step 1 You are buying an annuity plus a lump sum of $1,000. Find the PV of the interest payments:

1. Use $r/q = 10\%/2 = 5\%$ as the "interest rate."
2. Look up the PVIFA in Table A.4 for 20 periods at 5 percent, which is 12.4622.
3. Find the PV of the stream of interest payments:

$$\begin{aligned}\text{PV of the interest} &= \$50(\text{PVIFA})\\ &= \$50(12.4622)\\ &= \$623.11\end{aligned}$$

Step 2 Find the PV of the $1,000 maturity value:

1. Use $r/q = 10\%/2 = 5\%$ as the "interest rate."
2. Look up the PVIF in Table A.2 for 20 periods at 5 percent, which is 0.3769.
3. Find the PV of that value at maturity:

$$\begin{aligned}\text{PV of the maturity value} &= \$1{,}000(\text{PVIF})\\ &= \$1{,}000(0.3769) = \$376.90\end{aligned}$$

Step 3 Combine the two component PVs to determine the value of the bond:

$$\text{Bond value} = \$623.11 + \$376.90 = \$1{,}000.01$$

At 12 Percent Interest Repeating the process, we have:

Step 1 $12\%/2 = 6\% =$ the "interest rate."

$$\text{PVIFA from Table A.4} = 11.4699$$

$$\text{PVIF from Table A.2} = 0.3118$$

Step 2

$$\begin{aligned}\text{Bond value} &= \$50(11.4699) + \$1{,}000(0.3118)\\ &= \$573.50 + \$311.80\\ &= \$885.30\end{aligned}$$

Notice that the bond is worth less when the going rate of interest for investments of similar risk is 12 percent than when it is 10 percent. At a price of $885.30, this bond provides an annual rate of return of 12 percent; at a price of $1,000, it provides an annual return of 10 percent. If 10 percent is the coupon rate on a bond of a given degree of risk, then whenever interest rates in the economy rise to the point where bonds of this degree of risk have a 12 percent return, the price of our bond will decline to $885.30, at which price it will yield the competitive rate of return, 12 percent.

At 8 Percent Interest Using the same process produces the following results:

Step 1 $8\%/2 = 4\% =$ the "interest rate."

$$\text{PVIFA from Table A.4} = 13.5903$$

$$\text{PVIF from Table A.2} = 0.4564$$

Step 2 Bond value = \$50(13.5903) + \$1,000(0.4564)

= \$679.52 + \$456.40

= \$1,135.92

The bond is worth more than \$1,000 when the going rate of interest is less than 10 percent, because then it offers a yield higher than the going rate. Its price rises to \$1,135.92, where it provides an 8 percent annual rate of return. This calculation illustrates the fact that when interest rates in the economy decline, the prices of outstanding bonds rise.

Appropriate Compounding or Discounting Rates

Throughout the chapter, assumed compounding or discounting rates have been used in the examples. It is useful at this point to summarize what the appropriate interest rate for a particular investment might be.[6]

The starting point is, of course, the general level of interest rates (for each type of investment) in the economy as a whole, which is set by the interaction of supply and demand forces.

There is no single rate of interest in the economy; at any given time, there is an array of different rates. The lowest rates are set on the safest investments and the highest rates on the most risky ones. Usually, there is less risk on investments that mature in the near future than on longer-term investments, so higher rates are usually associated with long-term investments.

People who have money to invest can buy short-term United States government securities and incur no default risk whatever. However, they generally must accept a relatively low yield on investment. Those willing to assume a little more risk can invest in high-grade corporate bonds and get a higher fixed rate of return. And people willing to accept still more risk can move into common stocks to obtain variable (and, they hope, higher) returns (dividends plus capital gains) on investment. Still other alternatives are bank and savings and loan deposits, long-term government bonds, mortgages, apartment houses, land held for speculation, and various forms of international securities and investments.

Risk Premiums

With only a limited amount of money to invest, one must pick and choose among investments, the final selection involving a trade-off between risk and return. Suppose, for example, that you are indifferent about the choice of a five-year government bond yielding 10 percent a year, a five-year corporate bond yielding 12 percent, and a share of stock on which you can expect a 15 percent return. Given this situation, the government bond is assumed to be a riskless security, and a 2 percent risk premium is attached to the corporate bond, while a 5 percent risk premium is attached to the share of stock. Risk premiums, then, are the added returns that risky investments must command over less risky ones if there is to be a demand for them. (The concept of the risk premium is discussed in more detail in Chapters 14 and 16.)

[6] For convenience, in this chapter we speak of *interest rates*, which implies that only debt is involved. In later chapters the concept is broadened considerably, and the terms *rate of return* or *discount factor* are used in place of *interest rate*.

Opportunity Costs

Although there are many potential investments available in the economy at any given time, individual investors actively consider only a limited number of them. After making adjustments for risk differentials, they rank the various alternatives from most attractive to least attractive. Then, presumably, they put their available funds into the most attractive investment. If they are offered a new investment, they must compare it with the best of the existing alternatives. If they take the new investment, they must give up the opportunity of investing in the best of the old alternatives. *The yield on the best of the alternatives is defined as the opportunity cost of investing in the new alternative.* For example, suppose you have funds invested in an asset that pays 10 percent. Now someone offers you another investment of equal risk. To make the new investment, you must withdraw funds from the asset; therefore, 10 percent is the opportunity cost of the new investment.

Summary

A knowledge of compound interest and present value techniques is essential to an understanding of several important aspects of finance: capital budgeting, financial structure, security valuation, and many other topics.

The four basic equations with the notation that will be used throughout the book are:

1. $V_{r,n} = P_0\text{CVIF}(r, n)$

2. $P_{r,n} = V_{r,n}\text{PVIF}(r, n)$

3. $V_{r,t} = a\text{CVIFA}(r, t)$

4. $P_{r,t} = a\text{PVIFA}(r, t)$

The compound value ($V_{r,n}$), or the compound amount, is defined as the sum to which a beginning amount of principal (P_0) will grow over n years when interest is earned at the rate of r percent a year. The equation for finding compound value is:

$$V_{r,n} = P_0(1 + r)^n$$

Tables giving the compound value of $1 for a large number of different years and interest rates have been prepared. The compound value of $1 is called the compound value interest factor (CVIF), given in Appendix Table A.1.

The present value of a future payment ($P_{r,n}$) is the amount that, if we had it now and if we invested it at the specifed interest rate (r), would equal the future payment ($V_{r,n}$) on the date the future payment is due. For example, if a person were to receive $1,610 after five years and then decided 10 percent were the appropriate interest rate (called the *discount rate* when computing present values), then that person could find the present value of the $1,610 by applying the following equation:

$$P_{r,n} = V_{r,n}\left[\frac{1}{(1 + r)^n}\right] = \$1{,}610(0.6209) = \$1{,}000$$

The term in brackets is called the present value interest factor (PVIF), and values for it have been worked out in Appendix Table A.2.

An *annuity* is defined as a series of payments of a fixed amount (a) for a specifed number of years. The compound value of an annuity is the total amount one will have at the end of the annuity period if each payment is invested at a certain interest rate and is held to the end of the annuity period. For example, suppose we have a three-year, $1,000 annuity invested at 10 percent. There are formulas for annuities, but tables are available for the relevant interest factors. The CVIFA for the compound value of a three-year annuity at 10 percent is 3.3100, and it can be used to find the compound value of the illustrative annuity:

$$V_{r,t} = \text{Compound value of annuity} = \text{CVIFA}(r,t) \times \text{Annual receipt}$$
$$= 3.3100 \times \$1{,}000 = \$3{,}310$$

Thus, $3,310 is the compound value of the annuity.

The present value of an annuity is the lump sum we would need to have on hand today in order to be able to withdraw equal amounts (*a*) each year and end up with a balance exactly equal to zero at the end of the annuity period. For example, if we wish to withdraw $1,000 a year for three years, we could deposit $2,486.90 today in a bank account paying 10 percent interest, withdraw the $1,000 in each of the next three years, and end up with a zero balance. Thus, $2,486.90 is the present value of an annuity of $1,000 a year for three years when the appropriate discount rate is 10 percent. Again, tables are available for finding the present value of annuities. To use them, we simply look up the interest factor (PVIFA) for the appropriate number of years and interest rate, then multiply the PVIFA by the annual receipt:

$$P_{r,t} = \text{Present value of annuity} = \text{PVIFA}(r,t) \times \text{Annual receipt}$$
$$= 2.4869 \times \$1{,}000 = \$2{,}486.90$$

The four basic interest formulas can be used in combination to find such things as the present value of an uneven series of receipts. The formulas can also be transformed to find (1) the annual payments necessary to accumulate a future sum, (2) the annual receipts from a specified annuity, (3) the periodic payments necessary to amortize a loan, and (4) the interest rate implicit in a loan contract.

It is crucial to use the appropriate interest rate in working with compound interest problems. The true nature of the interest rates to be used with business problems can be understood only after examining the chapters dealing with the cost of capital. Risk premiums and opportunity costs are important considerations in determining the most attractive investments.

Questions

4.1 What kinds of financial decisions require explicit consideration of the interest factor?

4.2 Compound interest relationships are important for decisions other than financial ones. Why are they important to marketing managers?

4.3 Would you rather have a savings account that pays 5 percent interest compounded semiannually or one that pays 5 percent interest compounded daily? Why?

4.4 For a given interest rate and a given number of years, is the interest factor for the sum of an annuity greater or smaller than the interest factor for the present value of the annuity?

4.5 Suppose you are examining two investments, A and B. Both have the same maturity, but A pays a 6 percent return and B yields 5 percent. Which investment is probably riskier? How do you know?

Problems

4.1 Which amount is worth more at 9 percent: $1,000 today or $2,000 after eight years?

4.2 The current production target for the five-year plan of the Logo Company is to increase output by 8 percent a year. If the 1981 production is 3.81 million tons, what is the target production for 1986?

4.3 At a growth rate of 9 percent, how long does it take a sum to double?

4.4 a. What amount will be paid for a $1,000 ten-year bond that pays $40 interest semiannually ($80 a year) and that yields 10 percent, compounded semiannually?

b. What will be paid if the bond is sold to yield 8 percent?

c. What will be paid if semiannual interest payments are $50 and the bond yields 6 percent?

4.5 On December 31, Helen Ventor buys a building for $175,000, paying 20 percent down and agreeing to pay the balance in twenty equal annual installments that are to include principal plus 15 percent compound interest on the declining balance. What are the equal installments?

4.6 The Hull Company has established a sinking fund to retire a $900,000 mortgage that matures on December 31, 1990. The company plans to put a fixed amount into the fund each year for ten years. The first payment was made on December 31, 1981; the last will be made on December 31, 1990. The company anticipates that the fund will earn 10 percent a year. What annual contributions must be made to accumulate the $900,000 as of December 31, 1990?

4.7 You have just purchased a newly issued $1,000 five-year Malley Company bond at par. The bond (Bond A) pays $60 in interest semiannually ($120 a year). You are also negotiating the purchase of a $1,000 six-year Malley Company bond that returns $30 in semiannual interest payments and has six years remaining before it matures (Bond B).

a. What is the going rate of return on bonds of the risk and maturity of Malley Company's Bond A?

b. What should you be willing to pay for Bond B?

c. How will your answer to Part b change if Bond A pays $40 in semiannual interest instead of $60 but still sells for $1,000? (Bond B still pays $30 semiannually and $1,000 at the end of six years.)

4.8 You need $135,500 at the end of fourteen years. You know that the best you can do is to make equal payments into a bank account on which you can earn 6 percent interest compounded annually. Your first payment is to be made at the end of the first year.

a. What amount must you plan to pay annually to achieve your objective?

b. Instead of making annual payments, you decide to make one lump-sum payment today. To achieve your objective of $135,500 at the end of the fourteen-year period, what should this sum be? (You can still earn 6 percent interest compounded annually on your account.)

4.9 You can buy a note for \$11,300. If you buy it, you will receive ten annual payments of \$2,000, the first payment to be made one year from today. What rate of return, or yield, does the note offer?

4.10 You can buy a bond for \$1,000 that will pay no interest during its seven-year life but will have a value of \$2,502 when it matures. What rate of interest will you earn if you buy the bond and hold it to maturity?

4.11 A bank agrees to lend you \$1,000 today in return for your promise to pay back \$1,838.50 nine years from today. What rate of interest is the bank charging you?

4.12 If earnings in 1980 are \$1.99 a share, while eight years earlier (in 1972) they were \$1, what has been the rate of growth in earnings?

4.13 The Lowell Company's sales last year were \$1 million.

a. Assuming that sales grow 18 percent a year, calculate sales for each of the next six years.
b. Plot the sales projections.
c. If your graph is correct, your projected sales curve is nonlinear. If it had been linear, would this have indicated a constant, increasing, or decreasing percentage growth rate? Explain.

4.14 You are considering two investment opportunities, A and B. A is expected to pay \$300 a year for the first ten years, \$700 a year for the next fifteen years, and nothing thereafter. B is expected to pay \$1,000 a year for ten years and nothing thereafter. You find that other investments of similar risk to A and B yield 8 percent and 14 percent, respectively.

a. Find the present value of each investment. Show your calculations.
b. Which is the riskier investment? Why?
c. Assume that your rich uncle will give you a choice of A or B without cost to you and that you (1) must hold the investment for its entire life (cannot sell it), or (2) are free to sell it at its going market price. Which investment would you prefer under each of the two conditions?

4.15 The Hardy Company's common stock paid a dividend of \$1 last year. Dividends are expected to grow at a rate of 18 percent for each of the next six years.

a. Calculate the expected dividend for each of the next six years.
b. Assuming that the first of these six dividends will be paid one year from now, what is the present value of the six dividends? (Given the riskiness of the dividend stream, 18 percent is the appropriate discount rate.)
c. Assume that the price of the stock will be \$27 six years from now. What is the present value of this "terminal value"? Use an 18 percent discount rate.
d. Assume that you will buy the stock, receive the six dividends, then sell the stock. How much should you be willing to pay for it?
e. What would happen to the price of this stock if the discount rate declined because the riskiness of the stock declined? If the growth rate of the dividend stream increased?

APPENDIX 4A

SOME KEY COMPOUND INTEREST RELATIONSHIPS

Continuous Compounding

In Chapter 4 we implicitly assumed that growth occurs at discrete intervals—annually, semiannually, and so forth. For some purposes it is better to assume instantaneous, or *continuous*, growth. The relationship between discrete and continuous compounding is illustrated in Figure 4A.1. Figure 4A.1a shows the annual compounding case, where interest is added once a year; in Figure 4A.1b compounding occurs twice a year; in Figure 4A.1c interest is earned continuously.

We developed Equation 4.9 in Chapter 4 to allow for any number of compounding periods per year:

$$V_{r,n} = P_0\left(1 + \frac{r}{q}\right)^{qn} \tag{4.9}$$

where q is the number of times per year that compounding occurs. When banks or savings and loans calculate interest on a daily basis, the value of q is set at 365 and Equation 4.9 may be applied. Equation 4.9 can also be used to derive the equations for continuous compounding. As the number of compounding periods q increases and approaches infinity, compounding becomes instantaneous, or continuous. With

Figure 4A.1

Annual, Semiannual, and Continuous Compounding

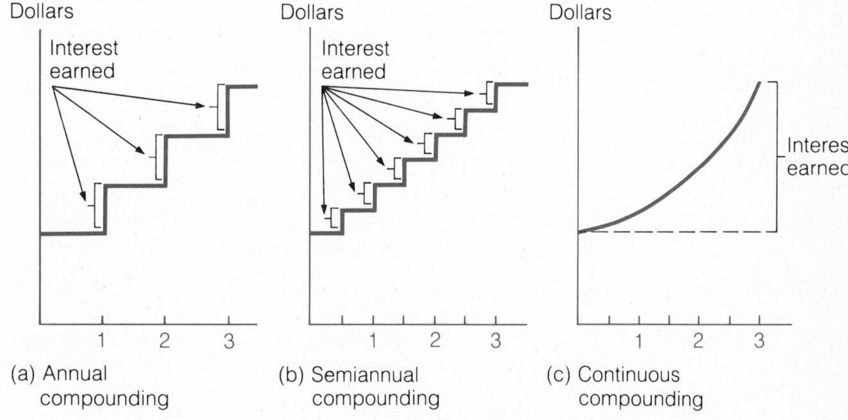

some algebraic manipulation, the exponent becomes *rn* and the term in the parentheses approaches 2.718, which is the value of *e*.[1] We can therefore express equation 4.9 as equation 4A.1 for the case of continuous compounding (or continuous growth).

$$V_{r,n} = P_0 e^{rn} \qquad \textbf{(4A.1)}$$

Interest factors (IF) can be developed for continuous compounding; developing the factors requires the use of natural, or Naperian, logarithms.[2] First, letting $P_0 = 1$, we can rewrite Equation 4A.1 as

$$V_{r,n} = e^{rn} \qquad \textbf{(4A.2)}$$

Setting Equation 4A.2 in log form and noting that *ln* denotes the log to the base *e*, we obtain

$$ln\ V_{r,n} = rn\ ln\ e$$

Since *e* is defined as the base of the system of natural logarithms, *ln e* must equal 1.0 (that is, $e^1 = e$, so $ln\ e = 1.0$). Therefore,

$$ln\ V_{r,n} = rn$$

One simply looks up the product *rn* in a table of natural logarithms and obtains the value $V_{r,n}$ as the antilog. For example, if $n =$ five years and $r = 10$ percent, the product is 0.50. Looking up this value in Appendix B at the end of the book, we find in this table of natural logs that 0.5 lies between 0.49470 and 0.50078, whose antilogs are 1.64 and 1.65, respectively. Interpolating, we find the antilog of 0.5 to be 1.648. Thus, 1.648 is the interest factor for a 10 percent growth rate compounded continuously for five years; $1 growing continuously at this compound rate would equal $1.648 after five years.

The $1.648 obtained for five years of *continuous* compounding compares closely with $1.629, the figure for semiannual compounding, and with the $1.611 obtained with annual compounding. Thus, continuous compounding does not produce values materially different from semiannual or annual compounding. The importance of continuous compounding is its convenience in analytical work.[3]

Continuous Discounting

Equation 4A.1 can be transformed into Equation 4A.3 and used to determine present values under continuous compounding.

$$PV = \frac{V_{r,n}}{e^{rn}} = V_{r,n} e^{-rn} \qquad \textbf{(4A.3)}$$

[1] The detailed steps in the derivation are presented in J. Fred Weston and Eugene F. Brigham, *Managerial Finance,* 7th ed. (Hinsdale, Ill.: Dryden Press, 1981), pp. 88–89.

[2] Recall that the logarithm of a number is the power, or exponent, to which a specified base must be raised to equal the number; that is, the log (base 10) of 100 is 2 because $(10)^2 = 100$. In the system of natural logs the base is $e \approx 2.718$.

[3] Continuous compounding is used extensively in theoretical work. In practice, the major use is by banks and savings and loan associations as a competitive tactic to raise the effective rate on deposits permitted by regulators.

Thus, if \$1,648 is due in five years and if the appropriate continuous discount rate r is 10 percent, the present value of this future payment is

$$PV = \frac{\$1{,}648}{1.648} = \$1{,}000$$

Continuous discounting of annuities results in a simple but useful relationship.

$$PV = \frac{a_0}{r - g} \tag{4A.4}$$

where a_0 is the initial amount received, r is the discount factor as before, and g is the rate at which the receipts are growing. Equation 4A.4 is the present value of a continuous stream of receipts growing at a rate g and discounted at rate r. This is the basic dividend valuation model, discussed further in Chapter 18.

Some Further Applications of Compound Interest Relationships

A problem that arises in finance in a number of forms is the following: An obligation of \$1,000 is to be paid in twenty days. If payment is made immediately, a \$20 discount is given and the payment required is only \$980. What is the rate of interest represented by the \$20 discount for payment 20 days earlier?

The basic problems can be formulated as: What do I earn by being able to settle an obligation P by a payment of $.98P$ by paying in advance by (20/365) of a year? The answer depends upon the compounding period used. This is illustrated for several different compounding periods.

Annual Compounding

The basic equation would be

$$P(.98)(1 + r)^{20/365} = P$$

What is the rate r that satisfies the equation? Divide through by $.98P$ to obtain

$$(1 + r)^{20/365} = 1/.98$$

Solving for r, we find

$$r = (1.020408)^{365/20} - 1$$

$$r = 44.58\%$$

Daily Compounding

With daily compounding, the basic equation is

$$P(.98)\left(1 + \frac{r}{365}\right)^{(20/365)365} = P$$

Dividing by $.98P$, we obtain

$$(1 + r/365)^{20} = 1.020408$$

$$(1 + r/365) = (1.020408)^{1/20}$$

$$r = 36.89\%$$

Thus with daily compounding rather than annual compounding the interest rate to equate the two sides of the equation is lower. We can predict that the interest rate will therefore be somewhat lower for continuous compounding.

Continuous Compounding

The basic equation is

$$P(.98)e^{r(20/365)} = P$$

$$r = (365/20)\ ln\ (1/.98)$$

$$= 18.25(.0202027)$$

$$r = 36.87\%$$

The solution for r does decline as expected. A simple approximation formula gives results similar to those obtained for continuous or daily compounding.

Simple Compounding

A compound interest relation can be approximated (when r is small and n is large) by the following:

$$(1 + r)^n = (1 + nr)$$

Now the basic equation can be written as

$$.98P[1 + r(20/365)] = P$$

Divide both sides by .98P to obtain

$$(20/365)r = (1/.98) - 1$$

$$(20/365)r = \left(\frac{1 - .98}{.98}\right)$$

$$r = \left(\frac{.02}{.98}\right)\left(\frac{365}{20}\right)$$

$$r = 37.24\%$$

This is the standard simplified textbook formula for calculating the interest return from taking a cash discount, presented in Chapter 12. The answer is $r = .020408(18.25) = 37.24\%$. Thus the standard simplified approximation method gives a result close to the answer obtained by daily or continuous compounding. The simple formula gives the same result as the more "complex" compounding methods. The relationships set out above provide a perspective on interest rate problems encountered throughout this book as well as in the work of the practicing financial manager.

PART 2

FINANCIAL ANALYSIS, PLANNING, AND CONTROL

The chapters of Part 2 discuss financial planning and control systems in firms. They provide the framework for planning the firm's growth and the development of financial controls for efficiency. Although these areas of finance do not have the sophistication of the formal models that will be used in later chapters, they are vital to the firm's healthy profitability. Chapter 5 examines the construction and use of the basic ratios of financial analysis; through this ratio analysis, we can pinpoint the firm's strengths and weaknesses.

Chapter 6 takes up financial forecasting: Given a projected increase in sales, how much money must the financial manager raise to support this level of sales? The statement of changes in financial position, or sources and uses of funds analysis, is also considered in a planning context.

Chapter 7 begins with the broad planning framework of the relations among revenues, volume, and profits in a breakeven analysis. The chapter then continues with a more detailed consideration of budget systems and controls for decentralized operations.

Finance deals, largely, with very specific questions. Should we lease or buy the new machine? Should we expand capacity at the Hartford plant? Should we raise capital this year by long-term or short-term debt or by selling stock? Should we go along with the marketing department, which wants to expand inventories, or with the production department, which wants to reduce them? Such specific questions, typical of those facing the financial manager, are considered in the remainder of the book. But Part 2 takes an overview of the firm. Because all particular decisions are made within the context of the firm's overall position, this overview is critical to an understanding of any individual proposal.

CHAPTER 5

FINANCIAL RATIO ANALYSIS

Planning is the key to the financial manager's success. Financial plans may take many forms, but any good plan must be related to the firm's existing strengths and weaknesses. The strengths must be understood if they are to be used to proper advantage, and the weaknesses must be recognized if corrective action is to be taken. For example, are inventories adequate to support the projected level of sales? Does the firm have too heavy an investment in accounts receivable, and does this condition reflect a lax collection policy? The financial manager can plan future financial requirements in accordance with the forecasting and budgeting procedures we will present in succeeding chapters, but the plan must begin with the type of financial analysis developed in this chapter.

Basic Financial Statements

Because ratio analysis employs financial data taken from the firm's balance sheet and income statement, it is useful to begin with a review of these accounting reports. For illustrative purposes, we shall use data taken from the Walker-Wilson Manufacturing Company, a manufacturer of specialized machinery used in the automobile repair business. Formed in 1961, when Charles Walker and Ben Wilson set up a small plant to produce certain tools they had developed while in the army, Walker-Wilson grew steadily and earned the reputation of being one of the best small firms in its line of business. In December 1978, both Walker and Wilson were killed in a crash of their private plane, and for the next two years the firm was managed by Walker-Wilson's accountant.

In 1980 the widows, who are the principal stockholders in Walker-Wilson, acting on the advice of the firm's bankers and attorneys, engaged David Thompson as president and general manager. Although Thompson is experienced in the machinery business, especially in production and sales, he does not have a detailed knowledge of his new company, so he has decided to conduct a careful appraisal of the firm's position and, on the basis of this position, to draw up a plan for future operations.

Balance Sheet

Walker-Wilson's balance sheet, given in Table 5.1, shows the value of the firm's assets, and of the claims on these assets, at two particular points in time, December 31, 1979, and December 31, 1980. The assets are arranged from top to bottom in order of decreasing liquidity; that is, assets toward the top of the column will be converted to cash sooner than those toward the bottom of the column. The top group of assets—cash, marketable securities, accounts receivable, and inventories,

Table 5.1

Walker-Wilson Company Illustrative Balance Sheet (Thousands of Dollars)

Assets		Dec. 31, 1979		Dec. 31, 1980
Cash		$ 52		$ 50
Marketable securities		175		150
Receivables		250		200
Inventories		355		300
Total current assets		$ 832		$ 700
Gross plant and equipment	$1,610		$1,800	
Less depreciation	400		500	
Net plant and equipment		1,210		1,300
Total assets		$2,042		$2,000

Claims on assets		Dec. 31, 1979		Dec. 31, 1980
Accounts payable		$ 87		$ 60
Notes payable (at 10%)		110		100
Accruals		10		10
Provision for federal income taxes		135		130
Total current liabilities		$ 342		$ 300
First mortgage bonds (at 8%)[a]		520		500
Debentures (at 10%)		200		200
Common stock (200,000 shares)	$ 600		$ 600	
Retained earnings	380		400	
Total net worth		980		1,000
Total claims on assets		$2,042		$2,000

[a] The sinking fund requirement for the mortgage bonds is $20,000 a year.

Table 5.2

Walker-Wilson Company Illustrative Income Statement for Year Ended December 31, 1980

Net sales		$3,000,000
Cost of goods sold		2,555,000
Gross profit		$ 445,000
Less operating expenses:		
Selling	$22,000	
General and administrative	40,000	
Lease payment on office building	28,000	90,000
Gross operating revenue		$ 355,000
Depreciation		100,000
Net operating income		$ 255,000
Other income and expense except interest		15,000
Earnings before interest and taxes		$ 270,000
Less interest expense:		
Interest on notes payable	$10,000	
Interest on first mortgage	40,000	
Interest on debentures	20,000	70,000
Net income before income tax		$ 200,000
Federal income tax (at 40%)		80,000
Net income, after income tax, available to common stockholders		$ 120,000
Earnings per share (EPS)		$ .60

which are expected to be converted into cash within one year—is defined as *current assets*. Assets in the lower part of the statement—plant and equipment, which are not expected to be converted to cash within one year—are defined as *fixed assets*.

The right side of the balance sheet is arranged similarly. Those items toward the top of the claims column will mature and have to be paid off relatively soon; those further down the column will be due in the more distant future. Current liabilities must be paid within one year; because the firm never has to "pay off" common stockholders, common stock and retained earnings represent "permanent" capital.

Income Statement

Walker-Wilson's income statement is shown in Table 5.2. Sales are at the top of the statement; various costs, including taxes, are deducted to arrive at the net income available to common stockholders.[1] The figure on the last line represents earnings per share (EPS), calculated as net income divided by number of shares outstanding.

Statement of Retained Earnings

Earnings can be paid out to stockholders as dividends or retained and reinvested in the business. Stockholders like to receive dividends, of course; but if earnings are plowed back into the business, the value of the stockholders' position in the company increases. Later in the book we shall consider the pros and cons of retaining earnings versus paying them out in dividends, but for now we are simply interested in the effects of dividends and retained earnings on the balance sheet. For this purpose, accountants use the statement of retained earnings, illustrated for Walker-Wilson in Table 5.3. Walker-Wilson earned $120,000 during the year, paid $100,000 in dividends to stockholders, and plowed $20,000 back into the business. Thus the retained earnings at the end of 1980, as shown both on the balance sheet and on the statement of retained earnings, is $400,000, which is $20,000 larger than the year-end 1979 figure.

Table 5.3

Walker-Wilson Company
Statement of Retained Earnings
for Year Ended December 31, 1980

Balance of retained earnings, December 31, 1979	$380,000
Plus net income, 1980	120,000
	$500,000
Less dividends to stockholders	100,000
Balance of retained earnings, December 31, 1980	$400,000

Relationships Among the Three Statements

It is important to recognize that the balance sheet is a statement of the firm's financial position *at a point in time*, whereas the income statement shows the results of operations *during an interval of time*. Thus, the balance sheet represents a snapshot of the firm's position on a given date, while the income statement is based on a flow concept, showing what occurred between two points in time.

[1] Note that net operating income (NOI) is adjusted for other non-operating income and expense to obtain earnings before interest and taxes (EBIT). If other income and expense are small, NOI and EBIT are approximately the same, as we shall usually assume in subsequent chapters.

The statement of retained earnings indicates how the retained earnings account on the balance sheet is adjusted between balance sheet dates. Since its inception, Walker-Wilson had retained a total of $380,000 by December 31, 1979. In 1980 it earned $120,000 and retained $20,000 of this amount. Thus, the retained earnings shown on the balance sheet for December 31, 1980, is $400,000.

A firm that retains earnings generally does so to expand the business—that is, to finance the purchase of assets such as plant, equipment, and inventories. As a result of operations in 1980, Walker-Wilson has $20,000 available for that purpose. Sometimes retained earnings are used to build up the cash account, but, as shown on the balance sheet, they are *not* cash. Through the years they have been invested in bricks and mortar and other assets, so they are not "available" for anything. The earnings *for the current year* may be available for investment, but the *past retained earnings* have already been employed.

Stated another way, the balance sheet item "retained earnings" simply shows how much of their earnings the stockholders, through the years, have elected to retain in the business. Thus, the retained earnings account shows the additional investment the stockholders as a group have made in the business over and above their initial investment at the inception of the company and through any subsequent issues of stock.

Basic Types of Financial Ratios

Each type of analysis has a purpose or use that determines the different relationships emphasized. The analyst may, for example, be a banker considering whether to grant a short-term loan to a firm. Bankers are primarily interested in the firm's near-term, or liquidity, position, so they stress ratios that measure liquidity. In contrast, long-term creditors place far more emphasis on earning power and operating efficiency. They know that unprofitable operations erode asset values and that a strong current position is no guarantee that funds will be available to repay a twenty-year bond issue. Equity investors are similarly interested in long-term profitability and efficiency. Management is, of course, concerned with all these aspects of financial analysis; it must be able to repay its debts to long- and short-term creditors as well as earn profits for stockholders.

It is useful to classify ratios into six fundamental types:

1. *Liquidity ratios*, which measure the firm's ability to meet its maturing short-term obligations
2. *Leverage ratios*, which measure the extent to which the firm has been financed by debt
3. *Activity ratios*, which measure how effectively the firm is using its resources
4. *Profitability ratios,* which measure management's effectiveness as shown by the returns generated on sales and investment
5. *Growth ratios*, which measure the firm's ability to maintain its economic position in the growth of the economy and industry
6. *Valuation ratios*, which measure the ability of management to create market values in excess of investment cost outlays. Valuation ratios are the most complete measure of performance in that they reflect the risk ratios (the

first two) and the returns ratios (the following three). Valuation ratios are of great importance since they relate directly to the goal of maximizing the value of the firm and shareholder wealth.

Specific examples of each ratio are given in the following sections, where the Walker-Wilson case history illustrates their calculation and use.

Liquidity Ratios

Generally, the first concern of the financial analyst is liquidity: Is the firm able to meet its maturing obligations? Walker-Wilson has debts totaling $300,000 that must be paid within the coming year. Can these obligations be satisfied? Although a full liquidity analysis requires the use of cash budgets (described in Chapter 7), ratio analysis, by relating the amount of cash and other current assets to the current obligations, provides a quick and easy-to-use measure of liquidity. Two commonly used liquidity ratios are presented here.

Current Ratio The current ratio is computed by dividing current assets by current liabilities. Current assets normally include cash, marketable securities, accounts receivable, and inventories; current liabilities consist of accounts payable, short-term notes payable, current maturities of long-term debt, accrued income taxes, and other accrued expenses (principally wages). The current ratio is the most commonly used measure of short-term solvency, since it indicates the extent to which the claims of short-term creditors are covered by assets that are expected to be converted to cash in a period roughly corresponding to the maturity of the claims.

The calculation of the current ratio for Walker-Wilson at year-end 1980 is shown below.

$$\text{Current ratio} = \frac{\text{Current assets}}{\text{Current liabilities}} = \frac{\$700{,}000}{\$300{,}000} = 2.3 \text{ times}$$

$$\text{Industry average} = 2.5 \text{ times}$$

The current ratio is slightly below the average for the industry, 2.5, but not low enough to cause concern. It appears that Walker-Wilson is about in line with most other firms in this particular line of business. Since current assets are near maturity, it is highly probable that they could be liquidated at close to book value. With a current ratio of 2.3, Walker-Wilson could liquidate current assets at only 43 percent of book value and still pay off current creditors in full.[2]

Although industry average figures are discussed later in the chapter, it should be stated at this point that the industry average is not a magic number that all firms should strive to maintain. In fact, some well-managed firms are above it, and other good firms are below it. However, if a firm's ratios are very far removed from the average for its industry, the analyst must be concerned about why this variance occurs; that is, a deviation from the industry average should signal the analyst to check further.

[2] (1/2.3) = .43, or 43 percent. Note that (.43)($700,000) ≈ $300,000, the amount of current liabilities.

Quick Ratio or Acid Test The quick ratio is calculated by deducting inventories from current assets and dividing the remainder by current liabilities. Inventories are typically the least liquid of a firm's current assets and the assets on which losses are most likely to occur in the event of liquidation. Therefore, this measure of the firm's ability to pay off short-term obligations without relying on the sale of inventories is important.

$$\text{Quick ratio or acid test} = \frac{\text{Current assets} - \text{Inventory}}{\text{Current liabilities}} = \frac{\$400,000}{\$300,000}$$

$$= 1.3 \text{ times}$$

$$\text{Industry average} = 1.0 \text{ times}$$

The industry average quick ratio is 1, so Walker-Wilson's 1.3 ratio compares favorably with other firms in the industry. Thompson knows that if the marketable securities can be sold at par and if he can collect the accounts receivable, he can pay off his current liabilities without selling any inventory.

Leverage Ratios

Leverage ratios, which measure the funds supplied by owners as compared with the financing provided by the firm's creditors, have a number of implications. First, creditors look to the equity, or owner-supplied funds, to provide a margin of safety. If owners have provided only a small proportion of total financing, the risks of the enterprise are borne mainly by the creditors. Second, by raising funds through debt, the owners gain the benefits of maintaining control of the firm with a limited investment. Third, if the firm earns more on the borrowed funds than it pays in interest, the return to the owners is magnified. For example, if assets earn 10 percent and debt costs only 8 percent, there is a 2 percent differential accruing to the stockholders. Leverage cuts both ways, however; if the return on assets falls to 3 percent, the differential between that figure and the cost of debt must be made up from equity's share of total profits. In the first instance, where assets earn more than the cost of debt, leverage is favorable; in the second, it is unfavorable.

Firms with low leverage ratios have less risk of loss when the economy is in a downturn, but they also have lower expected returns when the economy booms. Conversely, firms with high leverage ratios run the risk of large losses but also have a chance of gaining high profits. The prospects of high returns are desirable, but investors are averse to risk. Decisions about the use of leverage, then, must balance higher expected returns against increased risk.[3]

In practice, leverage is approached in two ways. One approach examines balance sheet ratios and determines the extent to which borrowed funds have been used to finance the firm. The other approach measures the risks of debt by income statement ratios designed to determine the number of times fixed charges are covered by operating profits. These sets of ratios are complementary, and most analysts examine both.

Total Debt to Total Assets The ratio of total debt to total assets, generally called the *debt ratio*, measures the percentage of total funds provided by creditors. Debt

[3] The problem of determining optimum leverage for a firm with given risk characteristics is examined extensively in Chapters 15 and 16.

includes current liabilities and all bonds. Creditors prefer moderate debt ratios, since the lower the ratio, the greater the cushion against creditors' losses in the event of liquidation. In contrast to the creditors' preference for a low debt ratio, the owners may seek high leverage to magnify earnings or because raising new equity means giving up some degree of control. If the debt ratio is too high, there is a danger of encouraging irresponsibility on the part of the owners. The owners' stake can become so small that speculative activity, if it is successful, will yield them a substantial percentage return. If the venture is unsuccessful, however, they will incur only a moderate loss because their investment is small.

$$\text{Debt ratio} = \frac{\text{Total debt}}{\text{Total assets}} = \frac{\$1{,}000{,}000}{\$2{,}000{,}000} = 50\%$$

$$\text{Industry average} = 33\%$$

Walker-Wilson's debt ratio is 50 percent; this means that creditors have supplied half the firm's total financing. Since the average debt ratio for this industry is about 33 percent, Walker-Wilson would find it difficult to borrow additional funds without first raising more equity capital. Creditors would be reluctant to lend the firm more money, and Thompson would probably be subjecting the stockholders to undue danger if he sought to increase the debt ratio even more by borrowing.[4]

Times Interest Earned The times-interest-earned ratio is determined by dividing earnings before interest and taxes (EBIT) from Table 5.2 by the interest charges. The ratio measures the extent to which earnings can decline without resultant financial embarrassment to the firm because of inability to meet annual interest costs. Failure to meet this obligation can bring legal action by the creditors, possibly resulting in bankruptcy. Note that the before-tax profit figure is used in the numerator. Because income taxes are computed after interest expense is deducted, the ability to pay current interest is not affected by income taxes.

$$\text{Times interest earned} = \frac{\text{Earnings before interest and taxes}}{\text{Interest charges}}$$

$$= \frac{\text{Profit before taxes} + \text{Interest charges}}{\text{Interest charges}}$$

$$= \frac{\$270{,}000}{\$70{,}000} = 3.9 \text{ times}$$

$$\text{Industry average} = 8.0 \text{ times}$$

Walker-Wilson's interest charges consist of three payments totaling $70,000 (see Table 5.2). The firm's gross income available for servicing these charges is $270,000, so the interest is covered 3.9 times. Since the industry average is 8 times,

[4] The ratio of debt to equity is also used in financial analysis. The debt to assets (B/A) and debt to equity (B/S) ratios are simply transformations of one another:

$$B/S = \frac{B/A}{1 - B/A} \quad \text{and} \quad B/A = \frac{B/S}{1 + B/S}$$

Both ratios increase as a firm of a given size (total assets) uses a greater proportion of debt, but B/A rises linearly and approaches a limit of 100 percent while B/S rises exponentially and approaches infinity.

the company is covering its interest charges by a minimum margin of safety and deserves only a poor rating. This ratio reinforces the conclusion based on the debt ratio that the company is likely to face some difficulties if it attempts to borrow additional funds.

Fixed Charge Coverage The fixed charge coverage ratio is similar to the times-interest-earned ratio, but it is somewhat more inclusive in that it recognizes that many firms lease assets and incur long-term obligations under lease contracts.[5] As we show in Chapter 22, leasing has become widespread in recent years, making this ratio preferable to the times-interest-earned ratio for most financial analyses. Fixed charges are defined as interest plus annual long-term lease obligations, and the fixed charge coverage ratio is defined as follows:

$$\text{Fixed charge coverage} = \frac{\text{Profit before taxes} + \text{Interest charges} + \text{Lease obligations}}{\text{Interest charges} + \text{Lease obligations}}$$

$$= \frac{\$200{,}000 + \$70{,}000 + \$28{,}000}{\$70{,}000 + \$28{,}000} = \frac{\$298{,}000}{\$98{,}000}$$

$$= 3.0 \text{ times}$$

$$\text{Industry average} = 5.5 \text{ times}$$

Walker-Wilson's fixed charges are covered 3.0 times, as opposed to an industry average of 5.5 times. Again, this indicates that the firm is somewhat weaker than creditors would prefer it to be, and it points up the difficulties Thompson would likely encounter if he attempted additional borrowing.

Cash Flow Coverage Suppose Walker-Wilson issued preferred stock which required payment of dividends of $12,000 per year and had to make annual payments of principal on its various debt obligations of $42,000 per year. To the numerator of the previous ratio we will add depreciation. To the denominator we shall add the two additional items on a before-tax basis. We divide each by $(1 - T)$ because neither is a tax-deductible expense. Hence the firm must have enough cash flow so that after taxes are paid, it can meet all cash flow obligations.

$$\text{Cash flow coverage} = \frac{\text{Cash inflows}}{\text{Fixed charges} + \dfrac{\text{Preferred stock dividends}}{(1 - T)} + \dfrac{\text{Debt repayment}}{(1 - T)}}$$

$$= \frac{\$298{,}000 + \$100{,}000}{\$98{,}000 + \$12{,}000/.6 + \$42{,}000/.6} = \frac{\$398{,}000}{\$188{,}000}$$

$$= 2.1 \text{ times}$$

While there are not generally published industry standards on this ratio, logic suggests that a cash coverage ratio of at least two times be achieved. This allows

[5] Generally, a long-term lease is defined as one that is at least three years long. Thus, rent incurred under a one-year lease would not be included in the fixed charge coverage ratio, but rental payments under a three-year or longer lease would be defined as fixed charges.

for a substantial decline in cash inflows before a cash solvency problem is encountered. Walker-Wilson meets this standard minimally.

Activity Ratios

Activity ratios measure how effectively the firm employs the resources at its command. These ratios all involve comparisons between the level of sales and the investment in various asset accounts. They presume that a "proper" balance should exist between sales and the various asset accounts—inventories, accounts receivable, fixed assets, and others. As we shall see in the following chapters, this is generally a good assumption.

Inventory Turnover The inventory turnover, defined as sales divided by inventory, is shown as follows:

$$\text{Inventory turnover} = \frac{\text{Sales}}{\text{Inventory}} = \frac{\$3{,}000{,}000}{\$300{,}000} = 10 \text{ times}$$

$$\text{Industry average} = 9 \text{ times}$$

Walker-Wilson's turnover of 10 times compares favorably with an industry average of 9 times. This suggests that the company does not hold excessive stocks of inventory; excess stocks are, of course, unproductive and represent an investment with a low or zero rate of return. The company's high inventory turnover also reinforces Thompson's faith in the current ratio. If turnover were low—say 3 or 4 times—Thompson would wonder if the firm were holding damaged or obsolete materials not actually worth their stated value.

Two problems arise in calculating and analyzing the inventory turnover ratio. First, sales are at market prices; if inventories are carried at cost, as they generally are, it is more appropriate to use cost of goods sold in place of sales in the numerator of the formula. However, established compilers of financial ratio statistics, such as Dun & Bradstreet, use the ratio of sales to inventories carried at cost. Therefore, to develop a figure that can be compared with those developed by Dun & Bradstreet it is necessary to measure inventory turnover with sales in the numerator, as we do here.

Second, sales occur over the entire year, whereas the inventory figure is for one point in time. This makes it better to use an average inventory, computed by adding beginning and ending inventories and dividing by 2. If it is determined that the firm's business is highly seasonal, or if there has been a strong upward or downward sales trend during the year, it is essential to make some such adjustment. Neither of these conditions holds for Walker-Wilson; to maintain comparability with industry averages, Thompson did not use the average inventory figure.

Average Collection Period The average collection period, which is a measure of the accounts receivable turnover, is computed in two steps: (1) annual sales are divided by 360 to get the average daily sales[6] and (2) daily sales are divided into

[6] Because information on credit sales is generally unavailable, total sales must be used. Since firms do not all have the same percentage of credit sales, there is a good chance that the average collection period will be somewhat in error. Also, note that in this illustration we have simplified the computation by using 360 rather than 365 as the number of days in a year. Both figures are used in the financial community, and the difference in results would not affect the decision involved.

accounts receivable to find the number of days' sales tied up in receivables. This is defined as the *average collection period*, because it represents the average length of time the firm must wait after making a sale before receiving payment. The calculations for Walker-Wilson show an average collection period of 24 days, slightly above the 20-day industry average.

$$\text{Sales per day} = \frac{\$3{,}000{,}000}{360} = \$8{,}333$$

$$\text{Average collection period} = \frac{\text{Receivables}}{\text{Sales per day}} = \frac{\$200{,}000}{\$8{,}333} = 24 \text{ days}$$

$$\text{Industry average} = 20 \text{ days}$$

This ratio can also be evaluated by comparison with the terms on which the firm sells its goods. For example, Walker-Wilson's sales terms call for payment within 20 days, so the 24-day collection period indicates that customers, on the average, are not paying their bills on time. If the collection period over the past few years had been lengthening while the credit policy had not changed, this would have been even stronger evidence that steps should be taken to expedite the collection of accounts receivable.

One additional financial tool should be mentioned in connection with accounts receivable analysis—the *aging schedule*, which breaks down accounts receivable according to how long they have been outstanding. The aging schedule for Walker-Wilson is given below.

Age of Account (Days)	Percent of Total Value of Accounts Receivable
0–20	50
21–30	20
31–45	15
46–60	3
Over 60	12
Total	100

The 24-day collection period looks bad by comparison with the 20-day sales term, and the aging schedule shows that the firm is having especially serious collection problems with some of its accounts: 50 percent are overdue, many for over a month; others pay quite promptly, bringing the average down to only 24 days. But the aging schedule shows this average to be somewhat misleading.

Fixed Assets Turnover The ratio of sales to fixed assets measures the turnover of plant and equipment.

$$\text{Fixed assets turnover} = \frac{\text{Sales}}{\text{Net fixed assets}} = \frac{\$3{,}000{,}000}{\$1{,}300{,}000} = 2.3 \text{ times}$$

$$\text{Industry average} = 5.0 \text{ times}$$

Walker-Wilson's turnover of 2.3 times compares poorly with the industry average of 5 times, indicating that the firm is not using its fixed assets to as high a percentage of capacity as are the other firms in the industry. Thompson should bear this in mind when his production people request funds for new capital investments.

Total Assets Turnover The final activity ratio, which measures the turnover of all the firm's assets, is calculated by dividing sales by total assets.

$$\text{Total assets turnover} = \frac{\text{Sales}}{\text{Total assets}} = \frac{\$3{,}000{,}000}{\$2{,}000{,}000} = 1.5 \text{ times}$$

$$\text{Industry average} = 2.0 \text{ times}$$

Walker-Wilson's turnover of total assets is well below the industry average. The company is simply not generating a sufficient volume of business for the size of its asset investment. Sales should be increased, or some assets should be disposed of, or both.

Profitability Ratios

Profitability is the net result of a large number of policies and decisions. The ratios examined thus far reveal some interesting things about the way the firm is operating, but the profitability ratios give final answers about how effectively the firm is being managed.

Profit Margin on Sales The profit margin on sales, computed by dividing net income after taxes by sales, gives the profit per dollar of sales.

$$\text{Profit margin} = \frac{\text{Net income}}{\text{Sales}} = \frac{\$120{,}000}{\$3{,}000{,}000} = 4\%$$

$$\text{Industry average} = 5\%$$

Walker-Wilson's profit margin is somewhat below the industry average of 5 percent, indicating that the firm's prices are relatively low, or that its costs are relatively high, or both.

Return on Total Assets The ratio of net profit to total assets measures the return on total investment in the firm, or the ROI (as it is frequently called).[7]

$$\text{Return on total assets} = \frac{\text{Net income}}{\text{Total assets}} = \frac{\$120{,}000}{\$2{,}000{,}000} = 6\%$$

$$\text{Industry average} = 10\%$$

Walker-Wilson's 6 percent return is well below the 10 percent average for the industry. This low rate results from the low profit margin on sales and from the low turnover of total assets.

[7] In calculating the return on total assets, it is sometimes desirable to add interest to net profits after taxes to form the numerator of the ratio. The theory is that since assets are financed by both stockholders and creditors, the ratio should measure the productivity of assets in providing returns to both classes of investors. We have not done so at this point because the published averages we use for comparative purposes exclude interest. Later in the book, however, when we deal with leverage decisions, we will add back interest. This addition has a material bearing on the value of the ratio for utilities (which have large amounts of fixed assets financed by debt), and the technically correct ratio is the one normally used for them.

Return on Net Worth The ratio of net profit after taxes to net worth measures the rate of return on the stockholders' investment.

$$\text{Return on net worth} = \frac{\text{Net income}}{\text{Net worth}} = \frac{\$120{,}000}{\$1{,}000{,}000} = 12\%$$

$$\text{Industry average} = 15\%$$

Walker-Wilson's 12 percent return is below the 15 percent industry average but not as far below as the return on total assets. In Chapter 7, where the du Pont method of analysis is introduced, we will see why this is so.

Growth Ratios

Growth ratios measure how well the firm is maintaining its economic position in the economy as a whole as well as in its own industry. During the recent period of inflation the interpretation of growth ratios has become more difficult. Since the early 1970s nominal growth rates have increased greatly. The growth of the economy as well as of industries and firms has reflected the inflation factor as well as the underlying (real) growth. Before the onset of persistent inflation in the late 1960s real growth rates were about 3 to $3\frac{1}{2}$ percent per year with an inflation rate of 2 to 3 percent. This made for a total growth rate in the 5-to-7 percent area. However, since the early 1970s the inflation rate has been in the range of 7 to 10 percent, while real growth has declined to 1 or 2 percent. Thus nominal growth has been from 8 to 12 percent while real growth has been much lower. Since reported figures are reflected in nominal terms, the growth rate reference standards we shall employ will include the inflation factor. However, as a part of the further internal analysis by business firms, a separation needs to be made between growth coming from the inflation influence alone (which just changes the measuring stick) and that coming from underlying real growth (which reflects the basic productivity of the economy).

The annual reports of business firms will generally include a section of historical data on selected financial items. These may be used to develop the growth and valuation ratios. The data for Walker-Wilson are presented in Table 5.4.

Table 5.4

Some Historical Data for Walker-Wilson Company

	1975	1976	1977	1978	1979	1980
Firm (in thousands)						
Sales	$2,100	$2,200	$2,500	$3,400	$3,200	$3,000
Net income	100	120	150	180	160	120
Per share						
Earnings	.50	.60	.75	.90	.80	.60
Dividends	.10	.12	.12	.12	.12	.12
Market price, common stock—high	5.00	7.00	8.00	9.00	5.00	6.00
low	4.00	5.00	6.00	7.00	4.00	3.00
average	4.50	6.00	7.00	8.00	4.50	4.50
Book value of common stock, year end	4.10	4.30	4.40	4.70	4.90	5.00

Table 5.5 **Growth Rate Data**

	Five-year growth rates, 1975–80	
	Walker-Wilson	Industry
Sales	7.4	7.2
Net income	3.7	7.8
Earnings per share	3.7	8.2
Dividends per share	3.7	6.4
Market price: average	0.0	2.0
Book value per share	4.0	7.0

From the basic data in Table 5.4 we have calculated the 5-year growth rates for six items for Walker-Wilson covering the years 1975 to 1980 in Table 5.5. We have calculated growth by dividing the last-period figure by the first-period figure, which gives a compound sum interest factor. Then by referring to the compound interest tables we can determine the growth rate represented by the ratio. We observe that the growth rate in sales for Walker-Wilson was about the same as for the industry. However, net income, which is the measure of the profitability performance of the firm, has grown at only about half the industry standard rate.

Next we turn to per-share growth analysis. First, we consider earnings per share, which reflect the methods by which the firm has financed its overall growth. Here again the growth rate is less than half that of the industry. Dividends per share have grown at the same rate as earnings per share. However, Table 5.4 shows that all of the dividend growth came in the first year while the earnings growth has been declining during the two most recent years.

Market price represents the results of the valuation of the firm's earnings. Market price growth for the industry as a whole has been weak, only 2 percent. But the market price change for Walker-Wilson has been zero. While its average price increased from $4.50 to $8 in the early years, it declined again to $4.50 in the last two years.

Book value per share indicates the resources in the company per share of stockholder investment. This grew at a 7 percent rate for the industry, but at only a 4 percent rate for Walker-Wilson. Again, the weakened performance of the last two years has pulled down the growth rate in the book value per share. Thus the growth performance of Walker-Wilson has been relatively weak, which should have some implications for the valuation ratios as well.

Valuation Ratios

Valuation ratios are the most comprehensive measures of performance for the firm in that they reflect the combined influence of risk ratios and return ratios. We have calculated two valuation ratios and summarized their patterns in Table 5.6.

We first analyzed trends in the price to earnings ratios. At the beginning of the period they were higher for the company than for the industry. However, by the end of the period the ratios were higher for the industry than for the company, reflecting the company's poor performance in the last two years.

Price to earnings ratios must be interpreted with caution. Note that between 1979 and 1980 the price-earnings ratio for the company rose from 5.6 to 7.5. However,

Table 5.6 **Valuation Ratios**

		1975	1976	1977	1978	1979	1980
Price to earnings ratios:	company	9.0	10.0	9.3	8.9	5.6	7.5
	industry	7.0	8.0	8.0	8.0	9.0	8.0
Market to book ratios:	company	1.1	1.4	1.6	1.7	0.9	0.9
	industry	0.9	1.0	1.0	1.2	1.1	1.0

the average market price of the company stock stayed at $4.50. The price-earnings ratio rose while earnings dropped only because the average price remained the same.

The market to book ratio is also an important valuation ratio. In a way it indicates the value that the financial markets attach to the management and the organization of the company as a going concern. In some sense book value represents the historical costs of brick and mortar—the physical assets of the company. A well-run company with strong management and an organization that functions efficiently should have a market value greater than or at least equal to the book value of its physical assets.

As we see from Table 5.6, in the early years the market to book ratio of the company exceeded 1.0. In fact, by 1978 it had become 1.7. The industry did not perform as well but in most years had a market to book ratio of at least 1.0. However, during the last two years, while the market to book ratio for the industry has remained at 1.0 or better, it has dipped below 1.0 for the company.

Summary of the Ratios

The individual ratios, which are summarized in Table 5.7, give Thompson a reasonably good idea of Walker-Wilson's main strengths and weaknesses. First, the company's liquidity position is reasonably good; its current and quick ratios appear to be satisfactory by comparison with the industry averages. Second, the leverage ratios suggest that the company is rather heavily indebted. With a debt ratio substantially higher than the industry average, and with coverage ratios well below the industry averages, it is doubtful that Walker-Wilson could do much additional debt financing except on relatively unfavorable terms. Even if Thompson could borrow more, to do so would be subjecting the company to the danger of default and bankruptcy in the event of a business downturn.

Turning to the activity ratios, the inventory turnover and average collection period both indicate that the company's current assets are pretty well in balance, but the low fixed asset turnover suggests that there has been too heavy an investment in fixed assets. This low turnover means, in effect, that the company probably could have operated with a smaller investment in fixed assets. Had the excessive fixed asset investment not been made, the company could have avoided some of its debt financing and would now have lower interest payments. This in turn would have led to improved leverage and coverage ratios.

The profit margin on sales is low, indicating that costs are too high or prices too low or both. In this particular case, the sales prices are in line with those of other

Table 5.7

Summary of Financial Ratio Analyses

Ratio	Formula for calculation	Calculation	Industry average	Evaluation
Liquidity				
Current	$\frac{\text{Current assets}}{\text{Current liabilities}}$	$\frac{\$700,000}{\$300,000} = 2.3$ times	2.5 times	Satisfactory
Quick ratio or acid test	$\frac{\text{Current assets} - \text{Inventory}}{\text{Current liabilities}}$	$\frac{\$400,000}{\$300,000} = 1.3$ times	1 time	Good
Leverage				
Debt to total assets	$\frac{\text{Total debt}}{\text{Total assets}}$	$\frac{\$1,000,000}{\$2,000,000} = 50$ percent	33 percent	Poor
Times interest earned	$\frac{\text{Earnings before taxes and interest charges}}{\text{Interest charges}}$	$\frac{\$270,000}{\$70,000} = 3.9$ times	8 times	Poor
Fixed charge coverage	$\frac{\text{Income available for meeting fixed charges}}{\text{Fixed charges}}$	$\frac{\$298,000}{\$98,000} = 3.0$ times	5.5 times	Poor
Activity				
Inventory turnover	$\frac{\text{Sales}}{\text{Inventory}}$	$\frac{\$3,000,000}{\$300,000} = 10$ times	9 times	Satisfactory
Average collection period	$\frac{\text{Receivables}}{\text{Sales per day}}$	$\frac{\$200,000}{\$8,333} = 24$ days	20 days	Satisfactory
Fixed assets turnover	$\frac{\text{Sales}}{\text{Fixed assets}}$	$\frac{\$3,000,000}{\$1,300,000} = 2.3$ times	5 times	Poor
Total assets turnover	$\frac{\text{Sales}}{\text{Total assets}}$	$\frac{\$3,000,000}{\$2,000,000} = 1.5$ times	2 times	Poor

Table 5.7 **Summary of Financial Ratio Analyses (*Continued*)**

Ratio	Formula for calculation	Calculation	Industry average	Evaluation
Profitability				
Profit margin on sales	$\frac{\text{Net income}}{\text{Sales}}$	$\frac{\$120{,}000}{\$3{,}000{,}000} = 4$ percent	5 percent	Fair
Return on total assets	$\frac{\text{Net income}}{\text{Total assets}}$	$\frac{\$120{,}000}{\$2{,}000{,}000} = 6$ percent	10 percent	Poor
Return on net worth	$\frac{\text{Net income}}{\text{Net worth}}$	$\frac{\$120{,}000}{\$1{,}000{,}000} = 12$ percent	15 percent	Fair
Growth				
Sales	$\frac{\text{Ending values}}{\text{Beginning values}} = CVIF_{r,5}$	$\frac{\$3{,}000}{\$2{,}100} = 1.4286;\ r = 7.4$ percent	7.2 percent	Satisfactor
Net income	$\frac{\text{Ending values}}{\text{Beginning values}} = CVIF_{r,5}$	$\frac{\$120}{\$100} = 1.2;\ r = 3.7$ percent	7.8 percent	Poor
Earnings per share	$\frac{\text{Ending values}}{\text{Beginning values}} = CVIF_{r,5}$	$\frac{\$0.60}{\$0.50} = 1.2;\ r = 3.7$ percent	8.2 percent	Poor
Dividends per share	$\frac{\text{Ending values}}{\text{Beginning values}} = CVIF_{r,5}$	$\frac{\$0.12}{\$0.10} = 1.2;\ r = 3.7$ percent	6.4 percent	Poor
Valuation				
Price to earnings ratio	$\frac{\text{Price}}{\text{Earnings}}$	$\frac{\$4.50}{\$0.60} = 7.5$ times	8 times	Fair
Market to book ratio	$\frac{\text{Market value}}{\text{Book value}}$	$\frac{\$4.50}{\$5.00} = 0.9$ times	1.0 times	Poor

firms; high costs are, in fact, the cause of the low margin. Further, the high costs can be traced to high depreciation charges and high interest expenses, both of which are in turn attributable to the excessive investment in fixed assets.

Returns on total investment and net worth are also below the industry averages. These relatively poor results are directly attributable to the low profit margin on sales, which lowers the numerators of the ratios, and the excessive investment, which raises the denominators.

Sales growth of Walker-Wilson is satisfactory in relation to the industry standard. However, all of the profitability growth measures are weak. Valuation relationships are also unfavorable. Additional perspective on the growth performance of Walker-Wilson is provided by the trend analysis, which supplements the single measure provided by the growth percentage.

Trend Analysis

While the preceding ratio analysis gives a reasonably good picture of Walker-Wilson's operation, it is incomplete in one important respect—it ignores the time dimension. The ratios are snapshots of the picture at one point in time, but there may be trends in motion that are in the process of rapidly eroding a relatively good present position. Conversely, an analysis of the ratios over the past few years may suggest that a relatively weak position is improving at a rapid rate.

The method of trend analysis is illustrated in Figure 5.1, which shows graphs of Walker-Wilson's sales, current ratio, debt ratio, fixed assets turnover, and return on net worth. The figures are compared with industry averages. Industry sales have been rising steadily over the entire period, and the industry average ratios have been relatively stable throughout. Thus, any trends in the company's ratios are due to its own internal conditions, not to environmental influences on all firms. In addition, Walker-Wilson's deterioration since the death of the two principal officers is quite apparent. Prior to 1978, the company grew more rapidly than the average firm in the industry; during the following two years, however, sales actually declined.

Walker-Wilson's liquidity position as measured by its current ratio has also gone downhill in the past two years. Although the ratio is only slightly below the industry average at the present time, the trend suggests that a real liquidity crisis may develop during the next year or two unless corrective action is taken immediately.

The debt ratio trend line shows that Walker-Wilson followed industry practices closely until 1978, when the ratio jumped to a full 10 percentage points above the industry average. Similarly, the fixed assets turnover declined during 1978, even though sales were still rising. The records reveal that the company borrowed heavily during 1978 to finance a major expansion of plant and equipment. Walker and Wilson had intended to use this additional capacity to generate a still higher volume of sales and to retire the debt out of expected high profits. Their untimely death, however, led to a decrease rather than an increase in sales, and the expected high profits that were to be used to retire the debt did not materialize. The analysis suggests that the bankers were correct when they advised Mrs. Walker and Mrs. Wilson of the need for a change in management.

Figure 5.1 **Illustration of Trend Analysis**

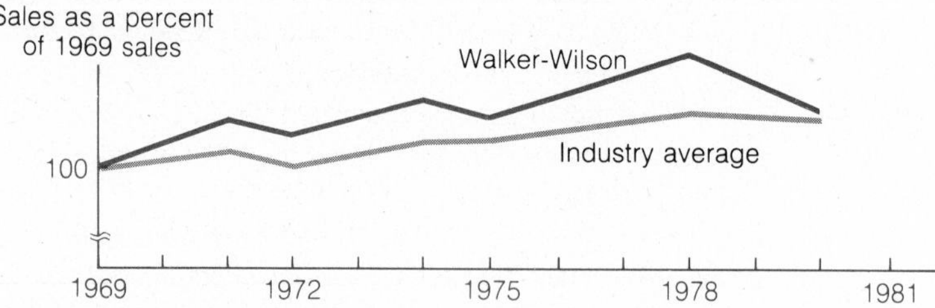

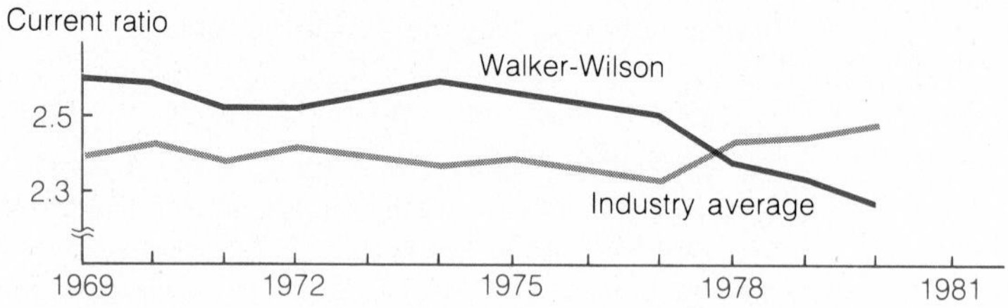

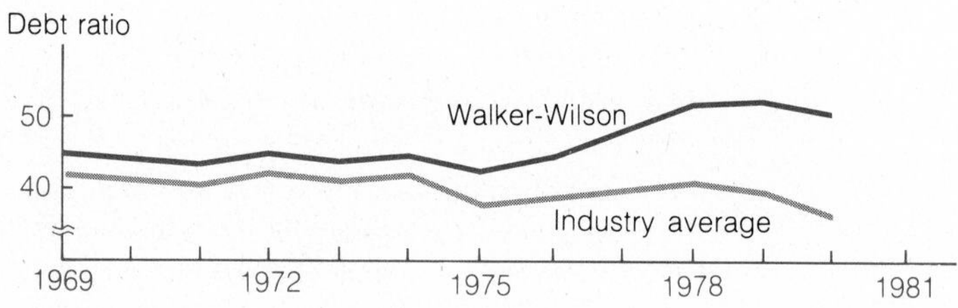

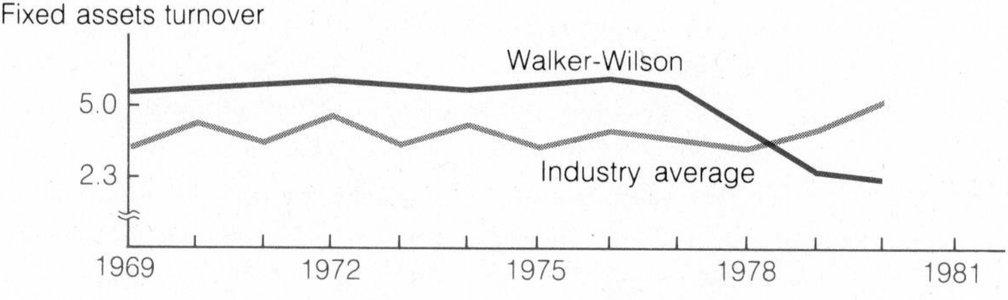

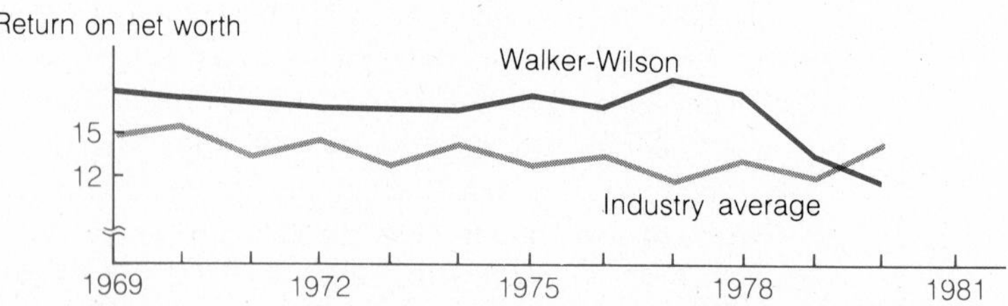

Sources of Comparative Ratios

In our analysis of the Walker-Wilson Company, we frequently used industry average ratios. Where are such averages obtained? Some important sources are listed below.

Dun & Bradstreet

Probably the most widely known and used of the industry average ratios are those compiled by Dun & Bradstreet. D&B provides fourteen ratios calculated for a large number of industries, samples and explanations of which are shown in Table 5.8. The complete data give the fourteen ratios, with the interquartile ranges, for 800 types of business activity based on their financial statements.[8] The compilations include 400,000 companies. The figures are also grouped by annual sales into three size categories. The comprehensive data are presented in *Key Business Ratios*.

Robert Morris Associates

Another group of useful ratios can be found in the annual *Statement Studies* compiled and published by Robert Morris Associates, the national association of bank loan officers. These are representative averages based on financial statements received by banks in connection with loans made. Ratios are calculated for manufacturing, wholesaling, retailing, contractors, and the finance industry. Asset items are all expressed as a percent of total assets. Income statement data are expressed as a percent of net sales. Data are presented for four size categories as well as for all of the firms in the industry. The industry names are related to the Standard Industrial Classification (SIC) codes of the U.S. Bureau of the Census. Sixteen ratios are presented as well as the total dollar amount of net sales and total assets for each category covered.

Quarterly Financial Report for Manufacturing Corporations

The Federal Trade Commission (FTC) publishes quarterly financial data on manufacturing companies. Both balance sheet and income statement data are developed from a systematic sample of corporations. The reports are published about six months after the financial data have been made available by the companies. They include an analysis by industry groups and by asset size, and financial statements in ratio form (or common-size analysis) as well. The FTC reports are a rich source of information and are frequently used for comparative purposes.

Individual Firms

Credit departments of individual firms compile financial ratios and averages on their customers in order to judge their ability to meet obligations and on their suppliers in order to evaluate their financial ability to fulfill contracts. The First National Bank of Chicago, for instance, compiles semiannual reports on the financial data for finance companies. NCR gathers data for a large number of business lines.

[8] The median and quartile ratios can be illustrated by an example. The median ratio of current assets to current debt of manufacturers of airplane parts and accessories, as shown in Table 5.8, is 2.30. To obtain this figure, the ratios of current assets to current debt for each of the 35 concerns were arranged in a graduated series, with the largest ratio at the top and the smallest at the bottom. The median ratio of 2.30 is the ratio halfway between the top and the bottom. The ratio of 4.40, representing the upper quartile, is one-quarter of the way down from the top (or halfway between the top and the median). The ratio 1.50, representing the lower quartile, is one-quarter of the way up from the bottom (or halfway between the median and the bottom).

Table 5.8 **Dun & Bradstreet Ratios for Selected Industries**

Line of Business (and number of concerns reporting)[a]	Current assets to current debt	Net profits on net sales	Net profits on tangible net worth	Net profits on net working capital	Net sales to tangible net worth	Net sales to net working capital
	Times	Per cent	Per cent	Per cent	Times	Times
2873	2.33	4.88	16.31	38.55	6.97	12.60
Agricultural Chemicals,	**1.63**	**2.56**	**9.03**	**21.39**	**4.08**	**7.00**
Nitrogenous (56)	1.27	1.03	4.33	6.48	2.27	3.83
3563	3.20	9.89	64.25	59.97	8.23	6.53
Air and Gas	**2.04**	**6.25**	**29.68**	**24.76**	**4.27**	**4.69**
Compressors (35)	1.49	2.27	8.14	8.87	3.08	2.88
3724	4.40	9.28	23.37	42.79	4.89	8.28
Airplane Parts	**2.30**	**6.75**	**20.30**	**26.40**	**3.11**	**5.38**
& Accessories (35)	1.50	5.23	14.11	19.53	2.07	3.25
2051	3.79	6.94	27.80	114.96	9.43	23.17
Bakery Products,	**1.75**	**3.20**	**17.23**	**34.39**	**6.42**	**12.12**
Bread, Cake (134)	1.05	1.30	6.65	−5.43	3.77	5.71
3312	2.54	6.92	34.22	35.48	7.62	11.63
Blast Furnaces and	**1.74**	**3.96**	**15.87**	**23.87**	**4.36**	**7.20**
Steel Mills (99)	1.43	2.23	7.67	13.59	2.89	4.55
2331	2.78	4.63	41.63	47.64	14.54	17.11
Blouses & Waists:	**1.75**	**2.37**	**21.04**	**22.00**	**8.13**	**9.41**
Women's & Misses' (285)	1.30	.86	7.01	4.37	4.97	5.02
2731	5.93	14.42	36.97	55.56	5.16	6.58
Book Publishing (270)	**2.58**	**6.60**	**17.70**	**24.20**	**2.62**	**2.94**
	1.58	3.18	6.99	7.03	1.19	1.54
2211	4.54	7.20	35.08	56.99	6.81	8.89
Broad Woven Fabrics,	**2.70**	**3.89**	**15.61**	**23.95**	**3.82**	**5.08**
Cotton (111)	1.71	1.56	8.57	7.92	2.57	3.57
2033	2.90	5.21	26.08	61.13	7.98	14.85
Canned Fruits &	**1.64**	**3.13**	**12.38**	**16.89**	**4.73**	**6.80**
Vegetables (108)	1.20	.89	2.75	3.58	2.88	3.53

[a] Standard Industrial Classification (SIC) categories
Source: "The Ratios," *Dun's Review* 116, November 1980. Reprinted by permission.

Trade Associations and Public Accountants

Financial ratios for many industries are compiled by trade associations and constitute an important source to be checked by a financial manager seeking comparative data. These averages are usually the best obtainable. In addition to balance sheet data, they provide detailed information on operating expenses, which makes possible an informed analysis of the firms' efficiency.

External Use of Financial Ratios

We have analyzed a rather long list of ratios, determining what each ratio is designed to measure. Sometimes it is unnecessary to go beyond a few of these calculations to determine that a firm is in very good or very bad condition, but often

Collection period	Net sales to inventory	Fixed assets to tangible net worth	Current debt to tangible net worth	Total debt to tangible net worth	Inventory to net working capital	Current debt to inventory	Funded debts to net working capital
Days	Times	Per cent	Per cent	Per cent	Per cent	Per cent	Per cent
77	14.4	126.0	168.9	208.9	146.8	275.4	204.9
49	**7.2**	**84.3**	**76.3**	**107.9**	**90.2**	**150.7**	**80.5**
24	5.3	42.8	49.3	61.1	49.1	88.9	22.7
54	12.0	63.9	134.7	158.4	171.3	126.0	58.4
41	**4.0**	**18.9**	**88.6**	**99.5**	**80.3**	**99.6**	**23.2**
28	3.8	10.3	34.3	37.4	35.1	66.4	1.8
68	20.0	95.3	114.3	163.6	90.2	306.8	163.8
54	**6.3**	**55.1**	**53.3**	**85.1**	**60.4**	**107.5**	**74.5**
29	4.5	22.4	23.8	36.1	13.4	54.5	32.6
28	59.9	150.5	113.5	208.5	66.6	484.3	185.1
20	**35.2**	**90.1**	**43.2**	**71.5**	**36.0**	**250.9**	**83.9**
11	21.2	49.1	13.6	25.4	6.8	126.8	1.5
50	15.5	122.4	125.5	125.5	193.3	120.3	191.8
43	**8.6**	**80.2**	**59.3**	**59.3**	**104.4**	**84.4**	**136.9**
35	5.5	39.7	39.7	36.6	66.3	40.0	86.3
56	19.0	42.5	237.7	261.5	143.4	262.4	70.5
34	**11.3**	**17.3**	**122.8**	**137.1**	**83.0**	**162.4**	**24.3**
15	6.9	5.7	50.9	60.3	41.4	97.9	10.7
90	10.0	60.7	108.2	163.0	90.8	181.5	100.4
49	**4.6**	**20.9**	**40.0**	**64.6**	**61.3**	**95.9**	**43.8**
28	2.8	6.5	12.8	22.7	29.9	40.0	9.8
64	16.4	76.0	113.4	131.5	104.1	157.6	92.3
41	**8.1**	**45.2**	**42.8**	**79.9**	**68.9**	**85.6**	**31.0**
23	5.4	20.5	18.5	28.9	36.4	48.8	11.9
33	7.9	106.0	187.0	261.5	321.5	134.9	132.5
22	**4.6**	**61.8**	**82.7**	**117.0**	**125.6**	**93.0**	**58.3**
16	3.1	32.4	30.8	48.5	67.2	63.3	12.9

what one ratio will not indicate, another may. Also, a relationship vaguely suggested by one ratio may be corroborated by another. For these reasons, it is generally useful to calculate a number of different ratios.

In numerous situations, however, a few ratios tell the story. For example, a credit manager who has a great many invoices flowing across her desk each day may limit herself to three ratios as evidence of whether the prospective buyer of goods will pay promptly. She may use (1) either the current or the quick ratio to determine how burdened the prospective buyer is with current liabilities, (2) the debt to total assets ratio to determine how much of the prospective buyer's own funds are invested in the business, and (3) any of the profitability ratios to determine whether the firm has favorable prospects. If the profit margin is high enough, it may justify the risk of dealing with a slow-paying customer (profitable companies are likely to grow and thus become better customers in the future). However, if the profit margin is low in relation to other firms in the industry, if the current ratio is low, and if the debt ratio is high, a credit manager probably will not approve a sale involving an extension of credit.[9]

Of necessity, the credit manager is more than a calculator and reader of financial ratios. Qualitative factors may override quantitative analysis. For instance, in selling to truckers, oil companies often find that the financial ratios are adverse and that if they based their decisions solely on financial ratios, they would not make sales. Or, to take another example, profits may have been low for a period, but if the customer understands why and can remove the cause of the difficulty, a credit manager may be willing to approve a sale to that customer. This decision is also influenced by the profit margin of the selling firm. If it is making a large profit on sales, it is in a better position to take credit risks than if its own margin is low. Ultimately, the credit manager must judge each customer on character and management ability, and intelligent credit decisions must be based on careful consideration of conditions in the selling firm as well as in the buying firm.

Use of Financial Ratios in Security Analysis

We have emphasized the use of financial analysis by the financial manager and by outside credit analysts. However, this type of analysis is also useful in security analysis—the analysis of the investment merits of stocks and bonds. When the emphasis is on security analysis, the principal focus is on judging the long-run profit potential of the firm. Profitability is dependent in large part on the efficiency with which the firm is run; because financial analysis provides insights into this factor, it is useful to the security analyst.

Some Limitations of Ratio Analysis

Although ratios are exceptionally useful tools, they do have limitations and must be used with caution. Ratios are constructed from accounting data, and these data are subject to different interpretations and even to manipulation. For example, two firms may use different depreciation methods or inventory valuation methods; depending on the procedures followed, reported profits can be raised or lowered. Similar differences can be encountered in the treatment of research and development expenditures, pension plan costs, mergers, product warranties, and bad-debt reserves. Further, if firms use different fiscal years, and if seasonal factors are important, this can influence the comparative ratios. Thus, if the ratios of two firms are to be compared, it is important to analyze the basic accounting data upon which the ratios were based and to reconcile any major differences.

A financial manager must also be cautious in judging whether a particular ratio is "good" or "bad" and in forming a composite judgment about a firm on the basis of a set of ratios. For example, a high inventory turnover ratio could indicate efficient

[9] Statistical techniques have been developed to improve the use of ratios in credit analysis. One such development is the discriminant analysis model reported by Edward I. Altman in "Financial Ratios, Discriminant Analysis, and the Prediction of Corporate Bankruptcy," *Journal of Finance* 23 (September 1968). Altman's model is discussed in Appendix B to this chapter. See also Edward I. Altman, Robert G. Haldeman, and P. Narayanan, "ZETA Analysis: A New Model to Identify Bankruptcy Risk of Corporations," *Journal of Banking and Finance* 1 (June 1977).

inventory management, but it could also indicate a serious shortage of inventories and suggest the likelihood of stock-outs. When financial ratio analysis indicates that the patterns of a firm depart from industry norms, this is not an absolutely certain indication that something is wrong with the firm. Such departures provide a basis for questions and further investigation and analysis. Additional information and discussions may establish sound explanations for the differences between the pattern for the individual firm and industry composite ratios. Or the differences may reveal forms of mismanagement calling for correction.

Conversely, conformance to industry composite ratios does not establish with certainty that the firm is performing normally and is managed well. In the short run, many tricks can be used to make a firm look good in relation to industry standards. The analyst must develop firsthand knowledge of the operations and management of the firm to provide a check on the financial ratios. In addition, the analyst must develop a sixth sense—a touch, a smell, a feel—for what is going on in the firm. Sometimes it is this kind of business judgment that uncovers weaknesses in the firm. The analyst should not be anesthetized by financial ratios that appear to conform with normality.

Ratios, then, are extremely useful tools. But as with other analytical methods, they must be used with judgment and caution, not in an unthinking, mechanical manner. Financial ratio analysis is a useful part of an investigation process. But financial ratios alone are not the complete answer to questions about the performance of a firm.

Summary

Ratio analysis, which relates balance sheet and income statement items to one another, permits the charting of a firm's history and the evaluation of its present position. It also allows the financial manager to anticipate reactions of investors and creditors and thus to gain insight into how attempts to acquire funds are likely to be received.

Ratios are classified into six basic types: liquidity, leverage, activity, profitability, growth, and valuation. Data from the Walker-Wilson Manufacturing Company are used to compute each type of ratio and to show how a financial analysis is made in practice. An almost unlimited number of ratios can be calculated, but in practice a limited number of each type is sufficient.

A ratio is not a meaningful number in and of itself; it must be compared with something before it becomes useful. The two basic kinds of comparative analysis are (1) trend analysis, which involves computing the ratio of a particular firm for several years and comparing the ratios over time to see if the firm is improving or deteriorating; and (2) comparisons with other firms in the same industry. These two comparisons are often combined in the graphic analysis illustrated in Figure 5.1.

Questions

5.1 "A uniform system of accounts, including identical forms for balance sheets and income statements, would be a most reasonable requirement for the SEC to impose on all publicly owned firms." Discuss this statement.

5.2 We have divided financial ratios into six groups: liquidity, leverage, activity, profitability, growth, and valuation. We could also consider financial analysis as being conducted by four groups of analysts: management, equity investors, long-term creditors, and short-term creditors.

a. Explain the nature of each type of ratio.

b. Explain the emphasis of each type of analyst in dealing with the ratios.

5.3 Why can norms with relatively well-defined limits be stated in advance for some financial ratios but not for others?

5.4 How does trend analysis supplement the basic financial ratio calculations and their interpretation?

5.5 Why should the inventory turnover figure be more important to a grocery store than to a shoe repair store?

5.6 How can a firm have a high current ratio and still be unable to pay its bills?

5.7 "The higher the rate of return on investment (ROI), the better the firm's management." Is this statement true for all firms? Explain. If you disagree with the statement, give examples of cases in which it might not be true.

5.8 What factors would you, as a financial manager, want to examine if a firm's rate of return (a) on assets or (b) on net worth was too low?

5.9 Profit margins and turnover rates vary from industry to industry. What industry characteristics account for these variations? Give some contrasting examples to illustrate your answer.

5.10 Which relation would you, as a financial manager, prefer: (a) a profit margin of 10 percent and a capital turnover of 2, or (b) a profit margin of 20 percent and a capital turnover of 1? Can you think of any firm with a relationship similar to (b)?

Problems

5.1 The Wagner Company has $2,400,000 in current assets and $950,000 in current liabilities. How much can its short-term debt (notes payable) increase without violating a current ratio of 2 to 1? (The funds from the additional notes payable will be used to increase inventory.)

5.2 Complete the balance sheet and sales information (fill in the blanks) for the Goodrich Company using the following financial data:

Debt/net worth: 1.5
Acid test ratio: 0.40
Total asset turnover: 1.5 times
Days' sales outstanding in accounts receivable: 20
Gross profit margin: 25 percent
Sales to inventory turnover: 5 times

Balance sheet

Cash	______	Accounts payable	______
Accounts receivable	______	Common stock	$10,000
Inventories	______	Retained earnings	$20,000
Plant and equipment	______	Total liabilities	
Total assets	______	and capital	______
Sales	______	Cost of goods sold	______

5.3 The following data were taken from the financial statements of the Wisconsin Furniture Company for the calendar year 1981. The norms given below are composite industry averages for the wood and upholstered furniture industry based on Dun & Bradstreet, Robert Morris Associates, and specific industry data.

a. Fill in the ratios for the Wisconsin Furniture Company.

b. Indicate by comparison with industry norms the possible errors in management policies reflected in these financial statements.

Wisconsin Furniture Company
Balance Sheet as of December 31, 1981

Assets		**Liabilities**	
Cash	$ 19,000	Accounts payable	$ 77,500
Receivables	180,000	Notes payable (at 9%)	36,000
Inventory	433,000	Other current liabilities	67,000
Total current assets	$632,000	Total current liabilities	$180,500
Net fixed assets	190,500	Long-term debt (at 10%)	200,000
		Net worth	442,000
Total assets	$822,500	Total claims on assets	$822,500

Wisconsin Furniture Company
Income Statement for Year Ended December 31, 1981

Sales		$1,315,000
Cost of goods sold:		
Material	$415,000	
Labor	360,000	
Heat, light, and power	45,000	
Indirect labor	52,000	
Depreciation	40,000	912,000
Gross profit		$ 403,000
Selling expense	$137,500	
General and administrative expense	195,000	332,500
Operating profit (EBIT)		$ 70,500
Less interest expense		23,000
Net profit before tax		47,500
Less federal income tax (at 40%)		19,000
Net profit		$ 28,500

Wisconsin Furniture Company

Ratio	Ratio	Industry norm
Current assets / Current liabilities	________	3.1 times
Debt / Total assets	________	45%
Times interest earned	________	4.8 times
Sales / Inventory	________	5.2 times

Wisconsin Furniture Company

Ratio	Ratio	Industry norm
Average collection period	______	46 days
Sales / Total assets	______	2.0 times
Net profit / Sales	______	2.8%
Net profit / Total assets	______	5.6%
Net profit / Net worth	______	10.2%

5.4 The following data were taken from the financial statements of Wheatland Pharmaceuticals Company, a wholesaler of drugs, drug proprietaries, and sundries, for the calendar year 1981. The norms given below are the industry averages for wholesale drugs, drug proprietaries, and sundries.

a. Fill in the ratios for Wheatland Pharmaceuticals Company.
b. Indicate by comparison with the industry norms the possible errors in management policies reflected in these financial statements.

Wheatland Pharmaceuticals Company Balance Sheet as of December 31, 1981 (Thousands of Dollars)

Assets		Liabilities	
Cash	$ 155	Accounts payable	$ 258
Receivables	672	Notes payable (at 8%)	168
Inventory	483	Other current liabilities	234
Total current assets	$1,310	Total current liabilities	$ 660
Net fixed assets	585	Long-term debt (at 7%)	513
		Net worth	722
Total assets	$1,895	Total claims on assets	$1,895

Wheatland Pharmaceuticals Company Income Statement for Year Ended December 31, 1981 (Thousands of Dollars)

Sales	$3,215	
Cost of goods sold	2,785	
Gross profit		$430
Operating expenses	230	
Depreciation expense	60	
Interest expense	49	
Total expenses		339
Net income before tax		$ 91
Taxes (at 40%)		36
Net income		$ 55

Wheatland Pharmaceuticals Company

Ratio	Ratio	Industry norm
Current assets / Current liabilities	______	2.0 times
Debt / Total assets	______	60%
Times interest earned	______	3.8 times
Sales / Inventory	______	6.7 times
Average collection period	______	35 days
Sales / Total assets	______	2.9 times
Net profit / Sales	______	1.2%
Net profit / Total assets	______	3.4%
Net profit / Net worth	______	8.3%

5.5 Richard Rutledge, a retired schoolteacher, holds a large number of shares of stock in the Bangor Corporation. The dividend payments from this stock make up a significant portion of Mr. Rutledge's income, so he was concerned when Bangor dropped its 1980 dividend to $1.25 per share from the $1.75 per share it had paid for the previous two years.

Mr. Rutledge gathered the information below for analysis to determine whether the financial condition of Bangor was indeed deteriorating.

Bangor Corporation Balance Sheets as of December 31

	1977	1978	1979	1980
Cash	$ 65,000	$ 76,250	$ 72,000	$ 40,000
Accounts receivable	284,000	401,600	439,000	672,000
Inventory	306,000	493,000	794,000	1,270,000
Total current assets	$655,000	$ 970,850	$1,305,000	$1,982,000
Land and building	95,000	126,150	138,000	125,000
Machinery	128,000	169,000	182,000	153,000
Other fixed assets	57,000	74,600	91,000	82,000
Total assets	$935,000	$1,340,600	$1,716,000	$2,342,000
Accounts and notes payable	$140,000	$ 152,700	$ 332,000	$ 633,240
Accruals	78,000	78,500	170,000	335,000
Total current liabilities	$218,000	$ 231,200	$ 502,000	$ 968,240
Long-term debt	81,000	304,250	304,290	408,600
Common stock	575,000	575,000	575,000	575,000
Retained earnings	61,000	230,150	334,710	390,160
Total liabilities and equity	$935,000	$1,340,600	$1,716,000	$2,342,000

Bangor Corporation Yearly Income Statements

	1978	1979	1980
Sales	$4,135,000	$4,290,000	$4,450,000
Cost of goods sold	3,308,000	3,550,000	3,560,000
Gross operating profit	$ 827,000	$ 740,000	$ 890,000
Gen. admin. & selling expense	318,000	236,320	256,000
Depreciation	127,000	159,000	191,000
Miscellaneous	64,000	134,000	318,000
Net income before taxes	$ 318,000	$ 210,680	$ 125,000
Taxes (40%)	127,000	84,270	50,000
Net income	$ 191,000	$ 126,410	$ 75,000
Number of shares outstanding	23,000	23,000	23,000
Per share data:			
EPS	$8.30	$5.50	$3.26
Cash dividend per share	$1.75	$1.75	$1.25
Market price (average)	$48\frac{7}{8}$	$25\frac{1}{2}$	$13\frac{1}{4}$

	Industry financial ratios (1980)[a]
Quick ratio	1.0
Current ratio	2.7
Inventory turnover[b]	7 times
Average collection period	32 days
Fixed asset turnover[b]	13.0 times
Total asset turnover[b]	2.6 times
Return on total assets	9%
Return on net worth	18%
Debt ratio	50%
Profit margin on sales	3.5%
P/E ratio	6 times

[a] Industry average ratios have been constant for the past four years.

[b] Based on year-end balance sheet figures

a. Calculate the key financial ratios for Bangor Corporation and plot trends in the firm's ratios against the industry averages.

b. What strengths and weaknesses are revealed by the ratio analysis?

APPENDIX 5A

EFFECTS OF CHANGING PRICE LEVELS

Immediately after World War II, with the removal of price controls that had held prices to arbitrary levels, there was a burst of inflation. Thereafter, prices increased at a rate of 2 to 3 percent per year until the escalation of hostilities in Southeast Asia in 1966, when inflation again erupted in the United States. In 1971, the United States departed from the convertibility of the dollar into gold, and the major nations adopted floating exchange rates in place of nominally fixed exchange rates. Double-digit inflation (as measured by the wholesale price index or consumer price index) has been a reality or a threat in the United States for more than a decade.

Inflation and the Measurement of Profitability

In an economy experiencing a high rate of price increases, the measurement of profitability becomes complicated. The times at which assets are purchased have a great impact on accounting profitability measures and on taxation. For example, Firm A purchased its assets in year 1, when their cost was $20 million, while Firm B purchased virtually identical assets five years later at a cost of $40 million. Let us assume that the assets will have an average twenty-year life, that both firms use straight-line depreciation, that the income before taxes for both firms is $5 million per year over the life of the assets, and that their tax rate is 50 percent. Let us compare the financial profiles of the two companies:

	Firm A	Firm B
Income before taxes and depreciation	$5,000,000	$5,000,000
Less depreciation expense	−1,000,000	−2,000,000
Income before taxes	$4,000,000	$3,000,000
Taxes (at 50%)	2,000,000	1,500,000
Net income after taxes	$2,000,000	$1,500,000
Average return on investment	20%	7.5%

Since the cost of the assets will be depreciated down to zero over their twenty-year lives, their average value is half the original cost. The net income after taxes is assumed to be constant for each year so that the average annual returns are 20 percent for Firm A and 7.5 percent for Firm B. But does Firm A really have a return almost three times greater than Firm B's? The replacement value of Firm A's assets is $40 million, on which the current depreciation expense would be $2 million per year, not $1 million. Is it correct for an investor to project Firm A's earning power into the future at 20 percent, or should the higher replacement cost of Firm A's assets that are being used up be taken into account? Should the tax-deductible depreciation expense for Firm A be $2 million per year rather than $1 million?

There are no easy answers to these questions, which arise because of the changing values of assets. Some people feel that Firm A is gaining windfall profits because it is using assets that it was able to purchase at lower than current costs. Others argue that Firm A is paying excessive taxes because the real depreciation expense should be doubled.

Inflation and Inventory Valuation Methods

The divergence between economic and accounting measures of profitability results from the valuation of both fixed assets and inventories. During periods of inflation the method of inventory valuation for income statements and balance sheets has a major impact on profitability measurement.

By comparing FIFO (first-in-first-out) and LIFO (last-in-first-out) inventory costing and valuation methods, Table 5A.1 illustrates the difficulty of obtaining a meaningful economic measure of profitability during a period of unstable prices. During such a period, Firms C and D each have two batches of inventory. The first batch of 100 units was acquired at a cost of $1 per unit; the second was acquired later at $1.50 per unit. Firm C uses the FIFO method, and Firm D uses the LIFO method. The income statement for each firm shows that it sold 100 units at $5 apiece. Since Firm C uses the FIFO method, it has figured the cost of goods sold (inventories used) as $100 (the cost of batch 1). Since Firm D uses the LIFO method, it has figured the cost of goods sold as $150 (the cost of batch 2). As a consequence, Firm C reports a net income of $100 and Firm D a net income of only $50.

However, the effects are reversed on the balance sheet, where Firm C carries inventories at $150 and Firm D at $100. On this basis, Firm C reports total assets of

Table 5A.1

Effects of FIFO and LIFO Inventory Costing and Valuation

Firm C (FIFO)			Firm D (LIFO)		
Income statement			*Income statement*		
Sales (100 at $5)		$ 500	Sales (100 at $5)		$500
Inventories used	$100		Inventories used	$150	
Other costs	300		Other costs	300	
Total costs		400	Total costs		450
Net income		$ 100	Net income		$ 50
Balance sheet			*Balance sheet*		
Inventories on hand		$ 150	Inventories on hand		$100
Other assets		850	Other assets		850
Total assets		$1,000	Total assets		$950
Return on assets		10%	Return on assets		5.3%

Note: Inventories for both companies are: batch 1—100 units at $1 per unit, for a total of $100; batch 2—100 units at $1.50 per unit, for a total of $150.

$1,000 and Firm D $950. The return on assets is thus 10 percent for Firm C and 5.3 percent for Firm D.

During a period of rising price levels, the use of LIFO results in an expense item on the income statement that is closer to the current replacement cost of items used from inventories. However, using LIFO also means that the balance sheet amount of inventory investment is carried at historical costs rather than current costs. Thus, although LIFO comes closer to a correct measure of *expenses* for the income statement, it results in an understatement of *investment* on the balance sheet. Conversely, if FIFO is used, the expense item on the income statement is understated and the balance sheet valuation of inventories is closer to current costs. The consequences are similar to those for depreciation based on historical acquisition costs versus current replacement costs.

Thus in a period of inflation, distortions will result from the use of the historical cost postulate. Assets are recorded at cost, but revenue and other expense flows are in dollars of different purchasing power. The amortization of fixed costs does not reflect the current cost of these assets. Furthermore, net income during periods when assets are held does not reflect the effects of management's decision to hold the assets rather than sell them. Assets are not stated on the balance sheet at their current values, so the firm's financial position cannot be accurately evaluated. When assets are sold, gains or losses are reported during that period even though these results reflect decisions in prior periods to hold the assets.

Proposals for Accounting Policies to Adjust for Inflation

As a consequence of a continued high rate of inflation, proposals have been made to modify accounting procedures to recognize that the traditional postulate of a stable measuring unit is no longer valid. In December 1974, the Financial Accounting Standards Board issued a proposed statement entitled "Financial Reporting in Units of General Purchasing Power." On March 23, 1976, the Securities and Exchange Commission issued Accounting Series Release No. 190. SEC Release 190 requires disclosure of replacement costs for inventory items and depreciable plant from registrants with $100 million or more (at historical cost) of gross plant assets and inventories constituting 10 percent or more of total assets.

In September 1979, the Financial Accounting Standards Board (FASB) issued Statement No. 33, *Financial Reporting and Changing Prices*. A related publication, *Illustrations of Financial Reporting and Changing Prices*, was issued in December 1979. FASB 33 requires major companies to disclose the effects of both general inflation (purchasing power) and specific price changes (current costs) as supplementary information in their published annual reports. FASB No. 33 applies to public enterprises having either (1) inventories and property, plant, and equipment (before deducting accumulated depreciation) amounting to more than $125 million, or (2) total assets amounting to more than $1 billion (after deducting accumulated depreciation). Statement No. 33 is effective for fiscal years ended on or after December 22, 1979.[1]

[1] In its Accounting Series Release No. 271, issued shortly after the publication of FASB No. 33, the Securities and Exchange Commission ruled that companies giving supplemental current-cost information in accordance with FASB No. 33 need not provide the SEC with replacement-cost information.

Effects of Adjustments for Inflation

Inflation-adjusted profits may be substantially below reported income. The nature of such impacts is indicated by Table 5A.2. In the building materials and paper and forest products industries the inflation-adjusted profits comprise about half the reported profits. For the steel industry, however, inflation-adjusted profits actually go from positive to negative. Thus if a steel company reported profits of $100 million, its inflation-adjusted profits would be −$39 million—a loss of $39 million.

Table 5A.2

The Varying Impact of Inflation on Profits

Industry	Inflation-adjusted profits[a] Percent of reported income 1974–78	1978
Computers	93%	90%
Retailers	81	82
Drugs	78	83
Food	71	71
Machinery	66	67
Chemicals	62	64
Industrial company composite	61	65
Autos	59	71
Building materials	51	51
Paper & forest products	48	49
Steel	−26	−39

[a] Net income less after-tax adjustments for inventory profits and the difference between reported depreciation and depreciation based on the replacement cost of plant and equipment.

Data: Reprinted by permission of Kidder, Peabody & Co. Inc., *Financial Quality Profile.*

Source: *BusinessWeek*, October 15, 1979, p. 69.

The impact of adjustments for inflation on the reports of individual companies can also be very substantial.[2] For example, in Table 5A.3 a five-year comparison is made for Shell Oil Company using historical costs, constant dollar costs, and a current cost basis. The historical cost basis of accounting represents traditional accounting methodology. The constant dollar basis adjusts for changes in the general level of prices using the Consumer Price Index as an indicator. The current cost basis takes into account the current values of specific assets related to their individual demand and supply conditions. For example, a drilling rig bought in 1975 for $500,000 would have increased in value by 38.2 percent if it kept up with the rise in the Consumer Price Index between 1975 and 1979. On this basis its value would have risen to $691,000. However, because of the great increase in drilling activity and the demand for drilling rigs, its value on a current cost basis could have risen to $900,000.

For Shell Oil in 1979, net income to shareholders' equity on a historical cost basis was 18.4 percent. On a constant dollar basis it was only 10.9 percent. Excluding

[2] For a detailed explanation of how the adjustments for inflation are made, see J. Fred Weston and Eugene F. Brigham, *Managerial Finance*, 7th ed., Appendix A to Chapter 7, "Adjustments for Changes in Price Levels."

Table 5A.3 **Adjusted Measures of Performance for Shell Oil Company, 1975–79**

Five-year comparisons (In December 1979 dollars)	1979	1978	1977	1976	1975
Revenues	$15,374	$13,081	$12,912	$12,551	$11,732
Constant dollar net income	$ 1,115	$ 840	$ 805	$ 778	$ 593
Cash dividends per share[a]	$ 2.22	$ 2.04	$ 1.98	$ 1.85	$ 1.80
Closing market price per share	$ 54.25	$ 36.54	$ 41.37	$ 52.02	$ 33.86
Consumer price index—end of year	229.9	202.9	186.1	174.3	166.3
Ratios					
Net income to shareholders' equity					
Historical cost basis	18.4%	15.1%	16.2%	18.2%	14.4%
Constant dollar basis	10.9%	8.8%	9.1%	9.7%	7.7%
Income from continuing operations to shareholders' equity					
Historical cost basis	18.4%	15.1%	16.2%	18.2%	14.4%
Constant dollar basis	7.6%	6.3%	7.4%	8.5%	6.0%
Current cost basis	5.1%	2.2%	—	—	—

[a] Per weighted average shares outstanding each year.

Source: Financial Accounting Standards Board, *Examples of the Use of FASB Statement No. 33, Financial Reporting and Changing Prices* (Special Report, Stamford, Connecticut, 1980), p. 40. Copyright by the Financial Accounting Standards Board, High Ridge Park, Stamford, Connecticut 06905 U.S.A. Reprinted with permission.

Table 5A.4 **Adjusted Measures of Performance for General Motors Corporation, 1975–79**

	1979	1978	1977	1976	1975
Net income as a percent of sales					
As reported	4.4%	5.5%	6.1%	6.2%	3.5%
In constant 1967 dollars	2.7	4.3	5.2	5.4	1.3
In current cost 1967 dollars	2.7				
Net income as a percent of stockholders' equity					
As reported	15.1%	20.0%	21.2%	20.2%	9.6%
In constant 1967 dollars	6.7	11.2	13.1	14.8	3.2
In current cost 1967 dollars	6.4				

Source: Financial Accounting Standards Boards, *Examples of the Use of FASB Statement No. 33, Financial Reporting and Changing Prices* (Special Report, Stamford, Connecticut, 1980), p. 40.

special gains and losses and special transactions, income from continuing operations to shareholders' equity was also 18.4 percent in 1979. However, on a constant dollar basis the ratio dropped to 7.6 percent, and on a current cost basis, it was only 5.1 percent.

Similar data are presented for General Motors Corporation in Table 5A.4. Net income as a percent of stockholders' equity as reported in 1979 was 15.1 percent. In constant 1967 dollars it was only 6.7 percent, while in current cost 1967 dollars it was 6.4 percent. Thus the adjusted return on stockholders' equity was less than half the levels reported on a historical cost basis.

Financial statements and financial ratio analysis are used to understand the past performance of a business firm as well as to lay a foundation for future projections. Traditional accounting methods assumed that the general price level was relatively stable. In addition, traditional accounting assumed that no major structural changes were taking place that caused the relative values of individual assets to change greatly. These assumptions were severely violated in the 1970s. It is, therefore, particularly important that methods be developed to make the appropriate adjustments in accounting data if they are to be used effectively in financial decision making.

APPENDIX 5B

USE OF FINANCIAL RATIOS IN DISCRIMINANT ANALYSIS

Financial ratios give an indication of the financial strength of a company. The limitations of ratio analysis arise from the fact that the methodology is basically *univariate*—that is, each ratio is examined in isolation. The combined effects of several ratios are based solely on the judgment of the financial analyst. Therefore, to overcome these shortcomings of ratio analysis, it is necessary to combine different ratios into a meaningful predictive model. Two statistical techniques, namely regression analysis and discriminant analysis, have been used for this purpose. *Regression analysis* uses past data to predict future values of a dependent variable, while *discriminant analysis* results in an index that allows classification of an observation into one of several a *priori* groupings.

Classification of Observations by Discriminant Analysis

The general problem of classification arises when an analyst has certain characteristics of an observation and wishes to classify that observation into one of several predetermined categories on the basis of these characteristics. For example, a financial analyst has on hand various financial ratios of a business enterprise and wishes to use these ratios to classify it as either a bankrupt firm or a nonbankrupt firm. Discriminant analysis is one statistical technique that allows such classification.

Basically, discriminant analysis consists of three steps:

1. Establish mutually exclusive group classifications. Each group is distinguished by a probability distribution of the characteristics.
2. Collect data for observations in the groups.
3. Derive linear combinations of these characteristics which "best" discriminate between the groups. (By "best," we mean the ones that minimize the probability of misclassification.)

Altman's Applications of Discriminant Analysis

Edward I. Altman used discriminant analysis to establish a model for predicting bankruptcy of firms.[1] His sample was composed of 66 manufacturing firms, half of which went bankrupt. From their financial statements one period prior to bankruptcy Altman obtained 22 financial ratios, of which five were found to contribute

[1] Edward I. Altman, "Financial Ratios, Discriminant Analysis and the Prediction of Corporate Bankruptcy," *Journal of Finance* 23 (Sept. 1968), pp. 589–609.

most to the prediction model. The discriminant function Z was found to be

$$Z = .012X_1 + .014X_2 + .033X_3 + .006X_4 + .999X_5 \tag{5B.1}$$

where

X_1 = Working capital/Total assets (in percent)

X_2 = Retained earnings/Total assets (in percent)

X_3 = EBIT/Total assets (in percent)

X_4 = Market value of equity/Book value of debt (in percent)

X_5 = Sales/Total assets (times)

Applications to Groups of Firms

We can illustrate how this discriminant function can be used by applying it to the group means reported by Altman for his groups of bankrupt and nonbankrupt firms.

	Group Means[2]	
	Bankrupt	Nonbankrupt
X_1	−6.1%	41.4%
X_2	−62.6%	35.5%
X_3	−31.8%	15.4%
X_4	40.1%	247.7%
X_5	1.5X	1.9X

The resulting Z values are as follows:

	X_1	X_2	X_3	X_4	X_5	Z
Z_{br} =	−.0732	− .8764	− 1.0494	+ .2406	+ 1.4985	= −0.2599
Z_{nbr} =	+.4968	+ .4970	+ .5082	+ 1.4862	+ 1.8981	= +4.8863

The largest contributor to group separation of the discriminant function was found to be the profitability ratio X_3, followed by X_5, X_4, X_2, and X_1, in that order. The model correctly classifies 95 percent of the total sample, the accuracy matrix being

Actual group membership	Predicted group membership: Bankrupt	Nonbankrupt
Bankrupt	31	2
Nonbankrupt	1	32

The zone of ignorance, that is, the range of Z values where misclassifications can be observed, lies between 1.81 and 2.67. To establish a guideline for classifying firms in this zone, a cut-off value for Z is chosen to be 2.675, the midpoint of the range of values of Z that results in minimal misclassifications. Thus a firm with a Z score of greater (less) than 2.675 is classified as a nonbankrupt (bankrupt) firm. We observe that the group means for bankrupt firms produced a Z value of −0.2599, while the group means for nonbankrupt firms produced a Z value of 4.8863. These results are consistent with the critical Z value of 2.675 which separates bankrupt and nonbankrupt firms.

By applying the above discriminant function to data obtained two to five years prior to bankruptcy, it was found that the model correctly classified 72 percent of

[2] E. I. Altman, *Corporate Bankruptcy in America* (Lexington, Mass.: Heath-Lexington Books, 1971), p. 65.

the initial sample two years prior to failure. A trend analysis shows that all five observed ratios $X_1, \ldots, X_5$ deteriorated as bankruptcy approached and that the most serious change in the majority of these ratios occurred between the third and second years prior to failure.

Application to an Individual Firm

The Altman model can also be applied to individual companies. For example, in Table 5B.1 the income statement and balance sheet for Chrysler Corporation are presented for the year ending December 31, 1979. These abbreviated financial statements provide the data needed to utilize the discriminant Z function presented in Equation 5B.1.

Table 5B.1

Chrysler Corporation Financial Statements

A. Chrysler Corporation income statement for year ended December 31, 1979 (in millions)

Revenues	$12,004
Costs (except depreciation and interest)	12,710
Depreciation	181
Interest expense, net	215
Income taxes (credit)	5
Net income	($1,097)

B. Chrysler Corporation balance sheet as of December 31, 1979

Current assets	$3,121	Current liabilities	$3,232	
Other assets	3,532	Long-term debt	1,597	
		Total debt		$4,829
		Preferred stock		219
		Common stock[a] (66.7 million shares)	417	
		Paid in capital	692	
		Retained earnings	496	
		Shareholders' equity		1,605
Total assets	$6,653	Total claims		$6,653

[a] Average price, 1979, was approximately $8.50.

Using the data on Chrysler we can make calculations of the five key financial ratios as presented in Table 5B.2. The data required for each ratio can be taken from the information in Table 5B.1.

Table 5B.2

Use of Chrysler Data in the Z Equation

$$X_1 = \frac{\text{Current assets less Current liabilities}}{\text{Total assets}} = \frac{3{,}121 - 3{,}232}{6{,}653} = -1.67\%$$

$$X_2 = \frac{\text{Retained earnings}}{\text{Total assets}} = \frac{496}{6{,}653} = 7.46\%$$

$$X_3 = \frac{\text{Earnings before interest and taxes}}{\text{Total assets}} = \frac{(887)}{6{,}653} = -13.33\%$$

$$X_4 = \frac{\text{Market value of equity}}{\text{Book value of debt}} = \frac{66.7 \times 8.50}{4{,}829} = \frac{567}{4{,}829} = 11.74\%$$

$$X_5 = \frac{\text{Sales}}{\text{Total assets}} = \frac{12{,}004}{6{,}653} = 1.8X$$

With the X values calculated in Table 5B.2, we can utilize Equation 5B.1 to calculate the Z value for Chrysler as of the end of 1979. This is done in Equation 5B.2.

$$Z = .012(-1.67) + .014(7.46) + .033(-13.33) + .006(11.74) + .999(1.8) \quad \textbf{(5B.2)}$$

$$Z = -.020 + .104 - .440 + .070 + 1.798$$

$$Z = 1.512$$

The resulting Z value is 1.512. Recall that the critical Z value that appeared to discriminate between bankrupt and nonbankrupt firms was 2.675. Chrysler's Z value of 1.512 is below the critical value and places it in the category of firms likely to go bankrupt. However, Chrysler's situation was not as bad as the group of bankrupt firms whose Z value was $-.26$. The intermediate result for Chrysler suggests that it was indeed in difficulty, but that even on a purely mechanical basis the loan guarantee might rescue Chrysler. Obviously, fundamental analysis of Chrysler's place in the dynamically changing automobile industry was required for a final decision. However, it is interesting to note that the discriminant analysis of Chrysler's position was consistent with the judgment that Chrysler was having problems but had some possibility of rescue in one form or another.

CHAPTER 6

FINANCIAL FORECASTING

Firms need assets to make sales; if sales are to be increased, assets must also be expanded. Growing firms require new investments—immediate investment in current assets and, as full capacity is reached, investment in fixed assets as well. New investments must be financed, and new financing carries with it commitments and obligations to service the capital obtained.[1] A growing, profitable firm is likely to require additional cash for investments in receivables, inventories, and fixed assets. Such a firm can have a cash flow problem, unless the required financing is identified on a timely basis.

The planning process is thus an integral part of the financial manager's job. As we will see in subsequent chapters, long-term debt and equity funds are raised infrequently and in large amounts, primarily because the cost per dollar raised by selling such securities decreases as the size of the issue increases. Because of these considerations, it is important that the firm have a working estimate of its total needs for funds for the next few years. It is therefore useful to examine methods of forecasting the firm's needs for funds, which is the subject of this chapter.

Approaches to Forecasting Financial Requirements

With the development of sophisticated computer models of the firm, very detailed procedures may be employed to forecast investment requirements. However, each builds on the basic methodologies presented here: the percent-of-sales method or the regression method. These two techniques and their more complex counterparts depend upon a number of relationships, particularly causality and stability.

Causality refers to what motivates investment in the various asset accounts. As we have seen in the previous illustrations, firms invest in fixed assets, such as plant and equipment, with the intention of producing goods to sell. It is hoped-for sales that cause investments in fixed assets to be made. As production gets underway, inventories of various kinds will be needed. When sales are made on credit, accounts receivable will be created. But for each type of investment, sales is the prime mover.

Although sales are the causal factor, the relationships can become complex because of the lead and lag timing involved. Clearly, investments in fixed assets

[1] "Servicing" capital refers to the payment of interest and principal on debt and to dividends on common stocks.

Figure 6.1 **Investments and Sales: Pfizer, Inc., 1973–79 (Dollar Amounts in Millions)**

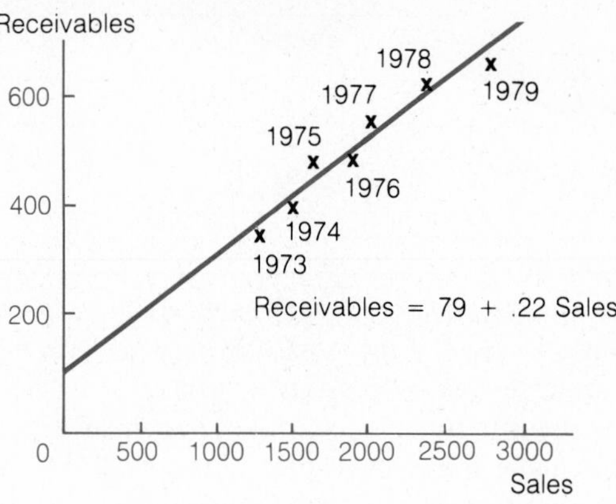

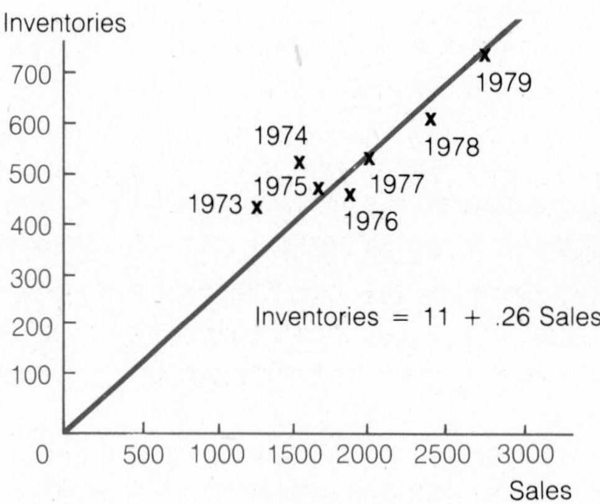

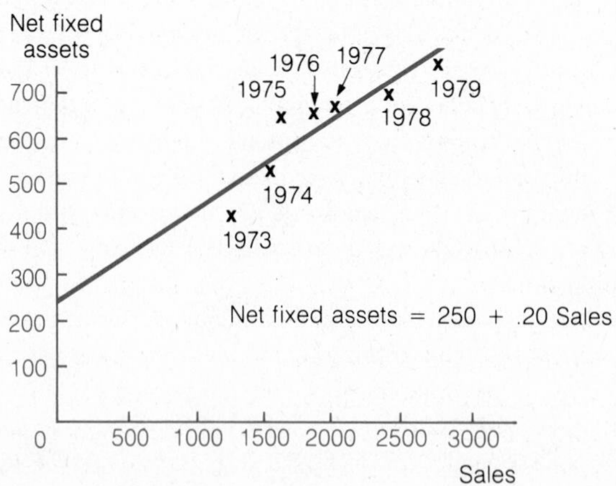

must be made before production starts, so fixed-asset investments *lead* sales. Investments in inventories of raw materials must be made to get production under way. Labor expenses transform raw materials into work-in-process and finally finished goods. Investments in all of these forms of inventories must be made before sales can be made, so inventory investments also lead sales. But the investment in accounts receivable does not occur until *after* sales are made. Hence receivables investments *lag* sales.

With shifts in the rate of sales growth, the interaction of these lead and lag relationships between investment in assets and sales levels can give rise to some complex patterns. For analysis of the intricate interaction effects between sales and investment requirements, the detailed computer models are useful. But for establishing broad patterns of relationships, relatively simple methodologies are adequate. In some respects they are superior to the complex models. Computer models become so complicated that it may be difficult to identify the forces driving the model.

In addition to identifying a basic causal variable such as sales, a forecasting model requires relative *stability* in the relationships. This second requirement is also generally met in financial models. For example, consider the three main asset items and sales for Pfizer, Inc., a pharmaceutical company, in Figure 6.1. The charts present the relationships graphically; we can see that the patterns are stable. The numerical calculations we have made further establish that the relationships meet the formal requirements of statistical significance. Whether the relationships between individual asset items and sales will be stable and significant will vary with companies and with individual assets. Our experience as well as the experience of many practicing financial executives will support the need for stability of relationships in any systematic forecasting procedure. The choice among the alternative methods can best be covered after the two basic alternative approaches are explained.

Percent-of-Sales Method

It is apparent from the preceding discussion that *the most important variable that influences a firm's financing requirements is its projected dollar volume of sales. A good sales forecast is an essential foundation for forecasting financial requirements.* In spite of its importance, we shall not discuss sales forecasting here; rather, we simply assume that a sales forecast has been made, and then estimate financial requirements on the basis of this forecast. The principal methods of forecasting financial requirements are described in this and the following sections.

The simplest approach to forecasting financial requirements expresses the firm's needs in terms of the percentage of annual sales invested in each individual balance sheet item. As an example, consider the Moore Company, whose balance sheet as of December 31, 1980, is shown in Table 6.1. The company's sales are running at about $500,000 a year, which is its capacity limit; the profit margin after tax on sales is 4 percent. During 1980, the company earned $20,000 after taxes and paid out $10,000 in dividends, and it plans to continue paying out half of net profits as dividends. How much additional financing will be needed if sales expand to

Table 6.1

The Moore Company
Balance Sheet
December 31, 1980

Assets		Liabilities	
Cash	$ 10,000	Accounts payable	$ 50,000
Receivables	85,000	Accrued taxes and wages	25,000
Inventories	100,000	Mortgage bonds	70,000
Fixed assets (net)	150,000	Common stock	100,000
		Retained earnings	100,000
Total assets	$345,000	Total liabilities and net worth	$345,000

Table 6.2

The Moore Company
Balance Sheet Items Expressed as a Percent of Sales
December 31, 1980

Assets		Liabilities	
Cash	2.0	Accounts payable	10.0
Receivables	17.0	Accrued taxes and wages	5.0
Inventories	20.0	Mortgage bonds	na*
Fixed assets (net)	30.0	Common stock	na*
		Retained earnings	na*
Total assets	69.0	Total liabilities and net worth	15.0

Assets as percent of sales	69.0
Less: Spontaneous increase in liabilities	15.0
Percent of each additional dollar of sales that must be financed	54.0

* Not applicable

$800,000 during 1981? The calculating procedure, using the percent-of-sales method, is explained below.[2]

First, isolate those balance sheet items that can be expected to vary directly with sales. In the case of the Moore Company, this step applies to each category of assets—a higher level of sales necessitates more cash for transactions, more receivables, higher inventory levels, and additional fixed plant capacity. On the liability side, accounts payable as well as accruals may be expected to increase with increases in sales. Retained earnings will go up as long as the company is profitable and does not pay out 100 percent of earnings, but the percentage increase is not constant. However, neither common stock nor mortgage bonds would increase spontaneously with an increase in sales.

The items that can be expected to vary directly with sales are tabulated as a percentage of sales in Table 6.2. For every $1.00 increase in sales, assets must

[2] We recognize, of course, that as a practical matter, business firms plan their needs in terms of specific items of equipment, square feet of floor space, and other factors, and not as a percentage of sales. However, the outside analyst does not have access to this information; the manager, even though he has the information on specific items, needs to check his forecasts in aggregate terms. The percent-of-sales method serves both these needs surprisingly well.

increase by \$.69; this \$.69 must be financed in some manner. Accounts payable will increase spontaneously with sales, as will accruals; these two items will supply \$.15 of new funds for each \$1.00 increase in sales. Subtracting the 15 percent for spontaneously generated funds from the 69 percent funds requirement leaves 54 percent. Thus, for each \$1.00 increase in sales, the Moore Company must obtain \$.54 of financing either from internally generated funds or from external sources.

In the case at hand, sales are scheduled to increase from \$500,000 to \$800,000, or by \$300,000. Applying the 54 percent developed in the table to the expected increase in sales leads to the conclusion that \$162,000 will be needed.

Some of that need will be met by retained earnings. Total revenues during 1981 will be \$800,000; if the company earns 4 percent after taxes on this volume, profits will amount to \$32,000. Assuming that the 50 percent dividend payout ratio is maintained, dividends will be \$16,000 and \$16,000 will be retained. Subtracting the retained earnings from the \$162,000 that was needed leaves a figure of \$146,000—this is the amount of funds that must be obtained through borrowing or by selling new common stock.

This process may be expressed in equation form, with EFR standing for external funds required.

$$\text{EFR} = \frac{A_c}{S}(\Delta S) + \frac{A_f}{S}(\Delta S) - \frac{B_s}{S}(\Delta S) - mb(S_1) \tag{6.1}$$

where:

$\frac{A_c}{S}$ = assets that increase spontaneously with total revenues or sales as a percent of total revenues or sales

$\frac{A_f}{S}$ = assets that increase in "lumps," requiring investment decisions by the firm as a percent of total revenues or sales

$\frac{B_s}{S}$ = those liabilities that increase spontaneously with total revenues or sales as a percent of total revenues or sales

S_1 = total revenues projected for next year

ΔS = change in total revenues or sales = $(S_1 - S)$

m = profit margin on sales

b = earnings retention ratio

For the Moore Company, then,

$$\begin{aligned} \text{EFR} &= .39(\$300{,}000) + .30(\$300{,}000) - .15(\$300{,}000) \\ &\quad - .04(.5)(\$800{,}000) \\ &= .54(\$300{,}000) - .02(\$800{,}000) \\ &= \$146{,}000 \end{aligned} \tag{6.1a}$$

The \$146,000 found by the formula method must, of course, equal the amount derived previously.

Figure 6.2 **The Relationship Between Asset Acquisitions and Sales Growth**

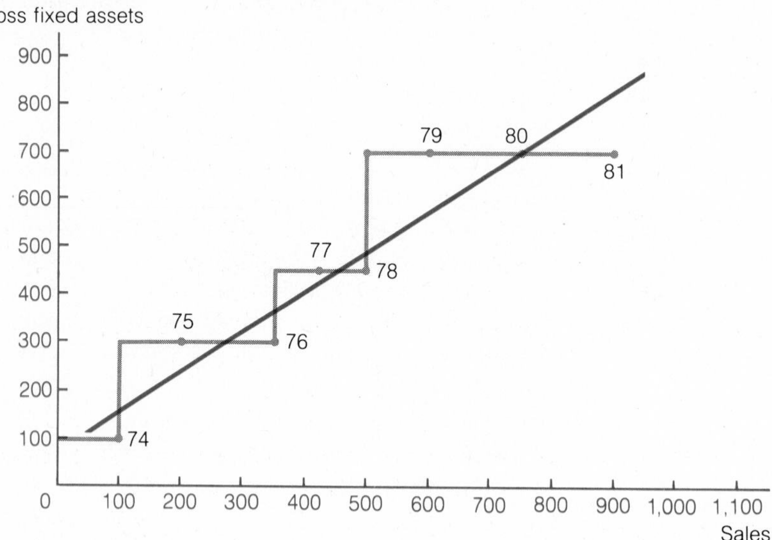

We recognize that investments in fixed assets may occur at intervals exceeding one year. The actual pattern may represent a set of "stairsteps," as shown in Figure 6.2. While the actual pattern is lumpy and uneven, the data by individual years may not be greatly different from a straight-line regression relationship as illustrated. In actual empirical measurements for individual companies, the relationship between fixed assets and sales is usually linear and statistically significant. The two asset groups can then be combined and EFR becomes as shown in equation 6.2, in which A stands for total assets.[3]

$$\text{EFR} = \frac{A}{S}(\Delta S) - \frac{B_s}{S}(\Delta S) - mb(S_1) \qquad \textbf{(6.2)}$$

In the above discussion of the relation between fixed assets and sales, Figure 6.2 utilizes gross fixed assets while the remainder of the discussion uses net fixed assets. In actual practice we do utilize gross, rather than net, fixed assets. However, in order to do this we need the requisite data, particularly the amount of fixed asset retirements each year. When gross fixed assets are used, the asset requirement percentage will be higher, but the annual depreciation expense will represent a "source of funds." But since we are using published data to illustrate the methodology and usually do not have information on asset retirements, we are forced to use net fixed assets rather than gross fixed assets in the relationships. The fundamental methodology, however, is not affected.

Notice what would have occurred if the Moore Company's sales forecast for 1981 had been only \$515,000, or a 3 percent increase. Applying the formula, we find

[3] These assertions are supported by the data patterns for most companies studied.

the external funds requirements as follows:

$$\begin{aligned}\text{External funds required} &= .54(\$15{,}000) - .02(\$515{,}000)\\ &= \$8{,}100 - \$10{,}300\\ &= (\$2{,}200)\end{aligned}$$

In this case, no external funds are required. In fact, the company will have $2,200 in excess of its requirements; it should therefore plan to increase dividends, retire debt, or seek additional investment opportunities. The example shows that while small percentage increases in sales can be financed through internally generated funds, larger percentage increases cause the firm to go into the market for outside capital. In other words, small rates of sales growth can be financed from internal sources, but higher rates of sales growth require external financing.

Of central concern in financial forecasting is an answer to the question, "What percentage of my firm's sales growth will require external financing?" This is an important question because its answer alerts financial management to the magnitude of the outside financing effort required. A compact equation can be derived to measure the percentage of external financing required (PEFR). To simplify, in Equation 6.2 let $(A/S - B_s/S) = I$. Note also that the new sales level S_1 equals $(1 + g)S$, where g is the growth rate in sales. The increase in sales can therefore be written

$$\Delta S = (1 + g)S - S = S(1 + g - 1) = gS$$

We can now write equation 6.2a, making the appropriate substitutions.

$$\text{EFR} = I\Delta S - mbS_1 \qquad \textbf{(6.2a)}$$

With some manipulation, we obtain Equation 6.3.[4]

$$\text{PEFR} = I - mb(1 + g)/g \qquad \textbf{(6.3)}$$

PEFR is the percentage of sales increase that will have to be financed from external sources. Recall that EFR was defined as the dollar amount of external financing required for a given amount of increase in sales. PEFR is a further step toward generalization. The PEFR expression assembles the factors for analyzing

[4] The proof is as follows: Begin with Equation 6.2a:

$$\text{EFR} = I\Delta S - mbS_1 \qquad \textbf{(6.2a)}$$

Use $\Delta S = gS$ and $S_1 = (1 + g)S$:

$$\text{EFR} = IgS - mb(1 + g)S \qquad \textbf{(6.2b)}$$

Divide by ΔS, or gS, which is the amount of the sales increase:

$$\frac{\text{EFR}}{\Delta S} = \text{PEFR} = \frac{IgS}{gS} - \frac{mb(1 + g)S}{gS}$$

With the appropriate cancellations and defining PEFR as EFR/ΔS, we have Equation 6.3:

$$\text{PEFR} = I - mb(1 + g)/g \qquad \textbf{(6.3)}$$

the relationships between the growth rate of sales and the percentage of sales growth that will have to be financed externally.

To illustrate, we can use the previous example for the Moore Company that was calculated in Equation 6.1a. EFR was \$146,000; the amount of sales growth was \$300,000; the PEFR is simply EFR expressed as a percentage of the amount of sales growth, or \$146,000/\$300,000 = 48.67 percent. We should get the same result using the compact PEFR formula in Equation 6.3. Recall that I is the financing requirements ratio to sales minus the spontaneous financing ratio to sales, or .69 minus .15 equals .54 for Moore. The profit margin on sales ratio, m, is .04 and the retention ratio is .5. The \$300,000 sales increase represents a 60 percent rate of growth in sales, g. We now insert these numbers into Equation 6.3 for calculating PEFR, the percentage of sales growth that will have to be financed externally.

$$\begin{aligned} \text{PEFR} &= .54 - .04(.5)(1.6)/(.6) \\ &= .54 - .02(2.667) \\ &= .4867 = 48.67\% \end{aligned} \tag{6.3a}$$

This is, of course, the same result obtained by simply taking the ratio of EFR to the amount of the sales increase. This is the way we could make the computation if we had already calculated EFR. However, the PEFR equation is more convenient if we are focusing on the percentage of sales growth and the possible impact of inflation on the rate of sales growth in inflated dollars.

For example, suppose that the sales growth expected for Moore were a 10 percent increase. We would now have:

$$\begin{aligned} \text{PEFR} &= .54 - .02(1.1)/(.1) \\ &= .54 - .22 \\ &= .32 = 32\% \end{aligned} \tag{6.3b}$$

Thus a drop in the rate of sales growth also decreases the extent to which external financing will be required. The rate at which the percentage of external financing changes with changes in the growth rate depends on the magnitudes of I and mb. For all manufacturing industries in the U.S., the key relationships are: $I = .5$, $m = .05$, $b = .60$.

Before the onset of inflation in the United States in 1966, the economy was growing at about 6 to 7 percent per annum. If a firm was in an industry that grew at the same rate as the economy as a whole and if a firm maintained its market share in its industry, the firm would be growing at 6 to 7 percent per annum as well. Let us see what the implications for external financing requirements would be. With a growth rate of 6 to 7 percent the percentage of an increase in sales that would have to be financed externally would be as follows:

$$\begin{aligned} \text{PEFR} &= .5 - (.05)(.6)(1.06)/(.06) \\ &= .50 - .53 = -.03 = -3\% \\ \text{PEFR} &= .5 - (.05)(.6)(1.07)/(.07) \\ &= .50 - .46 = .04 = 4\% \end{aligned}$$

Thus at a growth rate of 6 percent the percentage of external financing to sales growth would be −3 percent. In other words, the firm would have excess funds with which it could increase dividends or increase its investment in marketable securities. With a growth rate of 7 percent the firm would have a requirement of external financing of 4 percent of the sales increase.

Following 1966 the inflation rate in some years was in the double-digit range: that is, 10 percent or more. Suppose we add sufficient percentage points per annum of an inflation rate to the previous 6 to 7 percent growth rate to obtain a growth rate of 15 or 20 percent. Then the external financing requirements will be as follows:

$$\begin{aligned}\text{PEFR} &= .5 - .03(1.15)/(.15)\\ &= .50 - .23 = .27 = 27\%\\ \text{PEFR} &= .5 - .03(1.2)/(.2)\\ &= .50 - .18 = .32 = 32\%\end{aligned}$$

With a growth rate in sales of 15 percent, external financing rises to 27 percent of the firm's sales growth. If inflation caused the growth rate of sales to rise to 20 percent, then the external financing percentage rises to 32 percent.

The substantial increase in the growth rate of sales of firms measured in inflated dollars in recent years points up why external financing has become more important for firms. It underscores also why the finance function in firms has taken on increased importance in recent years. There is simply a much bigger job to be done, particularly in meeting requirements for external financing to maintain the sales growth of a firm. An inflation rate of 10 percent, for example, makes it necessary for a firm to raise external financing of 17 percent of its growth in sales of inflated dollars even if the real growth of the firm is zero.

The percent-of-sales method of forecasting financial requirements is neither simple nor mechanical, although an explanation of the ideas requires simple illustrations. Experience in applying the technique in practice suggests the importance of understanding (1) the basic technology of the firm and (2) the logic of the relation between sales and assets for the particular firm in question. A great deal of experience and judgment is required to apply the technique in actual practice.

The percent-of-sales method is most appropriately used for forecasting relatively short-term changes in financing needs. It is less useful for longer-term forecasting for reasons that are best described in connection with the analysis of the regression method of financial forecasting discussed in the next section.

Regression Method of Forecasting Financial Requirements

The percent-of-sales method assumes that a relatively constant relationship is maintained between sales and individual balance sheet and income statement items to be projected. The regression method is more general; it calculates average relationships and is more accurate if a constant term or large initial amount is involved. The essence of the regression method is seen by using a scatter diagram to visualize what is going on.

We will use data for the Standard Oil Company of California (SOCAL) to illustrate the basic concepts involved. Table 6.3 presents data on sales and inventories for

Table 6.3

Inventory-to-Sales Relationships for SOCAL for 1969–78

	Inventory (Y)	Sales (X)	Inventory to sales ratio (Y/X)
1969	403	4,560	.088
1970	461	4,962	.093
1971	506	5,728	.088
1972	507	6,477	.078
1973	665	8,480	.078
1974	1,087	17,924	.061
1975	1,165	17,524	.066
1976	1,278	20,181	.063
1977	1,438	21,752	.066
1978	1,216	24,106	.050

Source: Moody's *Industrials and Corporations*, 1973, 1979. Reprinted by permission.

the Standard Oil Company of California for 1969 through 1978. The data are graphed in Figure 6.3. Using a hand calculator, the "line of best fit for the points," or the regression line, was calculated to be:

$$\text{Inventories} = \$216 \text{ million} + .05 \text{ Sales}$$

This regression line was then drawn in on Figure 6.3. As can be seen, the points are all relatively close to the calculated regression line. The correlation coefficient between sales and inventories for these data is .9745, indicating that there is only a relatively small scatter of the actual data off the regression line.

Figure 6.3

Inventory-to-Sales Relationships for SOCAL for 1969–78

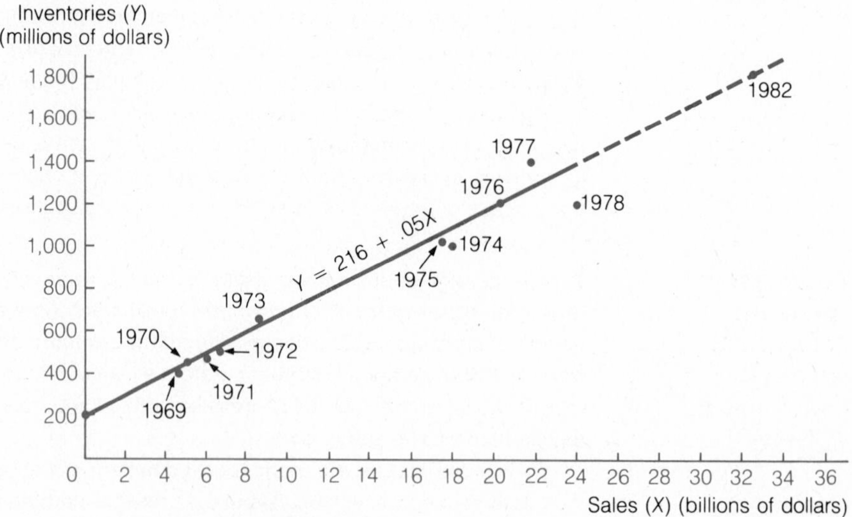

The relationship appears to be a straight line. A number of offsetting influences seem to be operating. From the economic order quantity formula to be discussed in Chapter 9, inventories increase with the square root of sales. This would cause the line to curve downward somewhat. The greater efficiencies in handling inventories, such as improved transportation, would also tend to cause the percentage of inventories to sales to decrease over time as sales increase. But the greater variety of products would cause inventories to rise as sales volume and product diversity increase. These influences appear to be counterbalancing since the actual data for SOCAL indicate that the straight line calculated is a very good fit to the data.

Suppose a sales forecast has been made for 1982 for SOCAL which projects that sales will increase at the same rate as they increased between 1974 and 1978, about 35 percent. This would result in sales of $32,543 for 1982. Given all the uncertainties of the international oil market, a sales forecast for 1982 would require a very comprehensive study. But our interest is in developing the relations between sales and inventories. Taking the sales forecast as given, what projection for inventories would be appropriate? Table 6.3 shows that the ratio of inventories to sales has been trending downward for SOCAL from over 9 percent in 1970 to 5 percent in 1978. But this result is mainly due to a mathematical relationship resulting from the positive amount of inventory as the intercept of the regression line. For example, consider the inventory to sales relationships for inventories forecast from the use of the regression line for the following sales levels.

Sales	Inventories	Ratio of inventories to sales
$ 5,000	$ 466	.0932
10,000	716	.0716
20,000	1,216	.0608
30,000	1,716	.0572

Note: Based on the use of the regression equation, Inventories = $216 + .05 Sales.

As sales rise, the ratio of inventories to sales declines from .0932 to .0572. Use of the ratio of .0932 based on a sales level of $5,000 million would have resulted in a forecast of inventories related to $30,000 million sales of $2,796 million instead of $1,716 million—an upside error of $1,080 million. This is due to the mathematical influence of the "base stock inventory" of $216 million in the regression equation. This "constant" has a greater influence when sales are small than when sales are large.

Thus if we had a sales forecast for 1982 in the case of SOCAL of $32,543 million, the forecast of inventories, using the regression line, would be $1,843 million. Using the ratio of inventories to sales, we might use the average ratio for 1974–78, which was .0612, giving an inventory projection of $1,992, which is greater by $149 million over the forecast using the regression method. If we used the low ratio for 1978, which was 5 percent, we would be $216 million lower than the projection by use of the regression method.

We have illustrated the use of the regression method as applied to one account—inventories. The same principles are involved in developing a forecasting equation for each account to be projected. This provides a basis for financial forecasts of the balance sheet and income statement, as well as other financial statements. The same procedures as illustrated for the percent-of-sales method would apply. The nature of the equations used in each method can be compared:

Percent-of-sales method: The account is a constant percent of sales.

Regression method: The account is equal on average to some absolute dollar amount plus a constant percent of sales.

The percent-of-sales method of projecting financing requirements will not be stable if the regression line for the data does not go through the origin. The regression method is seen to be superior to the percent-of-sales method of forecasting financial requirements, particularly for longer-term forecasts. When a firm is likely to have a base stock of inventory or fixed assets, the ratio of the item to sales declines as sales increase. In such cases, using historical relations between inventory and sales, for example, would set a "norm" or "control standard" that was too high as compared with the use of the regression method. This is an important difference between the two forecasting methods which is illustrated more completely in the following section.

Comparison of Forecasting Methods

Percent of Sales

The percent-of-sales method of financial forecasting assumes that certain balance sheet items vary directly with sales; that is, that the ratio of a given balance sheet item to sales remains constant. The postulated relationship is shown in Figure 6.4. *Notice that the percent-of-sales method implicitly assumes a linear relationship that passes through the origin.* The slope of the line representing the relationship may vary, but the line always passes through the origin. Implicitly, the relationship is established by finding one point, or ratio, such as that designated as X in Figure 6.4, and then connecting this point with the origin. Then, for any projected level of sales, the forecasted level of the particular balance sheet item can be determined.

Figure 6.4 **Percent of Sales**

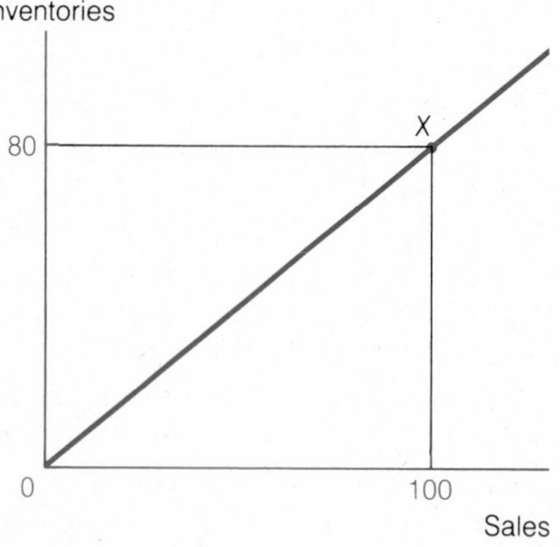

Scatter Diagram, or Regression Method

The scatter diagram method differs from the percent-of-sales method principally in that it does not assume that the line of relationship passes through the origin. In its simplest form, the scatter diagram method calls for calculating the ratio between sales and the relevant balance sheet item at two points in time, extending a line through these two points, and using the line to describe the relationship between sales and the balance sheet item. The accuracy of the regression is improved if more points are plotted, and the regression line can be fitted mathematically (by a technique known as the method of least squares) as well as drawn in by eye.

The scatter diagram method is illustrated in Figure 6.5, where the percent-of-sales relationship is also shown for comparison. The error induced by the use of the percent-of-sales method is represented by the gap between the two lines. At a sales level of 125, the percent-of-sales method would call for an inventory of 100 versus an inventory of only 90 using a scatter diagram forecast. *Notice that the error is very small if sales continue to run at approximately the current level, but the gap widens if the sales change is substantial.*

Because of the limitations of the percent-of-sales method, some have expressed skepticism of its practical worth. But note that it results in error only when the intercept term is large in relation to the magnitude of the periodic amounts of sales changes. Hence for short-term, month-to-month budgeting where the percentage sales changes are likely to be small, the error will be minimal. Furthermore, where the inflation component of growth is very large, the intercept term is likely to be small in relation to sales levels and changes in sales levels. Thus under a high rate of inflation there will not be a substantial difference between the percent-of-sales method and the regression method.

Figure 6.5

Scatter Diagram, or Simple Linear Regression

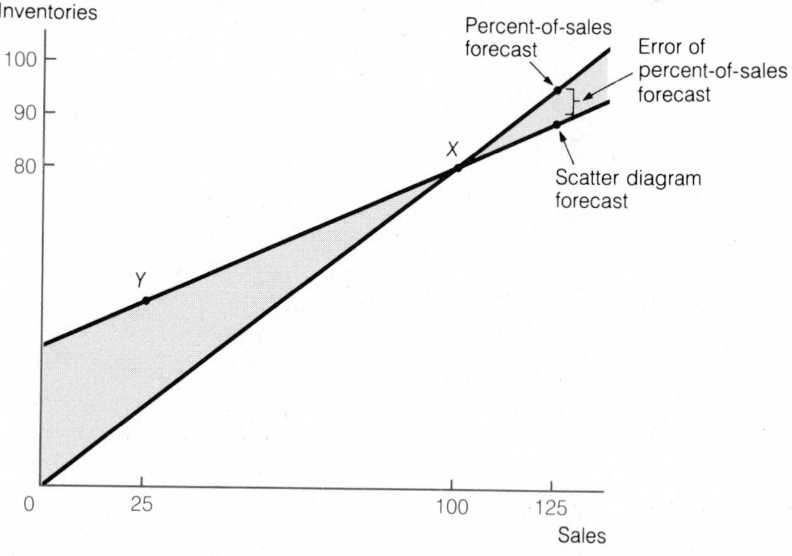

The other criticism leveled against both methods is that they are too simple compared to the highly complex and sophisticated analysis that takes place particularly on major capital investment decisions. In addition, in individual areas, such as forecasting receivables, it is argued that many factors are involved that may influence the relationship. These include the mix of sales to wholesalers versus retailers, the change in the mix of products sold which may have different payment periods, and so forth. However, we would urge that the percent-of-sales and regression methods are simple and inexpensive to apply. They provide a good basis for a review and check on the more complex and detailed methodologies that may be employed. In our own experience we have found that the perspective pro-

Table 6.4

Standard Oil Company of California Consolidated Statement of Changes in Financial Position, 1978

	1978
Sources of funds:	
Net income	$1,105,881,000
Depreciation, depletion, and amortization	621,533,000
Deferred income taxes	79,353,000
Undistributed income of unconsolidated companies	(37,073,000)
Funds provided by operations	1,769,694,000
Increases in long-term debt	27,724,000
Net book value of properties, plant, and equipment sold or retired	59,360,000
	1,856,778,000
Uses of funds:	
Additions to properties, plant, and equipment	1,049,673,000
Cash dividends	434,581,000
Reductions in long-term debt	264,458,000
Other net increase in investments and advances	7,589,000
Other—net	3,674,000
	1,759,975,000
Increase in working capital	$ 96,803,000
Analysis of changes in working capital:	
Increase (decrease) in current assets:	
Cash and marketable securities	$ 535,639,000
Receivables	614,143,000
Inventories	(221,310,000)
	928,472,000
(Increase) decrease in current liabilities:	
Accounts payable	(402,180,000)
Notes and loans payable	7,000,000
Current maturities of long-term debt	(208,239,000)
Federal and other taxes on income	(207,098,000)
Other	(21,152,000)
	(831,669,000)
Increase in working capital	$ 96,803,000

vided by these simple forecasting methods may sometimes uncover some very gross errors involved in the more complex methodologies. Since these techniques are simple and inexpensive to employ, they are useful methodologies for obtaining a broad overview of the relationships.

Statement of Changes in Financial Position

Financial forecasting is used to plan for financing requirements. The analysis of changes in the firm's financial position, also called *sources and uses of funds analysis*, performs an important role in this connection. If a firm requests a loan, the bank's loan officer will doubtless pose these questions: (1) What has the firm done with the money it has? (2) What will it do with the new funds? (3) How will it repay the loan? The sources and uses statement helps provide answers to these questions as well as to questions that other interested parties may have about the firm. This information can indicate whether the firm is making progress or whether problems are arising. The nature of this statement is conveyed by an actual illustration for the Standard Oil Company of California for 1978 (Table 6.4).

The main sources of funds were net income and depreciation. The main uses of funds were additions to properties, plant, and equipment. The excess of the sources of funds is related to the increase in working capital. One way to look at this is to recognize that the investment in current assets (a use of funds) exceeded the net increase in current liabilities (a source of funds) by $97 million, which just balanced the excess of "sources over uses of funds from other sources" of $97 million. Thus in practice, the sources and uses of funds are divided between those that do not affect current assets and current liabilities and those that do. For ease of presentation, we will not make this distinction in the procedures we describe. However, the format is perfectly general so that it could be modified as desired.

The Nature of Depreciation

Before constructing a sources and uses of funds statement, we shall discuss the nature of depreciation. *Depreciation* is an annual charge against income that reflects the cost of the equipment used in the production process. For example, suppose a machine with an expected useful life of ten years and no expected salvage value was purchased in 1978 for $100,000. This cost must be charged against production during the machine's ten-year life; otherwise, profits will be overstated. If the machine is depreciated by the straight-line method, the annual charge is $10,000. This amount is deducted from sales revenues, along with such other costs as labor and raw materials, to determine income. However, depreciation is not a cash outlay. Funds were expended back in 1978, so the depreciation charged against income each year is not a cash outlay, as are labor or raw materials payments.

To illustrate the significance of depreciation in cash flow analysis, consider the Dallas Fertilizer and Chemical Company, which has the following income statement for 1980:

Sales	$300,000,000
Costs excluding depreciation	$270,000,000
Depreciation	10,000,000
Net income before taxes	$ 20,000,000
Taxes	8,000,000
Net income after taxes	$ 12,000,000

Assuming that sales are for cash and that all costs except depreciation are paid in cash during 1980, how much cash is available from operations to pay dividends, retire debt, or make investments in fixed or current assets (or both)? The answer is $22 million, the sum of profit after taxes plus depreciation. The sales are all for cash, so the firm received $300 million in cash money. Its costs other than depreciation were $270 million, and these were paid in cash, leaving $30 million. Depreciation *is not* a cash charge—the firm does not pay out the $10 million of depreciation expenses—so $30 million of cash money is still left after depreciation. Taxes, on the other hand, are paid in cash, so $8 million for taxes must be deducted from the $30 million gross operating cash flow, leaving a net cash flow from operations of $22 million. Since $300 million flows in and $278 million flows out, $22 million must remain. This $22 million is, of course, exactly equal to net income after taxes plus depreciation: $12 million plus $10 million equals $22 million. As shown in the SOCAL example, depreciation is a non-cash charge which is added back to net income to arrive at something called *funds* (cash or working capital) generated by operations.

Sources and Uses of Funds Statement

Several steps are involved in constructing a sources and uses of funds statement. First, the changes in balance sheet items from one year to the next must be tabulated and then classified as either sources or uses of funds, according to the following

Table 6.5

Dallas Fertilizer and Chemical Company
Comparative Balance Sheets and
Sources and Uses of Funds
(Millions of Dollars)

Assets	Dec. 31, 1980		Dec. 31, 1981		Source	Use
Cash		$ 10		$ 5	$ 5	
Marketable securities		25		15	10	
Net receivables		15		20		$ 5
Inventories		25		35		10
Gross fixed assets	150		175			25
Less accumulated depreciation[a]	40		50		10	
Net fixed assets		110		125		
Total assets		$185		$200		
Liabilities						
Accounts payable		$ 10		$ 6		$ 4
Notes payable		15		10		5
Other current liabilities		10		14	4	
Long-term debt		60		70	10	
Preferred stock		10		10	—	—
Common stock		50		50	—	—
Retained earnings		30		40	10	
Total claims on assets		$185		$200	$49	$49

[a] The accumulated depreciation is actually a "liability" account (a contra-asset) that appears on the left side of the balance sheet. Note that it is deducted, not added, when totaling the column.

pattern:

1. *Source of funds* means either a decrease in asset items or an increase in liability items.
2. *Use of funds* means either an increase in asset items or a decrease in liability items.

Table 6.5 gives Dallas Chemical's comparative balance sheets for 1980 and 1981 along with net changes in each item, classified as to source or use.

The next step in constructing a sources and uses statement involves (1) making adjustments to reflect net income and dividends and (2) isolating changes in working capital (current assets and current liabilities). These changes are reflected in the sources and uses statement shown in Table 6.6. Net income in 1981 amounted to $12 million, and dividends of $2 million were paid. The $12 million is treated as a source, the $2 million as a use. The $10 million in retained earnings shown in Table 6.5 is deleted from Table 6.6 to avoid double counting. This statement of sources and uses of funds tells the financial manager that plant size was expanded, that fixed assets amounting to $25 million were acquired, that inventories and net receivables increased as sales increased, and that the firm needed funds to meet working capital and fixed assets demands.

Previously, Dallas had been financing its growth through bank credit (notes payable). In the present period of growth, management decided to obtain some

Table 6.6

Dallas Fertilizer and Chemical Company
Statement of Sources and Uses of Funds, 1981
(Millions of Dollars)

Sources	Amount		Percent	
Net income		$12	23.5	
Depreciation		10	19.6	
Decreases in working capital:				43.1
Reduction in cash	$ 5		9.8	
Sale of marketable securities	10		19.6	
Increase in other liabilities	4		7.9	
Total decrease in working capital		19		37.3
Increase in long-term debt		10		19.6
Total sources of funds		$51		100.0
Uses				
Increases in working capital:				
Inventory investment	$10		19.6	
Increase in receivables	5		9.8	
Reduction in notes payable	5		9.8	
Reduction in accounts payable	4		7.9	
Total increase in working capital		$24		47.1
Gross fixed assets expansion		25	49.0	
Dividends to stockholders		2	3.9	52.9
Total uses of funds		$51		100.0

financing from permanent sources—long-term debt. It obtained enough long-term debt not only to finance some of the asset growth but also to pay back some of its bank credit and to reduce accounts payable. In addition to the long-term debt, it obtained funds from earnings and from depreciation charges. Moreover, the firm had been accumulating marketable securities in anticipation of this expansion program, and some were sold to pay for new buildings and equipment. Finally, cash that had been accumulated in excess of the firm's needs was also worked down. In summary, this example illustrates how the sources and uses of funds statement can provide both a fairly complete picture of recent operations and a good perspective on the flow of funds within the company.

Pro Forma Sources and Uses of Funds Statement

A pro forma, or projected, sources and uses of funds statement can also be constructed to show how a firm plans to acquire and employ funds during some future period. In an earlier section of this chapter we discussed financial forecasting, which involves the determination of future sales, the level of assets necessary to generate these sales (the left side of the projected balance sheet), and the manner in which the assets will be financed (the right side of the projected balance sheet). Given the projected balance sheet and supplementary projected data on earnings, dividends, and depreciation, the financial manager can construct a pro forma sources and uses of funds statement to summarize the firm's projected operations over the planning horizon. Such a statement is obviously of much interest to lenders as well as to the firm's own management.

Summary

Firms need assets to make sales; if sales are to be increased, assets must also be expanded. The first section of this chapter illustrates the relationship between sales and asset requirements.

The most important causal variable in determining financial requirements is a firm's projected dollar volume of sales; a good sales forecast is an essential foundation for forecasting financial requirements. The two principal methods used for making financial forecasts are (1) the percent-of-sales method and (2) the regression method. The first has the virtue of simplicity—the forecaster computes past relationships between asset and liability items and sales, assumes these same relationships will continue, and then applies the new sales forecast to get an estimate of the financial requirements.

However, since the percent-of-sales method assumes that the balance-sheet-to-sales relationships will remain constant, it is only useful for relatively short-run forecasting. When longer-range forecasts are being made, the regression method is preferable because it allows for changing balance-sheet-to-sales relationships. Linear regression can be expanded to curvilinear regression, and simple regression to multiple regression. These more complex methods are useful in certain circumstances, but their increased accuracy must be balanced against the increased costs of using them.

The tools and techniques we have discussed in this chapter are generally used in the following manner: As a first step, one of the long-range forecasting techniques is used to make a long-run forecast of the firm's financial requirements over a 3- to 5-year period. This forecast is then used to make the strategic financing plans during the planning period. Long lead times are necessary when companies sell bonds or stocks; otherwise financial managers might be forced to go into the market for funds during unfavorable periods. In addition to the long-run strategic forecasting, the financial manager must also make accurate short-run forecasts to be sure that funds will be available to meet seasonal and other short-run requirements.

A statement of changes in financial position, commonly called the sources and uses of funds statement, indicates where cash came from and how it was used. When a firm is negotiating for a loan, one of the first areas of analysis is to determine how funds have been used in the past, what funds will be generated in the future, and how they will be used. The sources and uses of funds statement provides, on a historical basis, necessary background for determining the pattern of funds flows. The pattern of funds flows and the effects on the firm's working capital position may indicate that the firm is making progress or that problems are developing. The formulation of sources and uses data on a pro forma or projected basis is particularly important in providing a basis for analyzing what is likely to develop in future periods. Of particular interest is how the future funds flows will enable the firm to meet its interest and other payments schedules under alternative financing plans.

Questions

6.1 What should be the approximate point of intersection between the sales-to-asset regression line and the vertical axis (*Y*-axis intercept) for the following: inventory, accounts receivable, fixed assets? State your answer in terms of positive, zero, or negative intercept. Can you think of any accounts that might have a negative intercept?

6.2 How does forecasting financial requirements in advance of needs help financial managers perform their responsibilities more effectively?

6.3 Explain how a downturn in the business cycle could either cause a cash shortage for a firm or generate excess cash.

6.4 Explain this statement: To a considerable extent, current assets represent permanent assets.

6.5 Certain balance sheet items generally increase spontaneously with increases in sales. Which of the following items typically increase spontaneously?

a. Cash
b. Accounts receivable
c. Notes payable to banks
d. Accrued wages
e. Inventory
f. Mortgage bonds
g. Common stock
h. Retained earnings
i. Marketable securities

6.6 The following equation can, under certain assumptions, be used to forecast financial requirements:

$$\text{External funds required} = \frac{A}{S}(\Delta S) - \frac{B_s}{S}(\Delta S) - mb(S_1)$$

Under what conditions does the equation give satisfactory predictions, and when should it not be used?

6.7 Policy changes can alter the external financing requirements of a firm. For the changes below, will external financing requirements increase, decrease, or remain the same? (Answer in terms of the immediate, short-run effects of the policy change.)

a. The dividend payout ratio is decreased.
b. The firm decides to buy rather than to make certain components used in its products.
c. The firm lengthens the credit period to its customers from 30 to 60 days.
d. A nationwide television advertising campaign is begun.
e. Notes payable are paid off by issuing preferred stock.
f. Payroll is switched to a monthly rather than weekly basis.
g. A change to LIFO inventory accounting reduces the firm's tax liability.

6.8 Is it true that computerized corporate planning models were a fad during the 1960s, but, because of a need for flexibility in corporate planning, they have been dropped by most firms?

Problems

6.1 In 1980, the Dodd Company's total assets were $1.9 million. Sales, which were $3.8 million, will increase by 20 percent in 1981. The 1980 ratio of assets to sales will be maintained throughout 1981. Common stock amounted to $545,000 in 1980, and retained earnings were $500,000. Debt will increase by 10 percent in 1981, but common stock will remain unchanged; net profit after taxes will be 5 percent of sales, and no dividends will be declared or paid. What amount of new financing will be needed in 1981?

6.2 The Gabriel Company's 1980 balance sheet is shown below. Sales in 1980 totaled $3.5 million. The ratio of net profit to sales was 3 percent, with a dividend payout ratio of 60 percent of net income. Sales are expected to increase by 20 percent during 1981. No long-term debt will be retired. Using the percent-of-sales method, determine how much outside financing is required.

Gabriel Company
Balance Sheet as of December 31, 1980

Assets		**Liabilities**	
Cash	$ 52,500	Accounts payable	$ 35,000
Accounts receivable	122,500	Accruals	17,500
Inventory	262,500	Notes payable	122,500
Current assets	$ 437,500	Total current liabilities	$ 175,000
Fixed assets	1,312,500	Long-term debt	525,000
		Total debt	$ 700,000
		Capital stock	612,500
		Retained earnings	437,500
Total assets	$1,750,000	Total liabilities and net worth	$1,750,000

6.3 Given the following data on the Arcus Corporation, predict next year's balance sheet:

This year's sales: $50,000,000
Next year's sales: $57,500,000
After-tax profits: 5% of sales
Dividend payout: 45%
This year's retained earnings: $9,000,000
Cash as percent of sales: 5%
Receivables as percent of sales: 15%
Inventory as percent of sales: 20%
Net fixed assets as percent of sales: 35%
Accounts payable as percent of sales: 10%
Accruals as percent of sales: 15%
Next year's common stock: $12,000,000

Arcus Corporation
Balance Sheet as of December 31, 19XX

Assets		**Liabilities**	
Cash	______	Accounts payable	______
Accounts receivable	______	Notes payable	______
Inventory	______	Accruals	______
Total current assets	______	Total current liabilities	______
Fixed assets	______	Common stock	______
		Retained earnings	______
Total assets	______	Total liabilities	______

6.4 The Erie Supply Company is a wholesale steel distributor. It purchases steel in carload lots from more than twenty producing mills and sells to several thousand steel users. The items carried include sheets, plates, wire products, bolts, windows, pipe, and tubing.

The company owns two warehouses of 15,000 square feet each and is contemplating the erection of another warehouse of 20,000 square feet. The nature of the steel supply business requires that the company maintain large inventories to take care of customer requirements in the event of mill strikes or other delays.

In examining patterns from 1974 through 1979 the company found consistent relationships among the following accounts as a percent of sales.

Current assets: 60%
Net fixed assets: 30%
Accounts payable: 5%
Other current liabilities, including accruals and provision for income taxes but not bank loans: 5%
Net profit after taxes: 3%

The company's sales for 1980 were $3 million, and its balance sheet on December 31, 1980, is shown below. The company expects its sales to increase by $400,000 each year. If this level is achieved, what will the company's financial requirements be at the end of the five-year period? Assume that accounts not tied directly to sales (for example, notes payable) remain constant and that the company pays no dividends.

a. Construct a pro forma balance sheet for the end of 1985 using "additional financing needed" as the balancing item.
b. What are the crucial assumptions you made in your projection method?

Erie Supply Company
Balance Sheet as of December 31, 1980

Assets		**Liabilities**	
Current assets	$1,800,000	Accounts payable	$ 150,000
Fixed assets	900,000	Notes payable	400,000
		Other current liabilities	150,000
		Total current liabilities	$ 700,000
		Mortgage loan	300,000
		Common stock	550,000
		Retained earnings	1,150,000
Total assets	$2,700,000	Total liabilities and net worth	$2,700,000

6.5 One useful method of evaluating a firm's financial structure in relation to its industry is comparing it with financial ratio composites for the industry. A new firm, or one contemplating entering a new industry, may use such composites as a guide to its likely approximate financial position after the initial settling-down period.

The following data represent composite ratios for the frozen fruits and fruit juices industry for 1980:

Sales to net worth: 6.95 times
Current debt to net worth: 1.57 times
Total debt to net worth: 2.3 times
Current ratio: 1.2 times
Net sales to inventory: 5.8 times
Average collection period: 23 days
Fixed assets to net worth: 1.416 times

a. Complete the pro forma balance sheet (round to nearest thousand) for Sunlight Citrus, Inc., whose 1980 sales are $4 million.
b. What does the use of the financial ratio composites accomplish?
c. What other factors will influence the financial structure of the firm?

Sunlight Citrus, Inc.
Pro Forma Balance Sheet as of December 31, 1980

Cash	______	Current debt	______
Accounts receivable	______	Long-term debt	______
Inventory	______	Total debt	______
Current assets	______	Net worth	______
Fixed assets	______		
Total assets	______	Total liabilities and net worth	______

6.6 The following information is provided on the relationship between sales and inventory for the Wexler Company over the past six years.

Year	Sales (X)	Inventory (Y)
1975	$ 750,000	$100,000
1976	1,500,000	125,000
1977	2,250,000	150,000
1978	3,000,000	175,000
1979	3,750,000	200,000
1980	4,500,000	225,000

a. Plot these points on a graph with sales on the X-axis and inventory on the Y-axis.

b. What is the slope of the regression line?

c. What is the intercept?

d. Predict 1981 inventory if 1981 sales rise to $5,250,000.

6.7 The 1980 sales of Pyrotex, Inc., were $12 million. Common stock and notes payable are constant. The dividend payout ratio is 50 percent. Retained earnings as shown on the December 31, 1980, balance sheet were $60,000. The percent of sales in each balance sheet item that varies directly with sales is expected to be as follows:

	Percent
Cash	4
Receivables	10
Inventories	20
Net fixed assets	35
Accounts payable	12
Accruals	6
Profit rate (after taxes) on sales	3

a. Complete the balance sheet given below.

b. Suppose that in 1981 sales will increase by 10 percent over 1980 sales. How much additional (external) capital will be required?

c. What percentage of the sales growth must be financed externally?

d. Construct the year-end 1981 balance sheet. Set up an account for "financing needed" or "funds available."

e. What would happen to capital requirements under each of the following conditions:

1. The profit margin went from 3 percent to 6 percent? From 3 percent to 1 percent? Set up an equation to illustrate your answers.
2. The dividend payout rate was raised from 50 percent to 80 percent? Was lowered from 50 percent to 30 percent? Set up an equation to illustrate your answers.
3. Slower collections caused receivables to rise to 45 days of sales?

f. If the profit rate after taxes remains at 3 percent and the dividend payout rate remains at 50 percent, at what growth rate in sales will the external financing percentage be exactly zero?

Pyrotex, Inc.
Balance Sheet as of December 31, 1980

Cash	______	Accounts payable	______
Receivables	______	Notes payable	630,000
Inventory	______	Accruals	______
Total current assets	______	Total current liabilities	______
Fixed assets	______	Common stock	5,250,000
		Retained earnings	______
Total assets	______	Total liabilities and net worth	______

6.8 Jones Klein, a large plastics manufacturer, had the following balance sheet and income statement for 1980. (Also shown is the industry norm for each item based on various specific industry and composite financial data for 1980.) The industry norm for sales to assets is 2.1 times.

a. Given only the total sales figure of $1,190,500, project a balance sheet and income statement using the same format. Show liabilities below assets (round to hundreds).
b. For each item, compute the percent difference between actual and pro forma in the form (actual/pro forma)–1.
c. Comment on the difference between the actual and pro forma account based on the industry norms.

Jones Klein, Inc.
Balance Sheet as of December 31, 1980

Assets	Firm	Norm	Liabilities	Firm	Norm
Cash and securities	$162,800	7.8%	Accounts payable	$ 94,000	19.9%
Receivables	272,000	35.3	Notes payable	171,000	12.6
Inventories	122,800	23.2	Other current liabilities	149,000	16.7
Other current assets	22,600	1.9	Total current liabilities	$414,000	49.2
Total current assets	$580,200	68.2			
Net fixed assets	160,500	25.1	Long-term debt	77,400	11.3
Other tangible assets	37,400	6.7	Net worth	286,700	39.5
Total assets	$778,100	100.0%	Total claims on assets	$778,100	100.0%

Jones Klein, Inc.
Income Statement for Year Ended December 31, 1980

	Firm	Norm
Sales	$1,190,500	100.0%
Cost of goods sold	607,700	76.2
Gross profit	$ 582,800	23.8
Selling and administrative expense	485,000	18.0
Operating income	$ 97,800	5.8
Less interest expense	20,400	1.0
Net income before tax	$ 77,400	4.8
Less federal income tax	36,500	2.0
Net income	$ 40,900	2.8%

6.9 The consolidated balance sheets for the Simon Corporation at the beginning and end of 1980 are shown below. The company bought $225 million worth of fixed assets. The charge for current depreciation was $45 million. Earnings after taxes were $114 million, and the company paid out $30 million in dividends.

a. Fill in the amount of source or use in the appropriate column.

b. Prepare a percentage statement of sources and uses of funds.

c. Briefly summarize your findings.

Simon Corporation
Balance Sheets for Beginning and End of 1980 (Millions of Dollars)

	Jan. 1	Dec. 31	Source	Use
Cash	$ 45	$ 21	______	______
Marketable securities	33	0	______	______
Net receivables	66	90	______	______
Inventories	159	225	______	______
Total current assets	$303	$336	______	______
Gross fixed assets	$225	$450	______	______
Less reserve for depreciation	78	123	______	______
Net fixed assets	147	327	______	______
Total assets	$450	$663	______	______
Accounts payable	$ 45	$ 54	______	______
Notes payable	45	9	______	______
Other current liabilities	21	45	______	______
Long-term debt	24	78	______	______
Common stock	114	192	______	______
Retained earnings	201	285	______	______
Total claims on assets	$450	$663	______	______

CHAPTER 7

FINANCIAL PLANNING AND CONTROL

In the preceding chapter on financial forecasting the emphasis was on relating the level and rate of growth of sales to the firm's required investment in assets to support those sales. Investments in assets, in turn, give rise to financing requirements. In the present chapter we continue this planning framework. Here the emphasis is on profitability analysis, both in a broad long-term framework and also in connection with shorter-term forecasting, which is the focus of the budgeting process. In addition to long-range forecasts, the financial manager is concerned with short-term needs for funds. It is embarrassing for a corporate treasurer to "run out of money." Even though a bank loan can probably be negotiated on short notice, this plight may cause the banker to question the soundness of the firm's management and, accordingly, to reduce the company's line of credit or raise the interest rate. Therefore, attention must be given to short-term budgeting, with special emphasis on cash forecasting, or cash budgeting, as it is commonly called. Since modern business involves many large corporations with a number of individual divisions, the application of financial planning and control to divisions is also surveyed.

Four major areas are covered in this chapter:

1. Breakeven analysis, or profit planning
2. Operating leverage—the sensitivity of operating income to changes in the volume of operations
3. Cash forecasting and budgeting
4. Divisional control in a decentralized firm

These four topics are tied together by the framework of financial planning and control.

Financial Planning and Control Processes

Financial planning and control involve the use of projections based on standards and the development of a feedback and adjustment process to improve performance. This financial planning and control process involves forecasts and the use of several types of budgets. Budget systems are developed for every significant area of the firm's activities, as shown by Figure 7.1.

The production budget analyzes the use of materials, parts, labor, and facilities. Each of its major elements is likely to have its own budget as well: a materials budget, a personnel budget, and a facilities budget. To achieve sales of the products produced requires the use of a marketing budget. A budget is also developed to cover general office and executive requirements.

Figure 7.1 **Overview of the Financial Planning and Control Process**

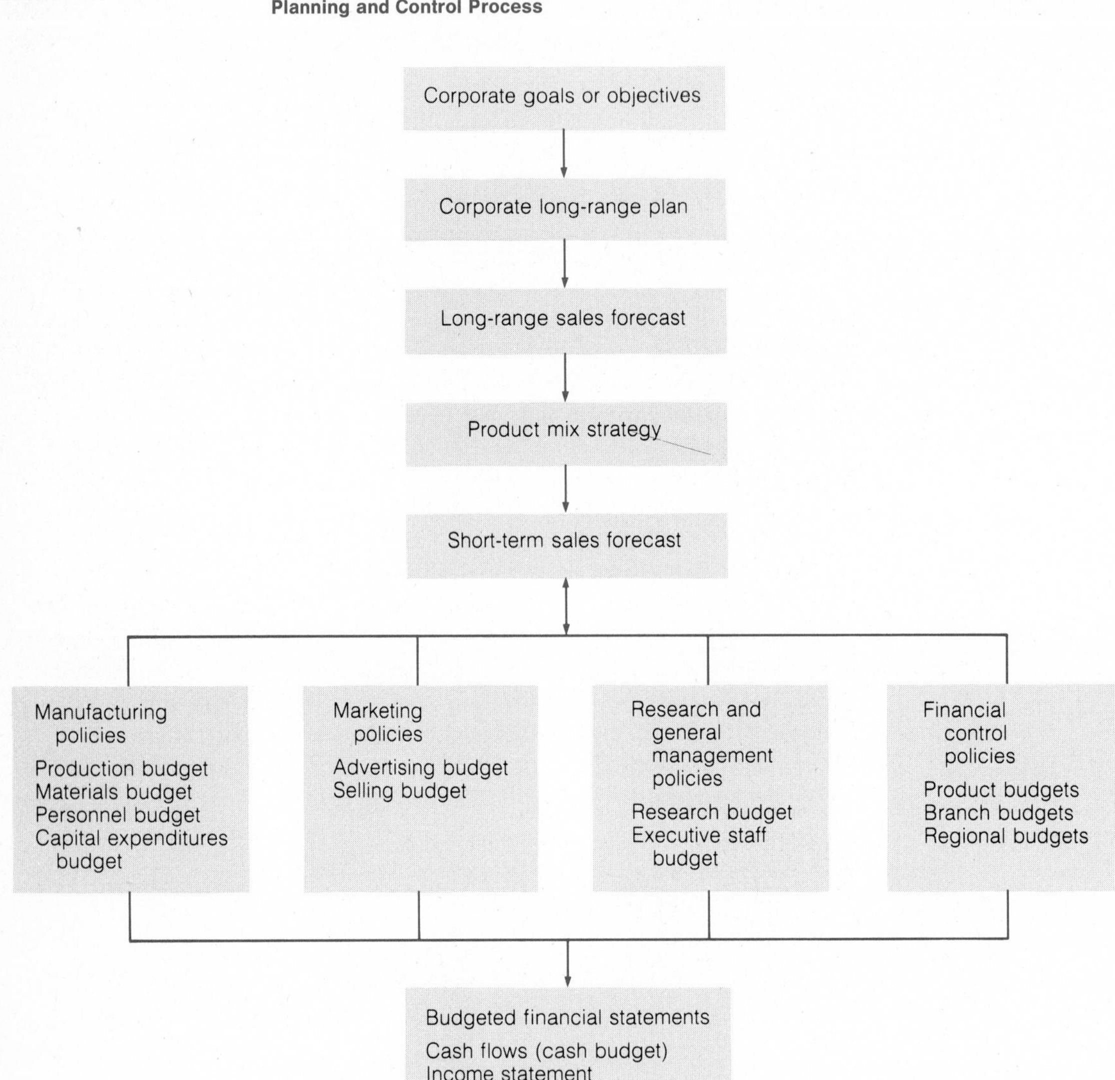

The results of projecting all these elements of cost are reflected in the budgeted (also called "pro forma" or "projected") income statement. Anticipated sales give rise to contemplation of the various types of investments needed to produce the products; these investments, plus the beginning balance sheet, provide the necessary data for developing the assets side of the balance sheet.

Assets must be financed, but first a cash flow analysis (the cash budget) is needed. The cash budget indicates the combined effects of the budgeted operations on the firm's cash flows. A positive net cash flow indicates that the firm has sufficient financing. However, if an increase in the volume of operations leads to a negative cash flow, additional financing is required. The longer the lead time in arranging for the required financing, the greater the opportunity for developing the required documentation and for working out arrangements with financing sources.

Financial planning and control seek to improve profitability, avoid cash squeezes, and improve the performance of individual divisions of a company. These areas represent the main sections covered in this chapter.

Breakeven Analysis

The relationships between the size of investment outlays and the required volume to achieve profitability are referred to as breakeven analysis or profit planning. Breakeven analysis is a device for determining the point at which sales will just cover costs. If all of a firm's costs were variable, the subject of breakeven volume would not come up. But since the level of total costs can be greatly influenced by the size of the fixed investments the firm makes, the resulting fixed costs will put the firm in a loss position unless a sufficient volume of sales is achieved.

If a firm is to avoid accounting losses its sales must cover all costs—those that vary directly with production and those that do not change as production levels change. Costs that fall into each of these categories are outlined in Table 7.1.

Table 7.1 **Fixed and Variable Costs**

Fixed costs[a]	Direct or variable costs
Depreciation on plant and equipment	Factory labor
Rentals	Materials
Salaries of research staff	Sales commissions
Salaries of executive staff	
General office expenses	

[a] Some of these costs—for example, salaries and office expenses—can be varied to some degree; however, firms are reluctant to reduce these expenditures in response to temporary fluctuations in sales. Such costs are often called *semivariable* costs.

The nature of breakeven analysis is depicted in Figure 7.2, the basic breakeven chart. The chart is presented on a unit basis, with units produced shown on the horizontal axis and income and costs measured on the vertical axis. Fixed costs of $40,000 are represented by a horizontal line; they are the same (fixed) regardless of the number of units produced. Variable costs are assumed to be $1.20 a unit. Units are assumed to be sold at $2 each, so the total income is pictured as a straight line, which must also increase with production. The slope (or rate of ascent) of the total revenue line is steeper than that of the total cost line. This must be true, because the firm is gaining $2 of revenue for every $1.20 paid out for labor and materials—the variable costs.

Figure 7.2 **Breakeven Chart**

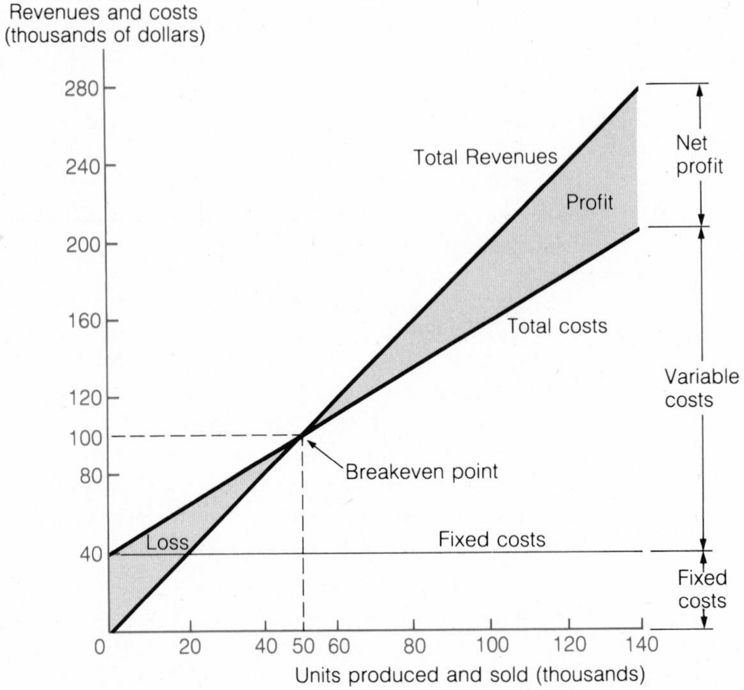

Until the breakeven point (found at the intersection of the total income and total cost lines), the firm suffers losses. After that point, it begins to make profits. Figure 7.2 indicates a breakeven point at a sales and cost level of $100,000 and a production level of 50,000 units.

Calculations of the breakeven point can also be carried out algebraically. From the data given, the firm's total revenue or sales function is

$$S = \$2Q$$

The total cost function is

$$TC = \$40{,}000 + \$1.20Q$$

At the breakeven quantity Q^*, total revenue and total cost are equal. So equating the sales and total cost functions,

$$\$2Q = \$40{,}000 + \$1.20Q$$

$$Q^* = 50{,}000$$

The relationships are clarified further by use of a contribution income statement for various levels of units sold, as shown by Table 7.2.

Table 7.2

Contribution Income Statement at Various Quantities of Units Sold

Units sold (Q)	20,000	40,000	50,000	80,000	100,000	200,000
Sales (S)	$40,000	$80,000	$100,000	$160,000	$200,000	$400,000
Total variable expenses (V)	24,000	48,000	60,000	96,000	120,000	240,000
Contribution margin (C)	16,000	32,000	40,000	64,000	80,000	160,000
Fixed operating expenses (F)	40,000	40,000	40,000	40,000	40,000	40,000
Net operating income (X)	($24,000)	($ 8,000)	—	$ 24,000	$ 40,000	$120,000

Note: $C = cQ$ and $X = cQ - F = C - F$

From Table 7.2 we can readily observe that the breakeven quantity is 50,000 units sold. The breakeven level of sales is $100,000. To develop these relationships algebraically, we define them as follows:

S^* = breakeven sales

Q^* = the breakeven quantity of units sold

P = selling price per unit

v = variable cost per unit

V = total variable costs = vQ

c = contribution margin per unit

C = total contribution margin = cQ

CR = contribution ratio = $\left(1 - \dfrac{V}{PQ}\right)$

We can then readily develop the breakeven quantity and the breakeven dollar volume of sales by beginning with the relationship that total revenues or sales equal total costs at breakeven. We then have the following:

Breakeven quantity = Q^*

$$P \cdot Q^* = vQ^* + F$$

$$P \cdot Q^* - vQ^* = F$$

$$Q^* = \frac{F}{P - v}$$

$$Q^* = \frac{F}{c} \qquad \textbf{(7.1a)}$$

Breakeven sales = S^*

$$S^* = F + V$$

$$= F + \frac{V \cdot S^*}{S^*}$$

$$S^* = PQ$$

$$S^* - \frac{V}{PQ} S^* = F$$

$$S^* = \frac{F}{1 - \dfrac{V}{PQ}}$$

$$S^* = \frac{F}{CR} \qquad \textbf{(7.1b)}$$

We can illustrate the calculation of both Q^* and S^* from the data of our numerical example.

$$Q^* = \frac{F}{c} \qquad\qquad S^* = \frac{F}{CR}$$

$$Q^* = \frac{\$40,000}{\$.80} \qquad\qquad \frac{V}{PQ} = .6 \text{ at all quantities sold}$$

$$Q^* = 50,000 \text{ units}$$

therefore,

$$CR = \left(1 - \frac{V}{PQ}\right) = .4$$

hence,

$$S^* = \frac{\$40,000}{.4} = \$100,000$$

Thus the breakeven quantity or breakeven sales volume can readily be calculated by use of the total fixed costs and a contribution margin relationship.

Limitations of Breakeven Analysis

Breakeven analysis is useful in studying the relations among volume, prices, and costs; it is thus helpful in pricing, cost control, and decisions about expansion programs. It has limitations, however, as a guide to managerial actions.

Linear breakeven analysis is especially weak in what it implies about the sales possibilities for the firm. Any linear breakeven chart is based on a constant sales price. Therefore, in order to study profit possibilities under different prices, a whole series of charts is necessary—one for each price.

Breakeven analysis may also be deficient with regard to costs. If sales increase to levels at which the existing plant and equipment are worked to capacity, additional workers are hired and overtime pay increases. All this causes variable costs to rise sharply. If additional equipment and plant are required, fixed costs are also increased. Finally, the products sold by the firm may change in quality and quantity. Such changes in product mix influence the level and slope of the cost function. Breakeven analysis is useful as a first step in developing the basic data required for pricing and for financial decisions. But more detailed analysis is required before final judgments can be made.

Applications of Breakeven Analysis

Used appropriately, breakeven analysis can shed light on a number of important business decisions. In general, breakeven analysis can be used by the firm in three separate but related ways. In new-product decisions, breakeven analysis helps determine how large sales of a new product must be for the firm to achieve profitability. Breakeven analysis can also be used as a broad framework for studying the effects of a general expansion in the level of operations. Finally, in analyzing programs to modernize and automate, where the firm would be operating in a more mechanized, automated manner and thus substituting fixed costs for variable costs, breakeven analysis helps analyze the consequences of shifting from variable costs to fixed costs. The key factor is the influence of volume changes on profitability when firms have different relationships between fixed and variable costs. Understanding these relationships involves understanding the idea of *operating leverage,* to which we now turn.

Operating Leverage

To a physicist, *leverage* implies the use of a lever to raise a heavy object with a small force. In business terminology, a high degree of leverage implies that a relatively small change in sales results in a large change in net operating income.

The significance of the degree of operating leverage is illustrated by Figure 7.3. Three firms—A, B, and C—with differing degrees of leverage are contrasted. Firm A has a relatively small amount of fixed charges; it does not have much automated equipment, so its depreciation cost is low. However, its variable cost line has a relatively steep slope, denoting that its variable costs per unit are higher than those of the other firms.

Firm B is considered to have a normal amount of fixed costs in its operations. It uses automated equipment (with which one operator can turn out a few or many units at the same labor cost) to about the same extent as the average firm in the industry. Firm B breaks even at a higher level of operations than does Firm A. At a production level of 40,000 units, B loses $8,000 but A breaks even.

Firm C has the highest fixed costs. It is highly automated, using expensive, high-speed machines that require very little labor per unit produced. With such an operation, its variable costs rise slowly. Because of the high overhead resulting from charges associated with the expensive machinery, Firm C's breakeven point is higher than that for either Firm A or Firm B. Once Firm C reaches its breakeven point, however, its profits rise faster than do those of the other firms.

Alternative operating leverage decisions can have a great impact on the unit cost position of each firm. When 200,000 units are sold, the average per unit cost of production for each firm, calculated by dividing total costs by the 200,000 units sold, is:

	Cost per unit
Firm A	$1.60
Firm B	$1.40
Firm C	$1.30

These results have important implications. At a high volume of operations of 200,000 units per period, Firm C has a substantial cost superiority over the other two firms and particularly over Firm A. Firm C could cut the price of its product to $1.50 per unit, which represents a level that would be unprofitable for Firm A, and still have more than a 13 percent ($.20/$1.50) return on sales. (The average pretax margin on sales for manufacturing firms is about 9 to 11 percent.) Another illustration of this idea is the difference in unit costs for Japanese versus U.S. steel companies. Most Japanese steel companies can produce 10 million tons or more per year, while only one or two U.S. steel companies can produce as much as 5 million tons per year. Operating at such a high capacity (in part due to the benefit of growth

Figure 7.3

Operating Leverage

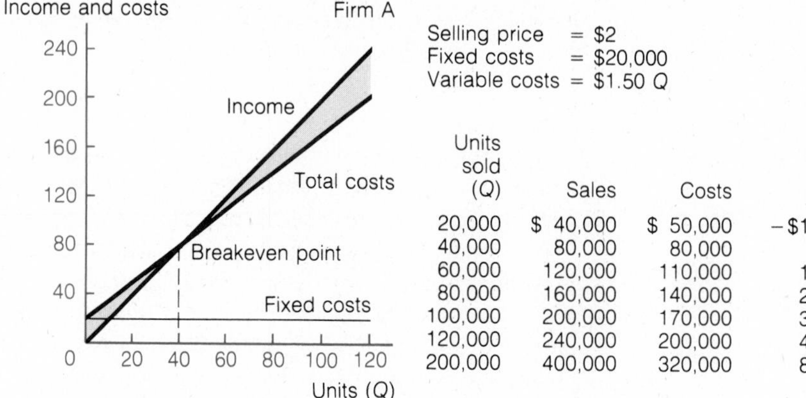

Selling price = $2
Fixed costs = $20,000
Variable costs = $1.50 Q

Units sold (Q)	Sales	Costs	Profit
20,000	$ 40,000	$ 50,000	−$10,000
40,000	80,000	80,000	0
60,000	120,000	110,000	10,000
80,000	160,000	140,000	20,000
100,000	200,000	170,000	30,000
120,000	240,000	200,000	40,000
200,000	400,000	320,000	80,000

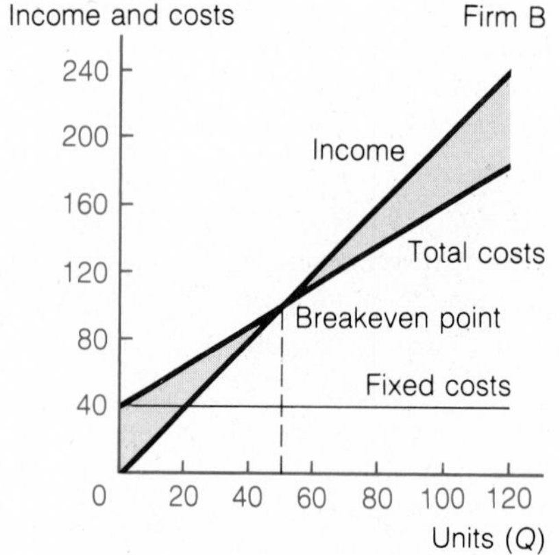

Selling price = $2
Fixed costs = $40,000
Variable costs = $1.20 Q

Units sold (Q)	Sales	Costs	Profit
20,000	$ 40,000	$ 64,000	−$ 24,000
40,000	80,000	88,000	− 8,000
60,000	120,000	112,000	8,000
80,000	160,000	136,000	24,000
100,000	200,000	160,000	40,000
120,000	240,000	184,000	56,000
200,000	400,000	280,000	120,000

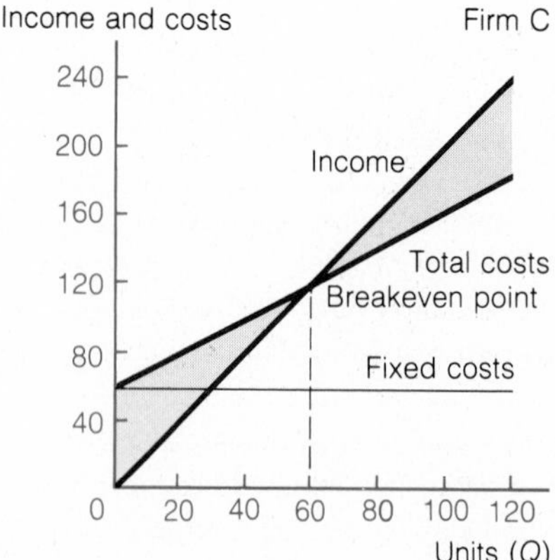

Selling price = $2
Fixed costs = $60,000
Variable costs = 1Q$

Units sold (Q)	Sales	Costs	Profit
20,000	$ 40,000	$ 80,000	−$ 40,000
40,000	80,000	100,000	− 20,000
60,000	120,000	120,000	0
80,000	160,000	140,000	20,000
100,000	200,000	160,000	40,000
120,000	240,000	180,000	60,000
200,000	400,000	260,000	140,000

through export sales), the Japanese companies have been able to sell steel in the United States at prices below the costs of the U.S. steel companies. While the total story is complex, the firms' operating leverage factor is an important influence on their relative costs per unit.

Degree of Operating Leverage

Operating leverage can be defined more precisely in terms of the way a given change in volume affects net operating income (NOI). To measure the effect on profitability of a change in volume, we calculate the *degree of operating leverage*. The degree of operating leverage is the ratio of the percentage change in operating income to the percentage change in units sold or in sales. Algebraically,

$$\text{Degree of operating leverage} = \frac{\text{Percentage change in operating income}}{\text{Percentage change in units sold or in sales}}$$

For Firm B in Figure 7.3, the degree of operating leverage (DOL_B) for a change in units of output from 100,000 to 120,000 is

$$DOL_B = \frac{\dfrac{\Delta\,\text{Income}}{\text{Income}}}{\dfrac{\Delta Q}{Q}} = \frac{\dfrac{\Delta X}{X}}{\dfrac{\Delta Q}{Q}}$$

$$= \frac{\dfrac{\$56{,}000 - \$40{,}000}{\$40{,}000}}{\dfrac{120{,}000 - 100{,}000}{100{,}000}} = \frac{\dfrac{\$16{,}000}{\$40{,}000}}{\dfrac{20{,}000}{100{,}000}}$$

$$= \frac{40\%}{20\%} = 2.0$$

Here ΔX is the increase in net operating income. Q is the quantity of output in units, and ΔQ is the increase in output.

Using the same equation, the degree of operating leverage at 100,000 units is 1.67 for Firm A and 2.5 for Firm C. Thus for a 10 percent change in volume, Firm C, the company with the most operating leverage, will experience a profit gain of 25 percent, while Firm A, the one with the least leverage, will have only a 16.7 percent profit gain. The profits of Firm C are more sensitive to changes in sales volume than those of Firm A. Thus the higher the degree of operating leverage, the more profits will fluctuate, both in an upward and downward direction, in response to changes in volume.

The degree of operating leverage of a firm has important implications for a number of areas of business and financial policy.[1] Firm C's high degree of operating

[1] The degree of operating leverage is a form of *elasticity concept* and thus is akin to the familiar price elasticity developed in economics. Since operating leverage is an elasticity, it varies depending on the particular part of the breakeven graph that is being considered. For example, in terms of our illustrative firms, the degree of operating leverage is greatest close to the breakeven point, where a very small change in volume can produce a very large percentage increase in profits simply because the base profits are close to zero near the breakeven point.

leverage suggests gains from increasing volume. Suppose Firm C could increase its quantity sold from 100,000 units to 120,000 units by cutting the price per unit to \$1.90. The equation for net operating income is

$$\begin{aligned}\text{Net operating income } (X) &= PQ - vQ - F \\ &= \$1.90(120{,}000) - (\$1)120{,}000 - \$60{,}000 \\ &= \$228{,}000 - \$120{,}000 - \$60{,}000 \\ &= \$48{,}000\end{aligned}$$

The equation shows that Firm C could increase its profits from \$40,000 at a volume of 100,000 to \$48,000 at a volume of 120,000. Thus a high degree of operating leverage suggests that an aggressive price policy may increase profits, particularly if the market is responsive to small price cuts.

On the other hand, Firm C's high degree of operating leverage tells us that the company is subject to large swings in profits as its volume fluctuates. Thus, if Firm C's industry is one whose sales are greatly affected by changes in the overall level of economic activity (as are, for example, the durable goods industries, such as machine tools, steel, and autos), its profits are subject to large fluctuations. Hence, the degree of financial leverage appropriate for Firm C to take on is lower than that for a firm with a lower degree of operating leverage and for industries whose sales are less sensitive to fluctuations in the level of the economy. (Financial leverage is discussed in Chapters 15 and 16.)

Cash Breakeven Analysis

Some of the firm's fixed costs are noncash outlays, and, for a period, some of its revenues may be in receivables. The cash breakeven chart for Firm B, constructed on the assumption that \$30,000 of the fixed costs from the previous illustration are depreciation charges and, therefore, a noncash outlay, is shown in Figure 7.4. Because fixed cash outlays are only \$10,000, the cash breakeven point is at 12,500 units rather than 50,000 units, which is the profit breakeven point.

An equation for the cash breakeven point based on sales dollars can be derived from the equation for the profit breakeven point. The only change is to reduce fixed costs by the amount of noncash outlays:

$$S^* = \frac{F - \text{Noncash outlays}}{CR}$$

If noncash outlays are very close to total fixed costs, the cash breakeven point approaches zero. The cash breakeven point based on units of output is comparable to the profit breakeven quantity, except that fixed costs must be adjusted for noncash outlays:

$$Q^* = \frac{F - \text{Noncash outlays}}{c}$$

Here again, if noncash outlays are very large, the cash breakeven point may be low, despite a large amount of fixed charges.

Figure 7.4 **Cash Breakeven Analysis**

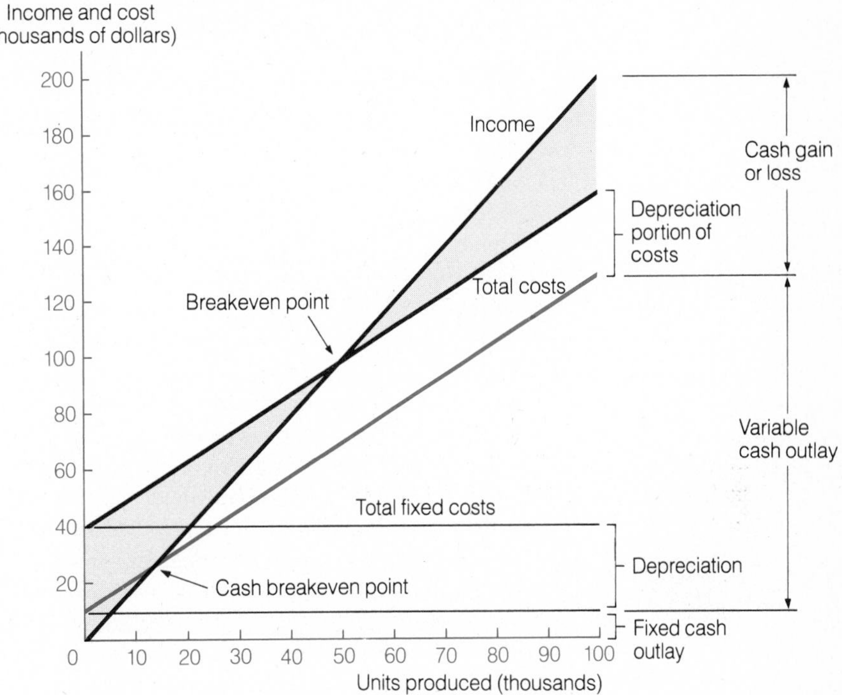

Cash breakeven analysis does not fully represent cash flows; for this a cash budget is required. But it is useful because it provides a picture of the flow of funds from operations. A firm may incur a level of fixed costs that will result in losses during business downswings but large profits during upswings. If cash outlays are small, even during periods of loss the firm may be able to operate above the cash breakeven point. Thus, the risk of insolvency (in the sense of being unable to meet cash obligations) is small. This allows a firm to reach out for higher profits through automation and operating leverage.

Cash Budgets

A natural extension of the ideas involved in cash breakeven analysis is a consideration of cash budgeting. The cash budget is a highly significant tool in the financial planning and control processes of business firms.

The cash budget indicates not only the total amount of financing required but its timing as well. It shows the amount of funds needed month by month, week by week, or even day by day; and it is one of the financial manager's most important tools. Because a clear understanding of the nature of cash budgeting is important, the process is described by means of an example that makes the elements of the cash budget explicit.

Marvel Toy is a medium-sized toy manufacturer. Sales are highly seasonal, the peak occurring in September, when retailers stock up for the Christmas season. All sales are on terms that allow a cash discount for payments made within thirty days; if the discount is not taken, the full amount must be paid in sixty days. However, Marvel, like most other companies, finds that some of its customers delay payment up to ninety days. Experience has shown that on 20 percent of the sales, payment is made within thirty days; on 70 percent it is made within sixty days, and on 10 percent it is made within ninety days.

Marvel's production is geared to future sales. Purchased materials and parts, which amount to 70 percent of sales, are bought the month before the company expects to sell the finished product. Its own purchase terms permit Marvel to delay payment on its purchases for one month. Thus, if August sales are forecast at $30,000, Marvel's purchases during July will amount to $21,000, which it will pay in August.

Wages and salaries, rent, and other cash expenses for Marvel are given in Table 7.3. The company also has a tax payment of $8,000 coming due in August. Its capital budgeting plans call for the purchase in July of a new machine tool costing $10,000, payment to be made in September. Assuming the company needs to keep a $5,000 cash balance at all times and has $6,000 on July 1, what are Marvel's financial requirements for the period July through December?

The cash requirements are worked out in the cash budget shown in Table 7.3. The top half of the table provides a worksheet for calculating collections on sales and payments on purchases. The first line in the worksheet gives the sales forecast for the period May through December (May and June sales are necessary to determine collections for July and August). The second line shows cash collections. The first line under this heading shows that 20 percent of the sales during any given month are collected that month. The second line shows the collections on the prior month's sales—70 percent of sales in the preceding month. The third line gives collections from sales two months earlier—10 percent of sales in that month. The collections are summed to find the total cash receipts from sales during each month under consideration.

With the worksheet completed, the cash budget itself can be considered. Receipts from collections are given on the top line. Next, payments during each month are summarized. The difference between cash receipts and cash payments is the net cash gain or loss during the month; for July, there is a net cash loss of $4,200. The initial cash on hand at the beginning of the month is added to the net cash gain or loss during the month to yield the cumulative cash that will be on hand if no financing is done; at the end of July, Marvel Toy will have cumulative cash equal to $1,800. The desired cash balance, $5,000, is subtracted from the cumulative cash balance to determine the amount of financing the firm needs if it is to maintain the desired level of cash. At the end of July, Marvel will need $3,200; thus loans outstanding will total $3,200 at that time.

The same procedure is used in the following months. Sales will expand seasonally in August; with increased sales will come increased payments for purchases, wages, and other items. Moreover, the $8,000 tax bill is due in August. Receipts from sales will go up too, but the firm will still be left with a $10,800 cash deficit during

Table 7.3

Marvel Toy Company
Worksheet and Cash Budget

Worksheet	May	June	July	Aug.	Sept.	Oct.	Nov.	Dec.
Sales (net of cash discounts)	$10,000	$10,000	$20,000	$30,000	$40,000	$20,000	$20,000	$10,000
Collections:								
First month (at 20%)	2,000	2,000	4,000	6,000	8,000	4,000	4,000	2,000
Second month (at 70%)		7,000	7,000	14,000	21,000	28,000	14,000	14,000
Third month (at 10%)			1,000	1,000	2,000	3,000	4,000	2,000
Total	$ 2,000	$ 9,000	$12,000	$21,000	$31,000	$35,000	$22,000	$18,000
Purchases (70% of next month's sales)	$ 7,000	$14,000	$21,000	$28,000	$14,000	$14,000	$ 7,000	
Payments (one month lag)		$ 7,000	$14,000	$21,000	$28,000	$14,000	$14,000	$ 7,000

Cash budget						
Receipts:						
Collections	$12,000	$21,000	$31,000	$35,000	$22,000	$18,000
Payments:						
Purchases	$14,000	$21,000	$28,000	$14,000	$14,000	$ 7,000
Wages and salaries	1,500	2,000	2,500	1,500	1,500	1,000
Rent	500	500	500	500	500	500
Other expenses	200	300	400	200	200	100
Taxes	—	8,000	—	—	—	—
Payment on machine	—	—	10,000	—	—	—
Total payments	$16,200	$31,800	$41,400	$16,200	$16,200	$ 8,600
Net cash gain (loss) during month	−$ 4,200	−$10,800	−$10,400	$18,800	$ 5,800	$ 9,400
Cash at start of month if no borrowing is done	6,000	1,800	−9,000	−19,400	−600	5,200
Cumulative cash (cash at start plus gains or minus losses)	$ 1,800	−$ 9,000	−$19,400	−$ 600	$ 5,200	$14,600
Less: Desired level of cash	−5,000	−5,000	−5,000	−5,000	−5,000	−5,000
Total loans outstanding to maintain $5,000 cash balance	$ 3,200	$14,000	$24,400	$ 5,600	—	—
Surplus cash	—	—	—	—	$ 200	$ 9,600

the month. The total financial requirements at the end of August will be $14,000—the $3,200 needed at the end of July plus the $10,800 cash deficit for August. Thus loans outstanding will total $14,000 at the end of August.

Sales peak in September, and the cash deficit during this month will amount to another $10,400. The total need for funds through September will increase to $24,400. Sales, purchases, and payments for past purchases will fall markedly in October; collections will be the highest of any month because they will reflect the high September sales. As a result, Marvel Toy will enjoy a healthy $18,800 cash surplus during October. This surplus can be used to pay off borrowings, so the need for financing will decline by $18,800 to $5,600.

Marvel will have another cash surplus in November, and this extra cash will permit the company to eliminate completely the need for financing. In fact, the company is expected to have $200 in surplus cash by the month's end, while another cash surplus in December will swell the amount of extra cash to $9,600. With such a large amount of unneeded funds, Marvel's treasurer will doubtless want to make investments in some interest-bearing securities or put the funds to use in some other way. (Types of investments for excess funds are discussed in Chapter 11.)

Control in Multidivision Companies

For organizational reasons, large firms are generally set up on a decentralized basis. For example, General Electric establishes separate divisions for heavy appliances, light appliances, power transformers, fossil fuel generating equipment, nuclear generating equipment, and so on. Each division is defined as a *profit center*, and each has its own investments—fixed and current assets, together with a share of such general corporate assets as research labs and headquarters buildings—and is expected to earn an appropriate return on them.

The corporate headquarters, or central staff, typically controls the various divisions by a form of the du Pont system.

Du Pont System of Financial Analysis

The du Pont system of financial analysis has achieved wide recognition in American industry, and properly so. It brings together the activity ratios and profit margin on sales and shows how these ratios interact to determine the profitability of assets. The nature of the system, modified somewhat, is set forth in Figure 7.5.

The bottom part of the figure develops the turnover ratio. It shows how current assets (cash, marketable securities, accounts receivable, and inventories) added to fixed assets give total investment. Total investment divided into sales gives the turnover of investment.

The upper part of the figure can develop the profit margin on sales. The individual expense items plus income taxes are subtracted from sales to produce net profits after taxes. Net profits divided by sales give the profit margin on sales. When the asset turnover ratio is multiplied by the profit margin on sales, the product is the return on total investment (ROI) in the firm. This can be seen from the following formula:

$$\frac{\text{Profit}}{\text{Sales}} \times \frac{\text{Sales}}{\text{Investment}} = \text{ROI}$$

Figure 7.5

Du Pont Chart for Divisional Control

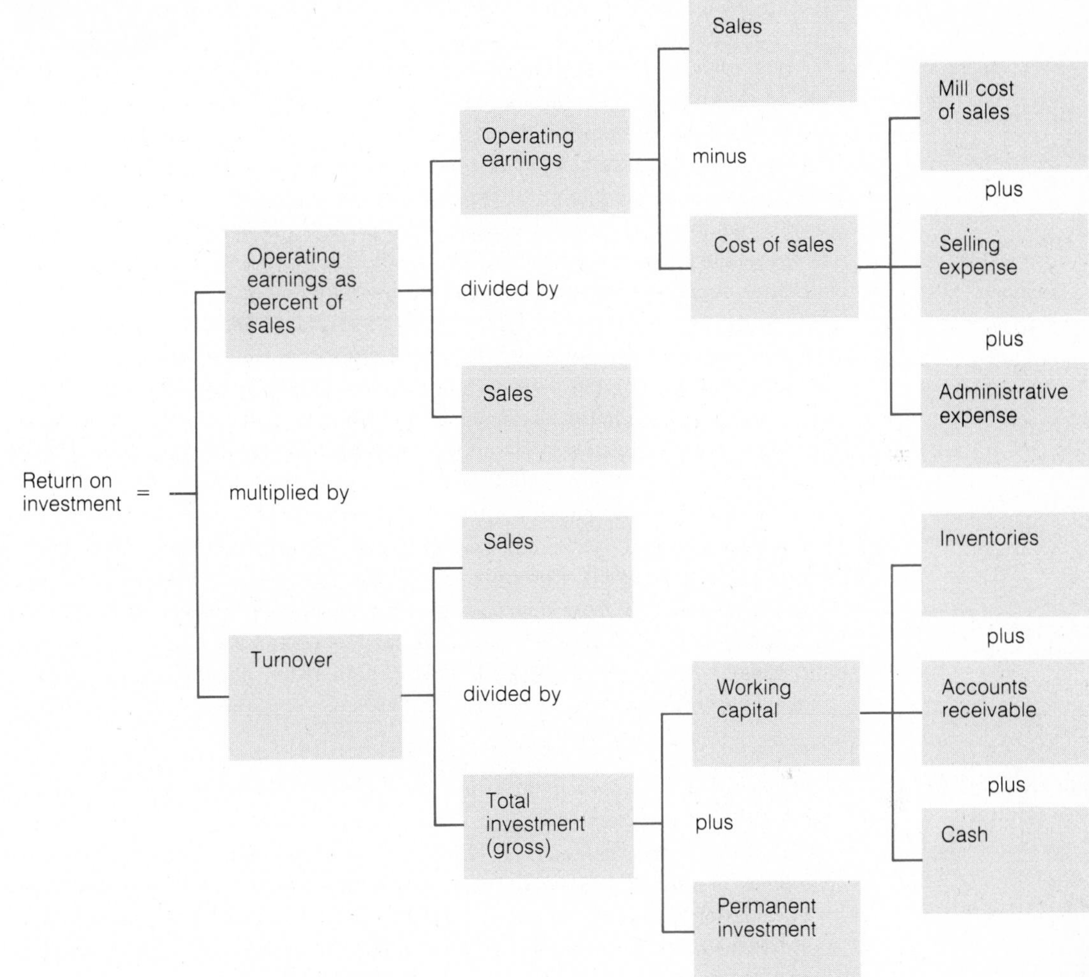

Would it be better to have a 5 percent margin on sales and a total asset turnover of 2 times or a 2 percent sales margin and a turnover of 5 times? It makes no difference; in either case the firm has a 10 percent return on investment. Actually, most firms are not free to make the kind of choice posed in this question. Depending on the nature of its industry, the firm *must* operate with more or fewer assets, and its turnover will depend on the characteristics of its particular line of business. In the case of a dealer in fresh fruits and vegetables, fish, or other perishable items, the turnover should be high—every day or two is most desirable. In contrast, some lines of business require heavy fixed investment or long production periods. A hydroelectric utility company, with its heavy investment in dams and transmission lines, requires heavy fixed investment; a shipbuilder or an aircraft producer needs a long production period. Such companies necessarily have a low asset turnover rate but a correspondingly higher profit margin on sales.

When the du Pont system is used for divisional control, the process is often called return on investment (ROI) control. Here return is measured by operating earnings—income before interest and taxes—as shown in Figure 7.5. Sometimes the earnings figure is calculated before depreciation, and total gross assets are measured before deduction of the depreciation reserve. Measurement on gross assets has the advantage of avoiding differences in ROI due to differences in the average age of the fixed assets. Older assets are more fully depreciated and have a higher depreciation reserve and lower net fixed asset amount. This causes the ROI on net total assets to be higher when fixed assets are older.

If a particular division's ROI falls below a target figure, then the centralized corporate staff helps the division's own financial staff trace back through the du Pont system to determine the cause of the substandard ROI. Each division manager is judged by the division's ROI and rewarded or penalized accordingly. Division managers are thus motivated to keep their ROI up to the target level. Their individual actions should in turn maintain the firm's ROI at an appropriate level.

In addition to its use in managerial control, ROI can be used to allocate funds to the various divisions. The firm as a whole has financial resources—retained earnings, cash flow from depreciation, and the ability to obtain additional debt and equity funds from capital markets. These funds can be allocated on the basis of the divisional ROIs, with divisions having high ROIs receiving more funds than those with low ones.

Pitfalls in the Use of ROI Control

Any system of divisional control runs the risk that executives will devise methods for "beating the system." Hence a number of problems can arise if ROI control is used without proper safeguards.[2] Since the divisional managers are rewarded on the basis of their ROI performance, it is absolutely essential for their morale that they feel their divisional ROI does indeed provide an accurate measure of relative performance. But ROI is dependent on a number of factors in addition to managerial competence; some of these factors are listed below.

1. *Depreciation.* ROI is very sensitive to depreciation policy. If one division is writing off assets at a relatively rapid rate, its annual profits—and hence its ROI—will be reduced.
2. *Book value of assets.* If an older division is using assets that have been largely written off, both its current depreciation charges and its investment base will be low. This will make its ROI high in relation to newer divisions.

[2] For a discussion of how to avoid the pitfalls of a static approach to ROI control and an emphasis on its use as a dynamic information feedback control process, see J. Fred Weston, "ROI Planning and Control: A Dynamic Management System," *Business Horizons*, August 1972, pp. 35–42.

3. *Transfer pricing.* In most corporations some divisions sell to other divisions. At General Motors, for example, the Fisher Body Division sells to the Chevrolet Division. In such cases the price at which goods are transferred between divisions has a fundamental effect on divisional profits. If the transfer price of auto bodies is set relatively high, then Fisher Body will have a relatively high ROI and Chevrolet a relatively low one.
4. *Time periods.* Many projects have long gestation periods, during which expenditures must be made for research and development, plant construction, market development, and the like. Such expenditures add to the investment base without a commensurate increase in profits for several years. During this period, a division's ROI can be seriously reduced; and without proper constraints, its manager may be improperly penalized. Given the frequency of personnel transfers in larger corporations, it is easy to see how the timing problem can keep managers from making long-term investments that are in the best interests of the firm.
5. *Industry conditions.* If one division is operating in an industry where conditions are favorable and rates of return are high, while another is in an industry suffering from excessive competition, the environmental differences may cause the favored division to look good and the unfavored one to look bad, quite apart from any differences in their managers. For example, Signal Companies' aerospace division could hardly have been expected to perform as well as their truck division did in 1973, when the entire aerospace industry suffered severe problems and truck sales soared. External conditions must be taken into account when appraising ROI performance.

Because of these factors, a division's ROI must be supplemented with other criteria for evaluating performance. For example, its growth rate in sales, profits, and market share (as well as its ROI) in comparison with other firms in its own industry has been used in such evaluations. Although ROI control has been used with great success in U.S. industry, the system cannot be used in a mechanical sense by inexperienced personnel. As with most other tools, it is helpful if used properly but destructive if misused.

Summary

The general theme of this chapter is the financial planning and control process. A number of analytical approaches are set forth to help implement financial planning and control. The relationship between investment outlays and the volume required to achieve profitability is referred to as breakeven analysis. Breakeven analysis focuses on the pattern of relations between total revenues and total costs. It is a method of relating fixed costs, variable costs, and total revenues to show the level of sales that must be attained if the firm is to operate at a profit. The analysis can be based on the number of units produced or on total dollar sales. It can be used for the entire company or for a particular product or division. With minor modifications, it can be put on a cash basis instead of a profit basis.

Operating leverage is defined as the extent to which fixed costs are used in operations. The degree of operating leverage (DOL), then, is the ratio of the percentage change in operating income to the percentage change in units sold or in sales. A firm's DOL is a precise measure of how much operating leverage the firm is employing. Breakeven analysis emphasizes the volume of sales the firm needs to be profitable. The degree of operating leverage measures how sensitive the firm's profits are to changes in the volume of sales. Both concepts measure the effects of the relative proportion of fixed costs in the total cost function of the firm.

The budgeting process provides more detailed analysis for the control of revenues and costs. A firm's budget is a detailed plan of how funds will be spent. A budget is a plan stated in terms of specific expenditures for specific purposes; it is used for both planning and control. Its overall purpose is to improve internal operations, thereby reducing costs and raising profitability. A budgeting system starts with a set of performance standards, or targets. The targets represent the firm's financial plan. The budgeted amounts are compared with the actual results. If there are differences, the reasons should be identified and appropriate adjustments in the firm's policies should be made. These changes include the correction of deficiencies and more aggressive pursuit of opportunities. This is the feedback and control part of the budget process. It is critical to achieving a high level of managerial performance.

Although the entire budget system is vital to corporate management, one aspect of the system is especially important to the financial manager—the cash budget. The cash budget is, in fact, the principal tool for making short-run financial forecasts. If used properly, it can pinpoint the funds that will be needed, when they will be needed, and when cash flows will be sufficient to retire the company's loans.

As a firm becomes larger, it is necessary for it to decentralize operations to some extent. But decentralized operations still require some centralized control. The principal tool used for such control is the return on investment (ROI) method. There are problems with ROI control; but if budgeting and ROI control are viewed as a communication system that aids the flow of information among managers of the firm, a dynamic interaction among managers can be developed. If the emphasis is on an informed interaction process, the results of operations as measured by ROI will be improved. Communication and motivation, the behavioral aspects of the budgeting process, cannot be overemphasized.

Questions

7.1 What benefits can be derived from breakeven analysis?

7.2 What is operating leverage? Explain how profits or losses can be magnified in a firm with high operating leverage as opposed to a firm without this characteristic.

7.3 What data are necessary to construct a breakeven chart?

7.4 What is the general effect of each of the following changes on a firm's breakeven point?

a. An increase in selling price with no change in units sold

b. A change from the leasing of a machine for $5,000 a year to the purchase of the machine for $100,000. The useful life of this machine will be twenty years, with no salvage value. Assume straight-line depreciation.
c. A reduction in variable labor costs

7.5 In what sense can depreciation be considered a source of funds?

7.6 Why is a cash budget important even when there is plenty of cash in the bank?

7.7 What is the difference between the long-range financial forecasting concept (for example, the percent-of-sales method) and the budgeting concept? How might they be used together?

7.8 Assume that a firm is making up its long-run financial budget. What period should this budget cover—one month, six months, one year, three years, five years, or some other period? Justify your answer.

7.9 Is a detailed budget more important to a large, multidivisional firm than to a small, single-product firm?

7.10 Assume that your uncle is a major stockholder in a multidivisional firm that uses a naive ROI criterion for evaluating divisional managers and that bases managers' salaries in large part on this evaluation. You can have the job of division manager in any division you choose. If you are a salary maximizer, what divisional characteristics will you seek? If, because of your good performance, you become president of the firm, what changes will you make?

Problems

7.1 The Bentley Corporation produces tea kettles, which it sells for $10. Fixed costs are $600,000 for up to 400,000 units of output. Variable costs are $7 per unit.
a. What is the firm's gain or loss at sales of 175,000 units? Of 300,000 units?
b. What is the breakeven point? Illustrate by means of a chart.
c. What is Bentley's degree of operating leverage at sales of 175,000 units? Of 225,000 units? Of 300,000 units?

7.2 For Pratt Industries the following relationships exist. Each unit of output is sold for $35; the fixed costs are $160,000; variable costs are $15 a unit.
a. What is the firm's gain or loss at sales of 6,000 units? Of 9,000 units?
b. What is the breakeven point? Illustrate by means of a chart.
c. What is Pratt's degree of operating leverage at sales of 6,000 units? Of 9,000 units?
d. What happens to the breakeven point if the selling price rises to $40? What is the significance of the change to financial management? Illustrate by means of a chart.
e. What happens to the breakeven point if the selling price rises to $40 but variable costs rise to $20 a unit? Illustrate by means of a chart.

7.3 For Ardell Industries the following relations exist. Each unit of output is sold for $100; the fixed costs are $312,500, of which $250,000 are annual depreciation charges; variable costs are $37.50 per unit.
a. What is the firm's gain or loss at sales of 4,000 units? Of 7,000 units?
b. What is the profit breakeven point? Illustrate by means of a chart.

c. What is the cash breakeven point? Illustrate by means of a chart.

d. Assume Ardell is operating at a level of 3,500 units. Are creditors likely to seek the liquidation of the company if it is slow in paying its bills?

7.4 The Ortho Company is planning to request a line of credit from its bank. The following sales forecasts have been made for parts of 1981 and 1982:

May 1981	$150,000
June	150,000
July	300,000
August	450,000
September	600,000
October	300,000
November	300,000
December	75,000
January 1982	150,000

Collection estimates obtained from the credit and collection department are as follows: collected within the month of sale, 5 percent; collected the month following the sale, 80 percent; collected the second month following the sale, 15 percent. Payments for labor and raw materials are typically made during the month following the month in which these costs are incurred. Total labor and raw materials costs are estimated for each month as follows:

May 1981	$ 75,000
June	75,000
July	105,000
August	735,000
September	255,000
October	195,000
November	135,000
December	75,000

General and administrative salaries will amount to approximately $22,500 a month; lease payments under long-term lease contracts will be $7,500 a month; depreciation charges will be $30,000 a month; miscellaneous expenses will be $2,250 a month; income tax payments of $52,500 will be due in both September and December; and a progress payment of $150,000 on a new research laboratory must be paid in October. Cash on hand on July 1 will amount to $110,000, and a minimum cash balance of $75,000 will be maintained throughout the cash budget period.

a. Prepare a monthly cash budget for the last six months of 1981.

b. Prepare an estimate of required financing (or excess funds)—that is, the amount of money the Ortho Company will need to borrow (or will have available to invest)—for each month during the period.

c. Assume that receipts from sales come in uniformly during the month (that is, cash receipts come in at the rate of 1/30 each day), but all outflows are paid on the fifth of the month. Will this have an effect on the cash budget (that is, will the cash budget you have prepared be valid under these assumptions)? If not, what can be done to make a valid estimate of financing requirements?

7.5 The board of directors of the San Jose Microprocessor Company has received numerous complaints from shareholders regarding the performance of the firm's management. In an effort to verify the validity of these complaints, the board has collected the information below.

a. Calculate the relevant financial ratios for San Jose Microprocessor.
b. Apply a du Pont chart analysis on San Jose and compare it to the du Pont chart analysis based on composite ratios for the industry as a whole.
c. Evaluate management's performance and list specific areas where improvement is needed.

San Jose Microprocessor Company
Balance Sheet as of December 31, 1980
(Thousands of Dollars)

Assets		**Liabilities**		
Cash	$ 90	Accounts payable	$450	
Marketable securities	$ 40	Notes payable (at 11%)	380	
Receivables	1,550	Other current liabilities	280	
Inventory	1,190	Total current liabilities		$1,110
Total current assets	$2,870	Long-term debt (at 9%)		880
Net fixed assets	1,130	Total liabilities		$1,990
		Net worth		2,010
Total assets	$4,000	Total claims on assets		$4,000

San Jose Microprocessor Company
Income Statement for Year Ended
December 31, 1980 (Thousands of Dollars)

Sales		$6,200
Cost of goods sold:		
Materials	$2,440	
Labor	1,540	
Heat, light, and power	230	
Indirect labor	370	
Depreciation	140	4,720
Gross profit		$1,480
Selling expenses	490	
General and administrative expenses	530	1,020
Operating profit		$ 460
Less interest expense		121
Net profit before taxes		$ 339
Less federal income taxes (assumed 45% rate)		152
Net profit		$ 187

Industry du Pont Analysis

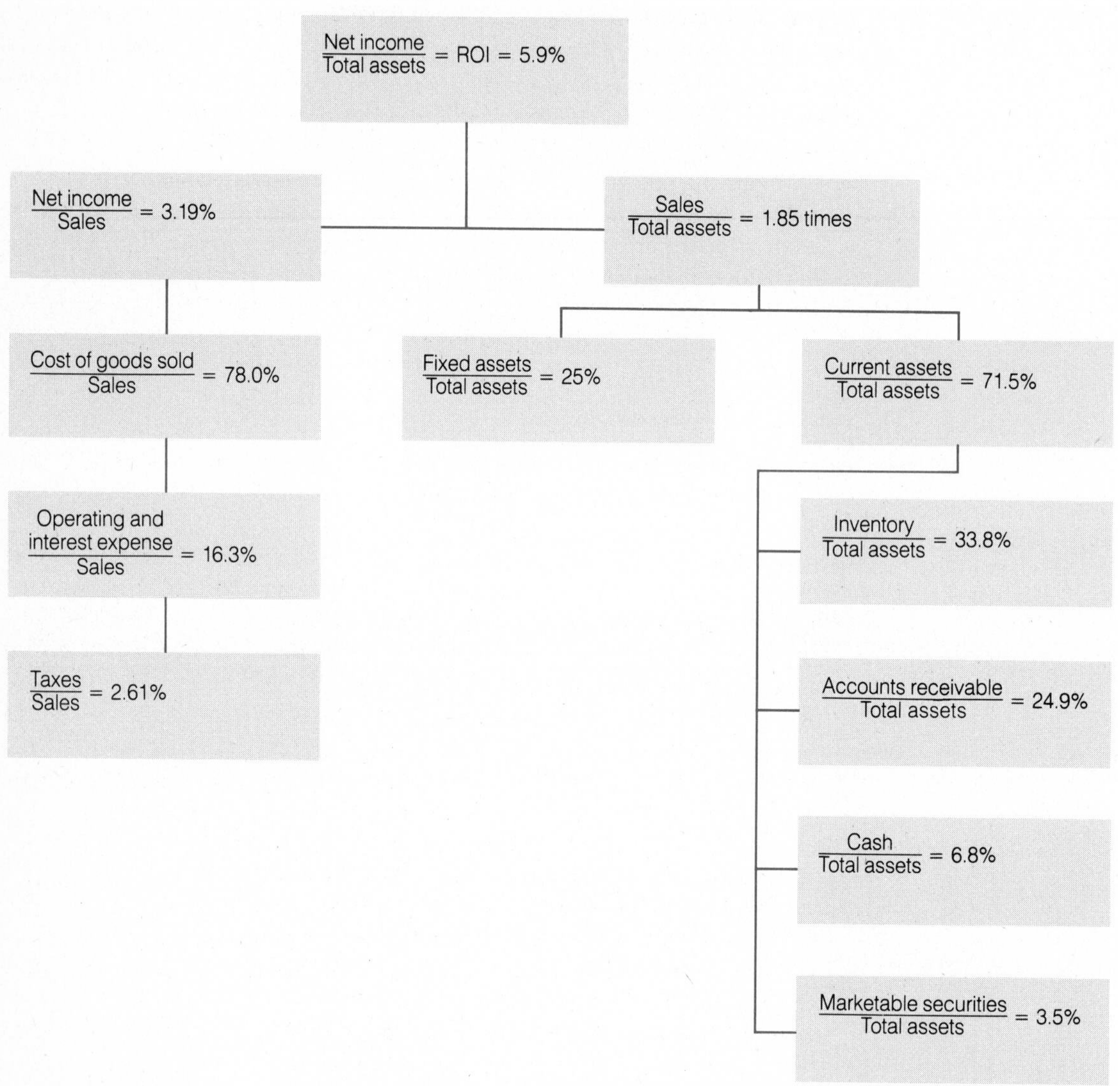

Key industry ratios:

Current ratio	2.2
Quick ratio	1.0
Debt/assets	50%
Times interest earned	5.2 times
Inventory turnover	5.1 times
Average collection period	52 days
Fixed asset turnover	9.25 times
Total asset turnover	1.85 times
Profit margin on sales	3.19%
Return on total assets	5.90%
Return on net worth	10.80%

7.6 Gulf and Eastern, Inc., is a diversified multinational corporation that produces a wide variety of goods and services, including chemicals, soaps, tobacco products, toys, plastics, pollution control equipment, canned food, sugar, motion pictures, and computer software. The corporation's major divisions were brought together in the early 1960s under a decentralized form of management; each division was evaluated in terms of its profitability, efficiency, and return on investments. This decentralized organization persisted through most of the decade, during which Gulf and Eastern experienced a high average growth rate in total assets, earnings, and stock prices.

Toward the end of 1975, however, those trends were reversed. The organization was faced with declining earnings, unstable stock prices, and a generally uncertain future. This situation persisted into 1976, but during that year a new president, Lynn Thompson, was appointed by the board of directors. Thompson, who had served for a time on the financial staff of I. E. du Pont, used the du Pont system to evaluate the various divisions. All showed definite weaknesses.

Thompson reported to the board that a principal reason for the poor overall performance was a lack of control by central management over each division's activities. She was particularly disturbed by the consistently poor results of the corporation's budgeting procedures. Under that system, each division manager drew up a projected budget for the next quarter, along with estimated sales, revenue, and profit; funds were then allocated to the divisions, basically in proportion to their budget requests. However, actual budgets seldom matched the projections; wide discrepancies occurred; and this, of course, resulted in a highly inefficient use of capital.

In an attempt to correct the situation, Thompson asked the firm's chief financial officer to draw up a plan to improve the budgeting, planning, and control processes. When the plan was submitted, its basic provisions included the following:

1. To improve the quality of the divisional budgets, the division managers should be informed that the continuance of wide variation between their projected and actual budgets would result in dismissal.
2. A system should be instituted under which funds would be allocated to divisions on the basis of their average return on investment (ROI) during the last four quarters. Since funds were short, divisions with high ROIs would get most of the available money.
3. Only about half of each division manager's present compensation should be received as salary; the rest should be in the form of a bonus related to the division's average ROI for the quarter.
4. Each division should submit to the central office for approval all capital expenditure requests, production schedules, and price changes. Thus the company would be recentralized.

a. 1. Is it reasonable to expect the new procedures to improve the accuracy of budget forecasts?
   2. Should all divisions be expected to maintain the same degree of accuracy?
   3. In what other ways might the budgets be made?

b. 1. What problems would be associated with the use of the ROI criterion in allocating funds among the divisions?

2. What effect would the period used in computing ROI (that is, four quarters, one quarter, two years, and so on) have on the effectiveness of this method?
3. What problems might occur in evaluating the ROI in the crude rubber and auto tires divisions? Between the sugar products and pollution control equipment divisions?

c. What problems would be associated with rewarding each manager on the basis of the division's ROI?

d. How well would the policy of recentralization work in this highly diversified corporation, particularly in light of the financial officer's three other proposals?

PART THREE

WORKING CAPITAL MANAGEMENT

Part 2 analyzed the firm's operations in an overall, aggregate framework. Now we must examine the individual aspects of the firm's financial decisions in more detail.

In Part 3, we focus on the top half of the balance sheet, studying current assets, current liabilities, and the relationship between these two sets of accounts. This type of analysis is commonly called *working capital management*.

Chapter 8 examines some general principles of overall working capital management. In the next three chapters we analyze the major current asset accounts. We begin with inventory models in Chapter 9 because all investments represent an inventory decision to some degree.

In Chapter 10, we analyze credit management decisions.

Chapter 11 covers several aspects of cash management, including cash gathering, cash disbursements, cash management models, and management of the firm's marketable securities portfolio. Since effective cash management can minimize financing requirements, a convenient bridge is provided to the fifth chapter on working capital management—short-term financing.

In broad perspective, working capital management represents the efforts of the firm to make adjustments to short-run changes. These represent the developments to which the firm must make prompt and effective responses. We take up these aspects of financial decision-making early, because they occupy the major portion of the financial manager's time and represent areas in which activity takes place on a continuing basis.

CHAPTER 8

WORKING CAPITAL POLICY

The term *working capital* is used in different ways by different writers. We take a practical approach by adopting the usage found in the annual reports of corporations where working capital is defined as current assets minus current liabilities. Thus working capital represents the firm's investment in cash, marketable securities, accounts receivable, and inventories less the current liabilities used to finance the current assets. Some refer to this measure as *net working capital*, but if working capital is what is left after taking account of current liabilities, it is redundant to add the term *net*. Working capital management is defined broadly to encompass all aspects of the administration of both current assets and current liabilities.

This chapter opens with a discussion of the nature of the cash flow cycle involved in working capital management. The issue of investment in current assets is treated next. After presenting some background on the relation between short-term and long-term interest rates, policies on the use of short-term versus long-term financing are considered. The chapter concludes with an analysis of the risk-return tradeoffs of aggressive versus conservative working capital management policies. This provides a framework for Chapters 9, 10, and 11, which treat decisions on investments in individual current assets; and for Chapter 12, which evaluates alternative sources of short-term financing.

Importance of Working Capital Management

Working capital management includes a number of aspects that make it an important topic for study:

1. Surveys indicate that the largest portion of a financial manager's time is devoted to the day-by-day internal operations of the firm, which can appropriately be subsumed under the heading of working capital management.
2. Characteristically, current assets often represent more than half the total assets of a business firm. Because they represent such a large investment and because this investment tends to be relatively volatile, current assets are worthy of the financial manager's careful attention.
3. Working capital management is particularly important for small firms. Although such firms can minimize their investment in fixed assets by renting or leasing plant and equipment, they cannot avoid investment in cash, receivables, and inventories. Further, because a small firm has relatively limited access to the long-term capital markets, it must necessarily rely heavily on trade credit and short-term bank loans, both of which affect working capital by increasing current liabilities.

4. The relationship between sales growth and the need to finance current assets is close and direct. For example, if the firm's average collection period is forty days and its credit sales are $1,000 a day, it has an investment of $40,000 in accounts receivable. If sales rise to $2,000 a day, the investment in accounts receivable rises to $80,000. Sales increases produce similar immediate needs for additional inventories and, perhaps, for cash balances. All such needs must be financed; and since they are so closely related to sales volume, it is imperative that the financial manager keep aware of developments in the working capital segment of the firm. Of course, continued sales increases require additional long-term assets, which must also be financed. However, fixed asset investments, while critically important to the firm in a strategic, long-run sense, generally have more lead time in financing than do current asset investments.

Cash Flow Cycle

An important aspect of working capital management is providing for the financing of increases in current assets required as the sales activity of the firm increases. Firms need assets to make sales; if sales are to be increased, assets must also be expanded. A growing firm is likely to need additional cash for immediate investment in receivables, inventories, and other current assets and, as full capacity is reached, in fixed assets as well. New investments must be financed, and new financing carries with it commitments and obligations to service the capital obtained. A growing firm can, therefore, have a cash flow problem. The nature of this problem, as well as the cause-and-effect relationship between assets and sales, is illustrated in the following discussion, in which we trace the consequences of a series of transactions.

Effects on the Balance Sheet

Two partners invest a total of $50,000 to create the Jonquil Dress Company. The firm rents a plant; equipment and other fixed assets cost $30,000. The resulting financial situation is shown by Balance Sheet 1.

Balance Sheet 1

Assets		**Liabilities**	
Current assets		Capital stock	$50,000
Cash	$20,000		
Fixed assets			
Plant and equipment	30,000		
Total assets	$50,000	Total liabilities and net worth	$50,000

Jonquil receives an order to manufacture 10,000 dresses. The receipt of an order in itself has no effect on the balance sheet, but in preparation for the manufacturing activity, the firm buys $20,000 worth of cotton cloth on terms of net 30 days. Without additional investment by the owners, total assets increase by $20,000, financed by the trade accounts payable to the supplier of the cotton cloth.

After the purchase, the firm spends $20,000 on labor for cutting the cloth to the required pattern. Of the $20,000 total labor cost, $10,000 is paid in cash and

$10,000 is owed in the form of accrued wages. These two transactions are reflected in Balance Sheet 2, which shows that total assets increase to $80,000. Current assets are increased; working capital—total current assets minus total current liabilities—remains constant. The current ratio declines to 1.67, and the debt ratio rises to 38 percent. The financial position of the firm is weakening. If it should seek to borrow at this point, Jonquil could not use the work in process inventories as collateral, because a lender could find little use for partially manufactured dresses.

Balance Sheet 2

Assets		**Liabilities**	
Current assets		Accounts payable	$20,000
Cash	$10,000	Accrued wages payable	10,000
Inventories		Total current liabilities	$30,000
Work in process			
Materials	20,000	Capital stock	50,000
Labor	20,000		
Total current assets	$50,000		
Fixed assets			
Plant and equipment	30,000		
Total assets	$80,000	Total liabilities and net worth	$80,000

In order to complete the dresses, the firm incurs additional labor costs of $20,000 and pays in cash. It is assumed that the firm desires to maintain a minimum cash balance of $5,000. Since the initial cash balance is $10,000, Jonquil must borrow an additional $15,000 from its bank to meet the wage bill. The borrowing is reflected in notes payable in Balance Sheet 3. Total assets rise to $95,000, with a finished goods inventory of $60,000. The current ratio drops to 1.4, and the debt ratio rises to 47 percent. These ratios show a further weakening of the financial position.

Balance Sheet 3

Assets		**Liabilities**	
Current assets		Accounts payable	$20,000
Cash	$ 5,000	Notes payable	15,000
Inventory		Accrued wages payable	10,000
Finished goods	60,000	Total current liabilities	$45,000
Total current assets	$65,000		
		Capital stock	50,000
Fixed assets			
Plant and equipment	30,000		
Total assets	$95,000	Total liabilities and net worth	$95,000

Jonquil ships the dresses on the basis of the original order, invoicing the purchaser for $100,000 within 30 days. Accrued wages and accounts payable have to be paid now, so Jonquil must borrow an additional $30,000 in order to maintain the $5,000 minimum cash balance. These transactions are shown in Balance Sheet 4. Note that in Balance Sheet 4, finished goods inventory is replaced by receivables, with the markup reflected as retained earnings. This causes the debt ratio to drop to 33 percent. Since the receivables are carried at the sales price, current assets increase to $105,000 and the current ratio rises to 2.3. Compared with the conditions reflected in Balance Sheet 3, most of the financial ratios show improvement. However, the absolute amount of debt is large.

Balance Sheet 4

Assets		**Liabilities**	
Current assets		Notes payable	$ 45,000
Cash	$ 5,000	Total current liabilities	$ 45,000
Accounts receivable	100,000	Capital stock	$ 50,000
Total current assets	$105,000	Retained earnings	40,000
		Total net worth	$ 90,000
Fixed assets			
Plant and equipment	30,000		
Total assets	$135,000	Total liabilities and net worth	$135,000

Whether the firm's financial position is really improved depends upon the creditworthiness of the purchaser of the dresses. If the purchaser is a good credit risk, Jonquil may be able to borrow further on the basis of the accounts receivable.

When the firm receives payment for the accounts receivable, it pays off the bank loan, and is in the highly liquid position shown by Balance Sheet 5. If a new order for 10,000 dresses is received, it will have no effect on the balance sheet, but a cycle similar to the one we have been describing will begin.

Balance Sheet 5

Assets		**Liabilities**	
Current assets		Capital stock	$50,000
Cash	$60,000	Retained earnings	40,000
Fixed assets			
Plant and equipment	30,000		
Total assets	$90,000	Total liabilities and net worth	$90,000

The cash flow cycle can be generalized from this example. An order that requires the purchase of raw materials is placed with the firm. The purchase in turn generates an account payable. As labor is applied, work-in-process inventories build up. To the extent that wages are not fully paid at the time labor is used, accrued wages will appear on the liability side of the balance sheet. As goods are completed, they move into finished goods inventories. The cash needed to pay for the labor to complete the goods may make it necessary for the firm to borrow.

Finished goods inventories are sold, usually on credit, which gives rise to accounts receivable. As the firm has not received cash, this point in the cycle represents the peak in financing requirements. If the firm did not borrow at the time finished goods inventories were at their maximum, it may do so as inventories are converted into receivables by credit sales. Income taxes, which were not considered in the example, can add to the problem. As accounts receivable become cash, short-term obligations can be paid off.

Managing the Cash Flow Cycle

We have just discussed the cash flow cycle as a process in which a firm requires investments in order to maintain the facilities for producing goods. The extent to which the firm is required to make investments in production and selling depends in part on the nature of the production cycle and on the terms on which it purchases its inputs and sells its finished goods. Richards and Laughlin have provided new insights on the management of cash flows by introducing the concept of a cash conversion cycle.[1] The cash conversion cycle is the net time interval between actual cash expenditures on a firm's purchase of productive resources and the recovery of cash receipts from product sales. Richards and Laughlin depict the cash conversion cycle in Figure 8.1, which shows that the cash flow financing period will be influenced by either expansion or contraction in any of the three liquidity flow measures: the inventory conversion period, the receivables conversion period, or the payments deferral period. Figure 8.1 illustrates the cash conversion cycle indicator of the firm's additional, nonspontaneous working capital financing requirements.

Figure 8.1

The Cash Conversion Cycle

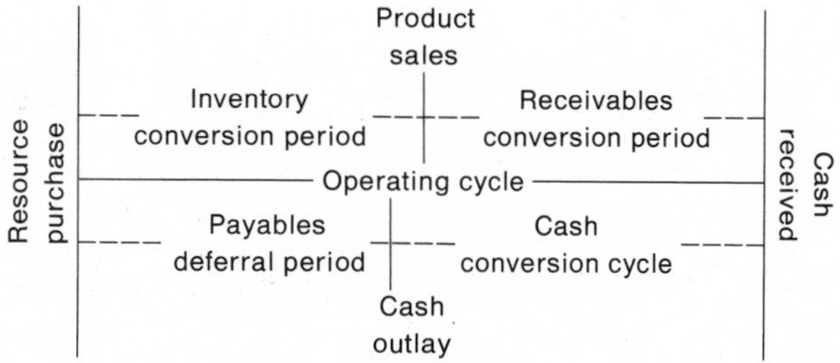

The significance of the cash conversion cycle analysis is demonstrated by the illustration Richards and Laughlin developed for the Martin Marietta Corporation. First, they summarized the income statement and balance sheet data for four years as shown in Table 8.1. Second, they contrasted the information conveyed by static liquidity ratios as compared with calculations of the cash conversion cycle by developing the material presented in Table 8.2.

Over the time period studied, a decline in the cash conversion cycle from 93 days to 64 days takes place. This indicates an associated reduction in the need for nonspontaneous financing over the period. A supplementary measure of the firm's liquidity reserve position calculates the ratio of working cash balances plus temporary cash investments (the firm's cash assets) to its total current assets. This ratio is rising, indicating that an increasing proportion of current assets are being held in the most liquid form. Increasing liquidity reserve investment joined with a shorter and more certain cash conversion cycle demonstrate an improving liquidity position.

In contrast, the current ratio is falling and the acid-test ratio rises then falls. The current ratio appears to give a wrong indicator of the change in liquidity position.

[1] Verlyn D. Richards and Eugene J. Laughlin, "A Cash Conversion Cycle Approach to Liquidity Analysis," *Financial Management,* 9 (Spring 1980) pp. 32–38. Used by permission.

Table 8.1

Selected Financial Data for Martin Marietta Corporation, 1975–1978 (000,000 omitted)

Year Ended December 31	1978	1977	1976	1975
Net sales	$1,758	$1,440	$1,213	$1,053
Cost of goods sold	$1,269	$1,030	$ 876	$ 774
Selling, general and administrative expense	192	161	142	132
Depreciation, depletion, and amortization	72	66	63	60
Total operating expense	$1,533	$1,257	$1,081	$ 966
Net operating income	$ 225	$ 183	$ 132	$ 87
Cash and short-term investments	$ 204	$ 158	$ 107	$ 46
Notes and accounts receivable	283	227	178	147
Inventories	199	209	199	186
Prepayments and other current assets	16	11	11	14
Total current assets	$ 702	$ 605	$ 495	$ 393
Accounts payable	$ 133	$ 106	$ 86	$ 78
Salaries, benefits, and payroll tax	72	48	37	33
Income taxes	210	151	88	36
Current maturities of long-term debt	14	16	16	14
Total current liabilities	$ 429	$ 321	$ 227	$ 161

Source: Years 1977 and 1978, Martin Marietta Corporation Annual Report to Stockholders, 1978. Years 1975 and 1976, Martin Marietta Corporation 10–K reports to the SEC.

Table 8.2

Liquidity Ratios and Cash Conversion Cycle for Martin Marietta Corporation, 1975–1978

	1978	1977	1976	1975
Static Ratios:				
Current Ratio	1.64	1.88	2.18	2.44
Acid-Test Ratio	1.14	1.20	1.26	1.20
Turnover Ratios:				
Receivables Turnover	6.21	6.34	6.81	7.16
Inventory Turnover	6.38	4.93	4.40	4.16
Payables Turnover[a]	7.13	7.73	8.28	8.16
Cash Conversion Cycle:				
Receivables Conversion Period	58 days	57 days	53 days	50 days
Inventory Conversion Period	56 days	73 days	82 days	87 days
Operating Cycle	114 days	130 days	135 days	137 days
Less: Payment Deferral Period	50 days	47 days	43 days	44 days
Cash Conversion Cycle	64 days	83 days	92 days	93 days
Supplementary Static Ratio:				
Cash Assets/Current Assets	0.29	0.26	0.22	0.12

[a] Cost of goods sold plus selling and general and administrative expense divided by accounts payable plus salaries, benefits, and payroll tax.

The acid-test ratio fails to convey a clear direction of change in the firm's operating cash flows. Thus the use of the conventional, static balance sheet liquidity ratios may potentially result in misinterpretation of the direction of change in the firm's liquidity position from one period to another.

Two broad decision areas are involved in evaluating whether trends in the firm's working capital position are favorable or unfavorable. The first is the analysis of the investments in current assets. The second is the use of short-term debt versus long-term debt. Both decision areas include a consideration of the relative costs and risks involved. To make this analysis requires some background on the term structure of interest rates, which we will look at next.

The Term Structure of Interest Rates

The *term structure of interest rates* describes the relationship between interest rates and loan maturity. When measuring the term structure, we generally use yields on United States government securities.[2] The term structure on other instruments, however, varies similarly.

Figure 8.2 shows the term structure of rates in two years, 1976 and 1980. In the lower curve for 1976 we see a pattern of rising yields. The shorter-term maturities carry lower rates of interest than the longer-term maturities. This rising yield structure has been characteristic of most years since 1930. The higher curve for 1980 shows a pattern which starts high, then declines until the fifth year, becoming relatively flat thereafter.

Figure 8.2

Term Structure of Rates on U.S. Government Securities 1976 and 1980

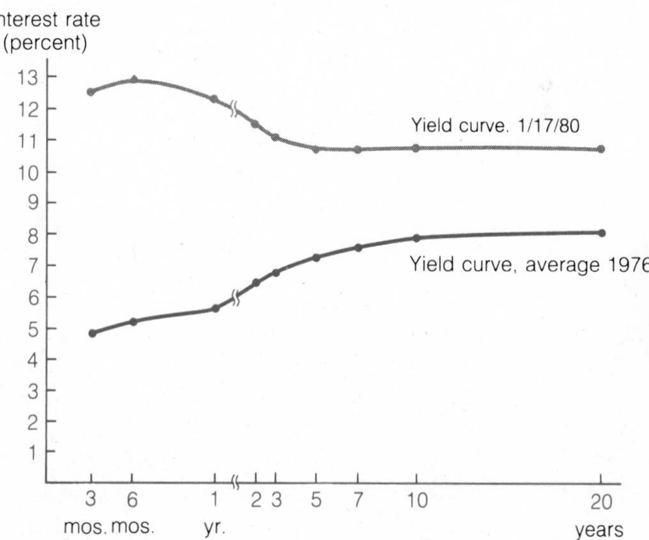

Source: 1/17/80: Salomon Brothers, *Bond Market Roundup*, Week Ending January 18, 1980. Reprinted by permission. 1976 *Federal Reserve Bulletin*, February 1978, p. A27.

[2] In discussing the term structure of interest rates, we are holding constant the risk of default. This is done by using government securities, which presumably have no default risk.

In addition to illustrating the changing term structure of interest rates, Figure 8.2 also reveals a shift in the "level of rates." Between 1976 and 1980, the interest rates on all government securities—long term and short term—increased. Such movements represent changes in the general level of interest rates.[3] The historical pattern of the relationship between long- and short-term interest rates is shown in Figure 8.3 for the period 1910 through 1979. The long-term rate is represented by the AAA bond rate—the rate on high-grade, long-term (25 years or more) corporate bonds; the short-term rate is represented by the rate on prime commercial paper—the four-to-six-month debt of top-quality firms.

Figure 8.3 **Long- and Short-Term Interest Rates Annually**

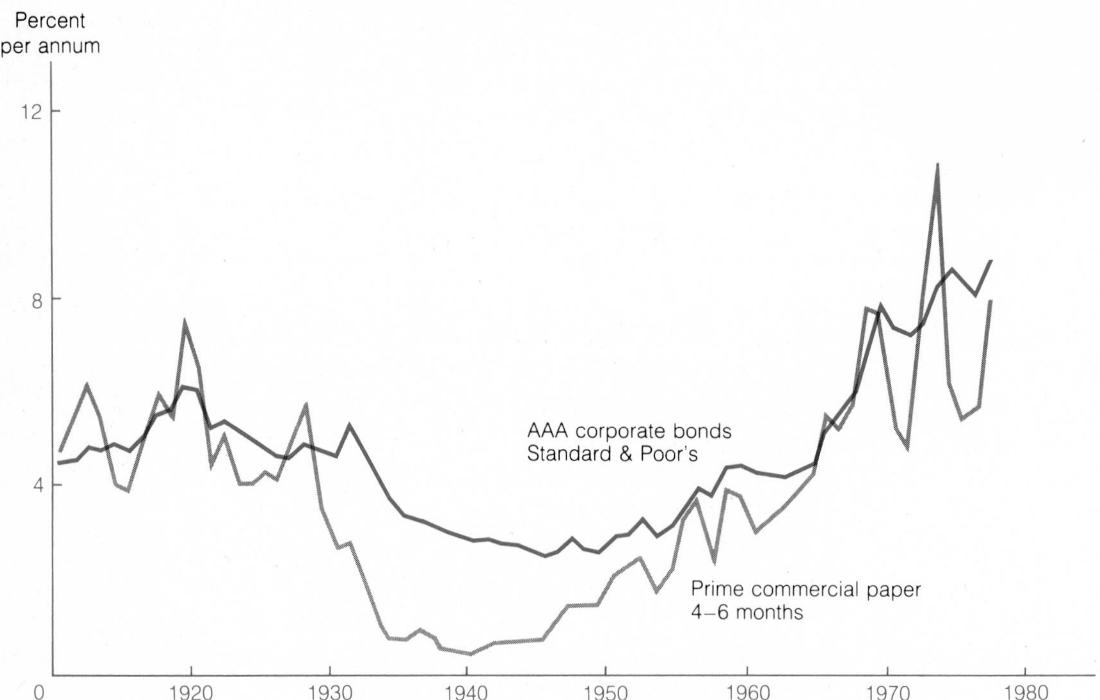

Source: Board of Governors of the Federal Reserve System, *1979 Historical Chart Book*, p. 96.

Three points should be made about the graph: (1) both long-term and short-term rates generally rose over the period; (2) short-term rates were more volatile than long-term rates; and (3) long-term rates were generally above short-term rates.

Except for a few months in the mid-1950s, the long-term rate was consistently above the short-term rate in all years from 1929 to 1966. However, in recent years

[3] In addition to the level and term structure of rates on a given class of securities—in this case, government securities—there is also the pattern of relationships among different classes of securities—for example, mortgages, government bonds, corporates, and bank business loans. The relationship among classes of securities is not discussed here. In general, movements in the term structure and level of rates are similar for most classes of securities.

Table 8.3

Hypothetical Relationship between Short-Term and Long-Term Interest Rates

	Situation A Expect Rising Rates			Situation B Expect Falling Rates		
Year	Long-Term (5-Year Note)	Short-Term (1-Year Note)	Intermediate-Term (3-Year Note)[a]	Long-Term (5-Year Note)	Short-Term (1-Year Note)	Intermediate-Term (3-Year Note)[a]
1	8%	6%	7%	8%	10%	9%
2		7			9	
3		8			8	
4		9			7	
5		10			6	

[a] Intermediate terms in this example could be anything between one and five years; for example, two-year notes, three-year notes, or four-year notes. Depending on the definition of intermediate term, different rates would emerge.

short-term rates have more often been above long-term rates. This occurred during 1966 and during parts of 1969, 1970, 1973, 1978, 1980, and 1981.

A brief summary of the expectations theory and the liquidity theory of the interest rate structure will help gain insights on the relations between short-term and long-term interest rates.[4]

Expections Theory

The expectations theory asserts that in equilibrium the long-term rate is a geometric average of today's short-term rate and expected short-term rates in the future. For continuous compounding, a simple arithmetic average may be used. The expectations theory is illustrated in Table 8.3 where "long term" is defined as five years. In situation A, the expected trend in short-term rates is upward—from 6 percent to 10 percent over five years. The long-term rate is thus 8 percent, the mean of that series; a lender could obtain an average yield of 8 percent on his investment either by lending long at 8 percent or by lending short at various increasing rates.

If the geometric average were used in Situation A, we would compute the current 5-year rate as $\sqrt[5]{1.06 \times 1.07 \times 1.08 \times 1.09 \times 1.10} - 1 = \sqrt[5]{1.468698} - 1 = 0.0799$, or 7.99%. The geometric measure of the 3-year note under A would be

$$\sqrt[3]{1.06 \times 1.07 \times 1.08} - 1 = \sqrt[3]{1.22494} - 1 = 0.06997,$$

or 7.0%.

The pattern is reversed in Situation B. There, the trend in short-term rates is expected to be downward. Again, however, the mean of the short-term rates is 8 percent, so 8 percent is the effective long-term rate. Under B, the 3-year rate would be $\sqrt[3]{1.10 \times 1.09 \times 1.08} - 1 = \sqrt[3]{1.29492} - 1 = 0.08997$, or 9.0%. Note that the results are approximately the same using either the simple or geometric averages for the data of the example presented.

The term structure of rates in year 1 under situations A and B is graphed in Figure 8.4. Expectations of rising rates produce an upward-sloping yield curve. With expectations of falling rates, the yield curve slopes down.

Liquidity Preference Theory

The future is inherently uncertain, and when uncertainty is considered, the pure expectations theory must be modified. To illustrate, let us consider a situation in which short-term rates are expected to remain unchanged in the future. In this case, the pure expectations theory predicts that short- and long-term bonds sell at equal yields. The liquidity preference theory, on the other hand, holds that long-term bonds must yield more than short-term bonds for two reasons. First, in a world of uncertainty, investors will generally prefer to hold short-term securities because they are more liquid in the sense that they can be converted to cash without danger of loss of principal. Investors will, therefore, accept lower yields on short-term securities. Second, borrowers react in exactly the opposite way from investors—business borrowers generally prefer long-term debt because short-term debt subjects a firm to the greater danger of having to refund debt under adverse conditions. Accordingly, firms are willing to pay a higher rate, other things held constant, for long-term than for short-term funds.

[4] Other somewhat arcane theories will not be described because they are not appropriate to the level of the present analysis.

Figure 8.4 **Term Structure of Rates under Two Hypothetical Situations**

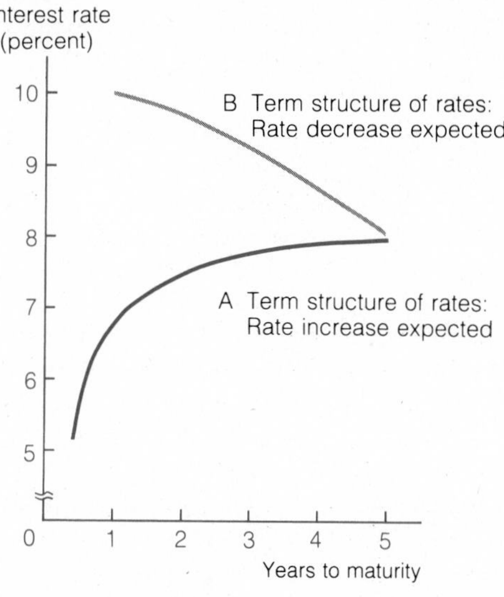

Figure 8.5 **Term Structure with Liquidity Preference**

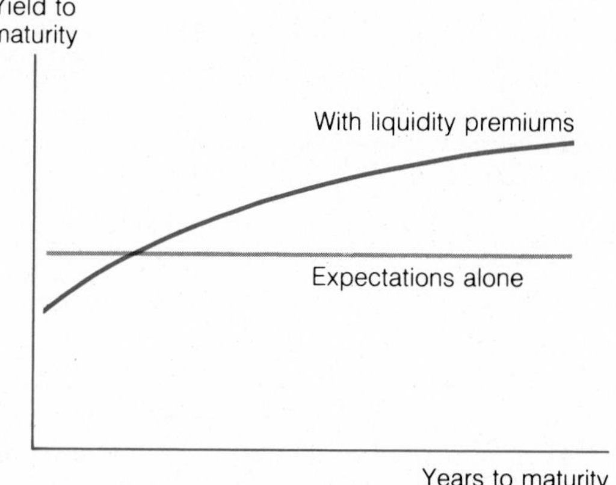

We see, then, that pressures on both the supply and demand sides—caused by liquidity preferences of both lenders and borrowers—will tend to make the yield curve slope upward. Figure 8.5 illustrates this effect.

Empirical Evidence

Empirical studies suggest that there is some validity to each of these theories. Specifically, recent work indicates that if lenders and borrowers have no reason to expect a change in the general level of interest rates, the yield curve will be upward-sloping because of liquidity preferences. (Under the expectations theory, the term structure of interest rates would be flat if there were no expectation of change in the level of short-term rates.) However, it is a fact that during periods of extremely high interest rates, the yield curve is downward-sloping; this proves that the expectations theory also operates. Each theory has an element of truth, and each must be taken into account in seeking to understand the changing patterns observed in the term structure of interest rates.

With this background on the relation between short-term and long-term interest rates, we can turn to the two main decision areas involved in working capital management. First we shall discuss current asset investments. Second we will analyze the use of short-term versus long-term debt.

Risk-Return Tradeoff for Current Asset Investments

Some of these ideas are illustrated in Figure 8.6, which shows the short-run relationship between the firm's current assets and output. The firm's fixed assets, assumed to be $50 million, cannot be altered in response to short-run fluctuations in output. Three alternative current asset policies are depicted. The line with the steepest slope represents a conservative policy. Under a conservative current asset policy, relatively large balances of cash and marketable securities are maintained, large amounts of inventories are kept on hand, and sales are stimulated by the use of a credit policy that provides liberal financing to customers and that results in a high level of accounts receivable. The lowest of the three lines on Figure 8.6 has the smallest slope, representing the most aggressive current asset policy in which holdings of cash, receivables, and inventories are sharply restricted. The intermediate line represents a middle-ground approach.

Current asset holdings are the highest at any output level under the conservative policy and the lowest under the aggressive policy. For example, at an output of

Figure 8.6

Relationship between Current Assets and Output

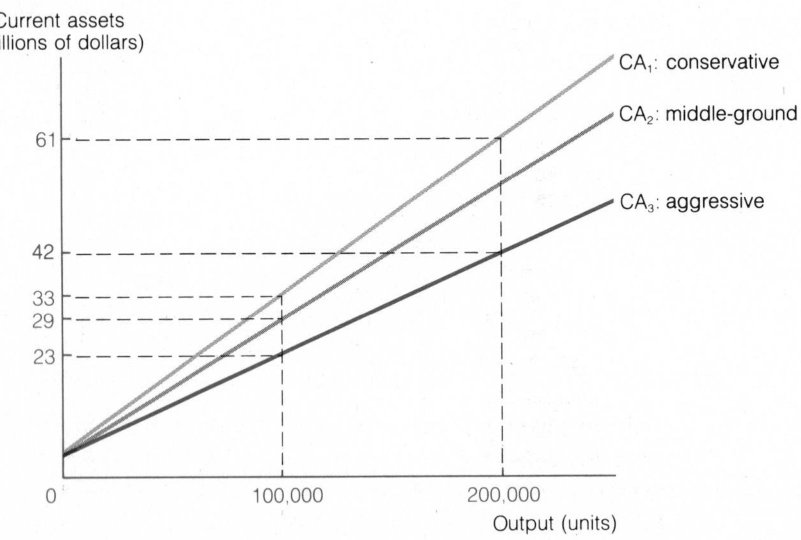

100,000 units, the conservative policy calls for $33 million of current assets versus only $23 million for the aggressive current asset policy. If demand for the firm's product increases and output increases to 200,000 units, current asset investments will also increase. Under the conservative policy, current assets will increase to $61 million, but under the aggressive policy, they rise to only $42 million. If it could forecast perfectly, a firm would hold exactly enough cash to make disbursements as required, exactly enough inventories to meet production and sales requirements, exactly the accounts receivable called for by an optimal credit policy, and no marketable securities unless the interest returns on such assets exceeded the cost of capital (an unlikely occurrence). The current asset holdings under the perfect foresight case would be the theoretical minimum for a profit-maximizing firm. Any larger holdings would increase the firm's assets without a proportionate increase in its returns, thus lowering its rate of return on investment. Any smaller holdings would mean the inability to pay bills on time, lost sales and production stoppages because of inventory shortages, and lost sales because of an overly restrictive credit policy.

When uncertainty is introduced into the picture, current asset management involves (1) determination of the minimum required balances of each type of asset and (2) addition of a safety stock to account for the fact that forecasters are imperfect. If a firm follows a conservative current asset policy, it is adding relatively large safety stocks. If it follows an aggressive policy, its safety stocks are minimal. The aggressive policy generally produces the highest expected returns on investment but, also, involves the greatest risk. However, the higher expected return, achieved by reduced investment in current assets, can be attenuated if the more restrictive asset management policies reduce sales levels below those that would be achieved under other policies. An example of this effect is presented in Table 8.4.

Table 8.4

Effects of Alternative Current Asset Policies on Rates of Return

Part A	Conservative	Middle-ground	Aggressive
Sales	$110,000,000	$105,000,000	$100,000,000
EBIT @ 15%	16,500,000	15,750,000	15,000,000
Current assets	70,000,000	55,000,000	40,000,000
Fixed assets	50,000,000	50,000,000	50,000,000
Total assets	$120,000,000	$105,000,000	$ 90,000,000
Rate of return on assets (EBIT/assets)	13.75%	15%	16.7%
Part B			
Sales	115,000,000	105,000,000	80,000,000
EBIT rate	15%	15%	12%
EBIT amount	17,250,000	15,750,000	9,600,000
Total assets	$120,000,000	$105,000,000	$ 90,000,000
Rate of return on assets (EBIT/assets)	14.4%	15%	10.7%

In Part A it is assumed that the less aggressive current asset investment policies stimulate sales to a slight degree by having more variety in inventory, fewer stock-out problems, and so forth. But still, the indicated rate of return on assets is highest for the current asset policy of greatest aggressiveness.

In Part B of Table 8.4 an alternative set of assumptions is illustrated. It is assumed that the aggressive current asset investment policy results in a larger adverse sales effect and also lowers the earnings rate. As a consequence, the most aggressive policy now results in the lowest indicated return on assets. It is assumed that the middle-road policy produces the same results as before. The results of the conservative policy are assumed to improve somewhat. Still the outcome for the middle-of-the-road policy represents the highest return on assets for the relationships postulated.

Table 8.4 illustrates the general idea that the kind of current asset policy a firm follows may result in a stimulus to sales and profitability or may result in negative effects on both the volume of sales and profitability.

In the real world, things are considerably more complex than this simple example suggests. For one thing, different types of current assets affect both risk and returns differently. Increased holdings of cash do more to improve the firm's risk posture than a similar dollar increase in receivables or inventories; idle cash penalizes earnings more severely than does the same investment in marketable securities. Generalizations are difficult when we consider accounts receivable and inventories, because it is difficult to measure either the earnings penalty or the risk reduction that results from increasing the balances of these items beyond their theoretical minimum levels.

Conservative versus Aggressive Working Capital Policies

Working capital policies involve decisions with respect to both current asset investments and the maturity structure of financing. As a framework for evaluating the use of short-term versus long-term financing, an overview relating asset structure and liability structure is first presented. The nature of the relationships involved is conveyed in Table 8.5, which presents the financial position of the Dow Chemical Company as of December 31, 1979. Current assets are $4,000 million and current liabilities are $2,600 million. Thus working capital totals $1,400 million. Since total assets are $10,000 million and current liabilities are $2,600 million, total long-term financing is $7,400 million. The difference between current assets and current liabilities—working capital—measures the amount by which current assets have been financed from long-term financing sources. A current ratio of two-to-one indicates that half the current assets are financed from long-term sources. The current ratio for Dow is somewhat over 1.5. Hence slightly more than one-third of Dow's current assets are financed from long-term sources.

Our analysis of the cash-flow cycle has demonstrated that as sales increase, the investment in cash, receivables, and inventories must grow proportionately. A steadily rising level of sales over the years will result in permanent increases in current assets. Although individual receivables accounts are paid off and individual inventory items become embodied in completed products and are sold, the continuous operations of the firm will result in rising investments in receivables and

Table 8.5

Financial Position of the Dow Chemical Company, December 31, 1979* (millions of dollars)

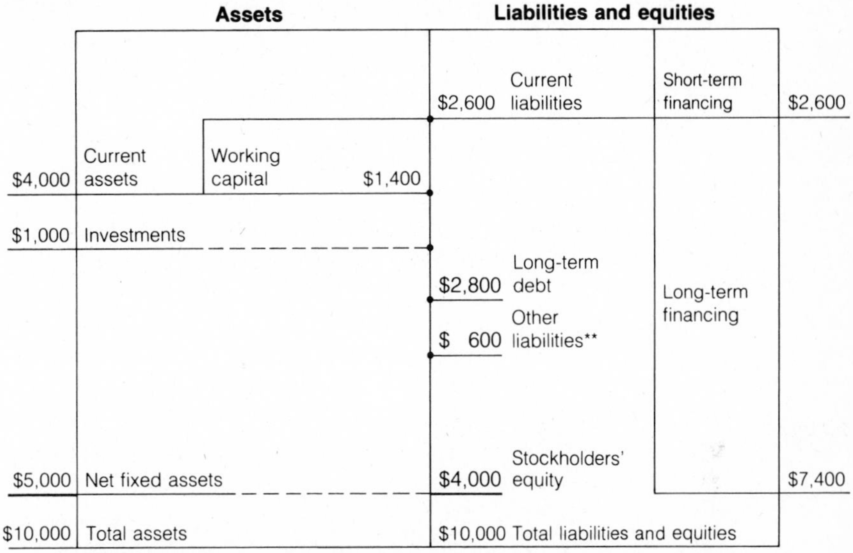

Assets				Liabilities and equities			
$4,000	Current assets	Working capital	$1,400	$2,600	Current liabilities	Short-term financing	$2,600
$1,000	Investments			$2,800	Long-term debt	Long-term financing	
				$ 600	Other liabilities**		
$5,000	Net fixed assets			$4,000	Stockholders' equity		$7,400
$10,000	Total assets			$10,000	Total liabilities and equities		

* The figures are rounded for convenience

** Other liabilities include deferred income taxes, $590 million, deferred employee benefits, $60 million; and minority interests in subsidiary companies, $50 million (representing holdings of stockholders' equity of companies in which Dow has a majority interest but in which others own a percentage of the stockholders' equity).

inventories as sales increase. Temporary seasonal fluctuations in sales would be followed by similar fluctuations in current asset requirements. Figures 8.7 through 8.9 illustrate three alternative patterns of relationships. In Figure 8.8 financing is matched to the permanence of assets. Current liabilities, such as accounts payable, accrued taxes, and wages, are related to the level of sales. As sales grow, these "spontaneous" current liabilities represent a component of "permanent" financing. Temporary changes in sales and assets give rise to fluctuations in "spontaneous" current liabilities and to changes in external short-term borrowing. As total permanent assets increase, they are financed by equity, long-term debt, and by the "permanent" portion of spontaneous current liabilities. At the limit, a firm can attempt to match the maturity structure of its assets and liabilities exactly.

An alternative policy would be an aggressive working capital management policy (Figure 8.9) in which all fixed assets are financed with long-term capital, but part of the permanent current assets are financed with short-term credit.[5] The dashed line could even have been drawn *below* the line designating fixed assets,

[5] Firms generally have some short-term credit in the form of "spontaneous" funds—accounts payable and accruals. Used in moderation, these constitute "free" capital, so virtually all firms employ at least some short-term credit at all times.

Figure 8.7

Conservative Working Capital Policy

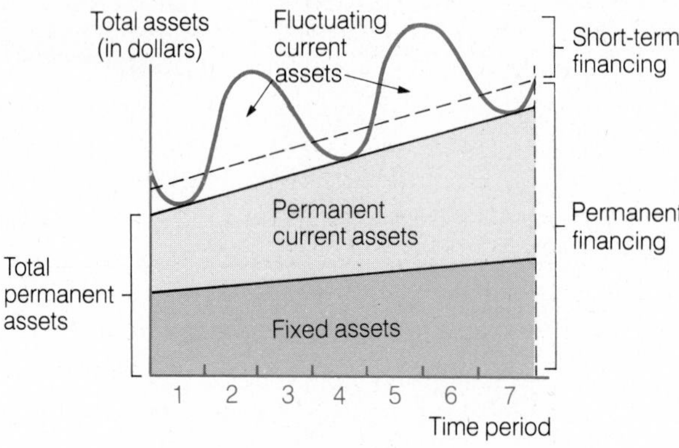

Figure 8.8

Average Working Capital Policy

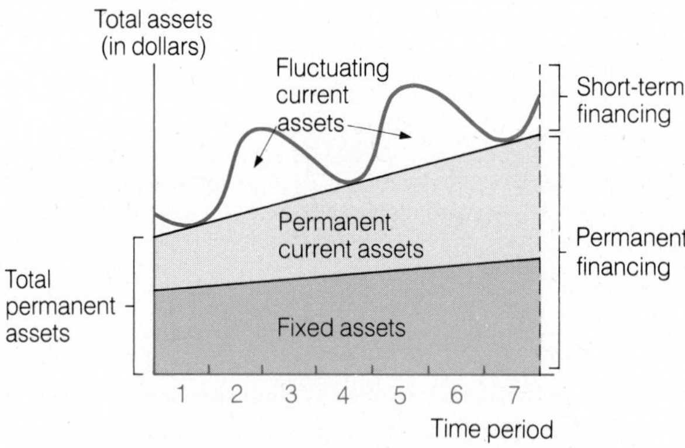

Figure 8.9

Aggressive Working Capital Policy

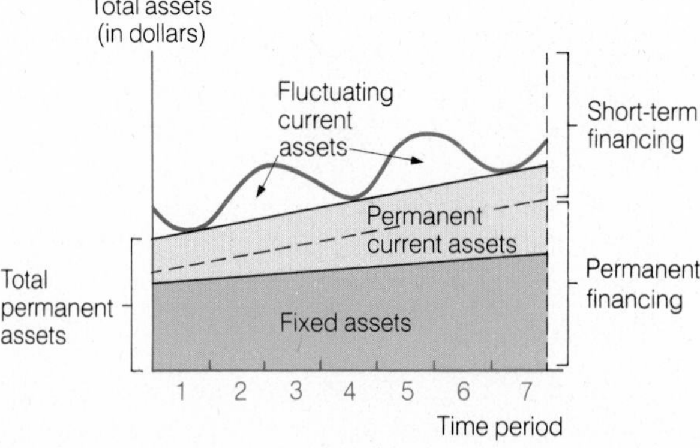

indicating that all the current assets and part of the fixed assets are financed with short-term credit; this would be a very aggressive policy.

Alternatively, as in Figure 8.7, the dashed line could be drawn *above* the line designating permanent current assets, indicating that permanent capital is being used to meet seasonal demands. In this case, the firm uses a small amount of short-term credit to meet its peak seasonal requirements, but it also meets part of its seasonal needs by "storing liquidity" in the form of marketable securities during the off-season. The humps above the dashed line represent short-term financing; the troughs below it represent short-term security holdings.

A basic policy decision in working capital management is the choice between the use of short-term versus long-term financing. To analyze this decision we shall first consider the relative costs and risks of these two financing methods.

Analysis of Relative Merits of Alternative Debt Maturities

The choice between short-term versus long-term debt involves an analysis of flexibility, costs, and risks.

Flexibility of Maturity Debt

If the need for funds is seasonal or cyclical, the firm may not want to commit itself to long-term debt. Such debt can be refunded, provided the loan agreement includes a call or prepayment provision; but even so, prepayment penalties can be expensive. Accordingly, if a firm expects its need for funds to diminish in the near future, or if it thinks there is a good chance that such a reduction will occur, it may choose short-term debt for flexibility.

A cash budget may be used to analyze the flexibility aspect of the maturity structure of debt. Flexibility may also be achieved with long-term debt. To illustrate: Suppose a firm invests in a major new project buying equipment with a ten-year life. The equipment will provide cash flows—depreciation plus profit—over its ten-year life. If the firm uses debt with a ten-year maturity to finance the equipment purchase, it may schedule the debt's retirement to the expected cash flows from the project.

The Cost of Short-term Versus Long-term Debt

Until the late 1960s, the cost of short-term debt was generally below the cost of long-term debt. Recall also that from the expectations theory, long-term borrowing is no different from a succession of short-term borrowings. If long-term rates reflect an average of future short-term rates, the use of long-term borrowing already reflects the short-term rates that are expected to be experienced in the future.

Some might argue that short-term borrowing rates may actually be lower in the future than the rates reflected in current long-term borrowings. This is possible, of course; but if it happens, it will be an unexpected, essentially random occurrence. As such, the unanticipated changes could go in either direction with equal probability, so no average gain or loss from unexpected changes in short-term rates can reasonably be argued.

However, to the extent that the liquidity preference theory of the term structure of interest rates dominates, short-term rates would be below long-term rates. From the standpoint of lenders there is less risk on a short-term loan because of the opportunity to reevaluate the loans more frequently as they come up for renewal. From the standpoint of borrowers, longer-term debt avoids the uncertainty of fluctuating short-term rates and the possibility of having to renew or refund debt under adverse money and capital market conditions.

The Risk-Return Tradeoff

Even when the cost of short-term debt is lower than that of long-term debt, its use is likely to entail greater risk. Thus we are again faced with a tradeoff between risk and rate of return. The nature of the risk-rate of return tradeoff relationships is illustrated in Table 8.6, Parts A and B.

We assume that the firm has $100 million in assets, half of which are held as fixed assets and half as current assets, and that it will earn 15 percent before interest and taxes on these assets. The debt ratio has been set at 50 percent, but the policy issue of whether to use short-term debt or long-term debt has not been determined.

In Part A of Table 8.6, short-term debt is assumed to cost 7 percent while long-term debt costs 9 percent. The return on equity will obviously be higher with greater use of short-term debt, since short-term debt is assumed to have lower costs.

On the other hand, in Part B of the table, a situation similar to that which occurred in early 1980 is illustrated. Short-term credit cost 15 percent or more; long-term debt, on the other hand, generally carried a yield of about 11 percent, though if it had been obtained even earlier, it could cost only 8–10 percent. The difference between the costs of short-term and long-term debt indicate the return on equity would be highest for the greatest use of long-term debt. Since short-term interest rates are subject to greater swings and greater volatility than the cost of long-term debt, the rate of return on equity fluctuates most widely for the aggressive policy under which short-term debt is used to the greatest degree.

Aside from interest rate fluctuations, there are also other risks for the firm employing a high proportion of short-term debt. When the time comes to renew its debt, general money and capital market conditions may be relatively tight. Then not only might short-term funds cost more, but worse, they might even be unavailable.

Let us consider still other risks of using a high proportion of short-term debt. For convenience, let us refer to the firm that uses a high proportion of short-term debt as Firm S and the firm using the higher proportion of long-term debt as Firm L. In addition to the risk of fluctuating interest charges, Firm S faces another risk vis-a-vis Firm L. Firm S may run into temporary difficulties that prevent it from being able to refund its debt. Remember that when Firm S's debt matures each year, the firm must negotiate new loans with its creditors, paying the going short-term rate. But suppose the loan comes up for renewal at a time when the firm is facing labor problems, a recession in demand for its products, extreme competitive pressures, or some other set of difficulties that has reduced its earnings.

The creditors will look at Firm S's ratios, especially the times-interest-earned and current ratios, to judge its creditworthiness. Firm S's current ratio is, of course,

Table 8.6

The Effect of Maturity Structure of Debt on Return on Equity (millions of dollars)

Part A	Conservative	Middle-ground	Aggressive
Current assets	$ 50.00	$ 50.00	$ 50.00
Fixed assets	50.00	50.00	50.00
Total assets	$100.00	$100.00	$100.00
Short-term credit (@ 7%)	$ --	$ 25.00	$ 50.00
Long-term debt (@ 9%)	50.00	25.00	--
Total debt (debt/assets = 50%)	$ 50.00	$ 50.00	$ 50.00
Equity	50.00	50.00	50.00
Total liabilities and net worth	$100.00	$100.00	$100.00
Earnings before interest and taxes (EBIT)	$ 15.00	$ 15.00	$ 15.00
Less interest	4.50	4.00	3.50
Taxable income	$ 10.50	$ 11.00	$ 11.50
Less taxes (@ 50%)	5.25	5.50	5.75
Earnings on common stock	$ 5.25	$ 5.50	$ 5.75
Rate of return on equity	10.5%	11.0%	11.5%
Current ratio	∞	2:1	1:1
Part B			
Current assets	$ 50.00	$ 50.00	$ 50.00
Fixed assets	50.00	50.00	50.00
Total assets	$100.00	$100.00	$100.00
Short-term credit (@ 15%)	$ --	$ 25.00	$ 50.00
Long-term debt (@ 10%)	50.00	25.00	--
Total debt (debt/assets = 50%)	$ 50.00	$ 50.00	$ 50.00
Equity	50.00	50.00	50.00
Total liabilities and net worth	$100.00	$100.00	$100.00
Earnings before interest and taxes (EBIT)	$15.00	$15.00	$15.00
Less interest	5.00	6.25	7.50
Taxable income	$10.00	$ 8.75	$ 7.50
Less taxes (@ 50%)	5.00	4.375	3.75
Earnings on common stock	$ 5.00	$ 4.375	$ 3.75
Rate of return on equity	10.0%	8.75%	7.5%
Current ratio	∞	2:1	1:1

always lower than that of Firm L, but in good times this is overlooked. If earnings are high, the interest will be well covered and lenders will tolerate a low current ratio. If, however, earnings decline, pulling down the interest coverage ratio, creditors will certainly reevaluate Firm S's creditworthiness. At the very least, because of the perceived increased riskiness of the company, creditors will raise the interest rate charged; at worst, they will refuse to renew the loan. In the latter event, the firm will be forced to raise the funds needed to pay off the loan by selling assets at bargain-basement prices, borrowing from other sources at exorbitant interest rates, or, in the extreme, going bankrupt.

Notice that if the firm follows a conservative policy of using all long-term debt, it need not worry about short-term temporary changes either in the term structure of interest rates or in its own EBIT. Its only concern is with its long-run performance, and its conservative financial structure may permit it to survive in the short run to enjoy better times in the long run.

On balance, many current liabilities arise because of the use of trade credit which is convenient and flexible. Other current liabilities are "spontaneous" accruals. Short-term bank borrowing may have the advantage of flexibility in meeting fluctuating needs for funds and for temporary use as longer-term financing arrangements are being worked out. Long-term debt involves a smaller degree of risk.

Summary

The cash flow cycle is determined by three basic liquidity flow measures. These are the inventory conversion period, the receivables conversion period, and the payments deferral period. The first two indicate how long the firm's funds are tied up, while the third indicates how long the firm uses the funds of suppliers of goods before cash payment is required. Taken together, they indicate the firm's non-spontaneous working capital financing requirements.

Working capital management decisions require an understanding of the term structure of interest rates, which is the relationship between interest rate levels and loan maturity. The expectations theory of the term structure states that current interest rates are an average of expected levels of interest rates in the future. The liquidity preference theory holds that long-term interest rates include a liquidity premium. The higher interest rates on longer-term maturities is said to be compensation to the investor for the loss of flexibility since the funds that are lent are tied up for a longer period of time.

Changes in the economy and in government policies will affect the supply and demand for funds, causing cyclical fluctuations above and below the long-run patterns described. When money market conditions are tight, short-term rates actually may be above long-term rates. When money market conditions are easy or relatively normal, short-term rates will be below long-term rates.

These interest rate relationships have important implications for working capital management. One basic issue is the extent of investment in current assets. This is in part a matter of the analysis of the profitability of investments in the individual asset accounts. Another aspect is the extent to which the firm provides for flexibility in meeting its future financial requirements by investments in marketable securities. Marketable securities are mainly forms of short-term or highly marketable financial instruments. On average we would expect that the return on marketable securities would be lower than the overall average return the firm earns on its business operations. The more cautious the firm is in holding marketable securities for liquidity purposes, the more it costs in terms of earning the firm's overall cost of capital. Thus there is a tradeoff between liquidity and profitability.

In addition, the cost of short-term funds fluctuates more widely than does the cost of long-term funds. If the expectations theory of the term structure holds, on average the cost of short-term funds would be equal to the cost of long-term funds. To the extent that the liquidity premium of the term structure holds, long-term funds will cost more than short-term funds on average.

But greater uncertainty is involved in using short-term financing over long-term financing. If short-term financing matures during a period of tight money conditions, funds may not be available or may be available only under very onerous conditions; so the use of short-term financing also involves a tradeoff. The cost of short-term funds is likely to be lower than the cost of long-term funds on average, but the risks of short-term financing are much greater. In addition, during a sustained period of time in which the monetary and fiscal authorities of the federal government seek to control inflation by limiting the growth rate of the monetary base or money supply, short-term rates may be "abnormally" above long-term rates.

Questions

8.1 How does the seasonal nature of a firm's sales influence the decision about the amount of short-term credit in the financial structure?

8.2 What is your reaction to this statement: Merely increasing the level of current asset holdings does not necessarily reduce the riskiness of the firm. Rather, the composition of the current assets, whether highly liquid or highly illiquid, is the important factor to consider.

8.3 What is the advantage of matching the maturities of assets and liabilities? What are the disadvantages?

8.4 There have been times when the term structure of interest rates has been such that short-term rates were higher than long-term rates. Does this necessarily imply that the best financial policy for a firm is to use all long-term debt and no short-term debt? Explain.

8.5 Assuming a firm's volume of business remained constant, would you expect it to have higher cash balances (demand deposits) during a tight-money period or an easy-money period? Does this situation have any ramifications for federal monetary policy?

Problems

8.1 Suppose that expected future short-term interest rates have the following alternative patterns:

Year	A	B	C	D
1	4%	8%	4%	8%
2	5	7	6	7
3	6	6	15	5
4	7	5	6	7
5	8	4	4	8

a. Using a simple arithmetic average, what is the current rate on a five-year note for each of the four patterns?
b. Using a geometric average, answer the same question as for Part a.
c. Optional:
   1. Calculate the current two-, three-, and four-year note yields using both the arithmetic and geometric averages, and graph the resulting yield curves in four graphs of two curves each.
   2. Is the height of the yield curve based on the arithmetic averages higher or lower than that based on the geometric averages?

8.2 The annual yield on a two-year bond is 11 percent. The yield on a one-year bond of comparable risk is 8 percent. Using the expectations theory, make a forecast of the interest rate on a one-year bond during the second year.

8.3 From the group of yield curves presented below, comment on the behavior of interest rates between January 15, 1980 and January 15, 1981.

Yields on U.S. Governent Securities

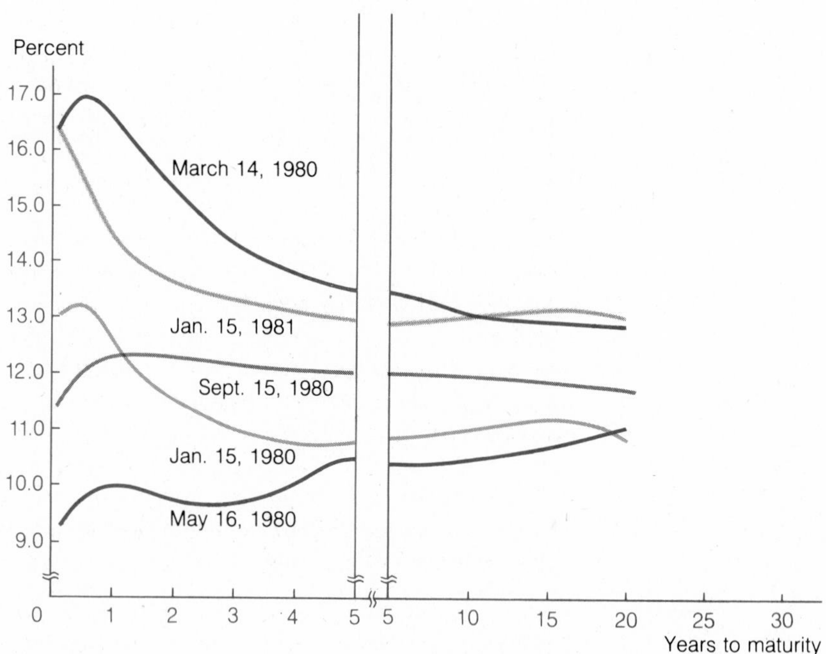

Source: Federal Reserve Bank of St. Louis, *U.S. Financial Data,* Week Ending Feb. 11, 1981.

8.4 From a recent issue of the *Federal Reserve Bulletin* or from another convenient source:

a. Construct a yield curve for the most recent monthly data for U.S. government securities, using money market rates for maturities of one year or less and the capital market rates for constant maturities for the maturities from two to twenty years.
b. Construct a yield curve for the average rates. Comment on any shifts you observe.
c. Next, add to the graph you developed in Part b the yield curve for the latest week available in the source you are using. Comment on any shifts in relation to 1980.
d. Why does the yield curve show only U.S. government security yields instead of including yields on commercial paper and corporate bonds?

8.5 For the Evergreen Bell Company, the average age of accounts receivable is 45 days, the average age of accounts payable is 40 days, and the average age of inventory is 65 days.

a. What is the length of the firm's cash conversion cycle?
b. If Evergreen's annual sales are $918,000, what is the firm's investment in accounts receivable?

8.6 The Warner Flooring Corporation is attempting to determine the optimal level of current assets for the coming year. Management expects sales to increase to approximately $1.2 million as a result of asset expansion presently being undertaken. Fixed assets total $500,000, and the firm wishes to maintain a 60 percent debt ratio. Warner's interest cost is currently 10 percent on both short-term debt and longer-term debt (which the firm uses in its permanent structure). Three alternatives regarding the projected current asset level are available to the firm: (1) an aggressive policy requiring current assets of only 45 percent of projected sales; (2) an average policy of 50 percent of sales in current assets; and (3) a conservative policy requiring current assets of 60 percent of sales. The firm expects to generate earnings before interest and taxes at a rate of 12 percent on total sales.

a. What is the expected return on equity under each current asset level? (Assume a 40 percent tax rate.)
b. In this problem, we have assumed that interest rates and the level of expected sales are independent of current asset policy. Is this a valid assumption?
c. How would the overall riskiness of the firm vary under each policy? Discuss specifically the effect of current asset management on demand, expenses, fixed charge coverage, risk of insolvency, and so on.

8.7 Three companies—Aggressive, Between, and Conservative—have different working capital management policies as implied by their names. For example, Aggressive employs only minimal current assets and finances almost entirely with current liabilities and equity. The "tight-ship" approach has a dual effect. It keeps total assets low, and this tends to increase return on assets. But for reasons such as stock-outs, total sales are reduced; and since inventory is ordered more frequently and in smaller quantities, variable costs are increased.

Condensed balance sheets for the three companies are presented below.

Balance Sheets

	Aggressive	Between	Conservative
Current assets	$150,000	$200,000	$300,000
Fixed assets	200,000	200,000	200,000
Total assets	$350,000	$400,000	$500,000
Current liabilities (at 12%)	$200,000	$100,000	50,000
Long-term debt (at 10%)	0	100,000	200,000
Total debt	$200,000	$200,000	$250,000
Equity	150,000	200,000	250,000
Total claims on assets	$350,000	$400,000	$500,000
Current ratio	0.75:1	2:1	6:1

The cost of goods sold functions for the three firms are as follows:

$$\text{Cost of goods sold} = \text{Fixed costs} + \text{Variable costs}$$

$$\text{Aggressive: Cost of goods sold} = \$200{,}000 + 0.70\ (\text{sales})$$

$$\text{Between: Cost of goods sold} = \$270{,}000 + 0.65\ (\text{sales})$$

$$\text{Conservative: Cost of goods sold} = \$385{,}000 + 0.60\ (\text{sales})$$

Because of the working capital differences, sales for the three firms under different economic conditions are expected to vary as indicated below:

	Aggressive	Between	Conservative
Strong economy	$1,200,000	$1,200,000	$1,200,000
Average economy	900,000	1,000,000	1,150,000
Weak economy	700,000	800,000	1,050,000

a. Make out income statements for each company for strong, average, and weak economies using the following pattern:

Sales
Less cost of goods sold
Earnings before interest and taxes (EBIT)
Less interest expense
Taxable income
Less taxes (at 40%)
Net income

b. Compare the rates of return (EBIT/assets and Return on equity). Which company is best in a strong economy? In an average economy? In a weak economy?

c. What considerations for management of working capital are indicated by this problem?

8.8 Indicate the effects of the transactions listed below on each of the following: total current assets, working capital, current ratio, and net profit. Use "+" to indicate an increase, "−" to indicate a decrease, and "0" to indicate no effect. State necessary assumptions and assume an initial current ratio of more than 1 to 1.

	Total current assets	Working capital[a]	Current ratio	Net profit
1. Cash is acquired through issuance of additional common stock.	______	______	______	______
2. Merchandise is sold for cash.	______	______	______	______
3. Federal income tax due for the previous year is paid.	______	______	______	______
4. A fixed asset is sold for less than book value.	______	______	______	______
5. A fixed asset is sold for more than book value.	______	______	______	______
6. Merchandise is sold on credit.	______	______	______	______
7. Payment is made to trade creditors for previous purchases.	______	______	______	______
8. A cash dividend is declared and paid.	______	______	______	______
9. Cash is obtained through short-term bank loans.	______	______	______	______
10. Short-term notes receivable are sold at a discount.	______	______	______	______
11. A profitable firm increases its fixed assets depreciation allowance account.	______	______	______	______
12. Marketable securities are sold below cost.	______	______	______	______
13. Uncollectable accounts are written off against the allowance account.	______	______	______	______
14. Advances are made to employees.	______	______	______	______
15. Current operating expenses are paid.	______	______	______	______
16. Short-term promissory notes are issued to trade creditors for prior purchases.	______	______	______	______
17. Ten-year notes are issued to pay off accounts payable.	______	______	______	______
18. A wholly depreciated asset is retired.	______	______	______	______
19. Accounts receivable are collected.	______	______	______	______
20. A stock dividend is declared and paid.	______	______	______	______
21. Equipment is purchased with short-term notes.	______	______	______	______
22. The allowance for doubtful accounts is increased.	______	______	______	______
23. Merchandise is purchased on credit.	______	______	______	______
24. The estimated taxes payable are increased.	______	______	______	______

[a] *Working capital* is defined as current assets minus current liabilities.

CHAPTER 9

INVENTORY

MODELS

The conventional sequence of chapters on working capital policy is to start with the most liquid current assets and to move to the least liquid—from cash to inventory management. However, inventory models provide the foundation for the analysis of investments in each type of current asset. It is more natural to begin with inventory models, which will be used in the subsequent analysis of investments in receivables, marketable securities, and then cash.

Inventory

Manufacturing firms generally have three kinds of inventories: (1) raw materials, (2) work in process, and (3) finished goods. The level of *raw materials inventory* is influenced by anticipated production, seasonality of production, reliability of sources of supply, and efficiency of scheduling purchases and production operations. *Work-in-process inventory* is strongly influenced by the length of the production period, which is the time between placing raw material in production and completing the finished product. Inventory turnover can be increased by decreasing the production period. One means of accomplishing this is to improve engineering techniques, thereby speeding up the manufacturing process. Another means is to buy items rather than make them.

The level of *finished goods inventory* is a matter of coordinating production and sales. The financial manager can stimulate sales by changing credit terms or by granting credit to marginal risks. But whether the goods remain on the books as inventories or as receivables, the financial manager has to finance them. Many times, firms find it desirable to make the sale so that they are one step nearer to realizing cash. The potential profits can outweigh the additional collection risk.

Our primary focus in this section is control of investment in inventories. Inventory models, developed as an aid in this task, have proved extremely useful in minimizing inventory costs. As our examination of the du Pont system in Chapter 7 showed, any procedure that can reduce the investment required to generate a given sales volume may have a beneficial effect on the firm's rate of return and hence on the value of the firm.

Determinants of the Size of Inventories

Although wide variations occur, inventory to sales ratios are generally concentrated in the 12 to 20 percent range, and inventory to total assets ratios are concentrated in the 16 to 30 percent range.

The major determinants of investment in inventory are (1) level of sales, (2) length and technical nature of the production processes, and (3) durability versus perishability (the style factors) in the end product. Inventories in the tobacco industry, for example, are large because of the long curing process. Similarly, in the machinery manufacturing industries, inventories are large because of the long work-in-process period. However, inventories are low in coal mining and in oil and gas production because no raw materials are used and the goods in process are small in relation to sales. In the canning industry, average inventories are large because of the seasonality of the raw materials.

With respect to durability and style factors, large inventories are found in the hardware and precious metals industries because durability is great and the style factor is small. Inventories are small in baking because of the perishability of the final product and in printing because the items are manufactured to order.

Within limits set by the economics of a firm's industry, there exists a potential for improvement in inventory control from the use of computers and operations research. Although the techniques are far too diverse and complicated for a complete treatment in this text, the financial manager should be prepared to use the contributions of specialists who have developed effective procedures for minimizing the investment in inventory.

An illustration of the techniques at the practical level is Harris Electronic's inventory system, which works like this: Tabulator cards are inserted in each package of five electronic tubes leaving Harris's warehouse. They are identified by account number, type of merchandise, and price of the units ordered. As the merchandise is sold, the distributor collects the cards and files the replacement order, without any paperwork, by simply sending in the cards.

Western Union Telegraph Company equipment accepts the punched cards and transmits information on them to the warehouse, where it is duplicated on other punched cards. A typical order of 5,000 tubes of varying types can be received in about seventeen minutes, assembled in about ninety minutes, and delivered to Boston's Logan Airport in an additional forty-five minutes. Orders from 3,000 miles away can be delivered within twenty-four hours, a saving of thirteen days (over other methods) in some cases.

Information on the order also goes into a computer, which keeps track of stock-on-hand data for each item. When an order draws the stock down below the *order point*, this triggers action in the production department, where additional units of the item are then manufactured for stock. In the next section, we will examine both the optimal order point and the number of units that should be manufactured—called the *economic ordering quantity* (*EOQ*).

Generality of Inventory Analysis

Managing assets of all kinds is basically an inventory problem; the same method of analysis applies to cash and fixed assets as to inventories themselves. First, a basic stock must be on hand to balance inflows and outflows of the items, the size of the stock depending on the patterns of flows, whether regular or irregular. Second, because the unexpected may always occur, it is necessary to have safety stocks on hand, representing the little extra to avoid the costs of not having enough to meet current needs. Third, additional amounts may be required to meet future growth needs; these are called *anticipation stocks*. Related to anticipation stocks is the recognition that there are optimum purchase sizes, defined as *economic ordering quantities*. In borrowing money, in buying raw materials for production,

Figure 9.1 **Determination of Optimal Investment in Inventory**

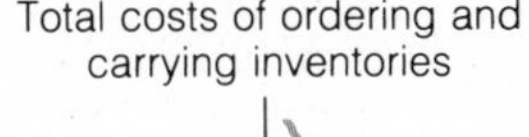

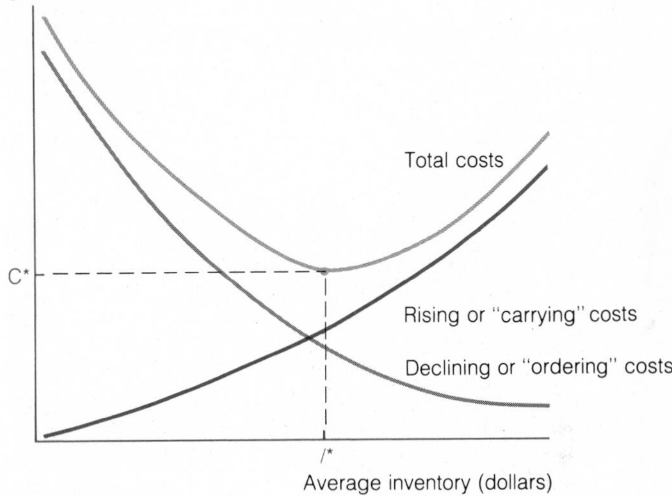

or in purchasing plants and equipment, it is cheaper to buy more than just enough to meet immediate needs.

With the foregoing as a basic foundation, we can develop the theoretical basis for determining the optimal investment in inventory, which is illustrated in Figure 9.1. Some costs rise with larger inventories; among these are warehousing costs, interest on funds tied up in inventories, insurance, and obsolescence. Other costs decline with larger inventories; these include the loss of profits resulting from sales lost because of lack of stock, costs of production interruptions caused by inadequate inventories, and possible purchase discounts.

The costs that decline with higher inventories are designated by the declining curve in Figure 9.1; those that rise with larger inventories are designated by the rising curve. The total costs curve is the total of the rising and declining curves, and it represents the total cost of ordering and holding inventories. At the point where the absolute value of the slope of the rising curve is equal to the absolute value of the slope of the declining curve (that is, where marginal rising costs are equal to marginal declining costs), the total costs curve is at a minimum. This represents the optimum size of investment in inventory.

Inventory Decision Models

The generalized statements in the preceding section can be made much more specific. In fact, it is usually possible to specify the curves shown in Figure 9.1, at least to a reasonable approximation, and actually to find the minimum point on the total costs curve. Since entire courses (in operations research programs) are devoted to inventory control techniques, and since a number of books have been written on the subject, we obviously cannot deal with inventory decision models in a very complete fashion. The model we illustrate, however, is probably the most widely used, even by quite sophisticated firms, and it can be readily expanded to encompass any desired refinements.

The numerical amounts and notation used in our inventory model example are:

A = average inventory = $Q/2$

C = carrying cost expressed as a percentage of inventory purchase price = 25%

CP = carrying cost expressed in dollars per unit of inventory = \$10

EOQ = economic order quantity

F = fixed costs of placing and receiving orders = \$5,400

K = total carrying costs = CPA

N = number of orders placed per year = U/Q

P = purchase price per unit of inventory = \$40

Q = order quantity

R = total ordering costs = $F + VN$

S = safety stock

T = total inventory costs = $K + R = CPA + F + VN$

U = annual usage in units = 3,600

V = variable cost per order of ordering, shipping, and receiving = \$125

This notation is independent of symbols used elsewhere in the book.

Nature of the Problem

Recalling Figure 9.1, we find (1) that some costs associated with inventories decline as inventory holdings increase, (2) that other costs rise, and (3) that the total inventory-associated cost curve has a minimum point. The purpose of the basic inventory model is to locate this minimum and the economic order quantity (EOQ) which will lead to minimum costs. We will assume that the Emerson Company expects to achieve a sales volume of 3,600 widgets during 1981 and that Emerson is quite confident of hitting this target. Further, these sales are expected to be evenly distributed over the year, so inventories will decline smoothly and gradually. Widgets are purchased for \$40 each. No inventory is on hand at the beginning of the year, and none will be held at year's end.

Under these circumstances, the Emerson Company could place one order for Q = 3,600 units at the start of the year. If it did, the average inventory for the year (A) would be equal to

$$A = \frac{Q}{2} = \frac{U}{2} = \frac{3{,}600}{2} = 1{,}800 \text{ units} \tag{9.1}$$

Since widgets cost \$40 each, the average investment in inventories is \$72,000.

Alternatively, Emerson would place two orders for 1,800 each, in which case average inventories would be

$$A = \frac{1{,}800}{2} = 900$$

or four orders of 900 each for an average inventory of 450, and so on. Inventory investment declines correspondingly.

We can see that average inventories are a function of the number of orders placed per year (N). Specifically, when the number of orders placed is incorporated into the calculation, Equation 9.1 becomes

$$A = \frac{U/2}{N} = \frac{U}{2N} = \frac{Q}{2} \tag{9.1a}$$

By ordering more frequently (increasing N), Emerson can reduce its average inventory further and further.

How far should inventory reductions be carried? Smaller inventories involve lower *carrying costs*—cost of capital tied up in inventories, storage costs, insurance, and so on—but, since smaller average inventories imply more frequent orders, they involve higher *ordering costs*. This is the tradeoff inherent in the inventory models.

Classification of Costs

The first step in the process of building an inventory model is to specify those costs that rise and those that decline with higher levels of inventory. Table 9.1 lists some typical costs associated with carrying inventories. The table classifies costs into three categories: those associated with holding inventories, those associated with running short of inventories, and those associated with ordering and receiving inventories.

Table 9.1 **Costs Associated with Inventories**

Carrying costs

1. Cost of capital tied up
2. Storage costs
3. Insurance
4. Property taxes
5. Depreciation and obsolescence

Costs of running short

1. Loss of sales
2. Loss of customer goodwill
3. Disruption of production schedules

Shipping, receiving, and ordering costs

1. Cost of placing order, including production setup costs
2. Shipping and handling costs
3. Quantity discounts lost

Although they may well be the most important element, we shall disregard the second category of costs—the costs of running short—at this point. These costs will be considered at a later stage, when we add "safety stocks" to the inventory model. Also, we shall disregard quantity discounts, although it is easy enough to adjust the basic model to include discounts.[1] The costs that remain for consideration at this stage are carrying costs and ordering costs.

Carrying Costs

Carrying costs generally rise in direct proportion to the average amount of inventory carried, and this is the case with the Emerson Company. For example, Emerson's required rate of return is 14 percent, and depreciation is estimated to amount to 5 percent per year. Adding these to Emerson's other costs of carrying inventory produces a total cost of 25 percent of the investment in inventory. Defining the percentage cost as C, we can, in general, find the total carrying costs as the percentage carrying cost (C) times the price per unit (P) times the average number of units (A):

$$\begin{aligned} K &= \text{total carrying costs} \\ &= CPA \end{aligned} \tag{9.2}$$

If Emerson elects to order only once a year, average inventories will be 3,600/2 = 1,800 units; the cost of carrying the inventory will be

$$0.25 \times \$40 \times 1{,}800 = \$18{,}000.$$

If the company orders twice a year and, hence, has average inventories that are half as large, total carrying costs will decline to $9,000, and so on.

In an unpublished study, the U.S. Department of Commerce estimated that, on the average, manufacturing firms have an annual cost of carrying inventories that equals 25 percent of original inventory cost. This percentage was broken down as follows:

Obsolescence	9.00%
Physical depreciation	5.00
Interest	7.00
Handling	2.50
Property taxes	0.50
Insurance	0.25
Storage	0.75
Total	25.00%

These costs obviously vary from situation to situation, but, with carrying costs of this order of magnitude, inventories deserve careful attention.

Shipping, Receiving, and Ordering Costs

Although carrying costs are entirely variable and rise in direct proportion to the average size of inventories, ordering costs consist of both a fixed and a variable component. The costs of a purchasing and receiving department are both fixed and variable. The personnel and space assigned to purchasing and receiving functions involve costs that are relatively fixed in total amount (F). In our example, this total is estimated to be $5,400. On the other hand, the cost of *placing* an order—interoffice memos, long-distance telephone calls, setting up a production run, and so on—are costs which vary depending on the number of orders. Their total is the

[1] See John F. Magee and Harlan C. Meal, "Inventory Management and Standards," *The Treasurer's Handbook*, J. Fred Weston and Maurice B. Goudzwaard, eds., (Homewood, Ill.: Dow Jones-Irwin, 1976).

cost of placing an order (V) times the number of orders placed (N). The company's per-order cost of ordering, shipping, and receiving, which we define as V, is $125.

Combining these components of ordering costs, we obtain the following equation for R, the total cost of placing and receiving orders:

$$R = F + VN \tag{9.3}$$

Where F = fixed ordering costs

V = cost per unit ordered

N = number of orders placed

To illustrate, if $V = \$125$, $U = 3{,}600$ and $A = 100$. $A = Q/2$, so $Q = 2A$ or 200 and $N = U/Q$ or $3{,}600/200 = 18$. Then R, the total ordering cost, is

$$R = \$5{,}400 + \$125(18) = \$7{,}650$$

Total Inventory Costs

Inventory carrying costs (K), defined in Equation 9.2, and ordering costs (R), defined in Equation 9.3, may be combined to find total inventory costs (T) as follows:

$$T = K + R$$
$$= CPA + F + VN \tag{9.4}$$

Recognizing that $A = Q/2$ and $N = U/Q$, Equation 9.4 may be rewritten as an explicit function of Q:

$$T = CP\left(\frac{Q}{2}\right) + V\left(\frac{U}{Q}\right) + F \tag{9.5}$$

$$= CP\left(\frac{Q}{2}\right) + VUQ^{-1} + F \tag{9.6}$$

Table 9.2

Costs Associated with Inventories Decisions

(1) Q	(2) Safety stock	(3) Average inv. $\left(\frac{Q}{2} + S\right)$	(4) Total carrying cost (K) (CPA)	(5) Fixed ordering cost (F)	(6) Variable ordering cost (VN)	(7) Total ordering cost (5) + (6)	(8) Total inventory cost (4) + (7)
100	0	50	$ 500	$5,400	$4,500	$9,900	$10,400
200	0	100	1,000	5,400	2,250	7,650	8,650
300	0	150	1,500	5,400	1,500	6,900	8,400
400	0	200	2,000	5,400	1,125	6,525	8,525
500	0	250	2,500	5,400	900	6,300	8,800
600	0	300	3,000	5,400	750	6,150	9,150

The pattern of carrying costs, ordering costs, and order size related to the above data is set forth in Table 9.2. The data from Table 9.2 are graphed in Figure 9.2.

Figure 9.2 **Determination of the Optimal Order Size**

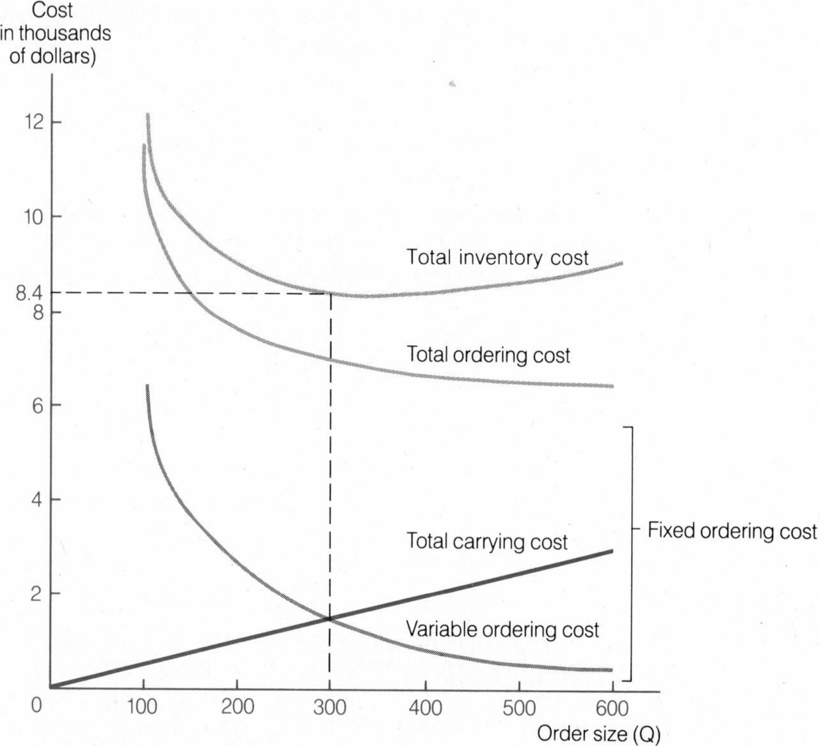

From both the table and figure we can determine the EOQ. We observe that the lowest total cost occurs at a quantity of 300 in Table 9.2. This is also the point at which total costs are at a minimum in Figure 9.2. The EOQ is at the intersection of the total carrying costs and the variable ordering costs.

We can also determine the optimal order quantity algebraically. This is the value of Q (quantity ordered) that minimizes T (total inventory costs). We find this optimal quantity, or the EOQ, by differentiating Equation 9.6 with respect to Q, and setting the derivative equal to zero, to obtain[2] the basic EOQ formula shown in equation 9.7.[2]

$$\text{EOQ} = \sqrt{\frac{2VU}{CP}} \tag{9.7}$$

[2] Proof: differentiate Equation 9.6 with respect to Q and set equal to zero, then solve for Q:

$$\frac{\partial T}{\partial Q} = \frac{CP}{2} - \frac{VU}{Q^2} = 0$$

$$\frac{CP}{2} = \frac{VU}{Q^2}$$

$$Q^2 = \frac{2VU}{CP}$$

$$Q = \sqrt{\frac{2VU}{CP}}$$

In the Emerson case, we find the EOQ to be

$$\begin{aligned} \text{EOQ} &= \sqrt{\frac{2(\$125)(3{,}600)}{(0.25)(\$40)}} \\ &= \sqrt{\frac{\$900{,}000}{\$10}} \\ &= \sqrt{90{,}000} \\ &= 300 \text{ units} \end{aligned}$$

If this quantity is ordered twelve times a year (3,600/300 = 12), or every thirty days, total costs of ordering and carrying inventories, calculated from Equation 9.5, will be:

$$\begin{aligned} T &= CP\left(\frac{Q}{2}\right) + V\left(\frac{U}{Q}\right) + F \\ &= \$10\left(\frac{300}{2}\right) + \$125\left(\frac{3{,}600}{300}\right) + \$5{,}400 \\ &= \$1{,}500 + \$1{,}500 + \$5{,}400 \\ &= \$8{,}400 \end{aligned}$$

That is the lowest possible cost of ordering and carrying the required amount of inventories.

Equation 9.7 gives us the optimum, or cost-minimizing, order quantity for given levels of usage (U), inventory carrying cost (C), and variable cost per order (V). Knowing the EOQ and continuing our assumption of zero beginning and ending inventory balances, we find the optimal average inventory as shown in equation 9.8.[3]

$$A = \frac{\text{EOQ}}{2} = \frac{300}{2} = 150 \qquad \textbf{(9.8)}$$

Emerson will thus have an average inventory investment of 150 units at $40 each, or $6,000.

Relationship between Sales and Inventories

Intuitively, we would suppose that the higher the ordering or processing costs, the less frequently orders should be placed. However, the higher the carrying costs of inventory, the more frequently stocks should be ordered. These two features are incorporated in the formula. Notice also that if Emerson's sales had been estimated at 7,200 units, the EOQ would have been 424, and the average inventory would have been 212 units instead of the 150 called for with sales of 3,600 units. Thus, a doubling of sales leads to less than a doubling of inventories. That is, in fact, a general rule: the EOQ increases with the *square root* of sales, so any increase in sales calls for a less-than-proportionate increase in inventories. The financial manager should keep this in mind when he is establishing standards for inventory control.

[3] If we maintain a "safety stock" of inventory to guard against shipping delays, unexpectedly heavy demand, and so on, then average inventories will be higher by this amount, and inventory costs will be higher by CP times this amount.

Extending the EOQ Model to Include "Safety Stocks"

The EOQ model assumes a predictable sales activity, a constant usage over the year, and an immediate replenishment of inventory stock.

The Emerson Company, with an annual demand of 3,600 units and an EOQ of 300 units, needs to order twelve times each year, or one order every 30 days. If the beginning and ending inventory balances are zero, the maximum inventory will be 300 units with an average of 150 units. The slope of the daily usage line is 10 units.

We can relax the assumption of instantaneous order and delivery. Let us assume Emerson requires 8 days to place an order and receive the delivery. In order not to interrupt its sales activities, Emerson must keep an 8-day stock, or 80 units, on hand whenever it places an order (daily usage × lead time = 10 × 8 = 80). The stock that is required to be on hand at the time of ordering is defined as the *order point*; whenever inventory falls below this point, a new order will be placed.[4] If Emerson's inventory control process is automated, the computer will generate an order when the stock on hand falls to 80 units. The implications of these assumptions are graphed in Figure 9.3.

Figure 9.3 **Demand Forecast with Certainty**

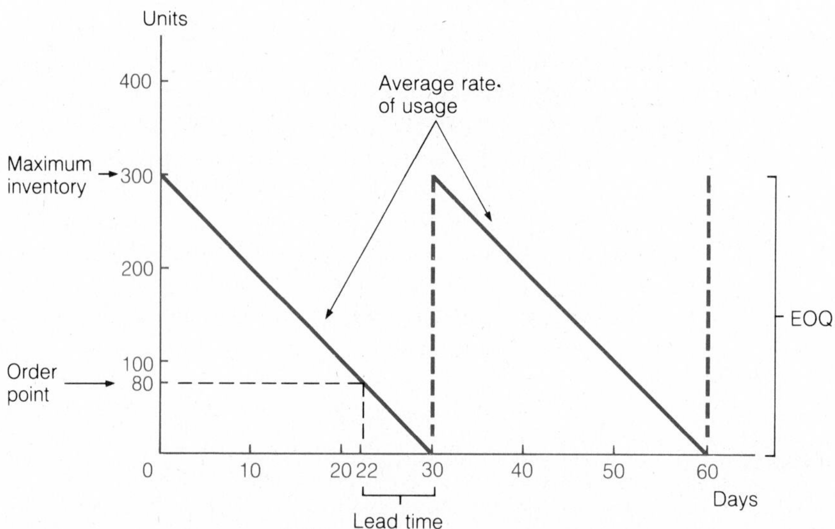

EOQ Model with Uncertainty

To this point we have assumed that usage (demand) is known with certainty and is uniform throughout time, and that the order lead time never varies. Either or both of these assumptions could be incorrect, so it is necessary to modify the

[4] If a new order must be placed before a previous order is received—that is, if the normal delivery lead time is longer than the time between orders—then what might be called a *goods in transit inventory* builds up. This complicates matters somewhat, but the simplest solution to the problem is to deduct goods in transit when calculating the order point. In other words, the order point would be calculated as Order point = Lead time × Daily usage − Goods in transit.

EOQ model to allow for this possibility. This modification generally takes the form of adding a *safety stock* to average inventories.

The amount of safety stock needed depends on the costs of a possible *stock-out* (inventory shortage) and the carrying costs of the additional inventories in the safety stock. At the optimal level of safety stock, the costs of a stock-out equal the costs of carrying additional inventory. Note that the greater the fluctuation in the rate of inventory usage, the greater the risk of a stock-out. Similarly, the greater the variability in the time required to receive deliveries, the greater the risk of a stock-out.

The costs of running out of inventory are important and vary with the nature of the business. For raw materials inventories, the production line will be interrupted if stock-outs occur. For continuous-process manufacturing, such as papermaking, substantial shutdowns and start-up costs would be involved. For finished goods, customer goodwill is lost by the inability to fill orders on schedule. This may cost immediate and future sales as well.

The probability of stock-outs times the estimated costs of stock-outs must be related to the costs of carrying additional inventories. These two influences are balanced in arriving at a decision on the amount of safety stock to carry. We can now consider the effect of safety stock on the EOQ analysis.

Continuing our previous example, let us assume that after evaluation of the factors influencing the size of safety stock, the size of the safety stock is set at 50. The determination of the EOQ with safety stock is illustrated by the materials in Table 9.3 and Figure 9.4.

From both Table 9.3 and Figure 9.4, we see that the EOQ remains at 300 units. The increase in total carrying costs resulting from the addition of a fixed amount for carrying the safety stock of 50 units at $10 per unit does not affect the cost minimizing quantity. The new order point will be (safety stock) plus (usage × lead time) = 50 + 10(8) = 130. When the inventory level hits 130 units, Emerson should reorder.

Note, however, that in Figure 9.4 the low point of the total inventory cost is no longer at the intersection of the variable ordering costs and the total carrying

Table 9.3 **Analysis of Inventory Costs Including Safety Stocks**

(1) Q	(2) Safety stock (S)	(3) Average inv. (A) $\left(\frac{Q}{2}+S\right)$	(4) Total carrying cost (K) (CPA)	(5) Fixed ordering cost (F)	(6) Variable ordering cost (VN)	(7) Total ordering cost (5) + (6)	(8) Total inventory cost (4) + (7)
100	50	100	$1,000	$5,400	$4,500	$9,900	$10,900
200	50	150	1,500	5,400	2,250	7,650	9,150
300	50	200	2,000	5,400	1,500	6,900	8,900
400	50	250	2,500	5,400	1,125	6,525	9,025
500	50	300	3,000	5,400	900	6,300	9,300
600	50	350	3,500	5,400	750	6,150	9,650

Figure 9.4 **Analysis of Inventory Costs with Safety Stocks**

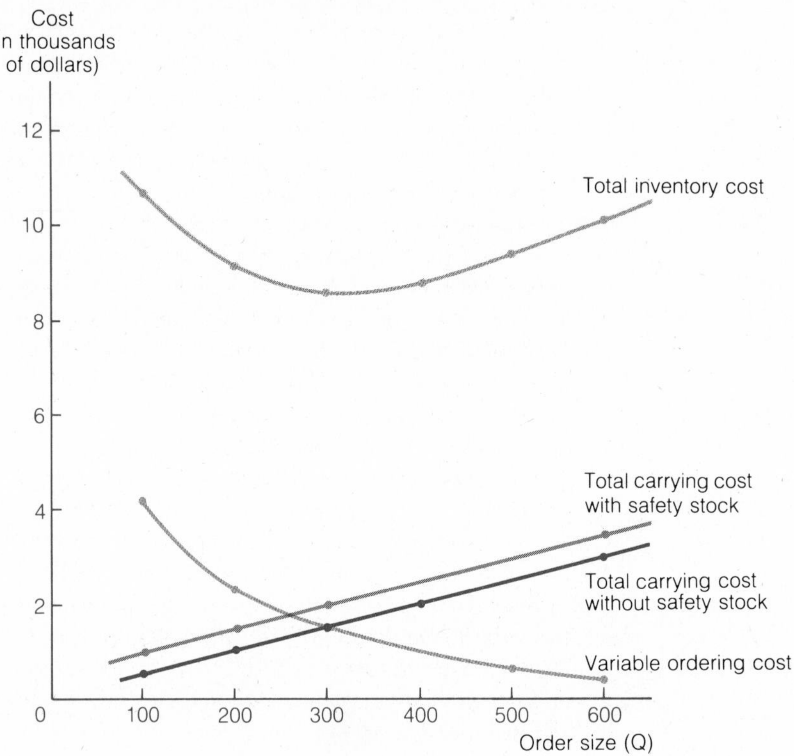

costs. When total carrying cost includes the costs of the safety stock, it lies above the total carrying cost without safety stock. The intersection point between the variable ordering costs and the total carrying costs is now to the left of the low point of the total inventory costs.

Effects of Inflation on EOQ

During inflation, formal models such as the EOQ may lose applicability. As freight costs rise, the cost of placing an order may increase rapidly. Purchase prices may also rise abruptly and repeatedly. Therefore, the values used in the EOQ equation may not remain constant for any appreciable length of time. If so, the optimal order quantity will not remain fixed. Some companies will need greater flexibility in the timing of their orders than that afforded by the "automatic order point." This is because they may be able to buy marginal production at reduced prices. Also, certain companies may stockpile inventories. This takes advantage of the opportunity to purchase supplies before major price increases and provides protection against shortages. Therefore, during periods of inflation and tight money, a firm may need more flexible inventory management as it attempts to take advantage of bargains and provide for future contingencies. The basic logic of the inventory model remains intact: Some costs will rise with larger inventories, and others will fall. Although an optimum is still there to be found, it may change and require repeated findings.

Summary

For a number of reasons, we have introduced the series of chapters on management of current assets with the inventory model. Inventories represent a substantial investment, making up a significant portion of the total assets of most business firms. They also perform an important role in the production cycle through to the sales of the final product.

Because of the great importance of inventory management and control, many new and sophisticated techniques have been developed in recent years. Inventory control usually involves some interaction with computer capability. The details of these new developments are the subject matter of specialized courses and publications. However, the fundamental principles involved in most approaches are illustrated by the economic order quantity (EOQ) framework which is the central focus of this chapter. The economic order quantity analysis illustrates the fundamental tradeoffs involved. Some costs increase by holding smaller quantities; other costs increase as larger quantities are held. The basic inventory model is general in concept and has a broad range of applicability.

Among the tools of inventory control, the economic order quantity provides a useful framework. The EOQ approach itself calls for determining the optimal size order to place on the basis of inventory usage, ordering costs, and carrying costs. In addition, under conditions of uncertainty (fluctuations in inventory use and delivery time) a safety stock must be provided for. The amount of safety stock used will influence the inventory level at which orders are placed, but will not change the EOQ.

The increased turbulence of the economy and the impact of inflation have altered traditional approaches to inventory management and control. Anticipated price changes of raw materials or finished goods may cause a firm to adjust the results provided by an EOQ analysis to take into account the dynamics of changes in the environment. In some situations, changes in the marketing outlook may alter inventory decisions.

Questions

9.1 Explain how a firm can reduce its investment in inventory by having its supplier hold raw materials inventories and its customers hold finished goods inventories. What are the limitations of such a policy?

9.2 What factors are likely to reduce the holdings of inventory in relation to sales in the future? What factors will tend to increase the ratio? What, in your judgment, is the net effect?

9.3 What are the probable effects of the following on inventory holdings?
a. Manufacture of a part formerly purchased from an outside supplier
b. Greater use of air freight
c. Increase, from 7 to 17, in the number of styles produced
d. Large price reductions to your firm from a manufacturer of bathing suits if the suits are purchased in December and January

9.4 Inventory decision models are designed to help minimize the cost of obtaining and carrying inventory. Describe the basic nature of the fundamental inventory control model, discussing specifically the nature of increasing costs, decreasing costs, and total costs. Illustrate your discussion with a graph.

9.5 Explain how the managers of the following departments might be expected to differ in their views of inventory levels for raw materials, work-in-process, and finished goods.

a. Production
b. Purchasing
c. Sales
d. Finance

9.6 The toy business is subject to large seasonal demand fluctuations. What effect would this have on inventory decisions of toy manufacturers and toy retailers?

Problems

9.1 You are given the following information:

Annual demand: 2,800 units
Cost per order placed: $5.25
Carrying cost: 20%
Price per unit: $30

a. Fill in the blanks in the table below.

Order size	35	56	70	140	200	2800
Number of orders	—	—	—	—	—	—
Average inventory	—	—	—	—	—	—
Carrying cost	—	—	—	—	—	—
Order cost	—	—	—	—	—	—
Total cost	—	—	—	—	—	—

b. What is the EOQ?

9.2 The Rosecrans Garden Center sells 90,000 bags of lawn fertilizer annually. Their optimal safety stock (on hand initially) is 1,000 bags. Each bag costs Rosecrans $1.50, inventory carrying costs are 20 percent and the cost of placing an order with its supplier is $15.

a. What is the economic order quantity?
b. What is the maximum inventory of fertilizer?
c. What will their average inventory be?
d. How often will the company order?

9.3 The following relationships for inventory purchase and storage costs have been established for the Kenyon Gyro Corporation.

1. Orders must be placed in multiples of 100 units.
2. Requirements for the year are 200,000 units.
3. The purchase price per unit is $2.50.
4. The carrying cost is 30 percent of the purchase price of goods.
5. The cost per order placed is $30.
6. Desired safety stock is 10,000 units (on hand initially).

7. Two weeks are required for delivery.
   a. What is the most economical order quantity?
   b. What is the optimal number of orders to be placed?
   c. At what inventory level should a reorder be made? (Hint: The inventory level should be sufficient to cover the amount used during delivery, plus the safety stock.)

9.4 The following relationships for inventory purchase and storage costs have been established for the Bradley Tool Corporation.

1. Requirements for the year are 500,000 units. (Use fifty weeks in a year for calculations.)
2. The purchase price per unit is \$0.80.
3. The carrying cost is 25 percent of the purchase price of goods.
4. The cost per order placed is \$45.
5. Desired safety stock is 10,000 units (on hand initially).
6. One week is required for delivery.
   a. What is the most economical order quantity? (Round to the 100s.)
   b. What is the optimal number of orders to be placed?
   c. At what inventory level should a reorder be made?
   d. If annual unit sales double, what is the percent increase in the EOQ? What is the elasticity of EOQ with respect to sales (percent change in EOQ/percent change in sales)?
   e. If the cost per order placed doubles, what is the percent increase in EOQ? What is the elasticity of EOQ with respect to cost per order?
   f. If the carrying cost declines by 50 percent, what is the elasticity of EOQ with respect to the change in carrying cost?
   g. If purchase price declines 50 percent, what is the elasticity of EOQ with respect to the change in purchase price?

CHAPTER 10

CREDIT MANAGEMENT AND POLICY

During a period of continued inflation, the need for external financing increases, as we demonstrated in Chapter 6. One important source of external financing is the normal time lag between when goods are received and when they have to be paid for. For the seller of the goods this results in accounts receivable; for the buyer of the goods this results in accounts payable. The subject is called *trade credit* and is a source of financing for buyers of goods and requires an investment in financing (i.e., represents a use of funds) for the sellers of goods.

With the persistence of inflation and efforts of the government to control inflation by tight monetary policies, interest rates have been high and periodically it is difficult to obtain financing. In these circumstances some firms may delay their payments beyond the normal credit period. For a given level of sales, a longer payment period causes the average collection period to increase and the amount of investment in accounts receivable by the selling firm to increase. Thus one of the consequences of the persistent inflation is to increase the importance of the role of credit and collection policies. In addition, some important new articles on credit policy have increased our understanding of how to analyze credit policy decisions. The subject of accounts receivables management has therefore taken on increased vitality.

Management of Accounts Receivable: Credit Policy

The level of accounts receivable is determined by the volume of credit sales and the average period between sales and collections. The average collection period is dependent partly on economic conditions (during a recession or a period of extremely tight money, for example, customers may be forced to delay payment) and partly on a set of controllable factors—*credit policy variables*. The major policy variables include (1) credit standards—the maximum riskiness of acceptable credit accounts; (2) credit period—the length of time for which credit is granted; (3) discounts given for early payment; and (4) the firm's collection policy. We will discuss each policy variable separately and in qualitative rather than quantitative terms; then we will illustrate the interaction of these elements and discuss the actual establishment of a firm's credit policy.

Credit Standards

If a firm makes credit sales to only the strongest customers, it will have few bad-debt losses. On the other hand, it will probably lose sales, and the profit it forgoes on these lost sales may be far greater than the costs it avoids. Determining the optimal credit standard involves relating the marginal costs of credit to the marginal profits on the increased sales.

Marginal costs include production and selling costs, but abstracting from them at this point we will consider only those costs associated with the "quality" of the marginal accounts, or *credit quality costs*. These costs include (1) default, or bad-debt losses; (2) higher investigation and collection costs; and (3) higher amounts and costs of capital tied up in receivables of less creditworthy accounts (who pay late).

Since credit costs and credit quality are correlated, it is important to be able to judge the quality of an account, and perhaps the best way to do this is in terms of the probability of default. Probability estimates are for the most part subjective; but credit rating is a well-established practice, and a good credit manager can make reasonably accurate judgments of the probability of default by different classes of customers.

Five C's of Credit To evaluate the credit risk, credit managers consider the five C's of credit: character, capacity, capital, collateral, and conditions. *Character* refers to the probability that a customer will try to honor obligations. This factor is of considerable importance because every credit transaction implies a promise to pay. Will the creditor make an honest effort to pay the debts, or is he or she likely to try to get away with something? Experienced credit managers frequently insist that the moral factor is the most important issue in a credit evaluation.

Capacity is a subjective judgment of the customer's ability to pay. It is gauged by the customer's past business performance record, supplemented by physical observation of the plant or store and business methods.

Capital is measured by the general financial position of the firm as indicated by a financial ratio analysis, with special emphasis on the tangible net worth of the enterprise.

Collateral is represented by assets offered by the customer as a pledge for security of the credit extended.

Finally, *conditions* refers to the impact of general economic trends on the firm or to special developments in certain areas of the economy that may affect the customer's ability to meet the obligation.

The five C's of credit represent the factors by which the credit risk is judged. Information on these items is obtained from the firm's previous experience with the customer, supplemented by a well-developed system of information-gathering.

By analyzing the five C's, credit managers try to formulate judgments of the total expected costs of granting credit to an account in relation to the expected increases in net revenues (positive cash flows) from sales produced by the credit extension. There are three main components of the costs of granting credit: (1) expected losses if the firm defaults—probability of default times the expected receivables investment; (2) accounts receivable carrying cost—expected receivables balance, which is proportional to time-to-pay, times the required return; and (3) collection costs—expenses involved in obtaining payment of receivables from the customer. Even if there only is a small probability of default, the prospective buyer may not be granted credit because he is expected to take a long time to pay, which will cause the costs of granting credit to be higher than the benefits.

An individual firm can translate its credit information into risk classes, grouped according to the probability of loss associated with sales to a customer. The combination of rating and supplementary information might lead to the following groupings of probable loss experience.

Risk class number	Probable loss ratio (in percentages)
1	None
2	0–$\frac{1}{2}$
3	Over $\frac{1}{2}$–1
4	Over 1–2
5	Over 2–5
6	Over 5–10
7	Over 10–20
8	Over 20

If the selling firm has a 20 percent margin over the sum of direct operating costs and all delivery and selling costs, and if it is producing at less than full capacity, it may adopt the following credit policies: selling on customary credit terms to groups 1 to 5; selling to groups 6 and 7 under more stringent credit terms, such as cash on delivery; and requiring advance payment from group 8. As long as the bad debt loss ratios are less than 20 percent, the additional sales are contributing something to overhead. However, the opportunity costs of the increased investment in receivables also must be taken into account in the analysis, as will be shown in the examples later in the chapter.

Statistical techniques, especially regression analysis and discriminant analysis, have been used with some success in judging creditworthiness.[1] These methods work best when individual credits are relatively small and a large number of borrowers are involved, as in retail credit, consumer loans, mortgage lending, and the like. As credit-card use and similar procedures build up, as computer use increases, and as credit records on individuals and small firms are developed, statistical techniques promise to become much more important than they are today.[2]

Obtaining Credit Information

In order to develop a file of credit information on each account, a firm's credit department gathers financial information by developing data from a number of sources.

Financial Statements The first step, of course, is to require the credit applicant to file financial statements. If it is a new account, financial statements for the three

[1] Discriminant analysis, discussed in Appendix B to Chapter 5, divides a sample into two or more components on the basis of a set of characteristics. The sample, for instance, might be loan applicants at a consumer loan company. The components into which they are classified might be those likely to make prompt repayment and those likely to default. The characteristics might be whether the applicant owns his or her home, how long the person has been with the current employer, level of income, and so on.

[2] It has been said that the biggest single deterrent to the increased automation of credit processes is George Orwell's classic book, *1984*, in which he described the social dangers of centralized files of information on individuals. Orwell's omnipresent watcher, Big Brother, is mentioned frequently in congressional sessions discussing mass storage of information relevant to credit analysis.

previous years may be requested. Typically the applicant firm will provide audited financial statements. Sometimes the applicant will submit income tax returns in lieu of other statements.

From financial statement data the credit management department can perform a financial ratio analysis of the kind described in Chapter 5. In evaluation of credit for relatively short-term purposes the emphasis is on liquidity, financial stability, debt capacity, and profitability. Continuing financial information is developed on the account by having it update its submission of financial statements on a regular basis. Thus with the aid of computer information systems the trend of the account can be analyzed as well as its relation to composites or standards for the line or lines of business in which it operates.

Credit Information Exchanges Typically credit managers selling to a particular industry will meet periodically to exchange credit experience. These activities may take place as a part of trade association activity or on an informal basis. In addition, credit exchange meetings may be arranged through local, regional, or national credit associations. Sometimes an industry association maintains credit information made available to all subscribing members. Or firms may make discreet inquiries of a prospective customer's other suppliers as to that customer's payment history. The expectation that firms will reciprocate in the exchange of information stimulates their cooperation.

Credit Interchange Bureaus The National Credit Interchange System is a more formal national network of local credit bureaus that exchange credit information on a reciprocal basis. The reports received are more factual than analytical. A fee is charged for each report. In addition, participating firms agree to provide credit information on their customers to their local credit bureau. This is an ongoing process by which general credit information is developed. In addition, private firms have developed compilations of credit bureau information. One supplier of such services is the TRW Corporation.

Dun & Bradstreet Dun & Bradstreet, Inc., provides a number of credit information services. It publishes a reference book with selected information including credit ratings and measures of overall strength for some 3 million firms located in the United States and Canada. The reference books are also available on a regional or state basis. The ratings present a measure of the owners' capital in the firm. Fifteen categories of capital size or financial strength are presented. The largest is $50 million and over; the smallest is under $5,000. The composite credit appraisal uses four numbers: "1" for high, "2" for good, "3" for fair, and "4" for limited. When a firm receives a fair or limited rating, there is something adverse either in its payment practices or in the trend of some key financial relationship such as liquidity or profitability.

When the credit department of the firm requires additional information, it can purchase a Business information Report from Dun & Bradstreet. The report covers the payment practices of the firm, its size measured by sales and net worth, number of employees, its present financial condition, and the trend in its financial condition. In addition, history is provided on the firm and its principal executives. Financial statements, banking relationships, and operating performance are also covered. Information is noted on special developments, changes in the business or business practices, updates of business activities, and any public filings such as lawsuits, tax liens, and judgments.

Information from Banks Another source of credit information is the customer's commercial bank. While the bank cannot disclose account balances and loan balances without the applicant's consent, some general information can be provided. Typically the bank will express the magnitude of the customer's account balance (for example, a "medium six-figure" balance). The extent to which the bank will disclose information will also depend in part on the credit firm's past dealings with the bank, and the personal relationships of the executives involved.

Analysis of Credit Information

The evaluation will start with a relatively standard financial ratio analysis with emphasis on the liquidity, leverage, and profitability ratios. The ratios will be compared to composites for the lines of business in which the firm operates. In addition, the analysis may become even more quantitative by employing some procedures for credit scoring. This represents an extension of the multiple discriminant analysis described in Appendix B to Chapter 5. The time trend analysis of ratios described in Chapter 5 will be particularly emphasized.

In addition to a general financial analysis some specific tests related to credit activity will be performed. Information on the payment practices of the prospective customer will be factored into the analysis. This is done by taking the accounts payable data from the financial statements and calculating an average age of accounts payable. This average payment period can then be used in two comparisons. The first one relates the actual payment period to the terms of credit. For example, if credit terms are net 30 days and the average payment period is 55 days, a slippage of 25 days is involved. The second comparison examines the customer's payment period against the average for its line of business. The average payment period might be 40 days. Continuing the assumption of credit terms of net 30 days, this represents a lag of 10 days as general practice and therefore "normal" in some sense. The additional 15 days beyond the 40 days represents a further "abnormal" lag by this particular customer.

Credit information may be used in a formal scoring and evaluation system. Or quantitative analysis will be combined with qualitative information on the prospective customer. Based on both kinds of information and the experience of the credit manager in dealing with similar situations, a number of decisions can be reached. One decision may be the approval or disapproval of a particular sale on the firm's standard credit terms. Also, a line of credit may be determined for this customer. One rule of thumb for a line of credit is a percentage of the customer's net worth (or "estimated financial strength") related to the number of its major suppliers. For example, if the credit-supplying firm has a general standard of trying to keep total trade credit below 60 percent of the customer's net worth and it is determined that there are four other major suppliers, then the credit limit may be established at no more than 12 percent of the customer's net worth (60% ÷ 5 total suppliers). Or, the figure may be set at 10 percent to provide a margin of safety and for fluctuations in the volume of business among the customer's major suppliers.

Counseling

Credit executives have a substantial positive function in a firm. They are not simply "heavies" whose job it is to bully delinquent accounts. The basic objective of credit management is to add value to the firm by contributing to an optimal amount of profitable sales. It is especially in the evaluation of credit information and in the collections functions that credit managers can perform a valuable role for the firm. If the potential borrower does not meet credit standards, one simple approach is to turn down the order. This could probably be justified by comparing probable gain with probable loss on the order. But in analyzing the applicant's credit information, the credit manager may have identified causes of or factors in the firm's poor financial performance that could alter the credit decision.

Similarly, when payments are delinquent, the temptation is to follow standard collections patterns. These include sending letters of increasing insistence, making phone calls, seeking intervention by the firm's legal department, using outside collection agencies, instigating lawsuits, etc. Such methods may succeed in collecting all or part of the money. But the credit manager's larger objective is to build a broad and increasing base of profitable sales.

A good credit manager will strive to learn the business of his firm's customers as well as (or better than) the executives of those firms. He should seek to keep current on their sales trends, management performance, liquidity, leverage, and profitability. The creative credit manager keeps abreast of all external factors affecting his customers' business and is in continuous communication with the large accounts. He should seek to serve as a valued sounding board for discussions of trends affecting his customers' industries as well as of important policy decisions in the individual firms. He should provide a source of counsel on important policy and decision areas affecting his customers' future well-being. To be sure, these recommendations reflect the ideal and must be compromised with practical considerations of time and cost. But to the degree that these potentials are realized, a credit manager can make an important contribution to his own firm. He can help his customers' businesses expand profitably and he can increase sales volume for his own firm. Thus the credit granting and collection functions can be part of an effective sales activity strategy.

Terms of Credit

The terms of credit specify the period for which credit is extended and the discount, if any, for early payment. For example, if a firm's credit terms to all approved customers are stated as "2/10, net 30," then a 2 percent discount from the stated sales price is granted if payment is made within ten days, and the entire amount is due thirty days from the invoice date if the discount is not taken. If the terms are stated "net 60," this indicates that no discount is offered and that the bill is due and payable sixty days after the invoice date.

If sales are seasonal, a firm may use seasonal dating. Jensen, Inc., a bathing-suit manufacturer, sells on terms of "2/10, net 30, May 1 dating." This means that the effective invoice date is May 1, so the discount can be taken until May 10, or the full amount must be paid on May 30, regardless of when the sale was made. Jensen produces output throughout the year, but retail sales of bathing suits are concentrated in the spring and early summer. Because of its practice of offering seasonal datings, Jensen induces some customers to stock up early, saving Jensen storage costs and also "nailing down sales."

Credit Period Lengthening the credit period stimulates sales, but there is a cost to tying up funds in receivables. For example, if a firm changes its terms from net 30 to net 60, the average receivables for the year may rise from $100,000 to $300,000—the increase caused partly by the longer credit terms and partly by the larger volume of sales. Determining the optimal credit period involves locating the point at which marginal profits on increased sales are exactly offset by the costs of carrying the higher amount of accounts receivable.

Cash Discounts The effect of granting cash discounts can be analyzed similarly. For example, if a firm changes its terms from "net 30" to "2/10, net 30," it may well attract customers who want to take discounts, thereby increasing gross sales. Also, the average collection period will be shortened, as some old customers pay more promptly to take advantage of the discount. Offsetting these benefits is the cost of the discounts taken. The optimal discount is established at the point where costs and benefits are exactly offsetting.

Collection Policy

Collection policy refers to the procedures the firm follows to obtain payment of past-due accounts. For example, it may send a letter to such accounts when they are ten days past due; it may use a more threatening letter, followed by a telephone call, if payment is not received within thirty days; and it may turn the account over to a collection agency after ninety days.

The collection process can be expensive in terms of both out-of-pocket expenditures and lost goodwill, but at least some firmness is needed to prevent an undue lengthening in the collection period and to minimize outright losses. Again, a balance must be struck between the costs and benefits of different collection policies.

Accounts Receivable versus Accounts Payable

Whenever goods are sold on credit, two accounts are created. An asset item called an *account receivable* appears on the books of the selling firm, and a liability item called an *account payable* appears on the books of the purchaser. At this point we are analyzing the transaction from the viewpoint of the seller, so we have concentrated on the type of variables under the seller's control. (In Chapter 12 we will examine the transaction from the viewpoint of the purchaser, discussing accounts payable as a source of funds and considering the cost of these funds vis-à-vis funds obtained from other sources.)

Evaluating Changes in Credit Policy

Changes in credit policy either increase sales and increase some costs, such as greater collection expenses, or decrease sales and decrease some costs, like lower bad-debt losses. A change in credit policy usually involves some additional benefits and some additional costs. The general rule is this: as long as positive benefits exceed costs, make the changes in credit policy. This principle is illustrated in the following examples.

The Wales Linen Company at present has total credit sales of $10 million per year. Its average collection period is 60 days. The current bad-debt loss ratio on these sales is 2 percent. Wales is considering a change in credit standards that would result in an increase in sales of $500,000 with an average collection period of 90 days and a bad-debt loss ratio on these incremental sales of 4 percent (since the new customers have lower financial ratings). Wale's ratio of variable costs to sales is 70 percent, and it can accommodate the incremental sales with existing capacity; for incremental sales, the other net working capital investment requirements are 30 percent of sales. The required rate of return on investment in receivables is 15 percent.

Table 10.1

Evaluating the Effects of a Change in Credit Standards

Part A Incremental investment		
1. Additional sales per day	$500,000/365	$ 1,370
2. Multiplied by average collection period on new sales	× 90	123,300
3. Opportunity costs of investment in receivables	.70(123,300)	86,310
4. Other working capital requirements for the incremental sales	$500,000(.3)	150,000
5. Total incremental investment from lowering credit standards	(3 + 4)	236,310
Part B Incremental profitability		
6. Contribution margin on incremental sales	.3($500,000)	$ 150,000
7. Less: increase in bad-debt losses	.04(500,000)	−20,000
8. Less: cost of funds in incremental investment	.15(236,310)	−35,447
9. Increase in net cash flows	(6 − 7 − 8)	$ 94,553

Table 10.1 analyzes the effects of the changed credit policy on investment profitability. The first issue relates to the measurement of the investment in receivables. If the sales were not made, the variable costs of producing the receivables would not be incurred. Hence, the variable cost ratio is multiplied by the invoice value of the receivables to measure the opportunity costs of investment in receivables. In a subsequent example in which the incremental receivables result from a longer collection period on existing sales, the incremental investment is measured at the full invoice value of the receivables.

Line 4 takes into account other working capital requirements related to the incremental sales. We have developed fully the basis for relating incremental investments to incremental sales in Chapter 6. Following the methodology of that chapter, the increase in sales would produce an increase in other current assets as well as receivables. Fixed assets would not be affected because we have assumed that the firm can handle the incremental sales with existing capacity. From the investment requirements for the other current assets, we deduct the spontaneous financing provided from current liabilities. We have used the estimate that the other net working capital investment requirements are 30 percent of sales.

In Part B, which deals with incremental profitability, we use the contribution margin on incremental sales rather than the net profit ratio. Here, we are measuring the contribution to cash flows from the incremental sales. Hence we do not take fixed costs into account.

Under the assumptions of this example it is profitable to relax the credit standards as described. This result, of course, depends on the data of the case and does not represent a general result.

In considering a change in credit terms, we return to the facts at the beginning of the preceding example, when the Wales firm had total credit sales of $10 million per year, an average collection period of 60 days, and a bad-debt loss ratio of 2 percent. Now Wales is considering a change in credit terms such that sales increase by $500,000, the average collection period increases to 70 days, and the new bad-debt loss ratio which applies to all sales—old and incremental—is 3 percent. Table 10.2 analyzes this change in credit terms.

Table 10.2

Wales Linen Company
Analysis of Changes in Credit Terms

Part A Incremental investment			
1. Old sales per day $10 million /365			$ 27,397
2. Multiplied by increase in average collection period on old sales	× 10		273,970
3. Additional sales per day $500,000/365			1,370
4. Multiplied by average collection period on new sales	× 70		95,900
5. Opportunity costs of investment in receivables .7(95,900)			67,130
6. Other working capital requirements for the incremental sales $500,000(.3)			150,000
7. Total incremental investment from lengthening credit terms (2 + 5 + 6)			491,100
Part B Incremental profitability			
8. Contribution margin on incremental sales .3(500,000)			$ 150,000
9. Bad-debt losses on new total sales	.03($10,500,000)	315,000	
Bad-debt losses on old total sales	.02($10,000,000)	200,000	
Increase in bad-debt losses			−115,000
10. Cost of funds in the incremental investment .15($491,100)			− 73,665
11. Increase in net cash flows (8 − 9 − 10)			($38,665)

The results indicated in Table 10.2 suggest that lengthening the credit terms would be unprofitable. Again, the results reflect the particular assumptions of the example. In Table 10.2 the measurement of the increase in old receivables due to the change in collection period on the old sales was carried at invoice value and not adjusted by the variable cost ratio. The reason is that the alternative is not to make the sales, in which case total cash flows would be decreased by the invoice amount of these sales. However, it will be noted that in lines 3 through 5 the investment in receivables due to the new sales measures the opportunity costs by the variable costs which would not otherwise have been incurred if the new sales had not been made. The logic of the other calculations in Table 10.2 is the same as for those in Table 10.1.

The foregoing examples illustrate the basic concepts involved and the appropriate methodology to employ. The actual implementation of changes in credit policy requires that some very difficult judgments be made, since estimating the changes in sales and costs associated with changes in credit policy involves some uncertainty.

For these reasons, firms usually move slowly toward optimal credit policies. One or two credit variables are changed slightly, the effect of the changes is observed, and a decision is made to change these variables even more or to retract them. Further, different credit policies are appropriate at different times, depending on economic conditions. Thus, credit policy is not a static, once-for-all-time decision. Rather, it is fluid, dynamic, and ever changing in its effort to reach a continually moving optimal target.

The Payments Pattern Approach to Receivables Management

Management of accounts receivable is an important aspect of working capital management for a firm that sells to customers on credit. The rate at which credit sales are converted into cash measures the efficiency of a firm's collection policy and the performance of its collection efforts. Two key issues facing the financial executive in accounts receivable management are the forecasting and control of accounts receivable. This chapter examines two methods widely used by corporations: the Days' Sales Outstanding (DSO) and the Aging Schedule (AS). Then, the discussion focuses on the payments pattern approach, which offers a better means of monitoring accounts receivable.

According to a survey by B. K. Stone, among the companies reporting the use of some systematic procedures to project accounts receivable, a great majority used a pro forma projection of DSO or some other ratio of receivables to a measure of sales.[3] AS is the method used most often in the control of receivables.

Days' Sales Outstanding

The average Days' Sales Outstanding (DSO) at a given time t is usually calculated as the ratio of receivables to a measure of daily sales.

$$\text{DSO}_t = \frac{\text{Total AR}_t}{\text{Daily Sales}}$$

The daily sales are obtained by averaging sales over a certain recent time period. The averaging period may be 30 days, 60 days, 90 days, and so on. Clearly DSO is affected by both the level of sales and the averaging period used.

In Table 10.3, we obtain the end-of-quarter DSO for three different sales patterns using three averaging periods. Total sales for the three quarters are identical; only their monthly distributions vary from quarter to quarter. The figures given in Table 10.3 give a confusing and misleading picture of the collection experience. The collection situation that the credit manager perceives depends on the averaging period selected in the calculation of daily sales. The signals range from deterioration through reasonable stability to improvement in collections. For example, during the third quarter, if the averaging period used is 30 days, DSO presents an alarming situation, whereas the same payment pattern would show an improvement if the averaging period were 90 days.

[3] Stone, B. K. "Payments-Pattern Approach to Forecasting and Control of Accounts Receivable," *Financial Management* 5 (1976), pp. 65–82. See also Lewellen, W. G., and Johnson, R. W. "Better Way to Monitor Accounts Receivable," *Harvard Business Review* 50 (May–June 1972), pp. 101–109.

Table 10.3 **DSO with Varying Sales Pattern and Varying Averaging Periods**

Month	Sales (in thousands)	Total receivables at end of quarter (in thousands)	Daily sales if averaging period is the most recent			End-of-quarter DSO (in days) if averaging period is		
			30 days	60 days	90 days	30 days	60 days	90 days
January	$60	$ 12						
February	60	36						
March	60	54						
		$102	$2	$2	$2	51	51	51
April	$30	$ 6						
May	60	36						
June	90	81						
		$123	$3	$2.50	$2	41	49	62
July	$90	$ 18						
August	60	36						
September	30	27						
		$ 81	$1	$1.50	$2	81	54	41

The Aging Schedule

The Aging Schedule (AS) is the percentage of end-of-quarter accounts receivable that are in different age groups. Here an age group refers to the period of time that receivables have been outstanding from the time of sales.

In Table 10.4 the aging schedules are derived from the same sales and collections data in Table 10.3. One can see from the calculations that the most recent month's sales always dominate the 0–30 days' age group. Consequently, rising sales (in second quarter) give the impression of improved payment experience while falling sales (in third quarter) suggest a worsened collection situation. Thus,

Table 10.4 **Aging Schedules**

Month	Sales (in thousands)	Total Receivables at end of quarter (in thousands)	Age group (in days)	Percent of total
January	$60	$ 12	61–90	12%
February	60	36	31–60	35
March	60	54	0–30	53
		$102		100%
April	$30	$ 6	61–90	5%
May	60	36	31–60	29
June	90	81	0–30	66
		$123		100%
July	$90	$18	61–90	22%
August	60	36	31–60	45
September	30	27	0–30	33
		$81		100%

seasonal variations in sales may send false signals to the credit manager even though the fluctuations are entirely normal. Furthermore, since the age groups are expressed in terms of percentages, an unusually high proportion of rapid payments made on the most recent month's sales results in higher percentages of old receivables although these may be normal in relation to the original sales. For example, in the third quarter, if the receivables from September sales were $10,000 because $20,000 had been paid instead of only $3,000, the proportions of receivables in the 0–30 days, 31–60 days, 61–90 days age groups would have been:

Month	Receivables	Age groups	Percent of total
July	$18	61–90	28%
August	36	31–60	56
September	10	0–30	16
	$64		100%

In this example, the exceptionally high collections on September sales (which are favorable to the firm) may actually communicate an erroneous signal to management that the aging schedule has deteriorated.

Thus the DSO and AS procedures may be unreliable in the forecasting and control of accounts receivable. The major deficiency of each method lies in its aggregation of sales and accounts receivable over a particular time period (a quarter in the above example). The payments pattern approach seeks to overcome these difficulties.

The Payments Pattern Methodology

A (monthly) payment pattern is defined by the proportions of credit sales in a given month that are paid in that month and in subsequent months. Table 10.5 gives the monthly cash flows and accounts receivable arising from $60,000 of credit sales in January. The payment pattern is given in the last column: 10 percent of January sales are paid during the month of sale, leaving 90 percent of sales in accounts receivable; in February, payment on January sales amounts to 30 percent of sales, leaving 60 percent of sales in accounts receivable; and so on until January sales are completely paid. A graphical representation of the payment pattern is given in Figure 10.1; the dotted rectangles and shaded rectangles represent respectively the accounts receivable proportions and the accumulated paid proportions of January sales at different points in time.

Table 10.5

Payment Pattern of $60,000 of Credit Sales in January

Month	Collections from January sales during month (in thousands)	Receivables from January sales outstanding at end of month (in thousands)	Receivables pattern (%)	Payment pattern (%)
January	$ 6	$54	90	10
February	18	36	60	30
March	24	12	20	40
April	12	0	0	20

Figure 10.1 **Graph of Payment Pattern for January Credit Sales**

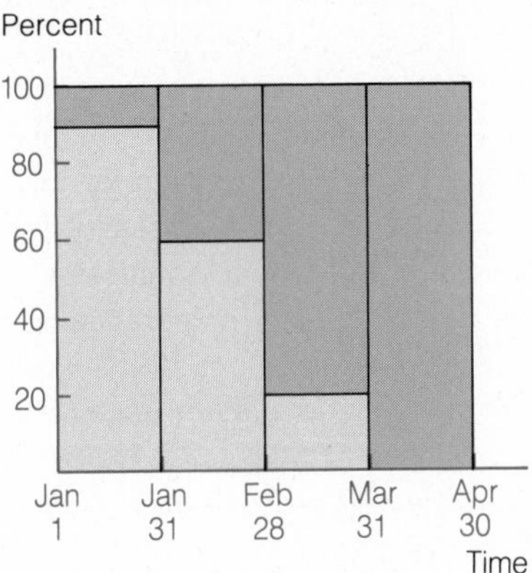

When the payment pattern remains the same in terms of percents collected and percents of original sales outstanding in various months, it is said to be constant. For example, using the same data as in Table 10.5, we observe a constant payment pattern (.1, .3, .4, .2)—these are the proportions paid in the month sales are made and in the three subsequent months—and consequently a constant accounts receivable pattern (.9, .6, .2)—in the same three subsequent months—as exhibited in Table 10.6.

In the payments pattern approach, accounts receivable are related to sales in the month of origin. As a consequence, the payments pattern approach, in contrast to DSO and AS, is not sales dependent. No matter what the sales pattern may be, the last column in Table 10.6 remains unchanged provided the payment pattern

Table 10.6 **Accounts Receivable as Percentages of Original Sales**

Month of origin	Sales during that month (in thousands)	Receivables at end of quarter (in thousands)	Percentage outstanding (receivables/sales in month of origin) (%)
January	$60	$ 12	20 (end of 3 months)
February	60	36	60 (end of 2 months)
March	60	54	90 (end of 1 month)
		$102	
April	$30	$ 6	20
May	60	36	60
June	90	81	90
		$123	
July	$90	$18	20
August	60	36	60
September	30	27	90
		$81	

is constant. Conversely, any change in payment behavior would be immediately reflected and recognized. Thus, the payment proportions and the balance proportions provide an efficient means of control for the credit manager. For example, assume that a firm's accounts receivable pattern was historically (.9, .6, .2). In early March, assume that the report on actual payments for January and February credit sales showed a current balance fraction for January sales of 0.70 versus the pro forma value of 0.60 and a balance fraction for February sales of 0.95 versus the pro forma value of 0.90. Because of two consecutive adverse and large deviations from the normal pattern, a problem is indicated.

The emphasis of the payments pattern approach is to relate receivables to the percent of sales of the given month. Control standards are developed from the percentages based on the payments pattern and corresponding receivables pattern.[4] The procedures proposed by Michael D. Carpenter and Jack E. Miller build upon the payments pattern concept to develop some additional evaluation relations. The key measure is the weighted DSO (WDSO). The changes in the WDSO or changes in the average daily sales (ADS) with the WDSO of the previous reference period enable Carpenter and Miller to calculate efficiency and volume variances in receivables. The resulting data enable the receivables manager to separate changes in collection experience from changes in sales patterns. He is thus better able to evaluate the current state of collections and receivables investment. Since he can distinguish between changes in credit experience and in sales volume, the credit manager can plan to work on changing collection performance or to alter the credit-related variables that influence the volume of sales. Or the changes in investments in receivables may guide the credit manager to arrange for changes in the required amount of financing.

Use of Computers in Credit Management

By nature credit management lends itself to the use of computer controls. Credit management involves the collection, compilation, storage, analysis, and retrieval of information. Since accurate information and fund flows are critical to good credit management, efficient information processing is important.

All of the accounts receivable materials can be organized into a computer record system giving the credit manager current information on the status of accounts. Records will include the date the account was opened, the amount currently owed, the customer's maximum credit line, and a record of the customer's past payments. The credit rating assigned to the customer by Dun & Bradstreet or other rating agencies can be noted. Periodically, the credit manager may draw off various types of analyses of the customer accounts. These may include the days' sales outstanding, the aging schedule, and a payments pattern analysis as described.

In addition, particular controls can be set up to monitor account delinquency. The computer can periodically flag past-due accounts for the credit manager's attention. The computer may be programmed to provide information on how close the account balance is to the established maximum line of credit. Such information

[4] Carpenter, Michael D., and Miller, Jack E. "A Reliable Framework for Monitoring Accounts Receivable," *Financial Management* 8 (Winter 1979), pp. 37–40.

provides the credit manager with the opportunity to contact the customer on a timely basis.

Indeed, the computer can be programmed to perform selected credit decisions. Based on credit limits set in advance, credit standards can be expressed quantitatively, and the computer can approve or reject credit applications, or flag them for further analysis. Aided by a computer, a relatively small staff can manage a greatly increased volume of credit activity.

In addition to information on individual accounts, the computer can provide the credit manager with information on groups of companies. Periodically, the credit manager may receive a summary of all receivable accounts with respect to each account individually and in total. Information can be provided on billings, payments, discounts taken, and amounts owed. In addition, the computer can prepare special reports to provide analytical information that may be useful in making credit decisions. For example, the payment history of companies in the same industry may be compared. Do companies in a particular industry tend to pay slowly during certain months of the year? If this appears to be a trend, the credit manager should analyze the economic factors that cause firms in a particular industry to respond in similar ways. On the other hand, if a customer performs differently from most firms in the industry, the credit manager can examine the circumstances behind that firm's behavior. The credit manager may also analyze any management or operating problems that may be developing in a firm, before the problems escalate, making the account a serious credit risk.

Using a computer increases both the amount and frequency of information available to the credit manager. This information facilitates interaction with the customer and enables the credit management department to communicate promptly and effectively with other divisions in its own company as well as with general management. Thus, the effectiveness of the credit department has been greatly enhanced by making feasible computer-generated information flows which otherwise would be too expensive and time consuming to develop.

Summary

Investment in accounts receivable is dependent on sales and on the firm's credit policy. The firm's credit policy, in turn, involves four controllable variables: credit standards, the length of the credit period, cash discounts, and collection policy. The significant aspect of credit policy is its effect on sales. A stringent policy will reduce bad-debt losses, but the profit forfeited on lost sales may be greater than the savings. An easy policy stimulates sales but involves costs of capital tied up in increased receivables, bad debts, discounts, and higher collection costs. The optimal credit policy is one in which marginal costs of credit are just offset by marginal profits on the increased sales.

In the evaluation of credit risk, a credit manager considers the five C's of credit: character, capacity, capital, collateral, and conditions. Based on internally developed information on the debtor's financial condition and payment history, and on external sources such as banks, credit associations, and credit-rating agencies (notably Dun & Bradstreet), the credit manager categorizes firms into risk classes based on probable loss experience. By relating this classification to the firm's gross profit margin, credit policies can be formulated for each risk class.

The balancing of costs and benefits applies to all aspects of credit management. Lengthening the credit period will stimulate sales, but also increase the amount of receivables to be financed. Increased cash discounts will speed collections but reduce receipts by the discounts taken. A tough collection policy to minimize past-due accounts may reduce bad-debt losses, but will involve expense in terms of both out-of-pocket expenditures and lost goodwill.

The creative credit manager will be well informed regarding the financial condition of his customers and may be able to act as a counselor in preventing or solving problems in the customer's business before they have an adverse effect on his credit standing.

The analysis of a change in credit policy involves quantifying its effects on both old and new customers to compare the incremental costs and incremental profits which are likely to result. By adjusting the variables and observing the effects, a firm moves toward the optimal credit policy appropriate to the economic conditions.

Two methods widely used by financial executives in the forecasting and control of accounts receivable are the Days' Sales Outstanding (DSO) and the Aging Schedule (AS). Both involve the aggregation of sales and accounts receivable over a particular time period and can result in misleading signals in the case of seasonal sales variations or an abnormal collection policy. The payments pattern approach enables the credit manager to monitor changes in the payment behavior by matching accounts receivable to sales in the month of origin. Changes in credit experience are thus separated from changes in sales volume. By examining changes in the payment and receivables balance proportions over time, the credit manager can better evaluate the current state of collections and receivables management.

Because of its needs for information analysis, storage, and retrieval, credit management is well suited to the use of computer controls. The effectiveness of a credit department can be greatly enhanced by the computer's ability to generate periodic reports and analyses, to monitor account performance, and even to make basic credit decisions.

Questions

10.1 Assume that a firm sells on terms of net 30 and that its accounts are, on the average, thirty days overdue. What will its investment in receivables be if its annual credit sales are approximately $720,000?

10.2 Evaluate this statement: It is difficult to judge the performance of many of our employees but not that of the credit manager. If the credit manager is performing perfectly, credit losses are zero; the higher our losses (as a percent of sales), the worse the performance.

10.3 Apco Corporation's 1981 sales were $990,000. In April 1981, the accounts receivable balance was $41,250; by July 1981, accounts receivable had more than doubled to $96,250. Calculate the Days' Sales Outstanding for each period. Did the increase necessarily represent a problem for Apco?

10.4 How would a new business go about setting up credit standards? Would its credit policies be likely to vary from those of established firms in the same line of business?

10.5 Explain how the credit terms of a firm's suppliers can affect the terms offered to the firm's customers.

Problems

10.1 Milburn Auto Parts is considering changing its credit terms from 2/10, net 30 to 3/15, net 30 in order to speed collections. At present, 60 percent of Milburn's customers take the 2 percent discount. Under the new terms, this number is expected to rise to 70 percent, reducing the average collection period from 22 to 18 days. Because the change does not involve a relaxation of credit standards, bad-debt losses are not expected to rise above their present 2 percent level. However, the more generous cash discount terms are expected to increase credit sales from $900,000 to $1,000,000 per year. Milburn's variable cost ratio is 80 percent, and its cost of accounts receivable is 15 percent.

a. What is the increase in gross profits?

b. What is the increase in discount costs?

c. What is the average balance in accounts receivable before and after the change?

d. What is the change in the cost of accounts receivable?

e. Evaluate the change.

10.2 Valley Distributors makes all sales on a credit basis. Once a year it routinely evaluates the creditworthiness of all its customers. The evaluation procedure ranks customers from 1 to 5, in order of increasing risk. Results of the ranking are as follows:

Category	Percentage of bad debts	Average collection period (days)	Credit decision	Annual sales lost due to credit restrictions
1	None	10	Unlimited credit	None
2	1.0	12	Unlimited credit	None
3	3.0	20	Limited credit	$360,000
4	9.0	60	Limited credit	$180,000
5	16.0	90	No credit	$720,000

The variable cost ratio is 75 percent. The ratio of net other working capital investment to sales is 40 percent. The opportunity cost of investment in receivables is 15 percent. What will be the effect on profitability of extending unlimited credit to each of the categories 3, 4, and 5?

10.3 Charles Roberts, the new credit manager of the Baskin Corporation, was alarmed to find that Baskin sells on credit terms of net 90 days, when industry-wide credit terms are net 30 days. On annual credit sales of $2,500,000 Baskin currently averages 95 days' sales in accounts receivable. Roberts estimates that tightening the credit terms to 30 days will reduce annual sales to $2,375,000, but that accounts receivable will drop to 35 days of sales, and that the savings on investment in accounts receivable should more than overcome any loss in profit.

Baskin's variable cost ratio is 85 percent, and the ratio of net other working capital investment to sales is 35 percent. If Baskin's opportunity cost of funds is 18 percent, should the change be made?

10.4 The Kenwood Corporation began doing business on January 1, 1981. Sales and end-of-quarter receivables for the first quarter are given below:

	Sales	End-of-quarter receivables
January	$20,000	$ 1,000
February	35,000	7,000
March	32,000	24,000
		$32,000

a. Calculate daily sales as of March 31, 1981, if the averaging period is the most recent 30, 60, and 90 days. (Assume 30 days per month.)

b. Calculate the end-of-quarter days' sales outstanding (DSO) if the averaging period is the most recent 30, 60, and 90 days. (Assume 30 days per month.)

c. The payment pattern on Kenwood's accounts receivable is constant at 0.25, 0.55, 0.15, 0.5. Prepare a schedule showing each month's collections and outstanding receivables through June 30, 1981 based on first quarter sales.

d. What is Kenwood's accounts receivable pattern?

e. Assuming that no sales are made after March 31, 1981, what will the accounts receivable balance be on April 30? On May 31?

f. Prepare aging schedules as of February 28, March 31, and April 30.

10.5 The Bickleigh Corporation has annual credit sales of $1,600,000. Current expenses for the collection department are $35,000, bad-debt losses are 1.5 percent, and the average collection period is 30 days. Bickleigh is considering easing its collection efforts such that collection expense will be reduced to $22,000 per year. The change is expected to increase bad-debt losses to 2.5 percent and to increase the average collection period to 45 days. In addition, sales are expected to increase to $1,625,000 per year.

Should Bickleigh relax collection efforts if the opportunity cost of funds is 16 percent, the variable cost ratio is 75 percent and the ratio of net other working capital investment to sales is 35 percent?

10.6 The Cranmere Company has annual credit sales of $3.9 million. Its average collection period is 30 days with a bad-debt loss ratio of 1 percent. Because persistent inflation has eroded the credit position of many of its customers, Cranmere is considering a reduction of its credit standards. As a result, incremental sales are expected to be $400,000, on which the average collection period would be 60 days and on which the bad-debt loss ratio would be 3 percent. The variable cost ratio to sales for Cranmere is 70 percent. The ratio of other net working capital requirements to sales is 25 percent. The required return on investment in receivables is 15 percent.

Evaluate the relaxation in credit standards Cranmere is planning.

10.7 Instead of relaxing credit standards, Cranmere is considering simply lengthening credit terms from net 20 to net 50, a procedure that would increase the average collection period from 30 to 60 days. Under this policy, Cranmere expects incremental sales to be $500,000. The bad-debt loss ratio will remain at 1, to rise to 3 percent on *all* sales. Assume all other returns hold. Evaluate the lengthening of credit terms Cranmere is considering.

CHAPTER 11

CASH AND MARKETABLE SECURITIES MANAGEMENT

Cash management has taken on increased importance in recent years. The generally higher level of interest rates has made the efficient management of cash more important. Recall that except for the temporary drop in short-term interest rates during May and June of 1980, the returns on short-term investments have been mostly in the 15 to 18% range since 1979. Cash assets are simply more valuable than they used to be. Financial managers have therefore developed new techniques of cash-gathering and disbursing systems to try to optimize the availability of funds and to reduce the interest costs of outside financing.

In addition, changing market characteristics and technologies present new environmental conditions, which an efficient cash management system must respond to. The changing market characteristics include shifts in the scale and sources of remittances; changes in the amount and conditions of cash discounts; changing services payments and charges by commercial banks; and the increasing international scope of business operations requiring the integration into cash management of the divisions operating in foreign countries. Changes have also occurred in the regulations of the Federal Reserve System.

Technological developments also require a reassessment of cash management procedures. Of greatest importance have been developments in the cost-efficiency of using high-speed information transmission systems and the use of the computer. One manifestation of these developments has been the growth of electronic funds transfer systems (EFTS). All these developments have influenced the nature of the cash management functions described in this chapter.

The Cash Management Function

Since liquid assets generally yield less than the average return of the firm, one issue in cash management is the risk-return tradeoff involved in determining the amount of liquid assets a firm will hold. Another issue is the division of the holdings in liquid assets between cash and marketable securities. The cash management function includes analysis of the investment in cash and marketable securities, the nature of efficient cash-gathering and disbursement systems, cash management models, and management of the investment in marketable securities.

Reasons for Holding Cash and Marketable Securities

Businesses (and individuals) have four primary reasons for holding cash: (1) the transactions motive, (2) the precautionary motive, (3) the speculative motive, and (4) compensating balance requirements.

Transactions Motive The transactions motive for holding cash is to enable the firm to conduct its ordinary business—making purchases and sales. In lines of business where billings can be cycled throughout the month (such as the utilities) cash inflows can be scheduled and synchronized with the need for the cash outflows. We expect the cash-to-revenues ratio and cash-to-total-assets ratio for such firms to be relatively low. In retail trade, by contrast, sales are more random, and a number of transactions may actually be conducted with physical currency. As a consequence, retail trade requires a higher ratio of cash to sales and of cash to total assets.

The seasonality of a business may give rise to a need for cash to purchase inventories. For example, raw materials may be available only during a harvest season and may be perishable, as in the food-canning business. Or sales may be seasonal, as they are in department stores (with peaks around the Christmas and Easter holidays), giving rise to an increase in cash needs.

Precautionary Motive The precautionary motive for holding cash relates primarily to the predictability of cash inflows and outflows. If the predictability is high, less cash need be held against an emergency or any other contingency. Another factor that strongly influences the precautionary motive is the ability to borrow additional cash on short notice. Borrowing flexibility is primarily a matter of the strength of the firm's relationships with banking institutions and other credit sources. The need for holding cash is satisfied in large part by having near-money assets such as short-term government securities.

Speculative Motive The speculative motive for holding cash is to enable the firm to accept profit-making opportunities that may arise. By and large, business accumulation of cash for speculative purposes is not widely found. Such accumulation is more common among individual investors.

Compensating Balance Requirements The commercial banking system performs many functions for business firms. Business firms pay for these services in part by direct fees and sometimes in part by maintaining compensating balances at the bank. Compensating balances represent the minimum levels that the firm agrees to maintain in its checking account with the bank. With this assurance, the bank can loan such funds on a longer basis, earning a return. This represents an indirect fee to the bank, and a fourth reason why a firm holds cash.

Specific Advantages of Adequate Cash

In addition to these general motives, sound working capital management requires maintenance of an ample amount of cash for several specific reasons:

1. It is essential that the firm have sufficient cash to take trade discounts. The payment schedule for purchases is referred to as the *term of the sale*. A commonly encountered billing procedure, or *term of trade*, is that of a 2 percent discount on a bill paid within ten days, with full payment required in thirty days regardless of whether the discount is taken. (This is usually stated as 2/10, net 30.) Since the net amount is due in thirty days, failure to take the discount means paying the extra 2 percent for using the money an additional twenty days. The following equation can be used for calculating

the cost, on an annual basis, of not taking discounts:[1]

$$\text{Cost} = \frac{\text{Discount percent}}{(100 - \text{Discount percent})} \times \frac{360}{(\text{Final due date} - \text{Discount period})}$$

The denominator in the first term (100 − Discount percent) equals the funds made available by not taking the discount. To illustrate, the cost of not taking a discount when the terms are 2/10, net 30 is computed:

$$\text{Cost} = \frac{2}{98} \times \frac{360}{20} = 0.0204 \times 18 = 36.72\%$$

This represents an annual interest rate of almost 37 percent. Most firms' cost of capital is substantially lower than 37 percent.

2. Since the current and acid test ratios are key items in credit analysis, it is essential that the firm, in order to maintain its credit standing, meet the standards of the line of business in which it is engaged. A strong credit standing enables the firm to purchase goods from trade suppliers on favorable terms and to maintain its line of credit with banks and other credit sources.
3. Ample cash is useful for taking advantage of favorable business opportunities, such as special offers from suppliers, that may come along from time to time.
4. The firm should have sufficient liquidity to meet emergencies, such as strikes, fires, or marketing campaigns of competitors.

Using the knowledge about the general nature of cash flows presented in Chapter 8, financial managers may be able to improve the inflow-outflow pattern of cash. They can do so by better synchronization of flows and by reduction of float, explained in the following sections.

Synchronization of Cash Flows

An example of synchronization demonstrates how cash flows can be improved through more frequent requisitioning of funds by divisional offices from the firm's central office. Some Gulf Oil Corporation divisional field offices, for instance, formerly requisitioned funds once a week; now the treasurer's office insists on daily requisitions, thus keeping cash on tap as long as four days more. On the basis of twenty offices, each requiring $1 million a week, the staggered requisitions free the equivalent of $40 million for one day each week. At 10 percent interest, this earns almost $570,000 a year.

[1] With daily compounding and 365 days in a year, the cost would be approximately the same:

$$P(.98)\left(1 + \frac{r}{365}\right)^{(20/365)(365)} = P$$

$$(.98)\left(1 + \frac{r}{365}\right)^{20} = 1$$

$$\left(1 + \frac{r}{365}\right)^{20} = \frac{1}{.98}$$

$$1 + \frac{r}{365} = (1.020408)^{1/20}$$

$$r = 36.89\%$$

Moreover, effective forecasting can reduce the firm's investment in cash. The cash flow forecasting at CIT Credit Corporation illustrates this idea. An assistant treasurer forecasts planned purchases of automobiles by the dealers. He estimates daily the number of cars shipped to the 10,000 dealers who finance their purchases through CIT. He then estimates how much money should be deposited in Detroit banks that day to pay automobile manufacturers. On one day he estimated a required deposit of $6.4 million; the actual bill for the day was $6.397 million, a difference of 0.05 percent. Although every firm cannot achieve such close forecasting, the system enables CIT to economize on the amount of money it must borrow and thereby keeps interest expense to a minimum. Hence the central importance of cash budgeting as a part of cash forecasting (discussed previously in Chapter 7) is demonstrated.

Managing the Firm's Cash Flows

Two major aspects of managing a firm's cash flows involve a cash-gathering system and the control of disbursements. The firm must consider both aspects of cash collections since it is both a seller and a buyer of goods. The lags which may favor it as a buyer of goods will work against the firm as a seller of goods. Float is the time lag while funds are in transit. Float is the interval between a buyer of goods writing a check and the point at which the seller has the use of the funds. A number of factors give rise to float.

Sources of Float

Whenever a customer mails a check, some amount of time passes before the check is received by the seller. This is called *mail-time float.* After the firm receives the check, processing time is involved in crediting the customer's account and in getting the check into the banking system. This kind of time lag is called *processing float.* A third type of lag, related to the clearing time within the banking system, is called *transit float.* The seller's bank may use the Federal Reserve System or a local clearinghouse for clearing its checks. The banks and clearinghouse mechanisms involved may have an availability schedule for checks involving specified distances, etc. The time required by the system to communicate the information needed to clear the checks may be longer or shorter than the availability schedule. Thus *availability time* may differ from *clear time.*

Considerable progress has been made by business firms and the banking system in an attempt to manage the clearing process efficiently. The development of an efficient cash-gathering system requires decisions with respect to (1) collection points, (2) bank-gathering systems, and (3) alternative methods of transferring funds.

Decentralized Collections

Mail-time float can be reduced by decentralizing collection points close to the location of the customer. For example, a sportshirt manufacturer in Los Angeles sells to customers throughout the United States. A check from a customer on the East Coast would take three to four days to reach the manufacturer in Los Angeles. The seller can process payments more rapidly by setting up collection points on the East Coast as well as in other areas where sales are made.

Field collections Since the firm is likely to have field sales offices in the major regions in which it sells, it can provide for direct collection by these units. As payments are received by the field office, they are recorded and deposited in a local bank (a field depository bank). Since the local offices are close to the customer, mail-time float is reduced.

Lockbox systems In a lockbox system, the selling firm directs its customers to mail payments to a post office box in a specified city. The firm arranges for a local bank to collect checks from the box, sometimes several times a day, and to deposit the checks to the firm's account. The bank begins the clearing process and notifies the firm that a check has been received. In this way the clearing process begins before the firm actually receives the check, reducing processing float. The bank charges the receiving firm for the services rendered. To determine whether a lockbox system is advantageous, the firm will compare the bank fees against the gains from reducing float.

Bank-Gathering System

Several categories of banks are used when a firm gathers cash. The general relationships are illustrated in Figure 11.1 for local depository banks, regional concentration banks, and a central bank. *Local depository banks* are those into which field collections are channeled. They are not necessarily limited to cities in which the firm has sales offices. A *regional concentration bank* is one to which a firm seeks to channel funds to have them available for disbursements. Firms usually

Figure 11.1

Cash-Gathering System of a National Company

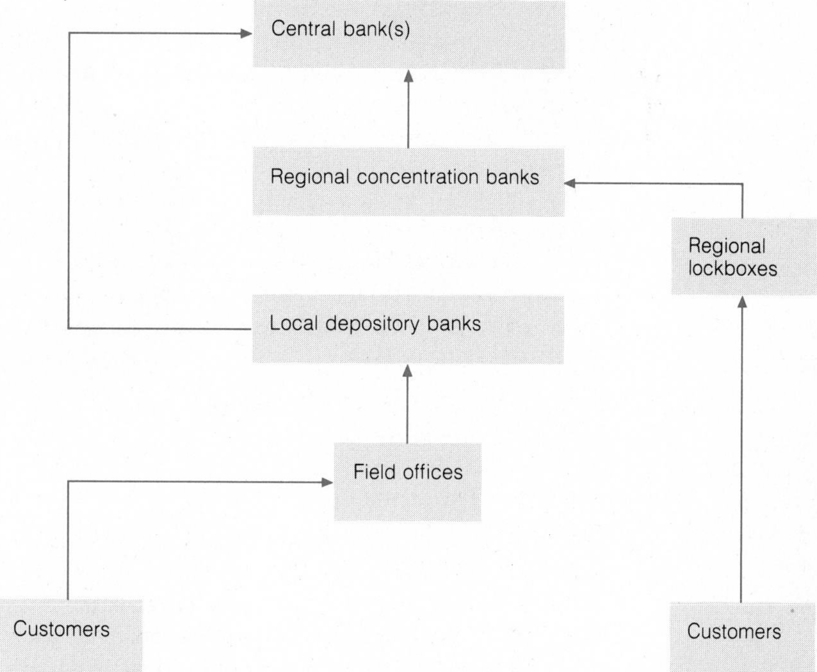

maintain a major disbursing account at such a bank. As illustrated in Figure 11.1, the regional concentration banks are part of the *concentration banking system* of the firm. Figure 11.1 also indicates that the regional concentration banks usually also handle a lockbox arrangement. Since a lockbox system uses data processing, check handling, and other banking services with substantial fixed costs and other expenses, there will be fewer regional concentration banks than local depository banks.

Some general guidelines for the selection of a concentration bank include the following:

1. The bank should be located in a Federal Reserve city serving the collection area (to reduce clearing float).
2. The bank should have access to the banking wire system.
3. The bank should be located so that it receives 80 percent or more of deposited checks one day after they are mailed.
4. The bank should be competitive with respect to its fees charged, including activity charges, compensating balance requirements, funds availability, and earnings credits.

The *central bank* is the overall control bank for the cash-gathering network. In an effort to avoid having various amounts of funds sitting idle in multiple bank accounts in different geographic regions, an effort will be made to move the funds into the central bank. A number of advantages may be achieved by centralizing the firm's pool of cash.

1. Better control can be achieved. The concentration banks prepare analytic reports monitoring the corporatewide movements of funds in and out of the central bank cash pool.
2. The amount of unused cash can be minimized. Target cash balance levels are set for each regional bank, taking into account necessary working levels of cash as well as compensating balance requirements. Cash in amounts over the target levels can be transferred regularly to concentration banks for deployment by the firm's top-level financial staff.
3. More efficient investment in marketable securities can be achieved. With information and cash focused in both the central bank and the concentration banks along with the firm's cash-forecasting system, the firm has continuing information on the amount of funds available for investment in marketable securities.

The concentration banking system developed by the firm seeks to mobilize its funds as efficiently as possible. In addition to a cash-gathering system, the firm needs to work out some policies and decision rules for the rapid transfer of funds. These rules are considered next.

Transfer Mechanisms

A transfer mechanism is a system for moving funds between accounts at different banks. The main transfer mechanisms are:

1. Depository transfer checks (DTC)
   a. Centralized company initiated
   b. Third-party assisted

2. Electronic depository transfer checks (EDTC)
   a. Centralized company initiated
   b. Third party assisted
3. Wire transfers
   a. Bank wire
   b. Federal reserve wire system

A *depository transfer check* (DTC) is a check restricted for deposit at a particular bank. Except for the deposit-only restriction, a DTC is an ordinary check. DTCs provide a means for moving funds from local depository banks into concentration banks. A DTC is payable only to the bank of deposit for credit to the firm's specific account. In a mail-based initiation procedure the local office or a company's field unit prepares the DTC and mails it with the deposit slip to a regional concentration bank which is often a "lockbox bank." This bank will subsequently transfer the funds to the central bank along with other checks received at the lockbox. The concentration bank credits the funds to the firm's account, placing the check into the clearing process. While this process is automatic in that no action is required by the firm's cash managers, funds availability is limited by postal and clearing times.

Under *centralized company-initiation* the firm's local representative phones a central company location with a report on deposits. The company accumulates the deposit data, developing a "DTC state image" on magnetic tape. This tape is sent or teleprocessed to the concentration bank which prepares the DTCs, entering them into the check-clearing system. In an electronics funds transfer system (EFTS), the company-managed central initiation may arise at point-of-sale (POS) terminals. Instead of a phone call the terminal link may be used to transmit the deposit data directly. Under a *third-party assisted initiation* the local offices of the company phone deposit information into a third-party deposit information gathering service. This specialized firm accumulates the deposit data, transmitting the deposit information to the company's concentration bank periodically for the preparation of DTCs.

A recent innovation in transfer mechanisms is the electronic image transfer via the automated clearinghouses developed by the Federal Reserve System. The electronic image transfer system is a combination of a wire and a DTC. As an electronic DTC it is referred to as an EDTC. It is paperless—like the wire—but involves a uniform one-day availability in clearing time with a lower cost than an ordinary check. The EDTC avoids the use of the mails. It may be initiated by central company management or by a third-party gathering service.

Wire transfer of funds between banks makes funds collected at one bank immediately available for use at another bank, even in a different city. It is the fastest way to move cash between banks, eliminating transit float. The bank wire method is a private wire service used and supported by about 300 banks in the United States. They use the bank wire system for transferring funds, exchanging credit information, and making securities transactions. The Federal Reserve wire system can be used by commercial banks that are members of the Federal Reserve System. However, commercial banks not on the bank wire or not members of the

Federal Reserve System can obtain access to the wire transfer system through their correspondent banks.

Wire transfers are typically initiated on a standing order basis. Company headquarters will make a written authorization to a local depository bank to transfer funds to the firm's concentration bank when the amount exceeds some target level such as $80,000. The use of standing instructions to transfer funds can be an effective way of managing complex cash-gathering systems, avoiding the need for daily communication with distant locations.

Comparing the Costs of Alternative Transfer Mechanisms

The use of a wire transfer is the quickest transfer mechanism but the most expensive. There is no delay on a wire transfer, but the typical cost range is $6 to $8. A mail depository transfer check (DTC) may cost only 40¢ to 50¢ but may involve delays from 2 to 7 days. An evaluation of the alternatives has conventionally involved a comparison of the value of the extra interest from the faster transfer related to the extra cost involved. The conventional cost comparisons are giving way to newer, more sophisticated programming techniques.[1] The conventional formula for the breakeven transfer size is as follows:

$$S^* = \Delta \text{COST} / I \, \Delta T \qquad \textbf{(11.1)}$$

where

S^* = the breakeven size of transfer above which the faster, higher cost mechanism is preferred

ΔCOST = the incremental cost of the faster mechanism

I = the applicable daily interest rate

ΔT = the difference in transfer time in days

If the cost difference between a wire and a DTC is $6, with a time difference of two days and an interest value of funds at the concentration bank of 0.03 percent per day, the breakeven transfer size would be:

$$S^* = \frac{\$6.00}{.0003(2)} = \$10{,}000 \qquad \textbf{(11.2)}$$

Thus on amounts above $10,000 a wire transfer would be used. If the time saved is only one day, the breakeven size is $20,000.

Another area of cost comparison is the issue of mail-based versus central initiation of fund transfers. For an extra cost of central initiation of $.60, a two-day saving of time, and the same daily 0.03 percent interest rate, the breakeven size is as follows:

$$S^* = \$.60/(.0003)(2) = \$1{,}000 \qquad \textbf{(11.3)}$$

This result suggests that switching to central initiation is advantageous for a deposit amount of over $1,000.

[1] This discussion is based on Bernell K. Stone and Ned C. Hill, "The Evaluation of Alternative Cash Transfer Mechanisms and Methods," *Proceedings of the Nineteenth Annual Meeting of the Southwestern Finance Association*, 1980, pp. 39–58.

Stone and Hill criticize the above conventional procedure on a number of grounds.[2] They argue that the conventional breakeven analysis assumes no value for funds in the depository bank. They observe that compensating balances are recognized by banks in assigning "service credits" to the firm in the bank's analysis of the profitability of the account and the need to make service charges to the company. Hence it is argued that the opportunity costs of not having funds in the concentration bank is not the full interest rate but rather the *difference* between the interest rate and the earnings credit rate at the depository bank.

They also point out that the choice of transfer alternatives will take time delays into account. For example, if all the deposits in a given depository bank are checks with a one-day availability delay, the depository bank then regards the funds as "available" in the sense of earning service credits. If the firm initiates the depository transfer checks (DTCs) on the same day the checks are deposited, the DTC arrives at the depository bank at the same time the checks become an available balance. But if the firm uses a wire, it would wait one day until the check deposits become an available balance before initiating the transfer. The "effective delay" (time difference in having funds available at the concentration bank) is zero because both the DTC and the wire provide an available balance at the concentration bank on the same day. Yet the DTC costs less.

Another distinction required for evaluating the alternative transfer mechanisms is a form of float which Stone and Hill term "dual balance." *Dual balance* refers to the balances resulting when the DTC clearing time is longer than the availability time specified. Dual balances involve only DTCs since both wires and EDTCs have the same clear time and availability time. For example, availability time at the concentration bank is one business day, but the actual DTC clearing time back to the depository bank upon which the DTC is written is *two* business days. Thus a $15,000 DTC deposited in the concentration bank on Tuesday would result in a $15,000 available balance addition at the concentration bank on Wednesday but with a $15,000 still not charged at the depository bank until Thursday. Thus the same $15,000 is an available balance in both the concentration bank and the depository bank on Wednesday—hence the term *dual balance*.

A number of other technical considerations including improvements in transfer practice need to be taken into account in evaluating the cost/benefit tradeoffs of alternative transfer mechanisms. These different tradeoffs plus the service credits earned by leaving some funds in the gathering system as compensating balances result in the use of a variety of transfer mechanisms under different circumstances. This is an area in which systematic decision models are still under development.

Managing Disbursements

Just as expediting the cash-gathering process conserves cash, effective management of disbursements accomplishes similar results by keeping cash on hand for longer periods. This is the "other side of the coin" of getting the money in as fast as possible. But as the Stone and Hill paper points out, banks are attempting to more accurately match costs and revenues on individual accounts. One effect of

[2] Stone and Hill, pp. 46–57.

this matching is a reduction in the gains from using float. Table 11.1 depicts a typical commercial checking account service charge analysis. In the earnings credit section, the customer is credited for the average collected balance at the interest rate of 5 percent. The collected balance is determined as the daily balance adjusted for the typical time it takes for the bank to collect on checks deposited. Thus, the estimated days of float will be low for a business dealing mostly with local customers and high for a business that receives payments from out-of-state customers. In this way the individual firm bears the cost of float directly. The expense part of the analysis is straightforward. In reality there are many more expense classifications than the few itemized here—among them lockbox charges, computer service billings, and required compensating balances.

In the illustration, the service charge to the firm is $10.98 after allowing for the earnings credit. In the event that the earnings credit exceeds the expenses, current regulations do not permit paying it to the depositor. But this regulation is under scrutiny and is likely to be changed in the near future.

The key point to remember is that the potential gains from using float are relative.[3] Even though banks have taken steps to reduce the gains, the company that deposits checks from customers promptly and delays bank clearing of checks it writes for as long as possible will still have a relative advantage from float.

Table 11.1

State National Bank
Commercial Service Charge Analysis
Mail Order Supply Company
September 1981

Earnings credit		
1 Days in month	31	
2 Less average days float	6	
3 Basis for earnings credit	25	
4 Average daily balance	$21,300.00	
5 Daily rate factor (at 5%)	0.000139	
6 Earnings credit (3 × 4 × 5)		$74.02
Service debits		
7 20 deposits (at $.25 each)	$ 5.00	
8 3,200 checks deposited (at $.02 each)	64.00	
9 200 checks written (at $.08 each)	16.00	
10 Total service debits (7 + 8 + 9)		85.00
Service charge (10 − 6)		$10.98

If a firm's own collection and clearing process is more efficient than that of the recipients of its checks—and this is often true of large, efficient firms—then the

[3] Modern technology is also reducing opportunities for using float. On October 1, 1981, the Clearing House Interbank Payment System (CHIPS)—an international electronic check transfer system—stopped settling accounts between banks on the next day. All settlements are now made by 6 p.m. on the same day and no messages ordering the transfer of funds from one bank to another are accepted after 4:40 p.m. A 16-hour float has been eliminated.

firm could show a negative balance on its own records and a positive balance on its bank's books. Some firms indicate that they *never* have positive accounting cash balances. One large manufacturer of construction equipment stated that, while its account according to its bank's records shows an average cash balance of about $2 million, its actual cash balance is *minus* $2 million; thus it has $4 million of float. Obviously, the firm must be able to forecast its positive and negative clearings accurately in order to make such heavy use of float.

Cash Management Models

In recent years, cash management has begun to receive increased emphasis, primarily in response to the high inflation rates that threaten to devalue any idle or unaccounted-for cash. Corporations are tightening their cash controls to ensure that cash will not be forgotten in a dormant bank account or distant subdivision. For example, Foremost-McKesson tightened internal controls and introduced an electronic funds transfer system, thereby gleaning an extra $30 million from operations. In order to protect its cash during an inflationary period, a firm must know exactly how much cash it has, and where it is. This explains the evolution of complicated cash management systems.

Interest in cash management is also being generated by the large number of firms expanding overseas. Floating exchange rates compel firms to develop worldwide cash control systems. A centralized cash management system is necessary to prevent large currency exchange losses. Even if a firm wishes to avoid currency speculation, it still must carefully monitor exposure to rate changes and develop an appropriate system of hedges and other means for reducing risk. In many firms, the cash manager takes full responsibility for covering exposure, determining daily or weekly exchange rates for use by all divisions and subsidiaries.

Several types of mathematical models have been developed to help determine optimal cash balances. An early model developed by William Baumol essentially applies the EOQ inventory model to cash management.[4] Ordering costs are represented by the clerical and transactions costs of making transfers between the investment portfolio and the cash account. The holding cost is the interest foregone on cash balances held. Assuming that expenditures occur continuously and that cash inflows come in lump sums at periodic intervals, the optimal size of the cash transfer is formulated as follows.

$$C^* = \sqrt{\frac{2bT}{i}}$$

where

C^* = the optimal size of the cash transfer

T = the total cash usage for the period of time involved

b = the fixed cost of the transaction in the purchase or sale of marketable securities

i = the applicable interest rate on marketable securities

[4] William J. Baumol, "The Transactions Demand for Cash: An Inventory Theoretic Approach," *Quarterly Journal of Economics* 66 (Nov. 1952), pp. 545–56.

The formula can be illustrated in a specific numerical example. The total demand for cash (T) over the period of time involved (one year) is \$1.8 million. The fixed cost of a transaction is \$25. The applicable interest rate is 10 percent.

Using the data in the formula we obtain:

$$C^* = \sqrt{\frac{2bT}{i}} = \sqrt{\frac{2(\$25)(\$1{,}800{,}000)}{.10}} = \$30{,}000$$

Having calculated C^*, the optimal amount of cash transfer, the average cash balance for the period will be

$$\frac{C^*}{2} = \frac{\$30{,}000}{2} = \$15{,}000$$

The total number of transactions or transfers required per year can also be readily determined.

$$\frac{\$1{,}800{,}000}{\$30{,}000} = 60, \text{ or somewhat more than 1 transaction per week}$$

Finally, the total cost per year of maintaining cash balances can be calculated.

$$TC = b\left(\frac{T}{C}\right) + i\left(\frac{C}{2}\right)$$

$$= \$25(60) + .10(\$15{,}000) = \$1{,}500 + \$1{,}500$$

$$= \$3{,}000$$

On the basis of the data of the example, the total cost is \$3,000 per year. Under the assumptions of the analysis this minimizes the costs of managing the inventory of cash.

Company Liquidity Policies in Practice

Liquidity policies of companies vary with their individual circumstances and needs. This is illustrated by the data in Table 11.2. First, the relationships for all manufacturing industries are shown as of the end of 1979. The total liquid assets held by all manufacturing industries at the end of 1979 were over \$70 billion. This represented 5.7 percent of total assets and 4.1 percent of revenues.

IBM had a lower ratio of cash to assets and revenues, but a much higher ratio of marketable securities. IBM required a higher cushion in marketable securities for a number of reasons. First, the introduction of a new line of computers involved many billions of dollars. Second, a shift in consumer patterns from buying to leasing involved substantial cash drains for IBM. This is because it costs just as much to manufacture a computer whether it is sold or leased and obviously the revenues from a lease represent only a fraction of the amount received on an outright sale.

In the final two columns of Table 11.2, the liquidity positions of Ford and Exxon are compared since Ford is in a depressed industry (automobiles) and Exxon is in a booming industry (petroleum). The percentage of liquid assets to either total assets or revenues does not differ greatly for the two companies. However, the breakdown between cash and marketable securities does differ. This is in part influenced by whether time deposits are classified as cash or as marketable securities. The overall liquidity ratio of Ford is relatively high, reflecting the un-

Table 11.2 **A Comparison of Liquidity Relationships, 1979**

Amounts	($) (in billions) All manufacturing	IBM	($) (in millions) Ford	Exxon
Cash	$44.9	$ 298	$1,127	$ 760
Marketable securities	26.3	3,473	1,066	3,748
Liquid assets	$71.2	$3,771	$2,193	$4,508
Percentage of total assets				
Cash	3.6%	1.2%	4.8%	1.8%
Marketable securities	2.1	14.2	4.5	9.0
Liquid assets	5.7%	15.4%	9.3%	10.8%
Percentage of revenues				
Cash	2.6%	1.3%	2.6%	1.2%
Marketable securities	1.5	15.2	2.4	5.8
Liquid assets	4.1%	16.5%	5.0%	7.0%
Total assets	$1,243	$24,530	$23,525	$41,531
Revenues	1,742	22,863	43,514	64,886

Source: FTC, *Quarterly Financial Reports*, company annual reports

certainty of the automobile industry. The liquidity ratios of Exxon are also on the high side, which may be due in part to the substantial exploration and investment programs planned by the major petroleum companies.

Management of the Marketable Securities Portfolio

In the framework of the firm's overall liquidity policies, the financial manager has a major responsibility for managing the firm's marketable securities portfolio. This involves choices among alternative financial assets.

Criteria for Selecting Securities

The applicable criteria for selection among the wide range of securities available include (1) financial risk, (2) interest rate risk, (3) purchasing power risk, (4) liquidity or marketability, (5) taxability, and (6) relative yields. Each will be considered in turn.

Financial Risk The greater the degree to which the price and returns of a security fluctuate, the greater the financial risk. Many factors may influence the size and frequency of a security's price changes. But the greater the fluctuations, the greater the risk that a loss may be incurred. In the extreme, the most serious unfavorable event is that the issuer cannot meet interest payments or principal payments—the risk of default. U.S. government securities do not carry the risk of default and are therefore considered "safer" than other securities. Bonds issued by state and local governments as well as corporate securities are considered to be subject to some degree of default risk. Rating agencies such as Moody's Investment Services and the Standard & Poor's Corporation assign quality ratings to securities. Among the factors influencing a security's rating is the degree of likelihood that default may occur. These quality assessments can and do change with time. For many years the securities of utility companies were regarded as of the highest quality with minimum risk of default. In recent years, however, utility securities have been downgraded to lower quality ratings.

Interest Rate Risk Changes in the general level of interest rates will cause the prices of securities to fluctuate. This is especially true of such securities as notes or bonds, which carry a fixed rate of interest. In general, the shorter the maturity of a debt instrument, the smaller the size of fluctuations in its price. A partial exception to this generalization should be noted. For deep-discount bonds (bonds selling at 20 to 30 percent below maturity value) with maturities of less than thirty years, the degree of fluctuation in their prices reaches a maximum around a maturity of about 15 to 18 years and then declines with longer maturities.

In general, long-term bonds are riskier than short-term securities for a firm's marketable securities portfolio. However, partly because of this risk differential, higher yields are more frequently available on long-term than on short-term securities; so again risk-return tradeoffs must be recognized.

Given the motives most firms have for holding marketable securities portfolios, generally it is not feasible for them to be exposed to a high degree of risk from interest rate fluctuations. Accordingly, firms usually confine their portfolios to securities with short maturities. Only if the securities are expected to be held for a long period and not be subject to forced liquidation on short notice will long-term securities be chosen. Additional protection from interest rate fluctuations is provided by the use of the interest rate futures markets described in the Appendix to this chapter.

Purchasing Power Risk Changes in general price levels will affect the purchasing power of both the principal and the income from investments in securities. The total return from a security is measured by the capital gain or loss plus the income yield. Varied relationships have developed for different types of assets during the prolonged inflation since the late 1960s in the United States. Bonds with fixed dollar amounts of income and a fixed dollar amount at maturity have declined in value as inflation has caused interest rates levels to rise. But common stocks whose dividends theoretically are not fixed in amount have also declined in value because the underlying earning power of corporations appears to have been impaired during the persistent inflation. The value of commodities such as gold and diamonds has risen in value even though they pay no interest or other forms of income. Real estate is a hybrid case in that rentals have not risen as fast as the general price level, but the values of homes and commercial properties have outpaced the rise in the general price level.

Liquidity or Marketability Risk The potential decline from a security's quoted market price when the security is sold is its liquidity or marketability risk. Liquidity risk is related to the breadth or thinness of the market for a security. U.S. Treasury bonds or AT&T securities will be more widely held and have greater liquidity than the securities of the Podunk Printing Company.

Taxability The tax position of a firm's marketable securities portfolio is influenced by the overall tax position of a firm. A firm with prior years' losses to carry forward can ignore taxability. A firm that pays the full 46 percent marginal corporate tax rate must take taxability into account. The market yields on a security will reflect the total demand and supply of tax influences. Yet the position of the individual firm may be different from the overall pattern. To the extent that a firm may have a need for tax protection different from the overall pattern of the market, it might find that taxability considerations are either favorable or unfavorable. A number of kinds of securities, such as the bonds of state and local governments, have varying degrees of tax exemption. In addition, securities that sell at a discount offer opportunities for taking returns in the form of capital gains rather than ordinary income.

Returns on Securities The higher the risk, the higher the required return. Thus in building a marketable securities portfolio, corporate treasurers must evaluate the risk-return tradeoffs. Since the motive for holding marketable securities is protection against uncertain and fluctuating inflows and outflows, the dominant policy is to choose relatively less risky alternatives at the sacrifice of some return. Accordingly, corporate treasurers will emphasize relatively short-term, highly liquid assets in constructing the marketable securities portfolio.

Investment Alternatives

The main kinds of investments meeting the objectives just set forth are listed in Table 11.3. These represent the highly liquid, short-term securities issued by the U.S. government and by the very strongest domestic and foreign banks and other business corporations.

Table 11.3

Alternative Marketable Securities for Investment[a]

	Approximate maturities[b]	Approximate yields[c]	
		April 1977	March 1981
U.S. Treasury bills	91–182 days	4.81%	13.52%
U.S. Treasury notes	1–5 years	6.41	13.14
U.S. Treasury bonds	Over 5 years	7.45	13.00
Negotiable certificates of deposit with U.S. and foreign banks	Varies, up to 3 years	5.35	12.63
Prime commercial paper	Varies, up to 270 days	4.70	14.00
Eurodollar bank time deposits	Varies, up to 1 year	5.18	15.16
Bonds of other domestic and foreign corporations (Aaa) in U.S. dollars	Varies, over 5 years	8.53	14.04

[a] The marketable securities listed in this table are only illustrative of a much larger range of available alternatives. For a more complete listing, including prices and yields, see Salomon Brothers, "Bond Market Roundup" and "International Bond Market Roundup," each published weekly.

[b] The maturities are those at issue date. For outstanding securities, maturities varying almost by day or week are available.

[c] Estimated yields for median maturities in the class.

The financial manager decides on a suitable maturity pattern for the holdings on the basis of how long the funds are to be held. The numerous alternatives can be selected and balanced in such a way that maturities and risks appropriate to the financial situation of the firm are obtained. Commercial bankers, investment bankers, and brokers provide the financial manager with detailed information on each of the forms of investment listed. Because the characteristics of investment outlets change with shifts in financial market conditions, it would be misleading to attempt to give detailed descriptions of them here. The financial manager should keep up to date on these characteristics and follow the principle of making investment selections that offer maturities, yields, and risks appropriate to the firm.

Effects of Inflation

Inflation devalues money very rapidly, making the careful investment of cash essential to the health of the firm. An improved cash management system keeps track of idle cash; but once this cash has been found, it can act as a hedge against inflation only if it is invested appropriately. During periods of tight money, neither small nor large firms can be confident of receiving bank loans to meet cash shortages. Therefore, it is imperative for them to keep cash reserves for future contingencies.

To protect these cash reserves against inflation, companies have begun to invest the funds aggressively, seeking higher yields. Idle cash is no longer merely

Table 11.4

International Business Machines Corporation and Subsidiary Companies Marketable Securities December 31, 1979 (Thousands of Dollars)

	Amount included in statement of financial position
U.S. government and its agencies	$1,295,677
State government securities	18,211
Other investments—U.S. institutions	177,891
Government securities—non-U.S. institutions	265,348
Other investments—non-U.S. institutions	48,345
Non-U.S. time deposits and other bank obligations:	
German marks	521,207
U.S. dollars	502,200
British pounds	100,058
Japanese yen	82,318
Swiss francs	74,205
Dutch guilders	60,323
Swedish kronor	55,730
Danish kroner	40,468
Other currencies	231,403
	1,667,912
Total	$3,473,384

Source: IBM Annual Report, 1979.

kept in the bank or invested exclusively in Treasury bills. Certificates of deposit, municipal securities, and commercial paper offer higher rates of return and are therefore gaining in popularity. Firms are even using foreign instruments. For example, NCR invests in commercial paper, the Euromarket, and both domestic and Japanese certificates of deposit to increase pretax earnings by about $1 million per year. Litton Industries invests part of its portfolio in Swiss franc- and German mark-denominated time deposits and in foreign certificates of deposit. AT&T trades Treasury bills, looking for the best yield, rather than holding them to maturity. Its other investments include commercial paper, bankers' acceptances, certificates of deposit, and overnight repurchase agreements. (Overnight repurchase agreements—repos—have a very short maturity, frequently no longer than one day. Therefore, they are especially appropriate for investing money that will be needed immediately.)

An example of the marketable securities portfolio of IBM as of December 31, 1979, is presented in Table 11.4. The largest single investment is in U.S. government and federal agency securities. It is of interest to note also that $1.67 billion of the marketable security investments were in foreign-denominated accounts. These included $500 million in foreign investments denominated in dollars, probably representing mostly Eurodollar deposits.

Summary

Recent high levels of interest rates have increased the importance of cash management, while at the same time advances in technology have changed the nature of the cash management function. Financial managers have developed new techniques for optimizing cash balances and determining the appropriate relation between holding cash and holding investments in marketable securities.

The four primary reasons for holding cash are the transactions motive, the precautionary motive, the speculative motive, and to satisfy bank compensating balance requirements. The two major aspects of a cash flow system involve the gathering and disbursement of cash, with the firm's objective to speed collections and legitimately slow disbursements.

Float arises from lags in the payment process (mail, processing, and bank clearing delays). Float is an advantage to the firm as a buyer and a disadvantage to the firm as a seller. An efficient cash-gathering system will focus on reducing negative mail float with decentralized collections and a lockbox system. The use of the lockbox also reduces processing time by starting checks through the bank clearing process before they have been recorded in the firm's accounting system.

A concentration banking system seeks to speed the cash-gathering process by mobilizing funds efficiently through a hierarchy of local depository banks, regional concentration banks, and a central bank. The local depository banks are used to channel field office collections. The concentration banks, which usually handle the lockbox arrangement, channel funds to a major disbursement account. A key element in the selection of concentration banks is their location relative to a firm's customers and to Federal Reserve System check-clearing facilities and their access to the bank wire system to facilitate the transfer of funds to the firm's central bank, where greater control can be exercised over a single cash pool.

The financial manager has a range of mechanisms from which to choose for the rapid transfer of funds and must balance speed against cost. The conventional model for the cost comparison arrives at a breakeven size of transfer (above which a more rapid, more expensive method would be preferred) by comparing the value of the extra interest which would be earned in the central bank with the incremental cost of the faster mechanism. This method has been criticized for failing to consider any other value for the funds than the interest foregone by not transferring them to the central bank. For example, balances left in the concentration banks can earn service credits, reducing the cost to the firm of using the bank's services. Timing considerations further complicate the cost-benefit analysis of transfer mechanisms, and systematic models which reflect these considerations are under development.

With respect to disbursements, several methods can be used to lengthen the payment period. However, banks seek to offset the gains from float; they attempt to charge for their services in such a way that firms bear the cost of the float directly.

An Electronic Funds Transfer System (EFTS) involves payment by consumers, business, and government through a network of data communications, whereby funds are immediately debited from the purchaser's bank account at the point of sale, without the use of a check. Because of the high fixed costs involved, the current cost per transaction in EFTS is relatively high, and will remain so until the volume of transactions increases substantially. However, with the expansion of the system nationwide, EFTS will significantly reduce float and further change the cash management function.

The performance of mathematical models designed to determine the optimal cash balance depends on how well the firm's patterns of cash flows conform to the assumptions of the model. The Baumol model applies the EOQ inventory model to cash management (with an assumption of continuous expenditures) to determine the economic quantity of cash to have on hand.

Companies' liquidity policies vary with individual circumstances and needs. In selecting the firm's portfolio of marketable securities, the financial manager must consider financial risk, interest rate risk, purchasing power risk, liquidity or marketability, taxability, and relative yields. The securities which have best suited the financial manager's objectives are short-term U.S. government issues, plus those of the very strongest domestic and foreign banks and corporations. The effects of inflation, however, with its rapid devaluation of the purchasing power of idle cash, have led firms to be somewhat more aggressive in seeking higher yields.

Questions

11.1 How can better methods of communication reduce the necessity for firms to hold large cash balances?

11.2 Discuss this statement: The highly developed financial system of the United States, with its myriad of different near-cash assets, has greatly reduced cash balance requirements by reducing the need for transactions balances.

11.3 Would you expect a firm with a high growth rate to hold more or fewer precautionary and speculative cash balances than a firm with a low growth rate? Explain.

11.4 Many firms that find themselves with temporary surplus cash invest these funds in Treasury bills. Since Treasury bills frequently have the lowest yield of any investment security, why are they chosen as investments?

11.5 Discuss the differences between financial risk and interest rate risk. Which has the greater effect on the selection of marketable securities?

11.6 Explain the possible effects on a firm's cash balance of each of the following factors (other things held constant):

a. The level of interest rates rises.
b. The cost of trading in marketable securities rises.
c. The cost of trading in marketable securities falls.
d. Sales forecasts are improved through the use of a more accurate forecasting technique.
e. A firm doing business exclusively on the West Coast transfers its checking account to a Florida bank.
f. A firm's research department has made a discovery with great market potential.

11.7 Discuss possible sources of resistance to a concentration banking system instituted in a decentralized firm.

Problems

11.1 Rutherford Associates is short on cash and is attempting to determine if it would be advantageous for them to forgo the discount on this month's purchases or to borrow funds to take advantage of the discount. The discount terms are 2/10, net 45.

a. What is the maximum annual interest rate that Rutherford Associates should pay on borrowed funds? Why?
b. What are some of the intangible disadvantages associated with forgoing the discount?

11.2 A firm issues checks in the amount of $1 million each day and deducts them from its own records at the close of business on the day they are written. On average, the bank receives and clears the checks (deducts them from the firm's bank balance) the evening of the fourth day after they are written; for example, a check written on Monday will be cleared on Friday afternoon. The firm's loan agreement with the bank requires it to maintain a $750,000 minimum average compensating balance; this is $250,000 greater than the cash safety stock the firm would otherwise have on deposit.

a. Assuming that the firm makes its deposit in the late afternoon (and the bank includes the deposit in the day's transactions), how much must the firm deposit each day to maintain a sufficient balance once it reaches a steady state?
b. How many days of float does the firm carry?
c. What ending daily balance should the firm try to maintain at the bank and on its own records?
d. Explain how float can help increase the value of the firm's common stock. Use a partial balance sheet and the du Pont system concept in your answer.

11.3 Aran, Inc., currently has a centralized billing system located in New York City. However, over the years its customers gradually have become less concentrated on the East Coast and now cover the entire United States. On average, it requires five days from the time customers mail payments until Aran is able to receive, process, and deposit their payments. To shorten this time, Aran is considering the installation of a lockbox collection system. It estimates that the system will reduce the time lag from customer mailing to deposit by three and one-half days. Aran has a daily average collection of $700,000.

a. What reduction in cash balances can Aran achieve by initiating the lockbox system?

b. If Aran has an opportunity cost of 8 percent, how much is the lockbox system worth on an annual basis?

c. What is the maximum monthly charge Aran can pay for the lockbox system?

11.4 The New York field office of the Metallux Corporation has sold a quantity of silver ingots for $15,000. Metallux wants to transfer this amount to its concentration bank in San Francisco as economically as possible. Two means of transfer are being considered.

1. A mail depository transfer check (DTC) costs $0.50 and takes 3 days.
2. A wire transfer costs $7.50 and funds are immediately available in San Francisco.

Metallux earns 14.5 percent annual interest on funds in its concentration bank. Which transfer method should be used?

11.5 Warrior Industries projects that cash outlays of $3,750,000 will occur uniformly throughout the forthcoming year. Warrior plans to meet these demands for cash by periodically selling marketable securities from its portfolio. The firm's marketable securities are invested to earn 12 percent, and the cost per transaction of converting funds to cash is $40.

a. Use the Baumol model to determine the optimal transaction size for transfers from marketable securities to cash.

b. What will be Warrior's average cash balance?

c. How many transfers per year will be required?

APPENDIX 11A

INTEREST RATE FUTURES AND RIDING THE YIELD CURVE

Forward Rates and Futures Rates

If the term structure of interest rates conforms to the unbiased expectations theory, the current long-term rate is a simple average of the present and expected future short-term rates for continuous compounding.

Table 11A.1 shows the long-term rates implied by an assumed sequence of expected future short-term rates.

Table 11A.1

Long-Term Rates Implied by Short-Term Rates

Year	One-year rates	Implied current long-term rates
1	6%	5-year, 8%; 4-year, 7.5% 3-year, 7%; 2-year, 6.5%
2	7%	
3	8%	
4	9%	
5	10%	

Table 11A.1 illustrates that with continuous compounding and under unbiased expectations, the current long-term rate is a simple arithmetic average of the expected future one-year rates. In equation form,

$$ {}_1R_5 = ({}_1r_1 + {}_2r_1 + {}_3r_1 + {}_4r_1 + {}_5r_1)/5 \tag{11A.1}$$

where ${}_1R_5$ is the 5-year rate at the beginning of year 1 and ${}_1r_1$, ${}_2r_1$, ${}_3r_1$, ${}_4r_1$, and ${}_5r_1$ are the 1-year rates at the beginnings of years 1, 2, 3, 4, and 5 respectively.

The one-period yield that is expected in the future has also been described as the *forward rate*. Under continuous compounding, the expected forward rates can be inferred simply and directly from the term structure of interest rates. An illustrative term structure of interest rates is set forth in Table 11A.2.

Table 11A.2 **Illustrative Term Structure of Interest Rates**

Term of the instrument	Yield to maturity
1 year	6%
2 years	6.5%
3 years	7%
4 years	7.5%
5 years	8%

The data from Table 11A.2 are graphed in Figure 11A.1.

Figure 11A.1 **A Graph of the Term Structure of Interest Rates**

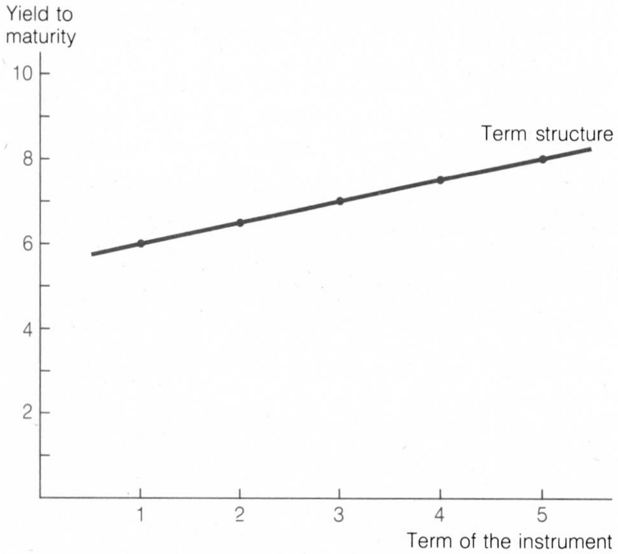

Formally, the relationship is as shown in Equation 11A.1:

$$_{n}r_{1} = n_{t}(R_{n}) - (n - 1)R_{n-1} \qquad \textbf{(11A.2)}$$

Using the data in Table 10A.2 we can calculate the implied forward rate at the beginning of the fifth year. The result is shown in Equation (11A.2a):

$$\begin{aligned} _{5}r_{1} &= 5(8) - 4(7.5) \\ &= 40 - 30 = 10 \end{aligned} \qquad \textbf{(11A.2a)}$$

Thus the implied forward rate for the fifth year is 10 percent. In a like manner we can calculate the implied forward rates for the other years as well. The results are shown in Table 11A.3.

Table 11A.3 **Forward Rates Implied by the Term Structure**

Year	Implied forward rates
1	6%
2	7
3	8
4	9
5	10

Forward rates are of importance because of their economic nature. The forward rate is the marginal return to an investment from holding or committing the investment for one additional time period. Thus the forward rate represents a return that will be realized over a future time period, if the expectations implied by the current term structure of interest rates are realized.

Another form of return from an investment held over a future time period is measured by the *futures rate*. Contracts can be made for transactions covering an investment in a financial instrument with a period of one year to be held during the second, third, fourth, or fifth year from the time period we have been analyzing. The yields on futures contracts for a series of years into the future would, in the absence of frictions or other types of market imperfections, be the same as the implied forward rates. The relationship between futures rates and implied forward rates in actuality is a matter of empirical testing. Divergences between the two sets of rates would offer possible profit-making opportunities. The relationship between futures and forward rates has taken on increased significance in recent years with the development of a market in interest rate futures next described.

The Establishment of an Interest Rate Futures Market

Interest rate futures are a relatively new development. In 1975 the Chicago Board of Trade established a contract for Government National Mortgage Association Securities (GNMAs). In 1976 the International Monetary Market (IMM) of the Chicago Mercantile Exchange introduced a contract for 90-day Treasury bills. In 1977 the Chicago Board of Trade extended trading to Treasury bond futures contracts.

The volume in these interest rate futures has grown substantially. For example, on an average day in 1979 futures contracts representing about $7\frac{1}{2}$ billion in three-months Treasury bills were traded on the International Monetary Market of the Chicago Mercantile Exchange. On an average day in 1979 at the Chicago Board of Trade (CBT) futures contracts representing almost $1 billion in long-term Treasury bonds were traded. Also, futures contracts representing more than $500 million in GNMAs changed hands on an average day.

The financial futures market operates as do other futures markets. One of the most active futures markets is for three-month Treasury bills at the IMM. Through this exchange a customer might buy a contract to take delivery of and pay for $1 million of three-month Treasury bills on March 20, 1981. There are eight contract delivery months on the IMM extending at quarterly intervals for about two years into the future.

The contract price is quoted as the difference between $100 and the discount rate on the bill in question. Thus a contract fixing a bill rate at 8.50 percent would be quoted at $91.50. The clearinghouse places itself between the buyer and the seller so that the buyer's contract is not with the seller but with the clearinghouse. Also, the seller's contract is with the clearinghouse and not with the original buyer. For the financial liability of the clearinghouse, the clearing member firms must meet deposits requirements on their contracts. For each purchase or sale of a three-month Treasury bill contract of $1 million on the IMM, the clearing member firm must post a margin of $1,200 which can be in the form of cash or a bank letter of credit. The clearing member firm in turn imposes an initial margin of at least $1,500 on the individual trader.

While the position is outstanding, the contract will be "marked-to-market" by the clearinghouse at the end of each business day. Either profits or losses are recorded, based on the position and price movements. Profits in the margin account may be withdrawn. If losses reduce the firm's margin below $1,200, the firm must make up the difference to the clearinghouse in cash before the next business day. The customer's margin account may fall below the initial $1,500, but if it falls below the $1,200 maintenance margin the account must be brought back up to the $1,500. There are also daily limits on the degree of price fluctuations. At the IMM, for example, no future trades in Treasury bills can involve prices more than 50 basis points above or below the final settlement price of the previous day. These margins may be temporarily increased if the daily limit restricts trading for a few days.

Use of the Futures Market to Hedge against Interest Rate Changes

The interest rate futures market can be used in a number of ways. In recent years interest rates have fluctuated widely within short periods of time. A corporate treasurer planning for meeting a future commitment or in process of raising additional capital may consider it important to nail down the interest rate applicable. The futures market makes this possible.

For example, on June 1, a treasurer is planning to issue $50 million of bonds with a 13-percent coupon. It will take her about three months to complete the paperwork with the financing source. The treasurer uses the interest rate futures market to hedge against the possibility of rising interest

On June 1, it is assumed that 20-year U.S. Treasury bonds have a market yield of 12 percent. The treasurer sells (short) $50,000,000 of the Treasury bonds for delivery in three months. Assuming an eight-percent coupon on the bonds, the amount of cash that will be realized is:

$$
\begin{aligned}
P &= \sum_{t=1}^{40} \frac{\$40}{(1.06)^t} + \frac{\$1{,}000}{(1.06)^{40}} \\
&= \$40(15.0463) + \$1{,}000(.0972) \\
&= \$601.85 + \$97.20 \\
P &= \quad \$699.05 \\
&\quad \times \ 50{,}000 \\
\textit{Total } P &= \$34{,}952{,}500
\end{aligned}
$$

Three months later, interest rate levels have risen by one percentage point to 13 percent on 20-year U.S. Treasury bonds with an 8-percent coupon. The bonds of the corporation now come onto the market and must also pay a higher coupon by 1 percent—14 percent, for example. But by having used the futures market, the effective interest cost on the corporate bonds will be less than 14 percent.

The treasurer can cover her commitment to deliver the 20-year U.S. Treasury bonds with a face amount of $50,000,000 by purchasing them in the current (spot) market. At the higher interest rate level, the purchase price of the U.S. Treasury bonds will be lower than the $34,952,500 received on the sale of the futures contract. It will be:

$$P = \sum_{t=1}^{40} \frac{\$40}{(1.065)^t} + \frac{\$1{,}000}{(1.065)^{40}}$$

$$= \$40(14.1455) + \$1{,}000(0.0805)$$

$$= \$565.82 + \$80.50$$

$$P = \$646.32$$

$$\times \; 50{,}000$$

$$\textit{Total } P = \$32{,}316{,}000$$

The difference between the amount received on the futures contract and the amount paid to cover it is a gain of $2,636,500. Expressed as a savings per half year, this is:

$$\$2{,}636{,}500/\text{PVIFA}\ (7\%,\ 40\ \text{yrs}) = \$2{,}636{,}500/13.3317 = \$197{,}762.$$

Dividing this amount by the 50,000 bonds to be issued, represents a saving of approximately $4 per bond every half year. Since the coupon on the corporate bonds is 14 percent, this is a $70 semi-annual coupon, reduced to $66 by the savings obtained by using the futures market. The effective rate of interest will now be:

$$\$1{,}000 = \sum_{t=1}^{40} \frac{\$66}{(1+r)^t} + \frac{\$1{,}000}{(1+r)^{40}}$$

$$r = 6.60\%$$

$$\text{Effective rate} = 13.2\%$$

Taking into account the gains from the use of the futures market in Treasury bonds, the effective rate of interest on the corporate bonds is reduced to 13.2 percent. If interest rate levels during the three-month period had fallen instead of risen, a loss on the use of the futures market would have been incurred. But the corporate bonds could have been sold at a lower interest cost. The treasurer could have reduced the effective cost of the corporate borrowing to offset the rise in interest rate levels exactly if she had sold a larger face amount of U.S. Treasury bonds in the futures market; but she cannot determine the exact amount she would have to sell without knowing how much interest rate levels would change (or rise as in this example). The use of the futures market in interest rates has enabled the treasurer to obtain protection against changing interest rate levels while the financing arrangements are made.

Riding the Yield Curve

As interest rates have risen in recent years, cash managers have tried to avoid holding idle cash. Rather, they have sought to obtain a return by investing cash balances. A substantial amount of such funds have been placed in very liquid, interest-earning marketable securities. U.S. Treasury bills have been used substantially as an investment instrument. The Treasury bills futures market has enabled investments in Treasury bills to be made in many alternative ways.

Suppose a cash manager has $1 million which is needed in 91 days to meet a commitment, and he invests in Treasury bills to earn interest during the 91 days. There are at least three alternative ways he can invest in the Treasury bills: (1) He can invest for a maturity of less than 91 days, planning to "roll over" the investment into other successive bills maturing at the end of 91 days. (2) He could buy a Treasury bill maturing in exactly 91 days. (3) He can buy a Treasury bill of maturity longer than 91 days with a plan of selling the bill at the end of 91 days. The strategy of purchasing bills of maturities longer than the planned holding period and selling them prior to maturity is referred to as *riding the yield curve.*

If the term structure of interest rates is positive, the longer maturity the cash manager can get into, the higher the yield will be. But the term structure itself reflects expectations of future supply and demand relationships, and these are subject to change. Risks may come from many sources. Changes may take place in the term structure of interest rates. The relation between the spot, forward, and futures rates may change. Among the investment alternatives that the cash manager may have for his available funds, there are different kinds and degrees of risk in relation to potential movements and changes in the money and capital markets.

Table 11A.4 **Illustrative Interest Rate Relations**

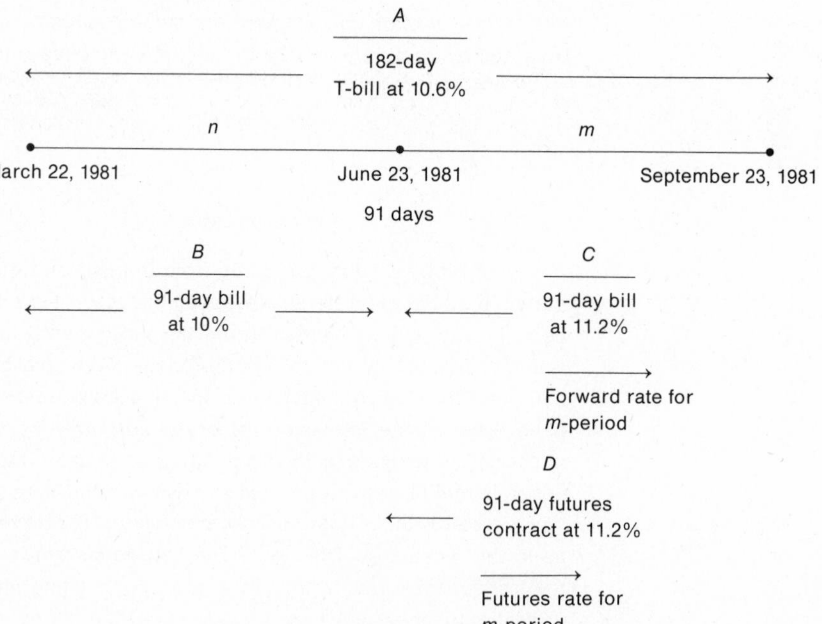

One alternative is simply to "match maturities." This would represent simply buying (under the previous example) a 91-day Treasury bill. The funds earn whatever Treasury bills earn during that 91-day period of time. Another alternative would be to ride the yield curve on an unhedged basis. An illustration would be to buy a 182-day Treasury bill with the intention of selling it at the end of 91 days. A third alternative would be to ride the yield curve in a hedged position. The data in Table 11A.4 illustrates this concept.

On March 22, 1981, buy the 182-day T-bill on a 10.6 percent basis at $947 simple interest. Sell a 91-day futures contract on a 11.2 percent basis at $972 simple interest. On June 23, 1981, deliver the 182-day T-bill with 91 days remaining to meet the futures contract requirement. The treasurer has locked in the 10.6 percent yield on the 182-day bill as compared with the lower 10 percent yield on the 91-day bill available on March 22, 1981.[1]

The differential gain from riding the yield curve in a hedged position results from the positive slope of the term structure curve and the relation between short-term and long-term rates, which reflects the unbiased expectations theory. Compared with simply taking a position in the 91-day T-bill, riding the yield curve in a hedged position requires two transactions and two commissions instead of one. The results also depend upon the commission levels in relation to the extent that the yield curve is positively sloped. Also, the higher relative purchases of the 182-day bill as compared to the 91-day bill will tend to drive up the price (and lower the yield) of the longer-term bill as compared to the shorter-term bill. The sale of the T-bill futures will tend to drive down their prices (and raise the required yields). The actions that were taken to benefit from the positively sloped term structure will tend to flatten the slope of the curve. In the light of the types of transactions described, it is not likely that opportunities for abnormal returns would persist.

[1] To verify the 10.6 percent yield, note that the treasurer paid out $947 for the 182-day T-bill, and took in $972 on the sale of the 91-day futures contract, for a net gain of $25 for the quarter during which the funds were at risk. On an investment of $947, this represents an annual return of 4($25/$947) = 10.6 percent.

CHAPTER 12

SHORT-TERM FINANCING

In Chapter 8 we discussed the maturity structure of the firm's debt and showed how this structure can affect both risk and expected returns. However, a variety of short-term credits are available to the firm, and the financial manager must know the advantages and disadvantages of each. Accordingly, the present chapter discusses the main forms of short-term credit, considering both the characteristics and the sources of this credit.

Short-term credit is defined as debt originally scheduled for repayment within one year. The three major sources of funds with short maturities, ranked in descending order by volume of credit supplied, are (1) trade credit among firms, (2) loans from commercial banks, and (3) commercial paper.

Trade Credit

In the ordinary course of events, a firm buys its supplies and materials on credit from other firms, recording the debt as an *account payable*. Accounts payable, or *trade credit*, is the largest single category of short-term credit, representing about 40 percent of the current liabilities of nonfinancial corporations.[1] This percentage is somewhat larger for small firms; because small companies may not qualify for financing from other sources, they rely rather heavily on trade credit.

Trade credit is a spontaneous source of financing in that it arises from ordinary business transactions. For example, suppose a firm purchases an average of $2,000 a day on terms of net 30. On the average it will owe 30 times $2,000, or $60,000, to its suppliers. If its sales and consequently its purchases double, accounts payable will also double—to $120,000. The firm will have spontaneously generated an additional $60,000 of financing. Similarly, if the terms of credit are extended from 30 to 40 days, accounts payable will expand from $60,000 to $80,000; thus lengthening the credit period, as well as expanding sales and purchases, generates additional financing.

Credit Terms

The terms of sales, or *credit terms*, describe the payment obligation of the buyer. The following discussion outlines the four main factors that influence the length of credit terms: the economic nature of the product, the seller's circumstances, the buyer's circumstances, and cash discounts.

[1] In Chapter 10, we discussed trade credit from the viewpoint of minimizing investment in current assets. In the present chapter we look at the other side of the coin—trade credit as a source of rather than a use of financing. In Chapter 10 the use of trade credit by customers resulted in an asset investment called *accounts receivable*. In the present chapter, the use of trade credit gives rise to short-term obligations, generally called *accounts payable*.

Economic Nature of the Product Commodities with high sales turnover are sold on relatively short credit terms; buyers resell the products rapidly, generating cash that enables them to pay the suppliers. Groceries have a high turnover, but perishability also plays a role. The credit extended for fresh fruits and vegetables might run from five to ten days, whereas the credit extended on canned fruits and vegetables would more likely be fifteen to thirty days. Terms for items that have a slow retail turnover, such as jewelry, may run six months or longer.

Seller Circumstances Financially weak sellers must require cash or exceptionally short credit terms. For example, farmers sell livestock to meat-packing companies on a cash basis. In many industries, variations in credit terms can be used as a sales promotion device. Although the use of credit as a selling device could endanger sound credit management, the practice does occur, especially when the seller's industry has excess capacity. Also, sellers with proprietary products could use their position to impose relatively short credit terms. However, the reverse appears more often in practice; that is, financially strong sellers are suppliers of funds to small firms.

Buyer Circumstances In general, financially sound retailers who sell on credit may, in turn, receive slightly longer terms from suppliers. Some classes of retailers regarded as selling in particularly risky areas (such as clothing) receive extended credit terms, but are offered large discounts to encourage early payment.

Cash Discounts A cash discount is a reduction in price based on payment within a specified period. The costs of not taking cash discounts often exceed the rate of interest at which the buyer can borrow, so it is important that a firm be cautious in its use of trade credit as a source of financing; it could be quite expensive. If the firm borrows and takes the cash discount, the period during which accounts payable remain on the books is reduced. The effective length of credit is thus influenced by the size of discounts offered. Credit terms typically express the amount of the cash discount and the date of its expiration, as well as the final due date. Earlier we noted that one of the most frequently encountered terms is 2/10, net 30. (If payment is made within ten days of the invoice date, a 2 percent cash discount is allowed. If the cash discount is not taken, payment is due thirty days after the date of invoicing.) The cost of not taking cash discounts can be substantial, as shown here.[2]

Credit terms	Cost of credit if cash discount not taken (percent)
1/10, net 20	36.36
1/10, net 30	18.18
2/10, net 20	73.47
2/10, net 30	36.73

[2] The method of calculating the effective interest rate of not taking cash discounts was described in Chapter 11. It is:

$$\text{Cost or effective interest rate} = \frac{\text{Discount percent}}{(100 - \text{Discount percent})} \times \frac{360}{(\text{Final due date} - \text{Discount period})}$$

If the actual payment date is later than the "due date," that would be used in the calculations.

Concept of Net Credit

Trade credit has double-edged significance for the firm. It is a source of credit for financing purchases, and it is a use of funds to the extent that the firm finances credit sales to customers. For example, if, on the average, a firm sells $3,000 worth of goods a day and has an average collection period of forty days, at any balance sheet date it will have accounts receivable of approximately $120,000.

If the same firm buys $2,000 worth of materials a day and the balance is outstanding for twenty days, accounts payable will average $40,000. The firm is thus extending net credit of $80,000—the difference between accounts receivable and accounts payable.

Large firms and well-financed firms of all sizes tend to be net suppliers of trade credit; small firms and undercapitalized firms of all sizes tend to be net users of trade credit. It is impossible to generalize about whether it is better to be a net supplier or a net user; the choice depends on the firm's circumstances and on the various costs and benefits of receiving and using trade credit.

Advantages of Trade Credit as a Source of Financing

Trade credit, a customary part of doing business in most industries, is convenient and informal. A firm that does not qualify for credit from a financial institution may receive trade credit because previous experience has familiarized the seller with the creditworthiness of the customer. The seller knows the merchandising practices of the industry and is usually in a good position to judge the business ability of the customer and the risk of selling on credit. The amount of trade credit fluctuates with the buyer's purchases, subject to any credit limits that may be operative.

Whether trade credit costs more or less than other forms of financing is a moot question. The buyer often does not have any alternative form of financing available, and the costs may be commensurate with the risks to the seller. But in some instances trade credit is used simply because the buyer does not realize how expensive it is. In such circumstances, careful financial analysis may lead to the substitution of alternative forms of financing.

At the other extreme, trade credit may represent a virtual subsidy or sales promotion device offered by the seller. The authors know, for example, of cases where manufacturers quite literally supplied *all* the financing for new firms by selling on credit terms substantially longer than those of the new company. In one instance a manufacturer, eager to obtain a dealership in a particular area, made a loan to the new company to cover operating expenses during the initial phases and geared the payment of accounts payable to cash receipts. Even in such instances, however, the buying firm must be careful that it is not really paying a hidden financing cost in the form of higher product prices than those elsewhere. Extending credit involves a cost to the selling firm, and this firm may well be raising its own prices to offset the "free" credit it extends.

Importance of Good Credit Relationships

During the persistent inflation and recurrent periods of tight money of the past decade, selling firms have raised their standards for extending trade credit to their customers. Since "cleaning up" accounts receivable is one way to obtain a more favorable liquidity position, suppliers are becoming more selective when extending trade credit. Therefore, it is important for a firm to earn the confidence of its suppliers. This can be achieved by showing good financial ratios and by paying promptly. But even if these indicators are unfavorable, a firm may be able to obtain trade credit by offering realistic plans for improving its situation. The experience of W. T. Grant Company is illustrative. For the fiscal year ended January 31, 1975, W. T. Grant showed an operating loss of $177 million. Top management announced policy changes, replaced key personnel, and offered security through inventory liens. Grant's suppliers continued to extend trade credit, some in amounts greater than $1 million. W. T. Grant lost another $111 million in the next six months and went bankrupt. But its experience shows that it is possible to achieve continuity in the supply of trade credit even in adversity when the credit relationship is well managed.

Short-Term Financing by Commerical Banks

Commercial bank lending, which usually appears on the balance sheet as *notes payable*, is second in importance to trade credit as a source of short-term financing. Banks occupy a key position in the short-term and intermediate-term money markets. Their influence is greater than it appears to be from the dollar amounts they lend because commercial banks provide pivotal, nonspontaneous funds. As a firm grows, it may seek to meet additional financing needs by borrowing from commercial banks. If the firm is not successful, either because it does not meet the bank's credit standards or because credit conditions are tight, the firm may be forced to restrict its activities, causing a slowdown in its rate of growth.

Characteristics of Loans from Commercial Banks

In the following sections, the main characteristics of lending patterns of commercial banks are briefly described.

Forms of Loans A single loan obtained from a bank by a business firm is not different in principle from a loan obtained by an individual. In fact, it is often difficult to distinguish a bank loan to a small business from a personal loan. The loan is obtained by signing a conventional promissory note. Repayment is made in a lump sum at maturity (when the note is due) or in installments throughout the life of the loan.

A *line of credit* is a formal or informal understanding between the bank and the borrower, setting a maximum loan balance the bank will extend to the firm. For example, the bank loan officer may indicate to a financial manager that the bank regards the firm as "good" for up to $300,000 for the forthcoming year. Subsequently, the financial manager tells the bank that it would like to "take down" the first $100,000. This amount is credited by the bank to the customer's checking account. The firm may subsequently borrow up to $200,000 additional on the basis of the line of credit.

If the firm does not use the total amount of the line, it may be required to pay a commitment fee of about one-half of one percent on the unused portion. The logic is that the bank has earmarked some of its lending ability for the use of this firm and has therefore incurred an opportunity cost of not having loaned the funds to another borrower. The commitment fee is a form of compensation to the bank.

The bank will notify the customer of interest payments due every ninety days. In addition, it is expected that the loan will be "cleaned up" by payment within a twelve-month period. This relates to the underlying theory of commercial bank lending—financing the temporary seasonal needs of a firm during the year. As the increased inventories or receivables of the borrowing firm are liquidated, it is expected that the firm will be able to repay its loan. As its seasonal needs for funds arise in the following year, the bank will again make a line of credit available to the firm if its repayment performance has been satisfactory.

Size of Customers Banks make loans to firms of all sizes. By dollar amount, the bulk of loans from commercial banks is obtained by firms with total assets of $5 million and more. But by number of loans, firms with total assets of $50,000 and less account for about 40 percent of bank loans.

Maturity Commercial banks concentrate on the short-term lending market. Short-term loans make up about two-thirds of bank loans by dollar amount, whereas *term loans* (loans with maturities longer than one year) make up about one-third.

Security If a potential borrower is a questionable credit risk, or if the firm's financing needs exceed the amount that the loan officer of the bank considers to be prudent on an unsecured basis, some form of security is required. More than half the dollar value of bank loans is secured. (The forms of security are described later in this chapter.) In terms of the number of bank loans, two-thirds are secured or endorsed by a third party who guarantees payment of the loan in the event the borrower defaults.

Compensating Balances Banks typically require that a regular borrower maintain an average checking account balance equal to 15 or 20 percent of the outstanding loan. These balances, commonly called *compensating balances*, are a method of raising the effective interest rate. For example, if a firm needs $80,000 to pay off outstanding obligations but must maintain a 20 percent compensating balance, it must borrow $100,000 in order to obtain the required $80,000. If the stated interest rate is 10 percent, the effective cost is actually 12.5 percent ($10,000 divided by $80,000).[3] These *loan* compensating balances are, of course, added to any *service* compensating balances (discussed in Chapter 11) that the firm's bank may require.

Repayment of Bank Loans Because most bank deposits are subject to withdrawal on demand, commercial banks seek to prevent firms from using bank credit for permanent financing. A bank may therefore require its borrowers to "clean up" their short-term bank loans for at least one month each year. If a firm is unable to become free of bank debt at least part of each year, it is using bank financing for permanent needs and should develop additional sources of long-term or permanent financing.

Cost of Commercial Bank Loans The cost of commercial bank loans is measured with reference to the prime rate. The *prime rate* is the charge to the banks' most

[3] Note, however, that the compensating balance is generally set as a minimum monthly average; if the firm maintains this average anyway, the compensating balance requirement does not entail higher effective rates.

creditworthy customers. The prime rate has fluctuated between $10\frac{3}{4}$ and 21 percent in recent years. The level reflects the state of tightness or ease in general money market conditions.

If the firm can qualify as a prime risk because of its size and financial strength, the rate of interest will be one-half to three-quarters of a percent above the rediscount rate charged by Federal Reserve banks to commercial banks. On the other hand, a small firm with below-average financial ratios may be required to pay an effective rate of interest of two or more points above the prime rate. In addition, a firm which does not meet high credit standards may have to provide collateral security to qualify for a loan.

"Regular" Interest Determination of the effective, or true, rate of interest on a loan depends on the stated rate of interest and the lender's method of charging interest. If the interest is paid at the maturity of the loan, the stated rate of interest is the effective rate of interest. For example, on a $20,000 loan for one year at 14 percent, the interest is $2,800.

$$\text{``Regular'' loan, interest paid at maturity} = \frac{\text{Interest}}{\text{Borrowed amount}}$$

$$= \frac{\$2{,}800}{\$20{,}000} = 14\%$$

Discounted Interest If the bank deducts the interest in advance (discounts the loan), the effective rate of interest is increased. On the $20,000 loan for one year at 14 percent, the discount is $2,800, and the borrower obtains the use of only $17,200. The effective rate of interest is 16.28 percent (versus 14 percent on a "regular" loan):

$$\text{Discounted loan} = \frac{\text{Interest}}{\text{Borrowed amount} - \text{Interest}} = \frac{\$2{,}800}{\$17{,}200} = 16.28\%$$

Another aspect is the need to adjust the amount borrowed because of the discount method of collecting interest or the compensating balance requirement. In the example above, if the firm wants to receive $20,000 and borrows on a discounted basis at 14 percent, it must borrow $20,000/(1 − 0.14) = $23,255.81. The amount of interest is then (0.14)($23,255.81) = $3,255.81, and the effective interest rate can be verified to be $3,255.81/$20,000 = 16.28%. The computations involving compensating balance requirements would use the same logic.

A further complication arises if the period of the loan is less than one year. In the example, suppose the loan is for 90 days. The discount penalty then will be smaller. The amount of interest that will be deducted from the $20,000 borrowed will be $2,800/4 = $700. The discounted annualized interest rate will be $2,800/$19,300 = 14.51 percent. This is a lower cost than the 16.28 percent because the amount of funds usable by the borrower is the $20,000 less only 3 months' interest rather than a full year's interest.

Installment Loan If the loan is repaid in twelve monthly installments but the interest is calculated on the original balance, then the effective rate of interest is even higher. The borrower has the full amount of the money only during the first month and by the last month has already paid eleven-twelfths of the loan. Thus the borrower of \$20,000 pays \$2,800 for the use of about half the amount received (\$20,000 or \$17,200 depending on the method of charging interest), since the *average* amount outstanding during the year is only \$10,000 or \$8,600. If interest is paid at maturity, the approximate effective rate on an installment loan is calculated as follows:[4]

$$\text{Interest rate on average amount of installment loan} = \frac{\$2{,}800}{\$10{,}000} = 28\%$$

Under the discounting method, the effective cost of the installment loan is over 32 percent:

$$\text{Interest rate on discounted installment loan} = \frac{\$2{,}800}{\$8{,}600} = 32.56\%$$

Here we see that interest is calculated on the *original* amount of the loan, not on the amount actually outstanding (the declining balance), and this causes the effective interest rate to be approximately double the stated rate. Interest is calculated by the installment method on most consumer loans (for example, automobile loans), but the installment method is not often used for business loans larger than about \$15,000.

Choice of Banks

Banks have direct relationships with their borrowers. There is much personal association over the years, and the business problems of the borrower are frequently discussed. Thus banks often provide informal management counseling services. A potential borrower seeking such a relationship should recognize the important differences among banks considered in the following discussion.

1. Banks have different basic policies toward risk. Some are inclined to follow relatively conservative lending practices; others engage in what are properly termed *creative banking practices*. The policies reflect partly the personalities of the bank officers and partly the characteristics of the bank's deposit liabilities. Thus a bank with fluctuating deposit liabilities in a static community tends to be a conservative lender. A bank whose deposits are growing with little interruption may follow liberal credit policies. A large bank with diversification over broad geographical regions or among several industries can obtain the benefit of combining and averaging risks. Thus marginal credit risks that may be unacceptable to a small bank or to a specialized unit bank can be pooled by a branch banking system to reduce the overall risks of a group of marginal accounts.
2. Some bank loan officers are active in providing counsel and in stimulating development loans to firms in their early and formative years. Certain banks even have specialized departments to make loans to firms expected to become growth firms. Bankers in such departments can provide much counseling to customers.

[4] More complicated formulas typically make some different assumptions about calculation of the average amount of funds made available to the borrower.

3. Banks differ in the extent to which they support a borrower's activities in bad times. This characteristic is referred to as the bank's *degree of loyalty*. Some banks put great pressure on a business to liquidate its loans when the firm's outlook becomes clouded, whereas others stand by the firm and work diligently to help it attain a more favorable condition.
4. Another characteristic in which banks differ is the degree of deposit stability. Instability arises not only from fluctuations in the level of deposits but also from the composition of deposits. Deposits can take the form of *demand deposits* (checking accounts) or *time deposits* (saving accounts, certificates of deposit, Christmas clubs). Total deposits tend to be more stable when time deposits are substantial. Differences in deposit stability go a long way toward explaining differences in the extent to which banks are willing or able to help borrowers work their way out of difficulties or even crises.
5. Banks differ greatly in the degree of loan specialization. Larger banks have separate departments specializing in different kinds of loans, such as real estate, installment, and commercial loans. Within these broad categories they may specialize by line of business, such as steel, machinery, or textiles. Smaller banks are likely to reflect the nature of the business and economic environment in which they operate. They tend to become specialists in specific lines, such as oil, construction, or agriculture. The borrower can obtain more creative cooperation and more active support at the bank that has the greatest experience and familiarity with the borrower's particular type of business. The financial manager should therefore choose a bank with care. The bank that is excellent for one firm may be unsatisfactory for another.
6. The size of a bank can be an important characteristic. Since the maximum loan a bank can make to any customer is generally limited to 10 percent of the bank's capital accounts (capital stock plus retained earnings), it generally is not appropriate for large firms to develop borrowing relationships with small banks.
7. With the heightened competition among commercial banks and other financial institutions, the aggressiveness of banks has increased. Modern commercial banks now offer a wide range of financial and business services. Most large banks have business development departments that provide counseling to firms and serve as intermediaries on a wide variety of their requirements.

Commercial Paper

Commercial paper, which consists of promissory notes of large firms, is sold primarily to other business firms, insurance companies, pension funds, and banks. Although the amounts of commercial paper outstanding are much smaller than bank loans outstanding, this form of financing has grown rapidly in recent years.

Maturity and Cost

Maturities of commercial paper generally vary from two months to one year, with an average of about five months. The rates on prime commercial paper vary, but they are generally about half a percent below those on prime business loans. And since compensating balances are not required for commercial paper, the *effective* cost differential is still wider.[5]

Use

The use of the open market for commercial paper is restricted to a comparatively small number of concerns that are exceptionally good credit risks. Dealers prefer to handle the paper of concerns whose net worth is $10 million or more and whose annual borrowing exceeds $1 million.

Advantages and Disadvantages

The commercial-paper market has some significant advantages:

1. It permits the broadest and the most advantageous distribution of paper.
2. It provides more funds at lower rates than do other methods.
3. The borrower avoids the inconvenience and expense of financing arrangements with a number of institutions, each of which requires a compensating balance.
4. Publicity and prestige accrue to the borrower as its product and paper become more widely known.
5. The commercial-paper dealer frequently offers valuable advice to clients.

A basic limitation of the commercial-paper market is that the size of the funds available is limited to the excess liquidity that corporations (the main suppliers of funds) have at any particular time. Another disadvantage is that a debtor who is in temporary financial difficulty receives little help because commercial-paper dealings are impersonal. Banks are much more personal and much more likely to help a good customer weather a temporary storm.[6]

Effects of Inflation

During periods of inflation and tight money, many commercial-paper sellers are pushed out of the market. Ryder System, a Florida trucking company, was forced to turn to bank loans for $10 million of financing during 1974 because they were able to find buyers for only $15 million of their commercial paper. Thus, during inflationary periods, firms may be forced to seek the more expensive bank loans since they can no longer sell the cheaper commercial paper. Bankers acceptances gain popularity during inflationary periods. A bankers acceptance is a draft drawn by an individual and accepted by a bank; it orders the bank to pay a specific sum to a third party at a particular time. Basically, it is a check whose payment is guaranteed by the bank's "acceptance." Bankers acceptances are an effective method of short-term financing since the drawer gains time before funds are due. The appeal of bankers acceptances, which are traded in an active secondary market,

[5] However, this factor is offset to some extent by the fact that firms issuing commercial paper are sometimes required by commercial-paper dealers to have unused bank lines of credit to back up their outstanding commercial paper, and fees must be paid on these lines.

[6] This point was emphasized dramatically in the immediate aftermath of the Penn Central bankruptcy. Penn Central had a large amount of commercial paper that went into default and embarrassed corporate treasurers who had been holding the paper as part of their liquidity reserves. Immediately after the bankruptcy, the commercial-paper market dried up to a large extent, and some companies that had relied heavily on this market found themselves under severe liquidity pressure as their commercial paper matured and could not be refunded.

results from two basic characteristics. First, they are safe. Since they usually finance the shipment and storage of goods, the inventory can be pledged as collateral. Return to investors is usually comparable to the return on a good certificate of deposit. During periods of inflation when investors become increasingly selective, a bankers acceptance may look safer than commercial paper or even the certificates of deposit of some banks. Second, when an acceptance is backed by readily marketable goods and a warehouse receipt has been issued, the acceptance is eligible for rediscount with the Federal Reserve.

Use of Security in Short-Term Financing

Given a choice, it is ordinarily better to borrow on an unsecured basis, since the bookkeeping costs of secured loans are often high. However, it frequently happens that a potential borrower's credit rating is not sufficiently strong to justify the loan. If the loan can be secured by some form of collateral to be claimed by the lender in the event of default, then the lender may extend credit to an otherwise unacceptable firm. Similarly, a firm that can borrow on an unsecured basis may elect to use security if it finds that this will induce lenders to quote a lower interest rate.

Several different kinds of collateral can be employed—marketable stocks or bonds, land or buildings, equipment, inventory, and accounts receivable. Marketable securities make excellent collateral, but few firms hold portfolios of stocks and bonds. Similarly, real property (land and buildings) and equipment are good forms of collateral, but they are generally used as security for long-term loans. The bulk of secured short-term business borrowing involves the pledge of short-term assets—accounts receivable or inventories.

In the past, state laws varied greatly with regard to the use of security in financing. By the late 1960s, however, most states had adopted the *Uniform Commercial Code* (UCC), which standardized and simplified the procedure for establishing loan security.

The heart of the UCC is the *security agreement*, a standardized document or form listing the specific pledged assets. The assets can be items of equipment, accounts receivable, or inventories. Procedures for financing under the UCC are described in the following sections.

Financing Accounts Receivable

Accounts receivable financing involves either the assigning of receivables or the selling of receivables (factoring). Assigning, or pledging, of accounts receivable is characterized by the fact that the lender not only has a lien on the receivables but also has recourse to the borrower (seller); if the person or firm that bought the goods does not pay, the selling firm must take the loss. In other words, the risk of default on the accounts receivable pledged remains with the borrower. Also, the buyer of the goods is not ordinarily notified about the pledging of the receivables. The financial institution that lends on the security of accounts receivable is generally either a commercial bank or one of the large industrial finance companies.

Factoring, or selling accounts receivable, involves the purchase of accounts receivable by the lender without recourse to the borrower (seller). The buyer of the goods is notified of the transfer and makes payment directly to the lender. Since the factoring firm assumes the risk of default on bad accounts, it must do the credit checking. Accordingly, factors provide not only money but also a credit department for the borrower. Incidentally, the same financial institutions that make loans against pledged receivables also serve as factors. Thus, depending on the circumstances and the wishes of the borrower, a financial institution will provide either form of receivables financing.

Procedure for Pledging Accounts Receivable

The financing of accounts receivable is initiated by a legally binding agreement between the seller of the goods and the financing institution. The agreement sets forth in detail the procedure to be followed and the legal obligations of both parties. Once the working relationship has been established, the seller periodically takes a batch of invoices to the financing institution. The lender reviews the invoices and makes an appraisal of the buyers. Invoices of companies that do not meet the lender's credit standards are not accepted for pledging. The financial institution seeks to protect itself at every phase of the operation. Selection of sound invoices is the essential first step. If the buyer of the goods does not pay the invoice, the lender still has recourse against the seller of the goods. However, if many buyers default, the seller may be unable to meet the obligation to the financial institution.

Additional protection afforded the lender is that the loan is generally for less than 100 percent of the pledged receivables; for example, the lender may advance the selling firm 75 percent of the amount of the pledged receivables.

The following example shows how accounts receivables financing works from the standpoint of the user. Rochester Electronics Company has annual credit sales of \$2 million. It has an average balance in accounts receivable of \$400,000; thus its receivables turn over 5 times per year. Rochester uses accounts receivables financing to provide needed funds. The financing arrangement specifies that a 15 percent reserve is to be deducted from the funds advanced to protect against returns on disputed items. The annual interest rate is 18 percent (the current bank prime rate plus 2 percent), charged on the amount of receivables less the reserve requirement, and deducted in advance.

The calculation of the effective interest rate is as follows:

$$\text{Average duration of advance} = 360/5 = 72 \text{ days}$$

$$\text{Periodic interest rate per advance} = 18\%/5 = 3.6\%$$

$$\text{Reserve} = (.15)(\$400{,}000) = \$60{,}000$$

$$\text{Interest charge} = (.036)(\$400{,}000 - \$60{,}000) = \$12{,}240$$

$$\text{Annual interest charge} = \$12{,}240 \times 5 = \$61{,}200$$

$$\text{Net amount received} = \$400{,}000 - \$60{,}000 - \$12{,}240 = \$327{,}760$$

$$\text{Effective interest rate} = \$61{,}200/\$327{,}760 = 18.7\%$$

The cost to Rochester is not affected by the reserve, since interest is paid only after deducting the reserve. However, the financing arrangement provides for deduction of the interest charge in determining the net amount received by Rochester. This raises the effective interest rate from the 18 percent nominal to the 18.7 percent level.

Procedure for Factoring Accounts Receivable

The procedure for factoring is somewhat different from that for pledging. Again, an agreement between the seller and the factor is made to specify legal obligations and procedural arrangements. When the seller receives an order from a buyer, a credit approval slip is written and immediately sent to the factoring company for a credit check. If the factor does not approve the sale, the seller generally refuses to fill the order. This procedure informs the seller, prior to the sale, about the buyer's creditworthiness and acceptability to the factor. If the sale is approved, shipment is made and the invoice is stamped to notify the buyer to make payment directly to the factoring company.

The factor performs three functions in carrying out the procedure outlined above: (1) credit checking, (2) lending, and (3) risk bearing. The seller can select various combinations of these functions by changing provisions in the factoring agreement. For example, a small- or medium-sized firm can avoid establishing a credit department. The factor's service may well be less costly than a department that has a capacity in excess of the firm's credit volume. Also, if the firm uses a part-time noncredit specialist to perform credit checking, the person's lack of education, training, and experience may result in excessive losses.

The seller may, for example, have the factor perform the credit-checking and risk-taking functions but not the lending function. In this situation, the following procedure is carried out on receipt of a $10,000 order. The factor checks and approves the invoices, and the goods are shipped on terms of net 30. Payment is made to the factor, who remits to the seller. But if the factor has received only $8,500 by the end of the credit period, it must still remit $10,000 to the seller (less the factor's fees, of course).

Now consider the more typical situation, where the factor performs a lending function by making payment in advance of collection. The goods are shipped, and even though payment is not due for thirty days, the factor immediately makes funds available to the seller. Suppose $10,000 worth of goods is shipped; the factoring commission for credit checking is $1\frac{1}{2}$ percent of the invoice price, or $150; and the interest expense is computed at the prime rate plus two percent—for example, a 15 percent annual rate on the invoice amount, or $125.[7] The seller's accounting entry is as follows:

Cash	$8,725	
Interest expense	125	
Factoring commission	150	
Reserve: Due from factor on collection of account	1,000	
Accounts receivable		$10,000

The $1,000 due from the factor on collection of the account is a 10 percent reserve established by the factor to cover disputes between sellers and buyers on damaged

[7] Since the interest is for only one month, we take one-twelfth of the stated rate, 15 percent, and multiply this by the $10,000 invoice price:

$$\frac{1}{12} \times 0.15 \times \$10{,}000 = \$125$$

Note that the effective rate of interest is really more than 15 percent, because a discounting procedure is used and the borrower does not get the full $10,000. In many instances, however, the factoring contract calls for interest to be computed on the invoice price *less* the factoring commission and the reserve account.

goods, goods returned by the buyer to the seller, and failure to make an outright sale of the goods. The amount is paid to the seller when the factor collects on the account.

Factoring is normally a continuous process rather than the single cycle described above. The seller of the goods receives orders and transmits the purchase orders to the factor for approval; on approval, the goods are shipped; the factor advances the money to the seller; the buyers pay the factor when payment is due; and the factor periodically remits any excess reserve to the seller of the goods. Once a routine is established, a continuous circular flow of goods and funds takes place among the seller, the buyers, and the factor. Thus, once the factoring agreement is in force, funds from this source are *spontaneous*.

Cost of Receivables Financing

Accounts receivable pledging and factoring services are convenient and advantageous, but they can be costly. The credit checking commission is 1 to 3 percent of the amount of invoices accepted by the factor, and the cost of money is reflected in the interest rate (somewhat above the prevailing prime rate) charged on the unpaid balance of the funds advanced by the factor. Where the risk to the factor is excessive, the factor purchases the invoices (with or without recourse) at discounts from face value.

Evaluation of Receivables Financing

It cannot be said categorically that accounts receivable financing is always either a good or a bad method of raising funds for an individual business. Among the advantages is, first, the flexibility of this source of financing. As the firm's sales expand and more financing is needed, a larger volume of invoices is generated automatically. Because the dollar amounts of invoices vary directly with sales, the amount of readily available financing increases. Second, receivables or invoices provide security for a loan that a firm might otherwise be unable to obtain. Third, factoring provides the services of a credit department that might otherwise be available to the firm only under much more expensive conditions.

Accounts receivable financing also has disadvantages. First, when invoices are numerous and relatively small in dollar amount, the administrative costs involved may render this method of financing inconvenient and expensive. Second, the firm is using a highly liquid asset as security. For a long time, accounts receivable financing was frowned on by most trade creditors; it was regarded as confession of a firm's unsound financial position. It is no longer regarded in this light, however, and many sound firms engage in receivables pledging or factoring. Still, the traditional attitude causes some trade creditors to refuse to sell on credit to a firm that is factoring or pledging its receivables, on the ground that this practice removes one of the most liquid of the firm's assets and, accordingly, weakens the position of other creditors.

Future Use of Receivables Financing

We will make a prediction at this point. In the future, accounts receivable financing will increase in relative importance. Computer technology is rapidly advancing toward the point where credit records of individuals and firms can be kept in computer memory units. Systems already have been devised whereby a retailer can insert an individual's magnetic credit card into a box and receive a signal showing whether the person's credit is good and whether a bank is willing to buy the receivable created when the store completes the sale. The cost of handling invoices will be greatly reduced from present-day costs because the new systems will be so highly automated. This will make it possible to use accounts receivable financing for very small sales, and it will reduce the cost of all receivables financing. The net result will be a marked expansion of accounts receivable financing.

Inventory Financing

A rather large volume of credit is secured by business inventories. If a firm is a relatively good credit risk, the mere existence of the inventory may be a sufficient basis for receiving an unsecured loan. If the firm is a relatively poor risk, the lending institution may insist on security, which often takes the form of a blanket lien against the inventory. Alternatively, trust receipts, field warehouse financing, or collateral certificates can be used to secure loans. These methods of using inventories as security are discussed below.

Blanket Inventory Lien

The blanket inventory lien gives the lending institution a lien against all inventories of the borrower. However, the borrower is free to sell the inventories; thus the value of the collateral can be reduced.

Trust Receipts

Because of the weaknesses of the blanket lien for inventory financing, another kind of security is often used—the trust receipt. A trust receipt is an instrument acknowledging that the borrower holds the goods in trust for the lender. On receiving funds from the lender, the borrowing firm conveys a trust receipt for the goods. The goods can be stored in a public warehouse or held on the borrower's premises. The trust receipt provides that the goods are held in trust for the lender or are segregated on the borrower's premises on behalf of the lender and that proceeds from the sale of such goods are transmitted to the lender at the end of each day. Automobile dealer financing is the best example of trust receipt financing.

One defect of this form of financing is the requirement that a trust receipt must be issued for specific goods. For example, if the security is bags of coffee beans, the trust receipts must indicate the bags by number. In order to validate its trust receipts, the lending institution must send someone to the borrower's premises to see that the bag numbers are correctly listed. Furthermore, complex legal requirements for trust receipts require the attention of a bank officer. Problems are compounded if borrowers are widely separated geographically from the lender. To offset these inconveniences, field warehousing is coming into wide use as a method of securing loans with inventory.

Field Warehouse Financing

Like trust receipts, field warehouse financing uses inventory as security. A public warehouse represents an independent third party engaged in the business of storing goods. Sometimes the warehouse is not practical because of the bulkiness of goods and the expense of transporting them to and from the borrower's premises. Field warehouse financing represents an economical method of inventory financing in which the "warehouse" is established on the borrower's premises. To provide inventory supervision, the lending institution employs a third party in the arrangement, the field warehousing company. This company acts as the control (or supervisory) agent for the lending institution.

Field warehousing is illustrated by a simple example. Suppose a potential borrower has stacked iron in an open yard on its premises. A field warehouse can be established if, say, a field warehousing concern places a temporary fence around the iron and erects a sign stating: "This is a field warehouse supervised and conducted by the Smith Field Warehousing Corporation."

The example illustrates the two elements in the establishment of a warehouse: (1) public notification of the field warehouse arrangement and (2) supervision of the warehouse by a custodian of the field warehouse concern. When the field warehousing operation is relatively small, the second condition is sometimes violated by hiring an employee of the borrower to supervise the inventory. This practice is viewed as undesirable by the lending institution because there is no control over the collateral by a person independent of the borrowing concern.[8]

The field warehouse financing operation is described best by a specific illustration. Assume that a tomato canner is interested in financing operations by bank borrowing. The canner has funds sufficient to finance 15 to 20 percent of operations during the canning season. These funds are adequate to purchase and process an initial batch of tomatoes. As the cans are put into boxes and rolled into the storerooms, the canner needs additional funds for both raw materials and labor.

Because of the canner's poor credit rating, the bank decides that a field warehousing operation is necessary to secure its loans. The field warehouse is established, and the custodian notifies the lending institution of the description, by number, of the boxes of canned tomatoes in storage and under his control. Thereupon the lending institution establishes for the canner a deposit on which it can draw. From this point on, the bank finances the operations. The canner needs only enough cash to initiate the cycle. The farmers bring more tomatoes; the canner processes them; the cans are boxed and the boxes put into the field warehouse; field warehouse receipts are drawn up and sent to the bank; the bank establishes further deposits for the canner on the basis of the receipts; and the canner can draw on the deposits to continue the cycle.

Of course, the canner's ultimate objective is to sell the canned tomatoes. As the canner receives purchase orders, it transmits them to the bank, and the bank directs the custodian to release the inventories. It is agreed that, as remittances are received by the canner, they will be turned over to the bank. These remittances pay off the loans made by the bank.

Typically, a seasonal pattern exists. At the beginning of the tomato harvesting and canning season, the canner's cash needs and loan requirements begin to rise, and they reach a maximum by the end of the canning season. It is hoped that, just before the new canning season begins, the canner has sold a sufficient volume to

[8] This absence of independent control was the main cause of the breakdown that resulted in the huge losses connected with loans to the Allied Crude Vegetable Oil Company headed by Anthony (Tino) DeAngelis. American Express Field Warehousing Company hired men from Allied's staff as custodians. Their dishonesty was not discovered because of another breakdown—the fact that the American Express touring inspector did not actually take a physical inventory of the warehouses. As a consequence, the swindle was not discovered until losses running into the hundreds of millions of dollars had been suffered. See Norman C. Miller, *The Great Salad Oil Swindle* (Baltimore: Penguin Books, 1965), pp. 72–77.

have paid off the loan completely. If for some reason the canner has had a bad year, the bank may carry the company over another year to enable it to sell off its inventory.

Acceptable Products In addition to canned foods, which account for about 17 percent of all field warehouse loans, many other product inventories provide a basis for field warehouse financing. Some of these are miscellaneous groceries, which represent about 13 percent; lumber products, about 10 percent; and coal and coke, about 6 percent.

These products are relatively nonperishable and are sold in well-developed, organized markets. Nonperishability protects the lender who has to take over the security. For this reason a bank will not make a field warehousing loan on perishables such as fresh fish. However, frozen fish, which can be stored for a long time, can be field warehoused. An organized market also aids the lender in disposing of inventory that it takes over. Banks are not interested in going into the canning or the fish business. They want to be able to dispose of an inventory quickly and with the expenditure of a minimum amount of their own time.

Cost of Financing The fixed costs of a field warehousing arrangement are relatively high; such financing is therefore not suitable for a very small firm. If a field warehouse company sets up the warehouse itself, it typically sets a minimum fixed charge, plus about 1 or 2 percent of the amount of credit extended to the borrower. Furthermore, the financing institution charges interest at a rate somewhat above the prevailing prime rate. The minimum size of an efficient warehousing operation requires an inventory of about $100,000.

Appraisal The use of field warehouse financing as a source of funds for business firms has many advantages. First, the amount of funds available is flexible because the financing is tied to the growth of inventories, which in turn is related directly to financing needs. Second, the arrangement increases the acceptability of inventories as loan collateral. Some inventories are not accepted by a bank as a security without a field warehousing arrangement. Third, the necessity for inventory control, safekeeping, and the use of specialists in warehousing has resulted in improved warehouse practices. The services of the field warehouse companies have often saved money for the firm, in spite of the financing costs mentioned above. The field warehouse company may suggest inventory practices that reduce both the number of people the firm has to employ and inventory damage and loss as well.

The major disadvantage of a field warehousing operation is the fixed cost element, which reduces the feasibility of this form of financing for small firms.

Collateral Certificates

A collateral certificate guarantees the existence of the amount of inventory pledged as loan collateral. It is a statement issued periodically to the lender by a third party, who certifies that the inventory exists and that it will be available if needed.

This method of bank financing is becoming increasingly popular, primarily because of its flexibility. First, there is no need for physical segregation or possesion of inventories. Therefore, collateral certificates can even be used to cover work-in-process inventories, facilitating more freedom in the movement of goods. Second, the collateral certificate can provide for a receivables financing plan, allowing financing to continue smoothly as inventories are converted into receivables. Third, the certificate issuer usually provides a number of services to simplify loan administration for both the borrower and the lender.

Summary

Short-term credit is debt originally scheduled for repayment within one year. The three major sources of short-term credit are trade credit among firms, loans from commercial banks, and commercial paper.

Trade credit (represented by accounts payable) is the largest single category of short-term credit; it is especially important for smaller firms. Trade credit is a *spontaneous source of financing* in that it arises from ordinary business transactions; as sales increase, so does the supply of financing from accounts payable.

Bank credit occupies a pivotal position in the short-term money market. Banks provide the marginal credit that allows firms to expand more rapidly than is possible through retained earnings and trade credit. A denial of bank credit often means that a firm must slow its rate of growth.

Bank interest rates are quoted in three ways—regular compound interest, discount interest, and installment interest. Regular interest needs no adjustment; it is correct as stated. Discount interest requires a small upward adjustment to make it comparable to regular compound interest rates. Installment interest rates require a large adjustment, and frequently the true interest rate is double the quoted rate for an installment loan.

Bank loans are personal in the sense that the financial manager meets with the banker, discusses the terms of the loan, and reaches an agreement that requires direct and personal negotiation. Commercial paper, however, although it is physically similar to a bank loan, is sold in a broad, impersonal market. A California firm might, for example, sell commercial paper to a manufacturer in the Midwest.

Only the very strongest firms are able to use the commercial-paper markets. The nature of these markets is such that the firm selling the paper must have a reputation so good that buyers of the paper are willing to buy it without any sort of credit check. Interest rates in the commercial-paper market are the lowest available to business borrowers.

The most common forms of collateral used for short-term credit are accounts receivable and inventories. Accounts receivable financing can be done either by pledging the receivables or by selling them outright (often called *factoring*). When the receivables are pledged, the borrower retains the risk that the person or firm owing the receivables will not pay; in factoring, this risk is typically passed on to the lender. Because factors take the risk of default, they investigate the purchaser's credit; therefore, factors can perform three functions: lending, risk bearing, and credit checking. When receivables are pledged, the lender typically performs only the first of these functions.

Loans can be secured by inventories under a number of arrangements. For certain kinds of inventory the technique known as *field warehousing* is used to provide security to the lender. Under a field warehousing arrangement, the inventory is physically controlled by a warehouse company, which releases the inventory only on order from the lending institution. Canned goods, lumber, steel, coal, and other standardized products are goods usually covered in field warehouse arrangements.

Questions

12.1 It is inevitable that firms will obtain a certain amount of their financing in the form of trade credit, which is (to some extent) a free source of funds. What are some other reasons for firms to use trade credit?

12.2 Discuss this statement: Commercial-paper interest rates are always lower than bank loan rates to a given borrower. Nevertheless, many firms perfectly capable of selling commercial paper employ higher-cost bank credit. Indicate (a) why commercial-paper rates are lower than bank rates and (b) why firms might use bank credit in spite of its higher cost.

12.3 Discuss this statement: Trade credit has an explicit interest rate cost if discounts are available but not taken. There are also some intangible costs associated with the failure to take discounts.

12.4 A large manufacturing firm that had been selling its products on a 3/10, net 30 basis changed its credit terms to 1/20, net 90. What changes might be anticipated on the balance sheets of the manufacturer and of its customers?

12.5 The availability of bank credit is more important to small firms than to large ones. Why?

12.6 What factors should a firm consider in selecting its primary bank? Would it be feasible for a firm to have a primary deposit bank (the bank where most of its funds are deposited) and a different primary loan bank (the bank where it does most of its borrowing)?

12.7 Indicate whether each of the following changes will raise or lower the cost of a firm's accounts receivable financing, and explain why.

a. The firm eases up on its credit standards in order to increase sales.
b. The firm institutes a policy of refusing to make credit sales if the amount of the purchase (invoice) is below $100. Previously, about 40 percent of all invoices were below $100.
c. The firm agrees to give recourse to the finance company for all defaults.
d. A firm that already has a recourse arrangement is merged into a larger, stronger company.
e. A firm without a recourse arrangement changes its terms of trade from net 30 to net 90.

12.8 Would a firm that manufactures specialized machinery for a few large customers be more likely to use a form of inventory financing or a form of accounts receivable financing? Why?

12.9 Discuss this statement: A firm that factors its accounts receivable will look better in a ratio analysis than one that assigns its receivables.

12.10 Why would it not be practical for a typical retailer to use field warehouse financing?

12.11 Describe an industry that might be expected to use each of the following forms of credit, and explain your reasons for choosing each one:

a. field warehouse financing
b. factoring
c. accounts receivable pledging
d. trust receipts
e. none of these

Problems

12.1 What is the equivalent annual interest rate that would be lost if a firm failed to take the cash discount under each of the following terms?

a. 1/15, net 30
b. 2/10, net 60
c. 3/10, net 60
d. 2/10, net 40
e. 1/10, net 40

12.2 Benton's Garden Shop is negotiating with Millstone Bank for a $12,000 one-year loan. Millstone has offered Benton the following alternatives:

1. A 16 percent annual interest rate, with no compensating balance and interest due at the end of the year
2. A 12 percent annual interest rate, with a 15 percent compensating balance requirement and interest due at the end of the year
3. An 11 percent annual interest rate, with a 10 percent compensating balance and the loan discounted
4. A 10 percent annual interest rate, with the loan to be repaid in 12 monthly installments, and interest due at the end of the year

Which alternative has the lowest effective interest rate?

12.3 Wagner Industries is having difficulty paying its bills and is considering foregoing its trade discounts on $250,000 of accounts payable. As an alternative, Wagner can obtain a sixty-day note with a 14 percent annual interest rate. The note will be discounted, and the trade credit terms are 2/10, net 60.

a. Which alternative has the lower effective cost?
b. If Wagner does not take its trade discounts, what conclusions may outsiders draw?

12.4 Because of crop failures last year, the San Joaquin Packing Company has no funds available to finance its canning operations over the next 6 months. It estimates that it will require $850,000 for inventory financing during the period. One alternative being considered is to establish a 6-month $1,000,000 line of credit with terms of 12 percent annual interest on the used portion, 1 percent commitment fee on the unused portion, and a $150,000 compensating balance at all times.

Expected inventory levels to be financed are:

Month	Amount
July 19X0	$150,000
August	600,000
September	850,000
October	600,000
November	350,000
December	0

Calculate the cost of the line of credit, including interest charges and commitment fees.

(Hint: Each month's borrowings will be $150,000 greater than the inventory level to be financed because of the compensating balance requirement.)

12.5 Because of the relative imperishability of canned vegetables, field warehouse financing would also be appropriate for the San Joaquin Packing Company in

Problem 12.4. The costs of the field warehousing alternative in this case would be a flat fee of $500, and 10 percent annual interest on all outstanding credit, plus 1 percent of the maximum amount of credit extended.

a. Calculate the total cost of the field warehousing operation.

b. Compare the cost of the field warehousing to the line of credit in Problem 12.4. Which alternative should San Joaquin choose?

12.6 The balance sheet of the Pacific Finance Corporation is shown here.

a. Calculate commercial paper as a percentage of short-term financing, as a percentage of total-debt financing, and as a percentage of all financing.

b. Why do finance companies such as Pacific Finance use commercial paper to such a great extent?

c. Why do they use both bank loans and commercial paper?

Pacific Finance Corporation
Balance Sheet
(millions of dollars)

Assets		**Liabilities**	
Cash	$ 75	Bank loans	$ 250
Net receivables	2,400	Commercial paper	825
Marketable securities	150	Others	375
Repossessions	5	Total due within a year	$1,450
Total current assets	$2,630	Long-term debt	1,000
Other assets	170	Total shareholders' equity	350
Total assets	$2,800	Total claims	$2,800

12.7 The Shelby Saw Corporation has fallen behind in its accounts payable. Although its terms of purchase are net 30 days, the current accounts payable balance represents 60 days' purchases. Shelby is seeking to increase bank borrowings in order to become current in meeting its trade obligations (that is, to reduce accounts payable to 30 days' purchases). The company's balance sheet is shown below:

Shelby Saw Corporation Balance Sheet

Assets		**Liabilities**	
Cash	$ 100,000	Accounts payable	$ 600,000
Accounts receivable	300,000	Bank loans	900,000
Inventory	1,400,000	Current liabilities	$1,500,000
Current assets	$1,800,000	Long-term debt	700,000
Fixed assets	1,200,000	Net worth	800,000
Total assets	$3,000,000	Total liabilities	$3,000,000

a. How much financing is required to eliminate past due accounts payable?

b. As a bank loan officer, would you make the loan? Explain.

12.8 Wilkins Manufacturing needs an additional $250,000 which it plans to obtain through a factoring arrangement. The factor would purchase Wilkins's accounts receivable and advance the invoice amount, less a 2 percent commission, on the invoices purchased each month. (Wilkins sells on terms of net 30 days.) In addition, the factor charges 16 percent annual interest on the total invoice amount, to be deducted in advance.

a. What amount of accounts receivable must be factored to net $250,000?

b. If Wilkins can reduce credit expenses by $1,500 per month, and avoid bad-debt losses of 3 percent on the factored amount, what is the total dollar cost of the factoring arrangement?

12.9 Sunlight Sailboats estimates that due to the seasonal nature of its business it will require an additional $200,000 of cash for the month of July. Sunlight has three options available to provide the needed funds. It can:

1. Establish a one-year line of credit for $200,000 with a commercial bank. The commitment fee will be 0.5 percent, and the interest charge on the used funds will be 15 percent per annum. The minimum time the funds can be used is thirty days.
2. Forego the July trade discount of 2/10, net 40 on $200,000 of accounts payable.
3. Issue $200,000 of thirty-day commercial paper at a 13.8 percent per annum interest rate.
4. Issue $200,000 of sixty-day commercial paper at a 14 percent per annum interest rate. Since the funds are required for only thirty days, the excess funds ($200,000) can be invested in 13 percent per annum marketable securities for the month of August. The total transaction fee on purchasing and selling the marketable securities is 0.5 percent of the fair value.

   a. Which financing arrangement results in the lowest cost?

   b. Is the source with the lowest expected cost necessarily the source to select? Why or why not?

12.10 The Morton Plastics Company manufactures plastic toys. It buys raw materials, manufactures the toys in the spring and summer, and ships them to a large number of department stores and toy stores by late summer or early fall. The company factors its receivables. If it did not, Morton's balance sheet would have appeared as follows:

Morton Company Pro Forma Balance Sheet
as of October 31, 19X0

Cash	$ 40,000	Accounts payable	$1,200,000
Receivables	1,200,000	Notes payable	800,000
Inventory	800,000	Accruals	80,000
Total current assets	$2,040,000	Total current debt	$2,080,000
		Mortgages	200,000
		Common stock	400,000
Fixed assets	800,000	Retained earnings	160,000
Total assets	$2,840,000	Total claims	$2,840,000

Morton provides advanced dating on its sales; thus its receivables are not due for payment until January 31, 19X1. Also, the company would have been overdue on some $800,000 of its accounts payable if the above situation actually existed.

Morton has an agreement with a factoring company which provides for a flat commission of 1.5 percent, plus interest at 3 points over the prime rate (15 percent) on the outstanding balance. It deducts a reserve of 15 percent for returned and damaged materials. Interest and commission are paid in advance. No interest is charged on the reserved funds or on the commission.

a. Show the balance sheet of Morton on October 31, 19X0, giving effect to the purchase of all the receivables by the factoring company and the use of the funds to pay accounts payable.
b. If the $1.2 million is the average level of outstanding receivables and if they turn over four times a year (hence the commission is paid four times a year), what are the total dollar costs of financing and the effective annual interest rate?
c. What are the advantages to Morton Plastics of using factoring, as opposed to pledging its receivables?

12.11 Linear Communications Corporation (LCC) develops and manufactures fiber optics technology, primarily laser equipment for use in telephone systems. Because of rapid sales growth over the past 4 years, LCC is experiencing a shortage of working capital; 35 percent of its accounts payable are overdue, and some of LCC's key suppliers are reluctant to extend further credit. Seventy-five percent of LCC's sales are to the 8 largest telephone companies in the United States. LCC's balance sheet, sales, and net profit for the past year are shown below.

Assets		**Liabilities**	
Cash	$ 47,520	Accounts payable*	$ 396,000
Receivables	528,000	Bank loans	316,800
Inventories	475,200	Accruals*	79,200
Total current assets	$1,050,720	Total current liabilities	$ 792,000
		Long-term debt	475,200
		Capital stock	158,400
Fixed assets	535,180	Retained earnings	160,300
Total assets	$1,585,900	Total liabilities and net worth	$1,585,900
Sales	$3,696,000		
Profit after taxes	221,760		

* Increases spontaneously with sales increases.

LCC's ratio of sales to receivables is 7 times. All sales are made on credit. LCC's management is deciding between receivables financing and factoring to raise needed funds.

Under the factoring arrangement, the factor would purchase all receivables and perform credit checking for a commission of 1 percent on average receivables, payable at the time the receivables are purchased.

The factor would require that a 10 percent reserve be set up for returns on disputed items. Interest would be charged at the rate of 16 percent on receivables *less* reserve and commission. This interest would be paid in advance, that is, deducted from any funds received from the factor.

With receivables financing there would be no commission to pay but the required reserve for disputed items would increase to 20 percent. The interest charged would be the same as under the factoring arrangement.

a. What is the average level of receivables given a sales level of $3,696,000?
b. What would be the average duration of advances based on a 360-day year?
c. How much cash would LCC actually receive under each of the financing alternatives?
d. Compare the total annual dollar cost under the two alternatives. Compare the effective annual interest rates.

PART FOUR

INVESTMENT

DECISIONS

Part Three dealt with the top portion of the firm's balance sheet—the current assets and liabilities. Now, in Part Four, we move down to the lower left side of the statement, focusing on the decisions involved in fixed asset acquisitions.

Capital budgeting—the planning of expenditures whose returns will extend beyond one year—is discussed in Chapter 13. Uncertainty about both the costs and the returns associated with a project is introduced in Chapter 14. Since projects differ in riskiness, that chapter develops methods of analysis which can be used to incorporate risk into the decision-making process. In considering the impact of risk, we develop the fundamental relations between risk and return.

CHAPTER 13

CAPITAL BUDGETING TECHNIQUES

Capital budgeting involves the entire process of planning expenditures whose returns are expected to extend beyond one year. The choice of one year is arbitrary, of course, but it is a convenient cutoff point for distinguishing between kinds of expenditures. Obvious examples of capital outlays are expenditures for land, buildings, and equipment, and for permanent additions to working capital associated with plant expansion. An advertising or promotion campaign or a research and development program is also likely to have an impact beyond one year, so they too can be classified as capital budgeting expenditures.

Capital budgeting is important for the future well-being of the firm; it is also a complex, conceptually difficult topic. As we shall see later in this chapter, the optimum capital budget—the level of investment that maximizes the present value of the firm—is simultaneously determined by the interaction of supply and demand forces under conditions of uncertainty. Supply forces refer to the supply of capital to the firm, or its *cost of capital schedule*. Demand forces relate to the investment opportunities open to the firm, as measured by the *stream of revenues* that will result from an investment decision. *Uncertainty* enters the decision because it is impossible to know exactly either the cost of capital or the stream of revenues that will be derived from a project.

To facilitate an exposition of the investment decision process, we have broken the topic down into its major components. In this chapter, we consider the capital budgeting process and the techniques generally employed by reasonably sophisticated business firms. Here our focus is on the time factor, and the compound interest concepts covered in the preceding chapters are used extensively. Uncertainty is explicitly and formally considered in Chapter 14, and the cost of capital concept is developed and related to capital budgeting in Chapters 15 and 16.

Significance of Capital Budgeting

A number of factors combine to make capital budgeting perhaps the most important decision with which financial management is involved. Further, all departments of a firm—production, marketing, and so on—are vitally affected by the capital budgeting decisions; so all executives, no matter what their primary responsibility, must be aware of how capital budgeting decisions are made. These points are discussed in this section.

Long-Term Effects

First and foremost, the fact that the results continue over an extended period means that the decision maker loses some flexibility. The firm must make a commitment into the future. For example, the purchase of an asset with an economic life of ten years requires a long period of waiting before the final results of the action can be known.

Asset expansion is fundamentally related to expected future sales. A decision to buy or to construct a fixed asset that is expected to last five years involves an implicit five-year sales forecast. Indeed, the economic life of a purchased asset represents an implicit forecast for the duration of the economic life of the asset. Hence, failure to forecast accurately will result in overinvestment or underinvestment in fixed assets.

An erroneous forecast of asset requirements can result in serious consequences. If the firm has invested too much in assets, it will incur unnecessarily heavy expenses. If it has not spent enough on fixed assets, two serious problems may arise. First, the firm's equipment may not be sufficiently modern to enable it to produce competitively. Second, if it has inadequate capacity, it may lose a portion of its share of the market to rival firms. To regain lost customers typically requires heavy selling expenses, price reduction, product improvements, and so forth.

Timing the Availability of Capital Assets

Another problem is to phase properly the availability of capital assets in order to have them come "on stream" at the correct time. For example, the executive vice president of a decorative tile company gave the authors an illustration of the importance of capital budgeting. His firm tried to operate near capacity most of the time. For about four years there had been intermittent spurts in the demand for its product; when these spurts occurred, the firm had to turn away orders. After a sharp increase in demand, the firm would add capacity by renting an additional building, then purchasing and installing the appropriate equipment. It would take six to eight months to have the additional capacity ready. At this point the company frequently found that there was no demand for its increased output: other firms had already expanded their operations and had taken an increased share of the market, with the result that demand for this firm had leveled off. If the firm had properly forecast demand and had planned its increase in capacity six months or one year in advance, it would have been able to maintain its market—indeed, to obtain a larger share of the market.

Good capital budgeting will improve the timing of asset acquisitions and the quality of assets purchased. This result follows from the nature of capital goods and their producers. Capital goods are not ordered by firms until they see that sales are beginning to press on capacity. Such occasions occur simultaneously for many firms. When the heavy orders come in, the producers of capital goods go from a situation of idle capacity to one in which they cannot meet all the orders that have been placed. Consequently, large backlogs accumulate. Since the production of capital goods involves a relatively long work-in-process period, a year or more of waiting may be involved before the additional modern capital goods are available. Furthermore, the quality of the capital goods, produced on rush order, may deteriorate. These factors have obvious implications for purchasing agents and plant managers.

Raising Funds

Another reason for the importance of capital budgeting is that asset expansion typically involves substantial expenditures. Before a firm spends a large amount of money, it must make the proper plans—large amounts of funds are not available automatically. A firm contemplating a major capital expenditure program may need to arrange its financing several years in advance to be sure of having the funds required for the expansion.

An Overview of Capital Budgeting

Capital budgeting is, in essence, an application of a classic proposition from the economic theory of the firm, namely, a firm should operate at the point at which its marginal revenue just equals its marginal cost. When this rule is applied to the capital budgeting decision, marginal revenue is taken to be the percentage rate of return on investments, while marginal cost is the firm's marginal cost of capital.

A simplified version of the concept is depicted in Figure 13.1(a). Here the horizontal axis measures the dollars of investment during a year, while the vertical axis shows both the percentage cost of capital and the rate of return on projects.

Figure 13.1

Illustrative Capital Budgeting Decision Process

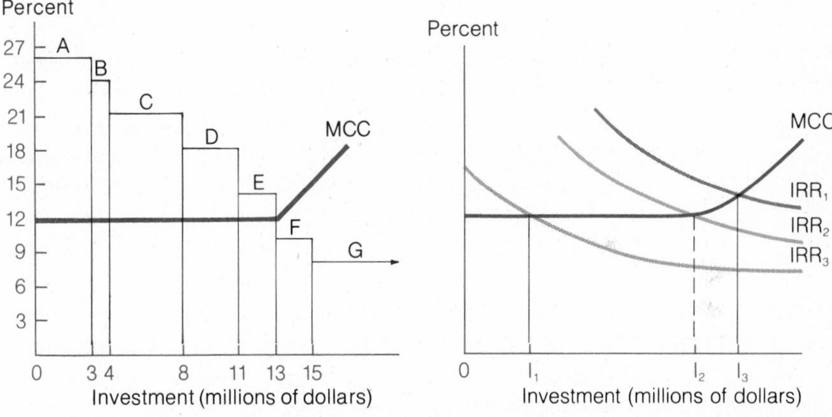

(a) Discrete investment projects

(b) Smoothed investment opportunity schedules

The projects are denoted by boxes—Project A, for example, calls for an outlay of $3 million and promises a 26 percent rate of return; Project B requires $1 million and yields about 24 percent; and so on. The last investment, Project G, simply involves buying 8 percent government bonds, which may be purchased in unlimited quantities. In Figure 13.1(b) the concept is generalized to show smoothed investment opportunity schedules (*IRR*), and three alternative schedules are presented.[1]

The curve *MCC* designates the marginal cost of capital, or the cost of each additional dollar acquired for purposes of making capital expenditures. As it is

[1] The investment opportunity schedules measure the rate of return on each project. The rate of return on a project is generally called the *internal rate of return* (*IRR*). This is why we label the investment opportunity schedules *IRR*. The process of calculating the *IRR* is explained later in this chapter.

drawn in Figure 13.1(a), the marginal cost of capital is constant at 12 percent until the firm has raised $13 million, after which the marginal cost of capital curve turns up.[2] To maximize profits, the firm should accept Projects A through E, obtaining and investing $13 million, and reject F, and G.

Notice that three alternative investment opportunity schedules are shown in Figure 13.1(b). IRR_1 designates relatively many good investment opportunities, while IRR_3 designates relatively few good projects. The three different curves could be interpreted as applying either to three different firms or to one firm at three different times. As long as the *IRR* curve cuts the *MCC* curve to the left of I_2—for example, at I_1—the marginal cost of capital is constant. To the right of I_2—for example, at I_3—the cost of capital is rising. Therefore, if investment opportunities are such that the *IRR* curve cuts the *MCC* curve to the right of I_2, the *actual* marginal cost of capital (a single point) varies, depending on the *IRR* curve. In this chapter we generally assume that the *IRR* curve cuts the *MCC* curve to the left of I_2. This permits us to assume that the cost of capital is constant. The assumption is relaxed in Chapter 16, where we show how the *MCC* varies with the amount of funds raised during a given year.

At the applied level, the capital budgeting process is much more complex than the preceding example suggests. Projects do not just appear; a continuing stream of good investment opportunities results from hard thinking, careful planning, and, often, large outlays for research and development. Moreover, some very difficult measurement problems are involved: The sales and costs associated with particular projects must be estimated, frequently for many years into the future, in the face of great uncertainty. Finally, some difficult conceptual and empirical problems arise over the methods of calculating rates of return and the cost of capital.

Business is required to take action, however, even in the face of the kinds of problems described; this requirement has led to the development of procedures that assist in making optimal investment decisions. One such procedure, forecasting, was discussed in Chapter 6; uncertainty is discussed in formal terms in the next chapter; and the important subject of the cost of capital is deferred to Chapter 16. The essentials of the other elements of capital budgeting are taken up in the remainder of this chapter.

Investment Proposals

Aside from the actual generation of ideas, the first step in the capital budgeting process is to assemble a list of the proposed new investments, together with the data necessary to appraise them. Although practices vary from firm to firm, proposals dealing with asset acquisitions are frequently grouped according to the following four categories:

1. Replacements
2. Expansion: additional capacity in existing product lines
3. Expansion: new product lines
4. Other (for example, pollution control equipment)

[2] The reasons for assuming this particular shape for the marginal cost of capital curve are explained in Chapter 16.

These groupings are somewhat arbitrary, and it is frequently difficult to decide the appropriate category for a particular investment. In spite of such problems, the scheme is used quite widely and, as we shall see, with good reason.

Ordinarily, replacement decisions are the simplest to make. Assets wear out or become obsolete, and they must be replaced if production efficiency is to be maintained. The firm has a very good idea of the cost savings to be obtained by replacing an old asset, and it knows the consequences of nonreplacement. All in all, the outcomes of most replacement decisions can be predicted with a high degree of confidence.

Examples of the second investment classification are proposals for adding more machines of the type already in use or the opening of new branches in a city-wide chain of food stores. Expansion investments are frequently incorporated in replacement decisions. To illustrate, an old, inefficient machine may be replaced by a larger, more efficient one.

A degree of uncertainty—sometimes extremely high—is clearly involved in expansion, but the firm at least has the advantage of examining past production and sales experience with similar machines or stores. When it considers an investment of the third kind, expansion into new product lines, little, if any, experience is available on which to base decisions. To illustrate, when Union Carbide decided to develop the laser for commercial application, it had very little idea of either the development costs or the specific applications lasers could have. Under such circumstances, any estimates must at best be treated as very crude approximations.

The "other" category is a catchall and includes intangibles; an example is a proposal to boost employee morale and productivity by installing a music system. Mandatory pollution control devices, which must be undertaken even though they produce no revenues, are another example of the "other" category. Major strategic decisions such as plans for overseas expansion or mergers might also be included here, but more frequently they are treated separately from the regular capital budget.

Administrative Aspects

Other important aspects of capital budgeting involve administrative matters. Approvals are typically required at higher levels within the organization as we move away from replacement decisions and as the sums involved increase. One of the most important functions of the board of directors is to approve the major outlays in a capital budgeting program. Such decisions are crucial for the future well-being of the firm.

The planning horizon for capital budgeting programs varies with the nature of the industry. When sales can be forecast with a high degree of reliability for ten to twenty years, the planning period is likely to be correspondingly long; electric ultilities are an example of such an industry. Also, when the product-technology developments in the industry require an eight-to-ten-year cycle to develop a new major product, as in certain segments of the aerospace industry, a correspondingly long planning period is necessary.

After a capital budget has been adopted, payments must be scheduled. Characteristically, the finance department is responsible for scheduling payments and for acquiring funds to meet payment schedule requirements. The finance department is also primarily responsible for cooperating with the members of operating divisions to compile systematic records on the uses of funds and the uses of equipment purchased in capital budgeting programs. Effective capital budgeting programs require such information as the basis for periodic review and evaluation of capital expenditure decisions—the feedback and control phase of capital budgeting, often called the *post audit review*.

The foregoing represents a brief overview of the administrative aspects of capital budgeting; the analytical problems involved are considered next.

Choosing among Alternative Proposals

In most firms there are more proposals for projects than the firm is able or willing to finance. Some proposals are good, others are poor, and methods must be developed for distinguishing between the good and the poor. Essentially, the end product is a ranking of the proposals and a cutoff point for determining how far down the ranked list to go.

In part, proposals are eliminated because they are mutually exclusive. Mutually exclusive proposals are alternative methods of doing the same job. If one piece of equipment is chosen to do the job, the others will not be required. Thus, if there is a need to improve the materials handling system in a chemical plant, the job may be done either by conveyer belts or by fork lifts. The selection of one method of doing the job makes it unnecessary to use the others; they are mutually exclusive items.

Independent items are pieces of capital equipment that are being considered for different kinds of projects or tasks. For example, in addition to the materials handling system, the chemical firm may need equipment to package the end product. The work would require a packaging machine, and the purchase of equipment for this purpose would be independent of the equipment purchased for materials handling.

To distinguish among the many items that compete for the allocation of the firm's capital funds, a ranking procedure must be developed. This procedure requires calculating the estimated benefits from the use of equipment and then translating the estimated benefits into a measure of the advantage of the purchase of the equipment. Thus, an estimate of benefits is required, and a method for converting the benefits into a ranking measure must be developed.

Measures of Cash Flows

It is especially important to use the correct concept of expected returns representing the future net cash flows. An illustration will help clarify some important relationships. A firm has the income statement shown in Table 13.1.

Expected net cash flows or expected future returns are equal to net operating income before deduction of payments to the financing sources—but after the deduction of applicable taxes and with depreciation added back.

$$\begin{aligned}\text{Expected returns} &= X(1 - \text{T}) + \text{Dep}\\ &= \$30{,}000(0.6) + \$15{,}000 = \$33{,}000 \qquad \textbf{(13.1)}\end{aligned}$$

Thus net operating income after taxes is figured before deduction of financial payments such as interest on debt and dividends to shareholders. Since interest

Table 13.1 **Illustrative Income Statement**

Sales	\$145,000
Operating costs (before depreciation)	100,000
Earnings before depreciation, interest, and taxes (EBDIT)	45,000
Depreciation expense (Dep)	15,000
Net operating income (X); (NOI); (EBIT)	30,000
Interest expense (Int)	5,000
Income before taxes	25,000
Taxes (T) at 40 percent	10,000
Net income (NI)	\$ 15,000

costs are included in the net operating income, they are included in the future returns from investments. We should note also that future returns can be defined on the most inclusive measure of income (EBDIT) as well as on EBIT or NI as shown below.

$$\begin{aligned}\text{Expected cash flows} &= (\text{EBDIT})(1 - \text{T}) + \text{TDep} \\ &= \$45{,}000(0.6) + 0.4(\$15{,}000) = \$33{,}000 \qquad \textbf{(13.2)}\end{aligned}$$

When we express EBDIT in terms of its components, we can readily demonstrate the equivalence of expected returns defined on EBDIT in Equation 13.2 with expected returns defined on EBIT, or X, in Equation 13.1. EBDIT is equal to X plus Dep, so we can write for Equation 13.2:

$$\begin{aligned}\text{Expected cash flows} &= X(1 - \text{T}) + \text{Dep}(1 - \text{T}) + \text{TDep} \\ &= X(1 - \text{T}) + \text{Dep} \qquad \textbf{(13.2a)}\end{aligned}$$

The last formulation of 13.2a is, of course, exactly Equation 13.1. Similarly, we can start with a net income formulation of expected returns.

$$\begin{aligned}\text{Expected cash flows} &= \text{NI} + (\text{Int})(1 - \text{T}) + \text{Dep} \\ &= \$15{,}000 + \$5{,}000(0.6) + \$15{,}000 = \$33{,}000 \qquad \textbf{(13.3)}\end{aligned}$$

Again we obtain the same numerical result as we did using Equation 13.1, and the logical equivalence is also readily established. We add back to NI what is required to reach X as follows:

$$\text{NI} + \text{T}(X - \text{Int}) + \text{Int} = X$$

We then change the combination of terms.

$$\begin{aligned}&\text{NI} + \text{T}X - \text{T}(\text{Int}) + \text{Int} = X \\ &\text{NI} + \text{Int}\ (1 - \text{T}) = X - \text{T}X \qquad \textbf{(13.3a)} \\ &\text{NI} + \text{Int}\ (1 - \text{T}) = X(1 - \text{T})\end{aligned}$$

Thus when Dep is added to both sides of 13.3a, we will have future returns defined on both net operating income (X) and on net income (NI).

Table 13.2 **Cash Flows with No Debt interest**

Sales	$145,000
Operating costs (except depreciation)	100,000
Earnings before depreciation, interest, and taxes (EBDIT)	45,000
Depreciation expense (Dep)	15,000
Net operating income (X); (NOI); (EBIT)	30,000
Taxes (T) at 40 percent	12,000
Net income (NI); $X(1 - T)$	$ 18,000

If a firm is not using debt as a part of its financing, it would not have interest expense, so its income statement would appear as in Table 13.2. The equivalent measures of future returns for Table 13.2 follow.

$$\text{Expected cash flows: } X(1 - \text{T}) + \text{Dep} = \$30{,}000(0.6) + \$15{,}000 = \$33{,}000$$

$$\text{Expected cash flows: EBDIT}(1 - \text{T}) + \text{TDep} = \$45{,}000(0.6) + 0.4(\$15{,}000) = \$33{,}000$$

$$\text{Expected cash flows: NI} + \text{Dep} = \$18{,}000 + \$15{,}000 = \$33{,}000$$

Again the expected returns defined on EBIT, EBDIT, or NI give the same result. Finally, in a number of theoretical studies, it is assumed that the firm is adding to its gross fixed assets an amount each year exactly equal to its depreciation expense. In the resulting models, cash outflows for the investment in new assets and the deduction for depreciation cancel out. We would then return to the income statement in Table 13.1, starting with EBIT. The relationships would be:

$$\text{Expected net cash flows} = X(1 - \text{T}) = \$30{,}000(0.6) = \$18{,}000$$

$$\text{Expected net cash flows} = \text{NI} + \text{Int}\,(1 - \text{T}) = \text{NI} + \text{Int}\,(1 - \text{T}) = \$15{,}000 + 0.6(\$5{,}000) = \$18{,}000$$

Whether cash flows are defined on a gross or a net basis, they reflect the uses of all sources of financing. Accordingly, when we discount future returns by the firm's cost of capital, the costs of all forms of financing utilized by the firm are already included in the cost of capital.[3]

Importance of Good Data

Most discussions of measuring the cash flows associated with capital projects are relatively brief, but it is important to emphasize this: *In the entire capital budgeting procedure, probably nothing is of greater importance than a reliable estimate of the cost savings or revenue increases that will be achieved from the prospective outlay of capital funds.* The increased output and sales revenue resulting from expansion programs are obvious benefits. Cost reduction benefits include changes in quality and quantity of direct labor; in amount and cost of scrap and rework time; in fuel costs; and in maintenance expenses, down time, safety, flexibility, and so

[3] The discussion of the cost of capital presented in Chapter 16 will demonstrate this concept.

on. So many variables are involved that it is obviously impossible to make neat generalizations. However, this should not minimize the crucial importance of the required analysis of the benefits derived from capital expenditures. Each capital equipment expenditure must be examined in detail for possible additional costs and savings.

All the subsequent procedures for ranking projects are no better than the data input—the old saying, "garbage in, garbage out," is certainly applicable to capital budgeting analysis. Thus, the data assembly process is not a routine clerical task to be performed on a mechanical basis. It requires continuous monitoring and evaluation of estimates by those competent to make such evaluations—engineers, accountants, economists, cost analysts, and other qualified persons.

After costs and benefits have been estimated, they are utilized for ranking alternative investment proposals. How this ranking is accomplished is our next topic.

Ranking Investment Proposals

The point of capital budgeting—indeed, the point of all financial analysis—is to make decisions that will maximize the value of the firm. The capital budgeting process is designed to answer two questions: (1) Which of several mutually exclusive investments should be selected? and (2) How many projects, in total, should be accepted?

Among the many methods used for ranking investment proposals, three are discussed here.[4]

1. *Payback method (or payback period)*: Number of years required to return the original investment
2. *Net present value (NPV) method*: Present value of future returns discounted at the appropriate cost of capital, minus the cost of the investment
3. *Internal rate of return (IRR) method*: Interest rate which equates the present value of future returns to the investment outlay

In the next sections of this chapter, the nature and characteristics of the three methods are illustrated and explained. To make the explanations more meaningful, the same data set is used to illustrate each procedure.

Payback Method

Assume that a firm is considering two projects. Each requires an investment of $1,000. The firm's marginal cost of capital is 10 percent.[5] The net cash flows (net operating income after taxes plus depreciation) from Investments A and B are shown in Table 13.3.

[4] A number of "average rate of return" methods have been discussed in the literature and used in practice. These methods are generally unsound. We discussed them in earlier editions, but they are deleted from this edition.

[5] A discussion of how the cost of capital is calculated is presented in Chapter 16. For now, the cost of capital should be considered as the firm's opportunity cost of making a particular investment. That is, if the firm does not make a particular investment, it saves the cost of this investment; and if it can invest these funds in another project that provides a return of 10 percent, then its opportunity cost of making the first investment is 10 percent.

Table 13.3 **Net Cash Flows**

Year	A	B
1	$500	$100
2	400	200
3	300	300
4	100	400
5	10	500
6	10	600

The *payback period* is the number of years it takes a firm to recover its original investment from net cash flows. Since the cost is $1,000, the payback period is two and one-third years for Project A and four years for Project B. If the firm were using a three-year payback period, Project A would be accepted, but Project B would be rejected.

Although the payback period is very easy to calculate, it can lead to the wrong decisions. As the illustration demonstrates, it ignores income beyond the payback period. If the project is one that matures in later years, the use of the payback period can lead to the selection of less desirable investments. Projects with longer payback periods are characteristically those involved in long-range planning—developing a new product or tapping a new market. These are the major strategic decisions that determine a firm's fundamental position, but they also involve investments that do not yield their highest returns for a number of years. This means that the payback method may be biased against the very investments that are most important to a firm's long-run success.

When we recognize the longer period over which an investment is likely to yield savings, we identify another weakness in the use of the payback method for ranking investment proposals: its failure to take into account the time value of money. To illustrate, consider two assets, X and Y, each costing $300 and each having the following cash flows:

Year	X	Y
1	$200	$100
2	100	200
3	100	100

Each project has a two-year payback; hence, each would appear equally desirable. However, we know that a dollar today is worth more than a dollar next year, so Project X, with its faster cash flow, is certainly more desirable.

The use of the payback period is sometimes defended on the grounds that returns beyond three or four years are fraught with such great uncertainty that it is best to disregard them altogether in a planning decision. However, this is clearly an unsound procedure. Some investments with the highest returns are those which may not come to fruition for many years. The new product cycle in industries involving advanced technologies may not have a payoff for eight or nine years. Furthermore, even though returns that occur after three, four, or five years may be highly uncertain, it is important to make a judgment about the likelihood of their occurring. To ignore them is to assign a zero probability to these distant receipts, a procedure that can hardly produce the best results.

Another defense of the payback method is that a firm that is short of cash must necessarily give great emphasis to a quick return of its funds so that they may be put to use in other places or in meeting other needs. However, this does not relieve the payback method of its many shortcomings, and there are better methods for handling the cash shortage situation.[6]

A third reason for using payback is that projects with faster paybacks typically have more favorable short-run effects on earnings per share. Firms that use payback for this reason are sacrificing future growth for current accounting income, and in general such a practice will not maximize the value of the firm. The discounted cash flow techniques discussed in the next section, if used properly, automatically give consideration to the present-earnings-versus-future-growth tradeoff and strike the balance that will maximize the firm's value.

The payback method is also used sometimes simply because it is so easy to apply. If a firm is making many small capital expenditure decisions, the costs of using more complex methods may outweigh the benefits of possibly "better" choices among competing projects. Thus, many electric utility companies with very sophisticated capital budgeting procedures use discounted cash flow techniques for larger projects, while using payback on certain small, routine replacement decisions. When these sophisticated companies do use the payback method, however, they generally do so only after special studies have indicated that the payback method will provide sufficiently accurate answers for the decisions at hand.

Finally, many firms use payback in combination with one of the discounted cash flow procedures described below. The NPV or IRR method is used to appraise a project's profitability, while the payback is used to show how long the initial investment will be at risk; that is, payback is used as a risk indicator. Recent surveys have shown that when larger firms use payback in connection with major projects, it is almost always used in this manner.

Net Present Value Method

When the flaws in the payback method were recognized, people began to search for methods of evaluating projects that would recognize that a dollar received immediately is preferable to a dollar received at some future date. This recognition led to the development of *discounted cash flow* (*DCF*) *techniques* to take account of the time value of money. One such discounted cash flow technique is called the *net present value method*, or sometimes simply the present value method. *To implement this approach, find the present value of the expected net cash flows of an investment, discounted at the cost of capital, and subtract from it the initial cost outlay of the project.*[7] If the net present value is positive, the project should be accepted; if negative, it should be rejected. If the two projects are mutually exclusive, the one with the higher net present value should be chosen.

[6] We interpret a cash shortage to mean that the firm has a high opportunity cost for its funds and a high cost of capital. We would consider this high cost of capital in the internal rate of return method or the net present value method, thus taking account of the cash shortage.

[7] If costs are spread over several years, this must be taken into account. Suppose, for example, that a firm bought land in 1978, erected a building in 1979, installed equipment in 1980, and started production in 1981. One could treat 1978 as the base year, comparing the present value of the costs as of 1978 to the present value of the benefit stream as of that same date.

The equation for the net present value (NPV) is

$$\text{NPV} = \left[\frac{F_1}{(1+k)^1} + \frac{F_2}{(1+k)^2} + \cdots + \frac{F_n}{(1+k)^n}\right] - I$$

$$= \sum_{t=1}^{n} \frac{F_t}{(1+k)^t} - I \quad \textbf{(13.4)}$$

Here F_1, F_2, and so forth, represent the net cash flows; k is the marginal cost of capital; I is the initial cost of the project; and n is the project's expected life.[8]

The net present values of Projects A and B are calculated in Table 13.4. Project A has an NPV of \$91, while B's NPV is \$403. On this basis, both should be accepted if they are independent, but B should be the one chosen if they are mutually exclusive. When a firm takes on a project with a positive NPV, the value of the firm increases by the amount of the NPV. In our example, the value of the firm increases by \$403 if it takes on Project B, but by only \$91 if it takes on Project A. Viewing the alternatives in this manner, it is easy to see why B is preferred to A, and it is also easy to see the logic of the NPV approach.

Table 13.4

Calculating the Net Present Value (NPV) of Projects with \$1,000 Cost

	Project A			Project B		
Year	Net cash flow	PVIF (10%)	PV of cash flow	Net cash flow	PVIF (10%)	PV of cash flow
1	\$500	0.9091	\$ 455	\$100	0.9091	\$ 91
2	400	0.8264	331	200	0.8264	165
3	300	0.7513	225	300	0.7513	225
4	100	0.6830	68	400	0.6830	273
5	10	0.6209	6	500	0.6209	310
6	10	0.5645	6	600	0.5645	339
	PV of inflows		\$1,091			\$1,403
	Less: cost		1,000			1,000
	NPV		\$ 91			\$ 403

Internal Rate of Return Method

The internal rate of return (IRR) is defined as the interest rate that equates the present value of the expected future cash flows, or receipts, to the initial cost outlay. The equation for calculating the internal rate of return is

$$\frac{F_1}{(1+R)^1} + \frac{F_2}{(1+R)^2} + \cdots + \frac{F_n}{(1+R)^n} - I = 0$$

$$\sum_{t=1}^{n} \frac{F_t}{(1+R)^t} - I = 0 \quad \textbf{(13.5)}$$

[8] The second equation is simply a shorthand expression in which sigma ($\sum$) signifies "sum up" or add the present values of N profit terms. If $t = 1$, then $F_t = F_1$ and $1/(1+k)^t = 1/(1+k)^1$; if $t = 2$, then $F_t = F_2$ and $1/(1+k)^1 = 1/(1+k)^2$; and so on until $t = n$, the last year the project provides any profits. The symbol $\sum_{t=1}^{n}$ simply says "Go through the following process: Let $t = 1$ and find the PV of F_1; then let $t = 2$ and find the PV of F_2. Continue until the PV of each individual profit has been found; then add the PVs of these individual profits to find the PV of the asset."

Here we know the value of I and also the values of F_1, F_2, . . . , F_n, but we do not know the value of R. Thus, we have an equation with one unknown, and we can solve for the value of R. Some value of R will cause the sum of the discounted receipts to equal the initial cost of the project, making the equation equal to zero, and that value of R is defined as the internal rate of return; that is, the solution value of R is the IRR.

Notice that the internal rate of return formula, Equation 13.5, is simply the NPV formula, Equation 13.4, solved for that particular value of k that causes the NPV to equal zero. In other words, the same basic equation is used for both methods, but in the NPV method the discount rate (k) is specified and the NPV is found, while in the IRR method the NPV is specified to equal zero and the value of R that forces the NPV to equal zero is found.

The internal rate of return may be found by trial and error. First, compute the present value of the cash flows from an investment, using an arbitrarily selected interest rate. (Since the cost of capital for most firms has been in the range of 10 to 15 percent, projects will hopefully promise a return of at least 10 percent. Therefore, 10 percent is a good starting point for most problems.) Then compare the present value so obtained with the investment's cost. If the present value is higher than the cost figure, try a higher interest rate and go through the procedure again. Conversely, if the present value is lower than the cost, lower the interest rate and repeat the process. Continue until the present value of the flows from the investment is approximately equal to its cost. The interest rate that brings about this equality is defined as the *internal rate of return.*[9]

This calculation process is illustrated in Table 13.5 for Projects A and B. First, the 10 percent interest factors are obtained from Table A.2 at the end of the book. These factors are then multiplied by the cash flows for the corresponding years, and the present values of the annual cash flows are placed in the appropriate columns. For example, the PVIF of 0.9091 is multiplied by $500, and the product, $455, is placed in the first row of Column A.

The present values of the yearly cash flows are then summed to get the investment's total present value. Subtracting the cost of the project from this figure gives the net present value. As the net present values of both investments are positive at the 10 percent rate, increase the rate to 15 percent and try again. *At this point the net present value of Investment A is zero, which indicates that its internal rate of return is 15 percent. Continuing, B is found to have an internal rate of return of approximately 20 percent.*[10]

What is so special about the particular discount rate that equates the cost of a project with the present value of its expected cash flows? Suppose that the weighted cost of all of the funds obtained by the firm is 10 percent. If the internal rate of

[9] In order to reduce the number of trials required to find the internal rate of return, it is important to minimize the error at each iteration. One reasonable approach is to make as good a first approximation as possible, then to "straddle" the internal rate of return by making fairly large changes in the interest rate early in the iterative process. In practice, if many projects are to be evaluated or if many years are involved, relatively inexpensive hand calculators can be used to solve for the internal rate of return.

Table 13.5 **Finding the Internal Rate of Return**

	Cash flows (F_t Values)		
	Year	F_A	F_B
I = Investment = \$1,000	1: F_1 =	\$500	\$100
	2: F_2 =	400	200
	3: F_3 =	300	300
	4: F_4 =	100	400
	5: F_5 =	10	500
	6: F_6 =	10	600

	10 percent			15 percent			20 percent		
		Present value			Present value			Present value	
Year	PVIF	A	B	PVIF	A	B	PVIF	A	B
1	0.9091	\$ 455	\$ 91	0.8696	\$ 435	\$ 87	0.8333	\$417	\$ 83
2	0.8264	331	165	0.7561	302	151	0.6944	278	139
3	0.7513	225	225	0.6575	197	197	0.5787	174	174
4	0.6830	68	273	0.5718	57	229	0.4823	48	193
5	0.6209	6	310	0.4972	5	249	0.4019	4	201
6	0.5645	6	339	0.4323	4	259	0.3349	3	201
Present value		\$1,091	\$1,403		\$1,000	\$1,172		\$924	\$991
Net present value = PV − I		\$ 91	\$ 403		\$ 0	\$ 172		\$(76)	\$ (9)

return on a particular project is 10 percent, the same as the cost of capital, the firm would be able to use the cash flow generated by the investment to repay the funds obtained, including the costs of the funds. If the internal rate of return exceeds 10 percent, the value of the firm increases. If the internal rate of return is less than 10 percent, taking on the project would cause a decline in the value of the firm. It is this breakeven characteristic that increases or decreases the value of the firm and makes the internal rate of return of particular significance.

Assuming that the firm uses a cost of capital of 10 percent, the internal rate of return criterion states that, if the two projects are independent, both should be accepted—they both do better than break even. If they are mutually exclusive, B ranks higher and should be accepted, while A should be rejected.

A more complete illustration of how the internal rate of return would be used in practice is given in Table 13.6. Assuming a 10 percent cost of capital, the firm should accept Projects 1 through 7, reject Projects 8 through 10, and have a total capital budget of \$10 million.

IRR for Level Cash Flows

If the cash flows from a project are level, or equal in each year, then the project's internal rate of return can be found by a relatively simple process. In essence, such a project is an annuity: The firm makes an outlay, I, and receives a stream

[10] The IRR can also be estimated graphically. First, calculate the NPV at two or three discount rates as in Table 13.5. Next, plot these NPVs against the discount rates—see Figure 13.2 in the next section for an example. The horizontal axis intercept is the IRR.

Table 13.6 **The Prospective Projects Schedule**

Nature of proposal	Amount of funds required	Cumulative total	IRR	
1. Purchase of leased space	$2,000,000	$ 2,000,000	23%	
2. Mechanization of accounting system	1,200,000	3,200,000	19	
3. Modernization of office building	1,500,000	4,700,000	17	
4. Addition of power facilities	900,000	5,600,000	16	
5. Purchase of affiliate	3,600,000	9,200,000	13	
6. Purchase of loading docks	300,000	9,500,000	12	
7. Purchase of tank trucks	500,000	10,000,000	11	
				10% cutoff
8. Installation of conveyor system	200,000	10,200,000	9	
9. Construction of new plant	2,300,000	12,500,000	8	
10. Purchase of executive aircraft	200,000	12,700,000	7	

of cash flow benefits, F, for a given number of years. The IRR for the project is found by applying Equation 4.6, presented in Chapter 4.

To illustrate, suppose a project has a cost of $10,000 and is expected to produce cash flows of $1,627 a year for ten years. The cost of the project, $10,000, is the present value of an annuity of $1,627 a year for ten years, so, applying Equation 4.5, we obtain

$$\frac{I}{F} = \frac{\$10{,}000}{\$1{,}627} = 6.1463 = PVIFA$$

Looking up PVIFA in Table A.4, across the ten-year row, we find it (approximately) under the 10 percent column. Accordingly, 10 percent is the IRR on the project. In other words, 10 percent is the value of R that would force Equation 13.5 to zero when F is constant at $1,627 for ten years and I is $10,000. This procedure works only if the project has constant annual cash flows; if it does not, the IRR must be found by trial and error or by using a calculator.

Basic Differences between the NPV and IRR Methods[11]

As noted above, the NPV method accepts all independent projects whose NPV is greater than zero, and ranks mutually exclusive projects by their NPV's, selecting the project with the higher NPV according to Equation 13.4:

$$\text{NPV} = \sum_{t=1}^{n} \frac{F_t}{(1+k)^t} - I \qquad \textbf{(13.4)}$$

The IRR method, on the other hand, finds the value of R that forces Equation 13.4 to equal zero:

$$\text{NPV} = \sum_{t=1}^{n} \frac{F_t}{(1+R)^t} - I = 0 \qquad \textbf{(13.5)}$$

[11] This section is relatively technical and may be omitted on a first reading without loss of continuity.

The IRR method calls for accepting independent projects where R, the internal rate of return, is greater than k, the cost of capital, and for selecting among mutually exclusive projects depending on which has the higher IRR.

It is apparent that the only structural difference between the NPV and IRR methods lies in the discount rates used in the two equations—all the values in the equations are identical except for R and k. Further, we can see that if $R > k$, then NPV > 0.[12] Accordingly, the two methods give the same accept-reject decisions for specific projects—if a project is acceptable under the NPV criterion, it is also acceptable if the IRR method is used.

However, under certain conditions the NPV and IRR methods can *rank* projects differently, and if mutually exclusive projects are involved or if capital is limited, then rankings can be important. The conditions under which different rankings can occur are as follows:

1. The cost of one project is larger than that of the other.
2. The timing of the projects' cash flows differs. For example, the cash flows of one project may increase over time, while those of the other decrease, or the projects may have different expected lives.

The first point can be seen by considering two mutually exclusive projects, L and S, of greatly differing sizes. Project S calls for the investment of $1.00 and yields $1.50 at the end of one year. Its IRR is 50 percent, and at a 10 percent cost of capital its NPV is $0.36. Project L costs $1 million and yields $1.25 million at the end of the year. Its IRR is only 25 percent, but its NPV at 10 percent is $136,375. The two methods rank the projects differently: $\text{IRR}_s > \text{IRR}_l$, but $\text{NPV}_l > \text{NPV}_s$. This is, of course, an extreme case, but whenever projects differ in size, the NPV and the IRR can give different rankings.[13]

The effect of differential cash flows is somewhat more difficult to understand, but it can be illustrated by an example. Consider two projects, A and B, whose cash flows over their three-year lives are given below:

	Cash Flow from Project	
Year	A	B
1	$1,000	$ 100
2	500	600
3	100	1,100

Project A's cash flows are higher in the early years, but B's cash flows increase over time and exceed those of A in later years. Each project costs $1,200, and

[12] This can be seen by noting that NPV = 0 only when $R = k$:

$$\text{NPV} = \sum_{t=1}^{n} \frac{F_t}{(1+k)^t} - I = \sum_{t=1}^{n} \frac{F_t}{(1+R)^t} - I = 0,$$

if and only if $R = k$. If $R > k$, then NPV > 0, and if $R < k$, then NPV < 0. We should also note that, under certain conditions, there may be more than one root to Equation 13.5; hence multiple IRR's are found.

[13] Projects of different size *could* be ranked the same by the NPV and IRR methods; that is, different sizes do not necessarily mean different rankings.

their NPVs discounted at the specified rates, are shown below:

	NPV	
Discount Rate	A	B
0%	$400	$600
5	292	390
10	197	213
15	114	64
20	38	(63)
24	(16)	(152)
32	(112)	(302)

At a zero discount rate, the NPV of each project is simply the sum of its receipts less its cost. Thus, the NPV of Project A at 0 percent is $1,000 + $500 + $100 − $1,200 = $400; that of Project B is $100 + $600 + $1,100 − $1,200 = $600. As the discount rate rises from zero, the NPVs of the two projects fall from these values.

The NPVs are plotted against the appropriate discount rates in Figure 13.2, a graph defined as a *present value profile*. Notice that the vertical axis intercepts are the NPVs when the discount rate is zero, while the horizontal axis intercepts show each project's IRR. The internal rate of return is defined as that point where NPV is zero; therefore, A's IRR is approximately 23 percent, while B's is approximately 17 percent. Because its largest cash flows come late in the project's life, when the discounting effects of time are most significant, B's NPV falls rapidly as the discount rate rises. However, since A's cash flows come early, when the impact of higher discount rates is not so severe, its NPV falls less rapidly as interest rates increase.

Notice that if the cost of capital is below 10 percent, B has the higher NPV but the lower IRR, while at a cost of capital above 10 percent A has both the higher

Figure 13.2 **Present Value Profile**

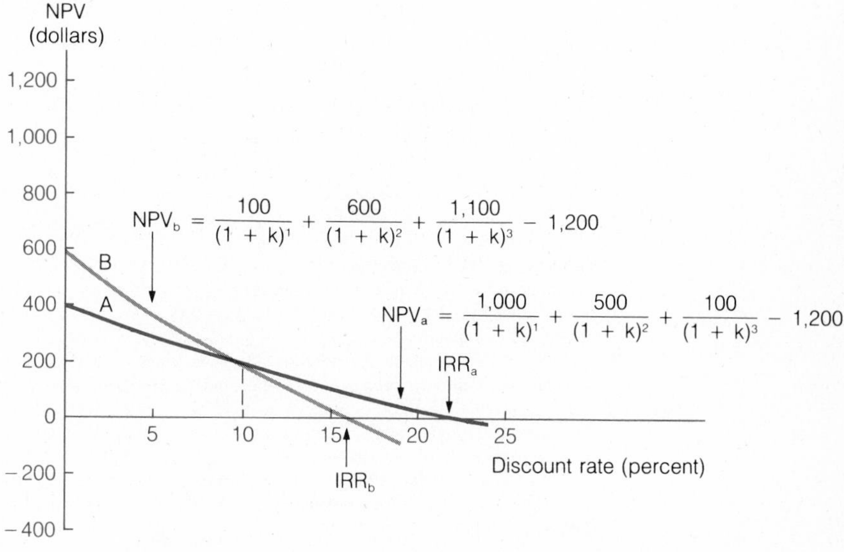

NPV and the higher IRR. We can generalize these results: Whenever the NPV profiles of two projects cross one another, a conflict will exist if the cost of capital is below the crossover rate. For our illustrative projects, no conflict would exist if the firm's cost of capital exceeded 10 percent, but the two methods would rank A and B differently if *k* were less than 10 percent.

How should such conflicts be resolved? For example, when the NPV and IRR methods yield conflicting rankings, which of two mutually exclusive projects should be selected? Assuming that management is seeking to maximize the value of the firm, the correct decision is to select the project with the higher NPV. After all, the NPVs measure the projects' contributions to the value of the firm, so the one with the higher NPV must be contributing more to the firm's value. This line of reasoning leads to the conclusion that firms should, in general, use the NPV method for evaluating capital investment proposals.[14] Recognizing this point, sophisticated firms generally rely on the NPV method. These firms often calculate (by computer) both the NPV and the IRR, but they rely on the NPV when conflicts arise among mutually exclusive projects.

Capital Budgeting Project Evaluation

Thus far the problem of measuring cash flows—the benefits used in the present value calculations above—has not been dealt with directly. This matter will now be discussed, and a few simple examples given. The procedures developed here can be used both for expansion and for replacement decisions.

Simplified Model for Determining Cash Flows[15]

One way of considering the cash flows attributable to a particular investment is to think of them in terms of comparative income statements. This is illustrated in the following example.

The Widget Division of the Culver Company, a profitable, diversified manufacturing firm, purchased a machine five years ago at a cost of $7,500. The machine had an expected life of fifteen years at time of purchase and a zero estimated salvage value at the end of the fifteen years. It is being depreciated on a straight line basis and has a book value of $5,000 at present. The division manager reports that, for $12,000 (including installation), a new machine can be bought which, over its ten-year life, will expand sales from $10,000 to $11,000 a year. Further, it will reduce labor and raw materials usage sufficiently to cut annual operating costs

[14] The question of *why* the conflict arises is an interesting one. Basically, it has to do with the reinvestment of cash flows—the NPV method implicitly assumes reinvestment at the marginal cost of capital (MCC), while the IRR method implicitly assumes reinvestment at the internal rate of return. For a value-maximizing firm, reinvestment at the MCC is the better assumption. The rationale is as follows: A value-maximizing firm will expand to the point where it accepts all projects yielding more than the MCC (these projects will have NPV > 0). How these projects are financed is irrelevant—the point is that they will be financed and accepted. Now consider the question of the cash flows from a particular project. If these cash flows are reinvested, at what rate will reinvestment occur? All projects that yield more than the cost of capital have already been accepted; thus, these cash flows can only be invested in physical assets yielding *less than* the MCC or be used in lieu of other capital with a cost of MCC. A rational firm will take the second alternative, so reinvested cash flows will save the firm the cost of capital. The effect of this is that cash flows are reinvested to yield the cost of capital, the assumption implicit in the NPV method.

[15] The procedure described in this section facilitates understanding of the capital investment analysis process, but the alternative worksheet illustrated in the next section is preferred for repeated calculations.

from $7,000 to $5,000. The new machine has an estimated salvage value of $2,000 at the end of ten years. The old machine's current market value is $1,000. Taxes are at a 40 percent rate and are paid quarterly, and the firm's cost of capital is 10 percent. Should Culver buy the new machine?

The decision calls for five steps: (1) estimating the actual cash outlay attributable to the new investment, (2) determining the incremental cash flows, (3) finding the present value of the incremental cash flows, (4) adding the present value of the expected salvage value to the present value of the total cash flows, and (5) seeing whether the NPV is positive or whether the IRR exceeds the cost of capital. These steps are explained further in the following sections.

Estimated Cash Outlay The net initial cash outlay consists of these items: (1) payment to the manufacturer, (2) proceeds from the sale of the old machine, and (3) tax effects. Culver must make a $12,000 payment to the manufacturer of the machine, but its next quarterly tax bill will be reduced because of the loss it will incur when it sells the old machine: Tax saving = (Loss)(Tax rate) = ($4,000)(0.4) = $1,600. The tax reduction will occur because the old machine, which is carried at $5,000, will be written down by $4,000 ($5,000 less $1,000 salvage value) immediately upon the purchase of the new one.

To illustrate, suppose the Culver Company's taxable income in the quarter in which the new machine is to be purchased would have been $100,000 without the purchase of the new machine and the consequent write-off of the old machine. With a 40 percent tax rate, Culver would have had to write a check for $40,000 to pay its tax bill. However, if it bought the new machine and sold the old one, it would take an operating loss of $4,000—the $5,000 book value on the old machine less the realized salvage value. (The loss is an operating loss, not a capital loss, because it is in reality simply recognizing that depreciation charges, an operating cost, were too low during the old machine's five-year life.)[16] With this $4,000 additional operating cost, the quarter's taxable income would be reduced from $100,000 to $96,000, and the tax bill from $40,000 to $38,400. This means, of course, that the firm's cash outflow for taxes would be $1,600 less *because* of the purchase of the new machine.

In addition, there would be a cash inflow of $1,000 from the sale of the old machine. The net result is that the purchase of the new machine would involve an immediate net cash outlay of $9,400, the cost used for capital budgeting purposes:

Invoice price of new machine	$12,000
Less: Tax savings	−1,600
Salvage of old machine	−1,000
Net cash outflow (cost)	$ 9,400

If additional working capital is required as a result of a capital budgeting decision, as would generally be true for expansion investments (as opposed to cost-reducing replacement investments), this factor must be taken into account. The amount of net working capital (additional current assets required as a result of the expansion

[16] If Culver traded in the old machine as partial payment for the new one, the loss would be added to the depreciable cost of the new machine, and there would be no immediate tax saving.

minus any spontaneous funds generated by the expansion) is estimated and added to the initial cash outlay. We assume that Culver will not need any additional working capital, so this factor is ignored in the example.

Annual Benefits Column 1 in Table 13.7 shows the Widget Division's estimated income statement as it would be without the new machine; Column 2 shows the statement as it would look if the new investment were made. (It is assumed that these figures are applicable for each of the next ten years; if this is not the case, then cash flow estimates must be made for each year.) Column 3 shows the differences between the first two columns.

Table 13.7

Comparative Accounting Income Statement Framework for Considering Cash Flows

	Without new investment (1)		With new investment (2)		Difference: (2) − (1) (3)	
Sales		$10,000		$11,000		$1,000
Operating costs	$7,000		$5,000		($2,000)	
Depreciation	500		1,000		500	
Interest charges	500		1,000		500	
Income before taxes		$ 2,000		$ 4,000		$2,000
Taxes (T = 0.4)		800		1,600		800
Income after taxes		$ 1,200		$ 2,400		$1,200
Dividends paid		600		1,200		600
Additions to retained earnings		$ 600		$ 1,200		$ 600

For capital budgeting analysis, the cash flows that are discounted are the net after-tax operating cash flows. The data in Table 13.7 represent accounting income and must be adjusted in order to be on a cash rather than accrual basis and also to exclude all payments to the sources of financing. In Table 13.7 depreciation is a noncash charge; interest charges and dividends paid are cash flows to the financing sources.

While depreciation is a noncash charge, it is deductible for computing income tax, and income tax payments are cash flows. The cash flows must include the depreciation tax benefits.

Table 13.8 shows the operating cash flows without the new investment, with the new investment, and the difference, or incremental flows.

The incremental cash flows can also be calculated using the following equation. Let ΔSales be the change in sales, ΔO the change in operating costs, ΔNOI the change in operating cash income, ΔDep the change in depreciation, and T the marginal corporate income tax rate. Then

$$\Delta\text{Cash flow} = \text{Change in after-tax operating cash income} + \text{Change in depreciation tax benefit}$$

$$\Delta F = \Delta\text{NOI}\,(1 - \text{T}) + \text{T}\Delta\text{Dep}$$

$$\Delta F = (\Delta\text{Sales} - \Delta\text{O})(1 - \text{T}) + \text{T}\Delta\text{Dep} \qquad \textbf{(13.6)}$$

$$\Delta F = [(\text{Sales}_2 - \text{Sales}_1) - (\text{O}_2 - \text{O}_1)](1 - \text{T}) + \text{T}(\text{Dep}_2 - \text{Dep}_1)$$

Table 13.8 **Net Operating Cash Flow Statement**

	Without new investment (1)	With new investment (2)	Difference or incremental flows: (2) − (1) (3)
Sales	\$10,000	\$11,000	\$1,000
Operating cash costs (O)[a]	7,000	5,000	(2,000)
Net operating cash income (NOI)[a]	\$ 3,000	\$ 6,000	\$3,000
Taxes (T = 0.4)	1,200	2,400	1,200
After-tax operating income: NOI (1 = T)	\$ 1,800	\$ 3,600	\$1,800
Depreciation tax benefit (T × Dep)	200	400	200
Net cash flows (*F*)	\$ 2,000	\$ 4,000	\$2,000

[a] Does not include depreciation as a cash cost since this is a cash flow statement and depreciation is not a cash cost.

or

$$\Delta F = [(\text{Sales}_2 - \text{Sales}_1) - (\text{O}_2 - \text{O}_1) - (\text{Dep}_2 - \text{Dep}_1)](1 - \text{T}) + (\text{Dep}_2 - \text{Dep}_1) \quad \textbf{(13.7)}$$

For the Widget Division analysis:

$$\begin{aligned} \Delta\text{Cash flow} &= [(\$11{,}000 - \$10{,}000) - (\$5{,}000 - \$7{,}000)](1 - 0.4) \\ &\quad + (0.4)(\$1{,}000 - \$500) \\ &= [\$1{,}000 - (-\$2{,}000)](0.6) + (0.4)(\$500) \\ \Delta F &= \$1{,}800 + \$200 = \$2{,}000 \end{aligned}$$

or

$$\Delta F = (\$1{,}000 + \$2{,}000 - \$500)(0.6) + \$500 = \$2{,}000$$

This \$2,000 result checks out with the bottom-line figure in the last column of Table 13.8. What happens if there is no change in sales? The equation is still valid, but ΔSales = 0. In this case, the problem is a simple replacement decision, with a new machine replacing an old one to reduce costs. The sales levels are the same with and without the investment and do not show up in the incremental column.

Finding the PV of the Benefits We have explained in detail how to measure the annual benefits. The next step is to determine the present value of the benefit stream. The interest factor for a ten-year, 10 percent annuity is found to be 6.1446 from Table A.4. This factor, when multiplied by the \$2,000 incremental cash flow, results in a present value of \$12,289.

Salvage Value The new machine has an estimated salvage value of \$2,000; that is, Culver expects to be able to sell the machine for \$2,000 after ten years of use. The present value of an inflow of \$2,000 due in ten years is \$771, found as \$2,000 × 0.3855. If additional working capital had been required and included in the initial cash outlay, this amount would be added to the salvage value of the machine because the working capital would be recovered if and when the project is abandoned.

Notice that the salvage value is a return of capital, not taxable income, so it is *not* subject to income taxes. Of course, when the new machine is actually retired ten years hence, it might be sold for more or less than the expected $2,000, so either taxable income or a deductible operating loss could arise, but $2,000 is the best present estimate of the new machine's salvage value.

Determining the Net Present Value The project's net present value is found as the sum of the present values of the inflows, or benefits, less the outflows, or costs:

Inflows: PV of annual benefits	$12,289
PV of salvage value, new machine	771
Less: Net cash outflow, or cost	(9,400)
Net present value (NPV)	$ 3,660

Since the NPV is positive, the project should be accepted.

Worksheet for Determining Cash Flows

Table 13.9 summarizes the five-step capital budgeting decision process described above. Using the Culver Company investment problem as an example, we first calculate the total outflows for the proposed project by subtracting from the cost of the new machine the sum of the funds received from the sale of the old machine plus the tax savings resulting from that sale. Recall that a $4,000 operating loss will occur if the old machine with a book value of $5,000 is sold for $1,000. Since the old machine is sold at a loss, the $1,000 received from the sale is not taxed. Only the *gain* on the sale of any asset is taxed. Further, the $4,000 loss is a tax deduction for next quarter's tax payment, and it results in a tax saving of $1,600.

Next, we calculate the net annual benefits, then find the present value of this benefit stream, which is $12,289, and we find the present value of the expected salvage value of the new machine, $771. Since salvage value is a *return of capital*, not taxable income, no taxes are deducted from the salvage value.

Finally, we sum up the PV of the inflows and then deduct the project cost to determine the NPV, $3,660 in this example. Since the NPV is positive, the project should be accepted.[17]

[17] Alternatively, the internal rate of return on the project could have been computed and found to be 18 percent. Because this is substantially in excess of the 10 percent cost of capital, the internal rate of return method also indicates that the investment should be undertaken. In this case, the *R* is found as follows:

$$\text{PV of benefit stream} + \text{PV of salvage} - \text{Cost} = 0$$

$$\sum_{t=1}^{10} \frac{\$2{,}000}{(1+R)^t} + \frac{\$2{,}000}{(1+R)^{10}} - \$9{,}400 = 0$$

$$\$2{,}000\ (\text{IF for PV of 10-year annuity}) + \$2{,}000\ (\text{PV of \$1 in 10 years}) - \$9{,}400 = 0$$

Try IFs for 18 percent:

$$\$2{,}000(4.4941) + \$2{,}000(0.1911) - \$9{,}400 = \$8{,}988 + \$382 - \$9{,}400 = \$-30,$$

which is very close to zero, indicating that the internal rate of return is approximately equal to 18 percent.

Table 13.9

Worksheet for Capital Budgeting Project Evaluation

1. *Project cost or initial outflows required to undertake the project*[a]	
Investment in new equipment	$12,000
Receipt from sale of old machine	(1,000)
Add (or subtract) the taxes (or tax savings) resulting from the gain (or loss) on the old machine: tax rate (T) times gain or loss	(1,600)
Total project cost	$ 9,400
2. *Calculation of annual benefits*[b]	
ΔSales	$ 1,000
Less: ΔO	(2,000)[c]
ΔDep	500
ΔTaxable income	$ 2,500
Less: ΔTax at 40%	1,000
ΔAfter-tax profits	$ 1,500
Plus: ΔDep	500
ΔCash flow	$ 2,000
3. *Present value of benefits*	
$\Delta F \times$ Interest factor	
$2,000 × 6.1446 =	$12,289
4. *Present value of expected salvage value*	
Expected salvage value × Interest factor $2,000 × 0.3855 =	$ 771
5. *Net present value*	
PV of inflows: Annual benefits	$12,289
Salvage	771
	$13,060
Less: Project cost	9,400
NPV	$ 3,660

[a] If project costs are incurred over a number of years, then the present value of project costs must be calculated.

[b] It should be noted that if the annual cash flows are not level, the annuity format cannot be used. Also note that if accelerated depreciation is used, the annuity format can almost never be used; in this case, cash flows are unlikely to be uniform from year to year. These restrictions might appear to present serious problems to practical applications in capital budgeting, but they seldom do. Most corporations have either computer facilities or time-sharing arrangements with computer service facilities that handle these nonannuity cases without difficulty.

[c] Refer to Equation 13.6. We are subtracting the change in cost from the change in sales: ΔO = $5,000 − $7,000 = −$2,000. Therefore, ΔSales − ΔO = $1,000 − (−$2,000) = $3,000.

Alternative Capital Budgeting Worksheet

Table 13.10 presents an alternative worksheet for evaluating capital projects. The top section shows net cash flows at the time of investment; since all these flows occur immediately, no discounting is required and the interest factor is 1.0. The lower section of the table shows future cash flows—benefits from increased sales and/or reduced costs, depreciation, and salvage value. These flows occur over time, so it is necessary to convert them to present values. The NPV as determined in the alternative format, $3,660, agrees with the figure as calculated in Table 13.9.

Table 13.10 **Alternative Worksheet for Capital Budgeting Project Evaluation**

	Amount before tax	Amount after tax[a]	Year event occurs	PV factor at 10%	PV
Outflows at time investment is made					
Investment in new equipment	$12,000	$12,000	0	1.0000	$12,000
Salvage value of old	(1,000)	(1,000)	0	1.0000	(1,000)
Tax effect of the sale[b]	(4,000)	(1,600)	0	1.0000	(1,600)
Increased working capital (if necessary)	c	—	0	1.0000	—
Total initial outflows (PV of costs)					$ 9,400
Inflows, or annual returns					
Benefits[d]	$ 3,000	$ 1,800	1–10	6.1446	$11,060
Depreciation on new (annual)[b]	1,000	400	1–10	6.1446	2,458
Depreciation on old (annual)[b]	(500)	(200)	1–10	6.1446	(1,229)
Salvage value on new	2,000	2,000	10	0.3855	771
Return of working capital (if necessary)	c	—	10	0.3855	—
Total periodic inflows (PV of benefits)					$13,060

NPV = PV of benefits less PV of cost = $13,060 − $9,400 = $3,660.

[a] Amount after tax equals amount before tax times T or (1 − T), where T = Tax rate.
[b] Deductions (tax loss and depreciation) are multiplied by T.
[c] Not applicable
[d] Benefits are multiplied by (1 − T).

Accelerated Depreciation

Thus far in our illustrations of capital budgeting, it has been assumed that straight line depreciation was used, thus enabling us to derive uniform cash flows over the life of the investment. Realistically, however, firms usually employ *accelerated depreciation* methods; when such is the case, it is necessary to modify the procedures outlined thus far. With accelerated depreciation, the deduction for depreciation expense is no longer a constant amount. It is, rather, larger in the earlier years and then declining. But for the entire period of a capital budgeting analysis, the present value of all of the accelerated depreciation tax deductions can be calculated.

Appendix C contains present value factors for accelerated depreciation. The factors in the table are developed as shown in the example in Table 13.11. In this example, we are interested in the factor for depreciation by the sum-of-years'-digits method over a five-year period with a 10 percent cost of capital. We first find the fraction of $1 that is charged to depreciation in each year, then discount that amount at 10 percent. The sum of the present values of the amounts received during the five years, shown in the product column, equals the accelerated depreciation factor (0.805 in this example).

To find the present value of the depreciation tax savings when an investment is depreciated by an accelerated method, we multiply the tax rate by the accelerated

Table 13.11

Calculation of the Accelerated Depreciation Factor

Year	Depreciation fraction applied to asset cost	Amount of depreciation	10% discount factor	Product
1	5/15	0.33333	0.9091	0.3030
2	4/15	0.26667	0.8264	0.2204
3	3/15	0.20000	0.7513	0.1503
4	2/15	0.13333	0.6830	0.0911
5	1/15	0.06667	0.6209	0.0414
	Totals 1.00	1.00000	Factor =	$0.8062 \approx 0.806$

depreciation factor by the amount to be depreciated. For $20,000 in depreciation:

$$\text{PV} = \text{T(accelerated depreciation PV factor)(I)}$$
$$= 0.4(0.806)(\$20{,}000) = \$6{,}448$$

Appendix C gives factors for both the sum-of-years'-digits and double declining balance depreciation methods, for various asset lives, and for different discount rates. The factor of 0.806 calculated in Table 13.11 can also be found in Appendix C—in the 10 percent column at Period 5.

We may utilize these accelerated depreciation factors to recalculate the Culver example, using the alternative, and somewhat streamlined, decision format shown in Table 13.12. The top section of the table presents the cash outflows at the time the investment is made. All these flows occur immediately, so no discounting is

Table 13.12

Calculations for Replacement Decision: Accelerated Depreciation

	Amount before tax	Amount after tax[a]	Year event occurs	PV factor at 10%	PV
Outflows at time investment is made					
Investment in new equipment	$12,000	$12,000	0	1.0000	$12,000
Salvage value of old	(1,000)	(1,000)	0	1.0000	(1,000)
Tax effect of the sale	(4,000)	(1,600)	0	1.0000	(1,600)
Total outflows (Present value of costs)					$ 9,400
Inflows, or annual returns					
Benefits	3,000	1,800	1–10	6.1446	$11,060
Depreciation on new (total)	10,000	4,000	1–10	0.7010	2,804
Depreciation on old (annual)	(500)	(200)	1–10	6.1446	(1,229)
Salvage value on new	2,000	2,000	10	0.3855	771
Total inflows (Present value of benefits)					$13,406
Present value of inflows less present value of outflows = $4,006					

[a] The "tax effect of the sale" and depreciation figures are multiplied by T, the tax rate, to obtain the after-tax figures, while the benefits are multiplied by (1 – T).

required, and the present value factor is 1.0. No tax adjustment is necessary on the invoice price of the new machine, but, as we saw above, the $4,000 loss on the old machine creates a $1,600 tax reduction, which is deducted from the price of the new machine. Also, the $1,000 salvage value on the old machine is treated as a reduction in cash outflows necessary to acquire the new machine. Notice that since the $1,000 is a recovery of capital investment, it is not considered to be taxable income; hence, no tax adjustment is made for the salvage value.

In the lower section of the table we see that net income before tax increases by $3,000 a year—a sales increase of $1,000 plus a cost reduction of $2,000. However, this amount is taxable, so with a 40 percent tax, the after-tax benefits are reduced to $1,800. This $1,800 is received each year for ten years, so it is an annuity. The present value of the annuity, discounted at the 10 percent cost of capital, is $11,060.

Cash inflows also come from the depreciation on the new machine—depreciation on the new machine totals $10,000, and the tax saving totals $4,000. In Table 13.12, we assume that the new investment is depreciated by the sum-of-years-digits method over a ten-year period; hence a factor of 0.701, taken from Appendix C, is applied to the after-tax depreciation figure of $4,000 to obtain a present value of $2,804 for the depreciation tax shelter.[18]

The old machine was being depreciated by the straight-line method; hence it provides a cash flow of $500 before taxes and $200 after taxes for ten years. Observe that the depreciation on the old machine is *subtracted* from the inflows section. The logic here is that, had the replacement *not* been made, the company would have had the benefit of the $500 depreciation each year for the next ten years. With the replacement, however, we take the depreciation on the new as a tax shelter, and the lost depreciation on the old as an opportunity cost.

When the present values of the inflows and outflows are summed, we obtain the project's NPV. In this example, the NPV is $3,942 versus $3,660 for the straight line text example. In general, NPVs are higher when accelerated depreciation is used, as the PV of the depreciation benefit is higher than it would be under straight line.

Capital Rationing

Ordinarily, firms operate as illustrated in Figure 13.1; that is, they take on investments to the point at which the marginal returns from investment just equal their estimated marginal cost of capital. For firms operating in this way, the decision process is as described above—they make those investments having positive net present values, reject those whose net present values are negative, and choose between mutually exclusive investments on the basis of the higher net present value. However, a firm will occasionally set an absolute limit on the size of its capital budget for any one year that is less than the level of investment it would undertake on the basis of the criteria described above.

The principal reason for such action is that some firms are reluctant to engage in external financing (borrowing or selling stock). One management, recalling the

[18] The terms *tax shelter* or *tax shield* are frequently used to denote the value of depreciation and other items which shelter or shield income from taxes.

plight of firms with substantial amounts of debt in the 1930s, may simply refuse to use debt. Another management, which has no objection to selling debt, may not want to sell equity capital for fear of losing some measure of voting control. Still others may refuse to use any form of outside financing, considering safety and control to be more important than additional profits. These are all cases of capital rationing, and they result in limiting the rate of expansion to a slower pace than would be dictated by "purely rational profit-maximizing behavior."[19]

Project Selection Under Capital Rationing

How should projects be selected under conditions of capital rationing? First, note that under conditions of true capital rationing, the firm's value is not being maximized—if management were maximizing, then it would move to the point where the marginal project's NPV was zero, and capital rationing as defined would not exist. So, if a firm uses capital rationing, it has ruled out value maximization. The firm may, however, want to maximize value *subject to the constraint that the capital ceiling is not exceeded.* Following constrained maximization behavior will, in general, result in a lower value than following unconstrained maximization, but some type of constrained maximization may produce reasonably satisfactory results. Linear programming is one method of constrained maximization that has been applied to capital rationing. To our knowledge, this method has not been widely applied, but much work is going on in the area, and linear programming may, in the future, prove useful in capital budgeting.

If a financial manager does face capital rationing and cannot get the constraint lifted, the manager's objective should be to select projects, subject to the capital rationing constraint, such that the sum of the projects' NPVs is maximized. Linear programming can be used, but there is really no practical alternative that will approximate the true maximum. Reasonably satisfactory results may be obtained by ranking projects by their internal rates of return and then, starting at the top of this list of projects, by taking investments of successively lower rank until the available funds have been exhausted. However, no investment with a negative NPV (or an internal rate of return below the cost of capital) should be undertaken.

A firm might, for example, have the investment opportunities shown in Table 13.13 and only $6 million available for investment. In this situation, the firm would probably accept Projects 1 through 4 and Project 6, ending with a capital budget

[19] We should make three points here. First, we *do not* necessarily consider a decision to hold back on expansion irrational. If the owners of a firm have what they consider to be plenty of income and wealth, then it might be quite rational for them to "trim their sails," relax, and concentrate on enjoying what they have already earned rather than on earning still more. Such behavior would not, however, be appropriate for a publicly owned firm.

The second point is that it is not correct to interpret as capital rationing a situation in which the firm is willing to sell additional securities at the going market price but finds that it cannot because the market will simply not absorb more of its issues. Rather, such a situation indicates that the cost-of-capital curve is rising. If more acceptable investments are indicated than can be financed, then the cost of capital being used is too low and should be raised.

Third, firms sometimes set a limit on capital expenditures, not because of a shortage of funds, but because of limitations on other resources, especially managerial talent. A firm might feel, for example, that its personnel development program is sufficient to handle an expansion of no more than 10 percent a year, then set a limit on the capital budget to insure that expansion is held to that rate. This is not *capital* rationing—rather, it involves a downward reevaluation of project returns if growth exceeds some limit; that is, expected rates of return are, after some point, a decreasing function of the level of expenditures.

Table 13.13 **The Prospective Projects Schedule**

Nature of proposal	Project's cost	Cumulative total of costs	Internal rate of return	PV of benefits	Project's NPV
1. Purchase of leased space	$2,000,000	$ 2,000,000	23%	$3,200,000	$1,200,000
2. Mechanization of accounting system	1,200,000	3,200,000	19	1,740,000	540,000
3. Modernization of office building	1,500,000	4,700,000	17	2,070,000	570,000
4. Addition of power facilities	900,000	5,600,000	16	1,125,000	225,000
5. Purchase of affiliate	3,600,000	9,200,000	13	4,248,000	648,000
6. Purchase of loading docks	300,000	9,500,000	12	342,000	42,000
7. Purchase of tank trucks	500,000	10,000,000	11	540,000	40,000
		cutoff			
8. Installation of conveyor system	200,000	10,200,000	9	186,000	(14,000)
9. Construction of new plant	2,300,000	12,500,000	8	2,093,000	(207,000)
10. Purchase of executive aircraft	200,000	12,700,000	7	128,000	(72,000)

of $5.9 million and a cumulative NPV of $2.6 million. Under no circumstances should it accept Projects 8, 9, or 10, as they all have internal rates of return of less than 10 percent (and also net present values less than zero).

Summary

Capital budgeting, which involves commitments for large outlays whose benefits (or drawbacks) extend well into the future, is of the greatest significance to a firm. Decisions in these areas will therefore have a major impact on the future well-being of the firm. This chapter focused on how capital budgeting decisions can be made more effective in contributing to the health and growth of a firm.The discussion stressed the development of systematic procedures and rules for preparing a list of investment proposals, for evaluating them, and for selecting a cutoff point.

The chapter emphasized that one of the most crucial phases in the process of evaluating capital budget proposals is obtaining a dependable estimate of the benefits that will be obtained from undertaking the project. It cannot be overemphasized that the firm must allocate to competent and experienced personnel the making of these judgments.

Determining Cash Flows The cash inflows from an investment are the incremental change in after-tax net operating cash income plus the incremental depreciation tax benefit; the cash outflow is the cost of the investment less the salvage value received on an old machine plus any tax loss (or less any tax savings) when the machine is sold.

Ranking Investment Proposals Three commonly used procedures for ranking investment proposals were discussed in the chapter: payback, net present value, and internal rate of return.

Payback is defined as the number of years required to return the original investment. Although the payback method is used frequently, it has serious conceptual weaknesses, because it ignores the facts (1) that some receipts come in beyond the payback period and (2) that a dollar received today is more valuable than a dollar received in the future.

Net present value is defined as the present value of future returns, discounted at the cost of capital, minus the cost of the investment. The NPV method overcomes the conceptual flaws noted in the use of the payback method.

Internal rate of return is defined as the interest rate that equates the present value of future returns to the investment outlay. The internal rate of return method, like the NPV method, meets the objections to the payback approach.

In most cases, the two discounted cash flow methods give identical answers to these questions: Which of two mutually exclusive projects should be selected? How large should the total capital budget be? However, under certain circumstances conflicts may arise. Such conflicts are caused by the fact that the NPV and IRR methods make different assumptions about the rate at which cash flows may be reinvested, or the opportunity cost of cash flows. In general, the assumption of the NPV method (that the opportunity cost is the cost of capital) is the correct one. Accordingly, our preference is for using the NPV method to make capital budgeting decisions.

Questions

13.1 A firm has $100 million available for capital expenditures. Suppose project A involves purchasing $100 million of grain, shipping it overseas, and selling it within a year at a profit of $20 million. The project has an IRR of 20 percent and an NPV of $9 million, and it will cause earnings per share (EPS) to rise within one year. Project B calls for the use of the $100 million to develop a new process, acquire land, build a plant, and begin processing. Project B, which is not postponable, has an NPV of $50 million and an IRR of 30 percent. But the fact that some of the plant costs will be written off immediately, combined with the fact that no revenues will be generated for several years, means that accepting project B will reduce short-run EPS.

a. Should the short-run effects on EPS influence the choice between the two projects?

b. How might situations such as the one described here influence a firm's decision to use payback as a screening criterion?

13.2 Are there conditions under which a firm might be better off if it were to choose a machine with a rapid payback rather than one with the largest rate of return?

13.3 Company X uses the payback method in evaluating investment proposals and is considering new equipment whose additional net after-tax earnings will be $150 a year. The equipment costs $500, and its expected life is ten years (straight-line depreciation). The company uses a three-year payback as its criterion. Should the equipment be purchased under the above assumptions?

13.4 What are the most critical problems that arise in calculating a rate of return for a prospective investment?

13.5 What other factors in addition to rate of return analysis should be considered in determining capital expenditures?

13.6 Would it be beneficial for a firm to review its past capital expenditures and capital budgeting procedures? Explain.

13.7 Fiscal and monetary policies are tools used by the government to stimulate the economy. Using the analytical devices developed in this chapter, explain how each of the following might be expected to stimulate the economy by encouraging investment:

a. A speedup of tax-allowable depreciation
b. An easing of interest rates
c. Passage of a new federal program giving more aid to the poor
d. An investment tax credit

Problems

13.1 Two pieces of equipment, a truck and an overhead pulley, are being considered in this year's capital budget. The projects are not mutually exclusive. The outlay for the truck is $9,869, and the outlay for the pulley is $17,845. The firm's cost of capital is 12 percent. Cash flows are shown below:

Year	Truck	Pulley
1	$3,300	$6,500
2	3,300	6,500
3	3,300	6,500
4	3,300	6,500
5	3,300	6,500

Calculate the IRR and NPV on each project, and indicate the correct adopt-reject decision for each.

13.2 You are choosing between a gas-powered and an electric-powered forklift truck for moving materials in the factory. Since they both perform the same function, you will choose only one. (They are mutually exclusive investments.) The electric-powered truck will cost more but be less expensive to operate. It will cost $16,628, while the gas-powered truck will cost $13,302. The cost of capital that applies to both investments is 10 percent. The life for both types of truck is estimated to be six years, during which the net cash flows for the electric-powered truck will be $5,000 per year and the net cash flows for the gas-powered truck will be $4,000 per year. Calculate the NPV and IRR on each type of truck and decide which to recommend for purchase.

13.3 Digital Systems Corporation has sales of $140,000 per year and net cash operating costs of $100,000 per year on Project A. The investment outlay (I) on the project is $100,000; its life ($N$) is ten years; the tax rate (T) is 40 percent. The applicable cost of capital (k) is 12 percent.

a. Present two formulations of the net cash flows (F) adjusted for depreciation tax shelter.
b. Calculate the net present value for Project A, using straight-line depreciation for tax purposes.

13.4 The Granger Shipyards is considering the replacement of a riveting machine with a new one that will increase the earnings before depreciation from $20,000 per year to $51,000 per year. The new machine will cost $100,000 and have an estimated life of eight years with no salvage value. The applicable corporate tax rate is 40 percent, and the firm's cost of capital is 12 percent. The old machine has been fully depreciated and has no salvage value. Should it be replaced by the new one?

13.5 Assume that Granger Shipyards (in Problem 13.4) will be able to realize an investment tax credit of 10 percent on the purchase of the new machine and that it will have a salvage value of $12,000. Assume further that the old machine has a book value of $40,000 and a remaining life of eight years. If replaced, the old machine can be sold now for $15,000. Should the machine replacement be made?

13.6 Bates Breweries is contemplating the replacement of one of its bottling machines with a newer and more efficient one. The old machine has a book value of $500,000 and a remaining useful life of five years. The firm does not expect to realize any return from scrapping the old machine in five years, but it can sell the machine now to another firm in the industry for $300,000.

The new machine has a purchase price of $1.1 million, an estimated useful life of five years, and an estimated salvage value of $100,000. It is expected to economize on electric power usage, labor, and repair costs and to reduce the number of defective bottles. In total, an annual saving of $200,000 will be realized if the new machine is installed. The company is in the 40 percent tax bracket, has a 10 percent cost of capital, and uses straight-line depreciation.

a. What is the initial cash outlay required for the new machine?
b. What are the cash flows in Years 1 to 5?
c. What is the cash flow from the salvage value in Year 5?
d. Should Bates Breweries purchase the new machine? Support your answer.
e. In general, how would each of the following factors affect the investment decision, and how should each be treated?
    1. The expected life of the existing machine decreases
    2. Capital rationing is imposed on the firm
    3. The cost of capital is not constant but is rising
    4. Improvements in the equipment to be purchased are expected to occur each year, and the result will be to increase the returns or expected savings from the new machine over the savings expected with this year's model for every year in the foreseeable future

13.7 Modigliani Milling is using a machine whose original cost was $72,000. The machine is two years old and has a current market value of $16,000. The asset is being depreciated over a twelve-year original life toward a zero estimated final salvage value. Depreciation is on a straight-line basis, and the tax rate is 40 percent.

Management is contemplating the purchase of a replacement that costs $75,000 and has an estimated salvage value of $10,000. The new machine will have a greater capacity, enabling annual sales to increase by $10,000 from $1 million to $1.01 million. Operating efficiencies with the new machine will also produce expected savings of $10,000 a year. Depreciation will be on a straight-line basis over a ten-year life, the cost of capital will be 10 percent, and a 40 percent tax rate will apply. The company's total depreciation costs are currently $120,000, and the total annual operating costs are $800,000.

a. Should the firm replace the asset? Use Equation 13.6 (showing the cash flow difference) to solve the problem.
b. How will your decision be affected if a second new machine is available that costs $140,000, has a $20,000 estimated salvage value, increases sales by $10,000 a year, and is expected to provide $25,000 in annual savings over its ten-year life? (There are now three alternatives: keep the old machine, replace it with a $75,000 machine, or replace it with a $140,000 machine.) Depreciation is still on a straight-line basis. For purposes of answering this question use both the NPV (which you must calculate) and the IRR (which you can assume to be 27 percent for the $75,000 project and 19 percent for the $140,000 project).
c. Disregarding the changes in Part b (that is, under the original assumption that one $75,000 replacement machine is available), how will your decision be affected if a new generation of equipment that will provide increased annual savings and have the same cost, asset life, and salvage value is expected to be on the market in about two years?
d. What factors in addition to the quantitative ones listed above are likely to require consideration in a practical situation?
e. How will your decision be affected if the asset lives of the various alternatives are not the same?

13.8 Twinkle Toy Company is considering the purchase of a new machine tool to replace an obsolete one. The machine being used for the operation has both a tax book value and a market value of zero; it is in good working order and will last, physically, for at least an additional fifteen years. The proposed machine will perform the operation so much more efficiently that Twinkle Toy engineers estimate that labor, material, and other direct costs of the operation will be reduced $4,500 a year if it is installed. The proposed machine costs $24,000 delivered and installed, and its economic life is estimated to be fifteen years with zero salvage value. The company expects to earn 12 percent on its investment after taxes (12 percent is the firm's cost of capital). The tax rate is 40 percent, and the firm uses straight-line depreciation.

a. Should Twinkle Toy buy the new machine?
b. Assume that the tax book value of the old machine is $6,000, that the annual depreciation charge is $400. The old machine still has a market value of zero. How do these assumptions affect your answer?

13.9 Each of two mutually exclusive projects involves an investment of $120,000. Cash flows (after-tax profits plus depreciation) for the two projects have a different time pattern, although the totals are approximately the same. Project M will yield high returns early and lower returns in later years. (It is a mining type of investment, and the expense of removing the ore is lower at the entrance to the mine, where there is easier access.) Project O yields low returns in the early years and higher returns in the later years. (It is an orchard type of investment, and it takes a number of years for trees to mature and be fully bearing.) The cash flows from the two investments are as follows:

Year	Project M	Project O
1	$70,000	$10,000
2	40,000	20,000
3	30,000	30,000
4	10,000	50,000
5	10,000	80,000

a. Compute the present value of each project when the firm's cost of capital is 0 percent, 6 percent, 10 percent, and 20 percent.
b. Compute the internal rate of return (IRR) for each project.
c. Graph the present value of the two projects, putting net present value (NPV) on the Y-axis and the cost of capital on the X-axis.
d. Can you determine the IRR of the projects from your graph? Explain.
e. Which project would you select, assuming no capital rationing and a constant cost of capital of 8 percent? Of 10 percent? Of 12 percent? Explain.
f. If capital were severely rationed, which project would you select?

CHAPTER 14

RISK AND INVESTMENT RETURN

In setting forth the basic concepts and procedures of capital budgeting, the preceding chapter did not consider the riskiness of alternative projects. Therefore, this chapter will add this missing dimension to capital budgeting analysis. The basic idea is that greater risk requires a higher return. Hence, the discount rate used in the analysis of projects with uncertain outcomes must include a risk adjustment factor, which requires that the applicable discount rate be increased. But a higher discount factor applied to a given cash flow stream results in a reduced present value. Thus it is also necessary to determine whether the new present value still exceeds the cost of the investment and thereby adds to the value of the firm. This depends on how much the discount rate is increased by the addition of a risk adjustment factor, and the amount of the risk adjustment factor depends on how risk is measured and how the risk adjustment factor is related to the risk measure.

The traditional measures of risk have been applied to individual projects in isolation. Newer approaches have recognized that individual projects can be combined with others into groups of projects, or portfolios. Viewing an individual project in its broader portfolio context changes the appropriate measure of risk to be applied. The derivation of the portfolio approach will be emphasized in this chapter, starting with a discussion of the traditional risk measures applied to individual projects so that the relationships between the different approaches can be seen.

The traditional measures of risk for projects in isolation are stated in terms of probability distributions. The tighter the probability distribution of expected future returns, the smaller the risk of a given project. The measure of tightness it utilizes is the standard deviation. The tighter the probability distribution, the smaller the standard deviation. However, the standard deviation must also be related to the expected return. The coefficient of variation is a measure of risk in which the standard deviation is normalized by dividing by the expected value, or mean.

Risk in Financial Analysis

The riskiness of an asset is defined in terms of the likely variability of future returns from the asset. For example, if one buys a $1 million short-term government bond expected to yield 8 percent, then the return on the investment, 8 percent, can be estimated quite precisely, and the investment is defined as relatively risk free. However, if the $1 million is invested in the stock of a company being organized to prospect for uranium in central Africa, then the probable return cannot be estimated precisely. The rate of return on the $1 million investment could range from minus

100 percent to some extremely large figure; because of this high variability, the project is defined as relatively risky. Similarly, sales forecasts for different products of a single firm might exhibit differing degrees of riskiness. For example, Union Carbide might be quite sure that sales of its Eveready batteries will range between 50 and 60 million for the coming year but be highly uncertain about how many units of a new laser measuring device will be sold during the year. Risk, then, is associated with project variability. The more variable the expected future returns, the riskier the investment. However, risk can be defined more precisely, and it is useful to do so. The definition requires a step-by-step development, and this constitutes the remainder of the section. Any investment decision—or, for that matter, almost *any* kind of business decision—implies a forecast of future events that is either explicit or implicit. Ordinarily, the forecast of annual cash flow is a single figure, or *point estimate*, frequently called the "most likely" or "best" estimate. For example, one might forecast that the cash flows from a particular project will be $500 a year for three years.

How good is this point estimate? That is, how confident is the forecaster of the predicted return—very certain, very uncertain, or somewhere in between? This degree of uncertainty can be defined and measured in terms of the forecaster's *probability distribution*—the probability estimates associated with each possible outcome. In its simplest form, a probability distribution could consist of just a few potential outcomes. For example, in forecasting cash flows, we could make an optimistic estimate, a pessimistic estimate, and a most likely estimate; or we could make high, low, and "best guess" estimates. We might expect our high, or optimistic, estimate to be realized if the national economy booms, our pessimistic estimate to hold if the economy is depressed, and our best guess to occur if the economy runs at a normal level.

Alternative outcome probabilities are fundamentally related to relative frequencies. If you flipped a fair coin for a large number of times (say 1,000), the probability is that it would turn up heads about 50 percent of the time and tails about 50 percent of the time. These percentages represent the relative frequencies of heads or tails. We also say that the probability of heads is 50 percent, or 0.5, and that the probability of tails is 50 percent, or 0.5. We note that the sum of the alternative probabilities is exactly 1.0 (0.5 + 0.5). The relative frequency from tossing coins is limited to heads or tails since those are the only alternatives. In the financial markets, many outcomes are possible.

Traditional Measures of Risk of Individual Projects

Risk is difficult to measure unambiguously. The traditional measures of risk have been applied to individual projects in isolation. Newer approaches have recognized that these projects can be combined with other projects into groups of projects, or portfolios. Viewing an individual project in its broader portfolio context changes the appropriate measure of risk to be applied. We will start with a discussion of the traditional measures of risk applied to individual projects so the relationships between the different approaches can be seen later.

The traditional measure of risk applied to individual projects is stated in terms of probability distributions such as those presented in Figure 14.1. The tighter the

Figure 14.1 Graph of Two Probability Distributions

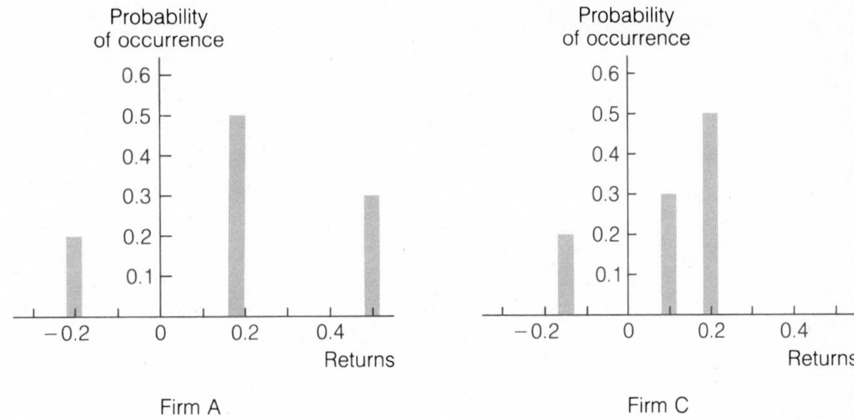

probability distribution of expected future returns, the smaller the risk of a given project. According to this view, Firm C is less risky than Firm A because each of the possible returns for C is closer to the expected return than is true for A.

Expected Return and Standard Deviation

Two measures developed from the probability distribution have been used as initial measures of return and risks. These are the mean and the standard deviation of the probability distribution. Calculations of the mean and standard deviation of returns for Firm A are shown in Table 14.1.

Table 14.1 Calculations of the Standard Deviation for Firm A

State of the Economy	P_s	$\tilde{R}_a$	$P_s\tilde{R}_a$	$(\tilde{R}_a - \bar{R}_a)$	$(\tilde{R}_a - \bar{R}_a)^2$	$P_s(\tilde{R}_a - \bar{R}_a)^2$
Down	0.2	−0.20	−0.04	−0.40	0.1600	0.0320
Average	0.5	0.18	0.09	−0.02	0.0004	0.0002
Up	0.3	0.50	0.15	0.30	0.0900	0.0270
			$\bar{R}_a = 0.20$			$\sigma_a^2 = 0.0592$
						$\sigma_a = 0.2433$

In equation form, the expected rate of return or mean return is:

$$\text{Expected rate of return } E(R_a) = \bar{R}_a = \sum_{s=1}^{S} P_s\tilde{R}_a \tag{14.1}$$

In Equation 14.1, the expected return is expressed either with the expectation operator, E, as $E(R_a)$ or with the bar as $\bar{R}_a$. It is simpler to use the bar, and we shall do so generally; but the forms can be used interchangeably. P_s is the probability of a state occurring, and $\tilde{R}_a$ is the associated return from Firm A under that state. Calculation of the expected return is the same as the calculation of the ordinary arithmetic mean of a frequency distribution. Here the frequency distribution is expressed by probabilities and so is called a *probability distribution*. In calculating an arithmetic mean, we sum the product of frequencies times associated values and divide by the number of frequencies (observations). We do essentially the same thing in calculating the weighted average here. We multiply each probability and associated return. We then total. We divide by the sum of the probabilities, which is one. We really have nothing further to do after we have multiplied by the probabilities and totaled:

$$\begin{aligned} \bar{R}_a &= P_1(\tilde{R}_{a_1}) + P_2(\tilde{R}_{a_2}) + P_3(\tilde{R}_{a_3}) \\ \bar{R}_a &= 0.2(-0.20) + 0.5(0.18) + 0.3(0.50) \qquad \textbf{(14.1a)} \\ \bar{R}_a &= -0.04 + 0.09 + 0.15 = 0.20 \end{aligned}$$

We have now calculated the expected return. We need to relate this return or reward to some measures of risk. We begin with the basic statistical measure of the dispersion of the probability distribution, the standard deviation, which is generally referred to by the Greek symbol σ (sigma). The standard deviation is the square root of the variance. The variance is computed by (1) calculating the deviations from the mean, (2) squaring the deviations, (3) summing the squared deviations, and (4) dividing by the total number of observations. For the probability distribution of returns, the probabilities total to 1, so this step is performed by multiplying the squared deviation by the probability before summing. The square root of the variance is the standard deviation. The general expression for the variance is shown in Equation 14.2.

$$\begin{aligned} \text{Variance} = \sigma_a^2 &= \sum_{s=1}^{S} P_s(\tilde{R}_a - \bar{R}_a)^2 \qquad \textbf{(14.2)} \\ \sigma_a^2 &= P_1(\tilde{R}_{a_1} - \bar{R}_a)^2 + P_2(\tilde{R}_{a_2} - \bar{R}_a)^2 + P_3(\tilde{R}_{a_3} - \bar{R}_a)^2 \end{aligned}$$

Using the data for Firm A, we have

$$\sigma_a^2 = 0.2(-0.40)^2 + 0.5(-0.02)^2 + 0.3(0.30)^2 = 0.0592$$

$$\sqrt{\sigma_a^2} = \sigma_a = 0.2433$$

These results reflect the calculations in Table 14.1.

We have now defined and set forth the procedures for calculating two parameters (summarizing measures) of the probability distributions of prospective returns: the mean and standard deviation. In general, these two measures enable us to sketch the full probability distribution. We make the further assumption that the probability distribution is continuous, implying that probabilities can be estimated for a large number of values so that we may draw an unbroken curve through all the indicated rates of return. For example, consider two assets, or investment opportunities, D and E, with the distribution of returns shown in Tables 14.2 and 14.3.

The probability distributions for Assets D and E from Tables 14.2 and 14.3 are graphed in Figure 14.2.

Table 14.2

Distribution of Returns from Asset D

Probability	Indicated return, $\tilde{R}_d$	
0.05	0.05	Mean = 0.1625
0.20	0.10	$\sigma_d = 0.063$
0.50	0.15	
0.20	0.25	
0.05	0.30	

Table 14.3

Distribution of Returns from Asset E

Probability	$\tilde{R}_e$	
0.03	−0.40	Mean = 0.0505
0.04	−0.30	$\sigma_e = 0.160$
0.06	−0.20	
0.08	−0.10	
0.10	0.00	
0.15	0.05	
0.20	0.10	
0.15	0.15	
0.10	0.20	
0.05	0.25	
0.04	0.30	

Figure 14.2

Graph of Continuous Probability Distributions

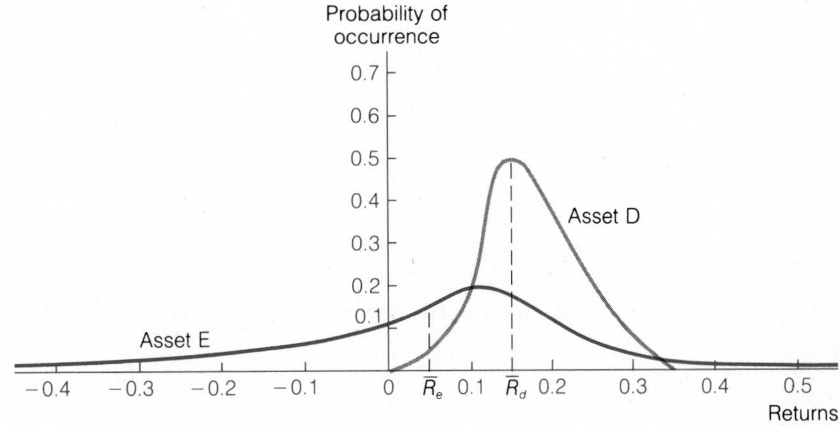

The graph of Asset D exhibits two features of a more favorable investment. First, it has a higher expected return. In addition, the frequency distribution is bunched closer together, indicating less dispersion, one of the measures of risk.

The Mean-Variance Criterion and Risk Aversion

From the data on Assets D and E it would appear that Investment D is preferable to Investment E. Investment D has a higher expected return and a lower standard deviation than does Investment E. This illustrates the fundamental basis for the mean-variance criterion: people prefer more return to less return and less risk to more risk. The mean-variance criterion is based on the general pattern that investors are, on average, averse to risk. In making investment decisions, a tradeoff between expected returns and risks is made. From this it would seem to follow that riskier securities would require higher expected returns than less risky securities. But that expectation covers only part of the story. We need to proceed further to consider more closely how risk is measured and to attempt to develop some quantitative relationships between levels of risk and required returns.

The Coefficient of Variation as a Measure of Risk

Asset D will be preferred to Asset E because it has a higher expected return and a lower standard deviation. But suppose we were comparing Assets G, H, and I with characteristics as shown in Table 14.4.

Table 14.4

Calculation of the Coefficient of Variation

	Expected return	Standard deviation of returns	Coefficient of variation (CV_j)
Asset G	0.12	0.10	0.83
Asset H	0.20	0.22	1.10
Asset I	0.15	0.10	0.67

Asset G has the same standard deviation of returns as Asset I, but it has a lower expected return. Asset H has both a higher expected return and a higher standard deviation than Asset I. Can we make comparisons of the relative risks of the different assets?

One procedure that can be used is to standardize the risk per unit of return. This is the concept of the coefficient of variation (CV), which is the standard deviation (σ_j) divided by the mean or expected return ($\bar{R}_j$):

$$CV_j = \frac{\sigma_j}{\bar{R}_j} \tag{14.3}$$

The measures of the coefficient of variation have been calculated in the final column of Table 14.4. By the criterion of the coefficient of variation, Asset I is less risky than Asset G, which in turn is less risky than Asset H. Thus although Asset G has the same standard deviation as Asset I, its standard deviation per unit of return is higher. Asset H has both a higher expected return and a higher standard deviation.

Its risk, as measured by the standard deviation per unit of return, is the highest of the three assets exhibited. If the standard deviation is to be used as a measure of risk for investments viewed in isolation, as individual investments, the normalization obtained by dividing through by the mean return to obtain the coefficient of variation should be used.

Risk in a Portfolio Framework

We have seen that the standard deviation is not a complete measure of risk, since the measure needs to be standardized per unit of return. In addition, another fundamental consideration that must be taken into account is that assets or investments are held not in isolation but jointly with other assets or investments. Hence, the riskiness of an asset can be influenced by the interaction of the pattern of its return with the patterns of return of the other assets it is held in combination with. This leads us to a consideration of portfolio risk.

To illustrate the basic idea, let us consider the pattern of returns for Firm B, as indicated by Table 14.5.

Table 14.5

Calculation of the Expected Return and Standard Deviation of Firm B

State of the economy	P_s	$\tilde{R}_b$	$P_s\tilde{R}_b$	$(\tilde{R}_b - \bar{R}_b)$	$(\tilde{R}_b - \bar{R}_b)^2$	$P_s(\tilde{R}_b - \bar{R}_b)^2$
Down	0.2	0.50	0.10	0.37	0.1369	0.02738
Average	0.5	0.18	0.09	0.05	0.0025	0.00125
Up	0.3	−0.20	−0.06	−0.33	0.1089	0.03267
			$\bar{R}_b = 0.13$			$\sigma_b^2 = 0.06130$
						$\sigma_b = 0.2476$

Firm B is assumed to have exactly the same returns as Firm A, but their state pattern is exactly reversed. When the state of the economy is strong, Firm B's earnings are negative; when the state of the economy is weak, its earnings are strong. We have taken an extreme illustration to emphasize the point. However, the example is not completely unrealistic: loan and finance companies tend to do better in a downturn, when people may need to borrow money. Also, the returns from gold mining companies have historically tended to move inversely with the general pattern of business activity.

We observe from Table 14.5 that the expected return from Firm B is 13 percent and the variability of its returns is about the same as for Firm A. The variance is about 6 percent, and the standard deviation is somewhat over 24 percent.

Now we want to examine what happens when we combine securities of A and B into a portfolio. A portfolio simply represents the practice among investors of having their funds in more than one asset: the combination of investment assets is called a *portfolio*. Here we have a two-asset portfolio. The first thing we seek to determine is how the returns *co-vary* between Firm A and Firm B. The calculations are shown in Table 14.6.

Table 14.6 **Covariance of Returns of Firm A with Returns of Firm B**

P_s	$(\tilde{R}_a - \bar{R}_a)(\tilde{R}_b - \bar{R}_b)$	$P_s(\tilde{R}_a - \bar{R}_a)(\tilde{R}_b - \bar{R}_b)$
0.2	$-0.40 \times 0.37 = -0.1480$	-0.0296
0.5	$-0.02 \times 0.05 = -0.0010$	-0.0005
0.3	$0.30 \times -0.33 = -0.0990$	-0.0297
	$\text{Cov}(\tilde{R}_a, \tilde{R}_b) =$	-0.0598
		≈ -0.06

For each of the firms, we simply take the deviations of the returns from the mean and multiply them, as shown in the second column of Table 14.6. We then multiply by the frequencies (in this case by the probabilities since we have probability distributions). Ordinarily, we would then divide by the sum of the frequencies, but for probabilities the sum is 1. Therefore, after multiplying the product of the deviation by the probabilities, we simply sum. We find that the covariance between the returns of Firms A and B is approximately −6 percent.

We can now proceed to analyze the prospective return and standard deviation for this two-security portfolio. Let us assume initially that the invested sums are distributed equally between Firm A and Firm B. In general, the return for a portfolio will be determined by the relationships set forth in Equation 14.4:

$$\bar{R}_p = w_a\bar{R}_a + w_b\bar{R}_b \tag{14.4}$$

Equation 14.4 indicates that the portfolio return is the proportion of each asset in the portfolio multiplied times its return summed over all assets in the portfolio. Using the expected returns previously calculated, we can determine the portfolio return from Equation 14.4a:

$$\bar{R}_p = 0.5\bar{R}_a + 0.5\bar{R}_b = 0.5(0.20) + 0.5(0.13) = 0.1 + 0.065 = 0.165 \tag{14.4a}$$

We now turn to the calculation of the portfolio standard deviation. The expression for the portfolio standard deviation when the portfolio is composed of two assets is shown in Equation 14.5:

$$\sigma_p = (w_a^2\sigma_a^2 + w_b^2\sigma_b^2 + 2w_aw_b\text{Cov}_{ab})^{1/2} \tag{14.5}$$

We illustrate the application of this expression in Equation 14.5a:

$$\begin{aligned}\sigma_p &= [0.25(0.06) + 0.25(0.06) + 2(0.25)(-0.06)]^{1/2} \\ &= (0.015 + 0.015 - 0.03)^{1/2} = 0\end{aligned} \tag{14.5a}$$

We observe that the portfolio's standard deviation has been reduced to zero. This is an extreme case, as the data assumed perfect inverse correlation between the returns for Firms A and B. In addition, the portfolios were equally weighted with the two securities. Although this is a special case, it does illustrate the power of diversification. Simply by combining the two assets in equal proportion, we eliminated risk as measured by the portfolio standard deviation.

We may also examine another aspect of the relationship between the two securities. This aspect is defined by the correlation between the returns from the two securities. It is another measure of how the returns co-vary. The measure is standardized so that the range of values for the correlation coefficient is constrained, limited between +1 and −1. The general expression for the covariance between two assets is set forth in Equation 14.6.

$$\text{Cov}(\tilde{R}_a, \tilde{R}_b) = \rho_{ab}\sigma_a\sigma_b \tag{14.6}$$

The nature of the correlation coefficient is indicated by the equation. When we solve for the correlation coefficient, we obtain Equation 14.6a:

$$\rho_{ab} = \frac{\text{Cov}(\tilde{R}_a, \tilde{R}_b)}{\sigma_a\sigma_b} \tag{14.6a}$$

As Equation 14.6a shows, the correlation coefficient is simply the covariance measure standardized by dividing by the product of the two standard deviations. Utilizing the data already developed, we can calculate the correlation coefficient between the returns for Assets A and B as shown in Equation 14.6b.

$$\rho_{ab} = \frac{-0.06}{(0.2433)(0.2476)} = \frac{-0.06}{0.06} = -1.0 \tag{14.6b}$$

But perfectly negative correlation between the returns from two securities is a rather extreme case. Let us therefore turn our attention to the more common pattern of relationships. In general, the returns from most securities tend to be positively correlated—but with a correlation coefficient that is something less than 1. Let us therefore consider Security C. The pattern of returns and the indicated expected return, variance, and standard deviation for Security C are shown in Table 14.7.

Table 14.7

Calculation of the Expected Return and Standard Deviation of Firm C

P_s	$\tilde{R}_c$	$P_s\tilde{R}_c$	$(\tilde{R}_c - \bar{R}_c)$	$(\tilde{R}_c - \bar{R}_c)^2$	$P_s(\tilde{R}_c - \bar{R}_c)^2$
0.2	−0.15	−0.03	−0.25	0.0625	0.01250
0.5	0.20	0.10	0.10	0.0100	0.00500
0.3	0.10	0.03	0.00	0.0000	0.00000
		$\bar{R}_c = 0.10$			$\sigma_c^2 = 0.01750$
					$\sigma_c = 0.1323$

The expected return for Firm C is 10 percent, and its standard deviation is about 13 percent. When Firm C is combined with Firm A, the portfolio return is 15 percent, shown by Equation 14.4b:

$$\bar{R}_p = 0.5\bar{R}_a + 0.5\bar{R}_c = 0.5(0.20) + 0.5(0.10) = 0.15 \tag{14.4b}$$

Next we seek to calculate the correlation coefficient between the two firms. To do this we need to calculate their covariance. The covariance is calculated in Table 14.8 in the same way that it was calculated for Firms A and B. The covariance between the two securities is approximately 2 percent.

Table 14.8 **Calculation of Covariance of Returns of Firm A with Returns of Firm C**

P_s	$(\tilde{R}_a - \bar{R}_a)(\tilde{R}_c - \bar{R}_c)$	$P_s(\tilde{R}_a - \bar{R}_a)(\tilde{R}_c - \bar{R}_c)$
0.2	$-0.40 \times -0.25 = 0.1000$	0.0200
0.5	$-0.02 \times 0.10 = -0.0020$	−0.0010
0.3	$0.30 \times 0.00 = 0.0000$	0.0000
		$\text{Cov}(\tilde{R}_a, \tilde{R}_c) = 0.0190$

We can then proceed to calculate the portfolio standard deviation as shown in Equation 14.7:

$$\begin{aligned} \sigma_p^2 &= 0.25(0.0592) + 0.25(0.01750) + 2(0.25)(0.0190) \\ &= 0.0148 + 0.004375 + 0.00950 = 0.028675 \qquad (14.7) \\ \sigma_p &= \sqrt{\sigma_p^2} = \sqrt{0.028675} = 0.169 \end{aligned}$$

The portfolio standard deviation is 16.9 percent. The simple average is (0.2433 + 0.1323)/2 = 18.8 percent. The portfolio standard deviation is below a straight average by 1.9 percentage points. It is below a straight average by the extent to which the correlation coefficient between the two securities is less than 1. In the present instance we can calculate the correlation between the returns from Firms A and C. This is shown in Equation 14.8:

$$\rho_{ac} = \frac{\text{Cov}(\tilde{R}_a, \tilde{R}_c)}{\sigma_a \sigma_c} = \frac{0.0190}{(0.2433)(0.1323)} = \frac{0.0190}{0.0322} = 0.59 \qquad (14.8)$$

The correlation coefficient between the returns from the two firms is 0.59. Since it is less than 1, it has the effect of bringing down the standard deviation for the portfolio to something below a straight average of standard deviations for the individual firms. Thus, combining individual securities into portfolios changes the nature of their riskiness.

Three influences reduce portfolio risk in relation to the standard deviation of individual securities in isolation: (1) the extent to which the correlation between the returns from the individual securities is less than 1, (2) the number of securities in the portfolio, and (3) the proportions or weights of the individual securities in the portfolio in relation to their correlations among one another. The effects of these three influences combined can be determined by relating individual securities to all securities—the market portfolio. We can obtain the most general relationship by relating the pattern of returns from an individual security to the pattern for the market as a whole. The *market as a whole* is defined as the portfolio of the total of all types of investment opportunities available.

We illustrate two methods for calculating the market parameters. One is based on historical data; the other uses probability estimates of market returns under alternative states. The market return is measured in the same way as returns to individual assets; it is the sum of the capital gain (loss) plus the dividend return for the period. The expected return and standard deviation for the market as a whole can also be calculated as we did for the individual securities by using a probability distribution of market returns. (This is shown later in Table 14.10.)

Much empirical work has been performed on the estimates of the market parameters. Some of the literature represents formal scholarly studies analyzing the empirical validity of the capital asset pricing model (described in a later section).[1] Other estimates of market parameters are available from such financial firms and services as Merrill Lynch, Pierce, Fenner & Smith; Wells Fargo Bank; and Value Line. The sophisticated methodologies utilized include analysis over a number of periods; typically the intervals are one month, but some services use intervals as short as one week or one day.

The nature of the sophisticated procedures for estimating the market parameters is conveyed by the data in Table 14.9, which provides an approximation to the market parameters for a seventeen-year period. The percent returns listed in Column 5 are obtained by adding the dividend yield in Column 4 to the capital gain calculated in Column 3 from the information on the Standard & Poor's 500 stock price index data listed in Column 2. Using the data in Column 5, we obtain the mean market return of approximately 8 percent over the period. Column 6 lists the deviations from the market return. In Column 7 the deviations are squared, then summed and divided by 15 to obtain the 0.0144 estimate of market variance.[2]

The risk-free return is estimated by use of the six-month Treasury bill rate. The averages for the years indicated are listed in Column 8. These average annual values are summed and divided by 16 to obtain an estimate of 5.1 percent for the risk-free return for the time period covered.

Studies of the market behavior over more extended time periods, utilizing monthly rather than annual intervals, suggest a range of about 9 to 11 percent for market returns. Thus our 8 percent dominated by the weak market in recent years is slightly low. Most previous studies of market parameters utilize at least 60 months of returns as compared with the 16 observations in Table 14.9. Of course, a large number of observations will reduce the variance measured, so the longer-term studies suggest that 1 percent is, on the average, a good estimate of market variance. Inspection of Column 8, which contains the risk-free return measures, indicates a range of from 3 percent to 8 percent. Thus the higher values of R_F have predominated in the later years. Hence, to make current estimates of the cost of equity or to make estimates for use for future periods, a 5 to 6 percent range of estimates of the risk-free return would be plausible.

[1] M. H. Miller and M. Scholes, "Rates of Return in Relation to Risk: A Re-examination of Some Recent Findings," in *Studies in the Theory of Capital Markets*, ed. M. C. Jensen (New York: Praeger, 1972), pp. 47–78; F. A. Black, M. C. Jensen, and M. Scholes, "The Capital Asset Pricing Model: Some Empirical Tests," in *Studies in the Theory of Capital Markets*, pp. 79–124; E. F. Fama and J. MacBeth, "Risk, Return and Equilibrium: Empirical Tests," *Journal of Political Economy* 81 (May–June 1973), pp. 607–36; I.I. Friend and M. Blume, "Measurement of Portfolio Performance under Uncertainty," *American Economic Review* 60 (September 1970), pp. 561–75; N. I. Jacob, "The Measurement of Systematic Risk for Securities and Portfolios: Some Empirical Results," *Journal of Financial and Quantitative Analysis* 6 (March 1971), pp. 815–34.

[2] We divide by 15 rather than 16 since one degree of freedom has been lost because the calculation of the variance involves the use of the mean return on the market, which has already been calculated.

Table 14.9 **Estimates of Market Parameters**

Year	S & P 500 price index	Percent change in price	Dividend yield	Percent return	Return deviation	Market variance	Risk-free return
(t)	P_t	$\frac{P_t}{P_{t-1}} - 1$	$\frac{D_t}{P_t}$	R_{Mt} (3) + (4)	$(R_{Mt} - \bar{R}_M)$ (5) − $\bar{R}_M$	$(R_{Mt} - \bar{R}_M)^2$ $(6)^2$	R_F
(1)	(2)	(3)	(4)	(5)	(6)	(7)	(8)
1	55.85						
2	66.27	0.1866	0.0298	0.2164	0.1371	0.018796	0.03
3	62.38	(0.0587)	0.0337	(0.0250)	(0.1043)	0.010878	0.03
4	69.87	0.1201	0.0317	0.1518	0.0725	0.005256	0.03
5	81.37	0.1646	0.0301	0.1947	0.1154	0.013317	0.04
6	88.17	0.0836	0.0300	0.1136	0.0343	0.001176	0.04
7	85.26	(0.0330)	0.0340	0.0010	(0.0783)	0.006131	0.04
8	91.93	0.0782	0.0320	0.1102	0.0309	0.000955	0.05
9	98.70	0.0736	0.0307	0.1043	0.0250	0.000625	0.05
10	97.84	(0.0087)	0.0324	0.0237	(0.0556)	0.003091	0.07
11	83.22	(0.1494)	0.0383	(0.1111)	(0.1904)	0.036252	0.06
12	98.29	0.1811	0.0314	0.2125	0.1332	0.017742	0.05
13	109.20	0.1110	0.0284	0.1394	0.0601	0.003612	0.05
14	107.43	(0.0162)	0.0306	0.0144	(0.0649)	0.004212	0.07
15	82.85	(0.2288)	0.0447	(0.1841)	(0.2634)	0.069380	0.08
16	85.17	0.0280	0.0431	0.0711	(0.0082)	0.000067	0.06
17	102.01	0.1977	0.0376	0.2353	0.1560	0.024336	0.06
				1.2682		0.215826	0.81

$R_F = 0.81/16 = 0.051$

$\bar{R}_M = 1.2682/16 = 0.0793 \approx 0.080$

$\text{Var}(R_M) = 0.215826/15 = 0.0144$

Sources: Columns 2 and 4 from individual issues of *Economic Report of the President*, and Column 8 from individual issues of the *Federal Reserve Bulletin*

The indicated return on the market in Table 14.10 is 9 percent. The variance of the market returns is approximately 1 percent, and the standard deviation of the market is 10 percent.

The pattern of data in Table 14.10 facilitates the calculation of the covariance of the returns on an individual security with the market returns. For each state of the

Table 14.10 **Calculation of Market Returns and Variance**

State of the economy	P_s	$\tilde{R}_M$	$P_s\tilde{R}_M$	$(\tilde{R}_M - \bar{R}_M)$	$(\tilde{R}_M - \bar{R}_M)^2$	$P_s(\tilde{R}_M - \bar{R}_M)^2$
Down	0.2	−0.10	−0.02	−0.19	0.0361	0.00722
Average	0.5	0.10	0.05	0.01	0.0001	0.00005
Up	0.3	0.20	0.06	0.11	0.0121	0.00363
			$\bar{R}_M = 0.09$			$\sigma_M^2 = 0.01090 \approx 0.01$
						$\sigma_M = 0.1044 \approx 0.1$

economy, the deviation of the return for each security from its mean is multiplied by the deviation of the market return from the mean return on the market. The probabilities of the alternative states are then multiplied by each of these products, and the results are summed. The calculations are shown in Table 14.11.

Table 14.11

Calculation of Covariances

Asset A

P_s	$(\tilde{R}_a - \bar{R}_a)(\tilde{R}_M - \bar{R}_M)$	$P_s(\tilde{R}_a - \bar{R}_a)(\tilde{R}_M - \bar{R}_M)$
0.2	$-0.40 \times -0.19 = 0.0760$	0.0152
0.5	$-0.02 \times 0.01 = -0.0002$	-0.0001
0.3	$0.30 \times 0.11 = 0.0330$	0.0099
		$\text{Cov}(\tilde{R}_a, \tilde{R}_M) = 0.0250$

Asset B

P_s	$(\tilde{R}_b - \bar{R}_b)(\tilde{R}_M - \bar{R}_M)$	$P_s(\tilde{R}_b - \bar{R}_b)(\tilde{R}_M - \bar{R}_M)$
0.2	$0.37 \times -0.19 = -0.0703$	-0.01406
0.5	$0.05 \times 0.01 = 0.0005$	0.00025
0.3	$-0.33 \times 0.11 = -0.0363$	-0.01089
		$\text{Cov}(\tilde{R}_b, \tilde{R}_M) = -0.02470$

Asset C

P_s	$(\tilde{R}_c - \bar{R}_c)(\tilde{R}_M - \bar{R}_M)$	$P_s(\tilde{R}_c - \bar{R}_c)(\tilde{R}_M - \bar{R}_M)$
0.2	$-0.25 \times -0.19 = 0.0475$	0.0095
0.5	$0.10 \times 0.01 = 0.0010$	0.0005
0.3	$0.0 \times 0.11 = 0.0000$	0.0000
		$\text{Cov}(\tilde{R}_c, \tilde{R}_M) = 0.0100$

With the covariances calculated in Table 14.11, we can readily calculate the beta for each asset, defined as:

$$\text{Beta of an asset} = \frac{[\text{Covariance with market returns}]}{[\text{Variance of the market returns}]}$$

We can utilize the data from the appropriate table to obtain:

$$\beta_j = \frac{\text{Cov}(R_j, R_M)}{\sigma_M^2}$$

$$\beta_a = \frac{0.0250}{0.01} = 2.5$$

$$\beta_b = \frac{-0.0247}{0.01} = -2.47 \qquad \textbf{(14.9)}$$

$$\beta_c = \frac{0.0100}{0.01} = 1.00$$

We have now constructed all of the building blocks to make use of some general market relationships between return and risk.

The Capital Asset Pricing Model (CAPM)

The riskiness of assets or securities held in portfolios can be measured by their contribution to the portfolio risk. This relationship is measured by the covariance of the asset or security returns with the returns on the market as a whole. From the portfolio approach to the measurement of risk, the capital asset pricing model (CAPM) sets forth a theory of the relationship between the risk of an asset and the required risk adjustment factor.[3]

The relationship is expressed in the security market line (SML) as:

$$\bar{R}_j = R_F + \lambda \, \text{Cov}(\tilde{R}_j, \tilde{R}_M) \tag{14.10}$$

$E(R_j) = \bar{R}_j =$ "Expected" return on Asset J ("expected" return *required* by the security market line relationships)

$R_F =$ Risk-free return

$\text{Cov}(\tilde{R}_j, \tilde{R}_M) =$ Covariance between the returns on Asset J and the returns on the market

$$\lambda = \text{Price of risk for securities} = \frac{\bar{R}_M - R_F}{\sigma_M^2}$$

In the above formulation, the market risk premium $(\bar{R}_M - R_F)$ is normalized by dividing it by the variance (a measure of market risk) of the market returns. Alternatively, the normalization can be applied to the covariance measure of the riskiness of the individual Asset J. The security market line (SML) is then expressed:

$$\bar{R}_j = R_F + (\bar{R}_M - R_F)\beta_j$$

where **(14.11)**

$$\beta_j = \text{Cov}(\tilde{R}_j, \tilde{R}_M)/\sigma_M^2$$

and is a measure of the volatility of the individual investment's returns relative to the market returns.

The Security Market Line (SML)

The logic of the security market line equation is that the required return on an investment is a risk-free return plus a risk adjustment factor. The risk adjustment factor is obtained by multiplying the risk premium required for the market return by the riskiness of the individual investment. If the returns on the individual investment fluctuate by exactly the same degree as the returns on the market as a whole, the beta for the security is 1. In this situation the required return on the individual investment is the same as the required return on the total market. If the variation in the returns of an individual investment is greater than the variation in the market returns, the beta of the individual investment is greater than 1, and its risk adjustment factor is greater than the risk adjustment factor for the market as a whole.

The relationship between the riskiness of an individual investment, as measured by its beta, and the risk adjustment factor is illustrated in Figure 14.3. The risk-free return is given as 6 percent. If we use 11 percent as the long-term average return on the market, the market risk premium is 11 percent minus 6 percent, which is

[3] See Weston and Brigham, *Managerial Finance,* 7th ed., pp. 456–92, for a formal development of the CAPM from the theory of portfolio choice.

Figure 14.3 **Graph of the Security Market Line**

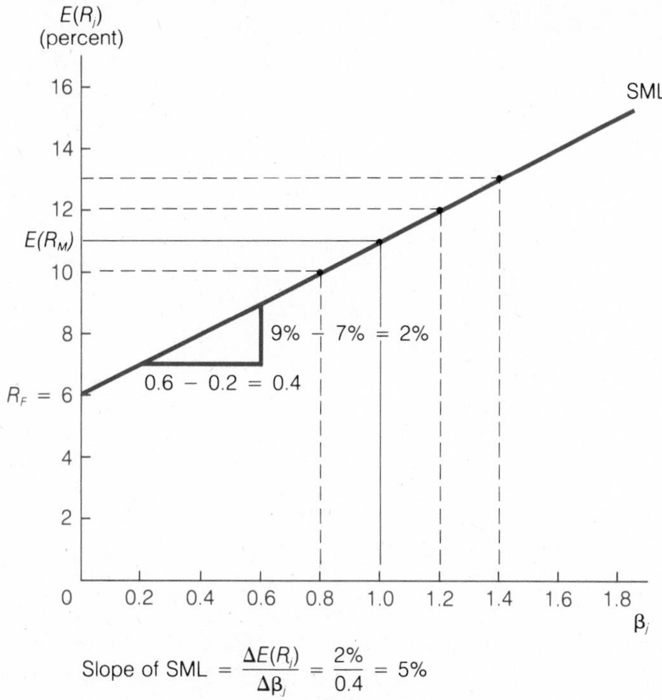

$$\text{Slope of SML} = \frac{\Delta E(R_j)}{\Delta \beta_j} = \frac{2\%}{0.4} = 5\%$$

5 percent, the slope of the SML. If the risk-free return is 6 percent, the required return on the market is 6 percent plus a risk adjustment factor of 5 percent, totaling 11 percent.

The required return on an individual investment depends on the size of its beta, which measures the variations in its returns in relation to the returns on the market. If the beta of an individual investment is 1.2, its risk adjustment factor is 1.2 times the market risk adjustment factor of 5 percent. The risk adjustment factor for the individual investment is therefore 6 percent, and its required return is 12 percent. If the beta measure of an investment is 1.4, its risk adjustment factor is 7 percent, and its required return is 13 percent. An investment with a beta of 0.8 has a risk adjustment factor of 4 percent and a required return of 10 percent.

Appraisal of the Use of the CAPM

The advantage of the use of the CAPM framework is that the security market line represents a theory of the relationship between risk and the required return on an investment. But it would be premature to discard the alternative approaches, particularly the use of the coefficient of variation as a measure of the riskiness of an individual investment. There are several reasons for keeping both approaches:

1. Some studies have found that the standard deviation does in fact have an influence on the required return of a security.

Figure 14.4 **Theoretical versus Statistical Estimates of the SML**

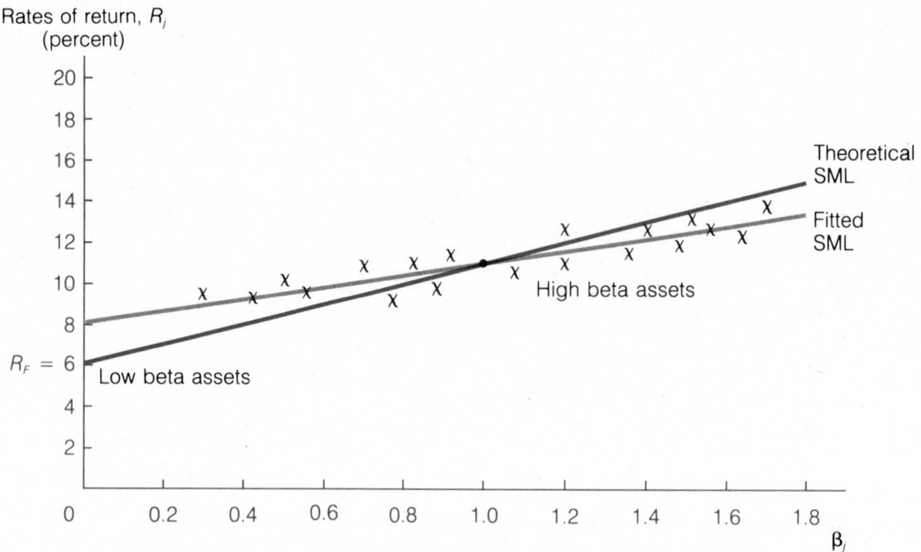

2. Empirical studies of the SML confirm a positive relationship between risk and return, but the observed SML appears to be tilted clockwise from the theoretical line, as shown in Figure 14.4. Low beta assets earn more than the CAPM would predict, and high beta assets earn less than the CAPM would predict.
3. The CAPM utilizes historical data, and all the terms in the SML can be different, depending on the time period selected for measurement. Thus, for some time periods, the average return on the market may be as low as 5 to 6 percent (or even negative). The risk-free rate may rise or fall, depending on the expected rate of inflation. Note, however, that if the rate of inflation causes the risk-free rate and market return to rise by the same number of percentage points, the market risk adjustment factor is unchanged. For example, suppose that with an expected rate of inflation of 3 percent per year, the risk-free rate is 5 percent and the market rate of return 10 percent. With an expected rate of inflation of 8 percent, the risk-free rate may rise to 10 percent and the market rate of return to 15 percent. In both cases, the market risk adjustment factor remains at 5 percent.
4. Richard Roll emphasizes the problems that may arise because we may not be using the true market portfolio in the empirical measurements.[4] Most studies have used an index composed mostly of U.S. common stock prices in measuring "the market index." However, this excludes other important

[4] Richard Roll, "A Critique of the Asset Pricing Theory's Tests," *Journal of Financial Economics* 4 (March 1977), pp. 129–76; and "Ambiguity When Performance is Measured by the Securities Market Line," *Journal of Finance* 33 (September 1978), pp. 1051–69.

assets, such as bonds, real estate, precious metals, foreign currencies and foreign securities, and human capital (wage and salary income). Roll demonstrates that small differences from the true market portfolio can cause biases in the measurement of beta and the expected returns. The Roll critique does not argue that the CAPM is invalid.[5] Rather, it emphasizes that the tests must be made and interpreted with great care.

5. The β for an individual security reflects industry characteristics and management policies that determine how returns fluctuate in relation to variations in overall market returns. If the general economic environment is stable, if industry characteristics remain unchanged, and if management policies have continuity, the measure of β will be relatively stable when calculated for different time periods. However, if these conditions do not exist, the value of β will vary as the characteristics of investments or securities change in their relationship to the total market.

Nevertheless, alternative measures of risk are subject to similar or even more serious limitations. The great attractiveness of the SML is that it provides a quantitative relationship between risk and required return. While the relationship is subject to some errors in measurement, at least we have a first approximation that may be used as a basis for further analysis. Further, while the SML estimates of the relationship between risk and return are subject to change over time, they provide one useful approach. SML measures must be combined with estimates reached through individual judgments to arrive at financial decisions. In formulating judgments, the alternative measures of risk—the standard deviation and its normalized from, the coefficient of variation—may also aid in the decision process.

Risk-Adjusted Investment Hurdle Rates

What we have been trying to explain is how to make an adjustment for risk in arriving at a discount rate to use in capital budgeting under uncertainty. This is a very difficult thing to do. We will describe some quantitative approaches, but this is an area in which ultimately the manager is required to make some subjective judgments.

The Risk-Adjustment Factor

The Security Market Line (SML) provides a formal relationship for measuring the risk adjustment subject to the qualifications we have noted in the previous section. The security market line can be expressed as a required return on an individual investment as depicted in Equation 14.12.

$$R_j^* = R_F + (\bar{R}_M - R_F)\beta_j \qquad \textbf{(14.12)}$$

Equation 14.12 states that the required return on an investment is a risk-free return plus a risk-adjustment factor. The risk-adjustment factor is the market risk premium (the expected return on the market, $\bar{R}_M$, less the risk-free return) multiplied (or weighted) by the riskiness of the individual investment as measured by its

[5] Particularly, the critique does not apply to the studies using "residual analysis" of the type employed in studies of the performance of merging firms. Roll, "A Reply to Mayers and Rice," *Journal of Financial Economics*, 7 (December 1979) pp. 391–400.

beta value. For example, the risk-free return may be measured by the return on government securities. Suppose this is 12 percent. The market risk premium measured over long periods of time has been about 5 percent. Suppose that the risk of Investment A is measured by a beta of 1.2. Then the required return on Investment A is 12 percent plus 6 percent equals 18 percent. The risk-adjustment factor is 6 percent. If the beta of Investment B were 1.4, the risk-adjustment factor would be 7 percent and the required return would be 19 percent.

We can now illustrate the application of the investment hurdle rate in capital budgeting decisions. Suppose that the systematic risk of Investment A is 1.2 so that the required rate of return R_a^* is 18 percent. Let us postulate further that required investment outlay, I_a is \$800 and that the expected cash flow from the investment, $\bar{X}_a$ is \$180. We can then make two types of comparisons. We can check whether the expected return exceeds the required return. The expected return is $\bar{X}_a/I_a =$ \$180/\$800 = 22.5 percent. Thus the expected return exceeds the required rate of return, so the project should be accepted.

A second test is the application of the fundamental NPV approach. The gross present value of the project $V_a = \bar{X}_a/R_a^*$ which is \$180/0.18 = \$1,000. Since the required investment outlay I_a is \$800, the project has a net present value of \$200 and should therefore be accepted. Thus we have solved the capital budgeting problem for a "perpetuity" of \$180 discounted at 18 percent.

We know that the world is not all that precise. But we may make the judgment that investment A would add value to the firm if other qualitative assessments also were positive. In addition, we may infer that Investment B is somewhat more risky than Investment A and we would probably apply a higher discount factor to Investment B than to Investment A.

Use of a Certainty-Equivalent Approach

Because discounting over a number of years results in a compounding effect of the risk premium, some analysts prefer to use a certainty equivalent discount rate and to adjust the expected cash flows in the numerator for risk. The use of the CAPM and the security market line (SML) lends itself to this approach as well. Recall that beta is the covariance of the investment's returns with the returns on the market divided by the variance of the market returns. The variance of the market returns averages about 1 percent. Hence if a firm has a beta of 1.2, its covariance with the market would be 1.2 multiplied by 1 percent or 0.012. Next we make use of the following definition:

$$E(R_j) = \frac{E(X_j)}{V_j}$$

This enables us to rewrite the security market line relationship as shown in Equation 14.13, which, after we rearrange terms, becomes Equation 14.13a.

$$\frac{E(X_j)}{V_j} = R_F + \lambda \operatorname{Cov}\left(\frac{X_j}{V_j}, R_M\right)$$

$$\frac{1}{V_j}[E(X_j) - \lambda \operatorname{Cov}(X_j, R_M)] = R_F \tag{14.13}$$

$$V_j = \frac{E(X_j) - \lambda \operatorname{Cov}(X_j, R_M)}{R_F} \tag{14.13a}$$

Equation 14.13a makes an adjustment to the numerator representing the investment returns. This adjustment converts the returns to a certainty equivalent amount. When this is done, the risk-free rate of return can be used as a discount rate. To illustrate what is involved, let us assume some values: Let $\overline{X}_j = \$180$; $\lambda = 5$; $\text{Cov}(X_j, R_M) = 12$; $R_F = 0.12$.

These values can then be utilized in Equation 14.13a as shown in Equation 14.14:

$$V_j = \frac{\$180 - 5(\$12)}{0.12} = \frac{\$180 - \$60}{0.12} = \frac{\$120}{0.12} = \$1{,}000. \qquad \textbf{(14.14)}$$

Thus we see that the risky returns are $180. The risk adjustment is $60. Hence, the certainty equivalent returns are $120. When we discount the certainty equivalent returns at the risk-free rate of 12 percent, we obtain a value for the investment of $1,000.

This shows that we can value an investment by using either a risk-adjusted discount rate or by adjusting the cash flows for risk and then applying a certainty-equivalent or risk-free discount rate to the risk-adjusted cash flows. If the cost to make this investment were $800, it would have a net present value (NPV) of $200. Again, we get the same capital budgeting result.

Another variation on the use of a risk-free discount rate is to convert the risky return to a certainty equivalent return by applying a certainty equivalent factor, ϕ. In the informal approaches to the treatment of risk the value of ϕ was formulated on a judgmental basis. However, with the use of the security market line we were able to develop a data-based estimate of ϕ. Using the information from the example above, we found that the certainty equivalent return was $120, while the risky return was $180. The ratio between the two is 0.667. Hence, we can take Equation 14.13a and, instead of subtracting the risk adjustment factor, multiply by the certainty equivalent factor, ϕ, as shown in Equation 14.15.

$$V_j = \frac{\phi E(X_j)}{R_F} \qquad \textbf{(14.15)}$$

When we insert the appropriate values, we again obtain a value of $1,000 for the asset:

$$V_j \frac{0.667(\$180)}{0.12} = \frac{\$120}{0.12} = \$1{,}000$$

This illustrates how the CAPM can provide a measure of the risk adjustment factor to calculate a certainty equivalent amount in the numerator to which the risk-free return in the denominator can be applied. We recognize that the computations of beta for individual assets are sometimes not statistically significant and often not stable over time. Nevertheless, the methodology described provides a starting point. In addition, a risk adjustment factor, taking other dimensions of risk into account as well as judgmental factors, may be used in estimating a project's net present value.

Illustrative Use of Risk-Adjusted Discount Rates

We have described a number of ways in which the adjustment for risk can be made in estimating a discount rate for use in making investment decisions under uncertainty. The CAPM approach represents a theory which formulates a quantitative relation between the measured amount of *systematic* risk of a project and the required return. But there is also some evidence that the total risk (including diversifiable risk) has some influence on the required (risk-adjusted) return. To the extent that this is true, the standard deviation which is a measure of the total risk of an investment and its normalized measure, $[\sigma_j/\bar{R}_j]$ the coefficient of variation, should also be taken into account. In the following example, we illustrate how this might be done. Along with the SML, the coefficient of variation can aid in the analysis of investment decisions under uncertainty. In addition, the use of these two alternative approaches to measuring the risk adjustment factor does not necessarily give conflicting results. This is the case even when one investment has a greater CV but a smaller beta. Assume that the risk-free rate is 6 percent and the expected market return is 11 percent. Consider two investments, I and J, for which the measures in Table 14.12 have been calculated.

Table 14.12

Return and Risk Estimates for Two Investment Projects

	Investment I	Investment J
Expected return ($\bar{R}$)	0.20	0.14
Standard deviation (σ)	0.80	0.42
Coefficient of variation (CV)	4.00	3.00
Beta (β)	1.50	2.00

If the financial manager uses the SML, the required returns for the two investments are

$$R_I^* = 0.06 + (0.11 - 0.06)1.5 = 0.135$$

$$R_J^* = 0.06 + (0.11 - 0.06)2.0 = 0.16$$

Using the CAPM, Investment I has a required return of 13.5 percent but an expected return of 20 percent; Investment J has a required return of 16 percent but an expected return of 14 percent. For Investment I the expected return exceeds the required return by 6.5 percentage points; for Investment J the expected return falls short of the required return by 2 percentage points.

But the coefficient of variation of Investment I is greater than the coefficient of variation of Investment J. Suppose the decision maker formulates a risk adjustment relationship based on the coefficient of variation, as in equation (14.16)

$$R^* = \text{Risk-free return} + 0.03\ \text{CV} \qquad \textbf{(14.16)}$$

We must acknowledge that the risk adjustment coefficient of 0.03 to apply to the coefficient of variation (CV) is purely illustrative. There is no theory or set of empirical materials which establishes its magnitude. However, decision makers must implicitly formulate some coefficient in choosing between the required risk adjustment factors to apply to investments with different CV's. We are simply quantifying their subjective judgments.

Using the CV as the basis for estimating the risk-adjustment factor, under the assumptions illustrated in equation 14.16, the required return for Investment I is

18 percent. The required return for Investment J is 15 percent. Investment I still exceeds its required return. Investment J still falls short of its required return. However, the decision is closer, because the expected return on Investment I is only 2 percentage points above its required return, while the expected return for Investment J is only 1 percentage point below its required return.

If the investments are mutually exclusive (for example, a gas- versus electric-powered forklift truck for handling materials in a factory), Investment I will probably be preferred to Investment J. But with the results so close, the financial manager may request that estimates of revenues, investment costs, maintenance costs, and all other factors that might affect the measures in Table 14.12 be reexamined and reworked. A sensitivity analysis of the critical factors affecting the level and variability of returns would be useful in estimating their influence on the measures in Table 14.12. Thus the use of both the CV and β approaches might result in better insights and decisions by the financial manager.

Management Science Approaches to Investment Under Uncertainty

The SML and CV approaches to estimating a risk adjustment factor for discounting the returns from a risky investment are useful as a first step in the quantification of return and risk relationships. In addition, a wide range of other approaches have been used. Some management science approaches involve further refinements of the risk adjustment measures. Other techniques, such as sensitivity analysis, decision trees, and simulation, combine quantitative and judgmental factors. These approaches are presented next.

Sensitivity Analysis

The NPV of a project will depend on such factors as quantity of sales, sales prices, input costs, and the like. If these values turn out to be favorable—if output and sales prices are high and costs are low—then profits, the realized rate of return, and the actual NPV will be high. Conversely, if poor results are experienced, then these three items will be low. Recognizing the causal relationships, business persons often calculate projects' NPVs under alternative assumptions, then see just how sensitive NPV is to changing conditions. To illustrate: A fertilizer company was comparing two types of phosphate plants. Fuel represents a major cost to the company. One plant used coal, which can be obtained under a long-term fixed cost contract; the other plant used oil, which must be purchased at current market prices. Considering present and projected future prices, the oil-fired plant looked better; it had a considerably higher NPV. However, oil prices are volatile; and if prices were to rise by more than the expected rate, this plant would be unprofitable. The coal-fired plant, on the other hand, had a lower NPV under the expected conditions; but this NPV was less sensitive to changing conditions in the energy market. The company finally selected the coal plant because the sensitivity analysis indicated it to be less risky.

The Use of Decision Tree Analysis

Important decisions are generally not made at one point in time; rather, they are made in stages. For example, a petroleum firm considering the possibility of expanding into agricultural chemicals may take the following steps: (1) spend \$100,000 for a survey of supply-demand conditions in the agricultural chemical industry; (2) if the survey results are favorable, spend $500,000 on a pilot plant to investigate production methods; and (3) depending on the costs estimated from the pilot study and the demand potential from the market study, either abandon the project, build a large plant, or build a small one. Thus the final decision actually is made in stages, with subsequent decisions depending on the results of previous ones.

The sequence of events can be shown as branches of a tree—hence the name *decision tree*. As an example, consider Figure 14.5. There it is assumed that the petroleum company has completed its industry supply-demand analysis and pilot plant study and has determined that it should proceed to develop a full-scale production facility. The firm must now decide whether to build a large plant or a small one. Probability estimates for the plant's products are 50 percent for high demand, 30 percent for medium demand, and 20 percent for low demand. Depending on demand, net cash flows (sales revenues minus operating costs, all discounted to the present) will range from $1.4 million to $8.8 million if a large plant is built, and from $1.4 million to $2.6 million if a small plant is built.

Figure 14.5 **Illustrative Decision Tree**

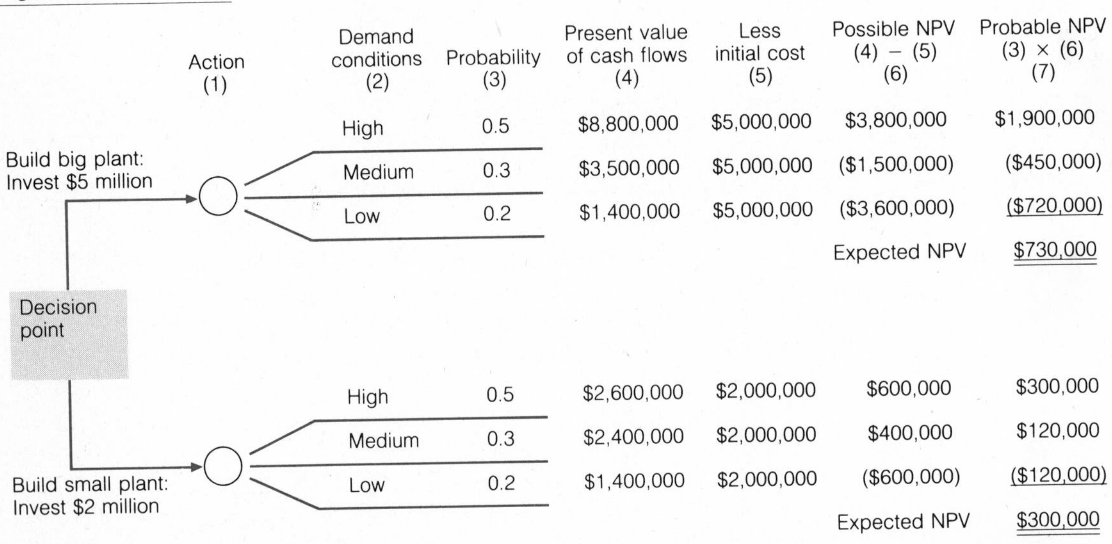

Action (1)	Demand conditions (2)	Probability (3)	Present value of cash flows (4)	Less initial cost (5)	Possible NPV (4) − (5) (6)	Probable NPV (3) × (6) (7)
Build big plant: Invest $5 million	High	0.5	$8,800,000	$5,000,000	$3,800,000	$1,900,000
	Medium	0.3	$3,500,000	$5,000,000	($1,500,000)	($450,000)
	Low	0.2	$1,400,000	$5,000,000	($3,600,000)	($720,000)
					Expected NPV	$730,000
Decision point						
Build small plant: Invest $2 million	High	0.5	$2,600,000	$2,000,000	$600,000	$300,000
	Medium	0.3	$2,400,000	$2,000,000	$400,000	$120,000
	Low	0.2	$1,400,000	$2,000,000	($600,000)	($120,000)
					Expected NPV	$300,000

The initial costs of the large and small plants are shown in Column 5; when these investment outlays are subtracted from the PV of cash flows, the result is the set of possible NPVs shown in Column 6. One (and only one) of these NPVs will actually occur. Finally, we multiply Column 6 by Column 3 to obtain Column 7, and the sums in Column 7 give the expected NPVs of the large and small plants.

Because the expected NPV of the large plant ($730,000) is larger than that of the small plant ($300,000), should the decision be to build the large plant? Perhaps, but not necessarily. Notice that the range of outcomes is greater if the large plant is built, with the possible NPVs (Column 6 in Figure 14.5 varying from $3.8 million to minus $3.6 million. However, a range of only $600,000 to minus $600,000 exists for the small plant. Since the required investments for the two plants are not the same, we must examine the coefficients of variation of the net present value possibilities in order to determine which alternative actually entails the greater risk. The coefficient of variation for the large plant's present value is 4.3, while that for the small plant is only 1.5.[6] Thus risk is greater if the decision is to build the large plant.

Computer Simulation Methods

The concepts embodied in decision tree analysis can be extended to computer simulation. To illustrate the technique, let us consider a proposal to build a new textile plant. The cost of the plant is not known for certain, although it is expected to run about $150 million. If no problems are encountered, the cost can be as low as $125 million, while an unfortunate series of events—such as strikes, unprojected increases in materials costs, and technical problems—could result in a cost as high as $225 million.

Revenues from the new facility, which will operate for many years, will depend on population growth and income in the region, competition, developments in synthetic fabrics research, and textile import quotas. Operating costs will depend on production efficiency, materials and labor cost trends, and the like. Since both sales revenues and operating costs are uncertain, annual profits are also uncertain.

Assuming that probability distributions can be assigned to each of the major cost and revenue determinants, a computer program can be constructed to simulate what is likely to happen. In effect, the computer selects one value at random from each of the relevant distributions, combines it with other values selected from the other distributions, and produces an estimated profit and net present value, or rate of return on investment. The particular profit and rate of return occur, of course, only for the particular combination of values selected during this trial. The computer goes on to select other sets of values and to compute other profits and rates of return repeatedly, for perhaps several hundred trials. A count is kept of the number of times each rate of return is computed; and when the computer runs are completed, the frequency with which the various rates of return occurred can be plotted as a frequency distribution.

The procedure is illustrated in Figures 14.6 and 14.7.[7] Figure 14.6 is a flow chart outlining the simulation procedure described above, while Figure 14.7 illustrates the frequency distribution of rates of return generated by such a simulation for two investments—X and Y—each with an expected cost of $20 million. The expected rate of return on Investment X is 15 percent and that on Investment Y is 20 percent. However, these are only the *average* rates of return generated by the computer; simulated rates range from 5 to 25 percent for Investment X and from −10 percent

[6] Using Equation 14.2 and the data on possible returns in Figure 14.5, the standard deviation of returns for the larger plant is found to be $3.155 million and for the smaller one $458,260. Dividing each of these standard deviations by the expected returns for their respective plant size gives the coefficents of variation.

[7] See also David B. Hertz, "Uncertainty and Investment Selection," in J. F. Weston and M. B. Goudzwaard, eds., *The Treasurer's Handbook* (Homewood, Ill.: Dow Jones-Irwin, 1976), Chapter 18, pp. 376–420.

Figure 14.6 **Simulation for Investment Planning**

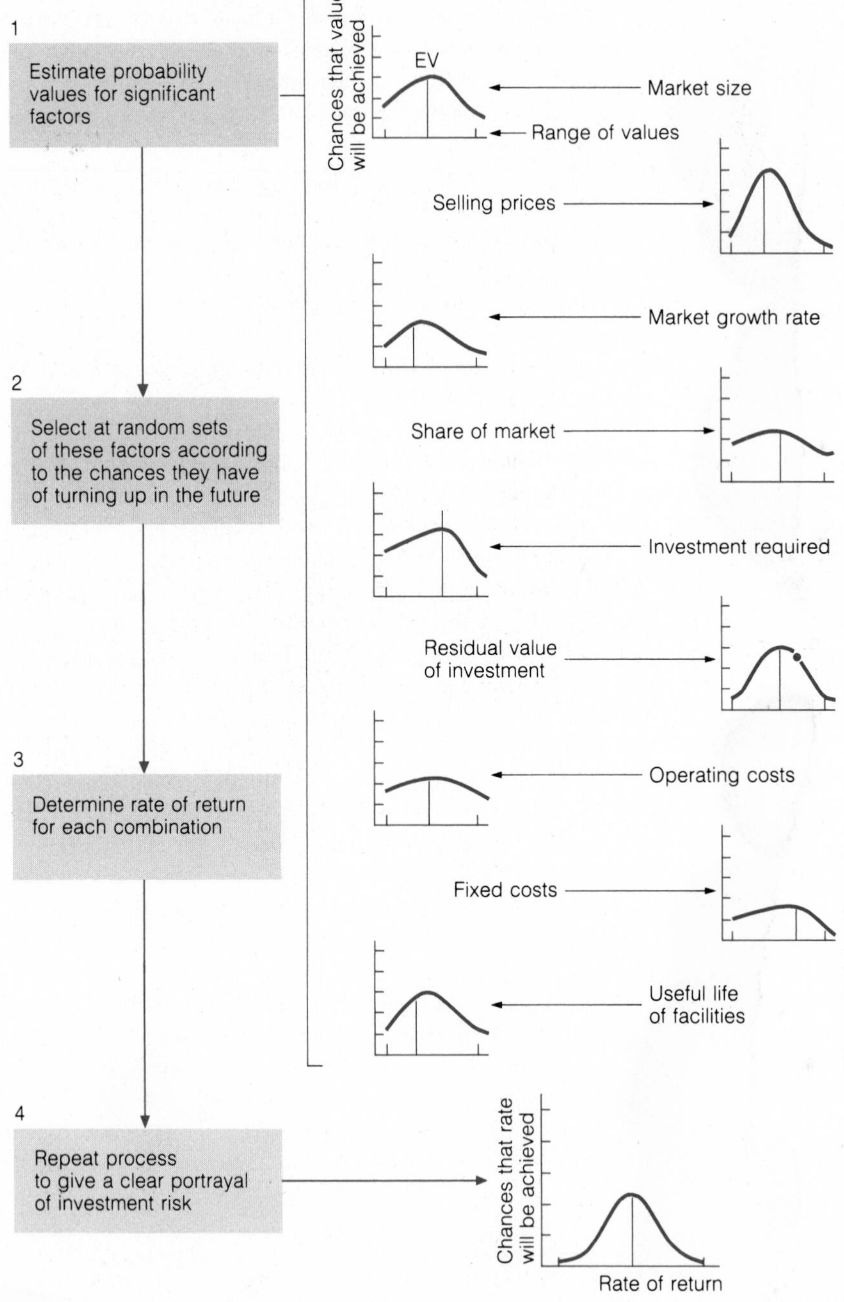

Figure 14.7

Expected Rates of Return on Investments X and Y

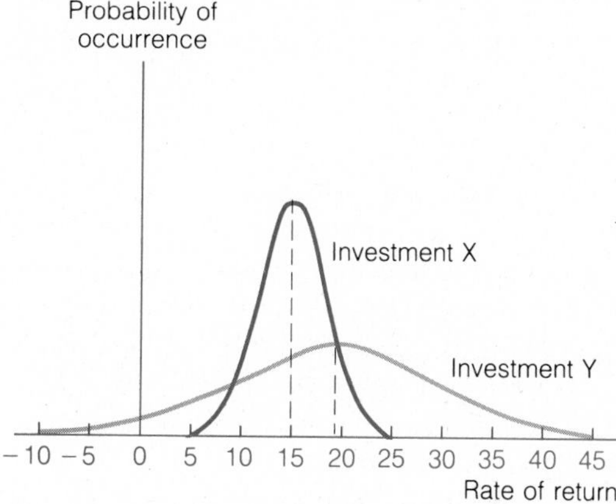

to +45 percent for Investment Y. The standard deviation generated for X is only 4 percentage points—68 percent of the computer runs had rates of return between 11 and 19 percent—while that for Y is 12 percentage points. Clearly, then, Investment Y is riskier than Investment X.

The computer simulation provides us with an estimate of both the expected returns on two projects and their relative risks. A decision about which alternative should be chosen can now be made, perhaps by using the risk-adjusted discount rate method or perhaps in an informal manner by the decision maker.

However, computer simulation is not always feasible for risk analysis. The technique involves obtaining probability distributions for a number of variables—investment outlays, unit sales, product prices, input prices, asset lives, and so on—and paying for a fair amount of programming and machine time. Therefore, full-scale simulation is not generally worthwhile except for large and expensive projects, such as major plant expansions or new-product decisions involving millions of dollars.

Summary

Two facts of life in finance are (1) that investors are averse to risk and (2) that at least some risk is inherent in most business decisions. Given investor aversion to risk and differing degrees of risk in different financial alternatives, it is necessary to consider risk in financial analysis.

Our first task is to define what we mean by risk; our second task is to measure it. The concept of *probability* is a fundamental element in both the definition and the measurement of risk. A *probability distribution* shows the probability of occurrence of each possible outcome, assuming a given investment is undertaken. The mean, or weighted average, of the distribution is defined as the *expected value* of the investment. The *coefficient of variation* of the distribution or, sometimes, the *standard deviation,* both of which measure the extent to which actual outcomes are likely to vary from the expected value, are used as measures of risk.

In appraising the riskiness of an individual capital investment, not only the variability of the expected returns of the project itself but also the correlation between expected returns on this project and the remainder of the firm's assets must be taken into account. This relationship is called the *portfolio effect* of the particular project. Favorable portfolio effects are strongest when a project is negatively correlated with the firm's other assets and weakest when positive correlation exists. Portfolio effects lie at the heart of the firm's efforts to diversify into product lines not closely related to the firm's main line of business.

The riskiness of a portfolio is measured by the standard deviation of expected returns. From any group of risky assets it is possible to develop an investment portfolio opportunity set in terms of risk and expected returns. Within the opportunity set there will be a smaller group of alternative portfolios that provide the maximum return for a given level of risk. This is the efficient set of portfolios. Given equal expected returns, a risk averse investor would choose the one that minimizes his risk.

The risk-return relationships for individual securities (imperfect portfolios) use the covariance of individual security returns with the market returns as the measure of risk. The relation between returns and the covariance for individual securities defines the security market line (SML).

Another way to describe the return-risk relationship is in terms of beta coefficients. β is simply the covariance standardized by the market variance. With risk expressed in this way, expected return can be stated as a β multiple of the market risk premium (expected return on the market less the risk-free rate) plus the risk-free rate. All factors except β are marketwide constants.

The SML is useful in quantifying the relationship between return and risk. However, its estimates are subject to change over time and have not been measured with precision. SML measures must be combined with judgmental estimates to arrive at financial decisions. In formulating judgments, the earlier measures of risk—the standard deviation and the coefficient of variation—will also aid in the analysis.

Thus we have two useful formal approaches to investment decisions under uncertainty. In addition, the formal approaches should be supplemented by techniques such as decision tree formulations, sensitivity analysis, and simulation of the consequences of alternative estimates of critical variables in the calculations. Simulation of possible outcomes enables us to determine the variations in the measures used in the formal approaches resulting from alternative estimates of critical input variables. Formal approaches, simulation with sensitivity analysis, and judgmental methods are all required in the effort to make sound investment decisions in a world in which outcomes are uncertain.

Questions

14.1 Define the following terms:

a. risk
b. uncertainty
c. probability distribution
d. expected value
e. standard deviation
f. market price of risk
g. covariance
h. correlation coefficient
i. beta
j. risk-adjusted discount rate

14.2 The probability distribution of a less risky expected return is more peaked than that of a risky return. What shape would the probability distribution have for completely certain returns? For completely uncertain returns?

14.3 What is the mean-variance approach to risk and uncertainty?

14.4 What is the coefficient of variation, and why is it used as a measure of risk?

14.5 Project A has an expected return of \$500 and a standard deviation of \$100. Project B also has a standard deviation of \$100 but an expected return of \$300. Which project is the more risky? Why?

14.6 How is the concept of risk measured when assets are viewed in the framework of the portfolio?

14.7 Assume that residential construction and industries related to it are countercyclical to the economy in general and to steel in particular. Does this negative correlation between steel and construction-related industries necessarily mean that a savings and loan association, whose profitability tends to vary with construction levels, would be less risky if it diversified by acquiring a steel distributor?

14.8 What is the relationship between covariance, the correlation coefficient, and the beta measure?

14.9 What is the basic underlying logic of the security market line equation?

14.10 What is the value of decision trees in managerial decision making?

14.11 In computer simulation, the computer makes a large number of trials to show what the various outcomes of a particular decision might be if the decision could be made many times under the same conditions. In practice, the decision will be made only once, so how can simulation results be useful to the decision maker?

14.12 Suppose that inflation causes the nominal risk-free return and the market return to rise by an equal amount. Will the market risk premium be affected?

Problems

14.1 The Barfield Company has a new investment project. The project returns are estimated as follows:

Year	Project return (R_j)
1981	0.10
1982	0.17
1983	0.24
1984	0.20
1985	0.14

Calculate:

a. The expected return on the investment

b. The variance of returns

c. The standard deviation of returns

d. The coefficient of variation of returns

Divide by 5 to calculate the expected return, and divide by 4 to calculate the variance. The variance calculation is dependent on the mean, and therefore one degree of freedom is lost.

14.2 Assuming the following probability distribution of market returns, calculate the $E(R_M)$, $\text{Var}(R_M)$, and σ_M.

State	Probability	Market return (R_M)
1	0.12	−0.10
2	0.26	0.15
3	0.44	0.20
4	0.18	0.25

14.3 Your firm is considering two mutually exclusive investment projects—Project A at a cost of $110,000 and Project B at a cost of $140,000. The planning division of your firm has estimated the following probability distribution of cash flows to be generated by each project in each of the next five years:

Project A		Project B	
Probability	Cash flow	Probability	Cash flow
0.2	$15,000	0.2	$10,000
0.6	30,000	0.6	40,000
0.2	35,000	0.2	60,000

a. Which of the projects is the riskier if the coefficient of variation is used as a measure of risk?

b. Each project's risk is different from that of the firm as a whole. The firm's management adjusts for risk by means of the formula:

$$R_j = R_F + 10\text{CV}$$

where:

R_j = Required rate of return on the jth project

R_F = Risk-free rate = 6 percent

CV = Coefficient of variation of the project's cash flows

What are the required rates of return on Projects A and B?

c. Which of the proposals, if either, should be accepted by the firm? Explain and support your answer. In calculating the NPVs, round the cost of capital figures calculated in Part b to the nearest whole number.

14.4 The McCoy Company has developed the following data regarding a project to add new production facilities.

State (s)	Probability (P_s)	Market return (R_M)	Project return (R_j)
1	0.05	−0.20	−0.30
2	0.25	0.10	0.05
3	0.35	0.15	0.20
4	0.20	0.20	0.25
5	0.15	0.25	0.30

Calculate:

a. The expected return on the project

b. The variance of the project returns

c. The standard deviation of project returns
d. The coefficient of variation of project returns
e. The covariance of the project returns with the market returns
f. The correlation coefficient between the project returns and the market returns

14.5 Based on the following historical market data, calculate the expected return on the market, the variance of the returns on the market, the standard deviation of the returns on the market, and the expected risk-free return.

Year	S & P 500 price index	Dividend yield	R_F
1	55.85		0.035
2	66.27	0.0298	0.032
3	62.38	0.0337	0.035
4	69.87	0.0317	0.039
5	81.37	0.0301	0.042
6	88.17	0.0300	0.051
7	85.26	0.0340	0.049
8	91.93	0.0320	0.056
9	98.70	0.0307	0.068
10	97.84	0.0324	0.065
11	83.22	0.0383	0.064
12	98.29	0.0314	0.086
13	109.20	0.0284	0.099
14	107.43	0.0306	0.119

14.6 The expected returns for two firms, A and B, are as follows:

State (s)	P_s	Return of Firm A	Return of Firm B
1	0.1	−0.05	−0.10
2	0.4	0.10	0.15
3	0.3	0.25	0.10
4	0.2	0.30	0.18

Firm A has a total investment in assets of $75,000,000, three times the size of Firm B.

Assume that a new firm, C, is formed through a merger between Firms A and B. The share of A and B in the portfolio represented by the new Firm C is based on the ratio of their total assets prior to the merger. Calculate:

a. The expected return and standard deviation of Firms A and B before the merger
b. The covariance—Cov(ab)—and correlation coefficient (ρ_{ab}) between the returns for Firms A and B before the merger
c. The expected return of Firm C, $\bar{R}_c$
d. The standard deviation of returns of firm C, σ_c

14.7 The expected return on IVO Corporation stock is 16 percent. The covariance of IVO's returns with the returns on the market is 0.0146. The expected return on the market is 14 percent, and the variance of market returns is 0.01. The risk-free rate is 8 percent.

a. What is the price of risk (λ) for IVO Corporation?
b. What is IVO's beta (β)?
c. Based on the expected return, is IVO stock a good investment?

14.8 Given the following facts (the investment cost of each project is equal)

S	P_s	R_{Ms}	Return to project 1	Return to project 2
1	0.1	−0.3	−0.4	−0.4
2	0.2	−0.1	−0.2	−0.2
3	0.3	0.1	0	0.6
4	0.4	0.3	0.7	0

Calculate:

a. The three means, the variances, the standard deviations, and the covariance of Project 1 with the market; covariance of Project 2 with the market; covariance of Project 1 with Project 2; the correlation coefficients ρ_{1M}, ρ_{2M}, and the correlation coefficient of Project 1 with Project 2.

b. Construct three portfolios, A, B, and C, of Projects 1 and 2 such that for portfolio A $w_1 = 25$ percent and $w_2 = 75$ percent; for portfolio B, $w_1 = 40$ percent and $w_2 = 60$ percent; for portfolio C, $w_1 = 75$ percent and $w_2 = 25$ percent. Calculate the expected return and standard deviation of each portfolio. Which portfolio would you select?

c. $R_F = 0.04$. Calculate the security market line. On a graph:
   1. Plot the security market line.
   2. Plot points for Project 1 and for Project 2.

d. If you had to choose between the two projects, which would you select?

14.9 The risk-free rate of return is 6 percent, and the market risk premium is 5 percent. The beta of the project under analysis is 1.8, with expected net cash flows after taxes estimated at $600 for five years. The required investment outlay on the project is $1,800.

a. What is the required risk-adjusted return on the project?

b. Should the project be accepted?

14.10 The Rowan Company is faced with two mutually exclusive investment projects. Each project costs $4,500, and each has an expected life of three years. Annual net cash flows from each project begin one year after the initial investment is made and have the following probability distributions:

Project A		Project B	
Probability	Cash flow	Probability	Cash flow
0.2	$4,000	0.2	$ 0
0.6	4,500	0.6	4,500
0.2	5,000	0.2	12,000

Rowan has decided to evaluate the riskier project at a 12 percent rate and the less risky project at a 10 percent rate.

a. What is the expected value of the annual net cash flows from each project?

b. What is the risk-adjusted NPV of each project?

c. If it were known that Project B was negatively correlated with other cash flows of the firm, while Project A was positively correlated, how should this knowledge affect the decision?

14.11 The Pierson Company is considering two mutually exclusive investment projects, P and Q. The risk and return estimates for these two investment projects are as follows:

	Project P	Project Q
Expected return ($\bar{R}$)	0.15	0.18
Standard deviation (σ)	0.50	0.75
Coefficient of variation (CV)	3.33	4.17
Beta (β)	1.80	1.40

Assume that the risk-free rate is 10 percent and the expected market return is 14 percent.

a. What would be the firm's decision if the SML analysis is used?

b. Suppose the firm has formulated a risk adjustment equation based on the coefficient of variation, such as:

$$\text{Required rate of return } (R^*) = R_F + 0.02\text{CV}$$

How would this adjustment equation affect the management's decision?

14.12 Your firm is considering the purchase of a tractor. It has been established that this tractor will cost $32,000, will produce revenues in the neighborhood of $10,000 (before taxes), and will be depreciated via straight line to zero in eight years. The board of directors, however, is having a heated debate as to whether the tractor can be expected to last eight years. Specifically, Wayne Brown insists that he knows of some that have lasted only five years. Tom Miller agrees with Brown but argues that it is more likely that the tractor will give eight years of service. Brown agrees. Finally, Laura Evans says she has seen some last as long as ten years. Given this discussion, the board asks you to prepare a sensitivity analysis to ascertain how important the uncertainty about the life of the tractor is. Assume a 40 percent tax rate on both income and capital loss, zero salvage value, and a cost of capital of 10 percent. (Hint: Depreciation is based on the expected life of the tractor and is not affected by the actual life.)

14.13 You have an investment opportunity for which the outlay and cash flows are uncertain. Analysis has produced the following subjective probability assessments:

Outlay		Annual cash flow	
Probability	Amount	Probability	Amount
0.4	$ 80,000	0.2	$14,000
0.3	100,000	0.5	16,000
0.2	120,000	0.3	18,000
0.1	140,000		

Let the cost of capital be 12 percent, life expectancy be ten years, and salvage value be zero.

a. Construct a decision tree for this investment to show probabilities, payoffs, and expected NPV.

b. Calculate the expected NPV, again using expected cash flow and expected outlay.

c. What is the probability of and the NPV of the worst possible outcome?
d. What is the probability of and the NPV of the best possible outcome?
e. Compute the probability that this will be a good investment.

14.14 The Fortuna Company is considering an investment opportunity which requires an outlay (I_j) of \$5,000. Fortuna has gathered the following information for analysis:

State	Probability (P_s)	R_M	Project cash flow (X_j)
1	0.2	−0.01	\$ 0
2	0.3	0.09	500
3	0.4	0.10	700
4	0.1	0.15	1,000

The risk-free rate is 6 percent.
a. What is the normalized market risk premium, lambda (λ)?
b. What is the project's expected risk-adjusted cash flow?
c. What is the certainty equivalent factor, ϕ?
d. What is the gross present value of the project, V_j?
e. What is the project's beta, β_j?
f. What is the project's required rate of return, R_j^*?
g. What is the project's expected rate of return, $\bar{R}_j$?
h. Should the project be accepted?

APPENDIX 14A

CAPITAL BUDGETING UNDER INFLATION

Since 1966, the United States has experienced persistent inflation. Double-digit rates of inflation have been experienced in a number of years. Even optimistic forecasts of the rates of future inflation are in the range of 7 to 9 percent per year. Inflation affects capital budgeting decisions in a number of ways. Here we shall discuss the effects of inflation on (1) the levels of required returns, (2) the adjustment of nominal returns to obtain real returns, and (3) capital budgeting computations.

Effects of Inflation on Required Returns

First we analyze the patterns of interest rates and returns before taking inflation into account. Three underlying infuences determine the levels of interest rates and returns: the real productivity rate in the economy, a positive differential for greater risk, and a positive differential for longer maturities. Here we will abstract from short-term demand and supply conditions, which sometimes push short-term interest rates above long-term interest rates. The real productivity rate is the basic rate of growth in the economy; it provides the sources of payment to savers for postponing their consumption from the present to the future. The basic real interest rate reflecting the productivity rate in the economy is 2.5 to 3 percent per annum. This is also the rate of interest on short-term government securities free of the risk of nonpayment at maturity. For longer-term government securities, the rate rises with the length of maturity, reflecting the greater risk of interest rate fluctuations. This adds 1.5 to 2 percent to the basic 2.5 to 3 percent interest rate.

For prime short-term business debt such as commercial paper, we add 1 to 1.5 percent to the government short-term debt rates. For longer-term corporate debt, we add about the same 1 to 1.5 percent differential to rates on longer-term government securities. Since common stocks of corporations carry still greater risk, we add risk adjustment premiums of 2 to 3 percentage points to the corporate bond rates.

To each of the interest rates and common stock returns we must also add a factor based on the expected rate of inflation, so that real returns are maintained after adjusting for inflation. Taking inflation into account, the pattern of rates appears something like this:

	Price level rise per year			
	Basic rates	2%	5%	10%
Short-term government bills	2.5–3%	4.5–5%	7.5–8%	12.5–13%
Long-term government bonds	4–5	6–7	9–10	14–15
Short-term business debt	3.5–4.5	5.5–6.5	8.5–9.5	13.5–14.5
Long-term corporate bonds	5–6.5	7–8.5	10–11.5	15–16.5
Common stocks of corporations	7–9.5	9–11.5	12–14.5	17–19.5

Thus nominal rates of interest and the required returns on investment will include an element for inflation. To the basic rates for different types of investment, an adjustment for inflation will be added. The magnitude of the adjustment will reflect the anticipated rate of future price level increases.

Calculation of Real Returns from Nominal Returns

One method of converting nominal returns into real returns is to simply deduct the inflation factor as illustrated above. Technically, however, we can be more precise. The correct procedures are illustrated by the data in Table 14A.1.

Table 14A.1

Calculation of Real Interest Rates on Short-term Business Debt

Year	One plus nominal returns (1)	Price index (P_t) (2)	$\frac{P_{t-1}}{P_t}$ (3)	One plus real rate of return (1) × (3) (4)
19X1		100		
19X2	1.10	106	0.94	1.03
19X3	1.11	114	0.93	1.03
19X4	1.12	124	0.92	1.03
19X5	1.13	136	0.91	1.03
19X6	1.14	151	0.90	1.03

The impact of inflation in recent years appears to have reduced real returns. It is doubtful whether the levels of real returns on common stocks, for example, have been maintained. The pattern of real returns is suggested by the data in Table 14A.2.

Table 14A.2

Calculation of Real Returns on Common Stocks

Year	One plus nominal returns (1)	Price index (P_t) (2)	$\frac{P_{t-1}}{P_t}$ (3)	One plus real rate of return (1) × (3) (4)
19X1		100		
19X2	1.10	102	0.98	1.08
19X3	1.11	106	0.96	1.07
19X4	1.12	116	0.91	1.02
19X5	1.13	130	0.89	1.01
19X6	1.14	148	0.88	1.00

We observe that while nominal returns have moved as high as 14 percent, real returns have been much lower. In one year, real returns dropped to zero. The impact of inflation has varied in different industries. The general impact of inflation on business earnings has been unfavorable for the following reasons. Firms in a given industry with fixed assets and inventories acquired at lower historical costs are able to offer severe price competition because they are operating from a lower historical cost basis. Since accounting is predominantly based on the expiration of historical costs, the higher current replacement costs of fixed assets and inventories may not be reflected in the prices charged by firms in industries such as paper, cement, and steel. As a consequence, even the nominal profits in inflated dollars reported by some individual companies may be severely depressed.

Capital Budgeting Under Inflation

We now describe how inflation should be taken into account in capital budgeting procedures. We shall use an example to illustrate concretely how the adjustment is made.[1]

Let us begin with the standard capital budgeting case in which inflation is absent. The expression for calculating the net present value of the investment is shown in Equation 14A.1.

$$\overline{\text{NPV}} = \sum_{t=1}^{n} \frac{\bar{F}_t}{(1+k)^t} - I \tag{14A.1}$$

The symbols used have the following meanings and values:

$\overline{\text{NPV}}$ = Expected net present value of the project

$\bar{F}_t$ = Expected net cash flows per year from the project = \$20,000

k = Cost of capital applicable to the risk of the project = 9 percent

n = Number of years the net cash flows are received = 5

I = Required investment outlay for the project = \$75,000

With the data provided, we can utilize Equation 14A.1 as follows:

$$\begin{aligned}\overline{\text{NPV}}_0 &= \sum_{t=1}^{n} \frac{\$20{,}000}{(1.09)^t} - \$75{,}000\\ &= \$20{,}000(3.8897) - \$75{,}000\\ &= \$77{,}794 - \$75{,}000\\ &= \$2{,}794\end{aligned}$$

We find that the project has an expected net present value of \$2,794; under the simple conditions assumed, we would accept the project. Now let us consider the effects of inflation. Suppose that inflation at an annual rate of 6 percent is expected to take place during the five years of the project. Since investment and security returns are based on expected future returns, the anticipated inflation rate will be reflected in the required rate of return on the project or the applicable cost of capital for the project. This relationship has long been recognized in financial

[1] For articles on this subject see J. C. Van Horne, "A Note on Biases in Capital Budgeting Introduced by Inflation," *Journal of Financial and Quantitative Analysis* 6 (January 1971), pp. 653–58; and P. L. Cooley, R. L. Roenfeldt, and It-Keong Chew, "Capital Budgeting Procedures under Inflation," *Financial Management* 4 (Winter 1975), pp. 18–27. Also see Cooley, Roenfeldt, and Chew's exchange with M. C. Findlay and A. W. Frankle in *Financial Management* 5 (Autumn 1976), pp. 83–90.

economics and is known as the *Fisher effect*. In formal terms we have:

$$(1 + k_j)(1 + \eta) = (1 + K_j), \qquad \textbf{(14A.2)}$$

where K_j is the required rate of return in nominal terms and η is the anticipated annual inflation rate over the life of the project. For our example, Equation 14A.2 would be:

$$(1 + 0.09)(1 + 0.06) = (1 + 0.09 + 0.06 + 0.0054)$$

If the cross product term 0.0054 is included in the addition, we would have 0.1554 as the required rate of return in nominal terms. However, since the cross product term is generally small and since both k_j, the required rate of return in real terms, and n, the anticipated inflation rate, are estimates, it is customary practice to make a simple addition of the real rate and the inflation rate. The required nominal rate of return K_j that would be used in the calculation would therefore be 15 percent.

It is at this point that some biases in capital budgeting under inflationary conditions may be introduced. The market data utilized in the estimated current capital costs will include the premium for anticipated inflation. But while the market remembers to include an adjustment for inflation in the capitalization factor, in the capital budgeting analysis the cash-flow estimates may fail to include an element to reflect future inflation. As a consequence, the analysis would appear as in the calculations below for $\overline{\text{NPV}}_1$.

$$\begin{aligned}\overline{\text{NPV}}_1 &= \sum_{t=1}^{n} \frac{\$20{,}000}{(1.09)^t(1.06)^t} - \$75{,}000 = \sum_{t=1}^{n} \frac{\$20{,}000}{(1.15)^t} - \$75{,}000 \\ &= \$20{,}000(3.3522) - \$75{,}000 \\ &= \$67{,}044 - \$75{,}000 = (\$7{,}956)\end{aligned}$$

It now appears that the project will have a negative net present value of almost \$8,000. With a negative net present value of substantial magnitude, the project would be rejected. However, a sound analysis requires that the anticipated inflation rate be taken into account in the cash flow estimates as well. Initially, for simplicity, let us assume that the same inflation rate of 6 percent is applicable to the net cash flows. We take this step in setting forth the expression for $\overline{\text{NPV}}_2$ as follows:

$$\overline{\text{NPV}}_2 = \sum_{t=1}^{n} \frac{\$20{,}000(1.06)^t}{(1.09)^t(1.06)^t} - \$75{,}000 = \sum_{t=1}^{n} \frac{\$20{,}000}{(1.09)^t} - \$75{,}000$$

Since the inflation factors are now in both the numerator and the denominator and are the same, they can be cancelled. The result for the calculation of $\overline{\text{NPV}}_2$ will therefore be the same as for $\overline{\text{NPV}}_0$ (a positive \$2,794). Thus when anticipated inflation is properly reflected in both the cash flow estimates in the numerator and the required rate of return from market data in the denominator, the resulting $\overline{\text{NPV}}$ calculation will be both in real and nominal terms. This was noted by M. Chapman Findlay III as follows: "Any properly measured, market-determined wealth concept is, simultaneously, *both nominal and real*. . . . Hence, $\overline{\text{NPV}}$, or any other wealth measure, gives the amount for which one can 'cash out' now (nominal) and also the amount of today's goods that can be consumed at today's prices (real)."[2] Thus if inflation is reflected in both the cash flow estimates and the required rate of return, the resulting $\overline{\text{NPV}}$ estimate will be free of inflation bias.

To this point we have purposely kept the analysis simple in order to focus on the basic principles involved, since controversy has erupted over certain issues. In applying these concepts, the anticipated inflation might be expected to affect the required rate of return and the cash flow estimates differently. Indeed, the components of the net cash flows, the cash outflows and the cash inflows, may themselves be influenced by the anticipated inflation to different magnitudes. These complications will not, however, change the basic method of analysis, only the specifics of the calculations. The nature of the more complex case is indicated by Equation 14A.3.

$$\overline{\text{NPV}}_0 = \sum_{t=1}^{n} \frac{[(\overline{\text{Inflows}})_t(1+\eta_I)^t - (\overline{\text{Outflows}})_t(1+\eta_O)^t](1-T)}{(1+K)^t} + \frac{(\overline{\text{Depr}})_t(T)}{(1+K)^t} \tag{14A.3}$$

The cash inflows may be subject to a different rate of inflation from the rate of inflation in the cash outflows, and both may differ from the anticipated rate of inflation reflected in the required rate of return in the denominator. Some illustrative data will demonstrate the application of Equation 14A.3.

Table 14A.3

Expected Net Cash Flows without Inflation Effects

	1	2	3	4	5
Expected cash inflows	\$40,000	\$50,000	\$60,000	\$70,000	\$80,000
Expected cash outflows	15,000	25,000	35,000	45,000	55,000
	25,000	25,000	25,000	25,000	25,000
Times (1 − Tax rate)	0.50	0.50	0.50	0.50	0.50
	12,500	12,500	12,500	12,500	12,500
Depreciation (Tax rate)	7,500	7,500	7,500	7,500	7,500
Expected net cash flows ($\overline{F}_t$)	\$20,000	\$20,000	\$20,000	\$20,000	\$20,000

Table 14A.3 sets forth data for expected cash flows without inflation effects. The pattern is a constant \$20,000 per year for five years as in the original example. In Table 14A.4 the estimates of expected net cash flows include inflation effects. The cash inflows are subject to a 7 percent inflation rate, while the cash outflows are subject to an 8 percent inflation rate. The resulting expected net cash flows are shown in the bottom line of the table. The required rate of return of 15 percent is assumed as before to reflect a 6 percent inflation rate.

The calculation of the expected net present value ($\overline{\text{NPV}}_3$) is shown in Table 14A.5. Taking all the inflation influences into account, $\overline{\text{NPV}}_3$ is a negative \$1,471.

[2] M. C. Findlay, "Reply," *Financial Management* 5 (Autumn 1976), pp. 83–90.

Table 14A.4 **Expected Net Cash Flows Including Inflation Effects**

	1	2	3	4	5
Expected cash inflows ($\eta = 7\%$)	$42,800	$57,245	$73,500	$91,756	$112,208
Expected cash outflows ($\eta = 8\%$)	16,200	29,160	44,090	61,223	80,812
	26,600	28,085	29,410	30,533	31,396
Times (1 − Tax rate)	0.50	0.50	0.50	0.50	0.50
	13,300	14,043	14,705	15,267	15,698
Depreciation (Tax rate)	7,500	7,500	7,500	7,500	7,500
Expected net cash flows ($\bar{F}_t$)	$20,800	$21,543	$22,205	$22,767	$ 23,198

Table 14A.5 **Calculation of $\overline{NPV}_3$**

Year	Cash Flow (1)	Discount Factor (15%) (2)	Present Value (1) × (2)
1	$20,800	0.8696	$18,088
2	21,543	0.7561	16,289
3	22,205	0.6575	14,600
4	22,767	0.5718	13,018
5	23,198	0.4972	11,534

$\overline{NPV}_3$ = $73,529 − $75,000
= ($1,471)

The project would be rejected. In this example, the inflationary forces on the cash outflows were greater than for the cash inflows. Some have suggested that this influence has been sufficiently widespread and that it accounts for the sluggish rate of capital investment in the United States since the early 1970s.

In the situation we illustrated initially, failure to take inflation into account in the expected cash flows resulted in an erroneous capital budgeting analysis. A project was accepted that, measured correctly, produced a negative NPV. There would be an unsound allocation of capital if the inflation-caused bias in the analysis had not been taken into account. In our more complex example, inflation caused the cash outflows to grow at a higher rate than the cash inflows. As a consequence, the expected net present value of the project was negative. Making the inflation adjustment does not always necessarily result in a negative net present value for the project—it simply results in a more accurate estimate of the net benefits from the project, positive or negative.

Problems

14A.1 In some recent years, the real rate of interest has been negative. Explain the possible reason for this and give a numerical example.

14A.2 In January 1981, the Windsor Corporation borrowed $1,000,000 at 16 percent interest to purchase a factory. During the year the factory increased in value by 20 percent; however, suppose the annual rate of inflation for 1981 was 14 percent. What has been the real cost of the borrowing?

14A.3 The Battersea Company manufactures plastic drinking glasses. The firm is considering investing $8,000 in a new machine that makes plastic wineglasses. The machine would have a four-year life and no salvage value. Production per year is estimated as follows: 200,000 units, 250,000 units, 200,000 units, 175,000 units. Production costs will be $0.50 per 50 glasses; 50 glasses can be sold at a price of $1.50.

Battersea uses straight-line depreciation and has a 12 percent cost of capital and a 40 percent tax rate.

a. Should Battersea purchase the new machine?

b. The financial vice president of Battersea is concerned that the above analysis has ignored the effects of inflation, estimated to be 14 percent annually over the life of the machine. Further, although the data for the first year are correct, the demand for plastic wineglasses is expected to grow, enabling Battersea to raise prices by 12 percent per year after the first year. Offsetting this, the price of plastic is expected to increase, raising production costs by 20 percent per year after the first year. Reevaluate the purchase decision, taking these factors into consideration.

14A.4 The finance department of the Jansen Corporation has estimated the firm's cost of capital at 18 percent based on the existing rate of inflation. Jansen is constructing a new plant and is trying to decide whether to install a coal- or natural-gas-powered production line. The basic cost of each system is $150,000; each has a 10-year life and no expected salvage value. The annual benefits of each system will be the same at $80,000. The coal-powered system will involve annual outflows of $20,000. Pollution control laws, however, require that a $15,000 scrubber system be installed if coal power is selected. The scrubber would also be depreciable over a 10-year life to a zero salvage value. The annual costs for the natural gas system are estimated at $15,000.

Jansen uses straight-line depreciation and has a 40 percent corporate tax rate.

a. Which system should Jansen choose?

b. If Jansen chooses the coal system, it can fix its expenses at the initial $20,000 per year through a long-term contract with its supplier. Such contracts are unavailable for natural gas, and the price of natural gas is expected to climb, raising outflows by 20 percent per year after the first year if gas is chosen. Which system should Jansen choose under these circumstances?

PART FIVE

COST OF CAPITAL AND VALUATION

Part Four developed the concepts needed for making investment decisions; in a number of places it made use of the applicable cost of capital. Part Five provides the basis for determining the relevant cost of capital and how it is influenced by financial decisions. It also examines financing decisions in the broad categories of debt versus equity. It attempts to determine the optimal financial structure—the financial structure that simultaneously minimizes the firm's cost of capital and maximizes its market value. Financing decisions and investment decisions are interdependent—the optimal financing plan and the optimal level of investment must be determined simultaneously—so Part Five also serves the important function of integrating the theory of capital budgeting with the theory of capital structure.

In Part Five, we come to the very heart of managerial finance. We analyze the factors affecting the firm's cost of capital and value. Chapter 15 analyzes the influence of capital structure decisions on the riskiness of the returns of a firm and hence on its required return. Chapter 16 discusses how the firm may move toward its goals of minimizing its cost of capital and maximizing its value. Chapter 17 discusses the role of dividend policy. Chapter 18 deals with valuation and how future revenue streams affect valuation.

CHAPTER 15

FINANCIAL STRUCTURE AND THE USE OF LEVERAGE

We have previously seen that operating leverage refers to the extent to which fixed operating costs are part of a firm's total operating costs. If all costs were variable (such as 80 percent of sales), the firm's pretax profits would equal 20 percent of sales. But if some costs are fixed, the firm suffers a loss until it achieves a volume of sales to cover both variable costs and the fixed costs. As volume increases beyond this breakeven point, profits increase because the fixed costs become smaller per unit of volume or sales made by the firm. So, operating leverage increases the volatility of profitability.

Financial leverage, similar in concept, refers to the use of debt in financing the firm. If all financing were owners' funds in the form of common stock dividend payments on the common stock would be made only if the firm had achieved some net income. But the interest on debt that is sold to obtain financing is a fixed financial charge that must be paid regardless of the level of the firm's earnings. The more debt that is used, the less money the owners need to put into the company. The owners are able to leverage the purchase of a larger amount of assets with a smaller investment of their own if debt financing is employed. The greater the use of debt, the greater the financial leverage and the greater the extent to which financial fixed costs are added to operating fixed costs.

The addition of more fixed costs increases the volatility of net returns to the common stockholders, and greater volatility means greater dispersion in the returns, or increased risk. Consequently, the use of financial leverage adds an element of risk to the cash flow streams. Quantifying the degrees of risk depends upon how risk is measured. As in Chapter 14, "Risk and Investment Return," we will use both the coefficient of variation and the beta measures.

In Chapter 16, we shall deal with the effects of financial leverage on the firm's cost of capital. At that point, we will have completed the analysis required to arrive at the cost of capital utilized in the capital budgeting decisions outlined in Chapter 13.

Financial Leverage

Some basic terms will be defined and will mean the same thing in all of the subsequent discussion. *Financial structure* refers to the way the firm's assets are financed. Financial structure is represented by the entire right-hand side of the balance sheet. It includes short-term debt, and long-term debt as well as shareholders' equity. *Capital structure* or the *capitalization* of the firm is the permanent financing represented by long-term debt, preferred stock, and shareholders' equity. Thus a firm's capital structure is only part of its financial structure. Shareholders' equity (SHE) includes common stock, paid-in or capital surplus, and the accumulated amount of retained earnings. If the firm has preferred stock it is added to the shareholders' equity and the two together may be termed the firm's *net worth*.

The key concept for this chapter is financial leverage, or the leverage factor. The *leverage factor* is the ratio of total debt (B) to total assets (TA) or to the total value (V) of the firm. When we refer to total assets (TA) we are referring to the total accounting book value of assets. Total value (V) refers to the total market value of all of the components of the firm's financial structure. While market values are used predominantly in developing financial theory, the leverage factor will also be defined with reference to accounting book values. For example, a firm having total assets of $100 million and total debt of $50 million would have a leverage factor of 50 percent. When we set forth the leverage relationships based on the ratio of debt to total assets, this necessarily implies what the ratio of debt to shareholders' equity (or in brief, the debt-to-equity ratio) will be. If we define the debt-to-equity ratio as B/S we can see that it is equal to $B/\text{TA} \div (1 - B/\text{TA})$. Thus if the ratio of debt to total assets is 50 percent, this means that the amount of debt is exactly equal to the amount of (shareholders') equity and the B/S ratio is equal to one. Or $B/\text{TA} = 0.5$ and, therefore, $B/S = [0.5 \div (1 - 0.5)] = 1$.

Finally, we should distinguish between business risk and financial risk. *Business risk* is the inherent uncertainty or variability of expected pretax returns on the firm's portfolio of assets. This kind of risk was examined in Chapter 14, where it

Table 15.1

Four Alternative Financial Structures, Universal Machine Company, Based on Book Values

Structure 1 ($B/S = 0\%$; $B/\text{TA} = 0\%$)			
		Total debt	$ 0
		Common stock ($10 par)	10,000
Total assets	$10,000	Total claims	$10,000
Structure 2 ($B/S = 25\%$; $B/\text{TA} = 20\%$)			
		Total debt	$ 2,000
		Common stock ($10 par)	8,000
Total assets	$10,000	Total claims	$10,000
Structure 3 ($B/S = 100\%$; $B/\text{TA} = 50\%$)			
		Total debt	$ 5,000
		Common stock ($10 par)	5,000
Total assets	$10,000	Total claims	$10,000
Structure 4 ($B/S = 400\%$; $B/\text{TA} = 80\%$)			
		Total debt	$ 8,000
		Common stock ($10 par)	2,000
Total assets	$10,000	Total claims	$10,000

was defined in terms of the probability distribution of returns on the firm's assets. *Financial risk* is the additional risk induced by the use of financial leverage.

The Nature of Financial Leverage

Perhaps the best way to understand the use of financial leverage is to analyze its impact on profitability and fluctuations in profitability under a range of leverage conditions. As an example, consider four alternative financial structures for the Universal Machine Company, a manufacturer of equipment used by industrial firms. The alternative balance sheets are displayed in Table 15.1.

Structure 1 uses no debt and consequently has a leverage factor of zero; Structure 2 has a leverage factor of 20 percent; Structure 3 has a leverage factor of 50 percent; and Structure 4 has a leverage factor of 80 percent.

The Impact of Financial Leverage

To understand the impact of financial leverage on the risk of the firm we first have to understand its impact on the degree of fluctuations in profitability. It will be demonstrated that greater leverage will produce greater volatility in profitability. This can be demonstrated algebraically, but the ideas can more readily be understood by a specific example which reflects a set of general relationships. Table 15.2 and Figure 15.1 provide the basic data and a graphical presentation of the relationships. Table 15.2 begins by considering a range of possible ratios of EBIT or NOI to total assets. Different levels of profitability as measured by the ratios of EBIT (or NOI) to total assets have effects which vary with alternative capital structures.

Figure 15.1

Financial Leverage Magnifies Variations in the Return on Equity

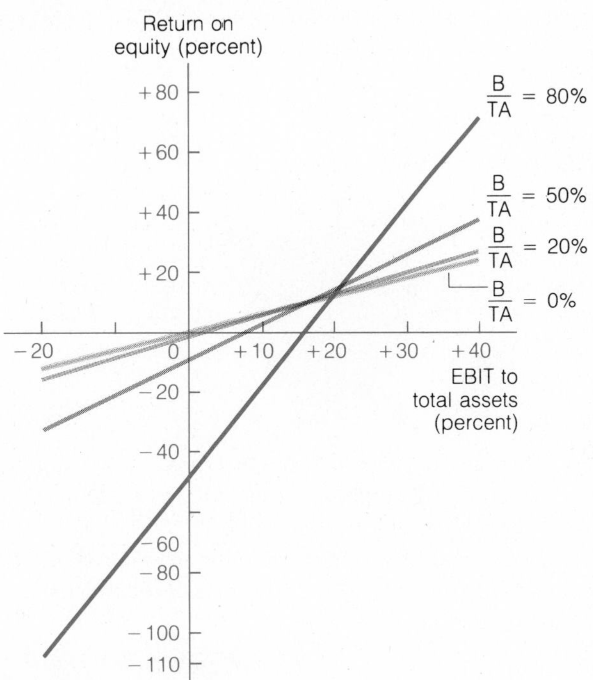

Table 15.2

Universal Machine, Financial Leverage, and Stockholders' Returns

Before-tax return on total assets	EBIT or NOI to total assets		
	−20%	20%	60%
Capital structure 1: *B*/TA = 0%			
EBIT or NOI	−$2,000	$2,000	$6,000
Less: interest	0	0	0
Earnings before taxes	−2,000	2,000	6,000
Less: income taxes (@ 40%)[a]	−800	800	2,400
Net income	−1,200	1,200	3,600
Return on stockholders' equity (ROE)	−12%	12%	36%
EPS on 1,000 shares	−$1.20	$1.20	$3.60
Capital structure 2: *B*/TA = 20%			
EBIT or NOI	−$2,000	$2,000	$6,000
Less: interest (@ 10%)	200	200	200
EBT	−2,200	1,800	5,800
Less: tax (@ 40%)[a]	−880	720	2,320
Net income	−1,320	1,080	3,480
Return on $8,000 equity (ROE)	−16.5%	13.5%	43.5%
EPS on 800 shares	−$1.65	$1.35	$4.35
Capital structure 3: *B*/TA = 50%			
EBIT or NOI	−$2,000	$2,000	$6,000
Less: interest (@ 14%)	700	700	700
EBT	−2,700	1,300	5,300
Less: tax (@ 40%)[a]	−1,080	520	2,120
Net income	−1,620	780	3,180
Return on $5,000 equity (ROE)	−32.4%	15.6%	63.6%
EPS on 500 shares	−$3.24	$1.56	$6.36
Capital structure 4: *B*/TA = 80%			
EBIT or NOI	−$2,000	$2,000	$6,000
Less: interest (@ 20%)	1,600	1,600	1,600
EBT	−3,600	400	4,400
Less: tax (@ 40%)[a]	−1,440	160	1,760
Net income	−2,160	240	2,640
Return on $2,000 equity (ROE)	−108%	12%	132%
EPS on 200 shares	−$10.80	$1.20	$13.20

[a] The tax calculations assume that losses are carried back or forward or otherwise utilized to produce tax credits.

Four different levels of financial leverage are illustrated in Table 15.2, the degree of financial leverage (*B*/TA) ranging from 0 to 80 percent. With zero leverage, the return on total assets after taxes [EBIT(1 − T)/TA] is 60 percent of the pretax rate of return on total assets because of the 40 percent corporate tax rate. With no leverage, the after-tax return on total assets is equal to the ratio of net income to shareholders' equity (NI/E = ROE).

With leverage, the amount of interest paid affects the relation between the after-tax return on total assets and the return on equity. The numerators of the two ratios have the following relationship:

$$(EBIT)(1 - T) = NI + (1 - T) \text{ Int Paid}$$

The amount of interest paid is rB, the interest rate (r) times the amount of debt outstanding (B). The rate of interest paid by Universal Machine is assumed to begin at 10 percent for the leverage factor of 20 percent. It is further assumed that the increased risk of rising leverage causes interest rates to rise. The increases in interest rates shown are purely illustrative.[1]

Table 15.2 shows that the higher the ratio of financial leverage employed, the greater the dispersion of returns. The pattern for the return on equity is summarized in Table 15.3. With no leverage, the range of the ROE is 48 percent. With an 80 percent leverage factor, the range of the ROE is 240 percent. Financial leverage magnifies the volatility of returns whether measured by net income, return on equity or earnings per share.

Table 15.3

Relation between Leverage Factors and Range of Returns

Leverage factor	Range of return on equity
0%	48%
20	60
50	96
80	240

These results are depicted in Figure 15.1. When none of the total assets are financed by debt, the ratio of the return on shareholders' equity to the return on total assets is a relatively flat line. But for the debt ratio B/TA (equal 80 percent), the line becomes steeper. This means that a small change in the ratio of EBIT to total assets produces a very large change in the ratio of net income to shareholders' equity. Thus greater financial leverage produces greater volatility in the return to equity.

Relationship of Financial Leverage to Operating Leverage

Chapter 7 showed that a firm has some degree of control over its production processes; it can, within limits, use either a highly automated production process with high fixed costs but low variable costs or a less automated process with lower fixed costs but higher variable costs. If a firm uses a high degree of operating leverage, its breakeven point is at a relatively high sales level, and changes in the sales level have a magnified (or "leveraged") impact on profits. Notice that financial leverage has exactly the same kind of effect on profits; the higher the leverage factor, the higher the breakeven sales volume and the greater the impact on profits from a given change in sales volume.

In Chapter 7 the *degree of operating leverage* was defined as the ratio of percentage change in net operating income (NOI = EBIT) associated with a given

[1] The relation between financial leverage and the cost of debt and equity capital is discussed in the following chapter.

percentage change in sales volume as shown in Equation 15.1:

$$\text{Degree of operating leverage (DOL)} = \frac{\text{\% change in EBIT}}{\text{\% change in sales}} \tag{15.1}$$

The summary income statement in Table 15.4 illustrates the impact of operating leverage alone. This is based on the Universal Machine's total cost structure in which fixed costs are $6,000 and variable costs are 20 percent of sales. The selling price per unit is $100. As sales in units rise from 50 to 150, the pretax return on total assets goes from a negative 20 percent to a positive 60 percent. Using the data from Table 15.4, as the sales in units increase from 100 to 150, the degree of operating leverage is:

$$\text{DOL} = \frac{\$4{,}000/\$2{,}000}{\$5{,}000/\$10{,}000} = \frac{200\%}{50\%} = 4$$

Thus a 10 percent increase in sales would result in a 40 percent increase in EBIT or NOI. This degree of operating leverage is relatively high.

Table 15.4

Illustration of Operating Leverage

The total cost structure of the firm is: Total costs = $6,000 + 0.2 Sales

Sales in units	50	100	150
Sales in dollars @ $100 per unit	$5,000	$10,000	$15,000
Fixed operating expenses	6,000	6,000	6,000
Variable operating expenses	1,000	2,000	3,000
Earnings before interest and taxes	−2,000	2,000	6,000
Before tax return on total assets	−20%	20%	60%

Degree of Financial Leverage (DFL)

Financial leverage takes over where operating leverage leaves off, further magnifying the effects on earnings per share of changes in the level of sales. For this reason, operating leverage is sometimes referred to as *first-stage leverage* and financial leverage as *second-stage leverage.* The *degree of financial leverage* is defined as the ratio of the percentage change in net income available to common stockholders that is associated with a given percentage change in earnings before interest and taxes (EBIT):

$$\text{DFL} = \frac{\text{\% change in net income}}{\text{\% change in EBIT}} \tag{15.2}$$

Thus using the data from Table 15.2 for Universal Machine with a leverage factor of 80 percent, at an output of 100 units and an EBIT of $2,000, the degree of financial leverage is:

$$\text{DFL} = \frac{(\$2{,}640 - \$240)/\$240}{(\$6{,}000 - \$2{,}000)/\$2{,}000} = \frac{1000\%}{200\%} = 5$$

Thus a 10 percent increase in EBIT would result in a 50 percent increase in net income.[2] If the leverage factor were only 20 percent, the degree of financial leverage would be:

$$\text{DFL} = \frac{(\$3{,}480 - \$1{,}080)/\$1{,}080}{(\$6{,}000 - \$2{,}000)/\$2{,}000} = \frac{222\%}{200\%} = 1.11$$

Thus the degree of financial leverage becomes 111 percent. Note that if there were no debt, the degree of financial leverage would be exactly 1. The use of debt will cause the degree of financial leverage to rise above 1.0 or above 100 percent. Thus the degree of financial leverage measures the magnification factor. If the degree of financial leverage is exactly one (or 100 percent) the multiplication factor is 1.0 and there is no degree of magnification in net income, return on equity, or earnings per share.

Combining Operating and Financial Leverage

Operating leverage causes a change in sales volume to have a magnified effect on EBIT. If financial leverage is superimposed on operating leverage, changes in EBIT have a magnified effect on NI, on ROE, and on EPS. Therefore, if a firm uses a considerable amount of both operating leverage and financial leverage, even small changes in the level of sales will produce wide fluctuations in NI, ROE, and EPS.

Equation 15.1 for the degree of operating leverage (DOL) can be combined with Equation 15.2 for the degree of financial leverage (DFL) to obtain the degree of combined leverage (DCL).

$$\begin{aligned} \text{DCL} &= \left(\frac{\%\text{ change in EBIT}}{\%\text{ change in sales}}\right)\left(\frac{\%\text{ change in net income}}{\%\text{ change in EBIT}}\right) \\ &= \frac{\%\text{ change in net income}}{\%\text{ change in sales}} \end{aligned} \tag{15.3}$$

The DOL at sales of $10,000 in Table 15.4 is 4 as calculated. Combined with a financial leverage factor of 80 percent, which represents a DFL of 5.0, the degree of combined leverage is 20. This is a very high degree of leverage; it indicates that a 10 percent change in sales would cause a 200 percent change in net income, return on equity, or earnings per share. The DOL of 4 combined with a DFL of 1.11 for the leverage factor of 20 percent would result in a degree of combined leverage of 4.44 times. In this case a 10 percent change in sales would result in a 44.4 percent change in NI, ROE, or EPS.

A number of different combinations of operating and financial leverage will produce the same combined leverage factor. Hence firms can make tradeoffs between operating and financial leverage. If a firm has a target degree of combined leverage and has high operating leverage because of the nature of its business, it can offset the degree of operating leverage by a lower degree of financial leverage. Alternatively, if the firm has a low degree of operating leverage, it might increase the degree of financial leverage to produce a target combined leverage.

[2] It can be demonstrated that the degree of financial leverage is unchanged whether it is measured by net income, return on equity or earnings per share as the measure in the numerator. For a demonstration see Weston and Brigham, *Managerial Finance*, Seventh Edition.

Financial Leverage and Risk

Let's examine the impact of different degrees of financial leverage on risk. We continue the theme of the relation between risk and return. We will use our two basic measures of risk, the coefficient of variation and the beta measure.

Returns under Alternative Levels of Sales

The first step is a consideration of possible alternative levels of sales and the appropriate probability assessments of each. This is a critical and difficult, yet unavoidable, step in the formulation. Regardless of what decision is taken, there is an implicit formulation of the probabilities. For example, suppose the decision would be to have very low operating leverage and very low financial leverage in order to "be conservative." There are two things wrong with this stance. It is conservative in the sense of limiting the firm's downside loss, but it is not conservative in the sense of having the firm take advantage of its opportunities and be a strong, healthy competitor. Low operating leverage and low financial leverage imply a forecast involving a high probability that a low level of sales may occur. On the other hand, if the firm employs a high degree of combined leverage, there is an implicit forecast of a high probability that sales will be very strong.

Hence the firm should do the best it can to assign probabilities to alternative future states-of-the-world in which sales will be at alternative levels. The probability distribution for future sales, constructed by Universal's marketing department in cooperation with representatives from the general staff group of top management, was based on their knowledge of present supply and demand conditions, along with estimates for future economic conditions and sales. The probable conditions range from "very poor" (due to a labor strike resulting from some very difficult labor negotiations currently under way) to "very good" (under an optimistic assessment of the future outlook).

The best judgments of the probabilities of alternative levels of future sales are presented in row 1 of Table 15.5. In addition, the cost structure from Table 15.4, Part B, is used to obtain the pretax return on total assets for each level of sales with its associated probability. The return on total assets in the bottom row of Table 15.5 is identical to the return on total assets in the top row of Table 15.2. Hence the measurement in Table 15.2 of the effects of alternative capital structures can be utilized in the subsequent analysis. The data will be used to calculate the two basic risk measures: the coefficient of variation (CV) and the beta (β), which is the covariance divided by the variance of market returns.

Table 15.5

Probabilities Associated with Alternative Sales Levels, UM Company

Probabilities	0.2	0.5	0.3
Sales	$5,000	$10,000	$15,000
Costs: (Table 15.4, Part B)			
Fixed costs	6,000	6,000	6,000
Variable costs (0.2S)	1,000	2,000	3,000
Total costs	7,000	8,000	9,000
Earnings before interest and taxes (EBIT)	−$2,000	$ 2,000	$ 6,000
Return on total assets	−20%	20%	60%

Table 15.6 **Calculation of Risk Measures for UM**

S	P_s	ROA	P_sROA	(ROA − $\overline{\text{ROA}}$)	(ROA − $\overline{\text{ROA}}$)^2	P_s(ROA − $\overline{\text{ROA}}$)^2
1	0.2	−0.20	−0.04	−0.44	0.1936	0.03872
2	0.5	0.20	0.10	−0.04	0.0016	0.00080
3	0.3	0.60	0.18	0.36	0.1296	0.03888
		$\overline{\text{ROA}}$ =	0.24			$\sigma^2 = 0.07840$

$$CV = \frac{\sigma}{\overline{\text{ROA}}} = \frac{0.28}{0.24} = 1.167 \qquad \sigma = 0.280$$

In Table 15.6, the expected returns on total assets and the standard deviation of those returns are calculated to obtain the coefficient of variation. The result is a coefficient of variation in the returns on total assets of 1.167, which indicates that there are about $1\frac{1}{6}$ units of dispersion per unit of expected return on total assets.

Table 15.7 utilizes the results of the return on equity calculations from Table 15.2 to measure the effects of leverage on risk as measured by the coefficient of variation. For financial structure 1, the return on equity has an expected return and

Table 15.7 **Effects of Leverage on UM's Risk Measures**

	S	P_s	ROE	P_sROE	(ROE − $\overline{\text{ROE}}$)	P_s(ROE − $\overline{\text{ROE}}$)^2
Structure 1	1	0.2	−0.12	−0.024	−0.264	0.0139
	2	0.5	0.12	0.060	−0.024	0.0003
	3	0.3	0.36	0.108	0.216	0.0140
				$\overline{\text{ROE}}$ = 0.144		$\sigma^2 = 0.0282$
			$CV = \frac{\sigma}{\overline{\text{ROE}}} = \frac{0.168}{0.144} = 1.167$			$\sigma = 0.168$
Structure 2	1	0.2	−0.165	−0.0330	−0.330	0.0218
	2	0.5	0.135	0.0675	−0.030	0.0005
	3	0.3	0.435	0.1305	0.270	0.0219
				$\overline{\text{ROE}}$ = 0.165		$\sigma^2 = 0.0442$
			$CV = \frac{0.21}{0.165} = 1.273$			$\sigma = 0.210$
Structure 3	1	0.2	−0.324	−0.0648	−0.528	0.0558
	2	0.5	0.156	0.0780	−0.048	0.0012
	3	0.3	0.636	0.1908	0.432	0.0560
				$\overline{\text{ROE}}$ = 0.204		$\sigma^2 = 0.1130$
			$CV = \frac{0.336}{0.204} = 1.647$			$\sigma = 0.336$
Structure 4	1	0.2	−1.08	−0.216	−1.320	0.3485
	2	0.5	0.12	0.060	−0.120	0.0072
	3	0.3	1.32	0.396	1.080	0.3499
				$\overline{\text{ROE}}$ = 0.240		$\sigma^2 = 0.7056$
			$CV = \frac{0.84}{0.24} = 3.500$			$\sigma = 0.840$

standard deviation which is (1 − T) times the corresponding measures for the return on assets. The resulting coefficient of variation for the return on equity with no leverage is exactly equal to the CV for the return on total assets. With no leverage, the CV risk measure is no different for the ROE than for the ROA.

However, with increased leverage, the CV is increased. The expected ROE also is increased. Thus both the expected ROE and its dispersion measures are increased by increased leverage.

The second basic measure of risk is the beta coefficient. Suppose that for the Universal Machine Company one of the financial services had calculated a beta of 1.568. This was associated with the degree of leverage for Universal Machine that resulted in a ratio of debt to equity of 20 percent based on market values. Assume further that the same financial services suggested that the appropriate security market line to apply is shown by Equation 15.4.

$$R_j^* = 0.09 + (0.05)\beta_j \qquad \textbf{(15.4)}$$

From the data provided, some estimates of the effect of changing leverage can be made. The following basic relationship between the unlevered beta and the levered beta can be employed.[3]

$$\beta_j = \beta_u[1 + (B/S)(1 - T)] \qquad \textbf{(15.5)}$$

where β_u is the unlevered beta, β_j is the levered beta, and B/S is the debt to equity ratio measured at market values. From the information provided, we can calculate the unlevered beta using the above expression. We would have:

$$1.568 = \beta_u[1 + .2(.6)] \qquad \textbf{(15.5a)}$$

With the information in Table 15.8, we can calculate β_u and the value of the other levered betas. First the table sets forth the ratio of debt to equity at book values for Universal Machine.

These are the alternative levels of leverage at book value that we have been using before. In Column (3) some estimated debt to equity market relationships are set forth that correspond to the financial structures measured at book value in Column (2). For financial structures 2 and 3 it is assumed that more leverage increases the market value of equity so that the ratio of debt to equity measured at market is lower than the ratio of debt to equity measured at book. For financial structure 4, where there is $4 of debt at book value to $1 of equity at book value, we judge that this degree of leverage is excessive. Because it is excessive, it results in a decline in the market value of equity. As a consequence the ratio of debt to equity at market values is shown to be greater than the ratio of debt to equity at book values.[4]

[3] M. E. Rubinstein, "A Mean-Variance Synthesis of Corporate Financial Theory," *Journal of Finance* 28 (March 1973), p. 178.

[4] We emphasize that these numbers used here are purely illustrative. There are formal methods that can be used by investment bankers, financial managers, and others to develop estimates of the ratio of debt to equity at market values. They are somewhat complex and are covered in *Managerial Finance*, 7th ed., pp. 587–672.

Table 15.8

Calculations of Leveraged Betas

(1)	(2)	(3)	(4)	(5)
	Ratio of debt to equity			
Financial structure	At book	At market	$[1 + (B/S)(1 - T)]$	β_j
1	0.00	0.00	1.00	1.400
2	0.25	0.20	1.12	1.568
3	1.00	0.60	1.36	1.904
4	4.00	5.00	4.00	5.600

Utilizing the leverage ratios at market in Column (3) and given the tax rate of 40 percent for Universal Machine, we can use the expression in Equation 15.5 to first calculate the β_u in 15.5a. We divide 1.568 by 1.12 to obtain 1.4 as the value of the unlevered beta. Column (4) provides the factors by which this unlevered beta is multiplied in order to obtain the levered betas. The resulting betas in Column (5) rise from the unlevered beta of 1.4 to a levered beta of 5.6. The indicated levered betas based on market value are plausible for the first three financial structures illustrated. The levered beta of 5.6 for financial structure 4 may seem to be unusually high. On the other hand, a leverage ratio of $4 of debt for $1 of equity is also extremely high. From a practical standpoint we would probably not actually observe a beta as high as 5.6 nor would we observe a debt ratio of $4 of debt to $1 of equity. The analysis is realistic and practical in indicating that such high debt ratios would not be observed because they would represent unduly high levels of financial risk.

Table 15.9

Relations between Expected and Required Returns for Alternative Beta Levels of UM

Financial structure	β_j	R^*	$\overline{ROE}$
1	1.400	0.1600	0.1440
2	1.568	0.1684	0.1650
3	1.904	0.1852	0.2040
4	5.600	0.3700	0.2400

SML: $R^* = .09 + .05\beta_j$

In Table 15.9 the leveraged betas that have been calculated are applied to the security market line to obtain the required rates of return. The required rates of return range from the 16 percent for an unlevered firm to 37 percent for the financial structure that we have indicated to be excessively top-heavy with debt. Under the assumptions reflected in the data patterns that we have employed, the results in

Table 15.9 suggest at least a tentative conclusion. For the leverage factors of financial structures 1, 2, and 4, the required return on equity is greater than the expected return on equity. For financial structure 3 with the debt to equity book ratio of 1, the expected return is greater than the required return. These results would indicate that financial structure 3 would be preferred to the alternatives.

Financial Leverage with Additional Investment

Thus far in the analysis we have varied leverage, holding constant the total amount of investment by the firm. In real-world decision making, it is often necessary to perform an analysis in which alternative leverage structures are considered along with financing that increases the firm's amount of investment and size of total assets. This aspect of combining the financing and leverage decisions will be developed by a continuation of the Universal Machine Company example. Universal's latest balance sheet is set forth in Table 15.10. Universal manufactures equipment used in industrial manufacturing. Its major product is a lathe used to trim the rough edges off sheets of fabricated steel. As is typically the case for producers of durable capital assets, the company's sales fluctuate widely, far more than does the overall economy. For example, during nine of the preceding twenty-five years, the company's sales have been below the breakeven point, so losses have been relatively frequent.

Table 15.10

Universal Machine Company Balance Sheet for Year Ended December 31, 1981 (Thousands of Dollars)

Cash	$ 300	Total liabilities having an average cost of 10%	$ 5,000
Receivables (net)	1,200		
Inventories	1,400		
Plant (net)	3,000	Common stock ($10 par)	5,000
Equipment (net)	4,100		
Total assets	$10,000	Total claims on assets	$10,000

Although future sales are uncertain, current demand is high and appears to be headed higher. Thus, if Universal is to continue its sales growth, it will have to increase capacity. A capacity increase involving $2 million of new capital is under consideration. James Watson, the financial vice president, learns that he can raise the $2 million by selling bonds with a 12 percent coupon or by selling 100,000 shares of common stock at a market price of $20 per share. Fixed costs after the planned expansion will be $6.4 million a year. Variable costs excluding interest on the debt will be 20 percent of sales.[5] The probability distribution for alternative future state-of-the-world, is the same as was set forth in the previous section analyzing the pure leverage decision for Universal.

Although Watson's recommendation will be given much weight, the final decision for the method of financing rests with the company's board of directors. Procedurally, the financial vice president analyzes the situation, evaluates all

[5] The assumption that variable costs will be a constant percentage of sales over the entire range of output is not valid, but variable costs are relatively constant over the output range likely to occur.

Table 15.11 **Profit Calculations at Various Sales Levels, Universal Machine Company (Thousands of Dollars)**

Probability of indicated sales	0.2	0.5	0.3
Sales	$5,000	$12,000	$20,000
Costs:			
Fixed	6,400	6,400	6,400
Variable (0.2S)	1,000	2,400	4,000
Total costs	7,400	8,800	10,400
Earnings before interest and taxes (EBIT)	−$2,400	$3,200	$9,600
Financing with bonds			
Earnings before interest and taxes	−$2,400	$3,200	$9,600
Less: interest (12% × $7,000)[a]	840	840	840
Earnings before taxes	−3,240	2,360	8,760
Less: income taxes (40%)	−1,296	944	3,504
Net income	−1,944	1,416	5,256
EPS on 500,000 shares[b]	−3.89	2.83	10.51
Return on equity	−38.9%	28.3%	105.1%
Expected EPS = $3.79			
Financing with stock			
Earnings before interest and taxes	−$2,400	$3,200	$9,600
Less: interest (10% × $5,000)	500	500	500
Earnings before taxes	−2,900	2,700	9,100
Less: income taxes (40%)	−1,160	1,080	3,640
Net income	−1,740	1,620	5,460
EPS on 600,000 shares[b]	−2.90	2.70	9.10
Return on equity	−24.8%	23.14%	78%
Expected EPS = $3.50			

[a] With higher leverage, the cost of debt rises to 12 percent on the new debt, and 12 percent represents the opportunity cost of the old debt as well.

[b] The EPS figures can also be obtained using the following formula:

$$\text{EPS} = \frac{(\text{Sales} - \text{Fixed costs} - \text{Variable costs} - \text{Interest})(1 - \text{Tax rate})}{\text{Shares outstanding}}$$

For example, at sales = $12 million:

$$\text{EPS}_{\text{bonds}} = \frac{(12 - 6.4 - 2.4 - 0.84)(0.6)}{0.5} = \$2.83$$

$$\text{EPS}_{\text{stock}} = \frac{(12 - 6.4 - 2.4 - 0.5)(0.6)}{0.6} = \$2.70$$

reasonable alternatives, comes to a conclusion, and then presents the alternatives with his recommendations to the board. For his own analysis, as well as for presentation to the board, Watson prepares the materials shown in Table 15.11.

The top third of the table calculates earnings before interest and taxes (EBIT) for different levels of sales ranging from $5 to $20 million. The firm suffers an operating loss until sales are $8 million, but beyond that point it enjoys a rapid rise in gross profit.[6]

The middle third of the table shows the financial results that will occur at the various sales levels if bonds are used. First, the $840,000 annual interest charges

[6] The breakeven sales are $S^* = \$6,400 + 0.2S^*$. Hence $S^* = \$8,000$ (in thousands).

($600,000 on existing debt plus $240,000 on the new bonds) are deducted from the earnings before interest and taxes. Next, taxes are taken out; and if the sales level is so low that losses are incurred, the firm receives a tax credit. Then, net profits after taxes are divided by the 500,000 shares outstanding to obtain earnings per share (EPS) of common stock.[7] The various EPS figures are multiplied by the corresponding probability estimates to obtain an expected EPS of $3.79.

The bottom third of the table calculates the financial results that will occur with stock financing. Net profit after interest and taxes is divided by 600,000—the original 500,000 shares plus the 100,000 new shares ($20 × 100,000 = $2 million)—to find earnings per share. Expected EPS is computed in the same way as for the bond financing.

Figure 15.2 shows the probability distribution of earnings per share. Stock financing has the tighter, more peaked distribution. We know from Table 15.3 that it will also have a smaller coefficient of variation than bond financing. Hence, stock financing is less risky than bond financing. However, the expected earnings per share are lower for stock than for bonds, so we are again faced with the kind of risk-return tradeoff that characterizes most financial decisions.

Figure 15.2

Probability Curves for Stock and Bond Financing

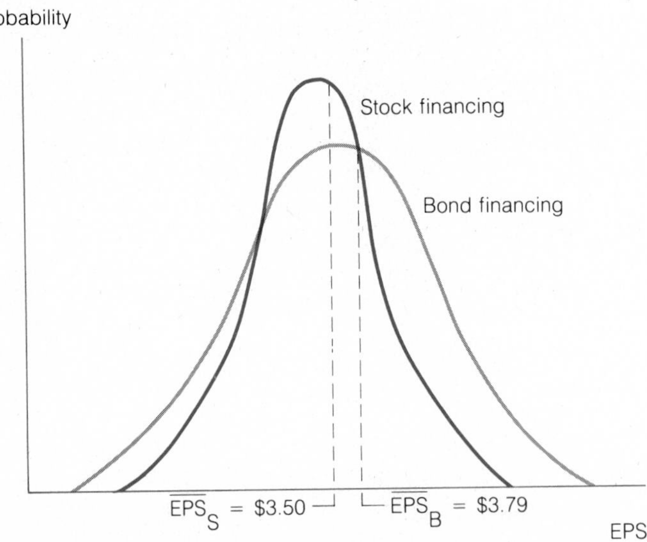

What choice should Watson recommend to the board? How much leverage should Universal Machine use? These questions cannot be answered at this point; the answers must be deferred until some additional concepts have been covered and the effects of leverage on the cost of both debt and equity capital have been examined.

[7] The number of shares initially outstanding can be calculated by dividing the $5 million common stock figure given on the balance sheet by the $10 par value.

Crossover Analysis

Another way of presenting the data on Universal's two financing methods is shown in Figure 15.3, depicting a crossover analysis.

At a low level of sales, the EPS using stock is much higher than the EPS when debt is used. The debt line has a steeper slope and rises faster, however, showing that earnings per share will go up faster with increases in sales if debt is used. The two lines cross at sales of \$11.175 million. Below that sales volume, the firm will be better off issuing common stock; above that level, debt financing will produce higher earnings per share.[8]

Figure 15.3

Earnings per Share for Stock and Debt Financing

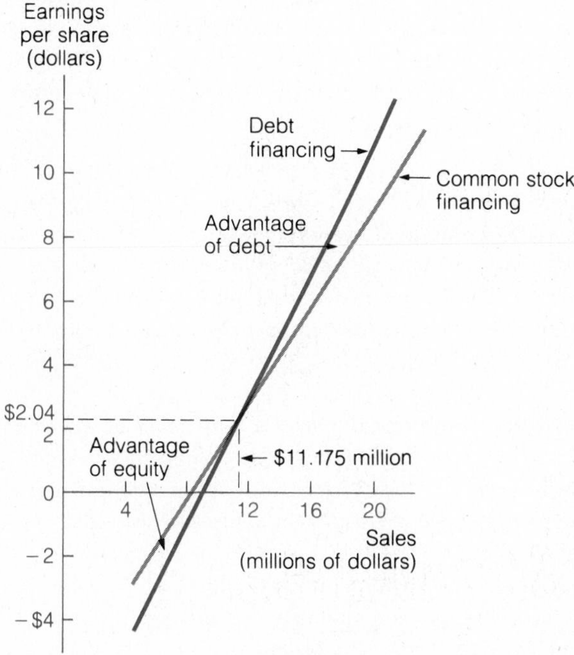

If Watson and his board of directors know with certainty that sales will never again fall below \$11.175 million, bonds are the preferred method of financing the asset increase. But they cannot know this for certain. In fact, they know that in previous years, sales have fallen below this critical level. Further, if any detrimental long-run

[8] Since the equation in this case is linear, the breakeven or indifference level of sales (S) can be found as follows:

$$\text{EPS}_S = \frac{(S - 6.4 - 0.2S - 0.5)(0.6)}{0.6} = \frac{(S - 6.4 - 0.2S - 0.84)(0.6)}{0.5} = \text{EPS}_B$$

$S = \$11.175$ and EPS $= \$2.04$

events occur, future sales may again fall well below $11.175 million. If sales continue to expand, however, there will be higher earnings per share from using bonds; and no officer or director will want to forego these substantial advantages.

Watson's recommendation and the directors' decision will depend on (1) each person's appraisal of the future and (2) each person's psychological attitude toward risk.[9] The pessimists, or risk averters, will prefer to employ common stock, while the optimists, or those less sensitive to risk, will favor bonds. This example, which is typical of many real-world situations, suggests that the major disagreements over the choice of forms of financing are likely to reflect uncertainty about the future levels of the firm's sales. The uncertainty in turn reflects the characteristics of the firm's environment—general business conditions, industry trends, and quality and aggressiveness of management.

The remainder of the chapter will discuss the key variables that influence judgments about the degree of financial leverage to employ. By getting into a consideration of more qualitative variables, we will have a more complete basis for arriving at decisions on the use of debt versus equity financing.

Factors Influencing Financial Structure

Thus far the discussion has only touched on the factors that are generally considered when a firm formulates basic policies relating to its financial structure. The more important of these financial structure determinants will now be treated. They are: (1) growth rate of future sales, (2) stability of future sales, (3) competitive structure of the industry, (4) asset structure of the firm, (5) control position and attitudes toward risk of owners and management, and (6) lenders' attitudes toward the firm and the industry.

Growth Rate of Sales

The future growth rate of sales is a measure of the extent to which the earnings per share of a firm are likely to be magnified by leverage. If sales and earnings grow at a rate of 8 to 10 percent a year, for example, financing by debt with limited fixed charges should magnify the returns to owners of the stock.[10] This can be seen from Figure 15.1.

However, the common stock of a firm whose sales and earnings are growing at a favorable rate commands a high price; thus it sometimes appears that equity financing is desirable. The firm must weigh the benefits of using leverage against the opportunity of broadening its equity base when it chooses between future financing alternatives. Such firms are expected to have a moderate to high level of debt financing.

Sales Stability

Sales stability and debt ratios are directly related. With greater stability in sales and earnings, a firm can incur the fixed charges of debt with less risk than when its sales and earnings are subject to periodic declines; in the latter instance it will

[9] Theory suggests that the decision should be based on stockholders' utility preferences. In practice, it is difficult to obtain such information as *data*, so decisions of this sort are generally based on the subjective judgment of the decision maker.

[10] Such a growth rate is also often associated with a high profit rate.

have difficulty meeting its obligations. The stability of the utility industry, combined with relatively favorable growth prospects, has resulted in high leverage ratios in that industry.

Competitive Structure

Debt-servicing ability is dependent on the profitability, as well as the volume, of sales. Hence, the stability of profit margins is as important as the stability of sales. The ease with which new firms can enter the industry and the ability of competing firms to expand capacity both influence profit margins. A growth industry promises higher profit margins, but such margins are likely to narrow if the industry is one in which the number of firms can be easily increased through additional entry. For example, the franchised fast-service food companies were a very profitable industry in the early 1960s, but it was relatively easy for new firms to enter this business and compete with the older firms. As the industry matured during the late 1960s and early 1970s, the capacity of the old and the new firms grew at an increased rate. As a consequence, profit margins declined.

Asset Structure

Asset structure influences the sources of financing in several ways. Firms with long-lived fixed assets, especially when demand for their output is relatively assured (for example, utilities), use long-term mortgage debt extensively. Firms that have their assets mostly in receivables and in inventory whose value is dependent on the continued profitability of the individual firm (for example, those in wholesale and retail trade) rely less on long-term debt financing and more on short-term financing.

Management Attitudes

The management attitudes that most directly influence the choice of financing are those concerning control of the enterprise and risk. Large corporations whose stock is widely owned may choose additional sales of common stock because such sales will have little influence on the control of the company.

In contrast, the owners of small firms may prefer to avoid issuing common stock in order to be assured of continued control. Because they generally have confidence in the prospects of their companies and because they can see the large potential gains to themselves resulting from leverage, managers of such firms are often willing to incur high debt ratios.

The converse can, of course, also hold; the owner-manager of a small firm may be *more* conservative than the manager of a large company. If the net worth of the small firm is, say, $1 million, and if it all belongs to the owner-manager, that individual may well decide that he or she is already prosperous enough and may elect not to risk using leverage in an effort to become still wealthier.

Lender Attitudes

Regardless of managements' analyses of the proper leverage factors for their firms, there is no question but that lenders' attitudes are frequently important—sometimes the most important—determinants of financial structures. In the majority of cases, the corporation discusses its financial structure with lenders and gives much weight to their advice. But when management is so confident of the future that it seeks to use leverage beyond norms for the industry, lenders may be unwilling to accept such debt increases. They emphasize that excessive debt reduces the credit standing of the borrower and the credit rating of the securities previously issued. The lenders' point of view has been expressed by a borrower (a financial vice president), who stated, "Our policy is to determine how much debt we can carry and still maintain an Aa bond rating, then use that amount less a small margin for safety."

Financial Structure in Practice

In this final section of the chapter, we shall indicate how the factors influencing the degree of financial leverage employed are reflected in actual practice among industries and firms. An overview of financial structures in a wide range of industries is set forth in Table 15.12. Financial structure is measured in the table by the ratio of common stockholders' equity to total capitalization, where total capitalization represents long-term financing. The ratio of shareholders' equity to total capitalization is used because some of the financing items that are not equity are not pure debt either—for example, preferred stock and deferred credits. Preferred stock usually has a limited, but not legally required, return and so is a method of leveraging common stock, but without risk of default. Deferred credits are mostly deferred tax obligations which pay no interest and generally increase in amount if a firm continues to grow and make investments in fixed assets.

The data in Table 15.12 show that, in general, manufacturing companies have lower leverage (a higher equity base) than do most utilities. Among the nonfinancials, air transport has the highest ratio of equity to total capitalization. Banking firms operate with a very low ratio of equity to total assets. For finance companies, the ratio of debt to equity is about 400 percent. (Equity to total assets = 0.2, so debt is 0.8 of total assets; debt to equity is 0.8/0.2, which equals 400 percent).

Within "All manufacturing", the amount of leverage employed depends upon how narrowly or broadly the industry is defined. Using the Federal Trade Com-

Table 15.12

Ratio of Common Stock Shareholders' Equity to Total Capitalization, All Manufacturing and Selected Utilities, 1978

	Percent
All manufacturing[a]	51.8
Electric utilities	37.2
Gas utilities	47.5
AT & T	44.4
Air transport	61.8
Railroads	34.6
Banking[a]	4.0
Savings & loans[a]	7.0
Finance companies[a]	20.0

[a] Ratio of equity to total assets.

Sources: *Industry Surveys* (New York: Standard & Poor's, 1979, 1980). Used by permission. Also Federal Trade Commission, *Quarterly Financial Reports* (Washington, D.C.: Government Printing Office, 1979).

mission's relatively broad classification of industries, we find that most industries fall within 4 to 5 percentage points of the all-manufacturing average. For the fourth quarter of 1979, when the all-manufacturing ratio of debt to total assets was 50 percent, the ratio for drugs and for instruments was about 40 percent. At the other end of the scale the total debt to total assets ratio for the aircraft and guided missiles industry was 66 percent. But with these three exceptions, most of the other industries were close to the all-manufacturing average.

However, when industries are defined more narrowly, as in the Dun & Bradstreet studies, much more variation is observed, as illustrated by Table 15.13,

Table 15.13

Ratio of Total Debt to Tangible Net Worth, Manufacturing, 1978

	Percent
Book publishing	50
Soap and other detergents	56
Mattresses and bedsprings	63
Malt liquors	65
Sawmills and planing mills	66
Sporting and athletic goods	69
Plumbing, heating, and air conditioning	76
Soft drinks: bottled and canned	76
Engineering and scientific instruments	77
Airplane parts and accessories	80
Paints and allied products	80
Concrete block and brick	80
Motor vehicle parts and accessories	80
Chemicals: alkalies and chlorine	85
Plastics materials and resins	90
Meat packing plants	90
Electric lamps	92
Office, computing, and accounting machines	93
Farm machinery and equipment	93
Metal stampings	93
Electric transformers	94
Work clothing: men's and boys'	95
Textile machinery	96
Grain mill products: flour	97
Suits and costs: men's and boys'	97
Agricultural chemicals, nitrogenous	105
Paperboard boxes: folding	107
Blast furnaces and steel mills	109
Dairy products: milk, fluid	110
Canned fruits and vegetables	111
Knit outerwear mills	112
Dresses: women's, misses', and juniors'	114
Paper mills, except building paper	118
Women's and misses' suits and coats	128
Petroleum refining	138
Household appliances	185

Source: "The Ratios," *Dun's Review*, October 1979. Reprinted by permission of Dun & Bradstreet.

which presents the ratio of total debt to tangible net worth for a sample of manufacturing industries in 1978. A wide range of debt to worth ratios is exhibited, the lowest being 50 percent for book publishing, and the highest 185 percent for household appliances. But within these wide variations many of the debt to tangible net worth ratios fall in the range of 90 to 100 percent. This corresponds to the 50 percent debt to total assets ratio for all manufacturing from the Federal Trade Commission data, which are equivalent to a debt to net worth ratio of 100 percent. Similarly, the Dun & Bradstreet data indicate that for most wholesaling industries the ratio of total debt to tangible net worth is in the 90 to 110 percent range. For retailing industries, the ratio is lower, falling mostly in the 50 to 70 percent range.

Leverage ratios vary among individual firms even more than among industries. In Table 15.14 the equity to total capitalization ratios for selected electric utility companies are presented. Even within this small sample a range of from 30 percent to over 40 percent is observed.

Table 15.14

Equity to Total Capitalization Ratios, Selected Electric Utility Companies, December 31, 1979

Company	Common stock and surplus to total capitalization (percent)
Central Illinois Public Service	32.4
Detroit Edison Company	31.4
Consolidated Edison of New Year	41.6
Montana Power Company	35.4
Dayton Power & Light	32.8
Middle South Utilities	30.0
American Electric Power	33.8

Source: *Moody's Handbook of Common Stocks* (New York: Moody's Investors Service, Spring 1981). Used by permission.

Among industrial companies, variations in leverage ratios are even wider. Table 15.15 presents the ratios of debt to total capitalization for the aerospace industry in 1978. Of course, the aerospace industry itself is highly diverse, encompassing airframe companies, general aviation firms, shipbuilding, propulsion, subcontractors, and diversified companies with some capabilities in electrical and electronics manufacturing. But even within a subgroup, one observes a range of debt to total capitalization as low as 3.7 percent for King Radio and as high as 79.9 percent for Aeronca Inc. Among the large airframe companies, debt-to-total-capitalization ratios near 5 percent are observed for Boeing and McDonnell Douglas. The ratio moves up toward 50 percent for Grumman and Lockheed, with Rockwell International in between. Thus, wide ranges in leverage ratios are observed among individual companies. The large differences in turn reflect a wide range of influences on financial leverage decisions. In the following chapters, we shall consider in greater depth the key influences (such as relative costs, risks, and control) in determining a basis for choosing between alternative forms and sources of financing.

Table 15.15 **Debt to Total Capitalization, Aerospace Industry, 1978**

Company	Percent
Diversified	
EG & G Inc.	14.8
Martin Marietta	13.3
Raytheon Co.	9.0
Signal Cos.	30.3
TRW Inc.	28.1
Teledyne Inc.	22.0
Subcontractors, Systems	
Aeronca Inc.	79.9
CCI Corp.	45.1
E-Systems	20.8
Fairchild Industries	16.5
Hazeltine Corp.	10.3
Heath Tecna Corp.	53.4
Hexcel Corp.	28.3
King Radio	3.7
Northrop Corp.	7.6
Pneumo Corp.	40.4
Rohr Industries	68.2
Sierracin Corp.	10.2
Simmonds Precision Prods.	25.9
TRE Corp.	17.6
VSI Corp.	10.6
Airframe	
Boeing Co.	5.3
Grumman Corp.	45.5
Lockheed Corp.	51.3
McDonnell Douglas	5.9
Rockwell Intl.	24.4
Propulsion, Engines	
Thiokol Corp.	9.1
United Technologies	28.9
General Aviation	
Bangor Punta	43.2
Cessna Aircraft	15.1
Gates Learjet	15.8
Shipbuilding	
Amer. Ship Building	31.1
General Dynamics	7.4
Todd Shipyards	69.3

Source: *Industry Surveys, Aerospace, Basic Analysis* (New York: Standard & Poor's, April 3, 1980), p. A35. Used by permission.

Summary

Financial leverage, which means using debt to boost rates of return on net worth over the returns on assets, is the primary topic covered in this chapter. Whenever the return on assets exceeds the cost of debt, leverage is favorable, and the return on equity is raised by using it. However, leverage is a two-edged sword, and if the returns on assets are less than the cost of debt, then leverage reduces the returns on equity. The more leverage a firm employs, the greater this reduction. As a result, leverage may be used to boost stockholder returns, but it is used at the risk of increasing losses if the firm's economic fortunes decline. Thus gains and losses are magnified by leverage; and the higher the leverage employed by a firm, the greater will be the volatility of its returns.

This chapter analyzed the effects of financial leverage by demonstrating the relationship between leverage and alternative risk measures. The alternative risk measures agree in demonstrating that with increased financial leverage the measure of risk increases as well. Using the security market line from the capital asset pricing model, a set of quantitative relationships between risk and required return can be illustrated. To the extent that the assumptions of the theory are valid and applicable, a basis is provided for measuring how beta increases with financial leverage. Then the required rate of return can be calculated using the SML. This could then be compared with the expected returns from the firm's activity or from an individual project. From this comparison can be developed a basis for a decision on how much financial leverage to utilize.

Using the coefficient of variation approach, we do not have a precise set of quantitative relationships between risk and required return. However, this measure of risk is consistent with the beta measure of risk in that both increase with increased financial leverage. The capital asset pricing model provides a precise set of relationships. The problem in applying the capital asset pricing model is that the parameters of the relationships may not be stable. In addition, the Roll critique argues that without a reliable market index the measure of beta itself may be subject to error. As in capital budgeting analysis, we recommend the calculation of alternative measures of risk. They are useful in providing a first-step basis for a quantitative analysis of a capital budgeting or financial structure decision. Ultimately, judgment will have to be exercised to arrive at a final decision.

In the following chapter the concepts developed to this point will be extended to the formal theory of the cost of capital. The way investors appraise the relative desirability of increased returns versus higher risks is seen to be a most important consideration—one that, in general, invalidates the theory that firms should strive for maximum earnings per share regardless of the risks involved.

Questions

15.1 How will each of the occurrences listed below affect a firm's financial structure, capital structure, and net worth?

a. The firm retains earnings of $100 during the year.
b. A preferred stock issue is refinanced with bonds.
c. Bonds are sold for cash.
d. The firm repurchases 10 percent of its outstanding common stock with excess cash.
e. An issue of convertible bonds is converted.

15.2 From an economic and social standpoint, is the use of financial leverage justifiable? Explain by listing some advantages and disadvantages.

15.3 Financial leverage and operating leverage are similar in one very important respect. What is this similarity, and why is it important?

15.4 How does the use of financial leverage affect the breakeven point?

15.5 Would you expect risk to increase proportionately, more than proportionately, or less than proportionately with added financial leverage? Explain.

15.6 What are some reasons for variations of debt ratios among the firms in a given industry?

15.7 Why is the following statement true? "Other things being the same, firms with relatively stable sales are able to incur relatively high debt ratios."

15.8 Why do public utility companies usually pursue a different financial policy from that of trade firms?

15.9 The use of financial ratios and industry averages in the financial planning and analysis of a firm should be approached with caution. Why?

Problems

15.1 The Corbin Company and the Hollister Company are identical except for their leverage ratios and the interest rate on debt. Each has $10 million in assets, each earned $2 million before interest and taxes in 1980, and each has a 40 percent corporate tax rate. Corbin, however, has a leverage ratio (B/TA) of 30 percent, and pays 10 percent interest on its debt, while Hollister has a 50 percent leverage ratio and pays 12 percent interest on debt.

a. Calculate the rate of return on equity (net income/equity) for each firm.

b. Observing that Hollister has a higher return on equity, Corbin's treasurer decides to raise the leverage ratio from 30 to 60 percent. This will increase Corbin's interest rate on debt to 15 percent. Calculate the new rate of return on equity for Corbin.

15.2 The Huston Company wishes to calculate next year's return on equity under different leverage ratios. Huston's total assets are $10 million, and its tax rate is 40 percent. The company is able to estimate next year's earnings for three possible states of the world. It estimates that 1981 earnings before interest and taxes will be $3 million with a 0.2 probability, $2 million with a 0.5 probability, and $500,000 with a 0.3 probability. Calculate Huston's expected return on equity, the standard deviation, and the coefficient of variation for each of the following leverage ratios:

Leverage (debt/total assets)	Interest rate
0%	—
10	10%
50	12
60	15

15.3 The beta for the Hanover Company is 0.8 if it employs no leverage, and its tax rate is 40 percent. The financial manager of Hanover uses the following expression to calculate the influence of leverage on beta:

$$\beta_j = \beta_u[1 + (B/S)(1 - T)]$$

a. Several alternative target leverage ratios are being considered. What will be the beta on the common stock of Hanover Company if the following alternative leverage ratios are employed—that is, $B/S = 0.4$? O.8? 1.0? 1.2? 1.6?
b. If the financial manager of Hanover uses the SML to estimate the required return on equity, what are the required rates of return on equity at each of the above leverage ratios? (The estimated risk-free return is 6 percent, and the market risk premium is 5 percent.)
c. The financial manager wants to keep the beta at 1.5 or below. What is the maximum leverage ratio which can be employed? What is the required rate of return on equity at this leverage ratio?

15.4 The Nordlund Company plans to raise a net amount of $240 million for new equipment financing and working capital. Two alternatives are being considered. Common stock may be sold to net $40 per share, or debentures yielding 10 percent may be issued. The balance sheet and income statement of the Nordlund Company prior to financing are given below:

The Nordlund Company Balance Sheet as of December 31, 1980 (Millions of Dollars)

Current assets	$ 800	Accounts payable	$ 150
Net fixed assets	400	Notes payable to bank	250
		Other current liabilities	200
		Total current liabilities	$ 600
		Long-term debt	250
		Common stock, $2 par	50
		Retained earnings	300
Total assets	$1,200	Total claims	$1,200

The Nordlund Company Income Statement for Year Ended December 31, 1980 (Millions of Dollars)

Sales	$2,200
Earnings before Interest and taxes (10%)	$ 220
Interest on debt	40
Earnings before taxes	$ 180
Tax (40%)	72
Net income after tax	$ 108

Annual sales are expected to be distributed according to the following probabilities:

Annual sales	Probability
$2,000	0.30
2,500	0.40
3,200	0.30

a. Assuming that earnings before interest and taxes remain at 10 percent of sales, calculate earnings per share under both the stock financing and the debt financing alternatives at each possible level of sales.
b. Calculate expected earnings per share under both debt and stock financing.

15.5 American Battery Corporation produces one product, a long-life rechargeable battery for use in small calculators. Last year 50,000 batteries were sold at $20 each. American Battery's income statement is shown below:

American Battery Corporation Income Statement for Year Ended December 31, 1981

Sales		$1,000,000
Less: variable costs	$400,000	
fixed costs	200,000	600,000
EBIT		$ 400,000
Less: interest		125,000
Net income before tax		$ 275,000
Less: income tax ($T = 0.40$)		$ 110,000
Net income		$ 165,000
EPS (100,000 shares)		$1.65

a. Calculate the following for American Battery's 1981 level of sales:
   1. the degree of operating leverage
   2. the degree of financial leverage
   3. the combined leverage effect

b. American Battery is considering changing to a new production process for manufacturing the batteries. Highly automated and capital intensive, the new process will double fixed costs to $400,000 but will decrease variable costs to $4 a unit. If the new equipment is financed with bonds, interest will increase by $70,000; if it is financed by common stock, total stock outstanding will increase by 20,000 shares. Assuming that sales remain constant, calculate for each financing method:
   1. earnings per share
   2. the combined leverage effect

c. Under what conditions would you expect American Battery to want to change its operations to the more automated process?

d. If sales are expected to increase, which alternative will have the greatest impact on EPS? Illustrate with an example.

15.6 You are given the following information about the Playmor Company which manufactures bowling balls:

Price	$35
Variable costs	$19 per unit
Fixed costs	$200,000
Debt (B)	$300,000
Interest rate	12%
T	40%

In 1981, Playmor's net income was $600,000.

a. How many bowling balls were sold in 1981?

b. Calculate the degrees of operating, financial and combined leverage for Playmor.

c. Suppose that Playmor restructures its balance sheet, increasing debt to $1 million. Prepare a pro forma income statement and calculate degree of the combined leverage assuming the same level of sales calculated in Part a.

15.7 The Hunter Corporation plans to expand assets by 50 percent. To finance the expansion, it is choosing between a straight 11 percent debt issue and common stock. Its current balance sheet and income statement are shown below:

Hunter Corporation Balance Sheet as of December 31, 1981

		Debt (at 8%)	$140,000
		Common stock, $10 par	350,000
		Retained earnings	210,000
Total assets	$700,000	Total claims	$700,000

Hunter Corporation Income Statement for Year Ended December 31, 1981

Sales	$2,100,000
Total costs (excluding interest)	1,881,600
Earnings before Interest and taxes	$ 218,400
Debt interest	11,200
Income before taxes	$ 207,200
Taxes (at 50%)	103,600
Net income	$ 103,600

Earnings per share: $\frac{\$103,600}{35,000} = \$2.96$

Price/earnings ratio: 10 ×[a]

Market price: 10 × $2.96 = $29.60

[a] The price/earnings ratio is the market price per share divided by earnings per share. It represents the amount of money an investor is willing to pay for $1 of current earnings. The higher the riskiness of a stock, the lower its P/E ratio, other things held constant.

If Hunter Corporation finances the $350,000 expansion with debt, the rate on the incremental debt will be 11 percent, and the price/earnings ratio of the common stock will be 8 times. If the expansion is financed by equity, the new stock can be sold at $25. The price/earnings ratio of all the outstanding common stock will remain at 10 times.

a. Assuming that earnings before interest and taxes (EBIT) is 10 percent of sales, what are the earnings per share at sales levels of $0; $700,000; $1,400,000; $2,100,000; $2,800,000; $3,500,000, and $4,200,000, when financing is with common stock? When financing is with debt? (Assume no fixed costs of production.)

b. Make a chart for EPS indicating the crossover point in sales (where EPS using bonds = EPS using stock).

c. Using the price/earnings ratio, calculate the market value per share of common stock for each sales level for both the debt and the equity financing.

d. Using data from Part c, make a chart of market value per share for the company indicating the crossover point.

e. Which form of financing should be used if the firm follows the policy of seeking to maximize

1. EPS?
2. market price per share?

f. Now assume that the following probability estimates of future sales have been made: 5 percent chance of $0, 7.5 percent chance of $700,000, 20 percent chance of $1,400,000, 35 percent chance of $2,100,000, 20 percent chance of $2,800,000, 7.5 percent chance of $3,500,000, and 5 percent chance of $4,200,000. Calculate expected values for EPS and market price per share under each financing alternative.
g. What other factors should be taken into account in choosing between the two forms of financing?
h. Would it matter if the presently outstanding stock was all owned by the final decision maker (the president) and that this represented his entire net worth? Would it matter if he was compensated entirely by a fixed salary? If he had a substantial number of stock options?

CHAPTER 16

THE COST OF CAPITAL

The cost of capital is a critically important topic for three reasons. First, as we saw in Chapters 13 and 14, capital budgeting decisions have a major impact on the firm, and proper capital budgeting requires an estimate of the cost of capital. Second, as we saw in Chapter 15, financial structure can affect both the size and the riskiness of the firm's earnings stream and hence the value of the firm. A knowledge of the cost of capital and how it is influenced by financial leverage is useful in making capital structure decisions. Finally, a number of other decisions—including those related to leasing, to bond refunding, and to working capital policy—require estimates of the cost of capital.[1]

This chapter first establishes that the cost of capital, calculated as a weighted average, is the rate of return which must be earned so that the value of the firm and the market price of its common stock do not decline. Second, it considers the cost of the individual components of the capital structure—debt, preferred stock, and equity. Because investors perceive different classes of securities as having different degrees of risk, there are variations in cost of the different types of securities. Third, it brings the individual component costs together to form a weighted cost of capital. Fourth, it illustrates the concepts developed in the earlier sections with an example of the cost of capital calculation for an actual company. Finally, it develops the interrelationship between the cost of capital and the investment opportunity schedule and discusses the simultaneous determination of the marginal cost of capital and the marginal return on investment.

Composite, or Overall, Cost of Capital

Suppose a particular firm's cost of debt is estimated to be 8 percent, its cost of equity 12 percent, and the decision has been made to finance next year's projects by selling debt. The argument is sometimes advanced that the cost of these projects is 8 percent because debt is being used to finance them. However, this position contains a basic fallacy. To finance a particular set of projects with debt implies that the firm is also using up some of its potential for obtaining new low-cost debt. As expansion occurs in subsequent years, the firm will find it necessary at some point to use additional equity financing to keep the debt ratio from becoming too large.

[1] The cost of capital is also vitally important in regulated industries, including electric, gas, telephone, and transportation. In essence, regulatory commissions seek to measure a utility's cost of capital, then set prices so the company will just earn this rate of return. If the estimate is too low, the company will not be able to attract sufficient capital to meet long-run demands for service, and the public will suffer. If the estimate is too high, customers will pay too much for service.

To illustrate: The firm in our example has an 8 percent cost of debt and a 12 percent cost of equity. In the first year it borrows heavily, using up its debt capacity in the process, to finance projects yielding 9 percent. In the second year it has projects available that yield 11 percent (well above the return on first-year projects), but it cannot accept them because they would have to be financed with 12 percent equity money. To avoid this problem, the firm should view itself as an ongoing concern, and its cost of capital should be calculated as a weighted average, or composite, of the various types of funds it uses: debt, preferred stock, and common equity.

Basic Definitions

Both students and financial managers are often confused about how to calculate and use the cost of capital. To a large extent, this confusion results from imprecise, ambiguous definitions; but a careful study of the following definitions will eliminate the confusion.

Capital (or financial) *components* are the items on the right-hand side of the balance sheet; they include various types of debt, preferred stock, and common equity. Any net increase in assets must be financed by an increase in one or more capital components.

Capital is a necessary factor of production; like any other factor, it has a cost. The cost of each component is defined as its *component cost.* For example, if a firm can borrow money at 8 percent, by definition, its component cost of debt is 8 percent.[2] This chapter will concentrate primarily on debt, preferred stock, retained earnings, and new issues of common stock. These are the capital structure components, and their component costs are identified by the following symbols:

k_b = Interest rate on firm's new debt = Component cost of debt, before tax

$k_b(1-T)$ = Component cost of debt, after tax, where T = Marginal tax rate; $k_b(1-T)$ = debt cost used to calculate the marginal cost of capital

k_{ps} = Component cost of preferred stock

k_r = Component cost of retained earnings (or internal equity)

k_e = Component cost of new issues of common stock (or external equity)

k_s = Required rate of return on common equity in general when no distinction is made between k_e and k_r, or when k_s represents a weighted average of incremental funds raised from retained earnings and from external equity

k = Weighted or composite cost of capital. If a firm raises new capital to finance asset expansion, and if it is to keep its capital structure in balance (that is, if it is to keep the same percentage of debt, preferred stock, and common equity funds), then it will raise part of new funds as debt, part as preferred stock, and part as common equity (with

[2] We will see later that there is an after-tax cost of debt; for now it is sufficient to know that 8 percent is the before-tax component cost of debt. (The effects of debt on the cost of equity will also be considered later.)

equity coming either from retained earnings or from the sale of new common stock).[3] Also, k is a marginal cost; it is the ratio of incremental financing costs to incremental funds raised per time period to finance an investment program.[4]

These definitions and concepts are explained in detail in the remainder of the chapter, which seeks to accomplish two goals: (1) to develop a marginal cost of capital schedule (k = MCC) that can be used in capital budgeting, and (2) to determine the mix of types of capital that will minimize the MCC schedule. If the firm finances so as to minimize its MCC, uses this MCC to calculate NPVs, and makes capital budgeting decisions on the basis of the NPV method, these actions will lead to a maximization of the prices of its securities.

Before-Tax Component Cost of Debt (k_b)

If a firm borrows $100,000 for one year at 10 percent interest, it must pay the investors who purchase the debt a total of $10,000 annual interest on their investment:

$$k_b = \text{Before-tax cost of debt} = \frac{\text{Interest}}{\text{Principal}} = \frac{\$10{,}000}{\$100{,}000} = 10\% \qquad \textbf{(16.1)}$$

For now, assume that the firm pays no corporate income tax (the effect of income taxes on the analysis of cost of capital is treated in a later section of the chapter). Under this assumption, the firm's dollar interest cost is $10,000, and its percentage cost of debt is 10 percent. As a first approximation, the component cost of debt is equal to the rate of return earned by investors, or the interest rate on debt. If the firm borrows and invests the borrowed funds to earn a return just equal to the interest rate, then the earnings available to common stock remain unchanged. This is demonstrated below.

Table 16.1 **Income Statement for the ABC Company**

	Before	After
Sales	$1,000,000	$1,014,000
Operating costs	900,000	904,000
Earnings before interest	$ 100,000	$ 110,000
Interest expense	—	10,000
Net income	$ 100,000	$ 100,000

The ABC Company has sales of $1 million, operating costs of $900,000, and no debt. Its income statement is shown in the Before column of Table 16.1. The firm borrows $100,000 at 10 percent and invests the funds in assets whose use causes

[3] Firms do try to keep their debt, preferred stock, and common equity in balance; they do not try to maintain any proportional relationship between the common stock and retained earnings accounts as shown on the balance sheet.

[4] The variable k also reflects the riskiness of the firm's various assets. If a firm uses risk-adjusted discount rates for different capital projects, the average of these rates weighted by the sizes of the various investments should equal k.

sales to rise by $14,000 and operating costs to rise by $4,000. Hence, profits before interest rise by $10,000. The new situation is shown in the After column. Earnings are unchanged, since the investment just earns its component cost of capital. Note that the cost of debt is the rate on new debt, not the rate on previously outstanding debt. In other words, we are interested in the cost of new debt, or the marginal cost of debt. The primary concern with the cost of capital is its use in a decision-making process—the decision whether to obtain capital to make new investments. Whether the firm borrowed at high or low rates in the past is irrelevant.[5]

Thus far we have used debt with a maturity of one year to focus on the basic concepts. But for multiple years, the yield to maturity is the basis for calculating the relevant cost of debt. As a practical matter, we could look in the financial section of a newspaper to obtain the coupon, maturity, and current price for a bond. For example, on February 5, 1980, Dow Chemical's 7.75% coupon bonds with a maturity date in 1999 closed at $72\frac{7}{8}$. The yield to maturity (with compounding semiannually) would be:

$$\$728.75 = \sum_{t=1}^{38} \frac{\$38.75}{(1+k_b)^t} + \frac{\$1{,}000}{(1+k_b)^{38}}$$

$$= \sum_{t=1}^{38} \frac{\$38.75}{(1.05615)^t} + \frac{\$1{,}000}{(1.05615)^{38}}$$

$$= \$603.55 + \$125.44$$

$$\$728.75 \cong \$728.99$$

The 5.615 percent was obtained by trial and error as the half-year interest rate that equates the present value of the coupons plus the maturity value to the current price of the bond. Thus the cost of nineteen-year maturity debt of Dow Chemical in early 1980 was 11.23 percent (that is, 5.615 percent times 2). An average of all long-term maturities would be the cost of long-term debt. Since Dow's long-term debt is rated mostly Aa quality, its cost of short-term debt would be based on the bank prime rate (at $15\frac{1}{4}$ percent on February 5, 1980) or the yield on four-month prime commercial paper (at 13.03 percent on February 1, 1980).

Preferred Stock

Preferred stock, described in detail in Chapter 21, is a hybrid between debt and common stock. Like debt, preferred stock carries a fixed commitment on the part of the corporation to make periodic payments; and in liquidation the claims of the preferred stockholders take precedence over those of the common stockholders. Failure to make the preferred dividend payments does not result in bankruptcy, however, as does nonpayment of interest on bonds. Thus, to the firm, preferred stock is somewhat riskier than common stock but less risky than bonds. Just the reverse holds for investors. To the investor, preferred is less risky than common but riskier than bonds. Thus an investor who is willing to buy the firm's bonds on

[5] Whether the firm borrowed at high or low rates in the past is, of course, important in terms of the effect of the interest charges on current profits, but it is not relevant for current decisions. For current financial decisions, only current interest rates are relevant.

the basis of a 10 percent interest return might, because of risk aversion, be unwilling to purchase the firm's preferred stock at a yield of less than 11 percent.[6] Assuming the preferred issue is a perpetuity that sells for $75 a share and pays an $8 annual dividend, its yield is calculated as follows:

$$\text{Preferred yield} = \frac{\text{Preferred dividend}}{\text{Price of preferred stock}} = \frac{d_{ps}}{p_{ps}} = \frac{\$8}{\$75} = 10.67\% \qquad \textbf{(16.2)}$$

Assuming the firm can sell additional preferred stock on the same yield basis, the cost of preferred is also 10.67 percent. In other words, as a first approximation, the component cost of preferred stock (k_{ps}) is equal to the return investors receive on the shares as calculated in Equation 16.2.

If the firm receives less than the market price of preferred stock when it sells new preferred, p_{ps} in the denominator of Equation 16.2 should be the net price received by the firm. Suppose, for example, the firm must incur a selling, or *flotation,* cost of $3 a share. In other words, buyers of the preferred issue pay $75 a share, but brokers charge a selling commission of $3 a share, so the firm nets $72 a share. The cost of new preferred to the firm is calculated in Equation 16.2a:

$$k_{ps} = \text{Cost of preferred} = \frac{d_{ps}}{p_{ps}} = \frac{\$8}{\$72} = 11.11\% \qquad \textbf{(16.2a)}$$

Using the net proceeds percentage, calculated by deducting the ratio of flotation costs to gross proceeds, the same result is obtained.

$$k_{ps} = \text{Cost of preferred} = \frac{\text{Preferred yield}}{(1 - \text{Flotation percentage})}$$

$$= \frac{10.67\%}{(1 - 0.04)} = 11.11\% \qquad \textbf{(16.2b)}$$

Most preferred stocks entitle their owners to regular, fixed dividend payments similar to bond interest. Although some preferred issues are eventually retired, most are perpetuities whose value is found as follows:

$$p_{ps} = \frac{d_{ps}}{k_{ps}}$$

In this case, d_{ps} is the dividend on the preferred stock, and k_{ps} is the appropriate capitalization rate for investments of this degree of risk. For example, General Motors has a preferred stock outstanding that pays a $3.75 annual dividend. The average annual yield on preferred stock in late 1946, when the stock was issued, was 3.79 percent. The GM preferred stock was a no par stock that sold at 100 to yield 3.75 percent at the issue date. The yield on a preferred stock is similar to that on a perpetual bond and is found by solving for k_{ps}. For the GM issue, the price of the stock for February 5, 1980, in newspaper market quotations was $37.25, and

[6] The 85 percent dividend credit makes preferred stock an attractive investment to other corporations, such as commercial banks and stock insurance companies. This pushes the yield down close to yields on bonds of similar companies.

its annual dividend is seen to be \$3.75. Thus the yield is 10.067 percent, calculated as follows:

$$k_{ps} = \frac{d_{ps}}{p_{ps}} = \frac{\$3.75}{\$37.25} = 10.067\%$$

Tax Adjustment

As they stand, the definitions of the *component costs of debt* and of *preferred stock* are incompatible when taxes are introduced into the analysis, because interest payments are a deductible expense, whereas preferred dividends are not. The following example illustrates the point.

The ABC Company can borrow \$100,000 at 10 percent, or it can sell 1,000 shares of \$10 preferred stock to net \$100 a share. Assuming a 46 percent tax rate, its before-investment situation is given in the Before column of Table 16.2. At what rate of return must the company invest the proceeds from the new financing to keep the earnings available to common shareholders from changing?

Table 16.2

Tax Adjustment for Cost of Debt

		Invest in assets yielding:		
	Before	10% Debt	10% Preferred	18.519% Preferred
Earnings before interest and taxes (EBIT)	\$100,000	\$110,000	\$110,000	\$118,519
Interest	—	−10,000	—	—
Earnings before taxes (EBT)	\$100,000	\$100,000	\$110,000	\$118,519
Taxes (at 46%) (T)	−46,000	−46,000	−50,600	−54,519
Preferred dividends	—	—	−10,000	−10,000
Available for common dividends	\$ 54,000	\$ 54,000	\$ 49,400	\$ 54,000

As can be seen from the tabulations in Table 16.2, if the funds are invested to yield 10 percent before taxes, earnings available to common stockholders are constant if debt is used, but they decline if the financing is with preferred stock. To maintain the \$54,000 net earnings requires that funds generated from the sale of preferred stock be invested to yield 18.519 percent before taxes or 10 percent after taxes.[7]

Since stockholders are concerned with after-tax rather than before-tax earnings, only the cost of capital *after* corporate taxes should be used. The cost of preferred stock is already on an after-tax basis as defined, but a simple adjustment is needed to arrive at the after-tax cost of debt. It is recognized that interest payments are tax deductible. In effect, the federal government pays part of a firm's interest charges. Therefore, the cost of debt capital is calculated as follows:

$$k_b(1 - T) = \text{After-tax cost of debt}$$
$$= \text{Before-tax cost} \times (1.0 - \text{Tax rate}) \quad \textbf{(16.3)}$$

Whenever the weighted cost of capital (k) is calculated, $k_b(1 - T)$—not k_b—is used.

[7] The 18.519 percent is found as follows: 10%/(1 − Tax rate) = 10%/0.54.

Example Before-tax cost of debt = 10 percent; tax rate = 46 percent; $k_b(1 - T)$ = after-tax cost = (0.10)(1 − 0.46) = (0.10)(0.54) = 5.40 percent.

Estimating the Rate of Return on a Stock

Let us now begin by calculating the rate of return you can expect if you purchase a stock at the current market price per share. To illustrate: The current price (p_0) of United Rubber Company common stock is $20. The stock is expected to pay a dividend (d_1) of $2 per share. Earnings, dividend and stock price are expected to grow at a rate (g) of 5 percent per year. The expected rate of return, defined as $\bar{k}_s$, is analogous to the internal rate of return on a capital project: $\bar{k}_s$ is the discount rate that equates the present value of the expected dividends, d_1, and the final stock price, p_1, to the present stock price, p_0:

$$p_0 = \frac{d_1 + p_1}{(1 + \bar{k}_s)} = \frac{d_1 + p_0(1 + g)}{(1 + \bar{k}_s)}$$

If United Rubber is selling for $20 per share, you can calculate $\bar{k}_s$ as follows:

$$\$20 = \frac{\$2 + \$20(1.05)}{(1 + \bar{k}_s)} = \frac{\$2 + \$21}{(1 + \bar{k}_s)}$$

$$\$20(1 + \bar{k}_s) = \$23$$

$$1 + k_s = 1.15$$

$$\bar{k}_s = 0.15 \text{ or } 15\%$$

Thus, if you expect to receive a $2 dividend and a year-end price of $21, your expected rate of return on the investment is 15 percent.

Notice that the expected rate of return, $\bar{k}_s$, consists of two components, an expected dividend yield and an expected capital gains yield:

$$\bar{k}_s = \frac{\text{Expected dividend}}{\text{Present price}} + \frac{\text{Expected increase in price}}{\text{Present price}}$$

$$= \frac{d_1}{p_0} + g \tag{16.7}$$

For United Rubber bought at a price of $20:

$$\bar{k}_s = \frac{\$2}{\$20} + \frac{\$1}{\$20} = 10\% + 5\% = 15\%$$

Given an expected rate of return of 15 percent, should you make the purchase? This depends on how the expected return compares with the required return. If $\bar{k}_s$ exceeds k_s^*, buy; if $\bar{k}_s$ is less than k_s^*, sell; and if $\bar{k}_s$ equals k_s^*, the stock price is in equilibrium and you should be indifferent.[8] Throughout the remainder of this book, we will assume that security markets are in equilibrium, with $k^* = \bar{k}$. Hence we shall generally use k (with the appropriate subscript) for the required return or

[8] Notice the similarity between this process and the IRR method of capital budgeting. The expected rate of return, $\bar{k}_s$, corresponds to the IRR on a project, and the required rate of return, k_s^*, corresponds to the cost-of-capital cutoff rate used in capital budgeting.

applicable discount rate unless we are directly contrasting the required return, k^*, with the expected return, k.

Cost of Retained Earnings (k_r)

The cost of preferred stock is based on the return that investors require if they are to purchase the preferred stock; the cost of debt is based on the interest rate investors require on debt issues, adjusted for taxes. The cost of equity obtained by retained earnings can be defined similarly.[9] It is k_r, the rate of return stockholders require on the firm's common stock. Why? The answer is that if the funds are invested at a lesser rate, the market price of the firm's stock will decline. In equilibrium, the expected and required rates of return must be equal, and the cost of retained earnings is the same as the rate of return on common equity. Substituting k_r for k_s in Equation 16.4, we obtain the required rate of return on common equity financed from retained earnings:

$$k_r = \frac{d_1}{p_0} + \text{Expected } g \tag{16.4a}$$

To illustrate, we return to the United Rubber (UR) example, a firm expected to earn \$3 a share and to pay a \$2 dividend during the coming year. The company's earnings, dividends, and stock price have all been growing at about 5 percent a year, and this growth rate is expected to continue indefinitely. The stock is in equilibrium and currently sells for \$20 a share. Using this information, the required rate of return on the stock in equilibrium can be computed using Equation 16.4a.

$$k_r = \frac{\$2}{\$20} + 5\% = 15\%$$

The expected growth rate for the price of the shares is 5 percent, which, on the \$20 initial price, should lead to a \$1 increase in the value of the stock, to \$21. Barring changes in the general level of stock prices, this price increase will be attained if UR invests the \$1 of retained earnings to yield 15 percent. However, if the \$1 is invested to yield only 10 percent, then earnings will grow by only 10 cents a share during the year, not by the expected 15 cents a share. The new earnings will be \$3.10, a growth of only 3.33 percent, rather than the expected \$3.15, or 5 percent increase. If investors believe that the firm will earn only 10 percent on retained earnings in the future and attain only a 3.33 percent growth rate, they will reappraise the value of the stock downward. Hence, UR will suffer a price decline if it invests equity funds—retained earnings—at less than its component cost of capital.

If UR refrains from making new investments and pays all its earnings in dividends, it will cut its growth rate to zero. However, the price of the stock will not

[9] The term *retained earnings* can be interpreted to mean the balance sheet item "retained earnings," consisting of all the earnings retained in the business throughout its history; or it can mean the income statement item "additions to retained earnings." The latter definition is used in this chapter. For our purpose, *retained earnings* refers to that part of current earnings not paid out in dividends but retained and reinvested in the business.

fall because investors will still get the required 15 percent rate of return on their shares:

$$k_r = \frac{d_1}{p_0} + g = \frac{\$3}{\$20} + 0 = 15\%,$$

All the return would come in the form of dividends, but the actual rate of return would match the required 15 percent.

This example demonstrates a fundamentally important fact. If a firm earns its required rate of return, k_r, then when it retains earnings and invests them in its operations, its current stock price will not change as a result of this financing and investment. However, if it earns less than k_r, the stock price will fall; and if it earns more, the stock price will rise.

Cost of New Common Stock, or External Equity Capital (k_e)

The cost of new common stock, or *external* equity capital, k_e, is higher than the cost of retained earnings, k_r, because of flotation costs involved in selling new common stock. What rate of return must be earned on funds raised by selling stock to make the action worthwhile? To put it another way, what is the cost of new common stock? The answer is found by applying the following formula:[10]

$$k_e = \frac{d_1}{p_0(1-f)} + g = \frac{d_1}{p_n} + g \tag{16.5}$$

$$= \frac{\text{Dividend yield}}{1 - \text{Flotation percentage}} + \text{Growth}$$

[10] The equation is derived as follows:

Step 1. The old stockholders expect the firm to pay a stream of dividends, d_t; this income stream is derived from existing assets. New investors likewise expect to receive the same stream of dividends, d_t. For new investors to obtain this stream without impairing that of the old investors, the new funds obtained from the sale of stock must be invested at a return high enough to provide a dividend stream whose present value is equal to the price the firm receives:

$$p_n = \sum_{t=1}^{\infty} \frac{d_t}{(1+k_e)^t} \tag{16.5a}$$

where:
p_n = Net price to the firm
d_t = Dividend stream to new stockholders
k_e = Cost of new outside equity

Step 2. If flotation costs are expressed as a percentage, f, of the gross price of the stock, p_0, we can express p_n as follows:

$$p_n = p_0(1-f)$$

Step 3. When growth is a constant, Equation 16.5a reduces to

$$p_n = p_0(1-f) = \frac{d_1}{k_e - g} \tag{16.5b}$$

Step 4. Equation 16.5b can be solved for k_e:

$$k_e = \frac{d_1}{p_0(1-f)} + g \tag{16.5}$$

Here f is the percentage cost of selling the issue, so $p_0(1 - f) = p_n$ is the net price received by the firm. For example, if p_0 is \$10 and f is 10 percent, then the firm receives \$9 for each new share sold; hence p_n is \$9. (Equations 16.4 and 16.5 are strictly applicable only if future growth is expected to be constant.)

For United Rubber, the cost of new outside equity is computed as follows:

$$k_e = \frac{\$2}{\$20(1 - 0.10)} + 5\% = 16.11\%$$

Investors require a return of $k_r = 15$ percent on UR's stock. However, because of flotation costs, UR must earn more than 15 percent on external stock-financed investments to provide this 15 percent. Specifically, if UR earns 16.11 percent on investments financed by new common stock issues, then earnings per share will not fall below previously expected earnings, the expected dividend can be maintained, the growth rate for earnings and dividends will be maintained, and (as a result of all this) the price per share will not decline. If UR earns less than 16.11 percent, then earnings, dividends, and growth will fall below expectations, causing the price of the stock to decline. Since the cost of equity capital is defined as the rate of return that must be earned to prevent the price of the stock from falling, we see that the company's cost of external equity, k_e, is 16.11 percent.[11]

Finding the Basic Required Rate of Return on Common Equity

The basic rate of return investors require on a firm's common equity, k_s, is a key quantity. This required rate of return is the cost of retained earnings, and it forms the basis for the cost of capital obtained from new stock issues. How is it estimated?

Our previous analysis suggests emphasis on two methods: the Security Market Line (SML) and the use of the Dividend Growth Model.

Using the SML, we would start with the basic relation:

$$k_s^* = R_F + (\bar{R}_M - R_F)\beta_j$$

$(\bar{R}_M - R_F)$ is the market risk premium, which has averaged about 5 percent. R_F is the risk-free rate measured by yields on government securities. The required return on equity is the risk-free return to which is added a risk adjustment factor. The risk adjustment factor is the market risk premium modified by a measure of the riskiness of the firm's common equity. If a firm's beta is greater than 1.0, the risk adjustment factor will be greater than the market risk premium.

In measuring R_F some argue for the use of short-term government securities. The purpose is to have numbers that are relatively free of interest rate risk and purchasing power risk. Others argue for the use of intermediate-term government securities (10 to 15 years), since the resulting cost of equity measures are used in decisions over a similar time horizon.

[11] The cost of external equity is sometimes defined as:

$$k_e = \frac{k_r}{1 - f}$$

This equation is correct if the firm's expected growth rate is zero (see Equation 16.5). In other cases it tends to overstate k_e.

A strength of this approach is that the market risk premium can be considered relatively stable at 5 to 6 percent for practical application. The risk-free rate can also be determined on a relatively objective basis. A weakness of the SML approach is that the reliability of the beta estimates has been questioned.[12] Richard Roll argues that because the total world market portfolio has not been identified and used in CAPM measurements, the resulting beta estimates may be subject to error. However, beta estimates are available from a number of financial research organizations and they can be used in a judgmental way as a guide to estimates of the cost of equity capital.

The second approach uses the dividend valuation model solved for the cost of common equity:

$$k_s^* = \frac{d_1}{p_0} + \text{Expected } g$$

Stockholder returns are derived from dividends and capital gains, and the total of the dividend yield plus the average growth rate over the past five to ten years can give an estimate of the total returns that stockholders expect in the future from a particular share of stock. For "normal" companies in "normal" times, past growth rates can be projected into the future, and the second method will give satisfactory results. However, if the company's growth has been abnormally high or low, either because of its own unique situation or because of general economic conditions, then investors will not project the past growth rate into the future, so Method 2 will not yield a good estimate of k_s^*. In this case, g must be estimated in some other manner. Security analysts regularly make earnings growth forecasts, looking at such factors as projected sales, profit margins, and competitive factors. Someone making a cost of capital estimate can obtain such analysts' forecasts and use them as proxy for the growth expectations of investors in general. Based on our own experience in estimating equity capital costs, we recognize that both careful analysis and very fine judgments are required in this process. It would be nice to pretend that these judgments are unnecessary and to specify an easy, precise way of determining the exact cost of equity capital. Unfortunately, this is not possible. Finance is in large part a matter of judgment, and we simply must face this fact.

The Effects of Leverage—the MM Propositions

Under a number of assumptions, Franco Modigliani and M. H. Miller (MM) have formulated some relationships between the cost of capital and capital structure.[13] The key assumptions are homemade leverage and no bankruptcy costs. *Homemade leverage* implies that personal and corporate leverage are perfect substitutes and

[12] R. W. Roll, "A Critique of the Asset Pricing Theory's Tests," *Journal of Financial Economics* 4 (March 1977), pp. 129–76. For a discussion of the issues, see the debate between Roll and Barr Rosenberg in Anise Wallace, "Is Beta Dead?", *Institutional Investor* XIV (July 1980), pp. 23–30.

[13] See F. Modigliani and M. H. Miller, "The Cost of Capital, Corporation Finance and the Theory of Investment," *American Economic Review* 48 (June 1958), pp. 261–97; and "The Cost of Capital, Corporation Finance and the Theory of Investment: Reply," *American Economic Review* 49 (September 1958), pp. 655–69; "Taxes and the Cost of Capital: A Correction" *American Economic Review* 53 (June 1963), pp. 433–43; and "Reply," *American Economic Review* 55 (June 1965), pp. 524–27.

that individuals can offset corporate leverage by personal leverage to eliminate any advantages (except corporate tax effects) of corporate leverage by arbitrage transactions. With no bankruptcy costs, firms can be formed, go bankrupt and be liquidated, be formed again, and so on, with very small transactions costs. Hence by diversification, investors can eliminate unsystematic risk, so that required returns will reflect only the systematic risk measured by covariance or the beta of the individual asset. A number of MM propositions then follow.

Proposition I states that the cost of capital of an unlevered firm is the after-tax net operating income divided by the value of the unlevered firm:

$$k_u = \frac{\bar{X}(1 - T)}{V_u} \tag{I}$$

It can also be shown that in the MM world, the following relationships hold:

$$V_L = V_u + TB \text{ and } S = V_L - B,$$

where B is the market value of the firm's debt. It follows then, that the weighted cost of capital for a levered firm would be:

$$k = \frac{\bar{X}(1 - T)}{V_L} \tag{Ia}$$

This is the same as Proposition I, except that the denominator is the value of the leveraged firm and the result is the weighted cost of capital. Proposition II, which can be derived from the foregoing, provides a measure of the cost of equity capital:

$$k_s = k_u + (k_u - k_b)(1 - T)(B/S) \tag{II}$$

Proposition II states that the cost of equity rises with leverage in a linear fashion, with the slope of the line equal to $(k_u - k_b)(1 - T)$, as shown in Figure 16.1.

Figure 16.1 **Cost of Equity Capital as a Function of Leverage**

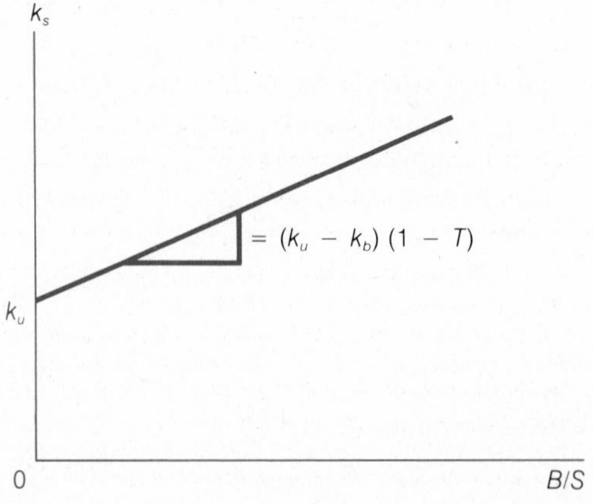

Finally, it can also be demonstrated that three formulations for measuring the weighted cost of capital give the same results. These are:

1. $k = k_b(1 - T)(B/V) + k_s(S/V)$

2. $k = \dfrac{\bar{X}(1 - T)}{V}$

3. $k = k_u(1 - TL)$ where $L = B/V$

(Note: From this point on, V is understood to be V_L, and the value of an unlevered firm will be designated V_u.) We can give content to these relationships by an illustrative example. We consider two alternative capital structures for the Stevens Company:

Stevens Company Balance Sheet, Unlevered

Total assets $1,000,000	Stockholders' equity $1,000,000

Stevens Company Balance Sheet, Levered

Total assets $1,000,000	Debt at 10%	$ 500,000
	Stockholders' equity	500,000
	Total claims	$1,000,000

The applicable corporate tax rate is 40 percent. The income statements for Stevens would reflect the two different capital structures.

Stevens Company Income Statements	Unlevered	Levered
Net operating income (X)	$200,000	$200,000
Interest on debt ($k_b B$)	—	50,000
Income before taxes ($X - k_b B$)	$200,000	$150,000
Taxes at 40% $T(X - k_b B)$	80,000	60,000
Net income ($X - k_b B$)(1 − T)	$120,000	$ 90,000

With the above accounting information, which represents data generally available in financial reports and financial manuals, we can apply the MM propositions. For an unlevered firm of similar characteristics to Stevens, we obtain a measure of the cost of capital for an unlevered firm, k_u, which we will assume to be 12 percent. All other relationships can now be computed.

Stevens' value as an unlevered firm would be:

$$V_u = \frac{\bar{X}(1 - T)}{k_u} = \frac{(\$200{,}000)0.6}{0.12} = \$1{,}000{,}000$$

We find that without leverage, the market value of Stevens is equal to the book value of its total assets. Next, consider Stevens as a levered firm. Its new value becomes:

$$V_L = V_u + TB = \$1{,}000{,}000 + 0.4(\$500{,}000) = \$1{,}200{,}000$$

Now the market value of Stevens exceeds the book value of its total assets. The market value of the equity, S, is:

$$S = V_L - B = \$1{,}200{,}000 - \$500{,}000 = \$700{,}000$$

The cost of equity capital of Stevens, unlevered, is equal to k_u, or 12 percent. As a levered firm, the cost of equity capital for Stevens can be calculated by two relationships:

$$k_s = k_u + (k_u - k_b)(1 - T)B/S \text{ or } k_s = \text{NI}/S$$

The first formulation is MM's Proposition II. The second is a conventional accounting relationship. We illustrate both:

$$\begin{aligned} k_s &= 0.12 + (0.12 - 0.10)(0.6)(5/7) \qquad & k_s &= \$90{,}000/\$700{,}000 \\ &= 0.12 + 0.0086 & k^s &= 12.86\% \\ &= 12.86\% \end{aligned}$$

The SML formulation of the cost of equity capital is:

$$k_s = R_F + (\bar{R}_M - R_F)\beta_u[1 + (B/S)(1 - T)]$$

(Recall from Chapter 15 that $\beta_u[1 + (B/S)(1 - T)] = \beta_L$.) For the Stevens example, let

$$R_F = 0.10,\ \bar{R}_M = 0.115, \text{ and } \beta_u = 1.333$$

We then have:

$$k_s = 0.10 + (0.115 - 0.10)1.333[1 + (5/7)(0.6)] = 0.1286 = 12.86\%$$

With leverage, the cost of equity capital has risen from 12 percent to 12.86 percent. What happens to the weighted cost of capital? We can employ all three formulations:

1. $k = k_b(1 - T)(B/V) + k_s(S/V)$ $\qquad k = 0.10(0.6)(5/12) + 0.128571(7/12)$
   $= 0.025 + 0.075 = 10\%$
2. $k = \dfrac{\bar{X}(1 - T)}{V_L}$ $\qquad k = \dfrac{\$120{,}000}{\$1{,}200{,}000} = 10\%$
3. $k = k_u(1 - TL)$ $\qquad k = 0.12[1 - 0.4(5/12)] = 0.12(5/6)$
   $= 10\%$

Each formulation gives a weighted cost of capital of 10 percent. The example illustrates that the use of leverage has increased the value of the firm from \$1,000,000 to \$1,200,000. The weighted cost of capital has been reduced from 12 percent to 10 percent. Thus under the MM propositions, the influence of the tax subsidy on debt is to increase the value of the firm and decrease its weighted cost of capital.

We believe that these kinds of results are applicable to the real world for companies like Kellogg and IBM, which until recent years had virtually no debt in their capital structures. With the relatively small fraction of total assets now represented by debt, this is still relatively non-risky debt. For the amount of debt financing that they have employed to date, the effects predicted by the MM propositions could be expected to hold. But when companies have leverage ratios with debt of one-half or more of total market value, the possibilities of bankruptcy costs are likely to result in some increase in the cost of debt and a rise in the cost of equity that is not linear but curved upward—increasing at an increasing rate as leverage is perceived to add to risks of bankruptcy costs and losses.

The Nature of Bankruptcy Costs

Bankruptcy costs take several forms. The most obvious are the legal, accounting, and other administrative costs associated with financial readjustments and legal proceedings. In addition to these direct costs, some costs of bankruptcy arise before the actual legal procedures of bankruptcy take place. As the operating performance of the firm deteriorates in relation to its fixed contractual obligations, or as the amount of debt increases in relation to the firm's equity for a given level of operating performance, the financial markets may become increasingly reluctant to provide additional financing. A number of costs arise as a result of increased evidence of financial inadequacy or failure on the part of the firm. These costs, in order of seriousness, include the following:

1. Financing under increasingly onerous terms, conditions, and rates, representing increased costs
2. Loss of key employees. If the firm's prospects are unfavorable, able employees and executives will seek alternative employment.
3. Loss of suppliers of the most salable types of goods. The suppliers may fear that they will not be paid or that the customer will not achieve sales growth in the future.
4. Loss of sales due to lack of confidence on the part of customers that the firm will be around to stand behind the product
5. Lack of financing under any terms, conditions, and rates to carry out favorable but risky investments because the overall prospects of the firm are not favorable in relation to its existing obligations
6. Need to liquidate fixed assets to meet working capital requirements (forced reduction in the scale of operations)
7. Formal bankruptcy proceedings, with the incurrence of legal and administrative costs. In addition, a receiver will be appointed to conduct the firm's operations, and this may involve a disruption of operations.

It is therefore clear that when indirect as well as direct bankruptcy costs are taken into account, they may be substantial. The costs of building up new organizations after old ones have been broken up represent substantial transactions costs in the creation and destruction of organizations.

Thus, we believe that the MM world applies for moderate amounts of leverage. However, we shall indicate how increased leverage is likely to cause departures from the MM relations. We present a further basis for this view in the following section.

Effects of Risky Leverage with Bankruptcy Costs

Effect of Leverage on the Cost of Equity

In Chapter 15, we used the Universal Machine Company case to demonstrate that for any given degree of business risk, the higher the debt ratio, the larger the measures of variability in earnings per share and return on equity. The higher the level of debt, the higher the fixed charges and the higher the probability of not being able to cover them. The inability to meet fixed charges may trigger a number of penalty clauses in the debt indentures (agreements) and lead to reorganization or bankruptcy (see Chapter 25), with attendant costs of attorneys and court proceedings. Even before such legal difficulties, the increasing risk of financial difficulties may result in the loss of key employees (who find positions with firms whose financial outlook is safer), in the reduced availability of goods from key suppliers, and in reduced financing.

Substantial bankruptcy costs will cause the relationship between leverage and the related risks of equity and debt to become curvilinear upward, thereby increasing the required returns on equity and debt. The required rate of return on equity is equal to the riskless rate plus a risk premium.

$$k_s = R_F + (\bar{R}_M - R_F)\beta_j = R_F + \rho \quad \textbf{(16.6)}$$

To separate the effects of operating and financial leverage, rho (ρ) can be divided into two components, ρ_1 and ρ_2. These components behave differently under the assumption of small bankruptcy costs versus large bankruptcy costs. Assuming that bankruptcy costs are small, we have the following relationships:

$$k_s = R_F + \rho_1 + \rho_2 = R_F + (\bar{R}_M - R_F)\beta_u + (\bar{R}_M - R_F)\beta_u(B/S)(1 - T) \quad \textbf{(16.7)}$$

Assuming no bankruptcy costs, ρ_1 is the premium for business risk. It is the beta for an unlevered firm, β_u, multiplied by the market risk premium $(\bar{R}_M - R_F)$. The value of ρ_1 depends on the nature of the firm's industry, its degree of operating leverage, etc. The variable ρ_2 represents the premium necessary to compensate stockholders for the increased risk caused by financial leverage. It is equal to ρ_1 multiplied by $B/S(1 - T)$. Therefore, if there are no bankruptcy costs, the required

Figure 16.2 **Illustrative Relationship Between the Cost of Equity and Financial Leverage**

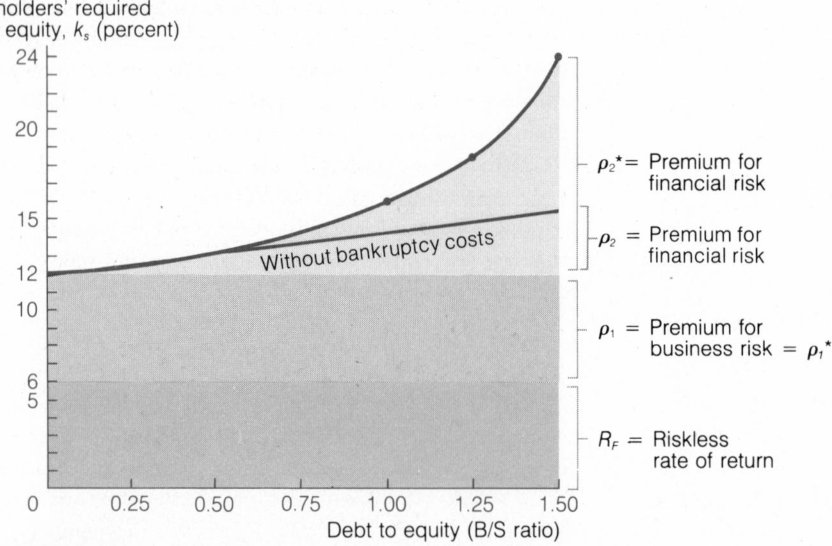

Note: The asterisk indicates that bankruptcy costs are substantial.

rate of return on equity increases linearly as the debt-equity ratio rises, as shown in Figure 16.2. The expression ρ_1 is simply the beta of an unlevered firm multiplied by the market risk premium, and ρ_2 is ρ_1 multiplied by B/S, as measured in Chapter 15, times $(1 - T)$.

With bankruptcy costs, however, the indexes of financial risk are likely to increase at an increasing rate when leverage passes some critical point and become curvilinear upward, as graphed in Figure 16.2. The required rate of return on equity is 12 percent if the company uses no debt, but k_s increases after debt passes some critical level and is 24 percent if the debt to value ratio is as high as 60 percent.[14] With leverage beyond 60 percent, it is likely that the required cost of equity is so high that the funds for all practical purposes are not available.

Effect of Leverage on the Component Cost of Debt

The component cost of debt is also affected by leverage. The higher the leverage ratio, the higher the cost of debt. Further, the cost of debt can be expected to rise at an increasing rate with leverage. To see why this is so, we can again consider the Universal Machine Company example. The more debt the firm has, the higher the interest costs; and the higher the interest charges, the greater the probability that earnings (EBIT) will not be sufficient to meet these charges. Creditors will perceive this increasing risk as the debt ratio rises, and they will begin charging a higher risk premium above the riskless rate, causing the firm's interest rate to rise. (Since creditors are risk averters and are assumed to have a diminishing marginal utility for money, they will demand that interest rates be increased to compensate for the increased risk.)

One other effect that may operate to raise interest rates at an increasing rate is the fact that a firm may need to use a variety of sources in order to borrow large amounts of funds in relation to its equity base. For example, a firm may be able to borrow from banks only up to some limit set by bank policy or bank examiner regulations. In order to increase its borrowings, the firm will have to seek other institutions, such as insurance companies and finance companies, that may demand higher interest rates than those charged by banks. Such an effect may tend to cause interest rates to jump whenever the firm is forced to find new lenders.

Table 16.3 shows the estimated relationships among leverage, the interest rate, and the after-tax cost of debt for Universal Machine Company. Assuming a 50 percent tax rate, the after-tax cost of debt is half the interest rate; these figures are also shown in Figure 16.3, where they are plotted against the debt ratio. In the example, Universal's cost of debt is constant until the debt to assets ratio passes 20 percent or \$2 million; then it begins to climb.

[14] This corresponds to a debt to equity ratio of 150 percent. In this example we assume that the risk-return tradeoff function has been estimated, perhaps in a subjective manner, by the financial manager. The precise specification of such risk-return functions is one of the more controversial areas of finance, and having attempted to measure them empirically ourselves, we can attest to the difficulties involved. However, even though the precise shape of the function is open to question, it is generally agreed (1) that the curve is upward sloping and (2) that some estimate, be it better or worse, is necessary if we are to obtain a cost of capital for use in capital budgeting. In this chapter our main concern is that the broad concepts be grasped.

Table 16.3

Effect of Leverage on the Cost of Debt for Universal Machine Company

Leverage (debt/assets)	Interest rate (k_b)	After-tax cost of debt $k_b(1-T)$
0%	10.0%	5.0%
10	10.0	5.0
20	10.0	5.0
30	10.8	5.4
35	11.0	5.5
40	12.0	6.0
50	16.0	8.0
60	27.0	13.5

Figure 16.3

After-Tax Cost of Debt for Universal Machine Company

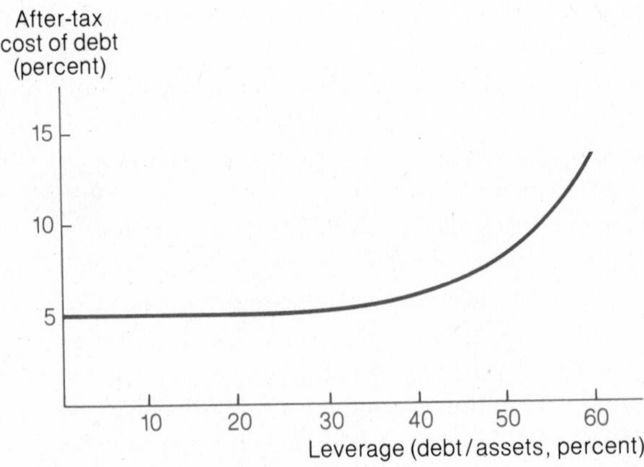

Combining Debt and Equity: Weighted Average, or Composite, Cost of Capital

Debt and equity can be combined to determine Universal Machine's average, or composite, cost of capital; Table 16.4 shows the calculations used to determine the weighted average cost. We shall assume conditions under which the cost of equity rises curvilinearly with leverage and the cost of debt is not constant. The average cost, together with the component cost of debt and equity, is plotted against the debt ratio at market value in Figure 16.4. Here the composite cost of capital is minimized when its debt ratio is approximately 35 percent, so Universal's optimal capital structure calls for about 35 percent debt and 65 percent equity.

Note that the average cost of capital curve is relatively flat over a fairly broad range. If Universal Machine's debt ratio is in the range of 20 to 40 percent, the average cost of capital cannot be lowered very much by moving to the optimal point. This appears to be a fairly typical situation, since almost any "reasonable" schedule for the component costs of debt and equity will produce a saucer-shaped average cost of capital schedule similar to that shown in Figure 16.4. This gives

Table 16.4

Calculation of Points on Average Cost of Capital Curve (Percent), or the Composite Cost of Capital for Different Capital Structures for Universal Machine Company

	Percent of total (1)	Component costs (2)	Weighted, or composite, cost: $k = (1) \times (2) \div 100$ (3)[a]
Debt	0%	5.00%	0.0%
Equity	100	12.00	12.0
	100		12.0
Debt	10	5.00	0.5
Equity	90	12.30	11.1
	100		11.6
Debt	20	5.00	1.0
Equity	80	12.75	10.2
	100		11.2
Debt	30	5.40	1.6
Equity	70	13.29	9.3
	100		10.9
Debt	35	5.50	1.9
Equity	65	13.50	8.8
	100		10.7
Debt	40	6.00	2.4
Equity	60	15.00	9.0
	100		11.4
Debt	50	8.00	4.0
Equity	50	18.00	9.0
	100		13.0
Debt	60	13.50	8.1
Equity	40	24.00	9.6
	100		17.7

[a] We divide by 100 to obtain percentages; figures are rounded to the nearest tenth.

financial managers a large degree of flexibility in planning their financing programs, permitting them to sell debt one year and equity the next in order to take advantage of capital market conditions and to avoid high flotation costs associated with small security issues.

Table 16.4 and Figure 16.4 are based on the assumption that the firm is planning to raise a given amount of new capital during the year. For a larger or smaller amount of new capital, some other cost figures may be applicable; the optimal capital structure may call for a different debt ratio, and the minimum average cost of capital (k) may be higher or lower.

Since interest on debt is deductible for tax purposes, the use of debt provides a tax shelter for some of the firm's cash flows. Hence the value of a firm increases with increases in debt if the only influence operating is the tax shelter effect of

Figure 16.4 **Cost of Capital Curves for Universal Machine Company**

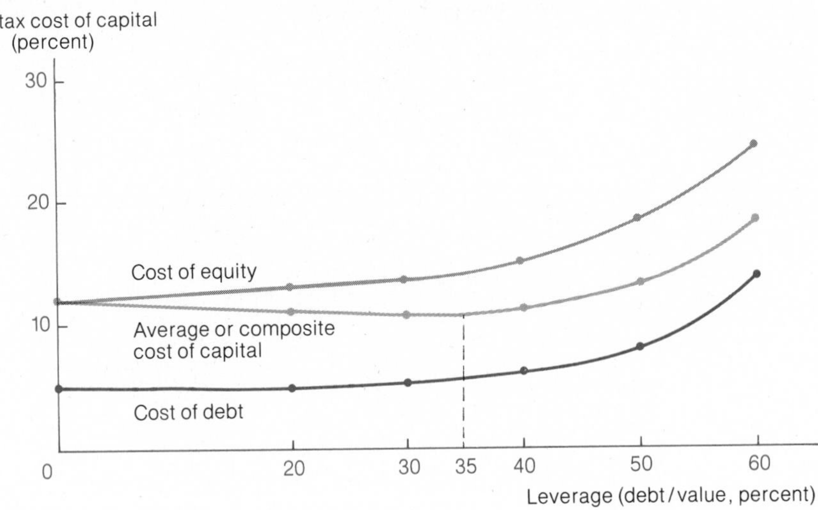

increased debt. But risks of rising bankruptcy costs will cause the value of a firm to fall at some level of increased leverage.

The existence of both tax shelter benefits of corporate debt and increased risks of rising bankruptcy costs with increased leverage will cause the value of the firm to behave as depicted in Figure 16.5. As the amount of debt in the financial structure increases, the present value of tax savings will initially cause the market value of the firm to rise. (The slope of the line will be equal to the corporate tax rate.) However, at some point, bankruptcy costs will cause the market value of the firm to be less than what it would have been if the only influence were corporate income taxes (Point B in Figure 16.5). Possible bankruptcy costs may become so large that the indicated market value of the firm actually begins to turn down (Point C in Figure 16.5.). This point represents the target leverage ratio at which the market value of the firm is maximized—the optimal financial structure.

We emphasize an important distinction in the circumstances postulated for the analysis. In one analysis, we hold the total amount of capital or of financing constant, changing only the mix of financing. We seek the optimal or target debt (leverage) ratio at which the (weighted) average cost of capital is at a minimum. This is the leverage ratio which maximizes the value of the firm. In a second framework for analysis, discussed in Chapter 15, we focus on related investment decisions, determining the size of the total capital budget in relation to the levels of the (weighted) marginal cost of capital. In this second context, the value of the firm is maximized when the size of the total capital budget is determined by the level of investment at which the marginal returns from investment are equal to the marginal cost of funds. After discussing the use of book versus market values, we shall discuss the measurement of the cost of capital in a specific case that illustrates the

Figure 16.5 **Influence of Debt on Market Value of the Firm**

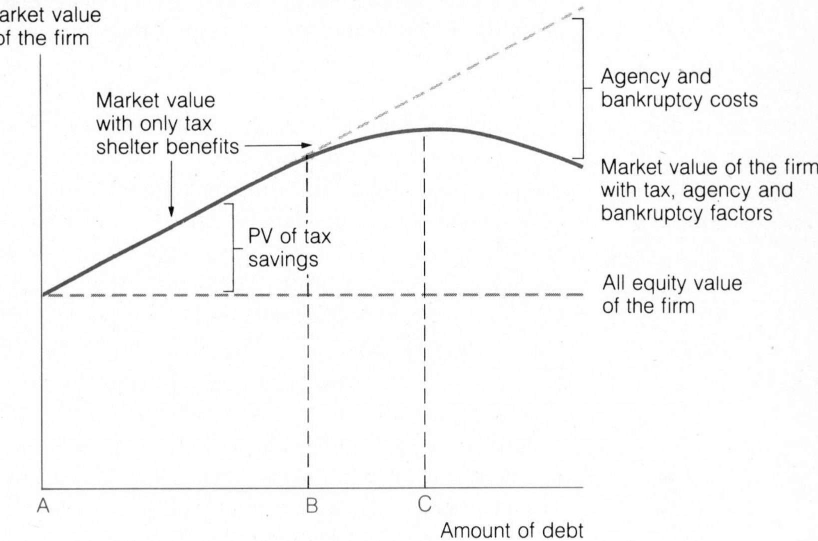

distinctions and appropriate applications of the concepts of the average cost of capital and the marginal cost of capital.

Book Rates and Market Weights

The correct principles to apply are now summarized. The basic issues are whether to use the actual historical financing costs of the firm and whether to use book or market values in calculating the proportions or weights of each source of financing. Financing costs must represent current opportunity costs, so the actual historical financing costs (reflected in the books) are not relevant. By the same reasoning, an average of past costs or an estimate of average expected future costs does not provide a correct measure of the current opportunity costs of funds.

With regard to weights or proportions of each source of financing, theory calls for the use of equilibrium market values. However, current market values may not be equilibrium values, so we do not necessarily apply the market values that we observe at a particular time. We should use those proportions or weights that represent the debt capacity of the firm appropriate for use in formulating the firm's target leverage proportions. A wide range of factors would have to be taken into consideration by the management of a firm in formulating its target leverage ratio. (Finance theory does not provide a precise theory for specifying a target leverage ratio.)

The future prospects of the firm represent an important factor to take into account—as well as the extent to which the future performance of the firm is subject to variability. These and other factors are reflected in the market value of the firm's equity shares and in the ratio of the market value of equity to its book value. In the example that follows we shall emphasize this principle: When the market to book ratio is greater than 1, the firm's prospects are viewed as relatively favorable, and a higher target leverage ratio is appropriate. When the market to book ratio is less than 1, the target leverage ratio will be relatively lower.

Calculating the Marginal Cost of Capital for an Actual Company

The concepts and procedures discussed above can be tied together by applying them to an actual company—the Continental Container Company. Continental Container is a large firm with assets of $950 million and sales of $1.5 billion in 1979. The analysis was made in late 1979 for use in planning for 1980 and for the three-year period 1980–1982. Dividends have been paid since 1923, even during the depression of the 1930s. On the basis of an indicated dividend rate of $2 and a current price of $20.00 a share, the dividend yield at the time of analysis is 10 percent.[15] Over the past ten years, earnings, dividends, and the price of the stock have grown at an annual rate of about 5 percent; all indications are that the same rate of growth will be maintained in the foreseeable future.[16] Since internally generated funds provide sufficient equity, only the costs of internal equity (found in this case to be the 10 percent dividend yield plus the 5 percent growth rate, or a total of 15 percent) need be considered.

The average interest rate on Continental Container's outstanding debt is 7.5 percent, but much of this debt was issued in earlier years, when interest rates were much lower than they are now. Current market yields (in the second half of 1979) on both long-term and short-term debt are about 11 percent, and approximately this rate will be associated with new debt issues. After a 46 percent income tax, the cost of debt is estimated to be 5.94 percent. The cost of preferred stock is stated to be 6.75 percent, but it was also issued when rates were low. On the basis of current market yields, the estimated cost of new preferred stock is 11 percent.

The right-hand side of Continental Container's balance sheet is given in Table 16.5. A large portion (24 percent) of the firm's funds are "free" in the sense that no interest is charged for them; accounts payable and accruals are in this class. Some argue that "free" capital should be included in the calculation of the overall cost of capital. Under certain circumstances this procedure is valid; usually, however, only "nonfree" capital need be considered.[17] Of this remaining capital

[15] Dividend yields on other companies at about the same time were: Ford Motor Company, 12%; Portland General Electric, 13%; Continental Group, 8.1%; American Can, 8.5%; and Safeway, 7.4%.

[16] Earnings per share for 1968 were $2.25, while EPS for 1978 were $3.65. Dividing $3.65 by $2.25 gives 1.62, which is the CVIF for ten years at 5 percent from Table A.1 at the end of the text. Thus EPS grew at a 5 percent rate over the ten-year period from 1968 through 1978. Dividends grew similarly, and security analysts are projecting a continuation of these rates.

[17] The primary justification for ignoring "free" capital is that in the capital budgeting process these spontaneously generated funds are netted out against the required investment outlay, then ignored in the cost of capital calculation. To illustrate: consider a retail firm thinking of opening a new store. According to customary practice, the firm should (1) estimate the required outlay, (2) estimate the net receipts (additions to profits) from the new store, (3) discount the estimated receipts at the cost of capital, and (4) accept the decision to open the new store only if the net present value of the expected revenue stream exceeds the investment outlay. The estimated accruals, trade payables, and other costless forms of credit are deducted from the investment to determine the "required outlay" before making the calculation. Alternatively, "free" capital could be costed in, and working capital associated with specific projects could be added in when determining the investment outlay. In most instances, the two procedures will result in similar decisions.

Table 16.5

Continental Container Company Right-Hand Side of Balance Sheet (Millions of Dollars)

	Amount	Percent	Nonfree funds only	
Payables and accruals	$186	19.6%		
Tax accruals	44	4.6		
Total "free" current funds	$230	24.2%		
Interest-bearing debt	$238	25.0%	$238	33.1%
Preferred stock	14	1.5	14	1.9
Common equity	468	49.3	468	65.0
Nonfree funds	$720	75.8%	$720	100.0%
Total financing	$950	100.0%		

structure, 33 percent is debt, 2 percent is preferred stock, and 65 percent is common equity. The financing proportions at market value have also been calculated. In connection with FASB Statement No. 33 requirements (discussed in Appendix A to Chapter 5), Continental has estimated the current value of its debt. In addition, market values of its preferred stock and common stock are readily available. The resulting proportions at market value were calculated as shown in Table 16.6. The current value of debt is 80 percent of its book value because interest rates have risen substantially above the average coupon rates on its debt. The even larger rise in preferred stock yields resulted in a market value of preferred at half the book value. Because of the moderate growth rate that Continental has experienced, the ratio of the market value of its stock to its book value is 0.9 to 1. At an earlier period, the ratio was 1.3 to 1, so the impact of that ratio is shown as the #2 percentages.

A member of the finance committee at Continental argued that a lower ratio of market value of equity to book value should support a lower leverage ratio and

Table 16.6

Continental Container Company Financing Proportions at Two Market/Book Ratios

	Market value of equity less than book #1 Market value		Market value of equity greater than book #2 Market value	
	Amount	Percent	Amount	Percent
Interest-bearing debt	$190	31%	$190	24%
Preferred stock	7	1	7	1
Common equity	421	68	608	75
	$618	100%	$805	100%

#1 Debt = 0.8 book debt
Preferred stock = 0.5 book preferred
Common equity = 0.9 book equity
#2 Common equity = 1.3 book equity

Table 16.7

Target Capital Structure Proportions Related to Market/Book Ratios

	#1 Target proportions	#2 Target proportions
Interest-bearing debt	29%	39%
Preferred stock	1	1
Common equity	70	60

a higher ratio would call for a higher target leverage ratio. His reasoning was that a market to book ratio of more than one for equity reflected profitable investment performance and opportunities. A low ratio of market to book reflected unfavorable investment opportunities. He argued further that from practical considerations, a firm whose market to book value of equity is 1.3 will be able to borrow more than a firm whose book value of equity is the same size, but whose market to book ratio is below 1. The market to book ratio is an index of the past and potential performance of the firm. These general performance capabilities of the firm should be reflected in its debt capacity and therefore the capital structure target formulated. Accordingly, he proposed that target capital structure proportions follow the pattern set forth in Table 16.7. He proposed that when the market value of equity was below book value, the target leverage ratio measured by market values should be lower. This reflected the greater risk attached to a firm whose performance resulted in a ratio of the market value of equity to book value of less than

Table 16.8

Calculation of the Weighted Cost of Capital with Different Leverage Targets

	Proportion (1)	Component cost (2)	Product: (1) × (2) (3)
Part A			
Actual book			
Interest-bearing debt	0.33	5.94%	1.96%
Preferred stock	0.02	11.00	0.22
Common equity	0.65	15.00	9.75
			$k = 11.93\%$
Part B			
Market equity to book above 1			
Interest-bearing debt	0.39	5.94%	2.32%
Preferred stock	0.01	11.00	0.11
Common equity	0.60	15.00	9.00
			$k = 11.43\%$
Part C			
Market equity to book below 1			
Interest-bearing debt	0.29	5.94%	1.72%
Preferred stock	0.01	11.00	0.11
Common equity	0.70	15.00	10.50
			$k = 12.33\%$

The financing mix was varied, but the total amount of capital raised was not. Since a marginal cost is the increment in cost as the total amount of financing is increased, varying the financing mix while holding the total amount of financing constant means that the relevant cost of capital is the weighted average cost of capital (WACC). We can say either that no marginal cost of capital is involved or that the marginal cost of capital is equal to the WACC (symbolized by k).

In the present analysis, Figure 16.6 portrays the effects of increasing the total amount of new financing while holding the financing mix fixed at the target proportions. Over the flat segment of the MCC curve, the average cost of capital is equal to the marginal cost of capital. When the marginal cost of capital begins to rise, the curve that is an average cost in relation to the MCC lies below the MCC. (If nine people who are all six feet tall come into a room in sequence, the average and marginal height will be 6 feet. If the tenth person entering is 7 feet tall, the marginal height will be 7 feet, but the average height will be 6.1 feet.) We exhibit only the MCC in Figure 16.6 because we are analyzing the determination of the total capital budget for a firm; hence the MCC is relevant as the investment hurdle rate. But recall that we are holding the financing mix at its optimal proportions, so the MCC for each amount of new financing is also the WACC for the optimal mix of financing that minimizes the level of the MCC curve. For these reasons, we again use k as the symbol for the cost of capital along the MCC curve.

Combining the MCC and the Investment Opportunity Schedules

Having developed the firm's MCC schedule and planned its financing mix so as to minimize the schedule, the financial manager's next task is to utilize the MCC in the capital budgeting process. How is this done? First, suppose that the k value in the flat part of the MCC schedule is used as the discount rate for calculating the NPV and that the total cost of all projects with NPV > 0 is less than the dollar amount at which the MCC schedule turns up. In this case, the value of k that was used is the correct one. For example, if Continental Container uses 12.33 percent as its cost of capital and finds that the acceptable projects total $45.7 million or less, then 12.33 percent is the appropriate cost of capital for capital budgeting.[19]

But suppose the acceptable projects total more than $45.7 million with a 12.33 percent discount rate. What do we do now? The most efficient procedure is given below.

Step 1 Calculate and plot the MCC schedule as shown in Figure 16.6.

Step 2 Ask the operating personnel to estimate the dollar volume of acceptable projects at a range of discount rates, say 17 percent, 16 percent, 15 percent, 14 percent, 13 percent, and 12 percent. There will thus be an estimate of the capital budget at a series of k values. For Continental Container, these values were estimated as follows:

Capital budget (in millions)	$30	$40	$50	$60	$70	$80
k	17%	16%	15%	14%	13%	12%

[19] We are, of course, not considering project risk; here we assume that the average riskiness of all projects undertaken is equal to the average riskiness of the firm's existing plant. Some projects may be riskier than average and therefore call for a risk-adjusted cost of capital greater than 12.33 percent, while others may be less risky than average and call for a cost of capital less than 12.33 percent.

Figure 16.7 **Interfacing the MCC and IRR Curves to Determine the Total Capital Budget for a Given Time Period**

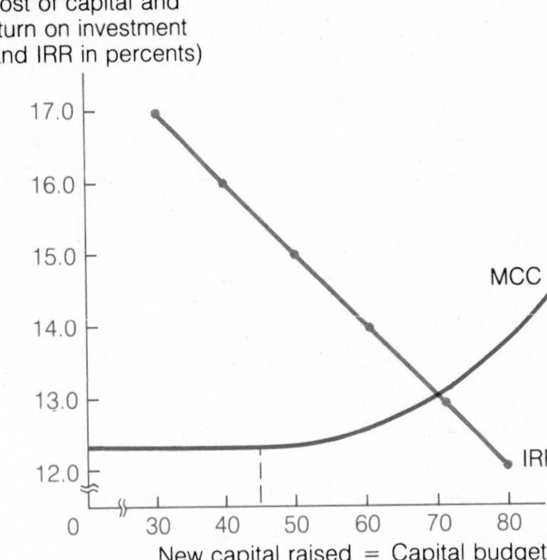

Step 3 Plot the capital budget points (k) as determined in Step 2 on the same graph as the MCC; this plot is labeled IRR in Figure 16.7.[20]

Step 4 The correct MCC for use in capital budgeting—assuming both the MCC and IRR curves are developed correctly—is the value at the intersection of the two curves, 13.2 percent. If this value of k is used to calculate NPVs, then projects totaling $68 million will have NPVs greater than zero. This is the capital budget that will maximize the value of the firm.

Dynamic Considerations

Conditions change over time; and when they do, the firm must make adjustments. First, the firm's individual situation may change. For example, as it grows and matures, its business risk may decline; this may in turn lead to an optimal capital structure that includes more debt. Second, capital market conditions may undergo a pronounced long-run change, making either debt or equity relatively favorable. This too may lead to a new optimal capital structure. Third, even though the long-run optimal structure remains unchanged, temporary shifts in the capital markets may

[20] To see why the capital budget line, k, is a type of IRR curve, consider the following:

1. The NPV of a project is zero if the project's IRR is equal to k.
2. If no projects have NPV ≥ 0 at $k = 15\%$, then no projects have IRR $\geq 15\%$.
3. If $20 million of projects have NPV ≥ 0 at $k = 14\%$, then these projects all have $14\% < \text{IRR} < 15\%$.
4. If the projects are completely divisible and if we examine very small changes in k, then we will have a continuous IRR curve. As it is, the curve labeled IRR in Figure 16.7 is an approximation. But the example does illustrate how an IRR curve can be developed even though a company uses the NPV capital budgeting method.

suggest that the firm use either debt or equity, departing somewhat from the optimal capital structure, then adjust back to the long-run optimum in subsequent years. Fourth, the supply and demand for funds varies from time to time, causing shifts in the cost of both debt and equity and, of course, in the marginal cost of capital. Because the financial markets have fluctuated so widely in recent years, it is necessary for firms to periodically reexamine their cost of capital.

Marketability and Rates of Return

So far, whenever we have discussed the required rate of return on securities, we have concentrated on two factors—the riskless rate of interest and the risk inherent in the security in question. However, we should note that investors also value flexibility, or maneuverability. An investor who becomes disenchanted with a particular investment or who needs funds for consumption or other investments finds it highly desirable to be able to liquidate current holdings. Other things being equal, the higher the liquidity, or marketability, the lower the investment's required rate of return. Accordingly, we expect to find listed stocks selling on a lower yield basis than over-the-counter stocks and widely traded stocks selling at lower yields than stocks with no established market. Since investments in small firms are generally less liquid than those in large companies, we have a reason for expecting to find higher required returns among smaller companies.

Large Firms versus Small Firms

Other significant differences in capital costs exist between large and small firms. These differences are especially pronounced for privately owned small firms. The same concepts are involved, and the methods of calculating the average and marginal cost of capital are similar; but some points of difference arise:

1. It may be difficult to obtain reliable estimates of equity capital costs for small, privately owned firms.
2. Tax considerations are generally quite important for privately owned companies, since owner-managers may be in the top personal tax brackets. This factor can cause the effective after-tax cost of retained earnings to be considerably lower than the after-tax cost of new outside equity.
3. Flotation costs for new security issues, especially new stock issues, are higher for small than for large firms (see Chapter 19).

Points 2 and 3 cause the marginal cost curves for small firms to rise rapidly once retained earnings are exhausted. However, when the new issue market is strong, the securities of small, new companies can be sold under very favorable conditions. Some dramatic recent examples can be cited. The prospectus of Genentech (dated October 14, 1980) shows that its EPS for 1979 was 2 cents per share. The offering price for raising $35 million was $35 per share. This represents a P/E ratio of 1,750 times. On its offering date the common stock rose to a high of $89, but thereafter began to decline toward the offering price. The pricing of Apple Computer was more "conservative." Its December 12, 1980, prospectus, offering common stock to the public at $22 per share to raise slightly over $100 million, shows an EPS for the year ending September 26, 1980, of 24 cents per share. The offering price represented a P/E ratio of 92 times. If the expected growth rate in earnings is high, the implied cost of capital could be high as well. But if the actual growth rate in earnings is smaller than expected, the return realized (the cost of capital actually paid by the company) by investors in small firms could be quite low.

Summary

The required rate of return on any security, k_j^*, is the minimum rate of return necessary to induce investors to buy or to hold the security; it is a function of the riskless rate of interest and the investment's risk characteristics:

$$\bar{k}_j^* = R_F + \rho_j = R_F + (\bar{R}_M - R_F)\beta_j$$

When graphed, this equation is called the security market line (SML). Because investors generally dislike risk, the required rate of return is higher on riskier securities. As a class, bonds are less risky than preferred stocks; and preferred stocks, in turn, are less risky than common stocks. The result is that the required rate of return is lowest for bonds, higher for preferred stocks, and highest for common stocks. Within each of these security classes, there are variations among the issuing firms' risks; hence, required rates of return vary among firms.

The *cost of debt*, $k_b(1 - T)$, is defined as the required yield to maturity on new increments of debt capital multiplied by (1 − Tax rate). The *preferred stock cost* to the company is the effective yield and is found as the annual preferred dividend divided by the net price the company receives when it sells new preferred stock. In equation form:

$$\text{Cost of preferred stock} = k_{ps} = \frac{\text{Preferred dividend}}{\text{Net price of preferred}}$$

The *cost of common equity* is defined as the minimum rate of return that must be earned on equity-financed investments to keep the value of the existing common equity unchanged. This required rate of return is the rate of return that investors expect to receive on the company's common stock—the dividend yield plus the capital gains yield. Sometimes, we assume that investors expect to receive about the same rates of return in the future that they have received in the past; in this case, we can estimate the required rate of return on the basis of actual historical returns.

Equity capital comes from two sources—retained earnings and the sale of new issues of common stock. The basic required rate of return (k_r) is used for the cost of retained earnings. However, new stock has a higher cost because of flotation costs associated with the sale of stock. The cost of new common stock issues is computed as follows:

$$\text{Cost of new stock} = k_e = \frac{\text{Dividend yield}}{1 - \text{Flotation percentage}} + \text{Growth}$$

New common stock is therefore more expensive than retained earnings.

If a firm has a high leverage ratio, increasing the proportion of debt will make the debt riskier because it increases the probability of bankruptcy. If bankruptcy costs are substantial, the value of the firm will rise, reach a peak, and then fall. The maximum point on this curve indicates a target debt ratio.

The first step in calculating the weighted average cost of capital, *k*, is to determine the cost of the individual capital components. The next step is to establish the proper set of weights to be used in the averaging process. The optimal capital structure varies from industry to industry, with more stable industries having optimal capital structures that call for the use of more debt than unstable industries. The market to book relation of a firm's common equity may also influence the target leverage ratio.

The *marginal cost of capital schedule,* defined as the cost of incremental funds raised during a period of time, is of interest for two reasons. First, the firm should finance in a manner that minimizes the MCC schedule; therefore, it must measure the MCC. Second, the MCC is the rate that should be used in the capital budgeting process. The firm should take on new capital projects only if the net present values are positive when evaluated at the marginal cost of capital.

The marginal cost of capital is constant over a range, then begins to rise. The rise is probably gradual rather than abrupt because firms make small adjustments in their target debt ratios, begin to use an assortment of securities, retain more of their earnings, and so on, as they reach the limit of internally generated equity funds.

Questions

16.1 Suppose that basic business risks to all firms in any given industry are similar.

a. Would you expect all firms in each industry to have approximately the same cost of capital?

b. How would the averages differ among industries?

16.2 Why are internally generated retained earnings less expensive than equity raised by selling stock?

16.3 Prior to the 1930s the corporate income tax was not very important, since the rates were fairly low. Also prior to the 1930s, preferred stock was much more important than it has been since that period. Is there a relationship between the rise of corporate income taxes and the decline in importance of preferred stock?

16.4 Describe how each of the following situations will affect the cost of capital to corporations in general.

a. The federal government solves the problem of business cycles (that is, cyclical stability is increased).

b. The Federal Reserve Board takes action to lower interest rates.

c. The cost of floating new stock issues rises.

16.5 The firm's covariance is 0.014, the risk-free rate is 10 percent, the market risk premium ($\bar{R}_M - R_F$) is 5 percent, and the variance of the market returns is 1 percent.

a. With no bankruptcy costs, what is the cost of capital, *k*, for an unlevered firm?

b. What is the beta of the firm?

16.6 Assume that the information in Question 16.5 is all on an after-tax basis, that the corporate tax rate is 50 percent, and that the firm has a debt to equity ratio of 50 percent, with a debt cost of 10 percent.

a. What is the new beta of the firm?
b. What is its return on equity?
c. What is the cost of capital for the levered firm?

16.7 An unlevered firm has a beta of 0.8. How much leverage can it employ if its corporate tax rate is 50 percent and it aims to have a beta of 1.2?

16.8 The formula $k_r = (d_1/p_0) + g$, where d_1 = expected current dividend, p_0 = the current price of a stock, and g = the past rate of growth in dividends, is sometimes used to estimate k_r, the cost of equity capital. Explain the implications of the formula.

16.9 What factors operate to cause the cost of debt to increase with financial leverage?

16.10 Explain the relationship between the required rate of return on common equity (k_s^*) and the debt ratio.

16.11 How will the various component costs of capital and the average cost of capital be likely to change if a firm expands its operations into a new, riskier industry?

16.12 The stock of XYZ Company is currently selling at its low for the year, but management feels that the stock price is only temporarily depressed because of investor pessimism. The firm's capital budget this year is so large that it is contemplating the use of new outside equity. However, management does not want to sell new stock at the current low price and is therefore considering a temporary departure from its "optimal" capital structure by borrowing the funds it would otherwise have raised in the equity markets. Does this seem to be a wise move? Explain.

16.13 Explain the following statement: The marginal cost of capital is an average in some sense.

Problems

16.1 The earnings, dividends, and stock price of the Abbott Company are expected to grow at 9 percent per year. Abbott's common stock sells for $30 per share, and the company will pay a year-end dividend of $2.40 per share. What is its cost of retained earnings?

16.2 The Crothers Company has a beta of 1.5. It has no debt in its capital structure.
a. The expected market rate of return is 14 percent and the risk-free rate is 6 percent. What is the cost of equity capital for Crothers?
b. Should Crothers accept a project that earns a rate of return of 15 percent and has a beta of 0.9?

16.3 The Graham Company's financing plans for next year include the sale of long-term bonds with a 9 percent coupon. The company believes it can sell the bonds at a price that will give a yield to maturity of 10 percent. If the tax rate is 40 percent, what is Graham's after-tax cost of debt?

16.4 The Brandon Company plans to issue 20-year bonds which have a 10 percent coupon, a par value of $1,000, and can be sold for $920. Interest is paid semiannually. Brandon's tax rate is 40 percent.
a. What is the after-tax cost of this debt to Brandon?
b. What would be the after-tax cost if this were a perpetual bond issue?

16.5 Infinity Industries has just issued some $100 par preferred stock with a 10 percent dividend. The stock is selling on the market for $96.17, and Infinity must pay flotation costs of 6 percent of the market price. What is the cost of the preferred stock for Infinity?

16.6 The Iversen Company earns $5 per share. The expected year-end dividend is $1.60, and price per share is $40. Iversen's earnings, dividends, and stock price have been growing at 8 percent per year, and this growth rate is expected to continue indefinitely. New common stock can be sold to net $38. What is Iversen's cost of retained earnings?

16.7 The Longwell Company is expected to pay a year-end dividend of $4.40. Longwell earns $7.70 per share, and its stock sells at $55 per share. Stock price, earnings, and dividends are expected to grow 6 percent per year indefinitely.

a. Calculate the stockholders' rate of return.
b. If the firm has a zero growth rate and pays out all its earnings as dividends, what is the stockholder's rate of return?

16.8 The Riley Company has $200 million in total net assets at the end of 1981. It plans to increase its production machinery in 1982 by $50 million. Bond financing, at an 11 percent rate, will sell at par. Preferred will have an 11.5 percent dividend payment and will be sold at a par value of $100. Common stock currently sells for $50 per share and can be sold to net $45 after flotation costs. There is $10 million of internal funding available from retained earnings. Over the past few years, dividend yield has been 6 percent and the firm's growth rate 8 percent. The tax rate is 40 percent. The present capital structure shown below is considered optimal:

Debt: 4% coupon bonds	$40,000,000	
7% coupon bonds	40,000,000	$ 80,000,000
Preferred stock		20,000,000
Common stock ($10 par)	$40,000,000	
Retained earnings	60,000,000	
Equity		100,000,000
		$200,000,000

a. How much of the $50 million must be financed by equity capital if the present capital structure is to be maintained?
b. How much of the equity funding must come from the sale of new common stock?
c. Calculate the component cost of:
   1. new debt
   2. new preferred stock
   3. retained earnings
   4. new equity
d. What is Riley's average cost of equity for 1982?
e. What would be Riley's weighted average cost of capital if only retained earnings were used to finance additional growth—that is, if only $20 million were raised?
f. What is the weighted average cost of capital when $50 million is raised?

g. What is the weighted average cost of capital on the $30 million raised over the $20 million?

16.9 The Tanner Company's cost of equity is 18 percent. Tanner's before-tax cost of debt is 12 percent, and its tax rate is 40 percent. Using the following balance sheet, calculate Tanner's after-tax weighted average cost of capital:

Assets		**Liabilities**	
Cash	$ 100	Accounts payable	$ 200
Accounts receivable	200	Accrued taxes due	200
Inventories	300	Long-term debt	400
Plant and equipment, net	1,800	Equity	1,600
Total assets	$2,400	Total liabilities	$2,400

16.10 Parnelli Products' stock is currently selling for $45 a share. The firm is earning $5 per share and is expected to pay a year-end dividend of $1.80.

a. If investors require a 12 percent return, what rate of growth must be expected for Parnelli?

b. If Parnelli reinvests retained earnings to yield the expected rate of return, what will be next year's EPS?

16.11 Bennett Company is considering payment of a $1 per share dividend. Stockholders can invest dividends to earn 18 percent; investors are taxed at 30 percent, and the brokerage costs on reinvestment are 3.5 percent. What rate of return must Bennett earn on retained earnings to equate incremental internal earnings to what stockholders would receive externally?

16.12 You are planning to form a new company, and you can use several different capital structures. Investment bankers indicate that debt and equity capital will cost the following under different debt ratios (debt/total assets):

Debt ratio	20% and below	21 to 40%	41 to 50%	51 to 65%
Before-tax cost of debt	8%	9%	11%	14%
Cost of equity capital	12	13	18	25

a. Assuming a 40 percent tax rate, what is the after-tax weighted cost of capital for the following capital structures?

	(1)	(2)	(3)	(4)	(5)	(6)	(7)	(8)
Debt	0%	20%	21%	40%	41%	50%	51%	65%
Equity	100	80	79	60	59	50	49	35

b. Which capital structure minimizes the weighted average cost of capital?

16.13 On January 1, 1981, the total assets of the Rossiter Company were $60 million. By the end of the year total assets are expected to be $90 million. (Assume there is no short-term debt.) The firm's capital structure, shown below, is considered to be optimal:

Debt (10% coupon bonds)	$24,000,000
Preferred stock (at 10.5%)	6,000,000
Common equity	30,000,000
	$60,000,000

New bonds will have an 11 percent coupon rate and will be sold at par. Preferred stock will have an 11.5 percent rate and will also be sold at par. Common stock, currently selling at $30 a share, can be sold to net the company $27 a share. Stockholders' required rate of return, estimated to be 12 percent, consists of a dividend yield of 4 percent and an expected growth of 8 percent. Retained earnings are estimated to be $3 million (ignoring depreciation). The marginal corporate tax rate is 40 percent.

a. Assuming all asset expansion (gross expenditures for fixed assets plus related working capital) is included in the capital budget, what is the dollar amount of the capital budget (ignoring depreciation)?
b. To maintain the present capital structure, how much of the capital budget must be financed by equity?
c. How much of the new equity funds needed must be generated internally? How much externally?
d. Calculate the cost of each of the equity components.
e. At what level of capital expenditures will there be a break in the MCC schedule?
f. Calculate the MCC both below and above the break in the schedule.
g. Plot the MCC schedule. Also, draw in an IRR schedule that is consistent with the MCC schedule and the projected capital budget.

16.14 The Austen Company has the following capital structure as of December 31, 1980:

Debt (at 8%)		$12,000,000
Preferred (at $8\frac{1}{2}$%)		4,000,000
Common stock	$ 4,000,000	
Retained earnings	12,000,000	
Common equity		16,000,000
Total capitalization		$32,000,000

Earnings per share have grown steadily from $0.93 in 1973 to $2 estimated for 1981. Expecting this growth to continue, the investment community applies a price/earnings ratio of 10 to yield a current market price of $20. Austen's last annual dividend was $1.25, and the company expects dividends to grow at the same rate as earnings. The addition to retained earnings for 1981 is projected at $4 million. The corporate tax rate is 40 percent.

Assuming that the capital structure relations set out above are maintained, new securities can be sold at the following costs:

Bonds: Up to and including $3 million of new bonds, 10 percent yield to investor on all new bonds

From $3.01 million to $6 million of new bonds, 10.5 percent yield to investor on this increment of bonds

Over $6 million of new bonds, 12 percent yield to investor on this increment of bonds

Preferred: Up to and including $1 million of preferred stock, 10 percent yield to investor on all new preferred stock

From $1.01 million to $2 million of preferred stock, 10.5 percent yield to investor on this increment of preferred stock

Over $2 million of preferred stock, 12.5 percent yield to investor on this increment of preferred stock

Common: Up to $4 million of new outside common stock, $20 a share less $2.50 a share flotation cost

Over $4 million of new outside common stock, $20 a share less $5 a share flotation cost on this increment of new common

a. At what dollar amounts of new capital will breaks occur in the MCC?

b. Calculate the MCC in the interval between each of these breaks; then plot the MCC schedule.

c. Discuss the breaking points in the marginal cost curve. What factors in the real world would tend to make the marginal cost curve smooth?

d. Assume now that Austen has the following investment opportunities:

1. It can invest any amount up to $4 million at a 15 percent rate of return.
2. It can invest an additional $8 million at a 13.7 percent rate of return.
3. It can invest still another $12 million at an 11.8 percent rate of return. Thus Austen's total potential capital budget is $24 million. Determine the size of the company's optimal capital budget for the year.

CHAPTER 17

DIVIDEND POLICY

Dividend policy determines the division of earnings between payments to stockholders and reinvestment in the firm. Retained earnings are one of the most significant sources of funds for financing corporate growth, but dividends constitute the cash flows that stockholders accrue. The factors that influence the allocation of earnings to dividends or retained earnings are the subject of this chapter.

Dividend Payments

Dividends are normally paid quarterly. For example, Liggett Group pays annual dividends of $2.50. In financial parlance we say that Liggett Group's regular quarterly dividend is 62.5 cents or that its regular annual dividend is $2.50. The management of a company such as Liggett Group conveys to stockholders, sometimes by an explicit statement in the annual report and sometimes by implication, an expectation that the regular dividend will be maintained if at all possible. Further, management conveys its belief that earnings will be sufficient to maintain the dividend.

Under other conditions, a firm's cash flows and investment needs may be too volatile for it to set a very high regular dividend. On the average, however, it needs a high dividend payout to dispose of funds not necessary for reinvestment. In such a case, the directors can set a relatively low regular dividend—low enough that it can be maintained even in low profit years or in years when a considerable amount of reinvestment is needed—and supplement it with an extra dividend in years when excess funds are available. General Motors, whose earnings fluctuate widely from year to year, has long followed the practice of supplementing its regular dividend with an extra dividend paid in addition to the regular fourth quarter dividend.

Payment Procedure

The actual payment procedure is of some importance, and the following is an outline of the payment sequence.

1. *Declaration date.* The directors meet, say, on November 15 and declare the regular dividend. On this date, they issue a statement similar to the following: "On November 15, 1981, the directors of the XYZ Company met and declared the regular quarterly dividend of 50 cents a share, plus an extra dividend of 75 cents a share, to holders of record on December 15, payment to be made on January 2, 1982."
2. *Holder-of-record date.* On December 15, the *holder-of-record-date*, the company closes its stock transfer books and makes up a list of the shareholders as of that date. If XYZ Company is notified of the sale and transfer of some stock before December 16, the new owner receives the dividend. If notification is received on or after December 16, the old stockholder gets the dividend.

3. *Ex dividend date.* Suppose Irma Jones buys 100 shares of stock from Robert Noble on December 13. Will the company be notified of the transfer in time to list her as the new owner and thus pay her the dividend? To avoid conflict, the brokerage business has set up a convention of declaring that the right to the dividend remains with the stock until four business days prior to the holder-of-record date; on the fourth day before the record date, the right to the dividend no longer goes with the shares. The date when the right to the dividend leaves the stock is called the *ex dividend date*. In this case, the ex dividend date is four days prior to December 15, or December 11. Therefore, if Jones is to receive the dividend, she must buy the stock by December 10. If she buys it on December 11 or later, Noble will receive the dividend. The total dividend, regular plus extra, amounts to $1.25, so the ex dividend date is important. Barring fluctuations in the stock market, we would normally expect the price of a stock to drop by approximately the amount of the dividend on the ex dividend date.
4. *Payment date.* The company actually mails the checks to the holders of record on January 2, the payment date.

Factors Influencing Dividend Policy

What factors determine the extent to which a firm will pay out dividends instead of retaining earnings? As a first step toward answering this question, we shall consider some of the factors that influence dividend policy.

Legal Rules

Although state statutes and court decisions governing dividend policy are complicated, their essential nature can be stated briefly. The legal rules provide that dividends must be paid from earnings—either from the current year's earnings or from past years' earnings as reflected in the balance sheet account "retained earnings."

State laws emphasize three rules: (1) the net profits rule, (2) the capital impairment rule, and (3) the insolvency rule. The *net profits rule* provides that dividends can be paid from past and present earnings. The *capital impairment rule* protects creditors by forbidding the payment of dividends from capital. (Paying dividends from capital would be distributing the investment in a company rather than its earnings.)[1] The *insolvency rule* provides that corporations cannot pay dividends while insolvent. (*Insolvency* is here defined, in the bankruptcy sense, as liabilities exceeding assets; and to pay dividends under such conditions would mean giving stockholders funds that rightfully belong to the creditors.)

Legal rules are significant in that they provide the framework within which dividend policies can be formulated. Within their boundaries, however, financial and economic factors have a major influence on policy.

Liquidity Position

Profits held as retained earnings (which show up on the right-hand side of the balance sheet) are generally invested in assets required for the conduct of the business. Retained earnings from preceding years are already invested in plant

[1] It is possible, of course, to return stockholders' capital; when this is done, however, the procedure must be clearly stated as such. A dividend paid out of capital is called a *liquidating dividend*.

and equipment, inventories, and other assets; they are not held as cash. Thus, even if a firm has a record of earnings, it may not be able to pay cash dividends because of its liquidity position. Indeed, a growing firm, even a very profitable one, typically has a pressing need for funds. In such a situation the firm may elect not to pay cash dividends.

If this point is not clear, refer again to Table 5.1—the Walker-Wilson Company's balance sheet. The retained earnings account shows $400,000, but the cash account shows only $50,000. Since some cash must be retained to pay bills, it is clear that Walker-Wilson's cash position precludes a dividend of even $50,000.

Need to Repay Debt

When a firm has sold debt to finance expansion or to substitute for other forms of financing, it is faced with two alternatives. It can refund the debt at maturity by replacing it with another form of security, or it can make provisions for paying off the debt. If the decision is to retire the debt, this will generally require the retention of earnings.

Restrictions in Debt Contracts

Debt contracts, particularly when long-term debt is involved, frequently restrict a firm's ability to pay cash dividends. Such restrictions, which are designed to protect the position of the lender, usually state that (1) future dividends can be paid only out of earnings generated *after* the signing of the loan agreement (that is, they cannot be paid out of past retained earnings), and (2) dividends cannot be paid when working capital (current assets minus current liabilities) is below a specified amount. Similarly, preferred stock agreements generally state that no cash dividends can be paid on the common stock until all accrued preferred dividends have been paid.

Rate of Asset Expansion

The more rapid the rate at which the firm is growing, the greater its needs for financing asset expansion. The greater the future need for funds, the more likely the firm is to retain earnings rather than pay them out. If a firm seeks to raise funds externally, natural sources are the present shareholders, who already know the company. But if earnings are paid out as dividends and are subject to high personal income tax rates, only a portion of them will be available for reinvestment.

Profit Rate

The rate of return on assets determines the relative attractiveness of paying out earnings in the form of dividends to stockholders (who will use them elsewhere) or using them in the present enterprise.

Stability of Earnings

A firm that has relatively stable earnings is often able to predict its future earnings. Such a firm is therefore more likely to pay out a higher percentage of its earnings than is a firm with fluctuating earnings. The unstable firm is not certain that in subsequent years the hoped-for earnings will be realized, so it is likely to retain a high proportion of current earnings. A lower dividend will be easier to maintain if earnings fall off in the future.

Access to the Capital Markets

A large, well-established firm with a record of profitability and stability of earnings has easy access to capital markets and other forms of external financing. A small, new, or venturesome firm, however, is riskier for potential investors. Its ability to raise equity or debt funds from capital markets is restricted, and it must retain more earnings to finance its operations. A well-established firm is thus likely to have a higher dividend payout rate than is a new or small firm.

Control

Another important variable is the effect of alternative sources of financing on the control situation in the firm. As a matter of policy, some corporations expand only to the extent of their internal earnings. This policy is defended on the ground that raising funds by selling additional common stock dilutes the control of the dominant group in that company. At the same time, selling debt increases the risks of fluctuating earnings to the present owners of the company. Reliance on internal financing in order to maintain control reduces the dividend payout.

Tax Position of Stockholders

The tax position of the corporation's owners greatly influences the desire for dividends. For example, a corporation closely held by a few taxpayers in high income tax brackets is likely to pay a relatively low dividend. The owners are interested in taking their income in the form of capital gains rather than as dividends, which are subject to higher personal income tax rates. However, the stockholders of a large, widely held corporation may be interested in a high dividend payout.

At times there is a conflict of interest in large corporations between stockholders in high income tax brackets and those in low tax brackets. The former may prefer to see a low dividend payout and a high rate of earnings retention in the hope of an appreciation in the capital stock of the company. The latter may prefer a relatively high dividend payout. The dividend policy in such firms may be a compromise between a low and a high payout—an intermediate payout ratio. If one group comes to dominate the company and sets, say, a low payout policy, those stockholders who seek income are likely to sell their shares over time and shift into higher-yielding stocks. Thus, to at least some extent, a firm's payout policy determines the type of stockholders it has—and vice versa. This has been called the "clientele influence" on dividend policy.

Tax on Improperly Accumulated Earnings

In order to prevent wealthy stockholders from using the corporation as an "incorporated pocketbook" by which they can avoid high personal income tax rates, tax regulations applicable to corporations provide for a special surtax on improperly accumulated income. However, Section 531 of the Revenue Act of 1954 places the burden of proof on the Internal Revenue Service to justify penalty rates for accumulation of earnings. That is, earnings retention is justified unless the IRS can prove otherwise.

General Dividend Patterns in the Economy

Table 17.1 presents after-tax profits, dividends, and the dividend payout ratios for the years 1946 to 1980. Payout ratios for selected time periods are also calculated. During 1946 to 1955, the postwar adjustment and the time of the Korean conflict, the payout was about 50 percent. The payout declined to 45 percent during the period of price stability from 1955 to 1966. During the first part of the inflationary period that began in 1966, the dividend payout remained near 45 percent. However, during the period of continued inflation and the rise in oil prices beginning in 1973, the dividend payout rose again to 49 percent.

Table 17.1

Dividend Payout Patterns 1946–1980 (Billions of Dollars)

	After-tax profits	Dividends	Dividend payout ratios
1946	$ 7.5	$ 5.6	0.75
1947	11.0	6.3	0.57
1948	17.0	7.0	0.41
1949	16.9	7.2	0.43
1950	16.0	8.8	0.55
1951	16.1	8.5	0.53
1952	16.7	8.5	0.51
1953	16.0	8.8	0.55
1954	17.5	9.1	0.52
1955	23.4	10.3	0.44
1956	21.8	11.1	0.51
1957	21.8	11.5	0.53
1958	19.5	11.3	0.58
1959	26.0	12.2	0.47
1960	24.9	12.9	0.52
1961	25.8	13.3	0.52
1962	32.6	14.4	0.44
1963	35.9	15.5	0.43
1964	41.2	17.3	0.42
1965	49.1	19.1	0.39
1966	51.4	19.4	0.38
1967	49.9	20.2	0.40
1968	50.0	22.0	0.44
1969	45.6	22.5	0.49
1970	37.2	22.5	0.60
1971	45.7	22.9	0.50
1972	55.0	24.4	0.44
1973	59.3	27.0	0.46
1974	43.3	29.9	0.69
1975	59.9	30.8	0.51
1976	74.3	37.4	0.50
1977	92.2	39.9	0.43
1978	102.5	44.6	0.44
1979	109.2	50.2	0.46
1980	101.6	56.0	0.55
Dividend payout patterns for selected periods			
1946–1955	$158.1	$ 80.1	0.51
1955–1966	373.4	168.3	0.45
1966–1972	334.8	153.9	0.46
1973–1980	642.3	315.8	0.49

Note that the second column shows corporate profits with inventory valuation and capital consumption adjustments.

Source: President's Council of Economic Advisers, *Economic Report of the President* (Washington, D.C.: Government Printing Office, January 1981), Table B-80

Table 17.2

Compound Annual Growth Rates in Selected Series, 1948–1980

	1948–1966	1966–1972	1973–1980
GNP	6.11%	7.64%	10.25%
After-tax profits	6.15	0.54	11.20
Dividends	5.83	4.04	10.98
CPI	1.67	4.32	9.22

Source: President's Council of Economic Advisers, *Economic Report of the President* (Washington, D.C.: Government Printing Office, 1981)

Another perspective is obtained by examining growth rate patterns for selected time periods, as shown in Table 17.2. The period from 1948 to 1966 was characterized by relative price stability in which the consumer price index (CPI) increased by less than 2 percent per annum. The GNP, after-tax profits, and dividends all grew at about a 6 percent rate. From 1966 to 1972, the CPI increased at a 4.32 percent per year rate, and GNP in nominal terms was growing at a 7.64 percent rate. After-tax profits were virtually flat, while dividends did not quite keep up with the inflation rate—the real dividend growth rate was slightly negative.

From 1973 to 1980, the CPI increased more than 9 percent per year. The GNP in nominal terms has grown at a rate of 10.25 percent per year, but at only about 1 percent per year in real terms. After-tax profit growth did keep up with the inflation rate, but real growth was below 2 percent per year for both after-tax profits and dividends.

Figure 17.1

Corporate Earnings After Taxes and Dividends (CPI Deflated), 1946–1980

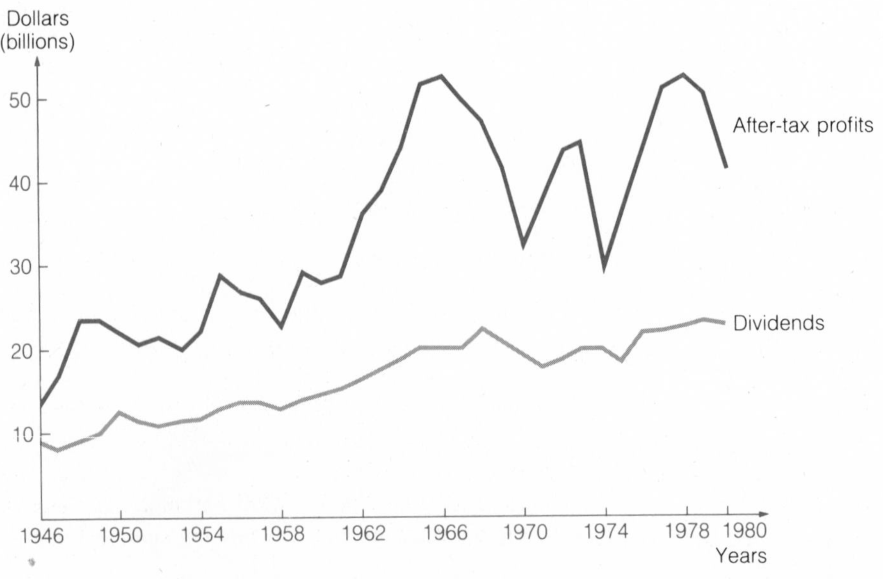

Because of the impact of inflation since 1966, it is useful to deflate both after-tax profits and dividends by the CPI. Deflated dividends increased at less than 1 percent per year from 1966 to 1980, while deflated after-tax profits actually decreased at a rate of 1.75 percent per year for the same time period. In spite of declining real profits, real dividends were relatively stable. This is also shown by Figure 17.1, which presents deflated after-tax profits and deflated dividends for the 1946-to-1980 period. Deflated dividends remained at about $20 billion from 1965 through 1975. Dividends moved up to about $23 billion for 1978 through 1980. But considerable stability in deflated dividends was exhibited for most of the 1966-to-1980 period. With the background of dividend patterns for the economy as a whole, we next turn to an examination of dividend policy at the level of the individual firm.

Dividend Policy Decisions

Most corporations seek to maintain a target dividend per share. However, dividends increase with a lag after earnings rise. That is, they are increased only after an increase in earnings appears clearly sustainable and relatively permanent. When dividends have been increased, strenuous efforts are made to maintain them at the new level. If earnings decline, the existing dividend generally is maintained until it is clear that an earnings recovery will not take place.

Figure 17.2

Dividends and Earnings Patterns for the Walter Watch Company

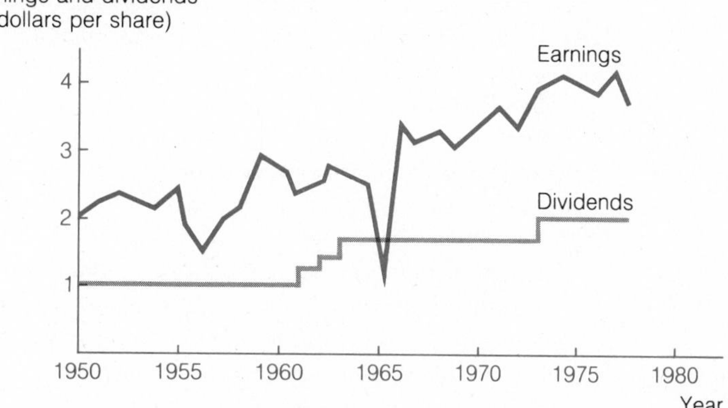

Figure 17.2 illustrates these ideas by showing the earnings and dividend patterns for the Walter Watch Company over a thirty-year period. Initially, earnings are $2 and dividends $1 a share, providing a 50 percent payout ratio. Earnings rise for four years, while dividends remain constant; thus the payout ratio falls during this period. During 1955 and 1956, earnings fall substantially; however, the dividend is maintained, and the payout ratio rises above the 50 percent target. During the period between 1956 and 1960, earnings experience a sustained rise. Dividends are held constant for a time, while management seeks to determine whether the

earnings increase is permanent. By 1961, the earnings gains seem permanent, and dividends are raised in three steps to reestablish the 50 percent target payout. During 1965 a strike causes earnings to fall below the regular dividend; expecting the earnings decline to be temporary, management maintains the dividend. Earnings fluctuate on a fairly high plateau from 1966 through 1972, during which time dividends remain constant. A new increase in earnings induces management to raise the dividend in 1973 to reestablish the 50 percent payout ratio.

Rationale for Stable Dividends

Like the great majority of firms, Walter Watch keeps its dividend at a relatively steady dollar amount but allows its payout ratio to fluctuate. Why does it follow such a policy?

Consider the stable dividend policy from the standpoint of the stockholders as owners of the company. Their acquiescence with the general practice must imply that stable dividend policies lead to higher stock prices on the average than do alternative dividend policies. Is this a fact? Does a stable dividend policy maximize equity values for a corporation? There has been no truly conclusive empirical study of dividend policy, so any answer to the question must be regarded as tentative. On logical grounds, however, there is reason to believe that a stable dividend policy does lead to higher stock prices. First, investors can be expected to value more highly dividends they are more sure of receiving, since fluctuating dividends are riskier than stable ones. Accordingly, the same average amount of dividends received under a fluctuating dividend policy is likely to have a higher discount factor applied to it than is applied to dividends under a stable dividend policy. In the terms used in Chapter 16, this means that a firm with a stable dividend will have a lower required rate of return—or cost of equity capital—than one whose dividends fluctuate.

Second, many stockholders live on income received in the form of dividends. These stockholders are greatly inconvenienced by fluctuating dividends, and they will likely pay a premium for a stock with a relatively assured minimum dollar dividend.

A third advantage of a stable dividend from the standpoint of both the corporation and its stockholders is the requirement of legal listing. *Legal lists* are lists of securities in which mutual savings banks, pension funds, insurance companies, and other fiduciary institutions are permitted to invest. One of the criteria for placing a stock on the legal list is that dividend payments are maintained. Thus legal listing encourages pursuance of a stable dividend policy.

On the other hand, if a firm's investment opportunities fluctuate from year to year, should it not retain more earnings during some years in order to take advantage of opportunities when they appear and increase dividends when good internal investment opportunities are scarce? This line of reasoning leads to a recommendation for a fluctuating payout for companies whose investment opportunities are unstable. However, the logic of the argument is diminished by recognizing that it is possible to maintain a reasonably stable dividend by using outside financing, including debt, to smooth out the differences between the funds needed for investment and the amount of money provided by retained earnings.

Alternative Dividend Policies

Before considering dividend policy at a theoretical level, it is useful to summarize the three major types of dividend policies:

1. *Stable dollar amount per share.* The policy of a stable dollar amount per share, followed by most firms, is the policy implied by the words *stable dividend policy.*
2. *Constant payout ratio.* Very few firms follow a policy of paying out a constant percentage of earnings. Since earnings fluctuate, following this policy necessarily means that the dollar amount of dividends will fluctuate. For reasons discussed in the preceding section, this policy is not likely to maximize the value of a firm's stock. Before its bankruptcy, Penn Central Railroad followed the policy of paying out half its earnings—"A dollar for the stockholders and a dollar for the company," as one director put it.
3. *Low regular dividend plus extras.* The low regular dividend plus extras policy is a compromise between the first two. It gives the firm flexibility, but it leaves investors somewhat uncertain about what their dividend income will be. If a firm's earnings are quite volatile, however, this policy may well be its best choice.

The relative merits of these three policies can be evaluated better after a discussion of the residual theory of dividends.

Residual Theory of Dividends

The earlier chapters on capital budgeting and the cost of capital indicated that the cost of capital schedule and the investment opportunity schedule generally must be combined before the cost of capital can be established. In other words, the optimum capital budget, the marginal cost of capital, and the marginal rate of return on investment are determined *simultaneously.* This section examines the simultaneous solution in the framework of what is called the *residual theory of dividends.*[2] The theory draws on materials developed earlier in the book—capital budgeting and the cost of capital—and serves to provide a bridge between these key concepts.

The starting point in the theory is that investors prefer to have the firm retain and reinvest earnings rather than pay them out in dividends if the return on reinvested earnings exceeds the rate of return the investors can obtain on other investments of comparable risk. If the corporation can reinvest retained earnings at a 20 percent rate of return, while the best rate stockholders can obtain if they receive earnings in the form of dividends is 10 percent, then stockholders prefer to have the firm retain the profits.

Chapter 16 showed that the cost of equity capital obtained from retained earnings is an *opportunity cost* that reflects rates of return open to equity investors. If a firm's stockholders can buy other stocks of equal risk and obtain a 10 percent dividend plus capital gains yield, then 10 percent is the firm's cost of retained

[2] "Residual" connotes *left over.* The residual theory of dividend policy implies that dividends are paid after internal investment opportunities have been exhausted.

earnings. The cost of new outside equity raised by selling common stock is higher because of the costs of floating the issue.

Most firms have an optimum debt ratio that calls for at least some debt, so new financing is done partly with debt and partly with equity. Debt has a different, and generally lower, cost than equity, so the two forms of capital must be combined to find the *weighted average cost of capital.* As long as the firm finances at the optimum point (using an optimum amount of debt and equity) and uses only internally generated equity (retained earnings), its marginal cost of each new dollar of capital is minimized.

Internally generated equity is available for financing a certain amount of new investment; beyond this amount, the firm must turn to more expensive new common stock. At the point where new stock must be sold, the cost of equity and, consequently, the marginal cost of capital rise.

These concepts, which were developed in Chapter 16, are illustrated in Figure 17.3. The firm has a marginal cost of capital of 10 percent so long as retained earnings are available; the marginal cost of capital begins to rise when new stock must be sold.

Figure 17.3 **The Marginal Cost of Capital**

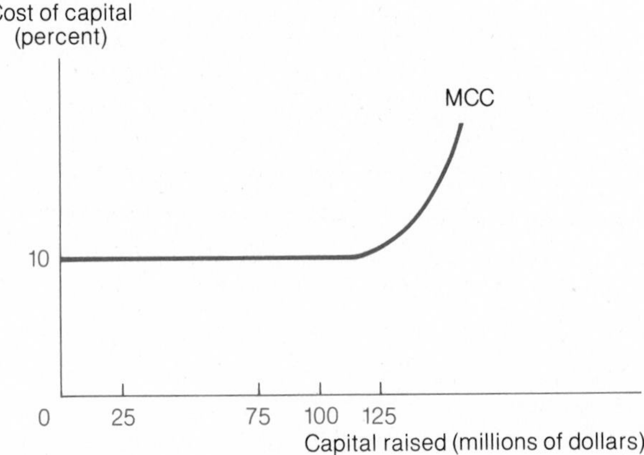

The hypothetical firm has \$50 million of earnings and a 50 percent optimum debt ratio. It can make net investments (investments in addition to asset replacements financed from depreciation) up to \$100 million—\$50 million from retained earnings plus \$50 million in new debt supported by the retained earnings if it does not pay dividends. Therefore, its marginal cost of capital is constant at 10 percent for up to \$100 million of capital. Beyond \$100 million, the marginal cost of capital begins rising as the firm begins to use more expensive new common stock.

Suppose the firm's capital budgeting department draws up a list of investment opportunities, ranked in the order of each project's IRR, and plots them on a graph. The investment opportunity curves of three different years—one for a good year (IRR_1), one for a normal year (IRR_2), and one for a bad year (IRR_3)—are shown

Figure 17.4

Investment Opportunities

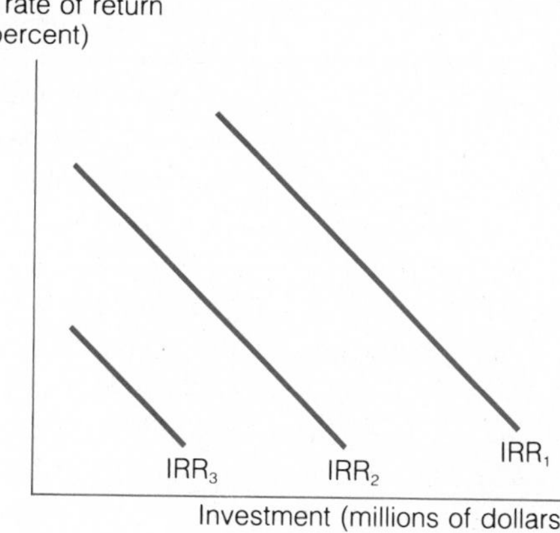

in Figure 17.4. The IRR_1 curve shows that the firm can invest more money, and at higher rates of return, than it can when the investment opportunities are those given by IRR_2 and IRR_3.

The investment opportunity schedule is now combined with the cost of capital schedule in Figure 17.5. The point where the investment opportunity curve cuts the cost of capital curve defines the proper level of new investment. When investment opportunities are relatively poor, the optimum level of investment is $25 million; when opportunities are about normal, it is $75 million; and when opportunities are relatively good, it is $125 million.

Consider the situation where IRR_1 is the appropriate schedule. Suppose the firm has $50 million in earnings and a 50 percent target debt ratio, so it can finance $100 million ($50 million earnings plus $50 million new debt) *if it retains all its*

Figure 17.5

Interrelationships Among Cost of Capital, Investment Opportunities, and New Investment

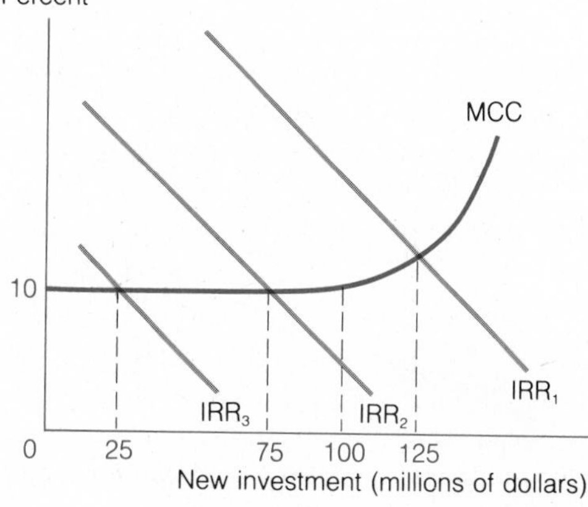

earnings. If it pays out part of the earnings in dividends, then it will have to begin using expensive new common stock sooner, so the cost of capital curve will rise sooner. This suggests that under the conditions of IRR_1 the firm should retain all its earnings and actually sell some new common stock in order to take advantage of its investment opportunities. Its payout ratio would thus be zero percent.

Under the conditions of IRR_2, however, the firm should invest only $75 million. How should this investment be financed? First, notice that if it retains the full amount of its earnings, $50 million, it will need to sell only $25 million of new debt. However, by doing this, the firm will move away from its target capital structure. To stay on target, the firm must finance the required $75 million half by equity (retained earnings) and half by debt—that is, $37.5 million by retained earnings and $37.5 million by debt. If the firm has $50 million in total earnings and decides to retain and reinvest $37.5 million, it must distribute the residual $12.5 million to its stockholders. In this case, the payout ratio is 25 percent ($12.5 million divided by $50 million).

Finally, under the bad conditions of IRR_3, the firm should invest only $25 million. Because it has $50 million in earnings, it could finance the entire $25 million out of retained earnings and still have $25 million available for dividends. Should this be done? Under the assumptions, this would not be a good decision, because it would move the firm away from its target debt ratio. To stay in the 50-50 debt/equity position, the firm must retain $12.5 million and sell $12.5 million of debt. When the $12.5 million of retained earnings is subtracted from the $50 million of earnings, the firm is left with a residual of $37.5 million—the amount that should be paid out in dividends. In this case the payout ratio is 75 percent.

Long-Run Viewpoint

A conflict apparently exists between the residual theory and the statement made in an earlier section that firms should and do maintain reasonably stable cash dividends. How can this conflict be reconciled?

A firm may have a target capital structure without being at that target at all times. In other words, it need not adjust its dividend each and every year. Firms do have target debt ratios, but they also have a certain amount of flexibility; they can be moderately above or below the target debt position in any year with no serious adverse consequences. This means that if an unusually large number of good investments are available in a particular year, the firm does not necessarily have to cut its dividend to take advantage of them; it can borrow somewhat more heavily than usual in that particular year without getting its debt ratio too far out of line. Obviously, however, this excessive reliance on debt cannot continue for too many years without seriously affecting the debt ratio, necessitating either a sale of new stock or a cut in dividends and an attendant increase in the level of retained earnings.

High and Low Dividend Payout Industries

Some industries are experiencing rapid growth in the demand for their products, a condition which obviously affords firms in the industries many good investment opportunities. Electronics, office equipment, and entertainment are examples of such industries in recent years. Other industries have experienced much slower growth and even declines. Examples of slow-growth industries are cigarette manufacturing and textiles. Still other industries are growing at about the same rate as the general economy; oil, food, and banking are representative.

The theory suggests that firms in rapidly growing industries should generally have IRR curves that are relatively far to the right on graphs such as Figure 17.5; for example, Xerox, Polaroid, and IBM might have investment schedules similar to IRR_1. The tobacco companies, on the other hand, could be expected to have investment schedules similar to IRR_3.

Each of these firms would, of course, experience shifts in investment opportunities from year to year, but the curves would *tend* to be in about the same part of the graph. In other words, firms such as Xerox would tend to have more investment opportunities than money, so we would expect them to have zero (or very low) payout ratios. Reynolds Tobacco, on the other hand, would tend to have more money than good investments, so we would expect it to pay out a relatively high percentage of earnings in dividends. These companies do, in fact, conform to our expectations.

Stock Dividends and Stock Splits

Another aspect of dividend policy is stock dividends and stock splits. A *stock dividend* is paid in additional shares of stock instead of in cash and simply involves a bookkeeping transfer from retained earnings to the capital stock account.[3] In a *stock split* there is no change in the capital accounts; instead, a larger number of shares of common stock is issued. In a two-for-one split, stockholders receive two shares for each one previously held. The book value per share is cut in half; and the par, or stated, value per share of stock is similarly changed.

From a practical standpoint there is little difference between a stock dividend and a stock split. The New York Stock Exchange considers any distribution of stock totaling less than 25 percent of outstanding stock to be a stock dividend and any distribution of 25 percent or more a stock split. Since the two are similar, the issues outlined below are discussed in connection with both stock dividends and stock splits.

Price Effects

The results of a careful empirical study of the effects of stock dividends are available and can be used as a basis for observations on their price effects.[4] (The findings of the study are presented in Table 17.3.) When stock dividends were associated with a cash dividend increase, the value of the company's stock six months after the ex dividend date had risen by 8 percent. When stock dividends were not accompanied by cash dividend increases, stock values fell by 12 percent during the subsequent six-month period.

[3] The transfer from retained earnings to the capital stock account must be based on market value. In other words, if a firm's shares are selling for $100 and it has 1 million shares outstanding, a 10 percent stock dividend requires the transfer of $10 million (100,000 × $100) from retained earnings to capital stock. Stock dividends are thus limited by the size of retained earnings. The rule was put into effect to prevent the declaration of stock dividends unless the firm has had earnings.

[4] C. Austin Barker, "Evaluation of Stock Dividends," *Harvard Business Review* 36 (July–August 1958), pp. 199–214. Barker's study has been replicated several times in recent years, and his results are still valid.

Table 17.3 **Price Effects of Stock Dividends**

	Prices at selected dates (in percentages)		
	Six months prior to ex dividend date	At ex dividend date	Six months after ex dividend date
Cash dividend increase	100	109	108
No cash dividend increase	100	99	88

The data in Table 17.3 seem to suggest that stock dividends are seen for what they are—simply additional pieces of paper—and that they are not perceived as representing true income. When they are accompanied by higher earnings and cash dividends, investors bid up the value of the stock. However, when they are not accompanied by such increases, the dilution of earnings and dividends per share causes the price of the stock to drop. The fundamental determinant is underlying earnings and dividend trends.

Similar results were developed more rigorously in the pioneering study by Eugene Fama, Lawrence Fisher, Michael Jensen, and Richard Roll using residual analysis, which measures differences from returns predicted by the security market line.[5] Positive abnormal returns were observed before the split. When the sample was divided between splits with dividend increases and those with decreases, a difference in post-split performance was observed. The dividend increase group showed slightly positive returns following the split. The poor dividend performance group experienced declines in cumulative average residuals until about a year after the split. The hypothesis suggested is that the splits and associated dividend experience convey a message about future changes in the firms' expected cash flows.

Table 17.4 **Effect of Stock Dividends on Stock Ownership**

	Percentage increase in ownership 1950–1953
Stock dividend, 25% and over	30
Stock dividend, 5–25%	17
All stock dividends	25
No stock dividends or splits	5

Source: C. Austin Barker, "Evaluation of Stock Dividends," *Harvard Business Review* 36 (July–August 1958), pp. 99–114.

Effects on Extent of Ownership

Table 17.4 shows the effect of stock dividends on common stock ownership during a four-year period. Large stock dividends resulted in the largest percentage increases in stock ownership. The use of stock dividends increased share ownership by 25 percent on the average. For companies and industries that did not offer

[5] Eugene Fama, Lawrence Fisher, Michael Jensen, and Richard Roll, "The Adjustment of Stock Prices to New Information," *International Economic Review* 10 (February 1969), pp. 1–21.

stock splits or stock dividends, the increase was only 5 percent. Furthermore, the degree of increase itself increased with the size of the stock dividend. This evidence suggests that regardless of the effect on the total market value of the firm, the use of stock dividends and stock splits effectively increases stock ownership by lowering the price at which shares are traded to a more popular range.

Stock Repurchases as an Alternative to Dividends

Treasury stock is the name given to common stock that has been repurchased by the issuing firm, and the acquisition of treasury stock represents an alternative to the payment of dividends. If some of the outstanding stock is repurchased, fewer shares will remain outstanding; and assuming that the repurchase does not adversely affect the firm's earnings, the earnings per share of the remaining shares will increase. This increase in earnings per share may result in a higher market price per share, so capital gains will have been substituted for dividends. These effects can be seen from the following example.

The National Development Corporation (NDC) earned $4.4 million in 1980; of this amount, 50 percent, or $2.2 million, has been allocated for distribution to common shareholders. There are currently 1.1 million shares outstanding, and the market value is $20 a share. NDC can use the $2.2 million to repurchase 100,000 of its shares through a tender offer for $22 a share, or it can pay a cash dividend of $2 a share.[6]

The effect of the repurchase on the EPS and market price per share of the remaining stock can be determined in the following way:

$$\text{Current EPS} = \frac{\text{Total earnings}}{\text{Number of shares}} = \frac{\$4.4 \text{ million}}{1.1 \text{ million}} = \$4 \text{ per share}$$

$$\text{Current P-E ratio} = \frac{\$20}{\$4} = 5 \text{ times}$$

$$\begin{array}{c}\text{EPS after repurchase} \\ \text{of 100,000 shares}\end{array} = \frac{\$4.4 \text{ million}}{1 \text{ million}} = \$4.40 \text{ per share}$$

$$\begin{array}{c}\text{Expected market price} \\ \text{after repurchase}\end{array} = (\text{P-E})(\text{EPS}) = (5)(\$4.40) = \$22 \text{ per share}$$

It can be seen from this example that investors will receive benefits of $2 a share in any case, in the form of either a $2 dividend or a $2 increase in stock price. The result occurs because of the assumptions that (1) shares can be repurchased at $22 a share, (2) total earnings will remain unchanged, and (3) the P-E ratio will remain constant. If shares could be bought for less than $22, the operation would be even better for *remaining* stockholders, but the reverse would hold if NDC paid

[6] Stock repurchases are commonly made in three ways. First, a publicly owned firm can simply buy its own stock through a broker on the open market. Second, it can issue a *tender,* under which it permits stockholders to send in ("tender") their shares to the firm in exchange for a specified price per share. When tender offers are made, the firm generally indicates that it will buy up to a specified number of shares within a specified time period (usually about two weeks); if more shares are tendered than the company wishes to purchase, then purchases are made on a pro rata basis. Finally, the firm can purchase a block of shares from one large holder on a negotiated basis. If the latter procedure is employed, care must be taken to ensure that the single stockholder does not receive preferential treatment.

more than $22 a share. Furthermore, the P-E ratio might change as a result of the repurchase operation—rising if investors viewed it favorably, falling if they viewed it unfavorably. Some factors that might affect P-E ratios are considered next.

Advantages of Repurchases from the Stockholders' Viewpoint

A number of possible advantages to stockholders may accrue from share repurchases. Gains earned on share repurchase are taxed at the long-term capital gains rate, assuming the investor has held the stock for at least the minimum one-year holding period and does not come under some special rules for large holders. Otherwise, the profits on share repurchase are taxed at the rates on ordinary personal income. Since the capital gains tax rates are in general only about one-half of the ordinary tax rates paid on dividends, this is clearly a benefit.

By reducing the equity base through share repurchase, while holding the level of debt the same, the debt to equity ratio of the firm has been increased. Tax shelter benefits and other advantages of increased leverage may therefore also benefit shareholders.

The stockholder has a choice: sell or not sell. The person who receives a dividend has to accept the payment and pay the tax.

A qualitative advantage advanced by market practitioners is that repurchase can often remove a large block of stock overhanging the market.

Advantages of Repurchases from Management's Viewpoint

Advantages to management of repurchases include the following: Studies have shown that dividends are sticky in the short run because managements are reluctant to raise them if the new dividend cannot be maintained in the future. Hence, if the excess cash flow is thought to be only temporary, management may prefer to "conceal" the distribution in the form of share repurchases rather than to declare a cash dividend that they believe cannot be maintained.

Repurchased stock can be used for acquisitions or released when stock options are exercised. Discussions with financial managers indicate that it is frequently more convenient and less expensive to use repurchased stock rather than newly issued stock for these purposes and when convertibles are converted or warrants exercised.

If directors have large holdings themselves, they may have especially strong preferences for repurchases rather than dividend payments because of the tax factor.

One interesting use of stock repurchases was Standard Products' strategy of repurchasing its own stock to thwart an attempted takeover. Defiance Industries attempted to acquire a controlling interest in Standard Products through a tender offer of $15 a share. Standard's management countered with a tender offer of its own at $17.25 a share, financed by $1.725 million in internal funds and by $3.525 million in long-term debt. This kept stockholders from accepting the outside tender offer and enabled Standard Products' management to retain control.

Repurchases can be used to effect large-scale changes in capital structure. For example, at one time American Standard had virtually no long-term debt outstanding. The company decided that its optimal capital structure called for the use of considerably more debt, but even if it financed *only* with debt it would have taken years to get the debt ratio up to the newly defined optimal level. So the company sold $22 million of long-term debt and used the proceeds to repurchase its common stock, thereby producing an instantaneous change in its capital structure.

Finally, treasury stock can be resold in the open market if the firm needs additional funds.

Disadvantages of Repurchases from the Stockholders' Viewpoint

Disadvantages to stockholders of repurchases include the following: Stockholders may not be indifferent to dividends and capital gains, and the price of the stock may benefit more from cash dividends than from repurchases. Cash dividends are generally thought of as being relatively dependable, and repurchases are not. Further, if a firm announces a regular, dependable repurchase program, the improper accumulation tax may become a threat.

The *selling* stockholders may not be fully aware of all the implications of a repurchase or may not have all pertinent information about the corporation's present and future activities. For this reason, firms generally announce a repurchase program before embarking on it.

The corporation may pay too high a price for the repurchased stock, to the disadvantage of remaining stockholders. If the shares are inactive, and if the firm seeks to acquire a relatively large amount of its stock, the price may be bid above a maintainable price and then fall after the firm ceases its repurchase operations.

By reducing the proportion of cash or marketable securities in the asset structure, the risk composition of the firm's assets and earnings may be increased. The P-E ratio may therefore drop.

Disadvantages of Repurchases from Management's Viewpoint

Disadvantages to management of repurchases include the following: Studies have shown that firms that repurchase substantial amounts of stock have poorer growth rates and investment opportunities than firms that do not. Thus some people feel that announcing a repurchase program is like announcing that management cannot locate good investment projects. One could argue that instituting a repurchase program should be regarded in the same manner as announcing a higher dividend payout, but if repurchases are regarded as indicating especially unfavorable growth opportunities, then they can have an adverse impact on the firm's image and on the price of its stock.

Repurchases may involve some risk from a legal standpoint. The SEC may raise serious questions if it appears that the firm is manipulating the price of its shares. Also, if the Internal Revenue Service can establish that the repurchases are primarily for the avoidance of taxes on dividends, then penalties may be imposed on the firm under the improper accumulation of earnings provision of the tax code. Actions have been brought against closely held companies under Section 531, but we know of no case where such an action has been brought against a publicly owned firm, even though some firms have retired over half their outstanding stock.

Conclusion on Stock Repurchases

When all the pros and the cons on stock repurchases are totaled, where do we stand? Our own conclusions can be summarized as follows: Repurchases on a regular, systematic, dependable basis (like quarterly dividends) are not feasible because of uncertainties about the tax treatment of such a program and about the market price of the shares, how many shares will be tendered, and so on. However, repurchases do offer some significant advantages over dividends, so the procedure should be given careful consideration on the basis of the firm's unique situation. They can be especially valuable to effect a significant shift in capital structure within a short period. Repurchases may increase the riskiness of the firm's assets and earnings. The latter two effects may represent a form of expropriation of bondholders.

Summary

Dividend policy determines the extent of internal financing by a firm. The financial manager decides whether to release corporate earnings from the control of the enterprise. Because dividend policy may affect such areas as the financial structure, the flow of funds, corporate liquidity, stock prices, and investor satisfaction, it is clearly an important aspect of financial management.

In theory, once the firm's debt policy and cost of capital have been determined, dividend policy should automatically follow. Under our theoretical model, dividends are simply a residual after investment needs have been met; if the residual policy is followed and if investors are indifferent to receiving their investment returns in the form of dividends or capital gains, stockholders are better off than they are under any other possible dividend policy. However, the financial manager simply does not have all the information assumed in the theory, and judgment must be exercised.

As a guide to financial managers responsible for dividend policy, the following is a summary of the major economic and financial factors influencing dividend policy: (1) rate of growth and profit level, (2) stability of earnings, (3) age and size of firm, (4) cash position, (5) need to repay debt, (6) control, (7) maintenance of a target dividend, (8) tax position of stockholders, (9) tax position of the corporation (including improper accumulation considerations).

Some of the factors listed lead to higher dividend payouts and some to lower payouts. It is not possible to provide a formula that can be used to establish the proper dividend payout for a given situation; this is a task requiring the exercise of judgment. But the considerations summarized above provide a checklist for guiding dividend decisions.

Empirical studies indicate a wide diversity of dividend payout ratios, not only among industries but also among firms in the same industry. Studies also show that dividends are more stable than earnings. Firms are reluctant to raise dividends in years of good earnings, and they resist dividend cuts as earnings decline. In view of investors' observed preference for stable dividends and of the probability that a cut in dividends is likely to be interpreted as forecasting a decline in earnings, stable dividends make good sense.

Neither stock dividends nor stock splits alone exert a major influence on prices. The fundamental determinant of the price of the company's stock is the company's earning power compared with the earning power of other companies. However, both stock splits and stock dividends can be used as effective instruments of financial policy. They are useful devices for reducing the price at which stocks are traded, and studies indicate that they tend to broaden the ownership of a firm's shares.

Stock repurchases have been used as an alternative to cash dividends. Although repurchases have significant advantages over dividends, they also have disadvantages; in particular they necessarily involve greater uncertainty than cash dividends. Generalizations about stock repurchases are difficult; each firm has its unique problems and conditions, and repurchase policy must be formulated within the context of the firm's characteristics and circumstances as a whole.

Questions

17.1 As an investor, would you rather invest in a firm with a policy of maintaining (a) a constant payout ratio, (b) a constant dollar dividend per share, or (c) a constant regular quarterly dividend plus a year-end extra when earnings are sufficiently high or corporate investment needs are sufficiently low? Explain your answer.

17.2 How would each of the following changes probably affect aggregate payout ratios? Explain your answer.

a. An increase in the personal income tax rate
b. A liberalization in depreciation policies for federal income tax purposes
c. A rise in interest rates
d. An increase in corporate profits
e. A decline in investment opportunities

17.3 Discuss the pros and cons of having the directors formally announce what a firm's dividend policy will be in the future.

17.4 Most firms would like to have their stock selling at a high P-E ratio and have extensive public ownership (many different shareholders). Explain how stock dividends or stock splits may be compatible with these aims.

17.5 What is the difference between a stock dividend and a stock split? As a stockholder, would you prefer to see your company declare a 100 percent stock dividend or a two-for-one split?

17.6 In theory, if we had perfect capital markets, we would expect investors to be indifferent about whether cash dividends were issued or an equivalent repurchase of stock outstanding were made. What factors might in practice cause investors to value one over the other?

17.7 Discuss the statement: The cost of retained earnings is less than the cost of new outside equity capital; consequently, it is totally irrational for a firm to sell a new issue of stock and to pay dividends during the same year.

17.8 Would it ever be rational for a firm to borrow money in order to pay dividends? Explain.

17.9 Unions have presented arguments similar to the following: "Corporations such as General Foods retain about half their profits for financing needs. If they financed by selling stock instead of by retaining earnings, they could cut prices substantially and still earn enough to pay the same dividend to their shareholders. Therefore, their profits are too high." Evaluate this statement.

Problems

17.1 The Arizona Engineering Company has $2 million of backlogged orders for its patented solar heating system. Management plans to expand production capacity by 30 percent with a $6 million investment in plant machinery. The firm wants to maintain a 45 percent debt to total asset ratio in its capital structure; it also wants to maintain its past dividend policy of distributing 20 percent of after-tax earnings. In 1980, earnings were $2.6 million. How much external equity must the firm seek at the beginning of 1981?

17.2 Warner Company expects next year's after-tax income to be $5 million. The firm's current debt-equity ratio is 80 percent. If Warner has $4 million of profitable investment opportunities and wishes to maintain its current debt-equity ratio with no external equity financing, how much should it pay out in dividends next year?

17.3 After a 3-for-1 stock split, Nevada Company paid a dividend of $4. This represents an 8 percent increase over last year's pre-split dividend. Nevada Company's stock sold for $80 prior to the split. What was last year's dividend per share?

17.4 The equity accounts of the Weller Company are shown below:

Common stock, par $10	$ 4,000,000
Paid-in surplus	3,000,000
Retained earnings	18,000,000
Total equity	$25,000,000

Weller's stock has a current market price of $50 per share.

a. Show the equity accounts of the Weller Company after the distribution of a 10 percent stock dividend.

b. Show the equity accounts of the Weller Company after a 2 for 1 stock split.

17.5 On June 30, the board of directors of Fulwell Corporation met and declared a special dividend of 85 cents a share to holders of record on August 15, payment to be made on September 1. You own 100 shares of Fulwell which you purchased in lots of 25 on each of the following dates: June 30, July 30, August 14, and September 1. What total dividends will you receive?

17.6 Some data related to the dividend policy of General Motors are presented below:

Year	Earnings per share EPS	Dividends per share DPS	P/E Ratio	Dividend yield on average price for the year
1971	$6.72	$3.40	12.2X	4.1%
1972	7.51	4.45	10.4	5.7
1973	8.34	5.25	7.8	8.1
1974	3.27	3.40	12.9	8.1
1975	4.32	2.40	10.5	5.3
1976	10.08	5.55	6.8	8.1
1977	11.62	6.80	6.0	9.7
1978	12.24	6.00	4.9	9.9
1979	10.04	5.30	5.7	9.2
1980	(2.65)	2.95	—	6.0

a. Calculate the dividend payout percentage for each year.

b. Calculate the dividend payout percentage for the 1971–1980 period as a whole.

c. Does GM appear to be following a stable dividend payout ratio or a policy of a stable dollar amount of dividends per year?

d. Comment on GM's dividend policy for 1980.

17.7 In 1980 the Vermont Company paid dividends totaling $1,125,000. For the past ten years, earnings have grown at a constant rate of 10 percent. After-tax income was $3,750,000 for 1980. However, in 1981, earnings were $6,750,000 with investment opportunities of $5,000,000. It is predicted that Vermont Company will not be able to maintain this higher level of earnings and will return to its previous 10 percent growth rate. Calculate dividends for 1981 if Vermont Company follows each of the following policies:

a. Its dividend payment is stable and growing.
b. It continues the 1980 dividend payout ratio.
c. It uses a pure residual dividend policy (30 percent of the $5,000,000 investment is financed with debt).
d. The investment in 1981 is financed 90 percent with retained earnings and 10 percent with debt. Any earnings not invested are paid out as dividends.
e. The investment in 1981 is financed 30 percent with external equity, 30 percent with debt, and 40 percent with retained earnings. Any earnings not invested are paid out as dividends.

17.8 Charleston Company stock earns $7 per share, sells for $30, and pays a $4 dividend per share. After a 2-for-1 split, the dividend will be $2.70 per share. By what percentage has the payout increased?

17.9 The directors of Northwest Lumber Supply have been comparing the growth of their market price with that of one of their competitors, Parker Panels. Their findings are summarized below.

Northwest Lumber Supply

Year	Earnings	Dividend	Payout	Price	P/E
1981	$4.30	$2.58	60%	$68	15.8
1980	3.85	2.31	60	60	15.6
1979	3.29	1.97	60	50	15.2
1978	3.09	1.85	60	42	13.6
1977	3.05	1.83	60	38	12.5
1976	2.64	1.58	60	31	11.7
1975	1.98	1.19	60	26	13.1
1974	2.93	1.76	60	31	10.6
1973	3.48	2.09	60	35	10.1
1972	2.95	1.77	60	30	10.2

Parker Panels

Year	Earnings	Dividend	Payout	Price	P/E
1981	$3.24	$1.94	60%	$70	21.6
1980	2.75	1.79	65	56	20.4
1979	2.94	1.79	61	53	18.0
1978	2.93	1.73	59	48	16.4
1977	2.90	1.65	57	44	15.2
1976	2.86	1.57	55	41	14.3
1975	2.61	1.49	57	35	13.4
1974	1.55	1.50	97	20	12.9
1973	2.24	1.50	67	34	15.2
1972	2.19	1.49	68	30	13.7

Both companies are in the same markets, and both are similarly organized (approximately the same degree of operating and financial leverage). Northwest has been consistently earning more per share; yet, for some reason, it has not been valued at as high a P/E ratio as Parker. What factors would you point out as possible causes for this lower market valuation of Northwest's stock?

CHAPTER 18

VALUATION

We now have the background to take up the subject of valuation. In Chapter 1, we noted that the goal of financial management is to maximize the value of the firm. We saw in Chapters 13 and 14 on capital budgeting that values are determined by applying a discount factor to a future stream of cash flows. The discount factor is determined by the basic business risk of the business activities of the firm, its degree of operating leverage, and the degree of financial leverage employed. In Chapter 16, we analyzed how the cost of capital is affected by the degree to which the firm employs financial leverage.

The other main element of valuation is the future revenue stream. Some aspects of the revenue stream were treated in the preceding chapter on dividend policy. In the present chapter, we can tie all of this together by consideration of how various characteristics of the pattern of the future revenue streams affect valuation.

Definitions of Value

While it may be difficult to ascribe monetary returns to certain kinds of assets—works of art, for instance—the fundamental characteristic of business assets is that they give rise to income flows. Sometimes these flows are easy to determine and measure; the interest return on a bond is an example. At other times, the cash flows attributable to the asset must be estimated, as was done in Chapters 13 and 14 in the evaluation of projects. Regardless of the difficulties of measuring income flows, it is the prospective income from business assets that gives them value.

Liquidating Value versus Going-Concern Value

Several different definitions of *value* exist in the literature and in practice; different definitions are appropriate at different times. The first distinction that must be made is that between liquidating value and going-concern value. *Liquidating value* is the amount that can be realized if an asset or a group of assets (the entire assets of a firm, for example) is sold separately from the organization that has been using them. If the owner of a machine shop decides to retire, he may auction off his inventory and equipment, collect his accounts receivable, and sell his land and buildings to a grocery wholesaler for use as a warehouse. The sum of the proceeds from each category of assets is the liquidating value of the assets. If the owner's debts are subtracted from this amount, the difference represents the liquidating value of his ownership in the business.

The *going-concern value* of a company is its worth as an operating business to another firm or individual. If this value exceeds the liquidating value, the difference represents the value of the organization as distinct from the value of the assets.[1]

[1] Accountants have termed this difference "goodwill," but "organization value" would be a more appropriate description.

Book Value versus Market Value

Book value, the accounting value at which an asset is carried, must also be distinguished from *market value*, the price at which the asset can be sold. If the asset in question is a firm, it actually has two market values—a liquidating value and a going-concern value. Only the higher of the two is generally referred to as the market value.

For stocks, book value per share is the firm's total common equity—common stock, capital or paid-in surplus, and accumulated retained earnings—divided by shares outstanding. Market value, what people will actually pay for a share of the stock, can be above or below book value. Nuclear Research, for example, has a book value of $8.27 per share and a market value of $25.50; West Virginia Railroad, on the other hand, has a book value of $112.80 and a market value of only $6.75. Nuclear Research's assets produce a high and rapidly growing earnings stream; West Virginia Railroad's assets are far less productive. Since market value depends on earnings, while book value reflects historical cost, it is not surprising to find deviations between book and market values in a dynamic, uncertain world.

Market Value versus Fair or Reasonable Value

The concept of fair or reasonable value (sometimes called *intrinsic value*) is widespread in the literature on stock market investments. Although the market value of a security is known at any given time, the security's fair value as viewed by different investors can differ. Graham, Dodd, and Cottle, authors of a leading investments text, define *fair value* as "that value which is justified by the facts; e.g., assets, earnings, dividends. . . . The computed [fair] value is likely to change at least from year to year, as the factors governing that value are modified."[2]

Although Graham, Dodd, and Cottle have developed this concept for security (that is, stock and bond) valuation, the idea applies to all business assets. It basically involves estimating the future net cash flows attributable to an asset; determining an appropriate capitalization, or discount, rate; and then finding the present value of the cash flows. This, of course, is exactly what was done in Chapters 13 and 14, where the concept of reasonable value was developed to help find the present value of investment opportunities.

The procedure for determining an asset's value is known as the *capitalization-of-income method of valuation*—a fancy name for the present value of a stream of earnings, discussed at length in Chapter 13. In going through the present chapter, keep in mind that *value, or the price of securities, is exactly analogous to the present value of assets* as determined in Chapters 13 and 14. From this point on, whenever the word *value* is used, it means the present value found by capitalizing expected future cash flows.

The next section applies these concepts to bond valuation; the two following sections treat the valuation of preferred and common stocks.

Bond Valuation

For bonds the expected cash flows are the annual interest payments plus the principal due when the bond matures. Depending on differences in the risk of default on interest or principal, the appropriate capitalization (or discount) rate applied to different bonds varies. A U.S. Treasury security, for example, has less

[2] B. Graham, D. L. Dodd, and S. Cottle, *Security Analysis* (New York: McGraw-Hill, 1961), p. 28.

risk than a security issued by a corporation; consequently, a lower discount (or capitalization) rate is applied to its interest payments. The actual calculating procedures employed in bond valuation are illustrated by the following examples.

Perpetual Bond

After the Napoleonic Wars (1814), England sold a huge bond issue, which it used to pay off many smaller issues that had been floated in prior years to pay for the war. Since the purpose of the new issue was to consolidate past debts, the individual bonds were called Consols. Suppose the bonds paid $100 interest annually to perpetuity. (Actually, interest was stated in pounds.) What would the bonds be worth under current market conditions?

First, note that the value v_b of any perpetuity is computed as follows:[3]

$$v_b = \frac{c}{(1+k_b)^1} + \frac{c}{(1+k_b)^2} + \cdots$$

$$= \frac{c}{k_b} \quad \textbf{(18.1)}$$

Here c is the constant annual interest in dollars and k_b the appropriate interest rate (or required rate of return) for the bond issue. Equation 18.1 is an infinite series of \$c a year, and the value of the bond is the discounted sum of the infinite series.

We know that the Consol's annual interest payment is $100; therefore, the only other thing we need in order to find its value is the appropriate interest rate. This is commonly taken as the going interest rate, or yield, on bonds of similar risk. Suppose we find such bonds to be paying 4 percent under current market conditions. Then the Consol's value is determined as follows:

$$v_b = \frac{c}{k_b} = \frac{\$100}{0.08} = \$1{,}250$$

[3] A perpetuity is a bond that never matures, that pays interest indefinitely. Equation 18.1 is simply the present value of an infinite series; its proof is demonstrated below. Rewrite Equation 18.1 as follows:

$$v_b = c\left[\frac{1}{(1+k_b)^1} + \frac{1}{(1+k_b)^2} + \cdots + \frac{1}{(1+k_b)^n}\right] \quad (1)$$

Multiply both sides of Equation 1 by $(1 + k_b)$:

$$v_b(1+k_b) = c\left[1 + \frac{1}{(1+k_b)^1} + \frac{1}{(1+k_b)^2} + \cdots + \frac{1}{(1+k_b)^{n-1}}\right] \quad (2)$$

Subtract Equation 1 from Equation 2, obtaining:

$$v_b(1 + k_b - 1) = c\left[1 - \frac{1}{(1+k_b)^n}\right] \quad (3)$$

As $n \rightarrow \infty$, $\frac{1}{(1+k_b)^n} \rightarrow 0$, so Equation 3 approaches

$$v_b k_b = c$$

and

$$v_b = \frac{c}{k_b}$$

If the going rate of interest rises to 10 percent, the value of the bond falls to $1,000 ($100/0.10). If interest rates continue rising, when the rate goes as high as 12 percent, the value of the Consol will be only $833.33. Values of this perpetual bond for a range of interest rates are given in the following table:

Current market interest rate	Current market value
4%	$2,500.00
6	1,666.67
8	1,250.00
10	1,000.00
12	833.33
14	714.29
16	625.00

Short-Term Bond

Suppose the British government issues bonds with the same risk of default as the Consols but with a three-year maturity. The new bonds also pay $100 interest and have a $1,000 maturity value. What will the value of these new bonds be at the time of issue if the going rate of interest is 8 percent? To find this value, we must solve Equation 18.2:

$$V_b = \frac{c_1}{(1 + k_b)^1} + \frac{c_2}{(1 + k_b)^2} + \frac{c_3 + M}{(1 + k_b)^3} \tag{18.2}$$

Here M is the maturity value of the bond. The solution is given in the following tabulation.[4]

Year	Receipt	8 percent discount factors	Present value
1	$100	0.9259	$ 92.59
2	$100	0.8573	85.73
1	$100 + $1,000	0.7938	873.18
		Bond value =	$1,051.50

At the various rates of interest used in the perpetuity example, this three-year bond will have the following values:

Current market interest rate	Current market value
4%	$1,166.51
6	1,106.90
8	1,051.50
10	1,000.00
12	951.99
14	907.17
16	865.30

[4] If the bond has a long maturity, twenty years for example, we would certainly want to calculate its present value by finding the present value of a twenty-year annuity and adding to it the present value of the $1,000 principal received at maturity. Special bond tables have been devised to simplify the calculation procedure. Note also that k_b frequently differs for the long- and short-term bonds; as we saw in Chapter 8, unless the yield to maturity curve is flat, long- and short-term rates differ.

Interest-Rate Risk

Figure 18.1 shows how the values of the long-term bond (the Consol) and the short-term bond change in response to changes in the going market rate of interest. Note how much less sensitive the short-term bond is to changes in interest rates. At a 10 percent interest rate, both the perpetuity and the short-term bonds are valued at $1,000. When rates rise to 16 percent, the long-term bond falls to $625, while the short-term bond falls only to $865. A similar situation occurs when rates fall below 10 percent. *This differential responsiveness to changes in interest rates depends on the required yield levels.* At the lower yields depicted in Figure 18.1, the longer the maturity of a security, the greater its price change in response to a given change in interest rates. This helps explain why corporate treasurers are reluctant to hold their near-cash reserves in the form of long-term debt instruments. These reserves are held at moderate interest levels for precautionary purposes, and treasurers are unwilling to sacrifice safety for a little higher yield on a long-term bond. However, for deep discount bonds at required yields of 10 percent or more, the further decline in price with higher required yields is at a lesser rate for longer-term bonds than for shorter-term bonds. This is depicted in Figure 18.2, where the value of the thirty-year bond falls less rapidly than the value of a twenty-year bond as required yields rise from 10 to 25 percent.

Figure 18.1

Values of Long-Term and Short-Term Bonds, 5 Percent Coupon Rate, at Different Market Interest Rates

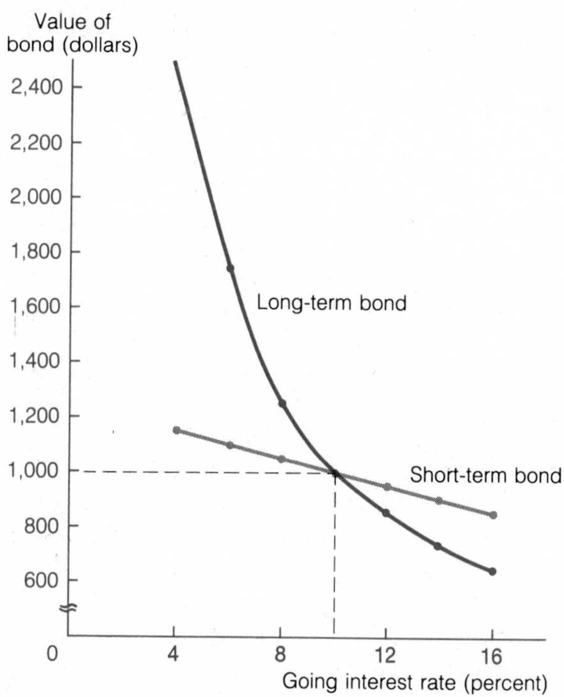

Figure 18.2 **Values of 20-Year and 30-Year Bonds at Required Yields of 10 to 25 Percent**

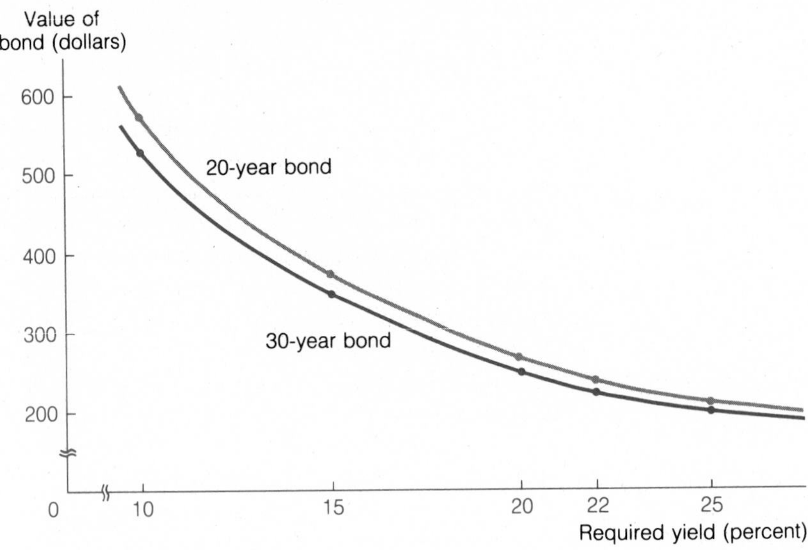

Preferred Stock Valuation

Most preferred stocks entitle their owners to regular, fixed dividend payments similar to bond interest. Although some preferred issues are eventually retired, most are perpetuities whose value is found as follows:

$$V_{ps} = \frac{d_{ps}}{k_{ps}} \tag{18.3}$$

In this case, d_{ps} is the dividend on the preferred stock, and k_{ps} is the appropriate capitalization rate for investments of this degree of risk. Recall the General Motors \$3.75 preferred stock issue discussed in Chapter 16. The GM preferred stock was a no par stock that sold at 100 to yield 3.75 percent at the issue date. On November 11, 1981, the \$3.75 preferred stock of General Motors closed at \$28. The yield on a preferred stock is similar to that on a perpetual bond and is found by solving Equation 18.3 for k_{ps}. For the GM issue, the current price of the stock is observed in newspaper market quotations to be \$28, and its annual dividend is seen to be \$3.75. Thus the yield is 13.4 percent, calculated as follows:

$$k_{ps} = \frac{d_{ps}}{V_{ps}} = \frac{\$3.75}{\$28} = 13.4\%$$

The valuation relationship expressed by Equation 18.3 is also implied. If we know the promised dividend payment on the preferred stock and its current yield, we can determine its value:

$$V_{ps} = \frac{\$3.75}{0.134} = \$28.$$

Common Stock Returns and Valuation

While the same principles apply to the valuation of common stocks as to bonds or preferred stocks, two features make their analysis more difficult. First is the degree of certainty with which receipts can be forecast. For bonds and preferred stocks, this presents little difficulty, since the interest payments or preferred dividends are known with relative certainty. However, in the case of common stocks, forecasting future earnings, dividends, and stock prices can be difficult. The second complicating feature is that, unlike interest and preferred dividends, common stock earnings and dividends are generally expected to grow, not remain constant. Hence, while standard annuity formulas can be applied, more difficult conceptual schemes must also be used.

Estimating the Value of a Stock: The Single-Period Case

The price today of a share of common stock, p_0, depends on the return investors expect to receive if they buy the stock, and the riskiness of these expected cash flows. The expected returns consist of two elements: (1) the dividend expected in each year t, defined as d_t, and (2) the price investors expect to receive when they sell the stock at the end of Year n, defined as p_n. The price includes the return of the original investment plus a capital gain (or minus a capital loss). If investors expect to hold the stock for one year, and if the stock price is expected to grow at the rate g, the valuation equation is:

$$p_0 = \frac{\text{Expected dividend} + \text{Expected price (Both at end of Year 1)}}{1.0 + \text{Required rate of return}}$$

$$= \frac{d_1 + p_1}{(1 + k_s)} = \frac{d_1 + p_0(1 + g)}{(1 + k_s)}, \qquad \textbf{(18.4)}$$

which results in Equation 18.5 after simplification.[5]

$$p_0 = \frac{d_1}{k_s - g} \qquad \textbf{(18.5)}$$

$$p_0 = \frac{d_1 + p_0(1 + g)}{(1 + k_s)} \qquad \textbf{(18.4)}$$

$$p_0(1 + k_s) = d_1 + p_0(1 + g)$$

$$p_0(1 + k_s - 1 - g) = d_1$$

$$p_0(k_s - g) = d_1$$

$$p_0 = \frac{d_1}{k_s - g} \qquad \textbf{(18.5)}$$

[5] Notice that this equation is developed for a one-year holding period. In a later section, we will show that it is also valid for longer periods, provided the expected growth rate is constant.

Equations 18.4 and 18.5 represent the present value of the expected dividends and the year-end stock price, discounted at the required rate of return. Solving Equation 18.5 gives the expected or intrinsic price for the stock. To illustrate: Suppose you are thinking of buying a share of United Rubber common stock and holding it for one year. You note that United Rubber earned $2.86 per share last year and paid a dividend of $1.90. Earnings and dividends have been rising at about 5 percent a year, on the average, over the last ten to fifteen years, and you expect this growth to continue. Further, if earnings and dividends grow at the expected rate, you think the stock price will likewise grow by 5 percent a year.

The next step is to determine the required rate of return on United Rubber stock. The current rate of interest on U.S. Treasury securities, R_F, is about 9 percent. But United Rubber is clearly more risky than government securities. Competitors can erode the company's market; labor problems can disrupt operations; an economic recession can cause sales to fall below the breakeven point; auto sales can decline, pulling down United Rubber's own sales and profits; and so on. Further, even if sales, earnings, and dividends meet projections, the stock price can still fall as a result of a generally weak market.

Given all these risk factors, you conclude that a 7 percent risk premium is justified, so you calculate your required rate of return on United Rubber's stock, k_s^*, as follows:

$$k_s^* = R_F + \rho = 9\% + 7\% = 16\%$$

Next, you estimate the dividend for the coming year, d_1, as follows:

$$d_1 = d_0(1 + g) = \$1.90(1.05) = \$2$$

Now you have the necessary information to estimate the fair value of the stock by the use of Equation 18.6:

$$p_0 = \frac{d_1}{k_s^* - g}$$

$$= \frac{\$2}{0.16 - 0.05} = \$18.18 \quad \textbf{(18.6)}$$

To you, $18.18 represents a reasonable price for United Rubber's stock. If the actual market price is less, you will buy it; if the actual price is higher, you will not buy it, or you will sell if you own it.[6]

[6] Notice the similarity between this process and the NPV method of capital budgeting described in Chapter 13. In the earlier chapter, we (1) estimated a cost of capital for the firm, which compares with estimating k_s^*, our required rate of return; (2) discounted expected future cash flows, which are analogous to dividends plus the future stock price; (3) found the present value of future cash flows, which corresponds the fair value of the stock; (4) determined the initial outlay for the project, which compares with finding the actual price of the stock; and (5) accepted the project if the PV of future cash flows exceeded the initial cost of the project, which is similar to comparing the fair value of the stock to its market price.

Factors Leading to Changes in Market Prices

Assume that United Rubber's stock is in equilibrium, selling at a price of $18.18 per share. If all expectations are exactly met, over the next year the price will gradually rise to $19.09 (5 percent). However, many different events can occur to cause a change in the equilibrium price of the stock. To illustrate the forces at work, consider again the stock price model, the set of inputs used to develop the price of $18.18, and a new set of assumed input variables:

	Variable Value	
	Original	New
Riskless rate (R_F)	9%	8%
Market risk premium ($\bar{R}_M - R_F$)	5%	6%
Index of stock's risk (β)	1.4	1.2
Expected growth rate (g)	5%	6%

The first three variables influence k_s^*, which declines as a result of the new set of variables from 16 to 15.2 percent:

$$\text{Original: } k_s^* = 9\% + (5\%)(1.4) = 16\%$$

$$\text{New: } k_s^* = 8\% + (6\%)(1.2) = 15.2\%$$

Using these values, together with the new d and g values, we find that p_0 rises from $18.18 to $21.85:

$$\text{Original: } p_0 = \frac{\$1.90(1.05)}{0.16 - 0.05} = \frac{\$2}{0.11} = \$18.18$$

$$\text{New: } p_0 = \frac{\$1.90(1.06)}{0.152 - 0.06} = \frac{\$2.01}{0.092} = \$21.85$$

At the new price, the expected and required rates of return are equal:

$$\bar{k}_s = \frac{\$2.01}{\$21.85} + 6\% = 9.2\% + 6\% = 15.2\% = k_s^*$$

as found above.

Evidence suggests that securities adjust quite rapidly to disequilibrium situations. Consequently, equilibrium ordinarily exists for any given stock, and in general the required and expected returns are equal. Stock prices certainly change, sometimes violently and rapidly; but this simply reflects changing conditions and expectations. There are, of course, times when a stock continues to react for several months to a favorable or unfavorable development, but this does not signify a long adjustment period; it merely shows that as more information about the situation becomes available, the market adjusts to the new information.

Valuation under Alternative Growth Patterns

To this point we have treated a single-period model of stock valuation, in which investors hold the stock for one year, receive one dividend, and then sell the stock at the end of the year. We now take up multiperiod stock valuation models.

According to generally accepted theory, stock prices are determined as the present value of a stream of cash flows. In other words, the capitalization of income procedure applies to stocks as well as to bonds and other assets. What are the cash flows that corporations provide to their stockholders? What flows do the markets in fact capitalize? A number of different models have been formulated, and at least four different categories of flows have been capitalized in alternative formulations: (1) the stream of dividends, (2) the stream of earnings, (3) the current earnings plus flows resulting from future investment opportunities, and (4) the discounting of cash flows as in capital budgeting models. Miller and Modigliani have demonstrated that these different approaches are equivalent and yield the same valuations.[7]

Since multiperiod valuation models are inherently complicated, we shall illustrate the methodology involved by using the least complicated one—the stream of dividends approach.[8] In this formulation, a share of common stock is regarded as similar to a perpetual bond or a share of perpetual preferred stock, and its value is established as the present value of its stream of dividends:

$$\begin{aligned}\text{Value of stock} = p_0 &= \text{PV of expected future dividends}\\ &= \frac{d_1}{(1+k_s)^1} + \frac{d_2}{(1+k_s)^2} + \cdots\\ &= \sum_{t=1}^{\infty} \frac{d_t}{(1+k_s)^t} \qquad \textbf{(18.7)}\end{aligned}$$

Unlike bond interest and preferred dividends, common stock dividends are not generally expected to remain constant in the future; hence the convenient annuity formulas cannot be used. This fact, combined with the much greater uncertainty about common stock dividends than about bond interest or preferred dividends, makes common stock valuation a more complex task than bond or preferred stock valuation.

Equation 18.7 is a general stock valuation model in the sense that the time pattern of d_t can be anything; that is, d_t can rise, fall, remain constant, or even fluctuate randomly, and Equation 18.7 will still hold. For many purposes, however, it is useful to estimate a particular time pattern for d_t and then develop a simplified (easier to evaluate) version of the stock valuation model expressed in Equation 18.7.

[7] See their "Dividend Policy, Growth, and the Valuation of Shares," *Journal of Business* 34 (October 1961).

[8] A more general free cash flow model of valuation under alternative growth patterns is presented in J. Fred Weston and Eugene F. Brigham, *Managerial Finance*, 7th ed. (Hinsdale, Ill.: The Dryden Press, 1981), pp. 120–131.

The following sections consider the special cases of zero growth, constant growth, and supernormal growth.

Stock Values with Zero Growth

Suppose the rate of growth is measured by the rate at which dividends are expected to increase. If future growth is expected to be zero, the value of the stock reduces to the same formula as that developed for a perpetual bond:

$$\text{Price} = \frac{\text{Dividend}}{\text{Capitalization rate}}$$

$$p_0 = \frac{d_1}{k_s} \tag{18.8}$$

Solving for k_s, we obtain:

$$k_s = \frac{d_1}{p_0} \tag{18.8a}$$

which states that the required rate of return on a share of stock that has no growth prospects is simply the dividend yield.

Normal, or Constant, Growth

Year after year, the earnings and dividends of most companies have been increasing. In general, this growth is expected to continue in the foreseeable future at about the same rate as the GNP. Thus, if such a company's current dividend is d_0, its dividend in any future year t will be $d_t = d_0(1 + g)^t$, where g = the expected rate of growth. For example, if United Rubber just paid a dividend of \$2.00 (d_0 = \$2.00) and its investors expect an 8 percent growth rate, the estimated dividend one year hence is d_1 = (\$2.00)(1.08) = \$2.16; two years hence is \$2.33; and five years hence is:

$$\begin{aligned} d_t &= d_0(1 + g)^t \\ &= \$2.00(1.08)^5 \\ &= \$2.94 \end{aligned}$$

Using this method of estimating future dividends, the current price, p_0, is determined as follows:

$$\begin{aligned} p_0 &= \frac{d_1}{(1 + k_s)^1} + \frac{d_2}{(1 + k_s)^2} + \frac{d_3}{(1 + k_s)^3} + \cdots \\ &= \frac{d_0(1 + g)^1}{(1 + k_s)^1} + \frac{d_0(1 + g)^2}{(1 + k_s)^2} + \frac{d_0(1 + g)^3}{(1 + k_s)^3} + \cdots \\ &= \sum_{t=1}^{\infty} \frac{d_0(1 + g)^t}{(1 + k_s)^t} \end{aligned} \tag{18.9}$$

If g is constant, Equation 18.9 can be simplified as follows:[9]

$$p_0 = \frac{d_1}{k_s - g} \tag{18.10}$$

Notice that the constant growth model expressed in Equation 18.10 is identical to the single-period model, Equation 18.5, developed in an earlier section.

A necessary condition for the constant growth model is that k_s be greater than g; otherwise, Equation 18.10 gives nonsense answers. If k_s equals g, the equation blows up, yielding an infinite price; If k_s is less than g, a negative price results. Since neither infinite nor negative stock prices make sense, it is clear that in equilibrium k_s must be greater than g.

Note that Equation 18.10 is sufficiently general to encompass the no-growth case described above. If growth is zero, this is simply a special case, and Equation 18.10 is equal to Equation 18.8.[10]

Supernormal Growth

Firms typically go through life cycles; during part of these cycles their growth is much faster than that of the economy as a whole. Automobile manufacturers in the 1920s and computer and office equipment manufacturers in the 1960s are examples. Figure 18.3 illustrates such supernormal growth and compares it with normal growth, zero growth, and negative growth.[11]

[9] The proof of Equation 18.10 is as follows. Rewrite Equation 18.9 as

$$p_0 = d_0\left[\frac{(1+g)}{(1+k_s)} + \frac{(1+g)^2}{(1+k_s)^2} + \frac{(1+g)^3}{(1+k_s)^3} + \cdots + \frac{(1+g)^n}{(1+k_s)^n}\right] \tag{1}$$

Multiply both sides of Equation 1 by $(1 + k_s)/(1 + g)$:

$$p_0\left[\frac{(1+k_s)}{(1+g)}\right] = d_0\left[1 + \frac{(1+g)}{(1+k_s)} + \frac{(1+g)^2}{(1+k_s)^2} + \cdots + \frac{(1+g)^{n-1}}{(1+k_s)^{n-1}}\right] \tag{2}$$

Subtract Equation 1 from Equation 2 to obtain:

$$p_0\left[\frac{(1+k_s)}{(1+g)} - 1\right] = d_0\left[1 - \frac{(1+g)^n}{(1+k_s)^n}\right]$$

$$p_0\left[\frac{(1+k_s)-(1+g)}{(1+g)}\right] = d_0\left[1 - \frac{(1+g)^n}{(1+k_s)^n}\right]$$

Assuming $k_s > g$, as $n \rightarrow \infty$, the term in brackets on the right side of the equation $\rightarrow$ 1.0, leaving:

$$p_0\left[\frac{(1+k_s)-(1+g)}{(1+g)}\right] = d_0$$

which simplifies to:

$$p_0(k_s - g) = d_0(1+g) = d_1$$

$$p_0 = \frac{d_1}{k_s - g}$$

[10] The logic underlying the analysis implicitly assumes that investors are indifferent betwsen dividend yield or capital gains. Empirical work has not conclusively established whether or not this is true.

[11] A negative growth rate represents a declining company (e.g., a mining company whose profits are falling because of a declining ore body).

Figure 18.3

A Comparison of Four Companies' Dividend Growth Rates

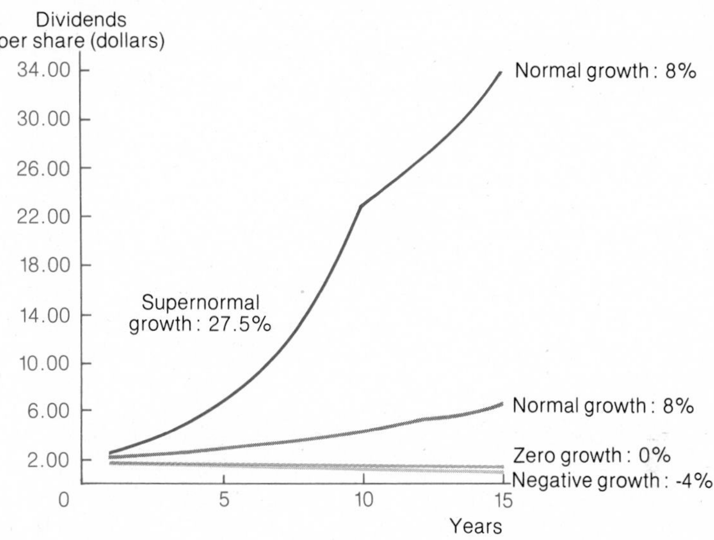

A hypothetical supernormal growth firm is expected to grow at a 27.5 percent rate for ten years, then to have its growth rate fall to 8 percent. The value of the firm with this growth pattern is determined by the following equation:

Present price = PV of dividends during supernormal growth period + Value of stock price at end of supernormal growth period discounted back to present

$$p_0 = \sum_{t=1}^{n} \frac{d_0(1 + g_s)^t}{(1 + k_s)^t} + \left(\frac{d_{n+1}}{k_s - g}\right)\left(\frac{1}{(1 + k_s)^n}\right) \tag{18.11}$$

where:

g_s = the supernormal growth rate

g = the normal growth rate

n = the period of supernormal growth

Working through an example will help make this clear. Consider a supernormal growth firm whose current dividend is \$2.00 (d_0 = \$2.00), with the dividend expected to increase by 27.5 percent a year for ten years and thereafter at 8 percent a year indefinitely. If stockholders' required rate of return is 16 percent on an investment with this degree of risk, what is the value of the stock? On the basis of the calculations in Table 18.1, the value is \$104.41, the present value of the dividends during the first ten years plus the present value of the stock at the end of the tenth year.

Table 18.1

Method of Calculating the Value of a Stock with Supernormal Growth

Assumptions:

a. Stockholders' capitalization rate is 16 percent ($k_s = 16\%$).

b. Growth rate is 27.5 percent for ten years, 8 percent thereafter ($g_s = 27.5\%$, $g = 8\%$, and $n = 10$).

c. The current dividend is \$2.00 ($d_0 = \$2.00$).

Step 1. Find present value of dividends during rapid growth period.

(1) Year	(2) Amount of dividend $\$2(1.275)^t$	(3) PVIF factor $1/(1.16)^t$	(4) Present value (2) × (3)
1	2.55	0.8621	2.20
2	3.25	0.7432	2.42
3	4.15	0.6407	2.66
4	5.29	0.5523	2.92
5	6.74	0.4761	3.21
6	8.59	0.4104	3.53
7	10.96	0.3538	3.88
8	13.97	0.3050	4.26
9	17.81	0.2630	4.68
10	22.71	0.2267	5.15
Present value of ten years' dividends			\$34.91

Step 2. Find present value of year 10 stock price.

a. Find value of stock at end of year 10:

$$p_{10} = \frac{d_{11}}{k_s - g} = \frac{\$22.71(1.08)}{0.08} = \$306.59$$

b. Discount p_{10} back to present:

$$PV = p_{10}\left(\frac{1}{1+k}\right)^{10} = \$306.59(0.2267) = \$69.50$$

Step 3. Sum to find total value of stock today:

$$p_0 = \$34.91 + \$69.50 = \$104.41$$

Comparing Companies with Different Expected Growth Rates

A comparison of four companies' illustrative dividend growth rates graphed in Figure 18.3 will help summarize this section. Using the valuation equations developed in this chapter, the conditions assumed in the preceding examples, and the additional assumptions that each firm had earnings per share of \$4.00 ($EPS_0 =$ \$4.00) during the preceding reporting period and paid out 50 percent of its reported earnings (therefore, that dividends per share, d_0, are \$2.00 for each company), we show prices, dividend yields, and price/earnings (P/E) ratios in Table 18.2.

Investors require and expect a return of 16 percent on each of the stocks. For the declining firm, this return consists of a relatively high current dividend yield combined with a capital loss amounting to 4 percent a year. For the no-growth

Table 18.2 **Prices, Dividend Yields, and Price/Earnings Ratios for 9 Percent Returns under Different Growth Assumptions**

		Price	Current dividend yield	P/E ratio[a]
Declining firm:	$p_0 = \frac{d_1}{k_s - g} = \frac{\$1.92}{0.16 - (-0.04)}$	\$ 9.60	20.8%	2.40
No-growth firm:	$p_0 = \frac{d_1}{k_s} = \frac{\$2.00}{0.16}$	12.50	16.0	3.13
Normal-growth firm:	$p_0 = \frac{d_1}{k_s - g} = \frac{\$2.16}{0.16 - 0.08}$	27.00	8.0	6.75
Supernormal-growth firm:	$p_0 =$ (See Table 18.1)	104.41	2.4	26.10

[a] The beginning of this example assumed that each company is earning \$4.00 initially. Divided into the various prices, this \$4.00 gives the indicated P/E ratios.

firm, there is neither a capital gain nor a capital loss expectation, so the 16 percent return must be obtained entirely from the dividend yield. The normal growth firm provides a relatively low current dividend yield but an 8 percent per year capital gain expectation. Finally, the supernormal growth firm has the lowest current dividend yield but the highest capital gain expectation.

What is expected to happen to the prices of the four firms' stocks over time? Three of the four cases are straightforward. The no-growth firm's price is expected to be constant ($p_t = p_{t+1}$); the declining firm is expected to have a falling stock price; and the normal-growth firm's stock is expected to grow at a constant rate, 8 percent. The supernormal growth case is more complex, but what is expected can be seen from the data in Table 18.1.

It can readily be shown that:

$$\sum_{t=1}^{n} \frac{(1+g_s)^t}{(1+k_s)^t} = (1+h)\,\frac{(1+h)^n - 1}{h}$$

where $\frac{(1+g_s)}{(1+k_s)} = (1+h)$ for ease of expression.[12]

[12] The calculation procedure for the summation expression is:

$$\sum_{t=1}^{n} \frac{d_0(1+g_s)^t}{(1+k_s)^t} = d_0\left(\frac{1+g_s}{1+k_s}\right)\sum_{t=1}^{n} \frac{(1+g_s)^{t-1}}{(1+k_s)^{t-1}}$$

Write out the summation expression:

$$\sum_{t=1}^{n}\left(\frac{1+g_s}{1+k_s}\right)^{t-1} = \left[1 + \left(\frac{1+g_s}{1+k_s}\right) + \cdots + \left(\frac{1+g_s}{1+k_s}\right)^{n-1}\right]$$

Let $\left(\frac{1+g_s}{1+k_s}\right) = (1+h)$. Then use the formula for the summation of a geometric progression over n periods and simplify:

$$S_n = \frac{r^n - 1}{r - 1} = \frac{(1+h)^n - 1}{1 + h - 1} = \frac{(1+h)^n - 1}{h}$$

The result is the sum of an annuity in which the discount factor is h, which equals $\left(\frac{1+g_s}{1+k_s}\right) - 1$.

For the example in Table 18.1, we have:

$$1 + h = \frac{(1 + g_s)}{(1 + k_s)} = \frac{1.275}{1.16} = 1.099138$$

$$(1 + h)^{10} = (1.099138)^{10} = 2.5735$$

$$(1 + h)^{10} - 1 = 1.5735$$

$$\frac{(1 + h)^{10} - 1}{h} = \frac{1.5735}{.099138} = 15.87 = \text{CVIFA}(9.9138\%, 10\text{ yrs.})$$

$$d_0(1 + h)(15.87) = \$2.00/1.099138(15.87) = \$34.89$$

The PV of the first ten years' dividends shown in Table 18.1 is $34.91, which is approximately the same. Note that the present price, p_0, is $104.41 and that the expected price in year 10, p_{10}, is $306.59. This represents an average growth rate of approximately 11.4 percent.[13] From year 11 on, the company's stock price and dividend are expected to grow at the normal rate, 8 percent.

The relationships among the P/E ratios, shown in the last column of Table 18.2, are similar to what can be intuitively expected—the higher the expected growth (all other things being equal), the higher the P/E ratio.[14]

The underlying determinants of the kind of growth in earnings, dividends, and value that will be experienced by a firm should be noted. The key relationship goes back to the discussion of capital budgeting in Chapter 13. If the earning rates on new investments are greater than the firm's cost of capital, net present value will be added to the firm. Its value will increase and it will be a growth company.

For a declining company, the earning rate on new investments is less than its cost of capital. For a no-growth company, the earnings rate on new investment is just equal to the firm's cost of capital. This sometimes creates confusion in the minds of even experienced financial executives. If the earnings rate on new investments is exactly equal to the firm's cost of capital, it can be demonstrated that the firm's earnings per share and value per share will not increase. Of course, the accounting measures of total assets and net income will increase, but no increase in market value per share can be expected to take place.

For the constant-growth company, the earning rates on new investments will exceed the firm's cost of capital. For the supernormal-growth company, the excess rate will be very high for a period of time before settling to some lower level.

So valuation ties back to how well the firm budgets its capital and how well it manages its cost of capital. The key to value growth is an earnings rate in excess of the firm's cost of capital. In the next section of this book, we will take up in greater detail how financing decisions can help hold down the firm's cost of capital and

[13] Found from a hand calculator or interpolation from Table A.1; $306.59/$104.41 = 2.9364, and this is approximately the CVIF for an 11.4 percent growth rate for a ten-year period.

[14] Differences in P/E ratios among firms can also arise from differences in the rates of return, k_s, that investors use in capitalizing the future dividend streams. If one company has a higher P/E ratio than another, this could be caused by a higher g, a lower k, or a combination of these two factors.

thereby contribute to the increases in value that represent a fundamental goal of financial management.

Summary

The different types of value defined are (1) liquidating value versus going-concern value, (2) book value versus market value, and (3) fair value versus current market price. The market value, or price, of a security is found by the capitalization-of-income method, which finds the present value of the security's stream of earnings in the same way that an asset's cash flows are discounted in capital budgeting. For bond valuation, the relevant cash flows are the periodic interest payments and the principal repaid at maturity, discounted by the required yield on the bond given its risk and maturity. The earnings stream for preferred stock consists of the regular fixed dividend payments discounted at the required rate of return. In terms of valuation, preferred stock is similar to a perpetual bond.

The valuation of common stock involves the same principles, but the returns to common stock consist of both the dividend yield and a capital gain expectation based on expected growth. Another complicating feature of common stock is the degree of uncertainty involved. Bond and preferred stock payments are relatively predictable, but forecasting common stock dividends and, even more, capital gains, is highly uncertain.

The fair value of a common share experiencing constant, "normal" growth can be found as

$$p_0 = \frac{d_1}{k_s - g}$$

where d_1 is the expected dividend, k_s is the risk-adjusted required rate of return, and g is the expected rate of growth. This model has general application for firms growing at a constant rate for an indefinite period, as well as for the special cases of the no-growth firm ($g = 0$) and the declining firm ($g < 0$). Similarly, given a stock's market price, its rate of return can be calculated as

$$k_s = \frac{d_1}{p_0} + g$$

Some companies may anticipate a temporary period of supernormal growth before leveling off to a more normal growth rate. In this case, the stock value consists of the present value of the dividends during the supernormal period plus the present value of the stock price at the end of the supernormal period discounted back to the present.

The required rate of return can be identical for companies experiencing each of these growth patterns, but the components of the return will vary. For the declining firm, the rate of return consists of a relatively high dividend yield less a capital loss expectation. For the no-growth firm, the dividend yield represents the entire return. For the firm with constant growth, the return is made up of both dividend yield and capital gain expectation. For the supernormal-growth firm, the dividend yield will be relatively low and the capital gain expectation relatively high.

Questions

18.1 Explain why a share of no-growth common stock is similar to a share of preferred stock. Use one of the equations developed in the chapter as part of your explanation.

18.2 Explain the importance in common stock valuation of:
a. current dividends
b. current market price
c. the expected future growth rate
d. the market capitalization rate

18.3 Suppose a firm's charter explicitly precludes it from ever paying a dividend. Investors know that this restriction will never be removed. Earnings for 1981 were \$1 a share, and they are expected to grow at the rate of 4 percent forever. If the required rate of return is 10 percent, what is the firm's theoretical P/E ratio?

18.4 Describe the factors that determine the market rate of return on a particular stock at a given point in time.

18.5 Explain how the following influence stock and bond prices:
a. interest rates
b. investor's aversion to risk

18.6 Most inheritance tax laws state that for estate tax purposes, property shall be valued on the basis of "fair market value." Describe how an inheritance tax appraiser might use the valuation principles discussed in this chapter to establish the value of:
a. shares of a stock listed on the New York Stock Exchange
b. shares representing 20 percent of a stock that is not publicly traded

Problems

18.1 The Jasper Baby Carriage Company has grown at a 6 percent annual rate over the past 10 years. Last year's annual dividend was \$2.00 per share. The appropriate capitalization rate for Jasper is 12 percent.
a. What is the market price per share?
b. Recent census information has caused the market to reevaluate its assessment of Jasper's growth potential to a negative 2 percent per year. What will be the market price of Jasper's stock?

18.2 Prosun Engineering has just developed a solar panel capable of generating 200 percent more electricity than any solar panel currently on the market. As a result, Prosun is expected to experience a 30 percent annual growth rate for the next 15 years. By the end of 15 years, other firms will have developed comparable technology, and Prosun's growth rate will slow to 8 percent per year indefinitely. Stockholders require a return of 12 percent on Prosun stock. The most recent annual dividend (d_0) was \$1.50 per share. What is the current price of Prosun stock?

18.3 After 6 years as vice president of a New York bank, Henry Thorson has decided to simplify his lifestyle and become a small-town shopkeeper.

He has found an apparently successful variety store in rural Pennsylvania for sale at a price of $120,000. The most recent balance sheet is given below:

Assets		Liabilities	
Cash	$ 18,000	Notes payable, bank	$ 6,000
Receivables, net	6,000	Accounts payable	12,000
Inventories	39,000	Accruals	3,000
Net fixed assets	42,000	Net worth	84,000
		Total liabilities and	
Total assets	$105,000	net worth	$105,000

Annual pre-tax earnings (after rent, interest, and salaries) have averaged $24,000 for the preceding 3 years. The store has been in business in the same community for 20 years, and has 6 years remaining on a 10-year lease. The purchase price includes all assets, except for cash, and Thorson would have to assume all debts.

a. Is the price of $120,000 reasonable?

b. What other factors should be considered in arriving at a purchase price?

c. What is the significance, if any, of the lease?

18.4 The Ellis Company is a small jewelry manufacturer. The company has been successful and has grown. Now, Ellis is planning to sell an issue of common stock to the public for the first time, and it faces the problem of setting an appropriate price on its common stock. The company feels that the proper procedure is to select firms similar to it, with publicly traded common stock, and to make relevant comparisons.

The commpany finds several jewelry manufacturers similar to it with respect to product mix, size, asset composition, and debt/equity proportions . Of these, Bonden and Seeger are most similar.

Relationships	Bonden	Seeger	(Ellis Totals)
Earnings per share 1980	$ 5.00	$ 8.00	$ 1,500,000
Average, 1974–1980	4.00	5.00	1,000,000
Price per share, 1980	48.00	65.00	—
Dividends per share, 1980	3.00	4.00	700,000
Average, 1974–1980	2.50	3.25	500,000
Book value per share	45.00	70.00	12,000,000

a. Calculate the per share data for Ellis assuming that 500,000 shares of stock will be sold.

b. Calculate the P/E, dividend yield, and market to book relations for Bonden and Seeger.

c. Apply the relationships in part b to the Ellis per share data to establish boundaries for the indicated market price for the Ellis stock.

d. Using the boundaries, and taking trend patterns into account, what is your recommendation for an issuing price for the Ellis stock?

18.5 An investor requires a 20 percent return on the common stock of the M Company. During its most recent complete year, the M Company stock earned $4 and paid $2 per share. Its earnings and dividends are expected to grow at a 32 percent rate for five years, after which they are expected to grow at 8 percent per year. At what value of M Company stock would the investor earn a required 20 percent return?

18.6 The Kubler Company has two issues of bonds outstanding. Both bear coupons of 7 percent, and the effective yield required on each is 12 percent. Bond A has a maturity of ten years and Bond B a maturity of twenty years. Both pay interest annually.
a. What is the price of each bond?
b. If the effective yield on each bond rises to 14 percent, what is the price of each bond?
c. Explain why the price of one bond falls more than the price of the other when the effective yield rises.

18.7 The Rush Company has two issues of bonds outstanding. Both bear coupons of 10 percent, and the effective yield required on each is 18 percent because of the uncertain future of the company. Bond C has a maturity of twenty years and Bond D a maturity of thirty years. Both pay interest annually.
a. What is the price of each bond?
b. If the effective yield on each bond rises to 24 percent, what is the price of each bond?
c. Explain why the price of one bond falls more than the price of the other when the effective yield rises.
d. Compare the results in this problem with the results in the previous problem.

18.8 What will be the yield to maturity of a perpetual bond with a $1,000 par value, an 8 percent coupon rate, and a current market price of $800? Of $1,000? Of $1,200? Assume interest is paid annually.

18.9 Assume that a bond has four years remaining to maturity and that interest is paid annually.
a. What will be the yield to maturity on the bond with a $1,000 maturity value, an 8 percent coupon interest rate, and a current market price of $825? Of $1,107?
b. Would you pay $825 for the bond if your required rate of return for securities in the same risk class was 10 percent ($k_b = 10\%$)? Explain.

18.10 The bonds of the Stanroy Corporation are perpetuities bearing a 9 percent coupon. Bonds of this type yield 8 percent. The par value of the bonds is $1,000.
a. What is the price of the Stanroy bonds?
b. Interest rate levels rise to the point where such bonds now yield 12 percent. What is the price of the Stanroy bonds now?
c. Interest rate levels drop to 9 percent. At what price do the Stanroy bonds sell?
d. How would your answers to parts a, b, and c change if the bonds had a definite maturity date of nineteen years?

PART SIX

LONG-TERM FINANCING DECISIONS

Part One covered the fundamental concepts of Managerial Finance. In Part Two, we developed materials for the analysis, planning, and control of the firm as a whole and for the control of decentralized divisions within the firm. Part Three considered the top half of the balance sheet, analyzing current assets, current liabilities, and the interactions between the two. In Part Four, we moved to the lower left side of the balance sheet, examining the process by which firms decide on investment in fixed assets. With the guidance of the concepts developed in Part Five on the cost of capital and valuation, we can now evaluate individual financing decisions.

Part Six deals with the lower right side of the balance sheet, considering the various types of funds available to the firm when it seeks long-term external capital. Within the framework of the relationship between financial structure and the cost of capital, decisions on individual financing episodes can be made to help the firm toward its objective of achieving an optimal mix of financing. Chapter 19 presents an overview of the institutional material essential to an understanding of the use of the financial markets by business firms. Chapter 20 analyzes the conditions under which common stock financing is used. Chapter 21 describes the nature of long-term debt and preferred stocks and their role in the financing of the firm. Chapter 22 analyzes leasing decisions. Chapter 23 discusses the nature and use of warrants, convertibles, and options.

CHAPTER 19

CAPITAL MARKETS: INSTITUTIONS AND BEHAVIOR

With the background of analysis of the major influences on the applicable cost of capital, we now turn to the objective of an optimal mix of financing that will result from individual financing decisions. This chapter deals with a number of aspects of the institutions and behavior of the capital markets business firms use in financing. We begin with an overview of the main sources of funds used by business corporations and an examination of the increasingly important practice of financing directly from such institutions as insurance companies and banks. We then turn to the investment banking mechanism by which the funds of individual investors are mobilized for use by business firms. The chapter includes an analysis of the relative costs of different methods of sale of new issues with particular attention to competitive versus negotiated securities offerings and a summary and discussion the implications of the securities laws for financing by business firms. The timing of financing decisions is analyzed in the light of theories of capital market efficiency.

Sources of Business Financing

An overview of the three broad sources of funds used by business corporations is presented in Table 19.1. The sources are internal cash flows, short-term external funds, and long-term external funds. The first two categories of financing were discussed in previous chapters. The third is the subject of this chapter, which provides an overview of the market mechanisms for raising long-term funds. The overview is intended as a framework for the discussion of individual forms of long-term financing, which are presented in the remaining chapters of this section.

The data in Table 19.1 show that internal financing provides more than 60 percent of the sources of funds for business corporations. External financing averages 36.5 percent of total sources. Of the external financing, long-term financing is more than two-thirds of the total. Short-term external financing is a kind of balance wheel, increasing as a source of financing when the economy is strong and decreasing during recessions. Long-term external financing now represents a market of more than $80 billion per year of net funds raised.

In making decisions about where and how to raise long-term funds, one important choice is between private sources and the public markets. Private financing represents funds obtained directly from one or a few individuals or financial institutions, such as banks, insurance companies, or pension funds.

Table 19.1

Sources of Funds for Business Corporations, 1972–1980 (Billions of Dollars)

	Internal cash flow		Short-term external funds		Long-term external funds		
	Amount	Percent	Amount	Percent	Amount	Percent	Total
1972	$ 87	60	$10	7	$47	33	$144
1973	102	57	32	18	45	25	179
1974	116	57	37	18	51	25	204
1975	119	76	(14)	(9)	52	33	157
1976	140	67	22	10	48	23	210
1977	155	66	29	12	52	22	236
1978	174	63	37	13	65	24	276
1979	200	62	45	14	78	24	323
1980	195	65	25	8	79	27	299

Source: Data from Donald E. Woolley and Beverly Lowen, *Credit and Capital Markets,1980* (New York: Bankers Trust Company, 1980), p. T26. Reprinted by permission. Woolley is senior vice president of Bankers Trust Company, and Lowen is senior economist of Bankers Trust Company.

Public financing uses investment bankers to sell securities to a large number of investors—both individuals and financial institutions. In the 1800s, before the development of broad financial markets, business firms were financed by a few wealthy individuals. One of the economic contributions of investment banking was to bring the general public into such financing by assembling smaller amounts of funds from larger numbers of sources and making the total available to business firms. By the 1930s, large pools of funds had been accumulated in insurance companies, pension funds, and commercial banks. This resulted in an increase in direct financing that bypassed to some degree the use of investment banking. Since direct financing is less complicated than public financing, it will be covered first in the chapter. Then the nature of investment banking will be discussed.

Direct Financing

Two major forms of direct long-term financing are term lending by commercial banks and insurance companies and the private placement of securities with insurance companies and pension funds. *Term loans* are direct business loans with a maturity of more than one year but less than fifteen years and with provisions for systematic repayment (amortization during the life of the loan). *Private placements* are direct business loans with a maturity of more than fifteen years.[1] Approximately half of such placements have been in the form of long-term promissory notes.[2] The distinction is, of course, arbitrary. Private placement differs

[1] This is the dividing line drawn by N. H. Jacoby and R. J. Saulnier, *Term Lending to Business* (New York: National Bureau of Economic Research, 1942), pp. 10–14 and Appendix B, pp. 143–47. See also the analysis in Avery B. Cohan, *Private Placements and Public Offerings* (Chapel Hill: School of Business Administration, University of North Carolina, 1961), pp. 2–5.

[2] E. Raymond Corey, *Direct Placement of Corporate Securities* (Cambridge, Mass: School of Business Administration, Harvard University, 1961), pp. 115–16.

from the term loan only in its arbitrary maturity length; this distinction becomes even fuzzier when we discover that some private placements call for repayment of a substantial portion of the principal within five to ten years.[3] Thus, term loans and private placements represent about the same kind of financing arrangements.

The total amount of bank term loans outstanding at the end of 1979 was $103 billion. The net amount of corporate debt sold on a private basis that remained outstanding at the end of 1979 was $145 billion. These two forms of direct financing sum to $248 billion. All corporate bonds outstanding at the end of 1979 totaled $431 billion. Hence direct financing was 58 percent of corporate bond funding.[4] These data establish that direct financing represents a major portion of long-term financing of business firms.

The central question of interest to financial managers is: What are the advantages and disadvantages of these two major sources of financing? The considerations that make direct financing of interest to borrowers can be shown under the heading of demand factors:

1. Term loans and private placements represent in part a shift by business firms from dependence on short-term bank borrowing to a greater utilization of longer-term financing. This shift helps businesses avoid the problem of unavailability of short-term loans during tight money periods.
2. Term loans and private placements were stimulated after 1934 by the increased cost and time involved in public offerings. The Securities Acts of 1933 and 1934 required that new financing go through a registration process and a twenty-day waiting period. Compiling data for the SEC registration statements increased the cost of public flotations, particularly for issues of less than $1 million, because the fixed costs were spread over small amounts.
3. A public offering takes time to prepare. There are registration statements to be written, underwriting agreements to be made, and a possible two-to-three-month waiting period before the offering can be made. A private placement or term loan can be taken care of in a matter of hours, especially where there is a continuing relationship between the insurance company or bank and the borrower.
4. If the securities of a public offering are widely held, it is more difficult to negotiate a modification in the indenture (loan agreement) provisions. If, for example, some of the terms of a direct loan have become onerous (not in the best interests of the borrower), the borrower can negotiate directly with the bank or the insurance company. It is much more difficult to contact thousands of bondholders to obtain agreement about modifying provisions of the bond issue.
5. The increased rates of corporate taxation in the 1930s made it more difficult for small and medium-sized firms to finance their growth with internal funds. It thus became necessary for them to turn to external sources, and direct longer-term loans represented one of these available sources. One study

[3] *Ibid.*, pp.120–21.

[4] Salomon Brothers, *1980 Prospects for the Credit Markets* (New York: Salomon Brothers, 1980), pp. 23–24.

observes that "the most important characteristic of the private placement market is that it serves as the major source of long-term debt financing for smaller, less financially secure companies."[5]

Characteristics of Term Loans and Private Placements

Most term loans are repayable on an amortized basis. Because this repayment, or amortization, schedule is a particularly important feature of such loans, it is useful to describe how it is determined. The purpose of amortization, of course, is to have the loan repaid gradually over its life rather than fall due all at once; this protects both the lender and the borrower against the possibility that the borrower will not make adequate provisions for retirement of the loan during its life. Amortization is especially important where the loan is for the purpose of purchasing a specific item of equipment; here the schedule of repayment will be geared to the productive life of the equipment, and payments will be made from cash flows resulting from use of the equipment.

To illustrate how the amortization schedule is determined, assume that a firm borrows $1,000 on a ten-year loan, that interest is computed at 8 percent on the declining balance, and that the principal and interest are to be paid in ten equal installments. What is the amount of each of the ten annual payments? To find this value we must use the present value concepts developed in Chapter 4.

First, notice that the lender advances $1,000 and receives in turn a ten-year annuity of *a* dollars each year. In Chapter 4 we saw that these receipts could be calculated as:

$$a = \frac{P_{r,t}}{\text{PVIFA}(r,t)}$$

where

$$a = \text{Annual receipt}$$

$$P_{r,t} = \text{Present value of the annuity}$$

$$\text{PVIFA}(r,t) = \text{Appropriate interest factor (found in Appendix Table A.4)}$$

Substituting the $1,000 for $P_{r,t}$ and the interest factor for a ten-year, 8 percent annuity—6.7101—for PVIFA(r, t), we find:

$$a = \frac{\$1{,}000}{6.7101} = \$149$$

Therefore, if the firm makes ten annual installments of $149 each, it will have retired the $1,000 loan and provided the lender an 8 percent return on the investment.

Table 19.2 breaks down the annual payments into interest and repayment components and proves in the process that level payments of $149 will, in fact, retire the $1,000 loan and give the lender an 8 percent return. This breakdown is important for tax purposes, because the interest payments are deductible expenses to the borrower and taxable income to the lender.

[5] E. Shapiro and C. R. Wolf, *The Role of Private Placements in Corporate Finance* (Cambridge, Mass.: School of Business Administration, Harvard University, 1972), p. 2.

Table 19.2 **Term Loan Schedule**

Year	Total payment	Interest[a]	Amortization repayment	Remaining balance
1	$149	$80	$ 69	$931
2	149	74	75	856
3	149	68	81	775
4	149	62	87	688
5	149	55	94	594
6	149	48	101	493
7	149	39	110	383
8	149	31	118	265
9	149	21	128	137
10	149	11	138	—

[a] Interest for the first year is 0.08 × $1,000 = $80; for the second year, 0.08 × $931 = $74; and so on.

Other Characteristics

Maturity For commercial banks, the term loan runs five years or less (typically three years). For insurance companies, typical maturities have been five to fifteen years. This difference reflects the fact that liabilities of commercial banks are shorter term than those of insurance companies. Banks and insurance companies occasionally cooperate in their term lending. For example, if a firm (usually a large one) seeks a fifteen-year term loan, a bank may take the loan for the first five years and an insurance company for the last ten years.

Collateral Commercial banks require security on about 60 percent of the volume and 90 percent of the number of term loans made. They take as security mainly stocks, bonds, machinery, and equipment. Insurance companies also require security on nearly one-third of their loans, frequently using real estate as collateral on the longer term ones.

Options In recent years institutional investors have increasingly taken compensation in addition to fixed interest payments on directly negotiated loans. The most popular form of additional compensation is an option to buy common stock, the option being in the form of detachable warrants permitting the purchase of the shares at stated prices over a designated period. (See Chapter 23 for more details on warrants.)

Terms of Loan Agreements

A major advantage of a term loan is that it assures the borrower of the use of the funds for an extended period. On a ninety-day loan, since the commercial bank has the option to renew or not renew, it has frequent opportunities to reexamine the borrower's situation. If it has deteriorated unduly, the loan officer simply does not renew the loan. On a term loan, however, the bank or insurance company has committed itself for a period of years. Because of this long-term commitment, restrictive provisions are incorporated into the loan agreement to protect the lender for the duration of the loan. The most important of these provisions (though by no means all of them) are listed below:

1. *Current ratio*. The current ratio must be maintained at some specified level—$2\frac{1}{2}$ to 1; 3 to 1; $3\frac{1}{2}$ to 1—depending on the borrower's line of business. Working capital must also be maintained at some minimum level.
2. *Additional long-term debt*. Typically, there are prohibitions against (a) incurring additional long-term indebtedness, except with the permission of the lender; (b) the pledging of assets; (c) the assumption of any contingent liabilities, such as guaranteeing the indebtedness of a subsidiary; and (d) the signing of long-term leases beyond specified amounts.
3. *Management*. The loan agreement may require (a) that any major changes in management personnel be approved by the lender; (b) that life insurance be taken out on the principals or key people in the business; and (c) that a voting trust be created or proxies be granted for a specified period to ensure that the management of the company will be under the control of the group on which the lender has relied in making the loan.
4. *Financial statements*. The lender will require the borrower to submit periodic financial statements for review.

Costs

Another major aspect of term loans is their cost. As with other forms of lending, the interest rate on these loans varies with the size of the loan and the quality of the borrower, reflecting also the fixed costs of making loans. Surveys show that on small term loans the effective interest rate may run to as much as six to eight percentage points above the prime rate. On loans of $1 million and more, term loan rates have been close to the prime rate.

The interest rate may be fixed for the life of the loan, or it may vary. Often the loan agreement specifies that the interest rate will be based on the average of the rediscount rate in the borrower's Federal Reserve district during the previous three months—generally 1 or 2 percent above the rediscount rate.[6] It may also be geared to the published prime rate charged by New York City banks.

On private placements, the interest rate generally runs from about ten to fifty basis points higher than that on comparable public issues. Empirical studies find the yield to maturity on the private placements to be about $\frac{1}{2}$ of 1 percent higher than on the public offerings. Thus, to some extent, the economies of using private placements are offset by their somewhat higher interest rates.

While direct long-term financing has grown to a substantial volume, public financing still predominates and is likely to continue doing so. Therefore, the institutions for long-term public financing are discussed next.

Investment Banking

In the U.S. economy, saving is done by one group of persons and investing by another. (*Investing* is used here in the sense of actually putting money into plant, equipment, and inventory, not in the sense of buying securities.) Savings are placed with financial intermediaries who, in turn, make the funds available to firms wishing to acquire plants and equipment and to hold inventories.

[6] The rediscount rate is the rate of interest at which a bank can borrow from a Federal Reserve bank.

One of the major institutions performing this channeling role is the *investment banking* institution. The term *investment banker* is somewhat misleading, since investment bankers are neither investors nor bankers. That is, they do not invest their own funds permanently; nor are they repositories for individuals' funds, as are commercial banks or savings banks. What, then, is the nature of investment banking?

The many activities of investment bankers can be described first in general terms and then with respect to specific functions. The traditional function of the investment banker has been to act as the middleman in channeling driblets of individuals' savings and funds into the purchase of business securities. The investment banker does this by purchasing and distributing the new securities of individual companies while performing the functions of underwriting, distribution of securities, and advice and counsel.

Underwriting

Underwriting is the insurance function of bearing the risks of adverse price fluctuations during the period in which a new issue of securities is being distributed. The nature of the investment banker's underwriting function can best be conveyed by example: A business firm needs $10 million. It selects an investment banker, holds conferences, and decides to issue $10 million of bonds. An underwriting agreement is drawn up. On a specific day, the investment banker presents the company with a check for $10 million (less commission). In return, the investment banker receives bonds in denominations of $1,000 each to sell to the public.

The company receives the $10 million before the investment banker has sold the bonds. Between the time the firm is paid the $10 million and the time the bonds are sold, the investment banker bears all the risk of market price fluctuations in the bonds. Conceivably, it can take the investment banker days, months, or longer to sell bonds. If the bond market collapses in the interim, the investment banker carries the risk of loss on the sale of the bonds.

There have been dramatic instances of bond market collapses within one week after an investment banker has bought $50 million or $100 million of bonds. For example, in the spring of 1974 an issue of New Jersey Sporting Arena bonds dropped $140 per $1,000 bond during the underwriting period, costing the underwriters an estimated $8 million. The issuing firm, however, does not need to be concerned about the risk of market price fluctuations while the investment banker is selling the bonds, since it has received its money. One fundamental economic function of the investment banker, then, is to underwrite the risk of a decline in the market price between the time the money is transmitted to the firm and the time the bonds are placed in the hands of their ultimate buyers. For this reason, investment bankers are often called *underwriters;* they underwrite risk during the distribution period.

Distribution

The second function of the investment banker is marketing new issues of securities. The investment banker is a specialist with a staff and organization to distribute securities and, therefore, the capacity to perform the physical distribution function more efficiently and more economically than can an individual corporation. A corporation that wished to sell an issue of securities would find it necessary to establish a marketing or selling organization—a very expensive and ineffective method of selling securities. The investment banker has a permanent, trained staff and dealer organization available to distribute securities. In addition, the investment banker's reputation for selecting good companies and pricing securities fairly builds up a broad clientele over time, and this further increases the efficiency with which securities can be sold.

Advice and Counsel

The investment banker, engaged in the origination and sale of securities, through experience becomes an expert adviser about terms and characteristics of securities that will appeal to investors. This advice and guidance is valuable. Furthermore, the person's reputation as a seller of securities depends on the subsequent performance of the securities. Therefore, investment bankers often sit on the boards of firms whose securities they have sold. In this way they can provide continuing financial counsel and increase the firm's probability of success.

Investment Banking Operation

Probably the best way to gain a clear understanding of the investment banking function is to trace the history of a new issue of securities.[7] Accordingly, this section describes the steps necessary to issue new securities.

Preunderwriting Conferences

First, the members of the issuing firm and the investment banker hold preunderwriting conferences at which they discuss the amount of capital to be raised, the type of security to be issued, and the terms of the agreement. Memorandums are written by the treasurer of the issuing company to the firm's directors and other officers describing proposals suggested at the conferences. Meetings of the board of directors of the issuing company are held to discuss the alternatives and to attempt to reach a decision.

At some point, the issuer enters an agreement with the investment banker that a flotation will take place. The investment banker then begins to conduct an underwriting investigation. If the company is proposing to purchase additional assets, the underwriter's engineering staff may analyze the proposed acquisition. A public accounting firm is called upon to make an audit of the issuing firm's financial situation and also helps prepare the registration statements in connection with these issues for the SEC.

A firm of lawyers is called in to interpret and judge the legal aspects of the flotation. In addition, the originating underwriter (who is the manager of the subsequent underwriting syndicate) makes an exhaustive investigation of the company's prospects.

When the investigations are completed, but before registration with the SEC is made, an underwriting agreement is drawn up by the investment banker. Terms of the tentative agreement may be modified through discussions between the

[7] The process described here relates primarily to situations where the firm doing the financing picks an investment banker, then negotiates over the terms of the issue. An alternative procedure, used extensively only in the public utility industry, is for the selling firm to specify the terms of the new issue, then to have investment bankers bid for the entire new issue with *sealed bids*. The very high fixed costs that an investment banker must incur to thoroughly investigate the company and its new issue rule out sealed bids except for the largest issues. The operation described in this section is called *negotiated underwriting*. Competition is keen among underwriters, of course, to develop and maintain working relations with business firms.

underwriter and the issuing company, but the final agreement will cover all underwriting terms except the price of the securities.

Registration Statement

A registration statement containing all relevant financial and business information on the firm then is filed with the SEC. The statutes set a twenty-day waiting period (which in practice may be shortened or lengthened by the SEC) during which the SEC staff analyzes the registration statement to determine whether there are any omissions or misrepresentations of fact. During the examination period, the SEC can file exceptions to the registration statement or can ask for additional information from the issuing company or the underwriters. Also during this period, the investment bankers are not permitted to offer the securities for sale, although they can print a preliminary prospectus with all the customary information except the offering price.

Pricing the Securities

The actual price the underwriter pays the issuer is not generally determined until the end of the registration period. There is no universally followed practice, but one common arrangement for a new issue of stock calls for the investment banker to buy the securities at a prescribed number of points below the closing price on the last day of registration. For example, in October 1977 the stock of Wilcox Chemical Company had a current price of $38 and had traded between $35 and $40 a share during the previous three months. The firm and the underwriter agreed that the investment banker would buy 200,000 new shares at $2.50 below the closing price on the last day of registration. The stock closed at $36 on the day the SEC released the issue, so the firm received $33.50 a share. Typically, such agreements have an escape clause that provides for the contract to be voided if the price of the securities falls below some predetermined figure. In the case of Wilcox, this *upset price* was set at $34 a share. Thus, if the closing price of the shares on the last day of registration had been $33.50, Wilcox would have had the option of withdrawing from the agreement.

This arrangement holds, of course, only for additional stock offerings of firms whose old stock was previously traded. When a company goes public for the first time, the investment banker and the firm negotiate a price in accordance with the valuation principles described in Chapter 18.

The investment banker has an easier job if the issue is priced relatively low, but the issuer of the securities naturally wants as high a price as possible. Some conflict on price therefore arises between the investment banker and the issuer. If the issuer is financially sophisticated and makes comparisons with similar security issues, the investment banker is forced to price close to the market.

Underwriting Syndicate

The investment banker with whom the issuing firm has conducted its discussions does not typically handle the purchase and distribution of the issue alone, unless the issue is a very small one. If the sums of money involved are large and the risks of price fluctuations are substantial, the investment banker forms a syndicate in an effort to minimize the amount of personal risk. A syndicate is a temporary association for the purpose of carrying out a specific objective. The nature of the arrangements for a syndicate in the underwriting and sale of a security through an investment banker can best be understood with the aid of Figure 19.1

Figure 19.1 **Diagram of Sales of $100 Million of Bonds through Investment Bankers**

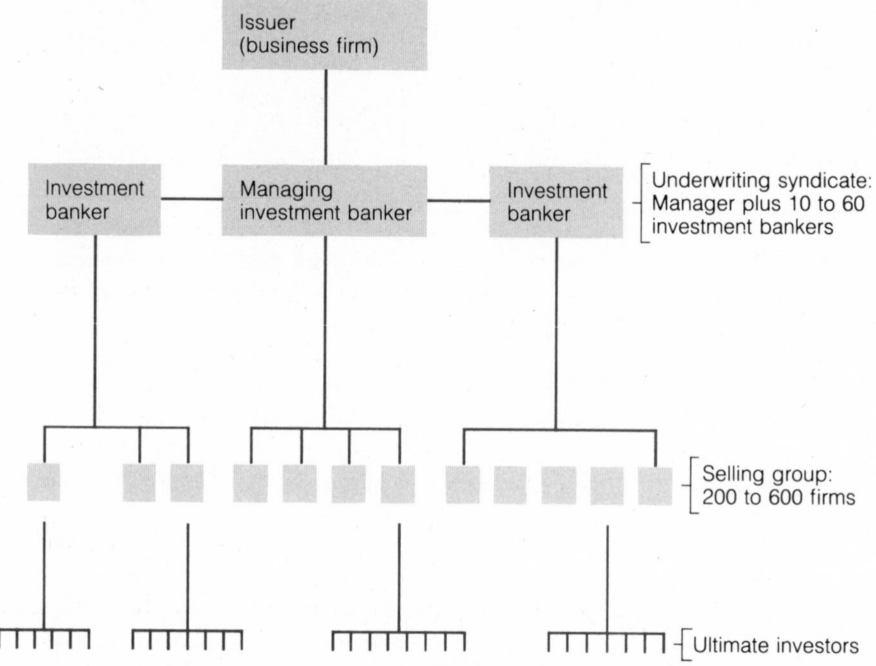

The managing underwriter invites other investment bankers to participate in the transaction on the basis of their knowledge of the particular kind of offering to be made and their strength and dealer contacts in selling securities of this type. Each investment banker has business relationships with other investment bankers and dealers and thus has a selling group composed of these people.

Some firms combine all these characteristics. For example, Merrill Lynch, Pierce, Fenner & Smith underwrites some issues and manages the underwriting of others. On still other flotations, it is invited by the manager to join in the distribution of the issue. It also purchases securities as a dealer, carries an inventory of those securities, and publishes lists of securities it has for sale. In addition to being a dealer, Merrill Lynch, of course, carries on substantial activity as a broker. An individual investment firm may also carry on all these functions.

There are also firms with a narrower range of functions—specialty dealers, specialty brokers, and specialty investment counselors. Thus, in the financial field, there is often specialization of financial functions. A *dealer* purchases securities outright, holds them in inventory, and sells them at whatever price can be gotten. The dealer may benefit from price appreciation or may suffer a loss on declines, as any merchandiser does. A *broker,* on the other hand, takes orders for purchases and transmits them to the proper exchange; the gain is the commission charged for the service.

Syndicates are used in the distribution of securities for three reasons:

1. A single investment banker may be financially unable to handle a large issue alone.
2. The originating investment banker may desire to spread the risk even if it is financially able to handle the issue alone.
3. The utilization of several selling organizations (as well as other underwriters) permits an economy of selling effort and expense and encourages nationwide distribution.

Participating underwriters and dealers are provided with full information on all phases of these financing transactions, and they share in the underwriting commission. Suppose that an investment banker buys $10 million worth of bonds to be sold at par, or $1,000 each. If this banker receives a two-point spread, the logical course is to buy the bonds from the issuer at 98; that is, the banker must pay the issuer $9.8 million for the issue of $10 million. Typically, on a two-point spread, the managing underwriter receives the first one-quarter of 1 percent for originating and managing the syndicate. Next, the entire underwriting group receives about 0.75 percent. Members of the selling group receive about 1 percent as a sales commission.

The manager of the underwriting group who makes a sale to an ultimate purchaser of the securities receives the 0.25 percent as manager, 0.75 percent as underwriter, and 1 percent as seller—the full 2 percent. If the manager wholesales some of the securities to members of the selling group who make the ultimate sale, they receive the 1 percent selling commission and the manager receives the other 1 percent for managing and underwriting the issue. If the issue is managed by one firm, underwritten by a second, and sold by a third, the 2 percent commission is divided, with 1 percent going to the selling firm, 0.75 percent to the underwriter, and 0.25 percent to the manager of the underwriting group.

Variations take place around these patterns. In early October 1979, IBM sold $500 million in seven-year notes and $500 million in twenty-five-year debentures; the commissions on the debentures were higher than those on the notes. On the notes, the total fee was $6.25 per note, representing about five-eighths of 1 percent of the selling price to buyers. The management fee was $1.25 and the underwriter fee was also $1.25, with a selling commission of $3.75. The total fee on the debentures was seven-eighths of 1 percent, or $8.75, with $1.75 to the managers, $2 to the underwriters, and $5 to the sellers.[8]

Ordinarily, each underwriter's liability is limited to the agreed-upon commitment. For example, an investment banker who participates in a $20 million offering and agrees to see to it that $5 million of the securities are sold is no longer responsible after the $5 million of securities are sold.

Selling Group

The selling group is formed primarily for the purpose of distributing securities; it consists of dealers, who take relatively small participations from the members of the underwriting group. The underwriters act as wholesalers; members of the

[8] W. Guzzardi, Jr., "The Bomb IBM Dropped on Wall Street," *Fortune*, November 19, 1979, p. 53.

selling group act as retailers. The number of investment banking houses in a selling group depends partly on the size of the issue. A selling group may have as many as three hundred to four hundred dealers. The operation of the selling group is controlled by the *selling group agreement,* which usually covers the following major points.

1. *Description of the issue.* The description is set forth in a report on the issue—the prospectus—which fully describes the issue and the issuer.
2. *Concession.* Members of the selling group subscribe to the new issue at a public offering price less the *concession* given to them as a commission for their selling service. The selling commission is generally greater than the sum of the managing and underwriting fees.
3. *Handling purchased securities.* The selling group agreement provides that no member of the selling group will be permitted to sell the securities below the public offering price. The syndicate manager invariably "pegs" the quotation in the market by placing continuous orders to buy at the public offering price. A careful record is kept of bond or stock certificate numbers so that repurchased securities can be identified with the member of the selling group who sold them. The general practice is to cancel the commission on such securities. Repurchased securities are then placed with other dealers for sale.[9]
4. *Duration of selling group.* The most common provision in selling group agreements is that the group has an existence of thirty days, subject to earlier termination by the manager. The agreement may be extended, however, for an additional eighty days by members representing 75 percent of the selling group.

Offering and Sale

After the selling group has been formed, the actual offering takes place. Publicity for the sale is given in advance of the offering date. Advertising material is prepared for release as soon as permitted. The actual day of the offering is chosen with a view to avoiding temporary congestion in the security market and other unfavorable events or circumstances.

The formal public offering is called *opening the books,* an archaic term reflecting ancient customs of the investment banking trade. When the books are opened, the manager accepts subscriptions to the issue from both selling group participants and outsiders who wish to buy. If the demand is great, the books may be closed immediately and an announcement made that the issue is oversubscribed; the issue is said to "fly out the window." If the reception is weak, the books may remain open for an extended period.

[9] Without these repurchase arrangements, members of the selling group could sell their share of the securities on the market instead of soliciting new purchasers. Since the pegging operation is going on, there will be a ready market for the securities; consequently, a penalty is necessary to avoid thwarting the syndicate operation.

Market Stabilization

During the period of the offering and distribution of securities, the manager of the underwriting group typically stabilizes the price of the issue. The duration of the price-pegging operation is usually thirty days. The price is pegged by placing orders to buy at a specified price in the market. The pegging operation is designed to prevent a cumulative downward movement in the price, which would result in losses for all members of the underwriting group. Since the manager of the underwriting group has the major responsibility, that person assumes the task of pegging the price.

If the market deteriorates during the offering period, the investment banker carries a substantial risk. For this reason, the pegging operation may not be sufficient to protect the underwriters. In one Pure Oil Company issue of $44 million of convertible preferred stock, only $1 million of shares were sold at the $100 offering price. At the conclusion of the underwriting agreement, initial trading took place at $74, incurring for the investment bankers a loss of over $11 million ($43 million × 26 percent). In the Textron issue of June 1967, the offering was reduced from $100 million to $50 million because of market congestion, and 5 percent of the bonds still were unsold after the initial offering. Other such cases can be cited.

IBM's October 1979 Debt Offering

The IBM debt offering of October 1979 provides an informative case study of the nature of modern investment banking and underwriting.[10] IBM's debt offering was called the largest in U.S. corporate history. It represented a combined offering by IBM of $500 million in seven-year notes and $500 million in twenty-five-year debentures (unsecured long-term debt) for a total of $1 billion. IBM's customary investment banker had been Morgan Stanley & Co. For this offering, IBM requested separate proposals from Morgan Stanley and from Salomon Brothers. It was reported that IBM's financial management was of the opinion that two managers would provide better execution of the sale and back it up with a larger amount of capital. John H. Gutfreund, Salomon Brother's managing partner, is quoted as stating, "A major corporation is best served by two sets of eyes and ears." Robert H. B. Baldwin, president of Morgan Stanley, is said to have responded, "You need only one brain surgeon."[11] Morgan Stanley dropped out as manager and Merrill Lynch became the co-manager, with an underwriting group totaling 227 members.

The Salomon and Morgan Stanley proposals had been presented to IBM early in September 1979. The ensuing discussions took place during a period when the prime rate was increased five times, reaching a level of 13.5 percent by September 28. The planned date for the offering was moved up from October 15 to the first week in October. A pricing meeting took place on October 3, 1979, with rapidly rising yields taking place in the money markets. Discussions centered around prices

[10] This summary is based on contemporaneous accounts in the financial press and in the later article by Guzzardi, "The Bomb IBM Dropped on Wall Street," pp. 52–56. Our assessment of the financing differs from the view expressed in the latter account.

[11] Guzzardi, "The Bomb IBM Dropped on Wall Street," p. 52.

based on a yield of seven basis points above Treasury notes for the IBM notes and twelve basis points above Treasury bonds for the IBM debentures. Taking the small price discounts into account, IBM was paying 9.62 percent for the seven-year notes and 9.41 percent for the twenty-five-year debentures. The underwriting spread or commission on the notes was five-eighths of 1 percent, or $6.25 per note. The underwriter fee on the debentures was seven-eighths of 1 percent, or $8.75 per debenture.

October 3 was a Wednesday. After the pricing meeting, which ended at 12:40 p.m., the market yield of Treasury bonds moved up during the afternoon by five basis points. The IBM offering began on Thursday, October 4. Also on Thursday the Treasury auctioned $2.5 billion of four-year notes yielding 9.79 percent, higher than the 9.62 percent for the IBM seven-year notes.

On Saturday, October 6, the Federal Reserve System announced an increase in its discount rate from 11 percent to 12 percent. A number of other credit-tightening policies, called "Draconian" in their severity, were implemented. As a result of the Fed's actions, by Tuesday, October 9, an additional increase in the prime rate was announced, with a rise of one full percent—to 14.5 percent. On Wednesday morning, October 10, the underwriting syndicate was disbanded. The price of both the notes and the debentures fell by about $5 each, with yields rising to 10.65 percent per note and 10.09 percent for the debentures.

When the syndicate was disbanded, it was estimated that $600 to $700 million of the issue had been sold. Using the mid-figure of $650 and applying the underwriting fees indicated revenues of about $5 million. When the market quotations dropped after the syndicate was disbanded, the losses on the $350 million sold at lower prices were estimated at around $15 million. The potential losses to individual underwriters were substantial. The two managers, Salomon and Merrill Lynch, each underwrote over $124 million. Morgan Stanley took $40 million. First Boston and Goldman Sachs each took $20 million.

Underwriting exposure must also take the practice of *swapping* into account. To sell institutional buyers a new issue, the seller takes in exchange (swaps) some other bonds that the institutions already own. The value placed on the bonds taken in exchange may have a substantial effect on the actual price received. Another aspect is the practice of hedging. When in a long position on bonds while interest rates are rising, the underwriter can take self-protective action by selling other issues short.

A controversy remains over whether the IBM issue was priced "too tight." During the month of September preceding the actual offering, the Federal funds rate, the prime rate, and the discount rate had all been increasing. The financial markets during the week of October 3, when the pricing decision was made, were hectic if not chaotic. Undoubtedly, the severe measures taken by the Federal Reserve System on Saturday, October 6, 1979, were in the air during the week.[12] For example, the October 5 *Wall Street Journal* reported, "Another negative development was the apparent decision by the Federal Reserve System to tighten its

[12] "Prices Drop Further as Record IBM Offer Encounters Surprising Buyer Resistance," *Wall Street Journal*, October 5, 1979, p. 37.

credit reins further and to push key short-term interest rates still higher." Whether the underwriters should have given themselves more cushion to avoid a subsequent price decline is a matter of judgment. From one standpoint, the price decline of $4 to $5 after disbanding the underwriting syndicate was relatively modest, given the sharply rising interest rates during the period and the Fed announcement on Saturday, October 6. Differences in judgment on this matter are likely, but such differences in judgment are what make markets.

The IBM offering illustrates a number of basic characteristics of investment banking. One is that the risks are real. Two, competition between investment bankers continues to be vigorous and tough. Three, a corporate issue of a well managed, prestigious firm which is taking on debt for the first time (and in moderate quantity in relation to its total assets) will be rated Aaa and priced close to Treasury issues. Fourth, the turbulence of the financial markets during the week of the offering made the task of the underwriters and the company a supremely difficult one. It demonstrated the great risk-taking and judgment required to make decisions in the face of an extremely volatile financial environment. Fifth, the episode illustrates the high drama, the considerable financial sophistication, and the continued great challenges that exist in the field of financial decision making.

Costs of Flotation

The cost of selling new issues of securities is put into perspective in Table 19.3. The table summarizes recent data on costs of flotation compiled by the SEC. Two important generalizations can be drawn from these data:

1. The cost of flotation for common stock is greater than for preferred stock, and the costs of both are greater than the cost of flotation for bonds.
2. The cost of flotation as a percentage of the gross proceeds is greater for small issues than for large ones.

The explanations for these relationships are found in the amount of risk involved and in the job of physical distribution. Bonds are generally bought in large blocks by relatively few institutional investors, whereas stocks are bought by millions of individuals. For this reason the distribution job for common stock is harder and the expenses of marketing it are greater. Similarly, stocks are more volatile than bonds, so underwriting risks are larger for stock than for bond flotations.

Reasons for the variation in cost with the size of issue are also easily found. First, certain fixed expenses are associated with any distribution of securities: the underwriting investigation, the preparation of the registration statement, legal fees, and so on. Since these expenses are relatively large and fixed, their percentage of the total cost of flotation runs high on small issues. Second, small issues are typically those of relatively less well-known firms, so underwriting expenses may be larger than usual because the danger of omitting vital information is greater. Furthermore, the selling job is more difficult; salespeople must exert greater effort to sell the securities of less well-known firms. For these reasons the underwriting commission, as a percentage of the gross proceeds, is relatively high for small issues.

Table 19.3

Costs of Flotation as a Percentage of Proceeds for Common Stock Issues, 1971–1975[a]

	Underwriting				Rights with standby underwriting				Rights	
Size of Issue (millions of dollars)	Number	Compensation as a percentage of proceeds	Other expenses as a percentage of proceeds	Total cost as a percentage of proceeds	Number	Compensation as a percentage of proceeds	Other expenses as a percentage of proceeds	Total cost as a percentage of proceeds	Number	Total cost as a percentage of proceeds
Under 0.50	0	—	—	—	0	—	—	—	3	8.99
0.50–0.99	6	6.96	6.78	13.74	2	3.43	4.80	8.24	2	4.59
1.00–1.99	18	10.40	4.89	15.29	5	6.36	4.15	10.51	5	4.90
2.00–4.99	61	6.59	2.87	9.47	9	5.20	2.85	8.06	7	2.85
5.00–9.99	66	5.50	1.53	7.03	4	3.92	2.18	6.10	6	1.39
10.00–19.99	91	4.84	0.71	5.55	10	4.14	1.21	5.35	3	0.72
20.00–49.99	156	4.30	0.37	4.67	12	3.84	0.90	4.74	1	0.52
50.00–99.99	70	3.97	0.21	4.18	9	3.96	0.74	4.70	2	0.21
100.00–500.00	16	3.81	0.14	3.95	5	3.50	0.50	4.00	9	0.13
Total/Average	484	5.02	1.15	6.17	56	4.32	1.73	6.05	38	2.45

[a] Issues are included only if the company's stock was listed on the NYSE, AMEX, or regional exchanges prior to the offering; any associated secondary distribution represents less than 10 percent of the total proceeds of the issue, and the offering contains no other types of securities. Source: From Clifford W. Smith, Jr., "Substitute Methods for Raising Additional Capital: Rights Offerings versus Underwritten Issues," *Journal of Financial Economics,* December 1977, Vol. 5, No. 3. By permission of North-Holland Publishing Company, Amsterdam.

Flotation costs are also influenced by whether or not the issue is a rights offering, and if it is, by the extent of the underpricing.[13] If rights are used, and if the underpricing is substantial, then the investment banker bears little risk of being unable to sell the shares. Further, very little selling effort is required in such a situation. These two factors enable a company to float new securities to its own stockholders at a relatively low cost. However, rights offerings without use of underwriters accounted for only 38 of the 578 issues sold (less than 7 percent) during the 1971–1975 period covered in Table 19.3.

Flotation Costs on Negotiated versus Multiple-Bidding Underwritings

The general practice is for a long-term relationship to develop between a business firm and its investment banker. The investment banking firm builds up a cumulative background of knowledge and understanding through its continuous counseling with the firm over a period of years. On a particular financing, the firm's historical investment banker already has considerable background knowledge. It takes much more time and expense for another investment banking firm to develop a comparable fund of knowledge. The business firm is therefore likely to look to its traditional investment banker on any new financing requirement. The terms and arrangements on any particular issue will be worked out in direct negotiations between the firm and its investment banker. These are called negotiated underwritings.

However, for public utility firms, more than one investment banker is likely to be competing for the business of underwriting a particular issue. The SEC Rule U-50 makes competitive bidding mandatory on new issues of securities by public utility holding companies. Whether required by law or not, it is more likely that competitive bidding will be used by public utilities than by industrial firms. The characteristics of public utilities are more uniform, with fewer special circumstances than for industrial firms in a wide variety of business activities. Also, as regulated industries, the utilities have long been required to provide substantial amounts of information on a relatively uniform basis. Hence the kinds of information that the historical investment banker develops for an industrial firm over a longer period of time are more easily developed for utility firms. The question of the relative costs of negotiated versus "competitive" underwritings has been raised.

The terms *negotiated* and *competitive* are sometimes misleading. Negotiated underwritings are as fully competitive as underwritings with bidding by more than one investment banker. The performance of the historical investment banker must assure the firm that no other investment banker could do the job better. Hence the presence of others waiting in the wings for the opportunity of displacing the historical investment banker assures that competition is as effective on single bids as on multiple bidding. Thus the empirical studies actually measure not only the effects of multiple bidding on the costs of underwriting but also the characteristics of the firms and the nature of the general financial market conditions that are likely to result in negotiated versus multiple bidding underwritings in particular cases.

[13] Rights offerings involve the sale of stock to existing stockholders. The topic is discussed in Chapter 20.

Regulation of Security Trading

The operations of investment bankers, exchanges, and over-the-counter markets described previously are significantly influenced by a series of federal statutes enacted during and after 1933. The financial manager is affected by these laws for several reasons:

1. Corporate officers are subject to personal liabilities.
2. The laws affect the ease and costs of financing and the behavior of the money and capital markets in which the corporation's securities are sold and traded.
3. Investors' willingness to buy securities is influenced by the existence of safeguards provided by these laws.

Securities Act of 1933

The first of the securities acts, the Securities Act of 1933, followed congressional investigations of the stock market collapse of 1929–1932. Motivating the act were (1) the large losses to investors, (2) the failures of many corporations on which little information had been provided, and (3) the misrepresentations that had been made to investors.

The basic objective of the Securities Act of 1933 is to provide for both *full disclosure* of relevant information and a *record of representations.* The act seeks to achieve these objectives by the following means:

1. It applies to all interstate offerings to the public in amounts of $1,500,000 or more. (Some exemptions are government bonds and bank stocks.)
2. Securities must be registered at least twenty days before they are publicly offered. The registration statement provides financial, legal, and technical information about the company. A prospectus summarizes this information for use in selling the securities. If information is inadequate or misleading, the SEC will delay or stop the public offering. (Obtaining the information required to review the registration statement may result in a waiting period that exceeds twenty days.)
3. After the registration has become effective, the securities can be offered if accompanied by the prospectus. Preliminary, or "red herring," prospectuses can be distributed to potential buyers during the waiting period.
4. If the registration statement or prospectus contains misrepresentations or omissions of material facts, any purchaser who suffers a loss can sue for damages. Liabilities and severe penalties can be imposed on the issuer and its officers, directors, accountants, engineers, appraisers, and underwriters and on all others who participated in preparing the registration statement.

Securities Exchange Act of 1934

The Securities Exchange Act of 1934 extends the disclosure principle applied to new issues by the Securities Act of 1933 to trading in already issued securities (the secondhand securities market). It seeks to accomplish this by the following measures:

1. It establishes the Securities and Exchange Commission. (The Federal Trade Commission had been administering the Securities Act of 1933.)
2. It provides for registration and regulation of national securities exchanges. Companies whose securities are listed on an exchange must file reports

similar to registration statements with both the SEC and the stock exchange and must provide periodic reports as well.

3. It establishes control over corporate "insiders." Officers, directors, and major stockholders of a corporation must file monthly reports of changes in holdings of the corporation's stock. Any short-term profits from such transactions are payable to the corporation.
4. It gives the SEC the power to prohibit manipulation by such devices as pools (aggregations of funds used to affect prices artificially), wash sales (sales among members of the same group to record artificial transaction prices), and pegging the market other than during stock flotations.
5. It gives the SEC control over the proxy machinery and practices.
6. It establishes control over the flow of credit into security transactions by giving the board of governors of the Federal Reserve System the power to control margin requirements.

Appraisal of Regulation of Security Trading

Why should security transactions be regulated? It can be argued that a great body of relevant knowledge is necessary to make an informed judgment of the value of a security. Moreover, security values are subject to many gyrations that influence stability and business conditions generally. Hence, social well-being requires that orderly markets be promoted. There are three primary objectives of regulation:

1. To protect investors from fraud and to provide them with a basis for informed judgments
2. To control the volume of bank credit to finance security speculation
3. To provide orderly markets in securities

Progress has been made on all three counts. There has been some cost in the increased time and expense involved in new flotations by companies, although the benefits seem worth their costs. The regulations are powerless to prevent investors from investing in unsound ventures or to prevent stock prices from skyrocketing during booms and plummeting during periods of pessimism. Still, requirements for increased information have been of value in preventing fraud and gross misrepresentations.

From the standpoint of the financial manager, regulation has a twofold significance. It affects both the costs of issuing securities and the riskiness of securities—and hence the rate of return investors require when they purchase stocks and bonds. As previous chapters have shown, these two factors have an important bearing on the firm's cost of capital and, through the capital budgeting process, on its investment decisions. Further, since business investment is a key determinant of employment and production in the economy, efficient capital markets have an important impact on all of society.

Efficient Capital Markets

One of the central issues in connection with the timing and selection of alternative forms and sources of financing is whether financial managers can "beat the market" if the capital markets are efficient in some sense. There is considerable disagreement in both theory and practice with regard to the questions raised. First let us consider what is involved in the nature of efficient markets.[14]

Forms of Capital Market Efficiency

Capital market efficiency has been defined in three forms. These are described as (1) weak-form efficiency, (2) semistrong-form efficiency, and (3) strong-form efficiency.[15]

The weak form of capital market efficiency holds that excess or abnormal returns cannot be earned on the basis of historical price or returns information. This argues that the historical pattern of prices or returns on stocks will not provide a basis for superior forecasting of future prices or returns.

The predictions of the weak form of financial market efficiency are in direct contradiction to the activity of chartists or technical analysts. Chartists argue that by observing the pattern of price or returns behavior, trading rules can be developed for achieving superior performance.

Studies of historical patterns of prices or returns have found that stock price changes over time are essentially independent of one another. Such findings of independence are consistent with weak-form efficiency, which argues that one cannot use past price or returns information to make superior predictions of future price or return patterns.

Semistrong-form efficient markets mean that investors cannot earn abnormal returns from trading rules based on publicly available information. Examples of public information include annual reports of companies, investment advisory data, ticker tape information, and articles and stories in newspapers and the financial press. Semistrong efficiency argues that existing prices reflect all public information, good or bad. All the information currently known to the market is already impounded in current market prices. Except for the predictable upward drift which constitutes part of the normal return on a security, prices change only when new information arrives.

Just as weak-form efficiency is associated with the activity of technical analysts, the implications of semistrong efficiency relate to the work of security analysts. Fundamental security analysis implies that the processing of public information will provide a basis for achieving superior performance. The semistrong efficiency theory, however, holds that the activity of fundamental analysis guarantees that security prices will in fact reflect processing of public information. This view argues that fundamental analysts will have returns commensurate with the ability with which they evaluate publicly available data. A highly able analyst will earn high returns; those of lesser ability will earn lower returns, as in most other fields of executive and managerial activity. The individual investor, unless trained to the same level as the professional analyst and able to commit as much time and study as the professional analyst, is not likely to do as well. There is considerable evidence to support the predictions of semistrong-form market efficiency theories.

[14] A more complete treatment of efficient capital markets is presented in T. E. Copeland and J. F. Weston, *Financial Theory and Corporate Policy* (Reading, Mass.: Addison-Wesley, 1979), pp. 196–248.

[15] Eugene F. Fama, "The Behavior of Stock Prices," *Journal of Business* 38 (January 1965), pp. 34–105, "Efficient Capital Markets: A Review of Theory and Empirical Work," *Journal of Finance* 25 (May 1970), pp. 383–417; and *Foundations of Finance* (New York: Basic Books, 1976).

Strong-form market efficiency holds that excess returns cannot be earned using any information source, regardless of whether or not it is publicly available. This implies that even corporate insiders will not, on average, be able to benefit from the information they receive ahead of the general public. The theory is that competition among those with inside information will result in equilibrium prices, quickly eliminating opportunities for abnormal returns. But the empirical studies on the strong-form of market efficiency have found that exceptional returns have been earned. They suggest that specialists on the major stock exchanges and officers and directors of firms may be accorded privileged information that can be used as a basis for earning above-average returns.

On balance, then, the evidence appears to be consistent with the achievement of both weak-form and semistrong-form market efficiency. However, empirical studies suggest that strong-form market efficiency is not achieved in practice.

Implications of Efficient Capital Markets

The evidence on the efficiency of financial markets has implications for investors, financial managers, and regulators. From the standpoint of investors, the evidence suggests that the appropriate strategy is deciding what risk level is preferred. A choice is made to invest in government bonds, savings accounts, common stocks, commodities, and so on. Market efficiency suggests that after a selection of the target level of risk, a well-diversified portfolio of investments will do as well as any other selection strategy.

From the standpoint of financial managers, efficient markets also have important implications. They mean, for example, that when investing in marketable securities, financial managers cannot expect to do better than the average. Prices largely reflect publicly available information, and the returns achieved should be consistent with the risks taken.

Particularly relevant for the kinds of financial policies with which we will be dealing in the remainder of the book are questions related to choosing between debt and equity financing and the timing of such financing. To gain from timing decisions requires the ability to make accurate predictions of the future. But the theory of efficient markets predicts that superior forecasting is not likely to be achieved. If prices and returns reflect all public information in an unbiased manner, current prices and returns represent a consensus about the future by the market as a whole. Of course, such consensus forecasts can be wrong, but since the error is as likely to be above as below the actual behavior of the market in the future, efforts to outjudge and market are as likely to be wrong as they are to be right.

Hence, those who support the efficient markets view argue that it is a waste of time for financial managers to try to outguess the market on interest rate trends and the relative cost of debt and equity funds. They recommend that financial managers focus on improving the operating efficiency and performance of their individual companies and forget about forecasting security prices.

Financial Planning in Efficient Markets

There are widespread misconceptions about what the notion of efficient markets implies. Some confuse it with the idea of perfect markets, which implies no frictions, complete costless knowledge, and atomistic buyers and sellers with no influence on prices. Others are agnostics with respect to efficient markets on other grounds. While they concede that the markets do reflect and impound all currently available information, they argue that the information which the market incorporates changes over time and that some of these changes may be anticipated.

Our position is pragmatic—that the financial markets are efficient in both the weak and the semistrong forms. As a practical matter, then, within the framework that they are not likely to beat the market on day-to-day movements, financial managers participate in the development of long-range investment and financing programs related to the long-range strategic planning of firms. Within these long-range plans, financial managers can make forecasts for investment programs and financial needs. Financing will be timed and related to the forms and sources that seem advantageous from a long-range planning perspective.

Emerging Trends

Important new developments are taking place in the financial markets, in commercial banking, and in investment banking. Some of these developments result from legislative changes, and others from fundamental shifts in the nature of the new international economic and financial relationships.

A major legislative change took place in the United States when the Depository Institutions Deregulation and Monetary Control Act of 1980 was passed. The new law directs the Federal Reserve to set new, lower reserve requirements, not only for its member banks, but for all commercial banks, savings banks, and savings and loan associations. The new reserve requirements will be phased in over three years for member banks and over seven years for other financial institutions. All deposit interest ceilings (such as the regulation limiting the interest rate that may be paid on time and savings deposits) will be phased out over six years. Under the law, depository institutions are permitted to offer interest-bearing checking accounts or negotiable order of withdrawal (NOW) accounts. Federally chartered savings and loan associations and savings banks are given new lending and investing powers, including the ability to make more types of consumer loans, offer credit cards, and invest in commercial paper and corporate debt.

The full impact of this legislation will not be apparent for some time. It can be predicted with confidence, however, that competition among the different types of financial institutions will increase. The artificial barriers to national operations by commercial banks also appear to be on their way toward relaxation and perhaps even elimination. Ironically, foreign banks may have greater flexibility in operating in the United States than domestic banks. The International Banking Act of 1978 established some guidelines for foreign banks operating in the United States and called upon the President of the United States to investigate whether U.S. banks have been under a competitive disadvantage with respect to foreign banks. It is expected that such a study will also give impetus to the development of interstate banking in some form.

Revolutionary developments also have occurred in investment banking. Investment banking has moved from its traditional business base in underwriting and brokerage activities toward insurance and commercial banking. Half the revenues of the large investment banking firms used to come from commissions until the Securities and Exchange Commission in 1975 ordered the end of fixed commission schedules. This was followed by competition for the big accounts of the institutional investors (insurance companies, pension funds, mutual funds, etc.). Commission rates were driven down and commission income dropped to less than 40 percent of revenues. Investment bankers have become more like commercial banks in that for the larger firms net interest revenues have ranged upward from 70 percent of pretax earnings.

Additional new sources of income for investment banking firms include credit cards and money market funds as well as counseling on corporate financing, ranging from cash management to mergers. Other important new activities that generate revenues are equity-based insurance policies; tax shelter programs in oil, real estate, etc.; stock options; commodities trading commissions; and participation in the interest rate futures markets.

Much of this new activity is facilitated by computer-assisted analysis; additionally, the tasks of office record keeping and reporting to customers have been computerized. As a result, the degree of operating leverage (DOL) of the investment banking firms has increased. (Here is another practical illustration of the importance of the concept discussed in both Chapters 7 and 15). This has occurred because the firms were shifting from the partly fixed costs of clerical workers to the almost completely fixed costs of computers. With higher operating leverage, recall that declines in volume have a greater adverse impact on profitability. As a consequence, the lower commission income (resulting from the abolition of fixed commission schedules) coupled with higher DOL places severe financial pressures on investment banking firms during periods of low income activity. To avoid financial disaster, numerous "mergers of necessity" have taken place as evident in the compound names of some of the surviving firms: Merrill Lynch White Weld Capital Markets Group; Blyth Eastman Paine Webber; Dean Witter Reynolds Inc.; and Smith Barney, Harris Upham & Co. In addition to mergers within the investment banking and brokerage business, mergers between different types of financial institutions have taken place. Bache and Co., once the eighth largest investment banking firm, was taken over by the Prudential Insurance Company of America. The American Express Company merged with Shearson Loeb Rhoades, the second largest investment banking firm in terms of brokerage business. The Bechtel consulting engineering company bought Dillion Read, an investment banking firm.

Many describe this trend as a movement toward financial services conglomerates. They point to other manifestations of these developments as well. It is commonplace for large industrial firms such as General Electric, Ford, or IBM to have a financial or credit affiliate or subsidiary. The National Steel Corporation owns the fourth largest publicly owned (rather than mutually owned) savings and loan holding company in the United States. By 1979, more than half the earnings of Household Finance Corporation (traditionally a consumer finance firm) came from sources other than financial operations.

Truly, the financial markets are experiencing fundamental changes. Laws are changing, but more important, the underlying economic and financial forces are exploding in many different directions. From the standpoint of managerial finance, these changes profoundly influence the investment and financing decisions of business firms.

All firms have become financial institutions to some degree. The range and types of investments made by manufacturing firms have greatly multiplied. In addition, the forms and sources of financing of business firms have also greatly changed in their variety and complexity.

Summary

Longer-term obligations are sold directly to investors or through the investment banking distribution systems. Two major forms of direct financing are term lending by commercial banks and the private placement of securities with insurance companies and pension funds. Term loans and private placements represent similar financing arrangements. Their advantages are avoidance of SEC registration procedures, flexibility in renegotiation of terms, and the assurance of availability of financing provided by long-term arrangements as compared with short-term bank borrowing.

Ordinarily, direct loans are retired by systematic repayments (amortization payments) over the life of the loan. Security, generally in the form of a chattel mortgage on equipment, is often employed, although the larger, stronger companies are usually able to borrow on an unsecured basis. Commercial banks typically make small short-term loans; life insurance companies and pension funds grant larger, longer-term loans.

Like rates on other credits, the cost of direct loans varies with the size of the loan and the strength of the borrower. For small loans to small companies, rates may be as high as 20 percent; for large loans to large firms, they will probably be close to the prime lending rate. Since these loans run for long periods, during which interest rates can change radically, many of them have variable interest rates, with the rate set at a certain level above the prime rate or above the Federal Reserve rediscount rate. Often, direct loans include a "kicker" in the form of warrants to purchase the borrower's equity securities near the price prevailing at the time of the loan transaction.

Another aspect of direct loans is the series of *protective covenants* contained in most loan agreements. The lender's funds are tied up for a long period, and during this time the borrower's situation can change markedly. For self-protection, the lender includes in the loan agreement stipulations that the borrower will maintain the current ratio at a specified level, limit acquisitions of additional fixed assets, keep the debt ratio below a stated amount, and so on. These provisions are necessary from the lender's point of view, but they restrict the borrower's actions.

The investment banker provides middleman services to both the seller and the buyer of new securities, helping plan the issue, underwriting it, and handling the job of selling the issue to the ultimate investor. The cost of this service to the issuer is related to the magnitude of the total job that must be performed to place the issue. The investment banker must also look to the interests of the brokerage customers; if these investors are not satisfied with the banker's products, they will deal elsewhere.

Flotation costs are lowest for bonds, higher for preferred stock, and highest for common stock. Larger companies have lower flotation costs than smaller ones for each type of security, and most companies can cut their stock flotation costs by issuing the new securities to stockholders through rights offerings. (These offerings are discussed in Chapter 20.)

The financial manager should be familiar with the federal laws regulating the issuance and trading of securities, because they influence liabilities and affect financing methods and costs. Regulation of securities trading seeks (1) to provide information that investors can utilize as a basis for judging the merits of securities, (2) to control the volume of credit used in securities trading, and (3) to provide orderly securities markets. The laws do not, however, prevent either purchase of unsound issues or wide price fluctuations. They raise the costs of flotation somewhat, but they also probably decrease the cost of capital by increasing public confidence in the securities markets.

Changes in the relative costs and availability of different forms and sources of financing raise questions as to the timing of decisions. The efficient markets theories are summarized to consider their implications for efforts by financial managers to "beat the market." Since the prices and returns prevailing at any point in the financial markets reflect all available historical and current public information, it is difficult for financial managers to achieve superior performance by judging that security market conditions may be better or worse in the future. However, government policies, which appear to overshoot at times and which do change, have great impact on the state of the financial markets. In addition, repetitive fluctuations are observed in financial market prices and return. These patterns tempt financial managers to judge that some periods are more favorable for financing of particular types than others.

Questions

19.1 State several advantages to a firm that lists its stock on a major stock exchange.

19.2 Would you expect the cost of capital of a firm to be affected if it changed its status from one traded over the counter to one traded on the New York Stock Exchange? Explain.

19.3 Evaluate the following position: Buying stocks is in the nature of true investment; stock is purchased in order to receive a dividend return on the invested capital. Short selling, on the other hand, is fundamentally a form of gambling; it is simply betting that a stock's price will decline. Consequently, if we do not wish to see Wall Street turned into a "Las Vegas," all short selling should be forbidden.

19.4 Evaluate the following statement: The fundamental purpose of the federal security laws dealing with new issues is to prevent investors, principally small ones, from sustaining losses on the purchase of stocks.

19.5 Suppose two similar firms are each selling $10 million of common stock. The firms are of the same size, are in the same industry, have the same leverage, and so on—except that one is publicly owned and the other is closely held.

a. Will their costs of flotation be the same?

b. If the issue were $10 million of bonds, would your answer be the same?

19.6 Define these terms: *brokerage firm, underwriting group, selling group,* and *investment banker.*

19.7 Each month the Securities and Exchange Commission publishes a report of the transactions made by the officers and directors of listed firms in their own companies' equity securities. Why do you suppose the SEC makes this report?

19.8 Prior to 1933, investment banking and commercial banking were both carried on by the same firm. In that year, however, the Banking Act required that these functions be separated. On the basis of your knowledge of investment banking and commercial banking, discuss the pros and cons of this forced separation.

19.9 Before entering a formal agreement, investment bankers carefully investigate the companies whose securities they underwrite; this is especially true of the issues of firms going public for the first time.

a. Since the bankers do not themselves plan to hold the securities but intend to sell them to others as soon as possible, why are they so concerned about making careful investigations?

b. Does your answer to the question have any bearing on the fact that investment banking is a very difficult field to break into? Explain.

19.10 a. If competitive bidding were required on all security offerings, would flotation costs be higher or lower?

b. Would the size of the issuing firm be material in determining the effects of required competitive bidding?

19.11 Since investment bankers price new issues in relation to outstanding issues, should a spread exist between the yields on the new and the outstanding issues? Discuss this matter separately for stocks and bonds.

19.12 What issues are raised by the increasing purchase of equities by institutional investors?

Problems

19.1 As the chief financial officer of XTZ Corporation, you are planning to sell $100 million of ten-year bonds to finance the construction of a hot-tub factory. The market rate of interest on debt of this quality and maturity is 12 percent. However, the total costs of the underwriting have been estimated to be 10.5 percent of the gross proceeds.

a. Calculate the effective cost of debt of this debt to your firm, before taxes. (Hint: Let the coupon rate be 12 percent so that the bonds will sell at face value; then solve for the IRR, which will make the future payments on the bond equal to the face value less 10.5 percent—that is, to $895 per bond.)

b. Your investment banker advises you that a 10 percent interest rate may be obtained by establishing a sinking fund provision whereby one-tenth of the debt principal will be retired at the end of each year. What is the effective cost of debt for this issue? (Underwriting costs remain at 10.5 percent.)

c. Why would an investment banker prefer you to finance by (b) rather than (a)?

19.2 If your firm sells preferred stock in the amount of $100 million, the total flotation expense will be about 11.5 percent of gross proceeds. If the going rate on preferred stock of the same quality as your firm's is 12 percent, what is the effective cost of the preferred stock issue? (Assume the stock will remain outstanding in perpetuity.)

19.3 The Fairmont Drilling Company was planning to issue $5 million of new common stock. In reaching the decision as to the form of offering, two alternatives were considered:

1. A rights offering, with out-of-pocket cost as a percentage of new capital at 1.4 percent
2. An underwriting, with out-of-pocket cost as a percentage of new capital at 7.0 percent

Fairmont chose the second alternative. Given the difference in cost, this choice seems paradoxical.

a. From Table 19.3, what proportion of issues this size are made by rights offerings instead of by underwriters?
b. Discuss the influence of other factors (in addition to direct costs cited) that must be taken into account in choosing between the two alternative methods of offering. In your answer consider the following as well as other factors that may occur to you:
   1. Timing of receipt of flows
   2. Risk
   3. Other internal benefits and costs
   4. Distribution
   5. Effect on stock price

19.4 Alfred Cognac is a senior partner of a prominent investment banking firm. He has the opportunity to invest in a potential acquisition candidate which will provide him with a $1 million profit if successful. He anticipates that there is a .90 probability of the acquisition occurring and that he will suffer no trading loss if it does not.

Mr. Cognac would be considered an insider by the SEC. If he profits from the transaction *and* the SEC finds out about it, he will be forced to resign his position and return all of his profits to the acquired company. He estimates that there is a .25 probability that he will be discovered. The loss of his job would cost him $400,000 per year for the next 10 years. His discount rate is 10 percent.

a. If Mr. Cognac's only concern is the maximization of his wealth, should he make the investment?
b. At what discount rate would Mr. Cognac be indifferent to his two alternatives?
c. What probability of SEC discovery would make him indifferent?

19.5 In March 1975, three executives of the Hughes Aircraft Company, one of the largest privately owned corporations in the world, decided to break away from Hughes and to set up a company of their own. The principal reason for this decision was capital gains; Hughes Aircraft stock is all privately owned, and the corporate structure makes it impossible for executives to be granted stock purchase options. Hughes's executives receive substantial salaries and bonuses, but this income is all taxable at normal tax rates, and no capital gains opportunities are available.

The three men, Jim Adcock, Robert Goddard, and Rick Aiken, have located a medium-size electronics manufacturing company available for purchase. All the stock of this firm, Baynard Industries, is owned by the founder, Joseph

Baynard. Although the company is in excellent shape, Baynard wants to sell it because of his failing health. A price of $5.7 million has been established, based on a price/earnings ratio of 12 and annual earnings of $475,000. Baynard has given the three prospective purchasers an option to purchase the company for the agreed price; the option is to run for six months, during which time the three men are to arrange financing with which to buy the firm.

Adcock has consulted with Jules Scott, a partner in the New York investment banking firm of Williams Brothers and an acquaintance of some years' standing, to seek his assistance in obtaining the funds necessary to complete the purchase. Adcock, Goddard, and Aiken each have some money available to put into the new enterprise, but they need a substantial amount of outside capital. There is some possibility of borrowing part of the money, but Scott has discouraged this idea. His reasoning is, first, that Baynard Industries is already highly leveraged, and if the purchasers were to borrow additional funds, there would be a very severe risk that they would be unable to service this debt in the event of a recession in the electronics industry. Although the firm is currently earning $475,000 a year, this figure could quickly turn into a loss in the event of a few canceled defense contracts or cost miscalculations.

Scott's second reason for discouraging a loan is that Adcock, Goddard, and Aiken plan not only to operate Baynard Industries and seek internal growth but also to use the corporation as a vehicle for making further acquisitions of electronics companies. This being the case, Scott believes that it would be wise for the company to keep any borrowing potential in reserve for use in later acquisitions. Scott proposes that the three partners obtain funds to purchase Baynard Industries in accordance with the figures shown in the following table.

Baynard Industries

Price paid to Joseph Baynard (12 × $475,000 earnings)			$5,700,000
Authorized shares		5,000,000	
Initially issued shares		1,125,000	
Initial distribution of shares:			
Adcock	100,000 shares at $1.00		$ 100,000
Goddard	100,000 shares at $1.00		100,000
Aiken	100,000 shares at $1.00		100,000
Williams Brothers	125,000 shares at $7.00		875,000
Public stockholders	700,000 shares at $7.00		4,900,000
	1,125,000		$6,075,000
Underwriting costs: 5% of $4,900,000		$ 245,000	
Legal fees, and so on, associated with issue		45,000	290,000
			$5,785,000
Payment to Joseph Baynard			5,700,000
Net funds to Baynard Industries			$ 85,000

Baynard Industries would be reorganized with an authorized 5,000,000 shares, with 1,125,000 to be issued at the time the transfer takes place and the other 3,875,000 to be held in reserve for possible issuance in connection with acquisitions. Adcock, Goddard, and Aiken would each purchase 100,000 shares at a price of $1 a share, the par value. Williams Brothers would purchase 125,000 shares at a price of $7. The remaining 700,000 shares would be sold to the public at a price of $7 a share.

Williams Brothers' underwriting fee would be 5 percent of the shares sold to the public, or $245,000. Legal fees, accounting fees, and other charges associated with the issue would amount to $45,000, for a total flotation cost of $290,000. After deducting the underwriting charges and the payment to Baynard from the gross proceeds of the stock sale, the reorganized Baynard Industries would receive funds in the amount of $85,000, which would be used for internal expansion purposes.

As a part of the initial agreement, Adcock, Goddard, and Aiken each would be given options to purchase an additional 80,000 shares at a price of $7 a share for one year. Williams Brothers would be given an option to purchase an additional 100,000 shares at $7 a share in one year.

a. What is the total flotation cost, expressed as a percentage of the funds raised by the underwriter? Does this charge seem reasonable in the light of published statistics on the cost of floating new issues of common stock?
b. Suppose that the three men estimate the following probabilities for the firm's stock price one year from now:

Price	Probability
$ 1	0.05
5	0.10
9	0.35
13	0.35
17	0.10
21	0.05

Assuming Williams Brothers exercises its options, calculate the following ratio based on the expected stock price (ignore time-discount effects):

$$\frac{\text{Financial benefits to Williams Brothers}}{\text{Funds raised by underwriter}}$$

Disregard Williams Brothers' profit on the 125,000 shares it bought outright at the initial offering. Comment on the ratio.
c. Are Adcock, Goddard, and Aiken purchasing their stock at a "fair" price? Should the prospectus disclose the fact that they would buy their stock at $1 a share whereas public stockholders would buy their stock at $7 a share?
d. Would it be reasonable for Williams Brothers to purchase its initial 125,000 shares at a price of $1?
e. Do you foresee any problems of control for Adcock, Goddard, and Aiken?
f. Would the expectation of an exceptionally large need for investment funds next year be a relevant consideration in deciding on the amount of funds to be raised now?

CHAPTER 20

COMMON STOCK FINANCING

Common equity or, if unincorporated firms are being considered, partnership or proprietorship interests constitute the first source of funds to a new business and the base of support for borrowing by existing firms. Accordingly, our discussion of specific forms of long-term financing will begin with an analysis of common stock.

Apportionment of Income, Control, and Risk

The nature of equity ownership depends on the form of the business or organization. The central problem of such ownership revolves around an apportionment of certain rights and responsibilities among those who have provided the funds necessary for the operation of the business. The rights and responsibilities attaching to equity consist of positive considerations (income potential and control of the firm) and negative considerations (loss potential, legal responsibility, and personal liability).

General Rights of Holders of Common Stock

The rights of holders of common stock in a business corporation are established by the laws of the state in which the corporation is chartered and by the terms of the charter granted by the state. Charters are relatively uniform on many matters, including collective and specific rights.

Collective rights Certain collective rights are usually given to the holders of common stock. Some of the more important rights allow stockholders to (1) amend the charter with the approval of the appropriate officials in the state of incorporation, (2) adopt and amend bylaws, (3) elect the directors of the corporation, (4) authorize the sale of fixed assets, (5) enter into mergers, (6) change the amount of authorized common stock, and (7) issue preferred stock, debentures, bonds, and other securities.

Specific rights Holders of common stock also have specific rights as individual owners: (1) the right to vote in the manner prescribed by the corporate charter, (2) the right to sell their stock certificates (their evidence of ownership) and in this way to transfer their ownership interest to other persons, (3) the right to inspect the corporate books,[1] and (4) the right to share residual assets of the corporation on dissolution. (However, the holders of common stock are last among the claimants to the assets of the corporation.)

[1] Obviously, a corporation cannot have its business affairs disturbed by allowing every stockholder to go through any records the stockholder wants to inspect. Furthermore, a corporation cannot wisely permit a competitor who buys shares of its common stock to look at all the corporation records. There must be, and there are, practical limitations to this right.

Apportionment of Income

Two important positive considerations are involved in equity ownership: income and control. The right to income carries the risk of loss. Control also involves responsibility and liability. In an individual proprietorship that uses funds supplied only by the owner, the owner has a 100 percent right to income and control and to loss and responsibility. As soon as the proprietor incurs debt, however, he or she has entered into contracts that limit the freedom to control the firm and to apportion the firm's income. In a partnership, these rights are apportioned among the partners in an agreed-upon manner. In the absence of a formal agreement, a division is made by state law. In a corporation, more significant issues arise concerning the rights of the owners.

Apportionment of Control

Through the right to vote, holders of common stock have legal control of the corporation. As a practical matter, however, in many corporations the principal officers constitute all, or a majority, of the members of the board of directors. In this circumstance the board may be controlled by the management rather than by the owners. However, numerous examples demonstrate that stockholders can reassert their control if they are dissatisfied with the corporation's policies. In recent years, proxy battles with the aim of altering corporate policies have occurred fairly often, and firms whose managers are unresponsive to stockholders' desires are subject to takeover bids by other firms.

Apportionment of Risk

Another consideration involved in equity ownership is risk: On liquidation, holders of common stock are last in the priority of claims. Therefore, the portion of capital they contribute provides a cushion for creditors if losses occur on dissolution. The equity-to-total-assets ratio indicates the percentage by which assets may shrink in value on liquidation before creditors will incur losses.

For example, compare two corporations, A and B, whose balance sheets are shown in Table 20.1. The ratio of equity to total assets in Corporation A is 80 percent. Total assets will therefore have to shrink by 80 percent before creditors will lose money. By contrast, in Corporation B the extent to which assets will have to shrink in value on liquidation before creditors lose money is only 40 percent.

Table 20.1 **Balance Sheets for Corporations A and B**

Corporation A				Corporation B			
		Debt	$ 20			Debt	$ 60
		Equity	80			Equity	40
Total assets	$100	Total claims	$100	Total assets	$100	Total claims	$100

Common Stock Financing

Before undertaking an evaluation of common stock financing, more of the important characteristics of such stock will be described: (1) the nature of voting rights, (2) the nature of the preemptive right, and (3) variations in the forms of common stock.

Nature of Voting Rights

For each share of common stock owned, the holder has the right to cast one vote at the annual meeting of stockholders or at such special meetings as may be called.

Proxy Provision is made for the temporary transfer of the right to vote by an instrument known as a *proxy*. The transfer is limited in its duration; typically it applies only to a specific occasion, such as the annual meeting of stockholders.

The SEC supervises the use of the proxy machinery and frequently issues rules and regulations to improve its administration. SEC supervision is justified for at least two reasons:

1. If the proxy machinery is left wholly in the hands of management, there is a danger that the incumbent management will be self-perpetuated.
2. If it is made easy for minority groups of stockholders and opposition stockholders to oust management, there is a danger that they will gain control of the corporation for temporary advantages or to place themselves or their friends in management positions.

Cumulative voting A method of voting that has come into increased prominence is cumulative voting. Cumulative voting for directors is required in twenty-two states, including California, Illinois, Michigan, Ohio, and Pennsylvania. It is permissible in eighteen, including Delaware, New Jersey, and New York. Ten states make no provision for it.

Cumulative voting permits multiple votes for a single director. For example, suppose six directors are to be elected. The owner of 100 shares can cast 100 votes for each of the six openings. Cumulatively, then, the stockholder has 600 votes. When cumulative voting is permitted, the stockholder can accumulate the votes and cast all of them for *one* director, instead of 100 each for *six* directors. Cumulative voting is designed to enable a minority group of stockholders to obtain some voice in the control of the company by electing at least one director to the board.

The nature of cumulative voting is illustrated by the use of the following formula:

$$req. = \frac{des.(N)}{\# + 1} + 1, \tag{20.1}$$

where:

$req.$ = Number of shares required to elect a desired number of directors

$des.$ = Number of directors stockholder desires to elect

N = Total number of shares of common stock outstanding and entitled to be voted[2]

$\#$ = Total number of directors to be elected

[2] An alternative that may be agreed to by the contesting parties is to define N as the number of shares *voted*, not *authorized to be voted*. This procedure, which in effect gives each group seeking to elect directors the same percentage of directors as their percentage of the voted stock, is frequently followed. When it is used, a group that seeks to gain control with a minimum investment must estimate the percentage of shares that will be voted and then obtain control of more than 50 percent of that number.

The formula can be made more meaningful by an example. The ABC company will elect six directors. There are fifteen candidates and 100,000 shares entitled to be voted. If a group desires to elect two directors, how many shares must it have?

$$req. = \frac{2 \times 100{,}000}{6 + 1} + 1 = 28{,}572$$

Observe the significance of the formula. Here, a minority group wishes to elect one-third of the board of directors. It can achieve its goal by owning less than one-third the number of shares of stock.[3]

Alternatively, assuming that a group holds 40,000 shares of stock in the company, how many directors can it elect following the rigid assumptions of the formula? The formula can be used in its present form or can be solved for *des.* and expressed as:

$$des. = \frac{(req. - 1)(\# + 1)}{N} \qquad \textbf{(20.2)}$$

Inserting the figures, the calculation is:

$$des. = \frac{39{,}999 \times 7}{100{,}000} = 2.8$$

The 40,000 shares can thus elect two and eight-tenths directors. Since directors cannot exist as fractions, the group can elect only two directors.

As a practical matter, suppose that in the above situation the total number of shares is 100,000; hence 60,000 shares remain in other hands. The voting of all 60,000 shares may not be concentrated. Suppose the 60,000 shares (cumulatively 360,000 votes) not held by the minority group are distributed equally among ten candidates—with 36,000 shares held by each candidate. If the minority group's 240,000 votes are distributed equally among each of six candidates, it can elect all six directors even though it does not have a majority of the stock.

Actually, it is difficult to make assumptions about how the opposition votes will be distributed. What is shown here is a good example of game theory. One rule in this theory is to assume that your opponents will do the worst they can do to you and to counter with actions to minimize the maximum loss. This is the kind of assumption followed in the formula. If the opposition concentrates its votes in the optimum manner, what is the best you can do to work in the direction of your goal? Other plausible assumptions can be substituted if there are sufficient facts to support alternative hypotheses about the opponents' behavior.

Preemptive Right

The preemptive right gives holders of common stock the first option to purchase additional issues of common stock. In some states, this right is made part of every corporate charter; in others, it is necessary to insert the right specifically in the charter.

[3] Note also that at least 14,286 shares must be controlled to elect one director. Any number less than that constitutes a useless minority.

The purpose of the preemptive right is twofold. First, it protects the power of control of present stockholders. If it were not for this safeguard, the management of a corporation under criticism from stockholders could prevent stockholders from removing it from office by issuing a large number of additional shares at a very low price and purchasing these shares itself. Management would thereby secure control of the corporation to frustrate the will of the current stockholders.

The second, and by far the more important, protection that the preemptive right affords stockholders concerns dilution of value. For example, assume that 1,000 shares of common stock, each with a price of $100, are outstanding—making the total market value of the firm $100,000. An additional 1,000 shares are sold at $50 a share—a total of $50,000—thereby raising the market value of the firm to $150,000. When the total market value is divided by the new total shares outstanding, a value of $75 a share is obtained. Thus selling common stock at below market value will dilute the price of the stock and will be detrimental to present stockholders and beneficial to those who purchase the new shares. The preemptive right prevents such occurrences. (This point is discussed at length later in the chapter.)

Forms of Common Stock[4]

Classified Classified common stock was used extensively in the late 1920s, sometimes in ways that misled investors. During that period Class A common stock was usually nonvoting, and Class B was usually voting. Thus promoters could control companies by selling large amounts of Class A stock while retaining Class B stock.

In more recent years there has been a revival of Class B common stock for sound purposes. It is used by small, new companies seeking to acquire funds from outside sources. Class A common stock is sold to the public and typically pays dividends; its holders have full voting rights. Class B common stock is retained by the organizers of the company, but dividends are not paid on it until the company has established its earning power. By the use of this classified stock, the public can take a position in a conservatively financed growth company without sacrificing income.

Founders' shares Founders' shares are somewhat like Class B stock except that they carry *sole* voting rights and typically do not confer the right to dividends for a number of years. Thus the organizers of the firm are able to maintain complete control of the operations in the firm's crucial initial development. At the same time, other investors are protected against excessive withdrawals of funds by owners.

[4] Besides *common stock*, accountants also use the term *par value* to designate an arbitrary value assigned when stock is sold. When a firm sells newly issued stock, it must record the transaction on its balance sheet. For example, suppose a newly created firm commences operations by selling 100,000 shares at $10 a share, raising a total of $1 million. This $1 million must appear on the balance sheet. But what will it be called? One choice is to assign the stock a "par value" of $10 and label the $1 million "common stock." Another choice is to assign a $1 par value and show $100,000 ($1 par value × 100,000 shares) as "common stock" and $900,000 as "paid-in surplus." Still another choice is to disregard the term *par value* entirely—that is, use no-par stock—and record the $1 million as "common stock." Since the choice is quite arbitrary for all practical purposes, more and more firms are adopting the last procedure and abolishing the term *par value*. Because there are quite enough useful concepts and terms in accounting and finance, we heartily applaud the demise of useless ones such as this.

Evaluation of Common Stock as a Source of Funds

Thus far, the chapter has covered the main characteristics of common stock (frequently referred to as equity shares). Now it will appraise this type of financing from the viewpoint of the issuer and from a social viewpoint.

From the Viewpoint of the Issuer

Advantages There are several advantages to the issuer of financing with common stock:

1. Common stock does not entail fixed charges. If the company generates the earnings, it can pay common stock dividends. In contrast to bond interest, however, there is no legal obligation to pay dividends.
2. Common stock carries no fixed maturity date.
3. Since common stock provides a cushion against losses of creditors, the sale of common stock increases the creditworthiness of the firm.
4. Common stock can at times be sold more easily than debt. It appeals to certain investor groups because (a) it typically carries a higher expected return than does preferred stock or debt; and (b) since it represents the ownership of the firm, it provides the investor with a better hedge against inflation than does straight preferred stock or bonds. Ordinarily, common stock increases in value when the value of real assets rises during an inflationary period.[5]
5. Returns from common stock in the form of capital gains are subject to the lower personal income tax rates on capital gains. Hence the effective personal income tax rates on returns from common stock may be lower than the effective tax rates on the interest on debt.

Disadvantages Disadvantages to the issuer of common stock include the following:

1. The sale of common stock extends voting rights or control to the additional stock owners who are brought into the company. For this reason, among others, additional equity financing is often avoided by small and new firms, whose owner-managers may be unwilling to share control of their companies with outsiders.
2. Common stock gives more owners the right to share in income. The use of debt may enable the firm to utilize funds at a fixed low cost, whereas common stock gives equal rights to new stockholders to share in the net profits of the firm.
3. As we saw in Chapter 19, the costs of underwriting and distributing common stock are usually higher than those for underwriting and distributing preferred stock or debt. Flotation costs for selling common stock are characteristically higher because (a) costs of investigating an equity security investment are higher than investigating the feasibility of a comparable debt security; and (b) stocks are more risky, which means equity holdings must be diversified, which in turn means that a given dollar amount of new stock must be sold to a greater number of purchasers than the same amount of debt.

[5] During the inflation of the last decade, the lags of product price increases behind the rise of input costs have depressed corporate earnings and increased the uncertainty of earnings growth, causing price-earnings multiples to fall.

4. As we saw in Chapter 16, if the firm has more equity or less debt than is called for in the optimum capital structure, the average cost of capital will be higher than necessary.
5. Common stock dividends are not deductible as an expense for calculating the corporation's income subject to the federal income tax, but bond interest is deductible. The impact of this factor is reflected in the relative cost of equity capital vis-à-vis debt capital.

From a Social Viewpoint

From a social viewpoint, common stock is a desirable form of financing because it renders business firms (a major segment of the economy) less vulnerable to the consequences of declines in sales and earnings. Common stock financing involves no fixed charges, the payment of which might force a faltering firm into reorganization or bankruptcy.

Use of Rights in Financing

If the preemptive right is contained in a firm's charter, then the firm must offer any new common stock to existing stockholders. If the charter does not prescribe a preemptive right, the firm has a choice of making the sale to its existing stockholders or to an entirely new set of investors. If it sells to the existing stockholders, the stock flotation is called a *rights offering*. Each stockholder is issued an option to buy a certain number of the new shares, and the terms of the option are contained on a piece of paper called a *right*. Each stockholder receives one right for each share of stock owned. The advantages and disadvantages of rights offerings are described in the following section.

Theoretical Relationships of Rights Offerings

Several issues confront the financial manager who is deciding on the details of a rights offering. The various considerations can be shown by the use of illustrative data on the Southeast Company, whose balance sheet and income statement are given in Table 20.2.

Table 20.2

Southeast Company Financial Statements before Rights Offering

Partial Balance Sheet

		Total debt (at 5%)	$ 40,000,000
		Common stock	10,000,000
		Retained earnings	50,000,000
Total assets	$100,000,000	Total liabilities and capital	$100,000,000

Partial Income Statement

Total earnings	$10,000,000
Interest on debt	2,000,000
Income before taxes	$ 8,000,000
Taxes (50% assumed)	4,000,000
Earnings after taxes	$ 4,000,000
Earnings per share (1 million shares)	$4
Market price of stock (price-earnings ratio of 25 assumed)	$100

Southeast earns $4 million after taxes and has 1 million shares outstanding, so earnings per share are $4. The stock sells at 25 times earnings, or for $100 a share. The company plans to raise $10 million of new equity funds through a rights offering and decides to sell the new stock to shareholders for $80 a share. The questions now facing the financial manager are:

1. How many rights will be required to purchase a share of the newly issued stock?
2. What is the value of each right?
3. What effect will the rights offering have on the price of the existing stock?

Number of Rights Needed to Purchase a New Share

As already mentioned, Southeast plans to raise $10 million in new equity funds and to sell the new stock at a price of $80 a share. Dividing the subscription price into the total funds to be raised gives the number of shares to be issued:

$$\text{Number of new shares} = \frac{\text{Funds to be raised}}{\text{Subscription price}} = \frac{\$10{,}000{,}000}{\$80}$$

$$= 125{,}000 \text{ shares}$$

The next step is to divide the number of new shares into the number of previously outstanding shares to get the number of rights required to subscribe to one share of the new stock. Note that stockholders always receive one right for each share of stock they own:

$$\begin{array}{c}\text{Number of rights needed to}\\ \text{buy a share of the stock}\end{array} = \frac{\text{Old shares}}{\text{New shares}} = \frac{1{,}000{,}000}{125{,}000} = 8 \text{ rights}$$

Therefore, a stockholder will have to surrender eight rights plus $80 to receive one of the newly issued shares. If the subscription price had been set at $95 a share, 9.5 rights would have been required to subscribe to each new share; if the price had been set at $10 a share, only 1 right would have been needed. If the number of new shares exceeds the number of old shares, the number of rights required to subscribe to each new share would be a fraction of 1. For example, if the number of old shares is 1,000,000 and 1,600,000 new shares are to be issued, the number of rights required to subscribe to each new share would be $\frac{5}{8}$ of 1 right. Trading in the rights would take place so that exact, not fractional, numbers of new shares could be purchased by the exercise of rights plus the required cash.

Value of a Right

It is clearly worth something to be able to pay less than $100 for a share of stock selling for $100. The right provides this privilege, so it must have a value. To see how the theoretical value of a right is established, we continue with the example of the Southeast Company, assuming that it will raise $10 million by selling 125,000 new shares at $80 a share.

Notice that the *market value* of the old stock was $100 million: $100 a share times 1 million shares. (The book value is irrelevant.) When the firm sells the new stock, it brings in an additional $10 million. As a first approximation, assume that the market value of the common stock increases by exactly this $10 million. Actually, the market value of all the common stock will go up by more than $10 million if investors think the company will be able to invest these funds at a yield substantially in excess of the cost of equity capital, but it will go up by less than $10 million if investors are doubtful of the company's ability to put the new funds to work profitably in the near future.

Under the assumption that market value exactly reflects the new funds brought in, the total market value of the common stock after the new issue will be $110 million. Dividing this new value by the new total number of shares outstanding, 1.125 million, gives a new market value of $97.78 a share. Therefore, after the financing has been completed, the price of the common stock will have fallen from $100 to $97.78.

Since the rights give the stockholders the privilege of paying only $80 for a share of stock that will end up being worth $97.78—thereby saving them $17.78—is $17.78 the value of each right? The answer is no, because eight rights are required to buy one new share. The $17.78 must be divided by 8 to get the value of each right. In the example, each one is worth $2.22.

Ex Rights

The Southeast Company's rights have a very definite value, and this value accrues to the holders of the common stock. But what happens if stock is traded during the offering period? Who will receive the rights—the old owners or the new? The standard procedure calls for the company to set a *holder of record date* and for the stock to go *ex rights* after that date. If the stock is sold prior to the ex rights date, the new owner receives the rights; if it is sold on or after the ex rights date, the old owner receives them. For example, on October 15, Southeast Company announces the terms of the new financing; the company states that rights will be mailed out on December 1 to stockholders of record as of the close of business on November 15. Anyone buying the old stock on or before November 15 will receive the rights; anyone buying the stock on or after November 16 will *not* receive them. Thus November 16 is the *ex rights date;* before November 16 the stock sells *rights on.* In the case of Southeast Company, the rights-on price is $100, and the ex rights price is expected to be $97.78.

Formula Value of a Right

Rights on Equations have been developed for determining the value of rights without going through all the procedures described above. While the stock is still selling rights on, the value at which the rights will sell when they are issued can be found by use of the following formula:

$$\text{Value of one right} = \frac{\text{Market value of stock, rights on} - \text{Subscription price}}{\text{Number of rights required to purchase 1 share} + 1}$$

$$v_r = \frac{p_0 - p^s}{\# + 1}, \tag{20.3}$$

where:

p_0 = Rights-on price of the stock

p^s = Subscription price

$\#$ = Number of rights required to purchase a new share of stock

v_r = Value of one right

Substituting the appropriate values for the Southeast Company:

$$v_r = \frac{\$100 - \$80}{8 + 1} = \frac{\$20}{9} = \$2.22$$

This agrees with the value of the rights found by the step-by-step analysis.

Ex rights Suppose you are a stockholder in the Southeast Company. When you return to the United States from a trip to Europe, you read about the rights offering in the newspaper. The stock is now selling ex rights for $97.78 a share. How can you calculate the theoretical value of a right? By using the following formula, which follows the logic described in preceding sections, you can determine the value of each right:

$$\text{Value of one right} = \frac{\text{Market value of stock, ex rights} - \text{Subscription price}}{\text{Number of rights required to purchase 1 share}}$$

$$v_r = \frac{p_e - p^s}{\#} \quad \textbf{(20.4)}$$

$$= \frac{\$97.78 - \$80}{8} = \frac{\$17.78}{8} = \$2.22$$

Here, p_e is the ex rights price of the stock.[6]

Effects on Position of Stockholders

Stockholders have the choice of exercising their rights or selling them. If they have sufficient funds and want to buy more shares of the company's stock, they will exercise the rights. If they do not have the money or do not want to buy more stock, they will sell the rights. In either case, provided the formula value of the rights

[6] We developed Equation 20.4 directly from the verbal explanation given in the immediately preceding section. Equation 20.3 was derived from Equation 20.4 as follows:

$$p_e = p_0 - v_r \quad \textbf{(20.5)}$$

Substituting Equation 20.5 into Equation 20.4:

$$v_r = \frac{p_0 - v_r - p^s}{\#} \quad \textbf{(20.6)}$$

Simplifying Equation 20.6:

$$v_r = \frac{p_0 - p^s}{\#} - \frac{v_r}{\#}$$

$$v_r + \frac{v_r}{\#} = \frac{p_0 - p^s}{\#}$$

$$v_r\left(\frac{\# + 1}{\#}\right) = \frac{p_0 - p^s}{\#}$$

$$v_r = \frac{p_0 - p^s}{\#} \cdot \frac{\#}{\# + 1}$$

$$v_r = \frac{p_0 - p^s}{\# + 1}$$

The result is Equation 20.3.

holds true, stockholders will neither benefit nor lose by the rights offering. This statement can be made clear by considering the position of an individual stockholder in the Southeast Company.

The stockholder has eight shares of stock before the rights offering. Each share has a market value of $100, so the stockholder has a total market value of $800 in the company's stock. If, after the rights offering, a shareholder exercises the rights, this individual will be able to purchase one additional share at $80—a new investment of $80. With a total investment of $880, the stockholder will own nine shares of the company's stock, which now has a value of $97.78 a share. The value of this stock will be $880, exactly what was invested in it.

Alternatively, by selling the eight rights, which have a value of $2.22 each, the holder will receive $17.76 and will thus have the original eight shares of stock plus $17.76 in cash. But the original eight shares of stock now have a market price of $97.78 a share. The $782.24 market value of this stock plus the $17.76 in cash is the same as the $800 market value of stock with which the investor began.

Oversubscription Privilege

Even though the rights are very valuable and should be exercised, some stockholders neglect to do so. Still, all the stock is sold because of the *oversubscription privilege* contained in most rights offerings. This privilege gives subscribing stockholders the right to buy, on a pro rata basis, all shares not taken in the initial offering. To illustrate: If Jane Doe owns 10 percent of the stock in Southeast Company, and if 20 percent of the rights offered by the company are not exercised (or sold) by the stockholders to whom they were originally given, then she can buy an additional 2.5 percent of the new stock.[7] Since this stock is a bargain—$80 for stock worth $97.78—Jane Doe and other stockholders will use the oversubscription privilege, thereby assuring the full sale of the new stock issue.

Relationship between Market Price and Subscription Price

We can now investigate the factors influencing the use of rights and, if they are used, the level at which the subscription price is set. The Southeast Company's articles of incorporation permit the firm to decide whether to use rights, depending on whether their use is advantageous to the firm and its stockholders. The financial vice-president of the company is considering three methods of raising the sum of $10 million:

1. The company could sell to the public, through investment bankers, additional shares at approximately $100 a share. The company would net approximately $96 a share; thus it would need to sell approximately 105,000 shares in order to cover the underwriting commission.
2. The company could sell additional shares through rights, using investment bankers and paying a commission of 1 percent on the total dollar amount of the stock sold plus an additional $\frac{3}{4}$ percent on all shares unsubscribed and taken over by the investment bankers. Allowing for the usual market pressure when common stock is sold, the new shares would be sold at a

[7] Eighty percent of the stock was subscribed. Since Jane Doe subscribed to 10/80, or 12.5 percent, of the stock that was taken, she can obtain 12.5 percent of the unsubscribed stock. Therefore, her oversubscription allocation is 12.5 percent × 20 = 2.5 percent of the new stock.

20 percent discount, or at $80. Thus 125,000 additional shares would be offered through rights. With eight rights, an additional share could be purchased at $80. Since stockholders are given the right to subscribe to any unexercised rights on a pro rata basis, only those shares not subscribed to on the original or secondary level are sold to the underwriters and subjected to the $\frac{3}{4}$ percent additional commission.

3. The company could sell additional shares through rights, at $10 a share, and not use investment bankers. The number of additional shares of common stock to be sold would be 1 million. For each right held, existing stockholders would be permitted to buy one share of the new common stock.

Method 1 uses investment bankers and no rights at all. In this circumstance the underwriting commission, or flotation cost, is approximately 4 percent. In Method 2, where rights are used with a small discount, the underwriting commission is reduced, because the discount removes much of the risk of not being able to sell the issue. The underwriting commission consists of two parts—1 percent on the original issue and an additional $\frac{3}{4}$ percent commission on all unsubscribed shares the investment bankers are required to take over and sell. Thus the actual commission ranges somewhere between 1 percent and $1\frac{3}{4}$ percent. Under Method 3, the subscription price is $10 a share. With such a large concession, the company does not need to use investment bankers at all, because the rights are certain to have value and to be either exercised or sold. Which of the three methods is superior?

Method 1 provides a wider distribution of the securities sold, thereby lessening any possible control problems. The investment bankers assure that the company will receive the $10 million involved in the new issue, and they give the firm ongoing financial counsel. The company pays for these services in the form of underwriting charges. After the issue, the stock price should be approximately $100.

Under Method 2, by utilizing rights, the company reduces its underwriting expenses and the unit price per share (from $100 to $97.78). Some stockholders may suffer a loss because they neither exercise nor sell their rights. Existing stockholders will buy some of the new shares, so the distribution is likely to be narrower than under Method 1. Because of the underwriting contract, the firm is assured of receiving the funds sought. Finally, investors often like the opportunity to purchase additional shares through rights offerings; thus their use may increase stockholder loyalty.

Method 3 involves no underwriting expense and results in a substantial decrease in the unit price of shares. Initially, however, the shares are less widely distributed than under either of the other two methods. Method 3 also has a large stock-split effect, which results in a much lower final stock price per share than under either of the other two methods.[8] Many people feel that there is an optimal stock price—one that will produce a maximum total market value of the shares—and that this price is generally in the range of $30 to $60 a share. If this is the feeling

[8] Stock splits were discussed in Chapter 17. Basically, a stock split is simply the issuance of additional shares to existing stockholders for *no* additional funds. Stock splits divide the "pie" into more pieces.

of Southeast's directors, they may believe that Method 3 will permit them to reach the more desirable price range while at the same time reducing flotation costs on the new issue. However, since the rights have a substantial value, any stockholder who fails either to exercise or to sell them will suffer a serious loss.

Table 20.3 **Summary of Three Methods of Raising Additional Money**

	Advantages	Disadvantages
Method 1	1. Wide distribution 2. Certainty of receiving funds	1. High underwriting costs
Method 2	1. Small underwriting costs 2. Lower unit price of shares 3. Certainty of receiving funds 4. Increased stockholder loyalty	1. Narrow distribution 2. Losses to forgetful stockholders
Method 3	1. No underwriting costs 2. Substantial decrease in unit price of shares 3. Increased stockholder loyalty	1. Narrow distribution 2. Severe losses to forgetful stockholders

The three methods are summarized in Table 20.3. The most advantageous method depends on the company's needs. For a company strongly interested in wide distribution of its securities, Method 1 is preferable. For a firm most interested in reducing the unit price of its shares and confident that the lower unit price will induce wide distribution, Method 3 is preferable. For a company whose needs are moderate in both directions, Method 2 may offer a satisfactory compromise. Whether rights will be used and the level of the subscription price both depend on the company's needs at a particular time.

Exercise of Rights

Interestingly enough, it is expected that a small percentage of stockholders will neglect to exercise or to sell their rights. In a recent offering, the holders of $1\frac{1}{2}$ percent of General Motors common stock did not exercise their rights. The loss experienced by these stockholders was $1.5 million. In a recent AT & T issue, the loss to shareholders who neglected to exercise their rights was $960,000.

Market Price and Subscription Price

Measured from the registration date for the new issue of the security, the average percentage by which the subscription prices of new issues were below their market prices has been about 15 percent in recent years. Examples of price concessions of 40 percent or more can be observed in a small percentage of issues, but the most frequently encountered discounts are from 10 to 20 percent.

Effect on Subsequent Behavior of Market Price

It is often said that issuing new stock through rights will depress the price of the company's existing common stock. To the extent that a subscription price in connection with the rights offering is lower than the market price, there will be a "stock-split effect" on the market price of the common stock. With the prevailing market price of Southeast Company's stock at $100 and a $10 subscription price, the new market price will probably drop to about $55.

But whether, because of the rights offering, the actual new market price will be $55 or lower or higher is unknown. Again, empirical analysis of the movement in stock prices during rights offerings indicates that generalization is not practical. What happens to the market prices of the stock ex rights and after the rights trading period depends on the future earnings prospects of the issuing company.

Advantages of Use of Rights in New Financing

The preemptive right gives shareholders the protection of preserving their pro rata share in the earnings and control of the company. It also benefits the firm. By offering new issues of securities to existing stockholders, the firm increases the likelihood of a favorable reception for the stock. By their ownership of common stock in the company, investors have already evaluated the company favorably. They may therefore be receptive to the purchase of additional shares.

Other factors can offset the tendency toward a downward pressure on the price of the common stock occurring at the time of a new issue.[9] With the increased interest in (and advantages afforded by) the rights offering, the "true" or "adjusted" downward price pressure may actually be avoided.

A related advantage is that the issuer's flotation costs associated with a rights offering are lower than the cost of a public flotation. The costs referred to here are cash costs. For example, the flotation costs of common stock issues during the period 1971 to 1975 were 6.17 percent on public issues compared with 2.45 percent on rights offerings.[10]

The financial manager can obtain positive benefits from underpricing. Since a rights offering is a stock split to a certain degree, it causes the market price of the stock to fall to a level lower than it otherwise would be. But stock splits can increase the number of shareholders in a company by bringing the price of a stock down to a more attractive trading level. Furthermore, a rights offering may be associated with increased dividends for the stock owners.[11]

In general, a rights offering can stimulate an enthusiastic response from stockholders and from the investment market as a whole, with the result that opportunities for financing become more attractive to the firm. Thus the financial manager may be able to engage in common stock financing at lower costs and under more favorable terms.

Choosing among Alternative Forms of Financing

A pattern of analysis can be formulated for choosing among alternative forms of financing. This framework applies to the decision choices involved in evaluating the other major forms of financing covered: various forms of debt, preferred

[9] The downward pressure develops because of an increase in the supply of securities without a necessarily equivalent increase in the demand. Generally it is a temporary phenomenon, and the stock tends to return to the theoretical price after a few months. Obviously, if the acquired funds are invested at a very high rate of return, the stock price benefits; if the investment does not turn out well, the stock price suffers.

[10] C. W. Smith, Jr., "Substitute Methods for Raising Additional Capital: Rights Offerings versus Underwritten Issues," *Journal of Financial Economics* 5 (December 1977), pp. 273–307.

[11] The increased dividends may convey information that the prospective earnings of the firm have improved and may result in a higher market price for the firm's stock.

stock, lease financing, and financing in international markets, among others. Thus the pattern of analysis has broad applications.

To make the application of the concepts more concrete, a case will be used to illustrate and exemplify the procedures involved. Stanton Chemicals, having estimated that it will need to raise \$200 million for an expansion program, discusses with its investment bankers whether it should raise the \$200 million through debt financing or through selling additional shares of common stock. The bankers are asked to make their recommendation to Stanton's board of directors using the information on industry financial ratios and the company's 1981 balance sheet and income statement found in Tables 20.4, 20.5, and 20.6, respectively.

Stanton's dividend payout has averaged about 30 percent of net income. At present, its cost of debt is 10 percent and its cost of equity 14 percent. If the additional funds are raised by debt, the cost of debt will be 12 percent, and the cost of equity will rise to 16 percent. If the funds are raised by equity, the cost of debt will remain at 10 percent, and the cost of equity will fall to 12 percent; new equity will initially be sold at \$9 per share.

Stanton's common stock is widely held; there is no strong control group. The market parameters are a risk-free rate of 6 percent and an expected return on the market of 11 percent. The debt will carry a maturity of ten years and will require a sinking fund of \$20 million per year in addition to the present \$20 million annual sinking fund requirement.

Table 20.4

Chemical Industry Financial Ratios

Current ratio: 2.0 times
Sales to total assets: 1.6 times
Current debt to total assets: 30%
Long-term debt to net worth: 40%
Total debt to total assets: 50%
Coverage of fixed charges: 7 times
Cash flow coverage: 3 times
Net income to sales: 5%
Return on total assets: 9%
Net income to net worth: 13%

Table 20.5

Stanton Chemicals Company Balance Sheet as of December 31, 1981 (Millions of Dollars)

Assets		Liabilities		
Total current assets	\$1,000	Notes payable (at 10%)	\$300	
Net fixed assets	800	Other current liabilities	400	
		Total current liabilities		\$ 700
		Long-term debt (at 10%)		300
		Total debt		\$1,000
		Common stock, par value \$1		100
		Paid-in capital		300
		Retained earnings		400
Total assets	\$1,800	Total claims on assets		\$1,800

Table 20.6

Stanton Chemicals Company Income Statement for Year Ended December 31, 1981 (Millions of Dollars)

	1981	Pro forma after financing
Total revenues	$3,000	$3,400
Depreciation expense	200	220
Other costs	2,484	2,820
Net operating income	$ 316	$ 360
Interest expense	60	
Net income before taxes	$ 256	
Income taxes (at 50%)	128	
Net income	$ 128	

In their analysis of which form of financing should be chosen, the investment bankers consider the following factors:

A. Risk

1. Financial structure
2. Fixed charge coverage
3. Coverage of cash flow requirements
4. Level of beta

B. Relative costs

1. Effects on market value per share of common stock
2. Effects on cost of capital

C. Effects on control

The solution proceeds as follows. First, the two forms of financing are examined with reference to the firm's risk as measured by its financial structure (see Table 20.7). Stanton fails to meet the industry standards on both the short-term and total debt ratios. If it finances with debt, its financial structure ratios will be further

Table 20.7

Stanton Financial Structure (Millions of Dollars)

	Present		Pro forma: Debt		Pro forma: Equity		Industry standard
	Amount	Percent	Amount	Percent	Amount	Percent	Percent
Current debt	$ 700	39	$ 700	35	$ 700	35	30
Long-term debt	300	17	500	25	300	15	20
Total debt	$1,000	56	$1,200	60	$1,000	50	50
Equity	800	44	800	40	1,000	50	
Total assets	$1,800	100	$2,000	100	$2,000	100	
Long-term debt to net worth		38		63		30	40

deficient. If it finances with equity, its long-term debt to net worth ratio will be strengthened, and it will meet the industry standard for the total debt to total assets ratio. Stanton should therefore seek to fund some short-term debt into longer-term debt in the future, and it should try to build up its equity base further from retained earnings.

Stanton's fixed charge coverage is analyzed next, in Table 20.8. The table shows that the company's fixed charge coverage is below the industry standard. The use of debt financing will further aggravate the weakness in this area. The use of equity financing will move the company toward the industry standard.

Table 20.8

Fixed Charge Coverage (Millions of Dollars)

		Pro forma		
	Present	Debt	Equity	Industry standard
Net operating income	$316	$360	$360	
Interest expenses	60	90[a]	60	
Coverage ratio	5.27	4.00	6.00	7.00

[a] See Table 20.10 and related discussion.

Stanton's cash flow coverage is analyzed in Table 20.9. To obtain the cash inflow, depreciation expense is added to net operating income. To obtain the cash outflow requirements, the before-tax sinking fund payment is added to the interest expenses. The sinking fund payments must be placed on a before-tax basis because they are not a tax-deductible expense.

The resulting cash flow coverage ratios appear satisfactory when measured against the industry standard of 3.00. However, this result has to be qualified by the recognition that a full analysis of cash flow coverage must consider other cash outflow requirements. These will include scheduled principal repayments on debt obligations, preferred stock dividends, payments under lease obligations, and probably some capital expenditures that are regarded as essential for the continuity of the firm. Within the broader definition of cash outflow requirements, Stanton's cash flow coverage would undoubtedly be lowered.

Table 20.9

Stanton's Cash Flow Coverage (Millions of Dollars)

		Pro forma		
	Present	Debt	Equity	Industry standard
Net operating income	$316	$360	$360	
Depreciation expense	200	220	220	
Cash inflow	$516	$580	$580	
Interest expense	60	90	60	
Sinking fund payments	20	40	20	
Before-tax sinking fund payments	40	80	40	
Cash outflow requirements	$100	$170	$100	
Cash flow coverage ratio	5.16	3.41	5.80	3.00

The next consideration is the effect of the various forms of financing on the level of the firm's beta. As indicated earlier, Stanton's cost of equity is at present 14 percent. Using the security market line and additional data on the market parameters already provided, Stanton's present level of beta can be determined as follows:

$$k_s = R_F + (\bar{R}_M - R_F)\beta$$

$$0.14 = 0.06 + (0.11 - 0.06)\beta$$

$$\beta = 1.6 \text{ at present}$$

Stanton's present level of beta is 1.6. As stated earlier, if the additional funds are raised by debt, the cost of equity will rise to 16 percent. The implied new beta will therefore be:

$$0.16 = 0.06 + (0.05)\beta$$

$$\beta = 2.0$$

Stanton's beta will rise to 2 with debt financing. With equity financing, the cost of equity will fall to 12 percent. The implied new beta will thus be 1.2.

Four measures of risk have been used to assess the effect of choosing between equity financing and debt financing. Each measure has covered different aspects of risk, and the results for Stanton have all pointed in the same direction. If debt financing is used, the financial structure ratios will be above the industry standards, the deficiency in the fixed charge coverage ratio will be further aggravated, and the cash flow coverage will decline toward the industry standard (and by a broader measure may even fall below it). The existing 1.6 beta level is relatively high. The use of debt financing will push the beta level to 2, which is high for an industrial firm. The use of equity financing will move the beta level toward the average beta level of the market, which is 1. Clearly, therefore, from the standpoint of the four different measures of risk, equity financing is the more favorable.

The next consideration is the relative costs of the different forms of financing. Relative costs are measured by the effects of each form of financing on the market value per share of common stock and by the effects on the firm's cost of capital. To apply these two criteria it is first necessary to calculate the amount of interest expense (in Table 20.10) for use in the income statements (Table 20.11).

Table 20.10

Calculation of the Amount of Debt Interest for Stanton (Millions of Dollars)

	No expansion		Expansion with debt		Expansion with equity	
Form of debt	Amount	Rate	Amount	Rate	Amount	Rate
$300 million short-term notes payable	$30	10%	$36	12%	$30	10%
$300 million existing long-term debt	30	10	30	10	30	10
$200 million new long-term debt			24	12		
Total interest expense	$60		$90		$60	

Table 20.11

Stanton's Income Statements (Millions of Dollars)

	No expansion	Expansion with debt	Expansion with equity
Net operating income	$316	$360	$360
Interest expense	60	90	60
Net income before taxes	$256	$270	$300
Income taxes (at 50%)	128	135	150
Net income	$128	$135	$150

The total amount of interest expense without expansion is $60 million. Interest expense will remain unchanged if the expansion is financed by equity funds. If the expansion is financed by long-term debt, the facts of the problem state that the cost of debt will rise to 12 percent. The opportunity cost of all debt funds is therefore 12 percent, and an argument can be made that all forms of debt should bear the higher 12 percent rate. However, the actual rate paid on the long-term debt will remain at 10 percent, while the short-term notes payable must be re-newed periodically at the higher 12 percent rate (as shown in Table 20.10). If the expansion is financed by debt, the total interest expense will be $90 million. The total interest expense amounts needed for the income statements in Table 20.11 are now available. With the information developed in the income statements, the market value of equity can be calculated (see Table 20.12).

Table 20.12

Stanton's Market Value of Equity (Millions of Dollars)

	No expansion	Expansion with debt	Expansion with equity
Net income (NI)	$128	$135	$150
Cost of equity (k_s)	0.14	0.16	0.12
Value of equity (S)	$914	$844	$1,250
Number of shares	100	100	122.2
Price per share	$9.14	$8.44	$10.23

The net income under each alternative is capitalized by the applicable cost of equity to obtain the total market value of equity. The price per share can also be determined. The total number of shares of common stock outstanding remains unchanged with no expansion or with expansion financed by debt. The facts of the case stated that if equity were sold, the price would be $9 per share; the $200 of new financing divided by the $9 equals 22.2 million shares. Thus the total number of shares is 122.2 million (the original 100 million plus the additional 22.2 million). The indicated new price per share of common stock is obtained by dividing the total value of equity by the total number of shares of common stock outstanding. The resulting new price per share declines with expansion by debt financing and increases with expansion by equity financing—which means that equity financing is more favorable than debt financing. If debt financing were used, the criterion of maximizing share price would recommend that the expansion program not be adopted.

This result can be checked further by calculating the total market value of the firm (see Table 20.13). The total market value is obtained by adding the amount of interest-bearing debt to the market value of equity. It is increased by expansion with either debt or equity. However, as shown in Table 20.12, the market price per share of common stock is decreased by expansion with debt.

Table 20.13

Stanton's Market Value (Millions of Dollars)

	No expansion	Expansion with debt	Expansion with equity
Market value of equity	$ 914	$ 844	$1,250
Amount of debt	600	800	600
Value of the firm	$1,514	$1,644	$1,850

The main reason for calculating the total market value of the firm is to determine the firm's capital structure proportions for use in the cost of capital calculations. The leverage ratios are calculated in Table 20.14.

Table 20.14

Calculation of Stanton's Leverage Ratios

	No expansion	Expansion with debt	Expansion with equity
Total debt	$ 600	$ 800	$ 600
Market value of the firm	$1,514	$1,644	$1,850
Debt to value ratio	0.40	0.49	0.32

The leverage ratio is increased if debt is employed but decreased if equity financing is employed. Using the capital structure proportions from Table 20.14, the weighted average cost of capital can be calculated:

	$k_b(1 - T)(B/V) + k_s(S/V) =$	k
No expansion	$0.10(0.5)(0.40) + 0.14(0.60) = 0.020 + 0.084 =$	10.4%
Expansion with debt	$0.12(0.5)(0.49) + 0.16(0.51) = 0.029 + 0.082 =$	11.1%
Expansion with equity	$0.10(0.5)(0.32) + 0.12(0.68) = 0.016 + 0.082 =$	9.8%

Expansion with debt will raise Stanton's cost of capital from 10.4 percent to 11.1 percent. Expansion with equity will lower the company's cost of capital from 10.4 percent to 9.8 percent. These results are consistent with the findings for the market value per share of common stock, where debt financing caused a decrease and equity financing an increase. Thus the cost of capital and market price per share of common stock criteria provide consistent findings. For example, we could also obtain the value of the firm using

$$V_L = \frac{X(1 - T)}{k_u} + TB$$

For the no expansion case, we have

$$k = k_b(1 - T)(L) + k_s(1 - L), \text{ where } L = B/V$$
$$= 0.10(0.5)(0.4) + 0.14(0.6)$$
$$= 0.02 + 0.084 = 0.104$$

Since $k = k_u(1 - TL)$,

$$0.104 = k_u(1 - 0.2),$$

and

$$k_u = 0.13$$

Hence,

$$V_L = \frac{\$316(0.5)}{0.13} + 0.5(\$600)$$
$$= \$1{,}515$$

The final item on the checklist of factors for evaluating alternative forms of financing is "effects on control." The problem states that the common stock is already widely held so that there is no control problem to militate against the use of equity financing.

The investment bankers summarize the evidence with respect to the two forms of financing as follows. Risks are already high and will be further increased if debt financing is used. As a result of this substantial increase in risk, the costs of both debt and equity funds will rise. With equity financing, the value per share of common stock is increased and the cost of capital reduced. There is no control issue. On the basis of all the factors considered, the common stock financing is recommended.

The Stanton case illustrates the application of a checklist of key factors to evaluate alternative forms of financing. Four measures of risk and several measures of costs to the firm (returns to investors) are employed. Relative costs of financing can be evaluated by reference to effects on market value per share of common stock, on the cost of capital, and on control of the firm. Thus the analysis is essentially a risk-return evaluation and reflects a basic theme that runs through all of the chapters of this book.

Summary

The explanations of common stock financing and of the advantages and disadvantages of external equity financing compared with the use of preferred stock and debt provide a basis for making sound decisions when a firm is considering common stock financing.

Rights offerings can be used effectively by financial managers. If the new financing associated with the rights represents a sound decision—one likely to result in improved earnings for the firm—a rise in stock values will probably result. The use of rights will permit shareholders to preserve their positions or improve them. However, if investors feel that the new financing is not well advised, the rights offering may cause the price of the stock to decline by more than the value of the rights. Because rights offerings are directed to existing shareholders, their use can reduce the costs of floating the new issue.

A major decision for financial managers in a rights offering is where to set the subscription price, or the amount of the concession from the existing market price of the stock. Formulas reflecting the static effects of a rights offering indicate that neither the company nor the stockholders gain or lose from the price changes. The rights offering has the effect of a stock split; that is, the level set for the subscription price reflects to a great degree the objectives and effects of a stock split.

The subsequent price behavior of the rights and the common stock in the associated new offering reflects the earnings and dividends prospects of the company as well as underlying developments in the securities markets. The new financing associated with the rights offering can be an indicator of prospective growth in the company's sales and earnings. The stock-split effects of the rights offering can be used to alter the company's dividend payments. The effects of these developments on the market behavior of the rights and the securities before, during, and after the rights trading period reflect the expectations of investors toward the outlook for the earnings of the firm.

A framework for decisions on choosing among various forms of financing is applied to the evaluation of common stock financing and can also be applied to the other forms of financing discussed in subsequent chapters.

Questions

20.1 By what percentage could total assets shrink in value on liquidation before creditors incur losses in each of the following cases:

a. Equity to total asset ratio of 50 percent
b. Debt to equity ratio of 50 percent
c. Debt to total asset ratio of 40 percent

20.2 How many shares must a minority group own in order to assure election of two directors if nine new directors will be elected and 200,000 shares are outstanding? Assume cumulative voting exists.

20.3 Should the preemptive right entitle stockholders to purchase convertible bonds before they are offered to outsiders?

20.4 What are the reasons for not letting officers and directors of a corporation make short sales in their company's stock?

20.5 It is frequently stated that the primary purpose of the preemptive right is to allow individuals to maintain their proportionate share of the ownership and control of a corporation.

a. Just how important do you suppose this consideration is for the average stockholder of a firm whose shares are traded on the New York or American stock exchange?
b. Is the preemptive right likely to be of more importance to stockholders of closely held firms? Explain.

20.6 How would the success of a rights offering be affected by a declining stock market?

20.7 What are some of the advantages and disadvantages of setting the subscription price on a rights offering substantially below the current market price of the stock?

20.8 a. Is a firm likely to get wider distribution of shares if it sells new stock through a rights offering or directly to underwriters?

b. Why would a company be interested in getting a wider distribution of shares?

Problems

20.1 The common stock of McLean Development Company is selling for $32 a share on the market. Stockholders are offered one new share at a subscription price of $20 for every three shares held. What is the value of each right?

20.2 United Appliance Company common stock is priced at $40 a share on the market. Notice is given that stockholders can purchase one new share at a price of $27.50 for every four shares held.

a. At approximately what market price will each right sell?

b. Why will this be the approximate price?

c. What effect will the issuance of rights have on the original market price?

20.3 Adele Jackson's total assets consist of 490 shares of Collingwood Corporation and $2,000 in cash. Collingwood now offers stockholders one additional share at a price of $20 for each 5 shares held. The current market price of the stock is $35.

a. What is the value of each right?

b. Prepare statements showing Jackson's total assets after the offering for each of these alternative courses of action.

1. She exercises all her rights.
2. She sells all her rights.
3. She sells 400 rights and exercises 90 rights.
4. She neither sells nor exercises the rights.

20.4 The Fuller Company has the following balance sheet and income statement:

The Fuller Company Balance Sheet before Rights Offering

		Total debt (6%)	$ 7,000,000
		Common stock (100,000 shares)	3,000,000
		Retained earnings	4,000,000
Total assets	$14,000,000	Total liabilities and capital	$14,000,000

The Fuller Company Income Statement

Earning rate: 10.5% *on total assets*	
Total earnings	$1,470,000
Interest on debt	420,000
Income before taxes	$1,050,000
Taxes (40% rate assumed)	420,000
Earnings after taxes	$ 630,000
Earnings per share	$6.30
Dividends per share (56% of earnings)	$3.53
Price/earnings ratio	15 times
Market price per share	$94.50

The company plans to raise an additional $5 million through a rights offering; the additional funds will continue to earn 10.5 percent. The price/earnings ratio is assumed to remain at 15 times, the dividend payout will continue to be 56 percent, and the 40 percent tax rate will remain in effect. (Do not attempt to use the formula given in the chapter. Additional information is given here that violates the "other things constant" assumption inherent in the formula.)

a. Assuming subscription prices of $25, $50, and $80 a share:
   1. How many additional shares of stock will have to be sold?
   2. How many rights will be required to purchase one new share?
   3. What will be the new earnings per share?
   4. What will be the new market price per share?
   5. What will be the new dividend per share if the dividend payout ratio is maintained?
b. Suppose you hold 100 shares of Fuller stock before the rights offering. After you exercise your rights, what is the value of your position?

20.5 As one of the minority shareholders of the Keane Corporation, you are dissatisfied with the current operations of the company. You feel that if you could gain membership on the company's board of directors, you could persuade the company to make improvements. The problem is that current management controls 75 percent of the stock, you control only 7 percent, and the balance is held by other minority shareholders. There is a total of 500,000 voting shares. Ten directors will be elected at the next annual stockholder meeting.

a. If voting is noncumulative, can you elect yourself director?
b. Suppose you are able to persuade all the minority shareholders that you should be elected. If voting is noncumulative, can they elect you?
c. If voting is cumulative, can you elect yourself director?
d. What percent of the minority shares other than your own will you need to have voted for you to be certain of election?
e. What is the number of directors the minority shareholders can elect with certainty?

20.6 The Frost Crop Food Company is engaged principally in the business of growing, processing, and marketing a variety of frozen vegetables. A major company in this field, it produces and markets high quality food at premium prices.

During each of the past several years the company's sales have increased and the needed inventories have been financed from short-term sources. The officers have discussed the idea of refinancing their bank loans with long-term debt or common stock. A common stock issue of 310,000 shares sold at this time (present market price $72 a share) will yield $21 million after expenses. The same sum can be raised by selling twelve-year bonds with an interest rate of 8 percent. (See financial ratios and statements below.)

a. Should Frost Crop Food refinance the short-term loans? Why?
b. If the bank loans should be refinanced, what factors should be considered in determining which form of financing to use?

Food Processing Industry Financial Ratios

Current ratio: 2.2 times
Sales to total assets: 2.0 times
Sales to inventory: 5.6 times
Average collection period: 22.0 days
Current debt/total assets: 25–30%
Long-term debt/total assets: 10–15%
Preferred/total assets: 0.5%
Net worth/total assets: 55–65%
Profits to sales: 2.3%
Net profits to total assets: 4.0%
Profits to net worth: 8.4%
Expected growth rate of earnings and dividends: 6.5%

Frost Crop Food Company Consolidated Balance Sheet as of March 31, 1980 (Millions of Dollars)[a]

Current assets	$141	Accounts payable	$12	
Fixed plant and equipment	57	Notes payable	36	
Other assets	12	Accruals	15	
		Total current liabilities		$ 63
		Long-term debt (at 5%)		63
		Preferred stock		9
		Common stock (par $6)	$12	
		Retained earnings	63	
		Shareholders' equity		75
Total assets	$210	Total claims on assets		$210

[a] The majority of harvesting activities do not begin until late April or May.

Frost Crop Food Company Consolidated Income Statement for Year Ended March 31 (Millions of Dollars)

	1977	1978	1979	1980
Net sales	$225.0	$234.6	$292.8	$347.1
Cost of goods sold	146.1	156.6	195.3	230.4
Gross profit	$ 78.9	$ 78.0	$ 97.5	$116.7
Other expenses	61.8	66.0	81.0	88.5
Operating income	$ 17.1	$ 12.0	$ 16.5	$ 28.2
Interest expense	3.3	4.2	5.7	9.3
Earnings before tax	$ 13.8	$ 7.8	$ 10.8	$ 18.9
Taxes	7.2	3.3	5.4	9.6
Net profit	$ 6.6	$ 4.5	$ 5.4	$ 9.3
Preferred dividend	0.3	0.3	0.3	0.3
Earnings available to common stock	$ 6.3	$ 4.2	$ 5.1	$ 9.0
Earnings per share	$3.15	$2.10	$2.55	$4.50
Cash dividends per share	$1.29	$1.44	$1.59	$1.80
Price range for common stock:				
High	$66.00	$69.00	$66.00	$81.00
Low	$30.00	$42.00	$51.00	$63.00

20.7 Inland Steel is planning an expansion program. It estimates that it will need to raise an additional $200 million. Inland discussed with its investment banker whether to raise the $200 million through debt financing or through selling additional shares of common stock. The banker's recommendation was based on the following background information. The dividend payout has averaged about 50 percent of net income. The cost of debt is 10 percent, and the cost of equity is 14 percent. If the additional funds are raised by debt, the cost of debt will be 12 percent and the cost of equity will rise to 16 percent. If the additional funds are raised by equity, the cost of debt will remain at 10 percent, and the cost of equity will fall to 12 percent. Equity will be sold at $9 per share. (See also the steel industry standards and Inland's balance sheet and income statement below.)

Steel Industry Standards

Long-term debt to shareholder's equity: 30%
Shareholders' equity to total assets: 55%
Fixed charge coverage: 7 times
Current ratio: 2.1 times
Return on net worth: 11%

Inland Steel Balance Sheet as of December 31, 1980 (Millions of Dollars)

Assets		**Liabilities**		
Total current assets	$ 600	Notes payable (at 10%)	$100	
Net fixed assets	1,200	Other current liabilities	100	
		Total current liabilities		$ 200
		Long-term debt (at 10%)		500
		Other liabilities		300
		Total debt		$1,000
		Common stock, par value $1		100
		Paid-in capital		300
		Retained earnings		400
Total assets	$1,800	Total claims on assets		$1,800

Inland Steel Income Statement for Year Ended December 31, 1980 (Millions of Dollars)

	Current year	With expansion, pro forma
Total revenues	$2,000	$2,400
Net operating income	231	260
Interest expense	60	———
Net income before taxes	$ 171	———
Income taxes (at 25%)	43	———
Net income to equity	$ 128	———

a. Make a financial risk analysis using financial structure ratios.
b. Complete the pro forma income statements under the two forms of financing, and compare fixed charge coverage under the two alternatives.
c. Calculate the market value of equity and the indicated market price per share before and after financing by the two methods.
d. Calculate the value of the firm and the *B/S*, *B/V*, and *S/V* percentages.
e. Calculate the weighted cost of capital at present and under the two financing alternatives.
f. Recommend the best form of financing for Inland.

CHAPTER 21

DEBT AND PREFERRED STOCK

There are many classes of fixed income securities: long-term and short-term, secured and unsecured, marketable and nonmarketable, participating and nonparticipating, senior and junior, and so on. Financial managers, with the counsel of investment bankers and other financial advisers, seek to package securities with characteristics that will make them attractive to the widest range of different types of investors. By relating the design of securities effectively to the tastes and needs of potential investors, financial managers can hold the firm's costs of financing to the lowest possible levels. This chapter deals with the two most important types of long-term, fixed-income securities—bonds and preferred stocks.

Instruments of Long-Term Debt Financing

An understanding of long-term forms of financing requires some familiarity with technical terminology. The discussion of long-term debt therefore begins with an explanation of several important instruments and terms.

Bond

Most people have had some experience with short-term promissory notes. A *bond* is simply a long-term promissory note.

Mortgage

A *mortgage* represents a pledge of designated property for a loan. Under a *mortgage bond,* a corporation pledges certain real assets as security for the bond. A mortgage bond is therefore secured by real property.[1] The pledge is a condition of the loan.

Debenture

A *debenture* is a long-term bond that is *not* secured by a pledge of any specific property. However, like other general creditor claims, it is secured by any property not otherwise pledged.

Indenture

The long-term relationship between the borrower and the lender of a long-term promissory note is established in a document called an *indenture.* In the case of an ordinary sixty- or ninety-day promissory note, few developments are likely to occur in the life or affairs of the borrower that will endanger repayment. The lender looks closely at the borrower's current position, because current assets are the main source of repayment. A bond, however, is a long-term contractual relationship between the bond issuer and the bondholder; over this extended period the bondholder has cause to worry that the issuing firm's position may change materially.

[1] There is also the *chattel mortgage*, which is secured by personal property; but this is generally an intermediate-term instrument. *Real property* is defined as real estate—land and buildings. *Personal property* is defined as any other kind of property, including equipment, inventories, and furniture.

In the ordinary common stock or preferred stock certificate or agreement, the details of the contractual relationship can be summarized in a few paragraphs. The bond indenture, however, can be a document of several hundred pages that discusses a large number of factors important to the contracting parties, such as: (1) the form of the bond and the instrument; (2) a complete description of property pledged; (3) the authorized amount of the bond issue; (4) detailed protective clauses, or *covenants,* which usually include limits on indebtedness, restrictions on dividends, and a sinking fund provision; (5) a minimum current ratio requirement; and (6) provisions for redemption or call privileges.

Trustee

Bonds are not only of long duration but also, usually, of substantial size. Before the rise of large aggregations of savings through insurance companies or pension funds, no single buyer was able to buy an issue of such size. Bonds were therefore issued in denominations of $1,000 each and were sold to a large number of purchasers. To facilitate communication between the issuer and the numerous bondholders, a trustee was appointed to represent the bondholders. The trustee is still presumed to act at all times for the protection of the bondholders and on their behalf.

Any legal person, including a corporation, is considered competent to act as a trustee. Typically, however, the duties of the trustee are handled by a department of a commercial bank.

Trustees have three main responsibilities:

1. They certify the issue of bonds. This duty involves making certain that all the legal requirements for drawing up the bond contract and the indenture have been carried out.
2. They police the behavior of the corporation in its performance of the responsibilities set forth in the indenture provisions.
3. They are responsible for taking appropriate action on behalf of the bondholders if the corporation defaults on payment of interest or principal.

It is said that in many corporate bond defaults in the early 1930s, trustees did not act in the best interests of the bondholders. They did not conserve the assets of the corporation effectively, and often they did not take early action, thereby allowing corporation executives to continue their salaries and to dispose of assets under conditions favorable to themselves but detrimental to the bondholders. In some cases, assets pledged as security for the bonds were sold, and specific security was thus no longer available. The result in many instances was that holders of mortgage bonds found themselves more in the position of general creditors than of secured bondholders.

As a consequence of such practices, Congress passed the Trust Indenture Act of 1939 in order to give more protection to bondholders. The act provides (1) that trustees must be given sufficient power to act on behalf of bondholders; (2) that the indenture must fully disclose rights and responsibilities and must not be deceptive; (3) that bondholders can make changes in the indenture; (4) that prompt, protective action be taken by the trustees for bondholders if default occurs; (5) that an arm's-length relationship exist between the issuing corporation and the trustee; and (6) that the corporation must make periodic reports to its trustee to enable that person to carry out the protective responsibilities.

Call Provision

A *call provision* gives the issuing corporation the right to call in the bond for redemption. The provision generally states that the company must pay an amount greater than the par value of the bond; this additional sum is defined as the *call premium*. The call premium is typically equal to one year's interest if the bond is called during the first year, and it declines at a constant rate each year thereafter. For example, the call premium on a $1,000 par value, twenty-year, 6 percent bond is generally $60 if called during the first year, $57 if called during the second year (calculated by reducing the $60, or 6 percent, premium by one-twentieth), and so on.

The call privilege is valuable to the firm but potentially detrimental to the investor, especially if the bond is issued in a period when interest rates are thought to be cyclically high. The problem for investors is that the call privilege enables the issuing corporation to substitute bonds paying lower interest rates for bonds paying higher ones. Consider a simple example of consols (bonds with no maturity). Suppose consols are sold to yield 10 percent when interest rates are high. If interest rates drop so that the consols yield 8 percent, the value of the bond theoretically could rise to $1,250. Suppose the issuing firm can call the bond by paying a $100 premium. The investor receives $1,100 for a bond whose market value will otherwise be $1,250. The callability of the bond will probably prevent its rising to the full $1,250 in the marketplace.

This disadvantage of the call privilege to the investor is supported by empirical data. Studies indicate that when interest rate levels are high, new issues of callable bonds must bear yields from one-quarter to one-half of 1 percent higher than the yields of noncallable bonds. If callability is deferred for five years (that is, if the issuer cannot exercise the call privilege until the bond has been outstanding for at least five years), in periods of relatively high interest rates, the yields for long-term bonds with five years of call deferment are about 0.13 percent lower than the yields for similar bonds that can be called immediately. During periods of relatively low interest rates, the discount for five years of deferment drops to about 0.04 percent from yields on fully callable bonds.[2] (The procedures for calculating when it is advantageous for the corporation to call or refund a bond or preferred stock issue are presented in Appendix A to this chapter.)

Sinking Fund

A *sinking fund* is a provision that facilitates the orderly retirement of a bond issue (or, in some cases, preferred stock issue). Typically, it requires the firm to buy and retire a portion of the bond issue each year. Sometimes the stipulated sinking fund payment is tied to the current year's sales or earnings, but usually it is a mandatory fixed amount. If it is mandatory, a failure to meet the payment causes the bond issue to be thrown into default and can lead the company into bankruptcy. Obviously, then, a sinking fund can constitute a dangerous cash drain on the firm.

[2] See F. C. Jen and J. E. Wert, "The Effects of Call Risk on Corporate Bond Yields," *Journal of Finance* 22 (December 1967), pp. 637–51; and G. Pye, "The Value of Call Deferment on a Bond: Some Empirical Results," *Journal of Finance* 22 (December 1967), pp. 623–36.

In most cases the bond trustee is given the right to handle the sinking fund in either of two ways:

1. It can call a certain percentage of the bonds at a stipulated price each year (for example, 2 percent of the original amount at a price of $1,050). The serial numbers of the actual bonds to be called are determined by a lottery.
2. To retire the required face amount of the bonds, it can buy the bonds on the open market.

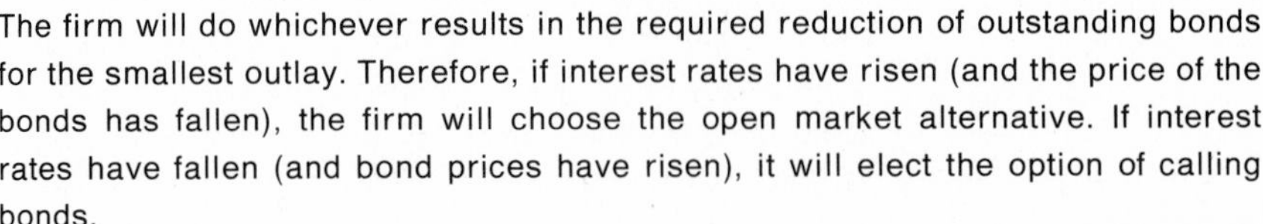

The firm will do whichever results in the required reduction of outstanding bonds for the smallest outlay. Therefore, if interest rates have risen (and the price of the bonds has fallen), the firm will choose the open market alternative. If interest rates have fallen (and bond prices have risen), it will elect the option of calling bonds.

The call provision of the sinking fund at times works to the detriment of bondholders. If, for example, the bond carries a 7 percent interest rate, and if yields on similar securities are 4 percent, the bond will sell for well above par. A sinking fund call at near par thus greatly disadvantages some bondholders.

On balance, securities that provide for a sinking fund and continuing redemption are likely to be offered initially on a lower yield basis than are securities without such a fund. Since sinking funds provide additional protection to investors, sinking fund bonds are likely to sell initially at higher prices; hence, they have a lower cost of capital to the issuer.

Funded Debt

Funded debt is simply long-term debt. A firm planning to "fund" its floating debt will replace short-term securities by long-term securities. *Funding* does not imply placing money with a trustee or other repository; part of the jargon of finance, it simply means "long-term."[3]

Secured Bonds

Secured long-term debt can be classified according to (1) the priority of claims, (2) the right to issue additional securities, and (3) the scope of the lien.

Priority of Claims

A senior mortgage has prior claims on assets and earnings. Senior railroad mortgages, for example, have been called the "mortgages next to the rail," implying that they have the first claim on the land and assets of the railroad corporations. A junior mortgage is a subordinate lien, such as a second or third mortgage. It is a lien or claim junior to others.

Right to Issue Additional Securities

Mortgage bonds can also be classified with respect to the right to issue additional obligations pledging already encumbered property.

[3] Tampa Electric Company provides a good example of funding. This company has a continuous construction program. Typically, it uses short-term debt to finance construction expenditures. However, once short-term debt has built up to about $75 million, the company sells a stock or bond issue, uses the proceeds to pay off its bank loans, and starts the cycle again. The high flotation costs of small security issues make this process desirable.

In the case of a *closed-end mortgage,* a company cannot sell additional bonds (beyond those already issued) secured by the property specified in the mortgage. For example, assume that a corporation with plant and land worth $5 million has a $2 million mortgage on these properties. If the mortgage is closed-end, no more bonds having first liens on this property can be issued. Thus a closed-end mortgage provides security to the bond buyer. The ratio of the amount of the senior bonds to the value of the property is not increased by subsequent issues.

If the bond indenture is silent on this point, it is called an *open-end mortgage.* Its nature can be illustrated by referring to the example cited above. Against property worth $5 million, bonds of $2 million are sold. If an additional first mortgage bond of $1 million is subsequently sold, the property has been pledged for a total of $3 million of bonds. If, on liquidation, the property sells for $2 million, the original bondholders will receive 67 cents on the dollar. If the mortgage had been closed-end, they would have been fully paid.

Most characteristic is the *limited open-end mortgage.* Its nature can be indicated by continuing the example. A first mortgage bond issue of $2 million, secured by the property worth $5 million, is sold. The indenture provides that an additional $1 million worth of bonds—or an additional amount of bonds to bring the total to 60 percent of the original cost of the property—can be sold. Thus the mortgage is open only to a certain point.

Scope of the Lien

Bonds can also be classified with respect to the scope of their lien. A lien is granted on certain specified property. When a *specific lien* exists, the security for a first or second mortgage is a specifically designated property. On the other hand, a *blanket mortgage* pledges all real property currently owned by the company. Real property includes only land and those things affixed thereto; thus a blanket mortgage is not a mortgage on cash, accounts receivables, or inventories, which are items of personal property. A blanket mortgage gives more protection to the bondholder than does a specific mortgage because it provides a claim on all real property owned by the company.

Unsecured Bonds

Debentures

The reasons for a firm's use of unsecured debt are diverse. Paradoxically, the extremes of financial strength and weakness may give rise to its use. Also, tax considerations and great uncertainty about the level of the firm's future earnings have given rise to special forms of unsecured financing. A *debenture* is an unsecured bond and, as such, provides no lien on specific property as security for the obligation. Debenture holders are therefore general creditors whose claim is protected by property not otherwise pledged. The advantage of debentures from the issuer's standpoint is that the property is left unencumbered for subsequent financing. However, in practice, the use of debentures depends on the nature of the firm's assets and its general credit strength.

A firm whose credit position is exceptionally strong can issue debentures; it simply does not need specific security. However, the credit position of a company may be so weak that it has no alternative to the use of debentures; all its property may already be encumbered. The debt portion of American Telephone & Telegraph's vast financing program since the end of World War II has been mainly through debentures. AT & T is such a strong institution that it does not have to provide security for its debt issues.

Debentures are also issued by companies in industries where it is not practical to provide a lien through a mortgage on fixed assets. Examples of such companies are large mail-order houses and finance companies, which characteristically do not have large fixed assets in relation to their total assets. Their assets are mainly in the form of inventories or receivables, which are not satisfactory security for a mortgage lien.

Subordinated Debentures

The term *subordinate* means below or inferior. Thus *subordinated debt* has claims on assets after unsubordinated debt in the event of liquidation. Debentures can be subordinated to designated notes payable—usually bank loans—or to any or all other debt. In the event of liquidation or reorganization, the debentures cannot be paid until senior debt *as named in the indenture* has been paid. Senior debt typically does not include trade accounts payable. How the subordination provision strengthens the position of senior debt holders is shown in Table 21.1.

Table 21.1

Illustration of Bankruptcy Payments to Senior Debt, Other Debt, and Subordinated Debt

Financial structure	Book value (1)	Percent of total debt (2)	Initial allocation (3)	Actual payment (4)	Percent of original claim satisfied (5)
$200 available for claims on liquidation					
Bank debt	$200	50%	$100	$150	75%
Other debt	100	25	50	50	50
Subordinated debt	100	25	50	0	0
Total debt	$400	100%	$200	$200	50%
Net worth	300				0
Total	$700				29%
$300 available for claims on liquidation					
Bank debt	$200	50%	$150	$200	100%
Other debt	100	25	75	75	75
Subordinated debt	100	25	75	25	25
Total debt	$400	100%	$300	$300	75%
Net worth	300				0
Total	$700				43%

Steps:

1. Express each type of debt as a percentage of total debt (Column 2).
2. Multiply the debt percentages (Column 2) by the amount available to obtain the initial allocations (Column 3).
3. The subordinated debt is subordinate to bank debt. Therefore, the initial allocation to subordinate debt is added to the bank debt allocation until it has been exhausted or until the bank debt is finally paid off (Column 4).

In Table 21.1, where $200 is available for distribution, the subordinated debt has a claim on 25 percent of $200, or $50. However, this claim is subordinated to the bank debt (the only senior debt) and is added to the $100 claim of the bank. As a consequence, 75 percent of the bank's original claim is satisfied.

Where $300 is available for distribution, the $75 allocated to the subordinated debt is divided into two parts; $50 goes to the bank, and the other $25 remains for the subordinated debt holders. In this situation, the senior bank debt holders are fully paid off, 75 percent of other debt is paid, and only 25 percent of subordinated debt is paid.

Subordination is frequently required. Alert credit managers of firms supplying trade credit or commercial bank loan officers typically insist on subordination, particularly where debt is owed to the principal stockholders or officers of a company. Often, subordinated debentures are also convertible into the common stock of the issuing company.

In comparison to subordinated debt, preferred stock suffers from the disadvantage that its dividends are not deductible as an expense for tax purposes. Subordinated debentures have been referred to as being like a special kind of preferred stock, the dividends of which *are* deductible as an expense for tax purposes. Subordinated debt has therefore become an increasingly important source of corporate capital.

The reasons for the use of subordinated debentures are clear. They offer a great tax advantage over preferred stock; yet they do not restrict the borrower's ability to obtain senior debt, as would be the case if all debt sources were on an equal basis.

The use of subordinated debentures is further stimulated by periods of tight money, when commercial banks tend to require a greater equity base for short-term financing. These debentures provide a greater equity cushion for loans from commercial banks or other forms of senior debt. Their use also illustrates the development of hybrid securities that emerge to meet the changing situations that develop in the capital market.

Income Bonds

Income bonds provide that interest must be paid only if the earnings of the firm are sufficient to meet the interest obligations. The principal, however, must be paid when due. Thus the interest itself is not a fixed charge. Income bonds historically have been issued because a firm has been in financial difficulties and its history suggests that it may be unable to meet a substantial level of fixed charges in the future. More generally, however, income bonds simply provide flexibility to the firm in the event that earnings do not cover the amount of interest that would otherwise have to be paid. Income bonds are like preferred stock in that the firm will not be in default if current payments on the obligations are not made. They have an additional advantage over preferred stock in that the interest is a deductible expense for corporate income tax computations, while the dividends on preferred stock are not.

The main characteristic and distinct advantage of the income bond is that interest is payable only if the company achieves earnings. Since earnings calculations are subject to differing interpretations, the indenture of the income bond carefully defines income and expenses. If it did not, litigation might result. Some income bonds are cumulative indefinitely (if interest is not paid, it accumulates, and it must be paid at some future date); others are cumulative for the first three to five years, after which they become noncumulative.

Income bonds usually contain sinking fund provisions to provide for their retirement. The annual payments to the sinking funds range between $\frac{1}{2}$ and 1 percent of the face amount of the original issue. Because the sinking fund payment requirements are typically contingent on earnings, a fixed cash drain on the company is avoided. Typically, income bondholders do not have voting rights when the bonds are issued. Sometimes bondholders are given the right to elect some specified number of directors if interest is not paid for a certain number of years.

Sometimes income bonds are convertible; there are sound reasons for convertibility if the bonds arise out of a reorganization. Creditors who receive income bonds in exchange for defaulted obligations have a less desirable position than they had previously. Since they have received something based on an adverse and problematical forecast of the company's future, it is appropriate that if the company does prosper, income bondholders are entitled to participate. When income bonds are issued in situations other than reorganization, the convertibility feature is likely to make the issue more attractive to prospective bond buyers.

Original Issue Discount Bonds

An interesting new development in bond financing is the use of the original issue, deep-discount bond (OID). They are sold at about 50 percent of face value, paying interest rates at about half the prevailing rates. For example, in March 1981 Martin Marietta sold 30-year bonds, A-rated, priced at $538.35 per $1,000 bond. The interest rate was 7 percent on face value, for an effective rate to maturity of 13.25 percent. Many other companies followed and by June 1981, issues totaling $2.5 billion in face value had been sold.

In about the same period, Pepsico privately placed a zero-coupon bond. In mid-1981, J. C. Penney pioneered the first public offering of a zero-interest, discount bond. Investors paid $322.47 for an 8-year bond of $1,000—an effective annual yield of 15.2 percent. Each year investors must pay taxes on one-eighth of the $667.53 increase that will take place. This is $83.44 per year. Hence the OID bonds are not attractive to individual investors. They are bought almost entirely by tax-exempt institutions, which do not pay taxes on the implicit interest.

There are two advantages to the issuer. First, the effective interest rate is lower. In May 1981, the investment banking firm Goldman Sachs sold two bonds for Archer-Daniels-Midland. One was a straight 30-year debenture with a yield of 16.08 percent and a 30-year deep-discount bond with an effective yield of 15.35 percent, which represents a yield 73 basis points lower. Second, there is a tax advantage. The issuing company deducts all the implicit interest, while actually paying only the coupon rate. This advantage varies with the effective corporate tax rate of the issuing firm.

The reason for the emergence of new instruments such as OIDs in 1981 is the persistence of high interest rates. Corporations have been financing at the very high interest rates, but at the same time seeking to shave the interest costs by innovative devices.

Characteristics of Long-Term Debt

From the viewpoint of long-term debt holders, debt is good in regard to risk, has limited advantages in regard to income, and is weak in regard to control. To elaborate:

1. In the area of risk, debt is favorable because it gives the holder priority both in earnings and in liquidation. Debt also has a definite maturity and is protected by the covenants of the indenture.
2. The bondholder has a fixed return; except in the case of income bonds, interest payments are not contingent on the company's level of earnings. However, debt does not participate in any superior earnings of the company, and gains are limited in magnitude. Bondholders actually suffer during inflationary periods. A twenty-year, 6 percent bond pays $60 of interest each year. Under inflation, the purchasing power of this $60 is eroded, causing a loss in real value to the bondholder.[4] Frequently, long-term debt is callable. If bonds are called, the investor receives funds that must be reinvested to be kept active.
3. In the area of control, the bondholder usually does not have the right to vote. However, if the bonds go into default, then bondholders in effect take control of the company.

From the viewpoint of long-term debt issuers, there are several advantages and disadvantages to bonds. The advantages include the following:

1. The cost of debt is definitely limited. Bondholders do not participate in superior profits (if earned).
2. Not only is the cost limited, but typically the expected yield is lower than that of common stock.
3. The owners of the corporation do not share their control when debt financing is used.
4. The interest payment on debt is deductible as a tax expense.
5. Flexibility in the financial structure of the corporation can be achieved by inserting a call provision in the bond indenture.

Disadvantages of bonds are as follows:

1. Debt is a fixed charge; if the earnings of the company fluctuate, it may be unable to meet the charge.
2. As seen in Chapters 15 and 16, higher risk brings higher capitalization rates on equity earnings. Thus, even though leverage is favorable and raises earnings per share, the higher capitalization rates attributable to leverage may drive the common stock value down.
3. Debt usually has a fixed maturity date, and the financial officer must make provision for repayment of the debt.
4. Since long-term debt is a commitment for a long period, it involves risk. The expectations and plans on which the debt was issued may change, and the debt may prove to be a burden. For example, if income, employment, the

[4] Recognizing this fact, investors demand higher interest rates during inflationary periods.

price level, and interest rates all fall greatly, the prior assumption of a large amount of long-term debt may have been an unwise financial policy. The railroads are always given as an example in this regard. They were able to meet their ordinary operating expenses during the 1930s but were unable to meet the heavy financial charges they had undertaken earlier, when their prospects looked more favorable than they turned out to be.

5. In a long-term contractual relationship, the indenture provisions are likely to be much more stringent than they are in a short-term credit agreement. Hence the firm may be subject to much more disturbing and crippling restrictions than if it had borrowed on a short-term basis or had issued common stock.
6. There is a limit on the extent to which funds can be raised through long-term debt. Generally accepted standards of financial policy dictate that the debt ratio shall not exceed certain limits. When debt goes beyond these limits, its cost rises rapidly.

Decisions on the Use of Long-Term Debt

When a number of methods of long-term financing are being considered, the following conditions favor the use of long-term debt:

1. Sales and earnings are relatively stable, or a large increase in future sales and earnings is expected to provide a substantial benefit from the use of leverage.
2. A substantial rise in the price level is expected in the future, making it advantageous for the firm to incur debt that will be repaid with cheaper dollars.
3. The existing debt ratio is relatively low for the line of business.
4. Management thinks the price of the common stock in relation to that of bonds is temporarily depressed.
5. Sale of common stock would involve problems of maintaining the existing control pattern in the company.

Decisions about the use of debt can also be considered in terms of the average cost of capital curve, as developed in Chapter 16. Firms have optimal capital structures, or perhaps optimal ranges, and the average cost of capital is higher than it need be if the firm uses other than an optimal amount of debt. The factors listed above all relate to the optimal debt ratio; some cause the optimal ratio to increase, and others cause it to decrease.

Whenever the firm contemplates raising new outside capital and chooses between debt and equity, it makes an implicit judgment about its actual debt ratio in relation to the optimal ratio. For example, consider Figure 21.1, which shows the assumed shape of the Longstreet Company's average cost of capital schedule. If Longstreet plans to raise outside capital, it must make a judgment about whether it is currently at Point A or Point B. If it decides that it is at A, it should issue debt; if it believes that it is at B, it should sell new common stock. This, of course, is a judgment decision; but all the factors discussed in this chapter must be considered in a qualitative way as well as on the basis of the formal analysis presented in Chapter 16.

Figure 21.1

The Longstreet Company's Average Cost of Capital Schedule

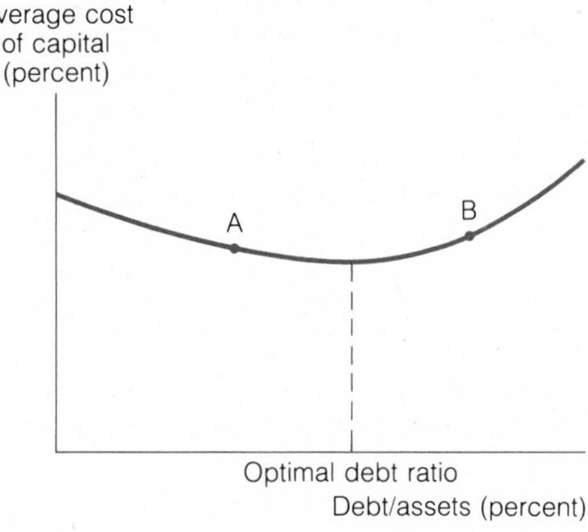

Nature of Preferred Stock

Preferred stock has claims and rights ahead of common stock but behind all bonds. The preference may be a prior claim on earnings, a prior claim on assets in the event of liquidation, or a preferential position with regard to both earnings and assets.

The hybrid nature of preferred stock becomes apparent when we try to classify it in relation to bonds and common stock. The priority feature and the (generally) fixed dividend indicate that preferred stock is similar to bonds. Payments to preferred stockholders are limited in amount, so that common stockholders receive the advantages (or disadvantages) of leverage. However, if the preferred dividends are not earned, the company can forego paying them without danger of bankruptcy. In this characteristic, preferred stock is similar to common stock. Moreover, failure to pay the stipulated dividend does not cause default of the obligation, as does failure to pay bond interest.

In some types of analysis, preferred stock is treated as debt. This occurs, for example, when the analysis is being made by a *potential stockholder* considering the earnings fluctuations induced by fixed charge securities. Suppose, however, that the analysis is by a *bondholder* studying the firm's vulnerability to failure brought on by declines in sales or income. Since the dividends on preferred stock are not a fixed charge (in the sense that failure to pay them represents a default of an obligation), preferred stock represents a cushion; it provides an additional equity base. For *stockholders,* it is a leverage-inducing instrument much like debt. For *creditors,* it constitutes additional net worth. Preferred stock can therefore be treated as either debt or equity, depending on the nature of the problem under consideration.[5]

[5] Accountants generally include preferred stock in the equity portion of the capital structure. But preferred is very different from common equity.

Major Provisions of Preferred Stock Issues

Because the possible characteristics, rights, and obligations of any specific security vary so widely, a point of diminishing returns is quickly reached in a descriptive discussion of the different kinds of securities. As economic circumstances change, new kinds of securities are manufactured. Their number and variety are limited chiefly by the imagination and ingenuity of the managers formulating the terms of the issues. It is not surprising, then, that preferred stock can be found in many forms. The following sections will look at the main terms and characteristics and examine the possible variations in relation to the circumstances in which they could occur.[6]

Priority in Assets and Earnings

Many provisions in a preferred stock certificate are designed to reduce the purchaser's risk in relation to the risk carried by the holder of common stock. Preferred stock usually has priority with regard to earnings and assets. Two provisions designed to prevent undermining this priority are often found. The first states that, without the consent of the preferred stockholders, there can be no subsequent sale of securities having a prior or equal claim on earnings. The second seeks to keep earnings in the firm. It requires a minimum level of retained earnings before common stock dividends are permitted. In order to assure the availability of liquid assets that can be converted into cash for the payment of dividends, the maintenance of a minimum current ratio may also be required.

Par Value

Unlike common stock, preferred stock usually has a par value; this value is a meaningful quantity. First, the par value establishes the amount due the preferred stockholders in the event of liquidation. Second, the preferred dividend is frequently stated as a percentage of the par value. For example, J. I. Case's preferred stock outstanding has a par value of $100 and a stated dividend of 7 percent of par. (It would, of course, be just as appropriate for the Case preferred stock to state simply that the annual dividend is $7; on many preferred stocks the dividends are stated in this manner rather than as a percentage of par value.)

Cumulative Dividends

Most preferred stock issues provide for cumulative dividends—that is, all past preferred dividends must be paid before common dividends can be paid. The cumulative feature is therefore a protective device. If the preferred stock were not cumulative, preferred and common stock dividends could be passed by for a number of years. The company could then vote a large common stock dividend but only the stipulated payment to preferred stock. Suppose that preferred stock with a par value of $100 carried a 7 percent dividend and that the company did not pay dividends for several years, thereby accumulating funds that would enable it to pay in total about $50 in dividends. It could pay a single $7 dividend to the preferred stockholders and a $43 dividend to the common stockholders. Obviously, this device could be used to evade the preferred position that the holders of preferred stock have tried to obtain. The cumulative feature prevents such evasion.[7]

[6] Much of the data in this section is taken from a study by Donald E. Fischer and Glenn A. Wilt, Jr., "Nonconvertible Preferred Stocks as a Financing Instrument, 1950–1965," *Journal of Finance* 23 (September 1968), pp. 611–24.

[7] Note, however, that compounding is absent in most cumulative plans. In other words, the arrearages themselves earn no return.

Large arrearages on preferred stock make it difficult to resume dividend payments on common stock. To avoid delays in beginning common stock dividend payments again, a compromise arrangement with the holders of common stock is likely to be worked out. A package offer is one possibility; for example, a recapitalization plan may provide for an exchange of shares. The arrearage will be wiped out by the donation of common stock with a value equal to the amount of the preferred dividend arrearage, and the holders of preferred stock will thus be given an ownership share in the corporation. In addition, resumption of current dividends on the preferred may be promised. Whether these provisions are worth anything depends on the future earnings prospects of the company.

The advantage to the company of substituting common stock for dividends in arrears is that it can start again with a clear balance sheet. If earnings recover, dividends can be paid to the holders of common stock without making up arrearages to the holders of preferred stock. The original common stockholders, of course, will have given up a portion of their ownership of the corporation.

Convertibility

Approximately 40 percent of the preferred stock that has been issued in recent years is convertible into common stock. For example, 1 share of a particular preferred stock could be convertible into 2.5 shares of the firm's common stock at the option of the preferred shareholder. (The nature of convertibility will be discussed in Chapter 23.)

Some Infrequent Provisions

Some of the other provisions occasionally encountered in preferred stocks include the following:

1. *Voting rights.* Sometimes preferred stockholders are given the right to vote for directors. When this feature is present, it generally permits the preferred stockholders to elect a *minority* of the board, say three out of nine directors. The voting privilege becomes operative only if the company has not paid the preferred dividend for a specified period, say six, eight, or ten quarters.
2. *Participating.* A rare type of preferred stock is one that participates with the common stock in sharing the firm's earnings. The following factors generally relate to participating preferred stocks: (a) the stated preferred dividend is paid first—for example, $5 a share; (b) next, income is allocated to common stock dividends up to an amount equal to the preferred dividend—in this case, $5; and (c) any remaining income is shared equally between the common and preferred stockholders.
3. *Sinking fund.* Some preferred issues have a sinking fund requirement. When they do, the sinking fund ordinarily calls for the purchase and retirement of a given percentage of the preferred stock each year.
4. *Maturity.* Preferred stocks almost never have maturity dates on which they must be retired. However, if the issue has a sinking fund, this effectively creates a maturity date.
5. *Call provision.* A call provision gives the issuing corporation the right to call in the preferred stock for redemption, as for bonds. If it is used, the call provision generally states that the company must pay an amount greater

than the par value of the preferred stock, the additional sum being defined as the *call premium*. For example, a $100 par value preferred stock might be callable at the option of the corporation at $108 a share.

Evaluation of Preferred Stock

There are both advantages and disadvantages to selling preferred stock. Among the advantages are these:

1. In contrast to bonds, the obligation to make fixed interest payments is avoided.
2. A firm wishing to expand because its earning power is high can obtain higher earnings for the original owners by selling preferred stock with a limited return rather than by selling common stock.
3. By selling preferred stock, the financial manager avoids the provision of equal participation in earnings that the sale of additional common stock would require.
4. Preferred stock also permits a company to avoid sharing control through participation in voting.
5. In contrast to bonds, it enables the firm to conserve mortgageable assets.
6. Since preferred stock typically has no maturity and no sinking fund, it is more flexible than bonds.

The disadvantages include the following:

1. Characteristically, preferred stock must be sold on a higher yield basis than that for bonds.[8]
2. Preferred stock dividends are not deductible as a tax expense, a characteristic that makes their cost differential very great in comparison with that of bonds.
3. As shown in Chapter 16, the after-tax cost of debt is approximately half the stated coupon rate for profitable firms. The cost of preferred, however, is the full percentage amount of the preferred dividend.[9]

In fashioning securities, the financial manager needs to consider the investor's point of view. Frequently it is asserted that preferred stocks have so many disadvantages to both the issuer and the investor that they should never be issued. Nevertheless, preferred stock is issued in substantial amounts. Preferred stock

[8] Historically, a given firm's preferred stock generally carried higher rates than its bonds because of the preferred's greater risk from the holder's viewpoint. However, as is noted below, the fact that preferred dividends are largely exempt from the corporate income tax has made preferred stock attractive to corporate investors. In recent years, high-grade preferreds on average have sold on a lower yield basis than high-grade bonds. As an example, on March 27, 1973, AT & T sold a preferred issue that yielded 7.28 percent to an investor. On that same date, AT & T bonds yielded 7.55 percent, or 0.27 percent more than the preferred. The tax treatment accounted for this differential; the *after-tax* yield to a corporate investor was greater on the preferred stock than on the bonds.

[9] By far the most important issuers of nonconvertible preferred stocks are the utility companies. For these firms, taxes are an expense for rate-making purposes—that is, higher taxes are passed on to the customers in the form of higher prices—so tax deductibility is not an important issue. This explains why utilities issue about 85 percent of all nonconvertible preferreds.

provides the following advantages to the investor:

1. It provides reasonably steady income.
2. Preferred stockholders have a preference over common stockholders in liquidation; numerous examples can be cited in which this senior position saved holders of preferred stock from losses incurred by holders of common stock.
3. Many corporations (for example, insurance companies) like to hold preferred stocks as investments because 85 percent of the dividends received on these shares is not taxable.

Preferred stock also has some disadvantages to investors:

1. Although the holders of preferred stock bear a substantial portion of ownership risk, their returns are limited.
2. Price fluctuations in preferred stock are far greater than those in bonds; yet yields on bonds are frequently higher than those on preferred stock.
3. The stockholders have no legally enforceable right to dividends.
4. Accrued dividend arrearages are seldom settled in cash comparable to the amount of the obligation that has been incurred.

Recent Trends

Because of the nondeductibility of preferred stock dividends as a tax expense, many companies have retired their preferred stock. Often debentures or subordinated debentures are offered to preferred stockholders in exchange, since the interest on the debentures is deductible as a tax expense.

When the preferred stock is not callable, the company must offer terms of exchange sufficiently attractive to induce these stockholders to agree to the exchange. Characteristically, bonds or other securities in an amount somewhat above the recent value of the preferred stock are issued in exchange. Sometimes bonds equal in market value to the preferred stock are issued along with additional cash or common stock to provide an extra inducement to the holders of preferred stock. At other times the offer is bonds equal to only a portion of the current market value of the preferred with an additional amount represented by cash or common stock that will bring the total offering to something over the preferred market value as of a recent date.

U.S. Steel's replacement of its 7 percent preferred stock in 1965 is a classic illustration of these exchange patterns. U.S. Steel proposed that its 7 percent preferred stock be changed into $4\frac{5}{8}$ percent thirty-year bonds at a rate of $175 principal amount of bonds for each preferred share. On August 17, 1965, when the plan was announced, the preferred stock was selling at $150. U.S. Steel also announced that the conversion would increase earnings available to common stock by $10 million yearly, or 18 cents a share at 1965 federal income tax rates; this was sufficient inducement to persuade the company to give the preferred stockholders the added $25 a share.

Decision Making on the Use of Preferred Stock

As a hybrid security, preferred stock is favored by conditions that fall between those favoring common stock and those favoring debt. When a firm's profit margin is high enough to more than cover preferred stock dividends, it is advantageous to employ leverage. However, if the firm's sales and profits are subject to considerable fluctuation, the use of debt with fixed interest charges may be unduly risky. Preferred stock can offer a happy compromise. Its use is strongly favored if the firm already has a debt ratio that is high in relation to the reference level maximum for the line of business.

Relative costs of alternative sources of financing are always important considerations. When the market prices of common stocks are relatively low, the costs of common stock financing are relatively high.

The costs of preferred stock financing follow interest rate levels more than common stock prices; in other words, when interest rates are low, the cost of preferred stock is also likely to be low. When the cost of fixed income instruments, such as preferred stock, are low and the costs of variable value securities, such as common stock, are high, the use of preferred stock is favored. Preferred stock may also be the desired form of financing whenever the use of debt will involve excessive risk, but the issuance of common stock will result in problems of control for the dominant ownership group in the company.

Rationale for Different Classes of Securities

At this point the following questions are likely to come to mind: Why are there so many different forms of long-term securities? Why is anybody ever willing to purchase subordinated bonds or income bonds? The answers to both questions can be

Figure 21.2

The Longstreet Company's Risk and Expected Returns on Different Classes of Securities

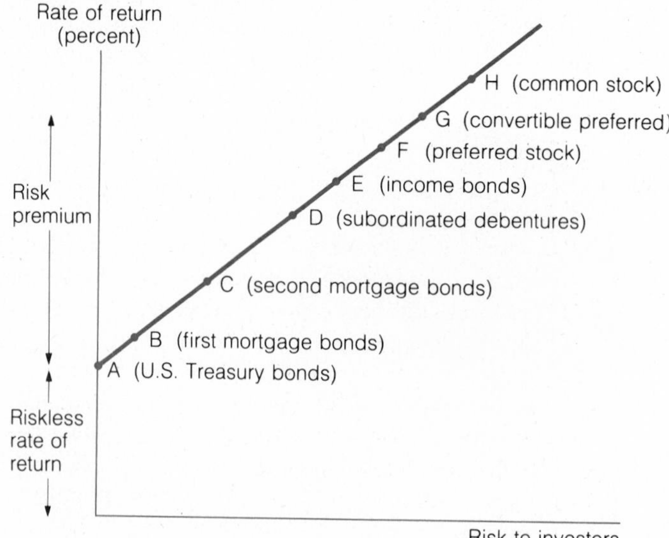

made clear by reference to Figure 21.2: The now familiar tradeoff function is drawn to show the risk and expected returns for the various securities of the Longstreet Company. Longstreet's first mortgage bonds are slightly riskier than U.S. Treasury bonds and sell at a slightly higher expected return. The second mortgage bonds are riskier yet and have a still higher expected return. Subordinated debentures income bonds, and preferred stocks all are increasingly risky and have increasingly higher expected returns. Longstreet's common stock, the riskiest security the firm issues, has the highest expected return of any of its offerings.

Why does Longstreet issue so many different classes of securities? Why not just offer one type of bond plus common stock? The answer lies in the fact that different investors have different risk-return tradeoff preferences, so if the company's securities are to appeal to the broadest possible market, Longstreet must offer as many as investors seem to want. Used wisely, a policy of selling differentiated securities can lower a firm's overall cost of capital below what it would be if it issued only one class of debt and common stock.

Summary

A *bond* is a long-term promissory note. A *mortgage bond* is secured by real property. An *indenture* is an agreement between the firm issuing the bond and the numerous bondholders, represented by a *trustee*.

Secured long-term debt differs with respect to (1) the priority of claims, (2) the right to issue additional securities, and (3) the scope of the lien provided. These characteristics determine the amount of protection provided to the bondholder by the terms of the security. Giving investors more security will induce them to accept a lower yield but will restrict the future freedom of action of the issuing firm.

The main classes of unsecured bonds are (1) *debentures*, (2) *subordinated debentures*, and (3) *income bonds*. Holders of debentures are unsecured general creditors. Subordinated debentures are junior in claim to bank loans. Income bonds are similar to preferred stock in that interest is paid only when earned.

The characteristics of long-term debt determine the circumstances under which it will be used when alternative forms of financing are under analysis. The cost of debt is limited, but it is a fixed obligation. Bond interest is an expense deductible for tax purposes. Debt carries a maturity date and may require sinking fund payments to prepare for extinguishing the obligation. Indenture provisions are likely to include restrictions on the freedom of action of the firm's management.

The nature of long-term debt encourages its use under the following circumstances:

1. Sales and earnings are relatively stable.
2. Profit margins are adequate to make leverage advantageous.
3. A rise in profits or the general price level is expected.
4. The existing debt ratio is relatively low.
5. Common stock price-earnings ratios are low in relation to the levels of interest rates.
6. Control considerations are important.
7. Cash flow requirements under the bond agreement are not burdensome.
8. Restrictions of the bond indenture are not onerous.

Even if seven of the eight factors favor debt, the remaining factor can swing the decision to the use of equity capital. The list of factors is thus simply a checklist of things to be considered when deciding on bonds versus stock; the actual decision is based on a judgment about the relative importance of the several factors.

The characteristics of preferred stock vary with the requirements of the situation under which it is used. However, certain patterns tend to remain. Preferred stocks usually have priority over common stocks with respect to earnings and claims on assets in liquidation. Preferred stocks are usually cumulative; they have no maturity but are sometimes callable. They are typically nonparticipating and offer only contingent voting rights.

The advantages to the issuer are limited dividends and no maturity. These advantages may outweigh the disadvantages of higher cost and nondeductibility of the dividends as an expense for tax purposes. But their acceptance by investors is the final test of whether they can be sold on favorable terms.

Companies sell preferred stock when they seek the advantages of financial leverage but fear the dangers of the fixed charges on debt in the face of potential fluctuations in income. If debt ratios or the cost of common stock financing are relatively high, the advantages of preferred stock are reinforced.

The use of preferred stock has declined significantly since the advent of the corporate income tax because preferred dividends are not deductible for income tax purposes, while bond interest payments are deductible. In recent years, however, there has been a strong shift back to a new kind of preferred stock—convertible preferred, used primarily in connection with mergers. If the stockholders of the acquired company receive cash or bonds, they are required to pay capital gains taxes on any gains they realize. If convertible preferred stock is given to the selling stockholders, this constitutes a tax-free exchange of securities. The selling stockholders can obtain a fixed income security and at the same time postpone the payment of capital gains taxes.

Questions

21.1 A sinking fund is set up in one of two ways:

a. The corporation makes annual payments to the trustee, who invests the proceeds in securities (frequently government bonds) and uses the accumulated total to retire the bond issue on maturity.

b. The trustee uses the annual payments to retire a portion of the issue each year, either calling a given percentage of the issue by a lottery and paying a specified price per bond or buying bonds on the open market, whichever is cheaper.

Discuss the advantages and disadvantages of each procedure from the viewpoint of both the firm and the bondholders.

21.2 Since a corporation often has the right to call bonds at will, do you believe individuals should be able to demand repayment at any time they so desire? Explain.

21.3 What are the relative advantages and disadvantages of issuing a long-term bond during a recession versus during a period of prosperity?

21.4 Missouri Pacific's $4\frac{3}{4}$ percent income bonds due in 2020 are selling for $770, while the company's $4\frac{1}{4}$ percent first mortgage bonds due in 2005 are selling for $945. Each has a $1,000 par value. Why do the bonds with the lower coupon sell at a higher price?

21.5 When a firm sells bonds, it must offer a package of terms acceptable to potential buyers. Included in this package are such features as the issue price, the coupon interest rate, the term of maturity, and sinking fund provisions. The package itself is determined through a bargaining process between the firm and the investment bankers who handle the issue. What particular features would you, as a corporate treasurer, be especially interested in having, and which would you be most willing to give ground on, under each of the following conditions:

a. You believe that the economy is near the peak of a business cycle.
b. Long-run forecasts indicate that your firm may have heavy cash inflows in relation to cash needs during the next five to ten years.
c. Your current liabilities are presently low, but you anticipate raising a considerable amount of funds through short-term borrowing in the near future.

21.6 Bonds are less attractive to investors during periods of inflation because a rise in the price level reduces the purchasing power of the fixed interest payments and of the principal. Discuss the advantages and disadvantages to a corporation of using a bond whose interest payments and principal would increase in direct proportion to increases in the price level (an inflation-proof bond).

21.7 If preferred stock dividends are passed for several years, the preferred stockholders are frequently given the right to elect several members of the board of directors. In the case of bonds that are in default on interest payments, this procedure is not followed. Why does the difference exist?

21.8 Preferred stocks are found in almost all industries, but one industry is the really dominant issuer of preferred shares. What is this industry, and why are firms in it so disposed to using preferred stock?

21.9 If the corporate income tax were abolished, would this raise or lower the amount of new preferred stock issued?

21.10 Investors buying securities have some expected or required rate of return in mind. Which would you expect to be higher—the required rate of return (before taxes) on preferred stocks or that on common stocks:

a. For individual investors?
b. For corporate investors (for example, insurance companies)?

21.11 Do you think the before-tax required rate of return is higher or lower on very high grade preferred stocks or on bonds:

a. For individual investors?
b. For corporate investors?

21.12 For purposes of measuring a firm's leverage, should preferred stock be classified as debt or as equity? Does it matter if the classification is being made (a) by the firm itself, (b) by creditors, or (c) by equity investors?

21.13 Explain what is meant by the term *yield to maturity* in reference to (a) bonds and (b) preferred stocks. Is it appropriate to talk of a yield to maturity on a preferred stock that has no specific maturity date?

21.14 A firm is seeking a term loan from a bank. Under what conditions would it want a fixed interest rate, and under what conditions would it want the rate to fluctuate with the prime rate?

Problems

21.1 Three years ago your firm issued some eighteen-year bonds with 10.5 percent coupon rates and a 10 percent call premium. You have called these bonds. The bonds originally sold at their face value of $1,000.

a. Compute the realized rate of return for investors who purchased the bonds when they were issued.

b. Given the rate of return in Part a, did investors welcome the call? Explain.

21.2 Net losses for the past two years have prevented the Hansen Company from paying the 7 percent dividend on its cumulative preferred stock issue. There are 20,000 shares of the $100 par preferred stock and 200,000 shares of common stock outstanding. This year Hansen has after-tax profits of $1,200,000, and the board of directors would like to declare a dividend on common stock. What is the largest dividend per share that can be declared?

21.3 On January 1, 1981, the loan officer of the Bay City Bank agreed to make a $600,000, five-year term loan to the Apkar Company, on the condition that any new debt issued by Apkar during the next five years must be subordinated to the Bay City loan. On June 1, 1981, Apkar sold $250,000 in subordinated debentures.

In spite of these two infusions of capital, the Apkar Company was forced into bankruptcy on September 12, 1981. Apkar's financial structure as of September 12 is given below:

Accounts payable	$ 400,000
Bank debt	600,000
Subordinated debentures	250,000
Total debt	$1,250,000
Net worth	850,000
Total claims	$2,100,000

a. What dollar amount and percent of Bay City's claim will be paid off if $500,000 is available for claims after liquidation of Apkar's assets?

b. What dollar amount and percent of Bay City's claim will be paid off if $800,000 is available for claims on liquidation?

c. What is the minimum amount available for claims that would completely pay off the bank debt?

21.4 In late 1981, the Coaltown Gas & Electric Company sought to raise $6 million for expansion of facilities and services. The company could have sold additional debt at 15 percent, preferred stock at 15 percent, or common stock at $35 per share. Growth in earnings and dividends was expected to be 8 percent per year. The following financial information is provided for analysis.

Public Utilities Financial Ratios

Current ratio: 1.0 times
Interest earned (before taxes): 4.0 times
Sales to total assets: 0.3 times
Average collection period: 28.0 days
Current debt/total assets: 5–10%
Long-term debt/total assets: 45–50%
Preferred/total assets: 10–15%
Common equity/total assets: 30–35%
Earnings before interest and taxes to total assets: 8.9%
Profits to common equity: 12.1%

Coaltown Gas & Electric Company Balance Sheet as of July 31, 1981 (Thousands of Dollars)

Assets		Liabilities	
Cash	$ 750	Current liabilities	$ 3,000
Receivables	1,500	Long-term debt (at 8%)	35,000
Materials and supplies	1,200	Preferred stock (at 10%)	6,000
Total current assets	$ 3,450	Common stock, $25 par value	10,000
Net property	56,550	Capital surplus	4,000
		Retained earnings	2,000
Total assets	$60,000	Total claims	$60,000

Coaltown Gas & Electric Company Income Statement for Year Ended July 31, 1981 (Thousands of Dollars)

	Current	Pro forma
Operating revenues	$18,900	$21,000
Operating expenses	12,000	13,400
Earnings before interest and taxes	$ 6,900	$ 7,600
Interest deduction	2,800	
Earnings before taxes	$ 4,100	
Income taxes (at 40%)	1,640	
Earnings after taxes	$ 2,460	
Preferred dividends	600	
Net income available to common	$ 1,860	
Earnings per share =	$4.65	
Expected dividends per share =	$3.50	

a. Calculate the following ratios and financial parameters for Coaltown:
   (1) EBIT/TA
   (2) Net income/Book value of common equity
   (3) P/E ratio
   (4) Earnings yield on common stock
   (5) Effective cost of new preferred stock
   (6) Effective cost of new debt
   (7) Cost of new equity

b. Prepare a financial risk analysis before the financing and under each of the financing alternatives. Compute the percentage of each capital component to total assets, the current ratio and the times interest earned for each.
c. Which financing method should Coaltown choose?

21.5 Carson Electronics, a leading manufacturer of electronic equipment, is planning an expansion program. It has estimated that it will need to raise an additional $100 million. Carson is discussing with its investment banker the alternatives of raising the $100 million through debt financing or through selling additional shares of common stock.

The prevailing cost of Aaa debt is 14 percent, while the prevailing cost of Baa debt is 15.8 percent. New equity would be sold at $10 per share. The corporate tax rate is 40 percent. Below are the industry's financial ratios (followed by Carson's balance sheet and income statement):

Electronics Industry Financial Ratios

Current ratio: 2.1 times
Sales to total assets: 1.8 times
Current debt to total assets: 30%
Long-term debt to net worth: 40%
Total debt to total assets: 50%
Coverage of fixed charges: 7 times
Net income to sales: 5%
Return on total assets: 9%
Net income to net worth: 12%

Carson Electronics Balance Sheet as of December 31, 1981 (Millions of Dollars)

Assets		Liabilities		
Total current assets	$ 600	Total current liabilities	$200	
Net fixed assets	400	Long-term debt (at 12%)	100	
		Total debt		$ 300
		Common stock, par value $1		100
		Additional paid-in capital		200
		Retained earnings		400
Total assets	$1,000	Total claims on assets		$1,000

Carson Electronics Income Statement for Year Ended December 31, 1981 (Millions of Dollars)

Total revenues	$2,000
Net operating income	312
Interest expense	12
Net income before taxes	$ 300
Income taxes (at 40%)	120
Net income to equity	$ 180

a. Estimate Carson Electronics' cost of equity capital by using the security market line. The risk-free rate is 10 percent, the expected return on the market is 15 percent, and the beta based on Carson's present leverage is 1.6.
b. What is the value of Carson's total equity? Its indicated price per share? The value of the firm?
c. On the basis of a cost of debt of 14 percent and the cost of equity that you have calculated, determine the weighted average cost of capital for Carson at the present time. (The company has no short-term interest-bearing debt.)
d. Calculate the new financial structure and coverage relationships for both debt and equity alternatives. (Assume that the same percentage of net operating income is earned on the increase in assets as was earned on the total assets before the financing.)
e. If Carson finances with debt, the cost of debt will be 14 percent, while the cost of equity will reflect the rise in β to 1.65. If the company finances with equity, the cost of debt will be 14 percent, while the cost of equity will reflect a drop in beta to 1.58. Compare the cost of equity under the two methods of financing.
f. Under each of the two methods of financing, what will be the total value of the equity, and what will be the new value per share of common stock?
g. Under the same assumptions as in the preceding questions, calculate the value of the firm under the two methods of financing.
h. Compare the weighted cost of capital under the two methods of financing.
i. Summarize your recommendation about which form of financing Carson should employ for raising the additional $100 million.

21.6 The Muir Company has 1 million shares of common stock outstanding, with a $10 par value, and has no debt in its capital structure. Muir's tax rate is 40 percent and annual earnings before interest and taxes are $2 million. It plans to increase debt, using the proceeds to retire stock over a period of 4 years, according to the schedule below. The interest rate indicated is applicable to the total amount of debt outstanding at the end of each year. Calculate earnings per share, price per share, and the leverage ratio, using both book and market values of equity, for the information given below:

Year	Debt (B) at year end	Interest rate (R_b)	Return on equity (R_s)
0	$ 0	—	12%
1	1,000,000	10%	12
2	3,000,000	10	13
3	5,000,000	11	16
4	6,000,000	14	20

Calculate price per share by dividing EPS by R_s. Next, calculate the number of shares of equity retired by dividing each amount of increase in debt by the share price resulting from the previous level of debt. (The number of equity shares retired is subtracted from the previous number of equity shares to obtain the number of shares of stock remaining for each year.)

APPENDIX 21A

REFUNDING A BOND OR A PREFERRED STOCK ISSUE

Suppose a company sells bonds or preferred stock at a time when interest rates are relatively high. Provided the issue is callable, as many are, the company can sell a new issue of low-yielding securities if and when interest rates drop and use the proceeds to retire the high-rate issue. This is called a *refunding operation*.

The decision to refund a security issue is analyzed in much the same manner as a capital budgeting expenditure. The costs of refunding—the investment outlay—are (1) the call premium paid for the privilege of calling the old issue and (2) the flotation costs incurred in selling the new issue. The annual receipts, in the capital budgeting sense, are the interest payments saved each year; for example, if interest expense on the old issue is $1 million while that on the new issue is $700,000, the $300,000 saving constitutes the annual benefit.

In analyzing the advantages of refunding, the recommended procedure is the net present value method—discounting the future interest savings back to the present and comparing the discounted value with the cash outlays associated with the refunding. In the discounting process, the after-tax cost of the new debt, not the average cost of capital, is used as the discount factor. The reason for this is that there is relatively little risk to the savings; their value is known with relative certainty (which is quite unlike most capital budgeting decisions).[1]

To provide a focus for the analysis, the presentation will make use of a case to exemplify the basic ideas. The Becker Company has a $50-million long-term bond issue outstanding, which has an additional ten years to maturity and bears a coupon interest rate of 12 percent. The interest payments are made semiannually. Financial market conditions have given the firm the opportunity of refinancing the debt with another ten-year bond but at the lower rate of 10 percent. The firm plans to use all debt financing for the proposed bond refunding project. The firm's applicable corporate tax rate is 40 percent. The relevant data on the old issue and

[1] A considerable amount of literature on refunding has appeared in recent years. That literature is summarized and critiqued in J. Fred Weston and Eugene J. Brigham, *Managerial Finance*, 7th. ed. (Hinsdale, Ill.: Dryden Press, 1981), pp. 835–44.

on the new refunding issue are summarized below:

	Old issue	New issue
Face amount	$50,000,000	$51,716,000
Interest rate (coupon rate)	$r_o = 12\%$	$r_1 = 10\%$
Life of bond	25 years	10 years
Maturity date	August 16, 1991	August 16, 1991
Flotation costs[a]	$750,000	$775,740
Net proceeds of sale	$49,250,000	$50,940,260
Date issued	August 16, 1966	August 16, 1981
Redemption date	August 16, 1981	—
Call price	$104	—

[a] Flotation costs on both the old and new issue are 1.5% of gross proceeds.

This is fundamentally a capital budgeting decision, so we shall present our analysis through a capital budgeting worksheet approach. A summary capital budgeting worksheet is presented in Table 21A.1. We shall discuss the reasoning behind the calculation of each item, keying the discussion to the numbered lines in Table 21A.1.

Table 21A.1

Capital Budgeting Worksheet Analysis of Bond Refunding

	Amount before tax	Amount after tax	Timing of event	Present value factor	Present value
Part A. After-Tax Refunding Costs					
1. Call premium	$2,000,000	$1,200,000	0	1.0	$1,200,000
2. Flotation costs on new issue	775,740	775,740	0	1.0	775,740
3. Tax savings on flotation costs of new issue	77,574	31,030	1 – 10	7.3601	(228,384)
4. Tax savings on flotation costs on old issue	300,000	120,000	0	1.0	(120,000)
Lost tax benefits on old flotation costs	30,000	12,000	1 – 10	7.3601	88,321
Present value of after-tax refunding costs					$1,715,677
Part B. Interest Savings					
5. Interest savings on new issue	$1,000,000	$600,000/2	1 – 20	14.8775	$4,463,250

Part A. After-Tax Refunding Costs

What is the investment required to refund the issue? There are four components to the required investment outlay: the call premium on the old issue, flotation costs on the new issue, tax savings on flotation costs on the new issue, and tax savings on flotation costs on the old issue.

Call Premium The call premium is 4 percent of face value as given by the bond indenture on the old issue. Since this is a tax-deductible expense, the actual cost is reduced by the company's tax rate of 40 percent.

$$\text{Before-tax call premium} = \text{Call rate} \times \text{Face amount}$$

$$\$2,000,000 = 0.04 \times \$50,000,000$$

$$\text{After-tax call premium} = \text{Before-tax call premium} \times (1 - \text{Tax rate})$$

$$\$1,200,000 = \$2,000,000 \times (1 - 0.40)$$

Although the Becker Company must expend \$2 million on the call premium, this is a deductible expense. Since the company is in a 40 percent tax bracket, it saved \$800,000 in taxes. The after-tax cost of the call is therefore only \$1,200,000.

Flotation Costs on the New Issue At 1.5 percent of \$51,716,000 we obtain \$775,740. This is the amount subject to tax deductions. The total amount is a current outflow. The tax savings are realized over the next ten years.

Tax Savings on Flotation Costs of New Issue For tax purposes, costs are amortized over the life of the new bond, or ten years. Assuming straight line amortization, the annual tax deduction is given by:

$$\text{Annual tax deduction} = \frac{\text{Flotation costs}}{\text{Life of bond (new issue)}}$$

$$\$77{,}574 = \frac{\$775{,}740}{10}$$

Since Becker Company is in the 40 percent tax bracket, it has a tax savings of \$31,030 a year (\$77,574 × 0.40) for ten years. This is an annuity of \$31,030 for ten years. The present value of the annuity is found by discounting at the after-tax cost of the new debt issue. The after-tax cost of debt is the before-tax interest rate times (one minus the tax rate), that is, 10.0 × 0.60, or 6 percent.

$$\begin{aligned}\text{PV of tax savings} &= \text{Annual after-tax savings} \times \text{PVIFA (6\%, 10 years)}\\ &= \$31{,}030(7.3601)\\ &= \$228{,}384\end{aligned}$$

The after-tax amount of new flotation costs is

New flotation costs	\$775,740
Less: PV of tax savings	228,384
PV of the new flotation costs, net of tax	\$547,356

Tax Savings on Flotation Costs on Old Issue The old issue has an unamortized flotation cost of \$750,000(10/25) = \$300,000. This can be recognized immediately as an expense, thus creating an after-tax savings of 0.4(\$300,000) = \$120,000. The firm will, however, lose a deduction of \$30,000 a year for ten years, or an after-tax benefit of \$12,000 a year. The present value of this lost benefit, discounted at 6 percent, is:

$$\begin{aligned}\text{PV of lost benefit} &= \$12{,}000 \times \text{PVIFA (6\%, 10 years)}\\ &= \$12{,}000 \times 7.3601\\ &= \$88{,}321\end{aligned}$$

The net after-tax effect of old flotation costs is

Tax savings on old flotation costs	\$120,000
Less: PV of lost benefits	88,321
Net after-tax effect of old flotation costs	\$ 31,679

The total of the four items is

1. Call premium	$1,200,000
2. Flotation costs on new issue	775,740
3. Tax savings on flotation cost on new issue	(228,384)
4. Tax savings on flotation costs on old issue	(31,679)
Present value of after-tax refunding costs	$1,715,677

In a capital budgeting sense, the $1,715,677 represents the investment outlay to obtain the interest savings on the new issue. These are covered in Part B of Table 21A.1.

Interest Savings on the New Issue The interest rate on the old issue was 12 percent. On the new issue, the interest rate will be 10 percent. Hence there is a savings of 2 percent on the $50,000,000 issue outstanding. The after-tax interest savings, therefore, are

Interest savings

$$\$50{,}000{,}000(0.02)(1-0.4) = \$600{,}000$$

Present value of interest savings

$$\$600{,}000/2 \times \text{PVIFA }(3\%, 20 \text{ periods}) = \$300{,}000(14.8775) = \$4{,}463{,}250$$

Since semiannual compounding is used, the annual savings and the 6 percent interest factor are divided by 2. The number of periods are multiplied by 2. The result is a total present value of interest savings of $4,463,250.

We can now make a net present value analysis of the refunding decision. The basic capital budgeting relationship is

$$\text{Present value of investment} = \text{Gross present value of benefits} - \text{Present value of costs}$$

For the refunding problem under analysis we have

$$\$2{,}747{,}573 = \$4{,}463{,}250 - \$1{,}715{,}677$$

Since the present value of the interest savings exceeds the after-tax refunding costs by a substantial amount, it will be profitable to refund the old bond issue.

Since the refunding operation is advantageous to the firm, it must be disadvantageous to bondholders; they must give up their 12 percent bonds and reinvest in bonds yielding 10 percent. This is a cost of the call provision to bondholders and explains why, at any given time, bonds with a call provision have lower prices than non-callable bonds. If the call privilege has been correctly priced, on average the exercise of this option by the firm simply compensates the firm for the higher interest rates that it paid because it had the call provision in the indenture of the bonds it sold. The firm paid an interest rate differential whose capitalized value is the value of the option privilege represented by the call provision.

Problems

21A.1 The Longmont Company has a $30 million long-term twenty-year bond issue outstanding which has an additional fifteen years to maturity and bears a coupon interest rate of 11.5 percent. The interest payments are made semiannually.

Financial market conditions have given the firm the opportunity of refinancing the debt with another fifteen-year bond but at a lower rate of 10 percent. The firm plans to use all debt financing for the proposed bond refunding project. The relevant data on the old issue and on the new refunding issue are summarized below:

	Old issue	New issue
Face amount	$30,000,000	$31,301,000
Interest rate	$r_0 = 11.5\%$	$r_1 = 10\%$
Life of bond	20 years	15 years
Maturity date	August 10, 1996	August 10, 1996
Flotation costs[a]	$600,000	—
Net proceeds of sale	$29,400,000	—
Date issued	August 14, 1976	August 10, 1981
Redemption date	August 10, 1981	—
Call price	$105	—

[a] Flotation costs on both the old and new issue are 2.0 percent of gross proceeds.

The firm's applicable corporate tax rate is 40 percent. The after-tax cost of debt is used as the discount factor in the analysis. Based on the data provided, evaluate the planned refunding issue.

21A.2 Ten years ago, the Tarman Company issued $850,000 in 20-year bonds with an 11 percent coupon, payable annually. The Tarman Company's bond rating has improved since that time, and the firm now has the opportunity to refund the debt with a 10-year bond issue at a 10 percent coupon, also payable annually. The refunding project would be financed exclusively by the new debt. Tarman has a 40 percent tax rate.

a. Evaluate the proposed refunding issue based on the data below.

	Old issue	New issue
Face amount	$850,000	$904,000
Interest rate	$r_0 = 11\%$	$r_1 = 10\%$
Life of bond	20 years	10 years
Maturity date	April 1, 1991	April 1, 1991
Flotation costs (3% of gross proceeds)	$25,500	—
Net proceeds of sale	$824,500	—
Date issued	March 15, 1971	April 1, 1981
Redemption date	April 1, 1981	—
Call price	$107	—

b. If the original bond issue had a 30-year maturity (and the new bond issue a 20-year maturity), would the decision in Part a be different?

APPENDIX 21B

FLOATING-RATE NOTES

When inflation forces interest rates to high levels, borrowers are reluctant to commit themselves to long-term debt. Yield curves are typically inverted at such times, with short-term interest rates higher than long-term. One factor is that borrowers would rather pay a premium for short-term funds than lock themselves into high long-term rates for two or three decades.

Two risks are faced by those who defer long-term borrowing in the hope that interest rates will soon fall. First, there is no assurance that rates will not rise even higher and remain at unexpectedly high levels for an indefinite period. If long-term rates rise to 15 percent, for example, debt that looked expensive at 12 percent will seem like a bargain to a borrower who passed it up in the hope of waiting out the rate crisis. Second, the short-term money may simply become unavailable.

The floating-rate note (FRN) was developed to decrease the risks of interest rate volatility at high levels.[1] In an FRN, the coupon rate varies at a given percentage above prevailing risk-free rates, which are determined by short- or long-term Treasury bill yields. The FRN rate is typically either fixed or guaranteed to exceed a stated minimum for an initial period, then adjusted at specified intervals to movements in the Treasury rates.

History of the FRN

FRNs were first issued in the United States by Citicorp in 1974. The rate was set at a minimum of 9.7 percent for ten months, then adjusted semiannually to 1 percent above the current three-month Treasury bill rate. Other firms followed Citicorp's lead. These early issues carried rates based on T-bill yields and most allowed investors to "put" the FRN to the issuer at face value after a given date.[2] Initial rates on the notes were well below the going rate on such short-term borrowing as commercial paper. In July 1974, the rate on three-month prime commercial paper was 11.9 percent, while Treasury bills of comparable maturity were yielding 7.6 percent. Because interest rates were generally expected to decline, borrowers hoped that FRNs would also cost less over the life of the notes than fixed-rate long-term debt.

Rates declined as predicted during the following two years, justifying the use of FRNs rather than fixed-rate debentures. However, many holders exercised their put options when other investments became more profitable, a situation which forced the borrowers to seek new funds after just a few years.

[1] See the excellent survey by Kenneth R. Marks and Warren A. Law, "Hedging against Inflation with Floating-Rate Notes," *Harvard Business Review* 58 (March–April 1980), pp. 106–112.

[2] A *call* gives the holder the option to buy at a specified price. For example, a security may be selling for $50, but the holder may have a call to buy it for $45. By symmetry, a *put* gives the owner the option to sell the security to the issuer at a specified price. For example, a bond may have a market price of $900, but the owner may own a put to sell the bond to the issuing corporation for $1,050.

When borrowers began to issue FRNs again in 1978, the put option was far less common. For that reason, and because high-yield certificates were newly available from savings institutions, the second round of FRNs was less well-suited to individual investors. Institutional investors found FRNs a valuable hedge against declines in the value of their bond portfolios, however. Because FRN's carry rates that vary with the market, their value tends to stay stable near the original price.

Strategies for Volatile Markets

The volatility of interest rates during 1979–80 again made decision making difficult for both borrowers and lenders. During one two-week period in October 1979, long-term Treasury bond yields rose 100 basis points from already high levels. In such a market, borrowers may avoid long-term debt in the expectation that interest rates will soon peak and begin to fall. With inflation continuing to rise, however, and with uncertainty about Federal Reserve moves and a probable recession, no one in late 1979 could be sure that interest rates would not continue their climb toward new record heights. But between March 28, 1980, and May 9, 1980, a period just slightly over one month, the yields on long-term Treasury securities fell 264 basis points.

The trend of innovations during the environment of rising interest rates during 1979 is indicated by the characteristics of individual issues that were offered. A FRN by Continental Illinois Corporation in April could be converted by the holder before May 1986 into fixed-rate 8.5 percent debentures; for the first time, a debt issue was convertible into another debt issue.

Additional new features appeared in the Gulf Oil Corporation issue of $250 million in May 1979. It was the second issue by a nonfinancial corporation, with Standard Oil (Indiana) first in 1974. The issue by Gulf was a thirty-year maturity with a coupon floating 35 basis points above the rate on the thirty-year constant maturity U.S. Treasury bond series published by the Federal Reserve Board. A *drop-lock* feature provided that the security would convert to a fixed rate of $8\frac{3}{8}$ percent if the yield on the Treasury bond series fell to 8 percent or below for three consecutive days.

In the Mellon National Corporation issue sold in June 1979, holders have the option to convert to fixed-rate debentures with a coupon of $8\frac{1}{2}$ percent. Mellon also has the right at its option to convert the securities to fixed-rate debentures whose rate would be the higher of $8\frac{1}{2}$ percent or 65 basis points above the rate on Treasury bonds at that time.

In late 1979, borrowers sought to devise ways to shield themselves against further interest rate increases while taking advantage of possible rate reductions. IBM found one solution in its twenty-five-year debenture offered in October 1979. Terms called for sinking fund payments beginning after the sixth year, with an option to boost the payments by 150 percent and a low call price of $102.50 at the first call date. The effect of these provisions was both to protect IBM against immediate interest rate increases and to allow early repayment if rates should fall within the first six years.

In the same month, Georgia-Pacific offered eight-year floating-rate notes designed to accomplish the same objectives. The interest rate on this more complicated offering was set at 12 percent for the first six months, at the higher of 12 percent or 75 basis points above the Treasury bill rate for the next six months, and then at spreads declining from 75 to 50 points above T-bills, with a minimum rate of 6 percent. Additional provisions allowed Georgia-Pacific to convert the notes to longer-term debentures during a stated period, with rates fixed at the higher of $8\frac{1}{2}$ percent or at least 40 points above long-term Treasury bond yields at the time of conversion. The purchaser also could exercise the right to convert the notes to $8\frac{1}{2}$ percent debentures at any time before maturity and could put the notes to Georgia-Pacific at face value after five years. Thus the Georgia-Pacific floating rate notes were puttable, callable, and convertible.

Characteristics of FRNs

The terms of FRNs are not fixed by law; a variety of features has been employed by issuing companies during the relatively short period FRNs have been available. Typical characteristics are:

1. *Convertibility.* Either to common stock or to fixed-rate notes or to both, at either the issuer's option, the holder's option, or both. The note may state particular dates or time periods when conversion is allowed and may set other conditions, such as a given Treasury bill rate at the time of conversion. The rate on the fixed-rate note may be preset or may depend on Treasury rates at conversion.
2. *Put option.* This feature allows the holder to redeem the note at face value, generally at stated times or under other given conditions.
3. *Minimum rate.* This feature prevents the note rate from floating below a stated minimum.
4. *Drop-lock rate.* If the note rate has dropped to a stated rate, it becomes locked at that rate until maturity.
5. *Sinking fund provision.* Permits the issuer to repay stated portions of the principal amount before maturity.
6. *Declining spread.* The spread between the note rate and the Treasury rate decreases by given amounts at specified times.
7. *Declining minimum rate.* The minimum rate decreases in a similar manner.
8. *Call option.* The issuer has the right to call the note, usually at a moderate premium, and sometimes within a short time after issuance.

Since certain features benefit the issuer while others favor potential buyers, the choice of terms for a particular offering influences the market value of the note. For example, convertibility at the issuer's option gives the issuer control over the cost of debt should Treasury rates remain at high levels; lenders will charge a premium for this right. Conversely, convertibility by the holder allows lenders to lock into higher rates of return if Treasury rates begin to fall. Lenders will accept a lower markup, or spread, over Treasury rates in return for this option. One important consideration for issuers is the complexity of the offering. If the FRN includes too many options, investors may conclude they are unable to evaluate it accurately and reduce the amount they are willing to pay.

Advantages for Issuers

The floating-rate note makes it possible for borrowers to obtain long-term funds when interest rates are generally high without locking into high rates for the entire life of the loan. The cost of debt will automatically fall when Treasury rates drop, and the issuer-convertibility features can be included as a hedge against the possibility that Treasury rates may continue to rise.

FRNs are particularly useful for financial institutions, which often hold a large percentage of assets bearing floating-rate returns. These institutions can issue FRNs to establish a constant spread between their return on investments and cost of debt. Nonfinancial companies whose revenues tend to vary more than their costs with the rate of inflation can also use FRNs to stabilize their cost-revenue spread. Capital-intensive companies, whose depreciation expenses vary little with inflation, are one example.

Advantages for Lenders

FRNs give investors two important guarantees during periods of high and unpredictable inflation:

1. Returns on investment will follow changes in Treasury rates.
2. Because FRN rates vary with the market, the market value of the note will remain relatively stable.

The convertibility and minimum rate features found in most FRNs give investors additional assurance and flexibility in an unstable investment environment.

Costs

When yield curves are inverted, the immediate costs of issuing FRNs based on short-term Treasury rates can be higher than ordinary fixed-rate long-term borrowing. In such periods, however, FRNs have tended to remain less expensive initially than short-term bank loans or commercial paper.

The long-term cost of selling FRNs depends on the movement of interest rates during the life of the notes. Borrowers issue FRNs when they expect current high rates to decline significantly within a short time and then remain at lower levels. If this occurs, the total cost of funding with FRNs falls below the cost for long-term fixed-rate notes. When rates have declined, the issuer can use the issuer-convertibility feature to ensure that total FRN costs remain low despite possible future rate increases.

While most FRNs have been tied to short-term T-bill rates, a few have been based on long-term Treasury bonds. One advantage of long-term-based FRNs is that long-term rates vary less than short-term rates. Borrowers may be willing to pay a premium for greater predictability of costs.

Floating-rate notes provide another illustration of the flexibility of financial markets and instruments. The increased volatility of fluctuations in interest rates has brought forth debt instruments with new types of provisions. Additional new efforts by lenders to achieve protection against inflation include a provision that the principal will also float—that it will be tied to the value of real assets such as oil or silver. Other inflation hedges by lenders include claims on equity such as warrants, convertibility into common stock, or add-on contingent interest fees based on some measure of company performance such as sales or income. Such hedges are added to a fixed interest rate that will be lower than it would otherwise have to be to provide protection against uncertain inflation. Thus the lender trades off some inflation protection against some near-term interest income.

CHAPTER 22

LEASE FINANCING

Prior to the 1950s, leasing was most often associated with real estate—land and buildings—but today it is possible to lease virtually any kind of fixed asset. We estimate that from 15 to 20 percent of all new capital equipment put in use by business each year is leased. In a number of respects, leasing is similar to borrowing. However, while debt or equity financing, as part of a general pool of financing sources, cannot be associated with specific assets, leasing is typically identified with individual assets.

Leasing simultaneously provides for the acquisition of assets and their financing. Its advantage over debt is that the lessor has a better position than a creditor if the user firm experiences financial difficulties. If the lessee does not meet the lease obligations, the lessor has a stronger legal right to take back the asset, because the lessor still legally owns it. A creditor, even a secured creditor, encounters costs and delays in recovering assets that have been directly or indirectly financed. Since the lessor has less risk than other financing sources used in acquiring assets, the riskier the firm seeking financing, the greater the reason for the supplier of financing to formulate a leasing arrangement rather than a loan. The relative tax positions of lessors and users of assets may also affect the lease versus own decision.

Types of Leases

Leases take several different forms, the most important of which are sale and leaseback, service or operating leases, and straight financial leases. These three major types of leases are described below.

Sale and Leaseback

Under a sale and leaseback arrangement, a firm owning land, buildings, or equipment sells the property to a financial institution and simultaneously executes an agreement to lease the property back for a certain period under specific terms.

Note that the seller, or *lessee,* immediately receives the purchase price put up by the buyer, or *lessor.* At the same time, the seller-lessee retains the use of the property. This parallel is carried over to the lease payment schedule. Under a mortgage loan arrangement, the financial institution receives a series of equal payments just sufficient to amortize the loan and to provide the lender with a specified rate of return on investment. Under a sale and leaseback arrangement, the lease payments are set up in the same manner. The payments are sufficient to return the full purchase price to the financial institution in addition to providing it with some return on its investment.

Operating Leases

Operating, or service, leases include both financing and maintenance services. IBM is one of the pioneers of the service lease contract. Computers and office copying machines, together with automobiles and trucks, are the primary types of equipment covered by operating leases. The leases ordinarily call for the lessor to maintain and service the leased equipment, and the costs of this maintenance are either built into the lease payments or contracted for separately.

Another important characteristic of the service lease is that it is frequently not fully amortized. In other words, the payments required under the lease contract are *not* sufficient to recover the full cost of the equipment. Obviously, however, the lease contract is written for considerably less than the expected life of the leased equipment, and the lessor expects to recover the cost either in subsequent renewal payments or on disposal of the equipment.

A final feature of the service lease is that it frequently contains a cancellation clause giving the lessee the right to cancel the lease and return the equipment before the expiration of the basic agreement. This is an important consideration for the lessee, who can return the equipment if technological developments render it obsolete or if it simply is no longer needed.

Financial Leases

A strict financial lease is one that does not provide for maintenance services, is not cancellable, and is fully amortized (that is, the lessor contracts for rental payments equal to the full price of the leased equipment). The typical arrangement involves the following steps:

1. The firm that will use the equipment selects the specific items it requires and negotiates the price and delivery terms with the manufacturer or distributor.
2. Next, the user firm arranges with a bank or leasing company for the latter to buy the equipment from the manufacturer or distributor, simultaneously executing an agreement to lease the equipment from the financial institution. The terms call for full amortization of the financial institution's cost, plus a return on its investment as lessor. The lessee generally has the option to renew the lease at a reduced rental on expiration of the basic lease, but does not have the right to cancel the basic lease without completely paying off the financial institution.

Financial leases are almost the same as sale and leaseback arrangements, the main difference being that the leased equipment is new and the lessor buys it from a manufacturer or a distributor instead of from the user-lessee. A sale and leaseback can thus be thought of as a special type of financial lease.

Internal Revenue Service Requirements for a Lease

The full amount of the annual lease payments is deductible for income tax purposes —provided the Internal Revenue Service agrees that a particular contract is a genuine lease and not simply an installment loan called a lease. This makes it important that the lease contract be written in a form acceptable to the IRS. Following are the major requirements for bona fide lease transactions from the standpoint of the IRS:

1. The term must be less than thirty years; otherwise the lease is regarded as a form of sale.
2. The rent must represent a reasonable return to the lessor—in the range of 7 to 12 percent on the investment.

3. The renewal option must be bona fide, and this requirement can best be met by giving the lessee the first option to meet an equal bona fide outside offer.
4. There must be no repurchase option; if there is, the lessee should merely be given parity with an equal outside offer.

Cost Comparison between Leasing and Owning for Financial Leases

We next consider the cost of owning versus the cost of leasing. The form of leasing to be analyzed will be a pure financial lease which is fully amortized, noncancellable, and without provision for maintenance services.

In concept, the first screening test is whether, from a capital budgeting standpoint, the project passes the investment hurdle rate. The second question is then whether leasing or some other method of financing is the least expensive method of financing the project.

Alternatively, it could be argued that we do not know what the cost of capital (and therefore the investment screening rate) is until we have determined the least expensive method of financing. Having determined this method, we can determine the applicable investment screening hurdle rate for the decision of whether to undertake the project from a capital budgeting standpoint.

To lay a foundation for the leasing versus owning cost comparison, the lessor's point of view will first be considered. The leasing company, or lessor, could be a commercial bank, a subsidiary of a commercial bank, or an independent leasing company. These various types of leasing companies are considered to be providing financial intermediation services of essentially the same kind. Each form of financial intermediary is considered to be providing a product, which represents a form of debt financing to the company that uses the equipment. Since the product (the debt instrument or lease) is an asset of the financial intermediary, its return must equal the intermediary's cost of capital. This is equivalent to the judgment that the financial intermediary's cost of capital, composed of both debt and equity capital, is approximately equal to the rate it charges on the debt (or equivalent) instruments that comprise its assets.

We can then proceed to calculate the required lease-rental charge that must be made by the lessor to obtain a fair rate of return for a lending position. To illustrate the analysis, assume the following data:

I_0 = Cost of an asset = \$20,000

Dep = Annual economic and tax depreciation charge

k_b = Before-tax cost of debt = 8%

T = Lessor's corporate tax rate = 40%

n = Economic life and tax depreciation life of the asset = 5 years

NPV_{LOR} = Net present value of the lease-rental income from the asset to the lessor

With the above facts, the equilibrium lease rental rate in a competitive market of lessors can be calculated. What has been posed is a standard capital budgeting question: What cash flow return from the use of an asset will earn the applicable cost of capital? The investment, or cost of the capital budgeting project, is $-I$. The return is composed of two elements: the cash inflow from the lease rental and the tax shelter from depreciation. The discount factor is the lessor's weighted cost of capital which, as we have indicated, will be equal to the applicable rate on debt instruments of the risk of the cash flows involved. As Stewart C. Myers, David A. Dill, and Alberto J. Bautista have pointed out, the weighted cost of capital of the financial intermediary is:

$$k_L = k_{uL}(1 - \lambda T) \tag{22.1}$$

For the financial intermediary, the lambda is the ratio of total debt to the value of the assets involved. Here we postulate that the all-equity financing rate for the lessor (k_{uL}) is 8.57 percent and lambda is 0.75. For the data assumed in the example, we would therefore have for the cost of capital of the lessor the amount shown in Equation 22.1a.

$$\begin{aligned} k_L &= k_{uL}(1 - \lambda T) \\ &= 8.57\%[1 - 0.75(0.4)] \\ &= 6\% \end{aligned} \tag{22.1a}$$

The after-tax weighted cost of capital to the lessor is 6 percent. We can verify the lessor's cost of capital computation:

$$\begin{aligned} k_L &= k_b(1 - T)(B/V) + k_s(S/V) \\ k_s &= k_u + (k_u - k_b)(B/S)(1 - T) \\ &= 0.0857 + (0.0857 - 0.08)(3)(0.6) \\ &= 0.0857 + 0.0103 \\ &= 0.096 \\ k_L &= 0.08(0.6)(0.75) + (0.096)(0.25) \\ &= 0.036 + 0.024 \\ &= 0.06 \end{aligned}$$

The uniform annual lease-rental required by the lessor can now be determined, therefore, by Equation 22.2:

$$\begin{aligned} \text{NPV}_{LOR} &= -I_0 + \sum_{t=1}^{n} \frac{L_t(1 - T) + T\text{Dep}_t}{(1 + k)^t} \\ &= -I_0 + \text{PVIFA}(6\%, 5 \text{ years})[L_t(1 - T) + T\text{Dep}_t], \end{aligned} \tag{22.2}$$

where:

L_t = Periodic lease payment

Dep_t = Amount of depreciation expense in period t = \$4,000 using straight-line depreciation and no salvage value

We can now solve for the equilibrium lease-rental rate required by the lessor by utilizing the data inputs we have provided, as shown in Equation 22.2a:

$$0 = -\$20{,}000 + (4.2124)[0.6L_t + 0.4(\$4{,}000)]$$
$$L_t = \$5{,}246 \qquad \textbf{(22.2a)}$$

Presented with a lease-rental rate of $5,246, the user firm takes this amount as an input in making a comparison of the cost of leasing with the cost of owning. Since both the lease payments and the foregone depreciation tax shields are risk-free, they can be discounted at the cost of debt. The before-tax cost of debt to the user is 10 percent. With a 40 percent tax rate, the after-tax rate is 6 percent. Since the debt cost is deductible to the user firm, the after-tax cost of debt is utilized. We can therefore substitute the numbers from our example into Equation 22.3.

$$\begin{aligned}\text{NPV(lease)} &= \text{I} - \text{PVIFA}(6\%, 5\text{ years})[L_t(1-T)] - \text{PVIFA}(6\%, 5\text{ years})[T\text{Dep}_t] \\ &= \$20{,}000 - 4.2124(\$5{,}246)(1-0.4) - 4.2124(0.4)(\$4{,}000) \\ &= \$20{,}000 - \$13{,}259 - \$6{,}740 \\ &= \$20{,}000 - \$19{,}999 \cong 0 \qquad \textbf{(22.3)}\end{aligned}$$

This result can also be expressed as the cost of owning versus the cost of leasing. The first and last terms on the right-hand side of the equation represent the cost of owning. The second term is the cost of leasing.

$$\text{Cost of owning} = I - \text{PVIFA}(6\%, 5\text{ years})[T\text{Dep}_t] = \$20{,}000 - \$6{,}740 = \$13{,}260$$

$$\text{Cost of leasing} = \text{PVIFA}(6\%, 5\text{ years})[L_t(1-T)] = \$13{,}259$$

Thus there is equilibrium between the lessor market and the user market. The lessor earns its cost of capital, which determines the lease-rental charge that it must make. At this lease-rental rate, the user is indifferent between owning or leasing the asset.

Note that in determining the lessor's cost of capital we started with the cost of equity that would be applicable to the debt instrument portfolio, or lease portfolio, of the financial intermediary. Given lambda as the appropriate leverage ratio for the lessor, we arrived at the after-tax cost of capital of the lessor. To earn its 6 percent after-tax cost of capital with a 40 percent tax rate, the financial intermediary must charge a 10 percent before-tax rate. This 10 percent rate represents the cost of debt borrowing or the implicit capital cost in the lease financing contract for the lessee's analysis. All the required conditions for an indifference result in the leasing market and the user market are obtained.

We have found that the present value of the cost of leasing and the cost of owning is $13,260. We next make a capital budgeting analysis to determine whether the project that requires the use of the asset should be undertaken. We determine that the net benefits of the project are $6,500 per year. These net cash flows are the same whether the firm owns or leases the asset. Given the indifference result above, the effect of the leverage on the cost of capital will also be the same under leasing or borrowing. In this example, the flows are capitalized at an assumed 12 percent cost of capital of the project. The present value of the benefits of the project will be:

$$\text{GPV} = \text{PVIFA}(12\%, 5\text{ years})[\$6{,}500(0.6)] = 3.6048(\$3{,}900) = \$14{,}059$$

The net present value of the project will be the GPV less the PV of costs, or $14,059 – $13,260, which equals $799. The project has a positive NPV and therefore should be accepted.

Next, we shall consider the use of accelerated depreciation. Appendix C of this book provides in convenient form the present value of depreciation for the sum-of-years'-digits and the double declining balance methods of depreciation over a range of values of the cost of capital. In the present example, the sum-of-years'-digits method of depreciation will be illustrated with the after-tax cost of capital of 6 percent for five years. The depreciation factor of 0.875 can be read directly from the table. Then Equation 22.2 can be solved for the uniform annual lease-rental rate required by the lessor:

$$\begin{aligned} 0 &= -\$20{,}000 + 4.2124(0.6L_t) + 0.4(\$20{,}000)(0.875) \\ 4.2124(0.6)L_t &= \$20{,}000 - \$7{,}000 \\ 2.5274L_t &= \$13{,}000 \\ L_t &= \$5{,}144 \end{aligned}$$

The resulting uniform annual lease-rental charge required by the lessor in order to earn its cost of capital of 6 percent is $5,144. Note that this is lower than the lease-rental of $5,246 required for the lessor to earn the cost of capital when straight-line depreciation was used. The reason is that with accelerated depreciation, the tax shelter comes in larger amounts in the earlier years, when the present value factors are higher. Thus, since the amount of tax shelter is increased, and since under competitive conditions the lease-rental moves to the level at which lessors earn their cost of capital, the lease-rental is reduced.

With accelerated depreciation, the lower required rental rate will be used in computing the cost of leasing:

$$\begin{aligned} \text{Cost of leasing} &= \text{PVIFA}(6\%, 5 \text{ years})[\$5{,}144(0.6)] \\ &= 4.2124(\$3{,}086) \cong \$13{,}000 \end{aligned}$$

The cost of owning should also use accelerated depreciation. It becomes:

$$\begin{aligned} \text{Cost of owning} &= I - [0.4(\$20{,}000)(0.875)] \\ &= \$20{,}000 - \$7{,}000 = \$13{,}000 \end{aligned}$$

The costs of leasing or owning decline from $13,260 to $13,000. The NPV from the project rises from $799 to $1,059. The increased NPV from the project results from the more favorable larger tax shelters provided by the accelerated depreciation. Given competition among the lessors, this results in a lower rental rate and a higher net present value of using the asset, regardless of whether the use is achieved through leasing (renting) or through buying and owning. But again, assuming competitive financial markets, the terms on which leasing versus owning are available to the user firm result in no advantage to one form of acquiring the use of the assets as compared with another. Only when some form of friction in the markets results in more favorable terms to lessees than to user-owners is there an advantage to leasing (and vice versa).

When an asset has an expected salvage value at the end of its useful life, the owner must include the present value of the salvage value in the analysis, whether the owner is a lessor or a user. At the time of the analysis, the future salvage value can only be an estimate. The risk that the actual salvage value may be less than anticipated must be accounted for in the discount factor used. Salvage value risk is associated with the asset and its use, not with the capital structure of the financial intermediary nor with the alternative financing opportunities available to the user firm. Therefore, the appropriate discount factor for both lessor and user is the cost of capital applicable to the risk in the use of the asset.

Using the same data as above (with straight-line depreciation), assume that salvage value is expected to be \$2,000. Recall that the cost of capital of the project was assumed to be 12 percent. The new annual lease rental rate required by the lessor can then be calculated using Equation 22.4:

$$\text{NPV}_{LOR} = 0 = -I_0 + \sum_{t=1}^{n} \frac{L_t(1 - T) + T\text{Dep}_t}{(1 + k)^t} + \frac{Z_n}{(1 + k_p)^n} \tag{22.4}$$

where:

$$Z_N = \text{Expected salvage value}$$

$$k_p = \text{Cost of capital of the project}$$

$$\text{Dep}_t = \text{Annual depreciation charge} = (\$20{,}000 - \$2{,}000)/5 = \$3{,}600$$

Substituting the numbers from our example, we can solve for L_t:

$$0 = -\$20{,}000 + \text{PVIFA}(6\%, 5 \text{ years})[L_t(1 - 0.4) + 0.4(\$3{,}600)] + \text{PVIF}(12\%, 5 \text{ years})(\$2{,}000)$$

$$0 = -\$20{,}000 + (4.2124)(0.6L_t + \$1{,}440) + (.5674)(\$2{,}000)$$

$$L_t = \$5{,}064$$

The lower lease rental charge resulting from the inclusion of salvage value in turn reduces the cost of leasing:

$$\begin{aligned}\text{Cost of leasing} &= \text{PVIFA}(6\%, 5 \text{ years})[0.6(\$5{,}064)] \\ &= 4.2124(\$3{,}038.4) \\ &= \$12{,}799\end{aligned}$$

The cost of owning will also be lower when adjusted for salvage value:

$$\begin{aligned}\text{Cost of owning} &= I - \text{PVIFA}(6\%, 5 \text{ years})(T\text{Dep}_t) \\ &\quad - \text{PVIF}(12\%, 5 \text{ years})Z_n \\ &= \$20{,}000 - \$6{,}066 - \$1{,}135 \\ &= \$12{,}799\end{aligned}$$

Thus the indifference result persists when salvage value is included in the analysis.

Similar reasoning may be applied to other uncertain flows involved in leasing; maintenance costs are an example. An important distinction must be made, however, in the analysis of costs as opposed to inflows. Using the higher project cost of capital as the discount rate instead of the after-tax cost of debt has the effect of reducing the present value of risky costs, when the logic of adjusting for greater risk requires a higher present value. Thus, risky costs must be discounted at a rate below the after-tax cost of debt. Determination of the appropriate lower rate can only be made subjectively on a judgmental basis. For example, with a 6 percent after-tax cost of debt and a 12 percent project cost of capital, a 4 percent discount rate might be applicable to the risk of maintenance expense.

Alternative Computation Procedures in the Leasing Analysis

Thus far we have made the leasing versus owning analysis using compact equations. The same results can be obtained when the flows are tabulated by years. To illustrate, we shall use the data from a previous example. The cost of the asset is $20,000, and the required lease-rental rate is calculated to be $5,246 under straight-line depreciation. The earlier analysis treated leasing and borrowing as substitutes; so under the owning analysis, the $20,000 is assumed to be borrowed at a 10 percent before-tax cost of debt by the user of the asset.

It is assumed that the loan of $20,000 is paid off at a level annual amount that covers annual interest charges plus amortization of the principal. The amount is an annuity that can be determined by the use of the present value of an annuity formula, shown in Equation 22.5:

$$\$20{,}000 = \sum_{t=1}^{n} \frac{a_t}{(1+k_b)^t}$$

$$a_t = \frac{\$20{,}000}{\text{PVIFA}(10\%,\ 5\text{ years})} \tag{22.5}$$

$$a_t = \frac{\$20{,}000}{3.7908} = \$5{,}276$$

Solving Equation 22.5 for the level annual annuity results in $5,276, which represents the principal plus interest payments set forth in Column 3 of Table 22.1. The sum of these five annual payments is shown to be $26,380, which represents repayment of the principal of $20,000 plus the sum of the annual interest payments. The interest payments of each year are determined by multiplying Column 2, the balance of principal owed at the end of the year, by 10 percent, the assumed cost of borrowing. The sum of the annual interest payments does, in fact, equal the total interest of $6,380 obtained by deducting the principal of $20,000 from the total of the five annual payments shown in Column 3.

Table 22.1 **Schedule of Debt Payments**

End of year (1)	Balance of principal owed at end of year (2)	Principal plus interest payments (3)	Annual interest 10% × (2): (4)	Reduction of principal (5)
1	$20,000	$5,276	$2,000	$ 3,276
2	16,724	5,276	1,672	3,604
3	13,120	5,276	1,312	3,964
4	9,156	5,276	916	4,360
5	4,796	5,276	480	4,796
Totals		$26,380	$6,380	$20,000

Table 22.2

Costs of Owning

End of year (1)	Loan payment (2)	Annual interest (3)	Depreciation (4)	Tax shield: [(3) + (4)]0.4 (5)	Cash flows after taxes: (2) – (5) (6)	Present value factor (at 6%) (7)	Present value of costs (8)
1	$ 5,276	$2,000	$ 4,000	$ 2,400	$ 2,876	0.9434	$ 2,713
2	5,276	1,672	4,000	2,269	3,007	0.8900	2,676
3	5,276	1,312	4,000	2,125	3,151	0.8396	2,646
4	5,276	916	4,000	1,966	3,310	0.7921	2,622
5	5,276	480	4,000	1,792	3,484	0.7473	2,603
Totals	$26,380	$6,380	$20,000	$10,552	$15,828		$13,260

A schedule of cash outflows for the borrow-own alternative is then developed to determine the present value of the after-tax cash flows. This is illustrated in Table 22.2.

The analysis of cash outflows begins with a listing of the loan payments, as shown in Column 2. Next, the annual interest payments from Table 22.1 are listed in Column 3. Since straight-line depreciation is assumed, the annual depreciation charges are $4,000 per year, as shown in Column 4. The tax shelter to the owner of the equipment is the sum of the annual interest plus depreciation multiplied by the tax rate. The amounts of the annual tax shield are shown in Column 5. Column 6 is cash flow after taxes, obtained by deducting Column 5 from Column 2.

Since the cost of borrowing is 10 percent, its after-tax cost with a 40 percent tax rate is 6 percent. The present value factors at 6 percent are listed in Column 7. They are multiplied by the after-tax cash flows to obtain Column 8, the present value of the after-tax costs of owning the asset.

The costs of leasing the asset can be obtained in a similar manner, as shown in Table 22.3. The uniform annual lease payments are shown in Column 2. By multiplying 0.6 times the Column 2 figures, the after-tax cost of leasing is obtained and shown in Column 3. The present value factors for 6 percent are listed in Column 4 and multiplied times the figures in Column 3. Column 5 presents the after-tax costs of leasing by year, which total to $13,260.

Table 22.3

Costs of Leasing

End of year (1)	Lease payments (2)	After-tax: 0.6 × (2) (3)	Present value factor (at 6%) (4)	Present value of costs: (3) × (4) (5)
1	$ 5,246	$ 3,147.6	0.9434	$ 2,970
2	5,246	3,147.6	0.8900	2,802
3	5,246	3,147.6	0.8396	2,643
4	5,246	3,147.6	0.7921	2,493
5	5,246	3,147.6	0.7473	2,352
Totals	$26,230	$15,738.0		$13,260

The result is the same as for the costs of owning. Thus in formulating the problem to make the positions of the lessors and users symmetrical, the indifference result between the costs of owning and the costs of leasing is obtained. A number of factors could change this result: differences in costs of capital, differences in applicable tax rates or usability of tax subsidies, differences in patterns of payments required under leasing versus owning, and so on. But in order to measure the effects of factors which cause the costs of leasing and owning to be different, it is helpful to start with an equality relation to understand better what is causing a divergence.

Use of an Internal Rate of Return Analysis

A related approach to analyzing the cost of leasing versus other sources of financing utilizes the internal rate of return. In this approach, the cost of leasing is the internal rate of return or discount rate that equates the present value of leasing payments—net of their tax shields plus the tax shields for depreciation and the investment tax credit that would be obtained if the asset were purchased—with the cost of the asset. In this method the cost of leasing includes not only the after-tax lease payments but the investment tax credit foregone and the depreciation tax deductions that otherwise would have been obtained if the asset had been purchased.

The cost of the asset avoided by leasing is treated as a cash inflow, while the costs of leasing just described are treated as cash outflows. A column of cash flows after taxes is calculated; it begins with a positive figure—the cost of the asset avoided—and then moves to negative figures representing the costs of leasing. A rate of discount that equates the negative cash flows with the positive cash flows in the column (6 percent in our example) is determined.

The discount rate is taken as a measure of the after-tax cost of lease financing. In the procedure, this after-tax cost is then compared with the after-tax cost of debt financing. In our example, the after-tax cost of debt financing is 6 percent, so the 6 percent after-tax cost of leasing is the same.

One of the advantages claimed for the approach is that it avoids the problem of having to determine a discount rate. However, this claim is illusory. The internal rate of return approach to the leasing comparison is fundamentally no different from the after-tax cost of debt method described in the previous section. Hence the internal rate of return analysis is equivalent to the more general framework presented here for analyzing the lease versus purchase decision.

A large number of factors potentially affect one or more of the critical variables in the lease versus purchase analysis. But we think it both theoretically correct and necessary from a practical standpoint to be able to identify what is causing the cost of leasing to be higher or lower than the cost of owning. The following section will consider some additional variables that may have an impact on the lease versus purchase decision.

Additional Influences on the Leasing versus Owning Decision

A number of other factors can influence the user firm's costs of leasing versus owning capital assets. These include: (1) different costs of capital for the lessor versus the user firm, (2) financing costs higher in leasing, (3) differences in maintenance costs, (4) the benefits of residual values to the owner of the assets, (5) the possibility of reducing obsolescence costs by the leasing firms, (6) the possibility of increased credit availability under leasing, (7) more favorable tax treatment, such as more rapid write-off, and (8) possible differences in the ability to utilize tax reduction opportunities. A number of arguments exist with respect to the advantages and disadvantages of leasing, given these factors. Many of the arguments carry with them implicit assumptions; thus their applicability to real world conditions is subject to considerable qualifications.

Different Costs of Capital

If the lessor has a lower cost of capital than the user, the cost of leasing is likely to be lower than the cost of owning and vice versa. However, it is difficult to formulate the conditions under which the cost of capital would be different except for differential tax effects. It is the risk of the project in which the asset is used that determines the applicable cost of capital. Why should the risk be different if the owner is a lessor rather than a user?[1]

Financing Costs Higher in Leasing

A similar view is that leasing always involves higher implicit financing costs. This argument is also of doubtful validity. First, in considering the lessee's credit rating, there may be no difference. Second, it is difficult to separate the money costs of leasing from the other services embodied in a leasing contract. If, because of its specialized operations, the leasing company can perform nonfinancial services (such as maintenance of the equipment) at a lower cost than the lessee or some other institution can perform them, then the effective cost of leasing may be lower than the cost of funds obtained from borrowing or other sources. The efficiencies of performing specialized services may thus enable the leasing company to operate by charging a lower total cost than the lessee would have to pay for the package of money plus services on any other basis.

Differences in Maintenance Costs

Another argument frequently encountered is that leasing may be less expensive because no explicit maintenance costs are involved. But this is because the maintenance costs are included in the lease-rental rate. The key question is whether the maintenance can be performed at a lower cost by the lessor or by an independent firm that specializes in performing maintenance on capital assets of the type involved. Whether the costs will differ if supplied by one type of specialist firm rather than another is a factual matter, depending on the industries and particular firms involved.

Residual Values

The lessor owns the property at the expiration of the lease. The value of the property when the lease expires is called the *residual value.* Superficially, it appears that where residual values are large, owning is less expensive than leasing. However, even this apparently obvious advantage of owning is subject to substantial qualification. On leased equipment, the obsolescence factor may be so great as to drive down residual values. If prospective future residual values appear favorable, competition between leasing companies and other financial sources (as well as competition among leasing companies themselves) will force leasing rates down

[1] Cf. Merton H. Miller and Charles W. Upton, "Leasing, Buying, and the Cost of Capital Services," *Journal of Finance* 31 (June 1976), pp. 762–67.

to the point at which the potentials of residual values are fully recognized in the leasing contract rates. Thus, the existence of residual values is unlikely to result in materially lower relative costs of owning.

However, in decisions about whether to lease or to own land, the obsolescence factor is involved only to the extent of deterioration in areas with changing population or use patterns. In a period of optimistic expectations about land values, there may be a tendency to overestimate their rates of increase. As a consequence, the current purchase of land may involve a price so high that the probable rate of return on owned land will be relatively small. Under this condition, leasing may well represent the more economical way of obtaining the use of land. Conversely, if the probable increase in land values is not fully reflected in current prices, it will be advantageous to own the land.

Thus it is difficult to generalize about whether residual value considerations are likely to make the effective cost of leasing higher or lower than the cost of owning. The results depend on whether the individual firm has opportunities to take advantage of over-optimistic or over-pessimistic evaluations of future value changes by the market as a whole and whether the firm or market is correct on average.

Obsolescence Costs

Neither residual values nor obsolescence rates can basically affect the cost of owning versus leasing. However, it is possible that certain leasing companies are well equipped to handle the obsolescence problem. For example, the Clark Equipment Company is a manufacturer, reconditioner, and specialist in materials handling equipment, with its own sales organization and system of distributors. This may enable Clark to write favorable leases for equipment. If the equipment becomes obsolete to one user, it may be satisfactory for other users with different materials handling requirements, and Clark is well situated to locate the other users. The situation is similar in computer leasing.

This illustration indicates how a leasing company, by combining lending with other specialized services, may reduce the social costs of obsolescence and increase effective residual values. By such operations the total cost of obtaining the use of such equipment is reduced. Possibly other institutions that do not combine financing and specialist functions (such as manufacturing, reconditioning, servicing, and sales) may, in conjunction with financing institutions, perform the overall functions as efficiently and at as low a cost as do integrated leasing companies. However, this is a factual matter depending on the relative efficiency of the competing firms in different lines of business and different kinds of equipment.

Differences in Tax Rates or Tax Subsidies

An advantage to leasing or to buying may occur when the tax rates of lessors and user firms are different. But even here unambiguous predictions are not always possible. The effects of differential taxes depend upon the relationships among earnings from the capital assets and their interactions with differential tax rates and tax subsidies.

But the inability of a user firm to utilize tax benefits such as the investment tax credit or accelerated depreciation may make it advantageous for it to enter a lease arrangement. In this situation, the lessor (a bank or a leasing company) can utilize the credit, and competition with other lessors may result in lower leasing rates.

For example, the investment tax credit (discussed in Chapter 3) can be taken only if the firm's profits and taxes exceed a certain level. If a firm is unprofitable, or if it is expanding so rapidly and generating such large tax credits that it cannot use them all, then it may be profitable for it to enter a lease arrangement. In this situation, the lessor (a bank or leasing company) can take the credit and give the lessee a corresponding reduction in lease charges. In recent years, railroads and airlines have been large users of leasing for this reason, as have industrial companies faced with similar situations. Anaconda, for example, financed most of the cost of a $138 million aluminum plant built in 1973 through a lease arrangement.[2] Anaconda had suffered a $365 million tax loss when Chile expropriated its copper mining properties, and the carry-forward of this loss would hold taxes down for years. Thus the firm could not use the tax credit associated with the new plant. By entering a lease arrangement, the company was able to pass the tax credit on to the lessors, who in turn gave it lower lease payments than would have existed under a loan arrangement. Anaconda's financial staff estimated that financial charges over the life of the plant would be $74 million less under the lease arrangement than under a borrow-and-buy plan.

Incidentally, the Anaconda lease was set up as a leveraged lease.[3] A group of banks and Chrysler Corporation provided about $38 million of equity and were the owner-lessors. They borrowed the balance of the required funds from Prudential, Metropolitan, and Aetna—large life insurance companies. The banks and Chrysler received not only the investment tax credit but also the tax shelter associated with accelerated depreciation on the plant. Such leveraged leases, often with wealthy individuals seeking tax shelters acting as owner-lessors, are an important part of the financial scene today and help explain why leasing has reached a total volume of over $100 billion.

Under the new 1981 tax law, a company can qualify as a "lessor" by purchasing a piece of equipment from the user of that equipment (for as little as 10 percent down with a note for the balance), and then leasing it back to the user for lease payments that are equal to the loan payments the company owes on the balance. Thus, while no money changes hands, the "lessor" company gains the tax advantages of leasing—investment tax credit, depreciation, and interest deductions.

Summary

Leasing has long been used in connection with the acquisition of equipment by railroad companies. In recent years, it has been extended to a wide variety of equipment.

The most important forms of lease financing are: (1) sale and leaseback, in which a firm owning land, buildings, or equipment sells the property and simultaneously executes an agreement to lease it for a certain period under specific terms; (2) service leases or operating leases, which include both financing and maintenance services, are often cancellable, and call for payments under the lease contract that may not fully recover the cost of the equipment; and (3) financial

[2] Peter Vanderwicken, "The Powerful Logic of the Leasing Boom," *Fortune*, November 1973, pp.136–40.

[3] Technically, a *leveraged lease* is one in which the financial intermediary (a bank or other lessor) uses borrowed funds to acquire the assets it leases.

leases, which do not provide for maintenance services, are not cancellable, and do fully amortize the cost of the leased asset during the basic lease contract period.

To understand the possible advantages and disadvantages of lease financing, the cost of leasing an asset must be compared with the cost of owning it. In the absence of major tax advantages and other "market imperfections," there should be no advantage to either leasing or owning an asset. Hence the recommended procedure is to first use a discount factor to obtain the result of no advantage to either leasing or owning. Then a wide range of factors that may influence the indifference result can be introduced: the different costs of capital for the lessor versus the user firm, differences in maintenance costs, the benefits of residual values to the owner, the possibility of reducing obsolescence costs by lessors, the possibility of increased credit availability under leasing, differential tax rates, and possible differences in utilizing tax reduction opportunities. Whether these other factors will actually give an advantage or disadvantage to leasing depends on the facts and circumstances of each transaction analyzed.

Questions

22.1 Discuss this position: The type of equipment best suited for leasing has a long life in relation to the length of the lease; is a removable, standard product that could be used by many different firms; and is easily identifiable. In short, it is the kind of equipment that could be repossessed and sold readily. However, we would be quite happy to write a ten-year lease on paper towels for a firm such as General Motors.

22.2 Leasing is often called a hedge against obsolescence. Under what conditions is this actually true?

22.3 Is leasing in any sense a hedge against inflation for the lessee? For the lessor?

22.4 One alleged advantage of leasing is that it keeps liabilities off the balance sheet, thus making it possible for a firm to obtain more leverage than it otherwise could. This raises the question of whether both the lease obligation and the asset involved should be capitalized and shown on the balance sheet. Discuss the pros and cons of capitalizing leases and related assets.

Problems

22.1 The Shelley Corporation plans to acquire new production machinery which will increase total assets by 25 percent. The firm's leverage ratio (B/S) is 0.80. If Shelley leases the equipment and capitalizes the lease, what will be the equity to total asset ratio (S/TA)?

22.2 a. The Clarkton Company produces industrial machines, which have five-year lives. Clarkton is willing to either sell the machines for $30,000 or to lease them at a rental that, because of competitive factors, yields a return to Clarkton of 6 percent—its cost of capital. What is the company's competitive lease rental rate? (Assume straight-line depreciation, zero salvage value, and $T = 40$ percent.)

b. The Stockton Machine Shop is contemplating the purchase of a machine exactly like those rented by Clarkton. The machine will produce net benefits of $10,000 per year. Stockton can buy the machine for $30,000 or rent it from

Clarkton at the competitive lease rental rate. Stockton's cost of debt is 10 percent, its cost of capital is 12 percent, and $T = 40$ percent. Which alternative is better for Stockton?

c. If Clarkton's cost of capital is 9 percent and competition exists among lessors, solve for the new equilibrium rental rate. Will Stockton's decision be altered?

22.3 The Bubbly Beverage Company needs a new bottling machine which costs $75,000, has an expected life of 5 years, and whose estimated salvage value is $8,000. Bubbly can purchase the machine by borrowing $75,000 repayable in 5 equal, annual installments at 14 percent interest. Alternatively, Bubbly can lease the machine for $25,000 a year. If owned, the cost of maintenance would be $3,000 per year. Assume straight-line depreciation, a 43 percent tax rate, and a 14 percent cost of debt. The cost of capital appropriate to the project's risk is 18 percent.

a. What is the present value of the after-tax cost of leasing for the 5-year period?
b. What are the yearly payments required to amortize the loan? What is the present value of these payments?
c. How are the yearly loan payments divided between interest and amortization of principal? What is the present value of the interest tax shelter?
d. What is the depreciation tax shelter under the borrow-purchase arrangement?
e. What is the present value (after-tax) of the maintenance costs? (Use a 6 percent discount rate for risky costs.)
f. What is the present value of the estimated salvage value?
g. What is the total net after-tax cost of the borrow-purchase alternative?
h. Which method of acquisition involves the lower net outflows?
i. What effects would accelerated depreciation have had on the decision?

22.4 The Nelson Company is faced with the decision of whether it should purchase or lease a new forklift truck. The truck can be leased on an eight-year contract for $5,800 a year, or it can be purchased for $26,000. The lease includes maintenance costs estimated at $200 per year. The salvage value of the truck after eight years is $2,000. The company uses straight-line depreciation. The company can borrow at 15 percent and has a 40 percent marginal tax rate and 12 percent cost of capital.

a. Analyze the lease versus purchase decision. The firm's cost of capital is applicable to the risk of the project. Discount maintenance costs at 7 percent.
b. What do your results imply about the lessor's cost of capital? What is the lessor's cost of capital?

22.5 The Bradley Steel Company seeks to acquire the use of a rolling machine at the lowest possible cost. The choice is either to lease one at $14,890 annually or to purchase one for $54,000. The company's cost of capital is 14 percent, its cost of debt is 10 percent, and its tax rate is 40 percent. The machine has an economic life of six years and no salvage value. The company uses straight-line depreciation. Which is the less costly method of financing?

22.6 The Scott Brothers Department Store is considering a sale and leaseback of its major property, consisting of land and a building, because it is thirty days late on 80 percent of its accounts payable. The recent balance sheet of Scott Brothers is shown below:

Scott Brothers Department Store
Balance Sheet as of December 31, 1981
(thousands of Dollars)

Assets		**Liabilities**	
Cash	$ 288	Accounts payable	$1,440
Receivables	1,440	Bank loans (at 8%)	1,440
Inventories	1,872	Other current liabilities	720
Total current assets	$3,600	Total current debt	$3,600
Land	1,152	Common stock	1,440
Building	720	Retained earnings	720
Fixtures and equipment	288		
Net fixed assets	2,160		
Total assets	$5,760	Total claims	$5,760

Profit before taxes in 1981 is $36,000; after taxes, $20,000. Annual depreciation charges are $57,600 on the building and $72,000 on the fixtures and equipment. The land and building could be sold for a total of $2.8 million. The annual net rental will be $240,000.

a. How much capital gains tax will Scott Brothers pay if the land and building are sold? (Assume all capital gains are taxed at a capital gains tax rate of 20 percent; that is, disregard such items as recapture of depreciation, tax preference treatment, and so on.)

b. Compare the current ratio before and after the sale and leaseback if the after-tax net proceeds are used to "clean up" the bank loans and to reduce accounts payable and other current liabilities.

c. If the lease had been in effect during 1981, what would Scott Brothers' profit for 1981 have been?

d. What are the basic financial problems facing Scott Brothers? Will the sale and leaseback operation solve them?

APPENDIX 22A

ACCOUNTING TREATMENT OF LEASES

Accounting for Leases

In November 1976, the Financial Accounting Standards Board issued its Statement of Financial Accounting Standards No. 13, *Accounting for Leases*. Like other FASB statements, the standards set forth must be followed by business firms if their financial statements are to receive certification by auditors. FASB Statement No. 13 has implications both for the utilization of leases and for their accounting treatment. The elements of FASB Statement No. 13 most relevant for financial analysis of leases are summarized below.

For some types of leases, this FASB statement requires that the obligation be capitalized on the asset side of the balance sheet with a related lease obligation on the liability side. The accounting treatment depends on the type of lease. The classification is more detailed than the two categories of operating and financial leases described above.

Table 22A.1

Types of Leases

From the standpoint of the lessee:

1. Capital leases
2. Operating leases (all leases other than capital leases)

From the standpoint of the lessor:

1. Sales-type leases
2. Direct financing leases
3. Leveraged leases
4. Operating leases (all leases other than the first three)

A lease is classified in Statement No. 13 as a capital lease if it meets one or more of four Paragraph 7 criteria:

1. The lease transfers ownership of the property to the lessee by the end of the lease term.
2. The lease gives the lessee the option to purchase the property at a price sufficiently below the expected fair value of the property that the exercise of the option is highly probable.
3. The lease term is equal to 75 percent or more of the estimated economic life of the property.
4. The present value of the minimum lease payments exceeds 90 percent of the fair value of the property at the inception of the lease. The discount factor to be used in calculating the present value is the implicit rate used by

the lessor or the lessee's incremental borrowing rate, whichever is lower. (Note that the lower discount factor represents a higher present value factor and therefore a higher calculated present value for a given pattern of lease payments. It thus increases the likelihood that the 90 percent test will be met and that the lease will be classified as a capital lease.)

From the standpoint of the lessee, if a lease is not a capital lease, it is classified as an operating lease.

From the standpoint of the lessor, four types of leases are defined: (1) sales-type leases, (2) direct financing leases, (3) leveraged leases, and (4) operating leases representing all leases other than the first three types. Sales-type leases and direct financing leases meet one or more of the four Paragraph 7 criteria and both of the Paragraph 8 criteria, which are:

1. Collectibility of the minimum lease payments is reasonably predictable.
2. No important uncertainties surround the amount of unreimbursable costs yet to be incurred by the lessor under the lease.

Sales-type leases give rise to profit (or loss) to the lessor—the fair value of the leased property at the inception of the lease is greater (or less) than its cost of carrying amount. Sales-type leases normally arise when manufacturers or dealers use leasing in marketing their products. Direct financing leases are leases other than leveraged leases for which the cost-of-carrying amount is equal to the fair value of the leased property at the inception of the lease. Leveraged leases are direct financing leases in which substantial financing is provided by a long-term creditor on a nonrecourse basis with respect to the general credit of the lessor.

For some types of leases, FASB Statement No. 13 requires that the obligation be capitalized on the asset side of the balance sheet with a related lease obligation on the liability side. The accounting treatment depends on the type of lease. The classification is more detailed than the two categories of operating and financial leases described in Chapter 22.

Accounting by Leases

For operating leases, rentals must be charged to expense over the lease term, with disclosures of future rental obligations in total as well as by each of the following five years. For lessees, capital leases are to be capitalized and shown on the balance sheet both as a fixed asset and a noncurrent obligation. Capitalization represents the present value of the minimum lease payments minus that portion of lease payments representing executory costs such as insurance, maintenance, and taxes to be paid by the lessor (including any profit return in such charges). The discount factor is as described in Paragraph 7(4)—the lower of the implicit rates used by the lessor and the incremental borrowing rate of the lessee.

The asset must be amortized in a manner consistent with the lessee's normal depreciation policy for owned assets. During the lease term, each lease payment is to be allocated between a reduction of the obligation and the interest expense to produce a constant rate of interest on the remaining balance of the obligation. Thus, for capital leases, the balance sheet includes the items in Table 22A.1.

Table 22A.2

Capitalization of Leases
Company X Balance Sheet

Assets	December 31, 1980	December 31, 1981	Liabilities	December 31, 1980	December 31, 1981
			Current:		
Leased property under capital leases, less accumulated amortization	XXX	XXX	Obligations under capital leases	XXX	XXX
			Noncurrent:		
			Obligations under capital leases	XXX	XXX

In addition to the balance sheet capitalization of capital leases, substantial additional footnote disclosures are required for both capital and operating leases. These include a description of leasing arrangements, an analysis of leased property under capital leases by major classes of property, a schedule by years of future minimum lease payments (with executory and interest costs broken out for capital leases), and contingent rentals for operating leases.

FASB Statement No. 13 sets forth requirements for capitalizing capital leases and for standardizing disclosures by lessees for both capital leases and operating leases. Lease commitments therefore do not represent "off–balance sheet" financing for capital assets, and standard disclosure requirements make general the footnote reporting of information on operating leases. Hence, the argument that leasing represents a form of financing that lenders may not take into account in their analysis of the financial position of firms seeking financing will be even less valid in the future than it is now.

It is unlikely that sophisticated lenders were ever fooled by off–balance sheet leasing obligations. However, the capitalization of capital leases and the standard disclosure requirements for operating leases will make it easier for general users of financial reports to obtain additional information on firms' leasing obligations. Hence, the requirements of FASB Statement No. 13 are useful. Probably, the extent of use of leasing will remain substantially unaltered, since the particular circumstances that have provided a basis for its use in the past are not likely to be greatly affected by the increased disclosure requirements.

CHAPTER 23

WARRANTS AND CONVERTIBLES

Thus far the discussion of long-term financing has dealt with the nature of common stock, preferred stock, various types of debt, and leasing. It has also explained how offering common stock through the use of rights can facilitate low-cost stock flotations. This chapter will show how the financial manager, through the use of warrants and convertibles, can make the company's securities attractive to an even broader range of investors. Therefore, it is important to understand the characteristics of these two types of securities.

Warrants

A *warrant* is an option to buy a stated number of shares of stock at a specified price. For example, Trans Pacific Airlines has warrants outstanding that give the warrant owners the right to buy one share of TPA stock at a price of $22 for each warrant held. Warrants generally expire on a certain date (TPA's warrants on December 1, 1983), although some have perpetual lives.

Formula Value of a Warrant

Warrants have a calculated, or formula, value and an actual value, or price, that is determined in the marketplace. The formula value is found by use of the following equation:

$$\text{Formula value} = \begin{pmatrix}\text{Market price of} \\ \text{common stock}\end{pmatrix} - \begin{pmatrix}\text{Option} \\ \text{price}\end{pmatrix} \times \begin{pmatrix}\text{Number of shares each} \\ \text{warrant entitles owner} \\ \text{to purchase}\end{pmatrix}$$

For instance, a TPA warrant entitles the owner to purchase one share of common stock at $22 a share. If the market price of the common stock is $64.50, the formula value of the warrant is obtained as follows:

$$(\$64.50 - \$22) \times 1.0 = \$42.50$$

The formula gives a negative value when the stock is selling for less than the option price. For example, if TPA stock is selling for $20, the formula value of the warrants is −$2. Since this makes no sense, the formula value is defined as zero when the stock is selling for less than the option price.

Actual Price of a Warrant

Generally, warrants sell above their formula values. When TPA stock was selling for $64.50, the warrants had a formula value of $42.50 but were selling at a price of $46.87. This represents a premium of $4.37 above the formula value.

A set of TPA stock prices, together with actual and formula warrant values, is given in Table 23.1 and plotted in Figure 23.1. At any stock price below $22, the

Table 23.1

Formula and Actual Values of TPA Warrants at Different Market Prices

	Value of warrant		
Price of stock	Formula price	Actual price	Premium
$ 0.00	$ 0.00	Not available	—[a]
22.00	0.00	$ 9.00	$9.00
23.00	1.00	9.75	8.75
24.00	2.00	10.50	8.50
33.67	11.67	17.37	5.70
52.00	30.00	32.00	2.00
75.00	53.00	54.00	1.00
100.00	78.00	79.00	1.00
150.00	128.00	Not available	—[a]

[a] Cannot be calculated

Figure 23.1

Formula and Actual Values of TPA Warrants at Different Common Stock Prices

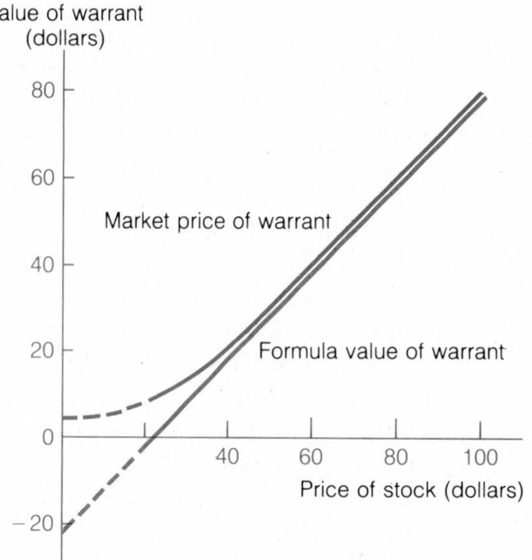

formula value of the warrant is zero; beyond $22, each $1 increase in the price of the stock brings with it a $1 increase in the formula value of the warrant. The actual market price of the warrant lies above the formula value at each price of the common stock. Notice, however, that the premium of market price over formula value declines as the price of the common stock increases. For example, when the common sold for $22 and the warrants had a zero formula value, their actual price, and the premium, was $9. As the price of the stock rises, the formula value of the warrants matches the increase dollar for dollar, but for a while the *market price* of the warrant climbs less rapidly and the premium declines. The premium is $9 when the stock sells for $22 a share, but it declines to $1 by the time the stock price has risen to $75 a share.

In the past, warrants have generally been used by small, rapidly growing firms as sweeteners when selling either debt or preferred stocks. Since such firms are frequently regarded by investors as highly risky, their bonds can be sold only if they are willing to accept extremely high rates of interest and very restrictive indenture provisions, to offer warrants, or to make the bonds convertible. In April 1970, however, AT & T raised $1.57 billion by selling bonds with warrants. This was the largest financing of any type ever undertaken by a business firm, and it marked the first use of warrants by a large, strong corporation.[1] It can safely be anticipated that other large firms will follow AT & T's lead.[2]

Giving warrants along with bonds enables investors to share in the company's growth if it does, in fact, grow and prosper; therefore, investors are willing to accept a lower bond interest rate and less restrictive indenture provisions. A bond with warrants has some characteristics of debt and some of equity. It is a hybrid security that provides the financial manager with an opportunity to expand the mix of securities, appealing to a broader group of investors and possibly lowering the firm's cost of capital.

Warrants can also bring in additional funds. If the company grows and prospers, causing the price of the stock to rise, the warrants are exercised and bring in needed funds. If the company is unsuccessful and cannot profitably employ additional money, the price of its stock will probably not rise sufficiently to induce exercise of the options.

Convertibles

Convertible securities are bonds or preferred stocks that are exchangeable into common stock at the option of the holder and under specified terms and conditions. The most important of the special features relates to how many shares of stock a convertible holder receives by converting. This feature is defined as the *conversion ratio,* and it gives the number of shares of common stock the holder of the convertible receives on surrender of the security. Related to the conversion ratio is the *conversion price*—the effective price paid for the common stock when conversion occurs. In effect, a convertible is similar to a bond with an attached warrant.

The relationship between the conversion ratio and the conversion price is illustrated by Adams Electric Company convertible debentures, issued at their $1,000 par value in 1975. At any time prior to maturity on July 1, 1995, a debenture holder can turn in the bond and receive in its place 20 shares of common stock; therefore, the conversion ratio is 20 shares for 1 bond. The bond has a par value of $1,000, so the holder is giving up this amount on conversion. Dividing the $1,000

[1] It is interesting to note that before the AT & T issue, the New York Stock Exchange had a policy against listing warrants. The NYSE's stated policy was that warrants could not be listed because they were "speculative" instruments rather than "investment" securities. When AT & T issued warrants, however, the exchange changed its policy and agreed to list warrants that met certain specifications.

[2] In fact, the number of warrant issues listed on the New York Stock Exchange stood at eleven at the end of 1979. See *1980 Fact Book* (New York: New York Stock Exchange, 1980), p. 33.

by the 20 shares received gives a conversion price of $50 a share:

$$\text{Conversion price} = \frac{\text{Par value of bond}}{\text{Shares received}} = \frac{\$1{,}000}{20} = \$50$$

The conversion price and conversion ratio are established at the time the convertible bond is sold. Generally, these values are fixed for the life of the bond, although sometimes a stepped-up conversion price is used. Litton Industries' convertible debentures, for example, were convertible into 12.5 shares until 1972, into 11.76 shares from 1972 until 1982, and into 11.11 shares from 1982 until they mature in 1987. The conversion price thus started at $80, rose to $85, then to $90. Litton's convertibles, like most, are callable at the option of the company.

Another factor that may cause a change in the conversion price and ratio is a standard feature of almost all convertibles—the clause protecting the convertible against dilution from stock splits, stock dividends, and the sale of common stock at low prices (as in a rights offering). The typical provision states that no common stock can be sold at a price below the conversion price and that the conversion price must be lowered (and the conversion ratio raised) by the percentage amount of any stock dividend or split. For example, if Adams Electric had a two-for-one split, the conversion ratio would automatically be adjusted to forty and the conversion price lowered to $25. If this protection were not contained in the contract, a company could completely thwart conversion by the use of stock splits and dividends. Warrants are similarly protected against dilution.

Like warrant option prices, the conversion price is characteristically set from 15 to 20 percent above the prevailing market price of the common stock at the time the convertible issue is sold. Exactly how the conversion price is established can best be understood after examining some of the reasons that firms use convertibles.

Advantages of Convertibles

Convertibles offer advantages to corporations as well as to individual investors. The most important of these advantages are discussed below.

A Sweetener when Selling Debt A company can sell debt with lower interest rates and less restrictive covenants by giving investors a chance to share in potential capital gains. Convertibles, like bonds with warrants, offer this possibility.

The Sale of Common Stock at Higher than Prevailing Prices Many companies actually want to sell common stock, not debt, but feel that the price of the stock is temporarily depressed. Management may know, for example, that earnings are depressed because of a strike but that they will snap back during the next year and pull the price of the stock up with them. To sell stock now would require giving up more shares to raise a given amount of money than management thinks is necessary. However, setting the conversion price 15 to 20 percent above the present market price of the stock will require giving up 15 to 20 percent fewer shares when the bonds are converted than would be required if stock was sold directly.

Notice, however, that management is counting on the stock's price rising above the conversion price to make the stock actually attractive in conversion. If the stock price does not rise and conversion does not occur, then the company is saddled with debt.

How can the company be sure that conversion will occur when the price of the stock rises above the conversion price? Characteristically, convertibles have a provision that gives the issuing firm the opportunity of calling the convertible at a specified price. Suppose the conversion price is $50, the conversion ratio is twenty, the market price of the common stock has risen to $60, and the call price on the convertible bond is $1,050. If the company calls the bond (by giving the usual notification of twenty days), bondholders can either convert into common stock with a market value of $1,200 or allow the company to redeem the bond for $1,050. Naturally, bondholders prefer $1,200 to $1,050, so conversion occurs. The call provision therefore gives the company a means of forcing conversion, provided that the market price of the stock is greater than the conversion price.

Disadvantages of Convertibles

From the standpoint of the issuer, convertibles have one possible disadvantage. Although the convertible bond does give the issuer the opportunity to sell common stock at a price 15 to 20 percent higher than it could otherwise be sold, if the stock greatly increases in price, the issuer may find that it would have been better off if it had waited and simply sold the common stock. Further, if the company truly wants to raise equity capital, and if the price of the stock declines after the bond is issued, then it is stuck with debt.

Analysis of Convertible Debentures

A *convertible security* is a hybrid, having some of the characteristics of common stocks and some of bonds or preferred stocks.[3] Investors expect to earn an interest yield as well as a capital gains yield. Moreover, the corporation recognizes that it incurs an interest cost and a potential dilution of equity when it sells convertibles. This section will develop a theoretical model to combine these two cost components and then will discuss the conditions under which convertibles should be used. Since an investor who purchases a convertible bond expects to receive interest plus capital gains, the total expected return is the sum of these two parts. The expected interest return is dependent primarily on the bond's coupon interest rate and the price paid for the bond, while the expected capital gains yield is dependent basically on (1) the relationship between the conversion price and the stock price at the time of issue and (2) the expected growth rate in the price of the stock. These two yield components will now be discussed.

Think of the graph in Figure 23.2 as showing the *ex ante*, or expected, relationships, starting now at Year $t = 0$ and projecting events into the future. (The symbols used in Figure 23.2 and the remainder of this chapter are listed in Table 23.2.)

The analysis of convertibles will be organized around four major aspects:

1. Conversion value
2. Straight bond value
3. Expected market value
4. Expected rate of return

[3] For further analysis of the issues treated in this section, see E. F. Brigham, "An Analysis of Convertible Debentures: Theory and Some Empirical Evidence," *Journal of Finance* 21 (March 1966), pp. 35–54.

Figure 23.2 **Model of a Convertible Bond**

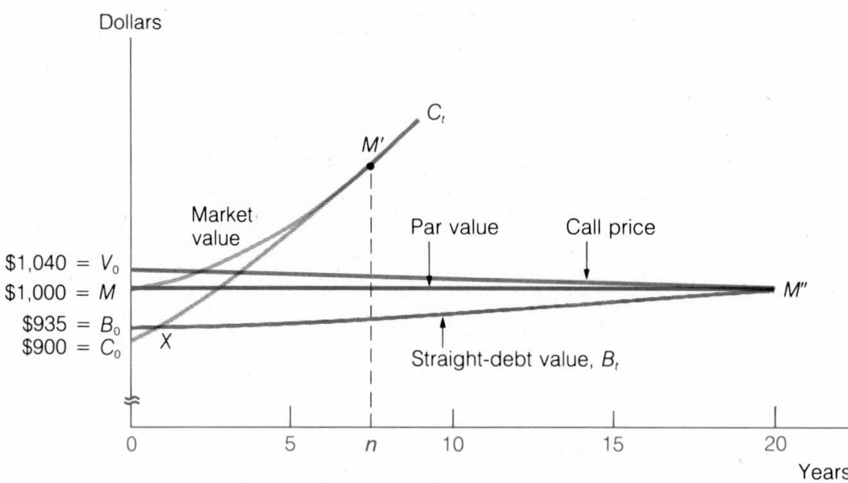

Table 23.2 **Summary of Symbols Used in Chapter 23 with Illustrative Values**

B_t = Straight debt value of a bond at time t
c = Dollars of interest paid each year = \$40
C_n = Conversion value = $p_0(1 + g)^n \#$
C_t = Conversion value at time t
g = Expected rate of growth of the stock's price = 4 percent
j = Time subscript from 1 to t^*
k_b = Market rate of interest on equivalent risk, nonconvertible debt issues = 4.5 percent
k_c = Internal rate of return, or expected yield, on the convertible
M = Price paid for the bond
M' = Market value of the convertible bond when its conversion value becomes equal to its market value
M'' = Maturity value
n = Number of years bond is expected to be held
\# = Conversion ratio, or number of shares received on conversion = 20
p_c = Conversion price = $M/\#$
p_0 = Current market price of the stock = \$45
t^* = Number of years remaining until maturity
T = Marginal corporate income tax rate
V_0 = Original call price of an option
X = Point at which the bond's conversion value rises above its straight debt value

Conversion Value

The hypothetical bond is a new issue that can be purchased for M = \$1,000; this initial price is also the par (and maturity) value. The bond is callable at the option of the corporation, with the call price originating at V_0 = \$1,040, somewhat above par, and declining linearly over the twenty-year term to maturity to M'' = \$1,000 at maturity.

At any point in time, the bond can be converted to stock; the value of the stock received on conversion is defined as the *conversion value* of the bond. The original conversion value (C_0) is established by multiplying the market price of the stock at the time of issue by the number of shares into which the bond can be converted (the conversion ratio). The stock price is expected to grow at a certain rate (g), causing the conversion value to rise at this same rate. This establishes the curve C_0C_t, which shows the expected conversion value at each point in time. All of this is expressed by Equation 23.1:

$$C_t = p_0(1 + g)^t \# \quad \textbf{(23.1)}$$

The initial conversion value of the bond, when $t = 0$, is simply $45 × 20, or $900. One year later it is expected to be $45(1.04)(20) = $936; after two years it is expected to rise to $973.44; and so on. Thus the expected conversion value curve is a function of the expected growth in the price of the stock.

Straight Debt Value

In addition to its value in conversion, the bond also has a straight debt value, B_t, defined as the price at which the bond would sell in any year t if it did not have the conversion option. At each point in time, B_t is determined by Equation 23.2:

$$B_t = \sum_{j=1}^{t^*} \frac{c}{(1 + k_b)^j} + \frac{M''}{(1 + k_b)^{t^*}} \quad \textbf{(23.2)}$$

Equation 23.2 is used to calculate the bond value, B_t, from each point t to the maturity date. To illustrate the use of the equation, B_t will be calculated at $t = 0$ and $t = 8$. First, note that $t = 0$ is the point in time when the bond is issued, while $t = 8$ means the bond is 8 years old and has 12 years remaining to maturity. So, for B_0, the summation term refers to an annuity of $40 per year for $t^* = 20 - 0 = 20$ years; while for B_8, the summation represents an annuity of $t^* = 20 - 8 = 12$ years:

$$\begin{aligned} B_0 &= \sum_{j=1}^{20} \frac{\$40}{(1.045)^j} + \frac{\$1{,}000}{(1.045)^{20}} \\ &= \$40(13.0079) + \$1{,}000(0.4146) \\ &= \$520.32 + \$414.60 = \$934.92 \\ B_8 &= \sum_{j=1}^{12} \frac{\$40}{(1.045)^j} + \frac{\$1{,}000}{(1.045)^{12}} \\ &= \$40(9.1186) + \$1{,}000(0.5897) \\ &= \$364.74 + \$589.70 = \$954.44 \end{aligned}$$

Thus B_t rises over time, and $B_{20} = \$1{,}000$.[4]

[4] In Equation 23.2, bond values are calculated at the beginning of each period, just after the last interest payment has been made. Most bonds (convertible and nonconvertible alike) are actually traded on the basis of a basic price, determined as in Equation 23.2, plus interest accrued since the last payment date. Thus, a person who bought this bond a few days before the end of Year 20 would pay approximately $1,000 plus $40 accrued interest, and the invoice from the broker would indicate these two components. Also, technically semiannual compounding should be used. However, we have used annual compounding here to focus on issues related to convertibility.

Expected Market Value

The convertible will never sell below its value as a straight bond. If it did, investors interested in buying debt instruments would see it as a bargain, start buying the bonds, and drive their value up to B_t. Similarly, the convertible can never sell below its conversion value. If it did, investors interested in the stock would buy the bonds, convert, and obtain shares at a bargain price; but they would drive the price of the convertible up to C_t in the process. Thus the lines C_0C_t and B_0M'' in Figure 23.2 serve as floors below which the market price of the bond cannot fall. The higher of these two floors dominates, with the discontinuous curve B_0XC_t forming the *effective market value floor.*

Ordinarily, convertibles sell at premiums over their bond and conversion value floors. For the illustrated bond, the expected market value is represented in Figure 23.2 by the curve MM', which lies above the effective floor (B_0XC_t) over most of the range but converges with B_0XC_t in Year *n*. The rationale behind this price action is developed in the following two sections.

Why the Market Value Exceeds the B_0XC_t Floor The spread between MM' and B_0XC_t, which represents the premium marginal investors are willing to pay for the conversion option, can be explained in several ways.[5] First, since the convertible bond can be converted into common stock if the company prospers and the stock price rises, it usually commands a premium over its value as straight debt (that is, the right of conversion has a positive value). Second, the convertible bond usually commands a premium over its conversion value because investors are able to reduce their risk exposure by holding convertibles. To illustrate: suppose someone buys the hypothetical bond for $1,000. At the time, it is convertible into 20 shares of stock with a market price of $45, giving a conversion value of $900. If the stock market turns sharply down and the stock price falls to $22.50 per share, the stock investor will suffer a 50 percent loss in value. The price of a convertible bond, however, will fall from $1,000 to the bond value floor (B_0M'' in Figure 23.2), which is at least $935. Hence, holding the convertible entails less risk than holding common stock, and this too causes convertibles to sell at a premium above their conversion value.[6]

Why the Market Value Approaches the Conversion Value The MM' curve in Figure 23.2 rises less rapidly than the C_0C_t curve, indicating that the market value approaches the conversion value as the conversion value increases. This is caused by three separate factors. First, and probably most important, the bondholders realize that the issue is callable; if it is in fact called, they have the option of either surrendering for redemption or converting. In the former case, they

[5] Marginal investors, often called "the market," are defined as those just willing to hold the bond at its going price. These investors are, in fact, the ones who actually determine the level of the bond's price.
[6] Two institutional factors may also contribute to convertible premiums. First, margin requirements are typically lower for convertibles than for stock; thus investors can speculate with less money in the convertible market than in the stock market. Second, certain institutional investors, such as life insurance companies, have more freedom to invest in convertibles than in stocks; so if these institutions want to invest in stocks to a greater extent than their regulators permit, they can expand stock holdings "through the back door" with convertibles.

receive the call price; in the latter, they receive stock with a value designated by C_t. If the market price of the bond is above both these values, the holder is in danger of a potential loss in wealth in the event of a call; this fact prevents wide spreads between MM' and B_0XC_t whenever the market value exceeds the call price.

The second factor driving MM' toward C_0C_t is related to the loss protection characteristic of convertibles. Barring changes in the interest rate on the firm's straight debt securities, the potential loss on a convertible is equal to the spread between MM' and B_0M''. Since this spread increases at high conversion values, the loss potential also increases, causing the premium attributable to the loss protection to diminish.

The third factor causing the gap between MM' and C_0C_t to close has to do with the relationship between the yield on a convertible and that on the common stock for which it can be exchanged. The yield on most common stocks consists of two components: a dividend yield and an expected capital gain yield. (The next section will show that convertibles also have two yield components, one from interest payments and one from capital gains.) After some point, the expected capital gain is the same for both instruments, but the current yield on the bond declines in comparison with that on the common stock because dividends on stocks whose prices are rising are typically also rising, while interest payments are fixed. This causes the gap between MM' and C_0C_t to close and would eventually lead to a negative premium except for the fact that voluntary conversion occurs first.

Expected Rate of Return on a Convertible

The purchaser of a convertible generally expects the price of the stock to rise, the conversion value to rise with the stock, and the conversion to take place after some period of time, say n years. Thus the purchaser expects first to receive a series of interest payments of \$$c$ per year for n years and then to have stock with a value equal to $C_n = p_0(1 + g)^n \#$. The expected rate of return on the convertible, k_c, is found by solving for it in Equation 23.3:

$$M = \sum_{t=1}^{n} \frac{c}{(1 + k_c)^t} + \frac{C_n}{(1 + k_c)^n} \tag{23.3}$$

The equation is purely definitional; it simply states that if an investor pays M dollars for a convertible bond, holds it for n years, and receives a series of interest payments plus a terminal value, then the return on the investment will be equal to k_c.[7]

The *ex ante* yield on a convertible (k_c) is probabilistic—dependent on a set of variables subject to probability distributions and hence itself a random variable. It is possible, however, to define each of the determinants of k_c in terms of its mean expected value; $E(g)$, for example, is the expected value of the growth rate in the stock's price over n years. For simplicity, $E(g)$ and other random variables are

[7] Three simplifications are made in this analysis. First, taxes are ignored. Second, the problem of reinvestment rates is handled by assuming that all reinvestment is made at the internal rate of return. Third, it is assumed that bondholders do not hold stock after conversion; they cash out, as do institutional investors precluded from holding common stock.

shortened to g, C_n, and so on. With the variables defined in this manner, it is possible to work sequentially to determine n from Equation 23.5, developed shortly, then to use n and C_n in Equation 23.3 to find a value of k_c (the return on a convertible bond) that makes Equation 23.3 hold. The determinants of C_n are (1) the corporation's policy in regard to calling the bond to force conversion; or (2) the investor's decision to hold the bond until it is called, to sell it, or to convert voluntarily. Corporate call policy and investor cash-out policy are therefore examined in the next two sections.

Corporate Call Policy Corporations issuing convertible bonds generally have policies regarding just how far up the C_0C_t curve they will allow a bond to go before calling to force conversion. These policies range from calling as soon as the company is "sure" conversion will take place (this generally means a premium of about 20 percent over the par value) to never calling at all. If the policy is never to issue a call, however, the firm generally relies on the dividend-interest differential to cause voluntary conversion.

It is apparent that call policy has a direct influence on the expected number of years a convertible will remain outstanding and therefore on the value of C_n. Naturally, expectations about call policy influence the expected rate of return on a convertible bond. Because of this, the issuing firm must take investor expectations into account. A policy in the apparent short-run interest of the corporation may penalize the investor with such a low effective actual yield that the firm will have difficulties when it subsequently attempts to market additional securities.[8] (This point is illustrated in one of the problems at the end of the chapter.)

Investor Cash-Out Policy Investor cash-out policy is similar to corporate call policy in that it sets a limit on how far up the C_0C_t curve investors are willing to ride. The decision is influenced by the interest-dividend relationship, by investors' aversion to risk (recall that risk due to a stock price decline increases as one moves up the C_0C_t curve), and by investors' willingness to hold securities providing low current yields. In general, it appears that investors are willing to ride higher up C_0C_t, given the dividend-interest relationship, than the firm is willing to let them ride; hence, corporate call policy generally supersedes investor cash-out policy. As already discussed, the path of the conversion value curve is traced out by Equation 23.1:

$$C_t = p_0(1 + g)^t\# \qquad \textbf{(23.1)}$$

Recognizing that $\# = M/p_c$, where p_c is defined as the initial conversion price of the shares, Equation 23.1 can be rewritten as:

$$C_t = \frac{p_0}{p_c}(1 + g)^t M \qquad \textbf{(23.4)}$$

[8] Some firms seek to encourage *voluntary conversion* rather than call to force conversion. One way of doing this is to include a provision for periodic stepped-up conversion prices; for example, Litton Industries' conversion price goes up every three years (so the number of shares received upon conversion goes down), and this stimulates voluntary conversion at the step-up date provided the conversion value of the bond is above the straight debt value. In addition, voluntary conversion occurs when the dividend yield on stock received on conversion exceeds the interest yield on the convertibles.

Setting Equation 23.4 equal to the C_n defined by corporate policy (in this case, $1,200 if a 20 percent premium is used) results in:

$$C_n = \frac{p_0}{p_c}(1+g)^n M = \$1{,}200 \quad \textbf{(23.5)}$$

$$\$1{,}200 = \frac{\$45}{\$50}(1.04)^n \$1{,}000 = \$900(1.04)^n$$

$$\frac{\$1{,}200}{\$900} = 1.333 = (1.04)^n$$

The 1.333 is the CVIF for the compound sum of $1 growing at 4 percent for n years. In the 4 percent column of Table A.1 at the end of the book, the factor 1.333 lies between the seventh and eighth years, so $n \approx 7\frac{1}{2}$ years.

This value of n (rounded to eight years for simplicity), together with the other known data, can now be substituted into Equation 23.3:

$$M = \sum_{t=1}^{n} \frac{c}{(1+k_c)^t} + \frac{C_n}{(1+k_c)^n}$$

$$\$1{,}000 = \sum_{t=1}^{8} \frac{\$40}{(1+k_c)^t} + \frac{\$1{,}200}{(1+k_c)^8}$$

$$= \$40(\text{PVIFA}) + \$1{,}200(\text{PVIF})$$

Using the interest factors for 6 percent:

$$\text{PV} = \$40(6.2098) + \$1{,}200(0.6274)$$

$$= \$248 + \$753 = \$1{,}001 \approx \$1{,}000$$

Therefore, k_c is 6 percent, so someone purchasing this convertible for $1,000 can expect to obtain a return of 6 percent on the investment.

The relationship among the coupon, purchase price, call policy and investor cash-out policy determines the return on an investment in a convertible security. This represents the cost of convertible debt. The required return or cost of convertible debt is composed of two parts. One is the interest return based on the coupon on the convertible debt. This is typically lower than the return on straight debt. The second component of return is based on the expected rise in the price of the common stock into which a conversion may be made. This component of return carries risk associated with a security junior to straight debt. Hence, the required return on convertibles would on average be higher than the cost of straight debt.

Decisions on the Use of Warrants and Convertibles

The Winchester Company, an electronic circuit and component manufacturer with assets of $12 million, illustrates a situation in which convertibles are useful. Winchester's profits were depressed as a result of its heavy expenditures on research and development for a new product. This situation had held down the growth rate of earnings and dividends; the price earnings ratio was only 18 times, as compared with an industry average of 22. At the then current $2 earnings per share and P/E of 18, the stock was selling for $36 a share. The Winchester family owned 70 percent of the 300,000 shares outstanding, or 210,000 shares. It wanted to retain majority control but could not buy more stock.

The heavy R & D expenditures had resulted in the development of a new type of printed circuit that management believed would be highly profitable. To build and equip new production facilities, $5 million was needed; and profits would not start to flow into the company for some eighteen months after construction on the new plant was started. Winchester's debt amounted to $5.4 million, or 45 percent of assets—well above the 25 percent industry average. Debt indenture provisions restricted the company from selling additional debt unless the new debt was subordinate to that outstanding.

Investment bankers informed J. H. Winchester, Jr., the financial vice president, that subordinated debentures could not be sold unless they were convertible or had warrants attached. Convertibles or bonds with warrants could be sold with a 5 percent coupon interest rate if the conversion price or warrant option price was set at 15 percent above the market price of $36—that is, at $41.40 a share. Alternatively, the investment bankers were willing to buy convertibles or bonds with warrants at a $5\frac{1}{2}$ percent interest rate and a 20 percent conversion premium, or a conversion (or exercise) price of $43.20. If the company wanted to sell common stock directly, it could net $33 a share.

Which of the alternatives should Winchester have chosen? If common stock were to be used, the company would have to sell 151,515 shares ($5 million divided by $33). Combined with the 90,000 shares held outside the family, this would amount to 241,515 shares versus the Winchester holdings of 210,000; thus the family would lose majority control if common stock were to be sold.

If the 5 percent convertibles or bonds with warrants were to be used and the bonds converted or the warrants exercised, 120,773 new shares would have been added. Combined with the old 90,000, the outside interest would then be 210,773, so again the Winchester family would lose majority control. However, if the $5\frac{1}{2}$ percent convertibles or bonds with warrants were to be used, then, after conversion or exercise, only 115,741 new shares would be created. In this case the family would have 210,000 shares versus 205,741 for outsiders; absolute control would be maintained.

In addition to assuring control, using the convertibles or warrants would also benefit earnings per share in the long run. The total number of shares would be less because fewer new shares would have to be issued to get the $5 million; thus earnings per share would be higher. Before conversion or exercise, however, the firm would have a considerable amount of debt outstanding. Adding $5 million would raise the total debt to $10.4 million against new total assets of $17 million, so the debt ratio would be over 61 percent versus the 25 percent industry average. This could have been dangerous. If delays were encountered in bringing the new plant into production, if demand did not meet expectations, if the company experienced a strike, or if the economy went into a recession, the company would be extremely vulnerable because of the high debt ratio.

Under these circumstances, Winchester decided to sell the $5\frac{1}{2}$ percent convertible debentures. Two years later, earnings climbed to $3 a share, the P/E ratio went to 20, and the price of the stock rose to $60. The bonds were called, but conversion of course occurred. After conversion, debt amounted to approximately $5.5 million against total assets of $17.5 million (some earnings had been retained), so the debt ratio was down to a more reasonable 31 percent.

Convertibles were chosen rather than bonds with warrants for the following reason. If a firm has a high debt ratio and its near-term prospects are favorable, it can anticipate a rise in the price of its stock and thus be able to call the bonds and force conversion. Warrants, on the other hand, have a stated life; and even if the price of the firm's stock rises, the warrants may not be exercised until near their expiration date. If, subsequent to the favorable period (during which convertibles can be called), the firm encounters less favorable developments and the price of its stock falls, the warrants may lose their value and may never be exercised. The heavy debt burden will then become aggravated. Therefore, the use of convertibles gives the firm greater control over the timing of future capital structure changes. This factor is of particular importance to the firm if its debt ratio is already high in relation to the risks of its line of business.

Reporting Earnings if Convertibles or Warrants Are Outstanding

Firms with convertibles or warrants outstanding are required to report earnings per share (EPS) in two ways: (1) *primary EPS*, which in essence is earnings available to common stock divided by the number of shares actually outstanding, and (2) *fully diluted EPS*, which shows what EPS would be if all warrants had been exercised or convertibles converted prior to the reporting date. For firms with large amounts of option securities outstanding, there can be a substantial difference between the two EPS figures. The purpose of the provision is, of course, to give investors more information on the firm's profit position.

Summary

Both warrants and convertibles are forms of options used in financing business firms. Their use is encouraged by an economic environment combining prospects of both boom or inflation and depression or deflation. The senior position of the securities protects against recessions, and the option feature offers the opportunity for participation in rising stock prices.

Both the convertibility privilege and warrants are used as sweeteners. The option privileges they grant can make it possible for small companies to sell debt or preferred stock that otherwise cannot be sold. For large companies, the sweeteners result in lower costs of the securities sold. In addition, the options provide for the future sale of the common stock at prices higher than can be obtained at present.

We focused on three central quantitative relationships conveyed by the first three equations developed in the chapter:

The conversion value

$$C_t = p_0(1 + g)^t \# \quad \mathbf{(23.1)}$$

The straight debt value

$$B_t = \sum_{j=1}^{t^*} \frac{c}{(1+k_b)^j} + \frac{M''}{(1+k_b)^{t^*}} \tag{23.2}$$

The expected return on a convertible

$$M = \sum_{t=1}^{n} \frac{c}{(1+k_c)^t} + \frac{C_n}{(1+k_c)^n} \tag{23.3}$$

In using Equation 23.3, the values of all terms are known except for k_c, which is obtained as the solution to the equation.

The conversion of bonds by their holders does not ordinarily bring additional funds to the company. However, the exercise of warrants does provide such funds. The conversion of securities results in reduced debt ratios, and the exercise of warrants strengthens the equity position but leaves the debt or preferred stock on the balance sheet. In comparing convertibles to senior securities carrying warrants, a firm with a high debt ratio should choose convertibles, while a firm with a moderate or low debt ratio should probably employ warrants.

Questions

23.1 Why do warrants typically sell at prices greater than their formula values?

23.2 Why do convertibles typically sell at prices greater than their formula values (the higher of the conversion value or straight debt value)? Would you expect the percentage premium on a convertible bond to be more or less than that on a warrant? (The percentage premium is defined as the market price minus the formula value, divided by the market price.)

23.3 What effect does the trend in stock prices (subsequent to issue) have on a firm's ability to raise funds through convertibles? Through warrants?

23.4 If a firm expects to have additional financial requirements in the future, would you recommend that it use convertibles or bonds with warrants? Why?

23.5 Evaluate the following statement: Issuing convertible securities represents a means by which a firm can sell common stock at a price above the existing market.

23.6 Why do corporations often sell convertibles on a rights basis?

23.7 Why might an investor prefer a bond with a warrant attached, over a convertible bond?

Problems

23.1 A convertible bond has a face value of $1,000 and a 10 percent coupon rate. It is convertible into stock of $50; that is, each bond can be exchanged for twenty shares. The current price of the stock is $43 per share.

a. If the price per share grows at 6 percent per year for five years, what will the approximate conversion value be at the end of five years?

b. If dividends on the stock are presently $2 per share, and if these also grow at 6 percent per year, will bondholders convert after five years, or will they tend to hold onto their bonds? Explain.

c. If the bonds are callable at a 10 percent premium, about how much would you lose per bond if the bonds were called before you converted? (Assume the same conversion value as in Part a above, at the end of five years.)

23.2 Warrants attached to a bond entitle the bondholder to purchase one share of stock at $10 per share. Compute the approximate value of a warrant if:

a. The market price of the stock is $9 per share
b. The market price of the stock is $12 per share
c. The market price of the stock is $15 per share
d. Each warrant entitles you to purchase two shares at $10, and the current price of the stock is $15 per share

23.3 The Schuller Chemical Company's net income for 1980 was $2,450,000. Schuller's capital stock consists of 500,000 shares of common stock, and 175,000 warrants, each good for buying two shares of common stock at $25. The warrants are protected against dilution; that is, the exercise price must be adjusted downward in the event of a stock dividend, or if Schuller sells common stock at less than the $25 exercise price. On June 1, 1981, Schuller issued rights to buy 1 new share of common stock for $15 for every 4 shares held. The market price of Schuller stock on June 1 was $45 per share.

a. Compute primary and fully diluted EPS as of December 31, 1980.
b. What is the theoretical value of the rights before the stock sells ex-rights?
c. What is the adjusted exercise price of the warrants after the rights offering? (Hint: Adjust the exercise price of the warrant so that the formula value of the warrant based on the ex-rights stock price is the same as the formula value before the rights offering.)
d. Net income for 1981 is $2,800,000. All of the rights and none of the warrants have been exercised. Compute primary and fully diluted EPS for 1981.

23.4 The Ironhill Manufacturing Company was planning to finance an expansion in the summer of 1981. The principal executives of the company were agreed that an industrial company such as theirs should finance growth by means of common stock rather than debt. However, they felt the price of the company's common stock did not reflect its true worth, so they were desirous of selling a convertible security. They considered a convertible debenture but feared the burden of fixed interest charges if the common stock did not rise in price to make conversion attractive. They decided on an issue of convertible preferred stock.

The common stock was selling at $48 a share. Management projected earnings for 1982 at $3.60 a share and expected a future growth rate of 12 percent a year. It was agreed by the investment bankers and management that the common stock would sell at 13.3 times earnings, the current price/earnings ratio.

a. What conversion price should be set by the issuer?
b. Should the preferred stock include a call price provision? Why?

23.5 The Durham Forge has the following balance sheet:

Balance Sheet 1

Current assets	$125,000	Current debt (free)	$ 50,000
Net fixed assets	125,000	Common stock, par value $2	50,000
		Retained earnings	150,000
Total assets	$250,000	Total claims	$250,000

Durham plans to sell $150,000 of debentures in order to finance its expected sales growth. It is trying to decide whether to sell convertible debentures or debentures with warrants. With spontaneous financing and retained earnings, next year's balance sheet is projected below:

Balance Sheet 2

Current assets	$250,000	Current debt	$100,000
Net fixed assets	250,000	Debentures	150,000
		Common stock, par value $2	50,000
		Retained earnings	200,000
Total assets	$500,000	Total claims	$500,000

The convertible debentures will pay 7 percent interest and will be convertible into 40 shares of common stock for each $1,000 debenture. The debentures with warrants will carry an 8 percent coupon and entitle each holder of a $1,000 debenture to buy 25 shares of common stock at $50.

a. Assume that convertible debentures are sold and that all are later converted. Show the new balance sheet, disregarding any changes in retained earnings.

Balance Sheet 3

		Current debt	______
		Debentures	______
		Common stock, par value $2	______
		Paid-in capital	______
		Retained earnings	______
Total assets	______	Total claims	______

b. Assume that instead of convertibles, debentures with warrants were issued. Assume further that the warrants were all exercised. Show the new balance sheet figures:

Balance Sheet 4

		Current debt	______
		Debentures	______
		Common stock, par value $2	______
		Paid-in capital	______
		Retained earnings	______
Total assets	______	Total claims	______

c. Durham's earnings before interest and taxes are 15 percent of total assets, its P/E ratio is 16 and its corporate tax rate is 40 percent. Prepare income statements corresponding to balance sheets 3 and 4. What is the effect of each alternative on Durham's EPS and market price per share?

d. Should Durham choose convertible debentures or debentures with warrants?

23.6 On July 2, 1981, it was announced that the Dana Corporation was issuing $150 million face amount of debt at $500 for each $1,000 face amount of securities. The debentures carry a $5\frac{7}{8}$ percent coupon, maturing in 2006. They are convertible until December 15, 1993, at $75.64 face amount of debentures for each common share. The common closed on July 2, 1981, at $32.

a. How many shares of common stock would be received upon conversion?
b. What is the conversion price based on the $500 issuing price of the bonds?
c. What premium percentage does this represent over the $32 common stock price?
d. What is the yield to maturity of the bonds based on the data given? (Assume semiannual compounding.)
e. Assume that the common stock of Dana increases in price by 10 percent per year and that the bonds sell at the higher of 12 percent above their conversion value or at their "intermediate face value" which is the $500 issue price increased by 4 percent per year. Assume that for a number of reasons, a purchaser of the bonds sells the bonds at the end of 10 years. Based on the higher of the two prices, what return has the investor earned?

23.7 The Printomat Company has grown rapidly during the past five years. Recently its commercial bank has urged the company to consider increasing permanent financing. Its bank loan under a line of credit has risen to $175,000, carrying 15 percent interest. Printomat has been thirty to sixty days late in paying trade creditors.

Discussions with an investment banker have resulted in the suggestion to raise $350,000 at this time. Investment bankers have assured the company that the following alternatives will be feasible (ignoring flotation costs):

1. Sell common stock at $7.
2. Sell convertible bonds at a 7 percent coupon, convertible into common stock at $8.
3. Sell debentures at a 7 percent coupon, each $1,000 bond carrying 125 warrants to buy common stock at $8.

Additional information is given in the company's balance sheet and income statement below:

Printomat Company Balance Sheet

		Current liabilities	$315,000
		Common stock, par $1	90,000
		Retained earnings	45,000
Total assets	$450,000	Total liabilities and capital	$450,000

Printomat Company Income Statement

Sales	$900,000
All costs except interest	810,000
Gross profit	$ 90,000
Interest	26,250
Profit before taxes	$ 63,750
Taxes (at 40%)	25,500
Profit after taxes	$ 38,250
Shares	90,000
Earnings per share	$0.43
Price/earnings ratio	17 times
Market price of stock	$7.31

Mary Anderson, the president, owns 70 percent of Printomat's common stock and wishes to maintain control of the company; 90,000 shares are outstanding.

a. Show the new balance sheet under each alternative. For alternatives 2 and 3, show the balance sheet after conversion of the debentures or exercise of warrants. Assume that half the funds raised will be used to pay off the bank loan and half to increase total assets.
b. Show Anderson's control position under each alternative, assuming that she does not purchase additional shares.
c. What is the effect on earnings per share of each alternative if it is assumed that profits before interest and taxes will be 20 percent of total assets?
d. What will be the debt ratio under each alternative?
e. Which of the three alternatives would you recommend to Anderson? Explain.

23.8 Vaught Engineering plans to sell a 6 percent coupon, $1,000 par value, twenty-year convertible bond issue. The bond is callable at $1,050 in the first year, and the call price declines by $2.50 each year thereafter. The bond may be converted into 18 shares of stock with a current market price for $46 per share. The stock price is expected to grow at a rate of 7 percent per year. Non-convertible bonds of the same risk as Vaught's would yield 9 percent. In the past, Vaught's policy has been to call convertible securities when the conversion value exceeds the call price by 20 percent.

a. Determine the straight-debt value (B_t) at $t = 0$, $t = 6$, and $t = 10$. Use these 3 points and the maturity value (M'') to graph the straight debt value of the convertible.
b. Graph the conversion value (C_t) on the same graph for $t = 0$, $t = 6$, $t = 10$, and $t = 20$.
c. What is the minimum the convertible can sell for at $t = 0$? At $t = 6$? At $t = 10$? Assume the stock value increases as predicted.
d. Show the call price of the debt on the same graph at $t = 0$, $t = 5$, $t = 6$, and $t = 10$.
e. In what year is the debt expected to be called?
f. On the graph, locate the maturity conversion value M', that is, C_t at the point where the expected call policy forces conversion. Draw a curve between the issue price M and M' with curvature similar to the C_t curve.
g. What would debt holders do if the bond was called at $t = 0$? At $t = 5$? At $t = 6$?
h. What return on investment is earned by bondholders who purchased the convertibles at par value on the date they were issued if the bonds are called in four years?

23.9 Olympic Lumber Company is planning to raise $10 million by selling convertible debentures. It recently sold an issue of non-convertible debentures yielding 10 percent. Investment bankers have informed the treasurer that she can sell convertibles at a lower interest yield; they have offered her these two choices:

A. $p_c = \$55.55$ (# = 18)
$c = \$70$ (7% coupon yield)
$M = \$1,000$
25-year maturity

B. $p_c = \$58.82$ ($\# = 17$)
   $c = \$80$ (8% coupon yield)
   $M = \$1{,}000$
   25-year maturity

In each case, the bonds are not callable for two years; but thereafter they are callable at $1,000. Investors do not expect the bonds to be called unless $C_t = \$1{,}354$; but they do expect the bonds to be called if $C_t = \$1{,}354$.

Olympic's current stock price (p_o) is $50, and its growth is expected to continue at an annual rate of 6 percent. Olympic's current dividend is $4.50 per share, so investors appear to have an expected (and required) rate of return of 15 percent ($k = d/p_o + g = \$4.50/\$50 + 6\%$) on investments as risky as the company's common stock. Olympic's tax rate is 40 percent.

a. Determine the expected yield on Bond A and on Bond B.
b. Do the terms offered by the investment bankers seem consistent? Which bond would an investor prefer? Which would Olympic's treasurer prefer?
c. Suppose the company decided on Bond A but wanted to step up the conversion price from $55.55 to $58.82 after ten years. Should this stepped-up conversion price affect the expected yield and the other terms on the bonds?
d. Suppose, contrary to investors' expectations, Olympic called the bonds after two years. What would the *ex post* (after-the-fact) effective yield be on Bond A? Would this early call affect the company's credibility in the financial markets?
e. Sketch out a rough graph similar to Figure 23.2 for Olympic. Use the graph to illustrate what would happen to the wealth position of an investor who bought Olympic bonds the day before the announcement of the unexpected two-year call.
f. Suppose the expected yield on the convertible had been less than that on straight debt (actually, it was higher). Would this appear logical? Explain.

APPENDIX 23A

OPTION PRICING MODELS (OPM)

Introduction to Options

Options are contracts that give their holder the right to buy (or sell) an asset at a predetermined price, called the *striking* or *exercise price*, for a given period of time. For example, on December 6, 1976, a call option on Dow Chemical common stock gave its holder the right to buy one share of common stock at an exercise price of $45 until July 1977. The price of a share of Dow was $$39\frac{1}{2}$ and the call option sold for $1.75. This would be referred to as an *out-of-the-money option*—the exercise price was more than the current price of the common stock. An *in-the-money option* has an exercise price that is less than the current price of the common stock. An option to buy the Dow common stock at $35 when the common was selling at $$39\frac{1}{2}$ would be an in-the-money option; it would sell for ($$39\frac{1}{2}$ – $35) = $$4\frac{1}{2}$ plus a premium of about $1.75, or at about $6.25.

In recent years option pricing models (OPM) have been derived which enable us to treat the variables discussed in Chapter 23 and in this appendix with numerical solutions.[1] These models are applicable to a wide range of option-type contracts, including the warrants and convertibles discussed in Chapter 23.

The considerable increase in interest in options and option pricing has been associated with the development of new options markets and important new theoretical developments. In April 1973, organized trading in call options began on the Chicago Board Options Exchange (CBOE), followed by call option trading on the American Stock Exchange (AMEX options); the path-breaking paper by Fischer Black and Myron Scholes appeared at about the same time. In addition to deriving the general equilibrium option pricing equation as well as conducting empirical tests, Black and Scholes suggested other implications of option pricing that have significance for many other important aspects of business finance.

Black and Scholes observed that option pricing principles can be used to value other complex contingent claim assets, such as the equity of a levered firm. From this viewpoint, the shareholders of a firm have a call that gives them the right to buy back the firm from the bondholders by paying the face value of the bonds at maturity or exercising other alternatives for buying the bonds. A number of important applications of the option pricing model were then made. As observed by Clifford Smith in his comprehensive review article, "the model is also applied by Merton (1974) to analyze the effects of risk on the value of corporate debt; by Galai

[1] F. Black and M. Scholes, "The Pricing of Options and Corporate Liabilities," *Journal of Political Economy* 81 (May–June 1973), pp. 637–54; Black and Scholes, "The Valuation of Option Contracts and a Test of Market Efficiency," *Journal of Finance* 27 (May 1972), pp. 339–417; and R. C. Merton, "Theory of Rational Option Pricing," *Bell Journal of Economics and Management Science* 4 (Spring 1973), pp. 141–83.

and Masulis (1976) to examine the effect of mergers, acquisitions, scale expansions, and spin-offs on the relative values of the debt and equity claims of the firm; by Ingersoll (1976) to value the shares of dual purpose funds; and by Black (1976) to value commodity options, forward contracts, and future contracts."[2]

Because of the large number of additional areas on which the option pricing models provide new insights, it is useful to develop an understanding of the basic ideas involved. First, some of the fundamental characteristics of the use of options will be developed. Second, some of the basic relationships will be developed in an intuitive way as a background for the presentation and application of the Black and Scholes option pricing model.

Basic Price Relations

An intuitive approach to option pricing is to consider the terminal call price under certainty.[3] Let C^* be the terminal call price, S^* the terminal stock price, and X_0 the exercise price of the option. The following relationship will obtain:

$$C^* = S^* - X_0$$

This is similar to the simple warrant formula. The call price will be equal to the difference between the stock price and the exercise price, or zero if the exercise price is greater than the stock price. Thus if the terminal stock price just before the expiration of a call is \$60 and the exercise price of the option is \$50, the terminal call price, C^*, will be \$10. In an equilibrium world of certainty, the return to all assets is equal to some rate, r. Hence, with continuous compounding, the terminal values of the stock price and option price may be written:

$$S_0^* = S_0 e^{rt^*} \text{ and } C_0^* = C_0 e^{rt^*}$$

Substituting, we have

$$C_0 e^{rt^*} = e^{rt^*} S_0 - X_0$$
$$C_0 = e^{-rt^*}[e^{rt^*} S_0 - X_0]$$
$$C_0 = e^{-rt^*} e^{rt^*} S_0 - e^{-rt^*} X_0$$
$$C_0 = S_0 - e^{-rt^*} X_0$$

Thus the value of a call is equal to the price of the stock less the exercise price discounted at r over the time of its remaining maturity period. This expression differs from the Black-Scholes pricing equation only in their multiplication of each of the terms on the right-hand side of the equation, S_0 and X_0, by probability factors. These probability terms reflect the uncertainty about the terminal prices of the stock. With this background, we can now turn to the Black-Scholes option pricing model.

Calculations of Options Values

In the Black-Scholes model, the derivation is based on the creation of a perfect hedge by simultaneously being long (short) in the underlying security and holding an opposite, short (long) position on a number of options. The return on a com-

[2] Clifford W. Smith, Jr., "Option Pricing: A Review," *Journal of Financial Economics* 3 (January–March 1976), p. 5.

[3] Based on the presentation in Smith, "Option Pricing."

pletely hedged position will then be equal to the risk-free return on the investment in order to eliminate arbitrage opportunities. A call option that can be exercised only on some future maturity date can then be evaluated by the following expressions:[4]

$$C_0 = S_0 N\text{ (dist. 1)} - X_0 e^{-R_F t^*} N\text{ (dist. 2)} \tag{23A.1}$$

$$\text{dist. } 1 = \frac{ln(S_0/X_0) + [R_F + (\sigma^2/2)]t^*}{\sigma\sqrt{t^*}} \tag{23A.2}$$

$$\text{dist. } 2 = \text{dist. } 1 - \sigma\sqrt{t^*} \tag{23A.3}$$

where:

C_0 = Option price or value of the option

S_0 = Current value of the underlying asset

X_0 = Exercise or striking price of the option

$N(\cdot)$ = Standardized normal cumulative probability density function

R_F = Riskless interest rate

σ^2 = Instantaneous rate of variance of percentage returns

t^* = Time to maturity or duration of the option[5]

The application of these expressions requires the use of cumulative probability distributions, that is, the area under the normal probability curve, found in Appendix D at the end of the book. Some specific numerical examples will illustrate the application of equations 23A.1 through 23A.3.

Suppose we are valuing a warrant to purchase a share of common stock. The following facts could be directly observed or estimated from market data:

$$S_0 = \$10$$
$$X_0 = \$10$$
$$t^* = 4 \text{ years}$$
$$R_F = 6\%$$
$$\sigma^2 = 9\%$$

The value of S could be read from the financial quotation page of a current newspaper. The exercise price of a warrant and its maturity, X_0 and t^*, respectively, are shown on the face of the warrant certificate. The risk-free rate can be estimated from the rates on short-term U.S. Treasury bills. The rate of variance can be estimated by taking the daily prices of the stock for one year, from which a variance of

[4] This is called a *European Option.* It is not unnatural to use a formula for the value of a European call option that can be exercised only at the maturity date of the option. R. C. Merton, in a purely probabilistic formulation for nondividend paying stocks, demonstrated that it is always advantageous to delay exercising a call option until the latest possible date: its maturity.

[5] Equations 23A.1 through 23A.3 can also be combined into one equation:

$$C_0 = S_0 \cdot N\left[\frac{ln(S_0/X_0) + (R_F + \sigma^2/2)t^*}{\sigma\sqrt{t^*}}\right] - e^{-R_F t^*} X_0 N\left[\frac{ln(S_0/X_0) + (R_F - \sigma^2/2)t^*}{\sigma\sqrt{t^*}}\right]$$

prices could be calculated.[6] We can now proceed to make the calculations as shown in Equations 23A.1a, 23A.2a, and 23A.3a.

$$C_0 = 10N\text{ (dist. 1)} - 10e^{-0.06(4)}N\text{ (dist. 2)} \tag{23A.1a}$$

$$\text{dist. } 1 = \frac{\ln(10/10) + [0.06 + (0.09/2)]4}{0.3(2)} \tag{23A.2a}$$

$$= \frac{(0.105)4}{0.6} = 0.7$$

$$\text{dist. } 2 = 0.7 - 0.3(2) = 0.1 \tag{23A.3a}$$

$$C_0 = 10(0.758) - 10(0.787)(0.5398)$$

$$= 7.58 - 4.25$$

$$= \$3.33$$

First, we calculate the value of the cumulative distribution function as shown in Equation 23A.2a. It should be noted that the logarithm is the natural logarithm. The *ln* of 10/10 or 1, the first term in the numerator, is zero. The value of dist. 1 is found to be 0.7. We use Appendix D at the end of this book to find the value of 0.7 in the *z* column. We find a value of 0.2580. This represents the shaded area in Figure 23A.1.

Since the formula calls for the cumulative distribution, we add the total area under the left-hand tail of the distribution, which has a value of 0.5000 exactly. Thus the value of dist. 1 equals 0.758, which is used in Equation 23A.1a. Because dist. 2 is related to dist. 1 by a simple relationship, we place 0.7 in 23A.2a to obtain a dist. 2 value of 0.1. In Appendix D at the end of the text, we find a value of 0.0398, to which we add 0.5 to obtain 0.5398 to use in Equation 23A.1a.

The evaluation of the $e^{-.06(4)}$ term involves continuous compounding. In Appendix A to Chapter 4 we described how Appendix Table B of natural logarithms at the end of this book could be used to perform continuous compounding. Looking in Appendix B for 0.24 and interpolating, we obtain 1.27125 for the future sum. We take the reciprocal to obtain the present value factor of 0.786627 or 0.787 used in Equation 23A.1a.[7] Performing the remaining calculations, we obtain $3.33 for the option price.

Next let us assume that the current price of the stock is $20 rather than $10. We now utilize Equations 23A.2b, 23A.3b, and 23A.1b.

$$\text{dist. } 1 = \frac{\ln(20/10) + 0.42}{0.6} = \frac{0.693 + 0.42}{0.6} = 1.86. \tag{23A.2b}$$

$$\text{dist. } 2 = 1.86 - 0.6 = 1.26. \tag{23A.3b}$$

$$C_0 = 20N\text{ (dist. 1)} - 10e^{-0.06(4)}N\text{ (dist. 2)}$$

$$= 20(0.9686) - 10(0.787)(0.8962)$$

$$= \$12.32 \tag{23A.1b}$$

[6] The model presented here assumes no dividend payments, so that dividends would be ignored in calculating the variance of the percentage value changes. This is precisely correct for non-cash-dividend paying stocks but only approximately correct for others.

[7] Many hand calculators are programmed for these logarithmic functions. We could also obtain an approximate result by using Table A.2 for the present value factors with annual compounding.

Figure 23A.1 **Graph of an Appendix D Value**

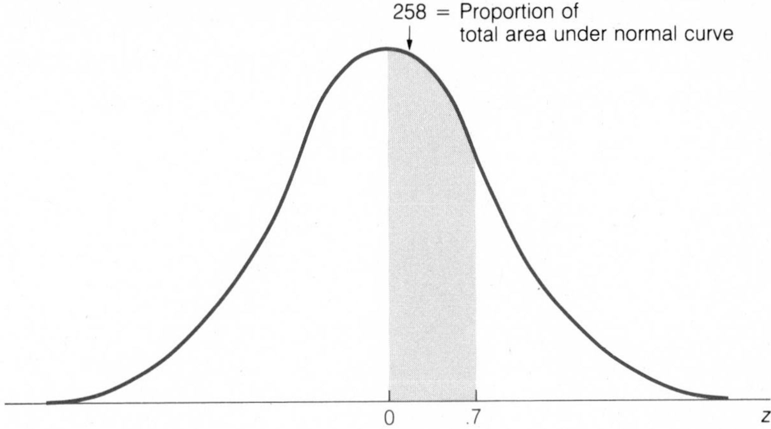

Proceeding as described before, we now obtain $12.32 as the value of the option. Thus we are enabled to derive the relationship for the predicted market value of the option as depicted in Figure 23.1. We will utilize another set of data to derive the values shown in Table 23A.1 to develop the lines shown in Figure 23A.2 for the

Table 23A.1 **Relations between the Values of an Option for a Range of Values of Stock Price and Option Maturity**[a]

t^* (1)	S_0 (2)	Change (percent) (3)	N (dist. 1) (4)	N (dist. 2) (5)	C_0 (6)	Change (percent) (7)	Ratio—percent change in option price to percent change in stock price (8)
4	2		0.0000[b]	0.0000[b]	$ 0.00[b]		
4	10		0.3246	0.1457	0.95		
4	20	100	0.7580	0.5398	6.66	601	6.0
4	30	50	0.9156	0.7811	15.17	128	2.6
4	40	33	0.9683	0.8953	24.64	62	1.9
4	60	50	0.9943	0.9733	44.34	80	1.6
9	10		0.6103	0.2676	$ 2.98		
9	20	100	0.8531	0.5596	10.54	254	2.5
9	30	50	0.9332	0.7257	19.53	85	1.7
9	40	33	0.9656	0.8212	29.05	49	1.5
9	60	50	0.9884	0.9147	48.64	67	1.3

[a] For $X_0 = \$20$, $R_F = 0.06$, and $\sigma^2 = 0.09$

[b] These values approach zero.

Figure 23A.2

The Relation between Option Value and Stock Price for a Given Exercise Price of the Option

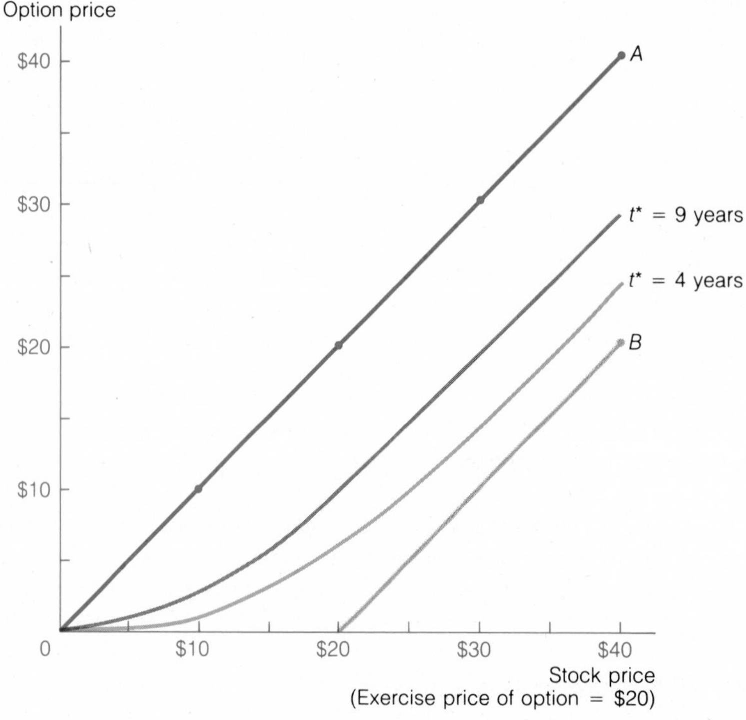

indicated market price of a warrant as a function of the following key variables:

S_0 = Price of the stock; varies from $2 to $60

t^* = Duration of the warrant; 4 or 9 years

X_0 = Exercise price of $20

Factors Influencing Options Values

A number of relationships can be observed from the patterns in Table 23A.1 and Figure 23A.2. The higher the price of the stock, the greater the value of the option for fixed values of the other variables. The longer the maturity of the option, the higher its value. Line A of the figure represents the maximum value of the option, since it cannot be worth more than the stock. Line B represents the minimum value of the option, corresponding to the formula value of the warrant given in Figure 23.1. Its value cannot be negative and will be no less than the formula value of an option given in Chapter 23.

The longer the maturity of the option, the closer it moves toward Line A, its maximum value. Conversely, the shorter the maturity of a warrant, the closer it moves toward its minimum value, Line B. In Figure 23.1, the market price of the TPA warrants is shown to be close to the formula value of a warrant that corresponds to Line B of Figure 23A.2. Hence it is likely that the remaining maturity of the TPA warrants is relatively short.

When the stock price is substantially higher than the exercise price, the option will have a high value and is almost certain to be exercised. The value of the option we have been computing is analogous to and can also be approximated by calculating the current price of a pure discount bond with a face value equal to the exercise price of the option and a maturity equal to the maturity of the option.[8] This current price is deducted from the current stock value to give the value of the option. For example, for a current stock value of \$60, an interest rate of 6 percent, and an option maturity of four years,

$$C_0 = 60 - 20e^{-0.24} = 60 - 20(0.787) = 60 - 15.74 = \$44.26$$

This result for the value of the option differs only slightly from the result of \$44.34, which we obtained using the option pricing model (OPM). The option has a high value and is likely to be exercised. On the other hand, if the price of the stock is considerably less than the exercise price of the option, such as the \$2 value in Table 23A.2, the option will have no value and will be likely to expire without being exercised.

We observe also that the curves depicting the value of an option as the stock price varies are concave from above and lie below the 45° line drawn from the origin (Line A). For an option of given maturity, any percentage change in the stock price will result in a larger percentage change in the option value. This is demonstrated by the percentage change columns in Table 23A.1 and by Column 8 of the same table, which presents the ratio of the percent change in the option price to the percent change in the stock price. For the longer maturity, the volatility of the option price is reduced somewhat. Also, at higher stock prices for a given maturity, the volatility of the option prices relative to the stock price changes is reduced.

Thus the use of the option pricing models enables us to quantify some fundamental patterns in the relationships between stock prices and the related option values. These relationships depend on the level of stock prices, the duration and exercise price of the option, the risk-free interest rate, and the variance of the percentage returns on the stock values.

Problems

23A.1 The current price of Anchor Corporation common stock is \$24 per share. Anchor also has warrants outstanding which enable the holder to buy one share of stock at a price of \$28. The warrants have four years to maturity. The instantaneous variance of returns on Anchor's common stock is 8 percent, and the risk-free rate is 12 percent.

a. Are these warrants in-the-money or out-of-the-money?

b. Using the option pricing model, determine the value of a warrant.

c. What would be the value of a warrant if the maturity were 5 years?

[8] The probability factors will approximate 1.

23A.2 The Thurston Corporation has options outstanding which permit the holder to buy one share of Thurston common stock at a price of $10. The current market price of Thurston stock is $15. The options have six months to maturity. The risk-free rate is 12 percent, and the instantaneous variance of returns on common stock is 16 percent.

a. Using the option pricing model, what is the value of the Thurston option?
b. Thurston's management decides to implement a new strategy which will reduce the instantaneous variance of returns on common stock from 16 percent to 9 percent. What is the effect on the price of the option?

PART SEVEN

INTEGRATED TOPICS IN MANAGERIAL FINANCE

The final chapters deal with important topics that bring together materials from a number of earlier sections of the book. Chapter 24 discusses the growth of firms through mergers and holding companies and seeks to explain the factors behind these developments. Chapter 25 considers the causes and possible remedies when firms encounter financial difficulties.

In Chapter 26, we apply many of the topics and concepts developed more generally in earlier chapters to the specific circumstances of a small firm. In Chapter 27, we extend the framework of financing into its international dimensions. A number of aspects of international business finance have been treated throughout the book, but in this chapter, some important areas of international business finance are developed more fully.

CHAPTER 24

MERGERS AND HOLDING COMPANIES

Growth is vital to the well-being of a firm. Growth is needed to compete for the best managerial talent by offering rapid promotions and broadened responsibilities. Without able executives, the firm is likely to decline and die. Much of the previous material dealing with analysis, planning, and financing has a direct bearing on the financial manager's potential contribution to the firm's growth. This chapter focuses on strategies for promoting growth through mergers and on the role of financial managers in evaluating prospective merger partners and making decisions on which parts of the company to sell off.

Mergers and Acquisitions

From a legal standpoint, there are many distinctions between types of mergers and combinations. Most generally, mergers mean any transaction that forms one economic unit from two or more previous ones. Two major forms of combination have been recognized in compiling data—mergers and acquisitions. In fact, the department of an investment banking firm engaged in providing advice on these activities is usually referred to as the "M & A (mergers and acquisitions) department." Another distinction is made, from an accounting standpoint, between a purchase and a pooling of interests (see the appendix to this chapter). A *purchase* generally refers to the acquisition of a much smaller entity which is absorbed into the acquiring firm. A *pooling of interests* represents the joining of two firms of not greatly unequal size, followed by operations in which their identities are continued to a considerable degree. But this distinction is made mainly from a financial accounting standpoint, while the more general distinction is between mergers and acquisitions. Examples of large *mergers* in recent years include the following:

Partners		Combined market value (in billions)	Year
Nabisco	Standard Brands	$2.0	1981
Dart Industries	Kraft	2.4	1980
Schering	Plough	1.4	1970

Examples of large *acquisitions* that occurred during the 1976–1981 period are these:

Buyer	Target	Price (in billions)	Year
Du Pont	Conoco	$7.5	1981
Elf-Aquitaine	Texasgulf	2.7*	1981
Fluor Corp.	St. Joe Minerals	2.0	1981
Standard Oil (Ohio)	Kennecott	2.3	1981
Shell Oil	Belridge Oil	3.7	1979
General Electric	Utah International	2.2	1976
Mobil	Marcor	1.6	1976

* For 63 percent interest

Tender Offers

A recent development in acquisition activity is the increased use of tender offers. In a tender offer, one party—generally a corporation seeking a controlling interest in another corporation—asks the stockholders of the firm it is seeking to control to submit, or tender, their shares in exchange for a specified price. The price is generally stated as so many dollars per share of acquired stock, although it can be stated in terms of shares of stock in the acquiring firm. Tender offers have been used for a number of years, but the pace greatly accelerated after 1965 and peaked in 1976 and 1977.

If one firm wishes to gain control over another, it typically seeks approval for the merger from the other firm's management and board of directors. An alternative approach is the "bear hug." In this approach, a company mails a letter to the directors of the takeover target announcing the acquisition proposal and requiring the directors to make a quick decision on the bid. If approval cannot be obtained, the acquiring company can appeal directly to stockholders by means of the tender offer, unless the management and directors of the target firm hold enough stock to retain control. The technique of going directly to the shareholders has been called a *Saturday night special*. The term implies that a gun has been aimed at the directors, since if the shareholders respond favorably to the tender offer, the acquiring company will gain control and have the power to replace the directors who have not cooperated in the takeover effort. (This is also referred to as a *hostile* takeover.) The target firm may seek to avoid being acquired or may seek to join with another firm with which it would rather be associated. The target firm may therefore seek to elicit an offer or tender from a partner it considers more desirable—a *white knight*.

The frequency of tender offers in the 1960s resulted in regulatory legislation. A law placing tender offers under full SEC jurisdiction became effective on July 29, 1968. Disclosure requirements written into the statute include the following:

1. The acquiring firm must give the management of the target firm and the SEC thirty days' notice of its intentions to make the acquisition.
2. When substantial blocks are purchased through tender offers or through open market purchases—that is, on the stock exchange—the beneficial owner of the stock must be disclosed, together with the name of the party

putting up the money for the transaction. Usually the stock is in the "street" name of the brokerage house that acts on behalf of the real (beneficial) owner.

In addition to the powers granted to the SEC to require disclosure of takeover intentions, certain tactics to prevent takeover can be used by the intended target. More than forty states have adopted antitakeover laws that can delay tender offers so that an alternative can be pursued. The takeover target may also utilize other legal tactics, such as court suits alleging that antitrust laws and other regulatory guidelines are being violated. Such tactics may forestall a takeover. For example, when Anderson, Clayton, & Co. made a bid for Gerber Products Co., the latter instituted a number of legal suits. After five months of legal maneuvers on both sides, Anderson, Clayton dropped its bid in September 1977. In another case, because Marshall Field and Co. threatened antitrust actions and announced its own acquisition program, Carter Hawley Hale dropped its 1978 takeover attempt. The Hart-Scott-Rodino Act of 1976, amending the antitrust laws, contains a provision that requires premerger notification to the FTC of large mergers. This provision became effective in July 1978.

As a consequence of the disclosure requirements in connection with intended tender offers, competition among bidders in takeover efforts may cause the acquisition price to rise well above the market price of the stock before the initial tender offer. This is illustrated by the Conoco story.

The Conoco Acquisition

During 1978, Conoco common stock traded in a relatively narrow range of $24 to $32. This range widened to $28–$50 in 1979 and to $41–$73 in 1980. In May 1981, Dome Petroleum made a tender offer of $65 per share for 14 million shares (13 percent) of Conoco common stock; Conoco termed the offer inadequate and took legal action to block the offer. On June 25, 1981, Seagram, the Canadian distiller, made a $73 per share tender offer for 41 percent of Conoco's stock. Conoco also opposed this bid. Conoco found a "white knight" in du Pont and on July 6, 1981, the firms announced an agreement to merge. The merger terms provided that du Pont would pay $87.50 per share in cash for 40 percent and trade 1.6 shares of du Pont common stock for the remaining 60 percent of Conoco shares, representing a total price of $7.3 billion.

On July 12, 1981, Seagram increased its offer to $85 per share for 51 percent of Conoco shares. On July 14 du Pont raised its offer to $85 in cash for the 40 percent and 1.7 du Pont shares for the remaining 60 percent, representing a total bid of $7.4 billion. On July 17, Mobil Oil entered the picture with a cash offer of $90 a share for half of Conoco's common stock and new Mobil preferred stock or debentures valued at $90 per Conoco common share for the remainder. On July 23, Seagram raised its offer to $92 cash. On July 27, Mobil increased its cash offer to $105 a share. On August 3, Mobil moved the cash offer to $115, and on the following day to $120 per share. Du Pont countered by raising its cash offer to $98 per share. At 3:45 A.M. on August 5, 1981, du Pont began purchasing the 55 percent of Conoco shares for which it held tenders.

The higher Mobil offer was clouded by investor uncertainty as to whether a Mobil-Conoco merger would lead to a protracted antitrust suit. In contrast, on July 31, 1981, the Department of Justice stated that the only possible antitrust problem it saw in the Conoco-du Pont merger stemmed from Conoco's joint venture in a petrochemical plant with Monsanto, a du Pont competitor. Du Pont quickly stated that any potential problem could be avoided since it was willing to either sell Conoco's share to Monsanto or to buy out Monsanto's interests; du Pont subsequently did buy out Monsanto.

The Conoco drama illustrates how competitive bids can push up the price of the target firm's stock. Another example is the earlier acquisition of Babcock and Wilcox by United Technologies. United Technologies (UT) bid $42 per share in March 1977 for Babcock & Wilcox (BW), whose common stock was then selling for less than $35 per share. UT is a producer of aircraft engines, rocket motors and engines, automotive and space equipment, helicopters, elevators, escalators, and other industrial equipment. BW mainly manufactured steam generating equipment, such as the massive boilers used in fossil fuel- and nuclear-powered turbine generator systems. In addition, it produced pollution control equipment and other equipment for the handling and transfer of heat. UT's 1976 sales were $5.2 billion, while BW's 1976 sales were $1.7 billion. Shortly after UT's tender offer, J. Ray McDermott & Co. (JRM) entered the contest. JRM, smaller than either of the other two companies, with sales of $1.2 billion in 1976, was mainly involved in the engineering, fabrication, and installation of facilities for the production of oil and gas. By May 1977, JRM announced that it had bought nearly 9 percent of BW's stock on the open market. BW proceeded to take legal action against both takeover rivals. In August 1977, UT upped its bid for BW to $48. Shortly thereafter, JRM bid $55, which the BW directors urged its shareholders to accept. A complicated series of counterbids ensued, with JRM winning the competition for a final price of $65 a share, nearly double the pre-tender market price.

In an example of a bid that might have been too high, Kennecott Copper was motivated by the fear of becoming a takeover target itself. In accordance with a requirement by the FTC of divestiture of Peabody Coal, Kennecott had agreed to a sale to a group of companies for $1.2 billion to be paid in installments. Since Kennecott was in the process of becoming cash-rich as it received installment payments for the purchase price, it wanted to utilize the cash. It sought to avoid being acquired by a company that might use debt to buy Kennecott and then use the cash flowing into Kennecott to pay off the debt.

Eaton Corporation, with 1976 revenues of $1.8 billion, had made, in early November 1977, an offer of $47 per share for the stock of the Carborundum Company, then selling at $33.25 per share. Eaton produces locks and other security systems as well as automotive parts and components. Carborundum, a leading producer of carbon products, other abrasives, and refractory and electric products, had 1976 revenues of $614 million. In mid-November, Kennecott made an offer to Carborundum of $66 per share. On November 17, it was announced that the directors of both companies had unanimously approved the offer. Some stockholders stated that they were stunned by this "squandering of Kennecott's cash." Others praised Kennecott for avoiding the "ridiculous newspaper auction that marked the Babcock & Wilcox battle."

Subsequently, in early 1981 Kennecott engaged in a battle with Curtiss-Wright Corporation (C-W), each firm trying to take over the other. An agreement was reached on January 28, 1981. Kennecott agreed to buy back 4.7 million of its shares from C-W for $168 million in cash; C-W had paid $110 million for this stock. Kennecott received $46 million in cash and C-W's Dorr-Oliver subsidiary in exchange for 1 million shares of C-W stock for which it had paid $112 million; C-W is said to have paid $70 million for Dorr-Oliver. The settlement left Teledyne Inc. with 57 percent of C-W stock. The C-W capitalization was cut in half with retirement of the shares redeemed from Kennecott.

The Kennecott saga reached its climax on March 13, 1981, when it was announced that its directors had approved a $1.77 billion cash offer from Standard Oil of Ohio (Sohio). Sohio agreed to pay $62 cash for each of Kennecott's 28.5 million shares. This was more than double Kennecott's closing price of $27.125 on Wednesday, March 11, 1981.

The episodes described are but a small sample of the many dramas that filled the pages of the financial press in the late 1970s and early 1980s. Some natural questions are: Why all this merger activity? What is its broader significance? These topics are considered next before taking up the discussion of the managerial finance aspects of merger.

Some Perspectives on Merger Activity

Merger and acquisition announcements in 1980 totaled 1,889 transactions. This was down 11 percent from 1979's 2,128 transactions.[1] The dollar volume of the transactions increased slightly from $43.5 billion to $44.3 billion. There was a trend toward an increase in the size of transactions as measured by the number with values of $100 million or more. In 1980, 94 announcements involved $100 million or more, compared with 83 in 1979, 80 in 1978, and 41 in 1977. During the first half of 1981, merger announcements totaled $35.7 billion, up 60 percent from the corresponding period in 1980.[2]

Basically, two viewpoints on the role of mergers are found. One view holds that mergers have undesirable effects. Proponents of this view are concerned that mergers may result in undue concentration of economic and political power and will increase monopoly elements in the economy.

Others hold that mergers are a part of the normal resource allocation and adjustment processes in the economy. They point out that while the total dollars involved in mergers are large in an absolute sense, they are small in a relative sense. The total dollar volume of merger activity in a given year is usually less than 2 percent of total corporate assets.[3]

Despite the high rate of merger activity in recent years, the average share of the four largest firms in the Census Bureau's classification of 450 industries has remained constant for two decades at about 40 percent. Similarly, the share of the largest 200 firms in the value added by all manufacturing firms has remained constant at (coincidentally) about 40 percent since the early 1960s. Proponents of

[1] *Wall Street Journal*, January 14, 1981, p. 48.

[2] *Wall Street Journal*, August 6, 1981, p. 1.

[3] J. Fred Weston, *Industrial Concentration, Mergers and Growth* (Washington, D.C.: U.S. Department of Commerce, 1981), vol. 2, Chapter IV.

the second view hold that mergers do not have a great impact on the economy one way or another. But then what motivates all of the merger activity observed in recent years? Here we take the view of the individual firms.

Motivations for Merger Activity

A tremendous amount of literature has been written on mergers in finance. Many aspects of mergers have been studied. This summary of the reasons for mergers will draw on the rich mine of empirical studies.[4]

Value Increases in Mergers

The many empirical studies of mergers agree in the finding that stockholders of acquired firms gain. The percentage of gain ranges from 10 to 20 percent over premerger market values. These studies suggest that on average either the acquired firms were not performing up to their potential or that some other economic benefits were achieved by the merger.

However, the shareholders of *acquiring* firms do not appear to achieve gains that are statistically significant. This suggests a competitive market for acquiring firms, and that competing bids result in merger gains going mainly to the acquired firms. Since the shareholders of acquired firms gain and the shareholders of acquiring firms do not lose, a net gain in value must be realized from the total merger activity. This supports the view that mergers are a part of the asset allocation process in the economy, whereby resources are moved to their most efficient uses.

Mergers in a Long-Range Strategic Planning Framework

In this framework mergers may be viewed as a part of the long-range and strategic planning processes of firms. Gains from mergers may come from a number of sources. These may include: (1) carryover of strong financial planning and control, (2) economies of scale, (3) complementary resources, (4) key specialist competence brought to a new situation, (5) excess cash, (6) unused debt capacity, (7) research and development (R & D) capability increased, and (8) a strong marketing organization more fully utilized.

Market Values versus Replacement Costs

A number of more specific influences have been operating during the late 1970s and early 1980s. One strong influence has been the sharp decline in the ratio of market values to the replacement costs of company assets. Thus to add capacity in a given line of business, it is cheaper to buy a company than to buy the brick and mortar to add physical assets. The fall in this ratio (market value to current replacement cost of assets) can be explained by either a decline in the profitability of firms or a rise in the discount rate used to capitalize the earnings streams into market values. Regardless of whether profitability has decreased, risk premiums have increased, or some combination of the two have been operating together, there is less disagreement on the result. A significant shift in the ratio of market values to replacement values has definitely occurred during the period of inflation. This ratio has been referred to as *Tobin's q-ratio*. During the period of price sta-

[4] Ibid., Chapter III.

bility in the years 1958 to 1965, the q-ratio rose from 0.681 in 1958 to 1.140 during 1965. With the onset of the period of inflation, the q-ratio began to decline. By 1981 it had fallen below 0.70. The main influence on the change in the q-ratio is, of course, the changes in the market values that make up the numerator of the ratio. The decline in the q-ratio would be consistent with a decline in real earnings rates, a rise in the required yields on equities, or some combination of both that may have appeared during the period of inflation.

Financing

Sometimes it is possible to finance an acquisition when it is not possible to finance internal growth. Building a large steel plant, for example, involves a large investment. Steel manufacturing capacity can be acquired more cheaply in a merger through an exchange of stock than by buying the facilities outright. Sellers are often more willing to accept the purchaser's stock in payment for the facilities sold than are the investors in a public offering, and the use of stock reduces cash requirements for the acquisition of assets.

In addition, merger activity has been supported by financing from commercial banking sources. The following indicates the lines of credit established by a number of large firms in the summer of 1981:

Company	Credit arranged	Banks
Mobil	$6.0 billion	Citicorp International heading a group of 41 banks
Pennzoil	$2.5 billion	Citibank heading a group of 24 banks
Seagram	$3.0 billion	Citibank, Manufacturers Hanover Trust, and Bank of Montreal leading 31 North American and European banks
Elf-Aquitaine	$1.9 billion	20 U.S. and Canadian banks
Du Pont	$3.0 billion	Chase Manhattan leading a syndicate of banks

Taxes

Without question, the high level of taxation helped stimulate merger activity in the postwar period. Studies have indicated that taxes appear to have been a major reason for the sale of about one-third of the firms acquired by merger. In some cases, inheritance taxes precipitated these sales; in others, the advantage of buying a company with a tax loss provided the motivation.

Terms of Mergers

For every merger actually consummated, a number of other potentially attractive combinations fail during negotiations. Negotiations may be broken off when it is revealed that the companies' operations are not compatible or when the parties are unable to agree on the merger terms. The most important of these terms is the price to be paid by the acquiring firm.

Effects on Price and Earnings

A merger carries the potential for either favorable or adverse effects on earnings, on market prices of shares, or on both. Previous chapters have shown that investment decisions should be guided by the effects on market values, and these effects should in turn be determined by the probable effects on future earnings and dividends. Future events are difficult to forecast, however, so both stockholders and managers attribute great importance to the immediate effects on earnings per share of a contemplated merger. Company directors will often state, "I do not know how the merger will affect the market price of the shares of my company, because so many forces influencing market prices are at work. But the effect on earnings per share can be seen directly."

An example will illustrate the effects of a proposed merger on earnings per share and thus suggest the kinds of problems likely to arise. Assume the following facts for two companies:

	Company A	Company B
Total earnings	$20,000	$50,000
Number of shares of common stock	5,000	10,000
Earnings per share of stock	$4	$5
Price-earnings ratio per share	15 times	12 times
Market price per share	$60	$60

Suppose the firms agree to merge, with B, the surviving firm, acquiring the shares of A by a one-for-one exchange of stock. The exchange ratio is determined by the market prices of the two companies. Assuming no increase in earnings, the effects on earnings per share are shown in the following tabulation:

	Shares of Company B owned after merger	Earnings per share	
		Before merger	After merger
A's stockholders	5,000	$4	$4.67
B's stockholders	10,000	5	4.67
Total	15,000		

Since total earnings are $70,000, and since a total of 15,000 shares will be outstanding after the merger has been completed, the new earnings per share will be $4.67. Earnings will increase by 67 cents for A's stockholders, but they will decline by 33 cents for B's.

The effects on market values are less certain. If the combined company sells at Company A's price-earnings ratio of 15, the market value per share of the new company will be $70. In this case, shareholders of both companies will have benefited. This result comes about because the combined earnings are now valued at a multiplier of 15, whereas prior to the merger one portion of the earnings was valued at a multiplier of 15 and another portion at a multiplier of 12. If, on the other hand, the earnings of the new company are valued at B's multiplier of 12, the indicated market value of the shares will be $56, and the shareholders of each company will have suffered a $4 dilution in market value.

Because the effects on market value per share are less certain than those on earnings per share, the impact on earnings per share tends to be given great weight in merger negotiations. The following analysis thus illustrates effects on earnings per share while recognizing that maximizing market value is the valid rule for investment decisions.

As shown below, if a merger takes place on the basis of earnings, neither earnings dilution nor earnings appreciation will take place:

	Shares of Company B owned after merger	Earnings per old share	
		Before merger	After merger
A's stockholders	4,000	$4	$4
B's stockholders	10,000	5	5
Total	14,000		

It is clear that the equivalent earnings per share after the merger are the same as before the merger.[5] The effect on market values, however, will depend on whether the 15-times multiplier of A or the 12-times multiplier of B prevails.

Quantitative Factors Affecting Terms of Mergers

Five factors have received the greatest emphasis in arriving at merger terms: (1) earnings and the growth of earnings, (2) dividends, (3) market values, (4) book values, and (5) net current assets. Analysis is typically based on the per-share values of the foregoing factors. The relative importance of each factor and the circumstances under which each is likely to be the most influential determinant in arriving at terms will vary. The nature of these influences is described below.

Earnings and Growth Rates Both expected earnings and capitalization rates as reflected in P/E ratios are important in determining the values that will be established in a merger. The analysis necessarily begins with historical data on the firms' earnings; their past growth rates, probable future trends, and variability are important determinants of the earnings multiplier, or P/E ratio, that will prevail after the merger.

The ways in which future earnings growth rates affect the multiplier can be illustrated by extending the preceding example. First, high P/E ratios are commonly associated with rapidly growing companies. Since Company A has the higher P/E ratio, it is reasonable to assume that its earnings will grow more rapidly than those of Company B. Suppose A's expected growth rate is 10 percent and B's is 5 percent. Looking at the proposed merger from the viewpoint of Company B and its stockholders, and assuming that the exchange ratio is based on present market prices, it can be seen that B will suffer a dilution in earnings when the merger occurs. However, B will be acquiring a firm with more favorable growth prospects; hence, its earnings after the merger should increase more rapidly than before. In this case, the new growth rate is assumed to be a weighted average of the growth rates of the individual firms—weighted by their respective total earnings before the merger. In the example, the new expected growth rate is 6.43 percent.

[5] On the basis of earnings, the exchange ratio is 4:5. That is, Company A's shareholders receive four shares of B stock for each five shares of A stock they own. Earnings per share of the merged company are $5. But, since A's shareholders now own only 80 percent of the number of their old shares, their equivalent earnings per *old* share are the same $4. For example, if one of A's stockholders formerly held 100 shares, that person will own only 80 shares of B after the merger; and the total earnings will be 80 × $5 = $400. Dividing the $400 total earnings by the number of shares formerly owned, 100, gives the $4 per *old* share.

Figure 24.1 **Effect of Merger on Future Earnings**

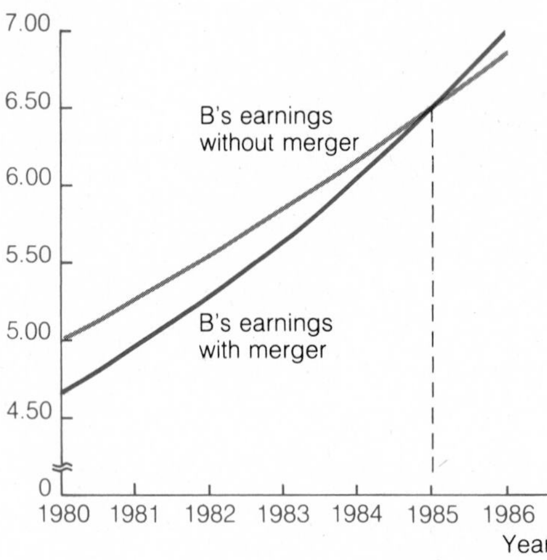

With the new growth rate it is possible to determine just how long it will take Company B's stockholders to regain the earnings dilution—that is, how long it will take earnings per share to revert to their premerger position as shown in Figure 24.1.[6] Without the merger, B will have initial earnings of \$5 a share, and these earnings will grow at a rate of 5 percent a year. With the merger, earnings will drop to \$4.67 a share, but the rate of growth will increase to 6.43 percent. Under these conditions, the earnings dilution will be overcome after five years; from the fifth year on, B's earnings will be higher, assuming the merger is consummated.

This same relationship can be developed from the viewpoint of the faster growing firm, for which there is an immediate earnings increase but a reduced rate of growth. Working through the analysis shows the number of years before the earnings accretion will be eroded.

It is apparent that the critical variables are (1) the respective rates of growth of the two firms; (2) their relative sizes, which determine the actual amount of the initial earnings per share dilution or accretion, as well as the new weighted average growth rate; (3) the firms' P/E ratios; and (4) the exchange ratio. These factors interact to produce the resulting pattern of earnings per share for the surviving

[6] The calculation could also be made algebraically by solving for n in the following equation:

$$E_1(1+g_1)^n = E_2(1+g_2)^n,$$

where:

E_1 and E_2 = Earnings before and after the merger, respectively

g_1 and g_2 = Growth rates before and after the merger, respectively

n = Breakeven number of years

company. It is possible to generalize the relationships somewhat; for the immediate purposes, it is necessary simply to note that in the bargaining process the exchange ratio is the variable that must be manipulated in an effort to reach a mutually satisfactory earnings pattern.[7]

Dividends Because they represent the actual income received by stockholders, dividends can influence the terms of merger. As Chapter 17 suggests, however, dividends are likely to have little influence on the market price of companies with a record of high growth and high profitability. Some companies have not yet paid cash dividends, but they nonetheless command market prices representing a high multiple of current earnings. However, for utility companies and for companies in industries where growth rates and profitability have declined, the dollar amount of dividends paid can have a relatively important influence on the market price of the stock. Dividends can therefore influence the terms on which these companies will be likely to trade in a merger.[8]

Market Values The price of a firm's stock reflects expectations about its future earnings and dividends, so current market values are expected to have a strong influence on the terms of a merger. However, the value placed on a firm in an acquisition is likely to exceed its current market price for a number of reasons:

1. If the company is in a depressed industry, its stockholders are likely to overdiscount the dismal outlook for the company. This will result in a very low current market price.
2. The prospective purchaser may be interested in the company for the contribution that it will make to the purchaser's company. Thus the acquired company may be worth more to an informed purchaser than it is in the general market.
3. Stockholders are offered more than current market prices for their stock as an inducement to sell.

For these reasons, the offering price is usually in the range of 10 to 20 percent above the market price before the merger announcement.

[7] Certain companies, especially the conglomerates, are reported to have used mergers to produce a "growth illusion" designed to increase the prices of their stocks. When a high P/E ratio company buys a low P/E ratio company, the earnings per share of the acquiring firm rise *because* of the merger. Thus mergers can produce growth in reported earnings for the acquiring firm. This growth by merger in turn can cause the acquiring firm to keep its high P/E ratio. With this ratio, the conglomerates can seek new low P/E merger candidates and thus continue to obtain growth through mergers. The chain is broken if (1) the merger activity slows, or (2) the P/E ratio of the acquiring firm falls. In 1968 and 1969 several large conglomerates reported profit declines caused by losses in certain of their divisions. This reduced the growth rate in EPS, which in turn led to a decline in the P/E ratio. A change in tax laws and antitrust suits against some conglomerate mergers also made it more difficult to consummate favorable mergers. These factors, along with tight money and depressed conditions in some industries, caused a further reduction in the P/E ratio and compounded the firms' problems. The net result was a drastic revaluation of conglomerate share prices, with such former favorites as LTV falling from a high of $169 to $7.50 and Litton Industries from $115 to $6.75.

[8] If a company that does not pay dividends on its stock is seeking to acquire a firm whose stockholders are accustomed to receiving dividends, the exchange can be on a "convertibles for common stock" basis. This will enable the acquired firm's stockholders to continue receiving income.

Book Value per Share Book value is generally considered to be relatively unimportant in determining the value of a company, since it represents only the historical investments made in the company—investments that may have little relation to current values or prices. At times, however, especially when it substantially exceeds market value, book value may well have an impact on merger terms. Book value is an index of the amount of physical facilities made available in the merger. Despite a past record of low earning power, it is always possible that, under effective management, a firm's assets may once again achieve normal earning power, in which case the market value of the company will rise. Because of the potential contribution of physical properties to improved future earnings, book value may have an influence on actual merger terms.

Net Current Assets per Share Net current assets (current assets minus current liabilities) per share are likely to have an influence on merger terms because they represent the amount of liquidity that can be obtained from a company in a merger. In the postwar textile mergers, net current assets were very high, and this was one of the characteristics making textile companies attractive to the acquiring firms. By buying a textile company, often with securities, an acquiring company was in a position to look for still other merger candidates, paying for new acquisitions with the just-acquired liquidity. Similarly, if an acquired company is debt-free, the acquiring firm may be able to borrow the funds required for the purchase, using the acquired firm's assets and earning power to pay off the loan after the merger or to provide security for renewing or even increasing the borrowing.[9]

Relative Importance of Quantitative Factors Attempts have been made to determine statistically the relative weights assigned to each of the above factors in actual merger cases. These attempts have been singularly unsuccessful. In one case, one factor seems to dominate; in another, some other determinant appears most important. This absence of consistent patterns among the quantitative factors suggests that qualitative forces are also at work.

Qualitative Influences: Synergy

Sometimes the most important influence on the terms of a merger is a business consideration not reflected at all in historical quantitative data. A soundly conceived merger is one in which the combination produces what may be called a *synergistic*, or "two-plus-two-equals-five," effect. By the combination, more profits are generated than could be achieved by the sum of the individual firms operating separately.

To illustrate: In the merger between Merck and Company and Sharp and Dohme, it was said that each company complemented the other in an important way. Merck had a good reputation for its research organization; Sharp and Dohme had an effective sales force. The combination of these two pharmaceutical companies added strength to both. Another example is the merger between Carrier Corporation

[9] By the same token, a firm seeking to *avoid* being acquired may reduce its liquid position and use up its borrowing potential.

and Affiliated Gas Equipment. The merger enabled the combined company to provide a complete line of air-conditioning and heating equipment. The merger between Hilton Hotels and Statler Hotels led to economies in the purchase of supplies and materials. One Hilton executive estimated that the savings accruing simply from the combined management of the Statler and Hilton hotels in New York amounted to $700,000 a year. The bulk of the savings was in laundry, food, advertising, and administrative costs.

The qualitative factors may also reflect other influences. The merger or acquisition may enable a company that lacks general management ability to obtain it from the other company. Another factor may be the acquisition of a technically competent scientific or engineering staff if one of the companies has fallen behind in the technological race. In such a situation, the company needing the technical competence possessed by the other firm may be willing to pay a substantial premium over previous levels of earnings, dividends, market values, or book values of the acquired firm.

The purpose of the merger may be to develop a production capability a firm does not possess. Some firms are strong in producing custom-made items with high performance characteristics; yet on entering new markets, these firms must make use of mass production techniques. If a firm has had no such experience, this skill may have to be obtained by means of a merger. Another firm may need to develop an effective sales organization. For example, some of the companies previously oriented to the defense market, such as those in aerospace, found that they had only a limited industrial sales organization; merger was the solution to the problem.

The foregoing are the kinds of qualitative considerations that may have an overriding influence on the actual terms of merger, and the value of such contributions is never easy to quantify. The all-encompassing question, of course, is how the factors will affect the contribution of each company to future market value of the combined operation. This historical data and qualitative considerations described, in addition to judgment and bargaining, combine to determine merger terms.

Holding Companies

In 1889, New Jersey became the first state to pass a general incorporation law permitting corporations to be formed for the sole purpose of owning the stocks of other companies. This law was the origin of the holding company. The Sherman Act of 1890, which prohibits combinations or collusion in restraint of trade, gave an impetus to holding company operations as well as to outright mergers, because companies could do as one company what they were forbidden to do as separate companies.

Many of the advantages and disadvantages of holding companies are no more than the advantages and disadvantages of large-scale operations already discussed in connection with mergers and consolidations. Whether a company is organized on a divisional basis or with the divisions kept as separate companies does not affect the basic reasons for conducting a large-scale, multiproduct, multiplant operation. However, the holding company form of large-scale operations has different advantages and disadvantages from those of completely integrated divisionalized operations.

Advantages of Holding Companies

Control with Fractional Ownership Through a holding company operation, a firm can buy 5, 10, or 50 percent of the stock of another corporation. Such fractional ownership may be sufficient to give the acquiring company effective working control of or substantial influence over the operations of the company in which it has acquired ownership. Working control is often considered to entail more than 25 percent of the common stock, but it can be as low as 10 percent if the stock is widely distributed. Also, control on a very slim margin can be held through friendship with large stockholders outside the holding company group. Sometimes holding company operations represent the initial stages of transforming an operating company into an investment company, particularly when the operating company is in a declining industry. When an industry's sales begin to decline permanently and the firm begins to liquidate its operating assets, it may use the liquid funds to invest in industries having a more favorable growth potential.

Isolation of Risks Because the various operating companies in a holding company system are separate legal entities, the obligations of any one unit are separate from those of the other units. Catastrophic losses incurred by one unit are therefore not transmitted as claims on the assets of the other units.

Although this is the customary generalization of the nature of a holding company system, it is not completely valid. In extending credit to one of the units of a holding company system, an astute financial manager or loan officer will require a guarantee or a claim on the assets of all the elements in the system. To some degree, therefore, the assets in the various elements are joined. The advantage remains to the extent that catastrophes occurring to one unit are not transmitted to the others.

Approval Not Required A holding company group that seeks to obtain effective working control of a number of companies may quietly purchase a portion of their stock. The operation is completely informal, and the permission or approval of the stockholders of the acquired company or companies is not required. Thus the guiding personalities in a holding company operation are not dependent on negotiations and approval of the other interest groups in order to obtain their objectives. This feature of holding company operations has, however, been limited somewhat by recent state law and SEC rules governing tender offers.

Disadvantages of Holding Companies

Partial Multiple Taxation Provided the holding company owns at least 80 percent of a subsidiary's voting stock, Internal Revenue Service regulations permit the filing of consolidated returns, in which case dividends received by the parent are not taxed. However, if less than 80 percent of the stock is owned, returns cannot be consolidated, although 85 percent of the dividends received by the holding company can be deducted. With a tax rate of 46 percent, this means that the effective tax on intercorporate dividends is 6.9 percent. This partial double taxation somewhat offsets the benefits of holding company control with limited ownership, but whether the penalty of 6.9 percent of dividends received is sufficient to offset the advantages is a matter that must be decided in individual situations.[10]

Ease of Enforced Dissolution In the case of a holding company operation that falls into disfavor with the U.S. Department of Justice, it is relatively easy to require dissolution of the relationship by disposal of stock ownership; for instance, in the late 1950s du Pont was required to dispose of its 23 percent stock interest in General Motors Corporation, acquired in the early 1920s. Because there was no fusion between the corporations, there were no difficulties, from an operating standpoint, in requiring the separation of the two companies. However, if complete amalgamation had taken place, it would have been much more difficult to break up the company after so many years, and the likelihood of forced divestiture would have been reduced.

Risks of Excessive Pyramiding Financial leverage effects in pyramiding magnify profits if operations are successful, but they also magnify losses. The greater the degree of pyramiding, the greater the degree of risk involved in any fluctuations in sales or earnings. This potential disadvantage of pyramiding operations through holding companies is discussed in the next section.

Leverage in Holding Companies

The problem of excessive leverage is worthy of further note, for the degree of leverage in certain past instances has been truly staggering. For example, in the 1920s, Samuel Insull and his group controlled electric utility-operating companies at the bottom of a holding company pyramid by a one-twentieth of 1 percent investment. As a ratio, this represents 1/2,000. In other words, $1 of capital at the top holding company level controlled $2,000 of assets at the operating level. A similar situation existed in the railroad field. It has been stated that Robert R. Young, with an investment of $254,000, obtained control of the Allegheny system, consisting of total operating assets of $3 billion.

The nature of leverage in a holding company system and its advantages and disadvantages are illustrated by the hypothetical example developed in Table 24.1.[11] As in the previous example, although this case is hypothetical, it illustrates actual situations. Half of the operating company's Class B common stock is owned by Holding Company 1; in fact, it is the only asset of Holding Company 1. Holding Company 2 holds as its total assets half of the Class B common stock of Holding Company 1. Consequently, $1,000 of Class B common stock of Holding Company 2 controls $2 million of assets at the operating company level. Further leverage could, of course, have been postulated in this situation by setting up a third company to own Class B common stock of Holding Company 2.

[10] The 1969 Tax Reform Law also empowers the Internal Revenue Service to prohibit the deductibility of debt issued to acquire another firm where the following conditions hold: (1) the debt is subordinated to a "significant portion" of the firm's other creditors; (2) the debt is convertible or has warrants attached; (3) the debt/assets ratio exceeds 67 percent; and (4) on a pro forma basis, the times interest earned ratio is less than 3. The IRS can use discretion in invoking this power.

[11] Corrections in computations were supplied by Dr. Narendra C. Bhandari, University of Baltimore.

Table 24.1

Leverage in a Holding Company System

Operating Company			
Total assets	$2,000,000	Debt	$1,000,000
		Preferred stock	150,000
		Common stock: Class A[a]	650,000
		Common stock: Class B	200,000
	$2,000,000		$2,000,000
Holding Company 1			
Class B common stock of operating company	$100,000	Debt	$ 50,000
		Preferred stock	10,000
		Common stock: Class A[a]	30,000
		Common stock: Class B	10,000
	$100,000		$100,000
Holding Company 2			
Class B common stock of Holding Company 1	$5,000	Debt	$2,000
		Preferred stock	1,000
		Common stock: Class A[a]	1,000
		Common stock: Class B	1,000
	$5,000		$5,000

[a] Class A common stock is nonvoting.

Table 24.2 shows the results of holding company leverage on gains and losses at the top level. In the first column, it is assumed that the operating company earns 12 percent before taxes on its $2 million of assets; in the second column it is assumed that the return on assets is 8 percent. The operating and holding companies are the same described in Table 24.1.

A return of 12 percent on the operating assets of $2 million represents earnings of $240,000. The debt interest of $40,000 is deducted from this amount, and the 50 percent tax rate applies to the remainder. The amount available to common stock after payment of debt interest, preferred stock dividends, and an 8 percent return to the nonvoting Class A common stock is $40,500. Assuming a $40,000 dividend payout, Holding Company 1, on the basis of its 50 percent ownership of the operating company, earns $20,000. If the same kind of analysis is followed through, the amount available to Class B common stock in Holding Company 2 is $4,455. This return is on an investment of $1,000, and it represents a return on the investment in Class B common stock of Holding Company 2 of about 445 percent. The power of leverage in a holding company system can indeed be great.

On the other hand, if a decline in revenues causes the pre-tax earnings to drop to 8 percent of the total assets of the operating company, the results will be disastrous. The amount earned under these circumstances will be $160,000. After deducting the bond interest, the amount subject to tax will be $120,000, and the tax will be $60,000. The after-tax but before-interest earnings will be $100,000. The total prior charges will be $99,500, leaving $500 available to Class B common stock. If all earnings are paid out in dividends to Class B common stock, the earnings of

Table 24.2 Results of Holding Company Leverage on Gains and Losses

	Earnings before interest and taxes at 12%	at 8%
Operating Company		
Earnings before interest and taxes	$240,000	$160,000
Less interest on debt (at 4%)	40,000	40,000
Earnings after interest	$200,000	$120,000
Less tax (at 50%)	100,000	60,000
After-tax earnings available for stockholders	$100,000	$ 60,000
Less: Preferred stock (at 5%)	7,500	7,500
Class A common stock (at 8%)	52,000	52,000
Earnings available to Class B common stock	$ 40,500	$ 500
Dividends to Class B common stock (by management decision)	40,000	500
Transferred to retained earnings	$ 500	$ 0
Holding Company 1		
Earnings before interest and taxes (received from the operating company)	$ 20,000	$ 250
Less 85% of dividends received	17,000	212
Intercorporate dividends subject to tax, before interest	$ 3,000	$ 38
Less interest on debt (at 4%)	2,000	2,000
Before-tax earnings	$ 1,000	[a]
Less tax (at 50%)	500	0
After-tax earnings	$ 500	$ 0
Amount of untaxed dividend	$ 17,000	[b]
After-tax earnings available to stockholders	$ 17,500	$ 0
Less: Preferred stock (at 5%)	500	0
Class A common stock (at 8%)	2,400	0
Earnings available to Class B common stock	$ 14,600	$ 0
Less dividends to Class B common stock (by management decision)	10,000	0
Transferred to reserves	$ 4,600	$ 0
Holding Company 2		
Earnings before interest and taxes (received from Holding Company 1)	$ 5,000	
Less 85% of dividends received	4,250	
Intercorporate dividends subject to tax, before interest	$ 750	
Less interest on debt (at 4%)	80	
Before-tax earnings	$ 670	
Less tax (at 50%)	335	
After-tax earnings	$ 335	
Amount of untaxed dividends	4,250	
After-tax earnings available to stockholders	$ 4,585	
Less: Preferred stock (at 5%)	50	
Class A common stock (at 8%)	80	
Earnings available to Class B common stock	$ 4,455	
Percentage return on Class B common stock	445.5%	

[a] Loss

[b] The available amount ($212) is used up by part of the interest charges.

Holding Company 1 will be $250. This is not enough to meet the debt interest. The holding company system will thus be forced to default on the debt interest of Holding Company 1 and, of course, Holding Company 2.

This example illustrates the potential for tremendous gains in a holding company system. It also illustrates that a small earnings decline on the assets of the operating companies will be disastrous.

Summary

Mergers have played an important part in the growth of firms, and since financial managers are required both to appraise the desirability of a prospective merger and to participate in evaluating the respective companies involved in it, this chapter has emphasized analysis of the terms of merger decisions.

The most important term to be negotiated in a merger arrangement is the price the acquiring firm will pay for the acquired one. The most important *quantitative* factors influencing the terms of a merger are (1) current earnings, (2) current market prices, (3) book values, and (4) net working capital. Qualitative considerations may suggest that *synergistic*, or "two-plus-two-equals-five," effects may be present to an extent sufficient to warrant paying more for the acquired firm than the quantitative factors suggest. Recently, the current replacement values of corporate assets have exceeded the market values of related corporate securities.

In mergers, one firm disappears. However, an alternative is for one firm to buy all or a majority of the common stock of another and to run the acquired firm as an operating subsidiary. When this occurs, the acquiring firm is said to be a *holding company*. A number of advantages arise when a holding company is formed, among them:

1. It may be possible to control the acquired firm with a smaller investment than necessary for a merger.
2. Each firm in a holding company is a separate legal entity, and the obligations of any unit are separate from the obligations of the other units.
3. Stockholder approval is required before a merger can take place. This is not necessary in a holding company situation.

There are also some disadvantages to holding companies, among them:

1. If the holding company does not own 80 percent of the subsidiary's stock and does not file consolidated tax returns, it is subject to taxes on 15 percent of the dividends received from the subsidiary.
2. The leverage effects possible in holding companies can subject the company to magnification of earnings fluctuations and related risks.
3. The antitrust division of the U.S. Department of Justice can much more easily force the breakup of a holding company situation than it can bring about the dissolution of two completely merged firms.

Questions

24.1 What are some of the potential benefits that can be expected by a firm that merges with a company in a different industry?

24.2 Distinguish between a holding company and an operating company. Give an example of each.

24.3 Which appears to be riskier—the use of debt in the holding company's capital structure or the use of debt in the operating company's capital structure? Explain.

24.4 Is the public interest served by an increase in merger activity? Give both pro and con arguments.

24.5 Is the book value of a company's assets considered the absolute minimum price to be paid for a firm? Explain. Is there any value that qualifies as an absolute minimum? Explain.

24.6 Discuss the situation in which Midwest Motors calls off merger negotiations with American Data Labs because the latter's stock price is overvalued. What assumption concerning dilution is implicit in the above situation?

24.7 There are many methods by which a company can raise additional capital. Can a merger be considered a means of raising additional equity capital? Explain.

24.8 Are the negotiations for merger agreements more difficult if the firms are in different industries or in the same industry? If they are about the same size or quite different in size? If the ages of the firms are about the same or if they are very different? Explain.

24.9 How would the existence of long-term debt in a company's financial structure affect its valuation for merger purposes? Could the same be said for any debt account regardless of its maturity? Explain.

24.10 During the merger activity of 1976–1981, cash was used by the acquiring company to a much greater extent than during the height of the conglomerate merger activity during 1967–1969. What are some reasons for the relatively greater use of cash in the acquisitions of the most recent period?

Problems

24.1 The Niles Company has agreed to merge with the Aruba Company. The following is information about the two companies prior to their merger:

	Aruba	Niles
Total earnings	$1,000,000	$750,000
Shares outstanding	1,000,000	250,000
P/E ratio	20 times	18 times

The Aruba Company will buy the Niles Company with a 4-for-1 exchange of stock. Combined earnings will remain at the premerger level.

a. What will be the effect on EPS for Aruba stockholders?

b. What will be the effect on EPS for premerger Niles Company stockholders?

24.2 The Brunner Company has agreed to merge with the Powell Company. The shareholders of Powell have agreed to accept half a share of Brunner for each of their Powell shares. The new company will have a P/E ratio of 40. Following is additional information about the merging companies.

	Brunner	Powell
P/E ratio	56	7
Shares outstanding	2,500,000	500,000
Earnings	$1,750,000	$700,000
Earnings per share	$.70	$1.40
Market value per share	$39.20	$9.80

a. After Brunner and Powell merge, what will the new price per share be, assuming that combined earnings remain the same?

b. Calculate the dollar and percent accretion in EPS for Brunner.

c. Calculate the dollar and percent dilution in EPS for Powell.

d. What is the effect on market price for each?

e. Assuming that Brunner has been growing at 24 percent per year, and Powell at 8 percent, what is the expected growth rate for the merged firm? (There are no synergistic effects.)

f. How long will it be before Powell's EPS recovers from the dilution caused by the merger? Illustrate by means of a graph showing premerger and post-merger EPS.

24.3 Dalton Company acquires Cory Company with a three-for-one exchange of stock. Following are data for the two companies:

	Dalton	Cory
Total earnings	$100,000,000	$1,000,000
Shares outstanding	80,000,000	800,000
Expected growth rate in earnings	10%	25%
P/E ratio	8 times	24 times

a. What is the basis for the three-for-one exchange ratio?

b. What is the new EPS for the premerger Dalton and Cory stockholders?

c. If Dalton's P/E ratio rises to 15, what is its new market price?

d. What merger concept does this problem illustrate?

24.4 Hempler Company merges with Rider Company on the basis of market values. Hempler pays one share of convertible preferred stock with a par value of $100 and an interest rate of 6 percent (convertible into 2 shares of Hempler's common stock) for each four shares of Rider Company. Following are more data:

	Hempler	Rider
Total earnings	$1,000,000	$400,000
Common shares outstanding	200,000	80,000
Expected growth rate in earnings	18%	6%
Dividends per share	$1.80	$1.80
P/E ratio	12 times	6 times
Dividend yield	3%	6%

a. 1. What are the new EPS and market price of Hempler if the P/E ratio remains at 12 times?

2. What are the new EPS and market price on a fully diluted basis?

b. Why might Rider Company shareholders agree to the acquisition?

24.5 You are given the following balance sheets:

Rocky Mountain Services Company
Consolidated Balance Sheet
(millions of dollars)

Cash	$1,500	Borrowings	$1,125
Other current assets	1,125	Common stock	1,875
Net property	1,875	Retained earnings	1,500
Total assets	$4,500	Total claims on assets	$4,500

White Lighting Company Balance Sheet
(millions of dollars)

Cash	$375	Net worth	$750
Net property	375		
Total assets	$750	Total net worth	$750

a. The holding company, Rocky Mountain, buys the operating company, White Lighting, with "free" cash of $750 million. Show the new consolidated balance sheet for Rocky Mountain after the acquisition.

b. Instead of buying White Lighting, Rocky Mountain buys Conner Company with free cash of $1.125 billion. Conner's balance sheet follows:

Conner Company Balance Sheet
(millions of dollars)

Cash	$ 750	Borrowings	$ 750
Net property	1,125	Net worth	1,125
Total assets	$1,875	Total claims on assets	$1,875

Show the new consolidated balance sheet for Rocky Mountain after acquisition of Conner.

c. What are the implications of your consolidated balance sheets for measuring the growth of firms resulting from acquisitions?

24.6 Fiscor is a holding company owning the entire common stock of Walter Company and Albright Company. The balance sheet for each subsidiary as of December 31, 1981, is identical to the following one:

Balance Sheet as of December 31, 1981
(millions of dollars)

Current assets	$ 7.50	Current liabilities	$ 1.25
Fixed assets, net	5.00	First mortgage bonds (at 9%)	5.00
		Common stock	5.00
		Retained earnings	1.25
Total assets	$12.50	Total claims on assets	$12.50

Each operating company earns 10 percent annually on total assets, before interest and taxes. The corporate tax rate for each is 40 percent.

a. What is the annual rate of return on each operating company's net worth (common stock plus retained earnings)?

b. Construct a balance sheet for Fiscor based on the following assumptions: (1) The only asset of the holding company is the common stock of the two subsidiaries, carried at par (not book) value. (2) The holding company has \$6.2 million of 8 percent coupon debt.

c. What is the annual rate of return on Fiscor's net worth assuming a 100 percent payout ratio for the subsidiaries?

d. If the subsidiaries' earnings rate before interest and taxes drops to 8 percent, what will be Fiscor's rate of return on net worth?

24.7 Every merger agreement is subject to negotiation between the companies involved. One significant indicator of the compensation received by the acquired company is the market price of each company's stock in relation to the merger terms. Some actual merger data are given in the table below.

Calculate the percent premium, or discount, received by the acquired company, using market prices as the criterion. Compare the results of your calculations on the basis of the stock prices two quarters previous with that of your results on the basis of the prices immediately preceding the merger. Which is the proper measure of the actual discount or premium received: the one indicated by the earlier stock prices or the one indicated by the stock prices immediately preceding the merger? Explain.

	Company	Terms	Market price two quarters before merger		Market price immediately preceding merger	
			A	B	A	B
1	A Celanese Corporation B Champlain Oil	2 shares of Celanese for every 3 shares of Champlain	62	34	67	42
2	A Cities Service Company B Tennessee Corporation	0.9 shares (2.25 pref.) for each Tenn. Corp. share (common)	65	48	61	55
3	A Ford Motor Company B Philco Corporation	1 share of Ford for every $4\frac{1}{2}$ shares of Philco	81	22	113	25
4	A General Telephone B Sylvania Electric	Share-for-share basis	52	46	69	69

24.8 To meet its growth objectives, Proxmore Manufacturing is planning to expand by acquisition. It has two potential candidates, Apex Corporation and Allied Engineering. The latest balance sheet for Proxmore and the latest income statements for Apex and Allied are given below, along with certain other statistical information. Both Apex and Allied have debt of \$50 million, at a before-tax cost of 10 percent. Assume that the weighted average cost of capital is 10 percent for Proxmore, 8 percent for Apex, and 12 percent for Allied. Assume also that the effective tax rate for all three companies is 40 percent.

Proxmore Manufacturing Balance Sheet as of December 31, 1981 (thousands of dollars)

Current assets	$125,000	Current liabilities	$ 50,000
Net fixed assets	150,000	Long-term debt (at 10%)	75,000
		Common equity	150,000
Total	$275,000	Total	$275,000

Income Statement for the Year Ending December 31, 1981 (thousands of dollars)

	Apex	Allied
NOI	$20,000	$30,000
Interest on debt (at 10%)	5,000	5,000
Earnings before taxes	15,000	25,000
Less tax at 40%	6,000	10,000
Net income	$ 9,000	$15,000

	NOI	EPS	Growth rate (percent)	Market price	Shares outstanding
Proxmore	$32.5M	$3.00	6.0	$45	5,000,000
Apex	20M	4.50	7.5	50	2,000,000
Allied	30M	5.00	2.0	42	3,000,000

a. Based on the above information, determine an appropriate price for Proxmore to pay for each acquisition candidate. Proxmore uses its own weighted average cost of capital in computing the value of an acquisition candidate by capitalizing NOI after tax.

b. Compute the price of each acquisition candidate, using each candidate's own weighted average cost of capital as the capitalization rate.

c. Which capitalization rate is most appropriate in determining the value of an acquisition candidate?

d. Given that Proxmore is forced to make a tender offer for the common stock of each of the two candidates at 20 percent above their current market value, compute the following:
   1. The exchange ratio based on a stock offering
   2. Proxmore's new earnings growth rate for next year after the acquisition of each company—Apex and Allied
   3. Proxmore's new EPS following each acquisition

e. Chart Proxmore's growth in EPS for the next ten years with and without each acquisition to illustrate the dilution effect of the purchase price computed in Part d.

APPENDIX 24A

FINANCIAL ACCOUNTING POLICIES IN MERGERS

After merger terms have been agreed upon, the financial manager must be familiar with the accounting principles for recording the financial results of the merger and for reflecting the initial effect on the earnings of the surviving firm. The financial statements of the survivor in a merger must follow the SEC's regulations. These regulations follow the recommendations of professional accounting societies on combinations, but interpretations of actual situations require much financial and economic analysis.

On August 2, 1970, the eighteen-member Accounting Principles Board (APB) of the American Institute of Certified Public Accountants issued Opinion 16 dealing with guidelines for corporate mergers and Opinion 17 dealing with goodwill arising from mergers. The recommendations, which became effective October 31, 1970, modify and elaborate previous pronouncements on the pooling of interests and purchase methods of accounting for business combinations. For reasons that will become clear later in this section, corporate managements generally prefer pooling. Six broad tests are used to determine whether the conditions for the pooling of interest treatment are met. If all of them are met, then the combination is, in a sense, a merger among equals, and the *pooling of interests* method can be employed. The six tests are:

1. The acquired firm's stockholders must maintain an ownership position in the surviving firm.
2. The basis for accounting for the assets of the acquired entity must remain unchanged.
3. Independent interests must be combined, each entity must have had autonomy for two years prior to the initiation of the plan to combine, and no more than 10 percent ownership of voting common stock can be held as intercorporate investments.
4. The combination must be effected in a single transaction; contingent payouts are not permitted in poolings but can be used in purchases.
5. The acquiring corporation must issue only common stock with rights identical to its outstanding voting common stock in exchange for substantially all the voting common stock of the other company (*substantially* is defined as 90 percent).
6. The combined entity must not intend to dispose of a significant portion of the assets of the combining companies within two years after the merger.

In contrast, a *purchase* involves (1) new owners; (2) an appraisal of the acquired firm's physical assets and a restatement of the balance sheet to reflect these new values; and (3) the possibility of an excess or deficiency of consideration given up vis-à-vis the book value of equity. Point 3 refers to the creation of goodwill. In a purchase, the excess of the purchase price paid over the book value (restated to reflect the appraisal value of physical assets) is set up as goodwill, and capital surplus is increased (or decreased) accordingly. In a pooling of interests, the combined total assets after the merger represent a simple sum of the asset contributions of the constituent companies.

In a *purchase,* if the acquiring firm pays more than the acquired net worth, the excess is associated either with tangible depreciable assets or with goodwill. Asset write-offs are deductible, but goodwill written off is not deductible for tax purposes, even though the new recommendations require that goodwill be written off over some reasonable period but no longer than forty years. This requires a write-off of at least 2.5 percent a year of the amount of goodwill arising from a purchase. Therefore, if a merger is treated as a purchase, reported profits will be lower than if it is handled as a pooling of interests. This is one of the reasons that pooling is popular among acquiring firms.

Previous to the issuance of APB Opinion 16, another stimulus to pooling was the opportunity to dispose of assets acquired at depreciated book values, selling them at their current values, and recording subsequent profits on sales of assets. Opinion 16 attempted to deal with this practice by the requirement that sales of

Table 24A.1 **Financial Treatment of a Purchase**

	Mammoth Company	Petty Company	Adjustments Debit	Adjustments Credit	Pro forma balance sheet
Assets					
Current assets	$ 80,000	$ 4,000			$ 84,000
Other assets	20,000	2,000			22,000
Net fixed assets	100,000	4,000			104,000
Goodwill			$54,000		54,000
Total assets	$200,000	$10,000			$264,000
Liabilities and Net Worth					
Current liabilities	$ 40,000	$ 4,000			$ 44,000
Long-term debt	20,000				20,000
Common stock	40,000	1,000	1,000	4,000	44,000
Capital surplus	20,000			56,000	76,000
Retained earnings	80,000	5,000	5,000		80,000
Total liabilities and net worth	$200,000	$10,000	$60,000	$60,000	$264,000
Explanation					
Par value per share, common stock	$4	$0.50			
Number of shares outstanding	10,000	2,000			
Book value per share	$14	$3			
Net income	$30,000	$2,000			
Earnings per share	$3	$1			
Price-earnings ratio	20 times	30 times			
Market value per share	$60	$30			

major portions of assets not be contemplated for at least two years after the merger has taken place. For example, suppose Firm A buys Firm B, exchanging stock worth $100 million for assets worth $100 million but carried at $25 million. After the merger, A could, before the change in rules, sell the acquired assets and report the difference between book value and the purchase price, or $75 million, as earned income. Thus mergers could be used in still another way to create an illusion of profits and growth.

Financial Treatment of a Purchase

The financial treatment of a purchase can best be explained by use of a hypothetical example.[1] The Mammoth Company has just purchased the Petty Company under an arrangement known as a *purchase*. The facts are as given in Table 24A.1, which also shows the financial treatment. The illustration conforms to the general nature of a purchase. Measured by total assets, the Mammoth Company is twenty times as large as Petty, while its total earnings are fifteen times as large. The terms of the purchase are one share of Mammoth for two shares of Petty, based on the prevailing market value of their shares of common stock. Thus, in terms of Mammoth's stock, Mammoth is giving to Petty's stockholders $30 of market value and $7 of book value for each share of Petty stock. Petty's market value is $30 a share, and its book value is $3 a share, for a total book value of equity of $6,000.[2] The total market value of Mammoth paid for Petty is $60,000. The goodwill involved can be calculated as follows:

Value given by Mammoth	$60,000
Book value of net worth of Petty purchased	6,000
Goodwill	$54,000

The $54,000 goodwill represents a debit in the adjustments column and is carried to the pro forma balance sheet. The pro forma balance sheet is obtained by simply adding the balance sheets of the constituent companies, together with adjustments.

A total value of $60,000 has been given by Mammoth for a book value of $6,000. This amount represents, in addition to the debt, a payment of $1,000 for the common stock of Petty, $5,000 for the retained earnings, and $54,000 for goodwill. The corresponding credit is the 1,000 shares of Mammoth given in the transaction at their par value of $4 a share, resulting in a credit of $4,000. The capital surplus of Mammoth is increased by $56,000 ($60,000 paid minus $4,000 increase in common stock). The net credit to the net worth accounts is $54,000, which balances the net debit to the asset accounts. When these adjustments are carried through to the pro forma balance sheet, total assets are increased from the uncombined total of

[1] The material in this section is technical and is generally covered in accounting courses.

[2] Under purchase accounting, the acquiring company "should allocate the cost of an acquired company to the assets acquired and liabilities assumed" (APB Opinion No. 16, p. 318, par. 87). A specific procedure is set forth. First, all identifiable assets acquired should be assigned a portion of the cost of the acquired company, normally equal to their fair (market or appraised) values at date of acquisition. Second, the excess of the cost of the acquired company over the sum of the amounts assigned to net assets should be recorded as goodwill. The sum of fair market values assigned may exceed the cost of the acquired company. If so, values otherwise assignable to noncurrent assets should be reduced by a proportionate part of the excess. If noncurrent assets are reduced to zero and some excess still remains, it should be set up as a deferred credit.

$210,000 to a new total of $264,000. Total tangible assets, however, still remain $210,000.

The effects on earnings per share for stockholders in each company are shown below:

Total earnings (before write-off of goodwill)	$32,000
Amortization of goodwill	1,350
Total net earnings	$30,650
Total shares	11,000
Earnings per share	$2.79
For Petty shareholders:	
New earnings per share	$1.40
Before-purchase earnings per old share	1.00
Accretion per share	$0.40
For Mammoth shareholders:	
Before-purchase earnings per share	$3.00
New earnings per share	2.79
Dilution per share	$0.21

Total earnings represent the combined earnings of Mammoth and Petty. Mammoth believes that the value reflected in goodwill will be permanent, but under APB Opinion 17, it is required to write off the goodwill account over a maximum of forty years. The annual charge of $1,350 is the goodwill of $54,000 divided by 40. The total amount of net earnings is therefore $30,650.

The total shares are 11,000 because Mammoth has given one share of stock for every two shares of Petty previously outstanding.[3] The new earnings per share are therefore $2.79. The calculation of earnings accretion or dilution proceeds on the same principles as the calculations set forth earlier. The results require two important comments, however.

Although the earnings accretion per share for Petty is 40 cents, the earnings dilution per share for Mammoth is relatively small, only 21 cents a share. The explanation is that the size of Mammoth is large in relation to that of Petty. This example also illustrates a general principle: When a large company acquires a small one, it can afford to pay a high multiple of earnings per share of the smaller company. In the present example, the price-earnings ratio of Petty is 30, whereas that of Mammoth is 20. If the acquiring company is large in relation to the acquired firm, it can pay the higher P-E ratio and yet suffer only small dilution in its earnings per share.

It is, however, unrealistic to assume that the same earnings on total assets will result after the merger. After all, the purpose of the merger is to achieve something that the two companies could not have achieved alone. When Philip Morris & Company purchased Benson & Hedges (the maker of Parliament, a leading filter-tip brand), it was buying the ability and experience of Benson & Hedges. By means of this merger, Philip Morris was able to make an entry into the rapidly growing filter cigarette business more quickly than it could otherwise have done. The combined earnings per share were expected to rise.

[3] After the one-for-two exchange, Petty shareholders have only half as many shares as before the merger.

In the Mammoth-Petty illustration, the earnings rate on the tangible assets of Mammoth is 15 percent and on the tangible assets of Petty 20 percent. Assume that the return on total tangible assets of the combined companies rises to 20 percent. The 20 percent of tangible assets of $210,000 equals $42,000; less the amortization of goodwill over forty years at $1,350 per year, the total is $40,650 net earnings. With the same total shares of 11,000 outstanding, the new earnings per share will be $3.70. Thus there will be an accretion of 85 cents for the Petty shareholders and an accretion of 70 cents for the Mammoth shareholders.

This illustrates another general principle: If the purchase of a small company adds to the earnings of the consolidated enterprise, earnings per share may increase for both participants in the merger. Even if the merger results in an initial dilution in earnings per share of the larger company, it may still be advantageous. The initial dilution can be regarded as an investment that will have a payoff at some future date in terms of increased growth in earnings per share of the consolidated company.

Treatment of Goodwill

In a purchase, goodwill is likely to arise; since it represents an intangible asset, its treatment is subject to the exercise of judgment. It will therefore be useful to set out a few generalizations on good practice in the treatment of goodwill.

1. When goodwill is purchased, it should not be charged to surplus immediately on acquisition. Instead it should be written off against income and should go through the income statement. Since goodwill is to be written off against income, it is not appropriate to write it off entirely on acquisition, because this will be of such magnitude that distortion of earnings for that year will result.
2. The general view is not to write off purchased goodwill by charges to capital surplus. Purchased goodwill is supposed to represent and to be reflected in a future rise of income. It should therefore be written off against income rather than against capital surplus.
3. When goodwill is purchased, an estimate should be made of its life. Annual charges based on the estimated life should then be made against income to amortize the goodwill over the estimated period of its usefulness.
4. Intangibles must be written off over a maximum of forty years, according to APB Opinion 17.

When goodwill is purchased, it should be treated like any other asset. It should be written off to the extent that the value represented by any part of it has a limited life, as is likely to be the situation. In a free enterprise economy, the existence of high profits represented by superior earning power attracts additional resources into that line of business. The growth of capacity and the increase in competition are likely to erode the superior earning power over time.

Financial Treatment of Pooling of Interests

When a business combination is a pooling of interests rather than a purchase, the accounting treatment is simply to combine the balance sheets of the two companies. Goodwill will not ordinarily arise in the consolidation.

The financial treatment can be indicated by another example, which reflects the facts as they are set forth in Table 24A.2. In order to focus on the critical issues, the balance sheets are identical in every respect. However, a difference in the amount and rate of profit after interest of the two companies is indicated.

Book value per share is $10. The amount of profit after interest and taxes is $42,000 for Company A and $21,000 for Company B. Earnings per share are therefore $3.50 and $1.75, respectively. The price-earnings ratio is 18 for A and 12 for B, so the market price of stock is $63 for A and $21 for B. The net working capital per share is $4.17 in each instance. The dividends per share are $1.75 for A and $0.875 for B. Assume that the terms of the merger will reflect either (1) earnings or (2) market price per share. In both cases it is assumed that A is the acquiring and surviving firm. If A buys B on the basis of earnings, it exchanges half a share of A's common stock for one share of B's common stock. The total number of shares of A common

Table 24A.2 **Financial Treatment of Pooling of Interests**

	Company A	Company B	Net adjustments on A's books: Debit	Net adjustments on A's books: Credit	Acquiring Company A's new balance sheets and earnings if the exchange basis is: Earnings 2/1	Price 3/1
Current assets	$100,000	$100,000			$200,000	$200,000
Fixed assets	100,000	100,000			200,000	200,000
Total assets	$200,000	$200,000			$400,000	$400,000
Current liabilities	$ 50,000	$ 50,000			$100,000	$100,000
Long-term debt	30,000	30,000			60,000	60,000
Total debt	80,000	80,000			160,000	160,000
Common stock, par value $5	60,000	60,000	$30,000[a]		90,000	
			$40,000[b]			80,000
Capital surplus	50,000	50,000		$30,000[a]	130,000	
				$40,000[b]		140,000
Retained earnings	10,000	10,000			20,000	20,000
Total claims on assets	$200,000	$200,000			$400,000	$400,000
			Ratios A/B			
Number of shares of stock	12,000	12,000			18,000	16,000
Book value	$10	$10	1.0			
Amount of profit after interest and taxes	$42,000	$21,000			$63,000	$63,000
Earnings per share	$3.50	$1.75	2.0		$3.50	$3.94
Price-earnings ratio	18	12				
Market price of stock	$63	$21	3.0			
Net working capital per share	$4.17	$4.17	1.0			
Dividends per share	$1.75	$0.875	2.0			
Shareholders' new EPS:						
Company A					$3.50	$3.94
Company B					$1.75	$1.31

[a] 2/1 ratio basis.
[b] 3/1 ratio basis.

stock that will be outstanding after the acquisition is 18,000, of which 6,000 will be held by the old stockholders of B. The new earnings per share in the now larger Firm A will be the total earnings of $63,000 divided by 18,000, which equals $3.50 per share. Thus the earnings for A remain unchanged. The old shareholders of B now hold half a share of A for each share of B held before the acquisition. Hence, their equivalent earnings per share from their present holdings of A shares are $1.75, the same as before the acquisition. The stockholders of both A and B have experienced no earnings dilution or accretion.

When the terms of exchange are based on market price per share, the terms of acquisition will be the exchange of one-third share of A stock for one share of B stock. The number of A shares is increased by the 4,000 exchanged for the 12,000 shares of B. The combined earnings of $63,000 are divided by 16,000 shares to obtain an increase in A's earnings per share to $3.94, which represents an earnings accretion of 44 cents per share for the A shareholders. The old B shareholders now hold one-third share of A for each share of B held before the acquisition. Their equivalent earnings are now $3.94 divided by 3, or $1.31, representing an earnings dilution of 44 cents per share.

The adjustment to the common stock account in surviving Firm A's balance sheet reflects the fact that only 6,000 shares of A are used to buy 12,000 shares of B when the acquisition is made on the basis of earnings. The net decrease of 6,000 shares times the par value of $5 requires a net debit of $30,000 to the common stock account of A ($60,000 + $60,000 − $30,000 = $90,000), with an offsetting increase of $30,000 in the capital surplus account of Firm A ($50,000 + $50,000 + $30,000 = $130,000). When the exchange is made on the basis of market values, only 4,000 shares of A are needed to acquire the 12,000 shares of B. Hence, the net decrease of 8,000 shares in the combined common stock account is $40,000, with an offsetting increase of the same amount in A's capital surplus.

The general principle is that when the terms of merger are based on the market price per share, and the price-earnings ratios of the two companies are different, earnings accretion and dilution will occur. The company with a higher P-E ratio will have earnings accretion; the company with the lower P-E ratio will suffer earnings dilution. If the sizes of the companies are greatly different, the effect on the larger company will be relatively small, whether in dilution or accretion. The effect on the smaller company will be relatively large.

Problems

24A.1 The Vorno Company has just acquired the Hondo Company in an exchange of stock, treating it as a purchase for merger accounting. Vorno paid a 20 percent premium over the market price of Hondo. Data on the two companies are given below.

a. Fill in the blanks, complete the adjustments and pro forma balance sheet columns, and show the journal entries for the stock purchase. Explain your journal entries.

b. Assuming that total earnings are unchanged, calculate whether earnings dilution or accretion occurs for each company.

c. Do the same on the assumption that earnings available to common stock rise to $160,000 for the combined company.

	Vorno	Hondo	Adjustments Debit	Adjustments Credit	Pro forma balance sheet
1. Current assets	$ 450,000	$ 7,000			______
2. Other assets	150,000	5,000			______
3. Fixed assets	400,000	13,000			______
4. Intangibles				______	______
Total assets	$1,000,000	$25,000			______
5. Current liabilities	200,000	10,000			______
6. Long-term debt	150,000	—			______
7. Common stock	200,000	5,000		______	______
8. Capital surplus	150,000	—		______	______
9. Retained earnings	300,000	10,000		______	______
Total claims	$1,000,000	$25,000			______
Par value	$5.00	$0.50			
Number of shares	______	______			
Earnings available to common stock	$120,000	$10,000			
Book value PER share	______	______			
Earnings per share	______	______			
Price/earnings ratio	10X	25X			
Market price per share	______	______			

24A.2 You are given the following data on two companies:

	Company I	Company II	Adjustments	Consolidated statement
Current assets	$56,000	$56,000		______
Fixed assets	34,000	34,000		______
Total assets	$90,000	$90,000		______
Current liabilities	$31,000	$31,000		______
Long-term debt	19,000	19,000		______
Total debt, 5%[a]	$50,000	$50,000		______
Common stock, par value $4	24,000	24,000	______	______
Capital surplus	11,000	11,000	______	______
Retained earnings	5,000	5,000	______	______
Total claims on assets	$90,000	$90,000		______

	Company I	Company II	Ratios			
1. Number of shares of stock	6,000	6,000			1.	______
2. Book value per share	______	______	1.	______	2.	______
3. Amount of profit before interest and taxes[b]	$24,583	$12,917			3.	______
4. Earnings per share	______	______	2.	______	4.	______
5. Price-earnings ratio	22.6	12				
6. Market price of stock	______	______	3.	______		
7. Working capital per share	______	______	4.	______		
8. Dividends per share, 50% payout	______	______	5.	______		
9. Exchange ratio	______	______	6.	______ (I/II)		
10. Equivalent earnings per old share	______	______				

[a] Average rate on interest bearing and non-interest bearing debt combined

[b] Assume a 40 percent tax rate

a. In your judgment, what would be a reasonable basis for determining the terms at which shares in Company I and in Company II would be exchanged for shares in a new company, III? What exchange ratio would you recommend and why?
b. Use the market price of stock relation as the basis for the terms of exchange of stock in the old company for stock in the new company (two shares of III for one share of I, and one-half share of III for one share of II). Then complete the calculations for filling in all the blank spaces, including the adjustments for making the consolidated statement. Treat this problem as a situation that the SEC and accountants would refer to as a pooling of interests.

CHAPTER 25

REORGANIZATION AND BANKRUPTCY

Thus far the text has dealt with issues associated mainly with the growing, successful enterprise. Not all businesses are so fortunate, however; so this chapter will examine financial difficulties—their causes and their possible remedies. The material is significant for the financial manager of successful, as well as potentially unsuccessful, firms. The successful firm's financial manager must know the firm's rights and remedies as a creditor and must participate effectively in efforts to collect from financially distressed debtors. The financial manager of a less successful firm must know how to handle the firm's affairs if financial difficulties arise. Such understanding can often mean the difference between loss of ownership of the firm and rehabilitation of the firm as a going enterprise.

Bankruptcy law in the United States underwent considerable change in 1979. The new 1979 law combines the procedures of Chapters X and XI of the previous laws into a single procedure. To understand the present bankruptcy law therefore requires a review of the previous procedures, which were modified and combined.

Some dramatic major bankruptcies have occurred in recent years. Most notable was the huge Penn Central Company, which involved total assets at the end of 1969 of almost $7 billion and total debts outstanding of over $4 billion. The W. T. Grant bankruptcy was also of substantial magnitude, involving $1.2 billion of assets. A number of bankruptcies have raised questions of impropriety. Illustrative is the Equity Funding Company bankruptcy, which involved writing up fictitious life insurance.

The instabilities of the early 1970s involved large commercial banks as well as nonfinancial enterprises. The Franklin National Bank, which failed in 1974, had reached an asset size of $5 billion and was the twentieth largest of the nation's more than 14,000 FDIC-insured banks. In the same year, the Beverly Hills Bancorp went into bankruptcy. Earlier, the U.S. National Bank of San Diego had to be taken over by the FDIC, and questions of fraud were raised in connection with its prior management. Even large foreign banks ran into difficulties in 1974. The failure of Bankhaus I. D. Herstatt, one of Germany's largest private banks, sent shock waves through the international money markets.

Failure

Failure can be defined in several ways, and some failures do not necessarily result in the collapse and dissolution of a firm.

Economic Failure

Failure in an economic sense usually signifies that a firm's revenues do not cover its costs. It can also mean that the rate of earnings on its historical cost of investment is less than the firm's cost of capital. It can even mean that the firm's actual returns have fallen below its expected returns. There is no consensus on the definition of failure in an economic sense.

Financial Failure

Although *financial failure* is a less ambiguous term than *economic failure,* it has two generally recognized aspects. A firm can be considered a failure if it cannot meet its current obligations as they fall due, even though its total assets may exceed its total liabilities. This is defined as *technical insolvency*. A firm is a failure, or *bankrupt*, if its total liabilities exceed a fair valuation of its total assets (that is, if the "real" net worth of the firm is negative).

Hereafter, when the word *failure* is used, it will mean both technical insolvency and bankruptcy.

Causes of Failures

Different studies assign the causes of failure to different factors. Dun & Bradstreet compilations assign these causes as follows.

Causes of failure, 1979	Percentage of total
Management incompetence	44.4
Lack of managerial experience	16.8
Unbalanced experience in sales, finance, production and the like	15.8
Lack of experience in line	14.9
Neglect	1.1
Disaster	0.6
Fraud	0.6
Reason unknown	5.8
Total	100.0

Source: Data from *The Business Failure Record* (New York: Dun & Bradstreet, 1981), p. 12. Used by permission of Dun & Bradstreet.

A number of other studies of failures can be generalized into the following groups.[1]

Cause of failure	Percentage of total
Management incompetence	60
Unfavorable industry trends	20
Catastrophes	10
Miscellaneous	10
Total	100

Both classifications include the effects of recessions but place the resulting failures in the category of managerial incompetence. This method is logical; managements should be prepared to operate in environments in which recessions occur and should frame their policies to cope with downturns as well as to benefit from

[1] See studies referred to in A. S. Dewing, *The Financial Policy of Corporations,* vol. 2, Book V (New York: Ronald Press, 1953), pp. 1265–81.

business upswings. Managements also should anticipate unfavorable industry trends.

A number of financial remedies are available to management when it becomes aware of the imminence or occurrence of insolvency. These remedies are described in subsequent sections.

The Failure Record

How widespread is business failure?[2] Is it a rare phenomenon, or does it occur fairly often? In recent times, about 10,000 to 12,000 firms a year have failed, but they represent less than one-half of 1 percent of all business firms. The failure rate rises during recession periods, when the economy is weakened and credit is tightened. (Among the large and well-known companies that went bankrupt during the 1970s were the Penn Central Transportation Company, Dolly Madison Industries, Four Seasons Nursing Centers, King Resources Company, Farrington Manufacturing Company, and W. T. Grant.)

Often, mergers or government intervention are arranged as alternatives to outright bankruptcy. Thus, in recent years, the Federal Home Loan Bank System has arranged the mergers of several very large "problem" savings and loan associations into sound institutions, and the Federal Reserve System has done the same thing for banks. Several government agencies, principally the U.S. Department of Defense, arranged to bail out Lockheed in 1970 to keep it from failing. The merger of Douglas Aircraft and McDonnell in the late 1960s was designed to prevent Douglas's failure. Similar instances could be cited for the securities brokerage industry in the late 1960s and early 1970s. In 1980 and 1981, loan guarantees were made by the federal government to keep credit flowing to Chrysler Corporation in the effort to keep it in business.

Why do government and industry seek to prevent the bankruptcy of larger firms? Three of the many reasons are (1) to prevent an erosion of confidence (in the case of financial institutions), (2) to maintain a viable supplier, and (3) to avoid disrupting a local community. Also, bankruptcy is an expensive process; so even when the public interest is not at stake, private industry has strong incentives to prevent it.

Extension and Composition

Extension and composition are discussed together because they both represent voluntary concessions by creditors. *Extension* postpones the date of required payment of past-due obligations. *Composition* voluntarily reduces the creditors' claims on the debtor. Both are intended to keep the debtor in business and to avoid court costs. Although creditors must absorb a temporary loss, the debtor's rehabilitation is often greater than if one of the formal procedures had been followed; and the hope is that a stable customer will emerge with long-run benefits to the creditors.

Procedure

A meeting of the debtor and the creditors is held. At the meeting, the creditors appoint a committee consisting of four or five of the largest creditors and one or two of the smaller ones. The meeting is typically arranged and conducted by an

[2] This section draws from Edward I. Altman, *Corporate Bankruptcy in America* (Lexington, Mass.: Heath Lexington Books, 1972), pp. 19–24.

adjustment bureau associated with the local credit managers' association or by a trade association.

After the first meeting, if it is judged that the case can be worked out, the bureau assigns investigators to make an exhaustive report. The bureau and the creditors' committee use the facts of the report to formulate a plan for adjustment of the claims. Another meeting between the debtor and the creditors is then held in an attempt to work out an extension or composition, or a combination of the two. Subsequent meetings may be required to reach final agreements.

Necessary Conditions

At least three conditions are usually necessary to make an extension or a composition feasible:

1. The debtor must be a good moral risk, in the sense of seeking to honor obligations and not diverting the business's assets to personal use and advantage.
2. The debtor must show ability to make a recovery.
3. General business conditions must be favorable to recovery.

Extension

Creditors prefer an extension because it provides for payment in full. The debtor buys current purchases on a cash basis and pays off the past-due balance over an extended time. In some cases, creditors may agree not only to extend the time of payment but also to subordinate existing claims to new debts incurred in favor of vendors extending credit during the period of the extension.

Of course, the creditors must have faith that the debtor will solve the problems. But because of the uncertainties involved, they will want to exercise controls over the debtor while waiting for their claims to be paid. For example, the creditors' committee may insist that an assignment of assets be executed, to be held in escrow in case of default. If the debtor is a corporation, the committee may require that stockholders transfer their stock certificates into an escrow account until the repayment called for under the extension has been completed. The committee may also designate a representative to countersign all checks, and it may obtain security in the form of notes, mortgages, or assignment of accounts receivable.

Composition

In a composition, a pro rata cash settlement is made. Creditors receive from the debtor a uniform percentage of the obligations—in cash. The cash received is taken as full settlement of the debt, even though the ratio may be as low as 10 percent. Bargaining occurs between the debtor and the creditors over the savings that result from avoiding bankruptcy: administration costs, legal fees, investigating costs, and so on. In addition to avoiding these costs, the debtor avoids the stigma of bankruptcy and thus may be induced to part with most of the savings that result from avoiding the bankruptcy.

Combination Settlement

Often the bargaining process results in a compromise involving both an extension and a composition. For example, the settlement may provide for a cash payment of 25 percent of the debt and six future installments of 10 percent each. Total payment thereby aggregates to 85 percent. Installment payments are usually evidenced by notes, and creditors also seek protective controls.

Appraisal of Voluntary Settlements

The advantages of voluntary settlements are informality and simplicity. Investigative, legal, and administrative expenses are held to a minimum. The procedure is the most economical and results in the largest return to creditors.

One possible disadvantage is that the debtor is left in control of the business. This situation may involve legal complications or erosion of assets still operated by the debtor. However, numerous controls are available to give the creditors protection.

A second disadvantage is that small creditors may take a nuisance role in that they may insist on payment in full. As a consequence, settlements typically provide for payment in full for claims under $50 or $100. If a composition is involved, and all claims under $50 are paid, all creditors will receive a base of $50 plus the agreed-on percentage of the balance of their claims.

Reorganization in General

Reorganization is a form of extension or composition of the firm's obligations. However, the legal formalities are much more involved than the procedures thus far described. Regardless of the legal procedure followed, reorganization processes have several features in common:

1. The firm is insolvent either because it is unable to meet cash obligations as they come due or because claims on the firm exceed its assets. Hence, some modifications in the nature or amount of the firm's obligations must be made. A scaling down of terms or amounts must be formulated. This procedure may represent scaling down fixed charges or converting short-term debt into long-term debt.
2. New funds must be raised for working capital and for property rehabilitation.
3. The operating and managerial causes of difficulty must be discovered and eliminated.

The procedures involved in effecting a reorganization are highly legalistic and, in fact, thoroughly understood only by attorneys who specialize in bankruptcy and reorganization. This section will therefore discuss only the general principles involved.

In essence, a reorganization is a composition, a scaling down of claims. In any composition, two conditions must be met:

1. The scaling down must be fair to all parties.
2. In return for the sacrifices, successful rehabilitation and profitable future operation of the firm must be feasible.

These are the standards of fairness and feasibility, which are analyzed further in the next section.

Financial Decisions in Reorganization

When a business becomes insolvent, a decision must be made whether to dissolve the firm through liquidation or to keep it alive through reorganization. Fundamentally, this decision depends on a determination of the value of the firm if it is rehabilitated versus the value of the sum of the parts if it is dismembered.

Liquidation values depend on the degree of specialization of the capital assets used in the firm and, hence, their resale value. In addition, liquidation itself involves costs of dismantling, including legal costs. Of course, successful reorganization also involves costs. Typically, better equipment must be installed, obsolete inventories must be disposed of, and improvements in management must be made. Often the greater indicated value of the firm in reorganization compared with its value in liquidation is used to force a compromise agreement among the claimants, even when they feel that their relative position has not been treated fairly in the reorganization plan.

Both the SEC and the courts are called upon to determine the fairness and feasibility of proposed plans of reorganization.[3] In developing standards of fairness in connection with such reorganizations, the courts and the SEC have adhered to two precedent-setting court decisions.[4]

Standards of Fairness

The basic doctrine of fairness states that claims must be recognized in the order of their legal and contractual priority. Junior claimants such as common stockholders can participate only to the extent that they make an additional cash contribution to the reorganization of the firm.

Carrying out this concept of fairness involves the following steps:

1. An estimate of future sales must be made.
2. An analysis of operating conditions must be made so that the future earnings on sales can be estimated.
3. A determination of the capitalization rate to be applied to these future earnings must be made.
4. The capitalization rate must be applied to the estimated future earnings to obtain an indicated value of the company's properties.
5. Provision for distribution to the claimants must be made.

Example of Reorganization and Standards of Fairness

The meaning and content of these procedures can be set out by the use of an actual example of reorganization—that of R. Hoe and Company, Inc.[5] The company was incorporated in 1909 and went public in 1924. Principally involved in the production of printing presses and saws and other woodcutting products, the company operated successfully until after 1965.[6]

At that point sales began growing at an accelerating rate. The rapid growth of sales and profits was accompanied by a rise in the price of Hoe common stock from $2 per share in 1965 to $48 per share in 1968. But the rapid sales growth put

[3] The federal bankruptcy laws specify that reorganization plans be worked out by court-appointed officials and be reviewed by the SEC.

[4] *Case* v. *Los Angeles Lumber Products Co.*, 308 U.S. 106 (1939) and *Consolidated Rock Products Co.* v. *du Boise*, 213 U.S. 510 (1940). *Securities and Exchange Commission, Seventeenth Annual Report* (Washington, D.C.: Government Printing Office, 1951), p. 130.

[5] This material is based on the *Securities and Exchange Commission Corporate Reorganization Release No. 319*, September 8, 1976.

[6] The early presses were made of wood, and R. Hoe began to manufacture saws to cut the wood.

a strain on the company's working capital. To remedy this, the firm issued new common stock in 1967 and 1968. In April 1969 it arranged additional financing in the form of a loan at high interest from James Talcott, Inc.

By this point the situation had already begun to deteriorate. Despite the new capital, Hoe continued having difficulty meeting its obligations. Not long after the loan from Talcott, the American Stock Exchange (ASE) suspended trading of Hoe stock because the company had failed to file audited financial statements for the previous year on a timely basis. Subsequently, Hoe reported a decline in earnings for 1968 and a loss for the first quarter of 1969. Trade creditors reacted by demanding payment on past-due accounts before shipping new supplies. The withdrawal of trade credit resulted in Hoe filing a petition on July 7, 1969, to reorganize under Chapter X of the Bankruptcy Act.

The bankruptcy trustee who was appointed was forced to deal with some urgent problems. Immediate working capital needs to continue the saw operation were met by renegotiation of contracts with printing press customers. The press operation was based on job orders from customers; but, because of the bankruptcy, no new orders were being received. By October 18, 1974, the trustee had formulated and then filed with the court a reorganization plan that was subsequently analyzed by the SEC. By court order, in 1975 the press business was sold for stock and notes to Wood Industries (a public company), and the loan from Talcott was settled for about $1 million.

Table 25.1

R. Hoe and Company, Inc.,
Balance Sheet as of December 31, 1975
(thousands of dollars)

Assets		Liabilities	
Cash and equivalents	$ 3,139	Current liabilities	$ 483
Receivables	925	Debts granted administration status	148
Inventory	3,476	Priority claims (taxes and wages)	390
Net plant	1,307	Unsecured claims	8,719
Investment in Wood Industries, Inc.	633	Total liabilities	$ 9,740
Other assets unrelated to saw division operations	826	Class A stock (436,604 shares, $15 liquidating value)	6,549
		Dividends in arrears on Class A stock	5,392
		Common stock (1,933,462 shares outstanding)	781
		Retained earnings deficit	−12,156
		Total stockholder equity	566
Total assets	$10,306	Total liabilities and equity	$10,306

Table 25.1 shows the R. Hoe balance sheet as of December 31, 1975—after settlement of the court orders. The trustee proposed an internal plan of reorganization under which Hoe would continue to operate the saw manufacturing business. New capitalization would consist only of 2.87 million shares of common stock. The

Table 25.2 **R. Hoe and Company, Inc., Trustee Valuation and Plan (thousands of dollars)**

Valuation

Going concern value of saw division		$ 9,688
Excess cash		2,609
Excess inventory		—
Nonoperating assets at present value		1,958
Value of tax loss carry-forward		2,840
Gross amount available for claims		$17,095
Less trustee administrative costs		2,000
Available for claims after trustee costs		$15,095
Priority claims paid in cash:		
Debts granted administrative status	$148	
Priority claims	390	
Interest on priority claims	215	
Total paid in cash		753
Available for remainder of claims		$14,342

Plan (Remainder of Claims Based on Shares Valued at $5)

		New shares		
	Amount of claims	Number of shares	Value	Percent of shares
Unsecured claims	$ 8,719			
Interest on unsecured claims	4,190			
Total	$12,909	2,581,800	$12,909	90%
Class A stockholders (436,604 shares)	11,941	286,600	1,433	10
Total value	$24,850	2,868,400	$14,342	100%

plan was based on a valuation of the firm at $15,095,000, payable to all creditors and to Class A stockholders. The valuation and plan are detailed in Table 25.2

All priority claims and trustee fees were to be paid in full with cash. Unsecured claims consisting primarily of current liabilities that existed prior to bankruptcy would receive one share of common stock for each $5 of claims. Class A stockholders would receive one share for each 1.523 shares of existing stock. Common stockholders would receive nothing, since the value of the firm was insufficient to meet creditors' claims, and Class A stock had a liquidation preference of $15 per share plus dividends in arrears.

In evaluating the proposal from the standpoint of fairness, the Securities and Exchange Commission began with an analysis of the prospective value of the company (Table 25.3). The SEC evaluated it at $2.3 million higher than the trustee had—primarily because of differences in beliefs about working capital needs and the going concern value of the firm. To determine going concern value, the trustee had used a P-E ratio of 11; but the SEC felt 12 would be more appropriate. The SEC also estimated future annual income at slightly higher than the trustee's estimate—$900,000 compared to $880,000.

Table 25.3

**R. Hoe and Company, Inc.,
SEC Evaluation of Fairness
(thousands of dollars)**

Valuation	Trustee valuation	SEC valuation
Going concern value of saw division	$9,688	$10,800
Excess cash	2,609	3,475
Excess inventory	—	1,000
Nonoperating assets at present value	1,958	1,536
Value of tax loss carry-forward	2,840	2,470
Gross amount available for claims	$17,095	$19,281
Less trust administration costs	2,000	1,848
Net value	$15,095	$17,433

Because of these differences, the SEC felt that the trustee's plan did not meet the standard of fairness. It therefore proposed an amended plan, under which the allocation to Class A stockholders would be increased, and unsecured creditors would receive one share of new common stock for each $5 value of claims (a total of 2.58 million shares)—the same as under the trustee's plan. (See Table 25.4.) The allocation to Class A stockholders was increased because of the SEC's higher estimated value of the firm. Under the new plan, Class A stockholders would receive one share for each 0.579 shares of their Class A stock. Again, common stockholders would receive nothing, since the value of the firm was insufficient to meet even the preferential claims.

Table 25.4

**SEC Amended Plan
(thousands of dollars)**

		New shares		
	Amount of claim	Number of shares	Value	Percent of shares
Unsecured claims:				
Principal	$ 8,719			
Interest	4,190			
Total	$12,909	2,581,800	$12,909	77%
Class A stockholders:				
436,604 shares	$11,941	754,200	3,771	23
Total value	$24,850	3,336,000	$16,680	100%

Note: Priority claims of $753,000 were to be paid as per the trustee's plan.

Standard of Feasibility

The primary test of feasibility is that the fixed charges on the income of the corporation after reorganization are amply covered by earnings or, if a value is established for a firm that is to be sold, that a buyer can be found at that price. Adequate coverage of fixed charges for a company that is to continue in operation generally requires an improvement in earnings, a reduction of fixed charges, or both.

Among the actions that have to be taken to improve the earning power of the company are the following:

1. Where the management has been inefficient and inadequate for the task, new talents and abilities must be brought into the company.
2. If inventories have become obsolete, they must be disposed of and the operations of the company streamlined.
3. Sometimes the plant and the equipment of the firm must be modernized before it can operate and compete successfully on a cost basis.
4. Reorganization may also require an improvement in production, marketing, advertising, and other functions to enable the firm to compete successfully.
5. It is sometimes necessary to develop new products so the firm can move from areas where economic trends have become undesirable into areas where the growth and stability potential is greater.

Application of Feasibility Tests

Referring again to R. Hoe and Company, the SEC observed that the company's failure had come about as the result of management attempts to expand the company faster than prudent working capital management would permit. With the sale of the printing press division by court order in 1975, the firm was left with the profitable saw division.

In the SEC's judgment, the critical element in the viability of the saw division was sufficient cash to carry out the SEC's plan and to provide adequate working capital. Under this plan, it was hoped that Hoe would emerge from Chapter X with normal current liabilities incident to its business and a simple and conservative capital structure, consisting only of current liabilities and common stock. Based on the December 31, 1975, balance sheet in Table 25.1, cash and equivalents would be $3,139,000 minus the $753,000 paid to priority claims, or a total of $2,386,000. This is nearly five times the $483,000 level of then-current liabilities.

The case study of R. Hoe and Company is a description of Chapter X proceedings. Proceedings under Chapter X were developed for large corporations with public investors in the bonds and common stock of the firm. In summary, a petition may be filed by the corporation to bring about a reorganization, or the petition can be filed by three or more creditors with claims aggregating $5,000 or over. A trustee, whose functions have been described, must be appointed by the court if liabilities involved exceed $250,000. The absolute priority rule must be followed so that senior creditors must be fully compensated before junior creditors and stockholders.

From the creditors' viewpoint, Chapter X proceedings are very inflexible and time-consuming. The operating control of the debtor firm is placed in a court-appointed trustee who sometimes does not have the technical knowledge to operate the debtor company successfully. Thus, creditors will suffer losses if the debtor company loses customers and operating efficiency under the trustee arrangement.

Chapter XI Proceedings

In contrast, Chapter XI proceedings are more flexible and informal. Chapter XI proceedings were devised for use with small corporations, partnerships, or individuals in cases involving no public participation in the financing or ownership of the firm. In Chapter XI proceedings, the debtor automatically receives the status of debtor in possession. Even after a bankruptcy referee is appointed by the court, the referee may grant an order of continuance which enables the debtor to continue operating the business. The referee can enjoin the creditors from legal action to recover debts by obtaining preference over other creditors and by property foreclosure. Payment schedules are worked out between the debtor and creditors, presented to the refereee for approval, and ultimately paid out to the creditors. From the creditors' standpoint, Chapter XI proceedings are much less time consuming. The debtors in possession have the opportunity to remain in control of the business, in the hope that they will be more successful than outsiders in reviving the firm and repaying its debts. Creditors are able to exert influence on the debtors. The creditors may even continue to grant credit to the debtor in helping the indebted firm achieve profitability again.

The New Bankruptcy Law

Under the bankruptcy law that became effective in 1979, Chapters X and XI are blended into a single procedure. Cases can be initiated on either a voluntary or involuntary basis. Involuntary petitions must be commenced only under Chapter VII, which deals with liquidation, or Chapter XI, which deals with reorganization. The debtor company remains in possession of its business and continues to operate it unless the court orders otherwise. Under a Chapter VII liquidation case, the court may appoint an interim trustee to operate the business to avoid loss. The debtor, however, may regain possession from the trustee by filing an appropriate bond as required by the court. The trustee has very broad powers and discretion if so authorized by the court. The trustee may retain or replace management as well as augment management with additional professionals. The trustee may also obtain additional financing on an unsecured credit basis.

The consolidated approach under the new bankruptcy law eliminates disputes over whether Chapter X or XI will be used. This speeds up the proceedings, reduces costs, and (it is hoped) shortens the time until the firm is operating profitably again. Since the debtor remains in control of the operations of the business, informal negotiations between the debtor company, the creditors, and the stockholders become more feasible. The absolute priority rule is relaxed under the new law. Negotiations may provide for a restructuring of debt involving rescaling (reducing the amount of obligations that will have to be paid) or time extensions (postponing the required payment dates for all or part of the obligations). Hence, claims from unsecured creditors and stockholders have an increased probability of realizing cash or receiving some contingent claims on the reorganized companies. If it can be established that claimants will receive as much as they would under a straight liquidation program, a reorganization plan can be approved by a vote of the parties who would be affected by it.

Since management will continue to be in control, the debtor and the large prime creditors will dominate the reorganization. Sometimes this means institutions such as banks and insurance companies will dominate the proceedings. It is said that the SEC loses a strong weapon under the new consolidated procedure. Formerly, the threat to convert a Chapter XI to a Chapter X made debtors and large creditors willing to make concessions to avoid such a conversion. Under the new bankruptcy law, the SEC can still sue to have a trustee appointed. However, to be successful in such a suit apparently will require demonstrating management incompetence.

Overall, the new bankruptcy law with respect to business firms provides for greater flexibility in the procedures. Greater flexibility avoids rigid processes that can often be very expensive and time consuming. On the other hand, greater flexibility may provide opportunities for increased leverage by some of the parties involved, and this may be to the detriment of other parties. Until we have more actual experience with the new bankruptcy law, it is not possible to make a definitive evaluation of its effectiveness.

Liquidation Procedures

Liquidation of a business occurs when the firm is worth more dead than alive. Assignment is a liquidation procedure that does not go through the courts, although it can be used to achieve full settlement of claims on the debtor. Bankruptcy is a legal procedure, carried out under the jurisdiction of special courts, in which a firm is formally liquidated and creditors' claims are completely discharged.

Assignment

Assignment (as well as bankruptcy) takes place when the debtor is insolvent and the possibility of restoring profitability is so remote that the enterprise should be dissolved. Assignment is a technique for liquidating a debt and yielding a larger amount to the creditors than is likely to be achieved in formal bankruptcy.

Technically, there are three classes of assignments: (1) common-law assignment, (2) statutory assignment, and (3) assignment plus settlement.

Common-Law Assignment Common law provides for an assignment whereby a debtor transfers the title to assets to a third person, known as an *assignee* or *trustee*. This person is instructed to liquidate the assets and to distribute the proceeds among the creditors on a pro rata basis.

Typically, an assignment is conducted through the adjustment bureau of the local credit managers' association. The assignee may liquidate the assets through a bulk sale—a public sale through an auctioneer. The auction is preceded by advertising so there will be a number of bids. Liquidation may also be by a piecemeal auction sale conducted on the premises of the assignor by a competent, licensed auctioneer. On-premises sales are particularly advantageous in the liquidation of large machine shops of manufacturing plants.

The common-law assignment, as such, does not discharge the debtor's obligations. If a corporation goes out of business and does not satisfy all its claims, there will still be claims against it; but in effect the corporation has ceased to exist. The people who have been associated with it can organize another corporation free of the debts and obligations of the previous one. Under a common-law assignment, the assignee, in drawing up the checks to pay the creditors, should write on each check the requisite legal language to make the payment a complete discharge of the obligation. The legal requirements for this process are technical and best carried out with the aid of a lawyer, but a statement that endorsement of the check represents acknowledgement of full payment for the obligation is essential.

Statutory Assignment Statutory assignment is similar in concept to common-law assignment. Legally, it is carried out under state statutes regulating assignment; technically, it requires more formality. The debtor executes an instrument of assignment, which is recorded and thereby provides notice to all third parties. The proceedings are handled under court order; the court appoints an assignee and supervises the proceedings, including the sale of the assets and the distribution of the proceeds. As with the common-law assignment, debtors are not automatically discharged from the balance of the obligations. They can discharge themselves, however, by printing the requisite statement on the settlement checks.

Assignment Plus Settlement Both the common-law and the statutory assignment may take place with recognition and agreement beforehand by the creditors that it will represent a complete discharge of obligation. Normally, the debtor communicates with the local credit managers' association. The association's adjustment bureau arranges a meeting of all the creditors, and a trust instrument of assignment is drawn up. The adjustment bureau is designated to dispose of the assets, which are sold through regular trade channels, by bulk sales, by auction, or by private sales. The creditors typically leave all responsibility for the liquidation procedure with the assignee—the adjustment bureau.

Having disposed of the assets and obtained funds, the adjustment bureau then distributes the proceeds pro rata among the creditors, designating on the check that this is in full settlement of the claims on the debtor. Ordinarily, a release is not agreed upon before the execution of the assignment. Instead, after full examination of the facts, the creditors' committee usually recommends granting a release following the execution of the assignment. If releases are not forthcoming, the assignor can, within four months of the date of the assignment, file a voluntary petition in bankruptcy. In this event, the assignment is terminated and the assignee must account for the assets, report to the trustee and the referee in bankruptcy, and deliver to the trustee all assets in the estate. (Usually, by that time, assets have been reduced to cash.)

Assignment has substantial advantages over bankruptcy. Bankruptcy through the courts involves much time, legal formalities, and accounting and legal expenses. Assignment saves the costs of bankruptcy proceedings, and it may save time as well. Furthermore, an assignee usually has much more flexibility in disposing of property than does a bankruptcy trustee. Assignees may be more familiar with the normal channels of trade; and since they take action quickly, before the inventories become obsolete, they may achieve better results.

Bankruptcy

Although the bankruptcy procedures need improvement, the Federal Bankruptcy Acts represent some major achievements:

1. They provide safeguards against fraud by the debtor during liquidation.
2. Simultaneously, they provide for an equitable distribution of the debtor's assets among the creditors.
3. Insolvent debtors can discharge all their obligations and start new businesses unhampered by a burden of prior debt.

Prerequisites for Bankruptcy

The debtor can file a voluntary petiton of bankruptcy; but if an involuntary petition is to be filed, three conditions must be met:

1. The total debts of the insolvent must be $1,000 or more.
2. If the debtor has fewer than twelve creditors, any single creditor can file the petition if the amount owed is $500 or more. If there are twelve or more creditors, the petition must be signed by three or more of them, each having provable total claims of at least $500.
3. Within the four preceding months, the debtor must have committed one or more of the following six acts of bankruptcy.

Acts of Bankruptcy

The six acts of bankruptcy can be summarized briefly:

1. *Concealment or Fraudulent Conveyance*. Concealment constitutes the hiding of assets with intent to defraud creditors. Fraudulent conveyance is transfer of property to a third party without adequate consideration and with intent to defraud creditors.
2. *Preferential Transfer*. A preferential transfer is the transfer of money or assets by an insolvent debtor to a creditor, giving that creditor a greater portion of the claim than other creditors would receive on liquidation.
3. *Legal Lien or Distraint*. If an insolvent debtor permits any creditor to obtain a lien on the property and fails to discharge the lien within thirty days, or if the debtor permits a landlord to distrain (to seize property that has been pledged as security for a loan) for nonpayment of rent, that person has committed an act of bankruptcy. By obtaining a lien, creditors can force an insolvent but obdurate debtor into bankruptcy.
4. *Assignment*. An act of bankruptcy likewise exists if a debtor makes a general assignment for the benefit of creditors. Again, this enables creditors who have become distrustful of the debtor in the process of assignment to transfer the proceedings to a bankruptcy court. As a matter of practice, creditors in common-law assignments typically require that a debtor execute a formal assignment document to be held in escrow and to become effective if informal and voluntary settlement negotiations fail. In the event of failure, the assignment becomes effective, and the creditors have the right to bring the case into bankruptcy court.
5. *Appointment of Receiver or Trustee*. If an insolvent debtor permits the appointment of a receiver or a trustee to take charge of the property, the debtor

has committed an act of bankruptcy. In this event, the creditors can remove a receivership or an adjustment proceeding to a bankruptcy court.

6. *Admission in Writing.* A debtor who admits in writing an inability to pay the debts and a willingness to be judged bankrupt has committed an act of bankruptcy. The reason for this sixth act of bankruptcy is that debtors are often unwilling to engage in voluntary bankruptcy because it carries the stigma of avoidance of obligations. Sometimes, therefore, negotiations with a debtor reach an impasse. Admission in writing is one of the methods of forcing the debtor to commit an act of bankruptcy and of moving the proceedings into a bankruptcy court, where the debtor will no longer be able to reject all plans for settlement.

Adjudication and the Referee

On the filing of the petition of involuntary bankruptcy, a subpoena is served on the debtor. There is usually no contest by the debtor, and the court adjudges the debtor bankrupt. On adjudication, the case is transferred by the court to a referee in bankruptcy, generally a lawyer appointed for a specified term by the judge of the bankruptcy court to act in the judge's place after adjudication.

In addition, on petition of the creditors, the referee in voluntary proceedings or the judge in involuntary proceedings can appoint a receiver, who serves as the custodian of the debtor's property until the appointment of a trustee. This arrangement was developed because a long period elapses between the date of the filing of a petition in bankruptcy and the election of a trustee at the first creditors' meeting. To safeguard the creditors' interests during this period, the court, through either the referee or the judge, can appoint a receiver in bankruptcy, who has full control until the trustee is appointed.

First Creditors' Meeting: Election of Trustee

At the first meeting of the creditors, a trustee is elected. If different blocks of creditors have different candidates for trustee, the election may become drawn out. Frequently, the trustee will be the adjustment bureau of the local credit managers' association. At this first meeting the debtor may also be examined for the purpose of obtaining necessary information.

Subsequent Procedures

The trustee and the creditors' committee act to convert all assets into cash. The trustee sends a letter to people owing the debtor money, warning that all past-due accounts will result in instant suit if immediate payment is not made. Appraisers are appointed by the courts to set a value on the property. With the advice of the creditors' committee and authorization of the referee, the merchandise is sold by approved methods. As in an assignment, auctions may be held.

Without the consent of the court, property cannot be sold at less than 75 percent of the value set by the court-appointed appraisers. Cash received from the disposition of the property is used first to pay all expenses associated with the bankruptcy proceedings, and then any remaining funds are paid to the claimants.

Final Meeting and Discharge

The trustee who has completed the liquidation and has sent out all the claimants' checks makes an accounting, which is reviewed by the creditors and the referee. The bankruptcy is then discharged, and the debtor is released from all debts.

If the hearings before the referee indicate the probability of fraud, the FBI is required to undertake an investigation. If fraud was not committed and the bankruptcy is discharged, the debtor is again free to engage in business. Since business is highly competitive in many fields, the debtor will probably not have great difficulty in obtaining credit again. Under the National Bankruptcy Act, however, a debtor cannot be granted a discharge more often than once every six years.

Priority of Claims on Distribution of Proceeds

The order of priority of claims in bankruptcy is as follows:

1. Costs of administering and operating the bankruptcy estate
2. Wages due workers if earned within three months prior to the filing of the petition in bankruptcy, the amount not to exceed $600 per person
3. Taxes due federal, state, county, or any other government agencies
4. Secured creditors, with the proceeds of the sale of specific property pledged for a mortgage
5. General or unsecured creditors—the claim consisting of the remaining balances after payment to secured creditors from the sale of specific property and including trade credit, bank loans, and debenture bonds. Holders of subordinated debt fall into this category, but they must turn over required amounts to the holders of senior debt.
6. Preferred stockholders
7. Common stockholders

An example will illustrate how this priority of claims works out. The balance sheet of a bankrupt firm is shown in Table 25.5. Assets total $90 million, and claims are

Table 25.5

Bankrupt Firm Balance Sheet (millions of dollars)

Current assets	$80.0	Accounts payable	$20.0
Net property	10.0	Notes payable (due bank)	10.0
		Accrued wages (1,400 at $500 each)	0.7
		U.S. taxes	1.0
		State and local taxes	0.3
		Current debt	$32.0
		First mortgage	$ 6.0
		Second mortgage	1.0
		Subordinated debentures[a]	8.0
		Long-term debt	$15.0
		Preferred stock	$ 2.0
		Common stock	26.0
		Capital surplus	4.0
		Retained earnings	11.0
		Net worth	$43.0
Total assets	$90.0	Total claims	$90.0

[a] Subordinated to $10 million notes payable to a commercial bank

those indicated on the right-hand side of the balance sheet. The subordinated debentures are subordinated to the notes payable to commercial banks.

Assume that the firm's assets are sold. These assets, shown in the balance sheet, are greatly overstated; they are worth much less than the $90 million at which they are carried. The following amounts are realized on liquidation:

Current assets	$28,000,000
Net property	5,000,000
Total assets	$33,000,000

The order of priority of payment of claims is shown by Table 25.6. Fees and expenses of administration are typically about 20 percent of gross proceeds, and in this example they are assumed to be $6 million. Next in priority are wages due workers, which total $700,000. The total amount of taxes to be paid is $1.3 million. Thus far, the total of claims paid from the $33 million is $8 million. The net proceeds of $5 million from the sale of fixed property is then paid on the first mortgage, leaving $20 million available to the general creditors.

The claims of the general creditors total $40 million. Since $20 million is available, each claimant will receive 50 percent of the claim before the subordination adjustment. This adjustment requires that the holders of subordinated debentures turn over to the holders of the notes to which they are subordinated all amounts received until the notes to which they are subordinated are satisfied. In this situation, the claim of the holders of notes payable is $10 million, but only $5 million is available; the deficiency is therefore $5 million. After transfer of $4 million by the holders of subordinated debentures, there remains a deficiency of $1 million, which will be unsatisfied. Note that 90 percent of the bank claim will be satisfied, whereas only 50 percent of other unsecured claims will be satisfied. These figures illustrate the usefulness of the subordination provision to the security to which the subordination is made. Since no other funds remain, the claims of the holders of preferred and common stocks are completely wiped out.

The order of priority can be altered by special subordination agreements. For example, in the W. T. Grant bankruptcy during the mid-1970s, the commercial banks had agreed to subordinate their loans to the amounts payable to trade creditors in order to induce suppliers of W. T. Grant to continue the flow of merchandise to the company. As a consequence, of the $400 million that appeared to be realizable from W. T. Grant, the order of priority seemed to be the following. First in line were the holders of the $24 million worth of senior debentures. Second, because of an unusual lien arrangement, came trade creditors, with $110 million owed. Third were the banks, which subordinated to the trade creditors $300 million of their $640 million loan to Grant, along with an additional $90 million loaned after the filing for reorganization. Next came junior debenture holders, with claims of $94 million. Last in line were the holders of unsecured debt, including $300 million in landlord claims and utility bills. In addition, it was estimated that administrative costs of the reorganization would total $30 million. There was also an unresolved Internal Revenue Service claim of $60 million plus interest. Further, there would

Table 25.6

Bankrupt Firm's Order of Priority of Claims (millions of dollars)

Distribution of Proceeds on Liquidation	
1. Proceeds of sales of assets	$33.0
2. Fees and expenses of administration of bankruptcy	6.0
3. Wages due workers earned three months prior to filing of bankruptcy petition	0.7
4. Taxes	1.3
5. Available after priority payments	$25.0
6. First mortgage, paid from sale of net property	5.0
7. Available to general creditors	$20.0

Claims of General Creditors

Class of creditor	Claim (1)	Application of 50 percent (2)	After subordination adjustment (3)	Percentage of original claims received (4)
Unsatisfied portion of first mortgage	$1.0	$0.5	$0.5	92%
Unsatisfied portion of second mortgage	1.0	0.5	0.5	50
Notes payable	10.0	5.0	9.0	90
Accounts payable	20.0	10.0	10.0	50
Subordinated debentures	8.0	4.0	0	0
	$40.0	$20.0	$20.0	56%

Notes:

1. Column 1 is the claim of each class of creditor. Total claims equal $40 million.
2. Line 7 in the upper section of the table shows that $20 million is available. This sum divided by the $40 million of claims indicates that general creditors will receive 50 percent of their claims shown in Column 1.
3. The debentures are subordinated to the notes payable; $4 million is transferred from debentures to notes payable in Column 3.
4. Column 4 shows the results of dividing the Column 3 figure by the original amount given in Table 25.5 except for first mortgage, where $5 million paid on sale of property is included. The 56 percent total figure includes the first mortgage transactions, that is: ($20,000,000 + $5,000,000) ÷ ($40,000,000 + $5,000,000) = 56%.

be legal fees estimated to run into the millions that would assume a priority status.[7]

Studies of the proceeds in bankruptcy liquidations reveal that unsecured creditors receive, on the average, about 15 cents on the dollar. Consequently,

[7] "Dividing What's Left of Grant's," *Business Week*, March 1, 1976, p. 21.

where assignment to creditors is likely to yield more, assignment is to be preferred to bankruptcy.

Summary

The major cause of a firm's failure is incompetent management. Bad managers should, of course, be removed as promptly as possible; if failure has occurred, a number of remedies are open to the interested parties.

The first question to be answered is whether the firm is better off dead or alive—whether it should be liquidated and sold off piecemeal or rehabilitated. Assuming the decision is made that the firm should survive, it must be put through what is called a *reorganization*. Legal procedures are always costly, especially in the case of a business failure. Therefore, if it is at all possible, both the debtor and the creditors are better off if matters can be handled on an informal basis rather than through the courts. The informal procedures used in reorganization are (1) extension, which postpones the date of settlement, and (2) composition, which reduces the amount owed.

If voluntary settlement through extension or composition is not possible, the matter is thrown into the courts. If the court decides on reorganization rather than liquidation, it will appoint a trustee (1) to control the firm going through reorganization and (2) to prepare a formal plan of reorganization. The plan, which must be reviewed by the SEC, must meet the standards of fairness to all parties and feasibility in the sense that the reorganized enterprise will stand a good chance of surviving instead of being thrown back into the bankruptcy courts.

The application of standards of fairness and feasibility can help determine the probable success of a particular plan for reorganization. The concept of fairness involves the estimation of sales and earnings and the application of a capitalization rate to the latter to determine the appropriate distribution to each claimant.

The feasibility test examines the ability of the new enterprise to carry the fixed charges resulting from the reorganization plan. The quality of management and the company's assets must be assured. Production and marketing may also require improvement.

Finally, where liquidation is treated as the only solution to the debtor's insolvency, the creditors should attempt procedures that will net them the largest recovery. Assignment of the debtor's property is the cheaper and the faster procedure. Furthermore, there is more flexibility in disposing of the property and thus larger returns. Bankruptcy provides formal procedures in liquidation to safeguard the debtor's property from fraud and to assure equitable distribution to the creditors. The procedure is long and cumbersome. Moreover, the debtor's property is generally poorly managed during bankruptcy proceedings unless the trustee is closely supervised by the creditors.

Questions

25.1 Discuss this argument, giving both pros and cons: A certain number of business failures is a healthy sign. If there are no failures, this is an indication (a) that entrepreneurs are overly cautious, hence not as inventive and as willing to take risks as a healthy, growing economy requires; (b) that competition is not functioning to weed out inefficient producers; or (c) that both situations exist.

25.2 How can financial analysis be used to forecast the probability of a given firm's failure? Assuming that such analysis is properly applied, will it always predict failure? Explain.

25.3 Why do creditors usually accept a plan for financial rehabilitation rather than demand liquidation of the business?

25.4 Would it be possible to form a profitable company by merging two companies, both of which are business failures? Explain.

25.5 Distinguish between a reorganization and a bankruptcy.

25.6 Would it be a sound rule to liquidate whenever the liquidation value is above the value of the corporation as a going concern? Discuss.

25.7 Why do liquidations usually result in losses for the creditors or the owners, or both? Would partial liquidation or liquidation over a period of time limit their losses? Explain.

25.8 Are liquidations likely to be more common for public utility, railroad, or industrial corporations? Why?

Problems

25.1 The final balance sheet of the bankrupt Scotshop Discount Stores is shown below:

Assets		Liabilities	
Current assets	$12,000,000	Accounts payable	$ 3,000,000
Net fixed assets	1,400,000	Notes payable (bank)	700,000
		Accrued wages (700 at $400 each)	280,000
		Taxes due	720,000
		Current liabilities	$ 4,700,000
		Mortgage	$ 1,000,000
		Subordinated debentures[a]	1,000,000
		Long-term debt	$ 2,000,000
		Preferred stock	$ 815,000
		Common stock	5,000,000
		Retained earnings	885,000
		Net worth	$ 6,700,000
Total assets	$13,400,000	Total claims	$13,400,000

[a] Subordinated to $700,000 notes payable to bank

Total legal fees and administrative expenses of the bankruptcy proceeding were $1,000,000. Upon liquidation of the firm's assets, only $5,000,000 was realized:

Current assets	$4,300,000
Net property	700,000
	$5,000,000

Prepare a schedule showing the distribution of the liquidation proceeds.

25.2 The financial statements of the Nova Publishing Company for 1980 are shown below:

Nova Publishing Company
Balance Sheet, as of
December 31, 1980
(thousands of dollars)

Current assets	$130,000	Current liabilities	$ 53,000
Investments	40,000	Advance payments for subscriptions	78,000
Net fixed assets	200,000	Reserves	8,000
Goodwill	14,000	$8 preferred stock, $100 par (1,500,000 shares)	150,000
		$9 preferred stock, no par (100,000 shares, callable at $110)	11,000
		Common stock, $1.50 par (8,000,000 shares)	12,000
		Retained earnings	72,000
Total assets	$384,000	Total claims	$384,000

Nova Publishing Company
Income Statement for Year
Ended December 31, 1980
(thousands of dollars)

Operating income		$194,400
Operating expenses		174,800
Earnings before income tax		19,600
Income tax (at 40 percent)		7,840
Income after taxes		11,760
Dividends on $8 preferred stock	$12,000	
Dividends on $9 preferred stock	900	12,900
Income available for common stock		−$1,140

A recapitalization plan is proposed in which each share of $8 preferred stock will be exchanged for a share of $2 preferred (stated value $20), plus $80 of stated principal in 8 percent subordinated income debentures with par value $1,000. The $9 preferred will be retired from cash.

a. Show the pro forma balance sheet (in thousands of dollars) giving effect to the recapitalization and showing the new preferred at its stated value and the common stock at par value.

b. Present the pro forma income statement (in thousands of dollars).

c. How much does the firm increase income available to common stock by the recapitalization?

d. How much less are the required pre-tax earnings after the recapitalization compared to before the change? (Required earnings are the amount necessary to meet fixed charges, debenture interest, and preferred dividends.)

e. How is the debt to net worth position of the company affected by the recapitalization?

f. Would you vote for the recapitalization if you were a holder of the $8 preferred stock?

25.3 The Positech Company produces precision instruments. The company's products, designed and manufactured according to specifications set out by its customers, are highly specialized. Declines in sales and increases in development expenses in recent years resulted in a large deficit at the end of 1980 (see the balance sheet and income data which follow):

Positech Company Balance Sheet as of December 31, 1980 (thousands of dollars)

Current assets	$375	Current liabilities	$450
Fixed assets	375	Long-term debt (unsecured)	225
		Capital stock	150
		Retained earnings (deficit)	−75
Total assets	$750	Total claims	$750

Positech Company Sales and Profits, 1976–1980 (thousands of dollars)

Year	Sales	Net profit after tax before fixed charges
1976	$2,625	$262.5
1978	2,400	225.0
1979	1,425	−75.0
1980	1,350	−112.5

Independent assessment led to the conclusion that the company would have a liquidation value of about $600,000. As an alternative to liquidation, management concluded that a reorganization was possible with the investment of an additional $300,000. Management was confident of the company's eventual success and stated that the additional investment would restore earnings to $125,000 a year after taxes and before fixed charges. The appropriate multiplier to apply is eight times. Management is negotiating with a local investment group to obtain the additional $300,000. If the funds are obtained, the holders of the long-term debt will be given half the common stock in the reorganized firm in place of their present claims.

Should the creditors agree to the reorganization, or should they force liquidation of the firm?

25.4 During the past several months, the American Industrial Products Company has had difficulty meeting its current obligations. Attempts to raise additional working capital have failed. To add to AIP's problems, its principal lenders, the First National Bank and the General Insurance Company, have been placing increased pressure on it because of its continued delinquent loan payments and apparent lack of fiscal responsibility.

The First National Bank is first mortgage holder on AIP's production facility and has a $1 million, unsecured revolving loan with AIP that is past due and on which certain restrictive clauses have been violated. The General Insurance Company is holding $5 million of AIP's subordinated debentures, which are subordinate to the notes payable.

Because of the bank's increasing concern for the long-term future of AIP, it has attached $750,000 of AIP's deposits. This action has forced the company into either reorganization or bankruptcy.

General Insurance has located a large manufacturing company that is interested in taking over AIP's operations. This company has offered to assume the $8 million mortgage, pay all back taxes, and pay $4.3 million in cash for the company.

AIP's estimated sales for 1980 are $20 million, its estimated earnings are $1,294,000, and its capitalization factor is 10 times. The company's balance sheet as of December 31, 1980, follows:

American Industrial Products Company
Balance Sheet as of December 31, 1980
(thousands of dollars)

Assets		Liabilities	
Current assets	$ 3,000	Accounts payable	$ 2,000
Net property, plant, and equipment	12,000	Taxes	200
Other assets	2,800	Notes payable to bank	250
		Other current liabilities	1,350
		Total current liabilities	$ 3,800
		Mortgage	8,000
		Subordinated debentures	5,000
		Common stock	1,000
		Paid-in capital	2,000
		Retained earnings	−2,000
Total assets	$17,800	Total liabilities and stockholders' equity	$17,800

a. Given all the data and the fact that AIP cannot be reorganized internally, show the effect of the reorganization plan on claims of AIP's creditors.
b. Based on the information in the paragraph preceding the balance sheet, test for the standard of fairness.
c. Comment on the actions of the bank in offsetting AIP's deposits.
d. Do you feel the bank and the insurance company were right in not advancing AIP additional money?

25.5 The Massey-Ferguson Company is a Canadian manufacturer of agricultural machinery. For the year ended October 31, 1978, the firm's net income was a negative $262 million (U.S. dollars). An abbreviated balance sheet and income statement for the year ended October 31, 1979, is presented below:

Massey-Ferguson Company of Canada, Ltd.
Income Statement for Year Ended
October 31, 1979 (thousands of U.S. dollars)

Revenues*	$3,125,000
Expenses (except interest)	2,930,000
Interest expense	164,000
Tax	cr 6,000
Net income	$ 37,000

Massey-Ferguson Company of Canada, Ltd.
Consolidated Balance Sheet as of
October 31, 1979 (thousands of U.S. dollars)

Assets		Liabilities and net worth		
Current assets	$1,935,000	Current liabilities	$1,509,000	
Other assets	810,000	Long-term debt	658,000	
		Total debt		$2,167,000
		Preferred stock	$ 96,000	
		Common stock**	177,000	
		Retained earnings	305,000	
		Net worth		$ 578,000
Total assets	$2,745,000	Total claims		$2,745,000

* Revenues include an extraordinary item of over $95 million, without which net income would be negative.
** 18,250,000 shares. Average stock price, 1979, was approximately $11.

Recall from Appendix B to Chapter 5 the Altman model of bankruptcy prediction utilizing discriminant analysis. Altman's discriminant function, Z, was found to be $Z = 0.012X_1 + 0.014X_2 + 0.033X_3 + 0.006X_4 + 0.999X_5$

X_1 = Working capital/Total assets (in percent)

X_2 = Retained earnings/Total assets (in percent)

X_3 = EBIT/Total assets (in percent)

X_4 = Market value of equity/Book value of debt (in percent)

X_5 = Sales/Total assets (times)

a. Apply the Altman model to the Massey-Ferguson data. What is the Z value for Massey-Ferguson?
b. Does it appear likely that the firm will go bankrupt?

CHAPTER 26

FINANCIAL MANAGEMENT IN THE SMALL FIRM

Small business is a key element of the U.S. economy. First, of the approximately 8.5 million firms in the United States, about 8.0 million are defined by the government as "small." Thus, small businesses are quantitatively important. Second, and of perhaps even greater significance, small businesses often serve as the vehicle through which ideas for new products and services make their way to the consuming public. Many of the large electronics firms of the 1970s were new, small businesses in the 1950s. Third, the very existence of small businesses, and the fact that new ones are continually being started, provides continuous stimulation to competition in the economy.

In some respects, there is no need to study small business finance as a separate topic—the same general principles apply to large and small firms alike. However, small firms face a somewhat different set of problems than larger businesses, and the goals of a small firm are likely to be oriented toward the aspirations of an individual entrepreneur rather than toward investors in general. Also, the characteristics of the money and capital markets create both problems and opportunities for small firms, and a special governmental agency, the Small Business Administration, exists to help small firms with their financing problems. For all these reasons, a chapter focusing directly on the small firm is useful in a book on financial management.

Life Cycle of the Firm

The life cycle of an industry or firm is often depicted as an S-shaped curve, as shown in Figure 26.1. The four stages in the life cycle are described as follows:

1. *Experimentation period.* Sales and profits grow slowly following the introduction of a new product or firm.
2. *High growth period.* The firm enjoys rapid growth of sales, high profitability, and acceptance of the product.
3. *Maturity.* The rate of growth of sales begins to slow down; growth is dependent in large part upon replacement demand.
4. *Decline.* The firm faces the appearance of substitute products, technological and managerial obsolescence, and saturation of demand for its goods.

Although it is an oversimplifcation, Figure 26.1 provides a useful framework for analysis. The hypothesis represented by the four-stage life-cycle concept is based on a number of assumptions. It assumes competent management in the

Figure 26.1 **Hypothetical Life Cycle of a Typical Firm**

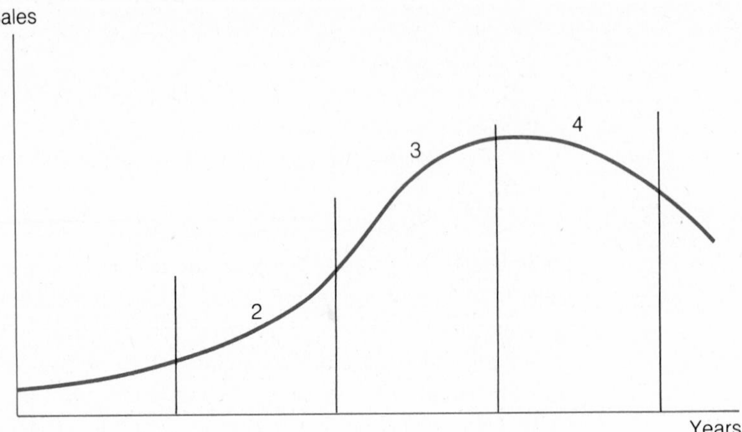

growth periods and insufficient management foresight prior to the decline phase. Obviously, one of management's primary goals is to prolong Phase 2, completely forestalling Phase 4; a great many firms are apparently successful in this endeavor.

The life cycle is substantially influenced by the form of organization a firm chooses—corporations have potentially long lives, while proprietorships obviously have finite lives. We shall discuss other aspects of the firm's life later, giving special attention to the financing forms employed at each stage.

Small Firms in Traditional Small Business Industries

Some firms are small because the nature of the industry enables small enterprises to operate competitively with large ones. Other firms are small primarily because they are new companies—either new entrants to established industries or entrepreneurial enterprises in developing industries. Since these two types of small firms face fundamentally different situations, they have vastly different problems and opportunities. Accordingly, it is useful to treat the two classes separately. We first discuss the small firm in the traditional small business industry, then consider the small firm with growth potential.

Characteristics of Traditional Small Firms

The industries or segments of industries in which small businesses predominate exhibit three common characteristics: (1) a localized market, (2) low capital requirements, and (3) relatively simple technology. Because these characteristics lead to heavy dependence on one person, problems often arise:

1. The manager may not possess the full range of skills required: A good salesperson is not necessarily able to handle employees well; a new business may have at the head a manager who does not yet understand the need for adequate accounting records, financial control systems, and the like.

2. In a small business with only one leader, the control system tends to be informal, direct, and personal; it often lacks formal, standardized controls. If the business grows, the span of responsibilities may become excessive for the entrepreneur.
3. Because of the entrepreneur's preoccupation with the pressing problems of day-to-day operations, planning for the future is often inadequate, so changes in the economic environment or competitive shifts can have severe impacts on the small firm.
4. A relatively high degree of managerial training, experience, and breadth are necessary, yet often lacking; preoccupied with the present, the characteristic small-firm entrepreneur simply does not plan for management succession. Dun & Bradstreet data on business failures indicate that a larger proportion of failures is caused by the lack of experienced management than by any other factor.

Profitability of Small Firms

The problems of a small business may be illustrated by some representative numbers. Most small independent "Mom and Pop" grocery stores have sales of less than $500 per day, but let us assume that a particular store is doing relatively well and has sales of $500 per day. Assume also that the store is open 365 days a year, so its sales for the year total $182,500. According to the *Statement Studies* of the Robert Morris Associates, grocery retailers have a profit margin on sales of about 1 percent after taxes: If our small firm makes 2 percent on sales—to include salaries—that would represent a total profit of only $3,650 for the year. The proprietors of small grocery stores typically work ten to twelve hours per day, six to seven days a week. Making calculations on the conservative side at ten hours a day for six days a week implies sixty hours of work a week. Assuming a two-week vacation, this would be fifty weeks in the year times sixty hours for a total of 3,000 hours. Three thousand hours divided into $3,650 yields about $1.22 per hour. This is well below the now-prevailing minimum wage for unskilled workers and does not include a return on invested capital.

The owners may suffer even more problems. The average net worth turnover ratio for retail grocery stores is fifteen times per year, so on sales of $182,500 the owner would probably need about $12,000 of his or her own capital. An owner will not usually have this much initial capital. As a consequence, the typical small firm incurs an inordinate amount of trade credit. It has a weak current ratio, it is slow in paying its bills, and if it is inefficient, what little capital it has is quickly eroded. For reasons such as these, one-third to one-half of all retail firms are discontinued within their first two years of life: The infant mortality rate is high indeed among small businesses!

In the face of these discouraging statistics, why do people open their own businesses? The reasons vary. One is the hope that they will beat the statistics and will be successful—any community, large or small, has a group of very successful owners of small businesses who, while perhaps not millionaires, can afford $250,000 homes, country clubs, and trips to Europe, not to mention sending their children to expensive colleges or universities. A second reason is the freedom of making one's own decisions, even if the price of this freedom is high. Third, a person may not regard time spent working in his or her own firm as drudgery; there is a wide variety of tasks to be performed in running a small enterprise, and the work can be both interesting and challenging.

Financing the Traditional Small Firm

The typical small business, even the successful one, cannot look to the general capital markets for funds. If the firm owns any real property, it may be able to obtain a mortgage from a bank or a savings and loan. Equipment may perhaps be purchased under a conditional sales contract or be leased. After the business has survived a few years, bank financing may be available on a seasonal basis, but not for permanent growth. Trade credit will, typically, represent the bulk of outside financing (that is, funds not supplied by the owner) available to the firm.

Financial ratio analysis must be of major and overriding importance to the small firm. Such analysis, on a regular basis, is essential to ascertain whether the firm is operating with the requisite managerial efficiency. Whereas a larger, stronger firm may have the financial strength to fall below its industry standards and still recover, the small firm has a smaller margin for error. Thus, anyone interested in a small firm is well advised to look at trends in its financial ratios and to compare them with industry standards.

Working capital management is of overwhelming importance for most small firms. Because the amount of funds available is limited, liquidity is crucial. Trade credit appears to be an easy way of obtaining funds, yet even trade credit is obtained on terms that generally call for payment within thirty days. Since inventories typically represent a large percentage of total assets, a small firm's inventory policy must also be stressed. Large firms usually offer credit, so to meet competition, small firms may also have to extend credit. The large firm is likely to have an established credit department, but how does the small firm evaluate credit risks? What volume of accounts receivable can be built up without endangering both the solvency and the liquidity of the business? All of these are critical questions for the manager of a small business.

Current liability management is also important for the small firm. Although trade credit is relatively easy to obtain, it is often very costly. If discounts are available but not taken, the effective interest expense of such credit can be extremely high—as we know, not taking discounts on terms of 2/10, net 30 implies a 37 percent interest rate. Also, there is a temptation to be a perpetually slow payer, but this involves dangers. Suppliers may refuse any credit whatever, or they may quote higher prices.

As the volume of operations becomes larger, the increased flow of funds through the firm may give the proprietor a false sense of affluence. Such a person may move to a larger home with a spacious yard and pool and buy the latest model car. Since the business is growing, the owner feels the firm can afford to take on more debt. But the owner may be bleeding the business or, at least, removing retained earnings that are really needed to finance growth.

Many traditional small-business industries are today being conducted under franchise arrangement. Franchising is a system whereby the training and experience required for a particular line of business are sold to the proprietor on a rental contract basis. Sometimes the franchise also includes a valuable trademark or calls for the supply of some key item. The franchiser may, through bulk buying, be able to sell supplies to the franchisee at lower costs than otherwise would be available. But, as many erstwhile franchise operators know, obtaining a franchise is not necessarily the road to riches—in many such arrangements, the owner of the franchised operation may be required to pay an excessive price for the trademark, specialty inputs and supplies, or managerial advice.

In summary, three areas of finance are of the utmost importance to firms in traditional small business industries. First, the proprietor of the traditional small business must rely on internal financing (retained earnings) to a greater extent than would the management of a larger firm. Second, to survive in the long run, the small business owner must be a somewhat better player of a relatively standardized game, in which financial ratio analysis can help the firm to excel. Third, working capital management is critical to the small entrepreneur; a small business owner who fails here will not remain solvent, and the firm will go out of business.

The Small Firm with Growth Potential

The second broad category of small business is the small firm with potential for substantial growth. Typically, such a firm has developed a new product or an innovative way of providing an old service. The electronics industry is a good example of the former, while franchised hamburgers and other food operations illustrate the latter. In this section, we discuss the financial aspects of such firms from inception until the business has matured enough to go public. The significant financial aspects of each stage of the firm's life cycle will be set out as a guide to the establishment and development of the new small business enterprise.

State 1: Experimentation Period

As indicated above and shown in Figure 26.1, the first stage of a firm's life cycle involves experimentation and simply getting itself firmly entrenched. During this period, management must lay the foundation for future growth, realizing that growth occurs either because the firm can increase its share of the market or because of industry expansion. Market share expansion is difficult because of the reaction of existing firms, and even if the industry is growing, management must recognize that every product and industry has a life cycle. Hence, supernormal growth, for whatever cause, will continue for only a finite period.

Even though the prospects of growth in an industry are favorable, there will be fluctuations. In addition, managers must be aware of the sales-to-capacity situation in the industry. For example, one of the most favorable growth industries in recent decades has been that of pleasure boats, which has generally grown at about the same rate as the growth in the population with incomes of over $12,000 per annum—10 to 12 percent per year. However, for a number of years capacity grew at a 20 percent rate, so after a point individual firms experienced the problem of excess capacity in spite of the favorable growth.

Particularly in new industries, it is important that the firm identify the techniques needed to succeed in the line of business. When the auto industry was maturing, dealership organizations and the availability of repair parts and service were the critical factors to the success of individual firms. In the computer industry, a backup of software, of marketing, and of maintenance service personnel was vital. In the aerospace industry, the essentials were technological capability and cost control.

Like the owner of a firm in a traditional small business industry, a growth industry entrepreneur must have a knowledge not only of a product and industry, but also of the standard administrative tools essential for effective management in any line of business. Financial planning and control processes are especially important. Financial ratio analysis should be used to develop standards for determining the broad outlines of the balance sheet and the income statement, as well as for guidelines to help isolate developing problem areas.

Stage 2: High Growth Period

After the firm's inception, a successful firm with growth potential will enter Stage 2 of its financial cycle. Here, the firm has achieved initial success—it is growing rapidly and is reasonably profitable. Cash flows and working capital management have become increasingly important. Also, at this stage the firm will have an extraordinary need for additional outside financing; this is shown in Table 26.1, which compares rapid and moderate growth firms. The growth company (Firm 1) expands from $800,000 in sales to $1.2 million in one year; Firm 2 grows by the same amount, but over a four-year period. The percentages in parentheses following the asset-liability accounts indicate the assumed relationships between asset items and the spontaneous sources of funds, which we discussed in Chapter 6 in the section on the percent of sales forecasting method. Note also that profits are assumed to be 6 percent of sales during the year, and that all earnings are retained. Let us further assume that notes payable are increased to cover the financing required—notes payable function as the balancing item. If the firm grows by 50 percent in one year,

Table 26.1

Financial Effects of Different Rates of Growth (thousands of dollars)

	Firm 1		Firm 2				
	Year 1	Year 2	Year 1	Year 2	Year 3	Year 4	Year 5
Sales	$800	$1,200	$800	$900	$1,000	$1,100	$1,200
Current assets (30%)	240	360	240	270	300	330	360
Fixed assets (20%)	160	240	160	180	200	220	240
Total Assets	$400	$ 600	$400	$450	$ 500	$ 550	$ 600
Accounts payable (10%)	80	120	80	90	100	110	120
Notes payable	96	172	96	79	56	27	(8)
Other accruals (3%)	24	36	24	27	30	33	36
Current liabilities	$200	$ 328	$200	$196	$ 186	$ 170	$ 148
Common stock	100	100	100	100	100	100	100
Retained earnings[a]	100	172	100	154	214	280	352
Net worth	$200	$ 272	$200	$254	$ 314	$ 380	$ 452
Total claims	$400	$ 600	$400	$450	$ 500	$ 550	$ 600
Key Ratios							
Current ratio (times)	1.2	1.1	1.2	1.4	1.6	1.9	2.4
Debt ratio (percentage)	50	55	50	44	37	31	25
Sales to total assets (times)	2	2	2	2	2	2	2
Profit to net worth (percentage)	24.0	26.5	24.0	21.3	19.1	17.4	15.9

[a] Profit is 6 percent of sales; retained earnings are equal to profit plus retained earnings from the previous year.

notes payable almost double. However, if the firm grows from $800,000 to $1.2 million over a four-year period, then notes payable not only do not increase at all, but they can actually be paid off. Hence, current liabilities decline from $200,000 to $148,000, while net worth increases from $200,000 to $452,000.

There is considerable doubt whether the growth firm could actually obtain short-term bank loans of the amount required. Such a large amount of short-term bank financing would cause its current ratio to drop to 1.1, and its debt ratio to rise to 55 percent. This situation develops even with the very favorable 24 percent rate of return on net worth. If the profit rate were lower, the firm's financing problem would be even more serious. When the firm uses four periods to achieve the same amount of growth, the financial ratios indicate a less risky situation. The current ratio never declines—it actually improves over the period. The debt ratio drops from 50 to 25 percent, which is very low compared with the average for all manufacturing firms.

If the rapid growth firm continues to grow at the 50 percent rate, the situation will further deteriorate, and it will become increasingly clear that the firm requires additional equity financing. The debt ratio will become much too high, yet the firm may well be reluctant to bring in additional outside equity money because the original owners are unwilling to share control. At this juncture, some financial pitfalls should be recognized and avoided. These are illustrated by the actual experiences of two individual small business owners who explained to the authors the difficulties they encountered. In one instance, the former owner of a firm described the problems that occurred after he obtained additional funds to support growth. He originally owned 100 percent of his company, but the firm needed capital. When two potential suppliers of the necessary funds each requested 30 percent ownership, the founder of the enterprise agreed, figuring that he would still have control with 40 percent, the largest block of the common stock. However, the two new equity owners joined forces, interfered with the creative management of the company, and caused it to fail. It may seem that this was a rather elementary error, since a person in business might be expected to look ahead to exactly this kind of move. However, production in new businesses tends to consume owner interest, and it is not uncommon for innovative entrepreneurs to fail as financial managers when more than one owner enters and changes the balance of power.

It is also an error to incur debt with an unrealistically short maturity. The former owner of another small firm borrowed on one- and two-year terms, but he failed to realize that if his firm continued to grow at a rapid rate, its needs for financing would increase, not decrease. Subsequently, he simply could not meet his debt maturities. It was convenient to borrow funds that were critically needed for growth on a relatively short-term basis, but when he was unable to make payments as the loans matured, he was forced to give up the controlling share of the equity. Thus, failure to plan properly again caused the founder to lose control of his company.

Stage 3: Growth to Maturity—Going Public

With favorable economic conditions and good management, the growth opportunities of Stage 2 will result in a relatively solid company with continued financing requirements. At this point, a full assessment of the critical step of going public must be made.

Going public represents a fundamental change in life-style in at least four respects:

1. The firm moves from informal, personal control to a system of formal controls, and the need for financial techniques such as ratio analysis and the du Pont system of financial planning and control greatly increases.
2. Information must be reported on a timely basis to the outside investors, even though the founders may continue to have majority control.
3. The firm must have a breadth of management in all the business functions if it is to operate its expanded business effectively.
4. The publicly owned firm typically draws on a board of directors to help formulate sound plans and policies; the board should include representatives of the public owners and other external interest groups to aid the management group in carrying out its broader responsibilities.

The timing of the decision to go public is also especially important, because small firms are more affected by variations in money market conditions than are larger companies. During periods of tight money and high interest rates, financial institutions, especially commercial banks, find that the quantity of funds demanded exceeds the supply available at legally permissible and conventionally acceptable rates. One important method employed to ration credit is to raise credit standards. During tight money periods, both a stronger balance sheet record and a longer and more stable record of profitability are required in order to qualify for bank credit. Since financial ratios for small and growing firms tend to be less strong, such firms bear the brunt of credit restraint. Obviously, the small firm that goes public and raises equity capital before a money squeeze is in a better position to ride it out. This firm has already raised some of its needed capital, and its equity cushion enables it to present a stronger picture to the banks, thus helping it to obtain additional capital in the form of debt.

The SEC has made a number of changes to make it easier for small firms to sell their stock to the public. Under Regulation A offerings, a firm is not required to meet standard SEC securities registration requirements. In 1978, the SEC raised the dollar ceiling for Regulation A offerings from $500,000 to $1.5 million. In late May 1979, the SEC announced that underwriters of Regulation A stock offerings will be able to use a preliminary offering circular as a sales tool, rather than waiting until a final offering circular has been cleared by the SEC staff. Securities firms had told the SEC that their inability to use the preliminary circular had hampered their ability to make firm underwriting commitments for such issues.

Also in May 1979, the SEC announced that a new and simplified registration form would be available to smaller firms with assets of less than $1 million and fewer than 500 shareholders. Such firms will be permitted to raise up to $5 million in the public market by using a new S-18 simplified registration form instead of the standard S-1. The companies may also register the sale at any of the commission's nine regional offices rather than in Washington only. This will enable them to use their local accounting and legal firms, holding down costs.

Venture Capital Financing

Small firms that have growth potential also have substantial financing needs associated with considerable risks. Their needs have led to the development of specialized venture capital financing sources. Some venture capital companies are organized as partnerships; others are more formal corporations termed *investment development companies*[1] The American Research and Development Corporation, one of the first investment development companies, is widely traded in the financial markets; it and other publicly owned investment companies permit individuals and institutions, such as insurance companies, to participate in the venture capital market. Other venture capital companies represent the activities of individuals or partnerships. From time to time the operations of these individual companies are described in the financial press. Notable examples are Arthur Rock and Charles Allen.[2]

When a new business makes an application for financial assistance from a venture capital firm, it receives a rigorous examination. Some development companies use their own staffs for this investigation, while others depend on a board of advisers acting in a consultative capacity. A high percentage of applications is rejected, but if the application is approved, funds are provided. Venture capital companies generally take an equity position in the firms they finance, but they may also extend debt capital. However, when loans are made, they generally involve convertibles or warrants or are tied in with the purchase of stock by the investment company.

Venture capital companies perform a continuing and active role in the enterprise. Typically, they do not insist on voting control, but they usually have at least one member on the board of directors of the new enterprise. The matter of control has *not* been one of the crucial considerations in investment companies' decisions to invest—indeed, if the management of a small business is not sufficiently strong to make sound decisions, the venture capital firm is not likely to be interested in the first place. However, the investment company does want to maintain continuous contact, provide management counsel, and monitor the progress of its investment.

Another distinctive contribution of the venture capital firm stems from its ownership by wealthy individuals. (Laurance Rockefeller, for example, is a leading venture capitalist.) For tax reasons, such people are interested in receiving their income in the form of capital gains rather than current income. They are, therefore, in a position to take larger risks. If they lose on the venture, the net after-tax loss is only a portion of the investment since they are in high personal income tax brackets. For example, a $100,000 loss "costs" only $25,000 for an investor who is in the 75 percent state-plus-federal tax bracket.[3] Their gains, if any, are in the form

[1] Under the Investment Company Act of 1940, investment development companies are defined as closed-end, nondiversified investment companies. Closed-end investment companies are like mutual funds, but they differ in that they are under no obligation to buy back the shares they have issued.

[2] See "Venture Capitalist with a Solid Intuition," *Business Week*, May 30, 1970, p. 102, for an article on Arthur Rock, and "Meet Charlie Allen," *Wall Street Journal*, August 4, 1970, for an article on Charles Allen.

[3] Special tax provisions make it possible to offset more than the regular $1,000 of ordinary income by capital losses if the losses are on small businesses as defined by the tax code.

of capital gains; they are therefore taxed at a rate lower than the rate on ordinary personal income. Thus, for the wealthy individual, the odds are in favor of making higher risk investments.

Another source of venture capital has been developed in recent years—large, well-established business firms.[4] A number of large corporations have invested both money and various types of know-how to start or to help develop small business firms. The owner of the small firm is usually a specialist, frequently a technically oriented person who needs both money and help in such administrative services as accounting, finance, marketing, and production. The small firm's owner contributes entrepreneurship, special talents, a taste for risk taking, and "the willingness to work 18 hours a day for peanuts." A number of major corporations have found that there is a mutual advantage for this form of venture capital investment.

Another important source of venture capital financing for small business is the Small Business Investment Company (SBIC). The Small Business Investment Company Act of 1958 empowered the Small Business Administration (SBA) to license and regulate SBICs and to provide them with financial assistance. A minimum of $150,000 in private capital is required for the licensing of an SBIC, and this amount can be doubled by selling subordinated debentures to the SBA (at interest rates generally below prevailing market rates).

In their operations, SBICs have followed two policies similar to investment development or venture capital companies. First, their investments are generally made by the purchase of convertible securities or bonds with warrants, thus giving the SBICs a residual equity position in the companies to which funds are provided. Second, SBICs emphasize management counsel, for which a fee is charged.[5]

In the early 1980s, there were over 300 SBICs with total resources of more than $1.1 billion. In addition, during the year 1971, Public Law 92-213 amended the Small Business Investment Company Act and clarified the SBA's authority to guarantee debentures issued by the SBICs, thus providing the SBIC industry with an expanded source of funding at interest rates somewhat below prevailing market levels.

The SBICs benefit from the aura of government sponsorship and the availability of long-term subordinated debt on attractive terms. Also, the spectacular success of one investment can assure the prosperity of an SBIC or other venture capital company.[6] When SBICs first appeared in the 1950s, these advantages gave rise to very optimistic expectations about SBICs' stock market values. Beginning in 1961, however, investors' appraisals of SBIC common stocks plunged, as it became clear that SBICs were not a guaranteed road to riches. To find and finance successful small businesses requires much work and considerable risks. There was indeed a weeding out of the weaker firms, and since the mid-1960s SBICs have achieved steady progress.

[4] "Venture Capital, Corporation Style," *Forbes*, August 1, 1970, pp. 41–42.

[5] The larger SBICs have staffs similar to those of holding companies or conglomerates; these staffs provide assistance, for a fee, to the firms in which the SBICs have invested.

[6] American Research and Development Company, for example, made over $100 million on the investment of a few thousand dollars in Digital Equipment Corporation.

Small Business Administration

To help small firms obtain capital, the federal government set up the Small Business Administration (SBA).[7] The SBA operates a number of different programs. One was discussed before in connection with the formation and growth of SBICs. Another, the "Business Loan Program," provides funds for construction, machinery, equipment, and working capital.[8] Loans under this program, which are available only when small businesses are unable to obtain funds on reasonable terms from private sources, are of two types: direct loans and participation loans. In a direct loan, the SBA simply makes a loan to a small business borrower. In a participation loan, the SBA lends part of the funds, while a bank or other private lending institution advances the balance. Under a participation loan, a portion of the funds advanced by the private party may be guaranteed by the SBA. The maximum amount the SBA may lend to any borrower is $350,000; this maximum applies to either a direct loan or to the SBA's portion of a participation loan.

Since SBA loans or guarantees are advantageous to the business recipient, the definition of what constitutes a small business is important. Actually, the definition varies somewhat, depending upon the industry. Any manufacturing concern is defined as small if it employs up to 250 people, while it is defined as large if it employs more than 1,000 people. Within this range, the SBA has different standards for different industries. A wholesale firm is classified as small if its annual sales are $5 million or less. Most retail businesses and service firms are defined as small if their total annual receipts are less than $1 million.[9]

Employee Stock Ownership Plans (ESOPs)

An Employee Stock Ownership Plan (ESOP) is a powerful financial tool that has been used primarily by smaller firms, but which can be useful at all stages of a firm's development. An ESOP is a profit sharing or pension plan whose primary objective is to invest in the securities of the employer company (but which is not limited to those securities).[10] ESOPs can be used to increase cash flow and to perform a number of financial transactions at a substantially reduced after-tax cost.

[7] The SBA also helps small companies obtain a share of government contracts, and it administers training programs of various types designed to help entrepreneurs of small businesses.

[8] In addition to the Business Loan Program, the SBA administers a number of other programs, including the following: (1) Equal Opportunity Loan Program, designed specifically for disadvantaged persons who wish to start or expand an existing business, (2) Development Company Loan Program, which is used to help attract businesses to geographic areas in need of economic stimulation, (3) Displaced Business Loan Program, designed to help small businesses which are forced to relocate because of urban renewal or similar events, (4) Disaster Loan Program, designed to aid both businesses and homeowners who suffer losses as a consequence of some natural disaster, (5) Lease Guarantee Program, designed to help small businesses to obtain rental space in the commercial real estate market, (6) Revolving Line-of-Credit Program designed to aid small building contractors, (7) Surety Bonding Program, designed to aid small businesses that must post performance bonds when seeking contracts, and (8) Minority Enterprise SBIC Program, which is designed to stimulate SBICs whose clients are minority-owned firms.

[9] Additional information on the SBA and its various programs may be obtained directly from the Small Business Administration, Washington, D.C., or from regional SBA offices.

[10] For a more complete discussion of the role of ESOPs, see Joseph K. Taussig, "ESOPS—A Creative Financial Alternative," in J. Fred Weston and Maurice B. Goudzwaard, eds., *Treasurer's Handbook* (Homewood, Ill: Dow Jones-Irwin, 1976), pp. 942–61.

The basic transaction involved is an annual, tax-deductible, company contribution to the plan. Since the benefits are not taxable to the employee until they are received, the ESOP represents a pool of untaxed dollars.

Sources of funds for the ESOP include:

1. Conversion of existing benefit plans to ESOPs—selling off the existing plan's securities to invest in the securities of the employer company results in an infusion of capital to the employer company, which should be approved by both management and labor, since this additional investment strengthens the company.
2. Corporate contributions—these represent the major predictable source of funds over the years. Firms may contribute a substantial portion of covered payroll to the plan, and thus it is not inconceivable that in labor-intensive industries all cash flow dollars from operations could be shielded from tax. The Tax Bill of 1981 further liberalized the provisions for ESOPs. Also, the predictability of the contributions over time can provide the basis for obtaining dollars from other sources in case of more immediate need.
3. Liquidation of assets—the trust administering the ESOP can liquidate assets for cash on the open market whenever it seems beneficial to do so.
4. Borrowing—lenders are beginning to be aware that a loan to an ESOP is a better-quality loan than one to the employer company in terms of risk and coverage. The ESOP loan is collateralized by stock in the company and guaranteed by the employer firm. Further, since the contributions to the ESOP are tax deductible, the firm need perform only half as well (given a 50 percent tax rate) in order to be able to repay the loan.
5. Insurance benefits—ESOPs can and do purchase life insurance on members and use the proceeds to buy what may be a large block of stock from the deceased's estate without financial strain on the corporation.

The transactions in which the pretax ESOP dollars can be most useful include:

1. Obtaining an immediate infusion of capital—an ESOP can provide the company with untaxed cash by taking stock or a note in exchange.
2. Increasing cash flow and doubling growth of net worth—contributions to ESOP can reduce taxable earnings, and thus retained earnings, to zero. However, when contributions are immediately used to purchase company stock, paid-in capital is increased and net worth grows faster than would have been the case without the contributions.

   To illustrate this point:

Ordinary Corporation	
1. Earnings before taxes	$1,000,000
2. Tax liability @ 40 percent	400,000
3. After-tax retained earnings (net worth and cash flow growth)	$ 600,000
ESOP Corporation	
1. Earnings before taxes and contributions	$1,000,000
2. Contributions	1,000,000
3. Taxable earnings	0

4. Taxes	0
5. Increases in paid-in capital when ESOP purchases stock (net worth and cash flow growth)	$1,000,000

Cash flow is increased by the reduction in taxes. A variation on this transaction is to contribute more than pretax earnings to the ESOP, resulting in a loss that will allow the firm to recapture past taxes paid. Cash flow is also increased by an additional 1 percent investment tax credit for firms with ESOPs.

3. Using tax dollars to meet obligations without impairing net worth growth—in this transaction, only a part of the firm's contribution to the ESOP is used to purchase company stock, with the remainder used to meet other obligations. The total amount of tax reduction is the same, net worth continues to grow through the addition to paid-in capital, and obligations are met with saved tax dollars.
4. Repaying loans or notes with pretax dollars—the untaxed contribution of the firm is used to pay off the debt of the ESOP. Firms should consider refinancing through their ESOPs even at a higher interest rate, since payments are made with pretax dollars. Thus both lenders and borrowers will benefit.
5. ESOP as market maker—because the ESOP is not prohibited from dealing in the stock of the employer company, it can create demand for the firm's stock.
6. Providing liquidity for the illiquid—ESOPs can purchase securities in several ways: directly from the firm, on the open market, or privately from individual investors, depending on where the best price is found. In the case of large blocks of stock or special classes of stock, the ESOP may provide liquidity for a stockholder who wishes to sell his stock without the firm having to buy the stock back with after-tax dollars impairing net worth.
7. Alternative to going public—the main reasons for going public are to raise equity capital and to provide liquidity, both of which can be done through an ESOP with more control over stock price fluctuations. The ESOP is also useful as a prelude to going public or to control the timing of an issue (i.e., the ESOP could purchase an issue when the funds are needed, but the market is weak, then resell the stock on the open market when the price improves).
8. Going private and tender offers—the ESOP can borrow the needed cash and accomplish the transaction at half the cost without impairing net worth.
9. Acquisitions and divestitures—again, the ESOP enables acquisitions and divestitures to be carried out with pretax dollars, using either the acquired or the acquiring firm's contributions.

A dramatic illustration of the role of an ESOP occurred in connection with an attempted hostile takeover of Continental Airlines by Texas International Airlines during the summer of 1981. One line of defense Continental used was to create an ESOP to sell 15.4 million new common shares, doubling the number of Continental shares outstanding, thereby cutting in half Texas International's holding of 48.5 percent. The new shares would have been paid for initially with a $185 million loan from a group of nine banks, with employees receiving shares over the subsequent seven years by foregoing portions of pay increases which would be used to pay off the loan.

Because Continental did not have an ESOP in place, it sought to move rapidly to defend against the takeover by Texas International. The company proposed to set up the ESOP and double the number of common shares outstanding without a shareholder vote on the action. The New York Stock Exchange stated that it would delist the Continental stock if shareholder approval were not obtained. The California State Corporation Commissioner's office also ruled against bypassing a shareholder vote.

These adverse developments were aggravated when, over the weekend of August 8–9, 1981, the banking group withdrew its pledge to lend the $185 million. The banks cited recessionary trends in the economy and the poor outlook for the airline industry, worsened by the air controllers' strike which had begun on August 3. These pressures were among the factors that led to the suicide of Continental's chairman and chief executive, Alvin L. Feldman, on Sunday, August 9.

If Continental had already established an ESOP prior to the summer of 1981, it might have been better able to use it to defend itself against the unwanted takeover by Texas International.

Some possible disadvantages of ESOPs may also be noted. Ownership dilution may occur unless the stock purchased by the ESOP is nonvoting stock or unless the ESOP invests in other securities of the firm, such as preferred stock or debt. Earnings reduction will result since the tax-deductible contribution reduces reported earnings. This could result in lower stock prices; alternatively, the ESOP contribution could be used partly to control growth and partly to support the price of the stock by increasing demand for it. An ESOP can be structured to minimize dilution. ESOPs can reduce the cost of most business transactions by the effective corporate tax rate.

Summary

The key factors relating to small business financing are summarized briefly in Table 26.2, which sets forth the financing patterns at the firm's four stages of development. In its formative stage, the new, small firm must rely most heavily on personal savings, trade credit, and government agencies. During its period of rapid growth, internal financing will become an important source of meeting its financing requirements, although continued reliance will be placed on trade credit.

Table 26.2

Financing Patterns at Four Stages of a Firm's Development

Stage	Financing pattern
1. Formation	Personal savings, trade credit, government agencies
2. High growth	Internal financing, trade credit, bank credit, venture capital
3. Growth to maturity	Going public, money and capital markets
4. Maturity and industry decline	Internal financing, share repurchase, diversification, mergers

At this stage, its record of accomplishment also makes it possible to obtain bank credit to finance seasonal needs; and if the loan can be paid off on an amortized basis over two or three years, the firm may qualify for a term loan as well. If it has the potential for really strong growth, the firm may also be able to attract equity from a venture capital company.

A particularly successful firm may reach the stage where going public becomes feasible—this leads to access to the broader money and capital markets, and it represents a true coming-of-age for the small firm. Even at this point, however, the firm must look ahead, analyzing its products and their prospects. Because every product has a life cycle, the firm must be aware that without the development of new products, growth will cease, and eventually the firm will decline. Accordingly, as product maturity approaches, the firm must plan for the possibility of share repurchases, mergers, or other longer-term strategies. The best time to look ahead and plan for this is while the firm has energy, momentum, and a high price-earnings ratio.

An employee stock ownership plan (ESOP) is a pension or profit-sharing plan allowed to invest in the employer company's securities. An ESOP represents a pool of untaxed dollars that a company can use to reduce the cost of almost any financial transaction. By diverting earnings through tax-deductible contributions to the ESOP, a firm can enhance its rate of growth. ESOPs can provide liquidity and equity capital as well as control over the timing of financing. ESOPs enable the employer firm to carry out transactions such as acquisitions, stock repurchases, and tender offer defenses at a lower after-tax cost basis. Disadvantages of ESOPs, such as ownership and earnings dilution, can be minimized through careful structuring, resulting in a plan that is beneficial to employees and employers alike.

In our coverage of small business financing, the major emphasis has been on providing a framework for analyzing financial needs and opportunities as the characteristics of the firm and its industry evolve. While this type of analysis cannot replace mature judgment, it can certainly aid such judgment and help financial managers of small businesses maximize their contributions to the successful development of small business enterprises.

Questions

26.1 A friend of yours has just developed a new product and plans to start a business to produce it. One of his goals is to maintain absolute control, but his own capital is limited. What are some of the ways he can reduce the amount of his initial outlay while still obtaining the use of an efficiently large plant?

26.2 Assume that you are starting a business of your own of the traditional small business type. Develop an outline of the kinds of decisions you will have to make in establishing and financing the small enterprise.

26.3 What are some sources of information on the past performance of a firm you are thinking of buying?

26.4 What influence does each of the following have on possible divergences between the goals and objectives of the managers who control a corporation and those of its stockholders?

a. Profit sharing plans
b. Executive compensation schemes
c. Employee stock option plans

Problems

26.1 Susan Smith plans to open the simplest of retail trade establishments, a grocery store with an emphasis on health foods. She has received an allowance from her parents for some years and has been able to save a little over $1,000. After making some inquiries, she has recognized that she must consider such things as location, potential flow of customer traffic, and present and potential competition. Also, she has realized that she must analyze the alternatives of buying or renting a store and buying or renting the equipment and fixtures she will need—counters, shelving, cash register, and the like. The store space she has in mind has not been occupied by a grocery before, so it lacks shelves and counters.

a. Should she buy or rent the store facilities?
b. How should she acquire the equipment and fixtures?
c. What kinds of questions is she likely to face with regard to choice of product line?
d. For planning purposes, assume a profit ratio of net income before taxes to sales of 4 percent and sales per day first of $100, then of $300, and finally of $500. In each situation, what are her earnings per hour before taxes, assuming that she works ten hours per day, seven days a week, for fifty weeks per year?
e. With a sales to net worth ratio of 15 times, what investment on her part is indicated at each level of sales? Comment on how she can raise the funds. Comment also on the implications of her withdrawing funds from the business.
f. What additional questions must she face if she sells on credit?
g. What critical problems are likely to occur if sales start at $500 per day?

26.2 The Biogene Corporation, a three-year-old genetic research firm, and the Corday Craft Company, a manufacturer of woodworking and needlecraft kits, had identical balance sheets as of December 31, 1980:

Current assets (25%)	$100,000	Accounts payable (9%)	$ 36,000
Fixed assets (20%)	80,000	Notes payable	12,000
		Other accruals (4%)	16,000
		Current liabilities	$ 64,000
		Common stock	$ 68,000
		Retained earnings	48,000
Total assets	$180,000	Total claims	$180,000

Both firms had 1980 sales of $400,000. The relationship to sales of the balance sheet items which increase spontaneously with sales is given by the percentages in parentheses. Both firms have an after-tax profit on sales of 5 percent. There the similarities end. Biogene expects sales to increase by 50 percent next year, while Corday expects its sales to increase by 50 percent over the next six years, for an annual growth rate of 7 percent.

Assume that common stock for each company will remain unchanged over the relevant period, that retained earnings consist entirely of accumulated profits, and that no dividends are paid.

a. Project the balance sheet position for Biogene Corporation for December 31, 1981, and for the Corday Company through 1986. (Use the item "financing requirements" as the balancing figure on an interim worksheet. Then, on the balance sheet assume that any financing required becomes an increase in notes payable, and that any excess funds will be used first to pay off notes payable. After notes payable are completely paid off, any remaining excess funds are invested in marketable securities.)
b. Calculate the following key ratios:
   1. Current ratio
   2. Debt ratio (total debt to net worth)
   3. Sales to total assets
   4. Sales to net worth
   5. Net income after taxes (profit) to sales
   6. Net income after taxes (profit) to net worth
c. Using the ratios calculated above, compare the effects of rapid and moderate growth on the financial position and related financial policies of the two firms.

CHAPTER 27

INTERNATIONAL BUSINESS FINANCE

International financial developments are having an increased effect on people because all parts of the world are now more closely linked together than ever before. Communications throughout the world take place within a matter of minutes or even seconds. Jet airplanes can take people anywhere within a matter of hours. Realignment of the relative values of different countries' currencies is continually occurring. These international financial developments have been helpful to some and harmful to others. Although the relationships are complex, the fundamentals presented here will provide a basis for understanding the new opportunities and threats that result from the increasingly dynamic international environment.

Changes in Relative Monetary Values in Recent Years

The changes in currency values that have taken place since 1965 are set forth in Table 27.1, which compares the values in relation to the U.S. dollar for two countries whose currencies have generally increased in strength and two whose currencies have declined in strength over recent years. In 1971 the major countries of the world departed from a policy of fixed exchange rates. But even before this formal recognition of realignment in currency values, changes had already been taking place. For years the ratio of the Japanese yen to the U.S. dollar was 360 to 1. By 1978 the number of yen required to equal one dollar had dropped to 194.60. The value of the yen in relation to the dollar increased by 86 percent from 1965 to 1978, falling back to a 71 percent increase by 1981. The value of the German mark was four marks to the dollar, but by 1981 it had dropped to slightly more than two marks to the dollar. Thus the dollar value of the mark increased from approximately 25 cents to about 46 cents—an increase of 84 percent.

For Mexico and Brazil, however, the changes have been in the opposite direction. During the 1960s the Mexican peso was worth 8 cents, and its ratio to the U.S. dollar was 12.5 to 1. In 1976 the peso was allowed to float against the dollar, and by 1978 the ratio of the peso to the dollar had moved to 22.72. Thus the value of the peso had shrunk to slightly over 4 cents, a decline of 45 percent from its previous value. For years Brazil has had a policy of periodically adjusting the value of its cruzeiro. Through these successive adjustments, by 1981 the value of the cruzeiro in relation to the dollar was only 1 percent of what it had been in 1965.

Thus changes in currency values in relation to the dollar have been very substantial—and in both directions. Almost every business firm has experienced some

This chapter utilizes materials developed jointly with Bart W. Sorge in J. Fred Weston and Bart W. Sorge, *International Managerial Finance* (Homewood, Ill.: Richard D. Irwin, 1972); and J. Fred Weston and Bart W. Sorge, *Guide to International Financial Management* (New York: McGraw-Hill, 1977).

Table 27.1 **Number of Foreign Currency Units per U.S. Dollar**

	1965	1970	1973	1975	1978	1979	1980	March 2, 1981
Japan X	360.90	357.60	280.00	305.15	194.60	239.70	215.45	211.00
E	0.00277	0.00280	0.00357	0.00328	0.00514	0.00417	0.00464	0.00474
Index	100	101	129	118	186	151	168	171
W. Germany X	4.00	3.65	3.70	2.62	1.83	1.73	1.76	2.16
E	0.2500	0.2740	0.2703	0.3817	0.5464	0.5780	0.5682	0.4630
Index	100	110	108	153	219	231	227	185
Mexico X	12.50	12.50	12.50	12.50	22.72	22.80	22.83	23.56
E	0.08	0.08	0.08	0.08	0.0440	0.0439	0.0438	0.0424
Index	100	100	100	100	55	55	55	53
Brazil X	0.89	2.47	6.22	9.07	20.92	42.53	51.45	71.57
E	1.1236	0.4049	0.1608	0.1103	0.0478	0.0235	0.0194	0.0140
Index	100	36	14	10	4	2	2	1

X = Number of FCs (foreign currency units) per dollar
E = Value of one FC (foreign currency unit) in dollars
Index: 1965 = 100
Sources: International Monetary Fund, *International Financial Statistics*, monthly issues; and "Foreign Exchange," *Wall Street Journal,* March 3, 1981.

of the effects of these changes on its operations. Its inputs may include imported materials, and its products may be exported or become part of an exported product. Some large companies have earned more than half their profits abroad. Even for smaller companies it is not uncommon to find that, if international sales can be developed to about one-fourth of total sales, then earnings from foreign sales or operations are likely to be as high as 40 to 50 percent of total earnings. International operations often enable the smaller firm to achieve better utilization of its investment in fixed plant and equipment.

Impact of Exchange Rate Fluctuations

A fundamental difference between international business finance and domestic business finance is that international transactions and investments are conducted in more than one currency. For example, when a U.S. firm sells goods to a French firm, the U.S. firm usually wants to be paid in dollars and the French firm usually expects to pay in francs. Because of the existence of a foreign exchange market in which individual dealers and many banks trade, the buyer can pay in one currency and the seller can receive payment in another.

Since different currencies are involved, a rate of exchange must be established between them. The conversion relationship of the currencies is expressed in terms of their price relationship. If foreign exchange rates did not fluctuate, it would make no difference whether firms dealt in dollars or any other currency. However, since exchange rates do fluctuate, firms are subject to exchange rate fluctuation risks if they have a net asset or net liability position in a foreign currency. When net claims exceed liabilities in a foreign currency, the firm is said to be in a "long" position, because it will benefit if the value of the foreign currency rises. When net liabilities exceed claims in regard to foreign currencies, the firm is said to be in a "short" position, because it will gain if the foreign currency declines in value.

Expressing Foreign Exchange Rates

The foreign exchange rate represents the conversion relationship between currencies and depends on demand and supply relationships between the two currencies. The foreign exchange rate is the price of one currency in terms of another. Exchange rates may be expressed in dollars per foreign currency unit or units of foreign currency per dollar. An exchange rate of \$.50 to FC1 shows the value of one foreign currency unit in terms of the dollar. We shall use E_0 to indicate the spot rate, E_f to indicate the forward rate at the present time, and E_1 to indicate the actual future spot rate corresponding to E_f. An exchange rate of FC2 to \$1 shows the value of the dollar in terms of the number of foreign currency units it will purchase. We will use the symbol X with corresponding subscripts to refer to the exchange rate expressed as the number of foreign currency units per dollar.

Measuring the Percentage of Devaluation or Revaluation

Assume that there has been a devaluation of the French franc from 3 per U.S. dollar to 4 per U.S. dollar. This can be expressed as the percentage change in the number of French francs required to purchase 1 U.S. dollar ($=D_{fd}$).

For example, where $X_0 = 3$ and $X_1 = 4$,

$$\%\text{ change} = (X_1 - X_0)/X_0 = (4-3)/3 = \tfrac{1}{3}, \text{ or } 33\tfrac{1}{3}\% = D_{fd}$$

There has been an increase of $33\frac{1}{3}$ percent in the number of French francs required to equal one U.S. dollar.

To show the percentage change in the dollar value of the franc ($=D_{df}$),

$$E_0 = \frac{1}{X_0} = \frac{1}{3} \text{ and } E_1 = \frac{1}{X_1} = \frac{1}{4}$$

Now the percentage change is given by

$$\%\text{ change} = (E_0 - E_1)/E_0 = \left(\frac{1}{X_0} - \frac{1}{X_1}\right)\Big/\frac{1}{X_0}$$

$$= (\tfrac{1}{3} - \tfrac{1}{4})/(\tfrac{1}{3}) = [(4-3)/12]/(\tfrac{1}{3}) = \tfrac{1}{4} = 25\% = D_{df}$$

There has been a 25% decrease in the value of the franc in terms of the U.S. dollar.

Summary of Exchange-Rate Relationships

D_{fd} is the change in value in terms of FC/\$:

$$D_{fd} = \frac{X_1 - X_0}{X_0} = \frac{\frac{1}{E_1} - \frac{1}{E_0}}{\frac{1}{E_0}} = \frac{E_0}{E_1} - 1 = \frac{E_0 - E_1}{E_1}$$

D_{df} is the change in value in terms of \$/FC:

$$D_{df} = \frac{E_0 - E_1}{E_0} = \frac{\frac{1}{X_0} - \frac{1}{X_1}}{\frac{1}{X_0}} = \frac{X_0}{X_0} - \frac{X_0}{X_1} = \frac{X_1 - X_0}{X_1}$$

Because of the risks of exchange rate fluctuations, transactions have developed in a forward, or futures, foreign exchange market. This market enables a firm to hedge in an attempt to reduce the risk. Individuals also speculate by means of transactions in the forward market. Forward contracts are normally for a thirty-, sixty-, or ninety-day period, although special contracts for longer periods can be arranged by negotiation.

The cost of this protection is the premium or discount of the forward contract over the current spot rate, which varies from 0 to 2 or 3 percent per year for currencies that are considered reasonably stable. For currencies undergoing devaluation in excess of 4 to 5 percent per year, the required discounts may be as high as 15 to 20 percent per year. When it is probable that future devaluations may exceed 20 percent per year, forward contracts are usually unavailable.

The magnitude of the premium or discount required depends on the forward expectations of the financial communities of the two countries involved and on the supply and demand conditions in the foreign exchange market. Since members of the financial communities are usually well-informed about the expected forward exchange values of their respective currencies, the premiums or discounts quoted are very closely related to the probable occurrence of changes in the exchange rates. As a result, the forward market is chiefly used as protection against *unexpected* changes in the foreign exchange value of a currency.

Three basic relationships will be treated:

1. Consistent foreign exchange rates
2. The Fisher effect
3. The interest rate parity theorem

Consistent Foreign Exchange Rates

Equilibrating transactions take place when exchange rates are not in proper relationship with one another. This will be illustrated by some examples with unrealistically rounded numbers that make the arithmetic of the calculations simple. The right direction of analysis will be obtained if the reader remembers the general maxim that arbitrageurs will seek to sell high and to buy low. First we will indicate the consistency of spot rates. Suppose the dollar value of the pound is $2 in New York City and $1.90 in London. The following adjustment actions would take place: In New York City sell £190 for $380. Pounds are sold in New York because the pound value is high there. In London sell $380 for £200. In London the dollar value is high in relation to the pound. Thus £190 sold in New York City for $380 can be used to buy £200 in London, a gain of £10. The sale of pounds in New York causes their value to decline and the purchase of pounds in London causes their value to rise until no further arbitrage opportunities remain. The same foreign exchange prices, assuming minimal transporation costs, would have to obtain in all locations.

The relations between two individual localities can be generalized across all countries. This is referred to as consistent cross rates. It works in the following fashion: Assume that the equilibrium relation between the dollar and the pound is $2 to £1 and that the dollar to franc rate is $.25 to fr. 1. Now, suppose that in New York City £.10 = fr. 1. The following adjustment process would take place. Sell $200 for £100 used to obtain fr. 1,000. The fr. 1,000 will buy $250. This is a $50 profit over the initial $200. Sell dollars for pounds and pounds for francs, since the pound is overvalued with respect to both the dollar to pound and dollar to franc relationships. Dollars will fall in relation to the pound and the pound will fall in relation to the franc until consistent cross rates obtain. If the relation were fr. 1 = £.125, consistent cross rates would obtain. Check using the following relation:

$$\$1 = £.5$$
$$£1 = \text{fr. } 8.00$$
$$\text{fr. } 1 = \$.25$$

The product of the right-hand sides of the three relationships must equal 1. Check thus: $0.5 \times 8 \times 0.25 = 1$. We have thus established consistency between foreign exchange rates.

The Fisher Effect

The Fisher effect holds for the relationship between interest rates and the anticipated rate of inflation. While it can also be regarded as purely a relationship for a domestic economy, it is utilized in developing some of the international relationships we will consider. The Fisher effect states that nominal interest rates rise to reflect the anticipated rate of inflation. The Fisher effect can be stated in a number of forms, as shown below:

$$\frac{P_0}{P_1} = \frac{1+r}{1+R_n}$$

$$1 + r = (1 + R_n)\frac{P_0}{P_1}$$

$$r = \left[(1 + R_n)\frac{P_0}{P_1}\right] - 1$$

$$R_n = \left[(1 + r)\left(\frac{P_1}{P_0}\right)\right] - 1$$

where:

P_0 = Initial price level

P_1 = Subsequent price level

$\frac{P_1}{P_0}$ = Rate of inflation

$\frac{P_0}{P_1}$ = Relative purchasing power of the currency unit

r = Real rate of interest

R_n = Nominal rate of interest

While the Fisher effect can be stated in a number of forms, its basic import can be conveyed by a simple numerical example. Over a given period of time, if the price index is expected to rise by 10 percent and the real rate of interest is 7 percent, then the current nominal rate of interest is:

$$R_n = [(1.07)(1.10)] - 1$$
$$= 17.7 \text{ percent}$$

Similarly if the nominal rate of interest is 12 percent and the price index is expected to rise by 10 percent over a given time period, the current real rate of interest is:

$$r = \left[1.12\left(\frac{100}{110}\right)\right] - 1$$

$$= 1.018 - 1 = 0.018 = 1.8 \text{ percent}$$

The Interest Rate Parity Theorem (IRPT)

The interest rate parity theorem is an extension of the Fisher effect to international markets. It holds that the ratio of the forward and spot exchange rates will equal the ratio of foreign and domestic gross interest rates. The formal statement of the interest rate parity theorem can be expressed as follows:

$$\frac{X_f}{X_0} = \frac{1 + R_{f0}}{1 + R_{d0}} = \frac{E_0}{E_f}$$

where:

X_f = Current forward exchange rate expressed as FC units per \$1

E_f = Current forward exchange rate expressed as dollars per FC1

X_0 = Current spot exchange rate expressed as FC units per \$1

E_0 = Current spot exchange rate expressed as dollars per FC1

R_{f0} = Current foreign interest rate

R_{d0} = Current domestic interest rate

Thus if the foreign interest rate is 15 percent while the domestic interest rate is 10 percent and the spot exchange rate is $X_0 = 10$, the predicted current forward exchange rate will be:

$$X_f = \frac{1 + R_{f0}}{1 + R_{d0}}(X_0)$$

$$= \frac{1.15}{1.10}(10)$$

$$= 10.45$$

For 90 days:

$$X_f = \frac{1.0375}{1.025}(10)$$

$$= 10.122$$

Thus the indicated foreign forward rate is 10.45 units of foreign currency per \$1. Thus the foreign forward rate is at a discount of 4.5 percent on an annual basis. If the time period of a transaction is ninety days, we have to rework the problem, first changing the interest rates to a quarterly basis. The discount on the ninety-day forward rate would now be 1.22 percent on the quarterly basis, since the ninety-day forward rate would be 10.122.

Alternatively, the example could be formulated for the effect on interest rates of expected changes in future foreign exchange rates. Here is a dynamic relationship that needs to be recognized: If the foreign exchange rate is expected to rise over a period of time, relative interest rates will reflect the rate of change expected in the foreign exchange rates. This is illustrated in Figure 27.1.

The figure shows that as the value of the foreign currency falls (the exchange rate expressed in the number of foreign currency units per dollar rises), the ratio

Figure 27.1 **Illustration of the Interest Rate Parity Theorem**

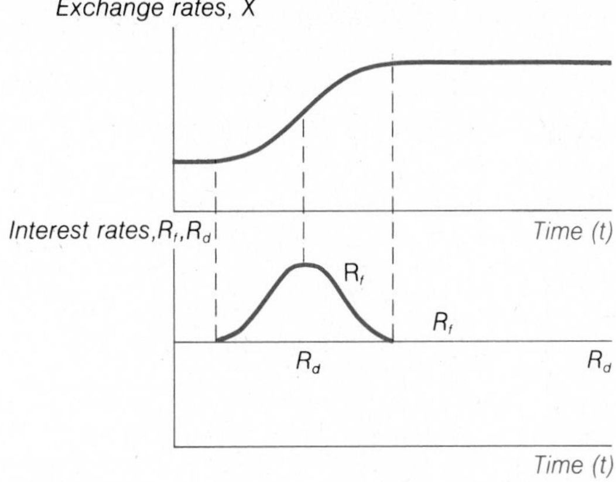

of foreign interest rates to domestic interest rates rises. At the inflection point of the rise in the expected number of foreign currency units per dollar, the ratio of foreign interest rates to domestic interest rates peaks. When the expected ratio of the number of foreign currency units per domestic currency unit levels off, then the former ratio of gross foreign interest rates to gross domestic interest rates is reestablished.

We could also use the interest rate parity theorem to express the results in terms of the interest rate parities required for given relationships between spot and future exchange rates. The transactions that result in interest rate parity are referred to as covered interest arbitrage. The basic facts of an arbitrage outflow situation are:

U.S. interest rate = 5%

German interest rate = 7%

Spot exchange rate \$1 = DM4

Forward exchange rate discount = 1%

The following arbitrage transaction will take place. In New York, borrow \$100,000 for ninety days ($\frac{1}{4}$ year) at 5 percent. The loan repayment at the end of ninety days is \$100,000 $[1 + (0.05 \times \frac{1}{4})]$ = \$101,250. At the spot exchange rate, convert the \$100,000 loan into DM400,000. In Germany, invest the DM400,000 for ninety days at 7 percent. Receive at the end of ninety days DM400,000 $[1+(0.07)\times\frac{1}{4})]$ = DM407,000.

A covering transaction is also made. To insure against adverse changes in the spot rate during the ninety-day investment period, sell investment proceeds forward. Since the forward exchange rate discount is 1 percent, then $4[1+(0.01\times\frac{1}{4})]$ = DM4.01 is required to exchange for \$1, in ninety days (forward). Sell investment proceeds forward; that is, contract to receive DM407,000 ÷ 4.01 = \$101,496.

$$\begin{aligned}\text{Arbitrage profits} &= \text{Investment receipts} - \text{Loan payments}\\ &= \$101{,}496 - \$101{,}250\\ &= \$246\end{aligned}$$

The arbitrage transaction increases the *demand* for currency in New York and increases the *supply* of funds in Germany. This raises the interest rate in New York and lowers it in Germany, thus narrowing the differential. The covering transaction increases the supply of German forward exchange, while the arbitrage investment action increases the demand for spot funds. Both forces tend to increase the forward exchange discount. The interest rate differential decreases and the forward rate discount increases until both are equalized.

An arbitrage inflow takes place when the forward exchange rate discount exceeds the interest rate differential. The basic facts are now:

$$\text{U.S. interest rate} = 5\%$$

$$\text{German interest rate} = 6\%$$

$$\text{Spot exchange rate DM4} = \$1$$

$$\text{Forward exchange rate discount} = 2\%$$

The arbitrage transaction involves borrowing in the foreign country. In Germany, borrow DM400,000 for ninety days at 6 percent. The loan repayment at the end of ninety days is DM400,000 $[1 + (0.06 \times \frac{1}{4})]$ = DM406,000. At the spot exchange rate, convert the DM400,000 loan into \$100,000. In New York, invest the \$100,000 for ninety days at 5 percent. Receive at the end of ninety days \$100,000 $[1 + (0.05 \times \frac{1}{4})]$ = \$101,250.

Again, a covering transaction would be made. To insure coverage for the loan repayment, buy DM406,000 forward. At a 2 percent forward exchange rate discount, it costs DM4$[1 + (0.02 \times \frac{1}{4})]$ = DM4.02 to buy \$1 forward. Thus, to repay DM400,000 requires DM406,000 ÷ 4.02 = \$100,995.

$$\begin{aligned} \text{Arbitrage profits} &= \text{Investment receipts} - \text{Loan repayments} \\ &= \$101{,}250 - \$100{,}995 \\ &= \$255 \end{aligned}$$

The arbitrage transaction increases the *demand* for DM and increases the *supply* of dollars. The U.S. interest rate decreases and the German rate rises; thus the differential increases. Covering transactions increase the spot supply of DM, thus decreasing the premium on forward DM. The interest rate differential and the forward exchange rate discount decrease until both rates are equalized.

As a result of the covered interest arbitrage transactions of the types described, the relationships depicted by the interest rate parity theorem would obtain. This relationship determines the home-currency cost that would be involved when a purchase or sale is made and a future payment or receipt is involved.

Risk Position of the Firm in Foreign Currency Units

The risk position of a firm in relation to possible fluctuations in foreign exchange rates can be clarified by referring to expected receipts or obligations in foreign currency units. If a firm is expecting receipts in foreign currency units (if it is "long" in the foreign currency units), its risk is that the value of the foreign currency units will fall (devaluing the foreign currency in relation to the dollar). If a firm is expecting to have obligations in foreign currency units (if it is "short" in the foreign currency units), its risk is that the value of the foreign currency will rise and it will have to buy the currency at a higher price.

Methods of Dealing with the Risk of a Decline in Foreign Currency Values

A brief example will illustrate methods of taking protective action against a decline in the value of a foreign currency. On September 1, 1981, the USP Company makes a sale of goods to a foreign firm; it will receive FC 380,000 (payment in local or foreign currency units) on December 1, 1981. The USP Company has incurred costs in dollars and wishes to make definite the amount of dollars it will receive on December 1. It is considering three alternatives to deal with the risk of exchange rate fluctuation. The first alternative is to enter the forward market to sell FC 380,000 for dollars at the ninety-day forward rate quoted on September 1, 1981. The company can then utilize the FC 380,000 it receives on December 1, 1981, to pay for the dollars it has contracted to buy at the ninety-day forward rate. Under this arrangement the company will receive a definite amount in dollars in December as determined by the forward rate on September 1.

The second alternative is to borrow now from a foreign bank the FC amount such that the principal plus interest will equal what the company will be receiving on December 1. The interest rate paid is 28 percent. By borrowing, the company will receive the FCs immediately, and with them it can immediately purchase dollars at the September spot rate. It can then invest the dollars received in the United States at an 8 percent interest rate. When the company receives the FC 380,000 in December, it can use the funds to liquidate the local currency loan incurred in September. (The effective tax rate in both countries is 40 percent.)

The third alternative is to make no attempt to cover the exchange risk involved in waiting the three months for receipt of the FC 380,000. Under this alternative, the USP Company will convert the FC 380,000 into dollars at whatever spot rate prevails on December 1, 1981.

The three alternatives will be analyzed for a pattern of actual spot and forward exchange rates on September 1, 1981, and the expected spot rate on December 1, 1981. First to be considered is the pattern of rates characteristic of countries subject to currency devaluation:

	September 1, 1981
Spot rate of foreign currency units per $1	FC 1.90
Ninety-day forward rate	FC 2.00
	December 1, 1981
Expected future spot rate	FC 2.10

The three alternatives can now be analyzed. The first alternative involves entering a forward contract in which the USP Company sells FC 380,000 for dollars at a rate of 2 FC to $1. Therefore, the company has contracted to receive $190,000. At the spot rate, it would have received $200,000, so a reduction of expected sales revenue of $10,000 has been incurred, providing a tax shelter of $4,000. Thus total receipts and taxes saved amounts to $194,000.

Under the second alternative, the USP Company borrows FC from a bank in the foreign country; the amount of FC plus interest equals the FC 380,000 that will be received in December. The company will have to pay interest at 28 percent on the loan obtained from the foreign bank. Since the loan is for ninety days, or one-fourth of a year, the 28 percent is divided by 4 to obtain 7 percent, which is then multiplied by $(1 - T)$, for a total of 4.2 percent, the after-tax interest rate. Since

$$1.042X = \text{FC } 380{,}000,$$

$$X = \text{FC } 364{,}683$$

At the spot exchange rate, the proceeds from the FC 364,683 divided by 1.90 equal $191,938 and this amount can be invested in the United States to earn an 8 percent annual rate for ninety days, or 2 percent times $(1 - T)$, which equals 1.2 percent. The proceeds of $191,938 times 1.012 equal $194,241. On December 1, 1981, USP will receive the FC 380,000, which it will use to repay the FC 380,000 principal plus interest on its FC loan.

Under the third alternative, on December 1, 1981, the FC 380,000 will be converted into dollars at the spot rate then in effect. This represents FC 380,000 divided by 2.10, or $180,952. The expected $180,952 involves a reduction in taxable sales revenue of $19,048, so net proceeds with the tax shelter are $180,952 plus 0.4 times $19,048, which equals $188,571.

The net proceeds received under the three alternatives are:

1.	Sell FC in forward market for dollars	$194,000
2.	Borrow FC and repay from FC received in future	194,241
3.	Receive dollars based on spot rate when FC funds received	188,571

Under the assumptions of this example, the second alternative provides the greatest amount of funds. But different degrees of uncertainty are associated with each of the three alternatives. The dollars to be received under the first two alternatives are certain, while those under the third are not.

Before the fact, it is not possible to state definitely which alternative will yield the largest number of dollars on December 1, 1981. It depends on the future level of the spot rate on that date. Suppose that the actual spot rate on that December 1 turns out to be exactly what it was on September 1, 1981. In this situation, the first two alternatives will be unchanged, but for the third alternative, 380,000 divided by 1.90 equals $200,000—making it the best choice. But under the original assumptions, the third alternative was the worst choice. Thus doing nothing under the new set of assumed data turns out to be the best course of action, although it is clearly the riskiest. The use of the forward market or borrowing and investing through the money markets will sometimes yield lower net proceeds than taking no protective actions whatsoever will do, but having an unprotected position with respect to foreign exchange rate fluctuations is the greatest risk.

Using the forward market or borrowing is a form of insurance taken out to protect against unexpected fluctuations in foreign exchange rates. Like other forms of insurance, the protection involves a cost. But the situation is similar to that of buying fire insurance on your house. You could save the money if you could be sure that a fire were not going to occur. If you have paid fire insurance for several years and no fire has occurred, you could have saved money by not buying the fire insurance. But you paid the money to protect against the loss that would have taken place if the unexpected fire had occurred. Similarly, the cost of forward hedging or borrowing is a form of insurance premium paid to avoid even larger losses.

Protection against Rising Values of Foreign Currencies

When a foreign currency is rising in value, the U.S. firm has a risk exposure if it is in a short position with respect to the foreign currency. This means that if the firm has payments to be made in foreign currency or has liabilities outstanding that are expressed in such units, a rise in the value of the foreign currency unit will require that more dollars be used to buy it after it has risen in value. Or, to put it another way, if the firm has future obligations that are expressed in foreign currency units, its risk exposure is from the potential rise in the value of those units.

To illustrate: On September 1, 1981, the INT Corporation made a purchase of goods from a foreign firm that will require the payment of FC 380,000 on December 1 of the same year. The corporation wishes to make definite the amount of dollars it will need to pay the FC 380,000 on that date. The foreign firm is in a country whose currency has been rising in relation to the dollar in recent years. The tax rate in both countries is 40 percent. The observed pattern of foreign exchange rates is as follows:

	September 1, 1981
Spot rate of foreign currency units per $1	FC 2.10
Ninety-day forward rate	FC 2.00
	December 1, 1981
Expected future spot rate	FC 1.90

The INT Corporation considers the three alternatives discussed earlier to deal with the risk of exchange rate fluctuations. However, the *direction* of actions is now different. The first alternative is to enter the forward market to *buy* FC 380,000 for dollars at the ninety-day forward rate in effect on September 1, 1981. The corporation can then utilize the FC 380,000 it will receive under the forward contract on December 1, 1981, to meet the obligation it has incurred to make a payment of FC 380,000 on that date.

The second alternative is to borrow an amount in dollars to exchange into FCs to buy foreign securities that, with interest, will equal FC 380,000 on December 1, 1981. The interest rate paid in the United States is 12 percent; the interest earned in the foreign country is 8 percent.

The third alternative is to make no attempt to cover the risk involved in waiting for three months to pay the foreign currency obligation in the amount of FC 380,000. Under this alternative, the corporation will need sufficient dollars to equal FC 380,000 at whatever spot rate prevails on December 1, 1981.

The effects of the three alternatives can be analyzed. The first alternative involves entering a forward contract in which the INT Corporation buys FC 380,000 for dollars at a rate of FC 2 to $1. Therefore, the corporation will spend $190,000 to meet the future foreign currency obligation in the amount of FC 380,000. At the spot rate, it would have had to make a payment of 380,000 divided by 2.10, or $180,952, which is $9,048 less than the $190,000. This increase in expenses represents a tax shelter, at the 40 percent tax rate, of $3,619. The $190,000 expended on the forward contract minus the tax shelter of $3,619 is equal to $186,381, which represents the net after-tax costs of meeting the foreign currency obligation of FC 380,000 due on December 1, 1981.

Under the second alternative, the INT Corporation borrows dollars from a bank in the United States in an amount which, with foreign income, will total FC 380,000 when the foreign obligation becomes due on December 1, 1981. The amount it borrows is:

$$(2.10)(1 + [0.08 \div 4]0.6)X = \text{FC } 380{,}000$$

$$(2.10)(1.012)X = \text{FC } 380{,}000$$

$$2.1252X = \text{FC } 380{,}000$$

$$X = \$178{,}807$$

Adding the interest expense, the total cost is 1.018 ($178,807) = $182,026.

Under the third alternative, on December 1, 1981, the FC 380,000 will be obtained by the use of dollars converted into the foreign currency at the spot rate then in effect. This will represent FC 380,000 divided by 1.90, or $200,000. However, under the September 1 spot rate, INT Corporation will have needed a dollar outlay of only $180,952 (FC 380,000 divided by 2.10). Therefore, the firm will have incurred an opportunity loss of $19,048, which will result in a tax shelter of 0.4($19,048), or $7,619. Hence, the after-tax costs are $192,381.

The amount of dollars to be paid under the three alternatives are:

1.	Buy FC in forward market	$186,381
2.	Borrow in the United States and invest in foreign country	182,026
3.	Pay dollars for FC based on expected future spot rate	192,381

Under the assumptions of this example, the second alternative involves the smallest outlay in dollars to meet the FC 380,000 obligation due on December 1,1981. The dollars that will have to be paid under the first and second alternatives are certain; under the third alternative, the total proceeds are uncertain. Before the fact, it is not possible to state definitely which alternative will cost the least amount of dollars to meet the obligation due on December 1, 1981. It depends on the future level of the spot rate on that date. For example, suppose that the actual spot rate on December 1 turns out to be exactly what it was on September 1. In that case the net cost of using the third alternative for arranging to meet the future FC obligation will be dollars based on the December 1, 1981, spot rate of FC 2.10—$180,952.

The third alternative is best here, while under the original assumptions it was the worst. But again, taking no protective action is clearly the riskiest method.

Monetary Balance

Firms must take protective actions not only in regard to future expected receipts or obligations but also against a long or short position in foreign currencies resulting from the balance sheet position of their foreign subsidiaries. In the example of USP Company, the sale of the goods for FC 380,000 represented an account receivable for the three months until the obligation was paid. Suppose, however, that the number of FCs per $1 had risen from 1.90 to 2.00. At 1.90 FCs per $1, the account receivable would have been worth $200,000 in U.S. currency. But at the lower value of the FCs, 2FC to $1, the account receivable would have been worth only $190,000. This represents a before-tax loss of $10,000 in the dollar value of the receivables.

Conversely, in the INT Corporation example, the firm had an account payable of FC 380,000. If the change in the FC value had been an upward one, from FC 2.00 to FC 1.90 per $1, the firm would have had a loss because the accounts payable expressed in dollars would have increased by $10,000. Hence the concept of monetary balance comes into consideration. *Monetary balance* involves avoiding either a net receivable or a net payable position. Monetary assets and liabilities are those items whose value, expressed in local currency, does not change with devaluation or revaluation. To illustrate:

Monetary assets	Monetary liabilities
Cash	Accounts payable
Marketable securities	Notes payable
Accounts receivable	Tax liability reserve
Tax refunds receivable	Bonds
Notes receivable	Preferred stock
Prepaid insurance	

What is referred to as a firm's monetary position is another way of stating the firm's position with regard to real assets. For example, the basic balance sheet equation can be written as follows:

$$\text{Monetary assets} + \text{Real assets} = \text{Monetary liabilities} + \text{Net worth}$$

Consider the following pattern of relationships:

	Monetary assets	+	Real assets	=	Monetary liabilities	+	Net worth
Firm A: Monetary creditor	$6,000		$4,000		$4,000		$6,000
Firm B: Monetary debtor	4,000		6,000		6,000		4,000

Firm A is a monetary creditor because its monetary assets exceed its monetary liabilities; its net worth position is negative with respect to its investment coverage of net worth by real assets. In contrast, Firm B is a monetary debtor because it has monetary liabilities that exceed its monetary assets; its net worth coverage by investment in real assets is positive. Thus the monetary creditor can be referred to as a firm with a negative position in real assets and the monetary debtor as a firm with a positive position in real assets. From the foregoing we can see that the following relationships are equivalent:

Firm A	(Long position in foreign currency)	≡ Monetary creditor	≡ Monetary assets exceed monetary liabilities	≡ Negative position in real assets	≡ Balance of receipts in foreign currency less obligations in foreign currency is *positive*
Firm B	(Short position in foreign currency)	≡ Monetary debtor	≡ Monetary liabilities exceed monetary assets	≡ Positive position in real assets	≡ Balance of receipts in foreign currency less obligations in foreign currency is *negative*

Thus, if Firm A has a long position in a foreign currency, on balance it will be receiving more funds in foreign currency, or it will have a net monetary asset position that exceeds its monetary liabilities in that currency. The opposite holds for Firm B, which is in a short position with respect to a foreign currency. Hence the analysis with respect to a firm with net future receipts or net future obligations can be applied also to a firm's balance sheet position. A firm with net receipts is a net monetary creditor. Its foreign exchange rate risk exposure is vulnerable to a decline in value of the foreign currency.

Conversely, a firm with future net obligations in foreign currency is in a net monetary debtor position. The foreign exchange risk exposure it faces is the possibility of an increase in the value of the foreign currency. The alternative methods of protection against foreign exchange fluctuations discussed earlier apply to the short or long balance sheet position a firm may have with respect to foreign currency.

In addition to the specific actions of hedging in the forward market or borrowing and lending through the money markets, other business policies can help the firm achieve a balance sheet position that minimizes the foreign exchange rate risk exposure to either currency devaluation or currency revaluation upward. Specifically, in countries whose currency values are likely to fall, local management of subsidiaries should be encouraged to follow these policies:

1. Never have excessive idle cash on hand. If cash accumulates, it should be used to purchase inventory or other real assets.
2. Attempt to avoid granting excessive trade credit or trade credit for extended periods. If accounts receivable cannot be avoided, an attempt should be made to charge interest high enough to compensate for the loss of purchasing power.
3. Wherever possible, avoid giving advances in connection with purchase orders unless a rate of interest is paid by the seller on these advances from the time the subsidiary—the buyer—pays them until the time of delivery, at a rate sufficient to cover the loss of purchasing power.

4. Borrow local currency funds from banks or other sources whenever these funds can be obtained at a rate of interest no higher than U.S. rates adjusted for the anticipated rate of devaluation in the foreign country.
5. Make an effort to purchase materials and supplies on a trade credit basis in the country in which the foreign subsidiary is operating, extending the final date of payment as long as possible.

The opposite policies should be followed in a country where a revaluation upward in foreign currency values is likely to take place. All these policies are aimed at a monetary balance position in which the firm is neither a monetary debtor nor a monetary creditor. Some firms take a more aggressive position. They seek to have a net monetary debtor position in a country whose exchange rates are expected fall and a net monetary creditor position in a country whose exchange rates are likely to rise.

International Financing

The general principles affecting financing decisions are the same for international financing as for domestic financing. However, the variables affecting international financing decisions are expanded, and the number of financing methods and sources is increased. The forms and sources of financing are similar in the different countries of the world, but important differences provide new pitfalls and additional opportunities. A wider range of alternatives must be evaluated in both quantitative and qualitative terms in choosing among alternative sources, forms, and localities of international financing. Financing in an international setting makes use of the increasingly important international financing markets—the Eurocurrency and Eurobond markets. The facilities of private lending institutions are augmented substantially by international lending agencies, national development banks, and other government agencies performing important functions in financing operations and projects.

Some financing operations are distinctive to international business finance. A form of commercial bank financing widely used in Europe is represented by overdrafts. An overdraft agreement permits a customer to draw checks up to some specified maximum limit in excess of the checking account balance. In contrast to U.S. practice, European overdrafts are provided for in previous loan agreements and have widespread use in normal banking relations.

Another form of financing—one that was until recent years much more widespread in Europe than in the United States—is the use of discounted *trade bills* in both domestic and foreign transactions. The increased use of bankers' acceptances in the United States has been associated with the growth of the movement of goods in international trade.

A third variation from U.S. financing practices found in Europe is the broad participation of commercial banks in medium- and long-term lending activities. In Europe, commercial banks carry on considerable activities of the kind that would be described as investment banking operations in the United States. This difference results from a legal requirement in the United States. The Banking Act of 1933 required the divestiture of investment banking operations by commercial banks.

A fourth practice distinctive to international financing relates to arbi-loans and link financing, both of which represent forms of equalizing the supply of and demand for loanable funds in relation to sensitive interest rate levels among different countries. Under *arbi-loans*, or international interest arbitrage financing, a borrower obtains loans in a country where the supply of funds is relatively abundant. The borrowed funds are then converted into another foreign currency needed by the firm. Simultaneously, the borrower enters into a forward exchange contract to protect itself on the reconversion of the new foreign currency into the original foreign currency that will be required at the time the loan must be repaid. Commercial banks are typically involved in arbi-loan transactions both as lenders and as intermediaries in the foreign exchange trading.

In *link financing*, the commercial banks take an even more direct role. A lender bank in the United States, for example, deposits funds with a bank in Mexico, the borrower's country, where interest rates are higher. This deposit may be earmarked for the specified borrower. The lender, of course, is expected to hedge its position in the foreign exchange markets, since it will be repaid in the currency of the country in which the bank deposit was made. The U.S. bank receives a rate that provides an interest differential after all additional expenses, such as the cost of hedging, are taken into consideration. The Mexican bank receives a commission for handling the transaction.

Expanding Role of U.S. Commercial Banks and Investment Bankers

Commercial banks have long performed an important role in export and import financing. They have increased the number of their foreign branches and have expanded their foreign operations and lending activities. They have also participated in consortiums with foreign merchant banks (banks that specialize in business lending) and investment banks for the conduct of all forms of international financing services.

Through their Edge Act corporations, by which they can make equity investments, commercial banks have participated for many years in the financing of international operations. Edge Act subsidiaries were provided for by amendments in 1916 and 1919 to the Federal Reserve Act of 1913. The amendments give U.S. commercial banks the authority to enter international markets and engage in certain operations that are prohibited in the United States. Edge Act subsidiaries can conduct all forms of international banking; they can issue or confirm letters of credit, finance foreign trade, engage in spot and foreign exchange transactions, and so on. Through these foreign banking subsidiaries and affiliates, direct investments in the form of both debt and equity can be made in commercial and industrial firms.

U.S. investment banking firms have actively participated in arranging Eurocurrency financing, mainly for their U.S. customers. They have developed joint participation activities with foreign merchant banks and with foreign investment banking houses. They have established offices in foreign countries and have participated in international underwriting groups that have developed the Eurobond market.

Commercial banks have become especially active in international project financing. This type of financing involves large investment projects, usually joint ventures between government and private enterprise that are financed by international and government sources as well as by private sources, often through a Eurodollar bank syndicate. International project financing is characterized by large investments for development activities such as the opening of a new mine, major drilling or exploration, or the establishment of a major chemical or pharmaceutical complex. Normally, there is more than one major equity owner of the project company itself. The equity owners collectively possess or arrange for the requisite operating, technical, marketing, and financial strengths needed for the project's success.

International project financing generally involves relatively high debt leverage. Since the projects provide output for international markets, debt is issued in several currencies. The sources of debt are commercial banks, export credit agencies, suppliers, product purchasers, international lending agencies, regional or national development banks, and local governments.

International investment bankers serve as project financial advisers, fitting together the various types of financing needed to meet the project's requirements. Each transaction typically includes various covenants related directly to the characteristics of the project.[1]

The Eurodollar System

The Eurodollar system, which operates as an international money market, was developed in the early 1950s as banks accepted interest bearing deposits in currencies other than their own. Most of the early activity occurred in Europe, where the predominant foreign currency used was the dollar (whose stability gave it the status of an international currency). Since the system is now worldwide, including many different currencies, it is often called the *Eurocurrency system*.

The flow process of the Eurodollar market can be illustrated as follows. A European firm holds a dollar deposit in a New York bank. It can hold the dollars in the form of a dollar deposit claim on its European bank by drawing a check on the New York bank and making a deposit in the European bank. The European bank can in turn make loans to other customers. Except for holding fractional reserves against its dollar deposit liabilities, the European bank has served as an intermediary in transferring the dollar balances in the United States from its depositors to its borrowers. Yet its depositors still hold claims in dollars.

The Eurobanks, including the foreign branches of many U.S. banks, accept Eurodollar deposits and lend out these funds. The transactions involve large amounts, and the spread between the interest rates on loans and the interest paid on deposits is usually small. This is a fast-action market in which most transactions are arranged over the phone or through cables, with the confirming documents sent later by mail.

Eurodollar loans are typically in multiples of $1 million and have maturities ranging from thirty days to five to seven years. If the borrower is known to the bank, a loan of less than a year can be arranged quickly. Eurodollar loans are typically unsecured, but there may be restrictions of other kinds placed on the borrowing activities of the firm receiving the loan. One form of Eurodollar loan is the floating

[1] For a more complete discussion, see Robert L. Huston, "Project Financing," in J. Fred Weston and Maurice B. Goudzwaard, eds., *The Treasurer's Handbook* (Homewood, Ill.: Dow Jones–Irwin, 1976).

rate revolving loan, sometimes referred to as a revolver or a roll-over credit. The rate on the loan is quoted as the percentage above the London interbank offer rate (LIBOR), and it reflects the rates on liquid funds that move among the money markets of the developed nations. The floating rate provision dampens borrowing based on speculation on future interest rates. Prime borrowers typically pay from three-eighths to three-quarters of 1 percent over the LIBOR, depending on maturity. Lines of credit are typically established for a given period not to exceed twelve months and can be renegotiated at the end of the period. There is usually a commitment fee of one-fourth of 1 percent to one-half of 1 percent on the unused portion of the line of credit. The Eurocurrency system contributes to increasing and redistributing the world supply of international reserves or liquid resources. It represents an important addition to the development of a competitive and unified international money market.

Eurobonds represent the longer-term range of maturities in the Eurocurrency market. They are offered for sale in more than one country through international syndicates of underwriting and selling banks, and they are typically denominated in a strong currency, such as the German mark. The U.S. dollar continues to be used, despite fluctuations in its value, because it is a principal transaction currency. A large pool of Eurodollars is also available. Sometimes Eurobonds are denominated for repayment in multiple currencies. The creditor can request payment of the interest and principal in any predetermined currency at a previously established parity.

Convertible Eurobonds were stimulated by the entry of U.S. firms into financing through the Eurobond market. The convertible Eurobonds of U.S. firms have the advantage of carrying relatively low interest rates. Also, the market is broad so that larger amounts can be sold. This represents a method of internationalizing the ownership of the common stock of U.S. multinational corporations that have large direct investments and operations in foreign countries. For the foreign investors the convertible Eurobonds have the advantage of a fixed rate of interest plus potential capital gains.

The Eurobond market has helped internationalize the local character of the capital markets in individual European countries by underwriting the sales of their securities to investors in a number of European countries. The market contributes to the international financial adjustment process by stimulating the outflow of funds from countries with balance of payments surpluses (such as Germany).

Working Capital Management in International Enterprise

International cash management involves minimizing the exposure of foreign-located funds to foreign exchange rate risk and avoiding prohibitions on the movement of funds from one country to another. Funds denominated in a foreign currency, particularly that of a developing country, are potentially subject to a decrease in value in terms of the home currency. The financial manager who hopes to avoid foreign exchange rate risk and prohibitions against the international movement of funds must continually assess political and economic trends in the countries of operation in order to anticipate changes that can have a detrimental effect.

The general principles that apply to the management of cash on an international basis are very similar to those used successfully by many firms on a domestic basis. Multinational firms try to speed up the collection of cash by having bank accounts in the banking system of each country. In many countries, customers pay their bills by requesting their bank or postal administration to deduct the amount owed from their account and to transfer it to the other firm's account.

Multinational commercial banks, particularly those that have branches or affiliates in a large number of countries, can be very helpful to multinational firms. Several of the larger U.S. multinational commercial banks have foreign departments whose sole purpose is to help U.S. multinational firms solve their problems of international cash management. An international bank can speed the flow of funds of a multinational firm and thereby decrease the exposure of these funds to foreign exchange rate risk. It can suggest the routing of the transfers as well as the national currency to be used. Although in the United States the average time between the initiation and completion of a financial transaction is two or three days, the time interval for foreign transactions can be as long as two or three weeks. The long delays unnecessarily tie up large amounts of funds and should be avoided. In this area, the multinational commercial banks are particularly helpful, since they can transfer funds from one country to another (provided government restrictions do not interfere) on a same-day basis if they have branches or affiliates in the two countries involved.

Increasingly, the arena for business finance is the global market. At the start of each day, the corporate treasurer determines whether to borrow or to lend in the international financial market. The investment decisions are made in both domestic and foreign countries.

The financial manager of the multinational corporate enterprise must consider the form and extent of protection against currency fluctuations on sales and purchases. If the firm has surplus cash, the financial manager must compare the returns from investing in the domestic money market with those from investing in the international market. Similarly, if short-term financing needs arise, the manager must make comparisons between domestic and foreign financing sources. Among the considerations are the advantages and disadvantages of using the impersonal international financial market versus those of developing long-term financing relations with international commercial banks or financial groups in the United States, London, Paris, Zurich, Bonn, and Tokyo.

Summary

International business transactions are conducted in more than one currency. If a firm is expecting receipts in foreign currency units, its risk is that the value of the foreign currency units will fall. If it has obligations to be paid in foreign currency units, its risk is that the value of the foreign currency will rise. To reduce foreign exchange risk, firms can engage in transactions in the forward foreign exchange market. They can also borrow at current spot exchange rates the amount of local currency needed for future transactions. These two forms of hedging are essentially insurance and therefore involve costs.

Firms also take protective action against long or short positions in foreign currencies resulting from the balance sheet position of their foreign subsidiaries. Monetary assets and liabilities are those items whose value, expressed in local currency, does not change with devaluation or revaluation. A firm seeks to have a net monetary creditor position in a country whose exchange rates are expected to rise and a net monetary debtor position in a country whose exchange rates are expected to fall. A monetary debtor position can be created by investing all excess cash, granting as little trade credit as possible, avoiding advances, and borrowing funds. A monetary creditor position can be developed by holding cash or cash equivalents, such as foreign securities, and by having receivables due in the foreign currency.

International financing broadens the range of fund sources. These sources include international and government institutions, Eurocurrency and Eurobond markets, overdrafts from European banks, discounted trade bills, and arbi-loans and link financing. Edge Act subsidiaries permit commercial banks to enter international markets and engage in operations from which they are prohibited in the United States. U.S. commercial banks and investment banking firms have become very active in international financing and related services.

International cash management involves minimizing exposure of foreign-located funds to exchange rate risks and avoiding restrictions on the movement of funds from one country to another. International banks provide many services that facilitate effective international working capital management by multinational firms.

Questions

27.1 What has been the impact of advances in the technology of transportation and communication on international trade and finance?

27.2 Why is the ratio of foreign earnings to a firm's total earnings likely to be greater than the ratio of its foreign sales to total sales?

27.3 If a firm has difficulty developing a product that will sell in the local domestic market, is it likely to have greater success in a foreign market? Explain.

27.4 What are monetary assets and liabilities (as contrasted with "real" or non-monetary assets and liabilities)?

27.5 What are arbi-loans and link financing?

27.6 What are some of the services provided by U.S. commercial banks to firms engaged in international operations or financing?

27.7 What are some of the services provided by U.S. investment banking firms to U.S. business firms engaged in international operations or financing?

27.8 What is the Eurocurrency system, and what economic functions does it perform?

27.9 Describe some major characteristics of Eurodollar loans.

27.10 In what respects are domestic working capital management and international working capital management similar and different?

27.11 What services can the multinational commercial bank perform to help the U.S. multinational operating firm solve its problems of international cash management?

27.12 What are some of the reasons that U.S. firms engage in financing abroad?

Problems

27.1 In 1978 the number of Japanese yen required to equal one U.S. dollar was 194.60. In March 1981, the U.S. dollar was worth 211 yen.

a. What is X_0 (1978)? What is X_1 (1981)?

b. What is E_0 (1978)? What is E_1 (1981)?

c. What is the percentage devaluation or revaluation of the yen in terms of the U.S. dollar?

d. What is the percentage devaluation or revaluation of the dollar in terms of the yen?

27.2 If the exchange rate between dollars and francs is fr. 5 = \$1, and between dollars and pounds is £1 = \$1.60, what is the exchange rate between francs and pounds?

27.3 The *Wall Street Journal* on March 5, 1981, listed the following information on the exchange rates between the dollar and the German mark:

$$X_0 = 2.1436 \text{ DM/\$}$$

$$E_0 = \$0.4665/\text{DM}$$

$$X_f \text{ (90 days)} = 2.1304 \text{ DM/\$}$$

$$E_f \text{ (90 days)} = \$0.4694/\text{DM}$$

The prime interest rate on that day was $18\frac{1}{2}$ percent.

a. What is implied about the German interest rate?

b. If the forward exchange rate was \$0.45/DM, what would be the German interest rate?

c. If the German interest rate was 12 percent, what would be the 90-day forward rate on Deutsche marks per dollar?

27.4 The Coret Company's subsidiary has monetary assets of FC 800,000 and monetary liabilities of FC 1,000,000. Calculate the gain or loss of the parent under the following two states of the world:

a. There has been a devaluation; the local currency has dropped from 20 FC per \$1 to 25 FC per \$1.

b. There has been a revaluation; the local currency has appreciated from 20 FC per \$1 to 15 FC per \$1.

27.5 Debussy Corporation exports a substantial amount of cosmetics each year and therefore has a great part of its assets invested in FC receivables. Monetary assets are FC 30,000,000, while monetary liabilities are FC 10,000,000. Calculate any gains or losses under the following two states of the world:

a. There is a revaluation from 4 FC per \$1 to 3 FC per \$1.

b. There is a devaluation from 4 FC per \$1 to 5 FC per \$1.

27.6 The MNC Corporation has a number of subsidiaries located in various Asian countries. These subsidiaries collect the equivalent of \$500,000 each month, and the funds are transferred to the company's cash center in Hong Kong. The average transfer time has been fourteen days. An international bank, eager to solicit business from MNC, has offered to handle the transfer of these funds at a guaranteed average transfer time of not more than two days. The company's opportunity cost is 15 percent.

a. How much is this service worth to the company?

b. What are the advantages and disadvantages of the arrangement?

27.7 Cartell International's principal manufacturing plant in Europe is located in Paris. In-transfer and temporarily idle funds have been routed to and through this office. However, since forward market quotations on the French franc have been weakening lately, the manager of the international division is planning to reroute temporarily idle cash funds to the office of the company's German subsidiary. The company has been protecting itself by entering into forward ninety-day contracts to purchase dollars with French francs at an annual discount of 5 to 6 percent. By comparison, ninety-day forward contracts can be obtained to buy dollars with Deutsche marks at a premium in relation to the present spot rate of 1.5 percent. Short-term interest rates in France are 7.5 percent and in West Germany approximately 7 per cent.

a. Should West Germany become the transfer center of the firm's international funds flow? What would be the cost or benefit of any change that might be suggested?
b. What requirements for an international financial center are considered important in locating a cash concentration center in a particular city? Why?

27.8 The treasurer of a company in Mexico borrowed $10,000 in dollars at a 15 percent interest rate when the exchange rate was 22 pesos to the dollar. His company paid the loan plus interest one year later, when the exchange rate was 25 pesos to the dollar.

a. What rate of interest was paid, based on the pesos received and paid by the treasurer?
b. Show how your result illustrates the interest rate parity theorem.

27.9 The treasurer of a company in Mexico is comparing two borrowing alternatives for a 180-day loan. He can borrow in U.S. dollars from a U.S. bank at a 15 percent interest rate or from a Mexican bank in pesos at a 25 percent interest rate. The spot exchange rate is 23.5 pesos to the dollar. The 180-day forward exchange rate is 25 pesos to the dollar.

a. What is the effective interest rate in pesos on the U.S. loan?
b. Verify your answer by use of the interest rate parity relationship.

27.10 The Kory Company has made a sale of construction equipment to a foreign firm and will receive FC 11,000,000 on May 31, 19X9. The company has incurred all of its expenses in dollars and needs to know the definite dollar amounts that it will receive on May 31, 19X9. The effective tax rate in both countries is 40 percent, and the expected future spot rate is 12 FC per dollar. The director of finance at Kory Company is considering three options to deal with the foreign exchange risk:

a. To enter the forward market to sell FC 11,000,000 for dollars at the ninety-day forward rate quoted on March 1, 19X9, which is 11 FC per dollar. Under this arrangement the Kory Company will receive a definite amount in dollars in May as determined by the forward rate on March 1, 19X9.
b. To borrow on March 1, 19X9, from a foreign bank an amount in foreign currency that, with interest, will equal the amount the Kory Company will be receiving on May 31, 19X9. The interest rate on the loan would be 32 percent. By borrowing, the company will receive FCs and, with the FCs received, can

immediately purchase dollars at the March 1, 19X9, spot rate, which is FC 10 per dollar. The dollars received can be invested in the United States at an interest rate of 12 percent. When the company receives the FC 11,000,000 on May 31, 19X9, it can liquidate the local currency loan plus interest.

c. To make no attempt to cover the exchange risk involved in waiting the three months for receipt of the FC 11,000,000. Under the third alternative, the company will convert the FC 11,000,000 into dollars at the spot rate of FC 12 per dollar that is expected to prevail on May 31, 19X9.

Which alternative should be chosen?

27.11 Rework Problem 27.10 assuming a foreign interest rate of 60 percent. Which alternative is the most attractive now? Explain.

27.12 On March 1, 19X9, the Burrows Company bought electronic equipment from a foreign firm that will require the payment of FC 900,000 on May 31, 19X9. The spot rate on March 1, 19X9, is FC 10 per dollar; the expected future spot rate is FC 8 per dollar; and the ninety-day forward rate is FC 9 per dollar. The U.S. interest rate is 12 percent, and the foreign interest rate is 8 percent. The tax rate for both countries is 40 percent. The Burrows Company is considering three alternatives to deal with the risk of exchange rate fluctuations:

a. To enter the forward market to buy FC 900,000 at the ninety-day forward rate in effect on March 1, 19X9.

b. To borrow an amount in dollars to buy the FC at the current spot rate. This money is to be invested in government securities of the foreign country; with the interest income, it will equal FC 900,000 on May 31, 19X9.

c. To wait until May 31, 19X9, and buy FCs at whatever spot rate prevails at that time.

Which alternative should the Burrows Company follow in order to minimize its cost of meeting the future payment in FCs? Explain.

27.13 The U.S.-based Polychem Corporation wishes to borrow $1,000,000 for a six-month period. The funds can be borrowed in the United States at a 16 percent annual rate. The financial vice-president feels that 16 percent is quite high, and finds that he can borrow in Swiss francs at an 8 percent annual rate. The spot value of Swiss francs is $.5120; the forward rate for a 180-day contract is $.5311. Is there an advantage to borrowing in Swiss francs at the 8 percent rate?

APPENDIX A

INTEREST TABLES

Table A.1

Compound Sum of $1
CVIF $(r, n) = (1 + r)^n$

Period	1%	2%	3%	4%	5%	6%	7%	8%	9%	10%	12%	14%	15%	16%	18%	20%	24%	28%	32%	36%
1	1.0100	1.0200	1.0300	1.0400	1.0500	1.0600	1.0700	1.0800	1.0900	1.1000	1.1200	1.1400	1.1500	1.1600	1.1800	1.2000	1.2400	1.2800	1.3200	1.3600
2	1.0201	1.0404	1.0609	1.0816	1.1025	1.1236	1.1449	1.1664	1.1881	1.2100	1.2544	1.2996	1.3225	1.3456	1.3924	1.4400	1.5376	1.6384	1.7424	1.8496
3	1.0303	1.0612	1.0927	1.1249	1.1576	1.1910	1.2250	1.2597	1.2950	1.3310	1.4049	1.4815	1.5209	1.5609	1.6430	1.7280	1.9066	2.0972	2.3000	2.5155
4	1.0406	1.0824	1.1255	1.1699	1.2155	1.2625	1.3108	1.3605	1.4116	1.4641	1.5735	1.6890	1.7490	1.8106	1.9388	2.0736	2.3642	2.6844	3.0360	3.4210
5	1.0510	1.1041	1.1593	1.2167	1.2763	1.3382	1.4026	1.4693	1.5386	1.6105	1.7623	1.9254	2.0114	2.1003	2.2878	2.4883	2.9316	3.4360	4.0075	4.6526
6	1.0615	1.1262	1.1941	1.2653	1.3401	1.4185	1.5007	1.5869	1.6771	1.7716	1.9738	2.1950	2.3131	2.4364	2.6996	2.9860	3.6352	4.3980	5.2899	6.3275
7	1.0721	1.1487	1.2299	1.3159	1.4071	1.5036	1.6058	1.7138	1.8280	1.9487	2.2107	2.5023	2.6600	2.8262	3.1855	3.5832	4.5077	5.6295	6.9826	8.6054
8	1.0829	1.1717	1.2668	1.3686	1.4775	1.5938	1.7182	1.8509	1.9926	2.1436	2.4760	2.8526	3.0590	3.2784	3.7589	4.2998	5.5895	7.2058	9.2170	11.703
9	1.0937	1.1951	1.3048	1.4233	1.5513	1.6895	1.8385	1.9990	2.1719	2.3579	2.7731	3.2519	3.5179	3.8030	4.4355	5.1598	6.9310	9.2234	12.166	15.916
10	1.1046	1.2190	1.3439	1.4802	1.6289	1.7908	1.9672	2.1589	2.3674	2.5937	3.1058	3.7072	4.0456	4.4114	5.2338	6.1917	8.5944	11.805	16.059	21.646
11	1.1157	1.2434	1.3842	1.5395	1.7103	1.8983	2.1049	2.3316	2.5804	2.8531	3.4785	4.2262	4.6524	5.1173	6.1759	7.4301	10.657	15.111	21.198	29.439
12	1.1268	1.2682	1.4258	1.6010	1.7959	2.0122	2.2522	2.5182	2.8127	3.1384	3.8960	4.8179	5.3502	5.9360	7.2876	8.9161	13.214	19.342	27.982	40.037
13	1.1381	1.2936	1.4685	1.6651	1.8856	2.1329	2.4098	2.7196	3.0658	3.4523	4.3635	5.4924	6.1528	6.8858	8.5994	10.699	16.386	24.758	36.937	54.451
14	1.1495	1.3195	1.5126	1.7317	1.9799	2.2609	2.5785	2.9372	3.3417	3.7975	4.8871	6.2613	7.0757	7.9875	10.147	12.839	20.319	31.691	48.756	74.053
15	1.1610	1.3459	1.5580	1.8009	2.0789	2.3966	2.7590	3.1722	3.6425	4.1772	5.4736	7.1379	8.1371	9.2655	11.973	15.407	25.195	40.564	64.358	100.71
16	1.1726	1.3728	1.6047	1.8730	2.1829	2.5404	2.9522	3.4259	3.9703	4.5950	6.1304	8.1372	9.3576	10.748	14.129	18.488	31.242	51.923	84.953	136.96
17	1.1843	1.4002	1.6528	1.9479	2.2920	2.6928	3.1588	3.7000	4.3276	5.0545	6.8660	9.2765	10.761	12.467	16.672	22.186	38.740	66.461	112.13	186.27
18	1.1961	1.4282	1.7024	2.0258	2.4066	2.8543	3.3799	3.9960	4.7171	5.5599	7.6900	10.575	12.375	14.462	19.673	26.623	48.038	85.070	148.02	253.33
19	1.2081	1.4568	1.7535	2.1068	2.5270	3.0256	3.6165	4.3157	5.1417	6.1159	8.6128	12.055	14.231	16.776	23.214	31.948	59.567	108.89	195.39	344.53
20	1.2202	1.4859	1.8061	2.1911	2.6533	3.2071	3.8697	4.6610	5.6044	6.7275	9.6463	13.743	16.366	19.460	27.393	38.337	73.864	139.37	257.91	468.57
21	1.2324	1.5157	1.8603	2.2788	2.7860	3.3996	4.1406	5.0338	6.1088	7.4002	10.803	15.667	18.821	22.574	32.323	46.005	91.591	178.40	340.44	637.26
22	1.2447	1.5460	1.9161	2.3699	2.9253	3.6035	4.4304	5.4365	6.6586	8.1403	12.100	17.861	21.644	26.186	38.142	55.206	113.57	228.35	449.39	866.67
23	1.2572	1.5769	1.9736	2.4647	3.0715	3.8197	4.7405	5.8715	7.2579	8.9543	13.552	20.361	24.891	30.376	45.007	66.247	140.83	292.30	593.19	1178.6
24	1.2697	1.6084	2.0328	2.5633	3.2251	4.0489	5.0724	6.3412	7.9111	9.8497	15.178	23.212	28.625	35.236	53.108	79.496	174.63	374.14	783.02	1602.9
25	1.2824	1.6406	2.0938	2.6658	3.3864	4.2919	5.4274	6.8485	8.6231	10.834	17.000	26.461	32.918	40.874	62.668	95.396	216.54	478.90	1033.5	2180.0
26	1.2953	1.6734	2.1566	2.7725	3.5557	4.5494	5.8074	7.3964	9.3992	11.918	19.040	30.166	37.856	47.414	73.948	114.47	268.51	612.99	1364.3	2964.9
27	1.3082	1.7069	2.2213	2.8834	3.7335	4.8223	6.2139	7.9881	10.245	13.110	21.324	34.389	43.535	55.000	87.259	137.37	332.95	784.63	1800.9	4032.2
28	1.3213	1.7410	2.2879	2.9987	3.9201	5.1117	6.6488	8.6271	11.167	14.421	23.883	39.204	50.065	63.800	102.96	164.84	412.86	1004.3	2377.2	5483.8
29	1.3345	1.7758	2.3566	3.1187	4.1161	5.4184	7.1143	9.3173	12.172	15.863	26.749	44.693	57.575	74.008	121.50	197.81	511.95	1285.5	3137.9	7458.0
30	1.3478	1.8114	2.4273	3.2434	4.3219	5.7435	7.6123	10.062	13.267	17.449	29.959	50.950	66.211	85.849	143.37	237.37	634.81	1645.5	4142.0	10143.
40	1.4889	2.2080	3.2620	4.8010	7.0400	10.285	14.974	21.724	31.409	45.259	93.050	188.88	267.86	378.72	750.37	1469.7	5455.9	19426.	66520.	*
50	1.6446	2.6916	4.3839	7.1067	11.467	18.420	29.457	46.901	74.357	117.39	289.00	700.23	1083.6	1670.7	3927.3	9100.4	46890.	*	*	*
60	1.8167	3.2810	5.8916	10.519	18.679	32.987	57.946	101.25	176.03	304.48	897.59	2595.9	4383.9	7370.1	20555.	56347.	*	*	*	*

* CVIF > 99,999

Table A.2

Present Value of $1

PVIF(r, n) = $(1 + r)^{-n}$

Period	1%	2%	3%	4%	5%	6%	7%	8%	9%	10%	12%	14%	15%	16%	18%	20%	24%	28%	32%	36%
1	.9901	.9804	.9709	.9615	.9524	.9434	.9346	.9259	.9174	.9091	.8929	.8772	.8696	.8621	.8475	.8333	.8065	.7813	.7576	.7353
2	.9803	.9612	.9426	.9246	.9070	.8900	.8734	.8573	.8417	.8264	.7972	.7695	.7561	.7432	.7182	.6944	.6504	.6104	.5739	.5407
3	.9706	.9423	.9151	.8890	.8638	.8396	.8163	.7938	.7722	.7513	.7118	.6750	.6575	.6407	.6086	.5787	.5245	.4768	.4348	.3975
4	.9610	.9238	.8885	.8548	.8227	.7921	.7629	.7350	.7084	.6830	.6355	.5921	.5718	.5523	.5158	.4823	.4230	.3725	.3294	.2923
5	.9515	.9057	.8626	.8219	.7835	.7473	.7130	.6806	.6499	.6209	.5674	.5194	.4972	.4761	.4371	.4019	.3411	.2910	.2495	.2149
6	.9420	.8880	.8375	.7903	.7462	.7050	.6663	.6302	.5963	.5645	.5066	.4556	.4323	.4104	.3704	.3349	.2751	.2274	.1890	.1580
7	.9327	.8706	.8131	.7599	.7107	.6651	.6227	.5835	.5470	.5132	.4523	.3996	.3759	.3538	.3139	.2791	.2218	.1776	.1432	.1162
8	.9235	.8535	.7894	.7307	.6768	.6274	.5820	.5403	.5019	.4665	.4039	.3506	.3269	.3050	.2660	.2325	.1789	.1388	.1085	.0854
9	.9143	.8368	.7664	.7026	.6446	.5919	.5439	.5002	.4604	.4241	.3606	.3075	.2843	.2630	.2255	.1938	.1443	.1084	.0822	.0628
10	.9053	.8203	.7441	.6756	.6139	.5584	.5083	.4632	.4224	.3855	.3220	.2697	.2472	.2267	.1911	.1615	.1164	.0847	.0623	.0462
11	.8963	.8043	.7224	.6496	.5847	.5268	.4751	.4289	.3875	.3505	.2875	.2366	.2149	.1954	.1619	.1346	.0938	.0662	.0472	.0340
12	.8874	.7885	.7014	.6246	.5568	.4970	.4440	.3971	.3555	.3186	.2567	.2076	.1869	.1685	.1372	.1122	.0757	.0517	.0357	.0250
13	.8787	.7730	.6810	.6006	.5303	.4688	.4150	.3677	.3262	.2897	.2292	.1821	.1625	.1452	.1163	.0935	.0610	.0404	.0271	.0184
14	.8700	.7579	.6611	.5775	.5051	.4423	.3878	.3405	.2992	.2633	.2046	.1597	.1413	.1252	.0985	.0779	.0492	.0316	.0205	.0135
15	.8613	.7430	.6419	.5553	.4810	.4173	.3624	.3152	.2745	.2394	.1827	.1401	.1229	.1079	.0835	.0649	.0397	.0247	.0155	.0099
16	.8528	.7284	.6232	.5339	.4581	.3936	.3387	.2919	.2519	.2176	.1631	.1229	.1069	.0930	.0708	.0541	.0320	.0193	.0118	.0073
17	.8444	.7142	.6050	.5134	.4363	.3714	.3166	.2703	.2311	.1978	.1456	.1078	.0929	.0802	.0600	.0451	.0258	.0150	.0089	.0054
18	.8360	.7002	.5874	.4936	.4155	.3503	.2959	.2502	.2120	.1799	.1300	.0946	.0808	.0691	.0508	.0376	.0208	.0118	.0068	.0039
19	.8277	.6864	.5703	.4746	.3957	.3305	.2765	.2317	.1945	.1635	.1161	.0829	.0703	.0596	.0431	.0313	.0168	.0092	.0051	.0029
20	.8195	.6730	.5537	.4564	.3769	.3118	.2584	.2145	.1784	.1486	.1037	.0728	.0611	.0514	.0365	.0261	.0135	.0072	.0039	.0021
25	.7798	.6095	.4776	.3751	.2953	.2330	.1842	.1460	.1160	.0923	.0588	.0378	.0304	.0245	.0160	.0105	.0046	.0021	.0010	.0005
30	.7419	.5521	.4120	.3083	.2314	.1741	.1314	.0994	.0754	.0573	.0334	.0196	.0151	.0116	.0070	.0042	.0016	.0006	.0002	.0001
40	.6717	.4529	.3066	.2083	.1420	.0972	.0668	.0460	.0318	.0231	.0107	.0053	.0037	.0026	.0013	.0007	.0002	.0001	*	*
50	.6080	.3715	.2281	.1407	.0872	.0543	.0339	.0213	.0134	.0085	.0035	.0014	.0009	.0006	.0003	.0001	*	*	*	*
60	.5504	.3048	.1697	.0951	.0535	.0303	.0173	.0099	.0057	.0033	.0011	.0004	.0002	.0001	*	*	*	*	*	*

* The factor is zero to four decimal places.

Table A.3

Sum on an Annuity of $1 per Period for *n* Periods

$$\text{CVIFA}(r,t) = \sum_{t=1}^{n} (1+r)^{t-1} = \frac{(1+r)^n - 1}{r}$$

Number of periods	1%	2%	3%	4%	5%	6%	7%	8%	9%	10%	12%	14%	15%	16%	18%	20%	24%	28%	32%	36%
1	1.0000	1.0000	1.0000	1.0000	1.0000	1.0000	1.0000	1.0000	1.0000	1.0000	1.0000	1.0000	1.0000	1.0000	1.0000	1.0000	1.0000	1.0000	1.0000	1.0000
2	2.0100	2.0200	2.0300	2.0400	2.0500	2.0600	2.0700	2.0800	2.0900	2.1000	2.1200	2.1400	2.1500	2.1600	2.1800	2.2000	2.2400	2.2800	2.3200	2.3600
3	3.0301	3.0604	3.0909	3.1216	3.1525	3.1836	3.2149	3.2464	3.2781	3.3100	3.3744	3.4396	3.4725	3.5056	3.5724	3.6400	3.7776	3.9184	4.0624	4.2096
4	4.0604	4.1216	4.1836	4.2465	4.3101	4.3746	4.4399	4.5061	4.5731	4.6410	4.7793	4.9211	4.9934	5.0665	5.2154	5.3680	5.6842	6.0156	6.3624	6.7251
5	5.1010	5.2040	5.3091	5.4163	5.5256	5.6371	5.7507	5.8666	5.9847	6.1051	6.3528	6.6101	6.7424	6.8771	7.1542	7.4416	8.0484	8.6999	9.3983	10.146
6	6.1520	6.3081	6.4684	6.6330	6.8019	6.9753	7.1533	7.3359	7.5233	7.7156	8.1152	8.5355	8.7537	8.9775	9.4420	9.9299	10.980	12.135	13.405	14.798
7	7.2135	7.4343	7.6625	7.8983	8.1420	8.3938	8.6540	8.9228	9.2004	9.4872	10.089	10.730	11.066	11.413	12.141	12.915	14.615	16.533	18.695	21.126
8	8.2857	8.5830	8.8923	9.2142	9.5491	9.8975	10.259	10.636	11.028	11.435	12.299	13.232	13.726	14.240	15.327	16.499	19.122	22.163	25.678	29.731
9	9.3685	9.7546	10.159	10.582	11.026	11.491	11.978	12.487	13.021	13.579	14.775	16.085	16.785	17.518	19.085	20.798	24.712	29.369	34.895	41.435
10	10.462	10.949	11.463	12.006	12.577	13.180	13.816	14.486	15.192	15.937	17.548	19.337	20.303	21.321	23.521	25.958	31.643	38.592	47.061	57.351
11	11.566	12.168	12.807	13.486	14.206	14.971	15.783	16.645	17.560	18.531	20.654	23.044	24.349	25.732	28.755	32.150	40.237	50.398	63.121	78.998
12	12.682	13.412	14.192	15.025	15.917	16.869	17.888	18.977	20.140	21.384	24.133	27.270	29.001	30.850	34.931	39.580	50.894	65.510	84.320	108.43
13	13.809	14.680	15.617	16.626	17.713	18.882	20.140	21.495	22.953	24.522	28.029	32.088	34.351	36.786	42.218	48.496	64.109	84.852	112.30	148.47
14	14.947	15.973	17.086	18.291	15.598	21.015	22.550	24.214	26.019	27.975	32.391	37.581	40.504	43.672	50.818	59.195	80.496	109.61	149.23	202.92
15	16.096	17.293	18.598	20.023	21.578	23.276	25.129	27.152	29.360	31.772	37.279	43.842	47.580	51.659	60.965	72.035	100.81	141.30	197.99	276.97
16	17.257	18.639	20.156	21.824	23.657	25.672	27.888	30.324	33.003	35.949	42.753	50.980	55.717	60.925	72.939	87.442	126.01	181.86	262.35	377.69
17	18.430	20.012	21.761	23.697	25.840	28.212	30.840	33.750	36.973	40.544	48.883	59.117	65.075	71.673	87.068	105.93	157.25	233.79	347.30	514.66
18	19.614	21.412	23.414	25.645	28.132	30.905	33.999	37.450	41.301	45.599	55.749	68.394	75.836	84.140	103.74	128.11	195.99	300.25	459.44	700.93
19	20.810	22.840	25.116	27.671	30.539	33.760	37.379	41.446	46.018	51.159	63.439	78.969	88.211	98.603	123.41	154.74	244.03	385.32	607.47	954.27
20	22.019	24.297	26.870	29.778	33.066	36.785	40.995	45.762	51.160	57.275	72.052	91.024	102.44	115.37	146.62	186.88	303.60	494.21	802.86	1298.8
21	23.239	25.783	28.676	31.969	35.719	39.992	44.865	50.422	56.764	64.002	81.698	104.76	118.81	134.84	174.02	225.02	377.46	633.59	1060.7	1767.3
22	24.471	27.299	30.536	34.248	38.505	43.392	49.005	55.456	62.873	71.402	92.502	120.43	137.63	157.41	206.34	271.03	469.05	811.99	1401.2	2404.6
23	25.716	28.845	32.452	36.617	41.430	46.995	53.436	60.893	69.531	79.543	104.60	138.29	159.27	183.60	244.48	326.23	582.62	1040.3	1850.6	3271.3
24	26.973	30.421	34.426	39.082	44.502	50.815	58.176	66.764	76.789	88.497	118.15	158.65	184.16	213.97	289.49	392.48	723.43	1332.6	2443.8	4449.9
25	28.243	32.030	36.459	41.645	47.727	54.864	63.249	73.105	84.700	98.347	133.33	181.87	212.79	249.21	342.60	471.98	898.09	1706.8	3226.8	6052.9
26	29.525	33.670	38.553	44.311	51.113	59.156	68.676	79.954	93.323	109.18	150.33	208.33	245.71	290.08	405.27	567.37	1114.6	2185.7	4260.4	8233.02
27	30.820	35.344	40.709	47.084	54.669	63.705	74.483	87.350	102.72	121.09	169.37	238.49	283.56	337.50	479.22	681.85	1383.1	2798.7	5624.7	11197.9
28	32.129	37.051	42.930	49.967	58.402	68.528	80.697	95.338	112.96	134.20	190.69	272.88	327.10	392.50	566.48	819.22	1716.0	3583.3	7425.6	15230.2
29	33.450	38.792	45.218	52.966	62.322	73.639	87.346	103.96	124.13	148.63	214.58	312.09	377.16	456.30	669.44	984.06	2128.9	4587.6	9802.9	20714.1
30	34.784	40.568	47.575	56.084	66.438	79.058	94.460	113.28	136.30	164.49	241.33	356.78	434.74	530.31	790.94	1181.8	2640.9	5873.2	12940.	28172.2
40	48.886	60.402	75.401	95.025	120.79	154.76	199.63	259.05	337.88	442.59	767.09	1342.0	1779.0	2360.7	4163.2	7343.8	22728.	69377.	*	*
50	64.463	84.579	112.79	152.66	209.34	290.33	406.52	573.76	815.08	1163.9	2400.0	4994.5	7217.7	10435.	21813.	45497.	*	*	*	*
60	81.669	114.05	163.05	237.99	353.58	533.12	813.52	1253.2	1944.7	3034.8	7471.6	18535.	29219.	46057.	*	*	*	*	*	*

* CVIFA > 99.999

Table A.4

Present Value of an Annuity of $1 per Period for n Periods

$$\text{PVIFA}(r,t) = \sum_{t=1}^{n} \frac{1}{(1+r)^t} = \frac{\left[1 - \frac{1}{(1+r)^n}\right]}{r}$$

Number of payments	1%	2%	3%	4%	5%	6%	7%	8%	9%	10%	12%	14%	15%	16%	18%	20%	24%	28%	32%
1	0.9901	0.9804	0.9709	0.9615	0.9524	0.9434	0.9346	0.9259	0.9174	0.9091	0.8929	0.8772	0.8696	0.8621	0.8475	0.8333	0.8065	0.7813	0.7576
2	1.9704	1.9416	1.9135	1.8861	1.8594	1.8334	1.8080	1.7833	1.7591	1.7355	1.6901	1.6467	1.6257	1.6052	1.5656	1.5278	1.4568	1.3916	1.3315
3	2.9410	2.8839	2.8286	2.7751	2.7232	2.6730	2.6243	2.5771	2.5313	2.4869	2.4018	2.3216	2.2832	2.2459	2.1743	2.1065	1.9813	1.8684	1.7663
4	3.9020	3.8077	3.7171	3.6299	3.5460	3.4651	3.3872	3.3121	3.2397	3.1699	3.0373	2.9137	2.8550	2.7982	2.6901	2.5887	2.4043	2.2410	2.0957
5	4.8534	4.7135	4.5797	4.4518	4.3295	4.2124	4.1002	3.9927	3.8897	3.7908	3.6048	3.4331	3.3522	3.2743	3.1272	2.9906	2.7454	2.5320	2.3452
6	5.7955	5.6014	5.4172	5.2421	5.0757	4.9173	4.7665	4.6229	4.4859	4.3553	4.1114	3.8887	3.7845	3.6847	3.4976	3.3255	3.0205	2.7594	2.5342
7	6.7282	6.4720	6.2303	6.0021	5.7864	5.5824	5.3893	5.2064	5.0330	4.8684	4.5638	4.2883	4.1604	4.0386	3.8115	3.6046	3.2423	2.9370	2.6775
8	7.6517	7.3255	7.0197	6.7327	6.4632	6.2098	5.9713	5.7466	5.5348	5.3349	4.9676	4.6389	4.4873	4.3436	4.0776	3.8372	3.4212	3.0758	2.7860
9	8.5660	8.1622	7.7861	7.4353	7.1078	6.8017	6.5152	6.2469	5.9952	5.7590	5.3282	4.9464	4.7716	4.6065	4.3030	4.0310	3.5655	3.1842	2.8681
10	9.4713	8.9826	8.5302	8.1109	7.7217	7.3601	7.0236	6.7101	6.4177	6.1446	5.6502	5.2161	5.0188	4.8332	4.4941	4.1925	3.6819	3.2689	2.9304
11	10.3676	9.7868	9.2526	8.7605	8.3064	7.8869	7.4987	7.1390	6.8052	6.4951	5.9377	5.4527	5.2337	5.0286	4.6560	4.3271	3.7757	3.3351	2.9776
12	11.2551	10.5753	9.9540	9.3851	8.8633	8.3838	7.9427	7.5361	7.1607	6.8137	6.1944	5.6603	5.4206	5.1971	4.7932	4.4392	3.8514	3.3868	3.0133
13	12.1337	11.3484	10.6350	9.9856	9.3936	8.8527	8.3577	7.9038	7.4869	7.1034	6.4235	5.8424	5.5831	5.3423	4.9095	4.5327	3.9124	3.4272	3.0404
14	13.0037	12.1062	11.2961	10.5631	9.8986	9.2950	8.7455	8.2442	7.7862	7.3667	6.6282	6.0021	5.7245	5.4675	5.0081	4.6106	3.9616	3.4587	3.0609
15	13.8651	12.8493	11.9379	11.1184	10.3797	9.7122	9.1079	8.5595	8.0607	7.6061	6.8109	6.1422	5.8474	5.5755	5.0916	4.6755	4.0013	3.4834	3.0764
16	14.7179	13.5777	12.5611	11.6523	10.8378	10.1059	9.4466	8.8514	8.3126	7.8237	6.9740	6.2651	5.9542	5.6685	5.1624	4.7296	4.0333	3.5026	3.0882
17	15.5623	14.2919	13.1661	12.1657	11.2741	10.4773	9.7632	9.1216	8.5436	8.0216	7.1196	6.3729	6.0472	5.7487	5.2223	4.7746	4.0591	3.5177	3.0971
18	16.3983	14.9920	13.7535	12.6593	11.6896	10.8276	10.0591	9.3719	8.7556	8.2014	7.2497	6.4674	6.1280	5.8178	5.2732	4.8122	4.0799	3.5294	3.1039
19	17.2260	15.6785	14.3238	13.1339	12.0853	11.1581	10.3356	9.6036	8.9501	8.3649	7.3658	6.5504	6.1982	5.8775	5.3162	4.8435	4.0967	3.5386	3.1090
20	18.0456	16.3514	14.8775	13.5903	12.4622	11.4699	10.5940	9.8181	9.1285	8.5136	7.4694	6.6231	6.2593	5.9288	5.3527	4.8696	4.1103	3.5458	3.1129
25	22.0232	19.5235	17.4132	15.6221	14.0939	12.7834	11.6536	10.6748	9.8226	9.0770	7.8431	6.8729	6.4641	6.0971	5.4669	4.9476	4.1474	3.5640	3.1220
30	25.8077	22.3965	19.6004	17.2920	15.3725	13.7648	12.4090	11.2578	10.2737	9.4269	8.0552	7.0027	6.5660	6.1772	5.5168	4.9789	4.1601	3.5693	3.1242
40	32.8347	27.3555	23.1148	19.7928	17.1591	15.0463	13.3317	11.9246	10.7574	9.7791	8.2438	7.1050	6.6418	6.2335	5.5482	4.9966	4.1659	3.5712	3.1250
50	39.1961	31.4236	25.7298	21.4822	18.2559	15.7619	13.8007	12.2335	10.9617	9.9148	8.3045	7.1327	6.6605	6.2463	5.5541	4.9995	4.1666	3.5714	3.1250
60	44.9550	34.7609	27.6756	22.6235	18.9293	16.1614	14.0392	12.3766	11.0480	9.9672	8.3240	7.1401	6.6651	6.2492	5.5553	4.9999	4.1667	3.5714	3.1250

APPENDIX B

NATURAL LOGARITHMS OF NUMBERS BETWEEN 1.0 AND 4.99

N	0	1	2	3	4	5	6	7	8	9
1.0	0.00000	.00995	.01980	.02956	.03922	.04879	.05827	.06766	.07696	.08618
.1	.09531	.10436	.11333	.12222	.13103	.13976	.14842	.15700	.16551	.17395
.2	.18232	.19062	.19885	.20701	.21511	.22314	.23111	.23902	.24686	.25464
.3	.26236	.27003	.27763	.28518	.29267	.30010	.30748	.31481	.32208	.32930
.4	.33647	.34359	.35066	.35767	.36464	.37156	.37844	.38526	.39204	.39878
.5	.40547	.41211	.41871	.42527	.43178	.43825	.44469	.45108	.45742	.46373
.6	.47000	.47623	.48243	.48858	.49470	.50078	.50682	.51282	.51879	.52473
.7	.53063	.53649	.54232	.54812	.55389	.55962	.56531	.57098	.57661	.58222
.8	.58779	.59333	.59884	.60432	.60977	.61519	.62058	.62594	.63127	.63658
.9	.64185	.64710	.65233	.65752	.66269	.66783	.67294	.67803	.68310	.68813
2.0	0.69315	.69813	.70310	.70804	.71295	.71784	.72271	.72755	.73237	.73716
.1	.74194	.74669	.75142	.75612	.76081	.76547	.77011	.77473	.77932	.78390
.2	.78846	.79299	.79751	.80200	.80648	.81093	.81536	.81978	.82418	.82855
.3	.83291	.83725	.83157	.84587	.85015	.85422	.85866	.86289	.86710	.87129
.4	.87547	.87963	.88377	.88789	.89200	.89609	.90016	.90422	.90826	.91228
.5	.91629	.92028	.92426	.92822	.93216	.93609	.94001	.04391	.94779	.95166
.6	.95551	.95935	.96317	.96698	.97078	.97456	.97833	.98208	.98582	.98954
.7	.99325	.99695	.00063[a]	.00430[a]	.00796[a]	.01160[a]	.01523[a]	.01885[a]	.02245[a]	.02604[a]
.8	1.02962	.03318[a]	.03674	.04028	.04380	.04732	.05082	.05431	.05779	.06126
.9	.06471	.06815	.07158	.07500	.07841	.08181	.08519	.08856	.09192	.09527
3.0	1.09861	.10194	.10526	.10856	.11186	.11514	.11841	.12168	.12493	.12817
.1	.13140	.13462	.13783	.14103	.14422	.14740	.15057	.15373	.15688	.16002
.2	.16315	.16627	.16938	.17248	.17557	.17865	.18173	.18479	.18784	.19089
.3	.19392	.19695	.19996	.20297	.20597	.20896	.21194	.21491	.21788	.22083
.4	.22378	.22671	.22964	.23256	.23547	.23837	.24127	.24415	.24703	.24990
.5	.25276	.25562	.25846	.26130	.26413	.26695	.26976	.27257	.27536	.27815
.6	.28093	.28371	.28647	.28923	.29198	.29473	.29746	.30019	.30291	.30563
.7	.30833	.31103	.31372	.31641	.31909	.32176	.32442	.32708	.32972	.33237
.8	.33500	.33763	.34025	.34286	.34547	.34807	.35067	.35325	.35584	.35841
.9	.36098	.36354	.36609	.36864	.37118	.37372	.37624	.37877	.38128	.38379
4.0	1.38629	.38879	.39128	.39377	.39624	.39872	.40118	.40364	.40610	.40854
.1	.41099	.41342	.41585	.41828	.42070	.42311	.42552	.42792	.43031	.43270
.2	.43508	.43746	.43984	.44220	.44456	.44692	.44927	.45161	.45395	.45629
.3	.45862	.46094	.46326	.46557	.46787	.47018	.47247	.47476	.47705	.47933
.4	.48160	.48387	.48614	.48840	.49065	.49290	.49515	.49739	.49962	.50185
.5	.50408	.50630	.50851	.51072	.51293	.51513	.51732	.51951	.52170	.52388
.6	.52606	.52823	.53039	.53256	.53471	.53687	.53902	.54116	.54330	.54543
.7	.54756	.54969	.55181	.55393	.55604	.55814	.56025	.56235	.56444	.56653
.8	.56862	.57070	.57277	.57485	.57691	.57898	.58104	.58309	.58515	.58719
.9	.58924	.59127	59331	.59534	.59737	.59939	.60141	.60342	.60543	.60744

[a] Add 1.0 to indicated figure.

APPENDIX C

TABLES OF ACCELERATED DEPRECIATION FACTORS

Sum-of-Years'-Digits Method (SYD) at Different Costs of Capital

Period	6%	8%	10%	12%	14%	15%	16%
1	—	—	—	—	—	—	—
2	—	—	—	—	—	—	—
3	0.908	0.881	0.855	0.831	0.808	0.796	0.786
4	0.891	0.860	0.830	0.802	0.776	0.763	0.751
5	0.875	0.839	0.806	0.775	0.746	0.732	0.719
6	0.859	0.820	0.783	0.749	0.718	0.703	0.689
7	0.844	0.801	0.761	0.725	0.692	0.676	0.661
8	0.829	0.782	0.740	0.702	0.667	0.650	0.635
9	0.814	0.765	0.720	0.680	0.643	0.626	0.610
10	0.800	0.748	0.701	0.659	0.621	0.604	0.587
11	0.786	0.731	0.683	0.639	0.600	0.582	0.565
12	0.773	0.715	0.665	0.620	0.581	0.562	0.545
13	0.760	0.700	0.648	0.602	0.562	0.543	0.526
14	0.747	0.685	0.632	0.585	0.544	0.525	0.508
15	0.734	0.671	0.616	0.569	0.527	0.508	0.491
16	0.722	0.657	0.601	0.553	0.511	0.492	0.475
17	0.711	0.644	0.587	0.538	0.496	0.477	0.460
18	0.699	0.631	0.573	0.524	0.482	0.463	0.445
19	0.688	0.618	0.560	0.510	0.468	0.449	0.432
20	0.677	0.606	0.547	0.497	0.455	0.436	0.419

Double Declining Balance Method (DDB) at Different Costs of Capital

Period	6%	8%	10%	12%	14%	15%	16%
1	—	—	—	—	—	—	—
2	—	—	—	—	—	—	—
3	0.920	0.896	0.873	0.851	0.831	0.821	0.811
4	0.898	0.868	0.840	0.814	0.789	0.777	0.766
5	0.878	0.843	0.811	0.781	0.753	0.739	0.727
6	0.858	0.819	0.783	0.749	0.718	0.704	0.689
7	0.840	0.796	0.756	0.720	0.687	0.671	0.656
8	0.821	0.774	0.731	0.692	0.657	0.641	0.625
9	0.804	0.753	0.708	0.667	0.630	0.614	0.597
10	0.787	0.733	0.685	0.643	0.605	0.588	0.571
11	0.771	0.714	0.664	0.620	0.582	0.564	0.547
12	0.755	0.696	0.644	0.599	0.559	0.541	0.524
13	0.740	0.678	0.625	0.579	0.539	0.521	0.504
14	0.725	0.661	0.607	0.560	0.520	0.501	0.484
15	0.711	0.645	0.590	0.542	0.502	0.483	0.466
16	0.697	0.630	0.573	0.526	0.485	0.466	0.450
17	0.684	0.615	0.558	0.510	0.469	0.451	0.434
18	0.671	0.601	0.543	0.495	0.454	0.436	0.419
19	0.659	0.587	0.529	0.480	0.440	0.422	0.405
20	0.647	0.574	0.515	0.467	0.427	0.409	0.392

APPENDIX D

TABLE OF AREAS UNDER THE NORMAL CURVE

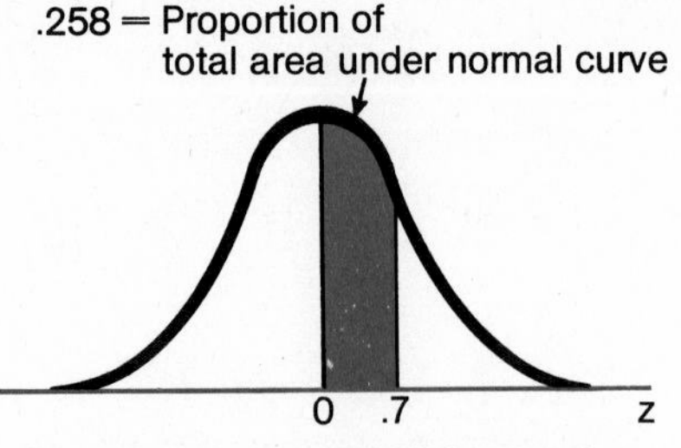

Graph of an Appendix Table D value

z	.00	.01	.02	.03	.04	.05	.06	.07	.08	.09
0.0	.0000	.0040	.0080	.0120	.0160	.0199	.0239	.0279	.0319	.0359
0.1	.0398	.0438	.0478	.0517	.0557	.0596	.0636	.0675	.0714	.0753
0.2	.0793	.0832	.0871	.0910	.0948	.0987	.1026	.1064	.1103	.1141
0.3	.1179	.1217	.1255	.1293	.1331	.1368	.1406	.1443	.1480	.1517
0.4	.1554	.1591	.1628	.1664	.1700	.1736	.1772	.1808	.1844	.1879
0.5	.1915	.1950	.1985	.2019	.2054	.2088	.2133	.2157	.2190	.2224
0.6	.2257	.2291	.2324	.2357	.2389	.2422	.2454	.2486	.2517	.2549
0.7	.2580	.2611	.2642	.2673	.2704	.2734	.2764	.2794	.2823	.2852
0.8	.2881	.2910	.2939	.2967	.2995	.3023	.3051	.3078	.3106	.3133
0.9	.3159	.3186	.3212	.3238	.3264	.3289	.3315	.3340	.3365	.3389
1.0	.3413	.3438	.3461	.3485	.3508	.3531	.3554	.3577	.3599	.3621
1.1	.3643	.3665	.3686	.3708	.3729	.3749	.3770	.3790	.3810	.3830
1.2	.3849	.3869	.3888	.3907	.3925	.3944	.3962	.3980	.3997	.4015
1.3	.4032	.4049	.4066	.4082	.4099	.4115	.4131	.4147	.4162	.4177
1.4	.4192	.4207	.4222	.4236	.4251	.4265	.4279	.4292	.4306	.4319
1.5	.4332	.4345	.4357	.4370	.4382	.4394	.4406	.4418	.4429	.4441
1.6	.4452	.4463	.4474	.4484	.4495	.4505	.4515	.4525	.4535	.4545
1.7	.4554	.4564	.4573	.4582	.4591	.4599	.4608	.4616	.4625	.4633
1.8	.4641	.4649	.4656	.4664	.4671	.4678	.4686	.4693	.4699	.4706
1.9	.4713	.4719	.4726	.4732	.4738	.4744	.4750	.4756	.4761	.4767
2.0	.4772	.4778	.4783	.4788	.4793	.4798	.4803	.4808	.4812	.4817
2.1	.4821	.4826	.4830	.4834	.4838	.4842	.4846	.4850	.4854	.4857
2.2	.4861	.4864	.4868	.4871	.4875	.4878	.4881	.4884	.4887	.4890
2.3	.4893	.4896	.4898	.4901	.4904	.4906	.4909	.4911	.4913	.4916
2.4	.4918	.4920	.4922	.4925	.4927	.4929	.4931	.4932	.4934	.4936
2.5	.4938	.4940	.4941	.4943	.4945	.4946	.4948	.4949	.4951	.4952
2.6	.4953	.4955	.4956	.4957	.4959	.4960	.4961	.4962	.4963	.4964
2.7	.4965	.4966	.4967	.4968	.4969	.4970	.4971	.4972	.4973	.4974
2.8	.4974	.4975	.4976	.4977	.4977	.4978	.4979	.4979	.4980	.4981
2.9	.4981	.4982	.4982	.4983	.4984	.4984	.4985	.4985	.4986	.4986
3.0	.4987	.4987	.4987	.4988	.4988	.4989	.4989	.4989	.4990	.4990

APPENDIX E

ANSWERS TO SELECTED END-OF-CHAPTER PROBLEMS

We present here some partial answers to selected end-of-chapter problems. For the most part, the answers given are only the final answers (or answers at intermediate steps to the more complex problems). Within limits, these answers will be useful to see if the student is on the right track toward solving the problem. The primary limitation, which must be kept in mind, is that some questions may have more than one solution, depending upon which of several equally plausible assumptions are made in working the problem. Also, many of the problems involve some verbal discussion as well as numerical calculations. We have not presented any of this discussion material here.

2.1 a. Investment A: $1,912.50, Investment B: $2,250; b. Investment A: $191.25, Investment B: $330.

2.2 a. $600 gain; b. $400 loss.

3.1 a. $16,300; b. 30%; c. 22.2%.

3.2 a. $8,250; b. 20%; c. 18.3%.

3.3 a. $37,330; b. 26.7%.

3.4 a. Marginal: 17%, Average: 17%; b. Marginal: 40%, Average: 26.75%; c. Marginal: 46%, Average: 44.08%; d. Marginal: 46%, Average: 45.98%.

3.5 1977: 0, 1978: 0, 1979: $5,250, 1980: $15,250, 1981: ($20,500).

3.6 a. 1. 1983: $6,151, 1984: $9,301, 1985: $12,901; 2. 1983: $7,637, 1984: $14,722, 1985: $22,818.

3.7 $16,250.

3.8 a. $1,000; b. Year 1: $2,080, Year 2: $1,248, Year 3: $748.80, Year 4: $461.60, Year 5: $461.60; c. Year 1: $1,666.70, Year 2: $1,333.30, Year 3: $1,000, Year 4: $666.70, Year 5: $333.30; d. Year 1: $1,364, Year 2: $1,273, Year 3: $1,091, Year 4: $818, Year 5: $454.

4.2 5.598 million tons.

4.3 8 years.

4.4 a. $875.39; b. $1,000.01; c. $1,297.58.

4.5 $22,366.72.

4.6 $56,472.

4.7 a. 12%; b. $748.51; c. $906.15.

4.8 a. $6,448; b. $59,932.

4.9 12%.

4.10 14%.

4.11 7%.

4.12 9%.

4.13 a. Year 1: $1,180,000, Year 2: $1,392,000, Year 3: $1,643,000, Year 4: $1,939,000, Year 5: $2,288,000, Year 6: $2,700,000.

4.14 a. A: $4,788, B: $5,216.

4.15 a. Year 1: $1.18, Year 2: $1.39, Year 3: $1.64, Year 4: $1.94, Year 5: $2.29, Year 6: $2.70; b. $6.00; c. $10; d. $16.

5.1 Maximum increase = $500,000.

5.2 Cash = $11,750, A/R = $6,250, Inventory = $22,500, Plant and equipment = $34,500, Accounts payable = $45,000.

5.3 a. Current assets/Current liabilities = 3.5, Debt/Total assets = 46%, Times interest earned = 3.1, Sales/Inventory = 3.0X, Average collection period = 49 days, Sales/Total assets = 1.6X, Net profit/Sales = 2.2%, Net profit/Total assets = 3.5%, Net profit/Net worth = 6.4%.

5.4 a. Current assets/Current liabilities = 2.0, Debt/Total assets = 62%, Times interest earned = 2.9, Sales/Inventory = 6.7X, Average collection period = 75 days, Sales/Total assets = 1.7X, Net profit/Sales = 1.7%, Net profit/Total assets = 2.9%, Net profit/Net worth = 7.6%.

5.5 1980: Quick ratio = 0.7, Current ratio = 2.0, Inventory turnover = 3.5X, Average collection period = 54 days, Fixed asset turnover = 12.4X, Total asset turnover = 1.9X, Return on total assets = 3%, Return on net worth = 8%, Debt ratio = 59%, Profit margin on sales = 1.7%, P/E ratio = 4X.

6.1 $66,500.

6.2 $289,100.

6.3 Cash = $2,875,000, A/R = $8,625,000, Inventory = $11,500,000, Fixed assets = $20,125,000, Accounts payable = $5,750,000, Notes payable = $6,168,750, Accruals = $8,625,000, Retained earnings = $10,581,250.

6.4 a. Current assets = $3,000,000, Fixed assets = $1,500,000, Accounts payable = $250,000, Other current liabilities = $250,000, Retained earnings = $1,780,000, Additional financing needed = $970,000.

6.5 a. Cash = $139,000, A/R = $256,000 Inventory = $690,000, Fixed assets = $816,000, Current debt = $904,000, Long-term debt = $421,000, Net worth = $576,000.

6.6 b. 0.033; c. $75,000; d. $250,000.

6.7 a. Cash = $480,000, Receivables = $1,200,000, Inventory = $2,400,000, Net fixed assets = $4,200,000, Accounts payable = $1,440,000, Accruals = $720,000, Retained earnings = $240,000; b. $414,000; c. 34.5%; d. Cash = $528,000, Receivables = $1,320,000, Inventory = $2,640,000, Net fixed assets = $4,620,000, Accounts payable: $1,584,000. Accruals: $792,000, Retained earnings = $438,000, Financing needed = $414,000; e. (1) (i) Funds needed = $216,000, (ii) Funds needed = $546,000; (2) (i) Funds needed = $532,800, (ii) Funds needed = $334,800, (3) Increases funds needed by $330,000; f. 3%.

6.8 a., b. *Balance Sheet:* Cash and securities: $44,000, 270%; Receivables: $200,000, 36%; Inventories: $132,000, −7%; Other current assets: $11,000, 105%; Net fixed assets: $142,000, 13%; Other tangible assets: $38,000, 2%; Accounts payable: $113,000, −17%; Notes payable: $71,000, 141%; Other current liabilities: $95,000, 57%; Long-term debt: $64,000, 21%; Net worth: $224,000, 28%. *Income Statement:* Sales: $1,190,500, 0%; Cost of goods sold: $907,000, −33%; Selling and administrative expense: $214,000, 127%; Interest expense: $12,000, 70%; Federal income tax: $24,000, 52%.

6.9 a. *Sources*: Cash = $24, Marketable securities = $33, Depreciation = $45, Accounts payable = $9, Other current liabilities = $24, Long-term debt = $54, Common stock = $78, Retained earnings = $84. *Uses:* Receivables = $24, Inventories = $66, Gross fixed assets = $225, Notes payable = $36.

7.1 a. (i) $75,000 loss, (ii) $300,000 gain; b. Q* = 200,000 units, S* = $2,000,000; c. (i) −7, (ii) 9, (iii) 3.

7.2 a. (i) $40,000 loss, (ii) $20,000 gain; b. Q* = 8,000 units, S* = $280,000; c. (i) −3, (ii) 9; d. Q* = 6,400 units, S* = $256,000; e. Q* = 8,000 units, S* = $320,000.

7.3 a. (i) $62,500 loss, (ii) $125,000 gain; b. Q* = 5,000 units, S* = $500,000; c. Q* = 1,000 units, S* = $100,000.

7.5 a. Current ratio = 2.6, Quick ratio = 1.5, Debt/Assets = 50%, Times interest earned = 3.8, Inventory turnover = 5.2X, Average collection period = 90 days, Fixed asset turnover = 5.49X, Total asset turnover = 1.55X, Profit margin on sales = 3.02%, Return on total assets = 4.68%, Return on net worth = 9.3%.

8.1 a. A: 6%, B: 6%, C: 7%, D: 7%; b. A: 5.99%, B: 5.99%, C: 6.92%, D: 6.99%; c. A: 2-year arithmetic mean = 4.5%, 2-year geometric mean = 4.499%; 3-year arithmetic mean = 5%, 3-year geometric mean = 4.997%; 4-year arithmetic mean = 5.5%, 4-year geometric mean = 5.494%; B: 2-year arithmetic mean = 7.5%, 2-year geometric mean = 7.499%; 3-year arithmetic mean = 7%, 3-year geometric mean = 6.997%; 4-year arithmetic mean = 7%, 3-year geometric mean = 6.997%; 4-year arithmetic mean = 6.5%, 4-year geometric mean = 6.494%; C: 2-year arithmetic mean = 5%, 2-year geometric mean = 4.995%; 3-year arithmetic mean = 8.33%, 3-year geometric mean = 8.23%, 4-year arithmetic mean = 7.75%, 4-year. geometric mean = 7.668%; D: 2-year arithmetic mean = 7.5%, 2-year geometric mean = 7.499%; 3-year arithmetic mean = 6.67%, 3-year geometric mean = 6.659%; 4-year arithmetic mean = 6.75%, 4-year geometric mean = 6.744%.

8.2 14.08%.

8.5 a. 70 days; b. $114,750.

8.6 a. Aggressive = 11.8%, Average = 10.6%, Conservative = 8.7%.

8.7 a. *Strong Economy:* Aggressive: CGS = $1,040,000, Interest = $24,000, Tax = $54,400; Between: CGS = $1,050,000, Interest = $22,000, Tax = $51,200; Conservative: CGS = $1,105,000, Interest = $26,000, Tax = $27,600. *Average Economy:* Aggressive: CGS = $830,000, Tax = $18,400; Between: CGS = $920,000, Tax = $23,200. Conservative: CGS = $1,075,000, Tax = $19,600. *Weak Economy:* Aggressive: CGS = $690,000, Tax = ($5,600); Between: CGS = $790,000, Tax = ($4,800); Conservative: CGS = $1,015,000, Tax = $3,600. b. *Strong Economy:* Aggressive: EBIT/Assets = 46%, Return on equity = 54%; Between: EBIT/Assets = 38%, Return on equity = 38%; Conservative: EBIT/Assets = 19%, Return on equity = 17%. *Average Economy:* Aggressive: EBIT/Assets = 20%, Return on equity = 18%; Between: EBIT/Assets = 20%, Return on equity = 17%; Conservative: EBIT/Assets = 15%, Return on equity = 12%. *Weak Economy:* Aggressive: EBIT/Assets = 3%, Return on equity = (6%); Between: EBIT/Assets = 3%, Return on equity = (4%); Conservative; EBIT/Assets = 7%, Return on equity: 2%.

9.1 b. 70.

9.2 a. 3,000; b. 4,000; c. 2,500; d. Every 12 days.

9.3 a. 4,000; b. 50; c. 13,962.

9.4 a. 15,000; b. 33; c. 20,000; d. 41% increase, elasticity = 0.41; e. 41% increase, elasticity = 0.41; f. Elasticity = −0.82; g. Elasticity = −0.82.

10.1 a. $20,000; b. $10,200; c. Before: $55,000, After: $50,004; d. $750 decrease.

10.2 Category 3: $55,350 increase, Category 4: $14,625 increase, Category 5: $1,350 increase.

10.4 a. 30 days: $1,067, 60 days: $1,117, 90 days: $967; b. 30 days: 30 DSO, 60 days: 29 DSO, 90 days: 33 DSO; d. 0.75, 0.20, 0.05; e. April 30: $8,150, May 31: $1,600.

10.5 Change in profitability = −$9,813.

10.6 Change in profitability = $86,001.

10.7 Change in profitability = −$29,751.

11.1 a. 20.99%.

11.2 a. $1,000,000; b. 4 days; c. Bank records: $750,000, Firm records: −$3,250,000.

11.3 a. $2,450,000; b. $196,000; c. $16,333.

11.4 Breakeven transfer size = $5,833.

11.5 a. $50,000; b. $25,000; c. 75.

12.1 a. 24.24%; b. 14.69%; c. 22.27%; d. 24.49%; e. 12.12%.

12.2 1. 16%; 2. 14.12%; 3. 13.92%; 4. 20%.

12.3 a. Trade discount: 14.69%, Loan: 14.33%.

12.4 Total cost = $35,249.

12.5 a. Total cost = $30,243.

12.6 a. 57% of short-term financing, 34% of total debt, 29% of total financing.

12.7 a. $300,000.

12.8 a. $258,621; b. Monthly cost = $639, Annual cost = $7,656.

12.9 a. 1. $3,416.67; 2. $4,000; 3. $2,300; 4. $3,500.

12.10 a. Reserve held by factor = $180,000, Interest paid in advance = $45,900, Total assets = $1,895,090, Accounts payable = $243,090, Retained earnings = $142,000; b. $252,360, 26.37%.

12.11 a. $528,000; b. 51 days; c. Factoring: $459,268, Receivables financing: $412,826; d. Factoring: $111,524, 24.28%; Receivables financing: $67,018, 16.23%.

13.1 Truck: NPV = $2,026.84, IRR = 20%; Pulley: NPV = $5,586.20, IRR = 24%.

13.2 Gas: NPV = $4,119.20, IRR = 20%; Electric: NPV = $5,148.50, IRR = 20%.

13.3 a. F = $28,000; b. NPV = $58,206.

13.4 NPV of replacement = $17,235.

13.5 NPV of replacement = $44,166.

13.6 a. $720,000; b. $160,000; c. $100,000 (PV = $62,090); d. NPV = −$51,382.

13.7 a. NPV of replacement = $37,419; b. NPV of machine 2 = $45,094.

13.8 a. NPV = −$1,251.59; b. NPV = $58.66.

13.9 a. Project M: 0%: $40,000, 6%: $22,220, 10%: $12,271, 20%: −$7,690; Project 0: 0%: $70,000, 6%: $31,811, 10%: $11,980, 20%: −$24,151; b. Project M: 15.78%; Project 0: 12.84%.

14.1 a. 0.17; b. 0.0029; c. 0.0539; d. 0.3171.

14.2 $E(R_M) = 0.16$, $\text{Var}(R_M) = 0.01$, $\sigma_M = 0.10$.

14.3 a. $\text{CV}_A = 0.242$, $\text{CV}_B = 0.421$; b. $R_A = 8.42\%$, $R_B = 10.21\%$; c. $\text{NPV}_A = \$1{,}795.60$, $\text{NPV}_B = \$4{,}050.40$.

14.4 a. 0.1625; b. 0.01871875; c. 0.1368; d. 0.8418; e. 0.01243752; f. 0.97342124.

14.5 $E(R_M) = 0.088$, $\text{Var}(R_M) = 0.01$, $\sigma_M = 0.10$, $E(R_F) = 0.06$.

14.6 a. $\bar{R}_a = 0.17$, $\bar{R}_b = 0.116$, $\sigma_a = 0.11$, $\sigma_b = 0.078$; b. $\text{Cov}(a, b) = 0.00508$, $\rho_{ab} = 0.592$, c. $\bar{R}_c = 0.1565$; d. $\sigma_c = 0.095$.

14.7 a. 6; b. 1.46; c. Required return = 0.1676.

14.8 a. $\bar{R}_M = 0.10$, $\text{Var}(R_M) = 0.04$, $\sigma_M = 0.2$, $\bar{R}_1 = 0.20$, $\text{Var}(R_1) = 0.18$, $\sigma_1 = 0.424$, $\bar{R} = 0.10$, $\text{Var}(R_2) = 0.122$, $\sigma_2 = 0.349$, $\text{Cov}(1, M) = 0.08$, $\rho_{1M} = 0.943$, $\text{Cov}(2, M) = 0.024$, $\rho_{2M} = 0.344$, $\text{Cov}(1, 2) = 0.004$, $\rho_{12} = 0.027$; b. Portfolio A: $\bar{R}_p = 0.125$, $\sigma_p = 0.285$, Portfolio B: $\bar{R}_p = 0.14$, $\sigma_p = 0.273$, Portfolio C: $\bar{R}_p = 0.175$, $\sigma_p = 0.332$; c. $R_j^* = 0.04 + 1.5\,\text{Cov}(R_j, R_M)$.

14.9 a. 15%; b. NPV = $211.32.

14.10 a. A: $4,500, B: $5,100; b. $\text{NPV}_A = \$6{,}691.05$, $\text{NPV}_B = \$7{,}749.18$.

14.11 a. $R_P^* = 0.172$, $R_Q^* = 0.156$; b. $R_P^* = 0.167$, $R_Q^* = 0.183$.

14.12 5-year life: NPV = −$209.60, 8-year life: NPV = $8,545.20, 10-year life: NPV = $13,403.40.

14.13 a. $\overline{\text{NPV}} = -\$8{,}470$; b. $\overline{\text{NPV}} = -\$8{,}467$; c. NPV = −$60,900, 2%; d. NPV = $21,700, 12%; e. 41%.

14.14 a. 8.70; b. $407; c. 0.7679; d. $6,783; e. 0.913; f. 7.8%; g. 10.5%.

14A.2 2%.

14A.3 a. NPV = $2,007; b. NPV = −$49.

14A.4 a. NPV(Coal) = $26,449, NPV(Gas) = $52,235; b. NPV(Gas) = $10,320.

15.1 a. ROE(Corbin) = 14.6%, ROE(Hollister) = 16.8%; b. ROE(Corbin) = 16.5%.

15.2 0% leverage: $\bar{R}_s = 0.105$, $\sigma = 0.054$, CV = 0.514; 10% leverage: $\bar{R}_s = 0.112$, $\sigma = 0.058$, CV = 0.518; 50% leverage: $\bar{R}_s = 0.14$, $\sigma = 0.108$, CV = 0.771; 60% leverage: $\bar{R}_s = 0.13$, $\sigma = 0.137$, CV = 1.05.

15.3 a., b. $B/S = 0.4$: $\beta = 0.99$, $R_s^* = 10.95\%$; $B/S = 0.8$: $\beta = 1.18$, $R_s^* = 11.90\%$; $B/S = 1.0$; $\beta = 1.28$, $R_s^* = 12.40\%$; $B/S = 1.2$: $\beta = 1.38$, $R_s^* = 12.90\%$; $B/S = 1.6$: $\beta = 1.57$, $R_s^* = 13.85\%$; c. $B/S = 1.458$, $R_s^* = 13.5\%$.

15.4 a. EPS(Debt) = \$3.28, \$4.48, \$6.16; EPS(Stock) = \$3.10, \$4.06, \$5.42; b. E[EPS(Debt)] = \$4.624, E[EPS(Stock)] = \$4.18.

15.5 a. (1) 1.5, (2) 1.45, (3) 2.18; b. Bonds: (1) \$1.23, (2) 3.90; Stock: (1) \$1.38, (2) 2.91.

15.6 a. 77,250; b. DOL = 1.19, DFL = 1.04, DCL = 1.24 c. DCL = 1.35.

15.7 a. EPS (Stock): −\$0.11, \$0.60, \$1.31, \$2.03, \$2.74, \$3.46, \$4.17; EPS (Debt): −\$0.71, \$0.29, \$1.29, \$2.29, \$3.29, \$4.29, \$5.29; c. Market value (Stock): N.A., \$6.00, \$13.10, \$20.30, \$27.40, \$34.60, \$41.70; Market value (Debt): NA, \$2.32, \$10.32, \$18.32, \$26.32, \$34.32, \$42.32; f. Stock financing: E(EPS) = \$2.03, Market price = \$20.30; Debt financing: E(EPS) = \$2.29, Market price = \$18.32.

16.1 17%.

16.2 a. 18%; b. $k_j^* = 13.2\%$.

16.3 6%.

16.4 a. 6.6%; b. 6.5%.

16.5 11%.

16.6 12%.

16.7 a. 14%; b. 14%.

16.8 a. \$25,000,000; b. \$15,000,000; c. (1) 0.066, (2) 0.115, (3) 0.14, (4) 0.147; d. 14.42%; e. 10.79%; f. 11%; g. 11.14%.

16.9 15.84%.

16.10 a. 8%; b. \$5.38.

16.11 12.2%.

16.12 a. (1) 12%, (2) 10.56%, (3) 11.40%, (4) 9.96%, (5) 13.33%, (6) 12.30%, (7) 16.53%, (8) 14.21%; b. Structure 4.

16.13 a. \$30,000,000; b. \$15,000,000; c. \$12,000,000; d. $k_e = 12.4\%$, $k_r = 12\%$; e. \$6,000,000; f. Below: 9.79%, Above: 9.99%.

16.14 a. At \$8,000,000 and \$16,000,000; b. Below break 1: 11.95%, Between break 1 and 2: 12.62%, Above break 2: 13.9%.

17.1 \$1,220,000.

17.2 \$2,760,000.

17.3 \$11.11.

17.4 a. Common stock, \$10 par = \$4,400,000, Paid-in surplus = \$4,600,000, Retained earnings = \$16,000,000; b. Common stock, \$5 par = \$4,000,000, Paid-in surplus = \$3,000,000, Retained earnings = \$18,000,000.

17.5 \$42.50.

17.6 a. 1971: 51%, 1972: 59%, 1973: 63%, 1974: 104%, 1975: 56%, 1976: 55%, 1977: 59%, 1978: 49%, 1979: 53%, 1980: n.a.; b. 71%.

17.7 a. \$1,237,500; b. \$2,025,000; c. \$3,250,000; d. \$2,250,000; e. \$4,750,000.

17.8 35%.

18.1 a. \$35.33; b. \$14.00.

18.2 \$468.69.

18.4 a. EPS, 1980 = \$3.00; Average EPS, 1974–80 = \$2.00; Dividends, 1980 = \$1.40; Average dividend, 1974–80 = \$1.00; Book value per share = \$24.00; b. *Bonden:* P/E, 1980 = 9.6; P/E, 1974–80 = 12; Dividend yield, 1980 = 6.25%; Dividend yield, 1974–80 = 5.21%; *Seeger:* P/E, 1980 = 8.13; P/E, 1974–80 = 13; Dividend yield, 1980 = 6.15%; Dividend yield, 1974–80 = 5%; c. High = \$28.80, Low = \$19.20.

18.5 \$42.42.

18.6 a. Bond A: \$717.51, Bond B: \$626.56; b. Bond A: \$634.83, Bond B: \$536.42.

18.7 a. Bond C: \$571.77, Bond D: \$558.68; b. Bond C: \$424.53, Bond D: \$417.61.

18.8 $800: 10%, $1,000: 8%, $1,200: 6.67%.

18.9 $825: 14%, $1,107: 5%.

18.10 a. $1,125; b. $750; c. $1,000.

19.1 a. 14.01%; b. 12.98%.

19.2 13.6%.

19.3 a. Pure rights offering: 8%.

19.4 b. 5.6%; c. 28.9%.

19.5 a. 5.02%.

20.1 $3.

20.2 a. $2.50.

20.3 a. $2.50; b. 1. Total assets = $19,150, 2. Total assets = $19,150, 3. Total assets = $19,150, 4. Total assets = $17,925.

20.4 *At $25 subscription price:* a. 1. 200,000, 2. 0.5, 3. $3.15, 4. $47.25, 5. $1.76; b. $14,175. *At $50 subscription price:* a. 1. 100,000, 2. 1, 3. $4.73, 4. $70.95, 5. $2.65; b. $14,190. *At $80 subscription price:* a. 1. 62,500, 2. 1.6, 3. $5.82, 4. $87.30, 5. $3.26; b. $14,186.

20.5 c. Required shares = 45,455; d. 11.6%; e. 2.

20.7 c. Share price: No expansion, $9.14; Debt financing, $8.13; Equity financing, $10.23; d. Value of the firm: No expansion, $1,514; Debt financing, $1,613; Equity financing, $1,850; e. No expansion, 11.4%; Debt financing, 12.5%; Equity financing, 10.6%.

21.1 a. 13.4%.

21.2 $3.90.

21.3 a. $340,000, 57%; b. $544,000, 91%; c. $882,353.

21.4 a. (1) 11.5%, (2) 11.6%, (3) 7.5X, (4) 13.3%, (5) 15%, (6) 9%, (7) 18%.

21.5 a. 18%; b. S = $1,000, p = $10, V = $1,100; c. 17.13%. *Debt financing:* e. 18.25%; f. S = $1,042, p = $10.42; g. V = $1,242; h. 16.67%. *Equity financing:* e. 17.90%; f. S = $1,110, p = $10.09; g. V = $1,210; h. 17.11%.

21.6 Year 0: EPS = $1.20, p = $10; Year 1: EPS = $1.27, p = $10.58; Year 2: EPS = $1.43, p = $11; Year 3: EPS = $1.64, p = $10.25; Year 4: EPS = $1.61, p = $8.05.

21A.1 NPV of refunding = $1,345,623.

21A.2 a. NPV of refunding = −$15,953; b. NPV of refunding = $4,797.

22.1 0.444.

22.2 a. $7,870; b. Cost of purchase = $19,890, Cost of leasing = $19,890; c. L_t = $8,854, Cost of leasing = $22,378.

22.3 a. $56,896; b. $21,846, $87,225; c. PV of interest tax shelter = $12,265; d. $23,006; e. $7,203; f. $3,497; g. $55,660; h. Advantage to owning = $1,236.

22.4 a. Cost of leasing = $19,261, Cost of owning = $19,744; b. 8.5%.

22.5 Cost of leasing = $43,931, Cost of owning = $36,298.

22.6 a. $185,600; b. Before: 1, After: 3.7; c. −$31,200.

23.1 a. $1,150.80; c. $50.80.

23.2 b. $2; c. $5; d. $10.

23.3 a. Primary EPS = $4.90, Fully-diluted EPS = $2.88; b. $6; c. $19; d. Primary EPS = $4.48, Fully-diluted EPS = $2.87.

23.5 a. Current debt = $100,000, Debentures = $0, Common stock = $62,000, Paid-in capital = $138,000, Retained earnings = $200,000; b. Current debt = $100,000, Debentures = $150,000, Common stock = $57,500, Paid-in capital = $180,000, Retained earnings = $200,000; c. Balance Sheet 3: EPS = $1.45, p = $23.20; Balance Sheet 4: EPS = $1.90, p = $30.40.

23.6 a. 13.22; b. $37.82; c. 18%; d. 12.4%; e. 17.6%.

23.7 a. Alternative 1: Long-term debt = $0, Common stock = $140,000, Paid-in surplus = $300,000; Alternative 2: Long-term debt = $0, Common stock = $133,750, Paid-in surplus = $306,250;

Alternative 3: Long-term debt = \$350,000, Common stock = \$133,750, Paid-in surplus = \$306,250; b. Original: 70%, Alternative 1: 45%, Alternative 2: 47%, Alternative 3: 47%; c. Original: \$0.43, Alternative 1: \$0.54, Alternative 2: \$0.56, Alternative 3: \$0.76; d. Original: 70%, Alternative 1: 22%, Alternative 2: 22%, Alternative 3: 50%.

23.8 a. B_0 = \$726.11, B_6 = \$766.37, B_{10} = \$807.46; b. C_0 = 828, C_5 = \$1,161, C_6 = \$1,243, C_{10} = \$1,629, C_{20} = \$3,204; c. t_0: \$828, t_6: \$1,243, t_{10}: \$1,629; d. t_0: \$1,050, t_5: \$1,037.50, t_6: \$1,035, t_{10}: \$1,025; e. Year 6; f. M' = \$1,243; h. <8%.

23.9 a. Bond A: 10.65%, Bond B: 11%; d. 7.54%.

23A.1 b. \$8.68; c. \$10.29.

23A.2 a. \$5.66; b. \$5.60.

24.1 a. \$0.125 decline; b. \$0.50 increase.

24.2 a. \$35.60; b. \$0.19, 27% accretion; c. \$0.955, 68% dilution; d. Brunner: \$3.60, 9.2% decline; Powell: \$8.00, 81.6% increase; e. 19%; f. 12 years.

24.3 b. Dalton: \$0.02, 1.6% dilution; Cory: \$2.44, 195% accretion; c. \$18.45.

24.4 a. 1. EPS = \$6.40, p = \$76.80; 2. EPS = \$5.83, p = \$69.96.

24.5 a. Cash = \$1,125, Net property = \$2,250, Total assets = \$4,500; b. Cash = \$1,125, Net property = \$3,000, Borrowing = \$1,875, Total assets = \$5,250.

24.6 a. 7.68%; b. Total assets = \$10,000,000, Debt = \$6,200,000, Net worth = \$3,800,000; c. 12.21%; d. 4.32%.

24.7 Two quarters before merger: 1. \$6.92, 20% premium; 2. \$10.50, 22% premium; 3. \$18, 18% discount; 4. \$6, 13% premium. Immediately preceding merger: 1. \$2.22, 5% premium; 2. \$0.10, 0.2% discount; 3. 0 premium; 4. 0 premium.

24.8 a. Apex: \$120 million, Allied: \$180 million; b. Apex: \$150 million, Allied: \$150 million; d. (1) Apex: 1.33, Allied: 1.12; (2) Apex: 6.6%, Allied: 4.0%; (3) Apex: \$3.13, Allied: \$3.59.

24A.1 a. Intangibles = \$285,000, Common stock = \$250,000, Capital surplus = \$400,000, Retained earnings = \$300,000, Total assets = \$1,310,000. *Vorno:* 40,000 shares, Book value per share = \$16.25, EPS = \$3, p = \$30. *Hondo:* 10,000 shares, Book value per share = \$1.50, EPS = \$1, p = \$25; b. Vorno: \$0.40 dilution, Hondo: \$1.60 accretion; c. Vorno: \$0.20 accretion, Hondo: \$2.20 accretion.

24A.2 b. Total assets = \$100,000, Common stock = \$60,000, Capital surplus = \$10,000.

25.1 Receipts after subordination adjustment Notes payable = \$700,000, Accounts payable = \$1,380,000, Subordinated debentures = \$82,000.

25.2 a. Current assets = \$119,000, Total assets = \$373,000, 8% subordinated income debentures = \$120,000, \$2 preferred stock = \$30,000; b. Interest expense = \$9,600, Earnings before tax = \$10,000, Tax = \$4,000, Preferred dividends = \$3,000, Income available to common = \$3,000; c. \$4.1 million; d. \$6.9 million less.

25.3 Liquidation value = \$600,000, Net value of reorganization = \$700,000.

25.5 a. Z = 1.772.

26.1 d. \$100: \$0.40/hr, \$300: \$1.20/hr, \$500: \$2.00/hr; e. \$100: \$2,333, \$300: \$7,000, \$500: 11,667.

26.2 a. Biogene balance sheet, 1981: Current assets = \$150, Fixed assets = \$120, Accounts payable = \$54, Notes payable = \$46, Other accruals = \$24, Common stock = \$68, Retained earnings = \$78. Corday balance sheet, 1986: Current assets = \$150, Marketable securities = \$77, Fixed assets = \$120, Accounts payable = \$54, Notes payable = \$0, Other accruals = \$24, Common stock = \$68, Retained earnings = \$201; b. *Biogene*, 1981: (1) 1.21X, (2) 85%, (3) 2.22X, (4) 4.11X, (5) 5%, (6) 21%; *Corday*, 1986: (1) 2.91X, (2) 29%, (3) 1.73X, (4) 2.23X, (5) 5%, (6) 11%

27.1 a. X_0 = 194.6 yen/\$, X_1 = 211 yen/\$; b. E_0 = \$0.005139/yen, E_1 = \$0.004739/yen; c. 7.78% devaluation; d. 8.42% revaluation.

27.2 £0.125/fr.

27.3 b. 33.8%; c. 2.1103DM/\$.

27.4 a. $2,000 gain; b. $3,333 loss.

27.5 a. $1,666,667 gain; b. $1,000,000 loss.

27.6 a. $30,000.

27.8 a. 30.68%.

27.9 a. 28.72%.

27.10 Net proceeds: Alternative a = $1,040,000, Alternative b = $1,068,511, Alternative c = $990,000.

27.11 Net proceeds: Alternative b = $1,027,339.

27.12 Net cost: Alternative a = $96,000, Alternative b = $90,533.60, Alternative c = $103,500.

GLOSSARY

A

Accelerated Depreciation Depreciation methods that write off the cost of an asset at a faster rate than the write-off under the straight line method. The three principal methods of accelerated depreciation are (a) sum-of-years'-digits, (2) double declining balance, and (3) units of production.

Accruals Continually recurring short-term liabilities; examples include accrued wages, accrued taxes, and accrued interest.

Aging Schedule A report showing how long accounts receivable have been outstanding

Amortization The repayment of the principal amount of a loan in installments during the life of the loan

Annuity A series of payments of a fixed amount for a specified number of years

Arbitrage The process of selling overvalued and buying undervalued assets so as to bring about an equilibrium where all assets are properly valued. One who engages in arbitrage is called an arbitrageur.

Arrearage Overdue payment; frequently, omitted dividends on preferred stocks

Assignment A relatively inexpensive way of liquidating a failing firm that does not involve going through the courts

B

Balloon Payment The final payment on a partially amortized debt, scheduled to be larger than all preceding payments

Banker's Acceptance A check drawn by a business firm whose payment is guaranteed by the bank's "acceptance" of it. It is especially important in foreign trade, because the seller of goods is less certain that the buyer's check (or draft) will actually have funds behind it.

Bankruptcy A legal procedure for formally liquidating a business, carried out under the jurisdiction of courts of law

Beta Coefficient A measure of the extent to which the returns on a given investment move with the stock market

Bond A long-term debt instrument

Book Value The accounting value of an asset. The book value of a share of common stock is equal to the shareholders' equity (common stock, paid-in surplus, and retained earnings) of the corporation divided by the number of shares of stock outstanding.

Breakeven Analysis An analytical technique for studying the relationship among fixed cost, variable cost, and profits

Budget Projected financial statements used to compare with actual performance to stimulate improvements in the use of company resources in a planning and control process

Business Risk The risk resulting from the nature of the products sold by the firm and from the degree of operating leverage employed

C

Call (1) An option to buy (or "call") an asset at a specified price within a specified period; (2) The process of redeeming a bond or preferred stock issue before its normal maturity

Call Premium The amount in excess of par value that a company must pay when it calls a security

Call Price The price that must be paid when a security is called. The call price is equal to the par value plus the call premium.

Capital Asset An asset with a life of more than one year that is not bought and sold in the ordinary course of business

Capital Asset Pricing Model (CAPM) A theory of asset pricing in which the return of an asset or security is the risk-free return plus a risk premium based on the excess of the return on the market over the risk-free rate multiplied by the asset's systematic risk (which cannot be eliminated by diversification).

Capital Budgeting The process of planning expenditures on assets whose returns are expected to extend beyond one year

Capital Gains Profits on the sale of capital assets held for twelve months or longer

Capital Losses Losses on the sale of capital assets

Capital Markets Financial transactions involving instruments with maturities greater than one year

Capital Rationing A situation in which a constraint is placed on the total amount of capital investments during a particular period

Capital Structure The permanent long-term financing of the firm represented by long-term debt, preferred stock, and net worth (net worth consists of capital, capital surplus, and retained earnings). Capital structure is distinguished from *financial structure*, which includes short-term debt plus all other liability accounts.

Capitalization Rate A discount rate used to find the present value of a series of future cash receipts; sometimes called discount rate

Carry-Back; Carry-Forward For income tax purposes, losses that can be carried back or forward to reduce average taxable income

Cash Budget A schedule showing cash flows (receipts, disbursements, and net cash) for a firm over a specified period

Cash Conversion Cycle The length of time between the purchase of raw materials and the collection of accounts receivable generated in the sale of the final product

Certainty Equivalents The amount of cash (or rate of return) that someone would require *with certainty* to make the recipient indifferent between this certain sum (or rate of return) and a particular uncertain, risky sum (or rate of return).

Certificate of Deposit (CD) A form of savings deposit which cannot be withdrawn before its maturity date. However, CDs are negotiable and are sold in an active secondary market before their maturity date.

Chattel Mortgage A mortgage on personal property (not real estate). A mortgage on equipment would be a chattel mortgage.

Coefficient of Variation (CV) Standard deviation divided by the mean

Collateral Assets used to secure a loan

Combined Leverage *See* Degree of Combined Leverage.

Commercial Paper Unsecured, short-term promissory note of a large firm. The rate of interest on commercial paper is typically somewhat below the prime rate of interest.

Commitment Fee The fee paid to a lender for a formal line of credit

Compensating Balance A required minimum checking account balance that a firm must maintain with a commercial bank. The required balance is generally equal to 15 to 20 percent of the amount of loans outstanding. Compensating balances raise the effective rate of interest on bank loans.

Composition An informal method of reorganization that voluntarily reduces creditors' claims on the debtor firm

Compound Interest An interest rate that is applicable when interest in succeeding periods is earned not only on the initial principal but also on the accumulated interest of prior periods. Compound interest is contrasted to *simple interest,* in which returns are not earned on interest received.

Conditional Sales Contract A method of financing new equipment by paying it off in installments over a one- to five-year period. The seller retains title to the equipment until payment has been completed.

Consol Bond A perpetual bond issued by England in 1814 to consolidate past debts; by extension, any perpetual bond

Consolidated Tax Return An income tax return that combines the income statement of several affiliated firms

Continuous Compounding (Discounting) The practice of adding interest continuously rather than at discrete points in time

Contribution Margin The difference between sales price per unit and variable costs per unit

Conversion Price The effective price paid for common stock when the stock is obtained by converting either convertible preferred stocks or convertible bonds. For example, if a $1,000 bond is convertible into 20 shares of stock, the conversion price is $50 ($1,000/20).

Conversion Ratio or **Conversion Rate** The number of shares of common stock that may be obtained by converting a convertible bond or share of convertible preferred stock

Convertibles Securities (generally bonds or preferred stocks) that are exchangeable at the option of the holder for common stock of the issuing firm

Correlation Coefficient A measure of the degree of relationship between two variables

Cost of Capital The discount rate that should be used in the capital budgeting process or in valuation computations

Coupon Rate The stated rate of interest on a bond

Covariance (Cov) The correlation between two variables multiplied by the standard deviation of each variable:

$$\text{Cov} = \rho_{xy}\sigma_x\sigma_y$$

Covenant Provisions contained in loan agreements. Covenants are designed to protect the lender and include such items as limits on total indebtedness, restrictions on dividends, minimum current ratio, and similar provisions.

Cumulative Dividends A protective feature on preferred stock that requires all past preferred dividends to be paid before any common dividends are paid

Cumulative Voting A method of voting for corporate directors which permits multiple votes for a single director. This can enable a minority group of shareholders to obtain some voice in the control of the company.

Cut-Off Point In the capital budgeting process, the minimum rate of return on acceptable investment opportunities

D

Debenture A long-term debt instrument that is not secured by a mortgage on specific property

Debt Ratio Total debt divided by total assets or total debt divided by net worth

Decision Tree A device for setting forth graphically the pattern of relationship between decisions and probability factors

Default The failure to fulfill a contract. Generally, default refers to the failure to pay interest or principal on debt obligations.

Degree of Combined Leverage (DCL) The ratio of the percentage change in net income (or net income to shareholders' equity or earnings per share) to the percentage change in sales

Degree of Financial Leverage (DFL) The ratio of the percentage change in net income to the percentage change in earnings before interest and taxes. *See also* Financial Leverage.

Degree of Operating Leverage (DOL) The ratio of the percentage change in earnings before interest and taxes to the percentage change in sales. *See also* Operating Leverage.

Devaluation The process of reducing the value of a country's currency stated in terms of other currencies. For example, the British pound might be devalued from $2.30 for one pound to $2.00 for one pound.

Discount Rate The interest rate used in the discounting process; sometimes called capitalization rate

Discounted Cash Flow Techniques Methods of ranking investment proposals, such as internal rate of return method and net present value method

Discounting The process of finding the present value of a series of future cash flows. Discounting is the reverse of compounding.

Discounting of Accounts Receivable Short-term financing where accounts receivable are used as security for the loan. Also called assigning or pledging accounts receivable.

Dividend Yield The ratio of the current dividend to the current price of a share of stock

Du Pont System A system of planning and control that emphasizes analysis of investments and cost elements for their effects on return on investment, asset turnover, and profit margins

E

EBIT Acronym for *earnings before interest and taxes*. Also net operating income (NOI).

Economical Ordering Quantity (EOQ) The optimum size of order which results in the least cost of purchasing and holding inventories

Edge Act Corporations Subsidiaries of U.S. banks which can conduct all forms of international banking, including investing in the equities of other companies

Efficient Market Hypothesis The theory that historical data on prices or returns plus other publicly available data are already reflected in current prices of assets or securities and cannot be used to earn above-average returns

Efficient Portfolio A portfolio which provides the highest expected return for a given level of risk, or the lowest amount of risk for a given level of expected return

EPS Acronym for *earnings per share*

Equity (S) The net worth of a business, consisting of capital stock, capital (or paid-in) surplus, earned surplus (or retained earnings), and occasionally, certain net worth reserves. *Common equity* is that part of the total net worth belonging to the common stockholders. *Total equity* would include preferred stockholders. The terms *net worth* and *common equity* are frequently used interchangeably.

Eurocurrency Bank deposits in one country denominated in the currency of another country—for example, U.S. dollar deposits in a French bank

Ex Dividend Date The date on which the right to the current dividend no longer accompanies a stock. (For listed stock, the ex dividend date is four working days prior to the date of record.)

Ex Rights Date The date on which stock purchase rights are no longer transferred to the purchaser of the stock

Exchange Rate The rate at which one currency can be exchanged for another—for example, $2.30 for one British pound

Excise Tax A tax on the manufacture, sale, or consumption of specified commodities

Exercise Price The price that must be paid for an asset when an option is exercised

Expected Return The mean value of the probability distribution of possible returns

Extension An informal method or reorganization in which the creditors voluntarily postpone the date of required payment on past-due obligations

External Funds Funds acquired through borrowing or by selling new common or preferred stock

F

Factoring A method of financing accounts receivable under which a firm sells its accounts receivable (generally without recourse) to a financial institution (the factor)

Federal Funds Deposits of member banks in the Federal Reserve Bank to meet reserve requirements. Sales of federal funds represent loans from one member bank to another, usually for overnight or over a weekend.

Field Warehousing A method of financing inventories in which a "warehouse" is established at the place of business of the borrowing firm

Financial Accounting Standards Board (FASB) A private (nongovernment) agency which functions as an accounting standards-setting body

Financial Intermediation Financial transactions which bring savings surplus units together with savings deficit units so that savings can be redistributed into their most productive uses

Financial Lease A lease that does not usually provide for maintenance services, is not cancellable, and is fully amortized over its life

Financial Leverage The ratio of total debt to total assets or of total debt to equity. There are other measures of financial leverage, especially those which relate cash inflows to required cash outflows. *See also* Degree of Financial Leverage.

Financial Markets Transactions in which the creation and transfer of financial assets and financial liabilities take place

Financial Risk That portion of total corporate risk, over and above basic business risk, that results from using debt

Financial Structure The entire right-hand side of the balance sheet—the way in which a firm is financed

Fisher Effect The excess of nominal interest rates over real (purchasing-power-adjusted) interest rates, reflecting the rate of anticipated inflation

Fixed Charges Costs that do not vary with the level of output, especially fixed financial costs such as interest, lease payments, and sinking fund payments

Float The time interval between the date on which the buyer writes a check and the date on which the seller has actual use of the funds. The term *float* is also used to refer to the amount of funds involved.

Floating Exchange Rates Exchange rates that are allowed to fluctuate in accordance with supply and demand

Flotation Cost The cost of issuing new stocks or bonds

Forward Contract A purchase or sale at a price specified now, with the transaction to actually take place at some future date. Can apply to commodities, foreign currencies, Treasury bills, and so on.

Fully Diluted EPS A figure that shows what earnings per share would be if all warrants had been exercised or convertibles converted prior to the reporting date

Funded Debt Long-term debt

Funding The process of replacing short-term debt with long-term securities (stocks or bonds)

G

General Purchasing Power Reporting A requirement of FASB Statement No. 33 that the current values of non-monetary items be adjusted by a general price index in the financial reports of major companies

Going-Concern Value The amount received when a firm is sold as an operating business. The excess over liquidating value is the value of the management organization operating the firm.

Goodwill Intangible assets of a firm established by the excess of the price paid for the going concern over its book value

H

Holder-of-Record Date The date on which a company closes its stock transfer books and makes up a list of the stockholders as of that date, to receive a future dividend payment

Holding Company A corporation operated for the purpose of owning the common stocks of other corporations

Hurdle Rate In capital budgeting, the minimum acceptable rate of return on a project; if the expected rate of return is below the hurdle rate, the project is not accepted. The hurdle rate should be the marginal cost of capital.

I

Improper Accumulation Earnings retained by a business for the purpose of enabling stockholders to avoid personal income taxes

Income Bond A bond that pays interest only to the extent that income is actually earned by a company

Incremental Cash Flow Net cash flow attributable to an investment project

Incremental Cost of Capital The weighted cost of the increment of capital raised during a specified time period

Indenture A formal agreement between the issuer of a bond and the bondholders

Insolvency The inability to meet maturing debt obligations

Interest Factor (IF) Numbers found in compound interest and annuity tables

Interest Rate Parity Theorem A theorem stating that the ratio of domestic forward to spot exchange rates expressed in foreign currency units per one domestic currency unit will equal the ratio of one plus foreign to one plus domestic interest rates

Internal Financing Funds available from the normal operations of the firm; internal financing is approximately equal to retained earnings plus depreciation.

Internal Rate of Return (IRR) The rate of return on an asset investment. The internal rate of return is calculated by finding the discount rate that equates the present value of future cash flows to the cost of the investment.

Intrinsic Value A valuation arrived at by the application of data inputs to a valuation theory or model. The resulting value may be compared with the prevailing market price.

Investment Banker A firm which underwrites and distributes new issues of securities

Investment Tax Credit A reduction in income tax liability that businesses are entitled to take for new investments in certain asset categories

J

Junior Securities Securities that have a lower priority in claims on assets and income than do other, senior, securities. For example, preferred stock is junior to debentures, but debentures are junior to mortgage bonds. Common stock is the most junior of all corporate securities.

L

Legal List A list of securities in which mutual savings banks, pension funds, insurance companies, and other fiduciary institutions are permitted to invest

Leverage Factor The ratio of debt to total assets or debt to equity

Lien A lender's claim on assets that are pledged for a loan

Line of Credit An arrangement whereby a financial institution (bank or insurance company) commits itself to lend up to a specified maximum amount of funds during a specified period

Liquidating Value The amount that could be realized if an asset or group of assets (the entire assets of a firm, for example) are sold separately from the organization that has been using them

Liquidity A firm's cash position and its ability to meet maturing obligations

Listed Securities Securities traded on an organized security exchange

Lock-Box Plan A procedure used to speed up collections and to reduce negative float

M

Margin The *profit margin* is the percentage of net income to sales.

Margin The buying of stocks or bonds on credit, known as *buying on margin*

Marginal Cost The cost of an additional unit. The marginal cost of capital is the cost of additional funds.

Marginal Efficiency of Capital A schedule showing the internal rate of return on investment opportunities

Marginal Revenue The increase in revenue produced by selling additional units

Market Portfolio The total of all investment opportunities available

Merger Any combination that forms one company from two or more previously existing companies

Money Market Financial markets in which funds are borrowed or lent for periods of less than one year. (The money market is distinguished from the capital market, which is the market for long-term funds.)

Monte Carlo Method A sensitivity analysis of the effects of using random combinations of probabilities applicable to two or more factors that affect the outcomes of business decisions

Mortgage A pledge of designated property as security for a loan

N

Net Present Value (NPV) Method The NPV is equal to the present value of future returns, discounted at the marginal cost of capital, minus the present value of the cost of the investment.

Net Worth The sum of shareholders' equity plus preferred stock

NOI Acronym for *net operating income,* same as EBIT; symbol *X* is also used

Nominal Interest Rate The contracted or stated interest rate, undeflated for price-level changes

Normal Probability Distribution A symmetrical, bell-shaped probability function

O

Objective Probability Distributions Probability distributions determined by relative frequencies

Operating Lease A lease in which the lessee has the option of cancelling without default. In contrast, a financial lease provides for a full payment of the lessor's projected investment and return over the life of the lease.

Operating Leverage The extent to which fixed costs are used in a firm's operation. Breakeven analysis is used to measure the extent to which operating leverage is employed. *See also* Degree of Operating Leverage.

OPM *See* Option Pricing Model.

Opportunity Cost The rate of return on the best alternative investment that is available. It is the highest return that will *not* be earned if the funds are invested in a particular project. For example, the opportunity cost of not investing in Bond A yielding 8 percent might be 7.99 percent, which could be earned on Bond B.

Option A contract that gives the holder the right to buy (or sell) an asset at a predetermined price for a given period of time

Option Pricing Model (OPM) The risk-free rate, the current value of the asset, the variance of returns, the exercise price, and the duration of an option are expressed in a formula from which the value of the option can be calculated.

Ordinary Income Income from the normal operations of a firm (specifically excludes income from the sale of capital assets)

Organized Security Exchanges Formal organizations having tangible, physical locations. Organized exchanges conduct an auction market in designated (listed) investment securities. The New York Stock Exchange is an example of an organized exchange.

Overdraft System A system in which a depositor may write checks in excess of his balance, with his bank automatically extending a loan to cover the shortage

Oversubscription Privilege In a rights offering, gives subscribing stockholders the right to buy, on a pro rata basis, all shares not taken in the initial offering

Over-the-Counter Market All facilities that provide for trading in unlisted securities; that is, those not listed on organized exchanges. The over-the-counter market is typically a telephone market, with most business conducted by phone.

P

Par Value The nominal value of a stock or bond

Payback Period The length of time required for the net revenues of an investment to return the cost of the investment

Payout Ratio The percentage of earnings paid out in the form of dividends

Pegging A market stabilization action taken by the manager of an underwriting group during the offering of new securities. The manager does this by continually placing orders to buy at a specified price in the market.

Perpetual Bond A bond that pays interest annually into perpetuity

Perpetuity A stream of future payments expected to continue forever

Pledging of Accounts Receivable Short-term borrowing from financial institutions where the loan is secured by accounts receivable. The lender may physically take the accounts receivable but typically has recourse to the borrower; also called discounting of accounts receivable.

Pooling of Interest An accounting method for combining the financial statements of firms that merge. Under the pooling-of-interest procedure, the assets of the merged firms are simply added to form the balance sheet of the surviving corporation.

Portfolio Combining assets to reduce risk by diversification

Portfolio Effect The extent to which the variation in returns on a combination of assets (a portfolio) is less than the simple average of the variations of the individual assets

Preemptive Right A provision contained in the corporate charter and bylaws that gives holders of common stock the right to purchase on a pro rata basis new issues of common stock (or securities convertible into common stock)

Present Value (PV) The value today of a future payment, or stream of payments, discounted at the appropriate discount rate

Present Value Profile A graph that plots a project's net present value (*y*-axis) against various discount rates (*x*-axis). The profile crosses the *x*-axis at the project's internal rate of return.

Price-Earnings Ratio (P-E) The ratio of price to earnings. Faster growing or less risky firms typically have higher P-E ratios than either slower growing or riskier firms.

Price-Level Adjustment A restatement of a financial statement to adjust for the effects of general or specific price-level changes, such as inflation

Primary EPS Earnings available to common stock divided by the number of shares actually outstanding, disregarding any unexercised warrants or unconverted convertibles

Prime Rate The rate of interest commercial banks charge borrowers with the highest credit ratings

Private Placement Financing directly from the source of funds without the use of an intermediary such as an investment banker

Pro Forma A projection. A pro forma financial statement shows how financial statements will look under specified assumptions. Pro forma statements may reflect historical relations or future projections.

Profit Center A unit of a firm with divisions that have identifiable cash flows and investments on which a rate of return on investment or other performance measures can be calculated

Profit Margin The ratio of net income to sales

Profit Planning *See* Breakeven Analysis.

Progressive Tax A tax that requires a higher percentage payment on higher incomes. The personal income tax structure in the United States is progressive.

Prospectus Information provided on a new security issue as a record of representations by the issuer to the prospective buyer

Proxy A document giving one person the authority or power to act for another. Typically, the authority in question is the power to vote shares of common stock.

Purchase Accounting A method of accounting that allows for a firm's goodwill value in a transaction (the premium, or discount, over the book value) to be set up as an asset of the surviving firm

Put An option to sell a specific security at a specified price within a designated period

R

Rate of Return The internal rate of return on an investment

Recourse Arrangement A term used in connection with accounts receivable financing. If a firm sells its accounts receivable to a financial institution under a recourse agreement and if the accounts receivable cannot then be collected, the selling firm must repurchase the account from the financial institution.

Rediscount Rate The rate of interest at which a bank may borrow from a Federal Reserve bank

Refunding Sale of new debt securities to replace an old debt issue

Regression Analysis A statistical procedure for predicting the value of one variable (dependent variable) on the basis of knowledge about one or more other variables (independent variables)

Reinvestment Rate The rate of return at which cash flows from an investment are reinvested. The reinvestment rate may or may not be constant from year to year.

Reorganization When a financially troubled firm goes through reorganization, its assets are restated to reflect their current market value, and its financial structure is restated downward to reflect reductions on the asset side of the statement. Under a reorganization, the firm continues in existence; this is contrasted to bankruptcy, in which the firm is liquidated and ceases to exist.

Replacement Cost Accounting A requirement under SEC Release No. 190 (1976) that large companies disclose the replacement costs of inventory items and depreciable plant; superseded by similar provisions in FASB Statement No. 33, issued in 1979

Required Rate of Return The rate of return necessary to avoid a decline in the value of a security

Residual Value The value of leased property at the end of the lease term

Retained Earnings That portion of earnings not paid out in dividends. The figure that appears on the balance sheet is the sum of the retained earnings for each year throughout the company's history.

Right A short-term option to buy a specified number of shares of a new issue of securities at a designated subscription price

Rights Offering A securities flotation offered to existing stockholders

Risk The degree of dispersion of future returns from their average expected value. Measured by the variance, standard deviation, or coefficient of variation of possible future returns.

Risk-Adjusted Discounted Rate The discount rate applicable for a particular risky (uncertain) stream of income; the riskless rate of interest plus a risk premium appropriate to the level of risk attached to the particular income stream

Risk-Free Rate Generally the return on short-maturity U.S. Treasury securities, on which there is little likelihood of variability or default

Risk Premium The difference between the required rate of return on a particular risky asset and the rate of return on a riskless asset with the same expected life

Risk-Return Tradeoff Function *See* Security Market Line.

S

Safety Stock An amount added to inventory holdings as a precautionary measure in the face of uncertainty as to delivery times and usage rates, and the cost of stock-outs

Sale and Leaseback An operation whereby a firm sells land, buildings, or equipment to a financial institution and simultaneously executes an agreement to lease the property back for a specified period under specific terms

Salvage Value The value of a capital asset at the end of a specified period. It is the current market price of an asset being considered for replacement in a capital budgeting problem.

Securities *See* Junior Securities; Senior Securities.

Securities and Exchange Commission (SEC) A federal government agency that supervises the operation of securities exchanges and related aspects of the securities business. Companies issuing securities must register with the SEC.

Security Agreement A standardized document or form which includes a description of the specific assets pledged for the purpose of a secured loan

Security Market Line (SML) The relationship between the required return on a security or investment and the product of its risk times a normalized market measure of risk.

Selling Group A group of securities brokers or dealers formed for the purpose of distributing a new issue of securities; part of the investment banking distribution process

Senior Securities Securities having claims on income and assets that rank higher than certain other, junior, securities. For example, mortgage bonds are senior to debentures, but debentures are senior to common stock.

Sensitivity Analysis Simulation analysis in which the values of causal variables are changed to determine the degree to which the results are related to the behavior of individual variables

Shareholders' Equity The common stock, paid-in surplus, and retained earnings of the corporation

Short Selling Selling a security that is not owned by the seller at the time of the sale. The seller borrows the security from a brokerage firm and must at some point repay the brokerage firm by buying the security on the open market.

Simulation Analysis of relationships by making assumptions in a model about the values of some of the variables and observing the effects on outcomes or results

Sinking Fund A fund set up for periodic payments, aimed at reducing or amortizing a financial obligation

Small Business Administration (SBA) A government agency organized to aid small firms with their financing and other problems

Spontaneous Financing Financing (for example, trade credit) which arises from ordinary business transactions

Standard Deviation (σ) A statistical term that measures the variability of a set of observations from the mean of the distribution

Stock Dividend A dividend paid in additional shares of stock rather than in cash; involves a transfer from retained earnings to the capital stock account

Stock Split An accounting action to increase the number of shares outstanding. For example, in a 3-for-1 split, three new shares are issued for each one formerly held.

Subjective Probability Distributions Probability distributions formulated by judgments not completely based on empirical evidence such as relative frequencies.

Subordinated Debenture A bond having a claim on assets only after specified senior claims have been paid off

Subscription Price The price at which a security may be purchased in a rights offering

Synergy The post-merger performance, in which the total is greater than the sum of its parts; derives from the interdependency of the activities of the firms

Systematic Risk That part of a security's risk that cannot be eliminated by diversification

T

Tangible Assets Physical assets (as opposed to intangible assets such as goodwill and the stated value of patents)

Tender Offer An offer to buy the stock of a firm at a specified price. Sometimes the offer is submitted for approval to the board of directors of the target company; or the offer may be made directly to the shareholders of the company.

Term Loan A loan generally obtained from a bank or an insurance company with a maturity greater than one year. Term loans are generally amortized; periodic repayments are made to reduce the outstanding amount of the loan over its life.

Term Structure of Interest Rates The relationship between interest rates and loan maturity

Terminal Value The value of an asset at a future time. The value of an asset today is the present value of its terminal value discounted at the appropriate rate.

Trade Credit Interfirm debt arising through credit sales and recorded as an account receivable by the seller and as an account payable by the buyer

Transfer Price The price used within a firm to record the "sale" of products or assets by one division to another

Treasury Stock Common stock that has been repurchased by the issuing firm

Trust Receipt An instrument acknowledging that the borrower holds certain goods in trust for the lender. Trust receipt financing is used in connection with the financing of inventories for automobile dealers, construction equipment dealers, appliance dealers, and other dealers in expensive durable goods.

Trustee The representative of bondholders who acts in their interest and facilitates communication between them and the issuer. Typically these duties are handled by a department of a commercial bank.

U

Underwriting (1) The entire process of issuing new corporate securities; (2) The insurance function of bearing the risk of adverse price fluctuations during the period in which a new issue of stock or bonds is being distributed

Underwriting Syndicate A syndicate of investment firms formed to spread the risk associated with the purchase and distribution of a new issue of securities. The larger the issue, the more firms typically are involved in the syndicate.

Unlisted Securities Securities that are traded in the over-the-counter market

Unsystematic Risk That part of a security's risk associated with random events; can be eliminated by proper diversification

V

Venture Capital Financing of a firm when its future outlook is highly uncertain. An example is the financing of a new small firm before it has established a performance record.

W

Warrant A long-term option to buy a stated number of shares of common stock at a specified price. The specified price is generally called the exercise price.

Weighted Cost of Capital A weighted average of the component costs of debt, preferred stock, and common equity. Also called the composite cost of capital.

Working Capital Refers to a firm's investment in short-term assets—cash, short-term securities, accounts receivable, and inventories. *Working capital* is defined as current assets minus current liabilities.

Y

Yield The rate of return on an investment; the internal rate of return

Yield to Maturity Based on a bond's coupon and price, the rate of return that is expected if a bond is held to maturity

INDEX

Summary of Key Formulas in *Essentials of Managerial Finance*
(Symbols are defined inside front cover)

I. Compound Interest
  A. Basic Relations
    1a. Compound sum:

$$V_{r,n} = P_0(1 + r)^n$$

    1b. Present value:

$$P_0 = V_{r,n}(1 + r)^{-n}$$

    2a. Sum of annuity:

$$V_{r,t} = [(1 + r)^n - 1]/r$$

    2b. Present value of annuity:

$$P_{r,t} = [1 - (1 + r)^{-n}]/r$$

  B. Bond Valuation
    1. Valuation of a perpetual bond:

$$B = \frac{c}{k_b}$$

    2. Valuation of bond of finite maturity:

$$B = \sum_{t=1}^{n} \frac{c_t}{(1 + k_b)^t} + \frac{M}{(1 + k_b)^n}$$

II. Capital Budgeting Relations
  A. Basic Capital Budgeting Relation—NPV

$$\text{NPV} = \sum_{t=1}^{n} \frac{F_t}{(1 + k)^t} - \text{I}$$

  B. Internal Rate of Return (R)

$$\text{NPV} = \sum_{t=1}^{N} \frac{F_t}{(1 + R)^t} - \text{I} = 0$$

III. Return and Risk
  A. Portfolios
    1. Expected return on a portfolio:

$$E(R_p) = w_1\bar{R}_1 + w_2\bar{R}_2 \cdots w_n\bar{R}_n$$

    2. Standard deviation of a portfolio (two-asset case):

$$\sigma_p = (w_a^2\sigma_a^2 + w_b^2\sigma_b^2 + 2w_a w_b \rho_{ab}\sigma_a\sigma_b)^{1/2}$$

  B. CAPM Relationships
    1. Security Market Line (SML):

$$\bar{R}_j = R_F + \lambda\text{Cov}(\tilde{R}_j, \tilde{R}_M)$$

$$\lambda = \frac{\bar{R}_M - R_F}{\sigma_M^2}$$

    2. $\bar{R}_j = R_F + (\bar{R}_M - R_F)\beta_j$
       where:

$$\beta_j = \text{Cov}(\tilde{R}_j, \tilde{R}_M)/\sigma_M^2$$

    3. CAPM valuation (certainty equivalent form):

$$V_j = \frac{E(\tilde{X}_j) - \lambda\text{Cov}(\tilde{X}_j, R_M)}{R_F}$$

IV. Cost of Capital Relationships
  A. Cost of Equity Capital

$$k_s = k_u + (k_u - k_b)(B/S)(1 - T)$$

  B. Weighted Cost of Capital
    1. $k_u = \dfrac{E(X)(1 - T)}{V_u}$ $\qquad k = \dfrac{E(X)(1 - T)}{V_L}$

    2. $k = k_b(1 - T)\dfrac{B}{V} + k_s\dfrac{S}{V}$

    3. $k = k_u[1 - T(B/V)]$